THIRD EDITION

DATABASE PRINCIPLES

fundamentals of design, implementation, and management

CARLOS CORONEL
STEVEN MORRIS
KEELEY CROCKETT
CRAIG BLEWETT

Australia • Brazil • Mexico • South Africa • Singapore • United Kingdom • United States

Database Principles: Fundamentals of Design, Implementation, and Management
Third Edition
US Authors: Carlos Coronel, Steven Morris
Adapters: Keeley Crockett, Craig Blewett

Publisher: Marinda Louw

Marketing Manager: Anna Reading

Senior Content Project Manager: Sue Povey

Manufacturing Manager: Eyvett Davis

Typesetter: SPi-Global

Cover Designer: Simon Levy Associates

Cover Image(s): ©Vijay Kumar/Getty Images

For product information and technology assistance, contact us at **emea.info@cengage.com**

For permission to use material from this text or product and for permission queries, email **emea.permissions@cengage.com**

British Library Cataloguing-in-Publication Data

A catalogue record for this book is available from the British Library.

ISBN: 978-1-4737-6804-8

Cengage Learning, EMEA
Cheriton House, North Way
Andover, Hampshire, SP10 5BE
United Kingdom

Cengage Learning is a leading provider of customized learning solutions with employees residing in nearly 40 different countries and sales in more than 125 countries around the world. Find your local representative at: **www.cengage.co.uk.**

Cengage Learning products are represented in Canada by Nelson Education, Ltd.

To learn more about Cengage platforms and services, register or access your online learning solution, or purchase materials for your course, visit **www.cengage.com.**

Printed in the United Kingdom by Ashford Colour Press Ltd.
Print Number: 03 Print Year: 2023

MIX
Paper from responsible sources
FSC www.fsc.org FSC® C011748

BRIEF CONTENTS

CONTENTS

Part V Database Transactions and Performance Tuning 632

Appendices (Available online)

PREFACE

We are excited to introduce the third edition of *Database Principles*, which is designed to provide a solid and practical foundation for the design, implementation and management of database systems. This foundation is built on the notion that, while databases are very practical things, their successful creation depends on understanding the important concepts that define them.

This edition is suitable for a first course in databases at undergraduate level and will also provide essential material for conversion postgraduate courses. Providing comprehensive and practical coverage of core database concepts, it is an ideal text not only for those studying database management systems in the context of computer science, but also those on courses in the areas of business technology, introductory data science and data analytics.

The Approach: Continued Emphasis on the Stages of Design

As the title suggests, *Database Principles: Design, Implementation, and Management* covers three broad aspects of database systems. However, for several important reasons, special attention is given to database design:

- The availability of excellent database software enables even database-inexperienced people to create databases and database applications. Unfortunately, the 'create without design' approach usually paves the way to any number of database disasters. In our experience, many, if not most, database system failures are traceable to poor design and cannot be solved with the help of even the best programmers and managers. Nor is better DBMS software likely to overcome problems created or magnified by poor design. Using an analogy, even the best bricklayers and carpenters can't create a good building from a bad blueprint.
- Most difficult problems associated with database system management seem to be triggered by poorly designed databases. It hardly seems worthwhile to use scarce resources to develop excellent and extensive database system management skills in order to exercise them on crises induced by poorly designed databases.
- Design provides an excellent means of communication. Clients are more likely to get what they need when database system design is approached carefully and thoughtfully. In fact, clients may discover how their organisations really function once a good database design is completed.
- Familiarity with database design techniques promotes one's understanding of current database technologies. For example, because data warehouses derive much of their data from operational databases, data warehouse concepts, structures, and procedures make more sense when the operational database's structure and implementation are understood.

Because the practical aspects of database design are stressed, we have covered design concepts and procedures in detail, making sure that the numerous end-of-chapter problems are sufficiently challenging for students to develop real and useful design skills. We also make sure that students understand the potential and actual conflicts between database design elegance, information requirements, and transaction processing speed. For example, it makes little sense to design databases that meet design elegance standards while they fail to meet end-user information requirements. Therefore, we explore the use of carefully defined trade-offs to ensure that the databases are capable of meeting end-user requirements while conforming to high design standards.

This edition retains the use of UML (Unified Modelling Language) notation for data modelling. Continual development by the Object Management Group has led to UML becoming an International Standard (UML 2.5.1 is available as the 2017 edition standard: ISO/IEC 19505-1 and 19505-2), which is continually reviewed. In keeping with the second edition, UML has continued to be used to produce entity relationship models within this third edition. However, as organisations still use both Chen and Crow's Foot notation approaches to data modelling in order to maintain legacy systems, it is important that familiarity is maintained. Appendix E, Comparison of ER Modelling Notations, contains coverage of both these notations.

CHANGES TO THE THIRD EDITION

In this third edition, we have added some new features and continued to strengthen the already strong database design coverage. Here are just a few of the highlights:

- To support the growth of Big Data and NoSQL technology, we have added a new Chapter 16: Big Data and NoSQL. The chapter focuses in greater depth on the characteristics of Big Data and the technologies that have been developed to support its use, including Hadoop and MongoDB.
- New and expanded coverage of data visualisation tools and techniques in Chapter 15, Databases for Business Intelligence.
- New and updated Business Vignettes to provide topical discussion points in the classroom.
- Coverage of MongoDB with hands-on exercises for querying MongoDB databases (Appendix Q).
- An additional appendix containing coverage of Neo4j with hands-on exercises for querying graph databases (Appendix R).

ACKNOWLEDGEMENTS

The publisher acknowledges the contribution of the following lecturers, who provided invaluable feedback on the second and third editions:

- Emilia Mwim, UNISA
- Patricia Alexander, University of Pretoria
- Judy van Biljon, UNISA
- Casper Wessels, Central University of Technology
- Theo Macdonald, University of the Free State
- Ismael Essop, University of Greenwich
- Chris Jakeman, Peterborough Regional College
- Andy Davies, Blackburn College
- Mick Ridley, University of Bradford
- Ray Turner, University of Essex
- Mark Green, Oxford Brookes University
- Duncan McPhee, University of Glamorgan

For this edition, I would like to say a special thanks to Pamela Quick, who previously worked as a Senior Lecturer in the School of Computing, Maths and Digital Technology at Manchester Metropolitan University. Her years of experience within the database field have been very valuable, specifically the coverage of relational algebra.

On this third edition, I have been lucky to work with a very patient, supportive and professional Publisher, Marinda Louw. Marinda provided fantastic support in answering all my emails. It has been a pleasure working with you.

Last, and certainly not least, thank you to my family (my ohana) for your patience and support.

Keeley Crockett
January 2020

ABOUT THE AUTHORS

Carlos Coronel is currently the Lab Director for the College of Business Computer Labs at Middle Tennessee State University. He has over 25 years of experience in various fields as a Database Administrator, Network Administrator, Web Manager and Technology Specialist, and has taught courses in Web development, database design and development, and data communications at the undergraduate and graduate levels.

Steven Morris completed his Bachelor of Science and PhD from Auburn University. He has taught Database Design and Development, Database Programming with Advanced SQL and PL/SQL, Systems Analysis and Design, and Principles of MIS at Middle Tennessee State University. Steven has published many articles, and currently serves on the review boards of several journals.

Dr Keeley Crockett is a Reader in Computational Intelligence in the School of Computing, Mathematics and Digital Technology at Manchester Metropolitan University. She gained a BSc Degree (Hons) in Computation from UMIST in 1993, and a PhD in the field of machine learning in 1998 entitled 'Fuzzy Rule Induction from Data Domains'. She has been teaching within the field of database systems and data engineering for 20 years to both undergraduate and postgraduate students. She leads the Computational Intelligence Research Lab, which has established a strong international presence for its research into Adaptive Psychological Profiling using artificial intelligence, fuzzy systems, and natural language dialogue systems. She has published over 125 refereed conference papers and journal articles in major international conferences and journals. She is an active volunteer in the IEEE undertaking many roles such as being a member of the IEEE Women in Engineering Leadership committee, and IEEE Women in Computational intelligence subcommittee among many other roles. Keeley is also proud to be a STEM Ambassador with a passion for outreach in computer science in rural schools.

Dr Craig Blewett has been researching and teaching in the area of Information Systems and Technology in South Africa for over 25 years. His Masters explored the application of Artificial Intelligence to database transaction management. His PhD, in education technology, resulted in the development of the Activated Classroom Teaching (ACT) model, a unique approach to teaching with technology. Craig is the founder of multiple technology companies and is the author of numerous books covering topics such as computer literacy, database systems, teaching with technology, running, and active living. He is also an internationally acclaimed speaker who is using his innovative approaches to help change education in our rapidly changing digital world.

WALK-THROUGH TOUR

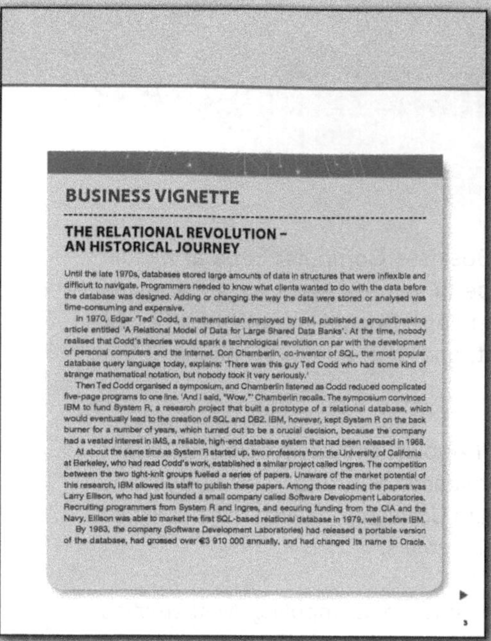

BUSINESS VIGNETTE

THE RELATIONAL REVOLUTION – AN HISTORICAL JOURNEY

Until the late 1970s, databases stored large amounts of data in structures that were inflexible and difficult to navigate. Programmers needed to know what clients wanted to do with the data before the database was designed. Adding or changing the way the data were stored or analysed was time-consuming and expensive.

In 1970, Edgar 'Ted' Codd, a mathematician employed by IBM, published a groundbreaking article entitled 'A Relational Model of Data for Large Shared Data Banks'. At the time, nobody realised that Codd's theories would spark a technological revolution on par with the development of personal computers and the Internet. Don Chamberlin, co-inventor of SQL, the most popular database query language today, explains: 'There was this guy Ted Codd who had some kind of strange mathematical notation, but nobody took it very seriously.'

Then Ted Codd organised a symposium, and Chamberlin listened as Codd reduced complicated five-page programs to one line. 'And I said, "Wow,"' Chamberlin recalls. The symposium convinced IBM to fund System R, a research project that built a prototype of a relational database, which would eventually lead to the creation of SQL and DB2. IBM, however, kept System R on the back burner for a number of years, which turned out to be a crucial decision, because the company had a vested interest in IMS, a reliable, high-end database system that had been released in 1968.

At about the same time as System R started up, two professors from the University of California at Berkeley, who had read Codd's work, established a similar project called Ingres. The competition between the two tight-knit groups fuelled a series of papers. Unaware of the market potential of this research, IBM allowed its staff to publish these papers. Among those reading the papers was Larry Ellison, who had just founded a small company called Software Development Laboratories. Recruiting programmers from System R and Ingres, and securing funding from the CIA and the Navy, Ellison was able to market the first SQL-based relational database in 1979, well before IBM.

By 1983, the company (Software Development Laboratories) had released a portable version of the database, had grossed over €3 910 000 annually, and had changed its name to Oracle.

3

Business Vignettes illustrate the part topics with a genuine scenario and show how the subject integrates with the real world.

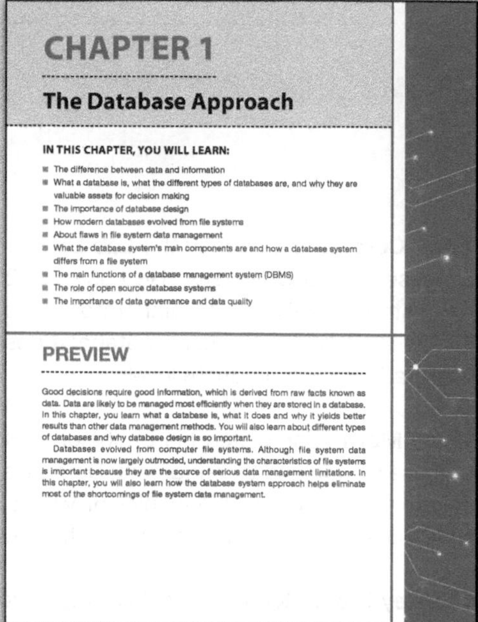

CHAPTER 1

The Database Approach

IN THIS CHAPTER, YOU WILL LEARN:

- The difference between data and information
- What a database is, what the different types of databases are, and why they are valuable assets for decision making
- The importance of database design
- How modern databases evolved from file systems
- About flaws in file system data management
- What the database system's main components are and how a database system differs from a file system
- The main functions of a database management system (DBMS)
- The role of open source database systems
- The importance of data governance and data quality

PREVIEW

Good decisions require good information, which is derived from raw facts known as data. Data are likely to be managed most efficiently when they are stored in a database. In this chapter, you learn what a database is, what it does and why it yields better results than other data management methods. You will also learn about different types of databases and why database design is so important.

Databases evolved from computer file systems. Although file system data management is now largely outmoded, understanding the characteristics of file systems is important because they are the source of serious data management limitations. In this chapter, you will also learn how the database system approach helps eliminate most of the shortcomings of file system data management.

Chapter Previews set the scene for the chapter and provide an overview of the chapter's contents.

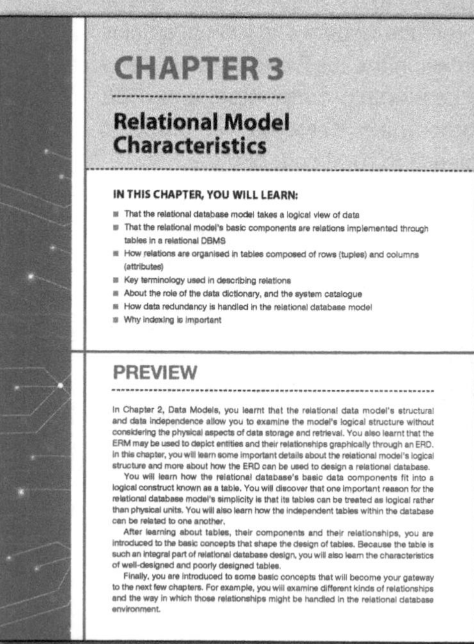

CHAPTER 3

Relational Model Characteristics

IN THIS CHAPTER, YOU WILL LEARN:

- That the relational database model takes a logical view of data
- That the relational model's basic components are relations implemented through tables in a relational DBMS
- How relations are organised in tables composed of rows (tuples) and columns (attributes)
- Key terminology used in describing relations
- About the role of the data dictionary, and the system catalogue
- How data redundancy is handled in the relational database model
- Why indexing is important

PREVIEW

In Chapter 2, Data Models, you learnt that the relational data model's structural and data independence allow you to examine the model's logical structure without considering the physical aspects of data storage and retrieval. You also learnt that the ERM may be used to depict entities and their relationships graphically through an ERD. In this chapter, you will learn some important details about the relational model's logical structure and more about how the ERD can be used to design a relational database.

You will learn how the relational database's basic data components fit into a logical construct known as a table. You will discover that one important reason for the relational database model's simplicity is that its tables can be treated as logical rather than physical units. You will also learn how the independent tables within the database can be related to one another.

After learning about tables, their components and their relationships, you are introduced to the basic concepts that shape the design of tables. Because the table is such an integral part of relational database design, you will also learn the characteristics of well-designed and poorly designed tables.

Finally, you are introduced to some basic concepts that will become your gateway to the next few chapters. For example, you will examine different kinds of relationships and the way in which those relationships might be handled in the relational database environment.

Learning Objectives appear at the start of each chapter to help you monitor your understanding and progress through each chapter. Each chapter also ends with a summary section that recaps the key content for revision purposes.

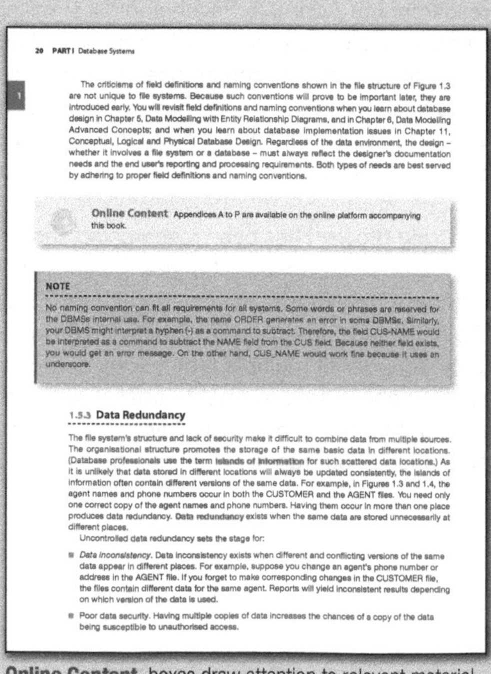

20 PART I Database Systems

1

The criticisms of field definitions and naming conventions shown in the file structure of Figure 1.3 are not unique to file systems. Because such conventions will prove to be important later, they are introduced early. You will revisit field definitions and naming conventions when you learn about database design in Chapter 5, Data Modelling with Entity Relationship Diagrams, and in Chapter 6, Data Modelling Advanced Concepts; and when you learn about database implementation issues in Chapter 11, Conceptual, Logical and Physical Database Design. Regardless of the data environment, the design – whether it involves a file system or a database – must always reflect the designer's documentation needs and the end user's reporting and processing requirements. Both types of needs are best served by adhering to proper field definitions and naming conventions.

Online Content Appendices A to P are available on the online platform accompanying this book.

NOTE

No naming convention can fit all requirements for all systems. Some words or phrases are reserved for the DBMSs internal use. For example, the name ORDER generates an error in some DBMSs. Similarly, your DBMS might interpret a hyphen (-) as a command to subtract. Therefore, the field CUS-NAME would be interpreted as a command to subtract the NAME field from the CUS field. Because neither field exists, you would get an error message. On the other hand, CUS_NAME would work fine because it uses an underscore.

1.5.3 Data Redundancy

The file system's structure and lack of security make it difficult to combine data from multiple sources. The organisational structure promotes the storage of the same basic data in different locations. (Database professionals use the term **islands of information** for such scattered data locations.) As it is unlikely that data stored in different locations will always be updated consistently, the islands of information often contain different versions of the same data. For example, in Figures 1.3 and 1.4, the agent names and phone numbers occur in both the CUSTOMER and the AGENT files. You need only one correct copy of the agent names and phone numbers. Having them occur in more than one place produces data redundancy. **Data redundancy** exists when the same data are stored unnecessarily at different places.

Uncontrolled data redundancy sets the stage for:

- *Data inconsistency*. Data inconsistency exists when different and conflicting versions of the same data appear in different places. For example, suppose you change an agent's phone number or address in the AGENT file. If you forget to make corresponding changes in the CUSTOMER file, the files contain different data for the same agent. Reports will yield inconsistent results depending on which version of the data is used.
- Poor data security. Having multiple copies of data increases the chances of a copy of the data being susceptible to unauthorised access.

Online Content boxes draw attention to relevant material on the online platform for this book.

Notes highlight important facts about the concepts introduced in the chapter.

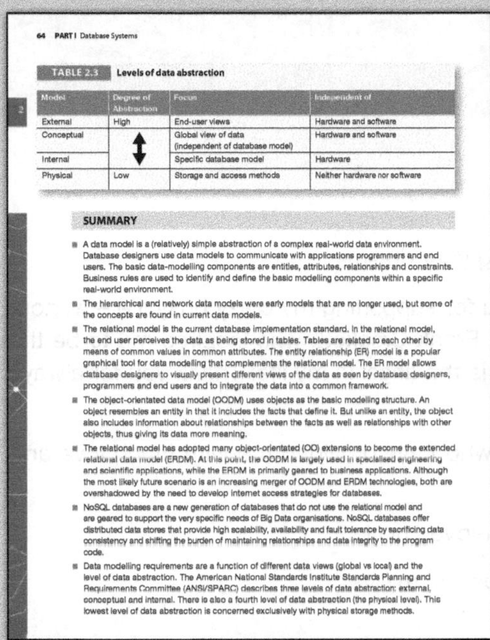

64 PART I Database Systems

TABLE 2.3 Levels of data abstraction

Model	Degree of Abstraction	Focus	Independent of
External	High	End-user views	Hardware and software
Conceptual	↕	Global view of data (independent of database model)	Hardware and software
Internal		Specific database model	Hardware
Physical	Low	Storage and access methods	Neither hardware nor software

SUMMARY

- A data model is a (relatively) simple abstraction of a complex real-world data environment. Database designers use data models to communicate with applications programmers and end users. The basic data-modelling components are entities, attributes, relationships and constraints. Business rules are used to identify and define the basic modelling components within a specific real-world environment.
- The hierarchical and network data models were early models that are no longer used, but some of the concepts are found in current data models.
- The relational model is the current database implementation standard. In the relational model, the end user perceives the data as being stored in tables. Tables are related to each other by means of common values in common attributes. The entity relationship (ER) model is a popular graphical tool for data modelling that complements the relational model. The ER model allows database designers to visually present different views of the data as seen by database designers, programmers and end users and to integrate the data into a common framework.
- The object-orientated data model (OODM) uses objects as the basic modelling structure. An object resembles an entity in that it includes the facts that define it. But unlike an entity, the object also includes information about relationships between the facts as well as relationships with other objects, thus giving its data more meaning.
- The relational model has adopted many object-orientated (OO) extensions to become the extended relational data model (ERDM). At this point, the OODM is largely used in specialised engineering and scientific applications, while the ERDM is primarily geared to business applications. Although the most likely future scenario is an increasing merger of OODM and ERDM technologies, both are overshadowed by the need to develop internet access strategies for databases.
- NoSQL databases are a new generation of databases that do not use the relational model and are geared to support the very specific needs of Big Data organisations. NoSQL databases offer distributed data stores that provide high scalability, availability and fault tolerance by sacrificing data consistency and shifting the burden of maintaining relationships and data integrity to the program code.
- Data modelling requirements are a function of different data views (global vs local) and the level of data abstraction. The American National Standards Institute Standards Planning and Requirements Committee (ANSI/SPARC) describes three levels of data abstraction: external, conceptual and internal. There is also a fourth level of data abstraction (the physical level). This lowest level of data abstraction is concerned exclusively with physical storage methods.

Summary Each chapter ends with a comprehensive summary that provides a thorough recap of the issues in each chapter, helping you to assess your understanding and revise key content.

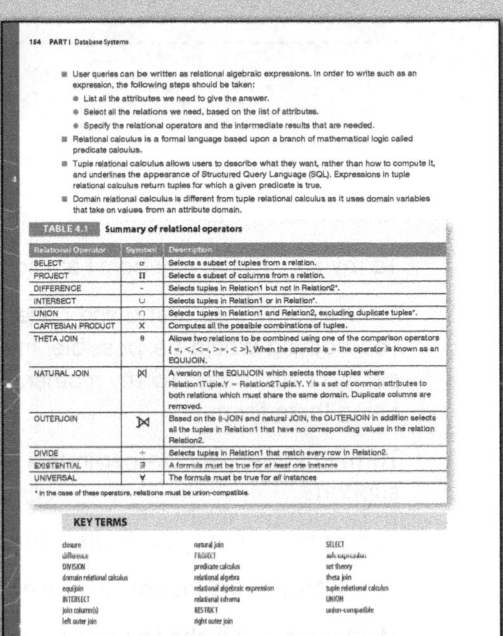

154 PART I Database Systems

- User queries can be written as relational algebraic expressions. In order to write such as an expression, the following steps should be taken:
  - List all the attributes we need to give the answer.
  - Select all the relations we need, based on the list of attributes.
  - Specify the relational operators and the intermediate results that are needed.
- Relational calculus is a formal language based upon a branch of mathematical logic called predicate calculus.
- Tuple relational calculus allows users to describe what they want, rather than how to compute it, and underlines the appearance of Structured Query Language (SQL). Expressions in tuple relational calculus return tuples for which a given predicate is true.
- Domain relational calculus is different from tuple relational calculus as it uses domain variables that take on values from an attribute domain.

TABLE 4.1 Summary of relational operators

Relational Operator	Symbol	Description
SELECT	σ	Selects a subset of tuples from a relation.
PROJECT	Π	Selects a subset of columns from a relation.
DIFFERENCE	-	Selects tuples in Relation1 but not in Relation2*.
INTERSECT	∪	Selects tuples in Relation1 or in Relation*.
UNION	∩	Selects tuples in Relation1 and Relation2, excluding duplicate tuples*.
CARTESIAN PRODUCT	X	Computes all the possible combinations of tuples.
THETA JOIN	θ	Allows two relations to be combined using one of the comparison operators {=, <, <=, >=, < >}. When the operator is = the operator is known as an EQUIJOIN.
NATURAL JOIN	⋈	A version of the EQUIJOIN which selects those tuples where Relation1Tuple.Y = Relation2Tuple.Y. Y is a set of common attributes to both relations which must share the same domain. Duplicate columns are removed.
OUTERJOIN	⟗	Based on the θ-JOIN and natural JOIN, the OUTERJOIN in addition selects all the tuples in Relation1 that have no corresponding values in the relation Relation2.
DIVIDE	÷	Selects tuples in Relation1 that match every row in Relation2.
EXISTENTIAL	∃	A formula must be true for *at least one* instance
UNIVERSAL	∀	The formula must be true for *all* instances

* In the case of these operators, relations must be union-compatible.

KEY TERMS

closure
difference
DIVISION
domain relational calculus
equijoin
INTERSECT
join column(s)
left outer join
natural join
PROJECT
predicate calculus
relational algebra
relational algebraic expression
relational schema
RESTRICT
right outer join
SELECT
[illegible]
set theory
theta join
tuple relational calculus
UNION
union-compatible

Key Terms are listed at the end of the chapter and explained in full in a Glossary at the end of the book, enabling you to find explanations of key terms quickly.

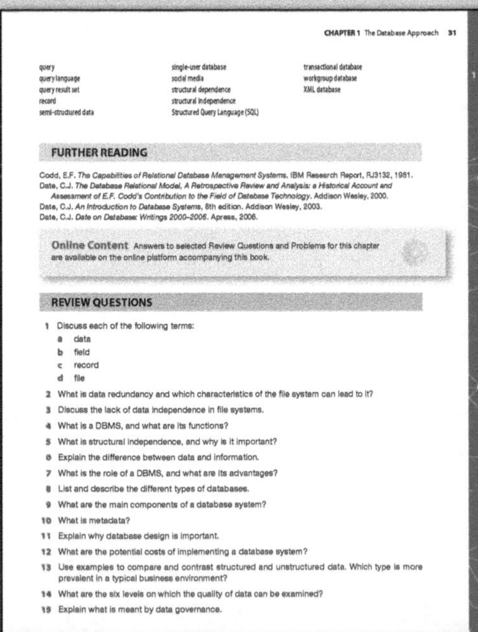

CHAPTER 1 The Database Approach 31

query
query language
query result set
record
semi-structured data
single-user database
social media
structural dependence
structural independence
Structured Query Language (SQL)
transactional database
workgroup database
XML database

FURTHER READING

Codd, E.F. *The Capabilities of Relational Database Management Systems*. IBM Research Report, RJ3132, 1981.
Date, C.J. *The Database Relational Model, A Retrospective Review and Analysis: a Historical Account and Assessment of E.F. Codd's Contribution to the Field of Database Technology*. Addison Wesley, 2000.
Date, C.J. *An Introduction to Database Systems*, 8th edition. Addison Wesley, 2003.
Date, C.J. *Date on Database: Writings 2000–2006*. Apress, 2006.

Online Content Answers to selected Review Questions and Problems for this chapter are available on the online platform accompanying this book.

REVIEW QUESTIONS

1 Discuss each of the following terms:
   a data
   b field
   c record
   d file
2 What is data redundancy and which characteristics of the file system can lead to it?
3 Discuss the lack of data independence in file systems.
4 What is a DBMS, and what are its functions?
5 What is structural independence, and why is it important?
6 Explain the difference between data and information.
7 What is the role of a DBMS, and what are its advantages?
8 List and describe the different types of databases.
9 What are the main components of a database system?
10 What is metadata?
11 Explain why database design is important.
12 What are the potential costs of implementing a database system?
13 Use examples to compare and contrast structured and unstructured data. Which type is more prevalent in a typical business environment?
14 What are the six levels on which the quality of data can be examined?
15 Explain what is meant by data governance.

Further Reading allows you to explore the subject further, and acts as a starting point for projects and assignments. **Review Questions** help reinforce and test your knowledge and understanding, and provide a basis for group discussions and activities.

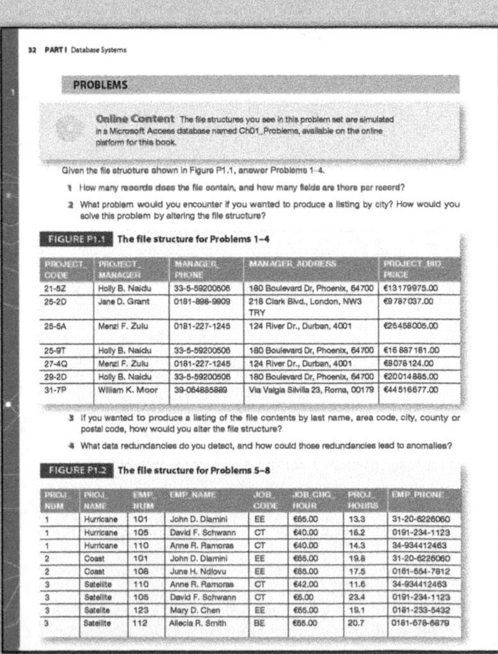

32 PART I Database Systems

PROBLEMS

Online Content The file structures you see in this problem set are simulated in a Microsoft Access database named Ch01_Problems, available on the online platform for this book.

Given the file structure shown in Figure P1.1, answer Problems 1–4.

1 How many records does the file contain, and how many fields are there per record?
2 What problem would you encounter if you wanted to produce a listing by city? How would you solve this problem by altering the file structure?

FIGURE P1.1 The file structure for Problems 1–4

PROJECT_CODE	PROJECT_MANAGER	MANAGER_PHONE	MANAGER_ADDRESS	PROJECT_BID_PRICE
21-5Z	Holly B. Naidu	33-5-59200506	180 Boulevard Dr, Phoenix, 64700	€13179975.00
25-2D	Jane D. Grant	0181-898-9909	218 Clark Blvd., London, NW3 TRY	€9787037.00
25-5A	Menzi F. Zulu	0181-227-1245	124 River Dr., Durban, 4001	€25458005.00
25-9T	Holly B. Naidu	33-5-59200506	180 Boulevard Dr, Phoenix, 64700	€16887181.00
27-4Q	Menzi F. Zulu	0181-227-1245	124 River Dr., Durban, 4001	€8078124.00
29-2D	Holly B. Naidu	33-5-59200506	180 Boulevard Dr, Phoenix, 64700	€20014885.00
31-7P	William K. Moor	39-064885889	Via Valgia Silvilla 23, Roma, 00179	€44516677.00

3 If you wanted to produce a listing of the file contents by last name, area code, city, county or postal code, how would you alter the file structure?
4 What data redundancies do you detect, and how could those redundancies lead to anomalies?

FIGURE P1.2 The file structure for Problems 5–8

PROJ_NUM	PROJ_NAME	EMP_NUM	EMP_NAME	JOB_CODE	JOB_CHG_HOUR	PROJ_HOURS	EMP_PHONE
1	Hurricane	101	John D. Dlamini	EE	€65.00	13.3	31-20-6226060
1	Hurricane	105	David F. Schwann	CT	€40.00	16.2	0191-234-1123
1	Hurricane	110	Anne R. Ramoras	CT	€40.00	14.3	34-934412463
2	Coast	101	John D. Dlamini	EE	€65.00	19.8	31-20-6226060
2	Coast	108	June H. Ndlovu	EE	€65.00	17.5	0161-554-7812
3	Satellite	110	Anne R. Ramoras	CT	€42.00	11.6	34-934412463
3	Satellite	105	David F. Schwann	CT	€6.00	23.4	0191-234-1123
3	Satelite	123	Mary D. Chen	EE	€65.00	19.1	0181-233-5432
3	Satellite	112	Allecia R. Smith	BE	€65.00	20.7	0181-678-6879

Problems become progressively more complex as students draw on the lessons learnt from the completion of preceding problems.

DEDICATION

To my son, Kona, of whom I am so proud – keep following your dreams.

To Craig, my best friend and patient husband. Thank you for supporting my crazy busy life – without you nothing would be possible. In memory of my father, Frank Crockett, who inspired me to be the person I am today. To my mother, Norma Crockett, who is the angel in my life. Thank you for always being there for me.

To my mother- and father-in-law Jackie and Bill Smith who have provided me with much love and support.

In memory of Leslie Crockett, a true gentleman and much-loved uncle.

To my family and friends, all of whom have painted rainbows in my life.

Much love and aloha to you all.

Keeley Crockett

DATABASE PRINCIPLES

Part I

DATABASE SYSTEMS

BUSINESS VIGNETTE

THE RELATIONAL REVOLUTION – AN HISTORICAL JOURNEY

Until the late 1970s, databases stored large amounts of data in structures that were inflexible and difficult to navigate. Programmers needed to know what clients wanted to do with the data before the database was designed. Adding or changing the way the data were stored or analysed was time-consuming and expensive.

In 1970, Edgar 'Ted' Codd, a mathematician employed by IBM, published a groundbreaking article entitled 'A Relational Model of Data for Large Shared Data Banks'. At the time, nobody realised that Codd's theories would spark a technological revolution on par with the development of personal computers and the internet. Don Chamberlin, co-inventor of SQL, the most popular database query language today, explains: 'There was this guy Ted Codd who had some kind of strange mathematical notation, but nobody took it very seriously.'

Then Ted Codd organised a symposium, and Chamberlin listened as Codd reduced complicated five-page programs to one line. 'And I said, "Wow,"' Chamberlin recalls. The symposium convinced IBM to fund System R, a research project that built a prototype of a relational database, which would eventually lead to the creation of SQL and DB2. IBM, however, kept System R on the back burner for a number of years, which turned out to be a crucial decision, because the company had a vested interest in IMS, a reliable, high-end database system that had been released in 1968.

At about the same time as System R started up, two professors from the University of California at Berkeley, who had read Codd's work, established a similar project called Ingres. The competition between the two tight-knit groups fuelled a series of papers. Unaware of the market potential of this research, IBM allowed its staff to publish these papers. Among those reading the papers was Larry Ellison, who had just founded a small company called Software Development Laboratories. Recruiting programmers from System R and Ingres, and securing funding from the CIA and the Navy, Ellison was able to market the first SQL-based relational database in 1979, well before IBM.

By 1983, the company (Software Development Laboratories) had released a portable version of the database, had grossed over €3 910 000 annually, and had changed its name to Oracle.

Spurred on by competition, IBM finally released SQL/DS, its first relational database, in 1980.[1] In 2008, a group of leading database researchers met in Berkeley and issued a report declaring that the industry had reached an exciting turning point and was on the verge of another database revolution.[2]

In 2010, Oracle acquired MySQL as part of its acquisition of Sun. It has since maintained the free open-source MySQL Community Edition while providing several versions (Standard Edition, Enterprise Edition and Cluster Edition) for commercial customers. In 2019, the release of MySQL Document Store brought together the SQL and the NoSQL languages, enabling developers to link SQL relational tables to schema-less NoSQL databases.[3] Oracle's latest offering is Oracle Database 19c, where the 'c' represents cloud; new versions now come out every year.

In our historical journey, we must also mention PostgreSQL, developed in1986 as part of the POSTGRES project at the University of California at Berkeley. PostgreSQL[4] is a free, open source, object-relational database that extends the traditional SQL language by allowing creation of new datatypes and functions, and the ability to write code in different programming languages. It is a strong competitor to MySQL, given that it has had over 33 years of active development.

Analysts, journalists and business leaders continually see new developments with data acquisition and its management, such as the explosion of unstructured data, the growing importance of business intelligence, and the emergence of cloud technologies, which may require the development of new database models. Although traditional relational databases meet rigorous standards for data integrity and consistency, they do not scale unstructured data as well as new database models such as NoSQL. NoSQL is also known as a non-relational database, which allows the storage and retrieval of unstructured data using a dynamic schema. A key question asked by database developers today is whether they need a NoSQL database or an SQL database for their application. For example, Twitter and Facebook, which do not require high levels of data consistency and integrity, have adopted NoSQL databases. In 2019, businesses are opting for SQL and NoSQL multiple database combinations, which suggests that one size does not fit all.

As of March 2019, the most popular database management systems worldwide were Oracle, MySQL, Microsoft SQL and PostgreSQL.[5] So, what is the future? Disruptive database technologies are required for business to remain competitive and the key is real-time data. Alternative database models such as cloud database platforms, which have the capability for real-time data analytics, are for certain. Big data has a role to play as additional data sources must be processed using data pipelines, all in accordance with the new General Data Protection Regulation (GDPR) data regulations. The relational model will survive, but it will also adapt at unprecedented speed.

---

1 'IBM and Oracle Trade Barbs over Databases', https://phys.org/news/2007-05-ibm-oracle-barbs-databases.html

2 Rakesh Agrawal et al.,'The Claremont Report on Database Research', http://db.cs.berkeley.edu/claremont/claremontreport08.pdf.

3 MySQL Editions, www.mysql.com/products/

4 PostgreSQL, www.postgresql.org/about/

5 Top 10 Databases for 2019, The Database Journal, www.databasejournal.com/features/oracle/slideshows/top-10-2019-databases.html

CHAPTER 1

The Database Approach

IN THIS CHAPTER, YOU WILL LEARN:

- The difference between data and information
- What a database is, what the different types of databases are, and why they are valuable assets for decision making
- The importance of database design
- How modern databases evolved from file systems
- About flaws in file system data management
- What the database system's main components are and how a database system differs from a file system
- The main functions of a database management system (DBMS)
- The role of open source database systems
- The importance of data governance and data quality

PREVIEW

Good decisions require good information, which is derived from raw facts known as data. Data are likely to be managed most efficiently when they are stored in a database. In this chapter, you learn what a database is, what it does and why it yields better results than other data management methods. You will also learn about different types of databases and why database design is so important.

Databases evolved from computer file systems. Although file system data management is now largely outmoded, understanding the characteristics of file systems is important because they are the source of serious data management limitations. In this chapter, you will also learn how the database system approach helps eliminate most of the shortcomings of file system data management.

1.1 DATA VS INFORMATION

To understand what drives database design, you need to understand the difference between data and information. **Data** are raw facts. The word *raw* indicates that the facts have not yet been processed to reveal their meaning. For example, suppose that you want to know what the users of a computer lab think of its services. Typically, you would begin by surveying users to assess the computer lab's performance. Figure 1.1, Panel (a), shows the Web survey form that enables users to respond to your questions. When the survey form has been completed, the form's raw data are saved to a data repository, such as the one shown in Figure 1.1, Panel (b). Although you now have the facts in hand, they are not particularly useful in this format – reading page after page of zeros and ones is not likely to provide much insight. Therefore, you transform the raw data into a data summary like the one shown in Figure 1.1, Panel (c). It is now possible to get quick answers to questions such as, 'What is the composition of our lab's customer base?' In this case, you can quickly determine that most of your customers are second-year undergraduates (38 per cent) and first-year undergraduates (32 per cent). And, because graphics can enhance your ability to extract meaning from data quickly, you show the data summary bar graph in Figure 1.1, Panel (d).

FIGURE 1.1 Transforming raw data into information

(a) Initial survey screen

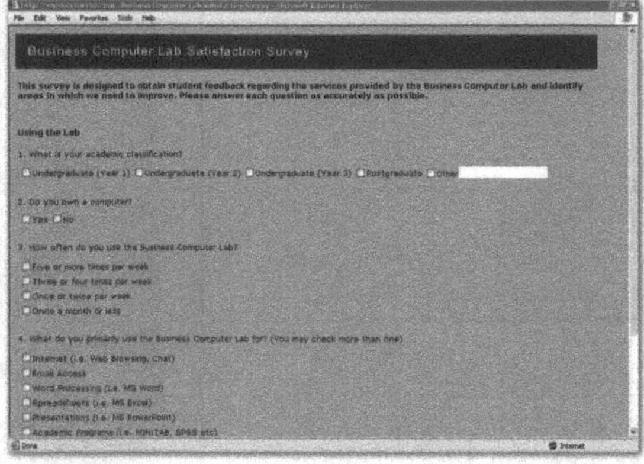

(b) Raw data

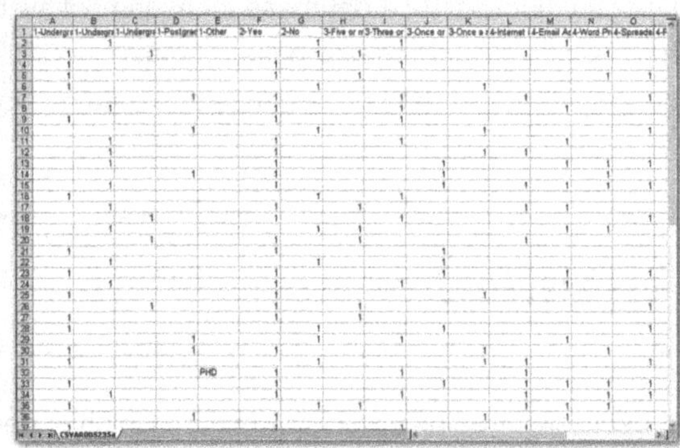

(c) Information in summary format

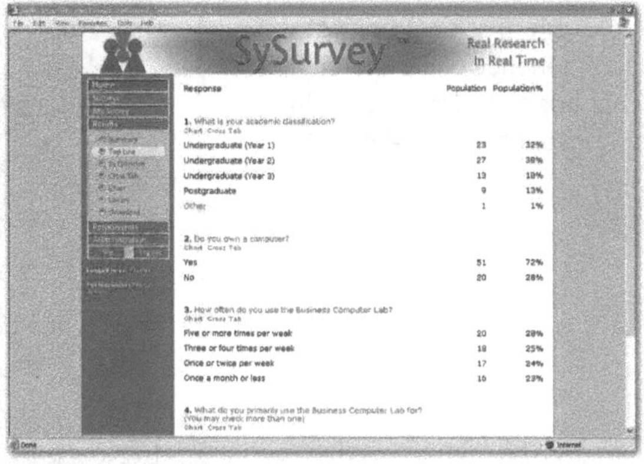

(d) Information in graphic format

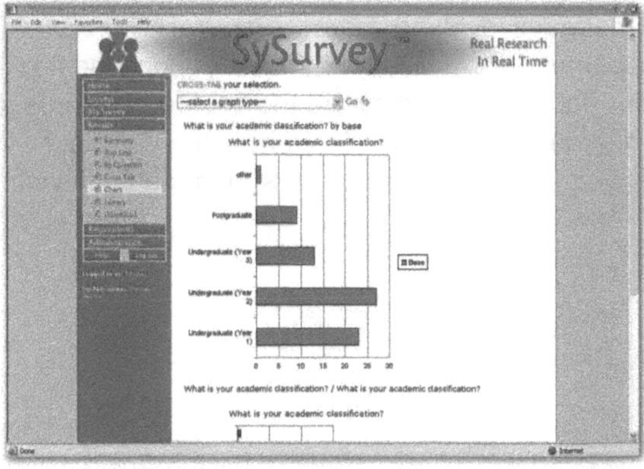

Information is the result of processing raw data to reveal its meaning. Data processing may be as simple as organising data to reveal patterns or as complex as making forecasts or drawing inferences using statistical modelling. Such information can then be used as the foundation for decision making. For example, the data summary for each question on the survey form can point out the lab's strengths and weaknesses, helping you to make informed decisions to better meet the needs of lab customers.

Raw data must be properly *formatted* for storage, processing and presentation. For example, the student classification in Figure 1.1, Panel (c) is formatted to show the results based on the classifications undergraduates years 1 to 3, postgraduates and a category 'other'. The respondents' yes/no responses may need to be converted to a Y/N format for data storage. More complex formatting is required when working with complex data types such as sounds, videos or images.

In this 'information age', production of accurate, relevant and timely information is the key to good decision making. In turn, good decision making is the key to business survival in a global market. We are now said to be entering the 'knowledge age'.[6] Data are the foundation of information, which is the bedrock of **knowledge** – that is, the body of information and facts about a specific subject. Knowledge implies familiarity, awareness and understanding of information as it applies to an environment. A key characteristic of knowledge is that 'new' knowledge can be derived from 'old' knowledge.

Let's summarise some key points:

- Data constitute the building blocks of information.
- Information is produced by processing data.
- Information is used to reveal the meaning of data.
- Accurate, relevant and timely information is the key to good decision making.
- Good decision making is the key to organisational survival in a global environment.

Timely and useful information requires accurate data. Such data must be generated properly, and they must be stored in a format that is easy to access and process. And, like any basic resource, the data environment must be managed carefully. **Data management** is a discipline that focuses on the proper generation, storage and retrieval of data. Given the crucial role that data play, it should not surprise you that data management is a core activity for any business, government agency, service organisation or charity.

1.1.1 Data Quality and Data Governance

The quality of the data within the database is essential if the organisation is to make accurate short- and long-term business decisions. Data must be fit for purpose and this often means that it can be used to develop new strategies which aim to increase the income generation of an organisation. **Data quality** can be examined at a number of different levels, including:

- Accuracy: Is the data accurate and has it been obtained from a verifiable source?
- Relevance: Is the data relevant to the organisation?
- Completeness: Is the required data being stored?
- Timeliness: Is the data updated frequently in order to meet the business requirements?

---

6 Peter Drucker coined the phrase 'knowledge worker' in 1959 in his book *Landmarks of Tomorrow*. In 1994, Ms Esther Dyson, Mr George Gilder, Dr George Keyworth and Dr Alvin Toffler introduced the concept of the 'knowledge age'.

- Uniqueness: Is the data unique and without redundancy?
- Unambiguous: Is the meaning of the data clear?

The above list is not exhaustive. Most countries will have their own laws on the storage of data which an organisation must adhere to. For example, the General Data Protection Regulation (GDPR), which governs collecting and processing data, became a legal requirement for all organisations in Europe from 25 May 2018. One of the major changes detailed in Article 22 of the GDPR includes the rights of an individual not to be subject to automated decision making, which includes profiling, unless explicit consent is given. Individuals who are subject to such decision making have the right to ask for an explanation of how the decision is reached and organisations must utilise appropriate mathematical and statistical procedures. South Africa has the Protection of Personal Information Act (POPIA) which was signed into law in 2013. POPIA promotes the protection of personal information by public and private bodies.

Data governance is the term used to describe a strategy or methodology defined by an organisation to safeguard data quality. Each organisation produces its own data governance strategy that will involve the development of a series of policies and procedures for managing availability, usability, quality, integrity and security of data within the organisation. For example, the strategy defines who owns the data within the organisation and who is authorised to create, update and delete new records in the database. Master Data Management (MDM) is a component of a data governance strategy that provides the technological foundation for implementation of the strategy. MDM ensures that data is consistent and accurate across all systems within an organisation and provides technology to allow the auditing, reporting and compliance of data.

Creating a data governance strategy is a complex and time-consuming task and will involve many people working at different levels within the organisation. Once the strategy has been developed and put into operation, it will take the organisation several months to ensure that all data complies with the strategy. Once in place, the polices and the procedures of the strategy should be regularly measured and monitored to ensure that they are being followed. This will allow continual monitoring of the data governance strategy to ensure that it is still relevant and up to date for the purpose of the organisation. Data profiling and data quality tools are often used as part of the monitoring process to keep track of data over time.

1.2 INTRODUCING THE DATABASE AND THE DBMS

Efficient data management typically requires the use of a computer database. A **database** is a shared, integrated computer structure that stores a collection of:

- end-user data, or raw facts of interest to the end user
- **metadata**, or data about data, through which the end-user data are integrated and managed.

The metadata provide a description of the data characteristics and the set of relationships that link the data found within the database. In a sense, a database resembles a very well-organised electronic filing cabinet in which powerful software, known as a *database management system*, helps manage the cabinet's contents. A **database management system (DBMS)** is a collection of programs that manages the database structure and controls access to the data stored in the database.

1.2.1 Role and Advantages of the DBMS

Figure 1.2 illustrates that the DBMS serves as the intermediary between the user and the database. The DBMS receives all application requests and translates them into the complex operations required to fulfil those requests. The DBMS hides much of the database's internal complexity from the application programs and users. The application program might be written by a programmer using a programming language such as Python, Visual Basic, C++ or Java, or it might be created through a DBMS utility program.

FIGURE 1.2 **The DBMS manages the interaction between the end user and the database**

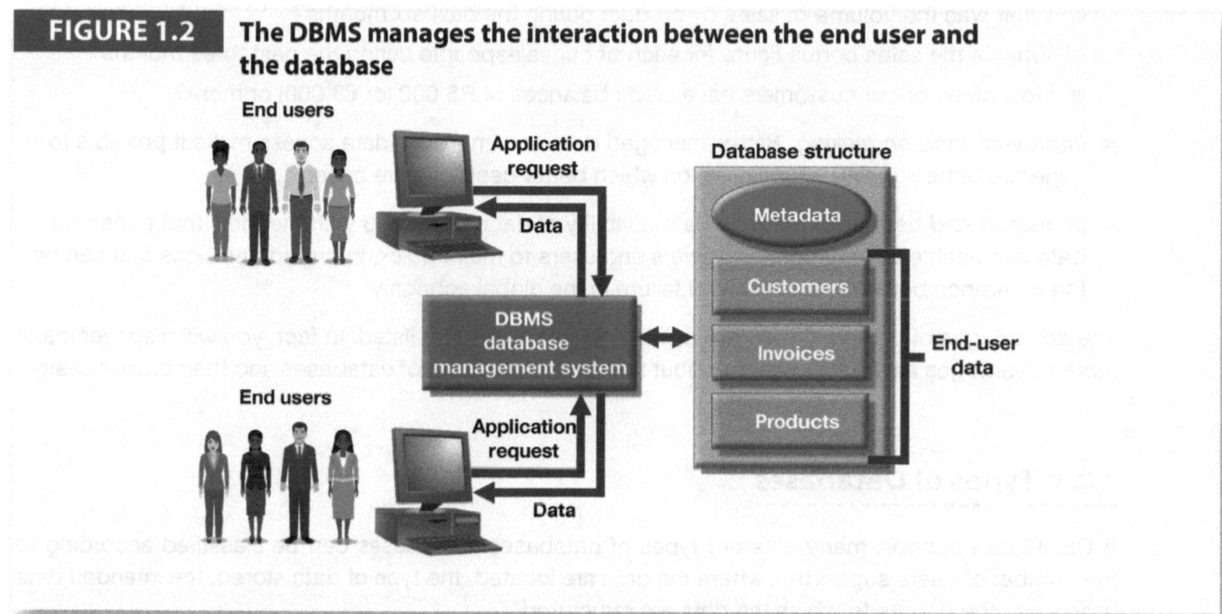

Having a DBMS between the end user's applications and the database offers some important advantages. First, the DBMS enables the data in the database *to be shared* among multiple applications or users. Second, the DBMS *integrates* the many different users' views of the data into a single all-encompassing data repository.

Because data are the crucial raw material from which information is derived, you need a good way of managing such data. As you will discover in this book, the DBMS helps make data management more efficient and effective. In particular, a DBMS provides advantages such as:

- *Improved data sharing*. The DBMS helps create an environment in which end users have better access to more and better-managed data. Such access makes it possible for end users to respond quickly to changes in their environment.
- *Better data integration*. Wider access to well-managed data promotes an integrated view of the organisation's operations and a clearer view of the big picture. It becomes much easier to see how actions in one segment of the company affect other segments.
- *Minimised data inconsistency*. **Data inconsistency** exists when different versions of the same data appear in different places. For example, data inconsistency exists when a company's sales department stores a sales representative's name as 'Thobile Cele' and the company's personnel department stores that same person's name as 'Bathobile M. Cele' or when the company's regional sales office shows the price of product X as R390.00 in South African currency and its national sales office shows the same product's price as R350.00. The probability of data inconsistency is greatly reduced in a properly designed database.
- *Improved data access*. The DBMS makes it possible to produce quick answers to ad hoc queries. From a database perspective, a **query** is a specific request for data manipulation (for example,

to read or update the data) issued to the DBMS. Simply put, a query is a question and an **ad hoc query** is a spur-of-the-moment question. The DBMS sends back an answer (called the **query result set**) to the application. For example, end users, when dealing with large amounts of sales data, might want quick answers to questions (ad hoc queries) such as:

- What was the volume of sales by product during the past six months?
- What is the sales bonus figure for each of our salespeople during the past three months?
- How many of our customers have credit balances of R5 000 (or €3 000) or more?

- *Improved decision making*. Better-managed data and improved data access make it possible to generate better-quality information, on which better decisions are based.
- *Increased end-user productivity*. The availability of data, combined with the tools that transform data into usable information, empowers end users to make quick, informed decisions that can be the difference between success and failure in the global economy.

The advantages of using a DBMS are not limited to the few just listed. In fact, you will discover many more advantages as you learn more about the technical details of databases and their proper design.

1.2.2 Types of Databases

A DBMS can support many different types of databases. Databases can be classified according to the number of users supported, where the data are located, the type of data stored, the intended data usage and the degree to which the data are structured.

The number of users determines whether the database is classified as single-user or multi-user. A **single-user database** supports only one user at a time. In other words, if user A is using the database, users B and C must wait until user A is done. A single-user database that runs on a personal computer is called a **desktop database**. In contrast, a **multi-user database** supports multiple users at the same time. When the multi-user database supports a relatively small number of users (usually fewer than 50) or a specific department within an organisation, it is called a **workgroup database**. When the database is used by the entire organisation and supports many users (more than 50, usually hundreds) across many departments, the database is known as an **enterprise database**.

Location might also be used to classify the database. For example, a database that supports data located at a single site is called a **centralised database**. A database that supports data distributed across several different sites is called a **distributed database**. The extent to which a database can be distributed, and the way in which such distribution is managed, is addressed in detail in Chapter 14, Distributed Databases.

The most popular way of classifying databases today, however, is based on how they will be used and on the time sensitivity of the information gathered from them. For example, transactions such as product or service sales, payments and supply purchases reflect critical day-to-day operations. Such transactions must be recorded accurately and immediately. A database that is designed primarily to support a company's day-to-day operations is classified as an **operational database**, also referred to as an **online transaction processing (OLTP)**, **transactional** or **production database**.

Typically, analytical databases comprise two main components: a data warehouse and an **online analytical processing (OLAP)** front end. The data warehouse is a specialised database that stores data in a format optimised for decision support. The data warehouse contains historical data obtained from the operational databases as well as data from other external sources. Online analytical processing is a set of tools that work together to provide an advanced data analysis environment for retrieving, processing and modelling data from the data warehouse. In recent times, this area of database application has grown in importance and usage, to the point that it has evolved into its own discipline: business intelligence. The term '**business intelligence**' describes a comprehensive approach to capturing and processing business data with the purpose of generating information to support business decision making. (See Chapter 15, Databases for Business Intelligence.)

Databases can also be classified to reflect the degree to which the data are structured. Unstructured data are data that exist in their original (raw) state – that is, in the format in which they were collected. Therefore, unstructured data exist in a format that does not lend itself to the processing that yields information. Structured data are the result of formatting unstructured data to facilitate its storage and use, and the generation of information. You apply structure (format) based on the type of processing that you intend to perform on the data. Some data might not be ready (unstructured) for some types of processing, but they might be ready (structured) for other types of processing. For example, the data value 37890 might refer to a postal code, a sales value or a product code. If this value represents a postal code or a product code and is stored as text, you cannot perform mathematical computations with it. On the other hand, if this value represents a sales transaction, it must be formatted as numeric.

To illustrate the concept of structure further, imagine a stack of printed paper invoices. If you merely want to store these invoices as images for future retrieval and display, you can scan them and save them in a graphic format. On the other hand, if you want to derive information such as monthly totals and average sales, such graphic storage would not be useful. Instead, you could store the invoice data in a (structured) spreadsheet format so that you can perform the requisite computations. Actually, most data you encounter are best classified as **semi-structured**. Semi-structured data have already been processed to some extent. For example, if you look at a typical Web page, the data are presented in a prearranged format to convey some information. The database types mentioned thus far focus on the storage and management of highly structured data. However, corporations are not limited to the use of structured data. They also use semi-structured and unstructured data. Just think of the valuable information that can be found in company emails, memos and documents such as procedures, rules and Web pages. Unstructured and semi-structured data storage and management needs are being addressed through a new generation of databases known as XML databases. **Extensible Markup Language (XML)** is a special language used to represent and manipulate data elements in a textual format. An **XML database** supports the storage and management of semi-structured XML data. XML databases will be discussed in more detail in Chapter 16, Database Connectivity and Web Technologies.

Analytical databases focus primarily on storing historical data and business metrics used exclusively for tactical or strategic decision making. Such analysis typically requires extensive 'data massaging' (data manipulation) to produce information on which to base pricing decisions, sales forecasts, market strategies and so on. Analytical databases allow the end user to perform advanced data analysis of business data using sophisticated tools.

In contrast, a **data warehouse** focuses primarily on storing data used to generate information required to make tactical or strategic decisions. Such decisions typically require extensive 'data massaging' (data manipulation) to extract information to formulate pricing decisions, sales forecasts, market positioning, etc. Most decisions supported by data are based on historical data obtained from operational databases. Additionally, the data warehouse can store data derived from many sources. To make it easier to retrieve such data, the data warehouse structure is quite different from that of a transactional database. The design, implementation and use of data warehouses are covered in detail in Chapter 15, Databases for Business Intelligence.

Table 1.1 compares features of several well-known database management systems.

TABLE 1.1 Types of databases

Product	Number Of Users			Data Location		Data Usage		XML
	Single User	Multi-user						
		Workgroup	Enterprise	Centralised	Distributed	Operational	Analytical	
MS Access	X	X		X		X		X
MS SQL Server	X[3]	X	X	X	X	X		X
IBM DB2	X[3]	X	X	X	X	X	X	X
MySQL	X	X	X	X	X	X	X	X
Oracle RDBMS	X[3]	X	X	X	X	X	X	X

All the database management systems shown in Table 1.1 (except MySQL) are provided by commercial vendors and require a significant investment from a company in order to buy the actual DBMS, its applications and ongoing support and maintenance. MySQL[7] is an **open source** database system which allows users to build and modify a database of their choice, distribute the database and improve the actual MySQL DBMS 'product'. The idea is that users can develop the database system for any purpose, look at the source code and make any improvements, which will then be released back to the general public.

The main benefit of open source software is that it is free to acquire and use the product itself. However, there will be costs involved in the development and ongoing support of the software. The term 'LAMP' is used to define the most popular open source software, namely: Linux, Apache Web server, MySQL DBMS and the Perl PHP/Python development languages. Together this software stack provides the basic building blocks for developing websites. Typically, open source database management system products such as MySQL and PostgreSQL[8] are easier to use than large-scale vendor DBMS products as they stick to the basic fundamental database principles. This makes them ideal for smaller companies and organisations to develop database-centred applications quickly. A disadvantage of open source software is that it does not provide the robust functionality and durability required by large-scale commercial systems.

With the emergence of the World Wide Web and internet-based technologies as the basis for the new 'social media' generation, great amounts of data are being stored and analysed. **Social media** refers to Web and mobile technologies that enable 'anywhere, anytime, always on' human interactions. Websites such as Google, Facebook, Instagram, Twitter and LinkedIn capture vast amounts of data about end users and consumers. These data grow exponentially and require the use of specialised database systems. Over the past few years, this new breed of specialised database has grown in sophistication and widespread usage. Currently, this new type of database is known as a NoSQL database. The term **NoSQL**[9] (Not only SQL) is generally used to describe a new generation of database management systems that is not based on the traditional relational database model. You will learn more about NoSQL in Chapter 16 Big Data and NoSQL.

---

7 mysql.com Available: www.mysql.com/

8 PostGres Available: www.postgresql.org/

9 NoSQL Available: http://nosql-database.org/

NOTE

Most of the database design, implementation and management issues addressed in this book are based on production (transactional) databases. The focus on production databases is based on two considerations. First, production databases are the databases most frequently encountered in common activities such as enrolling in a class, registering a car, buying a product or making a bank deposit or withdrawal. Second, data warehouse databases derive most of their data from production databases, and if production databases are poorly designed, the data warehouse databases based on them will lose their reliability and value as well.

1.3 WHY DATABASE DESIGN IS IMPORTANT

Database design refers to the activities that focus on the design of the database structure that will be used to store and manage end-user data. A good database – that is, a database that meets all user requirements – does not just happen; its structure must be designed carefully. In fact, database design is such a crucial aspect of working with databases that most of this book is dedicated to the development of good database design techniques. Even a good DBMS will perform poorly with a badly designed database.

Proper database design requires the database designer to identify precisely the database's expected use. Designing a transactional database emphasises accurate and consistent data and operational speed. The design of a data warehouse database recognises the use of historical and aggregated data. Designing a database to be used in a centralised, single-user environment requires a different approach from that used in the design of a distributed, multi-user database. This book emphasises the design of transactional, centralised, single-user and multi-user databases. Chapters 14 and 15 also examine critical issues confronting the designer of distributed and data warehouse databases.

A well-designed database facilitates data management and generates accurate and valuable information. A poorly designed database is likely to become a breeding ground for difficult-to-trace errors that may lead to bad decision making – and bad decision making can lead to the failure of an organisation. Database design is simply too important to be left to luck. That's why university students study database design, why organisations of all types and sizes send personnel to database design seminars, and why database design consultants often make an excellent living.

1.4 HISTORICAL ROOTS: FILES AND DATA PROCESSING

Understanding what a database is, what it does and the proper way to use it can be clarified by considering what a database is not. A brief explanation of the evolution of file system data processing can be helpful in understanding the data access limitations that databases attempt to overcome. Understanding these limitations is relevant to database designers and developers because database technologies do not make these problems magically disappear – database technologies simply make it easier to create solutions that avoid these problems. Creating database designs that avoid the pitfalls of earlier systems requires that the designer understands these problems and how to avoid them; otherwise, the database technologies are no better (and are potentially even worse!) than the technologies and techniques they have replaced.

1

1.4.1 Manual File Systems

To be successful, an organisation must develop systems for handling core business tasks. Historically, such systems were often manual, paper-and-pencil systems. The papers within these systems were organised to facilitate the expected use of the data. Typically, this was accomplished through a system of file folders and filing cabinets. As long as a collection of data was relatively small and an organisation's business users had few reporting requirements, the manual system served its role well as a data repository. However, as organisations grew and as reporting requirements became more complex, keeping track of data in a manual file system became more difficult. Therefore, companies looked to computer technology for help.

1.4.2 Computerised File Systems

Generating reports from manual file systems was slow and cumbersome. In fact, some business managers faced government-imposed reporting requirements that led to weeks of intensive effort each quarter, even when a well-designed manual system was used. Therefore, **a data processing (DP) specialist** was hired to create a computer-based system that would track data and produce required reports. Initially, the computer files within the file system were similar to the manual files. A simple example of a customer data file for a small insurance company is shown in Figure 1.3. (You will discover later that the file structure shown in Figure 1.3, although typically found in early file systems, is unsatisfactory for a database.)The description of computer files requires a specialised vocabulary. Every discipline develops its own terminology to enable its practitioners to communicate clearly. The basic file vocabulary shown in Table 1.2 will help you to understand subsequent discussions more easily.

Online Content The databases used in the chapters are available on the online platform accompanying this book. Throughout the book, Online Content boxes highlight material related to chapter content located on the online platform. Please see the prelims for details on how to access these useful resources.

TABLE 1.2 Basic file terminology

Term	Definition
Data	Raw facts, such as a telephone number, a birth date, a customer name and a year-to-date (YTD) sales value. Data have little meaning unless they have been organised in some logical manner. The smallest piece of data that can be recognised by the computer is a single character, such as the letter *A*, the number 5 or a symbol such as /. A single character requires 1 byte of computer storage.
Field	A character or group of characters (alphabetic or numeric) that has a specific meaning. A field is used to define and store data.
Record	A logically connected set of one or more fields that describes a person, place or thing. For example, the fields that constitute a record for a customer named J. D. Rudd might consist of J. D. Rudd's name, address, phone number, date of birth, credit limit and unpaid balance.
File	A collection of related records. For example, a file might contain data about vendors of ROBCOR Company, or a file might contain the records for the students currently enrolled at Gigantic University.

FIGURE 1.3 **Contents of the CUSTOMER file**

C_NAME	C_PHONE	C_ADDRESS	C_POSTCODE	A_NAME	A_PHONE	TP	AMT	REN
Alfred A. Ramas	32-3-8891367	Stationsplein 2, Sea Point, Cape Town	2880	Leah F. Hahn	27-21-410-7100	T1	€100.00	05-Apr-2018
Mpu K. Dlamini	0181-894-1238	Box 12A Rd, Highgate, Johannesburg	N6 4WE	Alex B. Alby	0161-228-1249	T1	€250.00	16-Jun-2018
Loli W. Ndlovu	32-3-8890340	Rijksweg 58, Pretoria	2880	Nkita F. Brown	27-12-410-7100	S2	€150.00	29-Jan-2018
Paul F. Olowski	31-20-6226060	Martin Rd, Westville, Durban	1018	Nkita F. Brown	27-21-410-7100	S1	€300.00	14-Oct-2018
Fatima Naidoo	0161-222-1672	Box 111 Dr., Chatsworth, Durban	M15 REE	Alex B. Alby	0181-228-1249	T1	€100.00	28-Dec-2018
Amy B. O'Brian	0181-442-3381	387 Troll Dr., Highgate, East London	N6 LOP	Menzi T. Ndlovu	0181-123-5589	T2	€850.00	22-Sep-2018
James G. Khumalo	33-5-59200506	19 East Block Street, Mitchells Plain	647000	Nkita F. Brown	27-21-410-7100	S1	€120.00	25-Mar-2018
Saajidah Mahraj	39-064885889	3 Baobab Street, Queenswood, Pretoria	00179	Menzi T. Ndlovu	0181-123-5589	S1	€250.00	17-Jul-2018
Anne G. Farriss	0181-382-7185	2119 Elm St., Parkview, Johannesburg	NW3 RTA	Alex B. Alby	0161-228-1249	T2	€100.00	03-Dec-2018
Olette K. Snyman	34-934412463	35 Libertas Avenue, Stellenbosch	08001	Menzi T. Ndlovu	0181-123-5589	S2	€500.00	14-Mar-2018

C_NAME = Customer name
C_PHONE = Customer phone
C_ADDRESS = Customer address
C_POSTCODE = Customer postcode
A_NAME = Agent name
A_PHONE = Agent phone
TP = Insurance type
AMT = Insurance policy amount, in thousands of euro
REN = Insurance renewal date

Using the proper file terminology given in Table 1.2, you can identify the file components shown in Figure 1.3. The CUSTOMER file shown in Figure 1.3 contains ten records. Each record is composed of nine fields: C_NAME, C_PHONE, C_ADDRESS, C_POSTCODE, A_NAME, A_PHONE, TP, AMT and REN. The ten records are stored in a named file. Because the file in Figure 1.3 contains customer data, its filename is CUSTOMER.

When business users wanted data from the computerised file, they sent requests for the data to the DP specialist. For each request, the DP specialist had to create programs to retrieve the data from the file, manipulate it in whatever manner the user had requested and present it as a printed report. If a request was for a report that had been run previously, the DP specialist could rerun the existing program and provide the printed results to the user. As other business users saw the new and innovative ways in which customer data were being reported, they wanted to be able to view their data in similar fashions. This generated more requests for the DP specialist to create more computerised files of other business data, which in turn meant that more data management programs had to be created, and more requests for reports. For example, the sales department at the insurance company created a file named SALES, which helped track daily sales efforts. The sales department's success was so obvious that the personnel department manager demanded access to the DP specialist to automate payroll processing and other personnel functions. Consequently, the DP specialist was asked to create the AGENT file shown in Figure 1.4. The data in the AGENT file were used to do electronic fund transfers (EFTs), keep track of taxes paid and summarise insurance coverage, among other tasks.

FIGURE 1.4 Contents of the AGENT file

A_NAME	A_PHONE	A_ADDRESS	POSTCODE	HIRED	YTD_PAY	YTD_IT	YTD_NI	YTD_SLS	DEP
Alex B. Alby	0161-228-1249	Deken Van Erpstraat 20, Best	5492	01-Nov-2001	€20 806.00	€5 201.00	€1 664.00	€103 963.00	3
Nkita F. Brown	27-21-410-7100	West Quay Road, Waterfront, Cape Town	8002	23-May-2004	€25 230.00	€6 308.00	€2 018.00	€108 844.00	0
Menzi T. Ndlovu	0181-123-5589	452 Elm St., Parkview, Johannesburg	2193	15-Jun-2003	€18 169.00	€4 542.00	€1 453.00	€99 548.00	2

A_NAME = Agent name
A_PHONE = Agent phone
A_ADDRESS = Agent address
POSTCODE = Agent postcode
HIRED = Agent date of hire

YTD_PAY = Year-to-date pay
YTD_IT = Year-to-date income tax paid
YTD_NI = Year-to-date national insurance paid
YTD_SLS = Year-to-date sales
DEP = Number of dependents

As the number of files increased, a small file system, like the one shown in Figure 1.5, evolved. Each file in the system used its own application programs to store, retrieve and modify data. And each file was owned by the individual or the department that commissioned its creation.

As the file system grew, the demand for the DP specialist's programming skills grew even faster, and the DP specialist was authorised to hire additional programmers. The size of the file system also required a larger, more complex computer. The new computer and the additional programming staff caused the DP specialist to spend less time programming and more time managing technical and human resources. Therefore, the DP specialist's job evolved into that of a **data processing (DP) manager**, who supervised a DP department. In spite of these organisational changes, however, the DP department's primary activity remained programming, and the DP manager inevitably spent much time as a supervising senior programmer and program troubleshooter.

FIGURE 1.5 A simple file system

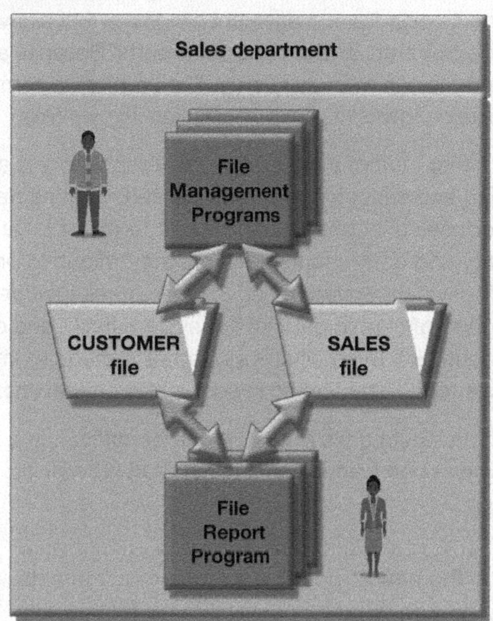

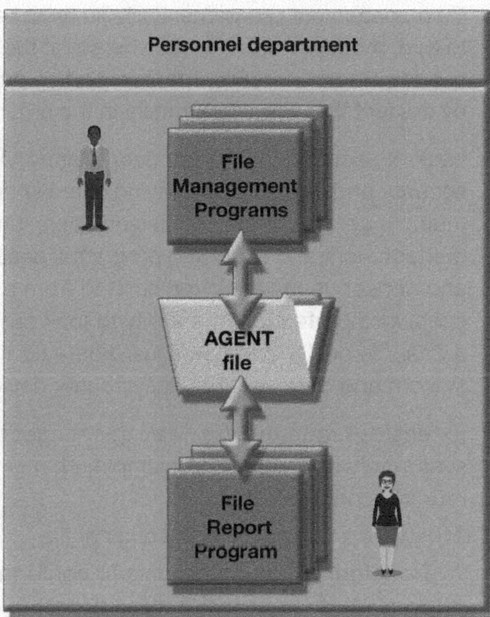

1.5 PROBLEMS WITH FILE SYSTEM DATA MANAGEMENT

The file system method of organising and managing data was a definite improvement on a manual system and served a useful purpose in data management for over two decades, a very long timespan in the computer era. Nonetheless, many problems and limitations became evident in this approach. A critique of the file system method serves two major purposes:

- Understanding the shortcomings of the file system enables you to understand the development of modern databases.
- Many of the problems are not unique to file systems. Failure to understand such problems is likely to lead to their duplication in a database environment, even though database technology makes it easy to avoid them.

The following problems severely challenge the types of information that can be created from the data as well as the accuracy of the information:

- Lengthy development times. The first and most glaring problem with the file system approach is that even the simplest data-retrieval task requires extensive programming. With the older file systems, programmers had to specify what must be done and how to do it. As you will learn in upcoming chapters, modern databases use a non-procedural data manipulation language that allows the user to specify what must be done without specifying how.
- Difficulty in getting quick answers. The need to write programs to produce even the simplest reports makes ad hoc queries impossible. DP specialists who work with mature file systems often receive numerous requests for new reports. They are often forced to say that the report will be ready 'next week' or even 'next month'. If you need the information now, getting it next week or next month will not serve your information needs.

- Complex system administration. System administration becomes more difficult as the number of files in the system expands. Even a simple file system with a few files requires creating and maintaining several file management programs. Each file must have its own file management programs that allow the user to add, modify and delete records; to list the file contents; and to generate reports. Because ad hoc queries are not possible, the file reporting programs can multiply quickly. The problem is compounded by the fact that each department in the organisation 'owns' its data by creating its own files.
- Lack of security and limited data sharing. Another fault of a file system data repository is a lack of security and limited data sharing. Data sharing and security are closely related. Sharing data among multiple geographically dispersed users introduces a lot of security risks. In terms of creating data management and reporting programs, security and data-sharing features are difficult to program and consequently are often omitted from a file system environment. Such features include effective password protection, the ability to lock out parts of files or parts of the system itself, and other measures designed to safeguard data confidentiality. Even when an attempt is made to improve system and data security, the security devices tend to be limited in scope and effectiveness.
- Extensive programming. Making changes to an existing file structure can be difficult in a file system environment. For example, changing just one field in the original CUSTOMER file would require a program that:
    1. Reads a record from the original file.
    2. Transforms the original data to conform to the new structure's storage requirements.
    3. Writes the transformed data into the new file structure.
    4. Repeats the preceding steps for each record in the original file.

In fact, any change to a file structure, no matter how minor, forces modifications in all of the programs that use the data in that file. Modifications are likely to produce errors (bugs), and additional time is spent using a debugging process to find those errors. Those limitations, in turn, lead to problems of structural and data dependence.

1.5.1 Structural and Data Dependence

A file system exhibits **structural dependence**; that is, access to a file is dependent on its structure. For example, adding a customer date-of-birth field to the CUSTOMER file shown in Figure 1.3 would require the five steps described in the previous section. Given this change, none of the previous programs will work with the new CUSTOMER file structure. Therefore, all of the file system programs must be modified to conform to the new file structure. In short, because the file system application programs are affected by change in the file structure, they exhibit structural dependence. Conversely, **structural independence** exists when it is possible to make changes in the file structure without affecting the application program's ability to access the data.

Even changes in file data characteristics, such as changing a field from integer to decimal, require changes in all programs that access the file. Because all data access programs are subject to change when any of the file's data storage characteristics change (that is, changing the data type), the file system is said to exhibit **data dependence**. Conversely, **data independence** exists when it is possible to make changes in the data storage characteristics without affecting the application program's ability to access the data.

The practical significance of data dependence is the difference between the **logical data format** (how the human being views the data) and the **physical data format** (how the computer 'sees' the data). Any program that accesses a file system's file must tell the computer not only what to do, but also how to do it. Consequently, each program must contain lines that specify the opening of a specific file type, its record specification and its field definitions. Data dependence makes the file system extremely cumbersome from a programming and data management point of view.

1

1.5.2 Field Definitions and Naming Conventions

At first glance, the CUSTOMER file shown in Figure 1.3 appears to have served its purpose well: requested reports could usually be generated. But suppose you want to create a customer phone directory based on the data stored in the CUSTOMER file. Storing the customer name as a single field turns out to be a liability because the directory must break up the field contents to list the last names, first names and initials in alphabetical order. Or suppose you want to get a customer listing by area code. Including the area code in the phone number field is inefficient.

Similarly, producing a listing of customers by city is a more difficult task than is necessary. From the user's point of view, a much better (more flexible) record definition would be one that anticipates reporting requirements by breaking up fields into their component parts. Thus, the CUSTOMER file's fields might be listed as shown in Table 1.3.

TABLE 1.3 Sample customer file fields

Field	Contents	Sample entry
CUS_LNAME	Customer last name	Ramas
CUS_FNAME	Customer first name	Alfred
CUS_INITIAL	Customer initial	A
CUS_AREACODE	Customer area code	1615
CUS_PHONE	Customer phone	0161-234-5678
CUS_ADDRESS	Customer street address or box number	123 Green Meadow Lane
CUS_CITY	Customer city	East London
CUS_COUNTY	Customer county/district	Eastern Cape
CUS_POSTCODE	Customer postcode	3001

Selecting proper field names is also important. For example, make sure that the field names are reasonably descriptive. In examining the file structure shown in Figure 1.3, it is not obvious that the field name REN represents the customer's insurance renewal date. Using the field name CUS_RENEW_DATE would be better for two reasons. First, the prefix CUS can be used as an indicator of the field's origin, which is the CUSTOMER file. Therefore, you know that the field in question yields a CUSTOMER property. Second, the RENEW_DATE portion of the field name is more descriptive of the field's contents. With proper naming conventions, the file structure becomes self-documenting. That is, by simply looking at the field names, you can determine which files the fields belong to and what information the fields are likely to contain.

Some software packages place restrictions on the length of field names, so it is wise to be as descriptive as possible within those restrictions. In addition, very long field names make it difficult to fit more than a few fields on a page, thus making output spacing a problem. For example, the field name CUSTOMER_INSURANCE_RENEWAL_DATE, while being self-documenting, is less desirable than CUS_RENEW_DATE.

Another problem in Figure 1.3's CUSTOMER file is the difficulty of finding desired data efficiently. The CUSTOMER file currently does not have a unique record identifier. For example, it is possible to have several customers named James G. Khumalo. Consequently, the addition of a CUS_ACCOUNT field that contains a unique customer account number would be appropriate.

1

The criticisms of field definitions and naming conventions shown in the file structure of Figure 1.3 are not unique to file systems. Because such conventions will prove to be important later, they are introduced early. You will revisit field definitions and naming conventions when you learn about database design in Chapter 5, Data Modelling with Entity Relationship Diagrams, and in Chapter 6, Data Modelling Advanced Concepts; and when you learn about database implementation issues in Chapter 11, Conceptual, Logical, and Physical Database Design. Regardless of the data environment, the design – whether it involves a file system or a database – must always reflect the designer's documentation needs and the end user's reporting and processing requirements. Both types of needs are best served by adhering to proper field definitions and naming conventions.

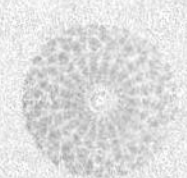

Online Content Appendices A to R are available on the online platform accompanying this book.

NOTE

No naming convention can fit all requirements for all systems. Some words or phrases are reserved for the DBMSs internal use. For example, the name ORDER generates an error in some DBMSs. Similarly, your DBMS might interpret a hyphen (-) as a command to subtract. Therefore, the field CUS-NAME would be interpreted as a command to subtract the NAME field from the CUS field. Because neither field exists, you would get an error message. On the other hand, CUS_NAME would work fine because it uses an underscore.

1.5.3 Data Redundancy

The file system's structure and lack of security make it difficult to combine data from multiple sources. The organisational structure promotes the storage of the same basic data in different locations. Database professionals use the term **islands of information** for such scattered data locations. As it is unlikely that data stored in different locations will always be updated consistently, the islands of information often contain different versions of the same data. For example, in Figures 1.3 and 1.4, the agent names and phone numbers occur in both the CUSTOMER and the AGENT files. You need only one correct copy of the agent names and phone numbers. Having them occur in more than one place produces data redundancy. **Data redundancy** exists when the same data are stored unnecessarily at different places.

Uncontrolled data redundancy sets the stage for:

- *Data inconsistency*. Data inconsistency exists when different and conflicting versions of the same data appear in different places. For example, suppose you change an agent's phone number or address in the AGENT file. If you forget to make corresponding changes in the CUSTOMER file, the files contain different data for the same agent. Reports will yield inconsistent results depending on which version of the data is used.
- *Poor data security*. Having multiple copies of data increases the chances of a copy of the data being susceptible to unauthorised access.

NOTE

Data that display data inconsistency are also referred to as data that lack data integrity. **Data integrity** is defined as the condition in which all of the data in the database are consistent with the real-world events and conditions. In other words,

- Data are *accurate*; there are no data inconsistencies.
- Data are *verifiable*; the data will always yield consistent results.

Data entry errors are more likely to occur when complex entries (such as 12-digit phone numbers) are made in several different files and/or recur frequently in one or more files. In fact, the CUSTOMER file shown in Figure 1.3 contains just such an entry error: the third record in the CUSTOMER file has a transposed digit in the agent's phone number (27-12-410-7100 rather than 27-21-410-1700).

It is possible to enter a non-existent sales agent's name and phone number into the CUSTOMER file, but customers are not likely to be impressed if the insurance agency supplies the name and phone number of an agent who does not exist. And should the personnel manager allow a non-existent agent to accrue bonuses and benefits? In fact, a data entry error such as an incorrectly spelled name or an incorrect phone number yields the same kind of data integrity problems.

- *Data anomalies*. The dictionary defines *anomaly* as 'an abnormality'. Ideally, a field value change should be made in only a single place. Data redundancy, however, fosters an abnormal condition by forcing field value changes in many different locations. Look at the CUSTOMER file in Figure 1.3. If agent Nikita F. Brown decides to get married and move, the agent name, address and phone are likely to change. Instead of making just a single name and/or phone/address change in a single file (AGENT), you also must make the change each time that agent's name, phone number and address occur in the CUSTOMER file. You could be faced with the prospect of making hundreds of corrections, one for each of the customers served by that agent! The same problem occurs when an agent decides to quit. Each customer served by that agent must be assigned a new agent. Any change in any field value must be correctly made in many places to maintain data integrity. A **data anomaly** develops when all of the required changes in the redundant data are not made successfully. The data anomalies found in Figure 1.3 are commonly defined as follows:
  - *Update anomalies*. If agent Nikita F. Brown has a new phone number, that number must be entered in each of the CUSTOMER file records in which Ms Brown's phone number is shown. In this case, only three changes must be made. In a large file system, such changes might occur in hundreds or even thousands of records. Clearly, the potential for data inconsistencies is great.
  - *Insertion anomalies*. For example, if only the CUSTOMER file existed, to add a new agent, you would also add a dummy customer data entry to reflect the new agent's addition. Again, the potential for creating data inconsistencies would be great.
  - *Deletion anomalies*. If you delete Amy B. O'Brian, Saajidah Maharaj and Olette K. Snyman, then you will also delete Menzi T. Ndlovu's agent data. Clearly, this is not desirable.

1.6 DATABASE SYSTEMS

The problems inherent in file systems make using a database system very desirable. Traditional file systems often made reference to several files such as the customer master file, the product master file and the transaction file, which were stored separately. However, unlike the file system,

1

the database consists of logically related data stored in a single logical data repository. (The 'logical' label reflects the fact that, although the data repository appears to be a single unit to the end user, its contents may actually be physically distributed among multiple data storage facilities and/or locations.) Since the database's data repository is a single logical unit, the database represents a major change in the way end-user data are stored, accessed and managed. The database's DBMS, shown in Figure 1.6, provides numerous advantages over file system management, shown in Figure 1.5, by making it possible to eliminate most of the file system's data inconsistency, data anomaly, data dependency and structural dependency problems. Better yet, the current generation of DBMS software stores not only the data structures, but also the relationships between those structures and the access paths to those structures, all in a central location. The current generation of DBMS software also takes care of defining, storing and managing all required access paths to those components.

Remember that the DBMS is just one of several crucial components of a database system. The DBMS may even be referred to as the database system's heart. However, just as it takes more than a heart to make a human being function, it takes more than a DBMS to make a database system function. In the sections that follow, you'll learn what a database system is, what its components are and how the DBMS fits into the database system picture.

FIGURE 1.6 **Contrasting database and file systems**

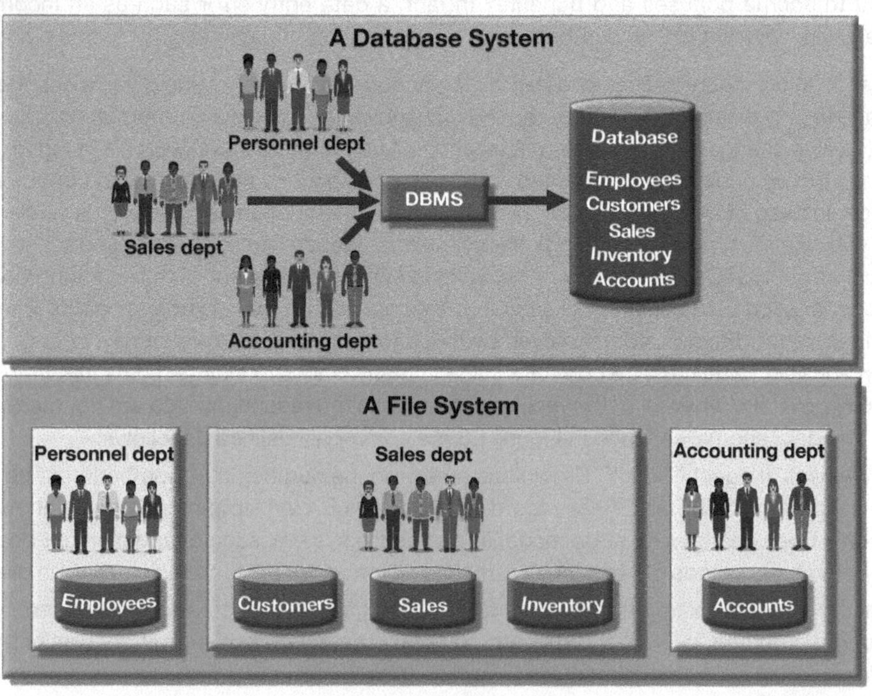

1.6.1 The Database System Environment

The term **database system** refers to an organisation of components that define and regulate the collection, storage, management and use of data within a database environment. From a general management point of view, the database system is composed of the five major parts shown in Figure 1.7: hardware, software, people, procedures and data.

Let's take a closer look at the five components shown in Figure 1.7:

- *Hardware*. Hardware refers to all of the system's physical devices – for example, computers (microcomputers, mainframes, workstations and servers), storage devices, printers, network devices (hubs, switches, routers and fibre optics) and other devices (automated teller machines, ID readers, etc.).

FIGURE 1.7 **The database system environment**

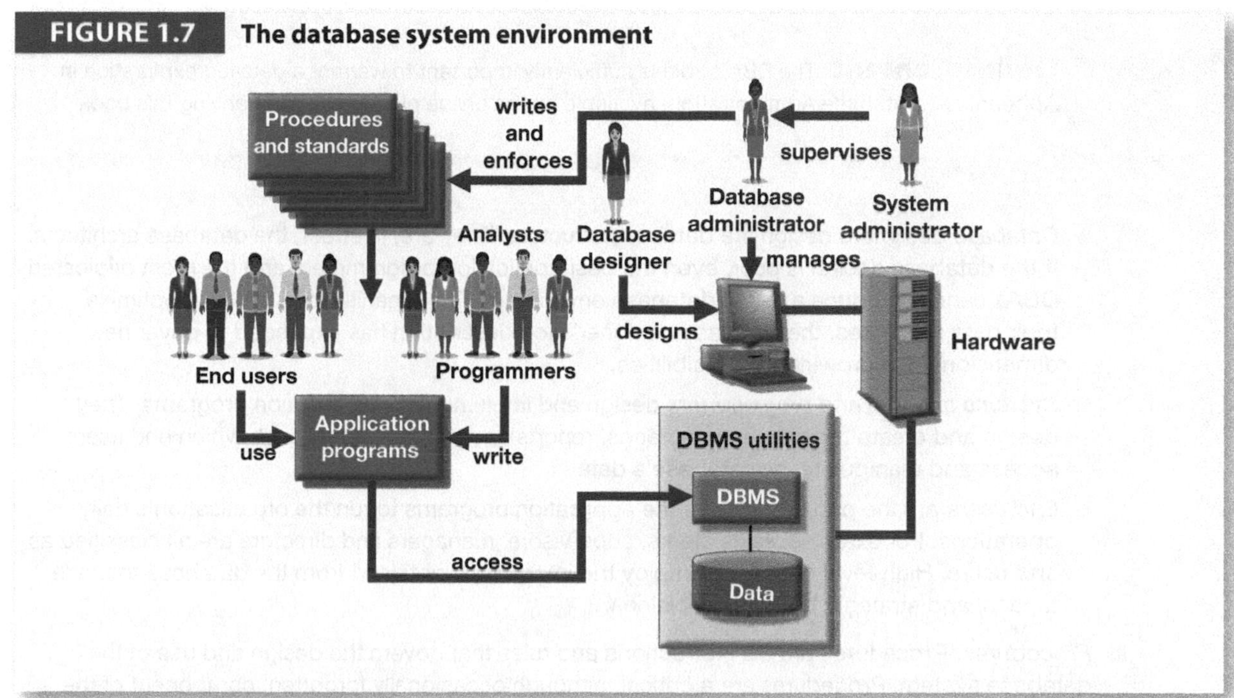

- *Software*. Although the most readily identified software is the DBMS itself, to make the database system function fully, three types of software are needed: operating system software, DBMS software, and application programs and utilities:
  - *Operating system software* manages all hardware components and makes it possible for all other software to run on the computers. Examples of operating system software include Microsoft Windows, Linux, Mac OS, UNIX and MVS.
  - *DBMS software* manages the database within the database system. Some examples of DBMS software include Microsoft Access and SQL Server, Oracle Corporation's Oracle and IBM's DB2.
  - *Application programs and utility software* are used to access and manipulate data in the DBMS and to manage the computer environment in which data access and manipulation take place. Application programs are most commonly used to access data found within the database, and to generate reports, tabulations and other information to facilitate decision making. Utilities are the software tools used to help manage the database system's computer components. For example, all of the major DBMS vendors now provide graphical user interfaces (GUIs) to help create database structures, control database access and monitor database operations.
- *People*. This component includes all users of the database system. On the basis of primary job functions, five types of users can be identified in a database system: systems administrators,

database administrators, database designers, systems analysts and programmers, and end users. Each user type, described below, performs both unique and complementary functions:

- *Systems administrators* oversee the database system's general operations.
- *Database administrators*, also known as DBAs, manage the DBMS and ensure that the database is functioning properly.

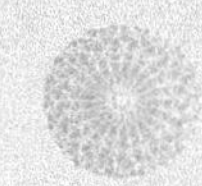

Online Content The DBA's role is sufficiently important to warrant a detailed exploration in Appendix K, Database Administration, available on the online platform accompanying this book.

- *Database designers* design the database structure. They are, in effect, the database architects. If the database design is poor, even the best application programmers and the most dedicated DBAs cannot produce a useful database environment. As organisations strive to optimise their data resources, the database designer's job description has expanded to cover new dimensions and growing responsibilities.
- *Systems analysts and programmers* design and implement the application programs. They design and create the data entry screens, reports and procedures through which end users access and manipulate the database's data.
- *End users* are the people who use the application programs to run the organisation's daily operations. For example, sales clerks, supervisors, managers and directors are all classified as end users. High-level end users employ the information obtained from the database to make tactical and strategic business decisions.

- *Procedures*. Procedures are the instructions and rules that govern the design and use of the database system. Procedures are a critical, although occasionally forgotten, component of the system. Procedures play an important role in a company because they enforce the standards by which business is conducted within the organisation and with customers. Procedures are also used to ensure that there is an organised way to monitor and audit both the data that enter the database and the information that is generated through the use of that data.
- *Data*. The word *data* covers the collection of facts stored in the database. Since data are the raw material from which information is generated, the determination of which data are to be entered into the database and how those data are to be organised is a vital part of the database designer's job.

A database system adds a new dimension to an organisation's management structure. Just how complex this managerial structure is depends on the organisation's size, its functions and its corporate culture. Therefore, database systems can be created and managed at different levels of complexity and with varying adherence to precise standards. For example, compare a local gym membership system with an insurance claims system. The gym membership system may be managed by two people, the hardware used is probably a single microcomputer, the procedures are probably simple and the data volume tends to be low. The insurance claims system is likely to have at least one systems administrator, several full-time DBAs and many designers and programmers; the hardware probably includes several mainframes at multiple locations; the procedures are likely to be numerous, complex and rigorous; and the data volume tends to be high.

In addition to the different levels of database system complexity, managers must also take another important fact into account: database solutions must be cost-effective as well as tactically and strategically effective. Producing a million-rand solution to a thousand-rand problem is hardly an example of good database system selection or of good database design and management. Finally, the database technology already in use is likely to affect the selection of a database system.

1.6.2 DBMS Functions

A DBMS performs several important functions that guarantee the integrity and consistency of the data in the database. Most of those functions are transparent to end users, and most can be achieved only through the use of a DBMS. They include data dictionary management, data storage management, data transformation and presentation, security management, multi-user access control, backup and recovery management, data integrity management, database access languages and application programming interfaces, and database communication interfaces.

- *Data dictionary management*. The DBMS stores definitions of the data elements and their relationships (metadata) in a **data dictionary.** In turn, all programs that access the data in the database work through the DBMS. The DBMS uses the data dictionary to look up the required data component structures and relationships, thus relieving you from having to code such complex relationships in each program. Additionally, any changes made in a database structure are automatically recorded in the data dictionary, thereby freeing you from having to modify all of the programs that access the changed structure. In other words, the DBMS provides data abstraction and it removes structural and data dependency from the system. (You will learn more about data abstraction in Chapter 2, Data Models). For example, Figure 1.8 shows an example of how Oracle's development tool SQL Developer presents the data definition for the CUSTOMER table.

FIGURE 1.8 **Illustrating metadata with Oracle's SQL Developer**

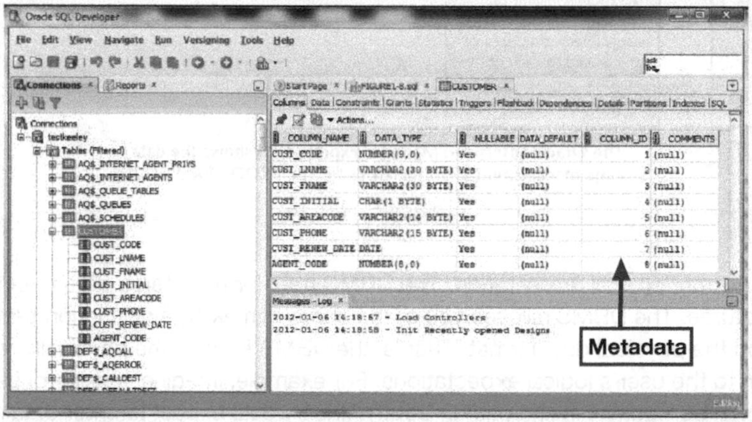

- *Data storage management*. The DBMS creates and manages the complex structures required for data storage, thus relieving you of the difficult task of defining and programming the physical data characteristics. A modern DBMS system provides storage not only for the data, but also for related data entry forms or screen definitions, report definitions, data validation rules, procedural code, structures to handle video and picture formats, etc. Data storage management is also important for database performance tuning. **Performance tuning** relates to the activities that make the database perform more efficiently in terms of storage and access speed. Although the user sees the database as a single data storage unit, the DBMS actually stores the database in multiple physical data files (see Figure 1.9). Such data files may even be stored on different storage media. Therefore, the DBMS doesn't have to wait for one disk request to finish before the next one starts. In other words, the DBMS can fulfil database requests concurrently. Data storage management and performance tuning issues are addressed in Chapter 13, Managing Database and SQL Performance.

FIGURE 1.9 Illustrating data storage management with Oracle

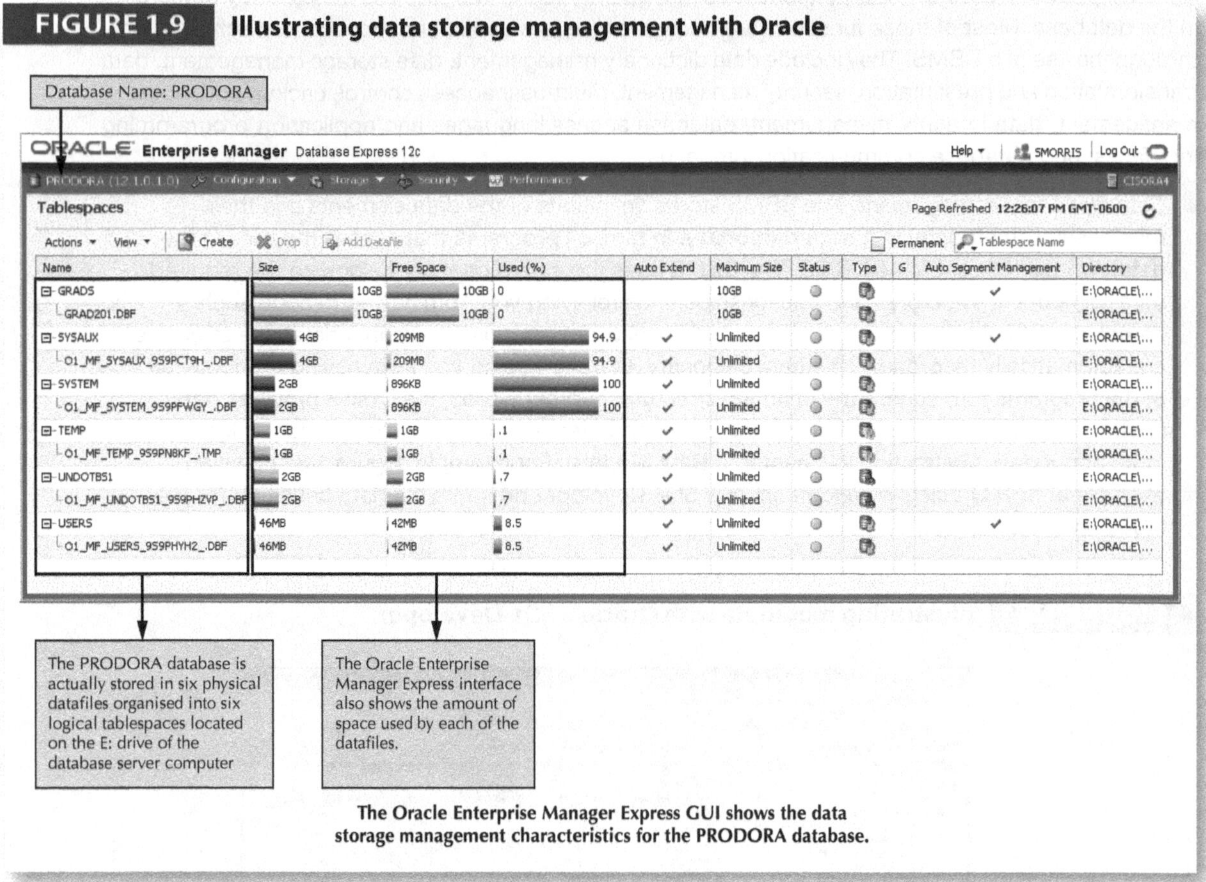

The Oracle Enterprise Manager Express GUI shows the data storage management characteristics for the PRODORA database.

- *Data transformation and presentation*. The DBMS transforms entered data to conform to required data structures. The DBMS relieves you of the chore of making a distinction between the logical data format and the physical data format. That is, the DBMS formats the physically retrieved data to make it conform to the user's logical expectations. For example, imagine an enterprise database used by a multinational company. An end user in South Africa would expect to enter data such as 11 July 2020 as '11/07/2020'. In contrast, the same date would be entered in the United States as '07/11/2020'. Regardless of the data presentation format, the DBMS must manage the date in the proper format for each country.

- *Security management*. The DBMS creates a security system that enforces user security and data privacy. Security rules determine which users can access the database, which data items each user can access and which data operations (read, add, delete or modify) the user can perform. This is especially important in multi-user database systems where many users access the database simultaneously. All database users may be authenticated to the DBMS through a username and password or through biometric authentication such as a fingerprint scan. The DBMS uses this information to assign access privileges to various database components, such as queries and reports.

Online Content Appendix K, Database Administration, examines data security and privacy issues in greater detail and is available on the online platform accompanying this book.

- *Multi-user access control*. To provide data integrity and data consistency, the DBMS uses sophisticated algorithms to ensure that multiple users can access the database concurrently without compromising the integrity of the database. Chapter 12, Managing Transactions and Concurrency, covers the details of the multi-user access control.
- *Backup and recovery management*. The DBMS provides backup and data recovery to ensure data safety and integrity. Current DBMS systems provide special utilities that allow the DBA to perform routine and special backup and restore procedures. Recovery management deals with the recovery of the database after a failure, such as a bad sector in the disk or a power failure. Such capability is critical to preserving the database's integrity. Appendix K, Database Administration, covers backup and recovery issues (see online platform).
- *Data integrity management*. The DBMS promotes and enforces integrity rules, thus minimising data redundancy and maximising data consistency. The data relationships stored in the data dictionary are used to enforce data integrity. Ensuring data integrity is especially important in transactional database systems. Data integrity and transaction management issues are addressed in Chapter 8, Beginning Structured Query Language, and Chapter 12, Managing Transactions and Concurrency.
- *Database access languages and application programming interfaces*. The DBMS provides data access through a query language. A **query language** is a non-procedural language—one that lets the user specify what must be done without having to specify how it is to be done. The DBMS also provides application programming interfaces to procedural languages such as COBOL, C, Java, Visual Basic.NET and C#. The DBMS also provides administrative utilities used by the DBA and the database designer to create, implement, monitor and maintain the database. **Structured Query Language (SQL)** is the de facto query language and data access standard supported by the majority of DBMS vendors. Chapter 8, Beginning Structured Query Language, and Chapter 9, Procedural Language SQL and Advanced SQL, address the use of SQL.
- *Database communication interfaces*. Current-generation DBMSs accept end-user requests via multiple, different network environments. For example, the DBMS might provide access to the database via the internet through the use of Web browsers such as Chrome, Firefox or Edge. In this environment, communications can be accomplished in several ways:
  - End users can generate answers to queries by filling in screen forms through their preferred Web browser.
  - The DBMS can automatically publish predefined reports on a website.
  - The DBMS can connect to third-party systems to distribute information via email or other productivity applications.

Database communication interfaces are examined in greater detail in Chapter 14, Distributed Databases, in Chapter 17, Database Connectivity and Web Technologies, and in Appendix H, Databases in e-Commerce (see online platform).

1

1.6.3 Managing the Database System: A Shift in Focus

The introduction of a database system provides a framework in which strict procedures and standards can be enforced. Consequently, the role of the human component changes from an emphasis on programming to a focus on the broader aspects of managing the organisation's data resources and on the administration of the complex database software itself.

The database system makes it possible to tackle far more sophisticated uses of the data resources as long as the database is designed accordingly. The kinds of data structures created within the database and the extent of the relationships among them play a powerful role in determining the effectiveness of the database system.

Although the database system yields considerable advantages over previous data management approaches, database systems do impose significant overheads. For example:

- *Increased costs*. Database systems require sophisticated hardware and software and highly skilled personnel. The cost of maintaining the hardware, software and personnel required to operate and manage a database system can be substantial.
- *Management complexity*. Database systems interface with many different technologies and have a significant impact on a company's resources and culture. The changes introduced by the adoption of a database system must be properly managed to ensure that they help advance the company's objectives. Given the fact that database systems hold crucial company data that are accessed from multiple sources, security issues must be assessed constantly.
- *System maintenance*. To maximise the efficiency of the database system, you must keep your system current. Therefore, you must perform frequent updates and apply the latest patches and security measures to all components. Since database technology advances rapidly, personnel training costs tend to be significant.
- *Vendor dependence*. Given the heavy investment in technology and personnel training, companies may be reluctant to change database vendors. As a consequence, vendors are less likely to offer pricing point advantages to existing customers and those customers may be limited in their choice of database system components.

1.7 PREPARING FOR YOUR DATABASE PROFESSIONAL CAREER

In this chapter, you were introduced to the concepts of data, information, databases and DBMSs. You also learnt that, regardless of what type of database you use (OLTP or OLAP), or what type of database environment you are working in (for example, Oracle, Microsoft or IBM), the success of a database system greatly depends on how well the database structure is designed.

Throughout this book, you will learn the building blocks that lay the foundation for your career as a database professional. Understanding these building blocks and developing the skills to use them effectively will prepare you to work with databases at many different levels within an organisation. A small sample of such career opportunities is shown in Table 1.4.

As you also learnt in this chapter, database technologies are constantly evolving to address new challenges such as large databases, semi-structured and unstructured data, increasing processing speed and lowering costs. While database technologies can change quickly, the fundamental concepts and skills do not. It is our goal that, after you learn the database essentials in this book, you will be ready to apply your knowledge and skills to work with traditional OLTP and OLAP systems as well as cutting-edge, complex database technologies such as:

TABLE 1.4 Database career opportunities

Job Title	Description	Sample Skills Required
Database developer	Creates and maintains database-based applications	Programming, database fundamentals, SQL
Database designer	Designs and maintains databases	Systems design, database design, SQL
Database administrator	Manages and maintains DBMS and databases	Database fundamentals, SQL, vendor courses
Database analyst	Develops databases for decision support reporting	SQL, query optimisation, data warehouses, data lakes
Database architect	Designs and implements database environments (conceptual, logical and physical)	DBMS fundamentals, data modelling, SQL, hardware knowledge
Database consultant	Helps companies leverage database technologies to improve business processes and achieve specific goals	Database fundamentals, data modelling, database design, SQL, DBMS, hardware, vendor-specific technologies
Database security officer	Implements security policies for data administration	DBMS fundamentals, database administration, SQL, data security technologies
Cloud Computing Data Architect	Design and implement the infrastructure for next-generation cloud database systems	Internet technologies, cloud storage technologies, data security, performance tuning, large databases, etc.
Data Scientist	Analyze large amounts of varied data to generate insights, relationships, and predictable behaviors	Data analysis, statistics, advanced mathematics, SQL, programming, data mining, machine learning, data visualization

- *Very large databases (VLDB).* Many vendors are addressing the need for databases that support large amounts of data, usually in the petabyte range. (A petabyte is more than 1 000 terabytes.) VLDB vendors include Oracle Exadata, IBM's Netezza, Greenplum, HP's Vertica and Teradata. VLDB are now being overtaken in market interest by Big Data databases.
- *Big Data databases.* Products such as Cassandra (Facebook) and Bigtable (Google) are using 'columnar database' technologies to support the needs of database applications that manage large amounts of 'non-tabular' data. See more about this topic in Chapter 2.
- *In-memory databases.* Most major database vendors also offer some type of in-memory database support to address the need for faster database processing. In-memory databases store most of their data in primary memory (RAM) rather than in slower secondary storage (hard disks). In-memory databases include IBM's solidDB and Oracle's TimesTen.
- *Cloud databases.* Companies can now use cloud database services to add database systems to their environment quickly, while simultaneously lowering the total cost of ownership of a new DBMS. A cloud database offers all the advantages of a local DBMS, but instead of residing within your organisation's network infrastructure, it resides on the internet. See more about this topic in Chapter 14.

We address some of these topics in this book, but not all – no single book can cover the entire realm of database technologies. This book's primary focus is to help you learn database fundamentals, develop your database design skills and master your SQL skills so you will have a head start in becoming a successful database professional. However, you first need to learn about the tools at your disposal. In the next chapter, you will learn different approaches to data management and how these approaches influence your designs.

SUMMARY

- Data are raw facts. Information is the result of processing data to reveal its meaning. Accurate, relevant and timely information is the key to good decision making, and good decision making is the key to organisational survival in a global environment.
- Data are usually stored in a database. To implement a database and to manage its contents, you need a database management system (DBMS). The DBMS serves as the intermediary between the user and the database. The database contains the data you have collected and 'data about data', known as metadata.
- Database design defines the database structure. A well-designed database facilitates data management and generates accurate and valuable information. A poorly designed database can lead to bad decision making, and bad decision making can lead to the failure of an organisation.
- Databases evolved from manual and then computerised file systems. In a file system, data are stored in independent files, each requiring its own data management programs. Although this method of data management is largely outmoded, understanding its characteristics makes database design easier to understand. Awareness of the problems of file systems can help you avoid similar problems with DBMSs.
- Some limitations of file system data management are that it requires extensive programming, system administration can be complex and difficult, making changes to existing structures is difficult, and security features are likely to be inadequate. Also, independent files tend to contain redundant data, leading to problems of structural and data dependency.
- Database management systems were developed to address the file system's inherent weaknesses. Rather than depositing data within independent files, a DBMS presents the database to the end user as a single data repository. This arrangement promotes data sharing, thus eliminating the potential problem of islands of information. In addition, the DBMS enforces data integrity, eliminates redundancy and promotes data security.
- Open source DBMS software allows users to develop the database system for any purpose, look at the source code and make any improvements, which will then be released back to the general public. Open source DBMSs such as MySQL are currently free to acquire and use, making them ideal for smaller companies and organisations to develop database-centred applications quickly.

KEY TERMS

ad hoc query
analytical database
business intelligence
centralised database
data
data anomaly
data dependence
data dictionary
data governance
data inconsistency
data independence
data integrity
data management
data processing (DP) manager
data processing (DP) specialist
data quality
data redundancy
data warehouse
database
database design
database management system (DBMS)
database system
desktop database
distributed database
enterprise database
Extensible Markup Language (XML)
field
file
information
islands of information
knowledge
logical data format
metadata
multi-user database
NoSQL
online analytical processing (OLAP)
online transaction processing (OLTP)
open source
operational database
performance tuning
physical data format
production database

query
query language
query result set
record
semi-structured
single-user database
social media
structural dependence
structural independence
Structured Query Language (SQL)
transactional database
workgroup database
XML database

FURTHER READING

Codd, E.F. *The Capabilities of Relational Database Management Systems*. IBM Research Report, RJ3132, 1981.

Date, C.J. *The Database Relational Model, A Retrospective Review and Analysis: a Historical Account and Assessment of E.F. Codd's Contribution to the Field of Database Technology*. Addison-Wesley, 2000.

Date, C.J. *An Introduction to Database Systems*, 8th edition. Addison-Wesley, 2003.

Date, C.J. *Date on Database: Writings 2000–2006*. Apress, 2006.

Online Content Answers to selected Review Questions and Problems for this chapter are available on the online platform accompanying this book.

REVIEW QUESTIONS

1 Discuss each of the following terms:
   a data
   b field
   c record
   d file
2 What is data redundancy and which characteristics of the file system can lead to it?
3 Discuss the lack of data independence in file systems.
4 What is a DBMS, and what are its functions?
5 What is structural independence, and why is it important?
6 Explain the difference between data and information.
7 What is the role of a DBMS, and what are its advantages?
8 List and describe the different types of databases.
9 What are the main components of a database system?
10 What is metadata?
11 Explain why database design is important.
12 What are the potential costs of implementing a database system?
13 Use examples to compare and contrast structured and unstructured data. Which type is more prevalent in a typical business environment?
14 What are the six levels on which the quality of data can be examined?
15 Explain what is meant by data governance.

PROBLEMS

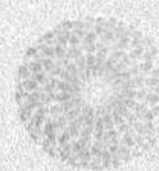

Online Content The file structures you see in this problem set are simulated in a Microsoft Access database named 'Ch01_Problems', available on the online platform for this book.

Given the file structure shown in Figure P1.1, answer Problems 1–4.

1 How many records does the file contain, and how many fields are there per record?

2 What problem would you encounter if you wanted to produce a listing by city? How would you solve this problem by altering the file structure?

FIGURE P1.1 The file structure for Problems 1–4

PROJECT_ CODE	PROJECT_ MANAGER	MANAGER_ PHONE	MANAGER_ADDRESS	PROJECT_BID_ PRICE
21-5Z	Holly B. Naidu	33-5-59200506	180 Boulevard Dr, Phoenix, 64700	€13 179 975.00
25-2D	Jane D. Grant	0181-898-9909	218 Clark Blvd., London, NW3 TRY	€9 787 037.00
25-5A	Menzi F. Zulu	0181-227-1245	124 River Dr., Durban, 4001	€25 458 005.00
25-9T	Holly B. Naidu	33-5-59200506	180 Boulevard Dr, Phoenix, 64700	€16 887 181.00
27-4Q	Menzi F. Zulu	0181-227-1245	124 River Dr., Durban, 4001	€8 078 124.00
29-2D	Holly B. Naidu	33-5-59200506	180 Boulevard Dr, Phoenix, 64700	€20 014 885.00
31-7P	William K. Moor	39-064885889	Via Valgia Silvilla 23, Roma, 00179	€44 516 677.00

3 If you wanted to produce a listing of the file contents by last name, area code, city, county or postal code, how would you alter the file structure?

4 What data redundancies do you detect, and how could those redundancies lead to anomalies?

FIGURE P1.2 The file structure for Problems 5–8

PROJ_ NUM	PROJ_ NAME	EMP_ NUM	EMP_NAME	JOB_ CODE	JOB_CHG_ HOUR	PROJ_ HOURS	EMP_PHONE
1	Hurricane	101	John D. Dlamini	EE	€65.00	13.3	31-20-6226060
1	Hurricane	105	David F. Schwann	CT	€40.00	16.2	0191-234-1123
1	Hurricane	110	Anne R. Ramoras	CT	€40.00	14.3	34-934412463
2	Coast	101	John D. Dlamini	EE	€65.00	19.8	31-20-6226060
2	Coast	108	June H. Ndlovu	EE	€65.00	17.5	0161-554-7812
3	Satellite	110	Anne R. Ramoras	CT	€42.00	11.6	34-934412463
3	Satellite	105	David F. Schwann	CT	€6.00	23.4	0191-234-1123
3	Satelite	123	Mary D. Chen	EE	€65.00	19.1	0181-233-5432
3	Satellite	112	Allecia R. Smith	BE	€65.00	20.7	0181-678-6879

5 Identify and discuss the serious data redundancy problems exhibited by the file structure shown in Figure P1.2.

6 Looking at the EMP_NAME and EMP_PHONE contents in Figure P1.2, which change(s) would you recommend?

7 Identify the different data sources in the file you examined in Problem 5.

8 Given your answer to Problem 7, which new files should you create to help eliminate the data redundancies found in the file shown in Figure P1.2?

FIGURE P1.3 **The file structure for Problems 9–10**

BUILDING_CODE	ROOM_CODE	TEACHER_LNAME	TEACHER_FNAME	TEACHER_INITIAL	DAYS_TIME
KOM	204E	Mbhato	Horace	G	MWF 8:00-8:50
KOM	123	Adam	Maria	L	MWF 8:00-8:50
LDB	504	Patroski	Donald	J	TTh 1:00-2:15
KOM	34	Hawkins	Anne	W	MWF 10:00-10:50
JKP	225B	Risell	James		TTh 9:00-10:15
LDB	301	Robertson	Jeanette	P	TTh 9:00-10:15
KOM	204E	Adam	Maria	I	MWF 9:00-9:50
LDB	504	Mbhato	Horace	G	TTh 1:00-2:15
KOM	34	Adam	Maria	L	MWF 11:00-11:50
LDB	504	Patroski	Donald	J	MWF 2:00-2:50

9 Identify and discuss the serious data redundancy problems exhibited by the file structure shown in Figure P1.3. (The file is meant to be used as a teacher class assignment schedule. One of the many problems with data redundancy is the likely occurrence of data inconsistencies – two different initials have been entered for the teacher named Maria Adam.)

10 Given the file structure shown in Figure P1.3, which problem(s) might you encounter if building KOM were deleted?

CHAPTER 2

Data Models

IN THIS CHAPTER, YOU WILL LEARN:

- Why data models are important
- About the basic data-modelling building blocks
- What business rules are and how they influence database design
- How the major data models evolved
- How data models can be classified by level of abstraction

PREVIEW

This chapter examines data modelling. Data modelling is the first step in the database design journey, serving as a bridge between real-world objects and the database that resides in the computer.

One of the most pressing problems of database design is that designers, programmers and end users see data in different ways. Consequently, different views of the same data can lead to database designs that do not reflect an organisation's actual operation, failing to meet end-user needs and data efficiency requirements. To avoid such failures, database designers must obtain a precise description of the nature of the data and the many uses of that data within the organisation. Communication among database designers, programmers and end users should be as free of ambiguities as possible. Data modelling clarifies such communications by reducing real-world complexities to more easily understood abstractions that define entities and the relations among them.

First, you will learn what some of the basic data-modelling concepts are and how current data models developed from earlier models. Tracing the development of those database models will help you understand the database design and implementation issues that are addressed in the rest of this book. Second, you will be introduced to a data modelling technique known as the entity relationship diagram (ERD). There are a number of ER model notation systems that are used to draw these diagrams. Within this chapter you will be briefly introduced to the unified modelling language (UML) notation. Whilst traditional ER model notations such as Chen and Crow's Foot notation are still common in legacy systems, UML is the new industry standard. Next, you will be introduced to the object-oriented model and the object relational model. Then, you will learn about the emerging NoSQL data model and how it is being used to fulfil the current need to manage very large social media data sets efficiently and effectively. Finally, you will also learn how different degrees of data abstraction help reconcile varying views of the same data.

2.1 THE IMPORTANCE OF DATA MODELS

Traditionally, database designers relied on good judgement to help them develop a good design. Unfortunately, good judgement is often in the eye of the beholder, and it often develops after much trial and error. Fortunately, **data models** (relatively simple representations, usually graphical, of more complex real-world data structures), bolstered by powerful database design tools, have made it possible to diminish the potential for errors in database design substantially. In general terms, a *model* is an abstraction of a more complex real-world object or event. A model's main function is to help you understand the complexities of the real-world environment. Within the database environment, a data model represents data structures and their characteristics, relationships, constraints and transformations.

NOTE

The terms *data model* and *database model* are often used interchangeably. In this book, the term *database model* will be used to refer to the implementation of a *data model* in a specific database system.

Data models can facilitate interaction among the designer, the applications programmer and the end user. A well-developed data model can even foster improved understanding of the organisation for which the database design is developed. This important aspect of data modelling was summed up neatly by a client whose reaction was as follows: 'I created this business, I worked with this business for years, and this is the first time I've really understood how all the pieces really fit together.'

The importance of data modelling cannot be overstated. Data constitute the most basic information units employed by a system. Applications are created to manage data and to help transform data into information. But data are viewed in different ways by different people. For example, contrast the (data) view of a company manager with that of a company clerk. Although the manager and the clerk both work for the same company, the manager is more likely to have an enterprise-wide view of company data than the clerk.

Even different managers view data differently. For example, a company director is likely to take a universal view of the data because he or she must be able to tie the company's divisions to a common (database) vision. A purchasing manager in the same company is likely to have a more restricted view of the data, as is the company's inventory manager. In effect, each department manager works with a subset of the company's data. The inventory manager is more concerned about inventory levels, while the purchasing manager is more concerned about the cost of items and about personal/business relationships with the suppliers of those items.

Applications programmers have yet another view of data, being more concerned with data location, formatting and specific reporting requirements. Basically, applications programmers translate company policies and procedures from a variety of sources into appropriate interfaces, reports and query screens.

The different users and producers of data and information often reflect the 'blindfolded people and the elephant' analogy: the blindfolded person who felt the elephant's trunk had quite a different view of the elephant from those who felt the elephant's leg or tail. What is needed is the ability to see the whole elephant. Similarly, a house is not a random collection of rooms; if someone is going to build a house, he or she should first have the overall view that is provided by blueprints. Likewise, a sound data environment requires an overall database blueprint based on an appropriate data model.

When a good database blueprint is available, it does not matter that an applications programmer's view of the data is different from that of the manager and/or the end user. Conversely, when a good database blueprint is not available, problems are likely to ensue. For instance, an inventory management program or an order entry system may not fit into the overall set of operational requirements, thereby costing the company thousands (or even millions).

Keep in mind that a house blueprint is an abstraction; you cannot live in the blueprint. Similarly, the data model is an abstraction; you cannot draw the required data out of the data model. Just as you are not likely to build a good house without a blueprint, you are equally unlikely to create a good database without first selecting an appropriate data model.

2.2 DATA MODEL BASIC BUILDING BLOCKS

The basic building blocks of all data models are entities, attributes, relationships and constraints. An **entity** is anything (a person, a place, a thing or an event) about which data are to be collected and stored. An entity represents a particular type of object in the real world. Entities may be physical objects, such as customers or products; but entities may also be abstractions, such as flight routes or musical concerts.

An **attribute** is a characteristic of an entity. For example, a CUSTOMER entity would be described by attributes such as customer last name, customer first name, customer phone, customer address and customer credit limit. Attributes are the equivalent of fields in file systems.

A **relationship** describes an association among entities. For example, a relationship exists between customers and agents that can be described as follows: an agent can serve many customers, and each customer may be served by one agent. Data models use three types of relationships: one-to-many, many-to-many and one-to-one. Database designers usually use the shorthand notations 1:*, *:* and 1:1, respectively. The following examples illustrate the distinctions among the three:

- **One-to-many (1:*) relationship.** A painter paints many different paintings, but each one of them is painted by only one painter. Thus, the painter (the 'one') is related to the paintings (the 'many'). Therefore, database designers label the relationship 'PAINTER paints PAINTING' as 1:*. (Note that entity names are often capitalised as a convention so they are easily distinguished.) Similarly, a customer (the 'one') may generate many invoices, but each invoice (the 'many') is generated by only a single customer. The 'CUSTOMER generates INVOICE' relationship would also be labelled 1:*.
- **Many-to-many (*:*) relationship.** An employee may learn many job skills, and each job skill may be learnt by many employees. Database designers label the relationship 'EMPLOYEE learns SKILL' as *:*. Similarly, a student can take many classes and each class can be taken by many students, thus yielding the *:* relationship label for the relationship expressed by 'STUDENT takes CLASS'.
- **One-to-one (1:1) relationship.** A retail company's management structure may require that each of its stores be managed by a single employee. In turn, each store manager, who is an employee, manages only a single store. Therefore, the relationship 'EMPLOYEE manages STORE' is labelled 1:1.

The preceding discussion identified each relationship in both directions; that is, relationships are bidirectional:

- *One* CUSTOMER can generate *many* INVOICEs.
- Each of the *many* INVOICEs is generated by only *one* CUSTOMER.

A **constraint** is a restriction placed on the data. Constraints are important because they help to ensure data integrity. Constraints are normally expressed in the form of rules; for example:

- The employee's salary must have values that are between 6 000 and 350 000.
- A student's grade must be between 0 and 100.
- Each class must have one and only one teacher.

How do you properly identify entities, attributes, relationships and constraints? The first step is to clearly identify the business rules of the environment you are modelling.

2.3 BUSINESS RULES

When database designers go about selecting or determining the entities, attributes and relationships that will be used to build a data model, they may start by gaining a thorough understanding of what types of data are in an organisation, how the data are used and in which time frames they are used. But such data and information do not, by themselves, yield the required understanding of the total business. From a database point of view, the collection of data becomes meaningful only when it reflects properly defined *business rules*. A **business rule** is a brief, precise and unambiguous description of a policy, procedure or principle within a specific organisation. In a sense, business rules are misnamed: they apply to *any* organisation, large or small – a business, a government unit, a religious group or a research laboratory – that stores and uses data to generate information.

Business rules, derived from a detailed description of an organisation's operations, help to create and enforce actions within that organisation's environment. Business rules must be rendered in writing and updated to reflect any change in the organisation's operational environment.

Properly written business rules are used to define entities, attributes, relationships and constraints. Any time you see relationship statements such as 'an agent can serve many customers, and each customer may be served by one agent', you are seeing business rules at work. You will see the application of business rules throughout this book, especially in the chapters devoted to data modelling and database design.

To be effective, business rules must be easy to understand and widely disseminated to ensure that every person in the organisation shares a common interpretation of the rules. Business rules describe, in simple language, the main and distinguishing characteristics of the data *as viewed by the company*. Examples of business rules are as follows:

- A customer may generate many invoices.
- An invoice is generated by only one customer.
- A training session cannot be scheduled for fewer than ten employees or for more than 30 employees.

Note that those business rules establish entities, relationships and constraints. For example, the first two business rules establish two entities, CUSTOMER and INVOICE, and a 1:* relationship between those two entities. The third business rule establishes a constraint: no fewer than ten people and no more than 30 people; two entities, EMPLOYEE and TRAINING; and a relationship between EMPLOYEE and TRAINING.

2.3.1 Discovering Business Rules

The main sources of business rules are company managers, policy makers, department managers and written documentation, such as a company's procedures, standards or operations manuals. A faster and more direct source of business rules is direct interviews with end users. Unfortunately, because perceptions differ, end users sometimes are a less reliable source when it comes to specifying business rules. For example, a maintenance department mechanic may believe that any mechanic can initiate a maintenance procedure, when actually only mechanics with inspection authorisation can perform such a task. Such a distinction may seem trivial, but it can have major legal consequences. Although end users are crucial contributors to the development of business rules, *it pays to verify end-user perceptions*. Too often, interviews with several people who perform the same job yield very different perceptions of what the job components are. While such a discovery may point to 'management problems', that general diagnosis does not help the database designer. The database designer's job is to reconcile such differences and verify the results of the reconciliation to ensure that the business rules are appropriate and accurate.

The process of identifying and documenting business rules is essential to database design for several reasons:

- They help standardise the company's view of data.
- They can be a communications tool between users and designers.
- They allow the designer to understand the nature, role and scope of the data.
- They allow the designer to understand business processes.
- They allow the designer to develop appropriate relationship participation rules and constraints, and to create an accurate data model.

Of course, not all business rules can be modelled. For example, a business rule that specifies that 'no pilot can fly more than ten hours within any 24-hour period' cannot be modelled. However, such a business rule can be enforced by application software.

2.3.2 Translating Business Rules into Data Model Components

Business rules set the stage for the proper identification of entities, attributes, relationships and constraints. In the real world, names are used to identify objects. If the business environment wants to keep track of the objects, there will be specific business rules for them. As a general rule, a noun in a business rule will translate into an entity in the model and a verb (active or passive) associating nouns will translate into a relationship among the entities. For example, the business rule 'a customer may generate many invoices' contains two nouns (*customer* and *invoices*) and a verb (*generate*) that associates the nouns. From this business rule, you could deduce that:

- 'Customer' and 'invoice' are objects of interest for the environment and should be represented by their respective entities.
- There is a 'generate' relationship between customer and invoice.

To properly identify the type of relationship, you should consider that relationships are bidirectional; that is, they go both ways. For example, the business rule 'a customer may generate many invoices' is complemented by the business rule 'an invoice is generated by only one customer'. In that case, the relationship is one-to-many (1:*). Customer is the '1' side, and invoice is the 'many' side.

As a general rule, to properly identify the relationship type, you should ask two questions:

- How many instances of B are related to one instance of A?
- How many instances of A are related to one instance of B?

For example, you could identify the relationship between student and class by asking two questions:

- How many classes can one student enrol in? Answer: Many classes.
- How many students can enrol in one class? Answer: Many students.

Therefore, the relationship between student and class is many-to-many (*:*). You will have many opportunities to determine the relationships between entities as you proceed through this book, and soon the process will become second nature.

2.4 THE EVOLUTION OF DATA MODELS

The quest for better data management has led to several different models that attempt to resolve the file system's critical shortcomings. These models represent schools of thought as to what a database is, what it should do, the types of structures that it should employ, and the technology that would be used to implement these structures. This section gives an overview of the major data models in roughly chronological order. You will discover that many of the 'new' database concepts and structures bear a remarkable resemblance to some of the 'old' data model concepts and structures. Table 2.1 traces the evolution of the major data models.

TABLE 2.1 Evolution of major data models

Generation	Time	Data Model	Examples	Comments
First	1960s–1970s	File system	VMS/VSAM	Used mainly on IBM mainframe systems Managed records, not relationships
Second	1970s	Hierarchical and network	IMS, ADABAS, IDS-II	Early database systems Navigational access
Third	Mid-1970s	Relational	DB2 Oracle MS SQL Server MySQL	Conceptual simplicity Entity relationship (ER) modelling and support for relational data modelling
Fourth	Mid-1980s	Object-oriented Object/relational (O/R)	Versant Objectivity/DB DB2 UDB Oracle 11g	Object/relational support for object data types Star Schema support for data warehousing Web databases become common
Fifth	Mid-1990s	XML Hybrid DBMS	dbXML Tamino DB2 UDB Oracle 11g MS SQL Server	Unstructured data support O/R model supports XML documents Hybrid DBMS adds object front end to relational databases Support large databases (terabyte size)
Emerging Models: NoSQL	Late 2000s to present	Key-value store Column store	SimpleDB (Amazon) Bigtable (Google) Cassandra (Apache)	Distributed, highly scalable High performance, fault tolerant Very large storage (petabytes) Suited for sparse data Proprietary API

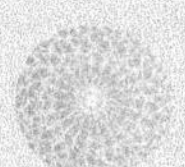

Online Content The hierarchical and network models are largely of historical interest, yet they do still contain some elements and features that interest current database professionals. The technical details of those two models are discussed in detail in Appendices I and J, respectively, on the accompanying online platform. Appendix G is devoted to the object-orientated (OO) model. However, given the dominant market presence of the relational model, most of the book focuses on that model.

2

2.4.1 Hierarchical and Network Models

The **hierarchical model** was developed in the 1960s to manage large amounts of data for complex manufacturing projects, such as the Apollo rocket that landed on the moon in 1969. The model's basic logical structure is represented by an upside-down tree. The hierarchical structure contains levels, or segments. A segment is the equivalent of a file system's record type. Within the hierarchy, a higher layer is perceived as the parent of the segment directly beneath it, which is called the child. The hierarchical model depicts a set of one-to-many (1:*) relationships between a parent and its children segments. (Each parent can have many children, but each child has only one parent.)

The **network model** was created to represent complex data relationships more effectively than the hierarchical model, to improve database performance and to impose a database standard. In the network model, the user perceives the network database as a collection of records in 1:* relationships. However, unlike the hierarchical model, the network model allows a record to have more than one parent. While the network database model is generally not used today, the definitions of standard database concepts that emerged with the network model are still used by modern data models:

- The **schema** is the conceptual organisation of the entire database as viewed by the database administrator.
- The **subschema** defines the portion of the database 'seen' by the application programs that actually produce the desired information from the data within the database.
- A **data manipulation language (DML)** defines the environment in which data can be managed and is used to work with the data in the database.
- A **schema data definition language (DDL)** enables the database administrator to define the schema components.

As information needs grew and more sophisticated databases and applications were required, the network model became too cumbersome. The lack of ad hoc query capability put heavy pressure on programmers to generate the code required to produce even the simplest reports. Although the existing databases provided limited data independence, any structural change in the database could still produce havoc in all application programs that drew data from the database. Because of the disadvantages of the hierarchical and network models, they were largely replaced by the relational data model in the 1980s.

2.4.2 The Relational Model

The **relational model** was introduced by E.F. Codd (of IBM) in 1970 in his landmark paper 'A Relational Model of Data for Large Shared Databanks'.[1] The relational model represented a major breakthrough for both users and designers. To use an analogy, the relational model produced an 'automatic transmission'

1 *Communications of the ACM*, pp. 377–387, June 1970.

database to replace the 'standard transmission' databases that preceded it. Its conceptual simplicity set the stage for a genuine database revolution.

In 1970, Codd's work was considered ingenious but impractical. The relational model's conceptual simplicity was bought at the expense of computer overhead; computers at that time lacked the power to implement the relational model. Fortunately, computer power grew exponentially, as did operating system efficiency. Better yet, the cost of computers diminished rapidly as their power grew. Today desktop and laptop computers, costing a fraction of what their mainframe ancestors did, can run relatively sophisticated relational database software provided by vendors such as Oracle, DB2, Informix, Ingres and other mainframe relational software vendors.

NOTE

The relational database model presented in this chapter is designed to introduce a more detailed discussion in Chapter 3, Relational Model Characteristics, and in Chapter 4, Relational Algebra and Calculus. In fact, the relational model is so important that it will serve as the basis for discussions in most of the remaining chapters.

The relational database model is implemented through a sophisticated **relational database management system (RDBMS)**. The RDBMS performs the same basic functions provided by the hierarchical and network DBMS systems, in addition to a host of other functions that make the relational database model easier to understand and implement.

Arguably the most important advantage of the RDBMS is its ability to hide the complexities of the relational model from the user. The RDBMS manages all of the physical details, while the user sees the relational database as a collection of tables in which data are stored and can manipulate and query data in a way that seems intuitive and logical.

Each **table** is a matrix, consisting of a series of row/column intersections. Tables, also called **relations**, are related to each other through the sharing of a field which is common to both entities. For example, the CUSTOMER table in Figure 2.1 might contain a sales agent's number that is also contained in the AGENT table.

Online Content This chapter's databases can be found on the accompanying online platform for this book. For example, the contents of the AGENT and CUSTOMER tables shown in Figure 2.1 are found in the database named 'Ch02_InsureCo'.

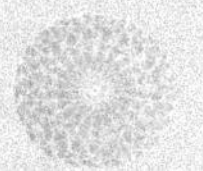

The common link between the CUSTOMER and AGENT tables enables you to match the customer to his or her sales agent even though the customer data are stored in one table and the sales representative data are stored in another table. For example, you can easily determine that customer Dunne's agent is Kubu Bhengani, because for customer Dunne, the CUSTOMER table's AGENT_CODE is 501, which matches the AGENT table's AGENT_CODE for Kubu Bhengani. Although the tables are independent of each other, you can easily associate the data between tables. The relational model provides a minimum level of controlled redundancy to eliminate most of the redundancies commonly found in file systems.

The relationship type (1:1, 1:* or *:*) is often shown in a relational schema, an example of which is depicted in Figure 2.2. A **relational diagram** is a representation of the relational database's entities, the attributes within those entities and the relationships between those entities.

2

FIGURE 2.1 Linking relational tables

Database name: Ch02_InsureCo Table name: AGENT (first six attributes)

AGENT_CODE	AGENT_LNAME	AGENT_FNAME	AGENT_INITIAL	AGENT_AREACODE	AGENT_PHONE
501	Bhengani	Kubu	B	0161	228-1249
502	Mbaso	Lethiwe	F	0181	882-1244
503	Okon	John	T	0181	123-5589

Link through AGENT_CODE

Table name: CUSTOMER

CUS_CODE	CUS_LNAME	CUS_FNAME	CUS_INITIAL	CUS_AREACODE	CUS_PHONE	CUS_RENEW_DATE	AGENT_CODE
10010	Ramas	Alfred	A	0181	844-2573	05-Apr-2018	502
10011	Dunne	Leona	K	0161	894-1238	16-Jun-2018	501
10012	Du Toit	Maelene	W	0181	894-2285	29-Jan-2018	502
10013	Pieterse	Jaco	F	0181	894-2180	14-Oct-2019	502
10014	Orlando	Myron		0181	222-1672	28-Dec-2019	501
10015	O'Brian	Amy	B	0161	442-3381	22-Sep-2019	503
10016	Brown	James	G	0181	297-1228	25-Mar-2018	502
10017	Williams	George		0181	290-2556	17-Jul-2019	503
10018	Padayachee	Vinaya	G	0161	382-7185	03-Dec-2019	501
10019	Moloi	Mlilo	K	0181	297-3809	14-Mar-2019	503

In Figure 2.2, the relational diagram shows the connecting fields (in this case, AGENT_CODE) and the relationship type, 1:*. In this example, the CUSTOMER represents the 'many' side because an AGENT can have many CUSTOMERs. The AGENT represents the '1' side because each CUSTOMER has only one AGENT.

A relational table stores a collection of related entities. In this respect, the relational database table resembles a file. However, there is one crucial difference between a table and a file: a table yields complete data and structural independence because it is a purely logical structure. How the data are physically stored in the database is of no concern to the user or the designer; the perception is what counts. And this property of the relational database model, explored in depth in the next chapter, became the source of a real database revolution.

Another reason for the relational database model's rise to dominance is its powerful and flexible query language. Relational algebra, which was defined by Codd in 1971, was the basis for many relational query languages and will be introduced in more detail in Chapter 4, Relational Algebra and Calculus. For most relational database software, the query language used is known as Structured Query Language (SQL). SQL is a 4GL that allows the user to specify what must be done without specifying how it must be done. The RDBMS uses SQL to translate user queries into instructions for retrieving the requested data. SQL makes it possible to retrieve data with far less effort than any other database or file environment.

FIGURE 2.2 **Relational diagram: a relational class diagram**

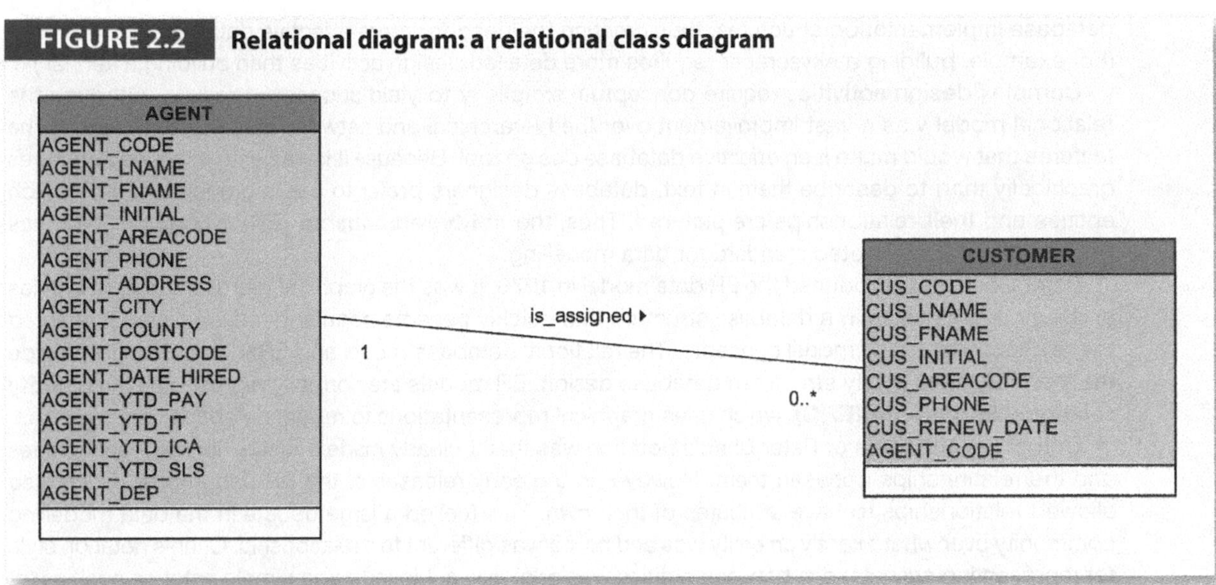

From an end-user perspective, any SQL-based relational database application involves three parts: a user interface, a set of tables stored in the database and the SQL 'engine'. Each of these parts is explained below:

- *The end-user interface.* Basically, the interface allows the end user to interact with the data (by auto-generating SQL code). Each interface is a product of the software vendor's idea of meaningful interaction with the data. You can also design your own customised interface with the help of application generators that are now standard in the database software arena.
- *A collection of tables stored in the database.* In a relational database, all data are perceived to be stored in tables. The tables simply 'present' the data to the end user in a way that is easy to understand. Each table is independent from another. Rows in different tables are related, based on common values in common attributes.
- *SQL engine.* Largely hidden from the end user, the SQL engine executes all queries or data requests. Keep in mind that the SQL engine is part of the DBMS software. The end user uses SQL to create table structures and to perform data access and table maintenance. The SQL engine translates all of those requests into the instructions necessary to perform such tasks – largely behind the scenes and without the end user's knowledge. Hence, it's said that SQL is a declarative language that tells what must be done but not how it must be done. (You will learn more about the SQL engine in Chapter 13, Managing Database and SQL Performance.)

  Because the RDBMS performs the behind-the-scenes tasks, it is not necessary to focus on the physical aspects of the database. Instead, the chapters that follow will concentrate on the logical portion of the relational database and its design. Furthermore, SQL is covered in detail in Chapter 8, Beginning Structured Query Language, and in Chapter 9, Procedural Language SQL and Advanced SQL.

2.4.3 The Entity Relationship Model

The conceptual simplicity of relational database technology triggered the demand for RDBMSs. In turn, the rapidly increasing transaction and information requirements created the need for more complex

2

database implementation structures, thus creating the need for more effective database design tools. (For example, building a skyscraper requires more detailed design activities than building a kennel.)

Complex design activities require conceptual simplicity to yield successful results. Although the relational model was a vast improvement over the hierarchical and network models, it still lacked the features that would make it an effective database *design* tool. Because it is easier to examine structures graphically than to describe them in text, database designers prefer to use a graphical tool in which entities and their relationships are pictured. Thus, the **entity relationship (ER) model**, or **ERM**, has become a widely accepted standard for data modelling.

Peter Chen first introduced the ER data model in 1976; it was the graphical representation of entities and their relationships in a database structure that quickly became popular because it *complemented* the relational database model concepts. The relational database model and ERM combined to provide the foundation for tightly structured database design. ER models are normally represented in an **entity relationship diagram (ERD)**, which uses graphical representations to model database components.

One of the strengths of Peter Chen's notation was that it clearly made a distinction between entities and the relationships between them. However in the early releases of the ER data model, Chen also allowed relationships to have attributes of their own. This fuelled a large debate in the data modelling community over what exactly an entity was and how it was different to a relationship. Chen's notation style for representing associations between entities was originally achieved using simple notation such as 'n' to indicate 'many'. When the basic data model components were introduced, three types of relationships among data were illustrated: one-to-many (1:M), many-to-many (M:N) and one-to-one (1:1). Relationships were represented by a diamond connected to the related entities through the relationship line. Whilst database designers adopted this model, more graphical versions of Chen's notation were developed, including one of the most common versions of the ERD, which uses the **Crow's Foot notation**.

NOTE

One of the more recent versions of Peter Chen's notations is known as *the Crow's Foot model*. The Crow's Foot notation was originally invented by Gordon Everest and later made popular by Clive Finkelstein[2] and James Martin. In Crow's Foot notation, graphical symbols were used instead of using the simple notation such as 'n' to indicate 'many' used by Chen. The label 'Crow's Foot' is derived from the three-pronged symbol used to represent the 'many' side of the relationship. Although there is a general shift towards the use of UML, many organisations today still use the Crow's Foot notation. This is particularly true in legacy systems which are running on obsolete hardware and software but are vital to the organisation. It is therefore important that you are familiar with both Chen's and Crow's Foot modelling notations.

More recently the **class diagram** component of the **Unified Modelling Language (UML)** has been used to produce entity relationship models. Although class diagrams have been developed as a part of the larger UML object-orientated design method, the notation is emerging as the industry data modelling standard. In this book the UML notation will therefore be used to model ERDs using relational concepts.

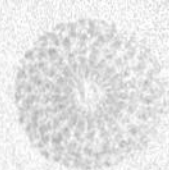

Online Content More in-depth coverage of the Crow's Foot notation is provided in Appendix E, Comparison of ER Modelling Notations, available on the online platform.

2 C. Finkelstein, *An Introduction to Information Engineering: From Strategic Planning to Information Systems*. Addison-Wesley, 1989.

NOTE

UML is an object-orientated modelling language sponsored by the Object Management Group (OMG®) and published as a standard in 1997. UML is the result of an effort headed by the OMG to develop a common set of object-orientated diagrams and notations (symbols and constructs) for the analysis, design and modeling of systems. Keep in mind that UML is not a methodology or procedure for developing databases. Rather, UML is a language that describes a set of diagrams and symbols that can be used to model a system graphically. The OMG® is an international not-for-profit software consortium that is setting standards in the area of distributed object computing, which includes UML. More details can be found on the website www.uml.org/

The ER model is based on the following components:

- *Entity*. Earlier in this chapter, an entity was defined as anything about which data are to be collected and stored. An entity is represented in the ERD by a rectangle, also known as an *entity box*. The name of the entity, a noun, is written in the centre of the rectangle. The entity name is generally written in capital letters and is written in the singular form: PAINTER rather than PAINTERS, or EMPLOYEE rather than EMPLOYEES. Usually, when applying the ERD to the relational model, an entity is mapped to a relational table. Each row in the relational table is known as an **entity instance** or **entity occurrence** in the ER model.

NOTE

A collection of like entities is known as an **entity set**. For example, you can think of the AGENT file in Figure 2.3 as a collection of three agents (*entities*) in the AGENT *entity set*. Technically speaking, the ERD depicts *entity sets*. Unfortunately, ERD designers use entity as a substitute for entity set, and this book will conform to that established practice when discussing any ERD and its components.

Each entity is described by a set of *attributes* that describes particular characteristics of the entity. For example, the entity EMPLOYEE will have attributes such as an employee number, a last name and a first name. (Chapter 5, Data Modelling with Entity Relationship Diagrams, explains how attributes are included in the ERD.)

- *Relationships.* Relationships describe associations among data. Most relationships describe associations between two entities. Within the basic data model, three types of relationships among data can be illustrated: one-to-many (1:*) many-to-many (*:*) and one-to-one (1:1). ERD modellers use the term **connectivity** to label the types of relationships. (The connectivities are written next to each entity box.) Relationships are represented by a relationship line that connects related entities. The name of the relationship, an active or passive verb, is written on the relationship line. For example, each of the company's DEPARTMENTs *has* many EMPLOYEEs; a PAINTER *paints* many PAINTINGs.

Figure 2.3 shows some basic ERDs that use the UML notation to illustrate these relationships and connectivities. As you examine the basic UML ERD in Figure 2.3, note that the entities and relationships may be presented horizontally or vertically. The location and the order in which the entities are presented in the ERD are immaterial; just remember to read a 1:* relationship from the '1' side to the '*' side.

2

FIGURE 2.3 The basic UML ERD

A One-to-Many (1..*) Relationship: A PAINTER can paint many PAINTINGs: each PAINTING is painted by one PAINTER.

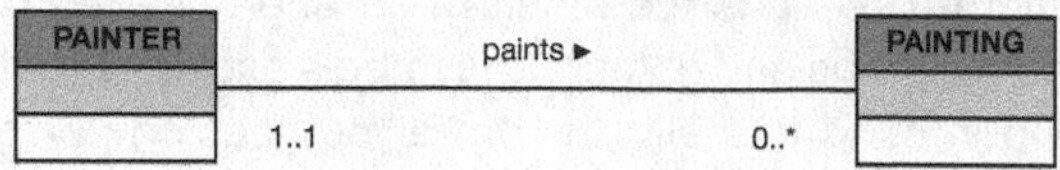

A Many-to-Many (*..*) Relationship: An EMPLOYEE can learn many SKILLs: each SKILL can be learned by many EMPLOYEEs.

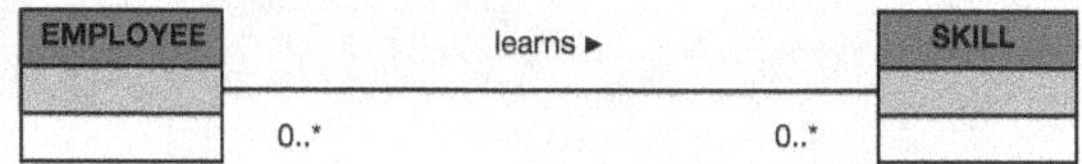

A One-to-Many (1..1) Relationship: An EMPLOYEE manages one STORE: each STORE is managed by one EMPLOYEE.

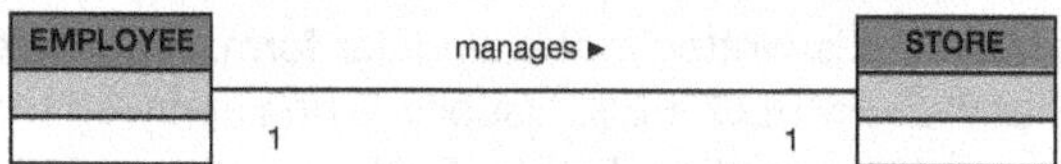

You should be aware that, typically, the UML class diagram was developed to model object classes and their associations. Because an object class is a collection of similar objects, a class is the equivalent of an entity set in the ER model. Likewise, an association is similar to a relationship where the degree of participation in a relationship is often referred to as multiplicities. The only major difference between a UML class and an ER entity is that a blank box is left in the drawing of the UML class to add the names of methods which are required when developing object-orientated systems. However, from a data modelling perspective this does not affect the structure of the data and you will use the UML notation to represent relational concepts only. Chapter 5, Data Modelling with Entity Relationship Diagrams, will introduce the concepts of both Crow's Foot notation and the Class Diagram notation in more detail.

Most database modelling tools let you select the UML model diagram option. Microsoft Visio Professional software was used to generate the UML class diagrams you will see in subsequent chapters.

NOTE

Many-to-many (*:*) relationships exist at a conceptual level, and you should know how to recognise them. However, you will learn in Chapter 3, Relational Model Characteristics, that *:* relationships are not appropriate in a relational model.

Online Content For a more detailed description of the Chen, Crow's Foot and other ER model notation systems, see Appendix E, Comparison of ER Model Notations, available on the online platform.

2

NOTE

For the purposes of illustration, Figure 2.6 shows alternative Crow's Foot models of the UML ERDs in Figure 2.4.

FIGURE 2.4 **The basic Crow's Foot ERD**

A One-to-Many (1:M) Relationship: A PAINTER can paint many PAINTINGs; each PAINTING is painted by one PAINTER.

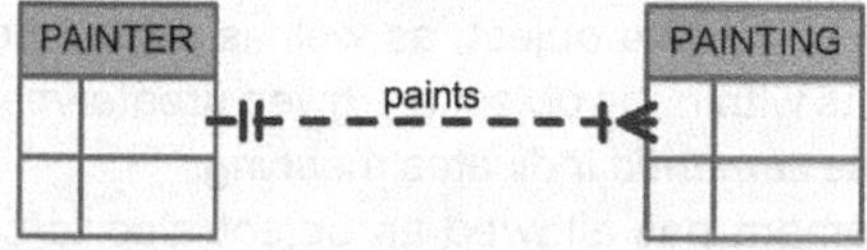

A Many-to-Many (M:N) Relationship: An EMPLOYEE can learn many SKILLs; each SKILL can be learnt by many EMPLOYEEs.

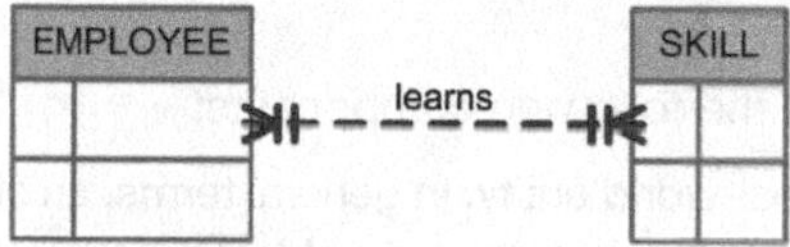

A One-to-One (1:1) Relationship: An EMPLOYEE manages one STORE; each STORE is managed by one EMPLOYEE.

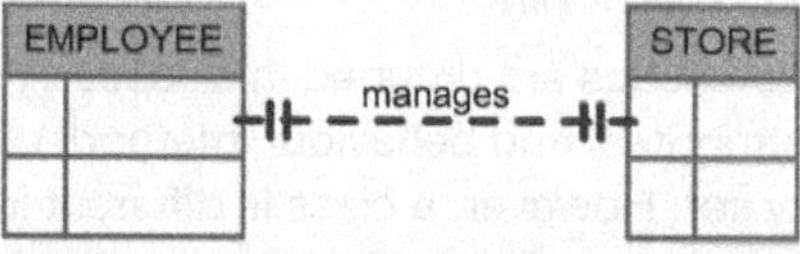

As you examine the basic Figure 2.4, note that the '1' is represented by a short line segment and the '*' is represented by the three-pronged 'Crow's Foot'. As with UML notation the entities and relationships may be presented horizontally or vertically and the order is again unimportant.

Its exceptional visual simplicity makes the ER model the dominant database modelling and design tool. Nevertheless, the search for better data modelling tools continues as the data environment continues to evolve.

2.4.4 The Object-Orientated (OO) Model

Increasingly complex real-world problems demonstrated a need for a data model that more closely represented the real world. In the **object-orientated data model (OODM)**, both data *and their relationships* are contained in a single structure known as an **object**. In turn, the OODM is the basis for the **object-orientated database management system (OODBMS)**.

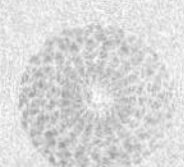

Online Content This chapter introduces only basic OO concepts. You'll have a chance to examine object-orientated concepts and principles in detail in Appendix G, Object-Oriented Databases, which can be found on the online platform.

2

An OODM reflects a different way to define and use entities. Like the relational model's entity, an object is described by its factual content. But quite *unlike* an entity, an object includes information about relationships between the facts within the object, as well as information about its relationships with other objects. Therefore, the facts within the object are given greater *meaning*. The OODM is said to be a **semantic data model** because *semantic* indicates meaning.

Subsequent OODM development has allowed an object also to contain all *operations* that can be performed on it, such as changing its data values, finding a specific data value and printing data values. As objects include data, various types of relationships and operational procedures, the object becomes self-contained, thus making the object – at least potentially – a basic building block for autonomous structures.

The OO data model is based on the following components:

- An object is an abstraction of a real-world entity. In general terms, an object may be considered equivalent to an ER model's entity. More precisely, an object represents only one individual occurrence of an entity. (The object's semantic content is defined through several of the items in this list.)
- Attributes describe the properties of an object. For example, a PERSON object includes the attributes Name, ID Number and Date of Birth.
- Objects that share similar characteristics are grouped in classes. A **class** is a collection of similar objects with shared structure (attributes) and behaviour (methods). In a general sense, a class resembles the ER model's entity *set*. However, a class is different from an entity set in that it contains a set of procedures known as *methods*. A class's **method** represents a real-world action such as *finding* a selected PERSON's name, *changing* a PERSON's name or *printing* a PERSON's address. In other words, methods are the equivalent of *procedures* in traditional programming languages. In OO terms, methods define an object's *behaviour*. (Some variants of the OO data model – such as the semantic object model – do not include methods in their representation.)
- Classes are organised in a *class hierarchy*. The **class hierarchy** resembles an upside-down tree in which each class has only one parent. For example, the CUSTOMER class and the EMPLOYEE class share a parent PERSON class. (Note the similarity to the hierarchical data model in this respect.)
- **Inheritance** is the ability of an object within the class hierarchy to inherit the attributes and methods of the classes above it. For example, two classes, CUSTOMER and EMPLOYEE, can be created as subclasses from the class PERSON. In this case, CUSTOMER and EMPLOYEE will inherit all attributes and methods from PERSON.

To illustrate the difference between the OO model and the ER model, examine their graphical representations in the simple invoicing problem shown in Figure 2.5.

As you examine Figure 2.5, note that:

- The OO data model represents an object as a box; all of the object attributes and relationships to other objects are included within the object box. The object representation of the INVOICE includes all related objects within the *same* object box. Note that the connectivities (1:1 and 1:*) indicate the relationship of the related objects to the INVOICE. For example, the 1:1 next to the CUSTOMER object indicates that each INVOICE is related to one and only one CUSTOMER. The 1:* next to the LINE object indicates that each INVOICE must contain at least one LINE but can also contain many LINEs.

2

FIGURE 2.5 **A comparison of the OO model and the ER model**

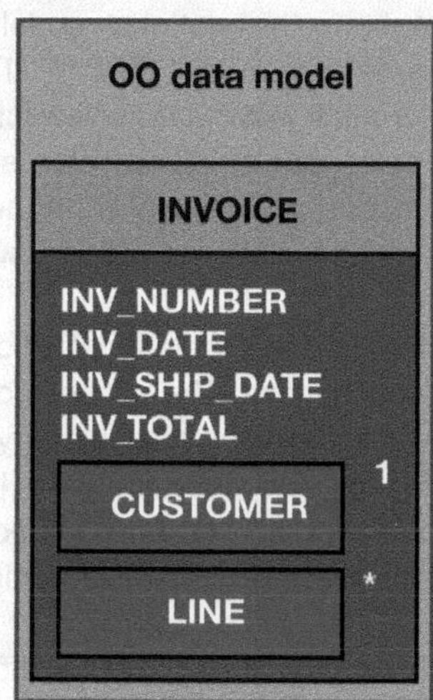

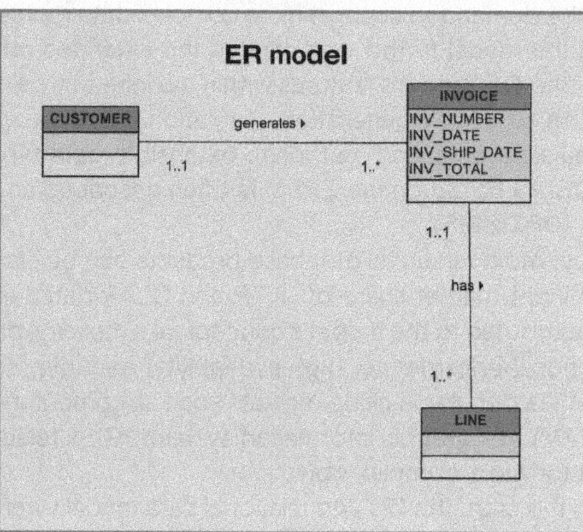

- The ER model uses three separate entities and two relationships to represent an invoice transaction. As customers can buy more than one item at a time, each invoice references one or more lines, one item per line. And because invoices are generated by customers, the data modelling requirements include a customer entity and a relationship between the customer and the invoice.

The OODM advances influenced many areas, from system modelling to programming. (Most contemporary programming languages have adopted OO concepts, including Java, Ruby, Perl, C# and Visual Studio) The added semantics of the OODM allowed for a richer representation of complex objects. This in turn enabled applications to support increasingly complex objects in innovative ways.

Online Content A useful comparison between the OO and ER model components can be found in Table G.3, located in Appendix G, Object-Orientated Databases, available on the online platform for this book.

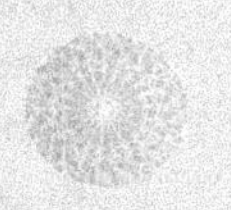

It is important to note that not all data models are created equal; some data models are better suited than others to some tasks. For example, *conceptual* models are better suited to high-level data modelling, while *implementation* models are better at managing stored data for implementation purposes. The entity relationship model is an example of a conceptual model, while the hierarchical and network models are examples of implementation models. At the same time, some models, such as the relational model and the OODM, could be used as both conceptual and implementation models.

2

2.4.5 Other Models

Facing the demand to support more complex data representations, the relational model's main vendors evolved the model further and created the **extended relational data model (ERDM)**. The ERDM adds many of the OO model's features within the inherently simpler relational database structure. The ERDM gave birth to a new generation of relational databases that support OO features such as objects (encapsulated data and methods), extensible data types based on classes and inheritance. That's why a DBMS based on the ERDM is often described as an **object relational database management system (ORDBMS)**.

Today, most relational database products can be classified as object relational, and they represent the dominant market share of OLTP and OLAP database applications. The success of the ORDBMS can be attributed to the model's conceptual simplicity, data integrity, easy-to-use query language, high transaction performance, high availability, security, scalability and expandability. In contrast, the OODBMS is popular in niche markets such as computer-aided drawing/computer-aided manufacturing (CAD/CAM), geographic information systems (GIS), telecommunications and multimedia, which require support for more complex objects.

From the start, the OO and relational data models were developed in response to different problems. The OO data model was created to address very specific engineering needs, not the wide-ranging needs of general data management tasks. The relational model was created with a focus on better data management based on a sound mathematical foundation. Given its focus on a smaller set of problem areas, it is not surprising that the OO market has not grown as rapidly as the relational data model market. However, large DBMS vendors such as Oracle readily promote their once relational DBMS now as object relational, with each new release adding new functionality. This gives organisations more choice and flexibility in the design and development of new database applications and in the integration with existing OO applications.

The use of complex objects received a boost with the internet revolution. When organisations integrated their business models with the internet, they realised its potential to access, distribute and exchange critical business information. This resulted in the widespread adoption of the internet as a business communication tool. Within this environment, Extensible Markup Language (XML) emerged as the de facto standard for the efficient and effective exchange of structured, semi-structured and unstructured data. Organisations that use XML data soon realised that they needed to manage large amounts of unstructured data such as word-processing documents, Web pages, emails and diagrams. To address this need, XML databases emerged to manage unstructured data within a native XML format. (See Chapter 17, Database Connectivity and Web Technologies). At the same time, ORDBMSs added support for XML-based documents within their relational data structure. Due to its robust foundation in broadly applicable principles, the relational model is easily extended to include new classes of capabilities, such as objects and XML.

Modelling spatial data for use in applications such as route optimisation (an ambulance finding the quickest route to a patient) or urban planning requires yet another type of data model. Spatial data comprises objects such as cities or forests that exist in a multi-dimensional space. Storing such data in a relational database would simply take up too much space and queries would be too long and complex to manage. A spatial database management system (SDBMS) is a database system with additional capabilities for handling spatial data. SDBMS include spatial data types (SDTs) in its data model and query language. For example the ability to model objects (forests, cities or rivers) in space using types such as POINT, LINE and REGION. The POINT data type refers to the object's centre point in the multi-dimensional space, the LINE data type is used to represent connections in multi-dimensional space, e.g. rivers or roads, and the REGION data type is a representation of an extent e.g. a lake in a 2-D space. In addition SDMS supports spatial indexing allowing the fast retrieval of objects in a specific area and efficient algorithms for supporting spatial joins. SDBMS are often used to support GIS applications – one of the most popular today being Google Earth.

Although relational and object relational databases address most current data processing needs, a new generation of databases has emerged to address some very specific data challenges found in some organisations.

2.4.6 Emerging Data Models: Big Data and NoSQL

Deriving usable business information from the mountains of Web data that organisations have accumulated over the years has become an imperative need. Web data in the form of browsing patterns, purchasing histories, customer preferences, behaviour patterns and social media data from sources such as Facebook, Twitter and LinkedIn have inundated organisations with combinations of structured and unstructured data. According to many studies, the rapid pace of data growth is the top challenge for organisations,[3] with system performance and scalability as the next biggest challenges. Today's information technology (IT) managers are constantly balancing the need to manage this rapidly growing data with shrinking budgets. The need to manage and leverage all these converging trends (rapid data growth, performance, scalability and lower costs) has triggered a phenomenon called 'Big Data'. **Big Data** refers to a movement to find new and better ways to manage large amounts of Web-generated data and derive business insight from it, while simultaneously providing high performance and scalability at a reasonable cost. (You will learn in more detail about NoSQL in Chapter 16 Big Data and NoSQL.)

The problem is that the relational approach does not always match the needs of organisations with Big Data challenges:

- It is not always possible to fit unstructured, social media data into the conventional relational structure of rows and columns.
- Adding millions of rows of multiformat (structured and non-structured) data on a daily basis will inevitably lead to the need for more storage, processing power and sophisticated data analysis tools that may not be available in the relational environment.
- Generally speaking, the type of high-volume implementations required in the RDBMS environment for the Big Data problem come with a hefty price tag for expanding hardware, storage and software licences.
- Data analysis based on OLAP tools has proven to be very successful in relational environments with highly structured data. However, mining for usable data in the vast amounts of unstructured data collected from Web sources requires a different approach.

There is no 'one-size-fits-all' cure to data management needs (although many established database vendors will probably try to sell you on the idea). For some organisations, creating a highly scalable, fault-tolerant infrastructure for Big Data analysis could prove to be a matter of business survival. The business world has many examples of companies that leverage technology to gain a competitive advantage, and others that miss it. Just ask yourself how the business landscape would be different if:

- MySpace had responded to Facebook's challenge in time.
- Blockbuster had reacted to the Netflix business model sooner.
- Barnes & Noble had developed a viable internet strategy before Amazon.

Therefore, it is not surprising that some organisations are turning to NoSQL databases to mine the wealth of information hidden in mountains of Web data and gain a competitive advantage.

---

3 See www.gartner.com/en/newsroom/press-releases/2019-02-18-gartner-identifies-top-10-data-and-analytics-technolo, 'Gartner Identifies Top 10 Data and Analytics Technology Trends for 2019', February 2019.

2

NOTE

Does this mean that relational databases don't have a place in organisations with Big Data challenges? No, relational databases remain the preferred and dominant databases to support most day-to-day transactions and structured data analytics needs. Each DBMS technology has its areas of application, and the best approach is to use the best tool for the job. In perspective, in September 2019, relational databases were still significantly the most dominant DDMS technology for businesses.

2.4.7 NoSQL Databases

Every time you search for a product on Amazon, send messages to friends via Facebook, watch a video on YouTube or search for directions in Google Maps, you are using a NoSQL database. As with any new technology, the term *NoSQL* can be loosely applied to many different types of technologies. However, this chapter uses **NoSQL** to refer to a new generation of databases that address the specific challenges of the Big Data era and have the following general characteristics:

- Not based on the relational model, hence the name NoSQL.
- Supports distributed database architectures.
- Provides high scalability, high availability and fault tolerance.
- Supports very large amounts of sparse data.
- Geared towards performance rather than transaction consistency.

Let's examine these characteristics in more detail.

NoSQL databases are not based on the relational model. In fact, there is no standard NoSQL data model. To the contrary, many different data models are grouped under the NoSQL umbrella, from document databases to graph stores, column stores and key-value stores. It is still too early to know which, if any, of these data models will survive and grow to become a dominant force in the database arena. However, the early success of products such as Amazon's SimpleDB, Google's Bigtable and Apache's Cassandra points to the *key-value stores* and *column stores* as the early leaders. The word *stores* indicates that these data models permanently store data in secondary storage, just like any other database. This added emphasis comes from the fact that these data models originated from programming languages (such as LISP), in which in-memory arrays of values are used to hold data.

The *key-value* data model is based on a structure composed of two data elements: a key and a value, in which every key has a corresponding value or set of values. The key-value data model is also referred to as the attribute-value or associative data model. To better understand the key-value model, look at the simple example in Figure 2.6.

Figure 2.6 shows the example of a small truck-driving company called Trucks-R-Us. Each of the three drivers has one or more certifications and other general information. Using this example, we can draw the following important points:

- In the relational model, every row represents a single entity occurrence and every column represents an attribute of the entity occurrence. Each column has a defined data type.
- In the key-value data model, each row represents one attribute of one entity instance. The 'key' column points to an attribute and the 'value' column contains the actual value for the attribute.

FIGURE 2.6 **A simple key-value representation**

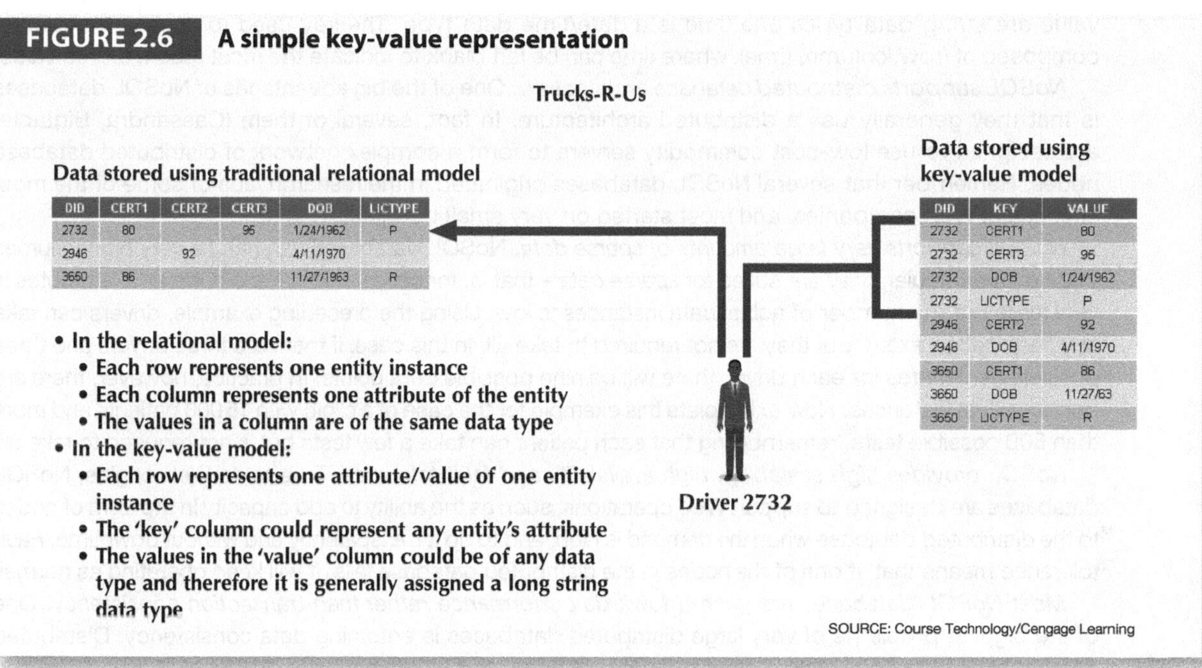

SOURCE: Course Technology/Cengage Learning

- The data type of the 'value' column is generally a long string to accommodate the variety of actual data types of the values placed in the column.
- To add a new entity attribute in the relational model, you need to modify the table definition. To add a new attribute in the key-value store, you add a row to the key-value store, which is why it is said to be 'schema-less'.
- NoSQL databases do not store or enforce relationships among entities. The programmer is required to manage the relationships in the program code. Furthermore, all data and integrity validations must be done in the program code (although some implementations have been expanded to support metadata).
- NoSQL databases use their own native application programming interface (API) with simple data access commands, such as *put*, *read* and *delete*. Because there is no declarative SQL-like syntax to retrieve data, the program code must take care of retrieving related data in the correct way.
- Indexing and searches can be difficult. Because the 'value' column in the key-value data model could contain many different data types, it is often difficult to create indexes on the data. At the same time, searches can become very complex.

As a matter of fact, you could use the key-value structure as a general data modelling technique when attributes are numerous but actual data values are scarce. The key-value data model is not exclusive of NoSQL databases; actually, key-value data structures could reside inside a relational database. However, because of the problems with maintaining relationships and integrity within the data, and the increased complexity of even simple queries, key-value structures would be a poor design for most structured business data.

Several NoSQL database implementations, such as Google's Bigtable and Apache's Cassandra, have extended the key-value data model to group multiple key-value sets into column families or column stores. In addition, such implementations support features such as versioning using a date/time stamp. For example, Bigtable stores data in the syntax of [row, column, time, value], where row, column and

2

value are string data types and time is a date/time data type. The key used to access the data is composed of (row, column, time), where time can be left blank to indicate the most recent stored value.

NoSQL supports distributed database architecture. One of the big advantages of NoSQL databases is that they generally use a distributed architecture. In fact, several of them (Cassandra, Bigtable) are designed to use low-cost commodity servers to form a complex network of distributed database nodes. Remember that several NoSQL databases originated in the research labs of some of the most successful Web companies, and most started on very small budgets!

NoSQL supports very large amounts of sparse data. NoSQL databases can handle very high volumes of data. In particular, they are suited for *sparse data* – that is, for cases in which the number of attributes is very large but the number of actual data instances is low. Using the preceding example, drivers can take any certification exam, but they are not required to take all. In this case, if there are three drivers and three possible certificates for each driver, there will be nine possible data points. In practice, however, there are only four data instances. Now extrapolate this example for the case of a clinic with 15 000 patients and more than 500 possible tests, remembering that each patient can take a few tests but is not required to take all.

NoSQL provides high scalability, high availability and fault tolerance. True to its Web origins, NoSQL databases are designed to support Web operations, such as the ability to add capacity in the form of nodes to the distributed database when the demand is high, and to do it transparently and without downtime. Fault tolerance means that, if one of the nodes in the distributed database fails, it will keep operating as normal.

Most NoSQL databases are geared towards performance rather than transaction consistency. One of the biggest problems of very large distributed databases is enforcing data consistency. Distributed databases automatically make copies of data elements at multiple nodes to ensure high availability and fault tolerance. If the node with the requested data goes down, the request can be served from any other node with a copy of the data. However, what happens if the network goes down during a data update? In a relational database, transaction updates are guaranteed to be consistent or the transaction is rolled back. NoSQL databases sacrifice consistency to attain high levels of performance. (See Chapter 12, Managing Transactions and Concurrency, to learn more about this topic.) Some NoSQL databases provide a feature called *eventual consistency*, which means that updates to the database will propagate through the system and eventually all data copies will be consistent. With eventual consistency, data are not guaranteed to be consistent across all copies of the data immediately after an update.

NoSQL is one of the hottest items in database technologies today. But, as you learnt in Chapter 1, it is only one of many emerging trends in data management. Whichever database technology you use, you need to be able to select the best tool for the job by understanding the pros and cons of each technology. The following section briefly summarises the evolution of data models and provides some advantages and disadvantages of each.

2.4.8 Data Models: A Summary

The evolution of DBMSs has always been driven by the search for new ways of modelling increasingly complex real-world data. A summary of the most commonly recognised data models is shown in Figure 2.7.

In the evolution of data models, there are some common characteristics that data models must have in order to be widely accepted:

- A data model must show some degree of conceptual simplicity without compromising the semantic completeness of the database. *It does not make sense to have a data model that is more difficult to conceptualise than the real world.*
- A data model must represent the real world as closely as possible. This goal is more easily realised by adding more semantics to the model's data representation. (Semantics concern the dynamic data behaviour, while data representation constitutes the static aspect of the real-world scenario.)

- Representation of the real-world transformations (behaviour) must be in compliance with the consistency and integrity characteristics of any data model.

FIGURE 2.7 The evolution of data models

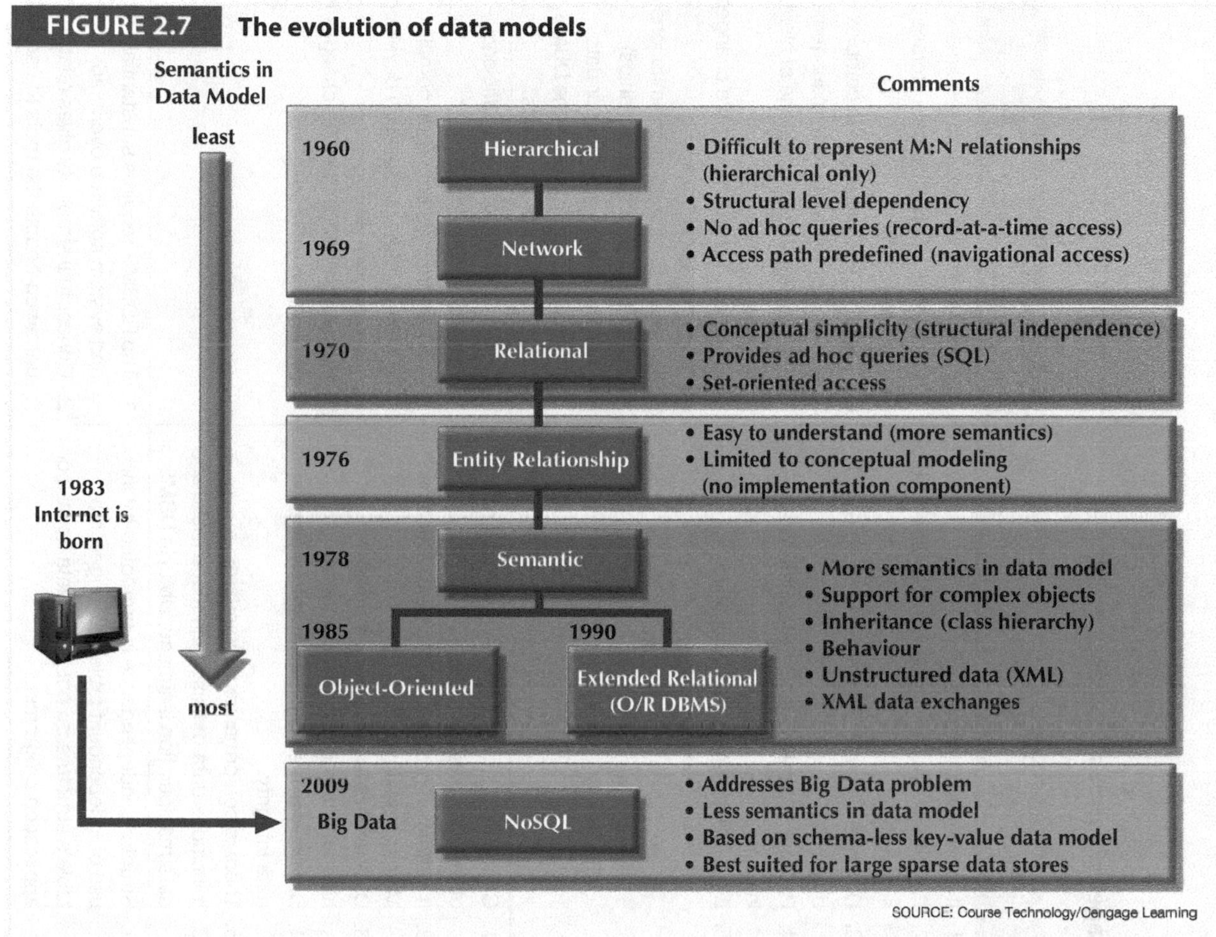

SOURCE: Course Technology/Cengage Learning

Each new data model capitalised on the shortcomings of previous models. The network model replaced the hierarchical model because the former made it much easier to represent complex (many-to-many) relationships. In turn, the relational model offered several advantages over the hierarchical and network models through its simpler data representation, superior data independence and easy-to-use query language; the relational model also emerged as the dominant data model for business applications. The OO data model introduced support for complex data within a rich semantic framework. The ERDM added many OO features to the relational model and allowed it to maintain strong market share within the business environment. In recent years, the Big Data phenomenon also has stimulated the development of alternative ways to model, store and manage data that represents a break with traditional data management.

It is important to note that not all data models are created equal; some data models are better suited than others for some tasks. For example, *conceptual* models are better suited to high-level data modelling, while *implementation* models are better for managing stored data for implementation purposes. The entity relationship model is an example of a conceptual model, while the hierarchical and network models are examples of implementation models. At the same time, some models, such as the relational model and the OODM, could be used as both conceptual and implementation models. Table 2.2 summarises the advantages and disadvantages of the various database models.

TABLE 2.2 Advantages and disadvantages of various database models

Data Model	Data independence	Structural Independence	Advantages	Disadvantages
Hierarchical	Yes	No	1. It promotes data sharing. 2. Parent/child relationship promotes conceptual simplicity. 3. Database security is provided and enforced by DBMS. 4. Parent/child relationship promotes data integrity. 5. It is efficient with 1:M relationships.	1. Complex implementation requires knowledge of physical data storage characteristics. 2. Navigational system yields complex application development, management, and use; requires knowledge of hierarchical path. 3. Changes in structure require changes in all application programs. 4. There are implementation limitations (no multiparent or M:N relationships). 5. There is no data definition or data manipulation language in the DBMS. 6. There is a lack of standards.
Network	Yes	No	1. Conceptual simplicity is at least equal to that of the hierarchical model. 2. It handles more relationship types, such as M:N and multiparent. 3. Data access is more flexible than in hierarchical and file system models. 4. Data owner/member relationship promotes data integrity. 5. There is conformance to standards. 6. It includes data definition language (DDL) and data manipulation language (DML) in DBMS.	1. System complexity limits efficiency – still a navigational system. 2. Navigational system yields complex implementation, application development and management. 3. Structural changes require changes in all application programs.
Relational	Yes	Yes	1. Structural independence is promoted by the use of independent tables. Changes in a table's structure do not affect data access or application programs.	1. The RDBMS requires substantial hardware and system software overhead. 2. Conceptual simplicity gives relatively untrained people the tools to use a good

			2. Tabular view substantially improves conceptual simplicity, thereby promoting easier database design, implementation, management and use. 3. Ad hoc query capability is based on SQL. 4. Powerful RDBMS isolates the end user from physical-level details and improves implementation and management simplicity.	system poorly and, if unchecked, it may produce the same data anomalies found in file systems. 3. It may promote islands of information problems as individuals and departments can easily develop their own applications.
Entity Relationship	Yes	Yes	1. Visual modelling yields exceptional conceptual simplicity. 2. Visual representation makes it an effective communication tool. 3. It is integrated with the dominant relational model.	1. There is limited constraint representation. 2. There is limited relationship representation. 3. There is no data manipulation language. 4. Loss of information content occurs when attributes are removed from entities to avoid crowded displays. (This limitation has been addressed in subsequent graphical versions.)
Object-Orientated	Yes	Yes	1. Semantic content is added. 2. Visual representation includes semantic content. 3. Inheritance promotes data integrity.	1. Slow development of standards caused vendors to supply their own enhancements, thus eliminating a widely accepted standard. 2. It is a complex navigational system. 3. There is a steep learning curve. 4. High system overhead slows transactions.
NoSQL	Yes	Yes	1. High scalability, availability and fault tolerance are provided. 2. It uses low-cost commodity hardware. 3. It supports Big Data. 4. Key-value model improves storage efficiency.	1. Complex programming is required. 2. There is no relationship support – only by application code. 3. There is no transaction integrity support. 4. In terms of data consistency, it provides an eventually consistent model.

2

2.5 DEGREES OF DATA ABSTRACTION

In the early 1970s, the **American National Standards Institute (ANSI)** Standards Planning and Requirements Committee (SPARC) defined a framework for data modelling based on degrees of data abstraction. To illustrate the meaning of data abstraction, consider the example of automotive design. A car designer begins by drawing the *concept* of the car that is to be produced. Next, engineers design the details that help transfer the basic concept into a structure that can be produced. Finally, the engineering drawings are translated into production specifications to be used on the factory floor. As you can see, the process of producing the car begins at a high level of abstraction and proceeds to an ever-increasing level of detail. The factory floor process cannot proceed unless the engineering details are properly specified, and the engineering details cannot exist without the basic conceptual framework created by the designer. Designing a usable database follows the same basic process. That is, a database designer starts with an abstract view of the overall data environment and adds details as the design comes closer to implementation. Using levels of abstraction can also be very helpful in integrating multiple (and sometimes conflicting) views of data as seen at different levels of an organisation.

The ANSI/SPARC architecture (as it is often referred to) defines three levels of data abstraction: external, conceptual and internal. You can use this framework to better understand database models, as shown in Figure 2.8. In the figure, the ANSI/SPARC framework has been expanded with the addition of a *physical* model to address physical-level implementation details of the internal model explicitly.

FIGURE 2.8 Data abstraction levels

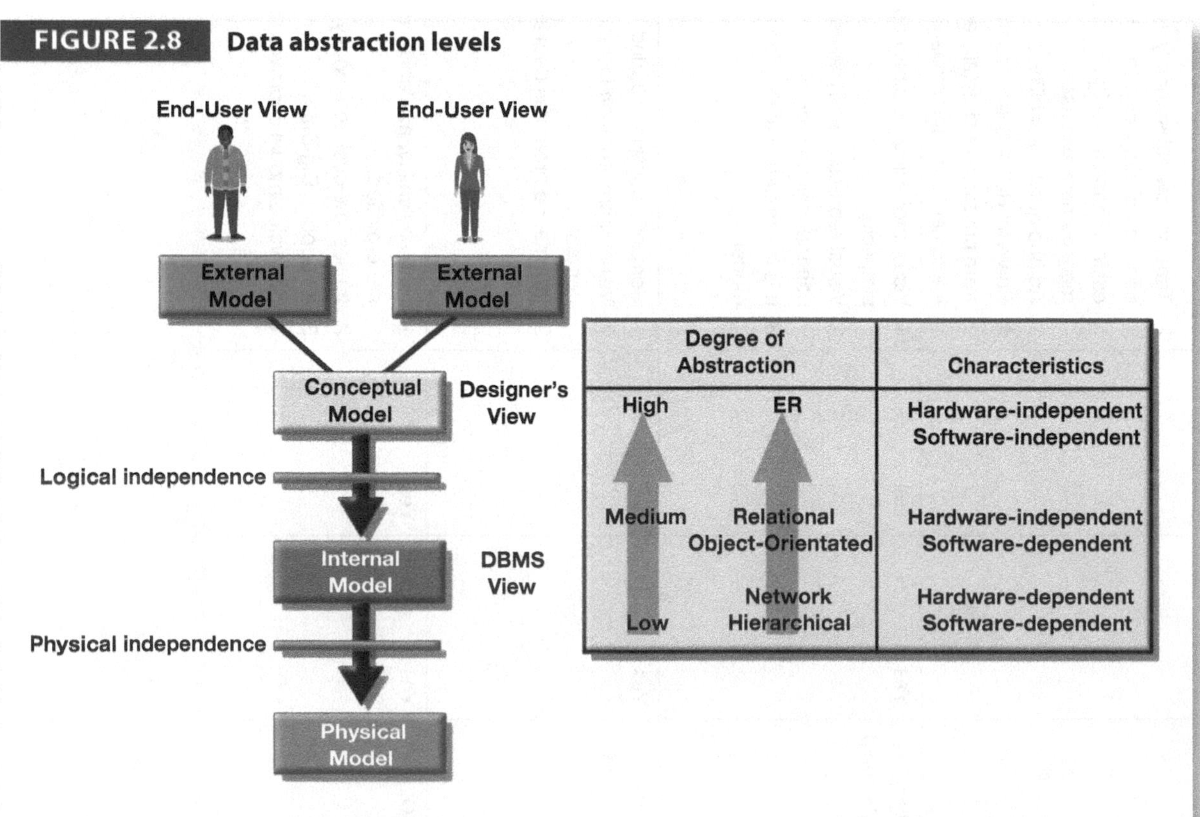

2.5.1 The External Model

The **external model** is the end users' view of the data environment. The term *end users* refers to people who use the application programs to manipulate the data and generate information. End users usually operate in an environment in which an application has a specific business unit focus. Companies are generally divided into several business units, such as sales, finance and marketing. Each business unit is subject to specific constraints and requirements, and each one uses a data subset of the overall data in the organisation. Therefore, end users working within those business units view their data subsets as separate from or external to those of other units within the organisation.

As data is being modelled, ER diagrams will be used to represent the external views. A specific representation of an external view is known as an **external schema**. To illustrate the external model's view, examine the data environment of Tiny University. Figure 2.9 (a) and (b) presents the external schemas for two Tiny University business units: student registration and class scheduling. Each external schema includes the appropriate entities, relationships, processes and constraints imposed by the business unit. Also note that, *although the application views are isolated from each other, each view shares a common entity with the other view*. For example, the registration and scheduling external schemas share the entities CLASS and COURSE.

Note the entity relationships represented in Figure 2.9. For example:

- A LECTURER may teach many CLASSes, and each CLASS is taught by only one LECTURER; that is, there is a 1:* relationship between LECTURER and CLASS.
- A CLASS may ENROL many students, and each student may ENROL in many CLASSes, thus creating a *:* relationship between STUDENT and CLASS. (You will learn about the precise nature of the ENROL entity in Chapter 5, Data Modelling with Entity Relationship Diagrams.)
- Each COURSE may generate many CLASSes, but each CLASS references a single COURSE. For example, there may be several classes (sections) of a database course having a course code of CIS-420. One of those classes may be offered on Mondays, Wednesdays and Fridays from 8:00 a.m. to 8:50 a.m., another may be offered on Mondays, Wednesdays and Fridays from 1:00 p.m. to 1:50 p.m., while a third may be offered on Thursdays from 6:00 p.m. to 8:40 p.m. Yet all three classes have the course code CIS-420.
- Finally, a CLASS requires one ROOM, but a ROOM may be scheduled for many CLASSes; that is, each classroom may be used for several classes: one at 9:00 a.m., one at 11:00 a.m., and one at 1:00 p.m., for example. In other words, there is a 1:* relationship between ROOM and CLASS.

The use of external views representing subsets of the database has some important advantages:

- It makes it easy to identify specific data required to support each business unit's operations.
- It makes the designer's job easy by providing feedback about the model's adequacy. Specifically, the model can be checked to ensure that it supports all processes as defined by their external models, as well as all operational requirements and constraints.
- It helps to ensure *security* constraints in the database design. Damaging an entire database is more difficult when each business unit works with only a subset of data.
- It makes application program development much simpler.

2

FIGURE 2.9 External models for Tiny University

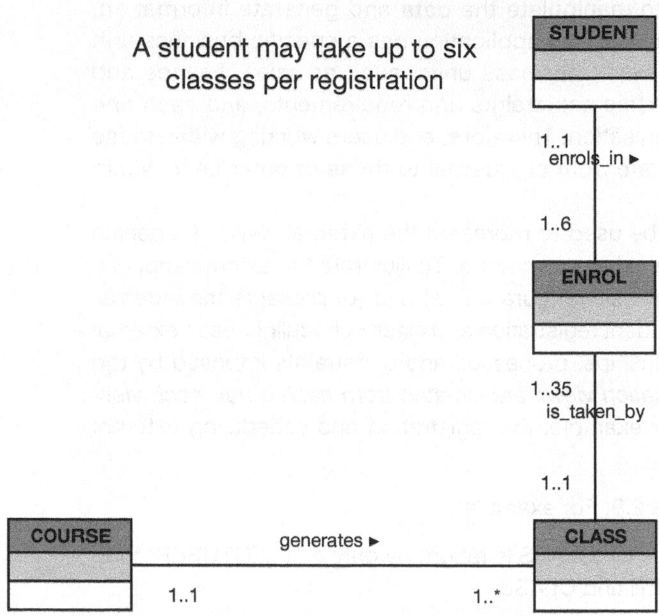

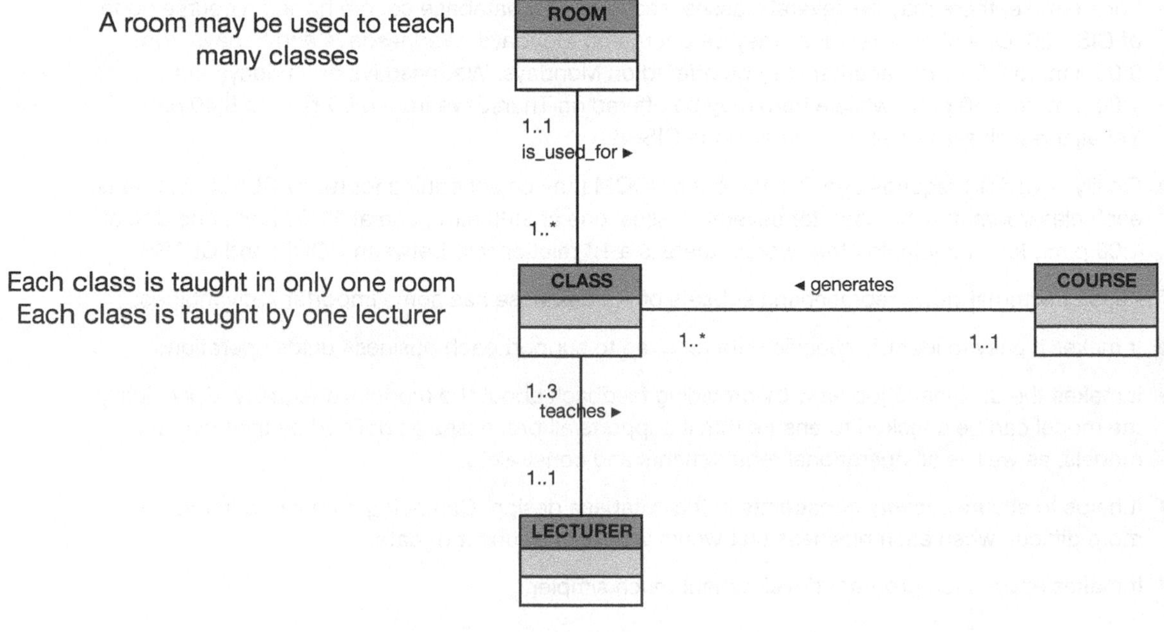

2.5.2 The Conceptual Model

Having identified the external views, a conceptual model is used, graphically represented by an ERD (Figure 2.10), to integrate all external views into a single view. The **conceptual model** represents a global view of the entire database. It is a representation of data as viewed by the entire organisation. That is, the conceptual model integrates all external views (entities, relationships, constraints and processes) into a single global view of the entire data in the enterprise, known as a **conceptual schema**. The conceptual schema is the basis for the identification and high-level description of the main data objects (avoiding any database model specific details).

The most widely used conceptual model is the ER model. Remember that the ER model is illustrated with the help of the ERD, which is, in effect, the basic database blueprint. The ERD is used to graphically *represent* the conceptual schema.

The conceptual model yields some very important advantages. First, it provides a relatively easily understood bird's-eye (macro-level) view of the data environment. For example, you can get a summary of Tiny University's data environment by examining the conceptual model presented in Figure 2.10.

Second, the conceptual model is independent of both software and hardware. **Software independence** means that the model does not depend on the DBMS software used to implement the model. **Hardware independence** means that the model does not depend on the hardware used in the implementation of the model. Therefore, changes in either the hardware or the DBMS software will have no effect on the database design at the conceptual level. Generally, the term **logical design** is used to refer to the task of creating a conceptual data model that could be implemented in any DBMS.

FIGURE 2.10 Conceptual model for Tiny University

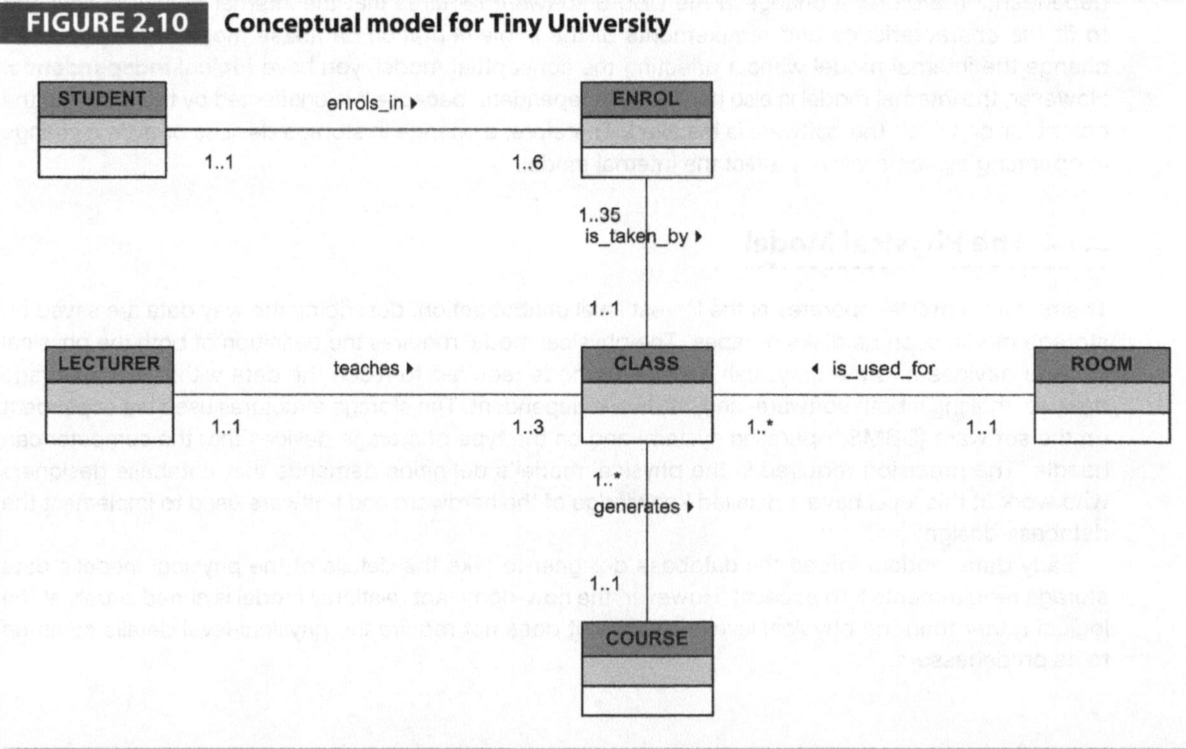

2.5.3 The Internal Model

Once a specific DBMS has been selected, the internal model maps the conceptual model to the DBMS. The **internal model** is the representation of the database as 'seen' by the DBMS. In other words, the internal model requires the designer to match the conceptual model's characteristics and constraints to those of the selected implementation model. An **internal schema** depicts a specific representation of an internal model, using the database constructs supported by the chosen database.

Since this book focuses on the relational model, a relational database was chosen to implement the internal model. Therefore, the internal schema should map the conceptual model to the relational model constructs. In particular, the entities in the conceptual model are mapped to tables in the relational model. Likewise, since a relational database has been selected, the internal schema is expressed using SQL, the standard language for relational databases. In the case of the conceptual model for Tiny University depicted in Figure 2.10, the internal model was implemented by creating the tables LECTURER, COURSE, CLASS, STUDENT, ENROL and ROOM. A simplified version of the internal model for Tiny College is shown in Figures 2.11 (a) and (b).

The development of a detailed internal model is especially important to database designers who work with hierarchical or network models because those models require very precise specification of data storage location and data access paths. In contrast, the relational model requires less detail in its internal model because most RDBMSs handle data access path definition *transparently*; that is, the designer need not be aware of the data access path details. Nevertheless, even relational database software usually requires data storage location specification, especially in a mainframe environment. For example, DB2 requires that the data storage group, the location of the database within the storage group, and the location of the tables within the database be specified.

Because the internal model depends on specific database software, it is said to be software-dependent. Therefore, a change in the DBMS software requires that the internal model be changed to fit the characteristics and requirements of the implementation database model. When you can change the internal model without affecting the conceptual model, you have **logical independence**. However, the internal model is also hardware-independent, because it is unaffected by the choice of the computer on which the software is installed. Therefore, a change in storage devices or even a change in operating systems will not affect the internal model.

2.5.4 The Physical Model

The **physical model** operates at the lowest level of abstraction, describing the way data are saved on storage media such as disks or tapes. The physical model requires the definition of both the physical storage devices and the (physical) access methods required to reach the data within those storage devices, making it both software- and hardware-dependent. The storage structures used are dependent on the software (DBMS, operating system) and on the type of storage devices that the computer can handle. The precision required in the physical model's definition demands that database designers who work at this level have a detailed knowledge of the hardware and software used to implement the database design.

Early data models forced the database designer to take the details of the physical model's data storage requirements into account. However, the now-dominant relational model is aimed largely at the logical rather than the physical level; therefore, it does not require the physical-level details common to its predecessors.

FIGURE 2.11 **An internal model for Tiny University**

CONCEPTUAL MODEL

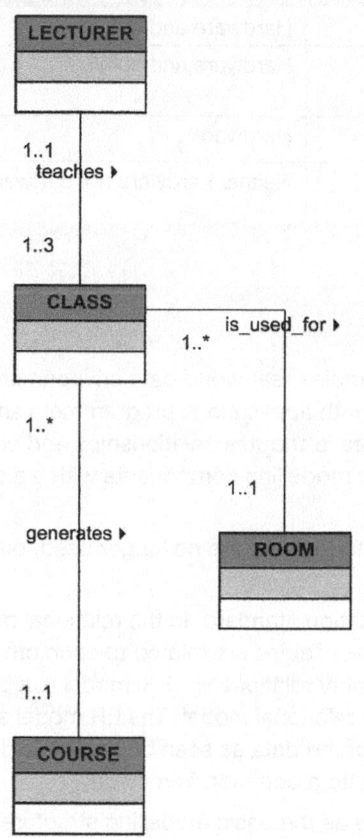

INTERNAL MODEL

```
CREATE TABLE LECTURER(
LECTURER_ID NUMBER PRIMARY KEY,
LECTURER_LNAME VARCHAR2(15),
LECTURER_INITIAL CHAR(1),
LECTURER_FNAME VARCHAR2(15),
..........);

CREATE TABLE CLASS(
CLASS_ID NUMBER PRIMARY KEY,
CRS_ID VARCHAR2(8) REFERENCES COURSE,
LECTURER_ID NUMBER REFERENCES LECTURER,
ROOM_ID VARCHAR2(8) REFERENCES ROOM,
..........);

CREATE TABLE ROOM(
ROOM_ID VARCHAR2(8) PRIMARY KEY,
ROOM_TYPE VARCHAR2(3),
..........);

CREATE TABLE COURSE(
CRS_ID VARCHAR2(8) PRIMARY KEY,
CRS_NAME VARCHAR2(25),
CRS_CREDITS NUMBER,
..........);
```

Although the relational model does not require the designer to be concerned about the data's physical storage characteristics, the *implementation* of a relational model may require physical-level fine-tuning for increased performance. Fine-tuning is especially important when very large databases are installed in a mainframe environment. Yet even such performance fine-tuning at the physical level does not require knowledge of physical data storage characteristics.

As noted earlier, the physical model is dependent on the DBMS, file level access methods and types of hardware storage devices supported by the operating system. When you can change the physical model without affecting the internal model, you have **physical independence**. Therefore, a change in storage devices or methods and even a change in operating system will not affect the internal model.

A summary of the levels of data abstraction is given in Table 2.3.

TABLE 2.3 Levels of data abstraction

Model	Degree of Abstraction	Focus	Independent of
External	High	End-user views	Hardware and software
Conceptual	↕	Global view of data (independent of database model)	Hardware and software
Internal		Specific database model	Hardware
Physical	Low	Storage and access methods	Neither hardware nor software

SUMMARY

- A data model is a (relatively) simple abstraction of a complex real-world data environment. Database designers use data models to communicate with applications programmers and end users. The basic data-modelling components are entities, attributes, relationships and constraints. Business rules are used to identify and define the basic modelling components within a specific real-world environment.
- The hierarchical and network data models were early models that are no longer used, but some of the concepts are found in current data models.
- The relational model is the current database implementation standard. In the relational model, the end user perceives the data as being stored in tables. Tables are related to each other by means of common values in common attributes. The entity relationship (ER) model is a popular graphical tool for data modelling that complements the relational model. The ER model allows database designers to visually present different views of the data as seen by database designers, programmers and end users and to integrate the data into a common framework.
- The object-orientated data model (OODM) uses objects as the basic modelling structure. An object resembles an entity in that it includes the facts that define it. But unlike an entity, the object also includes information about relationships between the facts as well as relationships with other objects, thus giving its data more meaning.
- The relational model has adopted many object-orientated (OO) extensions to become the extended relational data model (ERDM). At this point, the OODM is largely used in specialised engineering and scientific applications, while the ERDM is primarily geared to business applications. Although the most likely future scenario is an increasing merger of OODM and ERDM technologies, both are overshadowed by the need to develop internet access strategies for databases.
- NoSQL databases are a new generation of databases that do not use the relational model and are geared to support the very specific needs of Big Data organisations. NoSQL databases offer distributed data stores that provide high scalability, availability and fault tolerance by sacrificing data consistency and shifting the burden of maintaining relationships and data integrity to the program code.
- Data modelling requirements are a function of different data views (global vs local) and the level of data abstraction. The American National Standards Institute Standards Planning and Requirements Committee (ANSI/SPARC) describes three levels of data abstraction: external, conceptual and internal. There is also a fourth level of data abstraction (the physical level). This lowest level of data abstraction is concerned exclusively with physical storage methods.

2

KEY TERMS

American National Standards Institute (ANSI)
attribute
Big Data
business rule
class
class diagram
class hierarchy
conceptual model
conceptual schema
connectivity
constraint
Crow's Foot notation
data definition language (DDL)
data manipulation language (DML)
data models
entity
entity instance
entity occurrence
entity relationship (ER) model (ERM)
entity relationship diagram (ERD)
entity set
extended relational data model (ERDM)
external model
external schema
hardware independence
hierarchical model
inheritance
internal model
internal schema
logical design
logical independence
many-to-many (*:*) relationship
method
network model
NoSQL
object
object relational database management system (ORDBMS)
object-orientated data model (OODM)
object-orientated database management system (OODBMS)
one-to-many (1:*) relationship
one-to-one (1:1) relationship
physical independence
physical model
relational database management system (RDBMS)
relational diagram
relational model
relations
relationship
schema semantic data model
software independence
subschema table
Unified Modelling Language (UML)

FURTHER READING

Blaha, M. and Premerlani, W. *Object-Oriented Modelling and Design for Database Applications*. Prentice Hall, 1998.

Chen, P. 'The entity-relationship model towards a unified view of data', *ACM Transactions on Database Systems*, 1(1): 1976.

Codd, E.F. 'A relational model of data for large shared databanks', *Communications of the ACM*, pp. 377–387, 1970.

Codd, E.F. 'A database sublanguage founded on relational calculus', *Proceedings of the AIM SIGFIDET Conference on Data Description, Access and Control*, pp. 35–68, 1971.

Codd, E.F. *The Relational Model for Database Management*, Version 2. Addison-Wesley, 1990.

Lausen, G. and Vossen, G. *Models and Languages of Object Orientated Databases*. Addison-Wesley, 1998.

Oracle NoSQL Database Documentation, ORACLE, 2019 [online] Available: https://docs.oracle.com/en/database/other-databases/nosql-database/index.html

Thalheim, B. *Entity-Relationship Modelling Foundations of Database Technology*. Springer, 2000.

Online Content Answers to selected Review Questions and Problems for this chapter can be found on the online platform for this book.

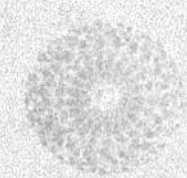

REVIEW QUESTIONS

1 Discuss the importance of data modelling.

2 What is a business rule, and what is its purpose in data modelling?

3 How would you translate business rules into data model components?

4 Describe the basic features of the relational data model and discuss their importance to the end user and the designer.

5. Explain how the entity relationship (ER) model helped produce a more structured relational database design environment.
6. Use the scenario described by 'A customer can make many payments, but each payment is made by only one customer' as the basis for an entity relationship diagram (ERD) presentation. Show your answer using UML class diagram notation.
7. Why is an object said to have greater semantic content than an entity?
8. What is the difference between an object and a class in the object-orientated data model (OODM)?
9. How would you model Question 6 with an OODM? (Use Figure 2.7 as your guide.)
10. What is an ERDM, and what role does it play in the modern (production) database environment?
11. What is a relationship, and which three types of relationships exist?
12. Give an example of each of the three types of relationships.
13. What is a table, and what role does it play in the relational model?
14. What is a relational diagram? Give an example.
15. What is connectivity? Draw ERDs to illustrate connectivity.
16. Describe the Big Data phenomenon.
17. What is sparse data? Give an example.
18. Define and describe the basic characteristics of a NoSQL database.
19. Describe the key-value data model.
20. Using the example of a medical clinic with patients and tests, provide a simple representation of how to model this example using the relational model and how it would be represented using the key-value modelling technique.
21. What is logical independence?
22. What is physical independence?

PROBLEMS

Use the contents of Figure 2.3 on p.46 to work Problems 1–5.

1. Write the business rule(s) that govern the relationship between AGENT and CUSTOMER.
2. Given the business rule(s) you wrote in Problem 1, create a basic UML class ERD.
3. If the relationship between AGENT and CUSTOMER were implemented in a hierarchical model, what would the hierarchical structure look like? Label the structure fully, identifying the root segment and the Level 1 segment.
4. If the relationship between AGENT and CUSTOMER were implemented in a network model, what would the network model look like? (Identify the record types and set.)
5. Using the ERD you drew in Problem 2, create the equivalent OO model. (Use Figure 2.7 on p. 55 as your guide.)

Using Figure P2.1 as your guide, answer Problem 6. The DealCo Class ERD shows the initial entities and attributes for the DealCo stores, located in two regions of the country.

2

FIGURE P2.1 **The DealCo class ERD**

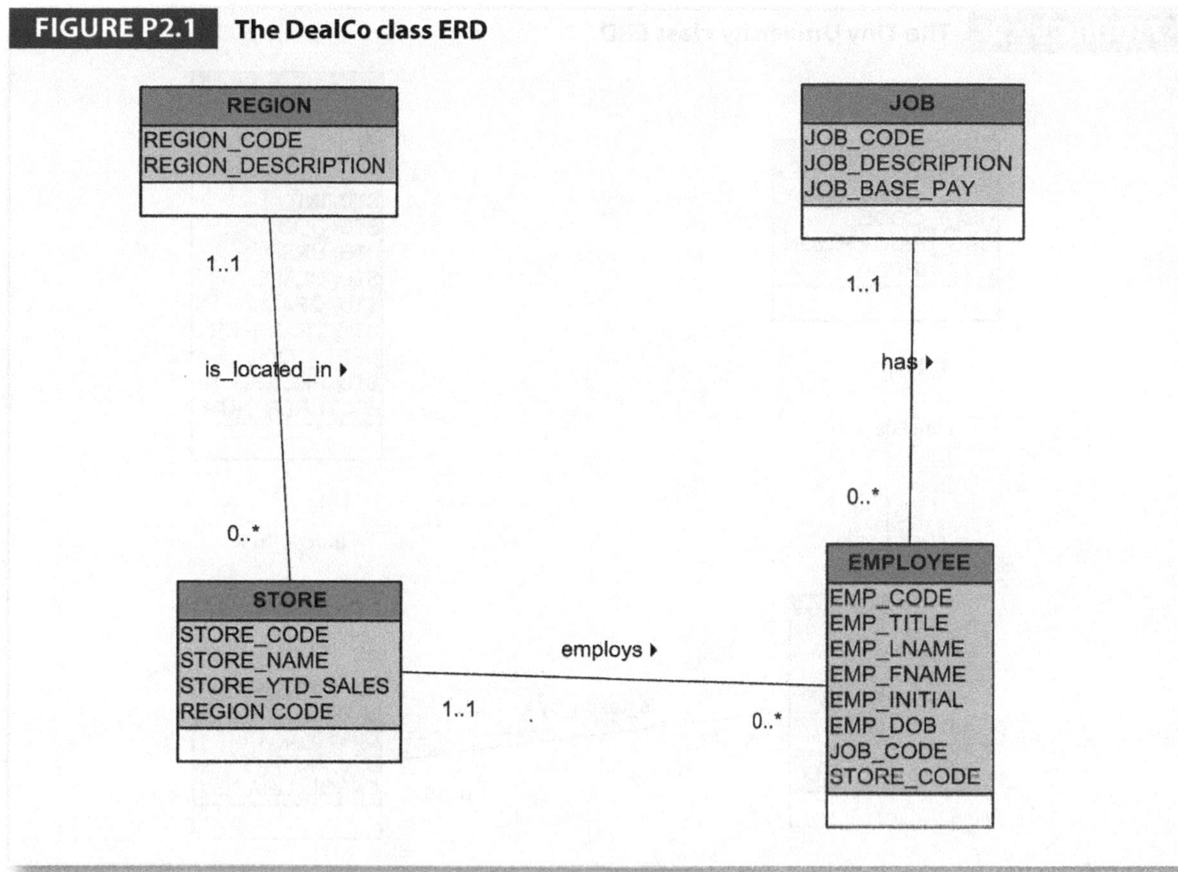

6 Identify each relationship type and write all of the business rules.

Using Figure P2.2 as your guide, answer Problems 7–9. The Tiny University class ERD shows the initial entities and attributes for Tiny University.

7 Identify each relationship type and write all of the business rules.

8 A hospital patient receives medications that have been ordered by a particular doctor. Because the patient often receives several medications per day, there is a 1:* relationship between PATIENT and ORDER. Similarly, each order can include several medications, creating a 1:* relationship between ORDER and MEDICATION.

   a Identify the business rules for PATIENT, ORDER and MEDICATION.

   b Create an ERD that depicts a relational database model to capture these business rules.

9 United Broke Artists (UBA) is a broker for not-so-famous artists. UBA maintains a small database to track painters, paintings and galleries. A painting is created by a particular artist and then exhibited in a particular gallery. A gallery can exhibit many paintings, but each painting can be exhibited in only one gallery. Similarly, a painting is created by a single painter, but each painter can create many paintings. Using PAINTER, PAINTING and GALLERY, in terms of a relational database:

   a Which tables would you create, and what would the table components be?

   b How might the (independent) tables be related to one another?

   c Draw the complete ERD.

2

FIGURE P2.2 **The Tiny University class ERD**

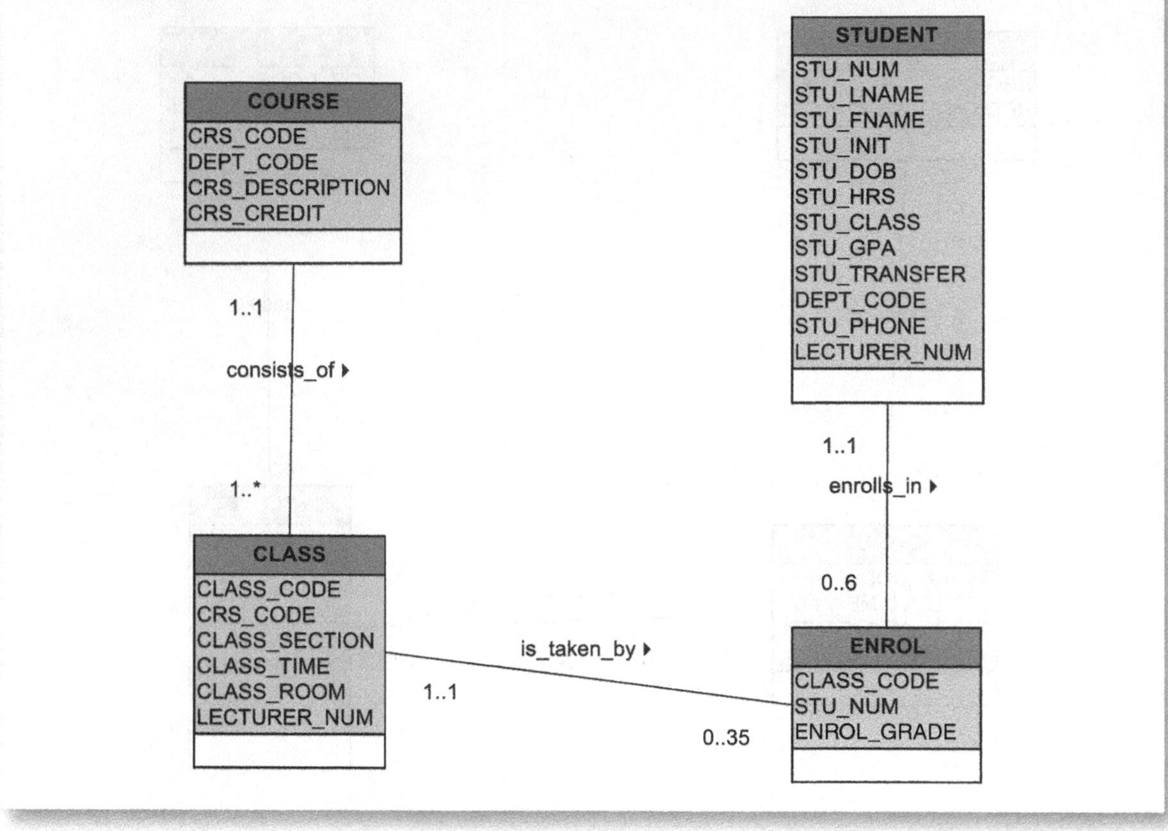

10 Using the ERD from Problem 9, create the relational schema. (Create an appropriate collection of attributes for each of the entities. Make sure you use the appropriate naming conventions to name the attributes.)

11 Describe the relationships (identify the business rules) depicted in the ERD shown in Figure P2.3.

12 Convert the ERD from Problem 11 into a UML class diagram.

13 Describe the relationships shown in the ERD in Figure P2.4.

14 Create a UML ERD for each of the following descriptions. (*Note:* The word *many* merely means 'more than one' in the database modelling environment.)

- **a** Each of the MegaCo Corporation's divisions is composed of many departments. Each of those departments has many employees assigned to it, but each employee works for only one department. Each department is managed by one employee, and each of those managers can manage only one department at a time.
- **b** During a period of time, a customer can rent many DVDs from the BigVid store. Each of the BigVid's DVDs can be rented to many customers during that period of time.
- **c** An airliner can be assigned to fly many flights, but each flight is flown by only one airliner.
- **d** The KwikTite Corporation operates many factories. Each factory is located in a region. Each region can be 'home' to many of KwikTite's factories. Each factory employs many employees, but each of those employees is employed by only one factory.
- **e** An employee may have earned many degrees, and each degree may have been earned by many employees.

FIGURE P2.3 The Crow's Foot ERD for Problem 11

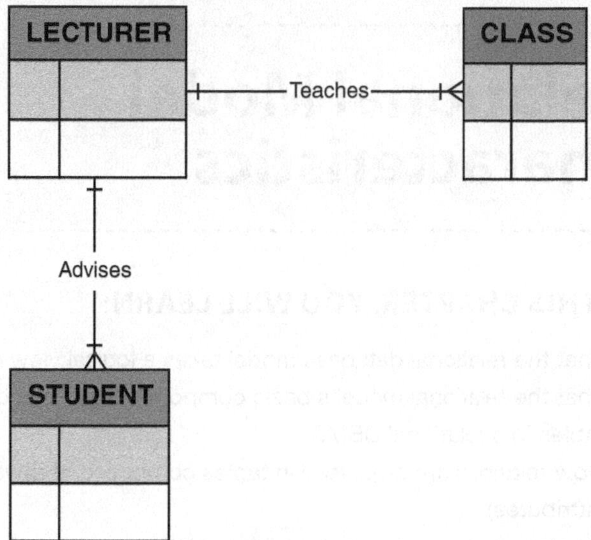

FIGURE P2.4 The UML ERD for Problem 13

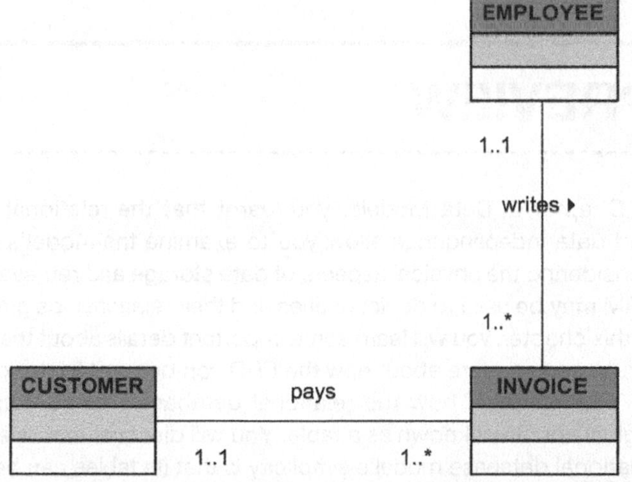

NOTE

Many-to-many (*:*) relationships exist at a conceptual level, and you should know how to recognise them. However, you will learn in Chapter 3, Relational Model Characteristics, that *:* relationships are not appropriate in a relational model.

CHAPTER 3

Relational Model Characteristics

IN THIS CHAPTER, YOU WILL LEARN:

- That the relational database model takes a logical view of data
- That the relational model's basic components are relations implemented through tables in a relational DBMS
- How relations are organised in tables composed of rows (tuples) and columns (attributes)
- Key terminology used in describing relations
- About the role of the data dictionary, and the system catalogue
- How data redundancy is handled in the relational database model
- Why indexing is important

PREVIEW

In Chapter 2, Data Models, you learnt that the relational data model's structural and data independence allow you to examine the model's logical structure without considering the physical aspects of data storage and retrieval. You also learnt that the ERM may be used to depict entities and their relationships graphically through an ERD. In this chapter, you will learn some important details about the relational model's logical structure and more about how the ERD can be used to design a relational database.

You will learn how the relational database's basic data components fit into a logical construct known as a table. You will discover that one important reason for the relational database model's simplicity is that its tables can be treated as logical rather than physical units. You will also learn how the independent tables within the database can be related to one another.

After learning about tables, their components and their relationships, you are introduced to the basic concepts that shape the design of tables. Because the table is such an integral part of relational database design, you will also learn the characteristics of well-designed and poorly designed tables.

Finally, you are introduced to some basic concepts that will become your gateway to the next few chapters. For example, you will examine different kinds of relationships and the way in which those relationships might be handled in the relational database environment.

NOTE

The relational model, introduced by E.F. Codd in 1970, is based on predicate logic and set theory. **Predicate logic**, used extensively in mathematics, provides a framework in which an assertion (statement of fact) can be verified as either true or false. For example, suppose that a student with a student ID of 12345678 is named Cela Nkosi. This assertion can easily be demonstrated to be true or false. *Set theory* is a mathematical science that deals with sets, or groups of things, and is used as the basis for data manipulation in the relational model. For example, assume that set A contains three numbers, 16, 24 and 77, represented as A(16, 24, 77). Furthermore, set B contains four numbers 44, 77, 90 and 11, represented as B(44, 77, 90, 11). Given this information, you can conclude that the intersection of A and B yields a result set with a single number, 77. This result can be expressed as $A \cap B = 77$. In other words, A and B share a common value, 77.

Based on these concepts, the relational model has three well-defined components:

- A logical data structure represented by the relational table, where data are stored (Sections 3.1, 3.2 and 3.4).
- A set of integrity rules to enforce that the data are and remain consistent over time (Sections 3.3, 3.5, 3.6 and 3.7).
- A set of operations that define how data are manipulated (Chapter 4, Relational Algebra and Calculus).

3

3.1 A LOGICAL VIEW OF DATA

In Chapter 1, The Database Approach, you learnt that a database stores and manages both data and metadata. You also learnt that the DBMS manages and controls access to the data and the database structure. Such an arrangement – placing the DBMS between the application and the database – eliminates most of the file system's inherent limitations. The result of such flexibility, however, is a far more complex physical structure. In fact, the database structures required by both the hierarchical and network database models often become complicated enough to diminish efficient database design. The relational data model changed all of that by allowing the designer to focus on the logical representation of the data and their relationships, rather than on the physical storage details. To use an automotive analogy, the relational database uses an automatic transmission to relieve you of the need to manipulate clutch pedals and gear levers. In short, the relational model enables you to view data *logically* rather than *physically*.

The practical significance of taking the logical view is that it serves as a reminder of the simple file concept of data storage. Although the use of a table, quite unlike that of a file, has the advantages of structural and data independence, a table does resemble a file from a conceptual point of view. Since you can think of related records as being stored in independent tables, the relational database model is much easier to understand than its hierarchical and network database predecessors. Greater logical simplicity tends to yield simpler and more effective database design methodologies.

As the table plays such a prominent role in the relational model, it deserves a closer look. Therefore, our discussion begins with an exploration of the details of table structure and contents.

NOTE

Relational database terminology is very precise. Unfortunately, file system terminology sometimes creeps into the database environment. Thus, rows are sometimes referred to as *records* and columns are sometimes labelled as *fields*. Occasionally, tables are labelled *files*. Technically speaking, this substitution of terms is not always appropriate; the database table is a logical rather than a physical concept, and the terms *file, record* and *field* describe physical concepts. Nevertheless, as long as you recognise that the table is actually a logical rather than a physical construct, you may (at the conceptual level) think of table rows as records and of table columns as fields. In fact, many database software vendors still use this familiar file system terminology.

3.1.1 Tables and Their Characteristics

The logical view of the relational database is facilitated by the creation of data relationships based on a logical construct known as a *table*. A table is perceived as a two-dimensional structure composed of rows and columns. As far as the table's user is concerned, *a table contains a group of related entities*, that is, an entity set; for that reason, the terms *entity set* and *table* are often used interchangeably. A table is also called a *relation* because the relational model's creator, E.F. Codd, used the term *relation* as a synonym for table. You can think of a table as a *persistent* relation, that is, a relation whose contents can be permanently saved for future use. Within the relational model, columns of tables are referred to as *attributes* and rows of tables are known as *tuples*.

NOTE

The concept of a relation is modelled on a mathematical construct and therefore must follow a certain restricted set of rules. For example, every relation within the database must have a distinct name. In mathematics, a relation is formally defined as:

Given a number of sets D_1, D_2, ..., D_n (which are not necessarily distinct), R is a relation on these n sets, it is a set of tuples each of which has its first element from D_1, second element from D_2 and so on.

Let's examine this formal definition with an example. Assume we have two sets ($n = 2$), one of students' last names (STU_LNAME) and one of the department codes (DEPT_CODE) where they have enrolled.

STU_LNAME {Ndlovu, Smithson, Le Roux, Ismail}
DEPT_CODE {BIOL, CIS, EDU}

Then a relation can be defined over the sets STU_LNAME and DEPT_CODE as:

R = {(Ndlovu, BIOL), (Smithson, CIS),(Le Roux, EDU),(Ismail, EDU)}

So, as you can see, a relation is simply a set of ordered pairs.

3

Table 3.1 shows the properties that a relation must conform to.

TABLE 3.1 Properties of a relation

1	A table is perceived as a two-dimensional structure composed of rows and columns.
2	Each table row (**tuple**) represents a single entity occurrence within the entity set and must be distinct. Duplicate rows are not allowed in a relation.
3	Each table column represents an attribute, and each column has a distinct name.
4	Each cell or column/row intersection in a relation should contain only an atomic value – that is, a single data value. Multiple values are not allowed in the cells of a relation.
5	All values in a column must conform to the same data format. For example, if the attribute is assigned an integer data format, all values in the column representing that attribute must be integers.
6	Each column has a specific range of values known as the **attribute domain.**
7	The order of the rows and columns is immaterial to the DBMS.
8	Each table must have an attribute or a combination of attributes that uniquely identifies each row.

Figure 3.1 shows two tables: COURSE and LECTURER. The LECTURER table conforms to all of the rules listed in Table 3.1 and hence constitutes a relation. The table COURSE however is not a relation because the COURSE_NAME column contains multiple values. For example CRS_CODE CIS-420 is associated with three COURSE_NAME values:

- Database Design and Implementation
- Introduction to Databases
- Data Modelling: An Introduction

3

FIGURE 3.1(a) The relation LECTURER

Table name: LECTURER

EMP_NUM	LECTURER_OFFICE	LECTURER_EXTENSION	LECTURER_HIGH_DEGREE
103	DRE 156	6783	PhD
104	DRE 102	5561	MA
105	KLR 229D	8665	PhD
106	KLR 126	3899	PhD
110	AAK 160	3412	PhD
114	KLR 211	4436	PhD
155	AAK 201	4440	PhD

FIGURE 3.1(b) The non-relational table COURSE

Table name: COURSE

CRS_CODE	COURSE_NAME
CIS-220	Introduction to Computer Science Assembly Language Programming
CIS-420	Database Design and Implementation Introduction to Databases Data Modelling: An Introduction
QM-261	Intro. to Statistics Statistical Applications

Applying the concepts of relations to database models allows us to define a relational schema for each entity. A **relational schema** is a textual representation of the database tables, where each table is described by its name followed by the list of its attributes in parentheses.

NOTE

A relational schema R can be formally defined as $R=\{a_1, a_2,...,a_n\}$ where $a_1...a_n$ is a set of attributes belonging to the relation.

For example, consider the database table LECTURER in Figure 3.1. The relational schema for LECTURER can be written as:

LECTURER(EMP_NUM, LECTURER_OFFICE, LECTURER_EXTENSION, LECTURER_HIGH_DEGREE)

3.1.2 Attributes and Domains

Each attribute is a named column within the relational table and draws its values from a **domain**. A domain is the set of possible values for this attribute. For example, an attribute called STU_CLASS, which stores the students' classification whilst at university, may have the following domain {UG1, UG2, UG3, PG, Other}, which means that STU_CLASS can only have one of these values within the database. The domain of values for an attribute should contain only atomic values and any one value should not be divisible into components. In addition, no attributes with more than one value are allowed. (These are often referred to as multi-valued attributes.) For example, the value of STU_CLASS could not be UG1 and UG2 at the same time. Each domain is also defined by its data type – for example, character string, number, date, etc.

The fundamental principle of the relational model is that relating different entities to one another is achieved by comparisons of their values. A pair of attribute values can only be meaningfully compared if their values are drawn from the same domains. For example, the columns STU_POSTCODE and LECT_POSTCODE may be in two different relational tables, but would share the common domain of all postal codes and could be compared. In contrast, it would be nonsense to try to match the attribute STU_NAME with STU_CLASS, even though the domains are defined by the data type (character string).

3.1.3 Degree and Cardinality

Degree and **cardinality** are two important properties of the relational model. A relation with *N* columns and *N* rows is said to be of degree *N* and cardinality *N*. The degree of a relation is the number of its attributes and the cardinality of a relation is the number of its tuples. The product of a relation's degree and cardinality is the number of attribute values it contains. Figure 3.2 shows the relational table DEPARTMENT with a degree of 4 and a cardinality of 4. The product of the relational table DEPARTMENT is 16 (4 * 4) and, as you can see in Figure 3.2, it contains 16 attribute values.

FIGURE 3.2 Degree and cardinality of the DEPARTMENT relation

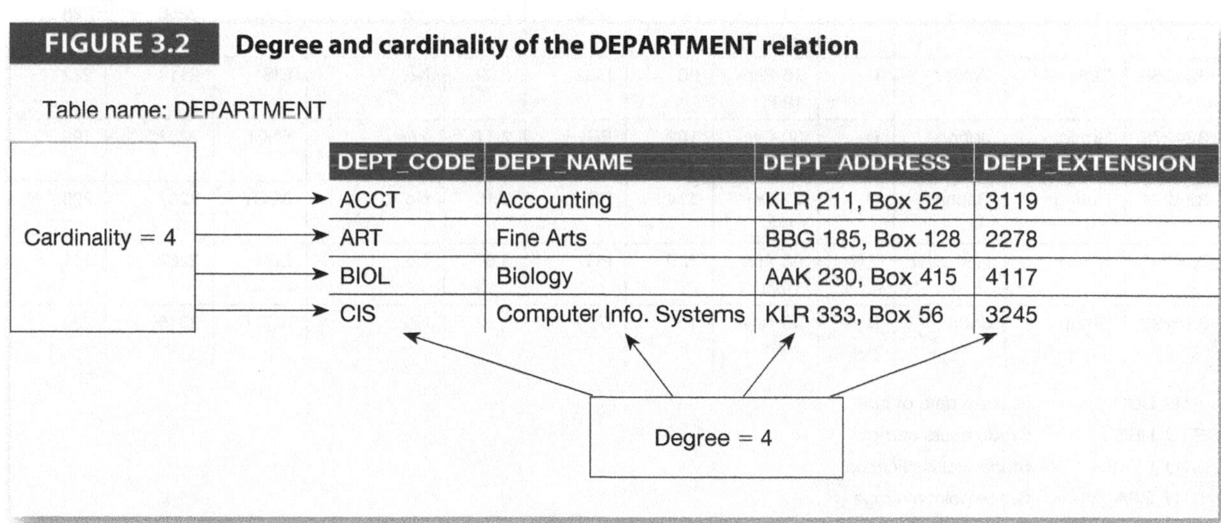

Table name: DEPARTMENT

DEPT_CODE	DEPT_NAME	DEPT_ADDRESS	DEPT_EXTENSION
ACCT	Accounting	KLR 211, Box 52	3119
ART	Fine Arts	BBG 185, Box 128	2278
BIOL	Biology	AAK 230, Box 415	4117
CIS	Computer Info. Systems	KLR 333, Box 56	3245

3

NOTE

The word **relation**, also known as a *dataset* in Microsoft Access, is based on the mathematical set theory from which Codd derived his model. Since the relational model uses attribute values to establish relationships among tables, many database users incorrectly assume that the term *relation* refers to such relationships. Many then incorrectly conclude that only the relational model permits the use of relationships.

3.1.4 Summary of Relational Characteristics

You will discover that the table view of data makes it easy to spot and define entity relationships, thereby greatly simplifying the task of database design. The tables shown in Figure 3.3 illustrate how the properties of a relation listed in Table 3.1 can be applied to a database table.

FIGURE 3.3 STUDENT table attribute values

Database name: Ch03_TinyUniversity

Table name: STUDENT

STU_NUM	STU_LNAME	STU_FNAME	STU_INIT	STU_DOB	STU_HRS	STU_CLASS	STU_GPA	STU_TRANSFER	DEPT_CODE	STU_PHONE	LECT_NUM
321452	Ndlovu	Amehlo	C	12-Feb-1999	42	UG3	2.84	No	BIOL	2134	205
324257	Smithson	Anne	K	15-Nov-2000	81	UG2	3.27	Yes	CIS	2256	222
324258	Le Roux	Dané		23-Aug-2000	36	UG3	2.26	Yes	ACCT	2256	228
324269	Oblonski	Walter	H	16-Sep-1996	66	UG2	3.09	No	CIS	2114	222
324273	Smith	John	D	30-Dec-1998	102	PG	2.11	Yes	ENGL	2231	199
324274	Katinga	Raphael	P	21-Oct-1999	114	PG	3.15	No	ACCT	2267	228
324291	Ismail	Hemalika	T	08-Apr-1999	120	PG	3.87	No	EDU	2267	311
324299	Smith	John	B	30-Nov-2001	15	UG1	2.92	No	ACCT	2315	230

STU_DOB = Student date of birth
STU_HRS = Credit hours earned
STU_CLASS = Student classification
STU_GPA = Grade point average
STU_PHONE = 4-digit campus phone extension
LECT_NUM = Number of the lecturer who is the student's advisor

Using the STUDENT table shown in Figure 3.3, you can draw the following conclusions corresponding to the points in Table 3.1:

1 The STUDENT table shown in Figure 3.3 is perceived to be a two-dimensional structure composed of eight rows (tuples) and twelve columns. The cardinality of STUDENT is therefore 8 and the degree is 12. You can also describe the table as being composed of eight records and twelve attributes (fields).

2 Each row in the STUDENT table describes a single entity occurrence within the entity set. (The entity set is represented by the STUDENT table.) Note that the row (entity or record) defined by STU_NUM = 321452 defines the characteristics (attributes or fields) of a student named Amehlo C. Ndlovu. For example, row 4 in Figure 3.3 describes a student named Walter H. Oblonski. Similarly, row 3 describes a student named Dané le Roux. Given the table contents, the STUDENT entity set includes eight distinct entities (rows).

3 Each column represents an attribute, and each column has a distinct name.

4 All of the values in a column match the entity's attribute characteristics. For example, the grade point average (STU_GPA) column contains only STU_GPA entries for each of the table rows. Data must be classified according to their format and function. Although various DBMSs can support different data types, most support at least the following:

   a *Numeric.* Numeric data are data on which you can perform meaningful arithmetic procedures. For example, STU_HRS and STU_GPA in Figure 3.3 are numeric attributes. On the other hand, STU_PHONE is not a numeric attribute because adding or subtracting phone numbers does not yield an arithmetically meaningful result.

   b *Character.* Character data, also known as text data or string data, can contain any character or symbol not intended for mathematical manipulation. In Figure 3.3, for example, STU_LNAME, STU_FNAME, STU_INIT, STU_CLASS and STU_PHONE are character, text or string attributes.

   c *Date.* Date attributes contain calendar dates stored in a special format known as the Julian date format. In Figure 3.3, STU_DOB is a data attribute.

   d *Logical.* Logical data can have only a true or false (yes or no) condition. For example, is a student a university transfer? In Figure 3.3, the STU_TRANSFER attribute uses a logical data format. Most, but not all, relational database software packages support the logical data format. Microsoft Access uses the label 'Yes/No data type' to indicate a logical data type whereas Oracle uses a data type known as Boolean, which can have values TRUE, FALSE and NULL.

5 The column's range of permissible values is known as its **domain**. Because the STU_GPA values are limited to the range 0–4, inclusive, the domain is [0,4].

6 The order of rows and columns is immaterial to the user.

7 Each table must have a primary key. In general terms, the **primary key (PK)** is an attribute (or a combination of attributes) that uniquely identifies any given row. In this case, STU_NUM (the student number) is the primary key. Using the data presented in Figure 3.3, observe that a student's last name (STU_LNAME) would not be a good primary key because it is possible to find several students whose last name is Smith. Even the combination of the last name and first name (STU_FNAME) would not be an appropriate primary key because, as Figure 3.3 shows, it is quite possible to find more than one student named John Smith.

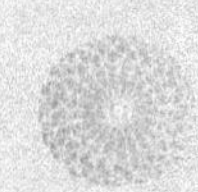

Online Content All of the databases used to illustrate the material in this chapter are found on the online platform for this book. The database names used in the folder match the database names used in the figures. For example, the source of the tables shown in Figure 3.3 is the 'Ch03_TinyUniversity' database.

3

3.2 KEYS

A **key** consists of one or more attributes that determine other attributes. (For example, an invoice number identifies all of the invoice attributes, such as the invoice date and the customer name.) One type of key, the primary key, has already been introduced. Given the structure of the STUDENT table shown in Figure 3.3, defining and describing the primary key seems simple enough. However, because the primary key plays such an important role in the relational environment, we will examine the primary key's properties more carefully. There are several other kinds of keys that warrant attention. In this section, you will also become acquainted with superkeys, candidate keys and secondary keys.

The key's role is based on a concept known as **determination**. In the context of a database table, the statement 'A determines B' indicates that if you know the value of attribute A, you can look up (determine) the value of attribute B. For example, knowing the STU_NUM in the STUDENT table (see Figure 3.3) means that you are able to look up (determine) that student's last name, grade point average, phone number and so on. The shorthand notation for 'A determines B' is A → B. If A determines B, C and D, you write A → B, C, D.

Therefore, using the attributes of the STUDENT table in Figure 3.3, you can represent the statement 'STU_NUM determines STU_LNAME' by writing:

STU_NUM → STU_LNAME

In fact, the STU_NUM value in the STUDENT table determines all of the student's attribute values. For example, you can write:

STU_NUM → STU_LNAME, STU_FNAME, STU_INIT

and

STU_NUM → STU_LNAME, STU_FNAME, STU_INIT, STU_DOB, STU_TRANSFER

In contrast, STU_NUM is not determined by STU_LNAME because it is quite possible for several students to have the last name Smith.

The principle of determination is very important because it is used in the definition of a central relational database concept known as functional dependence. The term **functional dependence** can be defined most easily this way: the attribute B is functionally dependent on A if A determines B. More precisely:

The output of the DIVIDE operation is a single column with the values of column B.

Using the contents of the STUDENT table in Figure 3.3, it is appropriate to say that STU_PHONE is functionally dependent on STU_NUM. For example, the STU_NUM value 321452 determines the STU_PHONE value 2134. On the other hand, STU_NUM is not functionally dependent on STU_PHONE because the STU_PHONE value 2267 is associated with two STU_NUM values: 324274 and 324291. (Apparently, some students share a phone.) Similarly, the STU_NUM value 324273 determines the STU_LNAME value Smith. But the STU_NUM value is not functionally dependent on STU_LNAME because more than one student may have the last name Smith.

The functional dependence definition can be generalised to cover the case in which the determining attribute values occur more than once in a table. Functional dependence can then be defined this way:[1]

> Attribute A determines attribute B (that is, B is functionally dependent on A) if all of the rows in the table that agree in value for attribute A also agree in value for attribute B.

Be careful when defining the dependency's direction. For example, Tiny University determines its student classification based on hours completed; these are shown in Table 3.2.

TABLE 3.2 Student classification

Hours completed	Classification
Fewer than 30	UG1
30–59	UG2
60–89	UG3
90 or more	PG

Therefore, you can write:

STU_HRS → STU_CLASS

However, the specific number of hours is not dependent on the classification. It is quite possible to find a third-year undergraduate (UG3) with 62 completed hours or one with 84 completed hours. In other words, the classification (STU_CLASS) does not determine one and only one value for completed hours (STU_HRS).

Keep in mind that it might take more than a single attribute to define functional dependence; that is, a key may be composed of more than one attribute. Such a multi-attribute key is known as a **composite key**.

Any attribute that is part of a key is known as a **key attribute**. For instance, in the STUDENT table, the student's last name would not be sufficient to serve as a key. On the other hand, the combination of last name, first name, initial and home phone is very likely to produce unique matches for the remaining attributes. For example, you can write:

STU_LNAME, STU_FNAME, STU_INIT, STU_PHONE → STU_HRS, STU_CLASS

or

---

1 *ISO-ANSI Working Draft Database Language/SQL Foundation (SQL3)*, Part 2, 29 August, 1994. This source was provided through the courtesy of Dr David Hatherly.

STU_LNAME, STU_FNAME, STU_INIT, STU_PHONE → STU_HRS, STU_CLASS, STU_GPA

or

STU_LNAME, STU_FNAME, STU_INIT, STU_PHONE → STU_HRS, STU_CLASS, STU_GPA, STU_DOB

3 Given the possible existence of a composite key, the notion of functional dependence can be further refined by specifying **full functional dependence**:

If the attribute (B) is functionally dependent on a composite key (A) but not on any subset of that composite key, the attribute (B) is fully functionally dependent on (A).

Within the broad key classification, several specialised keys can be defined. For example, a **superkey** is any key that uniquely identifies each row. In short, the superkey functionally determines all of the row's attributes. In the STUDENT table, the superkey could be any of the following:

STU_NUM

STU_NUM, STU_LNAME

STU_NUM, STU_LNAME, STU_INIT

In fact, STU_NUM, with or without additional attributes, can be a superkey even when the additional attributes are redundant.

A **candidate key** can be described as a superkey without redundancies, that is, a minimal superkey. Using this distinction, note that the composite key

STU_NUM, STU_LNAME

is a superkey, but it is not a candidate key because STU_NUM by itself is a candidate key! The combination

STU_LNAME, STU_FNAME, STU_INIT, STU_PHONE

might also be a candidate key, as long as you discount the possibility that two students share the same last name, first name, initial and phone number.

If the student's ID number had been included as one of the attributes in the STUDENT table in Figure 3.3 – perhaps named STU_ID – both it and STU_NUM would have been candidate keys, because either one would uniquely identify each student. In that case, the selection of STU_NUM as the primary key would be driven by the designer's choice or by end-user requirements. In short, the primary key is the candidate key chosen to be the unique row identifier. Note, incidentally, that a primary key is a superkey as well as a candidate key.

Within a table, each primary key value must be unique to ensure that each row is uniquely identified by the primary key. In that case, the table is said to exhibit **entity integrity**. To maintain entity integrity, a **null** 'value' (that is, no data entry at all) is not permitted in the primary key.

NOTE

A null does *not* mean a zero or a space. Pressing the keyboard's space bar creates a blank (or a space). A null is created when you press the keyboard's Enter key without making a prior entry of any kind. In other words, a null is no value at all.

Nulls can *never* be part of a primary key, and they should be avoided – to the greatest extent possible – in other attributes, too. There are rare cases in which nulls cannot be reasonably avoided when you are working with non-key attributes. For example, one of an EMPLOYEE table's attributes is likely to be the EMP_INITIAL. However, some employees do not have a middle initial. Therefore, some of the EMP_INITIAL 'values' may be null. You will also discover later in this section that there may be situations in which a null exists because of the nature of the relationship between two entities. In any case, even if nulls cannot always be avoided, they must be used sparingly. In fact, the existence of nulls in a table is often an indication of poor database design.

Nulls, if used improperly, can create problems, because they have many different meanings. For example, a null can represent:

- An unknown attribute value.
- A known, but missing, attribute value.
- A 'not applicable' condition.

Depending on the sophistication of the application development software, nulls can create problems when functions such as COUNT, AVERAGE and SUM are used. In addition, nulls can create logical problems when relational tables are linked.

Controlled redundancy makes the relational database work. Tables within the database share common attributes that enable the tables to be linked together. Note, for example, that the PRODUCT and VENDOR tables in Figure 3.4 share a common attribute named VEND_CODE. And note that the PRODUCT table's VEND_CODE value 232 occurs more than once, as does the VEND_CODE value 235. Because the PRODUCT table is related to the VENDOR table through these VEND_CODE values, the multiple occurrence of the values is *required* to make the 1:* relationship between VENDOR and PRODUCT work. Each VENDOR table VEND_CODE value is unique – the VENDOR is the '1' side in the VENDOR-PRODUCT relationship. But any given VENDOR table's VEND_CODE value may occur more than once in the PRODUCT table, thus providing evidence that PRODUCT is the '*' side of the VENDOR-PRODUCT relationship. In database terms, the multiple occurrences of the VEND_CODE values in the PRODUCT table are not redundant because they are *required* to make the relationship work. You should recall from Chapter 2, Data Models, that data redundancy exists only when there is *unnecessary* duplication of attribute values.

As you examine Figure 3.4, note that the VEND_CODE value in one table can be used to point to the corresponding value in the other table. For example, the VEND_CODE value 235 in the PRODUCT table points to vendor Henry Ortozo in the VENDOR table. Consequently, you discover that the product 'Houselite chain saw, 16 cm bar' is delivered by Henry Ortozo and that he can be contacted by calling 0181-899-3425. The same connection can be made for the product 'Steel tape, 12 m length' in the PRODUCT table.

Remember the naming convention – the prefix PROD was used in Figure 3.4 to indicate that the attributes 'belong' to the PRODUCT table. Therefore, the prefix VEND in the PRODUCT table's VEND_CODE indicates that VEND_CODE points to some other table in the database. In this case, the VEND prefix is used to point to the VENDOR table in the database.

As defined in section 3.1.1, a relational database can also be represented by a relational schema. The primary key attribute(s) is (are) underlined with the schema. You will see such schemas in Chapter 7, Normalising Database Designs. For example, the relational schema for Figure 3.4 would be shown as:

VENDOR (<u>VEND_CODE</u>, VEND_CONTACT, VEND_AREACODE, VEND_PHONE)

PRODUCT (<u>PROD_CODE</u>, PROD_DESCRIPT, PROD_PRICE, PROD_ON_HAND, VEND_CODE*)

3

FIGURE 3.4 An example of a simple relational database

Database name: Ch03_SaleCo

Table name: PRODUCT Primary key: PROD_CODE Foreign key: VEND_CODE

PROD_CODE	PROD_DESCRIPT	PROD_PRICE	PROD_ON_HAND	VEND_CODE
001278-AB	Claw hammer	€10.23	23	232
123-21UUY	Houselite chain saw, 16 cm bar	€150.09	4	235
QER-34256	Sledge hammer, 16 kg head	€14.72	6	231
SRE-657UG	Rat-tail file	€2.36	15	232
ZZX/3245Q	Steel tape, 12 m length	€5.36	8	235

link

VEND_CODE	VEND_CONTACT	VEND_AREACODE	VEND_PHONE
230	Shelly K. Smithson	7325	555-1234
231	James Johnson	0181	123-4536
232	Khaya Sibiya	7325	224-2134
233	Lindiwe Molefe	0113	342-6567
234	Nijan Pillay	0181	123-3324
235	Henry Ortozo	0181	899-3425

Table name: VENDOR

Primary key: VEND_CODE

Foreign key: none

The link between the PRODUCT and VENDOR tables in Figure 3.4 can also be represented by the relational diagram shown in Figure 3.5. In this case, the link is indicated by the line that connects the VENDOR and PRODUCT tables.

FIGURE 3.5 The UML entity relationship diagram for the CH03_SaleCo database

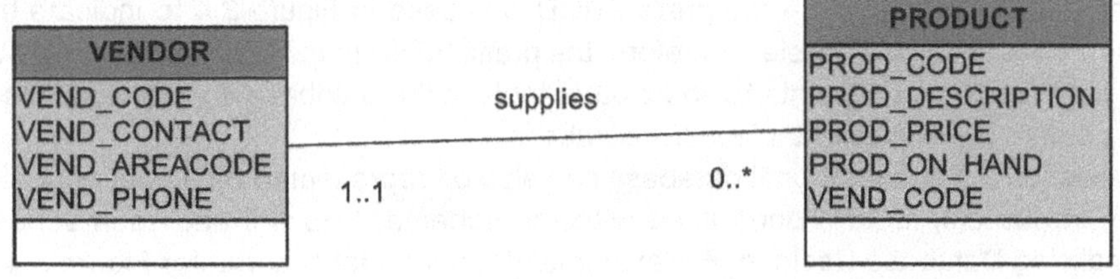

The relationship line in Figure 3.5 is created when two tables share an attribute with common values. More specifically, the primary key of one table (VENDOR) appears as the *foreign key* in a related table

(PRODUCT). A **foreign key (FK)** is an attribute whose values match the primary key values in the related table. For example, in Figure 3.5, the VEND_CODE is the primary key in the VENDOR table and it occurs as a foreign key in the PRODUCT table. Because the VENDOR table is not linked to a third table, the VENDOR table shown in Figure 3.4 does not contain a foreign key.

If the foreign key contains either matching values or nulls, the table(s) that make(s) use of that foreign key is (are) said to exhibit *referential integrity*. In other words, **referential integrity** means that, if the foreign key contains a value, that value refers to an existing valid tuple (row) in another relation. Note that referential integrity is maintained between the PRODUCT and VENDOR tables shown in Figure 3.4.

Finally, a **secondary key** is defined as a key that is used strictly for data retrieval purposes. Suppose customer data are stored in a CUSTOMER table in which the customer number is the primary key. Do you suppose that most customers will remember their number? Data retrieval for a customer can be facilitated when the customer's last name and phone number are used. In that case, the primary key is the customer number; the secondary key is the combination of the customer's last name and phone number. Keep in mind that a secondary key does not necessarily yield a unique outcome. For example, a customer's last name and home telephone number could yield several matches if several Smith family members were living at a residence with only one phone line. Similarly, the combination of last name and postal code could yield dozens of matches, which could then be searched for a specific match.

A secondary key's effectiveness in narrowing down a search depends on how restrictive that secondary key is. For instance, although the secondary key CUS_CITY is legitimate from a database point of view, the attribute values 'New York' or 'Paris' are not likely to produce a usable return unless you want to examine millions of possible matches. (Of course, CUS_CITY is a better secondary key than CUS_COUNTRY.)

Table 3.3 summarises the different relational database table keys.

TABLE 3.3 Relational database keys

Key type	Definition
Superkey	An attribute (or combination of attributes) that uniquely identifies each row in a table.
Candidate key	A minimal superkey. A superkey that does not contain a subset of attributes that is itself a superkey.
Primary key	A candidate key selected to uniquely identify all other attribute values in any given row. Cannot contain null entries.
Secondary key	An attribute (or combination of attributes) used strictly for data retrieval purposes.
Foreign key	An attribute (or combination of attributes) in one table whose values must either match the primary key in another table or be null.

3.3 INTEGRITY RULES

Relational database integrity rules are very important to good database design. Many (but by no means all) RDBMSs enforce integrity rules automatically. However, it is much safer to make sure that your application design conforms to the entity and referential integrity rules mentioned in this chapter. Those rules are summarised in Table 3.4.

The integrity rules summarised in Table 3.4 are illustrated in Figure 3.6.

3

3

TABLE 3.4 Integrity rules

Entity integrity	Description
Requirement	All primary key entries are unique, and no part of a primary key may be null.
Purpose	Each row will have a unique identity, and foreign key values can properly reference primary key values.
Example	No invoice can have a duplicate number, nor can it be null. In short, all invoices are uniquely identified by their invoice number.
Referential integrity	**Description**
Requirement	A foreign key may have either a null entry (as long as it is not a part of its table's primary key) or an entry that matches the primary key value in a table to which it is related. (Every non-null foreign key value *must* reference an *existing* primary key value.)
Purpose	It is possible for an attribute NOT to have a corresponding value, but it will be impossible to have an invalid entry. The enforcement of the referential integrity rule makes it impossible to delete a row in one table whose primary key has mandatory, matching, foreign key values in another table.
Example	A customer might not yet have an assigned sales representative (number), but it will be impossible to have an invalid sales representative (number).

Note the features of Figure 3.6 at the top of the next page.

1. *Entity integrity*. The CUSTOMER table's primary key is CUS_CODE. The CUSTOMER primary key column has no null entries, and all entries are unique. Similarly, the AGENT table's primary key is AGENT_CODE, and this primary key column also is free of null entries.
2. *Referential integrity*. The CUSTOMER table contains a foreign key AGENT_CODE, which links entries in the CUSTOMER table to the AGENT table. The CUS_CODE row that is identified by the (primary key) number 10013 contains a null entry in its AGENT_CODE foreign key, because Mr Jaco Pieterse does not yet have a sales representative assigned to him. The remaining AGENT_CODE entries in the CUSTOMER table all match the AGENT_CODE entries in the AGENT table.

To avoid nulls, some designers use special codes, known as **flags**, to indicate the absence of some value. Using Figure 3.6 as an example, the code -99 could be used as the AGENT_CODE entry of the fourth row of the CUSTOMER table to indicate that customer Jaco Pieterse does not yet have an agent assigned to him. If such a flag is used, the AGENT table must contain a dummy row with an AGENT_CODE value of -99. Thus, the AGENT table's first record might contain the values shown in Table 3.5.

TABLE 3.5 A dummy variable value used as a flag

AGENT_CODE	AGENT_AREACODE	AGENT_PHONE	AGENT_LNAME	AGENT_YTD_SALES
-99	0000	000-0000	None	€0.00

Chapter 5, Data Modelling with Entity Relationship Diagrams, discusses several ways in which nulls may be handled.

FIGURE 3.6 **An illustration of integrity rules**

Database name: Ch03_InsureCo
Table name: CUSTOMER
Primary key: CUS_CODE
Foreign key: AGENT_CODE

CUS_ CODE	CUS_ LNAME	CUS_ FNAME	CUS_ INITIAL	CUS_ AREACODE	CUS_ PHONE	CUS_RENEW_ DATE	AGENT_ CODE
10010	Ramas	Alfred	A	0181	844-2573	12-Mar-19	502
10011	Dunne	Leona	K	0161	894-1238	23-May-18	501
10012	Du Toit	Marlene	W	0181	894-2285	05-Jan-19	502
10013	Pieterse	Jaco	F	0181	894-2180	20-Sep-19	
10014	Orlando	Myron		0181	222-1672	04-Dec-18	501
10015	O'Brian	Amy	B	0161	442-3381	29-Aug-19	503
10016	Brown	James	G	0181	297-1228	01-Mar-19	502
10017	Williams	George		0181	290-2556	23-Jun-19	503
10018	Padayachee	Vinaya	G	1061	382-7185	09-Nov-19	501
10019	Moloi	Mlilo	K	0181	297-3809	18-Feb-19	503

Table name: AGENT
Primary key: AGENT_CODE
Foreign key: none

AGENT_CODE	AGENT_LNAME	AGENT_AREACODE	AGENT_PHONE	AGENT_YTD_SLS
501	Bhengani	0161	228-1249	€1 371 008.46
502	Mbaso	0181	882-1244	€3 923 932.59
503	Okon	0181	123-5589	€2 444 244.52

Other integrity rules that can be enforced in the relational model are the *NOT NULL* and *UNIQUE* constraints. The NOT NULL constraint can be placed on a column to ensure that every row in the table has a value for that column. The UNIQUE constraint is a restriction placed on a column to ensure that no duplicate values exist for that column.

3.4 THE DATA DICTIONARY AND THE SYSTEM CATALOGUE

The **data dictionary** provides a detailed accounting of all tables found within the user/designer-created database. Thus, the data dictionary contains at least all of the attribute names and characteristics for each table in the system. In short, the data dictionary contains metadata – data about data. Using the small database presented in Figure 3.6, you might picture its data dictionary as shown in Table 3.6.

3

TABLE 3.6 A sample data dictionary

Table Name	Attribute Name	Contents	Type	Format	Domain	Required	PK or FK	FK Referenced Table
CUSTOMER	CUS_CODE	Customer account code	CHAR(5)	99999	10000–99999	Y	PK	
	CUS_LNAME	Customer last name	VARCHAR2(20)	Xxxxxxxx	100–999	Y	FK	AGENT
	CUS_FNAME	Customer first name	VARCHAR2(20)	Xxxxxxxx		Y		
	CUS_INITIAL	Customer initial	CHAR(1)	X				
	CUS_RENEW_DATE	Customer insurance renewal date	DATE	dd-mmm-yyyy				
	AGENT_CODE	Agent code	CHAR(3)	999				
AGENT	AGENT_CODE	Agent code	CHAR(3)	999		Y	PK	
	AGENT_AREACODE	Agent area code	CHAR(4)	999	0.00–9 999 999.99	Y		
	AGENT_PHONE	Agent telephone number	CHAR(14)	999-9999		Y		
	AGENT_LNAME	Agent last name	VARCHAR2(20)	Xxxxxxxx		Y		
	AGENT_YTD_SLS	Agent year-to-date sales	NUMBER(9,2)	9 999 999.99		Y		

FK = Foreign key
PK = Primary key
CHAR = Fixed character length data (1–255 characters)
VARCHAR2 = Variable character length data (1–4 000 characters)
NUMBER = Numeric data (NUMBER(9,2) is used to specify numbers with two decimal places and up to nine digits, including the decimal places. Some RDBMSs permit the use of a MONEY or CURRENCY data type.)

NOTE

Telephone area codes are always composed of digits 0–9. Because area codes are not used arithmetically, they are most efficiently stored as character data. Also, the area codes are always composed of a maximum of four digits. Therefore, the area code data type is defined as CHAR(4). On the other hand, names do not conform to a standard length. Therefore, the customer first names are defined as VARCHAR2(20), thus indicating that up to 20 characters may be used to store the names. Character data are shown as left-justified.

NOTE

The data dictionary in Table 3.6 is an example of the *human* view of the entities, attributes and relationships. The purpose of this data dictionary is to ensure that all members of database design and implementation teams use the same table and attribute names and characteristics. The DBMS's internally stored data dictionary contains additional information about relationship types, entity and referential integrity checks and enforcement, and index types and components. This additional information is generated during the database implementation stage.

The data dictionary is sometimes described as 'the database designer's database' because it records the design decisions about tables and their structures.

Like the data dictionary, the **system catalogue** contains metadata. The system catalogue can be described as a detailed system data dictionary that describes all objects within the database, including data about table names, the table's creator and creation date, the number of columns in each table, the data type corresponding to each column, index filenames, index creators, authorised users and access privileges. Since the system catalogue contains all required data dictionary information, the terms *system catalogue* and *data dictionary* are often used interchangeably. In fact, current relational database software generally provides only a system catalogue, from which the designer's data dictionary information may be derived. The system catalogue is actually a system-created database whose tables store the user/designer-created database characteristics and content. Therefore, the system catalogue tables can be queried just like any user/designer-created table.

In effect, the system catalogue automatically produces database documentation. As new tables are added to the database, that documentation also allows the RDBMS to check for and eliminate homonyms and synonyms. In general terms, **homonyms** are similar-sounding words with different meanings, such as *sun* and *son*, or identically spelled words with different meanings, such as *fair* (meaning 'just') and *fair* (meaning 'festival'). In a database context, the word *homonym* indicates the use of the same attribute name to label different attributes. For example, you might use C_NAME to label a customer name attribute in a CUSTOMER table and also use C_NAME to label a consultant name attribute in a CONSULTANT table. To lessen confusion, you should avoid database homonyms; the data dictionary is very useful in this regard.

In a database context, a **synonym** is the opposite of a homonym and indicates the use of different names to describe the same attribute. For example, *car* and *auto* refer to the same object. Synonyms must be avoided. You will discover why using synonyms is a bad idea when you work through Problem 33 at the end of the chapter.

3.5 RELATIONSHIPS WITHIN THE RELATIONAL DATABASE

You already know that relationships are classified as one-to-one (1:1), one-to-many (1:*), and many-to-many (*:*). This section explores those relationships further, to help you apply them properly when you start developing database designs, focusing on the following points:

- The 1:* relationship is the relational modelling ideal. Therefore, this relationship type should be the norm in any relational database design.
- The 1:1 relationship should be rare in any relational database design.
- *:* relationships cannot be implemented as such in the relational model. Later in this section, you will see how any *:* relationship can be changed into two 1:* relationships.

NOTE

The UML class diagram represents relationships as associations among objects and can use the multiplicity element to represent *:* relationships directly. However, you will also learn how an association class is used to represent a *:* association between two classes in Chapter 5, Data Modelling with Entity Relationship Diagrams.

3.5.1 The 1:* Relationship

The 1:* relationship is the relational database norm. To see how such a relationship is modelled and implemented, consider the PAINTER paints PAINTING example that was used in Chapter 2. Compare the data models in Figure 3.7 with its implementation in Figure 3.8.

3

FIGURE 3.7 The 1:* relationship between PAINTER and PAINTING

PAINTER — paints ▸ — PAINTING

1..1 — 1..*

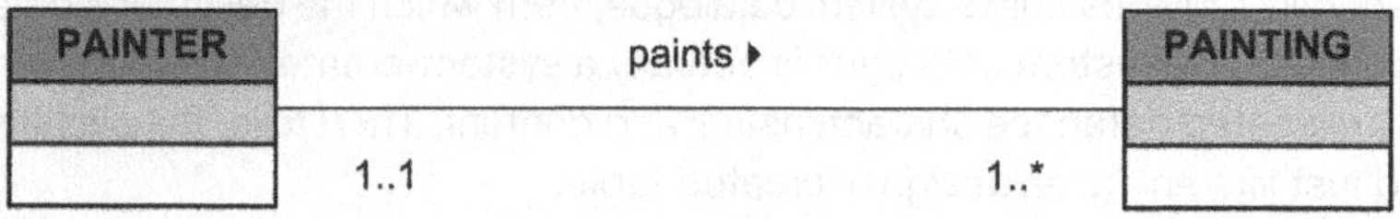

As you examine the PAINTER and PAINTING table contents in Figure 3.8, note the following features: each painting is painted by one and only one painter, but each painter could have painted many paintings. Note that painter 123 (Onele P. Najeke) has three paintings stored in the PAINTING table.

There is only one row in the PAINTER table for any given row in the PAINTING table, but there may be many rows in the PAINTING table for any given row in the PAINTER table.

FIGURE 3.8 The implemented 1:* relationship between PAINTER and PAINTING

Database name: Ch03_Museum
Primary key: PAINTER_NUM

Table name: PAINTER
Foreign key: none

PAINTER_NUM	PAINTER_LNAME	PAINTER_FNAME	PAINTER_INITIAL
123	Najeke	Onele	P
126	Itero	Julio	G

PAINTING_NUM	PAINTING_TITLE	PAINTER_NUM
1338	Dawn Thunder	123
1339	Vanilla Roses To Nowhere	123
1340	Tired Flounders	126
1341	Hasty Exit	123
1342	Plastic Paradise	126

Table name: PAINTING
Primary Key: PAINTING_NUM
Foreign Key: PAINTER_NUM

As we are using the UML notation, it is worth pointing out some of the different terminology that you may see when representing relationships amongst entities. In UML, relationships are also known as **associations** among entities. Associations have several characteristics:

- *Association name*. Each association has a name. Normally, the name of the association is written over the association line. In the example shown in Figure 3.7, the association name *paints* is written on the association line.
- *Association direction*. Associations also have a direction, represented by an arrow (→) pointing to the direction in which the relationship flows. In Figure 3.7, the arrow is shown pointing towards the PAINTING entity.
- *Role name*. The participating entities in the relationship can alternatively have role names instead of an association name. A role name expresses the role played by a given class in the relationship. Figure 3.7 does not show role names, as the association name *paints* is displayed. The role names represent the relationship 'as seen' by each entity (class); for example:

  A PAINTER *paints* a PAINTING, and each PAINTING *is_painted_by* a PAINTER.

  In this example the two role names would be *paints* and *is_painted_by*. As we are concentrating in this book on modelling relational concepts, we shall not use role names in modelling any relationships between entities.
- *Multiplicity*. **Multiplicity** refers to the number of instances of one entity (class) that are associated with one instance of a related entity (class). Multiplicity in the UML model provides the same information as the connectivity, cardinality and relationship participation constructs in the ER model. For example:

  One (and only one) PAINTER generates one to many PAINTINGs, and one PAINTING belongs to one and only one PAINTER.

NOTE

The one-to-many (1:*) relationship is easily implemented in the relational model by putting the primary key of the '1' side in the table of the 'many' side as a foreign key.

The 1:* relationship is found in any database environment. Students in a typical college or university will discover that each COURSE can generate many CLASSes but that each CLASS refers to only one COURSE. For example, an Accounting II course might yield two classes: one offered on Mondays, Wednesdays and Fridays (MWF) from 10:00 a.m. to 10:50 a.m. and one offered on Thursdays (Th) from 6:00 p.m. to 8:40 p.m. Therefore, the 1:* relationship between COURSE and CLASS might be described this way:

- Each COURSE can have many CLASSes, but each CLASS references only one COURSE.
- There will be only one row in the COURSE table for any given row in the CLASS table, but there can be many rows in the CLASS table for any given row in the COURSE table.
- Figure 3.9 maps the ERM (Entity Relationship Model) for the 1:* relationship between COURSE and CLASS.

3

FIGURE 3.9 **The 1:* relationship between COURSE and CLASS**

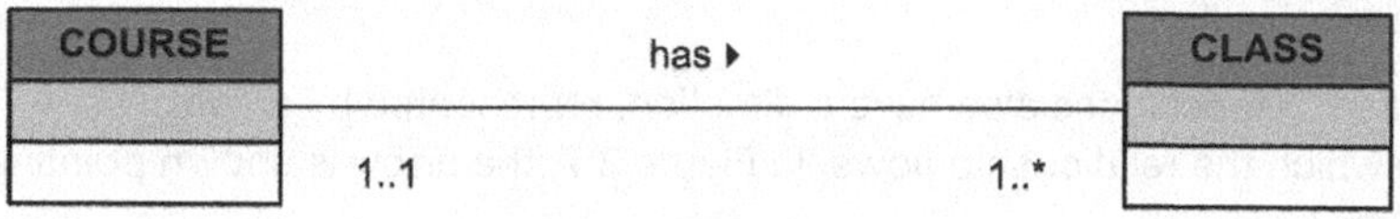

The 1:* relationship between COURSE and CLASS is further illustrated in Figure 3.10.

FIGURE 3.10 **The implemented 1:* relationship between COURSE and CLASS**

Database name: Ch03_TinyUniversity

Table name: COURSE

Primary key: CRS_CODE

Foreign key: none

CRS_CODE	DEPT_CODE	CRS_DESCRIPTION	CRS_CREDIT
ACCT-211	ACCT	Accounting I	3
ACCT-212	ACCT	Accounting II	3
CIS-220	CIS	Introduction to Computer Science	3
CIS-420	CIS	Database Design and Implementation	4
QM-261	CIS	Introduction to Statistics	3
QM-362	CIS	Statistical Applications	4

Table name: CLASS

Primary key: CLASS_CODE

Foreign key: CRS_CODE

CLASS_CODE	CRS_CODE	CLASS_SECTION	CLASS_TIME	CLASS_ROOM	LECT_NUM
10012	ACCT-211	1	MWF 8:00-8:50 a.m.	BUS311	105
10013	ACCT-211	2	MWF 9:00-9:50 a.m.	BUS200	105
10014	ACCT-211	3	TTh 2:30-3:45 p.m.	BUS252	342
10015	ACCT-212	1	MWF 10:00-10:50 a.m.	BUS311	301
10016	ACCT-212	2	Th 6:00-8:40 p.m.	BUS252	301
10017	CIS-220	1	MWF 9:00-9:50 a.m.	KLR209	228
10018	CIS-220	2	MWF 9:00-9:50 a.m.	KLR211	114
10019	CIS-220	3	MWF 10:00-10:50 a.m.	KLR209	228
10020	CIS-420	1	W 6:00-8:40 p.m.	KLR209	162
10021	QM-261	1	MWF 8:00-8:50 a.m.	KLR200	114
10022	QM-261	2	TTh 1:00-2:15 p.m.	KLR200	114
10023	QM-362	1	MWF 11:00-11:50 a.m.	KLR200	162
10024	QM-362	2	TTh 2:30-3:45 p.m.	KLR200	162

Using Figure 3.10, take a minute to review some important terminology. Note that CLASS_CODE in the CLASS table uniquely identifies each row. Therefore, CLASS_CODE has been chosen to be the primary key. However, the combination CRS_CODE and CLASS_SECTION will also uniquely identify each row in the class table. In other words, the *composite key* composed of CRS_CODE and CLASS_SECTION is a *candidate key.* Any candidate key must have the not null and unique constraints enforced. (You will see how this is done when you learn SQL in Chapter 8.)

Note in Figure 3.8, for example, that the PAINTER table's primary key, PAINTER_NUM, is included in the PAINTING table as a foreign key. Similarly, in Figure 3.10, the COURSE table's primary key, CRS_CODE, is included in the CLASS table as a foreign key.

3.5.2 The 1:1 Relationship

As the 1:1 label implies, in this relationship, one entity can be related to only one other entity, and vice versa. For example, one department chair – a lecturer – can chair only one department and one department can have only one department chair. The entities LECTURER and DEPARTMENT thus exhibit a 1:1 relationship. (You might argue that not all lecturers chair a department and lecturers cannot be *required* to chair a department. That is, the relationship between the two entities is optional. However, at this stage of the discussion, you should focus your attention on the basic 1:1 relationship. Optional relationships will be addressed in Chapter 5.) The basic 1:1 relationship is modelled in Figure 3.11, and its implementation is shown in Figure 3.12.

FIGURE 3.11 The 1:1 relationship between LECTURER and DEPARTMENT

As you examine the tables in Figure 3.12, note that there are several important features:

Each lecturer is a Tiny University employee. Therefore, the lecturer identification is through the EMP_NUM. (However, note that not all employees are LECTURERS – there's another optional relationship.)

The 1:1 LECTURER chairs DEPARTMENT relationship is implemented by having the EMP_NUM foreign key in the DEPARTMENT table. Note that the 1:1 relationship is treated as a special case of the 1:* relationship in which the 'many' side is restricted to a single occurrence. In this case, DEPARTMENT contains the EMP_NUM as a foreign key to indicate that it is the *department* that has a chair.

Also note that the LECTURER table contains the DEPT_CODE foreign key to implement the 1:* DEPARTMENT employs LECTURER relationship. This is a good example of how two entities can participate in two (or even more) relationships simultaneously.

Online Content If you open the 'Ch03_TinyUniversity' database available on the online platform accompanying this book you'll see that the STUDENT and CLASS entities still use LECT_NUM as their foreign key. LECT_NUM and EMP_NUM are labels for the same attribute, which is an example of the use of synonyms or different names for the same attribute.

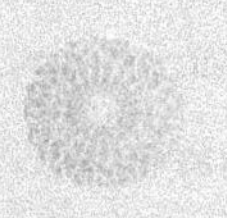

3

FIGURE 3.12 The implemented 1:1 relationship between LECTURER and DEPARTMENT

Database name: Ch03_TinyUniversity Table name: LECTURER

Primary key: EMP_NUM Foreign key: DEPT_CODE

EMP_NUM	DEPT_CODE	LECT_OFFICE	LECT_EXTENSION	LECT_HIGH_DEGREE
103	HIST	DRE 156	6783	PhD
104	ENG	DRE 102	5561	MA
105	ACCT	KLR 229D	8665	PhD
106	MKT/MGT	KLR 126	3899	PhD
110	BIOL	AAK 160	3412	PhD
114	ACCT	KLR 211	4436	PhD
155	MATH	AAK 201	4440	PhD
160	ENG	DRE 102	2248	PhD
162	CIS	KLR 203E	2359	PhD
191	MKT/MGT	KLR 409B	4016	DBA
195	PSYCH	AAK 297	3550	PhD
209	CIS	KLR 333	3421	PhD
228	CIS	KLR 300	3000	PhD
297	MATH	AAK 194	1145	PhD
299	ECON/FIN	KLR 284	2851	PhD
301	ACCT	KLR 244	4683	PhD
335	ENG	DRE 208	2000	PhD
342	SOC	BBG 208	5514	PhD
387	BIOL	AAK 230	8665	PhD
401	HIST	DRE 156	6783	MA
425	ECON/FIN	KLR 284	2851	MBA
435	ART	BBG 185	2278	PhD

The 1:* DEPARTMENT employs LECTURER relationship is implemented through the placement of the DEPT_CODE foreign key in the LECTURER table.

The 1:1 LECTURER chairs DEPARTMENT relationship is implemented through the placement of the EMP_NUM foreign key in the DEPARTMENT table.

Table name: DEPARTMENT

Primary key: DEPT_CODE

Foreign key: EMP_NUM

DEPT_ CODE	DEPT_NAME	SCHOOL_ CODE	EMP_ NUM	DEPT_ADDRESS	DEPT_ EXTENSION
ACCT	Accounting	BUS	114	KLR 211, Box 52	3119
ART	Fine Arts	A&SCI	435	BBG 185, Box 128	2278
BIOL	Biology	A&SCI	387	AAK 230, Box 415	4117
CIS	Computer Info. Systems	BUS	209	KLR 333, Box 56	3245
ECON/FIN	Economics/Finance	BUS	299	KLR 284, Box 63	3126
ENG	English	A&SCI	160	DRE 102, Box 223	1004
HIST	History	A&SCI	103	DRE 156, Box 284	1867
MATH	Mathematics	A&SCI	297	AAK 194, Box 422	4234
MKT/MGT	Marketing/Management	BUS	106	KLR 126, Box 55	3342
PSYCH	Psychology	A&SCI	195	AAK 297, Box 438	4110
SOC	Sociology	A&SCI	342	BBG 208, Box 132	2008

The preceding 'LECTURER chairs DEPARTMENT' example illustrates a proper 1:1 relationship. *In fact, the use of a 1:1 relationship ensures that two entity sets are not placed in the same table when they should not be.* However, the existence of a 1:1 relationship sometimes means that the entity components were not defined properly. It could indicate that the two entities actually belong in the same table!

As rare as 1:1 relationships should be, certain conditions absolutely *require* their use. For example, suppose you manage the database for a company that employs pilots, accountants, mechanics, clerks, salespeople, service personnel and more. Pilots have many attributes that the other employees don't have, such as licences, medical certificates, flight experience records, dates of flight proficiency checks and proof of required periodic medical checks. If you put all of the pilot-specific attributes in the EMPLOYEE table, you will have several nulls in that table for all employees who are not pilots. To avoid the proliferation of nulls, it is better to split the pilot attributes into a separate table (PILOT) that is linked to the EMPLOYEE table in a 1:1 relationship. Since pilots have many attributes that are shared by all employees – such as name, date of birth and date of first employment – those attributes would be stored in the EMPLOYEE table.

Online Content If you look at the 'Ch03_AviaCo' database on the online platform for this book, you will see the implementation of the 1:1 PILOT to EMPLOYEE relationship. This type of relationship will be examined in detail in Chapter 6, Data Modelling Advanced Concepts.

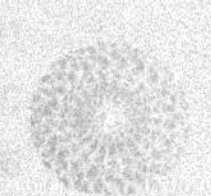

3.5.3 The *:* Relationship

A many-to-many (*:*) relationship is a more troublesome proposition in the relational environment. Traditionally in data modelling the *:* relationship can be implemented by breaking it up to produce a set of 1:* relationships. To explore the many-to-many (*:*) relationship, consider a rather typical college environment in which each STUDENT can take many CLASSes and each CLASS can contain many STUDENTs. The ERD model in Figure 3.13 shows this *:* relationship.

3

FIGURE 3.13 **The *:* relationship between STUDENT and CLASS**

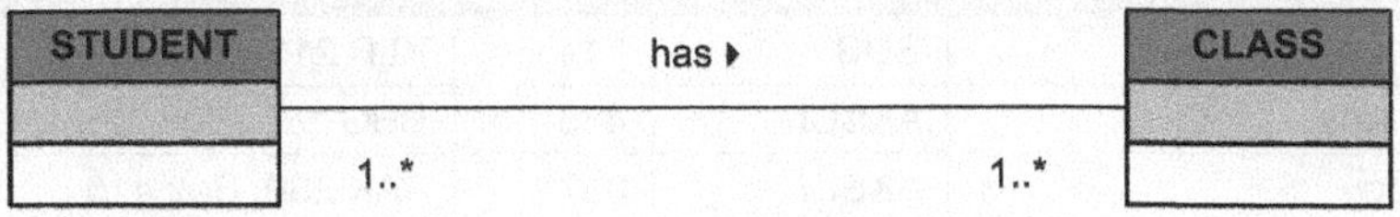

Note the features of the ERD in Figure 3.13:

- Each CLASS can have many STUDENTs, and each STUDENT can take many CLASSes.
- There can be many rows in the CLASS table for any given row in the STUDENT table, and there can be many rows in the STUDENT table for any given row in the CLASS table.

To examine the *:* relationship more closely, imagine a small university with two students, each of whom takes three classes. Table 3.7 shows the enrolment data for the two students.

TABLE 3.7 **Sample student enrolment data**

Student's Last Name	Selected Classes
Ndlovu	Accounting 1, ACCT-211, code 10014 Intro to Computer Science, CIS-220, code 10018 Intro to Statistics, QM-261, code 10021
Smithson	Accounting 1, ACCT-211, code 10014 Intro to Computer Science, CIS-220, code 10018 Intro to Statistics, QM-261, code 10021

Although the *:* relationship is logically reflected in Figure 3.13, it should *not* be implemented as shown in Figure 3.14 for two good reasons:

- The tables create many redundancies. For example, note that the STU_NUM values occur many times in the STUDENT table. In a real-world situation, additional student attributes such as address, classification, major and home phone would also be contained in the STUDENT table, and each of those attribute values would be repeated in each of the records shown here. Similarly, the CLASS table contains many duplications: each student taking the class generates a CLASS record. The problem would be even worse if the CLASS table included such attributes as credit hours and course description. Those redundancies lead to the anomalies discussed in Chapter 1.
- Given the structure and contents of the two tables, the relational operations become very complex and are likely to lead to system efficiency errors and output errors.

FIGURE 3.14 The *:* relationship between STUDENT and CLASS

Database name: Ch03_CollegeTry

Table name: STUDENT
Primary key: STU_NUM
Foreign key: none

STU_NUM	STU_LNAME	CLASS_CODE
321452	Ndlovu	10014
321452	Ndlovu	10018
321452	Ndlovu	10021
324257	Smithson	10014
324257	Smithson	10018
324257	Smithson	10021

Table name: CLASS
Primary Key: CLASS_CODE
Foreign Key: STU_NUM

CLASS_CODE	STU_NUM	CRS_CODE	CLASS_SECTION	CLASS_TIME	CLASS_ROOM	PROF_NUM
10014	321452	ACCT-211	3	TTh 2:30-3:45 p.m.	BUS252	342
10014	324257	ACCT-211	3	TTh 2:30-3:45 p.m.	BUS252	342
10018	321452	CIS-220	2	MWF 9:00-9:50 a.m.	KLR211	114
10018	324257	CIS-220	2	MWF 9:00-9:50 a.m.	KLR211	114
10021	321452	QM-261	1	MWF 8:00-8:50 a.m.	KLR200	114
10021	324257	QM-261	1	MWF 8:00-8:50 a.m.	KLR200	114

Fortunately, the problems inherent in the many-to-many (*:*) relationship can easily be avoided by creating a **composite entity** or **bridge entity**. Because such a table is used to link the tables that originally were related in a *:* relationship, the composite entity structure includes – as foreign keys – *at least* the primary keys of the tables that are to be linked. The database designer has two main options when defining a composite table's primary key: use the combination of those foreign keys or create a new primary key.

NOTE

In UML class diagrams, the multiplicity element can represent *:* relationships directly. Instead of using a composite entity, an **association class** is used to represent the association between two entities. We will explore the concept of an association class further in Chapter 5, Data Modelling with Entity Relationship Diagrams.

Remember that each entity in the ERD is represented by a table. Therefore, you can create the composite ENROL table shown in Figure 3.15 to link the tables CLASS and STUDENT. In this example, the ENROL table's primary key is the combination of its foreign keys CLASS_CODE and STU_NUM. But the designer could have decided to create a single-attribute new primary key such as ENROL_LINE, using a different line value to identify each ENROL table row uniquely. (Microsoft Access users might use the *Autonumber* data type to generate such line values automatically.)

FIGURE 3.15 Converting the *:* relationship into two 1:* relationships

Database name: Ch03_CollegeTry2

Table name: STUDENT
Primary key: STU_NUM
Foreign key: none

STU_NUM	STU_LNAME
321452	Ndlovu
324257	Smithson

Table name: ENROL
Primary key: CLASS_CODE+STU_NUM
Foreign keys: CLASS_CODE, STU_NUM

CLASS_CODE	STU_NUM	ENROLL_GRADE
10014	321452	C
10014	324257	B
10018	321452	A
10018	324257	B
10021	321452	C
10021	324257	C

Table name: CLASS
Primary key: CLASS_CODE
Foreign key: CRS_CODE

CLASS_CODE	CRS_CODE	CLASS_SECTION	CLASS_TIME	CLASS_ROOM	PROF_NUM
10014	ACCT-211	3	TTh 2:30-3:45 p.m.	BUS252	342
10018	CIS-220	2	MWF 9:00-9:50 a.m.	KLR211	114
10021	QM-261	1	MWF 8:00-8:50 a.m.	KLR200	114

Because the ENROL table in Figure 3.15 links two tables, STUDENT and CLASS, it is also called a **linking table**. In other words, a linking table is the implementation of a composite entity.

NOTE

In addition to the linking attributes, the composite ENROL table can also contain relevant attributes, such as the grade earned in the course. In fact, a composite table can contain any number of attributes that the designer wants to track. Keep in mind that the composite entity, *although it is implemented as an actual table*, is *conceptually* a logical entity that was created as a means to an end: to eliminate the potential for multiple redundancies in the original *:* relationship.

The linking table (ENROL) shown in Figure 3.15 yields the required *:* to 1:* conversion. Observe that the composite entity represented by the ENROL table must contain at least the primary keys of the CLASS and STUDENT tables (CLASS_CODE and STU_NUM, respectively) for which it serves as a connector. Also note that the STUDENT and CLASS tables now contain only one row per entity. The linking ENROL table contains multiple occurrences of the foreign key values, but those controlled redundancies are incapable of producing anomalies as long as referential integrity is enforced. Additional attributes may be assigned as needed. In this case, ENROL_GRADE is selected to satisfy a reporting requirement. Also note that the ENROL table's primary key consists of the two attributes CLASS_CODE and STU_NUM, because both the class code and the student number are needed to define a particular student's grade. Naturally, the conversion is reflected in the ERM, too. The revised relationship is shown in Figure 3.16.

FIGURE 3.16 **Changing the *:* relationship to two 1:* relationships**

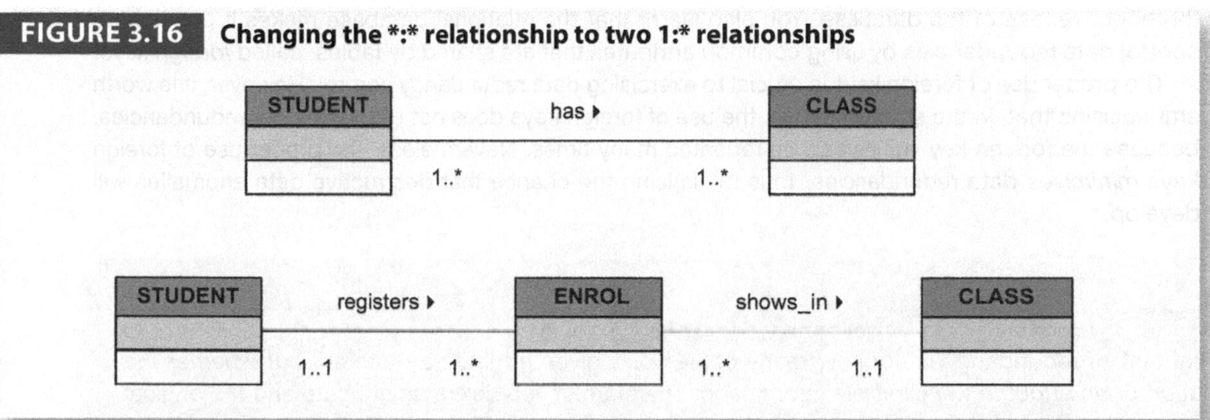

As you examine Figure 3.16, note that the composite entity named ENROL represents the linking table between STUDENT and CLASS.

The 1:* relationship between COURSE and CLASS was first illustrated in Figure 3.9 and Figure 3.10. With the help of this relationship, you can increase the amount of available information, even as you control the database's redundancies. Thus, Figure 3.16 can be expanded to include the 1:* relationship between COURSE and CLASS shown in Figure 3.17. Note that the model is able to handle multiple sections of a CLASS while controlling redundancies by making sure that all of the COURSE data common to each CLASS are kept in the COURSE table.

FIGURE 3.17 **The expanded entity relationship model**

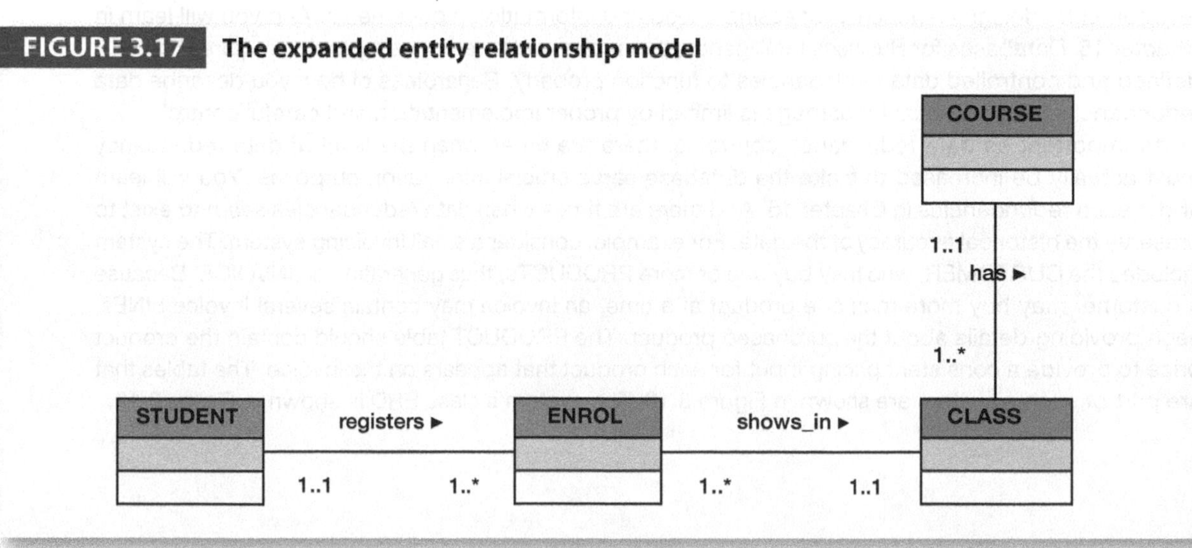

The ERD will be examined in greater detail in Chapter 5 to show you how it is used to design more complex databases. The ERD will also be used as the basis for the development and implementation of a realistic database design in Appendices B and C (see the online platform for this book).

3

3.6 DATA REDUNDANCY REVISITED

In Chapter 1 you learnt that data redundancy leads to data anomalies. Those anomalies can destroy the effectiveness of the database. You also learnt that the relational database makes it possible to control data redundancies by using common attributes that are shared by tables, called *foreign keys*.

The proper use of foreign keys is crucial to exercising data redundancy control. However, it is worth emphasising that, in the strictest sense, the use of foreign keys does not eliminate data redundancies, because the foreign key values can be repeated many times. Nevertheless, the proper use of foreign keys *minimises* data redundancies, thus minimising the chance that destructive data anomalies will develop.

NOTE

The real test of redundancy is *not* how many copies of a given attribute are stored, *but whether the elimination of an attribute will eliminate information*. Therefore, if you delete an attribute and the original information can still be generated through relational algebra, the inclusion of that attribute would be redundant. Given that view of redundancy, proper foreign keys are clearly not redundant in spite of their multiple occurrences in a table. However, even when you use this less restrictive view of redundancy, keep in mind that *controlled* redundancies are often designed as part of the system to ensure transaction speed and/or information requirements. Exclusive reliance on relational algebra to produce required information may lead to elegant designs that fail the test of practicality.

You will learn in Chapter 5 that database designers must reconcile three often contradictory requirements: design elegance, processing speed and information requirements. And you will learn in Chapter 15, Databases for Business Intelligence, that proper data warehousing design requires carefully defined and controlled data redundancies to function properly. Regardless of how you describe data redundancies, the potential for damage is limited by proper implementation and careful control.

As important as data redundancy control is, there are times when the level of data redundancy must actually be increased to make the database serve crucial information purposes. You will learn about such redundancies in Chapter 15. And there are times when data redundancies *seem* to exist to preserve the historical accuracy of the data. For example, consider a small invoicing system. The system includes the CUSTOMER, who may buy one or more PRODUCTs, thus generating an INVOICE. Because a customer may buy more than one product at a time, an invoice may contain several invoice LINEs, each providing details about the purchased product. The PRODUCT table should contain the product price to provide a consistent pricing input for each product that appears on the invoice. The tables that are part of such a system are shown in Figure 3.18. The system's class ERD is shown in Figure 3.19.

3

FIGURE 3.18 A small invoicing system

Database name: Ch03_SaleCo

Table name: CUSTOMER
Primary key: CUS_CODE
Foreign key: none

CUS_CODE	CUS_LNAME	CUS_FNAME	CUS_INITIAL	CUS_AREACODE	CUS_PHONE
10010	Ramas	Alfred	A	0181	844-2573
10011	Dunne	Leona	K	0161	894-1238
10012	Du Toit	Marlene	W	0181	894-2285
10013	Pieterse	Jaco	F	0181	894-2180
10014	Orlando	Myron		0181	222-1672
10015	O'Brian	Amy	B	0161	442-3381
10016	Brown	James	G	0181	297-1228
10017	Williams	George		0181	290-2556
10018	Padayachee	Vinaya	G	0161	382-7185
10019	Moloi	Mlilo	K	0181	297-3809

Table name: INVOICE
Primary key: INV_NUMBER
Foreign key: CUS_CODE

INV_NUMBER	CUS_CODE	INV_DATE
1001	10014	08-Dec-19
1002	10011	08-Dec-19
1003	10012	08-Dec-19
1004	10011	09-Dec-19

Table name: LINE
Primary key: INV_NUMBER + LINE_NUMBER
Foreign key: INV_NUMBER, PROD_CODE

INV_NUMBER	LINE_NUMBER	PROD_CODE	LINE_UNITS	LINE_PRICE
1001	1	123-21UUY	1	€150.09
1001	2	SRE-657UG	3	€2.36
1002	1	QER-34256	2	€14.72
1003	1	ZZX/3245Q	1	€5.36
1003	2	SRE-657UG	1	€2.36
1003	3	001278-AB	1	€10.23
1004	1	001278-AB	1	€10.23
1004	2	SRE-657UG	2	€2.36

Table name: PRODUCT

Primary key: PROD_CODE

Foreign key: none

PROD_CODE	PROD_DESCRIPT	PROD_PRICE	PROD_ON_HAND	VEND_CODE
001278-AB	Claw hammer	€10.23	23	232
123-21UUY	Houselite chain saw, 16 cm bar	€150.09	4	235
QER-34256	Sledge hammer, 16 kg head	€14.72	6	231
SRE-657UG	Rat-tail file	€2.36	15	232
ZZX/3245Q	Steel tape, 12 m length	€5.36	8	235

FIGURE 3.19 **The Class ERD for the invoicing system**

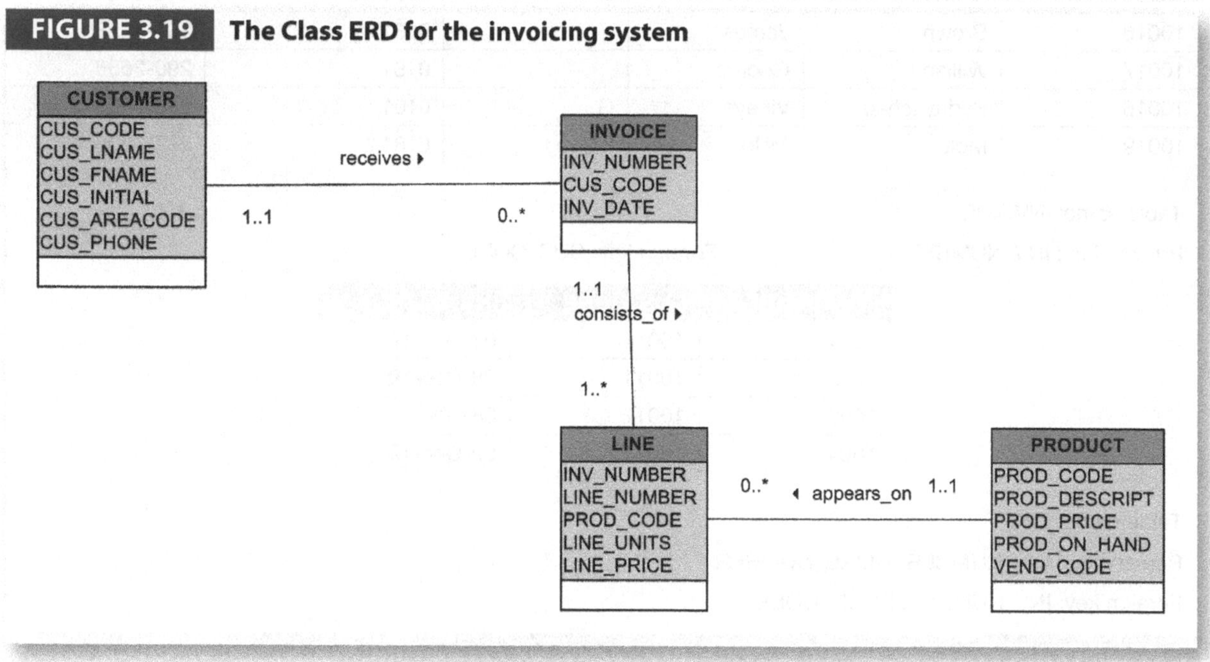

As you examine the tables in the invoicing system in Figure 3.18 and the relationships depicted in Figure 3.19, note that you can keep track of typical sales information. For example, by tracing the relationships among the four tables, you discover that customer 10014 (Myron Orlando) bought two items on 8 December, 2012 that were written to invoice number 1001: one Houselite chain saw with a 16-inch bar and three rat-tail files. (*Note*: Trace the CUS_CODE number 10014 in the CUSTOMER table to the matching CUS_CODE value in the INVOICE table. Next, take the INV_NUMBER 1001 and trace it to the first two rows in the LINE table; then match the two PROD_CODE values in LINE with the PROD_CODE values in PRODUCT.) Application software will be used to write the correct bill by multiplying each invoice line item's LINE_UNITS by its LINE_PRICE, adding the results, applying appropriate taxes, etc. Later, other application software might use the same technique to write sales reports that track and compare sales by week, month or year.

As you examine the sales transactions in Figure 3.18, you might reasonably suppose that the product price billed to the customer is derived from the PRODUCT table because that's where the product data are stored. *But why does that same product price occur again in the LINE table? Isn't that a data redundancy?* It certainly *appears* to be. But this time, the apparent redundancy is crucial to the system's success. Copying the product price from the PRODUCT table to the LINE table maintains the *historical accuracy of the transactions*. Suppose, for instance, that you fail to write the LINE_PRICE in the LINE table and that you use the PROD_PRICE (product price) from the PRODUCT table to calculate the sales revenue. Now suppose that the PRODUCT table's PROD_PRICE changes. This price change will be properly reflected in all subsequent sales revenue calculations. Unfortunately, the calculations of past sales revenues will now also reflect the new product price that was not in effect when the transaction took place! As a result, the revenue calculations for all past transactions will be incorrect, thus eliminating the possibility of making proper sales comparisons over time. On the other hand, if the price data are copied from the PRODUCT table and stored with the transaction in the LINE table, that price will always accurately reflect the transaction that took place *at that time*. You will discover that such planned 'redundancies' are common in good database design.

Finally, you might wonder why the LINE_NUMBER attribute was used in the LINE table in Figure 3.18. Wouldn't the combination of INV_NUMBER and PROD_CODE be a sufficient composite primary key – and, therefore, isn't the LINE_NUMBER redundant? Yes, the LINE_NUMBER is redundant, but this redundancy is quite commonly created by invoicing software that generates such line numbers automatically. In this case, the redundancy is not necessary. But given its automatic generation, the redundancy is not a source of anomalies. The inclusion of LINE_NUMBER also adds another benefit: the order of the retrieved invoicing data will always match the order in which the data were entered. If product codes are used as part of the primary key, indexing will arrange those product codes as soon as the invoice is completed and the data are stored. You can imagine the potential confusion when a customer calls and says, 'The second item on my invoice has an incorrect price' and you are looking at an invoice whose lines show a different order from those on the customer's copy!

3.7 INDEXES

Suppose you want to locate a particular book in a library. Does it make sense to look through every book in the library until you find the one you want? Of course not; you use the library's catalogue, which is indexed by title, topic and author. The index (in either a manual or a computer system) points you to the book's location, thereby making retrieval of the book a quick and simple matter. An **index** is an orderly arrangement used to access rows in a table logically.

Or suppose you want to find a topic, such as 'ER model', in this book. Does it make sense to read through every page until you stumble across the topic? Of course not; it is much simpler to go to the book's index, look up the phrase *ER model*, and read the page references that point you to the appropriate page(s). In each case, an index is used to locate a needed item quickly.

Indexes in the relational database environment work like the indexes described in the preceding paragraphs. From a conceptual point of view, an index is composed of an index key and a set of pointers. The **index key** is, in effect, the index's reference point. More formally, an index is an ordered arrangement of keys and pointers. Each key points to the location of the data identified by the key.

For example, suppose you want to look up all of the paintings created by a given painter in the Ch03_Museum database in Figure 3.8. Without an index, you must read each row in the PAINTING table and see if the PAINTER_NUM matches the requested painter. However, if you index the PAINTER table and use the index key PAINTER_NUM, you merely need to look up the appropriate PAINTER_NUM in the index and find the matching pointers. Conceptually speaking, the index would resemble the presentation depicted in Figure 3.20.

FIGURE 3.20 Components of an index

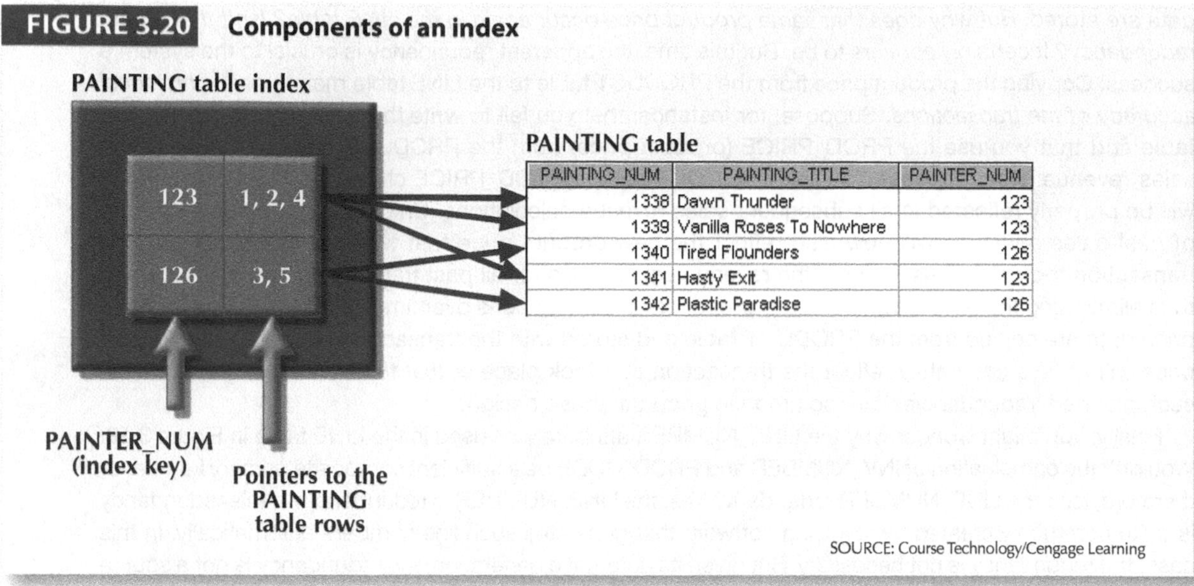

SOURCE: Course Technology/Cengage Learning

As you examine Figure 3.20, note that the first PAINTER_NUM index key value (123) is found in records 1, 2 and 4 of the PAINTING table. The second PAINTER_NUM index key value (126) is found in records 3 and 5 of the PAINTING table.

DBMSs use indexes for many different purposes. You just learnt that an index can be used to retrieve data more efficiently. But indexes can also be used by a DBMS to retrieve data ordered by a specific attribute or attributes. For example, creating an index on a customer's last name will allow you to retrieve the customer data alphabetically ordered by the customer's last name. Also, an index key can be composed of one or more attributes. For example, in Figure 3.18, you can create an index on VEND_CODE and PROD_CODE to retrieve all rows in the PRODUCT table ordered by vendor and within vendor, ordered by product.

Indexes play an important role in DBMSs for the implementation of primary keys. When you define a table's primary key, the DBMS automatically creates a unique index on the primary key column(s) you declared. For example, in Figure 3.18, when you declare CUS_CODE to be the primary key of the CUSTOMER table, the DBMS automatically creates a unique index on that attribute. A **unique index**, as its name implies, is an index in which the index key can have only one pointer value (row) associated with it. (The index in Figure 3.20 is not a unique index because the PAINTER_NUM has multiple pointer values associated with it. For example, painter number 123 points to three rows – 1, 2 and 4 – in the PAINTING table.)

Indexes are crucial in speeding up data access. They can be used to facilitate searching, sorting and even joining tables. The improvement in data access speed occurs because an index is an ordered set of values that contains the index key and pointers. A table can have many indexes, but each index is associated with only one table. The index key can have multiple attributes (composite index). Creating an index is easy. You will learn in Chapter 8 that a simple SQL command will produce any required index.

NOTE

You will learn more about how indexes can be applied to improve data access and retrieval in Chapter 11, Conceptual, Logical, and Physical Database Design.

3.8 CODD'S RELATIONAL DATABASE RULES

In 1985, Dr E.F. Codd published a list of 12 rules to define a relational database system.[2] The reason Dr Codd published the list was his concern that many vendors were marketing products as 'relational' even though those products did not meet minimum relational standards. Dr Codd's list, shown in Table 3.8, serves as a frame of reference for what a truly relational database should be. Bear in mind that even the dominant database vendors do not fully support all 12 rules.

TABLE 3.8 Dr Codd's 12 relational database rules

Rule	Rule Name	Description
1	**Information**	All information in a relational database must be logically represented as column values in rows within tables.
2	**Guaranteed Access**	Every value in a table is guaranteed to be accessible through a combination of table name, primary key value and column name.
3	**Systematic Treatment of Nulls**	Nulls must be represented and treated in a systematic way, independent of data type.
4	**Dynamic Online Catalogue Based on the Relational Model**	The metadata must be stored and managed as ordinary data, that is, in tables within the database. Such data must be available to authorised users, using the standard database relational language.
5	**Comprehensive Data Sub-language**	The relational database may support many languages. However it must support one well-defined declarative language with support for data definition, view definition, data manipulation (interactive and by program), integrity constraints, authorisation and transaction management (begin, commit and rollback).
6	**View Updating**	Any view that is theoretically updatable must be updatable through the system.
7	**High-Level Insert, Update and Delete**	The database must support set-level inserts, updates and deletes.
8	**Physical Data Independence**	Application programs and ad hoc facilities are logically unaffected when physical access methods or storage structures are changed.
9	**Logical Data Independence**	Application programs and ad hoc facilities are logically unaffected when changes are made to the table structures that preserve the original table values (changing order of column or inserting columns).
10	**Integrity Independence**	All relational integrity constraints must be definable in the relational language and stored in the system catalogue, not at the application level.
11	**Distribution Independence**	The end users and application programs are unaware of and unaffected by the data location (distributed vs local databases).
12	**Non-Subversion**	If the system supports low-level access to the data, there must not be a way to bypass the integrity rules of the database.
	Rule Zero	All preceding rules are based on the notion that, in order for a database to be considered relational, it must use its relational facilities exclusively to manage the database.

2 Codd, E.F., 'Is Your DBMS Really Relational?' and 'Does Your DBMS Run by the Rules?' *Computerworld*, 14 October and 21 October, 1985.

SUMMARY

- Tables are the basic building blocks of a relational database. A grouping of related entities, known as an entity set, is stored in a table. Conceptually speaking, the relational table is composed of intersecting rows (tuples) and columns. Each row represents a single entity, and each column represents the characteristics (attributes) of the entities.
- Keys are central to the use of relational tables. Keys define functional dependencies; that is, other attributes are dependent on the key and can, therefore, be found if the key value is known. A key can be classified as a superkey, a candidate key, a primary key, a secondary key or a foreign key.
- Each table row must have a primary key. The primary key is an attribute or a combination of attributes that uniquely identifies all remaining attributes found in any given row. Because a primary key must be unique, no null 'values' are allowed if entity integrity is to be maintained.
- Although the tables are independent, they can be linked by common attributes. Thus, the primary key of one table can appear as the foreign key in another table to which it is linked. Referential integrity dictates that the foreign key must contain values that match the primary key in the related table or must contain nulls.
- Once you know the relational database basics, you can concentrate on design. Good design begins by identifying appropriate entities and attributes, and the relationships among the entities. Those relationships (1:1, 1:* and *:*) can be represented using ERDs. The use of ERDs allows you to create and evaluate simple logical design. The 1:* relationships are most easily incorporated in a good design; you just have to make sure that the primary key of the '1' is included in the table of the 'many'.

KEY TERMS

associations
association class
attribute domain
bridge entity
candidate key
cardinality
composite entity
composite key
data dictionary
determination
domain
entity integrity
flags
foreign key (FK)
full functional dependence
functional dependence
homonyms
index
index key
key
key attribute
linking table
multiplicity
null
predicate logic
primary key (PK)
referential integrity
relation
relational schema
secondary key
superkey
synonym
system catalogue
tuple
unique index

FURTHER READING

Codd, E.F. *The Relational Model for Data Base Management: Version 2*. Addison-Wesley,1990.

Codd, E.F. 'Relational completeness of data base sublanguages' (presented at Courant Computer Science Symposia Series 6, 'Data Base Systems', New York City, NY, 24–25 May, 1971). 'IBM Research Report RJ987 (6 March 1972). Republished in Randall J. Rustin (ed.), *Data Base Systems: Courant Computer Science Symposia Series 6*. Prentice-Hall, 1972.

Date, C.J. *The Relational Database Dictionary*. O'Reilly, 2006.
Date, C.J. Darwen, H. *Databases, Types and the Relational Model*. Addison-Wesley, 2006.
Date, C.J. *Date on Database: Writings 2000–2006*. APress, 2006.
Date, C.J. *Database in Depth: The Relational Model for Practitioners*. O'Reilly, 2005.

Online Content All of the databases used in the questions and problems are available on the online platform accompanying this book. The database names used in the folder match the database names used in the figures. For example, the source of the tables shown in Figure Q3.1 is the 'Ch03_CollegeQue' database. Answers to selected Review Questions and Problems for this chapter are also available on the online platform.

REVIEW QUESTIONS

1 What is the difference between a database and a table?

2 What does it mean to say that a database displays both entity integrity and referential integrity?

3 Why are entity integrity and referential integrity important in a database?

4 What can a NULL value represent?

5 What is the domain of an attribute?

6 Create the basic ERD using UML notation for the database shown in Figure Q3.1.

FIGURE Q3.1 The Ch03_CollegeQue database tables

Database name: Ch03_CollegeQue

Table name: STUDENT

STU_CODE	LECT_CODE
100278	
128569	2
512272	4
531235	2
531268	
553427	1

Table name: LECTURER

LECT_CODE	DEPT_CODE
1	2
2	6
3	6
4	4

7 Create the basic ERD using UML notation for the database shown in Figure Q3.2.

FIGURE Q3.2 **The Ch03_TravelQue database tables**

Database name: Ch03_TravelQue

Table name: CUSTOMER

3

CUS_CODE	CUS_LNAME	CUS_EMAIL	CUS_MOBILE
24563	GARNETT	S.Garnett@yahoo.com	08703345671
24565	MWBAU	L.Mwbau@hotmail.com	08734566664

Table name: BOOKING

BOOKING_NO	PACKAGE_ID	BOOK_TOTAL_COST	BOOK_PAID	BOOK_DEP_DATE
24563	9910001	€956.00	Y	06-Jan-19
24565	9910001	€895.00	N	07-Sep-19
24563	9910003	€3056.00	N	05-Oct-19

Table name: PACKAGE_HOLIDAY

PACKAGE_ID	PACK_DESTINATION	PACK_OPERATOR	PACK_DURATION
9910001	Spain	Riveria Travel	7
9910002	USA	Mouse Holidays	14
9910003	Australia	Wallaby Tours	21

8 Suppose you have the ERD shown in Figure Q3.3. How would you convert this model into an ERD that displays only 1:* relationships? (Make sure you create the revised ERD.)

FIGURE Q3.3 **The UML Class ERD for question 6**

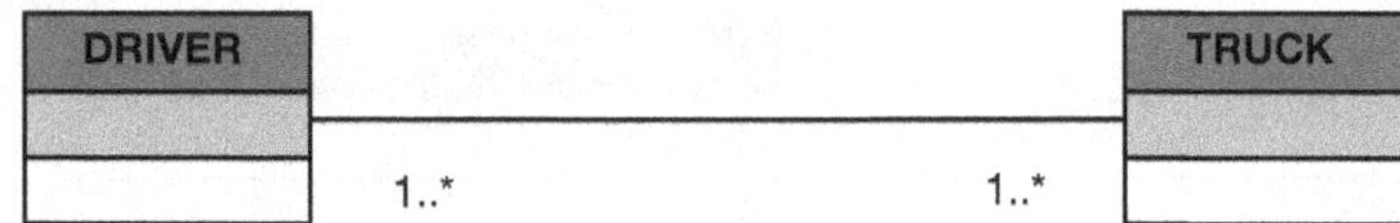

During some time interval, a DRIVER can drive many TRUCKS and any TRUCK can be driven by many DRIVERs.

9 What are homonyms and synonyms, and why should they be avoided in database design?

10 How would you implement a 1:* relationship in a database composed of two tables? Give an example.

11 Identify and describe the components of the table shown in Figure Q3.4, using correct terminology. Use your knowledge of naming conventions to identify the table's probable foreign key(s).

FIGURE Q3.4 The Ch03_NoComp database EMPLOYEE table

Database name: Ch03_NoComp

Table name: EMPLOYEE

EMP_NUM	EMP_LNAME	EMP_INITIAL	EMP_FNAME	DEPT_CODE	JOB_CODE
11234	Friedman	K	Robert	MKTG	12
11238	Zulu	D	Cela	MKTG	12
11241	Fontein		Juliette	INFS	5
11242	Theron	J	Emma	ENG	9
11245	Smithson	B	Bernard	INFS	6
11248	Washington	G	Oleta	ENGR	8
11256	McBride		Randall	ENGR	8
11257	Mazibuko	D	Fikile	MKTG	14
11258	Smith	W	William	MKTG	14
11260	Ratula	A	Katrina	INFS	5

12 Suppose you are using the database composed of the two tables shown in Figure Q3.5.

a Identify the primary keys.

b Identify the foreign keys.

c Create the ERM.

FIGURE Q3.5 The Ch03_Theatre database tables

Database name: Ch03_Theatre

Table name: DIRECTOR

DIR_NUM	DIR_LNAME	DIR_DOB
100	Broadway	12-Jan-75
101	Hollywoody	18-Nov-63
102	Goofy	21-Jun-72

Table name: PLAY

PLAY_CODE	PLAY_NAME	DIR_NUM
1001	Cat On a Cold, Bare Roof	102
1002	Hold the Mayo, Pass the Bread	101
1003	I Never Promised You Coffee	102
1004	Silly Putty Goes To Washington	100
1005	See No Sound, Hear No Sight	101
1006	Starstruck in Biloxi	102
1007	Stranger In Parrot Ice	101

d Suppose you wanted quick lookup capability to get a listing of all plays directed by a given director. Which table would be the basis for the INDEX table, and what would be the index key?

e What would be the conceptual view of the INDEX table that is described in Part d? Depict the contents of the conceptual INDEX table.

13 Suppose you are using the database to enable a museum to find the location of artefacts around the world. The database is composed of the three tables shown in Figure Q3.13.

a Identify the primary keys.

b Identify the foreign keys.

c Create the ERM.

FIGURE Q3.6 Table Name Artefact

Database name: Museum Database

ARTEFACT_ TRACK_ID	ARTEFACT_DESCRIPTION	ARTEFACT_ AGE	ARTEFACT_ VALUE	ARTEFCAT_ LOCATION_ID
10034	Greywacke Statue Tribute to Isis	664–525 BC	6000000	78343
10039	The Golden Rhinoceros of Mapungubwe	1075–1220	12100000	56432
10056	Pinner Qing Dynasty Vase	18th Century	85900000	23412
19002	Rosetta Stone	181 BC		23412

Table name: LOCATION

ARTEFACT_LOCATION_ID	ARTEFACT_COUNTRY
78343	FRANCE
56432	USA
23412	LONDON

d Suppose the museum database was to be expanded to include details of a curator who could be contacted to request to see an artefact. The details that need to be stored are a CURATOR_NO, CURATOR_NAME and CURATOR_CONTACT. A curator may be responsible for more than one location. Modify your ERM to include this information.

PROBLEMS

Use the database shown in Figure P3.1 to work Problems 1–7. Note that the database is composed of four tables that reflect these relationships:

- An EMPLOYEE has only one JOB_CODE, but a JOB_CODE can be held by many EMPLOYEEs.
- An EMPLOYEE can participate in many PLANs, and any PLAN can be assigned to many EMPLOYEEs.

Note also that the *:* relationship has been broken down into two 1:* relationships for which the BENEFIT table serves as the composite or bridge entity.

3

FIGURE P3.1 **The Ch03_BeneCo database tables**

Database name: Ch03_BeneCo

Table name: EMPLOYEE

EMP_CODE	EMP_LNAME	JOB_CODE
14	Rudell	2
15	Arendse	1
16	Ruellardo	1
17	Smith	3
20	Smith	2

Table name: JOB

JOB_CODE	JOB_DESCRIPTION
1	Clerical
2	Technical
3	Managerial

Table name: BENEFIT

EMP_CODE	PLAN_CODE
15	2
15	3
16	1
17	1
17	3
17	4
20	3

Table name: PLAN

PLAN_CODE	PLAN_DESCRIPTION
1	Term life
2	Stock purchase
3	Long-term disability
4	Dental

1 For each table in the database, identify the primary key and the foreign key(s). If a table does not have a foreign key, write *None* in the space provided.

Table	Primary Key	Foreign Key(s)
EMPLOYEE		
BENEFIT		
JOB		
PLAN		

2 Create the ERD using UML notation to show the relationship between EMPLOYEE and JOB.

3 Do the tables exhibit entity integrity? Answer yes or no; then explain your answer.

Table	Entity Integrity	Explanation
EMPLOYEE		
BENEFIT		
JOB		
PLAN		

4 Do the tables exhibit referential integrity? Answer yes or no; then explain your answer. Write *NA* (not applicable) if the table does not have a foreign key.

Table	Referential Integrity	Explanation
EMPLOYEE		
BENEFIT		
JOB		
PLAN		

5 Create the ERD using Crow's Foot notation to show the relationships among EMPLOYEE, BENEFIT, JOB and PLAN.

6 Create the ERD using UML class diagram notation to show the relationships among EMPLOYEE, BENEFIT, JOB and PLAN.

Use the database shown in Figure P3.2 to answer Problems 7–13.

FIGURE P3.2 The Ch03_StoreCo database tables

Database name: Ch03_StoreCo

Table name: EMPLOYEE

EMP_CODE	EMP_TITLE	EMP_LNAME	EMP_FNAME	EMP_INITIAL	EMP_DOB	STORE_CODE
1	Mr	Govender	Adimoolam	W	21-May-70	3
2	Ms	Ratula	Nancy		09-Feb-75	2
3	Ms	Greenboro	Lottie	R	02-Oct-67	4
4	Mrs	Rumpersfro	Jennie	S	01-Jun-77	5
5	Mr	Smith	Robert	L	23-Nov-65	3
6	Mr	Renselaer	Cary	A	25-Dec-71	1
7	Mr	Ogallo	Roberto	S	31-Jul-68	3
8	Ms	Van Blerk	Elandri	I	10-Sep-74	1
9	Mr	Eindsmar	Jack	W	19-Apr-61	2
10	Mrs	Jones	Rose	R	06-Mar-72	4
11	Mr	Broderick	Tom		21-Oct-78	3
12	Mr	Washington	Alan	Y	08-Sep-80	2
13	Mr	Smith	Peter	N	25-Aug-70	3
14	Ms	Smith	Sherry	H	25-May-72	4
15	Mr	Olenko	Howard	U	24-May-70	5
16	Mr	Archialo	Barry	V	03-Sep-66	5
17	Ms	Grimaldo	Jeanine	K	12-Nov-76	4
18	Mr	Rosenberg	Andrew	D	24-Jan-77	4
19	Mr	Bophela	Ingwe	F	03-Oct-74	4
20	Mr	Mckee	Robert	S	06-Mar-76	1
21	Ms	Baumann	Jennifer	A	11-Dec-80	3

Table name: STORE

STORE_CODE	STORE_NAME	STORE_YTD_SALES	REGION_CODE	EMP_CODE
1	Access Junction	€792 730.05	2	8
2	Database Corner	€1 123 370.04	2	12
3	Tuple Charge	€779 558.74	1	7
4	Attribute Alley	€746 209.16	2	3
5	Primary Key Point	€2 314 777.78	1	15

Table name: REGION

REGION_CODE	REGION_DESCRIPT
1	East
2	West

7 For each table, identify the primary key and the foreign key(s). If a table does not have a foreign key, write *None* in the space provided.

Table	Primary Key	Foreign Key(s)
EMPLOYEE		
STORE		
REGION		

8 Do the tables exhibit entity integrity? Answer yes or no; then explain your answer.

Table	Entity Integrity	Explanation
EMPLOYEE		
STORE		
REGION		

9 Do the tables exhibit referential integrity? Answer yes or no; then explain your answer. Write *NA* (not applicable) if the table does not have a foreign key.

Table	Referential Integrity	Explanation
EMPLOYEE		
STORE		
REGION		

10 Describe the type(s) of relationship(s) between STORE and REGION.

11 Create the ERD using UML notation to show the relationship between STORE and REGION.

3

12 Describe the type(s) of relationship(s) between EMPLOYEE and STORE. (*Hint*: Each store employs many employees, one of whom manages the store.)

13 Create the ERD using UML notation to show the relationships among EMPLOYEE, STORE and REGION.

Use the database shown in Figure P3.3 to answer Problems 14–18.

FIGURE P3.3 The Ch03_CheapCo database tables

Database name: Ch03_CheapCo

Table name: PRODUCT   Primary key: PROD_CODE

Foreign key: VEND_CODE

PROD_CODE	PROD_DESCRIPTION	PROD_STOCK_DATE	PROD_ON_HAND	PROD_PRICE	VEND_CODE
12-WW/P2	18 cm power saw blade	07-Apr-16	12	10.94	123
1QQ23-55	6 cm wood screw, 100	19-Mar-16	123	13.55	123
231-78-W	PVC pipe, 8 cm, 2.44 m	07-Dec-15	45	17.01	121
33564/U	Rat-tail file, 0.5 cm, fine	08-Mar-16	18	10.94	123
AR/3/TYR	Cordless drill, 0.6 cm	29-Nov-15	8	136.33	121
DT-34-WW	Philips screwdriver pack	20-Dec-15	11	118.40	123
EE3-67/W	Sledge hammer, 7 kg	25-Feb-16	9	114.21	121
ER-56/DF	Houselite chain saw, 40 cm	28-Dec-15	7	1186.04	125
FRE-TRY9	Jigsaw, 30 cm blade	12-Aug-15	67	11.15	125
SE-67-89	Jigsaw, 20 cm blade	11-Oct-15	34	11.07	125
ZW-QR/AV	Hardware cloth, 0.6 cm.	23-Apr-16	14	110.26	123
ZX-WR/FR	Claw hammer	01-Mar-16	15	17.07	121

Table name: VENDOR   Primary key: VEND_CODE

Foreign key: none

VEND_CODE	VEND_NAME	VEND_CONTACT	VEND_AREACODE	VEND_PHONE
120	Bargain Snapper, Inc.	Melanie T. Travis	0181	899-1234
121	Cut 'n' Glow Co.	Henry J. Olero	0181	342-9896
122	Rip & Rattle Supply Co.	Anne R. Morrins	0113	225-1127
123	Tools 'R' Us	Juliette G. McHenry	0161	546-7894
124	Trowel & Dowel, Inc.	George F. Frederick	0113	453-4567
125	Bow & Wow Tools	Bill S. Sedwick	0113	324-9988

14 For each table, identify the primary key and the foreign key(s). If a table does not have a foreign key, write *None* in the space provided.

Table	Primary Key	Foreign Key(s)
Product		
VENDOR		

15 Do the tables exhibit entity integrity? Answer yes or no; then explain your answer.

Table	Entity Integrity	Explanation
Product		
VENDOR		

16 Do the tables exhibit referential integrity? Answer yes or no; then explain your answer. Write *NA* (not applicable) if the table does not have a foreign key.

Table	Referential Integrity	Explanation
Product		
VENDOR		

17 Create the ERD using UML notation for this database.

18 Create the data dictionary for this database.

Use the database shown in Figure P3.4 to answer Problems 19–24.

FIGURE P3.4 The Ch03_TransCo database tables

Database name: Ch03_TransCo

Table name: TRUCK Primary key: TRUCK_NUM

Foreign key: BASE-CODE, TYPE_CODE

TRUCK_ NUM	BASE_ CODE	TYPE_ CODE	TRUCK_ KM	TRUCK_BUY_ DATE	TRUCK_SERIAL_ NUM
1001	501	1	32123.50	23-Sep-13	AA-322-12212-W11
1002	502	1	76984.30	05-Feb-12	AC-342-22134-Q23
1003	501	2	12346.60	11-Nov-13	AC-445-78656-Z99
1004		1	2894.30	06-Jan-14	WQ-112-23144-T34
1005	503	2	45673.10	01-Mar-13	FR-998-32245-W12
1006	501	2	193245.70	15-Jul-10	AD-456-00845-R45
1007	502	3	32012.30	17-Oct-11	AA-341-96573-Z84
1008	502	3	44213.60	07-Aug-12	DR-559-22189-D33
1009	503	2	10932.90	12-Feb-14	DE-887-98456-E94

Table name: BASE Primary key: BASE_CODE

Foreign key: none

BASE_CODE	BASE_CITY	BASE_PROVINCE	BASE_AREA_CODE	BASE_PHONE	BASE_MANAGER
501	Polokwane	Limpopo	0700	123-4567	Sibusiso Balisa
502	Cape Town	Western Cape	7100	234-5678	Clementine Daniels
503	Best	North Brabant	4567	345-6789	Maria J. Talindo
504	Durban	KwaZulu-Natal	4001	456-7890	Pragasen Khan

Table name: TYPE Primary key: TYPE_CODE

Foreign key: none

TYPE_CODE	TYPE_DESCRIPTION
1	Single box, double-axle
2	Single box, single-axle
3	Tandem trailer, single-axle

19 For each table, identify the primary key and the foreign key(s). If a table does not have a foreign key, write *None* in the space provided.

Table	Primary Key	Foreign Key(s)
TRUCK		
BASE		
TYPE		

20 Do the tables exhibit entity integrity? Answer yes or no; then explain your answer.

Table	Entity Integrity	Explanation
TRUCK		
BASE		
TYPE		

21 Do the tables exhibit referential integrity? Answer yes or no; then explain your answer. Write *NA* (not applicable) if the table does not have a foreign key.

Table	Referential Integrity	Explanation
TRUCK		
BASE		
TYPE		

22 Identify the TRUCK table's candidate key(s).

23 For each table, identify a superkey and a secondary key.

Table	Superkey	Secondary Key
TRUCK		
BASE		
TYPE		

24 Create the ERD using UML notation for this database.

FIGURE P3.5 **The Ch03_AviaCo database tables**

Database name: Ch03_AviaCo

Table name: CHARTER

CHAR_TRIP	CHAR_DATE	CHAR_PILOT	CHAR_COPILOT	AC_NUMBER	CHAR_DESTINATION	CHAR_DISTANCE	CHAR_HOURS_FLOWN	CHAR_HOURS_WAIT	CHAR_FUEL_GALLONS	CHAR_OIL_QTS	CUS_CODE
10001	05-Feb-20	104		2289L	CDG	936.00	5.1	2.2	354.1	1	10011
10002	05-Feb-20	101		2778V	BNA	320.00	1.6	0	72.6	0	10016
10003	05-Feb-20	105	109	4278Y	LHR	1 574.00	7.8	0	339.8	2	10014
10004	06-Feb-20	106		1484P	CPT	472.00	2.9	4.9	97.2	1	10019
10005	06-Feb-20	101		2289L	CDG	1 023.00	5.7	3.5	397.7	2	10011
10006	06-Feb-20	109		4278Y	CPT	472.00	2.6	5.2	117.1	0	10017
10007	06-Feb-20	104	105	2778V	LHR	1 574.00	7.9	0	348.4	2	10012
10008	07-Feb-20	106		1484P	TYS	644.00	4.1	0	140.6	1	10014
10009	07-Feb-20	105		2289L	LHR	1 574.00	6.6	23.4	459.9	0	10017
10010	07-Feb-20	109		4278Y	CDG	998.00	6.2	3.2	279.7	0	10016
10011	07-Feb-20	101	104	1484P	BNA	352.00	1.9	5.3	66.4	1	10012
10012	08-Feb-20	101		2778V	MOB	884.00	4.8	4.2	215.1	0	10010
10013	08-Feb-20	105		4278Y	TYS	644.00	3.9	4.5	174.3	1	10011
10014	09-Feb-20	106		4278Y	CDG	936.00	6.1	2.1	302.6	0	10017
10015	09-Feb-20	104	101	2289L	LHR	1 645.00	6.7	0	459.5	2	10016
10016	09-Feb-20	109	105	2778V	MQY	312.00	1.5	0	67.2	0	10011
10017	10-Feb-20	101		1484P	CPT	508.00	3.1	0	105.5	0	10014
10018	10-Feb-20	105	104	4278Y	TYS	644.00	3.8	4.5	167.4	0	10017

The destinations are indicated by standard three-letter airport codes. For example,

CDG = PARIS CHARLES DE GAULLE, FRANCE, LHR = LONDON HEATHROW, UNITED KINGDOM AND CPT = CAPE TOWN INTERNATIONAL, SOUTH AFRICA

Table name: AIRCRAFT

AC_NUMBER	MOD_CODE	AC_TTAF	AC_TTEL	AC_TTER
1484P	PA23-250	1833.10	1833.10	101.80
2289L	C-90A	4243.80	768.90	1123.40
2778V	PA31-350	7992.90	1513.10	789.50
4278Y	PA31-350	2147.30	622.10	243.20

AC_TTAF = Aircraft total time, airframe (hours)
AC_TTEL = Total time, left engine (hours)
AC_TTER = Total time, right engine (hours)

In a fully developed system, such attribute values would be updated by application software when the CHARTER table entries are posted.

Table name: MODEL

MOD_CODE	MOD_MANUFACTURER	MOD_NAME	MOD_SEATS	MOD_CHG_MILE
C-90A	Beechcraft	KingAir	8	€1.67
PA23-250	Piper	Aztec	6	€1.20
PA31-350	Piper	Navajo Chieftain	10	€1.47

Customers are charged per round-trip mile, using the MOD_CHG_MILE rate. The MOD_SEAT gives the total number of seats in the airplane, including the pilot and copilot seats. Therefore a PA31-350 trip that is flown by a pilot and copilot has six passenger seats available.

Table name: PILOT

EMP_ NUM	PIL_ LICENCE	PIL_RATINGS	PIL_MED_ TYPE	PIL_MED_ DATE	PIL_PT135_ DATE
101	ATP	ATP/SEL/MEL/Instr/CFII	1	20-Jan-20	11-Jan-20
104	ATP	ATP/SEL/MEL/Instr	1	18-Dec-19	17-Jan-20
105	COM	COMM/SEL/MEL/Instr/CFI	2	05-Jan-20	02-Jan-20
106	COM	COMM/SEL/MEL/Instr	2	10-Dec-19	02-Feb-20
109	COM	ATP/SEL/MEL/SES/Instr/ CFII	1	22-Jan-20	15-Jan-20

The pilot licences shown in the PILOT table include the ATP = Airline Transport Pilot and COM = Commercial Pilot. Businesses that operate on demand air services are governed by Part 135 of the Federal Air Regulations (FARs) that are enforced by the Federal Aviation Administration (FAA). Such businesses are known as 'Part 135 operators'. Part 125 operations require that pilots successfully complete flight proficiency checks every six months. The 'Part 135' flight proficiency check data is recorded in PIL_PT135_DATE. To fly commercially, pilots must have at least a commercial licence and a second-class medical certificate (PIL_MED_TYPE = 2).

The PIL_RATINGs include:

SEL = Single engine, land
SES = Single engine, sea
CFI = Certified flight instructor
MEL – Multi-engine, land
Instr. = Instrument
CFII = Certified flight instructor, instrument

Table name: EMPLOYEE

EMP_NUM	EMP_TITLE	EMP_LNAME	EMP_FNAME	EMP_INITIAL	EMP_DOB	EMP_HIRE_DATE
100	Mr.	Nkosi	Cela	D	15-Jun-52	15-Mar-98
101	Ms.	Naude	Amahle	G	19-Mar-75	25-Apr-96
102	Mr.	Vandam	Rhett		14-Nov-68	18-May-03
103	Ms.	Jones	Anne	M	11-May-84	26-Jul-09
104	Mr.	Lange	John	P	12-Jul-81	20-Aug-00
105	Mr.	Williams	Robert	D	14-Mar-85	19-Jun-13
106	Mrs.	Duzak	Jeanine	K	12-Feb-78	13-Mar-99
107	Mr.	Diante	Jorge	D	01-May-85	02-Jul-07
108	Mr.	Wiesenbach	Paul	R	14-Feb-76	03-Jun-03
109	Ms.	Travis	Elizabeth	K	18-Jun-71	14-Feb-16
110	Mrs.	Genkazi	Leighla	W	19-May-80	29-Jun-10

Table name: CUSTOMER

CUS_CODE	CUS_ LNAME	CUS_ FNAME	CUS_ INITIAL	CUS AREACODE	CUS_ PHONE	CUS_ BALANCE
10010	Ramas	Alfred	A	0181	844-2573	10.00
10011	Dunne	Leona	K	0161	894-1238	10.00
10012	Smith	Kathy	W	0181	894-2285	1559.73
10013	Pieterse	Jaco	F	0181	894-2180	1802.09
10014	Orlando	Myron		0181	222-1672	1420.15
10015	O'Brian	Amy	B	0161	442-3381	1633.19
10016	Brown	James	G	0181	297-1228	10.00
10017	Williams	George		0181	290-2556	10.00
10018	Padayachee	Vinaya	G	0161	382-7185	10.00
10019	Smith	Olette	K	0178	297-3809	1283.33

Use the database shown in Figure P3.5 to answer Problems 25–28. ROBCOR is an aircraft charter company that supplies on-demand charter flight services using a fleet of four aircraft. Aircraft are identified by a unique registration number. Therefore, the aircraft registration number is an appropriate primary key for the AIRCRAFT table.

The nulls in the CHARTER table's CHAR_COPILOT column indicate that a copilot is not required for some charter trips or for some aircraft. (Federal Aviation Administration (FAA) rules require a copilot on jet aircraft and on aircraft having a gross take-off weight over 5 500 kg. None of the aircraft in the AIRCRAFT table are governed by this requirement; however, some customers may require the presence of a copilot for insurance reasons.) All charter trips are recorded in the CHARTER table.

NOTE

Earlier in the chapter it was stated that it is best to avoid homonyms and synonyms. In this problem, both the pilot and the copilot are pilots in the PILOT table, but EMP_NUM cannot be used for both in the CHARTER table. Therefore, the synonyms CHAR_PILOT and CHAR_COPILOT were used in the CHARTER table.

Although the solution works in this case, it is very restrictive and it generates nulls when a copilot is not required. Worse, such nulls proliferate as crew requirements change. For example, if the AviaCo charter company grows and starts using larger aircraft, crew requirements may increase to include flight engineers and load masters. The CHARTER table would then have to be modified to include the additional crew assignments; such attributes as CHAR_FLT_ENGINEER and CHAR_LOADMASTER would have to be added to the CHARTER table. Given this change, each time a smaller aircraft flew a charter trip without the number of crew members required in larger aircraft, the missing crew members would yield additional nulls in the CHARTER table.

You will have a chance to correct those design shortcomings in Problem 27. The problem illustrates two important points:

- Don't use synonyms. If your design requires the use of synonyms, revise the design!
- To the greatest possible extent, design the database to accommodate growth without requiring structural changes in the database tables. Plan ahead and try to anticipate the effects of change on the database.

25 For each table, where possible, identify:

- **a** The primary key.
- **b** A superkey.
- **c** A candidate key.
- **d** The foreign key(s).
- **e** A secondary key.

26 Create the ERD using UML notation. (*Hint*: Look at the table contents. You will discover that an AIRCRAFT can fly many CHARTER trips, but each CHARTER trip is flown by one AIRCRAFT, that a MODEL references many AIRCRAFT, but each AIRCRAFT references a single MODEL, etc.)

27 Modify the ERD you created in Problem 26 to eliminate the problems created by the use of synonyms. (*Hint*: Modify the CHARTER table structure by eliminating the CHAR_PILOT and CHAR_COPILOT attributes; then create a composite table named CREW to link the CHARTER and EMPLOYEE tables. Some crew members, such as flight attendants, may not be pilots. That's why the EMPLOYEE table enters into this relationship.)

28 Create the ERD using UML notation for the design you revised in Problem 27. (After you have had a chance to revise the design, your instructor will show you the results of the design change, using a copy of the revised database named Ch03_AviaCo_2).

CHAPTER 4

Relational Algebra and Calculus

IN THIS CHAPTER, YOU WILL LEARN:

- What is meant by relational algebra and relational calculus
- How to manipulate database tables using relational set operators
- How the DBMS supports the key relational operators: select, project and join
- The different types of joins
- How to write queries using relational algebra expressions
- About tuple and domain relational calculus

PREVIEW

Relational algebra and relational calculus are the mathematical basis for 'relational databases' and were proposed by E.F. Codd in 1971 as the basis for defining the relational model. Codd proposed that the data should be modelled independently of how it would actually be used and that, to do this, data should be described both mathematically and minimally. In Chapter 2 we identified that one of the key components of the relational model was the concept of a relation, which allows data to be stored within the database in a structured manner. Relational algebra is a collection of formal operations acting on these relations that produce new relations as a result. The algebra is based on predicate logic and set theory and is described as a *procedural language*. *Predicate logic*, used extensively in mathematics, provides a framework in which an assertion (statement of fact) can be verified as either true or false. *Set theory* is a mathematical science that deals with sets, or groups of things, and is used as the basis for data manipulation in the relational model. Together, predicate logic and set theory provide an ideal basis for performing operations on relations in a database.

Once we have specified the relations in the database, the next important consideration is how to retrieve and modify data within a relation. This is usually achieved using a high-level data manipulation language (DML) such as SQL (Structured Query Language), which is relatively easy to understand. These DML languages have stemmed from relational algebra and relational calculus, which both provide the basic operations required by any DML. Languages such as SQL use a limited implementation of relational theory, and are often modified. In Chapter 8, Beginning Structured Query Language, you will learn how SQL commands can be used to accomplish relational algebra tasks.

Although relational algebra is not an easy language to understand, it is necessary to study the language to gain an understanding of the basic data manipulation operations. Essentially, relational algebra provides us with a formal description of how a relational database operates, and the mathematics that is necessary to retrieve and modify the data. Relational algebra and tuple relational calculus can both be used to express the same queries, which means that we have a relationally complete query language. We say a query language is relationally complete if any query that can be written in relational algebraic form can also be expressed by the query language. First, you will learn about the basic relational operators and how they can be used to manipulate data. Then, you will learn about how to write queries using relational algebraic expressions. Finally, you will explore how to write simple queries using both tuple and domain relational calculus.

4.1 RELATIONAL OPERATORS

Relational algebra defines the theoretical way of manipulating table contents through a number of relational operators. Codd originally defined eight relational operators, called SELECT (or RESTRICT), PROJECT, JOIN, PRODUCT, INTERSECT, UNION, DIFFERENCE and DIVIDE. The most important operators are SELECT, PROJECT and JOIN, which can be used to formulate relational algebra expressions to answer many user queries. The relational operators have the property of **closure**; that is, relational algebra operators are used on existing tables to produce new tables. The relational operators are classed as being *unary* or *binary*. Unary operators, such as SELECT and PROJECT, can be applied to one relation, whilst binary operators such as JOIN are applied on two relations.

In Chapter 3, Relational Model Characteristics, we learnt about a number of important concepts and properties of relations that are essential for understanding the relational model. In this chapter, we will build on these concepts to understand how relational algebra can be used to write queries. Within Chapter 3, we modelled a relation on a mathematical construct, which had to abide by a set of rules (Table 3.1). When applying relational operators to relations, we have to follow these rules in addition to those defined for each relational operator.

In the following sections you will learn about the theory associated with common relational operators and view some practical examples. Remember that the term *relation* is a synonym for table.

NOTE

To be considered minimally relational, the DBMS must support the key relational operators SELECT, PROJECT and JOIN. Very few DBMSs are capable of supporting all eight relational operators.

A NOTE ON SET THEORY

Set theory is one of the most fundamental concepts in mathematics.[1] The theory is based on the idea that *elements* have *membership* in a set. Given two sets, A and B, we say that *A* is a member of *B*, which can be written as $A \in B$. Alternatively, we can say that the set *B* contains *A* as its element. The elements of a set can be numbers, the names of students who enrolled in a course or the flight numbers of all the flights operated by an airline. Each set is then determined by its elements and each element in a set is unique. Venn diagrams[2] are a way of visually representing sets. Supposing we have the following two sets:

Set A = Students who take the Databases unit	{Sarah, Phinda, Paul, Hamzah, Mikla}
Set B = Students who take the Programming unit	{Paul, Mikla, Asanda, Kiki, Craig}

Some of the students in set A appear also in set B and vice versa. We can represent these facts using a Venn diagram as shown in Figure 4.1.

1 Karel Hrbacek and Thomas Jech, *Introduction to Set Theory*, third edn. Marcel Dekker, Inc., 1999.

2 John Venn (1880) 'On the Diagrammatic and Mechanical Representation of Propositions and Reasonings'. *Dublin Philosophical Magazine and Journal of Science* 9(59): 1–18.

4

FIGURE 4.1 **A simple Venn diagram**

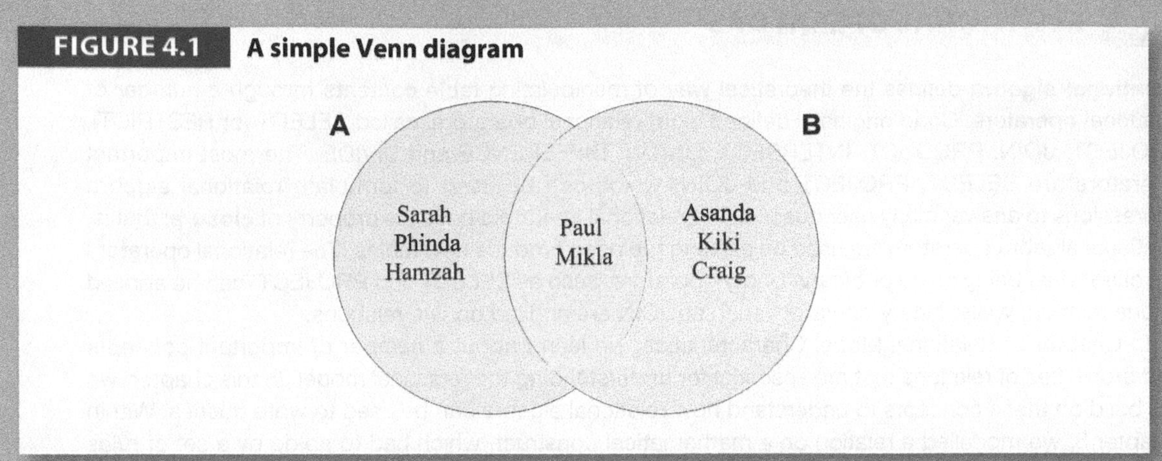

In Figure 4.1, the two circles represent the two sets A and B.The students who take both the Database and Programming units and who appear in both sets are Paul and Mikla. These will go in the overlapping sections of the two circles. Sarah, Phinda and Hamzah only take the Database unit, so these go only in the left-hand circle, whilst Asanda, Kiki and Craig only take the Programming unit and only appear in the right-hand circle.

We will be using Venn diagrams throughout this chapter to illustrate the three relational set operators: union, intersection and difference.

4.1.1 Selection

The relational operator **SELECT**, also known as **RESTRICT**, can be used to list all of the row values, or it can return only those row values that match a specified criterion. In other words, SELECT returns a horizontal subset of a relation.

The SELECT operator, denoted by σ_θ, is formally defined as:

$\sigma_\theta (R)$

or

$\sigma_{<criterion>} (RELATION)$

where $\sigma_\theta (R)$ is the set of specified tuples of the relation *R* and θ is the predicate (or criterion) to extract the required tuples.

NOTE

The Euro, denoted as €, became the official currency of 12 European member states in 2002. Today the Euro is used by more than 175 million Europeans in 19 of 28 EU member countries, as well as some countries that are not formally members of the EU.

Figure 4.2 (a) shows visually how rows within a relation are selected. An example of a relation that contains information about products which are sold in a store is shown in Figure 4.2 (b). Figure 4.2 (c) shows the effects of selecting all rows with no criteria. The criterion specified in Figure 4.2 (d) selects those rows only where the price is less than €2.00 and, in Figure 4.2 (e), only the row containing P_CODE 123456 is displayed.

FIGURE 4.2 The SELECT operator

Figure 4.2 (a) SELECTION

	Column 1	*Column 2*
Row 1		
Row 2		
Row 3		
Row 4		
Row 5		

Database name: Ch04_Relational_DB_Operators

Figure 4.2 (b) The PRODUCT Relation

P_CODE	P_DESCRIPT	PRICE
123456	Flashlight	€4.16
123457	Lamp	€19.87
123458	Box Fan	€8.68
213345	9 v battery	€1.52
254467	100 W bulb	€1.16
311452	Powerdrill	€27.64

Figure 4.2 (c) σ *(PRODUCT)*

P_CODE	P_DESCRIPT	PRICE
123456	Flashlight	€4.16
123457	Lamp	€19.87
123458	Box Fan	€8.68
213345	9 v battery	€1.52
254467	100 W bulb	€1.16
311452	Powerdrill	€27.64

Figure 4.2 (d) $\sigma_{price < 2.00}$ *(PRODUCT)*

P_CODE	P_DESCRIPT	PRICE
213345	9 v battery	€1.52
254467	100 W bulb	€1.16

Figure 4.2 (e) $\sigma_{p\_code = 123456}$ *(PRODUCT)*

P_CODE	P_DESCRIPT	PRICE
123456	Flashlight	€4.16

It is also possible to create more complex criteria by using the logical operators AND, OR and NOT. Figure 4.3 illustrates the use of the logical AND operator using the COURSE relation, which stores information about courses offered at Tiny University. Figure 4.3 (b) shows the new relation, which contains only the tuples where the DEPT_CODE is CIS and the CRS_CREDIT value is 4.

Online Content All of the databases used to illustrate the material in this chapter are found on the online platform for this book. The database names used in the folder match the database names used in the figures.

FIGURE 4.3 Selecting from the COURSE relation

Database name: Ch04_TinyUniversity

Figure 4.3 (a) the COURSE Relation

CRS_CODE	DEPT_CODE	CRS_DESCRIPTION	CRS_CREDIT
ACCT-211	ACCT	Accounting I	3
ACCT-212	ACCT	Accounting II	3
CIS-220	CIS	Introduction to Computer Science	3
CIS-420	CIS	Database Design and Implementation	4
QM-261	CIS	Intro. to Statistics	3
QM-362	CIS	Statistical Applications	4

Figure 4.3 (b) $\sigma_{dept\_code\ =\ 'CIS'\ AND\ crs\_credit\ =\ 4}(COURSE)$

CRS_CODE	DEPT_CODE	CRS_DESCRIPTION	CRS_CREDIT
CIS-420	CIS	Database Design and Implementation	4
QM-362	CIS	Statistical Applications	4

4.1.2 Projection

The PROJECT operator returns all values for selected attributes. In other words, PROJECT returns a vertical subset of a relation excluding any duplicates. The **PROJECT** operator, denoted by Π, is formally defined as:

$\Pi_{a1...an}(R)$

or

$\Pi_{<\text{List of attributes}>}$ (Relation)

where the projection of the relation *R*, denoted by $\Pi_{a1...an}(R)$ is the set of specified attributes $a_1...a_n$ of the relation *R*. Figure 4.4 (a) shows visually how columns within a relation are selected.

Figure 4.4 (b) shows a relation that stores information about products which are sold in a store. Figure 4.4 (c) shows the effect of applying the PROJECT relational operator on the PRODUCT relation, to create a new relation containing only the attribute PRICE. The two further examples in Figure 4.4 (d) and (e) illustrate the PROJECT operator. Notice that the order of attributes is maintained in the resulting relations.

4

FIGURE 4.4 **The PROJECT operator**

Database name: Ch04_Relational_DB_Operators

Figure 4.4 (a) PROJECTION

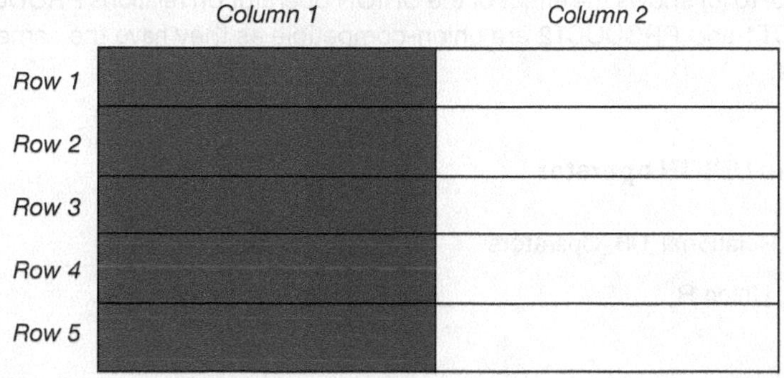

	Column 1	Column 2
Row 1		
Row 2		
Row 3		
Row 4		
Row 5		

Figure 4.4 (b) The PRODUCT relation

P_CODE	P_DESCRIPT	PRICE
123456	Flashlight	€4.16
123457	Lamp	€19.87
123458	Box Fan	€8.68
213345	9 v battery	€1.52
254467	100 W bulb	€1.16
311452	Powerdrill	€27.64

Figure 4.4 (c) Π_{price} (PRODUCT)

PRICE
€4.16
€19.87
€8.68
€1.52
€1.16
€27.64

Figure 4.4 (d) $\Pi_{p\_descript,price}$ (PRODUCT)

P_DESCRIPT	PRICE
Flashlight	€4.16
Lamp	€19.87
Box Fan	€8.68
9 v battery	€1.52
100 W bulb	€1.16
Powerdrill	€27.64

Figure 4.4 (e) $\Pi_{p\_code,price}$ (PRODUCT)

P_CODE	PRICE
123456	€4.16
123457	€19.87
123458	€8.68
213345	€1.52
254467	€1.16
311452	€27.64

4.1.3 UNION

The **UNION** set operator combines all tuples from two relations, excluding duplicate tuples. The relations must have the same attribute characteristics (the columns and domains must be identical) to be used in the UNION. When two or more tables share the same number of columns, i.e. have the same degree, and when they share the same (or compatible) domains, they are said to be **union-compatible**. The UNION operator, denoted by ∪, is formally defined as:

> The union of relations $R_1(a_1, a_2, \ldots, a_n)$ and $R_2(b_1, b_2, \ldots, b_n)$ denoted $R_1 \cup R_2$ with degree n, is the relation $R_3(c_1, c_2, \ldots, c_n)$ where for each i ($i = 1, 2..n$), a_i and b_i must have compatible domains.

The degree of R_3 is the same as that of R_1 and R_2. However the cardinality of R_3 is $a + b$, only if a and b are the cardinalities of R_1 and R_2 respectively, since there may not be duplicate tuples in R_1 and R_2. Figure 4.5 (a) visually shows $R_1 \cup R_2$.

Figure 4.5 (b) to (c) shows the effect of the UNION operator on relations PRODUCT1 and PRODUCT2. Both PRODUCT1 and PRODUCT2 are union-compatible as they have the same degree and share the same domains.

4

FIGURE 4.5 The UNION operator

Database name: Ch04_Relational_DB_Operators

Figure 4.5 (a) R_1 Union R_2

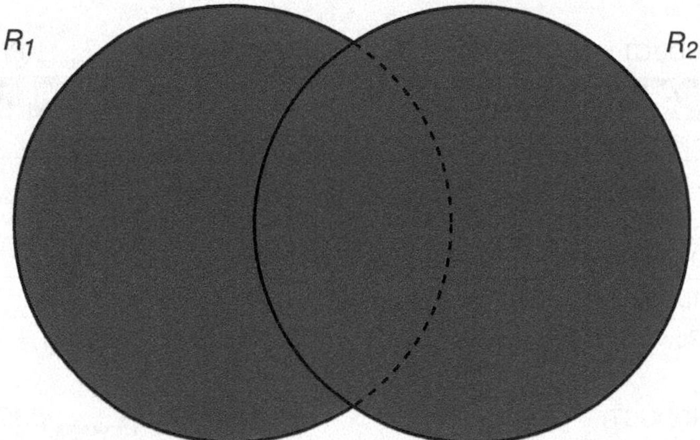

Figure 4.5 (b) The UNION_PRODUCT1 relation

P_CODE	P_DESCRIPT	PRICE
123456	Flashlight	€4.16
123457	Lamp	€19.87
123458	Box Fan	€8.68
213345	9 v battery	€1.52
254467	100 W bulb	€1.16
311452	Powerdrill	€27.64

Figure 4.5 (c) The UNION_PRODUCT2 relation

P_CODE	P_DESCRIPT	PRICE
345678	Microwave	€126.40
345679	Dishwasher	€395.00

Figure 4.5 (d) Result of UNION_PRODUCT1 ∪ UNION_PRODUCT2

P_CODE	P_DESCRIPT	PRICE
123456	Flashlight	€4.16
123457	Lamp	€19.87
123458	Box Fan	€8.68
213345	9 v battery	€1.52
254467	100 W bulb	€1.16
311452	Powerdrill	€27.64
345678	Microwave	€126.40
345679	Dishwasher	€395.00

Figure 4.6 shows the effects of the UNION operator when two relations contain duplicate tuples. Notice that only one additional tuple has been added in Figure 4.6 (c), as CRS_CODE = ACCT-211 already exists in the **COURSE_RELATION**.

FIGURE 4.6 The Union operator – COURSE ∪ COURSE2

Database name: Ch04_TinyUniversity

Figure 4.6 (a) The COURSE_RELATION

CRS_CODE	DEPT_CODE	CRS_DESCRIPTION	CRS_CREDIT
ACCT-211	ACCT	Accounting I	3
ACCT-212	ACCT	Accounting II	3
CIS-220	CIS	Introduction to Computer Science	3
CIS-420	CIS	Database Design and Implementation	4
QM-261	CIS	Intro. to Statistics	3
QM-362	CIS	Statistical Applications	4

Figure 4.6 (b) The COURSE2_RELATION

CRS_CODE	DEPT_CODE	CRS_DESCRIPTION	CRS_CREDIT
ACCT-211	ACCT	Accounting I	3
CIS-430	CIS	Advanced Databases	6

Figure 4.6 (c) Result of COURSE ∪ COURSE2

CRS_CODE	DEPT_CODE	CRS_DESCRIPTION	CRS_CREDIT
ACCT-211	ACCT	Accounting I	3
ACCT-212	ACCT	Accounting II	3
CIS-220	CIS	Introduction to Computer Science	3
CIS-420	CIS	Database Design and Implementation	4
QM-261	CIS	Intro. to Statistics	3
QM-362	CIS	Statistical Applications	4
CIS-430	CIS	Advanced Databases	6

If two relations are not **union-compatible**, then the UNION operator cannot be applied as the results would be invalid. For example, applying the UNION operator to the COURSE relation in Figure 4.6 (a) and the CLASS relation in 4.7 (a) is not allowed (COURSE ∪ CLASS). In order to get around this problem, the PROJECT operator could be used to restrict the columns in each relation over a common attribute. In the example, both relations COURSE and CLASS have a common attribute CRS_CODE. We could therefore write Π_{CRS_CODE} (COURSE) ∪ Π_{CRS_CODE} (CLASS) and obtain the resulting relation shown in Figure 4.7 (b).

4

FIGURE 4.7 The Union operator — not union-compatible example

Database name: Ch04_TinyUniversity

Figure 4.7 (a) the CLASS_RELATION

CLASS_CODE	CRS_CODE	CLASS_SECTION	CLASS_TIME	CLASS_ROOM	LECTURER_NUM
10012	ACCT-211	1	MWF 8:00-8:50 a.m.	BUS311	105
10013	ACCT-211	2	MWF 9:00-9:50 a.m.	BUS200	105
10014	ACCT-211	3	TTh 2:30-3:45 p.m.	BUS252	342
10015	ACCT-212	1	MWF 10:00-10:50 a.m.	BUS311	301
10016	ACCT-212	2	Th 6:00-8:40 p.m.	BUS252	301
10017	CIS-220	1	MWF 9:00-9:50 a.m.	KLR209	228
10018	CIS-220	2	MWF 9:00-9:50 a.m.	KLR211	114
10019	CIS-220	3	MWF 10:00-10:50 a.m.	KLR209	228
10020	CIS-420	1	W 6:00-8:40 p.m.	KLR209	162
10021	QM-261	1	MWF 8:00-8:50 a.m.	KLR200	114
10022	QM-261	2	TTh 1:00-2:15 p.m.	KLR200	114
10023	QM-362	1	MWF 11:00-11:50 a.m.	KLR200	162
10024	QM-362	2	TTh 2:30-3:45 p.m.	KLR200	162

Figure 4.7 (b) Result of Π_{CRS_CODE} (COURSE) $\cup$ Π_{CRS_CODE} (CLASS)

CRS_CODE
ACCT-211
ACCT-212
CIS-220
CIS-420
QM-261
QM-362

4.1.4 INTERSECT

The INTERSECT operator, denoted as ∩, returns only the tuples that appear in both relations. As was true in the case of UNION, the tables must be union-compatible to give valid results. For example, you cannot use INTERSECT if one of the attributes in the first table is numeric and the corresponding one in the second table is character-based. The **INTERSECT** operator is formally defined as:

> The intersect of relations $R_1(a_1, a_2, \ldots, a_n)$ and $R_2(b_1, b_2, \ldots, b_n)$ denoted $R_1 \cap R_2$ with degree n, is the relation $R_3(c_1, c_2, \ldots, c_n)$ that includes only those tuples of R_1 that also appear in R_2 where for each i ($i = 1, 2..n$), a_i and b_i must have compatible domains.

Figure 4.8 (a) visually shows $R_1 \cap R_2$.

The effect of applying the INTERSECT operator to the first name column (F_NAME) in two relations is shown in Figure 4.8 (d). Only Kuhle and Jorge appear in the final relation as they are the only two F_NAMEs that appear in both INTERSECT_RELATION_1 and INTERSECT_RELATION_2.

FIGURE 4.8 The INTERSECT operator

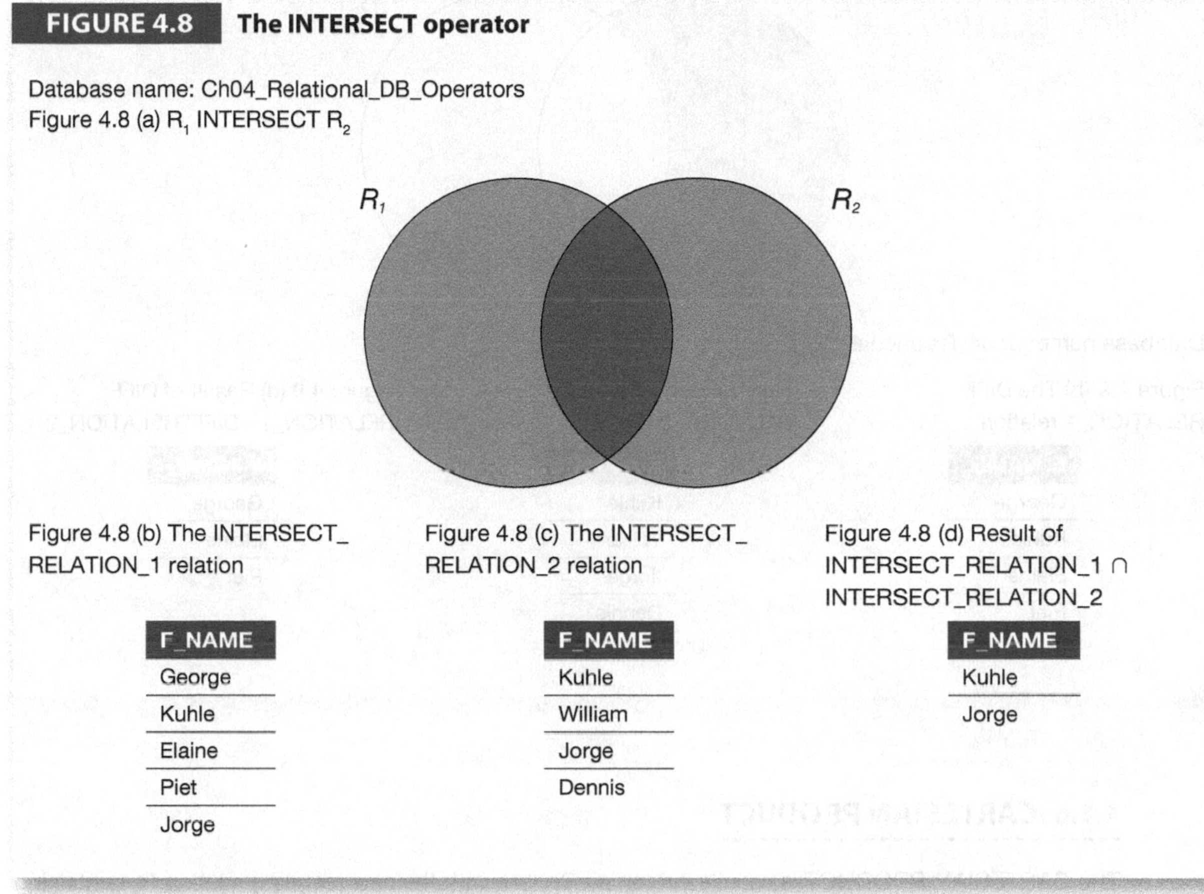

Database name: Ch04_Relational_DB_Operators

Figure 4.8 (a) R_1 INTERSECT R_2

Figure 4.8 (b) The INTERSECT_RELATION_1 relation

F_NAME
George
Kuhle
Elaine
Piet
Jorge

Figure 4.8 (c) The INTERSECT_RELATION_2 relation

F_NAME
Kuhle
William
Jorge
Dennis

Figure 4.8 (d) Result of INTERSECT_RELATION_1 ∩ INTERSECT_RELATION_2

F_NAME
Kuhle
Jorge

4.1.5 DIFFERENCE

The DIFFERENCE operator returns all tuples in one relation that are not found in the other relation; that is, it subtracts one relation from the other. The DIFFERENCE operator also requires that the two relations must be union-compatible. The **DIFFERENCE** operator is formally defined as:

> The difference of relations $R_1(a_1, a_2, \ldots, a_m)$ and $R_2(b_1, b_2, \ldots, b_m)$ denoted $R_1 - R_2$ with degree m, is the relation $R_3(c_1, c_2, \ldots, c_m)$ that includes all tuples that are in R_1 but not in R_2 where for each i ($i = 1,2..m$), a_i and b_i must have compatible domains.

Figure 4.9 (a) shows how *R1 – R2* can be visualised.

The effect of applying the DIFFERENCE operator to two relations is shown in Figure 4.9. The resulting relation in Figure 4.9 (c) shows only George, Elaine and Piet, as these are the only values of F_NAME that appear in DIFF_RELATION_1 and not in DIFF_RELATION_2. Note that A–B will not give the same result as B–A, i.e. the order of the relations are important in the DIFFERENCE operator.

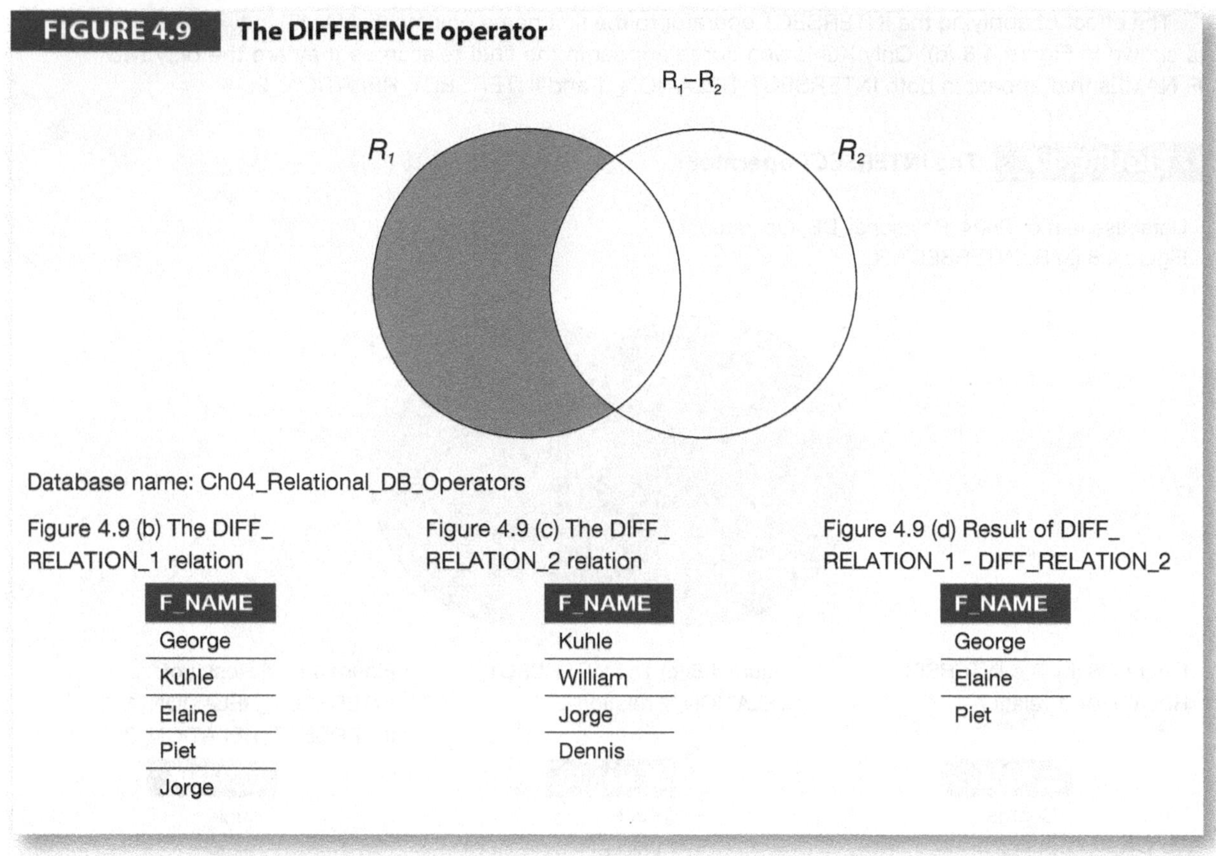

FIGURE 4.9 The DIFFERENCE operator

Database name: Ch04_Relational_DB_Operators

Figure 4.9 (b) The DIFF_RELATION_1 relation

F_NAME
George
Kuhle
Elaine
Piet
Jorge

Figure 4.9 (c) The DIFF_RELATION_2 relation

F_NAME
Kuhle
William
Jorge
Dennis

Figure 4.9 (d) Result of DIFF_RELATION_1 - DIFF_RELATION_2

F_NAME
George
Elaine
Piet

4.1.6 CARTESIAN PRODUCT

The CARTESIAN PRODUCT is usually written as $R_1 \times R_2$ with the new resulting relation R_3 containing all the attributes that are present in R_1 and R_2 along with all the possible combinations of tuples from both R_1 and R_2.

It can be formally defined as:

> The CARTESIAN PRODUCT of two relations $R_1(a_1, a_2, \ldots, a_n)$ with cardinality *i* and $R_2(b_1, b_2, \ldots, b_m)$ with cardinality *j* is a relation R_3 with degree $k = n + m$, cardinality *i*j* and attributes $(a_1, a_2, \ldots, a_n, b_1, b_2, \ldots, b_m)$. This can be denoted as $R_3 = R_1 \times R_2$.

Therefore, if one relation has six rows and four attributes and the other relation has three rows and two attributes, the CARTESIAN PRODUCT creates a new relation composed of $6 \times 3 = 18$ rows and $4 + 2 = 6$ attributes, i.e. the cardinality of the new relation would be 18 tuples and the degree would be 6. Figure 4.10 (c) shows how the CARTESIAN PRODUCT is used on combining the PRODUCT and LOCATION relations in Figures 4.10 (a) and (b) respectively.

You can see in Figure 4.10 (c) that the result of PRODUCT × LOCATION is a new relation with a cardinality of 18 (6×3) and a degree of 6 ($3 + 3$). The CARTESIAN PRODUCT is not a very useful operation by itself, as it combines many tuples that have no association with each other. However, if it is used in conjunction with the RESTRICT (SELECT) operator, it becomes a very important operator known as a JOIN.

FIGURE 4.10 The CARTESIAN PRODUCT

Database name: Ch04_Relational_DB_Operators

Figure 4.10 (a) The PRODUCT relation

P_CODE	P_DESCRIPT	PRICE
123456	Flashlight	€4.16
123457	Lamp	€19.87
123458	Box Fan	€8.68
213345	9 v battery	€1.52
254467	100 W bulb	€1.06
311452	Powerdrill	€27.64

Figure 4.10 (b) The LOCATION relation

STORE	AISLE	SHELF
23	W	5
24	K	9
25	Z	6

Figure 4.10 (c) PRODUCT X LOCATION

P_CODE	P_DESCRIPT	PRICE	STORE	AISLE	SHELF
123456	Flashlight	€4.16	23	W	5
123456	Flashlight	€4.16	24	K	9
123456	Flashlight	€4.16	25	Z	6
123457	Lamp	€19.87	23	W	5
123457	Lamp	€19.87	25	Z	6
123457	Lamp	€19.87	24	K	9
123458	Box Fan	€10.99	23	W	5
123458	Box Fan	€10.99	24	K	9
123458	Box Fan	€10.99	25	Z	6
213345	9 v battery	€1.52	23	W	5
213345	9 v battery	€1.52	24	K	9
213345	9 v battery	€1.52	25	Z	6
254467	100 W bulb	€1.16	23	W	5
254467	100 W bulb	€1.16	24	K	9
254467	100 W bulb	€1.16	25	Z	6
311452	Powerdrill	€27.64	24	W	5
311452	Powerdrill	€27.64	25	K	9
311452	Powerdrill	€27.64	26	Z	6

4.1.7 DIVISION

The DIVISION operation produces a new relation by selecting the tuples in one relation, R_1, that match every row in another relation, R_2. It is essentially the inverse of the CARTESIAN PRODUCT operation, just like the arithmetic divide is the inverse of multiplication. **DIVISION**, denoted by $R_1 \div R_2$, can be formally defined as:

> The DIVISION of two relations $R_1(a_1, a_2, \ldots, a_n)$ with cardinality *i* and $R_2(b_1, b_2, \ldots, b_m)$ with cardinality *j* is a relation R_3 with degree $k = n - m$ and cardinality i ÷ j.

4

Using the example shown in Figure 4.11, note that: Table 1 (Figure 4.11(a)) is 'divided' by Table 2 (Figure 4.11(b)) to produce Table 3 (Figure 4.11(c)). Tables 1 and 2 both contain the column CODE but do not share LOC. To be included in the resulting Table 3, a value in the unshared column (LOC) must be associated (in the dividing Table 2) with every value in Table 1. The only value associated with both A and B is 5.

FIGURE 4.11 The DIVISION operator

Database Name: Ch04_Relational_DB_Operators

Figure 4.11 (a) Division Table 1

CODE	LOC
A	5
A	9
A	4
B	5
B	3
C	6
D	7
D	8
E	8

Figure 4.11 (b) Division Table 2

CODE
A
B

Figure 4.11 (c) Result of Division Table 1 ÷ Division Table 2

LOC
5

4.2 JOINS

The JOIN operation is one of the essential operations of relational algebra. It is a binary operation that allows the user to combine two relations in a specified way. JOIN operations are the real power behind the relational database, allowing the use of independent tables linked by common attributes. The JOIN of two relations R_1 and R_2 is a restriction on their Cartesian product $R_1 \times R_2$ to meet a specified criterion. The join itself is defined on an attribute *a* of R_1 and an attribute *b* of R_2 where the attributes *a* and *b* share the same domain. A JOIN operator may be formally defined as:

> The join of two relations $R_1(a_1, a_2, \ldots, a_n)$ and $R_2(b_1, b_2, \ldots, b_m)$ is a relation R_3 with degree $k = n + m$ and attributes $(a_1, a_2, \ldots, a_n, b_1, b_2, \ldots, b_m)$ that satisfy a specific join condition.

In this section we will look at a number of different kinds of join operations including the THETA JOIN, EQUIJOIN, NATURAL JOIN, LEFT OUTER JOIN and RIGHT OUTER JOIN.

4.2.1 Theta Join and Equijoin

One of the most commonly used joins is known as an **equijoin**, which links tables on the basis of an equality condition that compares specified columns of each table. The outcome of the equijoin does not eliminate duplicate columns, and the condition or criterion used to join the tables must be explicitly defined. The equijoin takes its name from the equality comparison operator (=) used in the condition. If any other comparison operator is used the join is called a **theta join** denoted with the symbol θ (θ-join). So, theta represents a predicate that consists of one of the comparison operators { =, <, <=, >=, < >}. The equijoin is therefore one special type of theta join:

> Let $R_1(a_1, a_2, \ldots, a_n)$ and $R_2(b_1, b_2, \ldots, b_m)$ be relations that may have different schemas. Then the θ-join of R_1 and R_2 is denoted as $R_1 \bowtie_{\theta} R_2$ and the equijoin is denoted as $R_1 \bowtie_{R1.a = R2.b} R_2$.

It is also possible to express both the θ-join and the equijoin in terms of the restriction and Cartesian product operations. So, for example, the equijoin $R_1 \bowtie_{R1.a = R2.b} R_2$ may also be written as $\sigma_{R1.a = R2.b}(R_1 \times R_2)$.

Looking at the θ-join and the equijoin in this way allows us to create some simple rules, which will allow us to compute such joins on any two relations:

1. Compute $R_1 \times R_2$. This first performs a Cartesian product to form all possible combinations of the rows of R_1 and R_2.
2. Restrict the Cartesian product to only those rows where the values in certain columns match.

For example, suppose we wish to find out all students who take classes in each department at Tiny University. To answer this query, we must join together the two relations STUDENT-2 and DEPARTMENT-2 shown in Figure 4.12 (a) and (b). Following the two rules stated above, this will first involve finding the Cartesian product of the STUDENT-2 and DEPARTMENT-2 relations shown in Figure 4.12 (c). Then, we need to restrict the resulting relation in Figure 4.12 (c) to only those tuples that satisfy the join condition on the common columns of DEPT_CODE, which is found in both relations (Figure 4.12 (d)). In this case, this would be where STUDENT.DEPT_CODE = DEPARTMENT.DEPT_CODE. This query, which we will call STUDENT_IN_DEPT, can be written in relational algebra as:

$$\text{STUDENT\_IN\_DEPT} = \sigma_{STUDENT.DEPT\_CODE = DEPARTMENT.DEPT\_CODE}(STUDENT \times DEPARTMENT)$$

FIGURE 4.12 Equijoin example

Database name: Ch04_TinyUniversity

Figure 4.12 (a) The STUDENT-2 relation

STU_NUM	STU_LNAME	STU_FNAME	STU_DOB	DEPT_CODE
321452	Ndlovu	Amehlo	12 February 1992	BIOL
324257	Smithson	Anne	15 November 1997	CIS
324258	Le Roux	Dané	23 August 1986	ACCT
324269	Oblonski	Walter	16 September 1997	CIS
324273	Smith	John	30 December 1975	ENGL

Figure 4.12 (b) The DEPARTMENT-2 relation

DEPT_CODE	DEPT_NAME
ACCT	Accounting
BIOL	Biology
CIS	Computer Info. Systems
ENGL	English

Figure 4.12 (c) The Cartesian product (STUDENT × DEPARTMENT)

STU_NUM	STU_LNAME	STU_FNAME	STU_DOB	S.DEPT_CODE	D.DEPT_CODE	DEPT_NAME
321452	Ndlovu	Amehlo	12 February 1992	BIOL	ACCT	Accounting
321452	Ndlovu	Amehlo	12 February 1992	BIOL	BIOL	Biology
321452	Ndlovu	Amehlo	12 February 1992	BIOL	CIS	Computer Info. Systems
321452	Ndlovu	Amehlo	12 February 1992	BIOL	ENGL	English
324257	Smithson	Anne	15 November 1997	CIS	ACCT	Accounting
324257	Smithson	Anne	15 November 1997	CIS	BIOL	Biology
324257	Smithson	Anne	15 November 1997	CIS	CIS	Computer Info. Systems
324257	Smithson	Anne	15 November 1997	CIS	ENGL	English
324258	Le Roux	Dané	23 August 1986	ACCT	ACCT	Accounting
324258	Le Roux	Dané	23 August 1986	ACCT	BIOL	Biology
324258	Le Roux	Dané	23 August 1986	ACCT	CIS	Computer Info. Systems
324258	Le Roux	Dané	23 August 1986	ACCT	ENGL	English
324269	Oblonski	Walter	16 September 1993	CIS	ACCT	Accounting
324269	Oblonski	Walter	16 September 1993	CIS	BIOL	Biology
324269	Oblonski	Walter	16 September 1993	CIS	CIS	Computer Info. Systems
324269	Oblonski	Walter	16 September 1993	CIS	ENGL	English
324273	Smith	John	30 December 1975	ENGL	ACCT	Accounting
324273	Smith	John	30 December 1975	ENGL	BIOL	Biology

STU_NUM	STU_LNAME	STU_FNAME	STU_DOB	S.DEPT_CODE	D.DEPT_CODE	DEPT_NAME
324273	Smith	John	30 December 1975	ENGL	CIS	Computer Info. Systems
324273	Smith	John	30 December 1975	ENGL	ENGL	English

Figure 4.12 (d) the final relation STUDENT_IN_DEPT = $\sigma_{STUDENT.DEPT\_CODE\ =\ DEPARTMENT.DEPT\_CODE}$ *(STUDENT × DEPARTMENT)*

STU_NUM	STU_LNAME	STU_FNAME	STU_DOB	S.DEPT_CODE	D.DEPT_CODE	DEPT_NAME
321452	Ndlovu	Amehlo	12 February 1992	BIOL	BIOL	Biology
324257	Smithson	Anne	15 November 1997	CIS	CIS	Computer Info. Systems
324258	Le Roux	Dané	23 August 1986	ACCT	ACCT	Accounting
324269	Oblonski	Walter	16 September 1993	CIS	CIS	Computer Info. Systems
324273	Smith	John	30 December 1975	ENGL	ENGL	English

Notice in Figure 4.12 (c) that there are two columns called DEPT_CODE. This is due to the fact that both STUDENT-2 and DEPARTMENT-2 both contain a column of the same name. In this case DEPT_CODE also shares the same domain and provides referential integrity between the two relations. In order to distinguish between them, a prefix of S and D has been added to the name of these columns, i.e. S.DEPT_CODE and D.DEPT_CODE, to make them easier to read. You can also see these two common columns again in the resulting relation in Figure 4.12 (d) as the equijoin does not eliminate duplicate columns. Ideally, it would be far better not to show duplicate columns in the resulting relation, as equijoins are so common, so an operator called the **natural join** was defined.

4.2.2 The Natural Join

The natural join operation is the most common variant of the joins. The natural join operation requires that the two operant relations must have at least one common attribute, i.e. attributes that share the same domain. The common column(s) is (are) referred to as the **join column(s)**. The natural join is in fact an equijoin; however, in addition, we drop the duplicate attributes, so the resulting relation contains one less column than that of the equijoin.

Let R_1 be a relation having attributes (a_1, a_2,..., a_n, y), R_2 be another relation having attributes (b_1, b_2,..., b_m *y*) where *y* is a set of common attributes (join column(s)) that share the same domain. The natural join operator is defined as:

> The natural join of R_1 and R_2, denoted R_1 |×| R_2, consists of combining the tuples of R_1 and R_2 to build a new relation R_3, such that if $R_1Tuple \in R_1$, $R_2Tuple \in R_2$, and $R_1Tuple.y = R_2Tuple.y$, then $R_3Tuple = R_1Tuple.a_1, R_1Tuple.a_n, R_1Tuple.y, R_2Tuple.b_1, \ldots R_2Tuple.b_m$.

Note that the common set of attributes *y* appears only once in R_3; the notation $R_1Tuple.a_1$ corresponds to the a_1 attribute value of a tuple of R_1.

Although this definition appears to be quite complicated, the steps required to compute the natural join of two relations is quite straightforward and is the result of a three-stage process:

1 Compute $R_1 \times R_2$. This first performs a Cartesian product to form all possible combinations of the rows of R_1 and R_2.

2 Select those tuples where $R_1Tuple.y = R_2Tuple.y$. Only the rows are selected where the attribute values in the join column(s) are equal.

3 Perform a PROJECT operation on either $R_1.y$ or $R_2.y$ to the result of step (2), and call it y in the final relation. This is to ensure that the final relation results in a single copy of each attribute in the joining column, thereby eliminating duplicate columns. For example, if we joined the STUDENT and DEPARTMENT tables on the DEPT-CODE joining column, we would only want one column called DEPT_CODE in our final relation. Finally, project the rest of the attributes in R_1 and R_2 except y and drop the prefix R_1 and R_2 in the final relation.

Let us now apply these steps to an example. Figure 4.13 shows two relations called CUSTOMER and AGENT that will be used to illustrate the natural join operator.

FIGURE 4.13 The CUSTOMER and AGENT relations

Database name: Ch04_Relational_DB_Operators

Relation: CUSTOMER

CUS_CODE	CUS_LNAME	CUS_POSTCODE	AGENT_CODE
1132445	Strydom	4001	231
1217782	Adares	7550	125
1312243	Nokwe	678954	167
1321242	Reddy	2094	125
1542311	Smithson	1401	421
1657399	Vanloo	67543W	231

Relation: AGENT

AGENT_CODE	AGENT_PHONE
125	01812439887
167	01813426778
231	01812431124
333	01131234445

1 First, compute the Cartesian product of CUSTOMER and AGENT, i.e. CUSTOMER × AGENT. This operation will produce the results shown in Figure 4.14.

FIGURE 4.14 **Step 1: CUSTOMER X AGENT**

Database name: Ch04_Relational_DB_Operators

C.CUS_ CODE	C.CUS_ LNAME	C.CUS_ POSTCODE	C.AGENT_ CODE	A.AGENT_ CODE	A.AGENT_ PHONE
1132445	Strydom	4001	231	125	01812439887
1132445	Strydom	4001	231	167	01813426778
1132445	Strydom	4001	231	231	01812431124
1132445	Strydom	4001	231	333	01131234445
1217782	Adares	7550	125	125	01812439887
1217782	Adares	7550	125	167	01813426778
1217782	Adares	7550	125	231	01812431124
1217782	Adares	7550	125	333	01131234445
1312243	Nokwe	678954	167	125	01812439887
1312243	Nokwe	678954	167	167	01813426778
1312243	Nokwe	678954	167	231	01812431124
1312243	Nokwe	678954	167	333	01131234445
1321242	Reddy	2094	125	125	01812439887
1321242	Reddy	2094	125	167	01813426778
1321242	Reddy	2094	125	231	01812431124
1321242	Reddy	2094	125	333	01131234445
1542311	Smithson	1401	421	125	01812439887
1542311	Smithson	1401	421	167	01813426778
1542311	Smithson	1401	421	231	01812431124
1542311	Smithson	1401	421	333	01131234445
1657399	Vanloo	67543W	231	125	01812439887
1657399	Vanloo	67543W	231	167	01813426778
1657399	Vanloo	67543W	231	231	01812431124
1657399	Vanloo	67543W	231	333	01131234445

4

Notice in Figure 4.14 that we have prefixed each column with the starting letter of each relation. C.AGENT_CODE refers to the AGENT_CODE in the CUSTOMER relation whilst A.AGENT_CODE refers to the AGENT_CODE in the AGENT relation.

2 Select those tuples where $R_1Tuple.y = R_2Tuple.y$. To perform this step we must first identify the join column from the result of Step 1. In our example this is AGENT_CODE as it appears in both relations. Therefore we SELECT only the rows for which the AGENT_CODE values are equal, i.e. C.AGENT_CODE = A.AGENT.CODE. Figure 4.15 shows the results of Step 2.

3 Perform a PROJECT operation on either C.AGENT_CODE or A.AGENT_CODE to the result of Step 2 so that only one AGENT_CODE column appears in the final relation. Then project the rest of the attributes (CUS_CODE, CUS_LNAME, CUS_POSTCODE, AGENT_PHONE) and drop the prefix *C* and *A* in the final relation. The final relation is shown in Figure 4.16.

4

FIGURE 4.15 Step 2: Selecting rows where values in the join column match

Database name: Ch04_Relational_DB_Operators

Relation CUSTOMER X AGENT

Joining columns

C.CUS_CODE	C.CUS_LNAME	C.CUS_POSTCODE	C.AGENT_CODE	A.AGENT_CODE	A.AGENT_PHONE
1132445	Strydom	4001	231	125	01812439887
1132445	Strydom	4001	231	167	01813426778
1132445	Strydom	4001	231	231	01812431124
1132445	Strydom	4001	231	333	01131234445
1217782	Adares	7550	125	125	01812439887
1217782	Adares	7550	125	167	01813426778
1217782	Adares	7550	125	231	01812431124
1217782	Adares	7550	125	333	01131234445
1312243	Nokwe	678954	167	125	01812439887
1312243	Nokwe	678954	167	167	01813426778
1312243	Nokwe	678954	167	231	01812431124
1312243	Nokwe	678954	167	333	01131234445
1321242	Reddy	2094	125	125	01812439887
1321242	Reddy	2094	125	167	01813426778
1321242	Reddy	2094	125	231	01812431124
1321242	Reddy	2094	125	333	01131234445
1542311	Smithson	1401	421	125	01812439887
1542311	Smithson	1401	421	167	01813426778
1542311	Smithson	1401	421	231	01812431124
1542311	Smithson	1401	421	333	01131234445
1657399	Vanloo	67543W	231	125	01812439887
1657399	Vanloo	67543W	231	167	01813426778
1657399	Vanloo	67543W	231	231	01812431124
1657399	Vanloo	67543W	231	333	01131234445

The tuples shaded in blue are those where C.AGENT_CODE = A.AGENT.CODE. These are then selected to produce the results of Step 2.

C.CUS_CODE	C.CUS_LNAME	C.CUS_POSTCODE	C.AGENT_CODE	A.AGENT_CODE	A.AGENT_PHONE
1132445	Strydom	4001	231	231	01812431124
1217782	Adares	7550	125	125	01812439887
1312243	Nokwe	678954	167	167	01813426778
1321242	Reddy	2094	125	125	01812439887
1657399	Vanloo	67543W	231	231	01812431124

FIGURE 4.16 **Step 3: Final relation CUSTOMER |X| AGENT**

Database name: Ch04_Relational_DB_Operators

CUS_CODE	CUS_LNAME	CUS_POSTCODE	AGENT_CODE	AGENT_PHONE
1132445	Strydom	4001	231	01812431124
1217782	Adares	7550	125	01812439887
1312243	Nokwe	678954	167	01813426778
1321242	Reddy	2094	125	01812439887
1657399	Vanloo	67543W	231	01812431124

Note a few crucial features of the natural join operation:

- If no match is made between the tuples in the relation, the new relation does not include the unmatched tuple. In that case, neither AGENT_CODE 421 nor the customer whose last name is Smithson is included. Smithson's AGENT_CODE 421 does not match any entry in the AGENT table.
- The column on which the join was made – that is, AGENT_CODE – occurs only once in the new table.
- If the same AGENT_CODE were to occur several times in the AGENT table, a customer would be listed for each match. For example, if the AGENT_CODE 167 were to occur three times in the AGENT table, the customer named Nokwe who is associated with AGENT_CODE 167, would occur three times in the resulting table. (A good AGENT table cannot, of course, contain such a result because it would contain unique primary key values.)

4.2.3 The Outer Join

When using the theta join and the natural join, it is possible that some of the tuples in the joined relations do not have identical values for the common attributes. As a result these tuples will be 'lost'. If we require that all the tuples from the original tables are to be shown in the resulting relation, then it is necessary to have a join which keeps all the tuples in relation R_1 which have no corresponding values in the relation R_2. In these tuples, the attributes in the second relation R_2 will have null values. This type of join is known as the *outer join*, denoted by the symbol ⟕.

There are three common types of the outer join:

- ⟕ Left outer join – keeps data from the left-hand relation
- ⟖ Right outer join – keeps data from the right-hand relation
- ⟗ Full outer join – keeps data from both relations

As you will see, the steps for determining an outer join are very similar to those steps for computing a natural join, except that we also include data from the left or right side of the relation, depending on whether we are performing a left or right outer join.

The stages in determining a left outer join are:

1. Compute $R_1 \times R_2$. This first performs a Cartesian product to form all possible combinations of the rows of R_1 and R_2.

2 Select those tuples where $R_1Tuple.y = R_2Tuple.y$. Only the rows are selected where the attribute values in the join column(s) are equal.

3 Select those tuples in R_1 that do not have matching values in R_2, so $R_1Tuple.y <> R_2Tuple.y$.

4 Perform a PROJECT operation on either $R_1.y$ or $R_2.y$ to the result of Step 2, and call it simply *y* in the final relation. This is to ensure that the final relation results in a single copy of each attribute in the joining column, thereby eliminating duplicate columns. Finally, project the rest of the attributes in R_1 and R_2, except *y*, and drop the prefix R_1 and R_2 in the final relation.

4

For example, consider performing an outer join for the relations CUSTOMER and AGENT, which were defined in Figure 4.14.

A **left outer join**, CUSTOMER ⟕ AGENT, will return all of the tuples in the CUSTOMER relation, including those that do not have a matching value in the AGENT relation. The result of this join is shown in Figure 4.17. Notice that there is no AGENT_PHONE for the customer Smithson and a value of NULL has been entered in the AGENT_PHONE field.

A **right outer join**, CUSTOMER ⟖ AGENT, returns all of the tuples in the AGENT relation, including those that do not have matching values in the CUSTOMER relation. The result of this join is shown in Figure 4.18.

FIGURE 4.17 Left outer join : CUSTOMER ⟕ AGENT

Database name: Ch04_Relational_DB_Operators

CUS_CODE	CUS_LNAME	CUS_POSTCODE	AGENT_CODE	AGENT_PHONE
1132445	Strydom	4001	231	01812431124
1217782	Adares	7550	125	01812439887
1312243	Nokwe	678954	167	01813426778
1321242	Reddy	2094	125	01812439887
1657399	Vanloo	67543W	231	01812431124
1542311	Smithson	1401	421	NULL

FIGURE 4.18 Right outer join : CUSTOMER ⟖ AGENT

Database name: Ch04_Relational_DB_Operators

CUS_CODE	CUS_LNAME	CUS_POSTCODE	AGENT_CODE	AGENT_PHONE
1132445	Strydom	4001	231	01812431124
1217782	Adares	7550	125	01812439887
1312243	Nokwe	678954	167	01813426778
1321242	Reddy	2094	125	01812439887
1657399	Vanloo	67543W	231	01812431124
NULL	NULL	NULL	333	01131234445

So, regardless of the type of outer join, the two examples in Figures 4.17 and 4.18 have shown that the matched pairs would be retained and any unmatched values in the other relation would be left null. Outer joins are especially useful when you are trying to determine what value(s) in related tables cause(s) referential integrity problems – which are created when foreign key values do not match the primary key values in the related table(s). In fact, if you are asked to convert large spreadsheets or other non-database data into relational database tables, you will discover that the outer joins save you vast amounts of time and uncounted headaches when you encounter referential integrity errors after the conversions.

You may wonder why the outer joins are labelled *left* and *right*. The labels refer to the order in which the tables are listed in the SQL command. Chapter 8 will explore such joins.

4.3 CONSTRUCTING QUERIES USING RELATIONAL ALGEBRAIC EXPRESSIONS

The main purpose of relational algebra is to provide a way to create and manipulate relations (tables) in a database. The operations of relational algebra that you have just read about in the previous section are used to tell the DBMS how to build some required relation in terms of other relations. Relational calculus provides a notation for formulating the definition of the required relation in terms of those other relations. Relational algebra is often classed as a procedural language, whilst relational calculus is a non-procedural language and based on predicate logic. In 1972, Codd proposed one form of relational calculus known as tuple relational calculus and this was later followed by domain relational calculus in 1977 (Lacroix and Pirotte). Both versions were designed for use with relational databases. However, tuple relational calculus is equivalent to relational algebra in its expressive power and both provide the required base for specifying real database queries.

In this section, we will be focusing on applying relational algebra to formulate expressions using the main relation operators. There is no need in this book to examine the mathematical definitions, properties and characteristics behind relational calculus. For those who are interested there is a selection of material in the further reading section at the end of this chapter.

4.3.1 Building Queries

During the lifetime of a database, users will ask many different kinds of queries. Some will be asked over and over again, whilst others will be on the spur of the moment. The task of building a query involves breaking the query down into a number of smaller steps, where each step generates a set of intermediate results that are then used in the following steps of the query. Generally, when writing relational algebraic expressions to represent these queries, the order of execution of individual operations does not matter. This means that the results of the query will always be the same, but can be obtained by slightly different expressions. However, it is worth pointing out that the efficiency of a query is very important and that, in most DBMSs, the order of execution is determined by a *query optimiser*. The job of the query optimiser is to analyse the queries and find the most efficient way to access the data. You will discover more about the query optimiser in Chapter 13, Managing Database and SQL Performance.

In order to build a query using a **relational algebraic expression**, you should take the following steps:

1 List all the attributes we need to give the answer.

2 Select all the relations we need, based on the list of attributes.

3 Specify the relational operators and the intermediate results that are needed.

To learn how to build queries following these steps, we will now look at some examples based on a small database that stores information about the maintenance of cars (the ERD is shown in Figure 4.19). Each car is required to undergo an inspection each year to test whether it is roadworthy. After each inspection, a maintenance record is created and any repairs that are needed are recorded. A repair can require new parts to be purchased and fitted. If a car needs a repair, then the EVALUATION is set to FAIL until all the repairs are completed and then it is set to PASS. The tables representing this database are shown in Figure 4.20.

4

FIGURE 4.19 **The car inspection ERD**

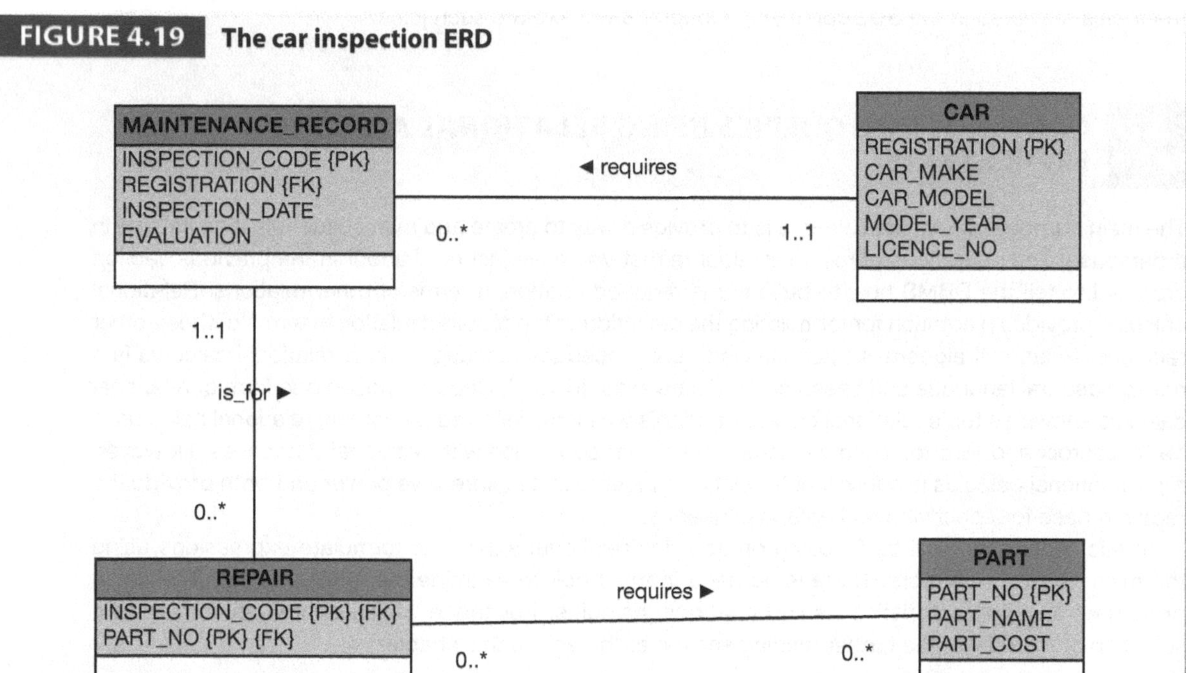

FIGURE 4.20 **The car inspection database**

Database name: Ch04_Car_Inspection

Table name: CAR

REGISTRATION	CAR_MAKE	CAR_MODEL	CAR_COLOUR	MODEL_YEAR	LICENCE_NO
3679MR82	Toyota	Corolla	Blue	2016	1967fr89768
E-TS865	Nissan	Micra	Red	2004	1973Smith121
PE57UVP	Peugeot	508	Blue	2017	1990bty3212
PISE567	Volkswagen	Eos	Lime	2016	DF-678-WV
ROMA482	Volkswagen	Golf GT	Black	2017	AQ-123-AV
Z-BA975	Peugeot	208	Black	2017	1980vrt7312

Table name: PART

PART_NO	PART_NAME	PART_COST
12390	Paint sealants	€14.95
12391	Wiper	€19.95
12392	Brake pads	€24.99
12393	Brake discs	€49.54
12395	Spark plugs	€0.99
12396	Airbag	€24.95
12397	Tyres	€25.00

Table name: MAINTENANCE_RECORD

INSPECTION_CODE	REGISTRATION	INSPECTION_DATE	EVALUATION
100036	PE57UVP	10/05/2018	FAIL
100390	ROMA482	01/09/2018	
106750	E-TS865	01/03/2016	PASS
122456	Z-BA975	03/10/2018	FAIL
145678	PISE567	30/09/2017	PASS
200450	E-TS865	21/02/2015	PASS
200456	E-TS865	01/04/2017	FAIL

Table name: REPAIR

INSPECTION_CODE	PART_NO
106750	12396
106750	12397
100036	12393
200450	12391
100036	12397
200450	12392
200456	12397

Example 1

Consider the following query asked by a user:

'List all information about cars where the model year is after 2016.'

To answer this query, you must first interpret that 'List all information about cars' means list all the attributes in the relation CAR. The user only wants to see information on cars where the attribute MODEL_YEAR > 2016. Using the relational operator SELECT we can write this query as a relational algebraic expression as:

$\sigma_{model\_year > 2016}(CAR)$

The resulting relation is shown in Figure 4.21.

FIGURE 4.21 **Result of $\sigma_{model\_year > 2016}$(CAR)**

REGISTRATION	CAR_MAKE	CAR_MODEL	CAR_COLOUR	MODEL_YEAR	LICENSE_NO
PE57UVP	Peugeot	508	Blue	2017	1990bty3212
ROMA482	Volkswagen	Golf GT	Black	2017	AQ-123-AV
Z-BA975	Peugeot	208	Black	2017	1980vrt7312

4

Example 2

Supposing the mechanic at the garage wishes to find out information about which parts are in stock. The following query is asked:

'Display all the part names and their prices where the cost of the part is greater than €20.00.'

This query requires only specific information about parts to be displayed, so we will need the relation which contains the attributes PART_NAME and PART_COST. Both are obviously in the relation PART. The attribute PART_COST will also be required to restrict the rows where PART_COST > €20.00 using the SELECT operator. The relational algebraic expression for this query is $\Pi_{part\_name}(\sigma_{part\_cost > 20.00}(PART))$

The resulting relation is shown in Figure 4.22.

FIGURE 4.22 **Result of $\Pi_{part\_name}(\sigma_{part\_cost > 20.00}$(PART))**

PART_NAME	PART_COST
Brake Pads	€24.99
Brake Discs	€49.54
Airbag	€24.95

Example 3

The final example will also use the natural join operator and show how we can write expressions when data is required from a number of different tables.

Consider the following query:

'List the car registration and model details and part numbers for all cars where the model year is 2017. where an inspection was carried out after 01/03/2018, which resulted in a part being required for a repair.'

This is a more complex query and will have to be broken down into a number of different stages, each one having a set of intermediate results. The first part of the query states that we need the attributes REGISTRATION and CAR_MODEL which are located in the CAR relation. Also, we are only interested in cars whose MODEL_YEAR is 2017. This information can be written using the following relational algebraic expression:

$\Pi_{registration,\ car\_model}(\sigma_{model\_year\ =\ 2017}(CAR))$

The result of applying this statement to the CAR table is shown in Figure 4.23.

FIGURE 4.23 **Result of $\Pi_{registration,\ car\_model}(\sigma_{model\_year\ =\ 2017}(CAR))$**

REGISTRATION	CAR_MODEL
PE57UVP	508
ROMA482	Golf GT
Z-BA975	208

4

The next part of this query requires information about inspections that were carried out after 01/03/2018. Information about inspections is stored in the MAINTENANCE_RECORD relation. The query is not asking for any specific attributes, so we will assume that 'information about inspections' means the values of all attributes in the MAINTENANCE_RECORD relation. However, we must restrict the query, by only selecting those tuples where the INSPECTION_DATE > 01/03/2018. This second part of the query can be written as:

$\sigma_{inspection\_date\ >\ '01/03/2018'}(MAINTENANCE\_RECORD)$

The result of applying this expression to the MAINTENANCE_RECORD table is shown in Figure 4.24.

FIGURE 4.24 **Result of $\sigma_{inspection\_date\ >\ '01/03/2018'}(MAINTENANCE\_RECORD)$**

INSPECTION_CODE	REGISTRATION	INSPECTION_DATE	EVALUATION
100036	PE57UVP	10/05/2018	FAIL
100390	ROMA482	01/09/2018	
122456	Z-BA975	03/10/2018	FAIL

We now have relational algebraic expressions for the first two parts of the query. The next stage is to join the rows from the resulting tables shown in Figures 4.23 and 4.24. This join operation is the now natural join operation, with the common column in both the CAR and MAINTENANCE_RECORD relations being REGISTRATION. This can be written as:

$TempR = \Pi_{registration,\ car\_model}(\sigma_{model\_year\ =\ 2017}(CAR))\ |\times|\ \sigma_{inspection\_date\ >\ '01/03/2018'}(MAINTENANCE\_RECORD)$

where *TempR* is a relation which stores the intermediate results.

The result of the natural join is shown using the three steps in Figure 4.25. Notice that the attributes have been prefixed with the letters M and C to show which relations they were originally from (MAINTENANCE_RECORD and CAR respectively).

4

FIGURE 4.25 The TempR relation

Step 1: Compute the Cartesian product: MAINTENANCE_RECORD X CAR.

M.INSPECTION_ CODE	M.REGISTRATION	M.INSPECTION_ DATE	M.EVALUATION	C.REGISTRATION	C.CAR_ MODEL
100036	PE57UVP	10/05/2018	FAIL	PE57UVP	508
100036	PE57UVP	10/05/2018	FAIL	ROMA482	Golf GT
100036	PE57UVP	10/05/2018	FAIL	Z-BA975	208
100390	ROMA482	01/09/2018		PE57UVP	508
100390	ROMA482	01/09/2018		ROMA482	Golf GT
100390	ROMA482	01/09/2018		Z-BA975	208
122456	Z-BA975	03/10/2018	FAIL	PE57UVP	508
122456	Z-BA975	03/10/2018	FAIL	ROMA482	Golf GT
122456	Z-BA975	03/10/2018	FAIL	Z-BA975	208

Step 2: SELECT only the rows for which the REGISTRATION values are equal, i.e. M. REGISTRATION = C. REGISTRATION.

Joining Columns

M.INSPECTION_ CODE	M.REGISTRATION	M.INSPECTION_ DATE	M.EVALUATION	C.REGISTRATION	C.CAR_ MODEL
100036	PE57UVP	10/05/2018	FAIL	PE57UVP	508
100390	ROMA482	01/09/2018		ROMA482	Golf GT
122456	Z-BA975	03/10/2018	FAIL	Z-BA975	208

Step 3: Perform a PROJECT on either C.REGISTRATION or M.REGISTRATION to the result of Step 2 and drop the prefixes C and M in the final relation. The table below shows the relation TempR, which has been created as a result of Step 3.

INSPECTION_CODE	REGISTRATION	INSPECTION_DATE	EVALUATION	CAR_MODEL
100036	PE57UVP	10/05/2018	FAIL	508
100390	ROMA482	01/09/2018		Golf GT
122456	Z-BA975	03/10/2018	FAIL	208

The next part of the query requires the information we have obtained so far to be restricted even further by only displaying information for cars where a part was needed for a repair. To find out this information we have to look to see if there is a PART_NO in the REPAIR relation, which corresponds to a specific INSPECTION_CODE in the MAINTENANCE_RECORD relation. The relation *TempR* already stores the intermediate results from the first part of our query, so we must now connect *TempR* to the REPAIR relation using a natural join on the INSPECTION_CODE column. This can be written as the expression:

$$QueryResult = TempR \; |\times| \; REPAIR$$

Figure 4.26 shows the result of performing this natural join operation and stores the results in a relation called *QueryResult*.

FIGURE 4.26 The QueryResult relation

The relation *TempR*

INSPECTION_CODE	REGISTRATION	INSPECTION_DATE	EVALUATION	CAR_MODEL
100036	PE57UVP	10/05/2018	FAIL	508
100390	ROMA482	01/09/2018		Golf GT
122456	Z-BA975	03/10/2018	FAIL	208

The relation *REPAIR*

INSPECTION_CODE	PART_NO
106750	12396
106750	12397
100036	12393
200450	12391
100036	12397
200450	12392
200456	12397

QueryResult = TempR |×| *REPAIR*

INSPECTION_CODE	REGISTRATION	INSPECTION_DATE	EVALUATION	CAR_MODEL	PART_NO
100036	PE57UVP	10/05/2018	FAIL	508	12393
100036	PE57UVP	10/05/2018	FAIL	508	12397

Finally, the original query requested that we only list 'the car registration, model details and part numbers'. This requires us to perform a PROJECT operation on the intermediate results in the *QueryResult* relation using the following expression:

$\Pi_{registration,\ car\_model,\ part\_no}(QueryResult)$

The final results of the query are shown in Figure 4.27.

FIGURE 4.27 Solution to example 3

REGISTRATION	CAR_MODEL	PART_NO
PE57UVP	508	12393
PE57UVP	508	12397

As you can see, it is possible to solve a complex query by breaking down the query into a number of smaller relational algebra expressions. The full expression for example 3 can be written as:

$\Pi_{registration,\ car\_model,\ part\_no}$ ((REPAIR) |×| ($\Pi_{registration,\ car\_model}(\sigma_{model\_year\ =\ 2018}(CAR))$ |×| $\sigma_{inspection\_date\ >\ '01/03/2018'}$(MAINTENANCE_RECORD)

4.4 RELATIONAL CALCULUS

Relational calculus is a formal language based upon a branch of mathematical logic called **predicate calculus**. There are two types of relational calculus, tuple relational calculus and domain relational calculus. **Tuple relational calculus** allows users to describe what they want, rather than how to compute it. In addition, it underlines the appearance of Structured Query Language (SQL), which you will learn about in Chapter 8. Domain relational calculus is different from tuple relational calculus as it uses domain variables that take on values from an attribute domain, rather than values for an entire tuple. In the following sections you will learn more about these two types of relational calculus.

NOTE

A NOTE ON PREDICATE CALCULUS

First-order logic or predicate calculus is a precise language that can be used to express queries. Predicates are words that describe certain relations and properties. In logic, a predicate has the form:

name_of_predicate(arguments).

Consider the following statements:

student(Alex)

studies(Alex, Database Systems)

In these two statements, *student* and *studies* are the names of the predicates. The statement *student(Alex)* has a value TRUE if Alex is a student, and a value FALSE if Alex is not a student.

Variables are used if we want to express the property of being a student, and not refer to a specific individual. So the above statements become:

student(x)

studies(x,y)

The expression *student(x)* is now referred to as a **predicate expression**. It has no predetermined truth value as the value of x is currently unknown. Variables in a predicate expression can take values within a certain **domain**. The domain of a predicate variable is the set of all values that can be substituted in the place of the variable.

When writing expressions in predicate calculus, we use a capital letter as the name of the predicate. For example:

P(x) represents a predicate with one variable x.

When x has a value we can say whether or not the expression is true or false. Every predicate has what is known as a Truth Set which is defined as:

$\{x \in D | P(x)\}$

So, a truth set of a predicate P(x) with a domain D is the set of all elements of D that make P(x) true when substituted for x. For example, consider the following predicate, *lecturer(x)*. The domain would be all people and the truth set would be all lecturers.

A formula in predicate calculus can comprise:

- Set of comparison operators: $<, \leq, >, \geq, =, \neq$
- Set of connectives: and ($\wedge$), or ($\vee$), not ($\neg$)
- Implication (=>) where x => y means: if x is true, then y is true.

4.4.1 Tuple Relational Calculus

Tuple relational calculus is a non-procedural query language which is used to describe what information is required from the database without giving a specific method for obtaining that information. When specifying a query in tuple relational calculus we say only which attributes are to be retrieved and not how the query is to be executed. This is in contrast to relational algebra, which provides a procedural way of writing the query and incorporates a strategy for executing the query through the way in which the operations are ordered. Relational algebra and tuple relational calculus can both be used to express the same queries, which means that we have a relationally complete query language. We say a query language is relationally complete if any query that can be written in relational algebraic form can also be expressed by the query language. Most relational query languages such as SQL are not only relationally complete, but also contain additional features like aggregate functions that allow more complex queries to be written.

4

In tuple relational calculus, we specify a number of tuple variables where each tuple variable ranges over a database table. The values of the tuple variables are the actual tuples in the table.

A query in the tuple relational calculus is expressed as:

$$\{t|P(t)\}$$

which represents the set of tuples, T, for which predicate, P, is true. Therefore, the results of this query are all tuples that satisfy the condition represented by predicate P.

For example, consider the car inspection database in Figure 4.20. If we wanted to write the following query 'Find all cars with a model_year >= 2018' using tuple relational calculus we would write:

$$\{t|t \in Car \wedge t.MODEL\_YEAR>=2018\}$$

This query means return the set of tuples, t, where t belongs to the Car relation and the model_year for year t is greater than 2018.

As you can see in the example, a query or expression in tuple relational calculus can also be written in the following extended form:

$$\{t_1.A_1, t_2.A_2, \ldots, t_n.A_n| P(t_1, \ldots, t_n, t_{n+1}, \ldots, t_{n+m})$$

where:

$t_1, \ldots, t_n, t_{n+1}, \ldots, t_{n+m}$ are tuple variables,
$A_1 \ldots A_n$ are attributes of the relation on which t_i ranges,
P is a predicate

A formula in tuple relational calculus consists of predicate calculus atoms. An atom has one of the following forms:

(i) *R(t)* where t is a tuple variable and R is a relation name.
(ii) t.*A oper s.B*
 where t and s are tuple variables,
 A and B are attributes and
 oper is a comparison operator.
(iii) t.*A oper const*
 where t is a tuple variable,
 A is an attribute,
 oper is a comparison operator, and
 const is a constant.

Each of these types of atoms evaluates to either TRUE or FALSE for a specific combination of tuples. Every atom has a truth value.

Tuple relational calculus formulae are either an atom or atoms or other formulae connected via the logical Boolean operators AND, OR, NOT (∧, ∨, ¬).

Existential and Universal Quantifiers

Tuple relational calculus formulae can contain existential (∃) and universal (∀) quantifiers. The role of these quantifiers is to constrain the variables of tuples in a single relation. Any variable that is not bound by a quantifier is said to be free. A tuple relational calculus expression may contain at most one free variable.

Consider the following two expressions:

∃ t ∈ R (P(t)) reads that there exists a tuple t in relation R such that predicate P (t) is true
∀ t ∈ R (P(t)) reads that P is true for all tuples t in relation R.

4

The existential (∃) quantifier states that a formula must be true for at least one instance, while the universal (∀) quantifiers state that the formula must be true for *all* instances.

4.4.2 Building a Tuple Relational Calculus Expression

To specify a tuple relational calculus expression, take the following steps:

(i) Specify the range relation R of each tuple variable t. In the form of R(t).
(ii) Specify a condition to select particular combinations of tuples.
(iii) Specify a set of attributes to be retrieved.

To learn how to build expressions, we will look at some examples based on a simple small database which stores information about customers at a bank. Customers can withdraw money and deposit money at any branch of the bank. The ERD is shown in Figure 4.28 and the relations (tables) representing this database are shown in Figure 4.29.

FIGURE 4.28

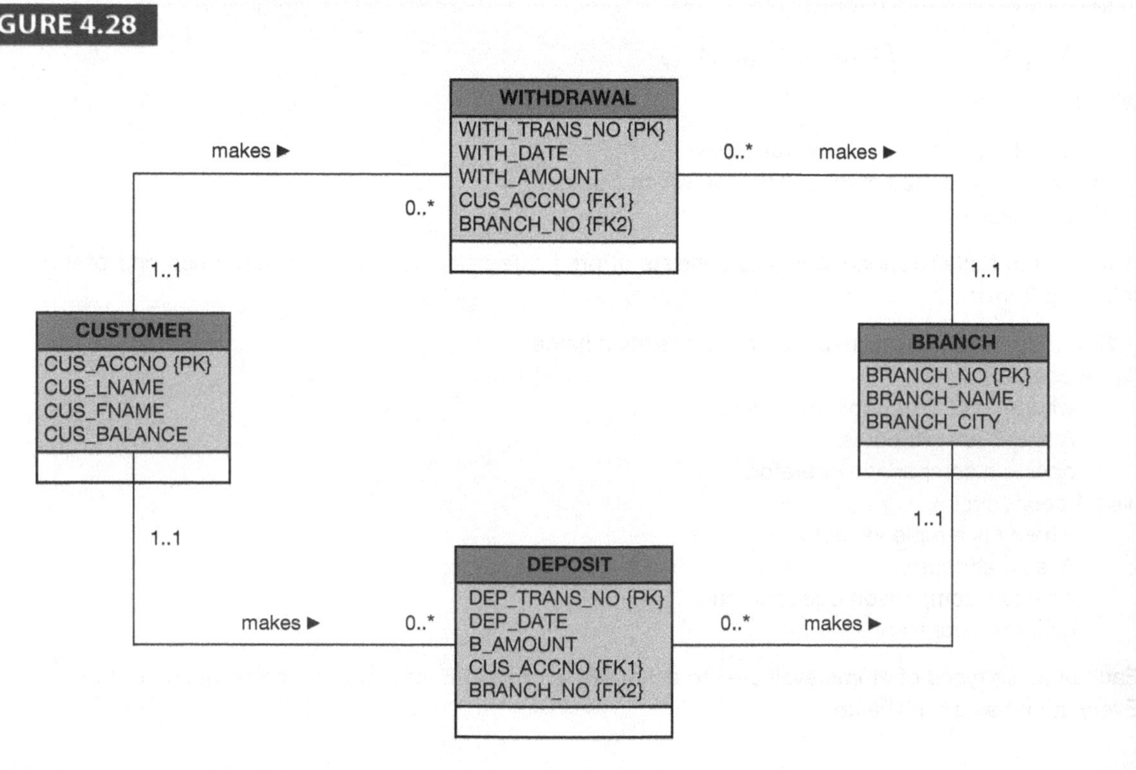

FIGURE 4.29

Relation: CUSTOMER

CUS_ACCNO	CUS_LNAME	CUS_FNAME	CUS_BALANCE
2465454	Emerson	Percy	1034
1012345	Adares	Constance	1865

Relation: BRANCH

BRANCH_NO	BRANCH_NAME	BRANCH_CITY
125	Monsuir	London
333	FirstStep	Paris
231	Cross_St	Rome

Relation: WITHDRAWAL

WITH_TRANS_NO	WITH_DATE	WITH_AMOUNT	CUS_ACCNO	BRANCH_NO
48887211	01-Jul-18	50	2465454	125
48867666	02-Jul-18	100	1012345	333
64446566	18-Jul-18	200	2465454	125
64443229	20-Jul-18	400	2465454	231

Relation: DEPOSIT

DEP_TRANS_NO	DEP_DATE	DEP_AMOUNT	CUS_ACCNO	BRANCH_NO
90000034	30-Jun-18	1000	2465454	125
90000780	30-Jun-18	1400	1012345	333

Example 1

Suppose we wanted to find out which customers had made any withdrawals over €200. We would write the following expression:

$\{w | w \in WITHDRAWAL(w) \wedge w.WITH\_AMOUNT >= 200\}$

This expression gives us all attributes from the WITHDRAWAL relation, but suppose we only want the last names of customers who have withdrawn €200 or more. CUS_LNAME exists in the CUSTOMER relation, which means we will have to perform a join on the CUSTOMER and WITHDRAWAL relations. The attribute CUS_ACCNO appears in both CUSTOMER and WITHDRAWAL and is used to join the two relations together as shown in the expression below:

$\{w.CUS\_LNAME | w \in WITHDRAWAL(w) \wedge (\exists c) (c \in CUSTOMER \wedge (c.CUS\_ACCNO = w.CUS\_ACCNO)$
$w.WITH\_AMOUNT >= 200\}$

In English, the above expression would read *display the names of all customers such that there exists a tuple in the relations WITHDRAWAL AND CUSTOMER for which the values of and for the CUS_ACCNO attribute are equal, and the value of the WITH_AMOUNT attribute is greater than or equal to €200.*

Example 2

Find all customers having made a deposit from branch in London.

{c| c ∈ CUSTOMER ∧ (∃d) (d ∈ DEPOSIT ∧ (c.CUS_ACCNO = d.CUS_ACCNO)
∧ (∃b) (b ∈ BRANCH (b.BRANCH_NO = d.BRANCH_NO) ∧ (b.BRANCH_CITY >= 'London'))))}

The above expression relies on joins existing between the CUSTOMER, BRANCH and DEPOSIT relations. As can be seen from Figure 4.29, the common column between DEPOSIT and CUSTOMER is CUS_ACCNO and between DEPOSIT and BRANCH the common attribute is BRANCH_NO.

4

NOTE

Safety of Expressions

It is possible to write tuple calculus expressions that generate infinite relations. For example, the expression

{ t | ¬ t ∈ R } results in an infinite relation if the domain of any attribute of relation R is infinite.

In order to solve this problem, the set of allowable expressions is restricted to safe expressions.

A **safe expression** is an expression { t | P(t) } in the tuple relational calculus that is classed as safe if every component of t appears in one of the relations, tuples, or constants that appear in tuple relational formula P.

For example, consider the following expression:

{ t | ¬ (t ∈ CUSTOMER) }

This expression is NOT safe as it reads *display all tuples that are NOT in the CUSTOMER relation*. It is not possible to have a customer tuple that does not appear in CUSTOMER.

4.4.3 Domain Relational Calculus

Domain relational calculus is classed as a non-procedural query language that is seen to be equivalent in power to tuple relational calculus. However, domain relational calculus is different from tuple relational calculus in that it uses domain variables that take on values from an attribute domain, rather than values for an entire tuple.

A general expression in domain relational calculus is of the form:

$$\{<x_1, x_2, \ldots, x_n> \mid P(x_1, x_2, \ldots, x_n)\}$$

Where $x_1, x_2, \ldots, x_n$ represent domain variables. P represents formulae composed of atoms, as was the case in tuple relational Calculus. Formulae are recursively defined, starting with simple atomic formulas that involve getting tuples from relations and making comparisons of attribute values. Bigger formulae are created using the logical connectives AND, OR and NOT.

A formula in domain relational calculus is constructed using the following rules:

(i) an atomic formula;

(ii) $\neg p, p \wedge q, p \vee q$ where p and q are formulas;

(iii) $\exists X (p(X))$ where X is a domain variable;

(iv) $\forall X (p(X))$ where X is a domain variable.

The use of quantifiers ∃x and ∀x in a formula is said to bind x. A variable that is not bound is said to be free. This means that, when writing expressions in domain relational calculus, the variables $x_1, x_2, \ldots, x_n$ must be the only free variables in the formulae $P(x_1, x_2, \ldots, x_n)$.

Let us take a look at some examples using the simple banking database shown in Figures 4.28 and 4.29.

Example 1

Find all customers with a balance greater than €500.

{CUS_ACCNO, CUS_LNAME,CUS_BALANCE| ((CUS_ACCNO, CUS_LNAME, CUS_BALANCE ∈ CUSTOMER) ∧ CUS_BALANCE > 500)}

In this formula, the condition CUS_ACCNO, CUS_LNAME, CUS_BALANCE customer, ensures that the domain variables CUS_ACCNO, CUS_LNAME and CUS_BALANCE are bound to the fields of the same CUSTOMER tuple. The term to the left of '|' means that every tuple that satisfies CUS_BALANCE > 500 should be included in the result set.

Example 2

Find all customers with a balance greater than €500 and who have deposited money at branch 125.

{CUS_ACCNO, CUS_LNAME, CUS_BALANCE| ((CUS_ACCNO, CUS_LNAME, CUS_BALANCE ∈ CUSTOMER) ∧ CUS_BALANCE > 500) ∧ ∃ DEPOSIT.BRANCH_NO (DEPOSIT.BRANCH_NO ∈ DEPOSIT) ∧ DEPOSIT.BRANCH_NO = CUSTOMER.BRANCH_NO ∧ CUSTOMER.BRANCH_NO = 125}

In this example, the existential quantifier ∃ has been used to to find a tuple in DEPOSIT that 'joins with' the CUSTOMERS tuple.

Example 3

List the branches where there have been no deposits.

{BRANCH_NO, BRANCH_NAME, BRANCH_CITY| ((({BRANCH_NO, BRANCH_NAME, BRANCH_CITY ∈ BRANCH) ∧ (∃ BRANCH.BRANCH_NO) BRANCH(BRANCH_NO, BRANCH_NAME, BRANCH_CITY) ∧ (∃ DEPOSIT.BRANCH_NO) (DEPOSIT.BRANCH_NO ∈ DEPOSIT) ∧ (DEPOSIT.BRANCH_NO = BRANCH.BRANCH_NO)}

SUMMARY

- One of the key components of the relational model is the relation, which allows data to be stored within the database in a structured manner.
- Relational algebra and relational calculus are the mathematical basis for 'relational databases'. Relational algebra is a collection of formal operations that act on relations to produce new relations as a result. Relational calculus (tuple relational calculus and domain relational calculus) provides a notation for formulating the definition of the required relation in terms of those other relations. Both relational algebra and tuple relational calculus provide the required operations for specifying real database queries, as they are formally both equivalent to each other.
- The relational model supports the eight relational algebra operators originally defined by Codd. These are known as SELECT (or RESTRICT), PROJECT, JOIN, PRODUCT, INTERSECT, UNION, DIFFERENCE and DIVIDE. The SELECT, PROJECT and JOIN operators are the ones that are most commonly used to retrieve information and form the basis for data manipulation languages such as SQL. A summary of these operators is shown in Table 4.1.

- User queries can be written as relational algebraic expressions. In order to write such as an expression, the following steps should be taken:
  - List all the attributes we need to give the answer.
  - Select all the relations we need, based on the list of attributes.
  - Specify the relational operators and the intermediate results that are needed.
- Relational calculus is a formal language based upon a branch of mathematical logic called predicate calculus.
- Tuple relational calculus allows users to describe what they want, rather than how to compute it, and underlines the appearance of Structured Query Language (SQL). Expressions in tuple relational calculus return tuples for which a given predicate is true.
- Domain relational calculus is different from tuple relational calculus as it uses domain variables that take on values from an attribute domain.

TABLE 4.1 Summary of relational operators

Relational Operator	Symbol	Description
SELECT	σ	Selects a subset of tuples from a relation.
PROJECT	Π	Selects a subset of columns from a relation.
DIFFERENCE	-	Selects tuples in Relation1 but not in Relation2*.
INTERSECT	$\cup$	Selects tuples in Relation1 or in Relation*.
UNION	$\cap$	Selects tuples in Relation1 and Relation2, excluding duplicate tuples*.
CARTESIAN PRODUCT	X	Computes all the possible combinations of tuples.
THETA JOIN	θ	Allows two relations to be combined using one of the comparison operators { =, <, <=, >=, < >}. When the operator is = the operator is known as an EQUIJOIN.
NATURAL JOIN	|X|	A version of the EQUIJOIN which selects those tuples where Relation1Tuple.Y = Relation2Tuple.Y. Y is a set of common attributes to both relations which must share the same domain. Duplicate columns are removed.
OUTERJOIN	⟗	Based on the θ-JOIN and natural JOIN, the OUTERJOIN in addition selects all the tuples in Relation1 that have no corresponding values in the relation Relation2.
DIVIDE	÷	Selects tuples in Relation1 that match every row in Relation2.
EXISTENTIAL	$\exists$	A formula must be true for *at least one* instance
UNIVERSAL	$\forall$	The formula must be true for *all* instances

* in the case of these operators, relations must be union-compatible.

KEY TERMS

closure
COURSE_RELATION
DIFFERENCE
DIVISION
domain
domain relational calculus
equijoin
INTERSECT
join column(s)
left outer join
natural join
predicate calculus
predicate expression
PROJECT
relational algebra
relational algebraic expression
RESTRICT
right outer join
safe expression
SELECT
set theory
theta join
tuple relational calculus
UNION
union-compatible

FURTHER READING

Codd, E.F. *A Relational Model of Data for Large Shared Data Banks*. CACM 13, No. 6, June 1970. Republished in Milestones of Research: Selected Papers 1958–1982. CACM 25th Anniversary Issue, CACM 26, No. 1, January 1983.

Codd, E.F. *Relational completeness of Data Base Sublanguages. Database Systems: 65–98*, Prentice Hall and IBM Research Report RJ 987, San Jose, California, 1972.

Date, C. J. *An Introduction to Database Systems, 8th edition*. Addison-Wesley, 2004.

Dietrich, S. *Understanding Relational Database Query Languages*, 1st edition. Prentice Hall, 2001.

Hrbacek, K. Jech, T. *Introduction to Set Theory*, 3rd edition. Marcel Dekker, Inc., 1999.

Lacroix, M. and Pirotte, A. *Domain-Oriented Relational Languages. Proceedings of the 3rd International Conference on Very Large Databases*, pp. 370–378, 1977.

Venn, J. 'On the Diagrammatic and Mechanical Representation of Propositions and Reasonings'. *Dublin Philosophical Magazine and Journal of Science* 9(59): 1–18, 1880.

Online Content Answers to selected Review Questions and Problems for this chapter are contained on the online platform accompanying this book.

REVIEW QUESTIONS

1 What are the main operations of relational algebra?

2 What is the Cartesian product? Illustrate your answer with an example.

3 What is the difference between PROJECTION and SELECTION?

4 Explain the difference between the natural join and the outer join.

5 What is the difference between tuple relational calculus and domain relational calculus?

6 Use the small database shown in Figure Q4.1 to illustrate the difference between a natural join, an equijoin and an outer join.

FIGURE Q4.1 The Ch04_UniversityQue database tables

Database name: Ch04_UniversityQue

Table name: STUDENT

STU_CODE	LECT_CODE
100278	
128569	2
512272	4
531235	2
531268	
553427	1

Table name: LECTURER

LECT_CODE	DEPT_CODE
1	2
2	6
3	6
4	4

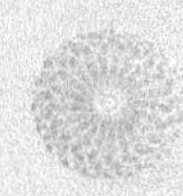

Online Content All of the databases used in the questions and problems are found on the online platform for this book. The database names used in the folder match the database names used in the figures. For example, the source of the tables shown in Figure Q4.1 is the 'Ch04_UniversityQue' database.

7 Using the relations shown in Figure Q4.2, compute the following relational algebra expressions:

 a TOUR_UK ∪ TOUR_EUROPE
 b TOUR_UK ∪ BOOKING
 c TOUR_UK ∩ TOUR_EUROPE
 d TOUR_UK – TOUR_EUROPE
 e TOUR_EUROPE – TOUR_UK
 f TOUR_UK X TOUR_EUROPE
 g $\sigma_{price\_brand\ =\ 'P2'}(TREK\_UK)$
 h $\Pi_{tour\_name,\ price\_band}(TREK\_EUROPE)$
 i $\Pi_{tour\_name}(\sigma_{price\_brand\ =\ 'P2'}(TREK\_UK))$
 j TREK_UK |X| BOOKING
 k TREK_EUROPE |X| BOOKING
 l BOOKING ⋈ TREK_EUROPE
 m $\Pi_{tour\_name,\ price\_band}(\sigma_{tour\_no\ =\ 'A1'\ or\ tour\_no\ =\ 'A2'}(TREK\_UK\ |X|\ TREK\_EUROPE))$

8 Using the relations shown in Figure Q4.2, compute the following tuple relational calculus expressions:

 a Find all bookings with a rating of 'S6'.
 b List the tour names offered by TREK_UK and TREK_EUROPE.

9 Using the relations shown in Figure Q4.2, compute the following domain relational calculus expressions:

 a Find all bookings with a rating of 'S7'.
 b List the tours from TREK_UK that have not yet been booked.

FIGURE Q4.2 The Ch04_Tours database tables

Database name: Ch04_Tours

Table name: TREK_UK

TOUR_NO	TOUR_NAME	PRICE_BAND
A1	TREK PERU	P2
A2	TREK ANDES	P2
A3	TREK EVEREST	P3
A4	TREK K2	P5

Table name: TREK_EUROPE

TOUR_NO	TOUR_NAME	PRICE_BAND
A3	TREK EVEREST	P3
A1	TREK K2	P4
A2	TREK ALPS	P9

Table name: BOOKING

TOUR_NAME	CUSTOMER_NO	RATING
TREK ANDES	C2	S5
TREK K2	C3	S6
TREK K2	C4	S7

FIGURE Q4.3 The Ch04_Vending database tables

Database name: Ch03_VendingCo

Table name: BOOTH

BOOTH_PRODUCT	BOOTH_PRICE
Chips	1.5
Cola	1.25
Energy Drink	2

Table name: MACHINE

MACHINE_PRODUCT	MACHINE_PRICE
Chips	1.25
Chocolate Bar	1
Energy Drink	2

Use Figure Q4.3 to answer Questions 10–14.

10 Write the relational algebra formula to apply a UNION relational operator to the tables shown in Figure Q4.3.

11 Create the table that results from applying a UNION relational operator to the tables shown in Figure Q4.3.

12 Write the relational algebra formula to apply an INTERSECT relational operator to the tables shown in Figure Q4.3.

13 Create the table that results from applying and INTERSECT relational operator to the tables shown in Figure Q4.3.

14 Using the tables in Figure Q4.3, create the table that results from MACHINE DIFFERENCE BOOTH.

PROBLEMS

The four relations shown in Figure P4.1 represent tables in a database which contains information about customers eating habits. The database tables store information about customers and the types of restaurants that they frequently visit. In addition, for each restaurant the types of cuisine which is served is recorded.

Use the relations shown in Figure P4.1 to write relational algebraic expressions for the following queries in Problems 1–12:

1. Display all information about restaurants where the restaurant price is equal to '€€€€'.
2. Find all the customers who frequently visit McDonalds.
3. List the names of all restaurants where it is possible to have fine dining.
4. Show the names of all customers who went to Claridges before 10 January 2008 or have spent more than €250 on the last bill.
5. Find the names and phone numbers of all customers who have visited fast food restaurants more than 40 times.

   Use the relations shown in Figure P4.1 to compute the following relational algebra expressions:

6. RESTAURANT X CUSINE
7. CUSTOMER |X| VISIT
8. CUSTOMER |X| VISIT |X| RESTAURANT

   Hint – When trying to solve this problem see how you can use your answer from Problem 7.

9. RESTAURANT ⟕ VISIT
10. $\Pi_{cus\_lname}(\sigma_{rest\_name\ =\ 'MacDonalds'}(\text{CUSTOMER |X| VISIT}))$
11. $\Pi_{rest\_name, last\_bill\_amount}(\text{VISIT})\ |X|\ (\sigma_{cus\_lname\ =\ 'Dunnes'}(\text{CUSTOMER}))$

Figure P4.2 shows a set of database tables that store information about student assessments at Tiny University. Use the relations shown in Figure P4.2 to write relational algebraic expressions for the following queries in Problems 12–20:

12. STUDENT-1 ∪ STUDENT-2
13. STUDENT-1 ∩ STUDENT-2
14. STUDENT-1 – STUDENT-2

FIGURE P4.1 The Ch04_Restaurant_Guide database tables

Database name: Ch04_Restaurant_Guide

Table name: CUSINE

TYPE	CATEGORY
American	FAST FOOD
French	FINE DINING
Chinese	BUFFET
South African	FINE DINING

Table name: CUSTOMER

CUS_CODE	CUS_LNAME	CUS_PHONE
10010	Ramas	844-2573
10011	Dunne	894-1238
10012	Smith	894-2285

Table name: RESTAURANT

REST_NAME	REST_LOCATION	REST_PRICE	REST_TYPE
McDonalds	The Hague	€	American
Claridges	London	€€€€€	French
Pompidou	Paris	€€€€	French
The Islands	Cape Town	€€€€	South African
Frankies	Milan	€€	American

Table name: VISIT

CUS_CODE	REST_NAME	NO_TIMES_VISITED	DATE_LAST_VISITED	LAST_BILL_AMOUNT
10010	The Islands	10	02/01/2018	€146.78
10011	McDonalds	87	30/12/2017	€7.98
10011	Claridges	1	01/01/2018	€520.22
10012	Pompidou	5	03/01/2017	€68.75
10012	McDonalds	32	04/01/2018	€12.75

15 STUDENT-1 |X| ASSESSMENT

16 STUDENT-2 $\bowtie$ ASSESSMENTS

17 Π_{stu_lname}(STUDENT-1 |X| ($\sigma_{exam\ mark > 60}$(ASSESSMENT)))

18 Π_{class_name}(CLASS) |X| ((ASSESSMENT) |X| ($\sigma_{stu\_lname = 'Vos'}$(STUDENT-1)))

19 Write a relational algebraic expression to find out the names of all students in STUDENT-1 who scored less than 60 in the Java_Prog exam.

20 To obtain a merit in a class, students must achieve 65 or over in both coursework and exam marks. Write a relational algebraic expression to show the names and numbers of all students in STUDENT-1 who have achieved a merit in their classes.

FIGURE P4.2 The Ch04_Student_Assess relations

Database name: Ch04_Student_Assess

Table name: STUDENT-1

STU_NUM	STU_LNAME	CRS_CODE
321452	Vos	Comp-600
324257	Smith	Eng-534
324258	Oblonski	Comp-600

Table name: CLASS

CLASS_CODE	CLASS_NAME
12	Databases
43	Info_Sys
46	Java_Prog

Table name: STUDENT-2

STU_NUM	STU_LNAME	CRS_CODE
324258	Oblonski	Comp-600
324787	Swithety	Comp-600

Table name: ASSESSMENT

STU_NUM	CLASS_CODE	EXAM_MARK	COURSE_WORK_MARK
321452	12	60	70
321452	46	50	60
324258	46	65	65
324457	43	0	70

21 Use the following relational schema to write relational algebra expressions for the following queries:

- a Show the names of all authors who have published books after 1st January 2019.
- b List the ISBNs of all books in stock.
- c Show all the stores in Belgium.
- d Find the ISBN of all stores that carry a non-zero quantity of every book in the BOOK relation.
- e Find the name and address of all stores that do not carry any books by 'Cornell'.

Relational schema
BOOK(ISBN, Author_name, Title, Publisher, Publish Date, Pages, Notes)
STORE(Store_No, Store_Name, Street, Country, Postcode)
STOCK(ISBN, Store_No, Price, Quantity)

22 Use the following relational schema to write relational algebra expressions for the following queries:

- a Show the Reservation_No and Total_cost of all flights that were paid before 21 December 2020.
- b List the last name of passengers travelling on flight number VO345.
- c Find the efficiency ratings of all planes, including in your answer the airline name for each plane.
- d List the Passport_No of passengers sitting in seats 36C, 38F and 42D on Flight_No V0667.

Relational schema
PASSENGER(Passenger_ID, Passenger_firstname, Passenger_lastname, Passport_No, Date_of_Birth)
FLIGHT(Flight_No, Airline_Name, Plane_Type)
RESERVATION(Reservation_No, passenger_ID, Flight_No, Seat_No, Flight_date, Date_paid, Total_Cost)
PLANE(Plane_type, Traveller_Capacity, Efficiency_Rating)

23 Using the relations shown in Figure P4.2, compute the following tuple relational calculus expressions:

- a Find the names of all students who are studying 'Comp-600'.
- b List all students who have course work and exam marks are both greater than 50.
- c List all students studying the class 'Java_Prog' and have taken the assessment.

24 Repeat Problem 7, but compute the expressions using domain relational calculus.

Part II

DESIGN CONCEPTS

BUSINESS VIGNETTE

USING DATA TO IMPROVE THE LIVES OF CHILDREN AND WOMEN

Over the past 20 years, UNICEF[1] has assisted charities, organisations and governments by providing data, analytics and insights to help improve the welfare of children and women worldwide. They are harnessing the Big Data available to them to make data work for children. In 2017, UNICEF released the Data for Children Strategic Framework, which has allowed it to expand its 'commitments in three areas that are essential for good data work: coordination, strategic planning and knowledge sharing'.[2] UNICEF currently holds data assets that have been generated from household surveys, global data advocacy and data provided by individual countries; the framework provides an opportunity to build a new data landscape to work within the data governance frameworks of individual countries and provide a 'gateway to reliable and open data and analysis on the situation of children and women worldwide'.[2]

UNICEF Data and Analytics teams work to ensure that the data collected is statistically sound by using Multiple Indicator Cluster Surveys (MICS).[3] Global databases are used to track children and women, and new methodologies and monitoring tools have been designed to enable successful data gathering on issues such as low birth weight, education and child labour. UNICEF houses the power of a modern data warehouse to enable data to be more accessible through interoperability, and data visualisation is achieved through the use of interactive maps and graphs. The ultimate aim is to put data into action.

1 UNICEF, available: https://data.unicef.org/about-us/

2 Data for Children Strategic Framework, available: https://data.unicef.org/resources/data-children-strategic-framework/

3 Multiple Indicator Cluster Surveys, available: http://mics.unicef.org/

One example project has been concerned with monitoring child health in Kenya, Swaziland and Uganda through the use of near real-time data and feedback from the community.[4] The aim of the project was to tackle the problems of decentralised health services in rural areas and report the impact to the communities. Data for Action has enabled mobile data collection using colour-coded scorecards, allowing health facilities to understand the quality, reach and impact of their delivery of care.[4] This, coupled with near-real time community feedback collected through many sources, including SMS messaging, has enabled impact to be measured and the ability for the community to recommend solutions.

Data for Action has also enabled UNICEF to provide education to child refugees in Lebanon.[4] The Ministry of Education and Higher Education (MEHE) and UNICEF came together in 2013 to provide free education to children, but due to the inadequate and poor-quality data received from a limited number of schools, it was impossible to determine the needs of the schools or the impact of the educational services being delivered. At this time, there was no Education Management Information System (EMIS) in Lebanon. During 2016, UNICEF and MEHE built an adaptive EMIS, which provided a way for schools to track a child's attendance, education history and periods when they were and weren't in school. Today, this system is in use in 355 schools.[4]

There are many examples where UNICEF's Data for Children Strategic Framework has successfully improved the lives of children. In Brazil, the Zika virus has caused severe distress and affected the well-being of women and children in at least 75 counties in South America. To raise awareness of prevention measures, Facebook and UNICEF teamed up to analyse social media conversations about Zika within Brazil. The anonymised data was used to develop a data-informed public communications campaign to raise awareness of the virus and provide prevention strategies.

These case studies are just the tip of the iceberg and demonstrate the impact of well architected databases to provide clean and robust data for data analytics and data mining purposes.

4 Using near real-time data and community feedback to support maternal, newborn and child health in East Africa, available: https://data.unicef.org/wp-content/uploads/2018/01/From-Insight-to-Action-November-2017.pdf

CHAPTER 5

Data Modelling with Entity Relationship Diagrams

IN THIS CHAPTER, YOU WILL LEARN:

- The main characteristics of entity relationship components
- How relationships between entities are defined and refined, and how those relationships are incorporated into the database design process
- How ERD components affect database design and implementation
- That real-world database design often requires the reconciliation of conflicting goals

PREVIEW

This chapter expands coverage of the data modelling aspect of database design. Data modelling is the first step in the database design journey, serving as a bridge between real-world objects and the database model that is implemented in the computer. Therefore, the importance of data modelling details, expressed graphically through entity relationship diagrams (ERDs), cannot be overstated.

Most of the basic concepts and definitions used in the entity relationship model (ERM) were introduced in Chapter 2, Data Models. For example, the basic components of entities and relationships and their representation should now be familiar to you. This chapter goes much deeper and broader, analysing the graphic depiction of relationships among the entities, and shows how those depictions help you summarise the wealth of data required to implement a successful design. Throughout this chapter, two case studies will be used to illustrate the different types of relationships amongst entities. One case study is based on an international travel company called ILoveHolidays, which owns a number of travel agents around the world. The second case study, known as Tiny University, is based on the internal structure of a university.

Finally, the chapter illustrates how conflicting goals can be a challenge in database design, possibly requiring you to make design compromises.

NOTE

As this book generally focuses on the relational model, you might be tempted to conclude that the ERM is exclusively a relational tool. Actually, conceptual models such as the ERM can be used to understand and design the data requirements of an organisation. Therefore, the ERM is independent of the database type. Conceptual models are used in the conceptual design of databases, while relational models are used in the logical design of databases. However, since you are now familiar with the relational model from the Chapter 3, the relational model is used extensively in this chapter to explain ER constructs and the way they are used to develop database designs.

5.1 THE ENTITY RELATIONSHIP (ER) MODEL

You should remember from Chapter 2, Data Models, and Chapter 3, Relational Model Characteristics, that the ERM forms the basis of an ERD. The ERD represents the conceptual database as viewed by the end user. ERDs depict the database's main components: entities, attributes and relationships. Because an entity represents a real-world object, the words *entity* and *object* are often used interchangeably. Thus, the entities (objects) of the ILoveHolidays database design developed in this chapter includes customers, bookings, employees, hotels and flights. The order in which the ERD components are covered in the chapter is dictated by the way the modelling tools are used to develop ERDs that can form the basis for successful database design and implementation.

Let's start by introducing a simple ERD, which has been created to model recipes within a cookery book and their ingredients. In Figure 5.1, BOOK, RECIPE, RECIPE_INGREDIENT and INGREDIENT are all examples of entities that would be identified during database design. By looking more closely at the ERD in Figure 5.1 we can find out some basic information about the relationships that exist between these entities, such as:

- a BOOK can contain at least one RECIPE, but may contain many RECIPEs
- a RECIPE requires at least one RECIPE_INGREDIENT, but may have many RECIPE_INGREDIENTs
- one INGREDIENT can be found in a number of RECIPE_INGREDIENTs but may not appear in any RECIPE_INGREDIENT.

You can also see in Figure 5.1 that each entity has a number of attributes. For example the entity BOOK contains an attribute called ISBN, which has the notation {PK} next to it. You will learn in this chapter that {PK} is used to denote an attribute that is the PRIMARY KEY of an entity, which is an attribute that identifies each instance of that entity. In this example, a book's ISBN is used to identify each different book uniquely. Likewise, FK is used to denote a FOREIGN KEY. We will use examples such as the one shown in Figure 5.1 to illustrate all the concepts of entity relationship modelling in this chapter.

FIGURE 5.1 A recipe ERD

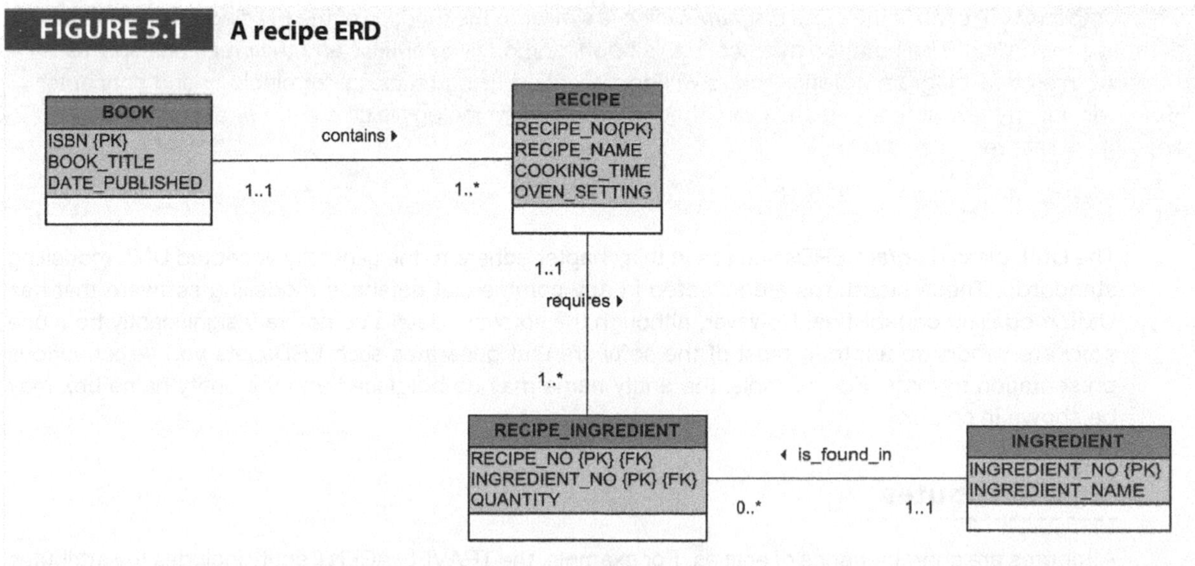

In Chapter 2, you learnt about the different notations used within ERDs, including the traditional Crow's Foot notation and the more contemporary UML notation. Within this chapter, we will continue to use UML notation to model ERDs, using relational concepts and terminology.

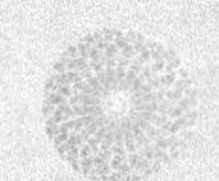

Online Content For a more detailed description of the Chen, Crow's Foot and other ER model notation systems, see Appendix E, Comparison of ER Modelling Notations, available on the online platform for this book.

5.1.1 Entities

5

An entity is an object of interest to the end user. In Chapter 2, you learnt that, at the ER modelling level, an entity actually refers to the *entity set* and not to a single entity occurrence. In other words, the word *entity* in the ERM corresponds to a table and not to a row in the relational environment. The ERM refers to a specific table row as an *entity instance* or *entity occurrence*. In UML notation, an entity is represented by a box that is subdivided into three parts:

- The top part is used to name the entity. The entity name, a noun, is usually written in capital letters.
- The middle part is used to name and describe the attributes.
- The bottom part is used to list the methods. Methods are used only when designing object-relational or object-orientated database models and therefore will be left blank in the examples within this book.

NOTE

One component of UML is the *class diagram,* which is similar to the function of the ER diagram in relational database modelling. The notation adopted in this book for modelling entities and their relationships, uses some of this class diagram notation, but it will be described using relational terminology and concepts. However, it is important that you are aware that in UML the terminology is different. For example, in UML, an entity is referred to as a **class**.

The UML class diagram ERDs you see in this chapter adhere to the generally accepted UML modelling standards. These standards are reflected in any commercial database modelling software that has UML modelling capabilities. However, although the software details do not vary significantly from one software vendor to another, most of the software that generates such ERDs lets you select various presentation formats. For example, the entity name may be boldfaced and the entity name box may be shown in colour.

5.1.2 Attributes

Attributes are characteristics of entities. For example, the TRAVEL_AGENT entity includes the attributes AGENT_ID, AGENT_NAME, AGENT_ADDRESS. In the UML model, the attributes are written in the attribute box below the entity rectangle (see Figure 5.2).

As you examine Figure 5.2, note that AGENT_ID, AGENT_NAME and AGENT_ADDRESS will require data entries, because of the assumption that all travel agents have an ID, name and address. However, if the travel agent has just been established, it might not have a phone number, email address and manager yet.

FIGURE 5.2 The attributes of the TRAVEL_AGENT entity

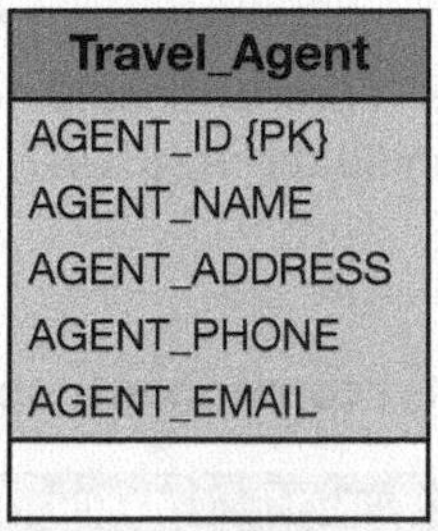

Travel_Agent
AGENT_ID {PK} AGENT_NAME AGENT_ADDRESS AGENT_PHONE AGENT_EMAIL

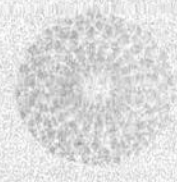

Online Content Microsoft Visio Professional was used to generate both the Crow's Foot ERDs and UML class diagrams in this and subsequent chapters. Appendix A, Designing Databases with Visio Professional: A Tutorial, available on the accompanying online platform, shows you how to create ERD models like the ones in this chapter.

Domains

Attributes have a domain. As you learnt in Chapter 3, a *domain* is the attribute's set of possible values. For example, the domain for the (numeric) attribute grade point average (GPA) is written (0,4) because the lowest possible GPA value is 0 and the highest possible value is 4. The domain for the (character) attribute GENDER consists of only two possibilities: M or F (or some other equivalent code). The domain for a company's date of hire attribute consists of all dates that fit in a range (for example, company startup date to current date).

Attributes may share a domain. For instance, an employee of a travel agency may also be a customer of the travel agency and share the same domain of all possible addresses. In fact, the data dictionary may let a newly declared attribute inherit the characteristics of an existing attribute if the same attribute name is used. For example, the TRAVEL_AGENT AND EMPLOYEE entities may each have an attribute named ADDRESS.

Identifiers (Primary Keys)

The ERM uses **identifiers** to uniquely identify each entity instance. In the relational model, such identifiers are mapped to primary keys in tables. Identifiers are underlined in the ERD. Key attributes are also underlined when writing the relational schema, using the notation introduced in Chapter 3.

TABLE NAME (KEY_ATTRIBUTE 1, ATTRIBUTE 2, ATTRIBUTE 3, ... ATTRIBUTE K)

For example, a CAR entity may be represented by:

CAR (CAR_REG, MOD_CODE, CAR_YEAR, CAR_COLOUR)

(REG is the standard acronym for vehicle registration number.)

Composite Primary Keys

Ideally, a primary key is composed of only a single attribute. For example, the table in Figure 5.3 uses a single-attribute primary key named PAYMENT_NO. However, it is possible to use a **composite key**, that is, a primary key composed of more than one attribute. For instance, the ILoveHolidays database administrator may decide to identify each PAYMENT entity instance (occurrence) by using a composite primary key composed of the combination of CUST_NO and INVOICE_NO instead of using PAYMENT_NO. Either approach uniquely identifies each entity instance. Given the current structure of the PAYMENT table shown in Figure 5.3, PAYMENT_NO is the primary key and the combination of CUST_NO and INVOICE_NO is a proper candidate key. If the PAYMENT_NO attribute is deleted from the PAYMENT entity, the candidate key (CUST_NO and INVOICE_NO) becomes an acceptable composite primary key.

5

FIGURE 5.3 The PAYMENT (entity) components and contents

PAYMENT_NO	CUST_NO	INVOICE_NO	AMOUNT_PAID	PAYMENT_TYPE	DATE_PAID
152675687	631304	152001	500	VISA	03-Apr-19
152342111	631304	152002	500	VISA	03-May-18
152887222	631304	152003	1000	VISA	03-June-19
152228445	712344	152010	350	American Express	24-May-19
152987877	712344	152011	550	VISA	01-Jul-19
152344223	901234	152132	2000	MasterCard	06-Jun-19
152334534	091234	152167	4329	MasterCard	02-Aug-19

If the PAYMENT_NO in Figure 5.3 is used as the primary key, the PAYMENT entity may be represented in shorthand form by: PAYMENT

(PAYMENT_NO, CUST_NO, INVOICE_NO, AMOUNT_PAID_PAYMENT, TYPE, DATE_PAID)

On the other hand, if PAYMENT_NO is deleted and the composite primary key is the combination of CUST_NO AND INVOICE_NO, the PAYMENT entity may be represented by:

(CUST_NO, INVOICE_NO, AMOUNT_PAID, PAYMENT_TYPE, DATE_PAID)
Note that *both* key attributes are underlined in the entity notation.

Composite and Simple Attributes

Attributes are classified as simple or composite. A **composite attribute**, not to be confused with a composite key, is an attribute that can be further subdivided to yield additional attributes. For example, the attribute ADDRESS can be subdivided into street, city, state and postal code. Similarly, the attribute PHONE_NUMBER can be subdivided into area code and exchange number. A **simple attribute** is an attribute that cannot be subdivided. For example, age, gender and marital status would be classified as simple attributes. To facilitate detailed queries, it is usually appropriate to change composite attributes into a series of simple attributes.

Single-Valued Attributes

A **single-valued attribute** is an attribute that can have only a single value. For example, a person can have only one ID number and a manufactured part can have only one serial number. *Keep in mind that* *a single-valued attribute is not necessarily a simple attribute*. For instance, a part's serial number, such as SE-08-02-189935, is single-valued, but it is a composite attribute because it can be subdivided into the region in which the part was produced (SE), the plant within that region (08), the shift within the plant (02) and the part number (189935).

Multivalued Attributes

Multivalued attributes are attributes that can have many values. For instance, a person may have several university degrees or a household may have several different phones, each with its own number. Similarly, a car's colour may be subdivided into many colours (that is, colours for the roof, body and trim). The ERD in Figure 5.4 contains all of the components introduced thus far. In the UML notation there is no support for primary keys. However, primary keys can be easily added to an attribute within the entity by adding the notation {PK} after the attribute(s) determined to be the primary key.

FIGURE 5.4 The multivalued attribute in an entity

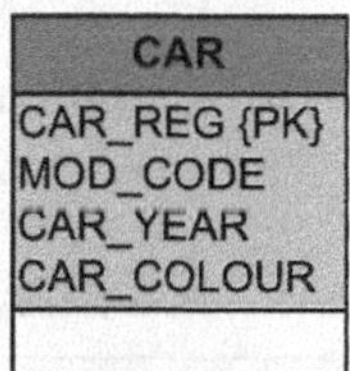

Resolving Multivalued Attribute Problems

Although the conceptual model can handle *:* relationships and multivalued attributes, *you should not implement them in the RDBMS*. Remember from Chapter 3, Relational Model Characteristics, that, in the relation table, each column/row intersection represents a single data value. So if multivalued attributes exist, the designer must decide on one of two possible courses of action:

1 Within the original entity, create several new attributes, one for each of the original multivalued attribute's components. For example, the CAR entity's attribute CAR_COLOUR can be split to create the new attributes CAR_TOPCOLOUR, CAR_BODYCOLOUR, and CAR_TRIMCOLOUR, shown in Figure 5.5, and assigned to the CAR entity.

FIGURE 5.5 Splitting the multivalued attribute into new attributes

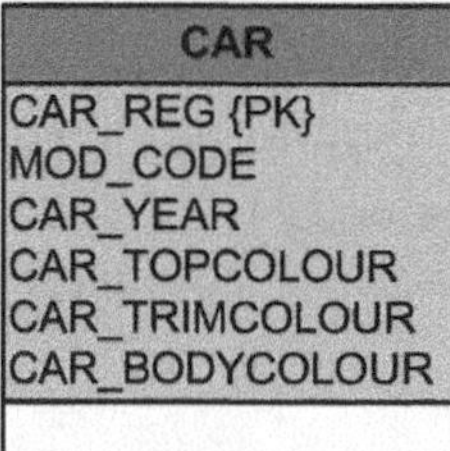

Although this solution seems to work, its adoption can lead to major structural problems in the table. For example, if additional colour components – such as a logo colour – are added for some cars, the table structure must be modified to accommodate the new colour section. In that case, cars that do not have such colour sections generate nulls for the non-existing components or their colour entries for those sections are entered as N/A to indicate 'not applicable'. (Imagine how the solution in Figure 5.5 – splitting a multivalued attribute into new attributes – would cause problems when it is applied to an employee entity containing employee degrees and certifications. If some employees have ten degrees and certifications while most have fewer or none, the number of degree/certification attributes would number ten and most of those attribute values would be null for most of the employees.) In short, although you have seen solution 1 applied, it is not an acceptable solution.

5

2 Create a new entity composed of the original multivalued attribute's components. (See Figure 5.6.) The new (independent) CAR_COLOUR entity is then related to the original CAR entity in a 1:* relationship. Note that such a change allows the designer to define colour for different sections of the car (see Table 5.1).

FIGURE 5.6 A new entity set composed of a multivalued attribute's components

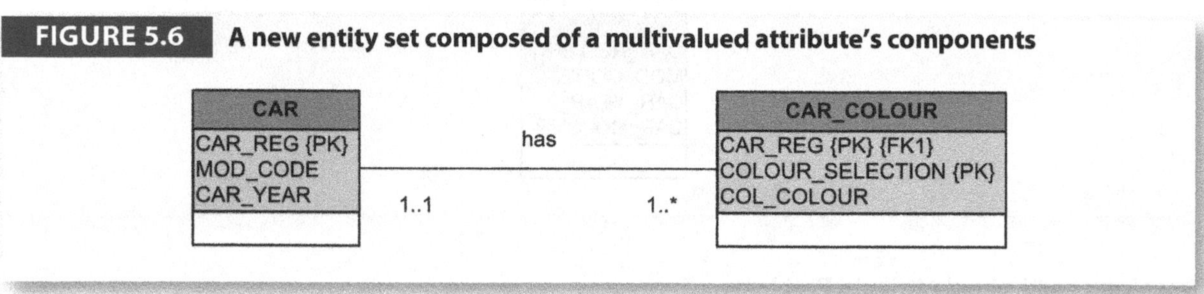

TABLE 5.1 Components of the multivalued attribute

Section	Colour
Top	White
Body	Blue
Trim	Gold
Interior	Blue

Using the approach illustrated in Table 5.1, you even get a fringe benefit: you are now able to assign as many colours as necessary without having to change the table structure. Note that the ERMs in Figure 5.5 (a) and (b) reflect the components listed in Table 5.1. This is the preferred way to deal with multivalued attributes. Creating a new entity in a 1:* relationship with the original entity yields several benefits: it is a more flexible, expandable solution, and it is compatible with the relational model!

Derived Attributes

Finally, an attribute may be classified as a derived attribute. A **derived attribute** is an attribute whose value is calculated (derived) from other attributes. The derived attribute need not be physically stored within the database; instead, it can be derived by using an algorithm. For example, an employee's age, EMP_AGE, may be found by computing the integer value of the difference between the current date and the EMP_DOB. If you use Microsoft Access, you would use INT((DATE() – EMP_DOB)/365).

If you use Oracle, you would use SYSDATE instead of DATE(). (You are assuming, of course, that the EMP_DOB was stored in the Julian date format.) Similarly, the total cost of an order line can be derived by multiplying the quantity ordered by the unit price. Or the estimated average speed can be derived by dividing trip distance by the time spent en route. In UML, derived attributes are prefixed with a '/', which can be seen on the attribute EMP_AGE in Figure 5.7.

FIGURE 5.7 Depiction of a derived attribute

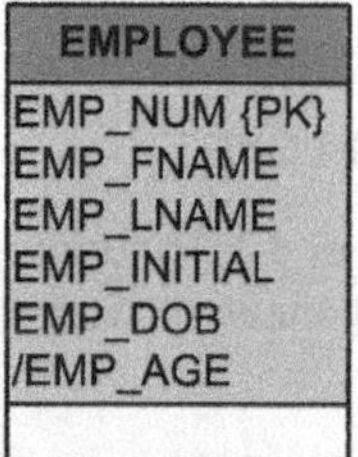

Derived attributes are sometimes referred to as *computed attributes*. A derived attribute computation could be as simple as adding two attribute values located on the same row, or it could be the result of aggregating the sum of values located on many table rows (from the same table or from a different table). The decision to store derived attributes in database tables depends on the processing requirements and the constraints placed on a particular application. The designer should be able to balance the design in accordance with such constraints. Table 5.2 shows the advantages and disadvantages of storing (or not storing) derived attributes in the database.

TABLE 5.2 Advantages and disadvantages of storing derived attributes

	Derived Attribute	
	Stored	**Not Stored**
Advantage	Saves CPU processing cycles Data value is readily available Can be used to keep track of historical data	Saves storage space Computation always yields current value
Disadvantage	Requires constant maintenance to ensure derived value is current, especially if any values used in the calculation change	Uses CPU processing cycles Adds coding complexity to queries

5.1.3 Relationships

A *relationship* is an association between entities. The entities that participate in a relationship are also known as **participants**. You should recall from Chapter 2, Data Models, that each relationship is identified by a name that is descriptive of the relationship. The relationship name is an active or passive verb; for example, a STUDENT *takes* a CLASS, a LECTURER *teaches* a CLASS, a DEPARTMENT *employs* a LECTURER, a DIVISION *is managed by* an EMPLOYEE, a CUSTOMER *makes* a BOOKING and an AIRCRAFT *is flown by* a CREW.

Relationships between entities always operate in both directions. That is, to define the relationship between the entities named CUSTOMER and INVOICE, you would specify that:

- A CUSTOMER may generate many INVOICEs.
- Each INVOICE is generated by one CUSTOMER.

Because you know both directions of the relationship between CUSTOMER and INVOICE, it is easy to see that this relationship can be classified as 1:*.

The relationship classification is difficult to establish if you know only one side of the relationship. For example, if you specify that:

A DIVISION is managed by one EMPLOYEE

5

you don't know if the relationship is 1:1 or 1:*. Therefore, you should ask the question 'Can an employee manage more than one division?' If the answer is yes, the relationship is 1:*, and the second part of the relationship is then written as:

An EMPLOYEE may manage many DIVISIONs.

If an employee cannot manage more than one division, the relationship is 1:1, and the second part of the relationship is then written as:

An EMPLOYEE may manage only one DIVISION.

NOTE

In UML class diagrams the relationship name is often referred to as an **association** *name.* Normally, the name of the association is written over the association line. Associations also have a direction, represented by an arrow (→) pointing in the direction in which the relationship flows. Alternatively, the association name may be replaced with role names. A role name expresses the role played by a given entity (class) in the relationship. Each relationship is usually described by two role names which represent the relationship 'as seen' by each class; for example:

A CUSTOMER *generates* an INVOICE and each INVOICE *belongs to* a CUSTOMER.

A VENDOR *supplies* a PRODUCT and each PRODUCT *is supplied by* a VENDOR.

In this chapter, all relationship names will be described using the singular association name, as it is the same as the relationship name used in traditional relational modelling.

5.1.4 Multiplicity

You learnt in Chapter 2 that entity relationships may be classified as one-to-one, one-to-many, or many-to-many. Multiplicity is the main constraint that exists on a relationship, which enables us to define the number of participants in that relationship. So, **multiplicity** refers to the number of instances of one entity that are associated with one instance of a related entity. Figure 5.8 illustrates how Visio shows multiplicity on an ERD using UML notation.

FIGURE 5.8 Multiplicity in an ERD

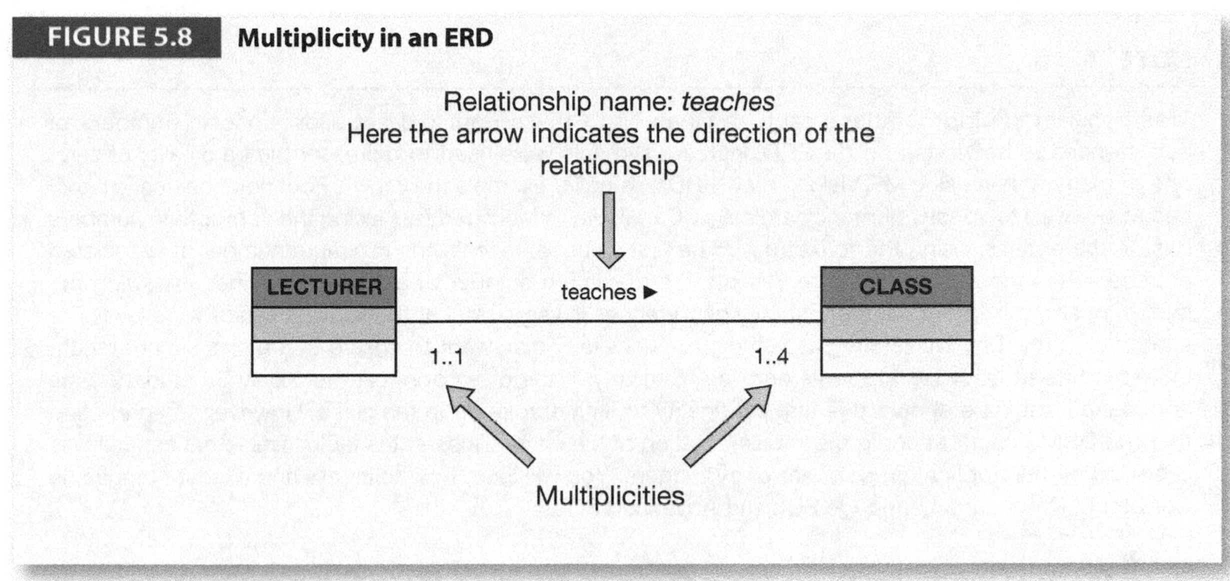

As you examine Figure 5.8, notice that the multiplicities represent the number of occurrences in the *related* entity. For example, the multiplicity (1..4) written next to the CLASS entity in the 'LECTURER teaches CLASS' relationship indicates that the LECTURER table's primary key value occurs at least once and no more than four times as foreign key values in the CLASS table. If the multiplicity had been written as (1..*), there would be no upper limit to the number of classes a lecturer might teach. Similarly, the multiplicity (1..1) written next to the LECTURER entity indicates that each class is taught by one and only one lecturer. That is, each CLASS entity occurrence is associated with one and only one entity occurrence in LECTURER.

If you examine multiplicity further, you will see that each numerical range actually describes two important constraints: **participation** and **cardinality**. The word *cardinality* is a common term used in traditional entity relationship modelling, and is used to express the maximum number of entity occurrences associated with one occurrence of the related entity. Participation determines whether all occurrences of an entity participate in the relationship or not. So, the multiplicity (1..4), written next to the CLASS entity in Figure 5.8, can be interpreted as follows:

- The '1' represents the participation and indicates that all lecturers must participate in the relationship and that it is mandatory.
- The '4' represents the cardinality, and indicates that one lecturer must teach at least one and up to four classes.

You will learn more about relationship participation in Section 5.1.8.

5

NOTE

Traditional modelling notations such as Chen and Crow's Foot did not allow specific numbers of occurrences to be written on the ERD. Instead, symbols were used to represent the cardinality of zero, one or many. When using MS Visio to draw ERDs, using for example the Crow's Foot notation, the text tool has to be used to specify numeric cardinality. Cardinality is indicated by placing the appropriate numbers beside the entities, using the format (x,y). The first value represents the minimum number of associated entities, while the second value represents the maximum number of associated entities. Knowing the minimum and maximum number of entity occurrences is very useful at the application software level. For example, in the Tiny University case study, the university may want to ensure that a class is not taught unless it has at least ten students enrolled. Similarly, if the classroom can hold only 30 students, the application software should use that cardinality to limit enrolment in the class. However, keep in mind that the DBMS cannot handle the implementation of the cardinalities at the table level – that capability is provided by the application software or by triggers. You will learn how to create and execute triggers in Chapter 9, Procedural Language SQL and Advanced SQL.

Multiplicities are established by very concise statements known as *business rules*. (Business rules were introduced in Chapter 2.) Such rules, derived from a precise and detailed description of an organisation's data environment, also establish the ERM's entities, attributes, relationships, cardinalities and constraints.

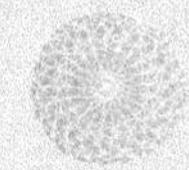

Online Content Since the careful definition of complete and accurate business rules is crucial to good design, their derivation is examined in detail in Appendix B, where you will undertake a real-life database design exercise for a university lab. The modelling skills you are learning in this chapter are applied in the development of a real database design in Appendices B and C (Global Tickets Ltd e-commerce database). In Appendices B and C you will be taken through all stages in the database design process from conceptual design and verification to logical and physical database design and implementation. (Both appendices are available on the online platform accompanying this book.)

Since business rules define the ERM's components, making sure that all appropriate business rules are identified is an important part of a database designer's job.

5.1.5 Existence Dependence

An entity is said to be **existence-dependent** if it can exist in the database only when it is associated with another related entity occurrence. In implementation terms, an entity is existence-dependent if it has a mandatory foreign key – that is, a foreign key attribute that cannot be null. For example, if an XYZ Corporation employee wants to claim one or more dependents for tax-withholding purposes, the relationship 'EMPLOYEE claims DEPENDENT' would be appropriate. In that case, the DEPENDENT entity is clearly existence-dependent on the EMPLOYEE entity, because it is impossible for the dependent to exist apart from the EMPLOYEE in the XYZ Corporation database.

If an entity can exist apart from one or more related entities, it is said to be **existence-independent**. (Sometimes designers refer to such an entity as a *strong* or *regular* entity.) For example, suppose that the XYZ Corporation uses parts to produce its products. Further, suppose that some of those parts are produced in-house and other parts are bought from vendors. In that scenario, it is quite possible for a PART to exist independently from a VENDOR in the relationship 'PART is supplied by VENDOR'. (After all, at least some of the parts are not supplied by a vendor.)

Therefore, PART is existence-independent from VENDOR.

5.1.6 Relationship Strength

The concept of relationship strength is based on how the primary key of a related entity is defined. To implement a relationship, the primary key of one entity appears as a foreign key in the related entity. For example, the 1:* relationship between VENDOR and PRODUCT in Chapter 3, Figure 3.5, is implemented by using the VEND_CODE primary key in VENDOR as a foreign key in PRODUCT. There are times when the foreign key is also a primary key component in the related entity. For example, in Figure 5.6, the CAR entity primary key (CAR_REG) appears as both a primary key component and a foreign key in the CAR_COLOUR entity. In this section, you will learn how different relationship strength decisions affect primary key arrangement in database design.

Weak (Non-Identifying) Relationships

A **weak relationship**, also known as a **non-identifying relationship**, exists if the PK of the related entity does not contain a PK component of the parent entity. By default, relationships are established by having the PK of the parent entity appear as a FK on the related entity. For example, suppose that the TRAVEL_AGENT and EMPLOYEE entities in the Travel Agent case study are defined as:

TRAVEL_AGENT(AGENT_ID, AGENT_NAME, AGENT_ADDRESS, AGENT_PHONE, AGENT_EMAIL)

EMPLOYEE(EMP_ID, AGENT_ID, EMP_LNAME, EMP_FNAME, EMP_PHONE, EMP_GRADE, PAYROLL_NO)

In this case, a weak relationship exists between TRAVEL_AGENT AND EMPLOYEE because the EMP_ID is the EMPLOYEE entity's PK, while the AGENT_ID in EMPLOYEE is only an FK. In this example, the EMPLOYEE PK did not inherit the PK component from the TRAVEL_AGENT entity. Figure 5.9 shows the weak relationship between TRAVEL_AGENT and EMPLOYEE. By examining Figure 5.9, you will see that the UML notation does not make a distinction between weak and strong relationships. UML class diagrams do not require the foreign key attribute to be added to the many side of the 1:* relationship. However, because the focus here is on the use of UML class diagrams to model relational databases, the foreign key attributes are shown in the class diagrams by adding {FK} after the attribute name.

FIGURE 5.9 A weak non-identifying relationship between TRAVEL AGENT and EMPLOYEE

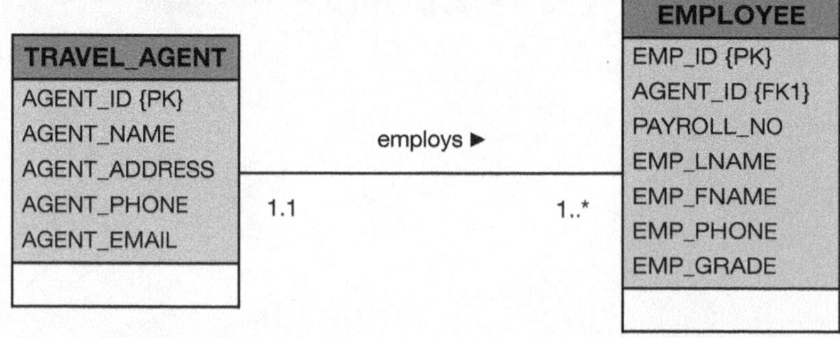

5

NOTE

If you are used to looking at relational diagrams such as the ones produced by Microsoft Access, you expect to see the relationship line *in the relational diagram* drawn from the PK to the FK. However, the relational diagram convention is not necessarily reflected in the ERD. In an ERD, the focus is on the entities and the relationships between them, rather than the way those relationships are anchored graphically. In fact, if design tools such as Visio Professional are used properly, the FKs are established *after* the relationship between the entities has been defined; so it is impossible to anchor the relationship line on the FK until *after* the FK has been created by the software. (This feature ensures that the FK attribute characteristics always properly match the attribute characteristics of the PK to which the FK points.) You can, of course, decide to move the relationship line anchor points after the update has been completed *but that decision clearly reflects choice, rather than necessity.* You will discover that the placement of the relationship lines in a complex ERD that includes both horizontally and vertically placed entities is largely dictated by the designer's decision to improve the readability of the design. (Remember that the ERD is used for communication between the designer(s) and end users.)

An example of the tables that exist in a weak relationship is shown in Figure 5.10.

FIGURE 5.10 **Weak (non-identifying) relationship between TRAVEL_AGENT and EMPLOYEE**

Database name: CH05_Travel_Agent

Table name: Travel_AGENT

Primary Key: AGENT_ID

AGENT_ID	AGENT_NAME	AGENT_ADDRESS	AGENT_PHONE	AGENT_EMAIL
1	Timeless Travel	Upper Keys Business Village, Cannock, Staffordshire, WS12 2HA, UK	0800 333 2233	timeless@travel.com
8	FlightLite	Anansi Park, Durbanville, 7550, Cape Town, SA	0860232425	info@flightlight.co.za
9	VILLANOVO	244 Rue De Rivoli 75001 Paris 222 Rue De Rivoli 75001 Paris, France	33170809753	enquire@villanovo.com.fr

Table name: EMPLOYEE
Primary Key: EMP_ID

EMP_ID	AGENT_ID	EMP_LNAME	EMP_FNAME	EMP_PHONE	EMP_GRADE	PAYROLL_NO
1239909	9	Meniur	Adele	044573322	Manager	NW445T
1239986	9	Vos	Astrid	049989900	Deputy Manager	NW211Q
1344255	9	Marin	Gaston	046656671	Staff	NW887L
1556743	9	Vulstrek	Henry	043343322	Staff	NW667P
4000566	1	Khoza	Buhle	087632343	Staff	CW990U
4000768	1	Fenyang	Abri	084544477	Staff	CW211R
4005655	1	Xu	Chang	088765676	Manager	CW223V
5009323	8	Lefu	Mosa	081231133	Manager	TY334Z

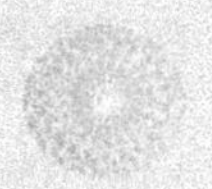

Strong (Identifying) Relationships

A **strong relationship**, also known as an **identifying relationship**, exists when the PK of the related entity contains a PK component of the parent entity. For example, the definitions of the TRAVEL_AGENT and EMPLOYEE entities:

TRAVEL_AGENT(AGENT_ID, AGENT_NAME, AGENT_ADDRESS, AGENT_PHONE, AGENT_EMAIL)

EMPLOYEE(AGENT_ID, PAYROLL_NO, EMP_LNAME, EMP_FNAME, EMP_PHONE, EMP_GRADE,)

indicate that a strong relationship exists between TRAVEL_AGENT and EMPLOYEE because the EMPLOYEE entity's composite PK is composed of AGENT_ID + PAYROLL_NO. (Note that the AGENT_ID in EMPLOYEE is *also* the FK to the TRAVEL_AGENT entity.)

Whether the relationship between TRAVEL_AGENT and EMPLOYEE is strong or weak depends on how the EMPLOYEE entity's primary key is defined. Figure 5.11 shows the strong relationship between TRAVEL_AGENT and EMPLOYEE.

Online Content All of the databases used to illustrate the material in this chapter are available on the online platform accompanying this book.

FIGURE 5.11 **STRONG (non-identifying) relationship between TRAVEL_AGENT and EMPLOYEE**

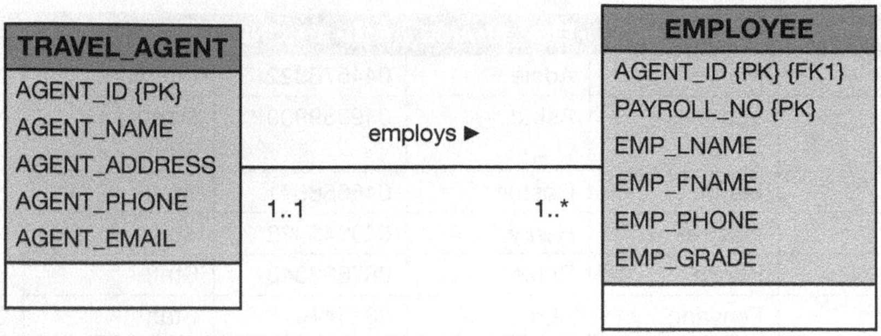

Database name: CH05_Travel_Agent

Table name: Travel_AGENT

Primary Key: AGENT_ID

AGENT_ID	AGENT_NAME	AGENT_ADDRESS	AGENT_PHONE	AGENT_EMAIL
1	Timeless Travel	Upper Keys Business Village, Cannock , Staffordshire, WS12 2HA, UK	0800 333 2233	timeless@travel.com
8	FlightLite	Anansi Park, Durbanville, 7550, Cape Town, SA	0860232425	info@flightlight.co.za
9	VILLANOVO	244 Rue De Rivoli 75001 Paris 222 Rue De Rivoli 75001 Paris, France	33170809753	enquire@villanovo.com.fr

Table name: EMPLOYEE

Primary Key: AGENT_ID AND PAYROLL_NO

Foreign Key: AGENT_ID

AGENT_ID	PAYROLL_NO	EMP_ID	EMP_LNAME	EMP_FNAME	EMP_PHONE	EMP_GRADE
9	NW445T	1239909	Meniur	Adele	044573322	Manager
9	NW211Q	1239986	Vos	Astrid	049989900	Deputy Manager
9	NW887L	1344255	Marin	Gaston	046656671	Staff
9	NW667P	1556743	Vulstrek	Henry	043343322	Staff
1	CW990U	4000566	Khoza	Buhle	087632343	Staff
1	CW211R	4000768	Fenyang	Abri	084544477	Staff
1	CW223V	4005655	Xu	Chang	088765676	Manager
8	TY334Z	5009323	Lefu	Mosa	081231133	Manager

Keep in mind that *the order in which the tables are created and loaded is very important*. For example, in the 'TRAVEL_AGENT employs EMPLOYEE' relationship (Figure 5.11), the TRAVEL_AGENT table must be created before the EMPLOYEE table. After all, it would not be acceptable to have the EMPLOYEE table's foreign key reference a TRAVEL_AGENT table that did not yet exist. In some DBMSs, this sequencing problem does not crop up until the data are loaded into the tables. In fact, *you must load the '1' side first in a 1:* relationship to avoid the possibility of referential integrity errors*, regardless of whether the relationships are weak or strong.

Remember that the nature of the relationship is often determined by the database designer, who must use professional judgement to determine which relationship type and strength best suit the database transaction, efficiency and information requirements. That point will often be emphasised in detail!

5.1.7 Weak Entities

A **weak entity** is one that meets two conditions:

1 It is existence-dependent; that is, it cannot exist without the entity with which it has a relationship.

2 It has a primary key that is partially or totally derived from the parent entity in the relationship.

For example, a company insurance policy may insure an employee and his/her dependants. For the purpose of describing an insurance policy, an EMPLOYEE may or may not have a DEPENDANT, but the DEPENDANT must be associated with an EMPLOYEE. Moreover, the DEPENDANT cannot exist without the EMPLOYEE; that is, a person cannot get insurance coverage at the XYZ Corporation as a *dependant* unless s(he) happens to be a dependant of an employee working for the XYZ Corporation. DEPENDANT is the weak entity in the relationship 'EMPLOYEE has DEPENDANT'.

An example of the weak entity DEPENDANT is shown in Figure 5.12.

A strong (identifying) relationship indicates that the related entity is weak. Such a relationship means that both conditions for the weak entity definition have been met – the related entity is existence-dependent, and the PK of the related entity contains a PK component of the parent entity.

As you examine the ERD in Figure 5.12, you will notice that there is no diagrammatic distinction between strong and weak entities when using the UML notation.

FIGURE 5.12 **A weak entity in an ERD**

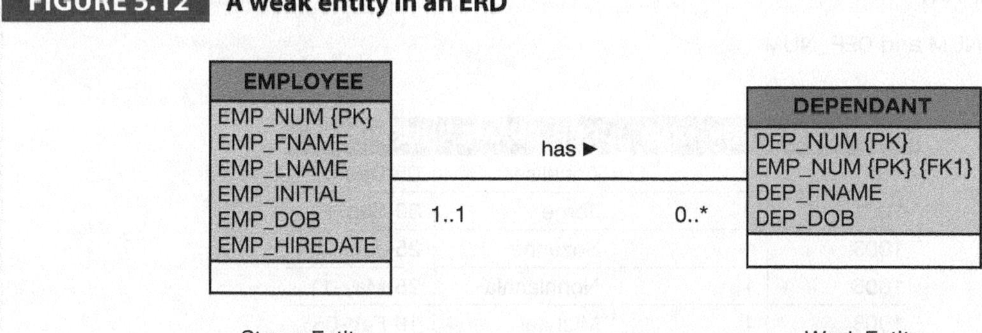

Remember that the weak entity inherits part of its primary key from its strong counterpart. For example, at least part of the DEPENDANT entity's key shown in Figure 5.12 was inherited from the EMPLOYEE entity:

EMPLOYEE (EMP_NUM, EMP_LNAME, EMP_FNAME, EMP_INITIAL, EMP_DOB, EMP_HIREDATE)

DEPENDANT (EMP_NUM, DEP_NUM, DEP_FNAME, DEP_DOB)

Figure 5.13 illustrates the implementation of the relationship between the weak entity (DEPENDANT) and its parent or strong counterpart (EMPLOYEE). Note that DEPENDANT's primary key is composed of two attributes, EMP_NUM and DEP_NUM, and that EMP_NUM was inherited from EMPLOYEE. Given this scenario and with the help of this relationship, you can determine:

Linda J. De Lange claims two dependants, Annelise and Jorge.

FIGURE 5.13 A weak entity in a strong relationship

Database name: CH05_ShortCo

Table name: EMPLOYEE

Primary key: EMP_NUM

EMP_NUM	EMP_LNAME	EMP_FNAME	EMP_INITIAL	EMP_DOB	EMP_HIREDATE
1001	De Lange	Linda	J	12-Mar-74	25-May-07
1002	Smithson	William	K	23-Nov-80	28-May-07
1003	Washington	Herman	H	15-Aug-78	28-May-07
1004	Chen	Lydia	B	23-Mar-84	15-Oct-08
1005	Johnson	Melanie		28-Sep-76	20-Dec-08
1006	Khumalo	Mandla	G	12-Jul-89	05-Jan-12
1007	O'Donnell	Peter	D	10-Jun-81	23-Jun-12
1008	Brzenski	Barbara	A	12-Feb-80	01-Nov-13

Table name: DEPENDANT

Primary keys: EMP_NUM and DEP_NUM

Foreign key: EMP_NUM

EMP_NUM	DEP_NUM	DEP_FNAME	DEP_DOB
1001	1	Annelise	05-Dec-07
1001	2	Jorge	30-Sep-12
1003	1	Suzanne	25-Jan-14
1006	1	Nonhlanhla	25-May-11
1008	1	Michael	19-Feb-05
1008	2	George	27-Jun-08
1008	3	Katherine	18-Aug-13

Keep in mind that the database designer usually determines whether an entity can be described as weak based on the business rules. An examination of the relationship between TRAVEL_AGENT and

EMPLOYEE in Figure 5.10 may cause you to conclude that EMPLOYEE is a weak entity to TRAVEL AGENT. After all, if you examine the EMPLOYEE rows in Figure 5.10, it seems clear that a EMPLOYEE cannot exist without being employed by a travel agency; so there is existence dependency. For example, employee Mosa Lefu cannot be an employee unless he is attached to an existing travel agent, in this case is the travel agent called 'FlightLite'. Note that the EMPLOYEE table's primary key is EMP_ID, which is not derived from the COURSE parent entity. That is, EMPLOYEE may be represented by:

EMPLOYEE(EMP_ID, AGENT_ID, EMP_LNAME, EMP_FNAME, EMP_PHONE, EMP_GRADE, PAYROLL_NO)

The second weak entity requirement has not been met; therefore, by definition, the EMPLOYEE entity in Figure 5.10 may not be classified as weak. On the other hand, if the EMPLOYEE entity's primary key had been defined as a composite key, composed of the combination AGENT_ID and PAYROLL_NO, EMPLOYEE could be represented by:

EMPLOYEE(AGENT_ID, PAYROLL_NO, EMP_LNAME, EMP_FNAME, EMP_PHONE, EMP_GRADE)

In that case, illustrated in Figure 5.11, the EMPLOYEE primary key is partially derived from TRAVEL_AGENT because AGENT_ID is the TRAVEL_AGENT table's primary key. Given this decision, EMPLOYEE is a weak entity by definition. (In Visio Professional Crow's Foot terms, the relationship between TRAVEL AGENT and EMPLOYEE is classified as strong, or identifying.) In any case, EMPLOYEE is always existence-dependent on TRAVEL_AGENT, *whether or not it is defined as weak*.

5.1.8 Relationship Participation

Participation in an entity relationship is either optional or mandatory. **Optional participation** means that one entity occurrence does not *require* a corresponding entity occurrence in a particular relationship. For example, consider the relationship between the two entities BOOKING and FLIGHT in Figure 5.14. In the 'BOOKING consists of FLIGHT' relationship, at least some bookings may not be for a flight. In other words, an entity occurrence (row) in the BOOKING table does not necessarily require the existence of a corresponding entity occurrence in the FLIGHT table. (Remember that each entity is implemented as a table.) Therefore, the FLIGHT entity is considered to be *optional* to the BOOKING entity.

In UML notation, an optional relationship between entities is shown by a 0..1 or 0..* multiplicity as illustrated in Figure 5.11. The existence of an *optionality* indicates that the minimum cardinality is 0 for the optional entity. (The term *optionality* is used to label any condition in which one or more optional relationships exist.)

FIGURE 5.14 **An optional FLIGHT entity in the relationship BOOKING consists of FLIGHT**

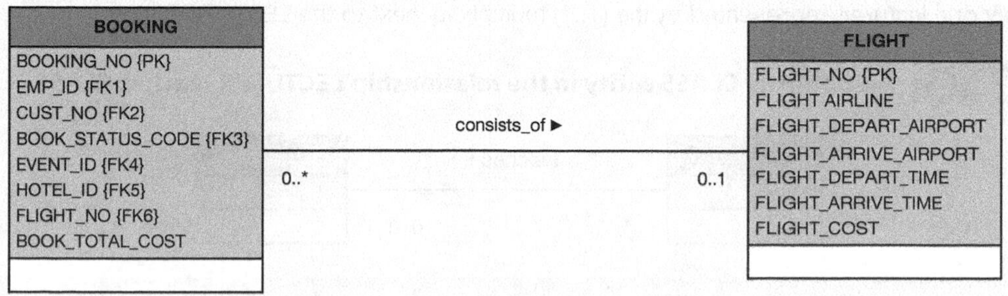

NOTE

Remember that the burden of establishing the relationship is always placed on the entity that contains the foreign key. In most cases, that will be the entity on the many side of the relationship.

Mandatory participation means that one entity occurrence *requires* a corresponding entity occurrence in a particular relationship. If no optionality symbol is depicted with the entity, the entity exists in a mandatory relationship with the related entity. The existence of a mandatory relationship indicates that the minimum cardinality is 1 for the mandatory entity.

5

NOTE

You may be tempted to conclude that relationships are weak when they occur between entities in an optional relationship and that relationships are strong when they occur between entities in a mandatory relationship. However, this conclusion is not warranted. Keep in mind that relationship participation and relationship strength do not describe the same thing. You are likely to encounter a strong relationship when one entity is optional to another. For example, the relationship between EMPLOYEE and DEPENDANT is clearly a strong one, but DEPENDANT is just as clearly optional to EMPLOYEE. After all, you cannot *require* employees to have dependents. And it is just as possible for a weak relationship to be established when one entity is mandatory to another. *The relationship strength depends on how the PK of the related entity is formulated, while the relationship participation depends on how the business rule is written*. For example, the business rules 'Each part must be supplied by a vendor' and 'A part may or may not be supplied by a vendor' create different optionalities for the same entities! Failure to understand this distinction may lead to poor design decisions that cause major problems when table rows are inserted or deleted.

Since relationship participation turns out to be an important component of the database design process, let's examine a few more scenarios. Suppose that Tiny University employs some lecturers who conduct research without teaching classes. If you examine the 'LECTURER teaches CLASS' relationship, it is quite possible for a LECTURER not to teach a CLASS. Therefore, CLASS is *optional* to LECTURER. On the other hand, a CLASS must be taught by a LECTURER. Therefore, LECTURER is *mandatory* to CLASS. Note that the ERD model shown in Figure 5.15 shows the multiplicity next to CLASS to be (0..3), thus indicating that a lecturer may teach no classes at all or as many as three classes. And each CLASS table row will reference one and only one LECTURER row – assuming each class is taught by one and only one lecturer, represented by the (1..1) multiplicity next to the LECTURER table.

FIGURE 5.15 An optional CLASS entity in the relationship LECTURER teaches CLASS

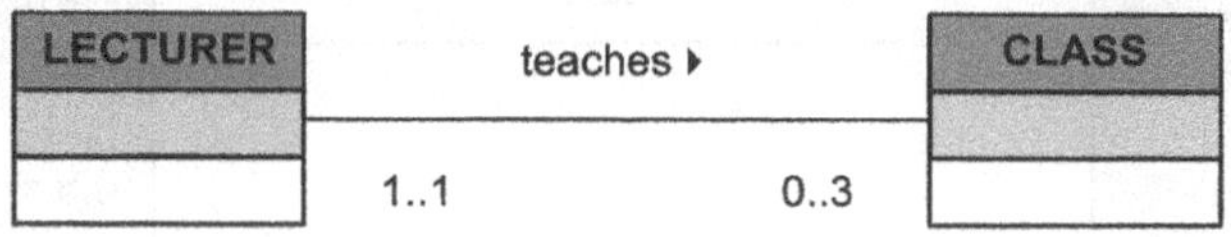

Failure to understand the distinction between *mandatory* and *optional* participation in relationships may yield designs in which awkward (and unnecessary) temporary rows (entity instances) must be created just to accommodate the creation of required entities. Therefore, it is important that you clearly understand the concepts of mandatory and optional participation.

It is also important to understand that the semantics of a problem may determine the type of participation in a relationship. For example, suppose that Tiny University offers several courses; each course has several classes. Note again the distinction between *class* and *course* in this discussion: a CLASS constitutes a specific offering (or section) of a COURSE. (Typically, courses are listed in the university's course catalogue, while classes are listed in the class schedules that students use to register for their classes.)

Analysing the CLASS entity's contribution to the 'COURSE generates CLASS' relationship, it is easy to see that a CLASS cannot exist without a COURSE. Therefore, you can conclude that the COURSE entity is *mandatory* in the relationship. Two scenarios for the CLASS entity may be written, shown in Figures 5.16 and 5.17. The different scenarios are a function of the semantics of the problem; that is, they depend on how the relationship is defined:

1 *CLASS is optional*. It is possible for the department to create the entity COURSE first and then create the CLASS entity after making the teaching assignments. In the real world, such a scenario is very likely; there may be courses for which sections (classes) have not yet been defined. In fact, some courses are taught only once a year and do not generate classes each semester.

FIGURE 5.16 CLASS is optional to COURSE

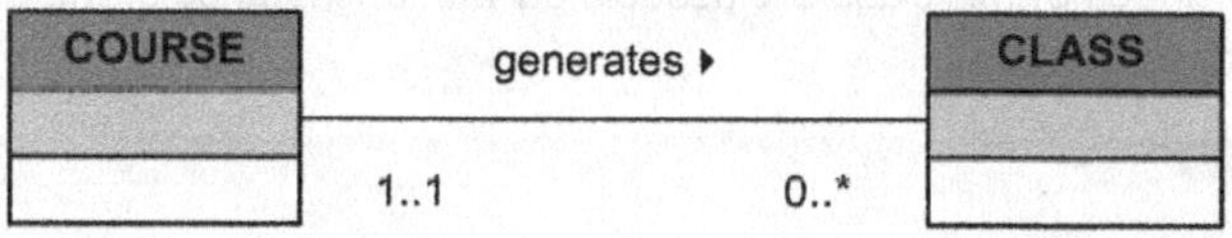

COURSE generates ▸ CLASS
1..1 0..*

2 *CLASS is mandatory*. This condition is created by the constraint that is imposed by the semantics of the statement 'Each COURSE generates one or more CLASSes'. In ER terms, each COURSE in the 'generates' relationship must have at least one CLASS. Therefore, a CLASS must be created as the COURSE is created in order to comply with the semantics of the problem.

FIGURE 5.17 COURSE and CLASS in a mandatory relationship

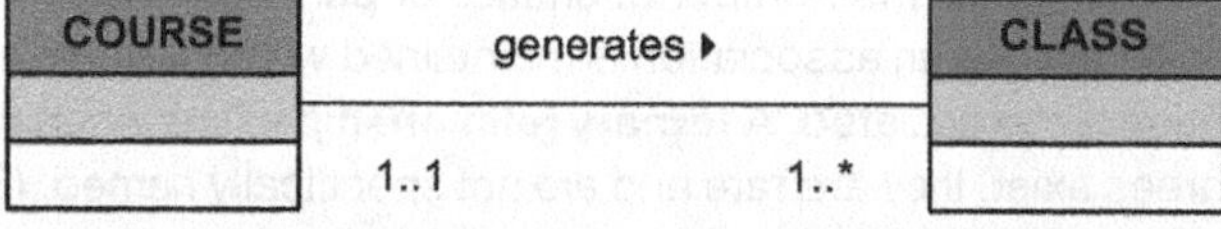

Keep in mind the practical aspects of the scenario presented in Figure 5.17. Given the semantics of this relationship, the system should not accept a course that is not associated with at least one class. Is such a rigid environment desirable from an operational point of view? For example, when a new COURSE is created, the database first updates the COURSE table, thereby inserting a COURSE entity that does not yet have a CLASS associated with it. Naturally, the apparent problem seems to be solved when CLASS entities are inserted into the corresponding CLASS table. However, because of the mandatory relationship, the system will be in temporary violation of the business rule constraint. For practical purposes, it would be desirable to classify the CLASS as optional in order to produce a more flexible design.

Finally, as you examine the scenarios presented in Figures 5.16 and 5.17, keep in mind the role of the DBMS. To maintain data integrity, the DBMS must ensure that the 'many' side (CLASS) is associated with a COURSE through the foreign key rules.

When you create a relationship in MS Visio using UML, the default relationship will be optional and 'many' on both sides. Table 5.3 shows the various multiplicities that are supported by the UML notation.

5

TABLE 5.3 Multiplicity

Multiplicity	Description
0..1	A minimum of zero and a maximum of one instance of this class are associated with an instance of the other related class (indicates an optional class).
0..*	A minimum of zero and a maximum of many instances of this class are associated with an instance of the other related class (indicates an optional class).
1..1	A minimum of one and a maximum of one instance of this class are associated with an instance of the other related class (indicates a mandatory class).
1..*	A minimum of one and a maximum of many instances of this class are associated with an instance of the other related class (indicates a mandatory class).
1	Exactly one instance of this class is associated with an instance of the other related class (indicates a mandatory class). In other words, equivalent to 1..1.
*	Many instances of this class are associated with an instance of the other related class. Equivalent to 0..*.

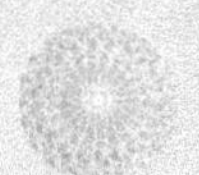

Online Content To learn how to define relationships properly with the help of MS Visio, see Appendix A, Designing Databases with Visio Professional: A Tutorial, available on the online platform for this book.

5.1.9 Relationship Degree

A **relationship degree** indicates the number of entities or participants associated with a relationship. A **unary relationship** exists when an association is maintained within a single entity. A **binary relationship** exists when two entities are associated. A **ternary relationship** exists when three entities are associated. Although higher degrees exist, they are rare and are not specifically named. (For example, an association of four entities is described simply as a *four-degree relationship*.) Figure 5.18 shows these types of relationship degrees using UML notation.

Unary Relationships

In the case of the unary relationship shown in Figure 5.18, an employee within the EMPLOYEE entity is the manager for one or more employees within that entity. In this case, the existence of the 'manages' relationship means that EMPLOYEE requires another EMPLOYEE to be the manager – that is, EMPLOYEE has a relationship with itself. Such a relationship is known as a **recursive relationship**. The different cases of recursive relationships will be explored in Section 5.1.10.

Binary Relationships

A binary relationship exists when two entities are associated in a relationship. Binary relationships are most common. In fact, to simplify the conceptual design, whenever possible, most higher-order (ternary and higher) relationships are decomposed into appropriate equivalent binary relationships. In Figure 5.18, the relationship 'a LECTURER teaches one or more CLASSes' represents a binary relationship.

FIGURE 5.18 Three types of relationship degree

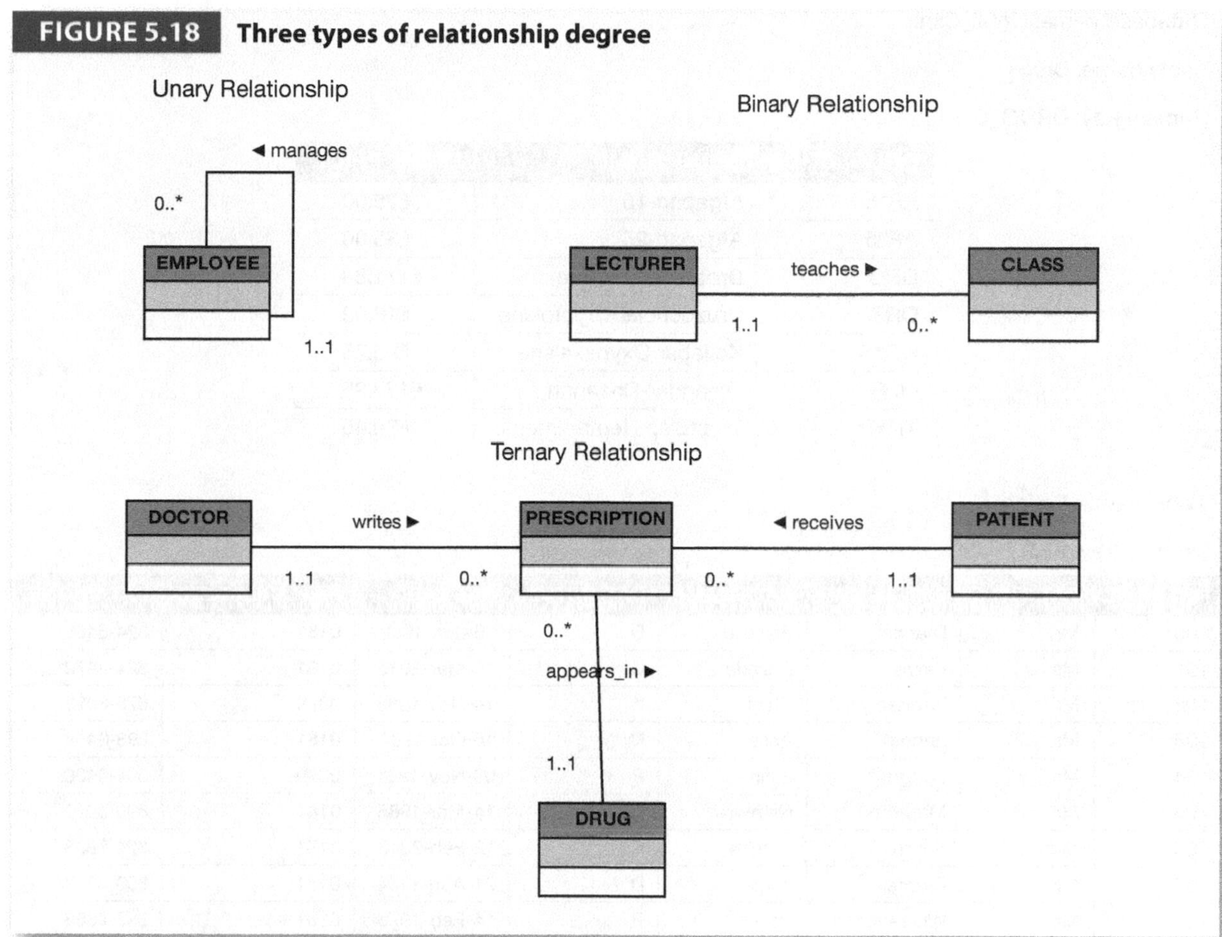

Ternary and Higher-Order Relationships

Although most relationships are binary, the use of ternary and higher-order relationships does allow the designer some latitude regarding the semantics of a problem. A ternary relationship implies an association among three different entities. For example, note the relationships (and their consequences) in Figure 5.18, which are represented by the following business rules:

- A DOCTOR writes one or more PRESCRIPTIONs.
- A PATIENT may receive one or more PRESCRIPTIONs.
- A DRUG may appear on one or more PRESCRIPTIONs. (To simplify this example, assume that the business rule states that each prescription contains only one drug. In short, if a doctor prescribes more than one drug, a separate prescription must be written for each drug.)

5

The reason why this is a ternary relationship and not three binary relationships is because the associate entity PRESCRIPTION reflects a single event or object that simultaneously includes all three parent entities (DOCTOR, PATIENT and DRUG).

FIGURE 5.19 The implementation of a ternary relationship

Database name: Ch05_Clinic

Table name: Drug

Primary key: DRUG_CODE

DRUG_CODE	DRUG_NAME	DRUG_PRICE
AF15	Afgapan-15	€25.00
AF25	Afgapan-25	€35.00
DRO	Droalene Chloride	€111.89
DRZ	Druzocholar Cryptolene	€18.99
KO15	Koliabar Oxyhexalene	€65.75
OLE	Oleander-Drizapan	€123.95
TRYP	Tryptolac Heptadimetric	€79.45

Table name: Patient

Primary key: PAT_NUM

PAT_NUM	PAT_TITLE	PAT_LNAME	PAT_FNAME	PAT_INITIAL	PAT_DOB	PAT_AREACODE	PAT_PHONE
100	Mr	Dlamini	Phindile	D	15-Jun-1952	0181	324-5456
101	Ms	Lewis	Rhonda	G	19-Mar-2015	0181	324-4472
102	Mr	Vandam	Rhett		14-Nov-1968	0879	675-8993
103	Ms	Jones	Anne	M	16-Oct-1984	0181	898-3456
104	Mr	Lange	John	P	08-Nov-1981	0879	504-4430
105	Mr	Mthembu	Nsizwa	D	14-Mar-1985	0181	890-3220
106	Mrs	Smith	Jeanine	K	12-Feb-2013	0181	324-7883
107	Mr	Diante	Jorge	D	21-Aug-1984	0181	890-4567
108	Mr	Wiesenbach	Paul	R	14-Feb-1976	0181	897-4358
109	Mr	Smith	George	K	18-Jun-1971	0879	504-3339
110	Mrs	Genkazi	Leighla	W	19-May-1980	0879	569-0093
111	Mr	Washington	Rupert	E	03-Jan-1976	0181	890-4925
112	Mr	Johnson	Edward	E	14-May-1971	0181	898-4387
113	Ms	Gounden	Melanie	P	15-Sep-1980	0181	324-9006
114	Ms	Brandon	Marie	G	02-Nov-1942	0879	882-0845
115	Mrs	Saranda	Hermine	R	25-Jul-1982	0181	324-5505
116	Mr	Smith	George	A	08-Nov-1975	0181	890-2984

Table name: Doctor

Primary keys: DOC_ID

DOC_ID	DOC_LNAME	DOC_FNAME	DOC_INITIAL	DOC_SPECIALTY
29827	Ndosi	Sipho	J	Dermatology
32445	Jorgensen	Annelise	G	Neurology
33456	Jali	Phakamile	A	Urology
33989	LeGrande	George		Paediatrics
34409	Washington	Dennis	F	Orthopaedics
36221	McPherson	Katye	H	Dermatology
36712	Dreifag	Herman	G	Psychiatry
38995	Minh	Tran		Neurology
40004	Chin	Ming	D	Orthopaedics
40028	Cele	Denise	L	Gynaecology

Table name: Prescription

Primary key: DRUG_CODE, DOC_ID and PAT_NUM, PRES_DATE

Foreign keys: DRUG_CODE, DOC_ID and PAT_NUM

DOC_ID	PAT_NUM	DRUG_CODE	PRES_DOSAGE	PRES_DATE
32445	102	DRZ	two tablets every four hours – 50 tablets total	12-Nov-19
32445	113	OLE	one teaspoon with each meal – 250 ml total	14-Nov-19
34409	101	KO15	one tablet every six hours – 30 tablets total	14-Nov-19
36221	109	DRO	two tablets with every meal – 60 tablets total	14-Nov-19
38995	107	KO15	one tablet every six hours – 30 tablets total	14-Nov-19

As you examine the table contents in Figure 5.18, note that it is possible to track all transactions. For instance, you can tell that the first prescription was written by doctor 32445 for patient 102, using the drug DRZ on 12 November 2019.

5.1.10 Recursive Relationships

As was previously mentioned, a *recursive relationship* is one in which a relationship can exist between occurrences of the same entity set. (Naturally, such a condition is found within a unary relationship.)

For example, a 1:* unary relationship can be expressed by 'an EMPLOYEE may manage many EMPLOYEEs, and each EMPLOYEE is managed by one EMPLOYEE'. As long as polygamy is not legal, a 1:1 unary relationship may be expressed by 'an EMPLOYEE may be married to one and only one other EMPLOYEE'. Finally, the *:* unary relationship may be expressed by 'a COURSE may be a prerequisite to many other COURSEs, and each COURSE may have many other COURSEs as prerequisites'. Those relationships are shown in Figure 5.20.

5

FIGURE 5.20 An ER representation of a recursive relationship

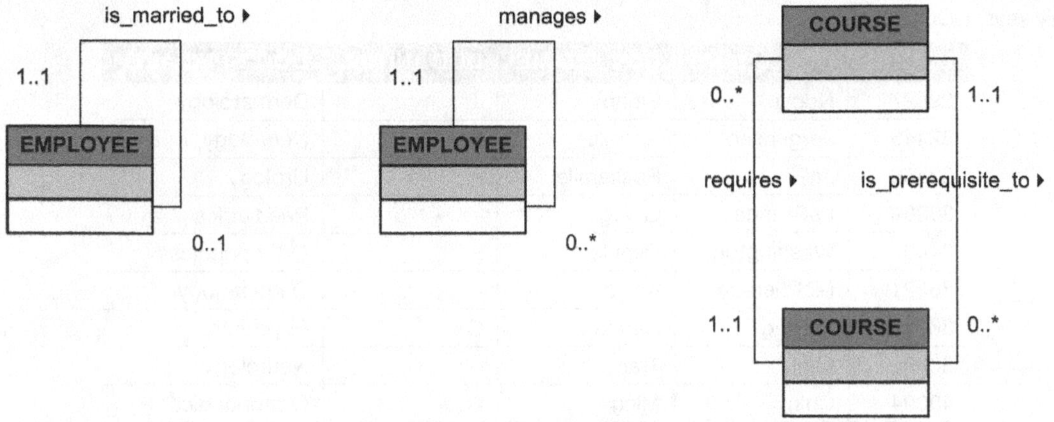

The 1:1 relationship shown in Figure 5.20 can be implemented in the single table shown in Figure 5.21. Note that you can determine that Nishok Singh is married to Vediga Singh, who is married to Nishok Singh. Anne Jones is married to Anton Shapiro, who is married to Anne Jones.

FIGURE 5.21 The 1:1 recursive relationship 'EMPLOYEE is married to EMPLOYEE'

Database name: Ch05_PartCo

Table name: EMPLOYEE_V1

EMP_NUM	EMP_LNAME	EMP_FNAME	EMP_SPOUSE
345	Singh	Nishok	347
346	Jones	Anne	349
347	Singh	Vediga	345
348	Delaney	Robert	
349	Shapiro	Anton	346

FIGURE 5.22 Another Unary relationship 'PART contains PART'

Database name: Ch05_PartCo

Table name: PART_V1

PART_CODE	PART_DESCRIPTION	PART_IN_STOCK	PART_UNITS_NEEDED	PART_OF_PART
AA21-6	2.5 cm washer, 1.0 mm rim	432	4	C-130
AB-121	Cotter pin, copper	1034	2	C-130
C-130	Rotor assembly	36		
E129	2.5 cm steel shank	128	1	C-130
X10	10.25 cm rotor blade	345	4	C-130
X34AW	2.5 cm hex nut	879	2	C-130

Unary relationships are common in manufacturing industries. For example, Figure 5.22 illustrates that a rotor assembly (C-130) is composed of many parts, but each part is used to create only one rotor assembly. Figure 5.22 indicates that a rotor assembly is composed of four 2.5 cm washers, two cotter pins, one 2.5 cm steel shank, four 10.25 cm rotor blades and two 2.5 cm hex nuts. The relationship implemented in Figure 5.21 thus enables you to track each part within each rotor assembly.

If a part can be used to assemble several different kinds of other parts and is itself composed of many parts, two tables are required to implement the 'PART contains PART' relationship. Figure 5.23 illustrates such an environment. Parts tracking is increasingly important as managers become more aware of the legal ramifications of producing more complex output. In fact, in many industries, especially those involving aviation, full parts tracking is mandatory.

FIGURE 5.23 Implementation of the *:* recursive 'PART contains PART' relationship

Database name: Ch05_PartCo

Table name: COMPONENT

COMP_CODE	PART_CODE	COMP_PARTS_NEEDED
C-130	AA21-6	4
C-130	AB-121	2
C-130	E129	1
C-131A2	E129	1
C-130	X10	4
C-131A2	X10	1
C-130	X34AW	2
C-131A2	X34AW	2

Table name: PART

PART_CODE	PART_DESCRIPTION	PART_IN_STOCK
AA21-6	2.5 cm washer, 1.0 mm rim	432
AB-121	Cotter pin, copper	1 034
C-130	Rotor assembly	36
E129	2.5 cm steel shank	128
X10	10.25 cm rotor blade	345
X34AW	2.5 cm hex nut	879

The *:* recursive relationship might be more familiar in a school environment. For instance, note how the *:* 'COURSE requires COURSE' relationship illustrated in Figure 5.20 is implemented in Figure 5.24. In this example, MATH-243 is a prerequisite to QM-261 and QM-362, while both MATH-243 and QM-261 are prerequisites to QM-362.

FIGURE 5.24 Implementation of the *:* recursive 'COURSE requires COURSE' relationship

Database name: Ch05_TinyUniversity

Table name: COURSE

CRS_CODE	DEPT_CODE	CRS_DESCRIPTION	CRS_CREDIT
ACCT-211	ACCT	Accounting I	3
ACCT-212	ACCT	Accounting II	3
CIS-220	CIS	Intro. to Computer Science	3
CIS-420	CIS	Database Design and Implementation	4
MATH-243	MATH	Mathematics for Managers	3
QM-261	CIS	Intro. to Statistics	3
QM-362	CIS	Statistical Applications	4

Table name: PREREQ

CRS_CODE	PRE_TAKE
CIS-420	CIS-220
QM-261	MATH-243
QM-362	MATH-243
QM-362	QM-261

Finally, the 1:* recursive relationship 'EMPLOYEE manages EMPLOYEE', shown in Figure 5.20, is implemented in Figure 5.25.

FIGURE 5.25 Implementation of the 1:* 'EMPLOYEE manages EMPLOYEE' recursive relationship

Database name: Ch05_PartCo

Table name: EMPLOYEE_V2

EMP_CODE	EMP_LNAME	EMP_MANAGER
101	Mazwai	102
102	Orincona	
103	Jones	102
104	Malherbe	102
105	Robertson	102
106	Deltona	102

5.1.11 Composite Entities

You should recall from Chapter 3, Relational Model Characteristics, that the relational model generally requires the use of 1:* relationships. (You should also recall that the 1..1 relationship has its place, but it should be used with caution and proper justification.) If *:* relationships are encountered, you must create a bridge between the entities that display such relationships. Recall that the *bridge entity* (also known as a *composite entity*) is composed of the primary keys of each of the entities to be connected. (An example of such a bridge is shown in Figure 5.26.)

FIGURE 5.26 Converting the *:* relationship into two 1:* relationships

Database name: CH05_Travel_Agent

Table name: BOOKING

BOOKING_ NO	EMP_ID	CUST_ NO	BOOK_ STATUS_ CODE	EVENT_ ID	HOTEL_ ID	FLIGHT_ NO	BOOK_ TOTAL_ COST	BOOKING_ DATE
204200	1239986	101	1				225	06/04/2019
301200	1239986	102	1				90	04/02/2019
401211	4000768	1099	2				185	25/05/2019

Table name: TOUR_BOOKING

TOUR_ID	BOOKING_NO	TOUR_DATE
1001	401211	06/07/2019
1002	401211	08/07/2019
1004	204200	03/08/2019
1005	301200	07/09/2019
1001	301200	28/09/2019

Table name: TOUR

TOUR_ ID	TOUR_ NAME	TOUR_DESCRIPTION	TOUR_ PRICE_ ADULT	TOUR_ PRICE_ CHILD	TOUR_ PRICE_ CON
1001	The Total London Experience	See the changing of the guards at Buckingham Palace, Covent Garden, the London Eye, St Paul's Cathedral, Westminster Abbey, the river Thames and more. Meeting Point: 4 Fountain Square. Daily at 08:45 a.m.	120	99	99
1002	London Gems	Visit the Tower of London and the Crown Jewels and go on a boat cruise on the River Thames. Meet 123–151 Buckingham Palace Road. Daily at 1:00 p.m.	65	50	55
1003	Big Bus City Tour	See nine attractions including the Eiffel Tower. Hop on and off in nine different places. Receive details of stops when booking.	26	20	20
1004	Paris Night Tour	Enjoy dinner at the 58 Tour Eiffel restaurant, located on the first floor of the Eiffel Tower, then take a relaxing scenic Seine River cruise. Departs daily at 6:15 p.m.	125	100	115
1005	Nairobi National Park Day Tour	Pick up from location/locations to be advised 7:45 p.m. Arrive at the Nairobi National Park for the game drive/park formalities. Go on escorted Safari Walk.	20	10	20

As you examine Figure 5.26, note that the composite TOUR_BOOKING entity is existence-dependent on the other two entities; its composition is based on the primary keys of the entities that are connected by the composite entity. The composite entity may also contain additional attributes that play no role in the connective process. For example, although the entity must be composed of at least the BOOKING and TOUR primary keys, it may also include any additional attributes, in this case the tour date which uniquely identifies the date on which that instance of the tour will take place for a specific booking.

Finally, keep in mind that the TOUR_BOOKING table's key (TOUR_ID and BOOKING_NO) is composed entirely of the primary keys of the BOOKING and TOUR tables. Therefore, no null entries are possible in the TOUR_BOOKING table's key attributes.

Implementing the small database shown in Figure 5.26 requires that you define the relationships clearly. Specifically, you must know the '1' and the '*' sides of each relationship, and you must know whether the relationships are mandatory or optional. For example, note the following points:

- A TOUR may exist even though no bookings have currently been made for it. Therefore, if you examine Figure 5.27, an optional multiplicity (0..*) should appear on the BOOKING side of the *:* relationship between BOOKING and TOUR.

FIGURE 5.27 The *:* relationship between BOOKING AND TOUR

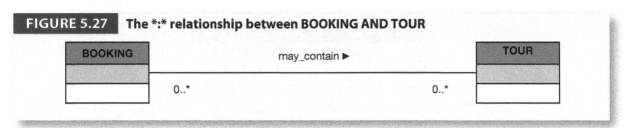

BOOKING — may_contain ▶ — TOUR (0..* / 0..*)

You might argue that, for a tour to exist, at least one BOOKING must be made. Therefore, TOUR is mandatory to BOOKING from a purely conceptual point of view. However, when a new tour is first offered, it will not have had the opportunity to be booked. Therefore, at least initially, TOUR is optional to BOOKING. Note that the practical considerations in the data environment help dictate the use of optionalities. If TOUR is *not* optional to BOOKING – from a database point of view – a booking must be made for the tour to allow it to be included in the database. But that's not how the process actually works. In short, the optionality reflects practice.

The ERD in Figure 5.28 shows that the *:* relationship between BOOKING and TOUR has been decomposed into two 1:* relationships through TOUR_BOOKING. In Figure 5.28, the optionalities have been transferred to TOUR_BOOKING. In other words, it now becomes possible for a TOUR not to occur in TOUR_BOOKING if no customer has actually booked that tour. Because a tour need not occur in TOUR_BOOKING, the TOUR_BOOKING entity becomes optional to BOOKING. And because the TOUR_BOOKING entity is created before any bookings have been made, the TOUR_BOOKING entity is also optional to BOOKING.

FIGURE 5.28 A composite entity in an ERD

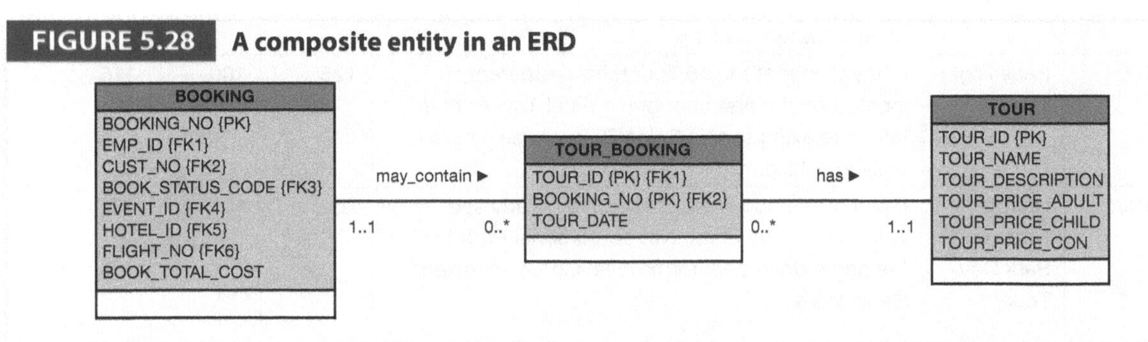

> **NOTE**
>
> In a UML class diagram, an association class is used to represent a *:* association between two entities. The association class exists within the context of the associated entities and, as in the ER model, the association class can have its own attributes. Figure 5.29 shows the use of an TOUR_BOOKING association class to represent the *:* relationship between BOOKING and TOUR. Note the multiplicities (0..*) on each side of the relationship, which indicate that both the participation of BOOKING and TOUR are optional.

FIGURE 5.29 An association class

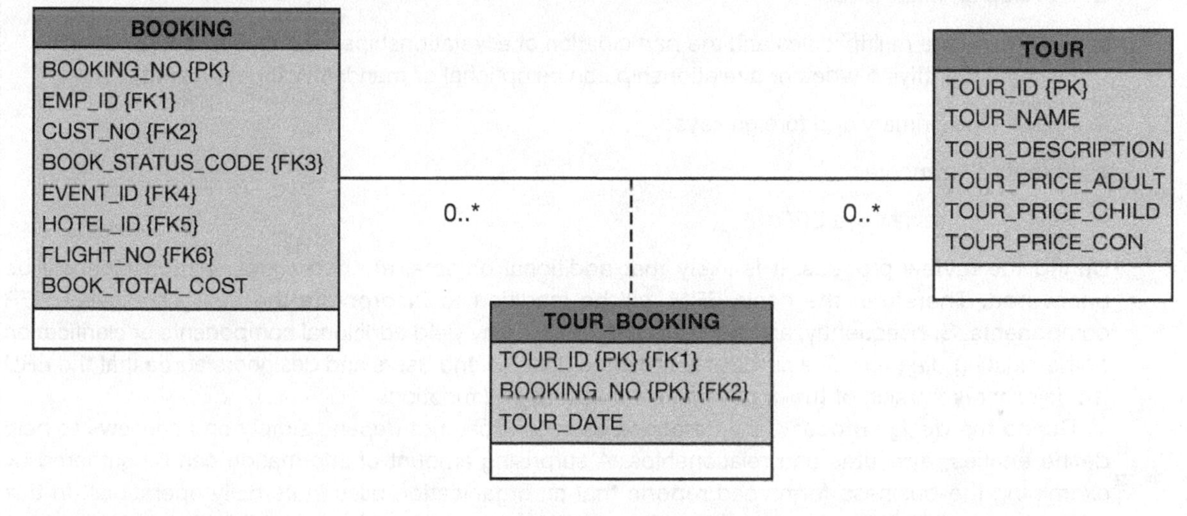

- As customers make bookings for specific tours, they will be entered into the TOUR_BOOKING entity. Naturally, if a customer books more than one tour, then that customers' booking number will appear more than once in TOUR_BOOKING. For example, note that BOOKING_NO = 401211 occurs twice in the TOUR_BOOKING table in Figure 5.26. On the other hand, each customer booking number occurs only once in the BOOKING entity. (Note that the BOOKING table in Figure 5.26 has only one that BOOKING_NO = 401211 entry.) Therefore, the relationship between BOOKING and TOUR_BOOKING is shown to be 1:* in Figure 5.28, with the * (shown as the multiplicity (0..*)) on the TOUR_BOOKING side.
- If you examine the tables shown in Figure 5.26, you will see that a tour can occur more than once in the TOUR_BOOKING table. For example, TOUR_ID = 1001 occurs twice in the TOUR_BOOKING table. However, TOUR_ID = 1001 occurs only once in the TOUR table to reflect that the relationship between TOUR_BOOKING and TOUR is 1:*. Note that, in Figure 5.28, the * (shown as the multiplicity (0..*)) is located on the TOUR_BOOKING side, while the 1 (shown as the multiplicity (1..1)) is located on the TOUR side.

5.2 DEVELOPING AN ER DIAGRAM

The process of database design is an iterative rather than a linear or sequential process. The verb *iterate* means 'to do again or repeatedly'. An **iterative process** is thus one based on repetition of processes and procedures. Building an ERD usually involves the following activities:

- Create a detailed narrative of the organisation's description of operations.
- Identify the business rules based on the descriptions of operations.
- Identify all main entities from the business rules.
- Identify all main relationships between entities from the business rules.
- Develop an initial ERD.
- Determine the multiplicities and the participation of all relationships. Remember, participation involves identifying whether a relationship can be optional or mandatory for each entity.
- Identify the primary and foreign keys.
- Identify all attributes.
- Revise and review the ERD.

During the review process, it is likely that additional objects, attributes and relationships will be uncovered. Therefore, the basic ERM will be modified to incorporate the newly discovered ER components. Subsequently, another round of reviews may yield additional components or clarification of the existing diagram. The process is repeated until the end users and designers agree that the ERD is a fair representation of the organisation's activities and functions.

During the design process, the database designer does not depend simply on interviews to help define entities, attributes and relationships. A surprising amount of information can be gathered by examining the business forms and reports that an organisation uses in its daily operations. In this section, we will use two case studies – Tiny University and ILoveHolidays – to show the interactive process involved in creating an ERD.

5.2.1 Tiny University Case Study

To start constructing an ERD, an initial interview is required with the Tiny University administrators. The interview process yields the following business rules:

1. Tiny University (TU) is divided into several schools: a school of business, a school of arts and sciences, a school of education, and a school of applied sciences. Each school is administered by a dean, who is a lecturer who has reached the grade of professor (LECT_GRADE has a value PROF). Keep in mind that each dean can administer only one school. Therefore, a 1:1 relationship exists between LECTURER and SCHOOL. Note that the multiplicity can be expressed by (1..1) for the entity LECTURER and by (0..1) for the entity SCHOOL. (The smallest number of deans per school is one, as is the largest number, and each dean is assigned to only one school.) However not all lecturers are deans, so we need to ensure that the entity SCHOOL has optional participation.
2. Each school is composed of several departments. For example, the school of business has an accounting department, a management/marketing department, an economics/finance department and a computer information systems department. Note again the cardinality rules: the smallest

number of departments operated by a school is one, and the largest number of departments is indeterminate (*). On the other hand, each department belongs to only a single school; thus, the multiplicity is expressed by (1..1). That is, the minimum number of schools that a department belongs to is one, as is the maximum number. Figure 5.30 illustrates these first two business rules.

NOTE

It is again appropriate to evaluate the reason for maintaining the 1:1 relationship between LECTURER and SCHOOL in the 'is dean of' relationship. It is worth repeating that the existence of 1:1 relationships often indicates a misidentification of attributes as entities. In this case, the 1:1 relationship could easily be eliminated by storing the dean's attributes in the SCHOOL entity. This solution also would make it easier to answer the queries, 'who is the school's dean?' and 'what are that dean's credentials?' The downside of this solution is that it requires the duplication of data that are already stored in the LECTURER table, thus setting the stage for anomalies. However, because each school is run by a single dean, the problem of data duplication is rather minor. The selection of one approach over another often depends on information requirements, transaction speed, and the database designer's professional judgement. In short, do not use 1:1 relationships lightly and make sure that each 1..1 relationship within the database design is defensible.

5

FIGURE 5.30 The first Tiny University segment

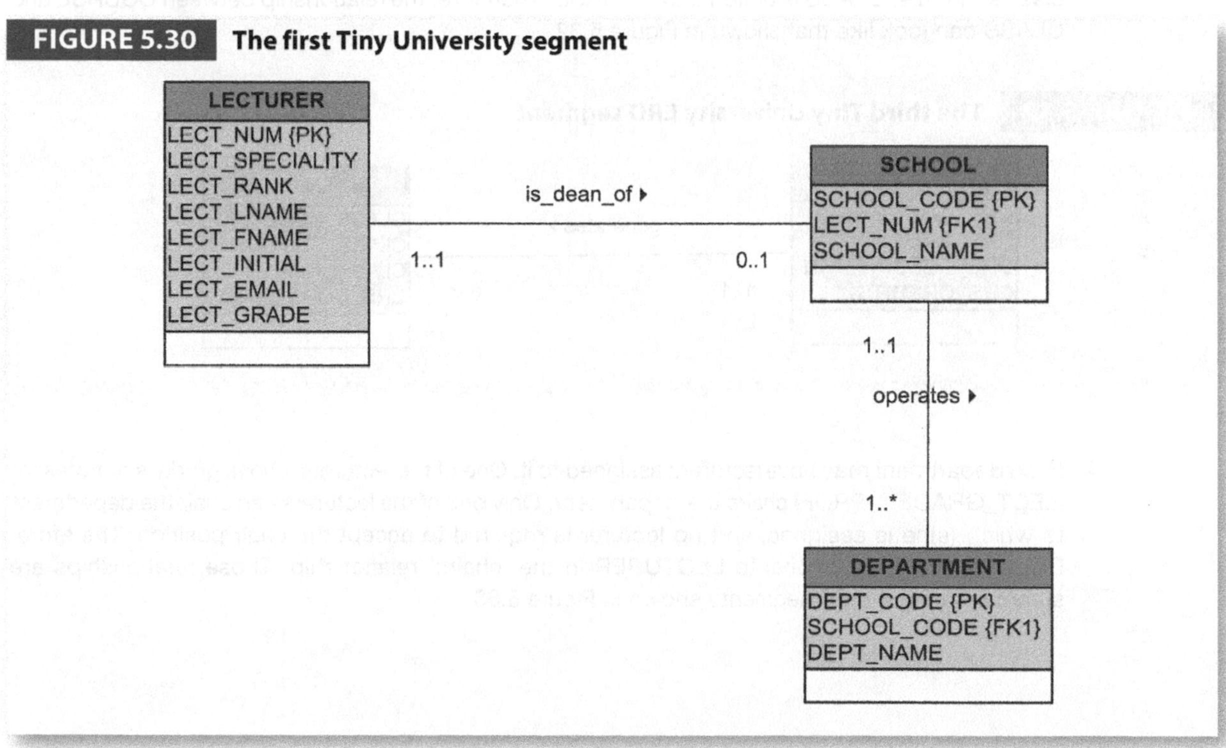

3 Each department may offer courses. For example, the management/marketing department offers courses such as Introduction to Management, Principles of Marketing, and Production Management. The ERD segment for this condition is shown in Figure 5.31. Note that this relationship is based on

the way Tiny University operates. If, for example, Tiny University had some departments that were classified as 'research only', those departments would not offer courses; therefore, the COURSE entity would be optional to the DEPARTMENT entity.

FIGURE 5.31 **The second Tiny University ERD segment**

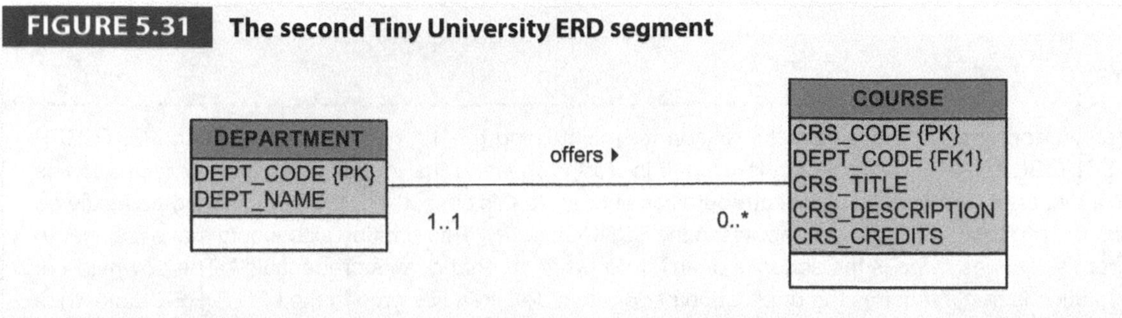

4 A CLASS is a section of a COURSE. That is, a department may offer several sections (classes) of the same database course. Each of those classes is taught by a lecturer at a given time in a given place. In short, a 1:* relationship exists between COURSE and CLASS. However, because a course may exist in Tiny University's course catalogue even when it is not offered as a class in a current class schedule, CLASS is optional to COURSE. Therefore, the relationship between COURSE and CLASS can look like that shown in Figure 5.32.

FIGURE 5.32 **The third Tiny University ERD segment**

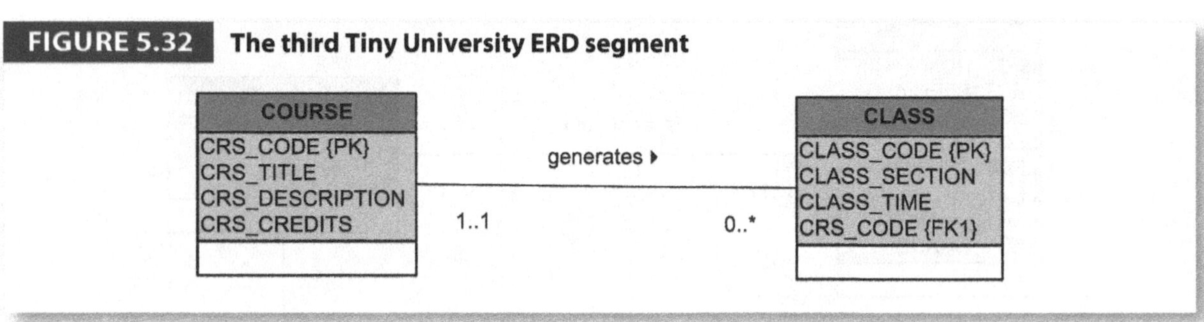

5 Each department may have lecturers assigned to it. One of the lecturers whose grade is a professor (LECT_GRADE = PROF) chairs the department. Only one of the lecturers can chair the department to which (s)he is assigned, and no lecturer is required to accept the chair position. Therefore, DEPARTMENT is optional to LECTURER in the 'chairs' relationship. Those relationships are summarised in the ER segments shown in Figure 5.33.

FIGURE 5.33 **The fourth Tiny University ERD segment**

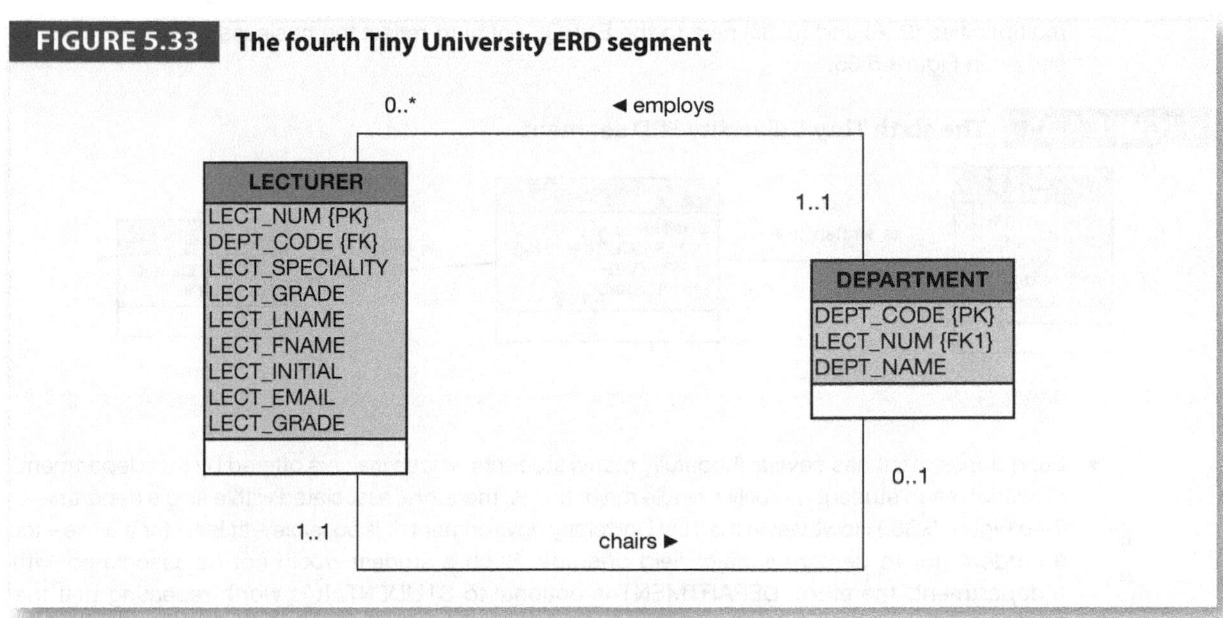

6 Each lecturer may teach up to four classes; each class is a section of a course. A lecturer may also be on a research contract and teach no classes at all. The ERD segments in Figure 5.34 depict those conditions.

FIGURE 5.34 **The fifth Tiny University ERD segment**

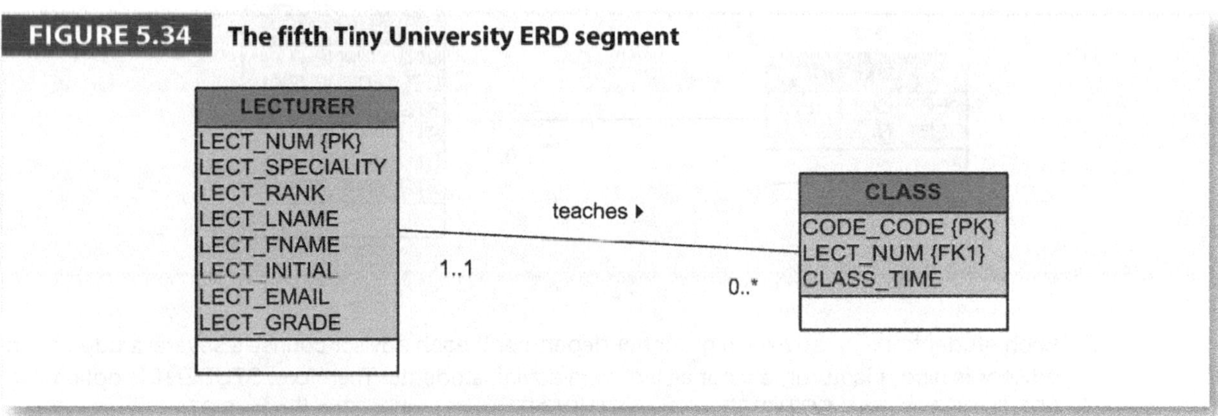

7 A student may enrol in several classes, but (s)he takes each class only once during any given enrolment period. For example, during the current enrolment period, a student may decide to take five classes – Statistics, Accounting, English, Database and History – but that student would not be enrolled in the same Statistics class five times during the enrolment period! Each student may enrol in up to six classes, and each class may have up to 35 students, thus creating a *:* relationship between STUDENT and CLASS. A CLASS can initially exist (at the start of the enrolment period) even though no students have enrolled in it, so STUDENT is optional to CLASS in the *:* relationship. This *:* relationship must be divided into two 1:* relationships, through the use of the ENROL entity shown in the ERD segment in Figure 5.35. But note that optional participation is shown next to ENROL. If a class exists that has no students enrolled in it, that class never occurs in the ENROL table. Note also that the ENROL entity is weak: it is existence-dependent, and its (composite) PK is composed of the PKs of the STUDENT and CLASS entities. You can add the

multiplicities (0..6) and (0..35) next to the ENROL entity to reflect the business rule constraints as shown in Figure 5.35.

FIGURE 5.35 **The sixth Tiny University ERD segment**

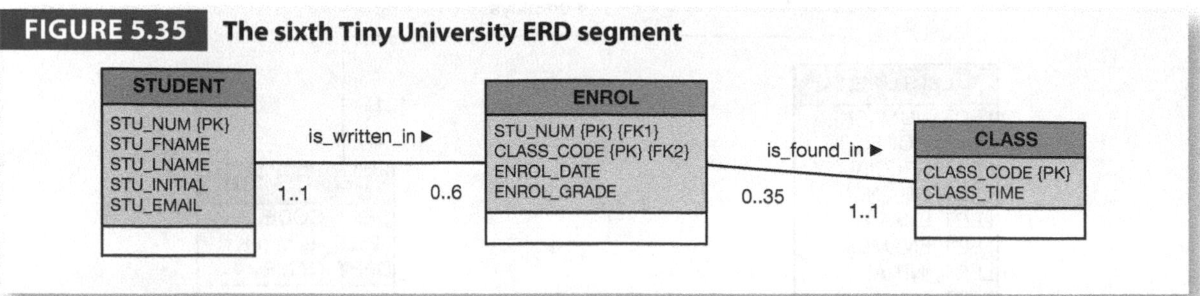

5

8 Each department has several (hopefully many) students whose major is offered by that department. However, each student has only a single major and is, therefore, associated with a single department. (See Figure 5.36.) However, in the Tiny University environment, it is possible – at least for a while – for a student not to declare a major field of study. Such a student would not be associated with a department; therefore, DEPARTMENT is optional to STUDENT. It is worth repeating that the relationships between entities and the entities themselves reflect the organisation's operating environment. That is, the business rules define the ERD components.

FIGURE 5.36 **The seventh Tiny University ERD segment**

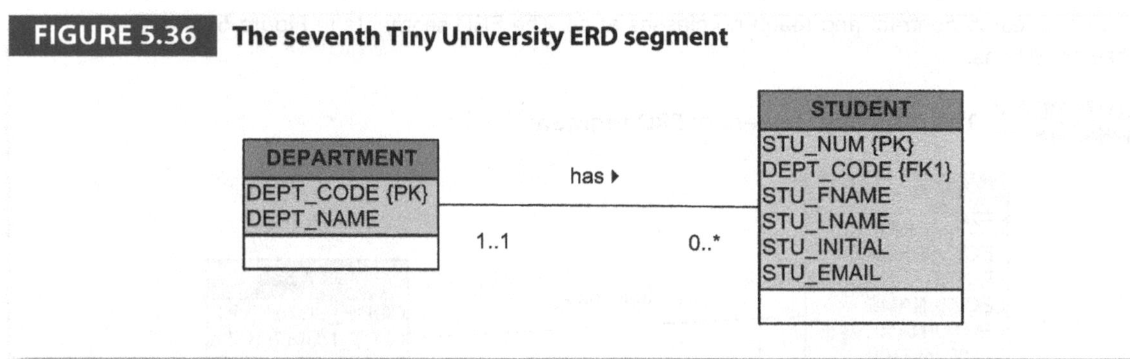

9 Each student has an advisor in his or her department; each advisor counsels several students. An advisor is also a lecturer, but not all lecturers advise students. Therefore, STUDENT is optional to LECTURER in the 'LECTURER advises STUDENT' relationship. (See Figure 5.37.)

FIGURE 5.37 **The eighth Tiny University ERD segment**

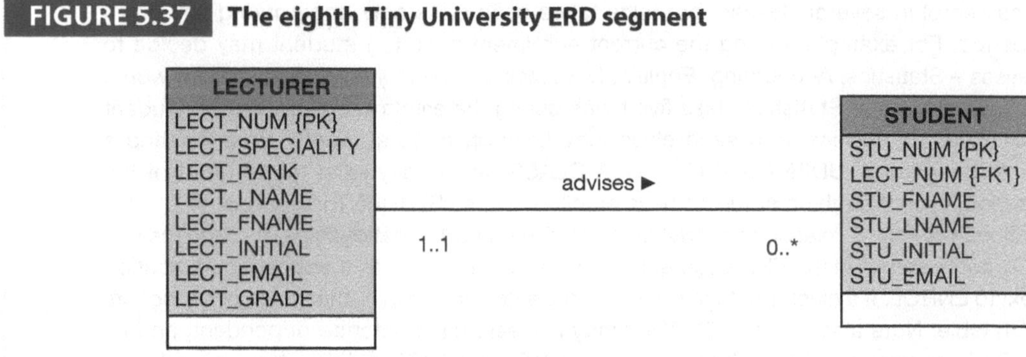

10 When you examine the CLASS entity in Figure 5.38, you'll note that this entity contains a ROOM_CODE attribute. Given the naming conventions, it is clear that ROOM_CODE is a FK to another entity. Clearly, because a class is taught in a room, it is reasonable to assume that the ROOM_CODE in CLASS is the FK to an entity named ROOM. In turn, each room is located in a building. So the last Tiny University ERD is created by observing that a BUILDING can contain many ROOMs, but each ROOM is found in a single BUILDING. (See Figure 5.38.) In this ERD segment, it is clear that some buildings do not contain (class) rooms. For example, a storage building might not contain any named rooms at all.

FIGURE 5.38 The ninth Tiny University ERD segment

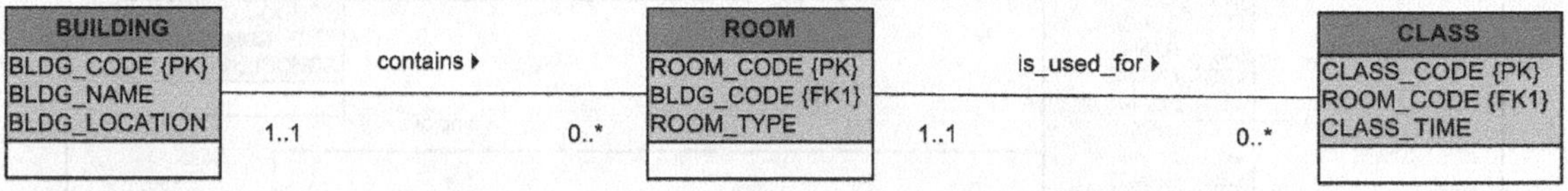

5

Using the preceding summary, you can identify the following entities:

SCHOOL COURSE

DEPARTMENT CLASS

ENROL (the bridge entity between STUDENT and CLASS)

LECTURER STUDENT

BUILDING ROOM

Once you have discovered the relevant entities, you can define the initial set of relationships among them. Next, you describe the entity attributes. Identifying the attributes of the entities helps you better understand the relationships among entities. Table 5.4 summarises the ERM's components, and names the entities and their relations.

TABLE 5.4 Components of the ERM

Entity	Relationship	Connectivity	Entity
SCHOOL	operates	1..*	DEPARTMENT
DEPARTMENT	has	1..*	STUDENT
DEPARTMENT	employs	1..*	LECTURER
DEPARTMENT	offers	1..*	COURSE
COURSE	generates	1..*	CLASS
LECTURER	is dean of	1..1	SCHOOL
LECTURER	chairs	1..1	DEPARTMENT
LECTURER	teaches	1..*	CLASS
LECTURER	advises	1..*	STUDENT
STUDENT	enrols in	1..*	CLASS
BUILDING	contains	1..*	ROOM
ROOM	is used for	1..*	CLASS

Note: ENROL is the composite entity that implements the relationship STUDENT enrols in CLASS.

You must also define the connectivity and cardinality for the just-discovered relations by querying the end user extensively. Having defined the ERM's components, you can now draw the ERD, or conceptual diagram, depicted in Figure 5.39. Actually, the entity attributes and their domains should also be displayed in the ERD. However, to avoid crowding the diagram, the entity attributes may be depicted separately.

FIGURE 5.39 The completed Tiny University ERD segment

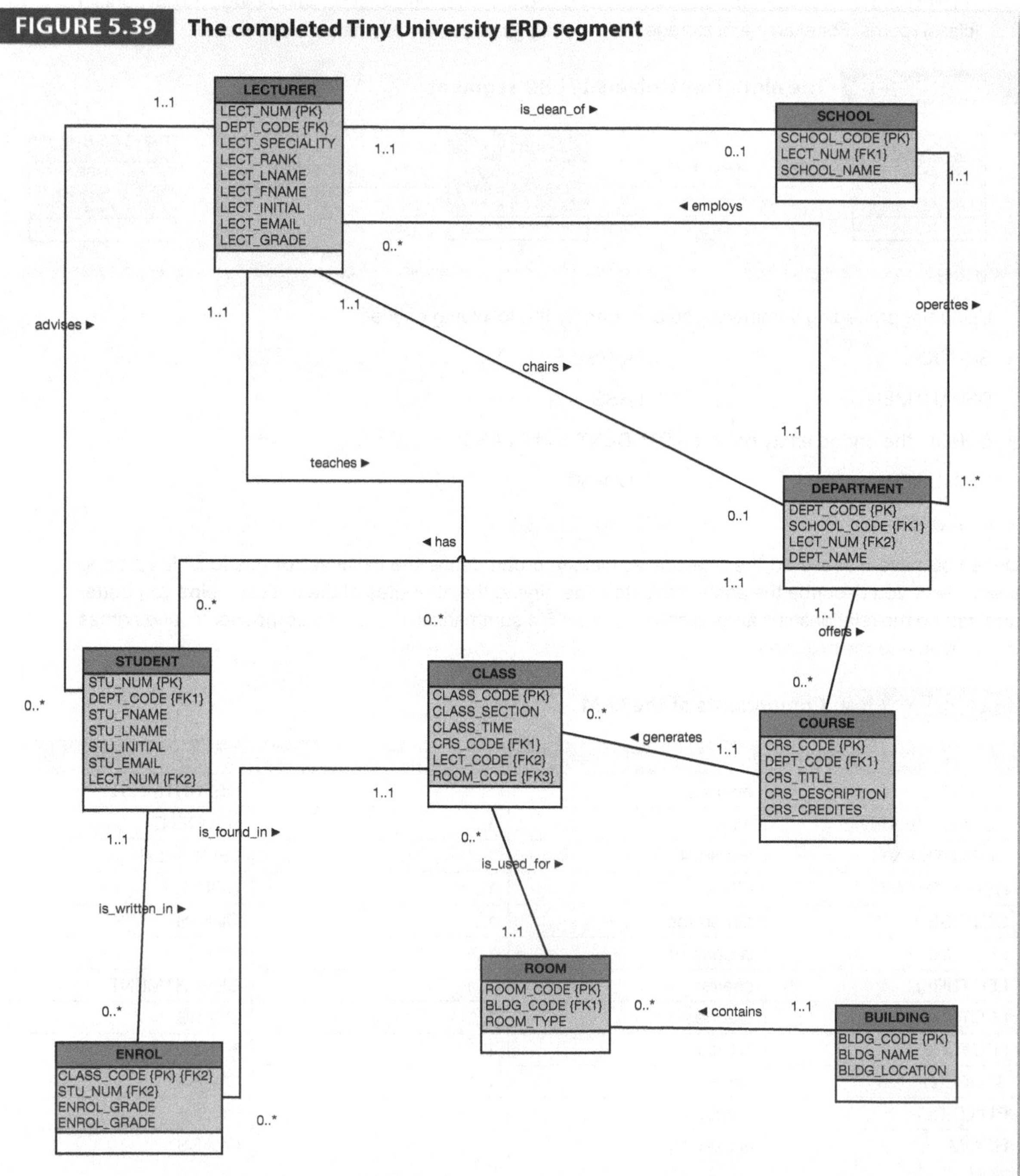

5.2.2 ILoveHolidays

ILoveHolidays is a small international company that owns a number of independent travel agencies in a number of countries. The travel agencies specialise in booking complete holidays, hotels, flights, tours and one-off events. They also offer information to customers on attractions and places of interest in a number of cities worldwide. From interviews with various stakeholders and employees, the following business rules have been established:

1 Each travel agent has a number of employees who each have an associated grade (Manager, Deputy Manager or Staff). Each travel agent must have one employee who takes the role of Manager. Therefore a 1:* mandatory relationship exists between TRAVEL_AGENT and EMPLOYEE. Figure 5.40 illustrates this first business rule.

FIGURE 5.40 **Segment 1: The TRAVEL_AGENT – EMPLOYEE relationship**

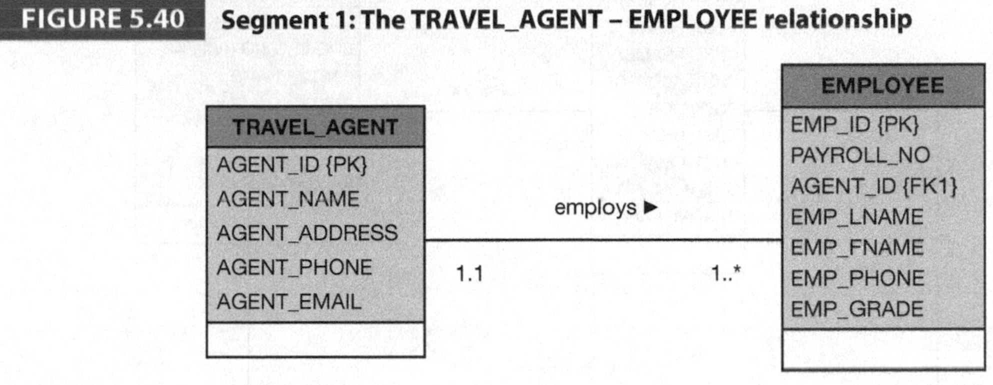

2 Each employee may make bookings on behalf of customers when they visit one of the travel agencies. However, some employees, such as the Manager, may be confined to back office duties and may not make a booking. This is why BOOKING is optional to EMPLOYEE. A booking can only exist if it has been made by an employee. The ERD segment is shown in Figure 5.41 and shows the 1:* relationship that exists between EMPLOYEE and BOOKING.

FIGURE 5.41 **Segment 2: The EMPLOYEE – BOOKING relationship**

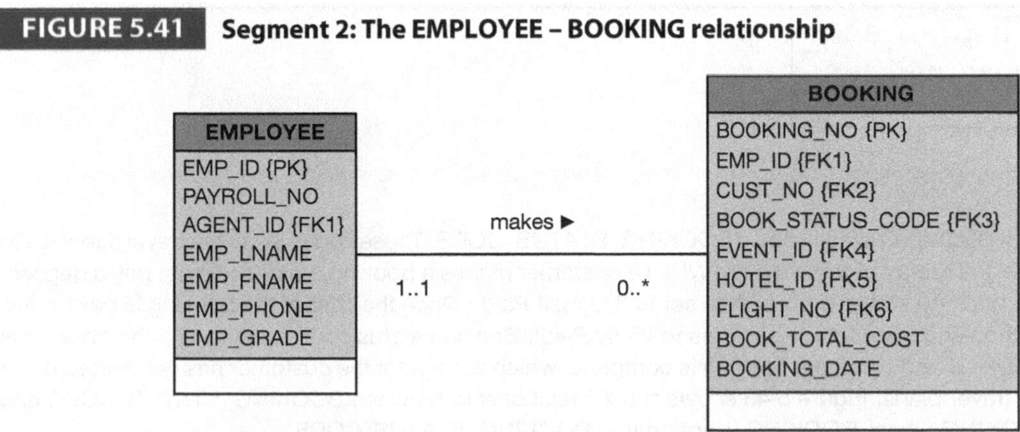

3 Figure 5.42 shows the relationships between the CUSTOMER, BOOKING and PARTY_MEMBERS entities. A customer can make one or more bookings at any of the travel agencies. The booking must be for at least the customer himself or herself but could also include other people such as family or friends. In this scenario the customer becomes the lead traveller and is responsible for the overall booking. This is represented by the 1:* relationship between CUSTOMER and PARTY_MEMBER where PARTY_MEMBERS is optional to CUSTOMER. Each booking is for only one customer and at the same time a booking may include 1 or more party members. The relationship between BOOKING and PARTY_MEMBERS is therefore 1:* and between BOOKING and CUSTOMER *:1.

FIGURE 5.42 **Segment 3: The CUSTOMER – BOOKING – PARTY_MEMBERS relationship**

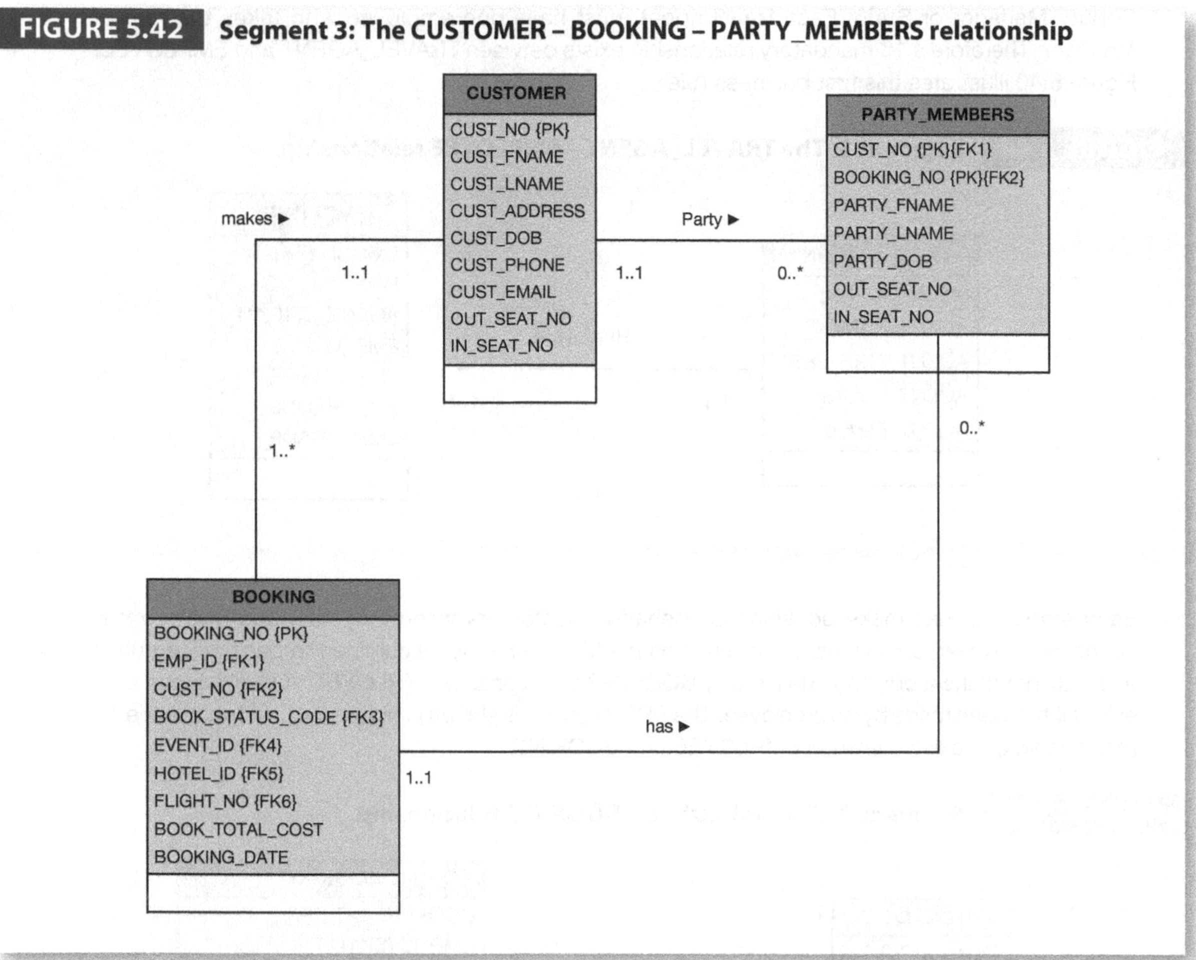

4 Each BOOKING is assigned a BOOKING_STATUS_CODE. These codes allow the travel agencies to track the status of the booking. When a customer makes a booking, he or she must pay a deposit. The booking status code is then set to 'Deposit Paid'. Once the cost of the booking is paid in full, the booking status code changes to 'Fully Paid'. Booking status codes also exist if the booking is cancelled and when the booking is complete, which is set after the customer has completed his or her travel plans. Figure 5.43 shows the 1:* relationship between BOOKING_STATUS_CODE and BOOKING where BOOKING is optional to BOOKING_STATUS_CODE.

FIGURE 5.43 Segment 4: The BOOKING – BOOKING_STATUS_CODE relationship

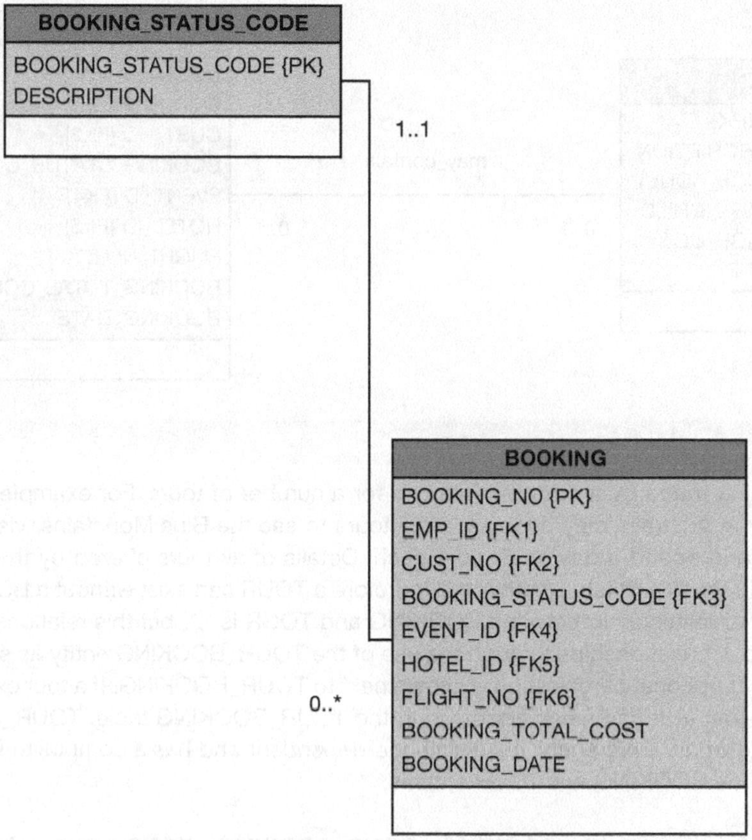

5

5 ILoveHolidays also sells tickets for a number of events such as the Monaco Grand Prix or the Wimbledon Tennis Championships. Figure 5.44 shows the relationship between EVENT and BOOKING. Both sides of the relationship allow for optional participation. That is because a booking may or may not be for an event and an event may or may not be booked by a customer. Regardless, the travel agencies will keep the details of all events offered within their database.

FIGURE 5.44 Segment 5: The BOOKING – EVENT relationship

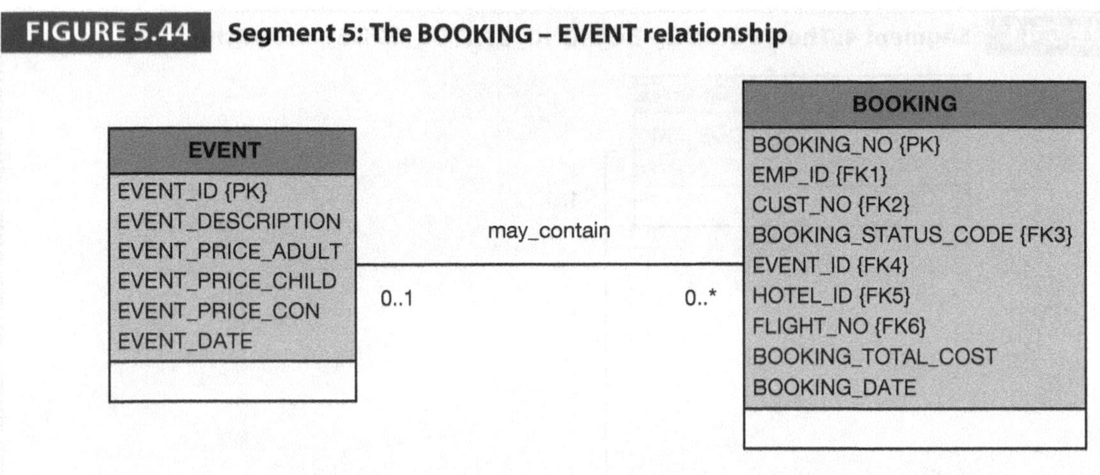

5

6 A booking made by a customer may be for a number of tours. For example, a customer visiting Sydney in Australia may book separate tours to see the Blue Mountains, visit the Sydney Opera House and spend a day on Bondi Beach. Details of all tours offered by the travel agencies are stored in the TOUR table (entity) and therefore a TOUR can exist without a BOOKING being made. The initial relationship between BOOKING and TOUR is *:*, but this relationship must be divided into two 1:* relationships through the use of the TOUR_BOOKING entity as shown in Figure 5.45. Note that optional participation is shown next to TOUR_BOOKING. If a tour exists that no one ever books, that tour can never appear in in the TOUR_BOOKING table. TOUR_BOOKING is also an example of a WEAK entity, it is existence-dependent and has a composite PK composed of the PKs of the BOOKING and TOUR entities.

FIGURE 5.45 Segment 6: The BOOKING – TOUR_BOOKING – TOUR relationship

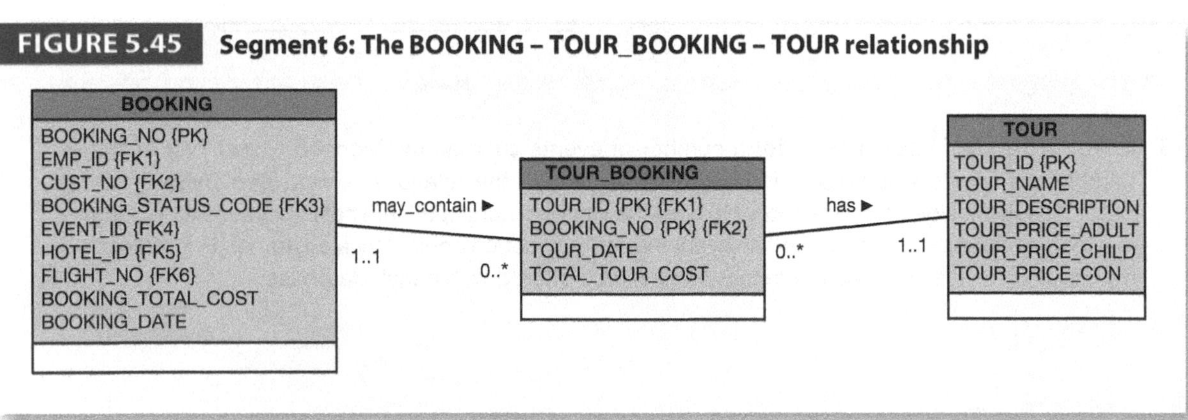

7 Figure 5.46 shows the relationship between TOUR, ATTRACT_TOUR and ATTRACTION. A tour may comprise visits to a number of attractions and at the same time different combinations of attractions may be offered on different tours. This means that, initially, a *:* relationship existed between TOUR and ATTRACTION, which needed to be resolved by the addition of the weak entity ATTRACT_TOUR. An attraction may exist without belonging to a tour and therefore the travel agencies would be able to provide information to the customer about the attraction such as travel instructions. This is a specific requirement of ILoveHolidays in order to provide additional help to customers and exceed expectations. Note that ATTRACT_TOUR has a composite PK comprising the PKs from TOUR and ATTRACTION.

FIGURE 5.46 **Segment 7: The TOUR – ATTRACT_TOUR – ATTRACTION relationship**

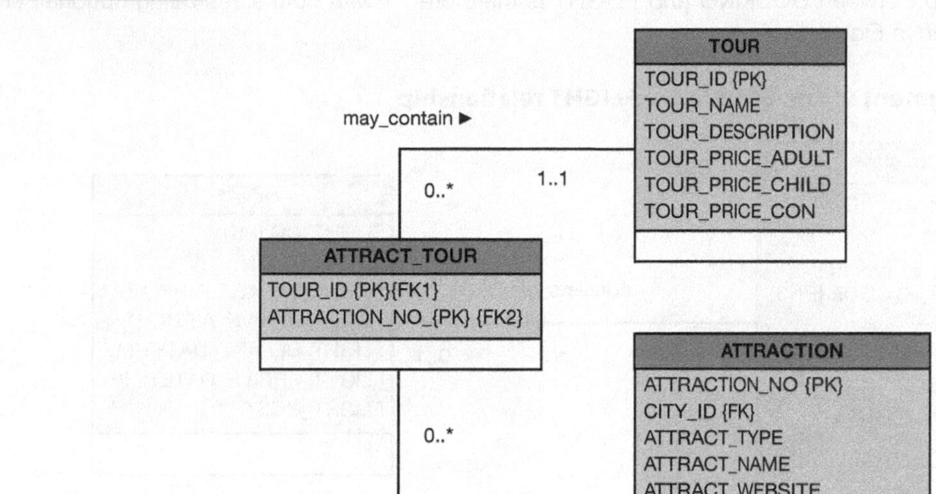

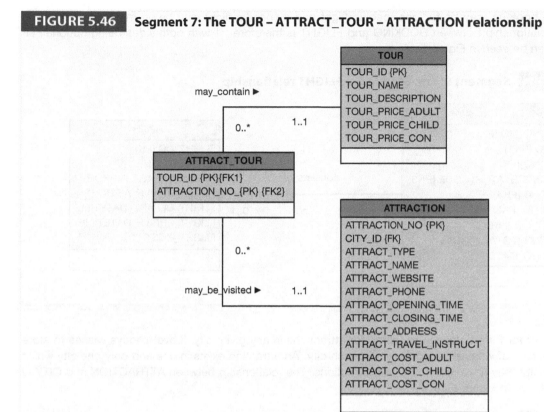

8 Each booking may be for one hotel. Hotels that exist in the HOTEL table may never be booked or may be booked on multiple occasions. This business rule is illustrated in Figure 5.47, which shows the relationship between the BOOKING and HOTEL entities. Note that both sides of the relationship are optional.

FIGURE 5.47 **Segment 8: The BOOKING – HOTEL relationship**

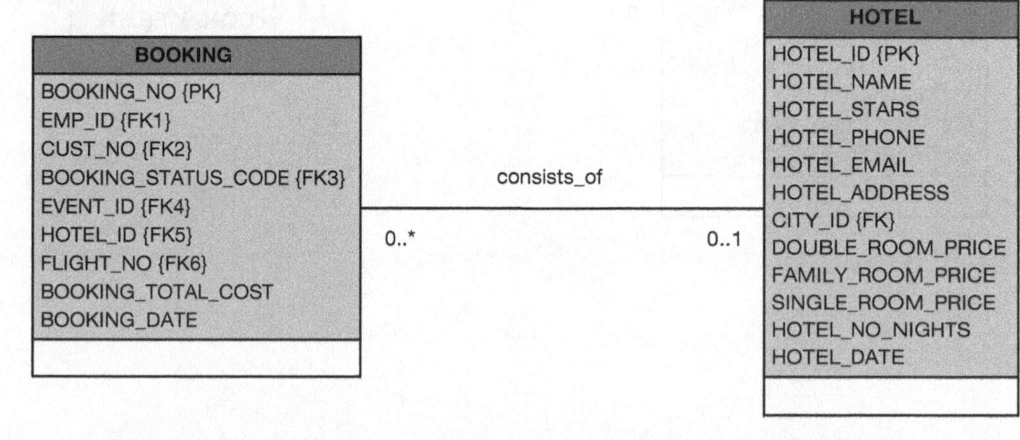

5

9 A booking may be for one specific flight and a specific flight may be on many bookings. The relationship between BOOKING and FLIGHT is therefore *:1 with both sides being optional, as can be seen in Figure 5.48.

FIGURE 5.48 Segment 9: The BOOKING – FLIGHT relationship

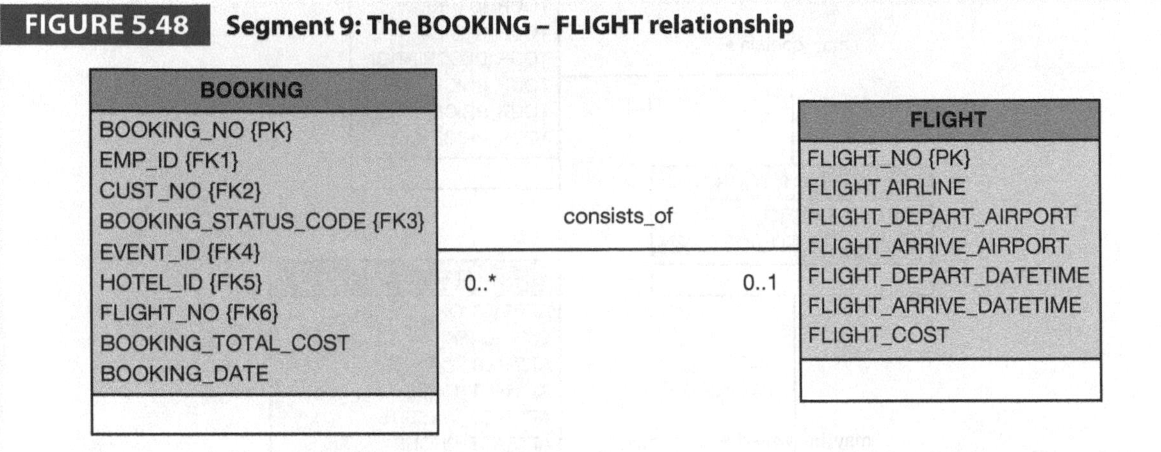

10 In order for employees to search for attractions in any given city, ILoveHolidays wishes to store details of what attractions exist in each city. An attraction exists in one and only one city whilst a city may have any number of attractions. The relationship between ATTRACTION and CITY is shown in Figure 5.49.

FIGURE 5.49 Segment 9: The ATTRACTION – CITY relationship

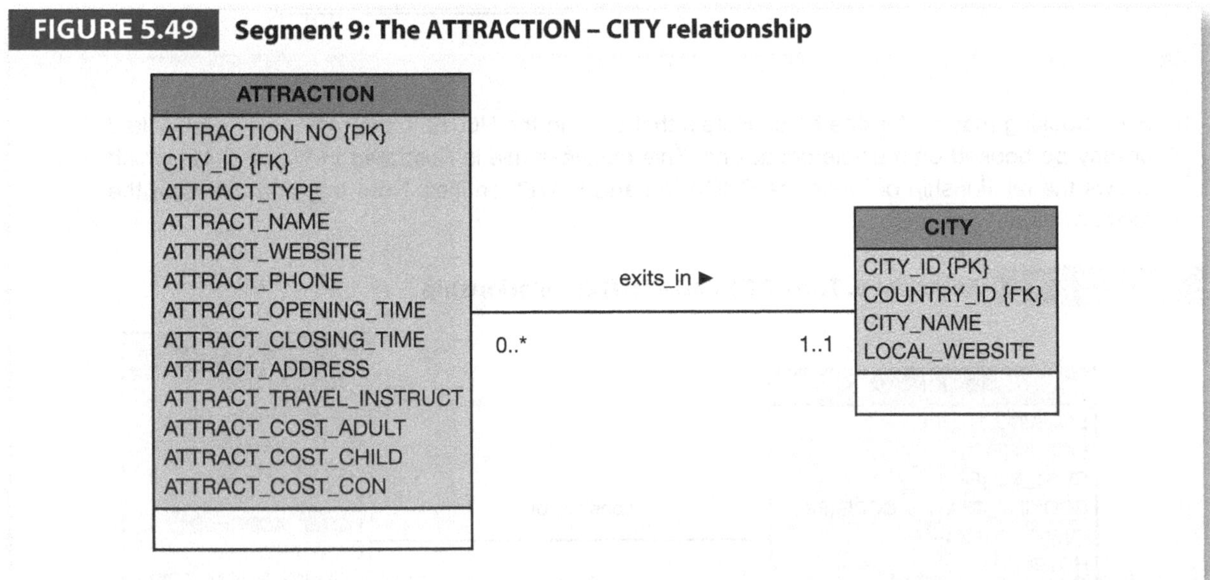

11 In order to deal with more detailed enquiries from customers about which cities to visit in a given country (for example, based upon the number of attractions in each city), it is necessary to model a relationship between cities and their associated country. One country has one or more cities whilst a city can only exist in one country (see Figure 5.50).

FIGURE 5.50 **Segment 10: The CITY – COUNTRY relationship**

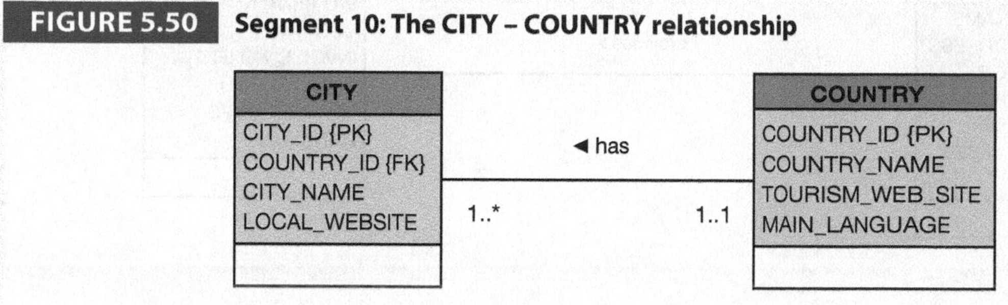

12 Each city where a customer would like to stay will hopefully have a selection of hotels that are available. To allow the travel agencies to search for hotels by city, two entities, HOTEL and CITY, are required. Figure 5.51 shows the 1:* relationship between CITY and HOTEL. Notice that HOTEL is optional in the relationship as a city may not have any hotels that are deemed good enough for the travel agencies to recommend (and therefore would not be included in the HOTEL table).

FIGURE 5.51 **Segment 11: The HOTEL – CITY relationship**

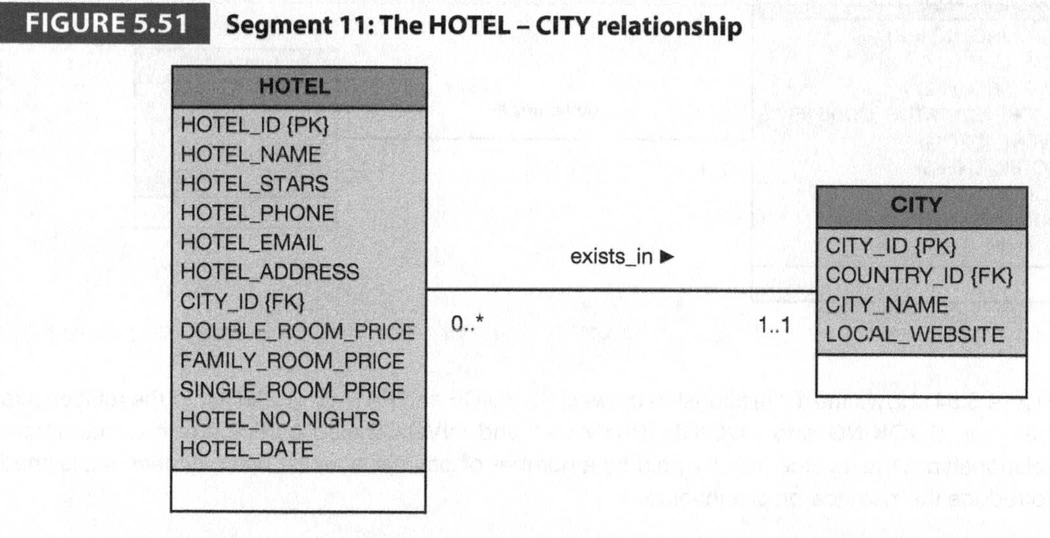

13 A customer makes at least one – or, in some cases, many – payments in order to pay off the total cost of their booking. The relationship between CUSTOMER and PAYMENT (shown in Figure 5.52) is mandatory on both sides as a customer must make at least one payment and one payment must be associated with a CUSTOMER.

5

FIGURE 5.52 **Segment 12: The CUSTOMER – PAYMENT relationship**

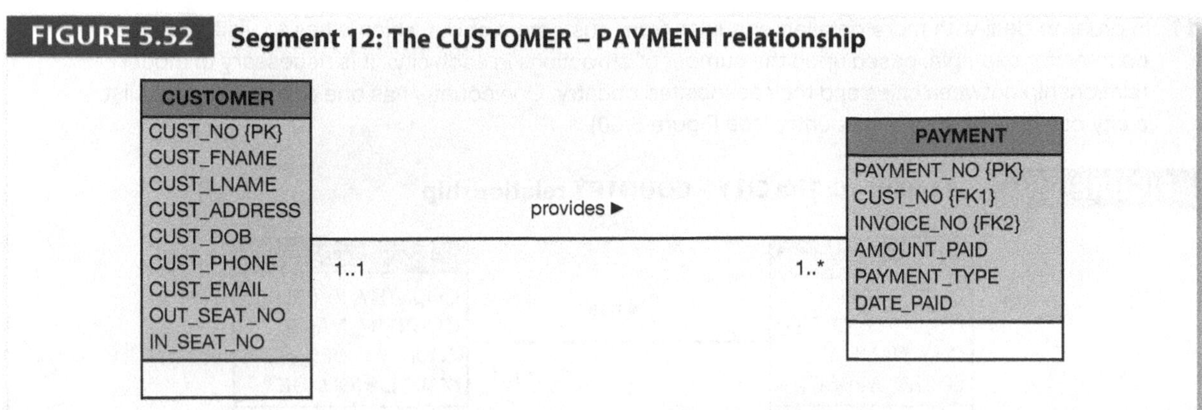

14 A booking will generate at least one invoice but may generate many invoices. This will depend on whether the customer chooses to pay for his or her booking all at once. In this case, only one invoice will be produced. Otherwise, several invoices may need to be generated for a specific booking. The 1:* mandatory relationship between BOOKING and INVOICE can be seen in Figure 5.53.

FIGURE 5.53 **Segment 13: The BOOKING – INVOICE relationship**

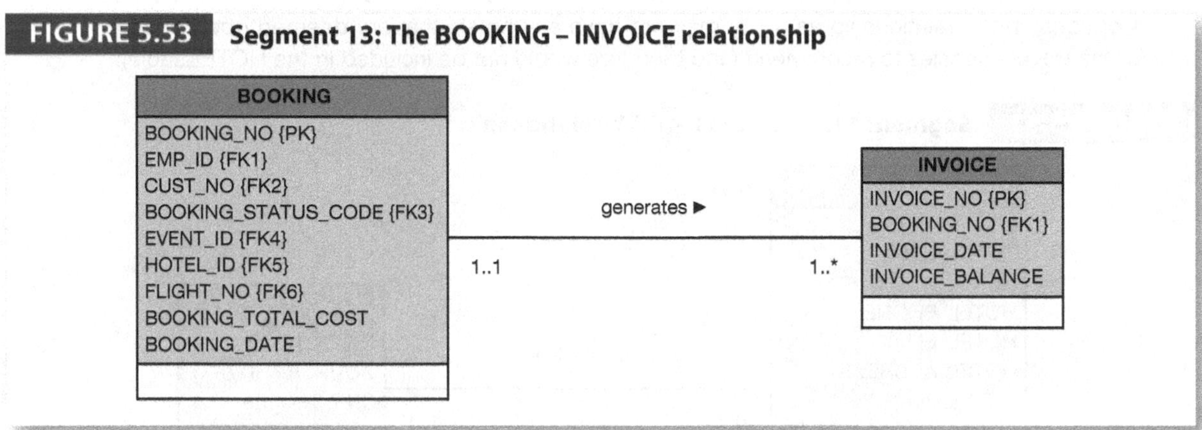

15 Figure 5.54 shows the 1:* relationship between INVOICE and PAYMENT. Similar to the relationship between BOOKING and INVOICE, PAYMENT and INVOICE also participate in a mandatory relationship. One invoice may be paid by a number of payments whilst one payment is assigned to reduce the balance on one invoice.

FIGURE 5.54 **Segment 14: The INVOICE – PAYMENT relationship**

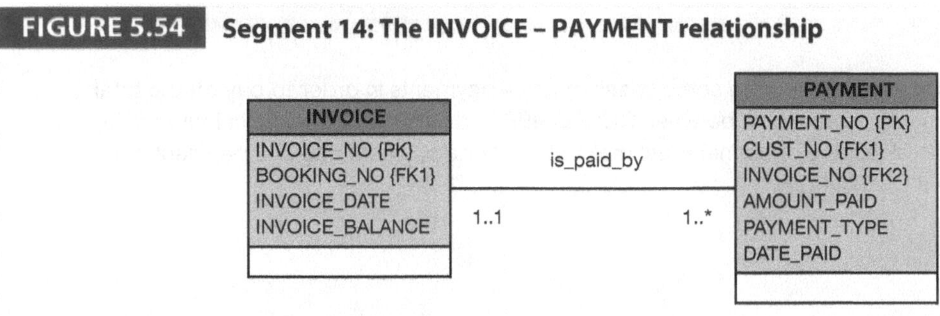

We have now completed all the segments of the ILoveHolidays ERD. Now that we have defined all the components, we can draw the completed conceptual ERD as shown in Figure 5.55.

FIGURE 5.55 Final ILoveHolidays ERD

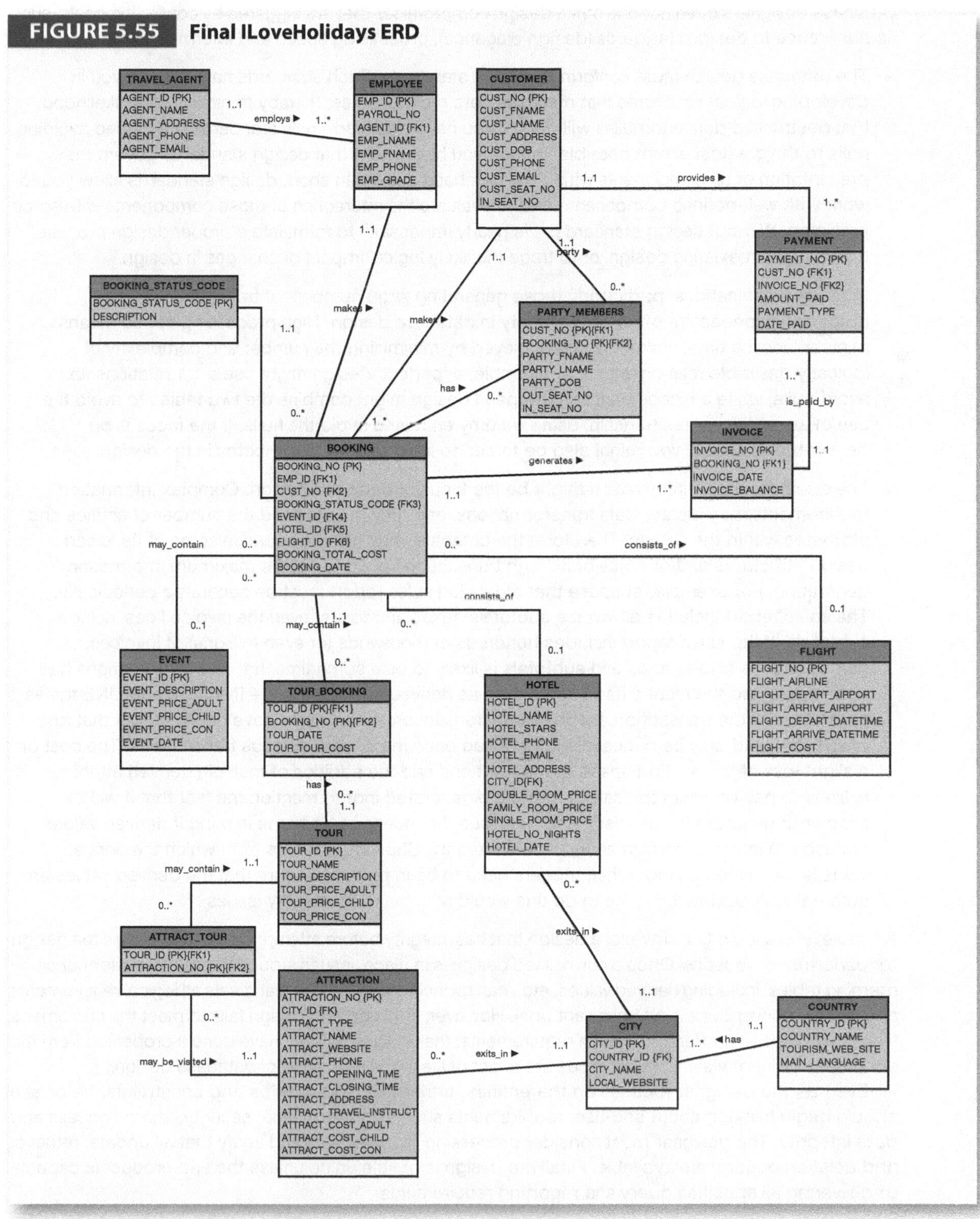

5.3 DATABASE DESIGN CHALLENGES: CONFLICTING GOALS

Database designers often need to make design compromises that are triggered by conflicting goals, such as adherence to design standards (design elegance), processing speed and information requirements.

- The database design must conform to design standards. Such standards have guided you in developing logical structures that minimise data redundancies, thereby minimising the likelihood that destructive data anomalies will occur. You have also learnt how standards prescribed avoiding nulls to the greatest extent possible. In fact, you have learnt that design standards govern the presentation of all components within the database design. In short, design standards allow you to work with well-defined components and to evaluate the interaction of those components with some precision. Without design standards, it is nearly impossible to formulate a proper design process, to evaluate an existing design, or to trace the likely logical impact of changes in design.
- In many organisations, particularly those generating large numbers of transactions, high processing speeds are often a top priority in database design. High processing speed means minimal access time, which may be achieved by minimising the number and complexity of logically desirable relationships. For example, a 'perfect' design might use a 1:1 relationship to avoid nulls, while a higher-transaction-speed design might combine the two tables to avoid the use of an additional relationship, using dummy entries to avoid the nulls. If the focus is on data-retrieval speed, you might also be forced to include derived attributes in the design.
- The quest for timely information might be the focus of database design. Complex information requirements may dictate data transformations, and they may expand the number of entities and attributes within the design. Therefore, the database may have to sacrifice some of its 'clean' design structures and/or some of its high transaction speed to ensure maximum information generation. For example, suppose that a detailed sales report must be generated periodically. The sales report includes all invoice subtotals, taxes and totals; even the invoice lines include subtotals. If the sales report includes hundreds of thousands (or even millions) of invoices, computing the totals, taxes and subtotals is likely to take some time. If those computations had been made and the results had been stored as derived attributes in the INVOICE and LINE tables at the time of the transaction, the real-time transaction speed might have declined, but that loss of speed would only be noticeable if there had been many simultaneous transactions. The cost of a slight loss of transaction speed at the front end and the addition of multiple derived attributes is likely to pay off when the sales reports are generated (not to mention the fact that it will be simpler to generate the queries). Another issue that needs to be borne in mind if derived values are used to improve performance, is data integrity. Should the values from which the derived value is calculated change, then triggers need to be in place to ensure that the derived values are automatically updated. Failing to do this would result in data integrity issues.

As a rule, you should first strive for a design that has integrity before attempting to denormalise the design for performance reasons. Once a normalised design is in place, issues around improving performance by merging tables, including derived values, etc., can be included. A design that meets all logical requirements and design conventions is an important goal. However, if this perfect design fails to meet the customer's transaction speed and/or information requirements, the designer will not have done a proper job from the end user's point of view. Compromises are a fact of life in the real world of database design.

Even as the designer focuses on the entities, attributes, relationships and constraints, he or she should begin thinking about end-user requirements such as performance, security, shared access and data integrity. The designer must consider processing requirements and verify that all update, retrieval and deletion options are available. Finally, a design is of little value unless the end product is capable of delivering all specified query and reporting requirements.

You are quite likely to discover that even the best design process produces an ERD that requires further changes, mandated by operational requirements. Such changes should not discourage you from using the process. ER modelling is essential in the development of a sound design that is capable of meeting the demands of adjustment and growth. Using ERDs yields perhaps the richest bonus of all: a thorough understanding of how an organisation really functions.

There are occasional design and implementation problems that do not yield 'clean' implementation solutions. To get a sense of the design and implementation choices a database designer faces, let's revisit the 1:1 recursive relationship 'EMPLOYEE is married to EMPLOYEE' first examined in Figure 5.21. Figure 5.56 shows three different ways of implementing such a relationship.

FIGURE 5.56 **Various implementations of the 1:1 recursive relationship**

Database name: Ch05_PartCo

Table name: EMPLOYEE_V1

First implementation

EMP_NUM	EMP_LNAME	EMP_FNAME	EMP_SPOUSE
345	Singh	Nishok	347
346	Jones	Anne	349
347	Singh	Vediga	345
348	Delaney	Robert	
349	Shapiro	Anton	346

Second implementation

Table name: EMPLOYEE

EMP_NUM	EMP_LNAME	EMP_FNAME
345	Singh	Nishok
346	Jones	Anne
347	Singh	Vediga
348	Delaney	Robert
349	Shapiro	Anton

Table name: MARRIED_V1

EMP_NUM	EMP_SPOUSE
345	347
346	349
347	345
349	346

5

Third implementation

Table name: MARRIAGE

MAR_NUM	MAR_DATE
1	04-Mar-13
2	02-Feb-09

Table name: MARPART

MAR_NUM	EMP_NUM
1	345
1	347
2	346
2	349

Table name: EMPLOYEE

EMP_NUM	EMP_LNAME	EMP_FNAME
345	Singh	Nishok
346	Jones	Anne
347	Singh	Vediga
348	Delaney	Robert
349	Shapiro	Anton

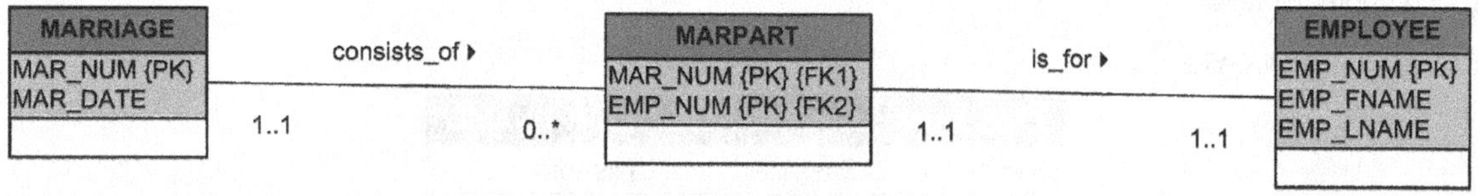

As you examine the EMPLOYEE_V1 table in Figure 5.56, note that this table is likely to yield data anomalies. For example, if Anne Jones divorces Anton Shapiro, two records must be updated – by setting the respective EMP_SPOUSE values to null – to properly reflect that change. If only one record is updated, inconsistent data occur. The problem becomes even worse if several of the divorced employees then marry each other. In addition, that implementation also produces undesirable nulls for employees who are *not* married to other employees in the company.

Another approach would be to create a new entity shown as MARRIED_V1 in a 1:* relationship with EMPLOYEE. (See Figure 5.56, second implementation.) This second implementation does eliminate the nulls for employees who are not married to somebody working for the same company. (Such employees would not be entered in the MARRIED_V1 table.) However, this approach still yields possible duplicate values. For example, the marriage between employees 345 and 347 may still appear twice, once as 345 347 and once as 347 345. (Since each of those permutations is unique the first time it appears, the creation of a unique index will not solve the problem.)

As you can see, the first two implementations yield several problems:

- Both solutions use synonyms. The EMPLOYEE_V1 table uses EMP_NUM and EMP_SPOUSE to refer to an employee. The MARRIED_V1 table uses the same synonyms.
- Both solutions are likely to produce inconsistent data. For example, it is possible to enter employee as 345 married to employee 347 and to enter employee 348 as married to employee 345.
- Both solutions allow data entries to show one employee married to several other employees. For example, it is possible to have data pairs such as 345 347 and 348 347 and 349 347 that will not violate entity integrity requirements because they are all unique.

A third approach would be to have two new entities MARRIAGE and MARPART in a 1:* relationship. MARPART contains the EMP_NUM foreign key to EMPLOYEE. (See the UML class diagram in Figure 5.38.) This third approach would be the preferred solution in a relational environment. But even this approach requires some fine-tuning. For example, to ensure that an employee occurs only once in any given marriage, you would have to use a unique index on the EMP_NUM attribute in the MARPART table.

As you can see, a recursive 1:1 relationship yields many different solutions with varying degrees of effectiveness and adherence to basic design principles. Your job as a database designer is to use your professional judgement to yield a solution that meets the requirements imposed by business rules, processing requirements and basic design principles.

Finally, document, document and document! Put all design activities in writing. Then review what you've written. Documentation not only helps you stay on track during the design process, but also enables you (or those following you) to pick up the design thread when the time comes to modify the design. Although the need for documentation should be obvious, one of the most vexing problems in database and systems analysis work is that the 'put it in writing' rule is often not observed in all of the design and implementation stages. The development of organisational documentation standards is a very important aspect of ensuring data compatibility and coherence.

SUMMARY

- The ERM uses ERDs to represent the conceptual database as viewed by the end user. The ERM's main components are entities, relationships and attributes. The ERD also includes connectivity and cardinality notations. An ERD can also show relationship strength, relationship participation (optional or mandatory), and degree of relationship (unary, binary, ternary, etc.).
- Multiplicity is the main constraint that exists on a relationship, which enables us to define the number of participants in that relationship, and refers to the number of instances of one entity that are associated with one instance of a related entity. Multiplicity describes two important constraints, known as participation and cardinality. Cardinality expresses the specific number of entity occurrences associated with an occurrence of a related entity. Participation determines whether all occurrences of an entity participate in the relationship or not. Participation is either mandatory or optional. Multiplicities are usually based on business rules.
- In the ERM, a *:* relationship is valid at the conceptual level. However, when implementing the ERM in a relational database, the *:* relationship must be mapped to a set of 1:* relationships through a composite entity.
- ERDs may be based on many different ERMs. However, regardless of which model is selected, the modelling logic remains the same. Because no ERM can accurately portray all real-world data and action constraints, application software must be used to augment the implementation of at least some of the business rules.

5

- Database designers, no matter how well they are able to produce designs that conform to all applicable modelling conventions, are often forced to make design compromises. Those compromises are required when end users have vital transaction speed and/or information requirements that prevent the use of 'perfect' modelling logic and adherence to all modelling conventions. Therefore, database designers must use their professional judgement to determine how and to what extent the modelling conventions are subject to modification. To ensure that their professional judgements are sound, database designers must have detailed and in-depth knowledge of data-modelling conventions. It is also important to document the design process from beginning to end, which helps keep the design process on track and allows for easy modifications in the future.
- The steps in creating an entity–relationship model are:
  1. Create a detailed narrative of the organisation's description of operations.
  2. Identify the business rules based on the descriptions of operations.
  3. Identify all main entities from the business rules.
  4. Identify all main relationships between entities from the business rules.
  5. Develop an initial ERD.
  6. Determine the multiplicities and the participation of all relationships. Remember, participation involves identifying whether a relationship can be optional or mandatory for each entity.
  7. Identify the primary and foreign keys.
  8. Identify all attributes.
  9. Revise and review the ERD.

KEY TERMS

association
binary relationship
cardinality
class
composite attribute
composite key
derived attribute
existence-dependent
existence-independent
identifiers
identifying relationship
iterative process
mandatory participation
multiplicity
multivalued attribute
non-identifying relationship
optional participation
participants
participation
recursive relationship
relationship degree
simple attribute
single-valued attribute
strong relationship
ternary relationship
unary relationship
weak entity
weak relationship

FURTHER READING

Chen, P. (ed.) *Entity-Relationship Approach: The Use of ER Concept in Knowledge Representation*. IEEE Computer Society and North-Holland, 1985.

Gordon, K. Modelling Business Information: Entity Relationship and Class Modelling for Business Analysts, BCS, 2.

Hernandez, M. J. *Database Design for Mere Mortals: A Hands-On Guide to Relational Database Design*. Addison-Wesley, 2003.

Larman, C. *Applying UML and Patterns: An Introduction to Object-Oriented Analysis and Design and Iterative Development*. Prentice Hall, 2004.

Patig, S. 'Evolution of entity-relationship modelling', *Journal of Data & Knowledge Engineering* 56(2): 122–138, Elsevier Science, February 2006.

Rumbaugh, J., Jacobson, I. and Booch, G. *The Unified Modelling Language Reference Manual*. Addison-Wesley, 2004.

Online Content Answers to selected Review Questions and Problems for this chapter are available on the online platform accompanying this book.

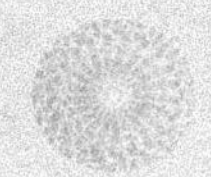

REVIEW QUESTIONS

1. Which two conditions must be met before an entity can be classified as a weak entity? Give an example of a weak entity.
2. What is a strong (or identifying) relationship?
3. Given the business rule 'an employee may have many degrees', discuss its effect on attributes, entities and relationships. (*Hint:* Remember what a multivalued attribute is and how it might be implemented.)
4. What is a composite entity and when is it used?

FIGURE Q5.1 **The conceptual model for question 5**

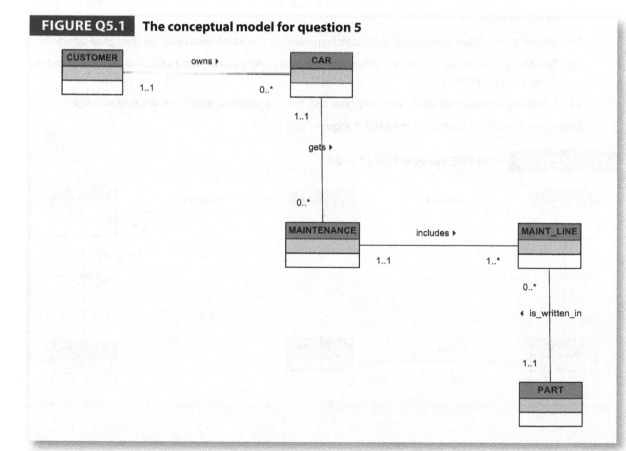

5 Suppose you are working within the framework of the conceptual model shown in Figure Q5.1. Given the conceptual model in Figure Q5.1:

- **a** Write the business rules that are reflected in it.
- **b** Identify all of the cardinalities.

6 What is a recursive relationship? Give an example.

7 How would you (graphically) identify each of the following ERM components in a UML model:

- **a** an entity?
- **b** the multiplicity (0:*)?

8 Discuss the difference between a composite key and a composite attribute. How would each be indicated in an ERD?

9 What two courses of action are available to a designer when he or she encounters a multivalued attribute?

10 What is a derived attribute? Give an example.

11 How is a relationship between entities indicated in an ERD? Give an example using UML notation.

12 Discuss two ways in which the 1:* relationship between COURSE and CLASS can be implemented. (*Hint:* Think about relationship strength.)

13 How is a composite entity represented in an ERD, and what is its function? Illustrate using the UML notation.

14 Which three (often conflicting) database requirements must be addressed in database design?

15 Briefly, but precisely, explain the difference between single-valued attributes and simple attributes. Give an example of each.

16 What are multivalued attributes, and how can they be handled within the database design?

Questions 17–20 are based on the ERD in Figure Q5.2.

FIGURE Q5.2 The ERD for questions 17–20

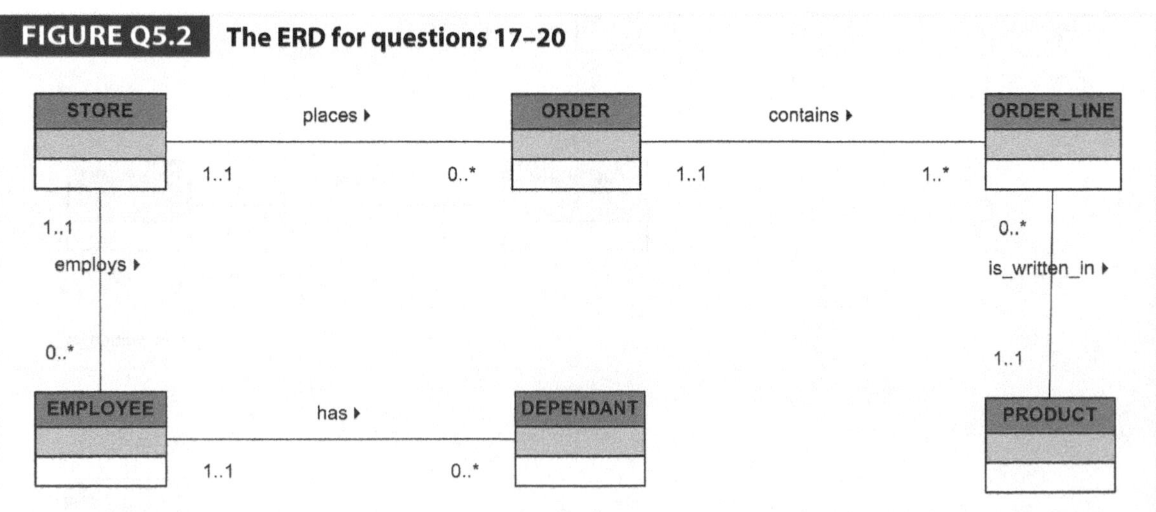

17 Write the ten cardinalities (multiplicities) that are appropriate for this ERD.

18 Write the business rules reflected in this ERD.

19 Which two attributes must be contained in the composite entity between STORE and PRODUCT? Use proper terminology in your answer.

20 Describe precisely the composition of the DEPENDANT weak entity's primary key. Use proper terminology in your answer.

21 The local city youth league needs a database system to help track children who sign up to play soccer. Data needs to be kept on each team, the children who will play on each team, and their parents. Also, data needs to be kept on the coaches for each team.

Draw a data model with the entities and attributes described here.

Entities required: Team, Player, Coach, and Parent

Attributes required:

Team: Team ID number, Team name, and Team colours

Player: Player ID number, Player first name, Player last name, and Player age

Coach: Coach ID number, Coach first name, Coach last name, and Coach home phone number

Parent: Parent ID number, Parent last name, Parent first name, Home phone number and Home address (Street, City, Province, and Postal code)

The following relationships must be defined:

- Team is related to Player.
- Team is related to Coach.
- Player is related to Parent.

Connectivities and participations are defined as follows:

- A Team may or may not have a Player.
- A Player must have a Team.
- A Team may have many Players.
- A Player has only one Team.
- A Team may or may not have a Coach.
- A Coach must have a Team.
- A Team may have many Coaches.
- A Coach has only one Team.
- A Player must have a Parent.
- A Parent must have a Player.
- A Player may have many Parents.
- A Parent may have many Players.

PROBLEMS

1 Using the following business rules, create the appropriate ERD using UML notation.

  a A company operates many departments.
  b Each department employs one or more employees.
  c Each of the employees may or may not have one or more dependants.
  d Each employee may or may not have an employment history.

2 Using the following business rules, create the appropriate ERD using UML notation:

  a A football team has at least 11 players and may have up to 40 players.
  b Each player may or may not play one or more games.
  c A minimum of 11 players and a maximum of 14 players may participate in one game.
  d A player may or may not score one or more goals.
  e Each game may have zero or more goals.

3 Using the following business rules, create an initial ERD using UML notation:

  a A musician makes at least one recording, but may over a period of time make many recordings.
  b One recording consists of at least three or more tracks.
  c A track can appear on more than one recording.

4 Revise the ERD you developed in Problem 3 and resolve any *:* relationships.

5 The Hudson Engineering Group (HEG) has contacted you to create a conceptual model whose application will meet the expected database requirements for the company's training programme. The HEG administrator gives you the description (see below) of the training group's operating environment. (*Hint:* Some of the following sentences identify the volume of data rather than cardinalities. Can you tell which ones?)

  The HEG has 12 instructors and can handle up to 30 trainees per class. HEG offers five 'advanced technology' courses, each of which may generate several classes. If a class has fewer than ten trainees, it will be cancelled. Therefore, it is possible for a course not to generate any classes. Each class is taught by one instructor. Each instructor may teach up to two classes or may be assigned to do research only. Each trainee may take up to two classes per year. Given that information, do the following:

  a Define all of the entities and relationships. (Use Table 5.4 as your guide.)
  b Describe the relationship between instructor and class in terms of cardinality, participation and existence-dependence.

6 Use the following business rules to create an ERD using UML notation. Write all appropriate multiplicities in the ERD.

  a A department employs many employees, but each employee is employed by one department.
  b Some employees, known as 'rovers', are not assigned to any department.
  c A division operates many departments, but each department is operated by one division.
  d An employee may be assigned many projects, and a project may have many employees assigned to it.
  e A project must have at least one employee assigned to it.

f One of the employees manages each department, and each department is managed by only one employee.

g One of the employees runs each division, and each division is run by only one employee.

7 During peak periods, Temporary Employment Corporation (TEC) places temporary workers in companies. TEC's manager gives you the following description of the business:

- TEC has a file of candidates who are willing to work.
- If the candidate has worked before, that candidate has a specific job history. (Naturally, no job history exists if the candidate has never worked.) Each time the candidate worked, one additional job history record was created.
- Each candidate has earned several qualifications. Each qualification may be earned by more than one candidate. (For example, it is possible for more than one candidate to have earned a BA degree or a Microsoft Network Certification. And clearly, a candidate may have earned both a BA and a Microsoft Network Certification.)
- TEC also has a list of companies that request temporaries.
- Each time a company requests a temporary employee, TEC makes an entry in the Openings folder. That folder contains an opening number, a company name, required qualifications, a starting date, an anticipated ending date, and hourly pay.
- Each opening requires only one specific or main qualification.
- When a candidate matches the qualification, he or she is given the job and an entry is made in the Placement Record folder. That folder contains an opening number, a candidate number, the total hours worked, etc. In addition, an entry is made in the job history for the candidate.
- An opening can be filled by many candidates, and a candidate can fill many openings.
- TEC uses special codes to describe a candidate's qualifications for an opening. The list of codes is shown in the table below.

CODE	DESCRIPTION
SEC-45	Secretarial work, at least 45 words per minute
SEC-60	Secretarial work, at least 60 words per minute
CLERK	General clerking work
PRG-PY	Programmer, Python
PRG-C++	Programmer, C++
DBA-ORA	Database Administrator, Oracle
DBA-DB2	Database Administrator, IBM DB2
DBA-SQLSERV	Database Administrator, MS SQL Server
SYS-1	Systems Analyst, level 1
SYS-2	Systems Analyst, level 2
NW-NOV	Network Administrator, Novell experience
WD-CF	Web Developer, ColdFusion

TEC's management wants to keep track of the following entities:

- COMPANY
- OPENING
- QUALIFICATION
- CANDIDATE
- JOB_HISTORY
- PLACEMENT

Given that information, do the following:

a Draw the ERD using UML notation for this enterprise.

b Identify all possible relationships.

c Identify the multiplicities (including the mandatory/optional dependencies) for each relationship.

d Resolve all *:* relationships.

8 The Gauteng Netball Conference (GNC) is an amateur netball association. Each town in the province has one team as its representative. Each team has a maximum of 14 players and a minimum of 11 players. Each team also has up to three coaches (offensive, defensive and physical training coaches). During the season, each team plays two games (home and visitor) against each of the other teams. Given those conditions, do the following:

a Identify the multiplicities of each relationship.

b Identify the type of dependency that exists between TOWN and TEAM.

c Identify the cardinality between teams and players and between teams and town.

d Identify the dependency between coach and team and between team and player.

e Draw the ERD to represent the GNC database.

9 Automata Inc. produces specialty vehicles by contract. The company operates several departments, each of which builds a particular vehicle, such as a limousine, a truck, a van or an RV.

When a new vehicle is built, the department places an order with the purchasing department to request specific components. Automata's purchasing department is interested in creating a database to keep track of orders and to accelerate the process of delivering materials.

The order received by the purchasing department may contain several different items. An inventory is maintained so that the most frequently requested items are delivered almost immediately. When an order comes in, it is checked to determine whether the requested item is in inventory. If an item is not in inventory, it must be ordered from a supplier. Each item may have several suppliers.

Using that functional description of the processes encountered at Automata's purchasing department, do the following:

a Identify all of the main entities.

b Identify all of the relations and multiplicities among entities.

c Identify the type of existence dependency in all relations.

d Give at least two examples of the types of reports that can be obtained from the database.

10 Create an ERD based on the UML notation, using the following requirements:

- An INVOICE is written by a SALESREP. Each sales representative can write many invoices, but each invoice is written by a single sales representative.
- The INVOICE is written for a single CUSTOMER. However, each customer can have many invoices.
- An INVOICE can include many detail lines (LINE), which describe the products bought by the customer.
- The product information is stored in a PRODUCT entity.
- The product's vendor information is found in a VENDOR entity.

> **NOTE**
>
> Limit your ERD to entities and relationships based on the business rules shown here. In other words, do *not* add realism to your design by expanding or refining the business rules. However, make sure you include the attributes that would permit the model to be successfully implemented.

11 Using the following brief summary of business rules for the ROBCOR catering service, draw the fully labelled ERD. Make sure you include all appropriate entities, relationships, connectivities and cardinalities.

Each dinner is based on a single entrée, but each entrée can be served at many dinners. A guest can attend many dinners, and each dinner can be attended by many guests. Each dinner invitation can be mailed to many guests, and each guest can receive many invitations.

12 Create an ERD using UML notation that can be implemented for a medical clinic, using at least the following business rules:

- A patient can make many appointments with one or more doctors in the clinic, and a doctor can accept appointments with many patients. However, each appointment is made with only one doctor, and each appointment references a single patient.
- Emergency cases do not require an appointment. However, for appointment management purposes, an emergency is entered in the appointment book as 'unscheduled'.
- If kept, an appointment yields a visit with the doctor specified in the appointment. The visit yields a diagnosis and, when appropriate, treatment.
- With each visit, the patient's records are updated to provide a medical history.
- Each patient visit creates a bill. Each patient visit is billed by one doctor, and each doctor can bill many patients.
- Each bill must be paid. However, a bill may be paid in many instalments, and a payment may cover more than one bill.
- A patient may pay the bill directly, or the bill may be the basis for a claim submitted to an insurance company.
- If the bill is paid by an insurance company, the deductible is submitted to the patient for payment.

13 Tiny University is so pleased with your design and implementation of its student registration/tracking system that it wants you to expand the design to include its car pool. A brief description of operations follows:

- Faculty members may use the vehicles owned by Tiny University for officially sanctioned travel. For example, the vehicles may be used by faculty members to travel to off-campus learning centres, to travel to locations at which research papers are presented, to transport students to officially sanctioned locations, and to travel for public service purposes. The vehicles used for such purposes are managed by Tiny University's TFBS (Travel Far But Slowly) Centre.
- Using reservation forms, each department can reserve vehicles for its faculty, who are responsible for filling out the appropriate trip completion form at the end of a trip. The reservation form includes the expected departure date, vehicle type required, destination and name of the authorised faculty member. When the faculty member arrives to pick up the vehicle, (s)he must sign a checkout form to log out the vehicle and pick up a trip completion form. (The TFBS employee who releases the vehicle for use also signs the checkout form.) The faculty member's trip completion form includes the faculty member's identification code, the vehicle's identification, the odometer readings at the start and end of the trip, maintenance complaints (if any), litres of fuel purchased (if any) and the Tiny University credit card number used to pay for the fuel. If fuel is purchased, the credit card receipt must be stapled to the trip completion form. Upon receipt of the faculty trip completion form, the faculty member's department is billed at a mileage rate based on the vehicle type (sedan, station wagon, panel van, minivan or minibus) used. (*Hint:* Do *not* use more entities than are necessary. Remember the difference between attributes and entities!)
- All vehicle maintenance is performed by TFBS. Each time a vehicle requires maintenance, a maintenance log entry is completed on a prenumbered maintenance log form. The maintenance log form includes the vehicle identification, a brief description of the type of maintenance required, the initial log entry date, the date on which the maintenance was completed and the identification of the mechanic who released the vehicle back into service. (Only mechanics who have an inspection authorisation may release the vehicle back into service.)
- As soon as the log form has been initiated, the log form's number is transferred to a maintenance detail form; the log form's number is also forwarded to the parts department manager, who fills out a parts usage form on which the maintenance log number is recorded. The maintenance detail form contains separate lines for each maintenance item performed, for the parts used and for identification of the mechanic who performed the maintenance item. When all maintenance items have been completed, the maintenance detail form is stapled to the maintenance log form, the maintenance log form's completion date is filled out and the mechanic who releases the vehicle back into service signs the form. The stapled forms are then filed, to be used later as the source for various maintenance reports.
- TFBS maintains a parts inventory, including oil, oil filters, air filters and belts of various types. The parts inventory is checked daily to monitor parts usage and to reorder parts that reach the 'minimum quantity on hand' level. To track parts usage, the parts manager requires each mechanic to sign out the parts that are used to perform each vehicle's maintenance; the parts manager records the maintenance log number under which the part is used.
- Each month, TFBS issues a set of reports. The reports include the mileage driven by vehicle, by department, and by faculty members within a department. In addition, various revenue reports are generated, by vehicle and department. A detailed parts usage report is also filed each month. Finally, a vehicle maintenance summary is created each month.

Given that brief summary of operations, draw the appropriate (and fully labelled) ERD. Use the UML ERD notation to indicate entities, relationships and multiplicities.

14 Using the following information, produce an ERD – based on the UML model – that can be implemented. Make sure you include all appropriate entities, relationships and multiplicities:

- EverFail company is in the quick oil change and lube business. Although customers bring in their cars for what is described as 'quick oil changes', EverFail also replaces windshield wipers, oil filters and air filters, subject to customer approval. The invoice contains the charges for the oil and all parts used, and a standard labour charge. When the invoice is presented to customers, they pay cash, use a credit card or write a cheque. EverFail does not extend credit. EverFail's database is to be designed to keep track of all components in all transactions.
- Given the high parts usage of the business operations, EverFail must maintain careful control of its parts (oil, wipers, oil filters and air filters) inventory. Therefore, if parts reach their minimum on-hand quantity, the parts in low supply must be reordered from an appropriate vendor. EverFail maintains a vendor list, which contains vendors actually used and potential vendors.
- Periodically, based on the date of the car's service, EverFail mails updates to customers. EverFail also tracks each customer's car mileage.

15 Create a complete ERD that can be implemented in the relational model using the following description of operations. Hot Water (HW) is a small start-up company that sells spas. HW does not carry any stock. A few spas are set up in a simple warehouse so customers can see some of the models available, but any products sold must be ordered at the time of the sale:

- HW can get spas from several different manufacturers.
- Each manufacturer produces one or more different brands of spas.
- Each and every brand is produced by only one manufacturer.
- Every brand has one or more models.
- Every model is produced as part of a brand. For example, Meerkat Bay Spas is a manufacturer that produces Big Blue Meerkat spas, a premium-level brand, and Lazy Lizard spas, an entry-level brand. The Big Blue Meerkat brand offers several models, including the BBI-6, an 81-jet spa with two 6 hp motors, and the BBI-10, a 102-jet spa with three 6 hp motors.
- Every manufacturer is identified by a manufacturer code. The company name, address, area code, phone number and account number are kept in the system for every manufacturer.
- For each brand, the brand name and brand level (premium, mid-level, or entry-level) are kept in the system.
- For each model, the model number, number of jets, number of motors, horsepower per motor, suggested retail price, HW retail price, dry weight, water capacity, and seating capacity must be kept in the system.

16 United Helpers is a non-profit organisation that provides aid to people after natural disasters. Based on the following brief description of operations, create the appropriate fully labelled ERD:

- Volunteers carry out the tasks of the organisation. The name, address and telephone number are tracked for each volunteer. Each volunteer may be assigned to several tasks, and some tasks require many volunteers. A volunteer might be in the system without having been assigned a task yet. It is possible to have tasks that no one has been assigned. When a volunteer is assigned to a task, the system should track the start time and end time of that assignment.

- Each task has a task code, task description, task type and task status. For example, there may be a task with task code '101', a description of 'answer the telephone', a type of 'recurring', and a status of 'ongoing'. Another task might have a code of '102', a description of 'prepare 5 000 packages of basic medical supplies', a type of 'packing', and a status of 'open'.
- For all tasks of type 'packing', there is a packing list that specifies the contents of the packages. There are many packing lists to produce different packages, such as basic medical packages, child-care packages, and food packages. Each packing list has an ID number, a packing list name and a packing list description, which describes the items that should make up the package. Every packing task is associated with only one packing list. A packing list may not be associated with any tasks, or it may be associated with many tasks. Tasks that are not packing tasks are not associated with any packing list.
- Packing tasks result in the creation of packages. Each individual package of supplies produced by the organisation is tracked, and each package is assigned an ID number. The date the package was created and its total weight are recorded. A given package is associated with only one task. Some tasks (such as 'answer the phones') will not produce any packages, while other tasks (such as 'prepare 5 000 packages of basic medical supplies') will be associated with many packages.
- The packing list describes the ideal contents of each package, but it is not always possible to include the ideal number of each item. Therefore, the actual items included in each package should be tracked. A package can contain many different items, and a given item can be used in many different packages.
- Each item that the organisation provides has an item ID number, item description, item value and item quantity on hand stored in the system. Along with tracking the actual items that are placed in each package, the quantity of each item placed in the package must be tracked as well. For example, a packing list may state that basic medical packages should include 100 bandages, 4 bottles of iodine and 4 bottles of hydrogen peroxide. However, because of the limited supply of items, a given package may include only 10 bandages, 1 bottle of iodine, and no hydrogen peroxide. The fact that the package includes bandages and iodine needs to be recorded along with the quantity of each item included. It is possible for the organisation to have items that have not been included in any package yet, but every package will contain at least one item.

17 Luxury-Oriented Scenic Tours (LOST) provides guided tours to groups of visitors to the Cape Town area. In recent years, LOST has grown quickly and is having difficulty keeping up with all of the various information needs of the company. The company's operations are as follows:

- LOST offers many different tours. For each tour, the tour name, approximate length (in hours), and fee charged is needed. Guides are identified by an employee ID, but the system should also record a guide's name, home address, and date of hire. Guides take a test to be qualified to lead specific tours. It is important to know which guides are qualified to lead which tours and the date on which they completed the qualification test for each tour. A guide may be qualified to lead many different tours. A tour can have many different qualified guides. New guides may or may not be qualified to lead any tours, just as a new tour may or may not have any qualified guides.
- Every tour must be designed to visit at least three locations. For each location, a name, type and official description are kept. Some locations (such as Table Mountain) are visited by more than one tour, while others (such as District Six) are visited by a single tour. All locations are visited by at least one tour. The order in which the tour visits each location should be tracked as well.

- When a tour is actually given, that is referred to as an 'outing'. LOST schedules outings well in advance so they can be advertised and so employees can understand their upcoming work schedules. A tour can have many scheduled outings, although newly designed tours may not have any outings scheduled. Each outing is for a single tour and is scheduled for a particular date and time. All outings must be associated with a tour. All tours at LOST are guided tours, so a guide must be assigned to each outing. Each outing has one and only one guide. Guides are occasionally asked to lead an outing of a tour even if they are not officially qualified to lead that tour. Newly hired guides may never have been scheduled to lead any outings. Tourists, called 'clients' by LOST, pay to join a scheduled outing. For each client, the name and telephone number are recorded. Clients may sign up to join many different outings, and each outing can have many clients. Information is kept only on clients who have signed up for at least one outing, although newly scheduled outings may not have any clients signed up yet.

  a Create an ERD to support LOST operations.

  b The operations provided state that it is possible for a guide to lead an outing of a tour even if the guide is not officially qualified to lead outings of that tour. Imagine that the business rules instead specified that a guide is never, under any circumstances, allowed to lead an outing unless he or she is qualified to lead outings of that tour. How could the data model in Part a be modified to enforce this new constraint?

NOTE

Problems 18 and 19 may be used as the basis for class projects. These problems illustrate the challenge of translating a description of operations to a set of business rules that will define the components of an ERD that can be successfully implemented. These problems can also be used as the basis for discussions about the components and contents of a proper description of operations. One of the things you must need to learn if you want to create databases that can be successfully implemented, is to separate the generic background material from the details that directly affect database design. You must also keep in mind that many constraints cannot be incorporated into the database design; instead, such constraints are handled by the applications software. Although the description of operations in Problem 18 deals with a Web-based business, the focus should be on the *database* aspects of the design, rather than on its interface and the transaction management details. In fact, the argument can easily be made that the existence of Web-based businesses has made database design more important than ever. (You might be able to get away with a bad database design if you sell only a few items per day, but the problems of poorly designed databases are compounded as the number of transactions increases.)

18 Use the following descriptions of the operations of RC_Models Company to complete this exercise.

RC_Models Company sells its products – plastic models (aircraft, ships and cars) and 'add-on' decals for those models – through its internet website (*www.rc_models.com*). Models and decals are available in scales that vary from 1/144 to 1/32.

Customers use the website to select the products and to pay by credit card. If a product is not currently available, it is placed on back order at the customer's discretion. (Back orders are not charged to a customer until the order is shipped.) When a customer completes his or her transactions, the invoice is printed and the products listed on the invoice are pulled from inventory for shipment. (The invoice includes a shipping charge.) The printed invoice is enclosed in the shipping container. The customer credit card charges are transmitted to the CC Bank, at which RC_Models Company maintains a commercial account. (*Note:* The CC Bank is *not* part of the RC_Models database.)

RC_Models Company tracks customer purchases and periodically sends out promotional materials. Because management at RC_Models Company requires detailed information to conduct its operations, numerous reports are available. Those reports include, but are not limited to, customer purchases by product category and amount, product turnover and revenues by product and customer. If a product has not recorded a sale within four weeks of being stocked, it is removed from inventory and scrapped.

Many of the customers on the RC_Models customer list have bought RC_Models products. However, RC_Models Company also has purchased a copy of the *FineScale Modeler* magazine subscription list to use in marketing its products to customers who have not yet bought from RC_Models Company. In addition, customer data are recorded when potential customers request product information.

RC_Models Company orders its products directly from the manufacturers. For example, the plastic models are ordered from Tamiya, Academy, Revell/Monogram and others. Decals are ordered from Aeromaster, Tauro, WaterMark and others. (*Note:* Not all manufacturers in the RC_Models Company database have received orders.) All orders are placed via the manufacturers' websites, and the order amounts are automatically handled through RC_Models' commercial bank account with the CC Bank. Orders are automatically placed when product inventory reaches the specified minimum quantity on hand. (The number of product units ordered depends on the minimum order quantity specified for each product.)

a Given that brief and incomplete description of operations for RC_Models Company, write all applicable business rules to establish entities, relationships, optionalities and multiplicities. (*Hint:* Use the following three business rules as examples, writing the remaining business rules in the same format.)

- A customer may generate many invoices.
- Each invoice is generated by only one customer.
- Some customers have not (yet) generated an invoice.

b Draw the fully labelled and implementable ERD based on the business rules you wrote in Part a of this problem. Include all entities, relationships, optionalities and multiplicities.

19 Use the following description of the operations of the RC_Charter2 Company to complete this exercise.

The RC_Charter2 Company operates a fleet of aircraft under the FAR Part 135 (air taxi or charter) certificate of the Federal Air Regulations (FARs) that are enforced by the FAA. The aircraft are available for air taxi (charter) operations within the United States and Canada.

Charter companies provide so-called unscheduled operations – that is, charter flights take place only after a customer reserves the use of an aircraft to fly at a customer-designated date and time to one or more customer-designated destinations, transporting passengers, cargo or some combination of passengers and cargo. A customer can, of course, reserve many different charter flights (trips) during any time frame. However, for billing purposes, each charter trip is reserved by one and only one customer. Some of RC_Charter2's customers do not use the company's charter operations; instead, they purchase fuel, use maintenance services or use other RC_Charter2 services. (*Note:* This database design will focus on the charter operations only.)

Each charter trip yields revenue for the RC_Charter2 Company. This revenue is generated by the charges a customer pays upon the completion of a flight. The charter flight charges are a function of aircraft model used, distance flown, waiting time, special customer requirements and crew expenses. The distance mileage charges are computed by multiplying the round-trip miles by the model's charge per mile. Round-trip miles are based on the actual navigational path flown. The sample route traced in Figure P5.1 illustrates the procedure. Note that the number of round-trip miles is calculated to be 130 + 200 + 180 + 390 = 900.

FIGURE P5.1 **Round-trip mile determination**

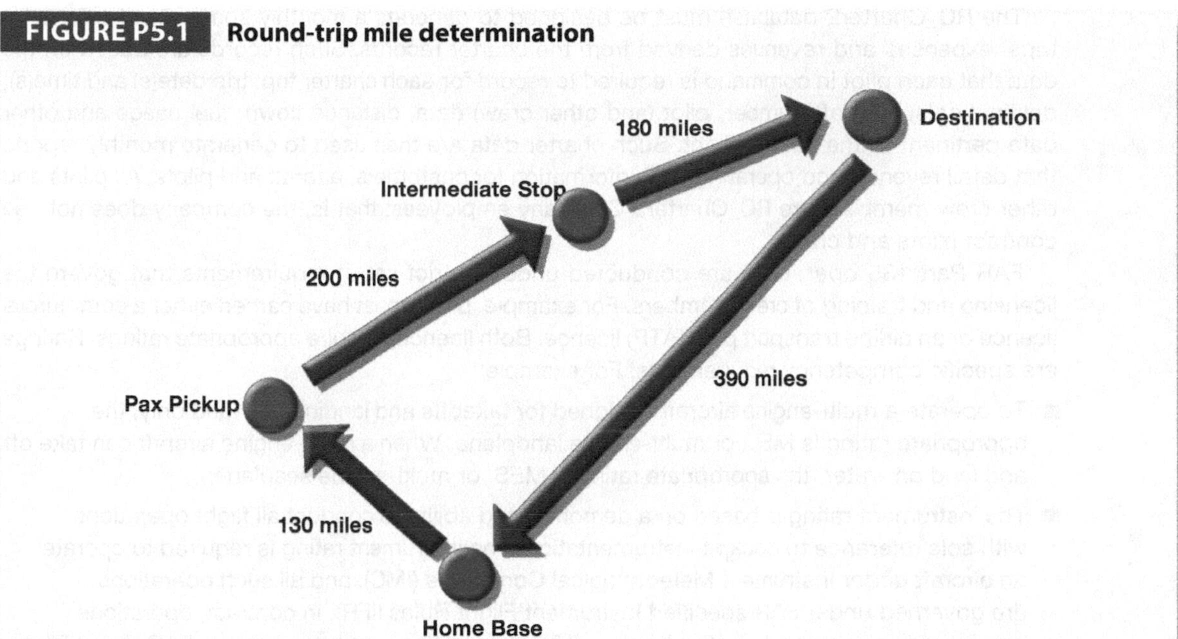

Depending on whether a customer has RC_Charter2 credit authorisation, he or she may:

- Pay the entire charter bill upon the completion of the charter flight.
- Pay a part of the charter bill and charge the remainder to the account. The charge amount may not exceed the available credit.
- Charge the entire charter bill to the account. The charge amount may not exceed the available credit.

Customers may pay all or part of the existing balance for previous charter trips. Such payments may be made at any time and are not necessarily tied to a specific charter trip. The charter mileage charge includes the expense of the pilot(s) and other crew required by FAR 135. However, if customers request *additional* crew *not* required by FAR 135, those customers are charged for the crew members on an hourly basis. The hourly crew-member charge is based on each crew member's qualifications.

The database must be able to handle crew assignment. Each charter trip requires the use of an aircraft, and a crew flies each aircraft. The smaller piston engine-powered charter aircraft require a crew consisting of only a single pilot. Larger aircraft – that is, aircraft having a gross takeoff weight of 5 500 kg or more – and jet-powered aircraft require a pilot and a copilot, while some of the larger aircraft used to transport passengers may require flight attendants as part of the crew. Some of the older aircraft require the assignment of a flight engineer, and larger cargo-carrying aircraft require the assignment of a loadmaster. In short, a crew can consist of more than one person and not all crew members are pilots.

The charter flight's aircraft waiting charges are computed by multiplying the hours waited by the model's hourly waiting charge. Crew expenses are limited to meals and overnight expenses such as hotel/motel charges and ground transportation.

The RC_Charter2 database must be designed to generate a monthly summary of all charter trips, expenses and revenues derived from the charter records. Such records are based on the data that each pilot in command is required to record for each charter trip: trip date(s) and time(s), destination(s), aircraft number, pilot (and other crew) data, distance flown, fuel usage and other data pertinent to the charter flight. Such charter data are then used to generate monthly reports that detail revenue and operating cost information for customers, aircraft and pilots. All pilots and other crew members are RC_Charter2 Company employees; that is, the company does not use contract pilots and crew.

FAR Part 135 operations are conducted under a strict set of requirements that govern the licensing and training of crew members. For example, pilots must have earned either a commercial licence or an airline transport pilot (ATP) licence. Both licences require appropriate ratings. Ratings are specific competency requirements. For example:

- To operate a multi-engine aircraft designed for takeoffs and landings on land only, the appropriate rating is MEL, or multi-engine landplane. When a multi-engine aircraft can take off and land on water, the appropriate rating is MES, or multi-engine seaplane.
- The instrument rating is based on a demonstrated ability to conduct all flight operations with sole reference to cockpit instrumentation. The instrument rating is required to operate an aircraft under Instrument Meteorological Conditions (IMC), and all such operations are governed under FAR-specified Instrument Flight Rules (IFR). In contrast, operations conducted under 'good weather' or *visual* flight conditions are based on the FAR Visual Flight Rules (VFR).
- The type rating is required for all aircraft with a takeoff weight of more than 5 500 kg or for aircraft that are purely jet-powered. (If an aircraft uses jet engines to drive propellers, that aircraft is said to be turboprop-powered. A turboprop – that is, a turbo propeller-powered aircraft – does not require a type rating unless it meets the 5 500 kg weight limitation.)

Although pilot licences and ratings are not time-limited, exercising the privilege of the licence and ratings under Part 135 requires both *a current medical certificate and a current Part 135 checkride*. The following distinctions are important:

- The medical certificate may be Class I or Class II. The Class I medical is more stringent than the Class II, and it must be renewed every six months. The Class II medical must be renewed yearly. If the Class I medical is not renewed during the six-month period, it automatically reverts to a Class II certificate. If the Class II medical is not renewed within the specified period, it automatically reverts to a Class III medical, which is not valid for commercial flight operations.
- A Part 135 checkride is a practical flight examination that must be successfully completed every six months. The checkride includes all flight manoeuvres and procedures specified in Part 135.

Non-pilot crew members must also have the proper certificates in order to meet specific job requirements. For example, loadmasters need an appropriate certificate, as do flight attendants. In addition, crew members such as loadmasters and flight attendants who may be required in operations that involve large aircraft (more than a 5 500 kg takeoff weight and passenger numbers over 19) are also required periodically to pass a written and practical exam. The RC_Charter2 Company is required to keep a complete record of all test types, dates and results for each crew member, as well as pilot medical certificate examination dates.

In addition, all flight crew members are required to submit to periodic drug testing; the results must be tracked, too. (Note that non-pilot crew members are not required to take pilot-specific tests such as Part 135 checkrides. Nor are pilots required to take crew tests such as loadmaster and flight attendant practical exams.) However, many crew members have licences and/or certifications in several areas. For example, a pilot may have an ATP and a loadmaster certificate. If that pilot is assigned to be a loadmaster on a given charter flight, the loadmaster certificate is required. Similarly, a flight attendant may have earned a commercial pilot's licence. Sample data formats are shown in the table below.

PART A Tests

Test code	Test description	Test frequency
1	Part 135 Flight Check	6 months
2	Medical, Class 1	6 months
3	Medical, Class 2	12 months
4	Loadmaster Practical	12 months
5	Flight Attendant Practical	12 months
6	Drug test	Random
7	Operations, written exam	6 months

Part B Results

Employee	Test code	Test date	Test result
101	1	12-Nov-18	Pass-1
103	6	23-Dec-18	Pass-1
112	4	23-Dec-18	Pass-2
103	7	11-Jan-19	Pass-1
112	7	16-Jan-19	Pass-1
101	7	16-Jan-19	Pass-1
101	6	11-Feb-19	Pass-2
125	2	15-Feb-19	Pass-1

Part C Licences and Certificates

Licence or Certificate	Licence or Certificate Description
ATP	Airline Transport Pilot
Comm	Commercial licence
Med-1	Medical certificate, class 1
Med-2	Medical certificate, class 2
Instr	Instrument rating
MEL	Multi-engine land aircraft rating
LM	Loadmaster
FA	Flight attendant

5

Part D Licences and Certificates Held by Employees		
Employee	**Licence or Certificate**	**Date Earned**
101	Comm	12-Nov-03
101	Instr	28-Jun-04
101	MEL	9-Aug-04
103	Comm	21-Dec-05
112	FA	23-Jun-12
103	Instr	18-Jan-06
112	LM	27-Nov-15

Pilots and other crew members must receive recurrency training appropriate to their work assignments. *Recurrency training* is based on an FAA-approved curriculum that is job-specific. For example, pilot recurrency training includes a review of all applicable Part 135 flight rules and regulations, weather data interpretation, company flight operations requirements and specified flight procedures. The RC_Charter2 Company is required to keep a complete record of all recurrency training for each crew member subject to the training.

The RC_Charter2 Company is required to maintain a detailed record of all crew credentials and all training mandated by Part 135. *The company must keep a complete record of each requirement and of all compliance data.*

To conduct a charter flight, the company must have a properly maintained aircraft available. A pilot who meets all of the FAA's licensing and currency requirements must fly the aircraft as Pilot in Command (PIC). For those aircraft that are powered by piston engines or turboprops and have a gross takeoff weight under 5 500 kg, single-pilot operations are permitted under Part 135 as long as a properly maintained autopilot is available. However, even if FAR Part 135 permits single-pilot operations, many customers require the presence of a copilot who is capable of conducting the flight operations under Part 135.

The RC_Charter2 operations manager anticipates the lease of turbojet-powered aircraft, and those aircraft are required to have a crew consisting of a pilot and copilot. Both pilot and copilot must meet the same Part 135 licensing, ratings and training requirements.

The company also leases larger aircraft that exceed the 5 500 kg gross takeoff weight. Those aircraft can carry the number of passengers that requires the presence of one or more flight attendants. If those aircraft carry cargo weighing over 5 500 kg, a loadmaster must be assigned as a crew member to supervise the loading and securing of the cargo. *The database must be designed to meet the anticipated additional charter crew assignment capability.*

a Using this incomplete description of operations, write all applicable business rules to establish entities, relationships, optionalities and multiplicities. (*Hint:* Use the following five business rules as examples, writing the remaining business rules in the same format.)

- A customer may request many charter trips.
- Each charter trip is requested by only one customer.
- Some customers have not (yet) requested a charter trip.
- An employee may be assigned to serve as a crew member on many charter trips.
- Each charter trip may have many employees assigned to it to serve as crew members.

b Draw the fully labelled and implementable ERD based on the business rules you wrote in Part a of this problem. Include all entities, relationships, optionalities and multiplicities.

CHAPTER 6

Data Modelling Advanced Concepts

IN THIS CHAPTER, YOU WILL LEARN:

- About the extended entity relationship (EER) model's main constructs
- How entity clusters are used to represent multiple entities and relationships
- The characteristics of good primary keys and how to select them
- How to use flexible solutions for special data modelling cases

PREVIEW

In the previous chapters, you learnt how to use entity relationship diagrams (ERDs) to properly create a data model. In this chapter, you will learn about the extended entity relationship (EER) model. The EER model builds on ER concepts and adds support for entity supertypes, subtypes and entity clustering.

Most current database implementations are based on relational databases. As the relational model uses keys to create associations among tables, it is essential to learn the characteristics of good primary keys and how to select them. Primary key selection is too important to be left to chance, which is why this chapter covers critical aspects of primary key identification and placement.

Focusing on practical database design, this chapter also illustrates some special design cases that highlight the importance of flexible designs, proper identification of primary keys and placement of foreign keys. (Flexible designs are designs that can be adapted to meet the demands of changing data and information requirements.) Data modelling is a vital step in the development of databases, providing a good foundation for successful application development. (You should know the mantra: good database applications cannot be based on bad database designs, and no amount of outstanding coding can overcome the limitations of poor database design.)

To help you carry out data modelling tasks, the chapter concludes with a database modelling checklist that outlines basic data modelling principles.

6.1 THE EXTENDED ENTITY RELATIONSHIP MODEL

As the complexity of the data structures being modelled has increased, and as application software requirements have become more stringent, there has been an increasing need to capture more information in the data model. The **extended entity relationship model (EERM)**, sometimes referred to as the enhanced entity relationship model, is the result of adding more semantic constructs to the original entity relationship (ER) model. As you might expect, a diagram using this model is called an **EER diagram (EERD)**. In the following sections, you will learn about the main EER model constructs – entity supertypes, entity subtypes and entity clustering – and see how they are represented in ERDs. Following on from Chapter 5, Data Modelling with Entity Relationship Diagrams, this chapter will use UML notation to produce EER diagrams.

6.1.1 Entity Supertypes and Subtypes

In the real world, most businesses employ people with a wide range of skills and special qualifications. In fact, data modellers find many ways to group employees based on employee characteristics. For instance, a retail company would group employees as salaried and hourly employees, while a university would group employees as faculty, staff and administrators.

The grouping of employees to create various *types* of employees provides two important benefits:

- It avoids unnecessary nulls in the employee attributes when some employees have characteristics that are not shared by other employees.
- It enables a particular employee type to participate in relationships that are unique to that employee type.

To illustrate those benefits, let's explore the case of an aviation business. The aviation business employs pilots, mechanics, secretaries, accountants, database managers and many other types of employees. Figure 6.1 illustrates how pilots share certain characteristics with other employees, such as a last name (EMP_LNAME) and hire date (EMP_HIRE_DATE). On the other hand, many pilot characteristics

FIGURE 6.1 **Nulls created by unique attributes**

EMP_NUM	EMP_LNAME	EMP_FNAME	EMP_INITIAL	EMP_LICENCE	EMP_RATINGS	EMP_MED_TYPE	EMP_HIRE_DATE
100	Nkosi	Cela	T				15-Mar-98
101	Lewis	Marcos		ATP	SEL/MEL/Instr/CFII	1	25-Apr-99
102	Vandam	Jean					20-Dec-03
103	Jones	Victoria	R				28-Aug-13
104	Lange	Edith		ATP	SEL/MEL/Instr	1	20-Oct-07
105	Williams	Gabriel	U	COM	SEL/MEL/Instr/CFI	2	08-Nov-07
106	Naidu	Theeban		COM	SEL/MEL/Instr	2	05-Jan-14
107	Diante	Venite	L				02-Jul-07
108	Shenge	Mhambi					18-Nov-05
109	Travis	Brett	T	COM	SEL/MEL/SES/Instr/CFII	1	14-Apr-11
110	Genkazi	Stan					01-Dec-13

are not shared by other employees. For example, unlike other employees, pilots must meet special requirements such as flight hour restrictions, flight checks and periodic training. Therefore, if all employee characteristics and special qualifications were stored in a single EMPLOYEE entity, you would have a lot of nulls or you would have to make a lot of needless dummy entries. In this case, special pilot characteristics such as EMP_LICENCE, EMP_RATINGS and EMP_MED_TYPE will generate nulls for employees who are not pilots. In addition, pilots participate in some relationships that are unique to their qualifications. For example, not all employees can fly aircraft; only employees who are pilots can participate in the 'employee flies aircraft' relationship.

Based on the preceding discussion, you would correctly deduce that the PILOT entity stores only those attributes that are unique to pilots and that the EMPLOYEE entity stores attributes that are common to all employees. Based on that hierarchy, you can conclude that PILOT is a *subtype* of EMPLOYEE and that EMPLOYEE is the *supertype* of PILOT. In modelling terms, an **entity supertype** is a generic entity type that is related to one or more **entity subtypes**, where the entity supertype contains the common characteristics and the entity subtypes contain the unique characteristics of each entity subtype. In the next section, you will learn how the entity supertypes and subtypes are related in a specialisation hierarchy.

6.1.2 Specialisation Hierarchy

Entity supertypes and subtypes are organised in a specialisation hierarchy. The **specialisation hierarchy** depicts the arrangement of higher-level entity supertypes (parent entities) and lower-level entity subtypes (child entities). Figure 6.2 shows the specialisation hierarchy formed by an EMPLOYEE supertype and three entity subtypes – PILOT, MECHANIC and ACCOUNTANT. The specialisation hierarchy reflects the 1:1 relationship between EMPLOYEE and each of its subtypes. For example, a PILOT subtype occurrence is related to one instance of the EMPLOYEE supertype, and a MECHANIC subtype occurrence is related to one instance of the EMPLOYEE supertype.

NOTE

In UML notation, subtypes are called *subclasses* and supertypes are known as *superclasses*. UML notation also enables you to represent specialisation hierarchies, which are referred to in UML as **class generalisation hierarchies.** A **class hierarchy** resembles an upside-down tree in which each child class has only one parent class. Each child class 'is a' subclass of another (supertype) class. Throughout this chapter we will use the terms *subtype* and *supertype* in all discussions.

The terminology and symbols in Figures 6.2 will be explained as you continue through the chapter.

The relationships depicted within the specialisation hierarchy are sometimes described in terms of 'IS-A' relationships. For example, a pilot *is an* employee, a mechanic *is an* employee, and an accountant *is an* employee. It is important to understand that, within a specialisation hierarchy, a subtype can exist only within the context of a supertype and every subtype can have only one supertype to which it is directly related. However, a specialisation hierarchy can have many levels of supertype/subtype relationships – that is, you can have a specialisation hierarchy in which a supertype has many subtypes; in turn, one of the subtypes is the supertype to other lower-level subtypes.

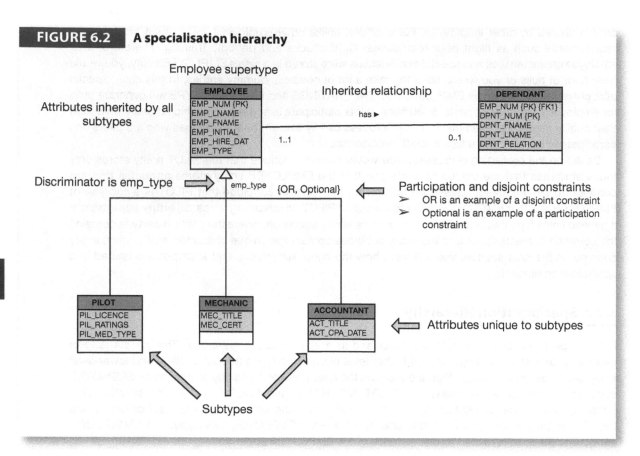

FIGURE 6.2 **A specialisation hierarchy**

Employee supertype

Inherited relationship

Attributes inherited by all subtypes

EMPLOYEE
EMP_NUM {PK}
EMP_LNAME
EMP_FNAME
EMP_INITIAL
EMP_HIRE_DAT
EMP_TYPE

has ▸ 1..1 0..1

DEPENDANT
EMP_NUM {PK} {FK1}
DPNT_NUM {PK}
DPNT_FNAME
DPNT_LNAME
DPNT_RELATION

Discriminator is emp_type

emp_type {OR, Optional}

Participation and disjoint constraints
- OR is an example of a disjoint constraint
- Optional is an example of a participation constraint

PILOT
PIL_LICENCE
PIL_RATINGS
PIL_MED_TYPE

MECHANIC
MEC_TITLE
MEC_CERT

ACCOUNTANT
ACT_TITLE
ACT_CPA_DATE

Attributes unique to subtypes

Subtypes

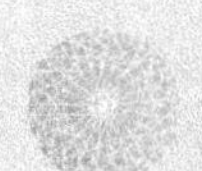

Online Content This chapter covers only specialisation hierarchies. The EER model also supports specialisation *lattices* where a subtype can have multiple parents (supertypes). However, those concepts are better covered under the object-oriented model in Appendix G, Object-Orientated Databases. The appendix is available on the online platform for this book.

As you can see in Figure 6.2, specialisation hierarchies enable the data model to capture additional semantic content (meaning) into the ERD. A specialisation hierarchy provides the means to:

- Support attribute inheritance.
- Define a special supertype attribute known as the subtype discriminator.
- Define disjoint/overlapping constraints and complete/partial constraints.

The following sections will cover such characteristics and constraints in more detail.

6.1.3 Inheritance

The property of **inheritance** enables an entity subtype to inherit the attributes and relationships of the supertype. As discussed earlier, a supertype contains those attributes that are common to all of its subtypes. In contrast, subtypes contain only the attributes that are unique to the subtype. For example,

Figure 6.2 illustrates that pilots, mechanics and accountants all inherit the employee number, last name, first name, middle initial, hire date and so on. However, Figure 6.2 also illustrates that pilots have attributes that are unique; the same is true for mechanics and accountants. *One important inheritance characteristic is that all entity subtypes inherit their primary key attribute from their supertype.* Note in Figure 6.2 that the EMP_NUM attribute is the primary key for each of the subtypes, but it is not shown in the subtype.

At the implementation level, the supertype and its subtype(s) depicted in the specialisation hierarchy maintain a 1:1 relationship. For example, the specialisation hierarchy lets you replace the undesirable EMPLOYEE table structure in Figure 6.1 with two tables – one representing the supertype EMPLOYEE and the other representing the subtype PILOT. (See Figure 6.3.)

FIGURE 6.3 The EMPLOYEE – PILOT supertype – subtype relationship

Table name: EMPLOYEE

EMP_NUM	EMP_LNAME	EMP_FNAME	EMP_INITIAL	EMP_HIRE_DATE	EMP_TYPE
100	Nkosi	Cela	T	15-Mar-98	
101	Lewis	Marcos		25-Apr-99	P
102	Vandam	Jean		20-Dec-03	A
103	Jones	Victoria	R	28-Aug-13	
104	Lange	Edith		20-Oct-07	P
105	Williams	Gabriel	U	08-Nov-07	P
106	Naidu	Theeban		05-Jan-14	P
107	Diante	Venite	L	02-Jul-07	M
108	Shengi	Mhambi		18-Nov-05	M
109	Travis	Brett	T	14-Apr-11	P
110	Genkazi	Stan		01-Dec-13	A

Table name: PILOT

EMP_NUM	PIL_LICENCE	PIL_RATINGS	PIL_MED_TYPE
101	ATP	SEL/MEL/Instr/CFII	1
104	ATP	SEL/MEL/Instr	1
105	COM	SEL/MEL/Instr/CFI	2
106	COM	SEL/MEL/Instr	2
109	COM	SEL/MEL/SES/Instr/CFII	1

Entity subtypes inherit all relationships in which the supertype entity participates. For example, Figure 6.2 shows the EMPLOYEE entity supertype participating in a 1:* relationship with a DEPENDANT entity. Through inheritance, all subtypes are also able to participate in that relationship. In specialisation hierarchies with multiple levels of supertype/subtypes, a lower-level subtype inherits all of the attributes and relationships from all of its upper-level supertypes.

6.1.4 Subtype Discriminator

A **subtype discriminator** is the attribute in the supertype entity that determines to which entity subtype each supertype occurrence is related. As seen in Figure 6.2, the subtype discriminator is the employee type (EMP_TYPE).

It is common practice to show the subtype discriminator and its value for each subtype in the ER diagram, as seen in Figure 6.2. However, not all ER modelling tools follow that practice. In Figure 6.2, the discriminator was added in MS Visio by using the UML generalisation properties.

It's important to note that the default comparison condition for the subtype discriminator attribute is the equality comparison. However, there may be situations in which the subtype discriminator is not necessarily based on an equality comparison. For example, based on business requirements, you may create two new pilot subtypes, PIC (pilot-in-command) qualified and copilot qualified only. A PIC-qualified pilot will be anyone with more than 1 500 PIC flight hours. In this case, the subtype discriminator would be 'Flight_Hours' and the criteria would be > 1500 or <= 1500, respectively.

NOTE

When creating a specialisation hierarchy using UML notation in MS Visio, you should use the generalisation object to connect the subtype entity to the supertype entity. The subtype discriminator is typed into the field called **discriminator** through the UML **generalisation properties box**.

Online Content For a tutorial on using MS Visio to create a specialisation hierarchy, see Appendix A, Designing Databases with Visio Professional: A Tutorial, available on the online platform for this book.

6.1.5 Disjoint and Overlapping Constraints

An entity supertype can have disjoint or overlapping entity subtypes. For example, in the aviation example, an employee can be a pilot or a mechanic or an accountant. Assume that one of the business rules dictates that an employee cannot belong to more than one subtype at a time; that is, an employee cannot be a pilot and a mechanic at the same time. **Disjoint subtypes**, also known as **non-overlapping subtypes**, are subtypes that contain a *unique* subset of the supertype entity set; in other words, each entity instance of the supertype can appear in only one of the subtypes. When using UML notation, a disjoint relationship is represented by an 'OR', and an overlapping constraint is represented by an 'AND'.

For example, in Figure 6.2, an employee (supertype) who is a pilot (subtype) can appear only in the PILOT subtype, not in any of the other subtypes. You can see that when using MS Visio to produce ERDs using UML notation, the disjoint subtype is indicated by placing the word 'OR' in brackets.

On the other hand, if the business rule specifies that employees can have multiple classifications, the EMPLOYEE supertype may contain *overlapping* job classification subtypes. **Overlapping** or **non-disjoint subtypes** are subtypes that contain non-unique subsets of the supertype entity set; that is, each entity instance of the supertype may appear in more than one subtype. For example, in a university environment, a person may be an employee or a student or both. In turn, an employee may be a lecturer as well as an administrator. Because an employee also may be a student, STUDENT and EMPLOYEE are overlapping subtypes of the supertype PERSON, just as LECTURER and ADMINISTRATOR are overlapping subtypes of the supertype EMPLOYEE. Figure 6.4 illustrates how these overlapping subtypes are represented in UML notation by placing the word 'AND' in brackets.

FIGURE 6.4 **Specialisation hierarchy with overlapping subtypes**

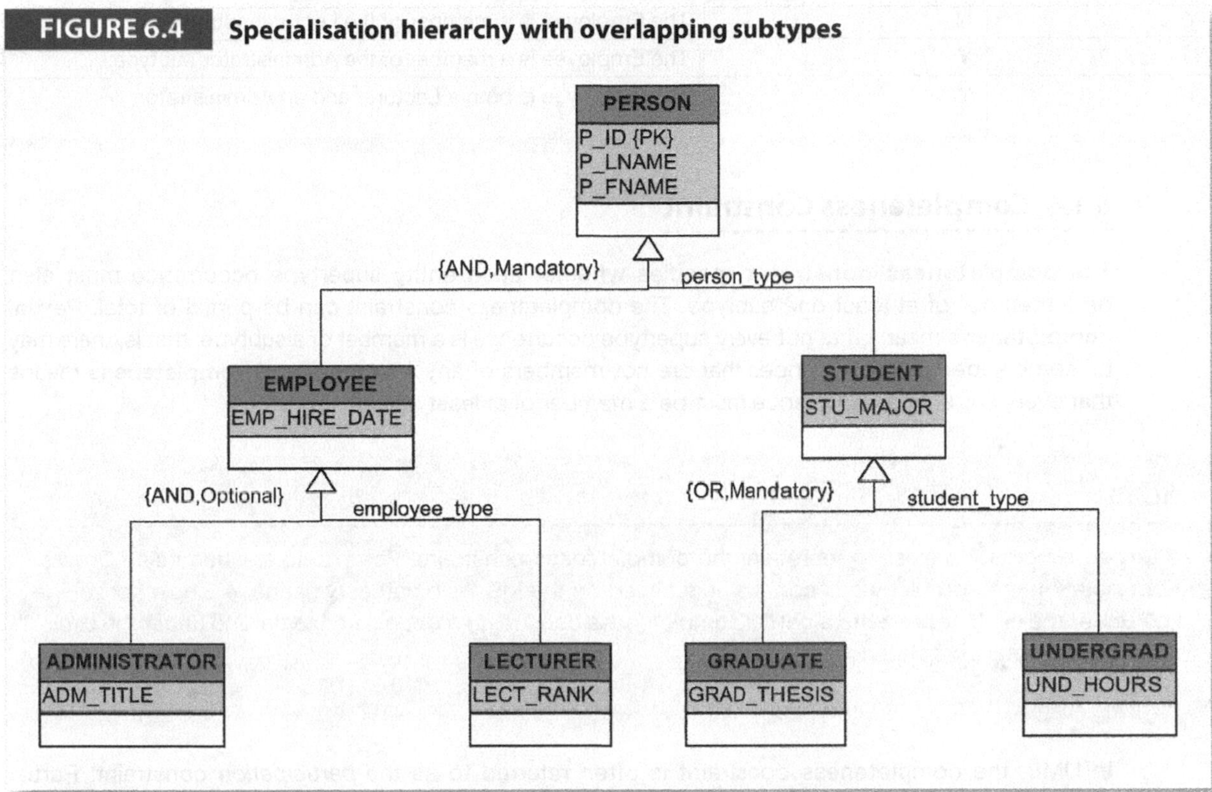

It is common practice to show the disjoint/overlapping symbols in the ERD. (See Figure 6.2 and Figure 6.4.) However, not all ER modelling tools follow that practice. For example, when using UML notation, MS Visio does not show the disjoint/overlapping constraints. Therefore, the MS Visio text tool was used to manually add the 'OR' and 'AND' constraints in Figures 6.2 and 6.4.

NOTE

Alternative notations exist for representing disjoint/overlapping subtypes. For example, Toby J. Teorey popularised the use of *G* and *G*s to indicate disjoint and overlapping subtypes.

As you learnt earlier in this section, the implementation of disjoint subtypes is based on the value of the subtype discriminator attribute in the supertype. However, *implementing* overlapping subtypes requires the use of one discriminator attribute for each subtype. For example, in the case of the Tiny University database design you saw in Chapter 5, Data Modelling with Entity Relationship Diagrams, a lecturer can also be an administrator. Therefore, the EMPLOYEE supertype would have the subtype discriminator attributes and values shown in Table 6.1.

TABLE 6.1 Discriminator attributes with overlapping subtypes

Discriminator Attributes		Comment
Lecturer	Administrator	
Y	N	The Employee is a member of the Lecturer subtype.
N	Y	The Employee is a member of the Administrator subtype.
Y	Y	The Employee is both a Lecturer and an Administrator.

6.1.6 Completeness Constraint

6

The **completeness constraint** specifies whether each entity supertype occurrence must also be a member of at least one subtype. The completeness constraint can be partial or total. **Partial completeness** means that not every supertype occurrence is a member of a subtype; that is, there may be some supertype occurrences that are not members of any subtype. **Total completeness** means that every supertype occurrence must be a member of at least one subtype.

NOTE

Alternative notations exist to represent the completeness constraint. For example, when using Crow's Foot notation the completeness constraint is based on the MS Visio category shape. A single horizontal line under the circle represents a partial completeness constraint; a double horizontal line under the circle represents a total completeness constraint.

In UML, the completeness constraint is often referred to as the *participation* constraint. Partial completeness as described above is represented by 'Optional' participation whilst total completeness is represented by 'Mandatory' participation. This representation can be seen in Figures 6.2 and 6.4.

Given the disjoint/overlapping subtypes and completeness constraints, it is possible to have the specialisation hierarchy constraint scenarios shown in Table 6.2. The UML notation is shown in brackets.

TABLE 6.2 Specialisation hierarchy constraint scenarios

Type	Disjoint Constraint {OR}	Overlapping Constraint {AND}
Partial {Optional}	Supertype has optional subtypes. Subtype discriminator can be null. Subtype sets are unique.	Supertype has optional subtypes. Subtype discriminators can be null. Subtype sets are not unique.
Total {Mandatory}	Every supertype instance is a member of a (at least one) subtype. Subtype discriminator cannot be null. Subtype sets are unique.	Every supertype instance is a member of a (at least one) subtype. Subtype discriminators cannot be null. Subtype sets are not unique.

6.1.7 Specialisation and Generalisation

You can use different approaches to develop entity supertypes and subtypes. For example, you can first identify a regular entity, and then identify all entity subtypes based on their distinguishing characteristics. You also can start by identifying multiple entity types and then later extract the common characteristics of those entities and create a higher-level supertype entity.

Specialisation is the top-down process of identifying lower-level, more specific entity subtypes from a higher-level entity supertype. Specialisation is based on grouping unique characteristics and relationships of the subtypes. In the aviation example, you used specialisation to identify multiple entity subtypes from the original employee supertype. *Generalisation* is the bottom-up process of identifying a higher-level, more generic entity supertype from lower-level entity subtypes. Generalisation is based on grouping common characteristics and relationships of the subtypes. For example, you might identify multiple types of musical instruments: piano, violin and guitar. Using the generalisation approach, you could identify a 'string instrument' entity supertype to hold the common characteristics of the multiple subtypes.

6.1.8 Composition and Aggregation

So far we have looked at how to model relationships between entities using 'IS-A' relationships. Suppose we have two entities, one called DEPARTMENT and one called UNIVERSITY. The relationship between the two could be described as a 'part_of' or 'has_a' relationship as the DEPARTMENT entity is a part_of the UNIVERSITY entity. This type of relationship is known as **aggregation**, whereby a larger entity can be composed of smaller entities. A special case of aggregation is known as **composition**. This is a much stronger relationship than aggregation, since when the parent entity instance is deleted, all child entity instances are automatically deleted. Consider the two entities BUILDING and ROOM, where BUILDING is the parent entity and ROOM is the child entity. A ROOM is 'part_of' a BUILDING and if the building was destroyed then all the rooms would also be destroyed.

TABLE 6.3 Aggregations and compositions

UML Construct	UML Symbol	Description
Aggregation	◇————	This type of association represents a 'part_of' or 'has_a' type of relationship (that is, an entity that is formed as a collection of other entity). An aggregation indicates that the dependent (child) entity instance has an optional association with the strong (parent) entity instance. When the parent entity instance is deleted, the child entity instances are not deleted. The aggregation association is represented by an empty diamond in the side of the parent entity.
Composition	◆————	This type of association represents a special case of the aggregation association. A composition indicates that a dependent (child) entity instance has a mandatory association with a strong (parent) entity instance. When the parent entity instance is deleted, all child entity instances are automatically deleted. The composition association is represented with a filled diamond in the side of the parent object instance. This is the equivalent of a weak entity in the ER model.

There is no ability to model such relationships using Crow's Foot notation, as the concept of aggregation and composition is a much more contemporary approach, which has been developed through the UML notation. In particular, the UML class diagrams use aggregation and composition to indicate the strength of dependency between two entities participating in an relationship. Table 6.3 summarises the main characteristics of the aggregation and composition UML constructs.

The UML standard guides the use of the aggregation and composition constructs as follows:

- An *aggregation construct* is used when an entity is composed of (or is formed by) a collection of other entities, but the entities are independent of each other. That is, the relationship can be classified as a 'has_a' relationship type. For example, a team has many players, or a band has many musicians.
- A *composition construct* is used when two entities are associated in an aggregation association with a strong identifying relationship. That is, deleting the parent deletes the children instances. For example, an invoice contains invoice lines, or an order contains order lines.

Examine the relationships depicted in Figure 6.5 to help you understand the use of aggregation and composition.

6

FIGURE 6.5 Aggregation and composition

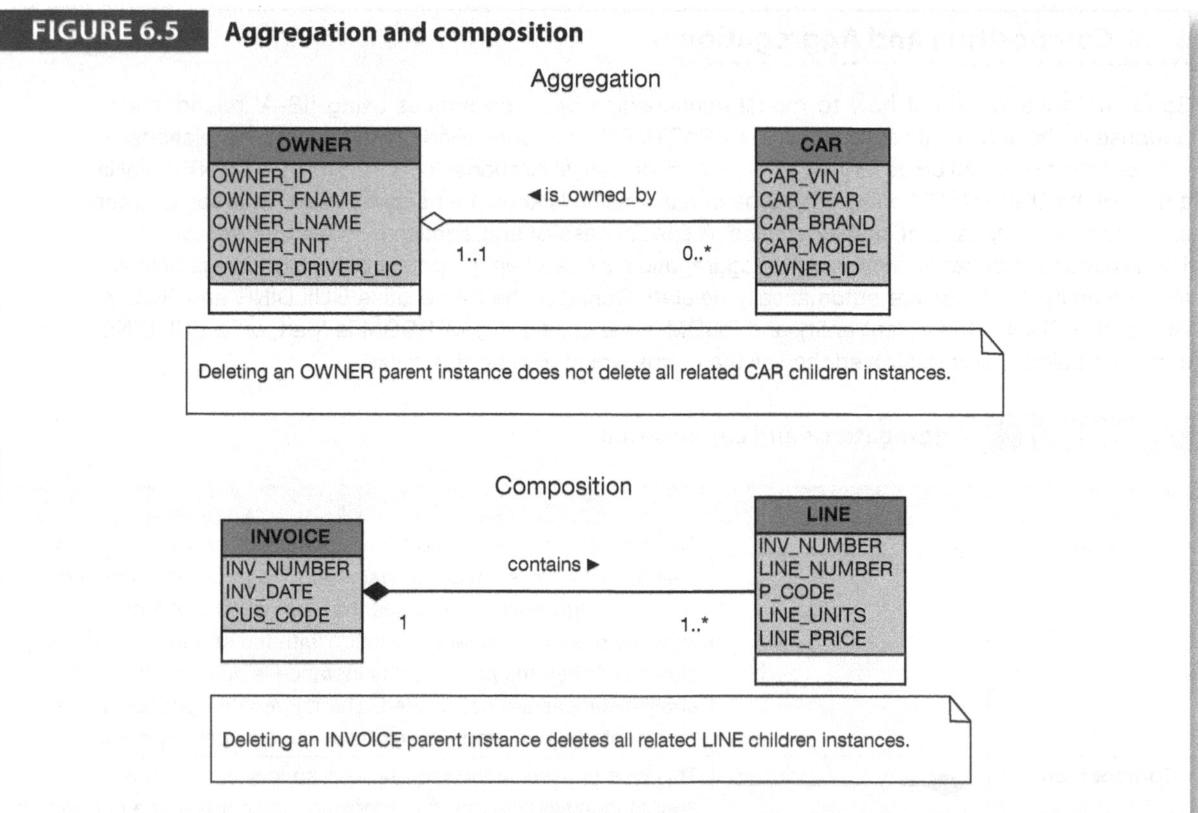

6.2 ENTITY CLUSTERING

Developing an ER diagram entails the discovery of possibly hundreds of entity types and their respective relationships. Generally, the data modeller will develop an initial ERD containing a few entities. As the design approaches completion, the ERD will contain hundreds of entities and relationships that crowd the diagram to the point of making it unreadable and inefficient as a communication tool. In those cases, you can use entity clusters to minimise the number of entities shown in the ERD.

An **entity cluster** is a 'virtual' entity type used to represent multiple entities and relationships in the ERD. An entity cluster is formed by combining multiple interrelated entities into a single abstract entity object. An entity cluster is considered 'virtual' or 'abstract' in the sense that it is not actually an entity in the final ERD; the entity cluster is a temporary entity used to represent multiple entities and relationships, with the purpose of simplifying the ERD and thus enhancing its readability.

Figure 6.6 illustrates the use of entity clusters based on the Tiny University example that was first introduced in Chapter 5, Data Modelling with Entity Relationship Diagrams. Note that the ERD contains two entity clusters:

- OFFERING grouping the COURSE and CLASS entities and relationships.
- LOCATION grouping the ROOM and BUILDING entities and relationships.

Note also that the ERD in Figure 6.6 does not show attributes for the entities. When using entity clusters, the key attributes of the combined entities are no longer available. Without the key attributes, primary key inheritance rules change. In turn, the change in the inheritance rules can have undesirable consequences, such as changes in relationships – from identifying to non-identifying or vice versa – and the loss of foreign key attributes from some entities. To eliminate those problems, the general rule is to *avoid the display of attributes when entity clusters are used*.

FIGURE 6.6 Tiny University ERD using entity clusters

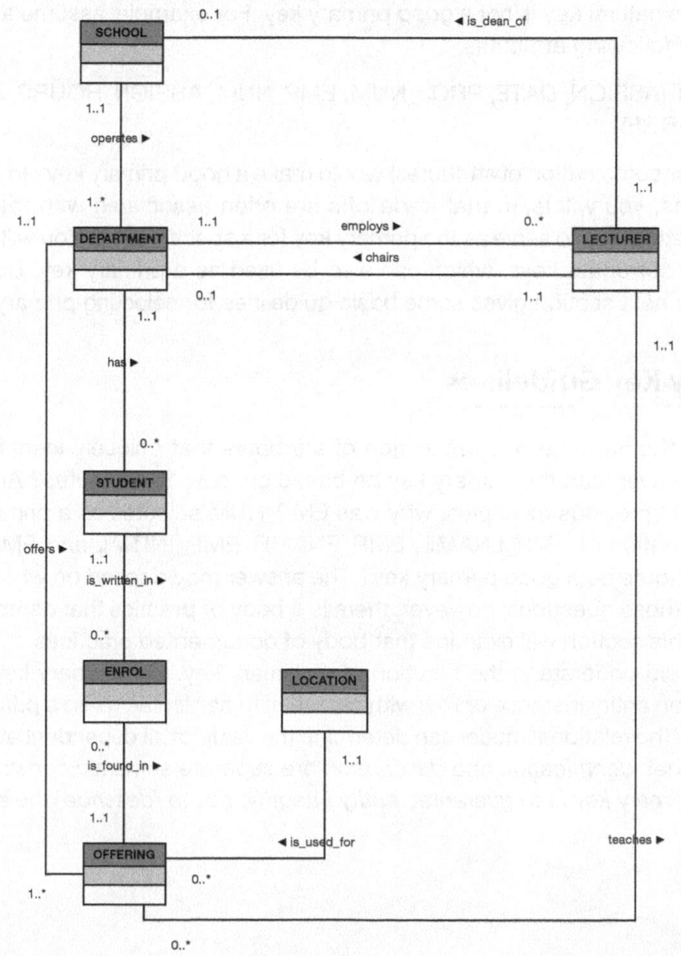

6.3 ENTITY INTEGRITY: SELECTING PRIMARY KEYS

Arguably, the most important characteristic of an entity is its primary key (a single attribute or some combination of attributes) used to uniquely identify each entity instance. The primary key's function is to guarantee entity integrity. Furthermore, primary keys and foreign keys work together to implement relationships in the relational model. Therefore, the importance of properly selecting the primary key has a direct bearing on the efficiency and effectiveness of database implementation.

6.3.1 Natural Keys and Primary Keys

The concept of a unique identifier is commonly encountered in the real world. For example, you use class (or section) numbers to register for classes, invoice numbers to identify specific invoices, account numbers to identify credit cards, and so on. Those examples illustrate natural identifiers or keys. A **natural key** or **natural identifier** is a real-world, generally accepted identifier used to distinguish – that is, uniquely identify – real-world objects. As its name implies, a natural key is familiar to end users and forms part of their day-to-day business vocabulary.

Usually, a data modeller uses a natural identifier as the primary key of the entity being modelled, assuming that the entity *has* a natural identifier. Generally, most natural keys make acceptable primary key identifiers. However, there are occasions when the entity being modelled does not have a natural primary key or the natural key is not a *good* primary key. For example, assume an ASSIGNMENT entity composed of the following attributes:

ASSIGNMENT (ASSIGN_DATE, PROJ_NUM, EMP_NUM, ASSIGN_HOURS, ASSIGN_CHG_HOUR, ASSIGN_CHARGE)

Which attribute (or combination of attributes) would make a good primary key? In Chapter 7, Normalising Database Designs, you will learn that trade-offs are often associated with the selection of different combinations of attributes to serve as the primary key for a specific table. You will also learn in Chapter 7 about the use of surrogate keys, which can also be used as a primary key. But what makes a good primary key? The next section gives some basic guidelines for selecting primary keys.

6.3.2 Primary Key Guidelines

A primary key is the attribute or combination of attributes that uniquely identifies entity instances in an entity set. However, can the primary key be based on, say, 12 attributes? And just how long can a primary key be? In previous examples, why was EMP_NUM selected as a primary key of EMPLOYEE and not a combination of EMP_LNAME, EMP_FNAME, EMP_INITIAL and EMP_DOB? Can a single 256-byte text attribute be a good primary key? The answer may depend on whom you ask. There is no single answer to those questions; however, there is a body of practice that database experts have built over the years. This section will examine that body of documented practices.

First, you should understand the function of a primary key. The primary key's main function is to uniquely identify an entity instance or row within a table. In particular, given a primary key value – that is, the determinant – the relational model can determine the value of all dependent attributes that 'describe' the entity. Note that *identification* and *description* are separate semantic constructs in the model. *The function of the primary key is to guarantee entity integrity, not to 'describe' the entity.*

Second, primary keys and foreign keys are used to implement relationships among entities. However, the implementation of such relationships is done mostly behind the scenes, hidden from end users. In the real world, end users identify objects based on the characteristics they know about the objects. For example, when shopping at a grocery store, you select products by taking them from a store display shelf and reading the labels, not by looking at the stock number. It's only natural for database applications to mimic the human selection process as much as possible. Therefore, database applications should let the end user choose among multiple descriptive narratives of different objects while using primary key values behind the scenes. Keeping those concepts in mind, look at Table 6.4, which summarises desirable primary key characteristics.

TABLE 6.4 Desirable primary key characteristics

PK Characteristic	Rationale
Unique values	The PK must uniquely identify each entity instance. A primary key must be able to guarantee unique values. It cannot contain nulls.
Nonintelligent	The PK should not have embedded semantic meaning. An attribute with embedded semantic meaning is probably better used as a descriptive characteristic of the entity rather than as an identifier. In other words, a student ID of 650973 would be preferred over Smith, Martha L. as a primary key identifier.
No change over time	If an attribute has semantic meaning, it may be subject to updates. This is why names do not make good primary keys. If you have Vickie Smith as the primary key, what happens when she gets married and decides to change her surname to her husband's surname? If a primary key is subject to change, the foreign key values must be updated, thus adding to the database workload. Furthermore, changing a primary key value means that you are basically changing the identity of an entity.
Preferably single-attribute	A primary key should have the minimum number of attributes possible. Single-attribute primary keys are desirable but not required. Single-attribute primary keys simplify the implementation of foreign keys. Having multiple-attribute primary keys can cause primary keys of related entities to grow through the possible addition of many attributes, thus adding to the database workload and making (application) coding more cumbersome.
Preferably numeric	Unique values can be better managed when they are numeric because the database can use internal routines to implement a counter-style attribute that automatically increments values with the addition of each new row. In fact, most database systems include the ability to use special constructs, such as Autonumber in Microsoft Access, to support self-incrementing primary key attributes.
Security complaint	The selected primary key must not be composed of any attribute(s) that might be considered a security risk or violation. For example, using an ID number as a PK in an EMPLOYEE table is not a good idea.

6

6.3.3 When to Use Composite Primary Keys

In the previous section, you learnt about the desirable characteristics of primary keys. For example, you learnt that the primary key should use the minimum number of attributes possible. However, that does *not* mean that composite primary keys are not permitted in a model. In fact, composite primary keys are particularly useful in two cases:

- As identifiers of composite entities, where each primary key combination is allowed only once in the *:* relationship.
- As identifiers of weak entities, where the weak entity has a strong identifying relationship with the parent entity.

To illustrate the first case, let us consider two examples. For the first example, assume that you have a STUDENT entity set and a CLASS entity set. In addition, assume that those two sets are related in a *:* relationship via an ENROL entity set in which each student/class combination may appear only once in the composite entity. Figure 6.7 shows the ERD to represent such a relationship using UML notation. As shown in Figure 6.7, the composite primary key automatically provides the benefit of ensuring that there cannot be duplicate values – that is, it ensures that the same student cannot enrol more than once in the same class.

FIGURE 6.7 The *:* relationship between STUDENT and CLASS

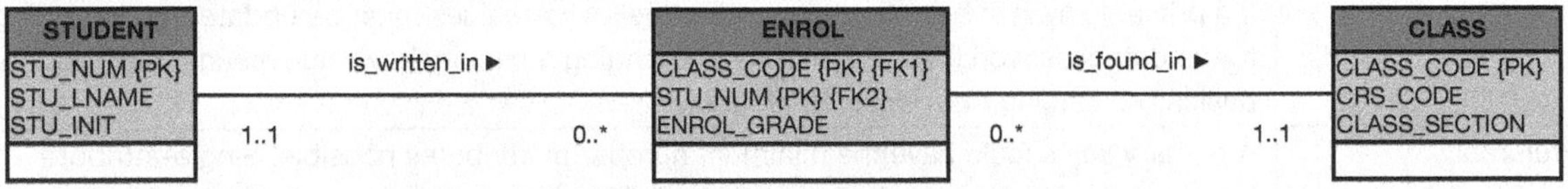

Table name: STUDENT

STU_NUM	STU_LNAME	STU_FNAME	STU_INIT
321452	Ndlovu	Amehlo	C
324257	Smithson	Anne	K
324258	Le Roux	Dané	
324269	Oblonski	Walter	H
324273	Smith	John	D
324274	Katinga	Raphael	P
324291	Ismail	Hemalika	T
324299	Smith	John	B

Table name: ENROL

CLASS_CODE	STU_NUM	ENROL_GRADE
10014	321452	C
10014	324257	B
10018	321452	A
10018	324257	B
10021	321452	C
10021	324257	C

Table name: CLASS

CLASS_CODE	CRS_CODE	CLASS_SECTION
10012	ACCT-211	1
10013	ACCT-211	2
10014	ACCT-211	3
10015	ACCT-212	1
10016	ACCT-212	2
10017	CIS-220	1
10018	CIS-220	2
10019	CIS-220	3
10020	CIS-420	1
10021	QM-261	1
10022	QM-261	2
10023	QM-362	1
10024	QM-362	2
10025	MATH-243	1

The second example shown in Figure 6.8 further illustrates the use of composite primary keys. The entities TOUR and BOOKING are related by a *:* relationship via the TOUR_BOOKING entity in which a booking/tour combination can only appear once in the TOUR_BOOKING entity.

In the second case, a weak entity in a strong identifying relationship with a parent entity is normally used to represent one of two situations:

1. *A real-world object that is existent-dependent on another real-world object*. Those types of objects are distinguishable in the real world. A dependant and an employee are two separate people who exist independently of each other. However, such objects can exist in the model only when they relate to each other in a strong identifying relationship. For example, the relationship between EMPLOYEE and DEPENDANT is one of existence dependency in which the primary key of the dependant entity is a composite key that contains the key of the parent entity.

FIGURE 6.8 The *:* relationship between BOOKING and TOUR

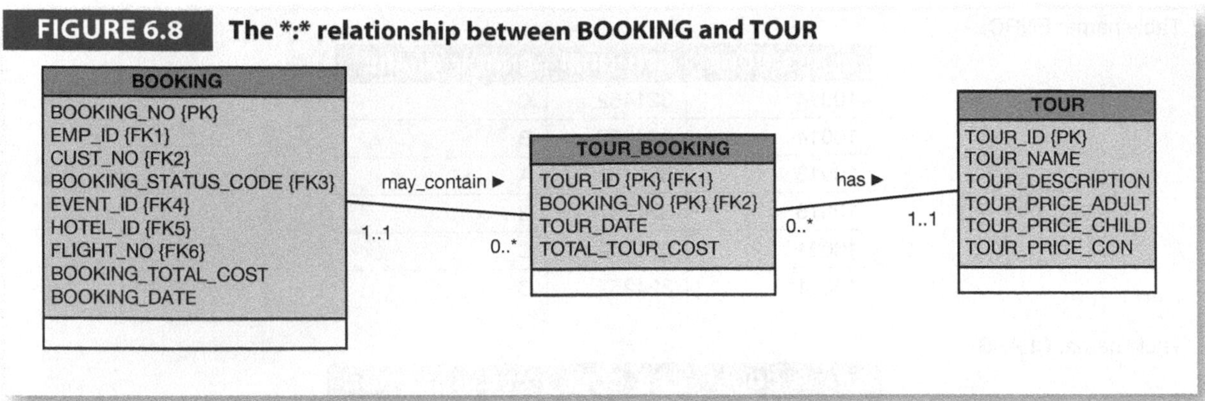

6

2 *A real-world object that is represented in the data model as two separate entities in a strong identifying relationship*. For example, the real-world invoice object is represented by two entities in a data model: INVOICE and LINE. Clearly, the LINE entity does not exist in the real world as an independent object, but rather as part of an INVOICE.

In both situations, having a strong identifying relationship ensures that the dependent entity can exist only when it is related to the parent entity. In summary, the selection of a composite primary key for composite and weak entity types provides benefits that enhance the integrity and consistency of the model.

6.3.4 When to Use Surrogate Primary Keys

There are some instances when a primary key doesn't exist in the real world or when the existing natural key may not be a suitable primary key. For example, consider the case of a park recreation facility that houses rooms for small parties. The manager of the facility keeps track of all events, using a folder with the format shown in Table 6.5.

TABLE 6.5 Data used to keep track of events

Date	Time_Start	Time_End	Room	Event_Name	Party_Of
17/06/19	11:00AM	2:00PM	Allure	Ndlovu Wedding	60
17/06/19	11:00AM	2:00PM	Bonanza	Adams Office	12
17/06/19	3:00PM	5:30PM	Allure	Naidoo Family	15
17/06/19	3:30PM	5:30PM	Bonanza	Adams Office	12
18/06/19	1:00PM	3:00PM	Bonanza	Scouts	33
18/06/19	11:00AM	2:00PM	Allure	March of Dimes	25
18/06/19	11:00AM	12:30PM	Bonanza	Naidoo Family	12

Given the data shown in Table 6.5, you would model the EVENT entity as:

EVENT(DATE, TIME_START, TIME_END, ROOM, EVENT_NAME, PARTY_OF)

What primary key would you suggest? In this case, there is no simple natural key that could be used as a primary key in the model. Based on the primary key concepts you learnt about in previous chapters, you might suggest one of these options:

(DATE, TIME_START, ROOM) or (DATE, TIME_END, ROOM)

Assume you select the composite primary key (DATE, TIME_START, ROOM) for the EVENT entity. Next, you determine that one EVENT may use many RESOURCEs (such as tables, projectors, PCs and stands) and that the same RESOURCE may be used for many EVENTs. The RESOURCE entity would be represented by the following attributes:

RESOURCE (RSC_ID, RSC_DESCRIPTION, RSC_TYPE, RSC_QTY, RSC_PRICE)

Given the business rules, the *:* relationship between RESOURCE and EVENT would be represented via the EVNTRSC composite entity, with a composite primary key as follows:

EVNTRSC (DATE, TIME_START, ROOM, RSC_ID, QTY_USED)

You now have a lengthy four-attribute composite primary key. What would happen if the EVNTRSC entity's primary key were inherited by another existence-dependent entity? At this point, you can see that the composite primary key could make the implementation of the database and program coding unnecessarily complex.

As a data modeller, you may have noticed that the EVENT entity's selected primary key may not work well, given the primary key guidelines you learnt about in Table 6.4. In this case, the EVENT entity's selected primary key contains embedded semantic information and is formed by a combination of date, time and text data columns (that is, attributes with several different data types). In addition, the selected primary key would cause lengthy primary keys for existence-dependent entities. The solution to the problem is to use a numeric single-attribute surrogate primary key.

Surrogate primary keys are accepted practice in today's complex data environments. Surrogate primary keys are especially helpful when there is no natural key, when the selected candidate key has embedded semantic contents, or when the selected candidate key is too long or cumbersome. However, there is a trade-off: if you use a surrogate key, you must ensure that the candidate key of the entity in question performs properly through the use of 'unique index' and 'not null' constraints.

6.4 DESIGN CASES: LEARNING FLEXIBLE DATABASE DESIGN

Data modelling and design require skills that are acquired through experience. In turn, experience is acquired through practice – regular and frequent repetition, applying the concepts learnt to specific and different design problems. This section will present four special design cases that highlight the importance of flexible designs, proper identification of primary keys and placement of foreign keys.

NOTE

In describing the different modelling concepts throughout this book, the focus has been – and continues to be – on relational models. Also, given the focus on the practical nature of database design, all design issues are addressed with the implementation goal in mind. Therefore, there is no sharp line of demarcation between design and implementation.

At the pure conceptual stage of the design, foreign keys are not part of an ER diagram – the ERD displays only entities and relationships. Entities are identified by identifiers that may become primary keys. During design, the modeller attempts to understand and define the entities and relationships. Foreign keys are the mechanism through which the relationship *designed* in an ERD is *implemented* in a relational model. If you use MS Visio Professional as your modelling tool, you will discover that this book's methodology is reflected in the Visio modelling practice.

6

6.4.1 Design Case #1: Implementing 1:1 Relationships

Foreign keys work with primary keys to properly implement relationships in the relational model. The basic rule is very simple: put the primary key of the 'one' side (the parent entity) on the 'many' side (the dependent entity) as a foreign key. However, where do you place the foreign key when you are working with a 1:1 relationship? For example, assume the case of a 1:1 relationship between EMPLOYEE and DEPARTMENT based on the business rule 'one EMPLOYEE is the manager of one DEPARTMENT, and one DEPARTMENT is managed by one EMPLOYEE'. In that case, there are two options for selecting and placing the foreign key:

Place a foreign key in both entities. That option is derived from the basic rule you learnt in Chapter 5, Data Modelling with Entity Relationship Diagrams. Place EMP_NUM as a foreign key in DEPARTMENT and DEPT_ID as a foreign key in EMPLOYEE. However, that solution is not recommended as it would create duplicated work and it could conflict with other existing relationships. (Remember that DEPARTMENT and EMPLOYEE also participate in a 1:* relationship – one department employs many employees.)

Place a foreign key in one of the entities. In that case, the primary key of one of the two entities appears as a foreign key on the other entity. That is the preferred solution, but there is a remaining question: *which* primary key should be used as a foreign key? The answer to that question is found in Table 6.6.

Table 6.6 shows the rationale for selecting the foreign key in a 1:1 relationship based on the relationship properties in the ERD.

TABLE 6.6 Selection of foreign key in a 1:1 relationship

Case	ER Relationship Constraints	Action
I	One side is mandatory and the other side is optional.	Place the PK of the entity on the mandatory side in the entity on the optional side as a FK and make the FK mandatory.
II	Both sides are optional.	Select the FK that causes the fewest number of nulls or place the FK in the entity in which the (relationship) role is played.
III	Both sides are mandatory.	See Case II or consider revising your model to ensure that the two entities do not belong together in a single entity.

Figure 6.9 illustrates the 'EMPLOYEE manages DEPARTMENT' relationship. Note that, in this case, EMPLOYEE is mandatory to DEPARTMENT. Therefore, EMP_NUM is placed as the foreign key in DEPARTMENT. Alternatively, you might argue that the 'manager' role is played by the EMPLOYEE in the DEPARTMENT.

FIGURE 6.9 A 1:1 relationship between DEPARTMENT and EMPLOYEE

A one-to-one (1:1) relationship: An EMPLOYEE manages zero or one DEPARTMENT; each DEPARTMENT is managed by one EMPLOYEE

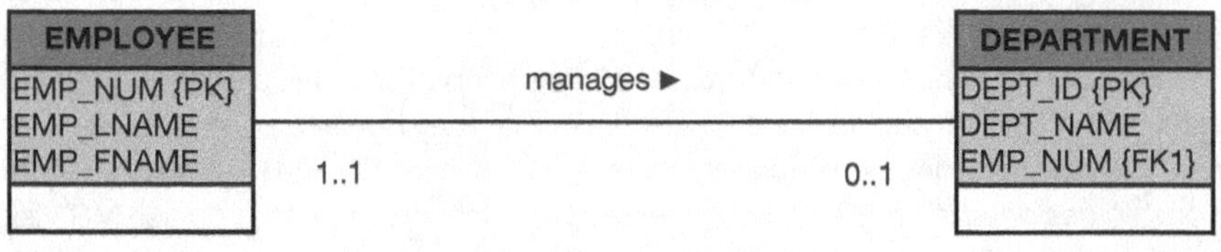

As a designer, you need to recognise that 1:1 relationships exist in the real world and, therefore, they should be supported in the data model. In fact, a 1:1 relationship is used to ensure that two entity sets are not placed in the same table. In other words, EMPLOYEE and DEPARTMENT are clearly separate and unique entity types that do not belong together in a single entity. If you group them together in one entity, what would be the name of that entity?

6.4.2 Design Case #2: Maintaining History of Time-Variant Data

Company managers generally realise that good decision making is based on the information that is generated through the data stored in databases. Such data reflect current as well as past events. In fact, company managers use the data stored in databases to answer questions such as, How do the current company profits compare to those of previous years and what are XYZ product's sales trends? In other words, the data stored on databases reflect not only current data, but also historic data.

Normally, data changes are managed by replacing the existing attribute value with the new value, without regard to the previous value. However, there are situations when the history of values for a given attribute must be preserved. From a data modelling point of view, **time-variant data** refer to data whose values change over time and for which you *must* keep a history of the data changes. You could argue that all data in a database are subject to change over time and are, therefore, time variant. However, some attribute values, such as your date of birth or your ID number, are not time variant. On the other hand, attributes such as your student grades or your bank account balance are subject to change over time. Sometimes the data changes are externally originated and event driven, such as a product price change. On other occasions, changes are based on well-defined schedules, such as the daily stock quote 'open' and 'close' values.

In any case, keeping the history of time-variant data is equivalent to having a multivalued attribute in your entity. To model time-variant data, you must create a new entity in a 1:* relationship with the original entity. This new entity will contain the new value, the date of the change, and whatever other attribute is pertinent to the event being modelled. For example, if you want to keep track of the current manager as well as the history of all department managers over time, you could create the model shown in Figure 6.10.

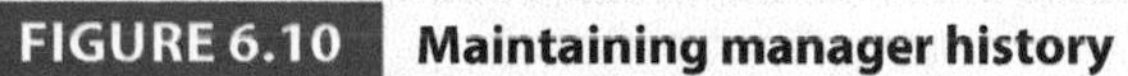

FIGURE 6.10 Maintaining manager history

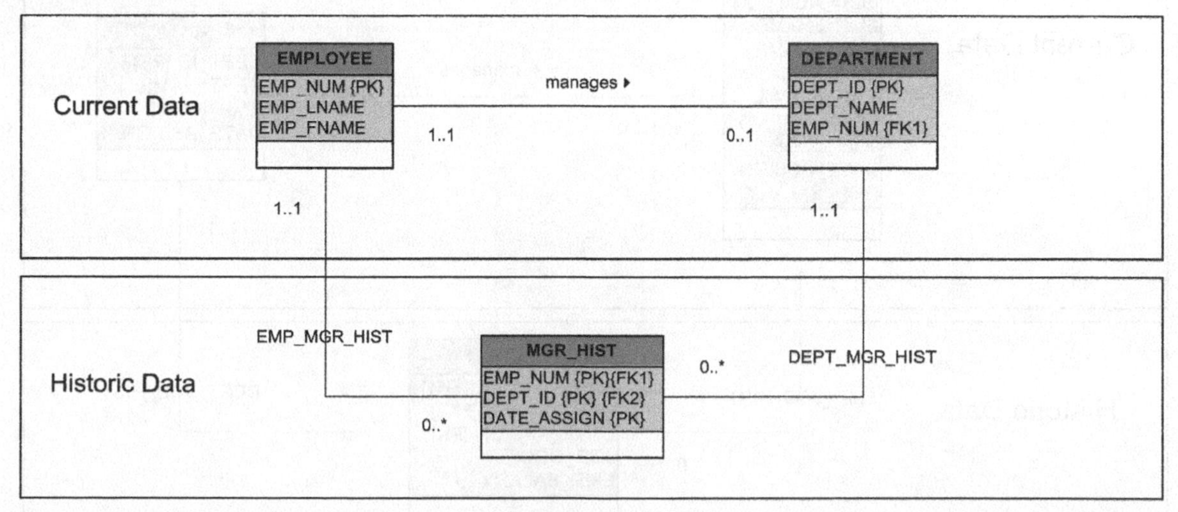

As you examine Figure 6.10, note that the MGR_HIST entity has a 1:* relationship with EMPLOYEE and a 1:* relationship with DEPARTMENT to reflect the fact that, over time, an employee could be the manager of many different departments and a department could have many different employee managers. Because you are recording time-variant data, you must store the DATE_ASSIGN attribute in the MGR_HIST entity to provide the date on which the employee (EMP_NUM) became the manager of the department. The primary key of MGR_HIST permits the same employee to be the manager of the same department, but on different dates. If that scenario is not the case in your environment – if, for example, an employee is the manager of a department only once – you could make DATE_ASSIGN a non-prime attribute in the MGR_HIST entity.

Note in Figure 6.10 that the 'manages' relationship is optional in theory and redundant in practice. At any time, you could find out who the manager of a department is by retrieving the most recent DATE_ASSIGN date from MGR_HIST for a given department. On the other hand, the ERD in Figure 6.10 differentiates between current data and historic data. The *current* manager relationship is implemented by the 'manages' relationship between EMPLOYEE and DEPARTMENT. Additionally, the historic data are managed through EMP_MGR_HIST and DEPT_MGR_HIST. The trade-off with that model is that each time a new manager is assigned to a department, there will be two data modifications: one update in the DEPARTMENT entity and one insert in the MGR_HIST entity.

6

The flexibility of the model proposed in Figure 6.10 becomes more apparent when you add the 1:* 'one department employs many employees' relationship. In that case, the PK of the '1' side (DEPT_ID) appears in the 'many' side (EMPLOYEE) as a foreign key. Now suppose you would like to keep track of the job history for each of the company's employees. In that case, you would keep track of the department, the job code, the date assigned and the salary for each employee. To accomplish that task, you would modify the model in Figure 6.9 by adding a JOB_HIST entity. Figure 6.11 shows the use of the new JOB_HIST entity to maintain the employee's history.

FIGURE 6.11 Maintaining job history

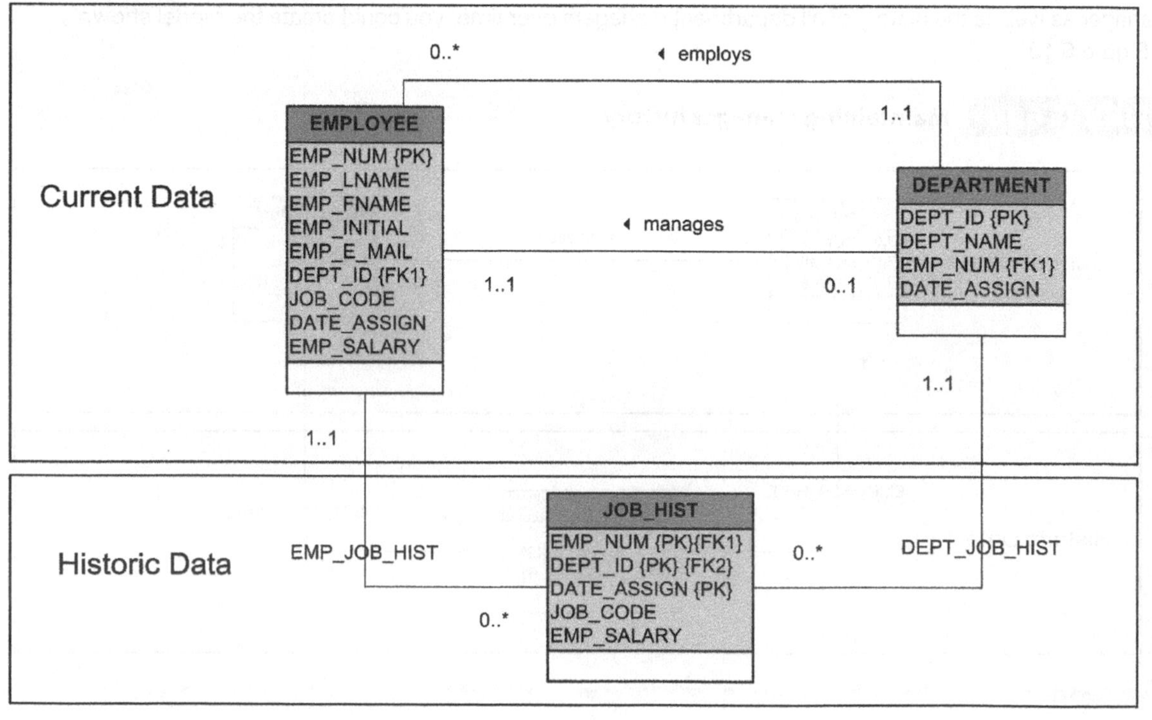

Again, it is worth emphasising that the 'manages' and 'employs' relationships are theoretically optional and redundant in practice. You can always find out where each employee works by looking at the job history and selecting only the most current data row for each employee. However, as you will discover in Chapter 8, Beginning Structured Query Language (SQL), and in Chapter 9, Procedural Language SQL and Advanced SQL, finding where each employee works is not a trivial task. Therefore, the model represented in Figure 6.11 includes the admittedly redundant but unquestionably useful 'manages' and 'employs' relationships to separate current data from historic data.

6.4.3 Design Case #3: Fan Traps

Creating a data model requires proper identification of the data relationships among entities. However, due to miscommunication or incomplete understanding of the business rules or processes, it is not uncommon to misidentify relationships among entities. Under those circumstances, the ERD may contain a design trap. A **design trap** occurs when a relationship is improperly or incompletely identified and, therefore, is represented in a way that is not consistent with the real world. The most common design trap is known as a *fan trap*.

A **fan trap** occurs when you have one entity in two 1:* relationships to other entities, thus producing an association among the other entities that is not expressed in the model. For example, assume the football league has many divisions. Each division has many players, and each division has many teams. Given those 'incomplete' business rules, you might create an ERD that looks like the one shown in Figure 6.12.

FIGURE 6.12 **Incorrect ERD with fan trap problem**

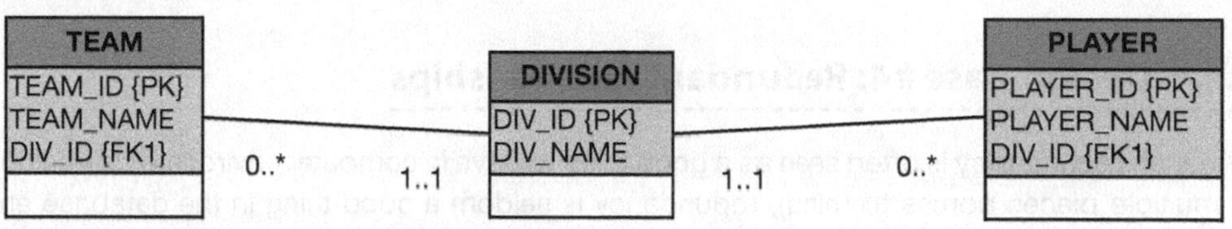

As you can see in Figure 6.12, DIVISION is in a 1:* relationship with TEAM and in a 1:* relationship with PLAYER. Although that representation is semantically correct, the relationships are not properly identified. For example, there is no way to identify which players belong to which team. Figure 6.12 also shows a sample instance relationship representation for the ERD. Note that the DIVISION instances relationship lines fan out to the TEAM and PLAYER entity instances, thus the 'fan trap' label.

Figure 6.13 shows the correct ERD after the fan trap has been eliminated. Note that, in this case, DIVISION is in a 1:* relationship with TEAM. In turn, TEAM is in a 1:* relationship with PLAYER. Figure 6.13 also shows the instance relationship representation after eliminating the 'fan trap'.

FIGURE 6.13 **Corrected ERD after removal of the fan trap**

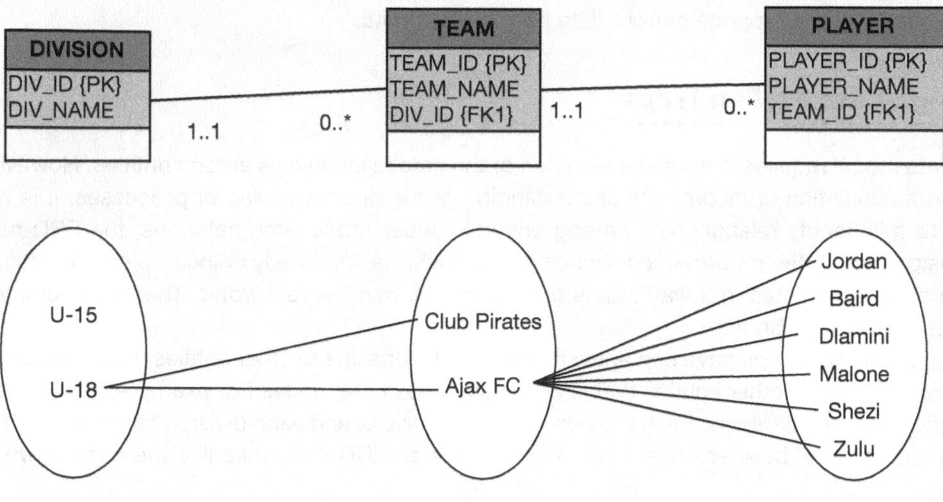

Given the design in Figure 6.13, note how easy it is to see which players play for which team. However, to find out which players play in which division, you first need to see which teams belong to each division; then you need to find out which players play on each team. In other words, there is a transitive relationship between DIVISION and PLAYER via the TEAM entity.

6.4.4 Design Case #4: Redundant Relationships

Although redundancy is often seen as a good thing to have in computer environments (multiple backups in multiple places comes to mind), redundancy is seldom a good thing in the database environment. (As you learnt in Chapter 3, Relational Model Characteristics, redundancies can cause data anomalies in a database.) Redundant relationships occur when there are multiple relationship paths between related entities. The main concern with redundant relationships is that they remain consistent across the model. However, it is important to note that some designs use redundant relationships as a way to simplify the design.

An example of redundant relationships was first introduced in Figure 6.10 during the discussion on maintaining history of time-variant data. However, the use of the redundant 'manages' and 'employs' relationships was justified by the fact that such relationships were dealing with current data rather than historic data. Another more specific example of a redundant relationship is represented in Figure 6.14.

In Figure 6.14, note the transitive 1:* relationship between DIVISION and PLAYER through the TEAM entity set. Therefore, the relationship that connects DIVISION and PLAYER is, for all practical purposes, redundant. (So too is the additional attribute DIV_ID in PLAYER.) In that case, the relationship could be safely deleted without losing any information-generation capabilities in the model.

FIGURE 6.14 **A redundant relationship**

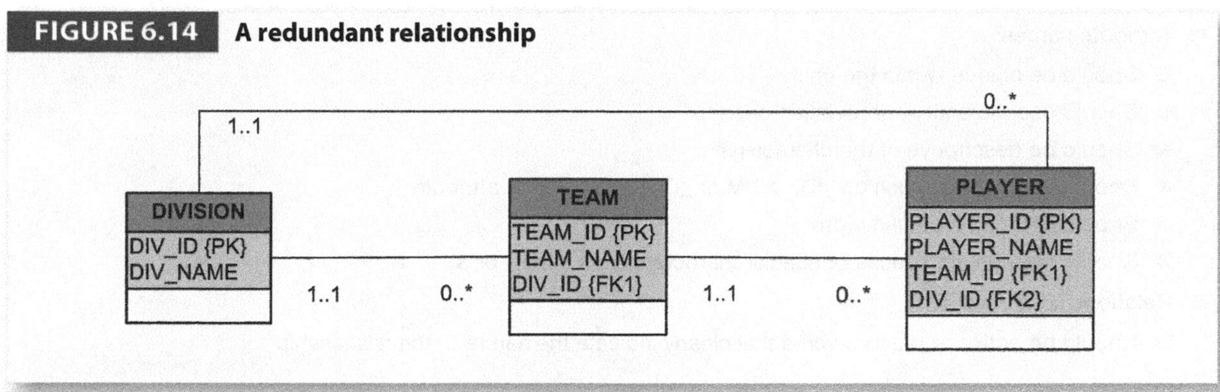

6

6.5 DATA MODELLING CHECKLIST

Data modelling translates a specific real-world environment into a data model that represents the real-world data, users, processes and interactions. You have learnt in this chapter how the EERM enables the designer to add more semantic content to the model. You have also learnt about the trade-offs and intricacies in the selection of primary keys and the modelling of time-variant data. The modelling techniques you have learnt thus far give you the tools needed to produce successful database designs. However, just as any good pilot uses a checklist to ensure that all is in order for a successful flight, the data modelling checklist shown in Table 6.7 will help ensure that you perform data modelling tasks successfully. (The data modelling checklist in Table 6.7 is based on the concepts and tools you have learnt, beginning in Chapter 3 – the relational model, the entity relationship model, normalisation and the extended entity relationship model.) Therefore, it is assumed that you are familiar with the majority of terms and labels used in the checklist, such as *synonyms, aliases* and *relationships*.

TABLE 6.7 **Data modelling checklist**

BUSINESS RULES

- Properly document and verify all business rules with the end users.
- Ensure that all business rules are written precisely, clearly and simply. The business rules must help identify entities, attributes, relationships and constraints.
- Identify the source of all business rules and ensure that each business rule is accompanied by the reason for its existence and by the date and person(s) responsible for the business rule's verification and approval.

DATA MODELLING

Naming Conventions: All names should be limited in length (database-dependent size).

- Entity names:
  - Should be nouns that are familiar to business and should be short and meaningful
  - Should include abbreviations, synonyms and aliases for each entity
  - Should be unique within the model
  - For composite entities, may include a combination of abbreviated names of the entities linked through the composite entity

- Attribute names:
  - Should be unique within the entity
  - Should use the entity abbreviation or prefix
  - Should be descriptive of the characteristic
  - Should use suffixes such as _ID, _NUM or _CODE for the PK attribute
  - Should not be a reserved word
  - Should not contain spaces or special characters such as @, ! or &
- Relationship names:
  - Should be active or passive verbs that clearly indicate the nature of the relationship

Entities:

- All entities should represent a single subject
- All entities should be in 3NF or higher (covered in Chapter 7, Normalising Database Designs)
- The granularity of the entity instance is clearly defined
- The PK is clearly defined and supports the selected data granularity

Attributes:

- Should be simple and single-valued (atomic data)
- Should include default values, constraints, synonyms and aliases
- Derived attributes should be clearly identified and include source(s)
- Should not be redundant, unless they are required for transaction accuracy or for maintaining a history or are used as a foreign key

Relationships:

- Should clearly identify relationship participants
- Should clearly define participation and cardinality rules

ER Diagram:

- Should be validated against expected processes: inserts, updates and deletions
- Should evaluate where, when, and how to maintain a history
- Should not contain redundant relationships except as required (see attributes)
- Should minimise data redundancy to ensure single-place updates

SUMMARY

- The extended entity relationship (EER) model adds semantics to the ER model via entity supertypes, subtypes and clusters. An entity supertype is a generic entity type that is related to one or more entity subtypes.
- A specialisation hierarchy depicts the arrangement and relationships between entity supertypes and entity subtypes. Inheritance allows an entity subtype to inherit the attributes and relationships of the supertype. Subtypes can be disjoint or overlapping. A subtype discriminator is used to determine to which entity subtype the supertype occurrence is related. The subtypes can exhibit partial or total completeness. There are basically two approaches to developing a specialisation hierarchy of entity supertypes and subtypes: specialisation and generalisation.

- An entity cluster is a 'virtual' entity type used to represent multiple entities and relationships in the ERD. An entity cluster is formed by combining multiple interrelated entities and relationships into a single abstract entity object.
- Natural keys are identifiers that exist in the real world. Natural keys do not necessarily make good primary keys. Primary keys should have these characteristics: They must have unique values, they should be non-intelligent, they must not change over time, and they are preferably numeric and composed of a single attribute.
- Composite keys are useful to represent *:* relationships and weak (strong-identifying) entities.
- Surrogate primary keys are useful when there is no natural key that makes a suitable primary key, when the primary key is a composite primary key with multiple different data types, or when the primary key is too long to be usable.
- In a 1:1 relationship, place the PK of the mandatory entity as a foreign key in the optional entity, place it in the entity that causes the least number of nulls, or place it where the role is played.
- Time-variant data refers to data whose values change over time and whose requirements mandate that you keep a history of data changes. To maintain the history of time-variant data, you must create an entity containing the new value, the date of change and any other time-relevant data. This entity maintains a 1:* relationship with the entity for which the history is to be maintained.
- A fan trap occurs when you have one entity in two 1:* relationships to other entities and there is an association among the other entities that is not expressed in the model. Redundant relationships occur when there are multiple relationship paths between related entities. The main concern with redundant relationships is that they remain consistent across the model.
- Aggregation and composition are used to represent 'has_a' or 'part_of' relationships between entities.
- The data modelling checklist provides a way for the designer to check that the ERD meets a set of minimum requirements.

6

KEY TERMS

aggregation
completeness constraint
composition
design trap
disjoint subtypes (non-overlapping subtypes)
EER diagram (EERD)
entity cluster
entity subtype
entity supertype
extended entity relationship model (EERM)
fan trap
inheritance
natural key (natural identifier)
overlapping (non-disjoint) subtypes
partial completeness
specialisation hierarchy
subtype discriminator
time-variant data
total completeness

FURTHER READING

Advances in Conceptual Modelling – Theory and Practice, *Lecture Notes in Computer Science*, Volume 4231, Springer, 2006.

Booch, G. *Unified Modelling Language User Guide*, Addison-Wesley, 2005.

Gordon, K. *Modelling Business Information: Entity Relationship and Class Modelling for Business Analysts*. British Computer Society, 2017.

Hernandez, M. J. *Database Design for Mere Mortals: A Hands-On Guide to Relational Database Design*. Addison-Wesley, 2003.

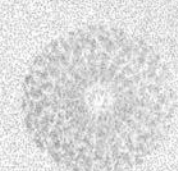

Online Content Answers to selected Review Questions and Problems for this chapter are available on the online platform accompanying this book.

REVIEW QUESTIONS

1 What is an entity supertype and why is it used?

2 What kinds of data would you store in an entity subtype?

3 What is a specialisation hierarchy?

4 What is a subtype discriminator? Given an example of its use.

5 What is an overlapping subtype? Give an example.

6 What is the difference between partial completeness and total completeness?

7 What is an entity cluster, and which advantages are derived from its use?

8 Which primary key characteristics are considered desirable? Explain *why* each characteristic is considered desirable.

9 Under which circumstances would composite primary keys be appropriate?

10 What is a surrogate primary key, and when would you use one?

11 When implementing a 1:1 relationship, where should you place the foreign key if one side is mandatory and one side is optional? Should the foreign key be mandatory or optional?

12 What are time-variant data, and how would you deal with such data from a database design point of view?

13 What is the most common design trap, and how does it occur?

PROBLEMS

1 AVANTIVE Corporation is a company specialising in the commercialisation of automotive parts. AVANTIVE has two types of customers: retail and wholesale. All customers have a customer ID, a name, an address, a phone number, a default shipping address, a date of last purchase and a date of last payment. Retail customers have the credit card type, credit card number, expiration date and email address. Wholesale customers have a contact name, contact phone number, contact email address, purchase order number and date, discount percentage, billing address, tax status (if exempt) and tax identification number. A retail customer cannot be a wholesale customer and vice versa. Given that information, create the ERD containing all primary keys, foreign keys and main attributes.

2 AVANTIVE Corporation has five departments: administration, marketing, sales, shipping and purchasing. Each department employs many employees. Each employee has an ID, a name, a home address, a home phone number, a salary and a tax ID. Some employees are classified as sales representatives, some as technical support and some as administrators. Sales representatives receive a commission based on sales. Technical support employees are required to be certified in

their areas of expertise. For example, some are certified as drivetrain specialists; others, as electrical systems specialists. All administrators have a title and a bonus. Given that information, create the ERD containing all primary keys, foreign keys and main attributes.

3 AVANTIVE Corporation operates under the following business rules:

- AVANTIVE keeps a list of car models with information about the manufacturer, model and year. AVANTIVE keeps several parts in stock. A part will have a part ID, description, unit price and quantity on hand. A part can be used for many car models, and a car model has many parts.
- A retail customer normally pays by credit card and is charged the list price for each purchased item. A wholesale customer normally pays via purchase order with terms of net 30 days and is charged a discounted price for each item purchased. (The discount varies from customer to customer.)
- A customer (retail or wholesale) can place many orders. Each order will have an order number, a date, a shipping address, a billing address and a list of part codes, quantities, unit prices and extended line totals. Each order also has a sales representative ID (an employee) to identify the person who made the sale, an order subtotal, an order tax total, a shipping cost, a shipping date, an order total cost, an order total paid and an order status (open, closed or cancel).

Using that information, create the complete ERD containing all primary keys, foreign keys and main attributes.

4 In Chapter 5, Data Modelling with Entity Relationship Diagrams, you saw the creation of the Tiny University database design. That design reflected such business rules as 'a lecturer may advise many students' and 'a lecturer may chair one department'. Modify the design shown in Figure 5.39 to include these business rules:

- An employee could be staff or a lecturer or an administrator.
- A lecturer may also be an administrator.
- Staff employees have a work level classification, such as Level I and Level II.
- Only lecturers can chair a department. A department is chaired by only one lecturer.
- Only lecturers can serve as the dean of a school. Each of the university's schools is served by one dean.
- A lecturer can teach many classes.
- Administrators have a position title.

Given that information, create the complete ERD using UML class diagram notation, containing all primary keys, foreign keys and main attributes.

5 Tiny University wants to keep track of the history of all administrative appointments (date of appointment and date of termination). (*Hint*: Time variant data are at work.) The Tiny University chancellor may want to know how many deans worked in the School of Business between 1 January, 2000 and 1 January, 2018 or who the dean of the School of Education was in 2010. Given that information, create the complete ERD containing all primary keys, foreign keys and main attributes.

6 Some Tiny University staff employees are information technology (IT) personnel. Some IT personnel provide technology support for academic programmes. Some IT personnel provide technology infrastructure support. Some IT personnel provide technology support for academic programmes and technology infrastructure support. IT personnel are not lecturers. IT personnel are required to take periodic training to retain their technical expertise. Tiny University tracks all IT personnel

training by date, type and results (completed vs not completed). Given that information, create the complete ERD containing all primary keys, foreign keys and main attributes.

7 The FlyRight Aircraft Maintenance (FRAM) division of the FlyRight Company (FRC) performs all maintenance for FRC's aircraft. Produce a data model segment that reflects the following business rules:

- All mechanics are FRC employees. Not all employees are mechanics.
- Some mechanics are specialised in engine (EN) maintenance. Some mechanics are specialised in airframe (AF) maintenance. Some mechanics are specialised in avionics (AV) maintenance. (Avionics are the electronic components of an aircraft that are used in communication and navigation.) All mechanics take periodic refresher courses to stay current in their areas of expertise. FRC tracks all courses taken by each mechanic – date, course type, certification (Y/N) and performance.
- FRC keeps a history of the employment of all mechanics. The history includes the date hired, date promoted, date terminated and so on. (*Note:* The 'and so on' component is, of course, not a real-world requirement. Instead, it has been used here to limit the number of attributes you will show in your design.)

Given those requirements, create the ERD segment using UML notation.

8 You have been asked to create a database design for the BoingX Aircraft Company (BAC), which has two products: TRX-5A and TRX-5B HUD (heads-up display) units. The database must enable managers to track blueprints, parts and software for each HUD, using the following business rules:

- For simplicity's sake, you may assume that the TRX-5A unit is based on two engineering blueprints and that the TRX-5B unit is based on three engineering blueprints. You are free to make up your own blueprint names.
- All parts used in the TRX-5A and TRX-5B are classified as hardware. For simplicity's sake, you may assume that the TRX-5A unit uses three parts and that the TRX-5B unit uses four parts. You are free to make up your own part names.

NOTE

Some parts are supplied by vendors, while others are supplied by the BoingX Aircraft Company. Parts suppliers must be able to meet the technical requirements specification (TRSs) set by the BoingX Aircraft Company. Any parts supplier that meets the BoingX Aircraft Companys TRSs may be contracted to supply parts. Therefore, any part may be supplied by multiple suppliers and a supplier can supply many different parts.

- BAC wants to keep track of all part price changes and the dates of those changes.
- BAC wants to keep track of all TRX-5A and TRX-5B software. For simplicity's sake, you may assume that the TRX-5A unit uses two named software components and that the TRX-5B unit also uses two named software components. You are free to make up your own software names.
- BAC wants to keep track of all changes made in blueprints and software. Those changes must reflect the date and time of the change, the description of the change, the person who authorised the change, the person who actually made the change and the reason for the change.
- BAC wants to keep track of all HUD test data by test type, test date and test outcome.

Given those requirements, create the ERD segment using UML notation.

9 Given the following business scenario, create a Crow's Foot ERD using a specialisation hierarchy, if appropriate. Granite Sales Company keeps information on employees and the departments in which they work. For each department, the department name, internal mail box number and office phone extension are kept. A department can have many assigned employees, and each employee is assigned to only one department. Employees can be salaried, hourly, or work on contract. All employees are assigned an employee number, which is kept along with the employee's name and address. For hourly employees, hourly wages and target weekly work hours are stored; for example, the company may target 40 hours/week for some employees, 32 for others, and 20 for others. Some salaried employees are salespeople who can earn a commission in addition to their base salary. For all salaried employees, the yearly salary amount is recorded in the system. For salespeople, their commission percentage on sales and commission percentage on profit are stored in the system. For example, John is a salesperson with a base salary of R500 000 per year plus a 2 per cent commission on the sales price for all sales he makes, plus another 5 per cent of the profit on each of those sales. For contract employees, the beginning date and end date of their contracts are stored along with the billing rate for their hours.

CASE STUDIES

1 Sedgefield Bike Rentals is a small family-owned business located in Sedgefield, South Africa. Tourists regularly visit the area to admire the countryside and cycle around the area's beautiful coastline. The main business of Sedgefield Bike Rentals is in acquiring bikes to hire to tourists, maintaining those bikes to ensure a good working order and selling on bikes that are no longer suitable for hiring.

Create a complete ERD to support the business needs described below:

- Every bike has a bike record and is identified by a unique number. For each bike, the model, manufacturer, and type (e.g. mountain or road) is recorded along with the size (e.g. INFANT, CHILD, TEENAGER, ADULT, etc.). After a bike has reached the end of its lifespan (typically three years but dependent on usage) it is sold on to a dealer. The price it is sold for and the date are also recorded in the bike record.
- Sedgefield Bike Rentals has a number of dealers they sell to on a regular basis and maintain a list that contains the dealers contact information. A dealer may or may not purchase a bike depending on its condition. If the bike is in poor condition then it is not offered to a dealer and just scrapped.
- Each bike is associated with a class size code that is used to determine standard rates for the period of hire (half day or full day). The class sizes of bike are {INFANT, CHILD_YOUNG, CHILD_OLD, TEENAGER, STANDARD_ADULT and LARGE_ADULT}. For each class size, a unique code is assigned, along with the half-day and full-day rates.
- After a bike has been returned, it is checked to ensure that it is still in good working order. If a fault is noticed, it is recorded in the Bike Maintenance Log. A description of the fault and the date on which it was noticed is recorded. When the bike has been repaired, the action that was taken and the date are also recorded. For example, a typical problem is that new tyres are required. Over its lifespan, a bike will undergo maintenance on a regular basis. However, it is possible that a bike may never need maintenance.
- Customers make a request to hire bikes by either telephoning Sedgefield Bike Rentals or by simply walking into the shop. If a customer agrees to hire a bike, his or her name, address and contact details are recorded. A customer can rent one or more bikes at a given time.

- For each bike that is rented, a rental record is created. This contains the rental date, the time the bike was taken out, the time it was due back and the actual time it was returned. In addition, the amount of rent paid is recorded, which is determined through the class size code. Each rental record is associated with only one customer. A bike can be rented out any number of times or may never be rented.
- When a bike is being maintained, an employee of Sedgefield Bike Rentals will be responsible for ordering additional bike parts that are required. Typically orders are placed on Fridays each week, for delivery on Mondays. An employee may place any number of orders. An order consists of an order number, order date, a subtotal of the order, any associated delivery costs and a grand order total. Only one employee can be associated with placing one order but over time employees can place many orders.
- A order can be made for many parts and parts can be ordered on multiple occasions. Each part is identified by a unique number, a part description and part cost. An order must be for at least one part but can often contain a request for several of the same parts, e.g. three Explorer mountain bike large saddles.

- A particular part can always be obtained from any number of manufacturers. If a part is not in stock with one manufacturer, others can be checked to see if they have the part in stock. Sedgefield Bike Rentals keep a list of manufacturers they use on a regular basis. For each manufacturer, the following information is recorded: the name, address, telephone number and email address.
- Each order is placed with one manufacturer and a manufacturer may supply parts via orders to Sedgefield Bike Rentals on a regular basis.

2 The *Journal of E-commerce Research Knowledge* is a prestigious information systems research journal. It uses a peer-review process to select manuscripts for publication. Only about 10 per cent of the manuscripts submitted to the journal are accepted for publication. A new issue of the journal is published each quarter. Create a complete ERD to support the business needs described below:

- Unsolicited manuscripts are submitted by authors. When a manuscript is received, the editor assigns it a number and records some basic information about it in the system, including the title of the manuscript, the date it was received and a manuscript status of 'received'. Information about the author(s) is also recorded, including each author's name, mailing address, email address and affiliation (the author's school or company). Every manuscript must have an author. Only authors who have submitted manuscripts are kept in the system. It is typical for a manuscript to have several authors. A single author may have submitted many different manuscripts to the journal. Additionally, when a manuscript has multiple authors, it is important to record the order in which the authors are listed in the manuscript credits.
- At her or his earliest convenience, the editor will briefly review the topic of the manuscript to ensure that its contents fall within the scope of the journal. If the content is not appropriate for the journal, the manuscript's status is changed to 'rejected' and the author is notified via email. If the content is within the scope of the journal, then the editor selects three or more reviewers to review the manuscript. Reviewers work for other companies or universities and read manuscripts to ensure their scientific validity. For each reviewer, the system records a reviewer number, name, email address, affiliation and areas of interest. Areas of interest are predefined areas of expertise that the reviewer has specified. An area of interest is identified by an IS code and includes a description (for example, IS2003 is the code for 'database modelling'). A reviewer can have many areas of interest, and an area of interest can be

associated with many reviewers. All reviewers must specify at least one area of interest. It is unusual, but possible, to have an area of interest for which the journal has no reviewers. The editor will change the status of the manuscript to 'under review' and record which reviewers received the manuscript and the date it was sent to each reviewer. A reviewer will typically receive several manuscripts to review each year, although new reviewers may not have received any manuscripts yet.

- The reviewers will read the manuscript at their earliest convenience and provide feedback to the editor. The feedback from each reviewer includes rating the manuscript on a ten-point scale for appropriateness, clarity, methodology and contribution to the field, as well as a recommendation for publication (accept or reject). The editor will record all of this information in the system for each review received, along with the date on which the feedback was received. Once all of the reviewers have provided their evaluations, the editor will decide whether to publish the manuscript and change its status to 'accepted' or 'rejected'. If the manuscript will be published, the date of acceptance is recorded.
- Once a manuscript has been accepted for publication, it must be scheduled. For each issue of the journal, the publication period (autumn, winter, spring, summer), publication year, volume and number are recorded. An issue will contain many manuscripts, although the issue may be created in the system before it is known which manuscripts will be published in that issue. An accepted manuscript appears in only one issue of the journal. Each manuscript goes through a typesetting process that formats the content, including fonts, font size, line spacing, justification and so on. Once the manuscript has been typeset, its number of pages is recorded in the system. The editor will then decide which issue each accepted manuscript will appear in and the order of manuscripts within each issue. The order and the beginning page number for each manuscript must be stored in the system. Once the manuscript has been scheduled for an issue, the status of the manuscript is changed to 'scheduled'. Once an issue is published, the print date for the issue is recorded, and the status of each manuscript in that issue is changed to 'published'.

3 Global Computer Solutions (GCS) is an information technology consulting company with many offices located throughout Europe and South Africa. The company's success is based on its ability to maximise its resources, that is, its ability to assign highly skilled employees to work on projects according to region. To better manage its projects, GCS has contacted you to design a database so that GCS managers can keep track of their customers, employees, projects, project schedules, assignments and invoices.

   The GCS database must support all of GCS's operations and information requirements. A basic description of the main entities follows:

   - The *employees* working for GCS have an employee ID, an employee last name, a middle initial, a first name, a region and a date of hire.
   - Valid *regions* are as follows: Northern Europe (NE), Eastern Europe (EE), Western Europe (WE), Southern Europe (SE) and South Africa (SA).
   - Each employee has many skills, and many employees have the same skill.
   - Each *skill* has a skill ID, description and rate of pay. Valid skills are as follows: data entry I, data entry II, systems analyst I, systems analyst II, database designer I, database designer II, C I, C II, C++ I, C++ II, Python I, Python II, Java I, Java II, ASP I, ASP II, Oracle DBA, MS SQL Server DBA, network engineer I, network engineer II, web administrator, technical writer and project manager. The following table shows an example of the skills inventory.

Skill	Employee
Data Entry I	Seaton Amy; Williams Josh; Khoza Buhle
Data Entry II	Williams Josh; Seaton Amy
Systems Analyst I	Craig Brett; Sewell Beth; Robbins Erin; Bush Emily; Zebras Steve
Systems Analyst II	Chandler Joseph; Burklow Shane; Robbins Erin
DB Designer I	Yarbrough Peter; Smith Mary
DB Designer II	Yarbrough Peter; Pascoe Jonathan
C I	Kattan Chris; Epahnor Victor; Summers Anna; Ellis Maria
C II	Kattan Chris; Epahnor Victor, Nkosi Cela
C++ I	Smith Jose; Nokwi Londe; Cope Leslie
C++ II	Nokwi Londe; Bible Hanah
Python I	Zebras Steve; Ellis Maria
Python II	Zebras Steve; Pieterse Jaco
Java I	Duarte Miriam; Bush Emily
Java II	Ismail Hemalika; Pieterse Jaco
ASP I	Duarte Miriam; Bush Emily
ASP II	Duarte Miriam; Pieterse Jaco
Oracle DBA	Smith Jose; Pascoe Jonathan
SQL Server DBA	Yarbrough Peter; Smith Jose
Network Engineer I	Ismail Hemalika; Smith Mary
Network Engineer II	Ismail Hemalika; Smith Mary
Web Administrator	Ismail Hemalika; Smith Mary; Pieterse Jaco
Technical Writer	Kilby Surgena; Bender Larry
Project Manager	Paine Brad; Mudd Roger; Kenyon Tiffany; Connor Sean

- GCS has many *customers*. Each customer has a customer ID, customer name, phone number and region.
- GCS works by *projects*. A project is based on a contract between the customer and GCS to design, develop and implement a computerised solution. Each project has specific characteristics such as the project ID, the customer to which the project belongs, a brief description, a project date (that is, the date on which the project's contract was signed), a project start date (an estimate), a project end date (also an estimate), a project budget (total estimated cost of project), an actual start date, an actual end date, an actual cost and one employee assigned as manager of the project.
- The actual cost of the project is updated each Friday by adding that week's cost (computed by multiplying the hours each employee worked times the skill's rate of pay) to the actual cost.
- The employee who is the manager of the project must complete a *project schedule*, which is, in effect, a design and development plan. In the project schedule (or plan), the manager must determine the tasks that will be performed to take the project from beginning to end. Each task has a task ID, a brief task description, the task's starting and ending date, the type of skill needed, and the number of people (with the required skills) required to complete

the task. General tasks are initial interview, database and system design, implementation, coding, testing, and final evaluation and sign-off. For example, GCS would have the project schedule shown in the next table.

Project ID:1	Description: Sales Management System			
Company: See Rocks		Contract Date: 12/2/2019	Region: WE	
Start Date: 1/3/2019		End Date: 1/7/2019	Budget: R375 000	
Start Date	**End Date**	**Task Description**	**Skill(s) Required**	**Quantity Required**
1/3/13	6/3/19	Initial Interview	Project Manager	1
			Systems Analyst II	1
			DB Designer I	1
11/03/13	15/03/19	Database Design	DB Designer I	1
11/03/13	12/04/19	System Design	Systems Analyst II	1
			Systems Analyst I	2
18/03/13	22/03/19	Database Implementation	Oracle DBA	1
25/03/13	20/05/19	System Coding and Testing	C I	2
			C II	1
			Oracle DBA	1
25/03/13	07/06/19	System Documentation	Technical Writer	1
10/06/13	14/06/19	Final Evaluation	Project Manager	1
			Systems Analyst II	1
			DB Designer I	1
			Cobol II	1
17/06/13	21/06/19	On-Site System Online and Data Loading	Project Manager	1
			Systems Analyst II	1
			DB Designer I	1
			C II	1
01/07/13	01/07/19	Sign-Off	Project Manager	1

- Assignments: GCS pools all of its employees by region, and from this pool, employees are assigned to a specific task scheduled by the project manager. For example, for the first project's schedule, you know that for the period 01/03/19 to 06/03/19 a systems analyst II, a database designer I and a project manager are needed. (The project manager is assigned when the project is created and remains for the duration of the project.) Using that information, GCS searches the employees who are located in the same region as the customer, matching the skills required and assigning them to the project task.
- Each project schedule task can have many employees assigned to it, and a given employee can work on multiple project tasks. However, an employee can work on only one project task at a time. If an employee is already assigned to work on a project task from 20/02/19 to 03/03/19, (s)he cannot work on another task until his/her current assignment is closed (ends). The date on which an assignment is closed does not necessarily match the ending date of the project schedule task because a task can be completed ahead of (or behind) schedule.

Project ID:1	Description: Sales Management System					
Company: See Rocks		Contract Date: 12/2/2019		As of: 29/03/19		
Scheduled				Actual assignments		
Project Task	**Start Date**	**End Date**	**Skill**	**Employee**	**Start Date**	**End Date**
Initial Interview	1/3/19	6/3/19	Project Mgr. Sys. Analyst II DB Designer I	101 – Connor S. 102 – Cele S. 103 – Pillay M.	01/03/19 01/03/19 01/03/19	06/03/13 06/03/13 06/03/13
Database Design	11/03/19	15/03/19	DB Designer I	104 – Pillay M.	11/03/19	14/03/13
System Design	11/03/19	12/04/19	Sys. Analyst II Sys. Analyst I Sys. Analyst I	105 – Cele S. 106 – Hemalika I. 107 – Zebras S.	11/03/19 11/03/19 11/03/19	
Database Implementation	18/03/19	22/03/19	Oracle DBA	108 – Smith J.	15/03/19	19/03/13
System Coding & Testing	25/03/19	20/05/19	Cobol I Cobol I Cobol II Oracle DBA	109 – Summers A. 110 – Ellis M. 111 – Epahnor V. 112 – Smith J.	21/03/19 21/03/19 21/03/19 21/03/19	
System Documentation	25/03/19	07/06/19	Tech. Writer	113 – Kilby S.	25/03/19	
Final Evaluation	10/06/19	14/06/19	Project Mgr. Sys. Analyst II DB Designer I Cobol II			
On-Site System Online and Data Loading	17/06/19	21/06/19	Project Mgr. Sys. Analyst II DB Designer I Cobol II			
Sign-Off	01/07/19	01/07/19	Project Mgr.			

(*Note:* The assignment number is shown as a prefix of the employee name; for example, 101, 102.) Assume that the assignments shown previously are the only ones existing as of the date of this design. The assignment number can be whatever number matches your database design.

- Given all of the preceding information, you can see that the assignment associates an employee with a project task, using the project schedule. Therefore, to keep track of the *assignment*, you require at least the following information: assignment ID, employee, project schedule task, date assignment starts and date assignment ends (which could be any dates as some projects run ahead of or behind schedule). A sample assignment form is shown on page 267.
- The hours an employee works are kept in a *work log* containing a record of the actual hours worked by an employee on a given assignment. The work log is a weekly form that the employee fills out at the end of each week (Friday) or at the end of each month. The form contains the date (of each Friday of the month or the last day of the month if it doesn't fall on a Friday), the assignment ID, the total hours worked that week (or up to the end of the month), and the number of the bill to which the work log entry is charged. Obviously, each work log entry can be related to only one bill. A sample list of the current work log entries for the first sample project is shown in the following table.

Employee Name	Week Ending	Assignment Number	Hours Worked	Bill Number
Cele S.	01/03/19	1-102	4	xxx
Connor S.	01/03/19	1-101	4	xxx
Smith M.	01/03/19	1-103	4	xxx
Cele S.	08/03/19	1-102	24	xxx
Connor S.	08/03/19	1-101	24	xxx
Smith M.	08/03/19	1-103	24	xxx
Cele S.	15/03/19	1-105	40	xxx
Hemalika I.	15/03/19	1-106	40	xxx
Pillay J.	15/03/19	1-108	6	xxx
Pillay M.	15/03/19	1-104	32	xxx
Zebras S.	15/03/18	1-107	35	xxx
Cele S.	22/02/19	1-105	40	
Hemalika I.	22/02/19	1-106	40	
Ellis M.	22/02/19	1-110	12	
Mbaso V.	22/02/19	1-111	12	
Pillay J.	22/02/19	1-108	12	
Pillay J.	22/02/19	1-112	12	
Summers A.	22/02/19	1-109	12	
Zebras S.	22/02/19	1-107	35	
Cele S.	22/02/19	1-105	40	
Hemalika I.	29/03/19	1-106	40	
Ellis M.	29/03/19	1-110	35	
Mbaso V.	29/03/19	1-111	35	
Kilby S.	29/03/19	1-113	40	
Smith J.	29/03/19	1-112	35	
Summers A.	29/03/19	1-109	35	
Zebras S.	29/03/19	1-107	35	

(*Note:* xxx represents the bill ID. Use the one that matches the bill number in your database.)

- Finally, every 15 days a *bill* is written and sent to the customer, totalling the hours worked on the project for that period. When GCS generates a bill, it updates, using the bill number, the work-log entries that are part of that bill. In summary, a bill can refer to many work log entries and each work log entry can be related to only one bill. GCS sent one bill on 15/03/19 for the first project (Xerox), totalling the hours worked between 01/02/19 and 15/03/19. Therefore, you can safely assume that there is only one bill in this table and that bill covers the work-log entries shown in the above form.

Your assignment is to create a database that will fulfil the operations described in this problem. The minimum required entities are employee, skill, customer, region, project, project schedule, assignment, work log and bill. (There are additional required entities that are not listed.)

- Create all of the required tables and create all of the required relationships.
- Create the required indexes to maintain entity integrity when using surrogate primary keys.
- Populate the tables as needed (as indicated in the sample data and forms).

4 'Martial Arts R Us' (MARU) needs a database. MARU is a martial arts school with hundreds of students. The database must keep track of all the classes that are offered, who is assigned to teach each class, and which students attend each class. Also, it is important to track the progress of each student as they advance. Create a complete Crow's Foot ERD for these requirements:

- Students are given a student number when they join the school. The number is stored along with their name, date of birth, and the date they joined the school.
- All instructors are also students, but clearly not all students are instructors. In addition to the normal student information, for all instructors, the date that they start working as an instructor must be recorded along with their instructor status (compensated or volunteer).
- An instructor may be assigned to teach any number of classes, but each class has one and only one assigned instructor. Some instructors, especially volunteer instructors, may not be assigned to any class.
- A class is offered for a specific level at a specific time, day of the week, and location. For example, one class taught on Mondays at 5:00 p.m. in Room 1 is an intermediate-level class. Another class taught on Mondays at 6:00 p.m. in Room 1 is a beginner-level class. A third class taught on Tuesdays at 5:00 p.m. in Room 2 is an advanced-level class.
- Students may attend any class of the appropriate level during each week, so there is no expectation that any particular student will attend any particular class session. Therefore, the attendance of students at each individual class meeting must be tracked.
- A student will attend many different class meetings, and each class meeting is normally attended by many students. Some class meetings may not be attended by any students. New students may not have attended any class meetings yet.
- At any given meeting of a class, instructors other than the assigned instructor may show up to help. Therefore, a given class meeting may have a head instructor and many assistant instructors, but it will always have at least the one instructor who is assigned to that class. For each class meeting, the date of the class and the instructors' roles (head instructor or assistant instructor) need to be recorded. For example, Mr Jones is assigned to teach the Monday, 5:00 p.m., intermediate class in Room 1. During a particular meeting of that class, Mr Jones was the head instructor and Ms Khumalo served as an assistant instructor.
- Each student holds a rank in the martial arts. The rank name, belt colour, and rank requirements are stored. Most ranks have numerous rank requirements, but each requirement is associated with only one particular rank. All ranks except white belt have at least one requirement.
- A given rank may be held by many students. While it is customary to think of a student as having a single rank, it is necessary to track each student's progress through the ranks. Therefore, every rank that a student attains is kept in the system. New students joining the school are automatically given the rank of white belt. The date that a student is awarded each rank should be kept in the system. All ranks have at least one student who has achieved that rank at some time.

5 Global Unified Technology Sales (GUTS) is moving towards a 'bring your own device' (BYOD) model for employee computing. Employees can use traditional desktop computers in their offices. They can also use a variety of personal mobile computing devices such as tablets, smartphones and laptops. The new computing model introduces some security risks that GUTS is attempting to address. The company wants to ensure that any devices connecting to their servers are properly

registered and approved by the Information Technology department. Create a complete ERD to support the business needs described below:

- Every employee works for a department that has a department code, name, mail box number, and phone number. The smallest department currently has 5 employees, and the largest department has 40 employees. This system will only track in which department an employee is currently employed. Very rarely, a new department can be created within the company. At such times, the department may exist temporarily without any employees. For every employee, an employee number and name (first, last, and middle initial) are recorded in the system. It is also necessary to keep each employee's title.
- An employee can have many devices registered in the system. Each device is assigned an identification number when it is registered. Most employees have at least one device, but newly hired employees might not have any devices registered initially. For each device, the brand and model need to be recorded. Only devices that are registered to an employee will be in the system. While unlikely, it is possible that a device could transfer from one employee to another. However, if that happens, only the employee who currently owns the device is tracked in the system. When a device is registered in the system, the date of that registration needs to be recorded.
- Devices can be either desktop systems that reside in a company office or mobile devices. Desktop devices are typically provided by the company and are intended to be a permanent part of the company network. As such, each desktop device is assigned a static IP address, and the MAC address for the computer hardware is kept in the system. A desktop device is kept in a static location (building name and office number). This location should also be kept in the system so that, if the device becomes compromised, the IT department can dispatch someone to remediate the problem.
- For mobile devices, it is important also to capture the device's serial number, which operating system (OS) it is using, and the version of the OS. The IT department is also verifying that each mobile device has a screen lock enabled and has encryption enabled for data. The system should support storing information on whether or not each mobile device has these capabilities enabled.
- Once a device is registered in the system, and the appropriate capabilities are enabled if it is a mobile device, the device may be approved for connections to one or more servers. Not all devices meet the requirements to be approved at first, so the device might be in the system for a period of time before it is approved to connect to any server. GUTS has a number of servers, and a device must be approved for each server individually. Therefore, it is possible for a single device to be approved for several servers but not for all servers.
- Each server has a name, brand, and IP address. Within the IT department's facilities are a number of climate-controlled server rooms where the physical servers can be located. Which room each server is in should also be recorded. Further, it is necessary to track which operating system is being used on each server.
- Some servers are virtual servers and some are physical servers. If a server is a virtual server, then the system should track which physical server it is running on. A single physical server can host many virtual servers, but each virtual server is hosted on only one physical server. Only physical servers can host a virtual server. In other words, one virtual server cannot host another virtual server. Not all physical servers host a virtual server.
- A server will normally have many devices that are approved to access the server, but it is possible for new servers to be created that do not yet have any approved devices. When a

6

device is approved for connection to a server, the date of that approval should be recorded. It is also possible for a device that was approved for a server to lose its approval. If that happens, the date that the approval was removed should be recorded. If a device loses its approval, it may regain that approval at a later date if whatever circumstance that lead to the removal is resolved.

- A server can provide many user services, such as email, chat, homework managers, and others. Each service on a server has a unique identification number and name. The date that GUTS began offering that service should be recorded. Each service runs on only one server although new servers might not offer any services initially. Client-side services are not tracked in this system, so every service must be associated with a server.
- Employees must get permission to access a service before they can use it. Most employees have permissions to use a wide array of services, but new employees might not have permission on any service. Each service can support multiple approved employees as users, but new services might not have any approved users at first. The date on which the employee is approved to use a service is tracked by the system. The first time an employee is approved to access a service, the employee must create a username and password. This will be the same username and password that the employee will use for every service for which the employee is eventually approved.

6

CHAPTER 7

Normalising Database Designs

IN THIS CHAPTER, YOU WILL LEARN:

- What normalisation is and what role it plays in the database design process
- About the normal forms 1NF, 2NF, 3NF, BCNF and 4NF
- How normal forms can be transformed from lower normal forms to higher normal forms
- That normalisation and ER modelling are used concurrently to produce a good database design
- That some situations require denormalisation to generate information efficiently

PREVIEW

Good database design must be matched to good table structures. In this chapter, you will learn to evaluate and design good table structures to control data redundancies, thereby avoiding data anomalies. The process that yields such desirable results is known as normalisation.

In order to recognise and appreciate the characteristics of a good table structure, it is useful to examine a poor one. Therefore, the chapter begins by examining the characteristics of a poor table structure and the problems it creates. You will then learn how to correct a poor table structure. This methodology will yield important dividends: you will know how to design a good table structure and how to repair an existing poor one.

You will discover not only that data anomalies can be eliminated through normalisation, but also that a properly normalised set of table structures is actually less complicated to use than an unnormalised set. In addition, you will learn that the normalised set of table structures more faithfully reflects an organisation's real operations.

7.1 DATABASE TABLES AND NORMALISATION

Having good relational database software is not enough to avoid the data redundancy discussed in Chapter 1, The Database Approach. If the database tables are treated as though they are files in a file system, the relational database management system (RDBMS) never has a chance to demonstrate its superior data-handling capabilities.

The table is a basic building block in the database design process. Consequently, the table's structure is of great interest. Ideally, the database design process explored in Chapter 5, Data Modelling with Entity Relationship Diagrams, yields good table structures. Yet it is possible to create poor table structures even in a good database design. So, how do you recognise a poor table structure, and how do you produce a good table? The answer to both questions is based on normalisation. **Normalisation** is a process for evaluating and correcting table structures to minimise data redundancies, thereby reducing the likelihood of data anomalies. The normalisation process involves assigning attributes to tables based on the concept of determination you learned about in Chapter 3, Relational Model Characteristics.

Normalisation works through a series of stages called *normal forms*. The first three stages are described as first normal form (1NF), second normal form (2NF) and third normal form (3NF). From a structural point of view, 2NF is better than 1NF and 3NF is better than 2NF. For most business database design purposes, 3NF is as high as you need to go in the normalisation process. (Actually, you will discover in Section 7.3 that properly designed 3NF structures also meet the requirements of fourth normal form (4NF).)

Although normalisation is a very important database design ingredient, you should not assume that the highest level of normalisation is always the most desirable. Generally, the higher the normal form, the more relational join operations are required to produce a specified output and the more resources are required by the database system to respond to end-user queries. A successful design must also consider end-user demand for fast performance. Therefore, you will occasionally be expected to *denormalise* some portions of a database design in order to meet performance requirements. (**Denormalisation** produces a lower normal form; that is, a 3NF will be converted to a 2NF through denormalisation.) However, *the price you pay for increased performance through denormalisation is greater data redundancy*.

7.2 THE NEED FOR NORMALISATION

The normalisation process can be illustrated with a business application, the simplified database activities of a construction company that manages several building projects. Each project has its own project number, name, employees assigned to it and so on. Each employee has an employee number, name and job classification, such as engineer or computer technician.

The company charges its clients by billing for the hours spent on each contract. The hourly billing rate is dependent on the employee's position. (For example, one hour of computer technician time is billed at a different rate from one hour of engineer time.) Periodically, a report is generated that contains the information displayed in Table 7.1.

TABLE 7.1 **A sample report layout**

Proj. Num.	Project Name	Employee Number	Employee Name	Job Class	Chg/ Hour	Hours Billed	Total Charge
15	Evergreen	103	Mzwandile E. Baloyi	Elec. Engineer	€67.55	23.8	€1 607.69
		101	John G. News	Database Designer	€82.95	19.4	€1 609.23
		105	Alice K. Johnson*	Database Designer	€82.95	35.7	€2 961.32
		106	William Smithfield	Programmer	€26.66	12.6	€335.92
		102	Kavyara H. Moonsamy	Systems Analyst	€76.43	23.8	€1 819.03
				Subtotal			**€8 333.19**
18	Amber Wave	114	Annelise Jones	Applications Designer	€38.00	25.6	€972.80
		118	James J. Frommer	General Support	€14.50	45.3	€656.85
		104	Noxolo K. Maseki*	Systems Analyst	€76.43	32.4	€2 476.33
		112	Darlene M. Smithson	DSS Analyst	€36.30	45.0	€1 633.50
				Subtotal			**€5 739.48**
22	Rolling Tide	105	Alice K. Johnson	Database Designer	€82.95	65.7	€5 449.82
		104	Noxolo K. Maseki	Systems Analyst	€76.43	48.4	€3 699.21
		113	Delbert K. Joenbrood*	Applications Designer	€38.00	23.6	€896.80
		111	Geoff B. Wabash	Clerical Support	€21.23	22.0	€467.06
		106	William Smithfield	Programmer	€28.24	12.8	€361.47
				Subtotal			**€10 874.36**
25	Starflight	107	Maria D. Alonzo	Programmer	€28.24	25.6	€722.94
		115	Travis B. Bawangi	Systems Analyst	€76.43	45.8	€3 500.49
		101	John G. News*	Database Designer	€82.95	56.3	€4 670.09
		114	Annelise Jones	Applications Designer	€38.00	33.1	€1 257.80
		108	Krishshanth B. Khan	Systems Analyst	€76.43	23.6	€1 803.75
		118	James J. Frommer	General Support	€14.50	30.5	€442.25
		112	Darlene M. Smithson	DSS Analyst	€36.30	41.4	€1 502.82
				Subtotal			**€13 900.14**
				Total			**€38 942.09**

Note: * indicates project leader.

The subtotals and total charge in Table 7.1 are derived attributes and, at this point, not stored in the table.

The easiest short-term way to generate the required report might seem to be a table whose contents correspond to the reporting requirements. (See Figure 7.1.)

Online Content The databases used to illustrate the material in this chapter are available on the online platform accompanying this book.

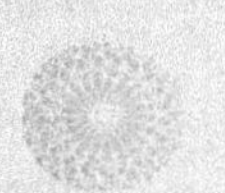

7

FIGURE 7.1 **Tabular representation of the report format**

Database name: Ch07_ConstructCo

Table name: RPT_FORMAT

PROJ_NUM	PROJ_NAME	EMP_NUM	EMP_NAME	JOB_CLASS	CHG_HOUR	HOURS
15	Evergreen	103	Mzwandile E. Baloyi	Elect. Engineer	€67.55	23.80
		101	John G. News	Database Designer	€82.95	19.40
		105	Alice K. Johnson *	Database Designer	€82.95	35.70
		106	William Smithfield	Programmer	€26.66	12.60
		102	Kavyara H. Moonsamy	Systems Analyst	€76.43	23.80
18	Amber Wave	114	Annelise Jones	Applications Designer	€38.00	24.60
		118	James J. Frommer	General Support	€14.50	45.30
		104	Noxolo K. Maseki *	Systems Analyst	€76.43	32.40
		112	Darlene M. Smithson	DSS Analyst	€36.30	44.00
22	Rolling Tide	105	Alice K. Johnson	Database Designer	€82.95	64.70
		104	Noxolo K. Maseki	Systems Analyst	€76.43	48.40
		113	Delbert K. Joenbrood *	Applications Designer	€38.10	23.60
		111	Geoff B. Wabash	Clerical Support	€21.23	22.00
		106	William Smithfield	Programmer	€28.24	12.80
25	Starflight	107	Maria D. Alonzo	Programmer	€28.24	24.60
		115	Travis B. Bawangi	Systems Analyst	€76.43	45.80
		101	John G. News *	Database Designer	€82.95	56.30
		114	Annelise Jones	Applications Designer	€38.00	33.10
		108	Krishshanth B. Khan	Systems Analyst	€76.43	23.60
		118	James J. Frommer	General Support	€14.50	30.50
		112	Darlene M. Smithson	DSS Analyst	€36.30	41.40

As you examine the data in Figure 7.1, note that it reflects the assignment of employees to projects. Apparently, an employee can be assigned to more than one project. For example, Darlene Smithson (EMP_NUM = 112) has been assigned to two projects: Amber Wave and Starflight. Given the structure of the data set, each project includes only a single occurrence of any one employee. Therefore, knowing the PROJ_NUM and EMP_NUM value will let you find the job classification and its hourly charge. In addition, you will know the total number of hours for which each employee worked on each project. (The total charge – a derived attribute whose value can be computed by multiplying the hours billed and the charge per hour – has not been included in Figure 7.1. No structural harm is done if this derived attribute is included.)

Unfortunately, the structure of the data set in Figure 7.1 does not conform to the requirements discussed in Chapter 3, Relational Model Characteristics, nor does it handle data very well.

1 The project number (PROJ_NUM) is apparently intended to be a primary key (PK) or at least a part of a PK, but it contains nulls. (Given the preceding discussion, you know that PROJ_NUM + EMP_NUM will define each row.)

2 The table entries invite data inconsistencies. For example, the JOB_CLASS value 'Elect. Engineer' might be entered as 'Elect.Eng.' in some cases, 'El. Eng.' in others, and 'EE' in still others.

3 The table displays data redundancies. Those data redundancies yield the following anomalies:

   a *Update anomalies*. Modifying the JOB_CLASS for employee number 105 requires (potentially) many alterations, one for each EMP_NUM = 105.

   b *Insertion anomalies*. Just to complete a row definition, a new employee must be assigned to a project. If the employee is not yet assigned, a phantom project must be created to complete the employee data entry.

   c *Deletion anomalies*. Suppose that only one employee is associated with a given project. If that employee leaves the company and the employee data are deleted, the project information will also be deleted. To prevent the loss of the project information, a fictitious employee must be created just to save the project information.

In spite of those structural deficiencies, the table structure *appears* to work; the report is generated with ease. Unfortunately, the report may yield different results depending on what data anomaly has occurred. For example, if you want to print a report to show the total 'hours worked' value by the job classification 'Database Designer', that report will not include data for 'DB Design' and 'Database Design' data entries. (Such reporting anomalies drive managers up the proverbial wall – and cannot be fixed through programming.) The only solution to avoid these anomalies is to ensure that the database has design integrity. For example, codes could be used for job classification that are looked up from another table. In other words, they are a foreign key in this table.

Even if very careful data entry auditing can eliminate most of the reporting problems (at a high cost), it is easy to demonstrate that even a simple data entry becomes inefficient. Given the existence of update anomalies, suppose Darlene M. Smithson is assigned to work on the Evergreen project. The data entry clerk must update the PROJECT file with the entry:

15 Evergreen 112 Darlene M. Smithson DSS Analyst €36.30 0.0

to match the attributes PROJ_NUM, PROJ_NAME, EMP_NUM, EMP_NAME, JOB_CLASS, CHG_HOUR and HOURS. (When Ms Smithson has just been assigned to the project, she has not yet worked, so the total number of hours worked is 0.0.)

Each time an existing employee is assigned to a project, some data entries (such as PROJ_NAME, EMP_NAME and CHG_HOUR) are unnecessarily repeated. Imagine the data entry chore when 200 or 300 table entries must be made! Note that the entry of the employee number should be sufficient to identify Darlene M. Smithson, her job description and her hourly charge. Because there is only one person identified by the number 112, that person's characteristics (name, job classification and so on) should not have to be typed in each time the main file is updated. Unfortunately, the structure displayed in Figure 7.1 does not make allowances for that possibility.

The data redundancy evident in Figure 7.1 leads to wasted disk space. What's more, data redundancy produces data anomalies. For example, suppose the data entry clerk had entered the data as:

15 Evergeen 112 Darla Smithson DCS Analyst €36.30 0.0

At first glance, the data entry appears to be correct. But is Evergeen the same project as Evergreen? And is DCS Analyst supposed to be DSS Analyst? Is Darla Smithson the same person as Darlene M. Smithson? Such confusion is a data integrity problem that was caused because the data entry failed to conform to the rule that all copies of redundant data must be identical.

The possibility of introducing data integrity problems caused by data redundancy must be considered when a database is designed. The relational database environment is especially well suited to helping the designer overcome those problems.

NOTE

Remember that the naming convention makes it easy to see what each attribute stands for and what its likely origin is. For example, PROJ_NAME uses the prefix PROJ to indicate that the attribute is associated with the PROJECT table, while the NAME component is self-documenting, too. However, keep in mind that name length is also an issue, especially in the prefix designation. For that reason, the prefix CHG was used rather than CHARGE. (Given the database's context, it is not likely that that prefix will be misunderstood.)

7.3 THE NORMALISATION PROCESS

In this section, you learn how to use normalisation to produce a set of normalised tables to store the data that will be used to generate the required information. The objective is to create tables that have the following characteristics:

- Each table represents a single subject. For example, a course table will contain only data that directly pertains to courses. Similarly, a student table will contain only student data.
- No data item will be *unnecessarily* stored in more than one table. The reason for this requirement is to ensure that the data are updated in only one place.
- All attributes in a table are dependent on the primary key – the entire primary key and nothing but the primary key.

To accomplish the objective, the normalisation process takes you through the steps that lead to successively higher normal forms. The most common normal forms and their basic characteristics are listed in Table 7.2. You will learn the details of these normal forms in the indicated sections.

TABLE 7.2 Normal forms

Normal Form	Characteristic	Section
First normal form (1NF)	Table format; no repeating groups and PK identified	7.3.1
Second normal form (2NF)	1NF and no partial dependencies	7.3.2
Third normal form (3NF)	2NF and no transitive dependencies	7.3.3
Boyce-Codd normal form (BCNF)	Every determinant is a candidate key (special case of 3NF)	7.6.1
Fourth normal form (4NF)	3NF and no independent multivalued dependencies	7.6.2

Even higher-level normal forms exist. However, normal forms such as the fifth normal form (5NF) and domain-key normal form (DKNF) are not likely to be encountered in a business environment and are mainly of theoretical interest. Some very specialised applications, such as statistical research, may require normalisation beyond the 4NF, but those applications fall outside the scope of most business operations. Since this book focuses on practical applications of database techniques, the higher-level normal forms are not covered.

7.3.1 Conversion To First Normal Form

Because the relational model views the data as part of a table or collection of tables in which all key values must be identified, the data depicted in Figure 7.1 might not be stored as shown. Note that Figure 7.1 contains what is known as repeating groups. A **repeating group** derives its name from the fact that multiple entries of the same type can exist for any *single* key of an attribute key. These entries, or repeating groups, will have identical structures but may consist of several fields. In Figure 7.1, note that each project number (PROJ_NUM) can reference a group of related data entries. For example, the Evergreen project (PROJ_NUM = 15) is associated with five entries, one for each person working on the project. Those entries are related because they each have a PROJ_NUM whose value is 15. Each time a new record is entered for another person who works on the Evergreen project, the number of entries in the repeating group grows by one.

A relational table must not contain repeating groups. The existence of repeating groups provides evidence that the RPT_FORMAT table in Figure 7.1 fails to meet even the lowest normal form requirements, thus reflecting data redundancies.

Normalising the table structure will reduce the data redundancies. If repeating groups do exist, they must be eliminated by making sure that each row defines a single entity. In addition, the dependencies must be identified to diagnose the normal form. Identification of the normal form will let you know where you are in the normalisation process. The normalisation process starts with a simple three-step procedure.

Step 1: Eliminate the Repeating Groups

Start by presenting the data in a tabular format, where each cell has a single value and there are no repeating groups. To eliminate the repeating groups, eliminate the nulls by making sure that each repeating group attribute contains an appropriate data value. This change converts the table in Figure 7.1 to 1NF in Figure 7.2.

FIGURE 7.2 A table in first normal form

Database name: Ch07_ConstructCo

Table name: DATA_ORG_1NF

DATA_ORG_1NF

PROJ_NUM	PROJ_NAME	EMP_NUM	EMP_NAME	JOB_CLASS	CHG_HOUR	HOURS
15	Evergreen	103	Mzwandile E. Baloyi	Elect. Engineer	€67.55	23.80
15	Evergreen	101	John G. News	Database Designer	€82.95	19.40
15	Evergreen	105	Alice K. Johnson *	Database Designer	€82.95	35.70
15	Evergreen	106	William Smithfield	Programmer	€26.66	12.60
15	Evergreen	102	Kavyara H. Moonsamy	Systems Analyst	€76.43	23.80
18	Amber Wave	114	Annelise Jones	Applications Designer	€38.00	24.60
18	Amber Wave	118	James J. Frommer	General Support	€14.50	45.30

DATA_ORG_1NF						
PROJ_NUM	**PROJ_NAME**	**EMP_NUM**	**EMP_NAME**	**JOB_CLASS**	**CHG_HOUR**	**HOURS**
18	Amber Wave	104	Noxolo K. Maseki *	Systems Analyst	€76.43	32.40
18	Amber Wave	112	Darlene M. Smithson	DSS Analyst	€36.30	44.00
22	Rolling Tide	105	Alice K. Johnson	Database Designer	€82.95	64.70
22	Rolling Tide	104	Noxolo K. Maseki	Systems Analyst	€76.43	48.40
22	Rolling Tide	113	Delbert K. Joenbrood *	Applications Designer	€38.00	23.60
22	Rolling Tide	111	Geoff B. Wabash	Clerical Support	€21.23	22.00
22	Rolling Tide	106	William Smithfield	Programmer	€28.24	12.80
25	Starflight	107	Maria D. Alonzo	Programmer	€28.24	24.60
25	Starflight	115	Travis B. Bawangi	Systems Analyst	€76.43	45.80
25	Starflight	101	John G. News *	Database Designer	€82.95	56.30
25	Starflight	114	Annelise Jones	Applications Designer	€38.00	33.10
25	Starflight	108	Krishshanth B. Khan	Systems Analyst	€76.43	23.60
25	Starflight	118	James J. Frommer	General Support	€14.50	30.50
25	Starflight	112	Darlene M. Smithson	DSS Analyst	€36.30	41.40

Step 2: Identify the Primary Key

The layout in Figure 7.2 represents more than a mere cosmetic change. Even a casual observer will note that PROJ_NUM is not an adequate primary key because the project number does not uniquely identify one row of the table and hence does not identify all of the remaining entity (row) attributes. For example, the PROJ_NUM value 15 can identify any one of five employees. To maintain a proper primary key that will *uniquely* identify any attribute value, the new key must be composed of a *combination* of PROJ_NUM and EMP_NUM. This is called a composite primary key. For example, using the data shown in Figure 7.2, if you know that PROJ_NUM = 15 and EMP_NUM = 103, the entries for the attributes PROJ_NAME, EMP_NAME, JOB_CLASS, CHG_HOUR, and HOURS can only be Evergreen, Mzwandile E. Baloyi, Elect. Engineer, €67.55 and 23.8, respectively.

Step 3: Identify All Dependencies

The identification of the PK in Step 2 means that you have already identified the following dependency:

PROJ_NUM, EMP_NUM → PROJ_NAME, EMP_NAME, JOB_CLASS, CHG_HOUR, HOURS

That is, the PROJ_NAME, EMP_NAME, JOB_CLASS, CHG_HOUR and HOURS values are all dependent on – that is, they are determined by – the combination of PROJ_NUM and EMP_NUM. There are additional dependencies. For example, the project number on its own identifies (determines) the project name. In other words, the project name is dependent on the project number. You can write that dependency as:

PROJ_NUM → PROJ_NAME

Also, if you know an employee number, you also know that employee's name, that employee's job classification and that employee's charge per hour. Therefore, you can identify the dependency shown next:

EMP_NUM → EMP_NAME, JOB_CLASS, CHG_HOUR

However, given the previous dependency components, you can see that knowing the job classification means knowing the charge per hour for that job classification. In other words, you can identify one last dependency:

JOB_CLASS → CHG_HOUR

The dependencies you have just examined can also be depicted with the help of the diagram shown in Figure 7.3. Because such a diagram depicts all dependencies found within a given table structure, it is known as a **dependency diagram**. Dependency diagrams are very helpful in getting a bird's-eye view of all of the relationships among a table's attributes, and their use makes it less likely that you will overlook an important dependency. The diagram below shows two types of dependencies: partial dependencies and transitive dependencies. Partial dependencies are where a non-key attribute can be determined by part of the primary key. Transitive dependencies are when one non-key attribute determines another non-key attribute.

FIGURE 7.3 **First normal form (1NF) dependency diagram**

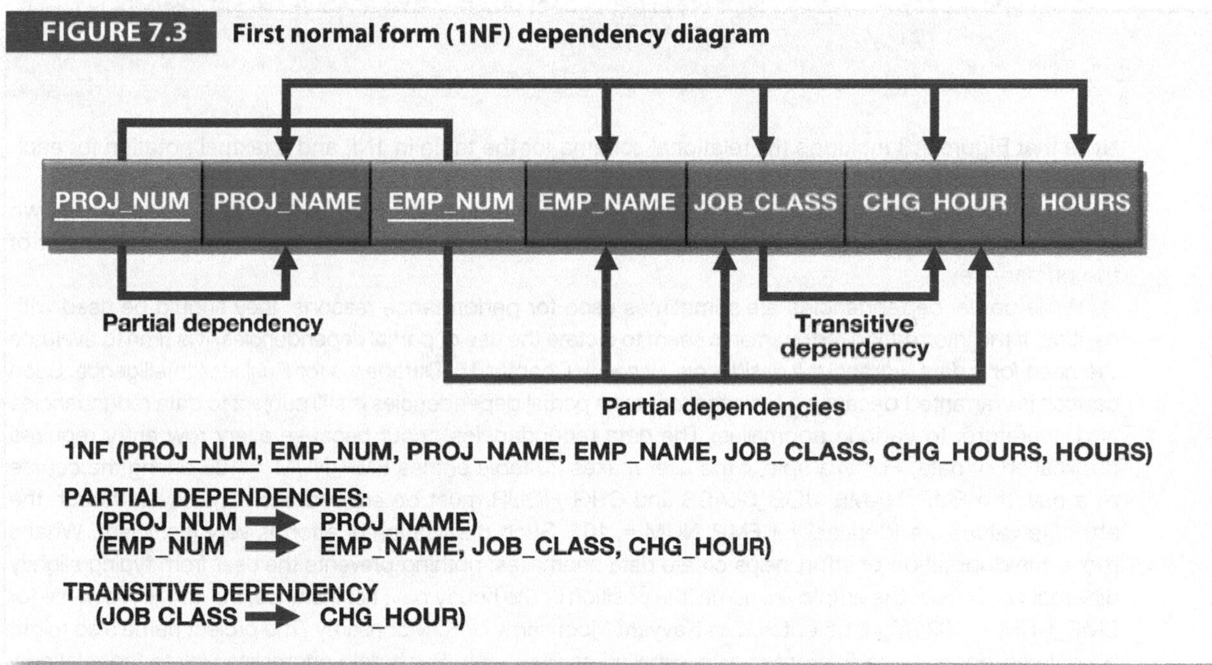

As you examine Figure 7.3, note the following dependency diagram features:

1. The primary key attributes are bold, underlined and shaded in a different colour.
2. The arrows above the attributes indicate all desirable dependencies, that is, dependencies that are based on the primary key. In this case, note that the entity's attributes are dependent on the *combination* of PROJ_NUM and EMP_NUM.
3. The arrows below the dependency diagram indicate less desirable dependencies. Two types of such dependencies exist:
   a. *Partial dependencies*. You need to know only the PROJ_NUM to determine the PROJ_NAME; that is, the PROJ_NAME is dependent on only part of the primary key. And you need to know only the EMP_NUM to find the EMP_NAME, the JOB_CLASS and the CHG_HOUR. A dependency based on only a part of a composite primary key is called a **partial dependency**.

b *Transitive dependencies*. As you examine Figure 7.3, note that CHG_HOUR is dependent on JOB_CLASS. Because neither CHG_HOUR nor JOB_CLASS is a prime attribute – that is, neither attribute is at least part of a key – the condition is known as a transitive dependency. (In other words, a **transitive dependency** is a dependency of one non-prime attribute on another non-prime attribute.) The problem with transitive dependencies is that they still yield data anomalies.

NOTE

Partial and transitive dependencies are important concepts when performing normalisation. To recap:

- Partial dependency refers to attributes that are only dependent on part of the composite primary key.
- Transitive dependency is when an attribute is dependent on any other attribute except the primary key.

7

Note that Figure 7.3 includes the relational schema for the table in 1NF and a textual notation for each identified dependency.

All relational tables satisfy the 1NF requirements. The problem with the 1NF table structure shown in Figure 7.3 is that it contains partial dependencies – that is, dependencies based on only a part of the primary key.

While partial dependencies are sometimes used for performance reasons, they should be used with caution. If the information requirements seem to dictate the use of partial dependencies, it is time to evaluate the need for a data warehouse design, discussed in Chapter 15, Databases for Business Intelligence. Such caution is warranted because a table that contains partial dependencies is still subject to data redundancies and, therefore, to various anomalies. The data redundancies occur because every row entry requires duplication of data. For example, if the user makes 20 table entries EMP_NUM = 105 during the course of a day, the EMP_NAME, JOB_CLASS and CHG_HOUR must be entered each time even though the attribute values are identical for EMP_NUM = 105. Such duplication of effort is very inefficient. What's more, the duplication of effort helps create data anomalies; nothing prevents the user from typing slightly different versions of the employee name, the position or the hourly pay. For instance, the employee name for EMP_NUM = 102 might be entered as Kavyara Moonsamy or K. Moonsamy. The project name also might be entered correctly as Evergreen or misspelled as Evergeen. Such data anomalies violate the relational database's integrity and consistency rules.

NOTE

The term **first normal form (1NF)** describes the tabular format in which:

- All of the key attributes are defined.
- There are no repeating groups in the table. In other words, each row/column intersection contains one and only one value, not a set of values.
- All attributes are dependent on the primary key.

7.3.2 Conversion To Second Normal Form

Fortunately, the relational database design can be improved easily by converting the database into a format known as the second normal form (2NF). The 1NF-to-2NF conversion is simple. Starting with the 1NF format displayed in Figure 7.3, you do the following:

Step 1: Write Each Key Component on a Separate Line

Write each of the composite primary key's components on a separate line; then write the original (composite) key on the last line. For example:

PROJ_NUM

EMP_NUM

PROJ_NUM EMP_NUM

Each component will become the key in a new table. In other words, the original table is now divided into three tables (PROJECT, EMPLOYEE and ASSIGNMENT).

Step 2: Assign Corresponding Dependent Attributes

Use Figure 7.3 to determine those attributes that are dependent on other attributes. The dependencies for the original key components are found by examining the arrows below the dependency diagram shown in Figure 7.3. In other words, the three new tables (PROJECT, EMPLOYEE and ASSIGNMENT) are described by the following relational schemas:

PROJECT (PROJ_NUM, PROJ_NAME)

EMPLOYEE (EMP_NUM, EMP_NAME, JOB_CLASS, CHG_HOUR)

ASSIGNMENT (PROJ_NUM, EMP_NUM, ASSIGN_HOURS)

As the number of hours spent on each project by each employee is dependent on both PROJ_NUM and EMP_NUM in the ASSIGNMENT table, you place those hours in the ASSIGNMENT table as ASSIGN_HOURS.

NOTE

The ASSIGNMENT table contains a composite primary key composed of the attributes PROJ_NUM and EMP_NUM. Any attribute that is at least part of a key is known as a **prime attribute** or a **key attribute**. Therefore, both PROJ_NUM and EMP_NUM are prime (or key) attributes. Conversely, a **non-prime attribute**, or a **non-key attribute**, is not even part of a key.

The results of Steps 1 and 2 are displayed in Figure 7.4. At this point, most of the anomalies discussed earlier have been eliminated. For example, if you now want to add/change/delete a PROJECT record, you need to go only to the PROJECT table and add/change/delete only one row.

A partial dependency can exist only when a table's primary key is composed of several attributes, so a table whose primary key consists of only a single attribute is automatically in 2NF when it is in 1NF.

Figure 7.4 still shows a transitive dependency, which can generate anomalies. For example, if the charge per hour changes for a job classification held by many employees, that change must be made for *each* of those employees. If you forget to update some of the employee records that are affected by the charge per hour change, different employees with the same job description will generate different hourly charges.

FIGURE 7.4 **Second normal form (2NF) conversion results**

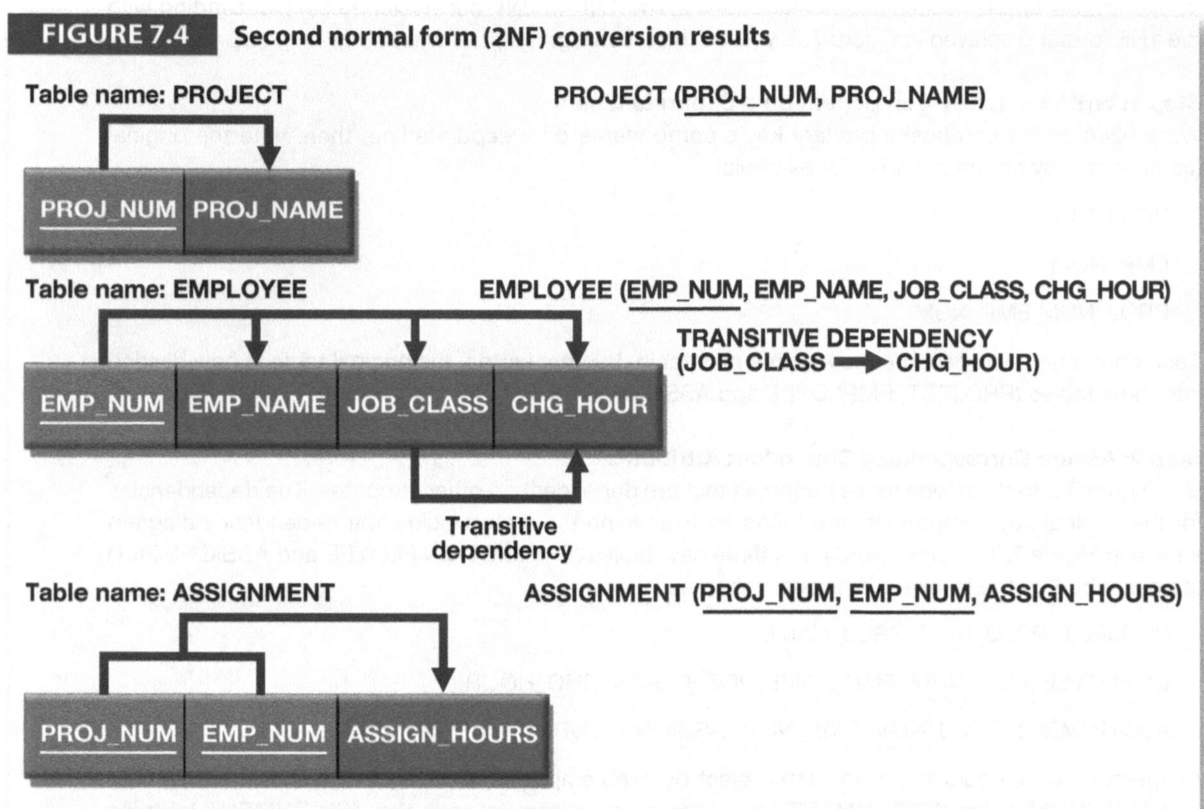

7

NOTE

A table is in **second normal form (2NF)** when:

- It is in 1NF.

and

- It includes no partial dependencies; that is, no attribute is dependent on only a portion of the primary key.
- (It is still possible for a table in 2NF to exhibit transitive dependency; that is, one or more attributes may be functionally dependent on non-key attributes.)

7.3.3 Conversion To Third Normal Form

The data anomalies created by the database organisation shown in Figure 7.4 are easily eliminated by completing the following three steps:

Step 1: Identify Each New Determinant

For every transitive dependency, write its determinant as a PK for a new table. (A **determinant** is any attribute whose value determines other values within a row.) If you have three different transitive dependencies, you will have three different determinants. Figure 7.4 shows a table that contains only one transitive dependency. Therefore, write the determinant for this transitive dependency as:

JOB_CLASS

Step 2: Identify the Dependent Attributes

Identify the attributes that are dependent on each determinant identified in Step 1 and identify the dependency. In this case, you write:

JOB_CLASS $\rightarrow$ CHG_HOUR

Name the table to reflect its contents and function. In this case, JOB seems appropriate.

Step 3: Remove the Dependent Attributes from Transitive Dependencies

Eliminate all dependent attributes in the transitive relationship(s) from each of the tables that have such a transitive relationship. In this example, eliminate CHG_HOUR from the EMPLOYEE table shown in Figure 7.4 to leave the EMPLOYEE table dependency definition as:

EMP_NUM $\rightarrow$ EMP_NAME, JOB_CLASS

Note that the JOB_CLASS remains in the EMPLOYEE table to serve as the FK.

Draw a new dependency diagram to show all of the tables you have defined in Steps 1–3. Check the new tables as well as the tables you modified in Step 3 to make sure that each table has a determinant and that no table contains inappropriate dependencies.

When you have completed Steps 1–3, you will see the results in Figure 7.5. (The usual procedure is to complete Steps 1–3 by simply drawing the revisions as you make them.)

In other words, after the conversion has been completed, your database contains four tables:

PROJECT (PROJ_NUM, PROJ_NAME)

EMPLOYEE (EMP_NUM, EMP_NAME, JOB_CLASS)

JOB (JOB_CLASS, CHG_HOUR)

ASSIGNMENT (PROJ_NUM, EMP_NUM, ASSIGN_HOURS)

Note that this conversion has eliminated the original EMPLOYEE table's transitive dependency; the tables are now said to be in third normal form (3NF).

NOTE

A table is in **third normal form (3NF)** when:

- It is in 2NF.

and

- It contains no transitive dependencies.

7

FIGURE 7.5 Third normal form (3NF) conversion results

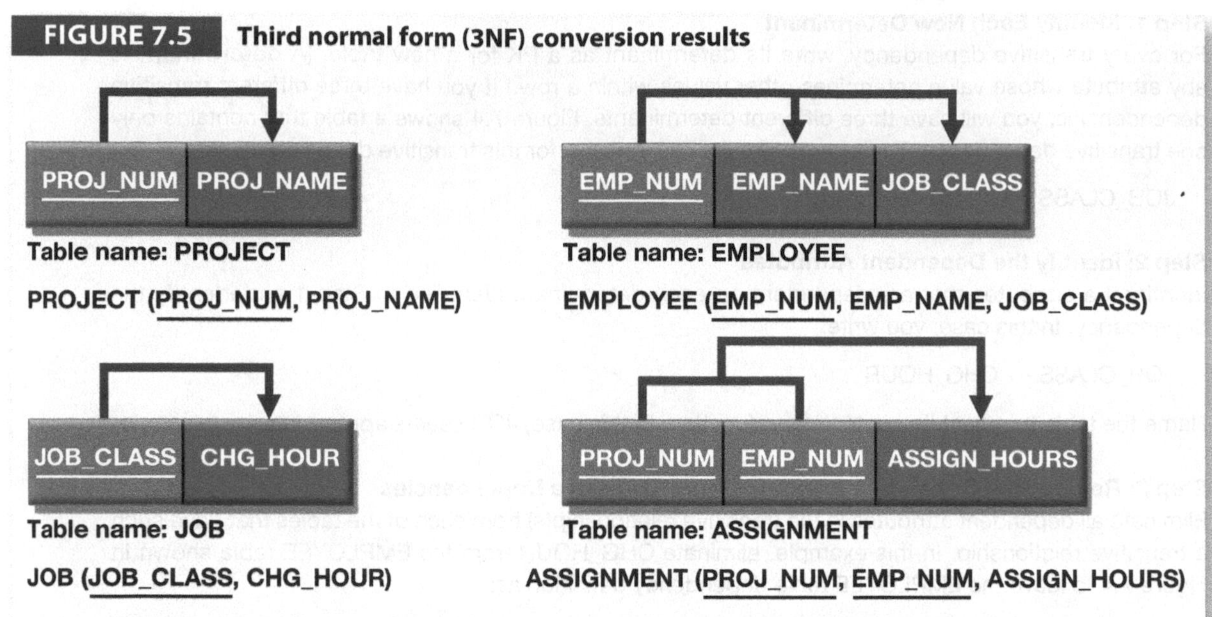

7

7.4 IMPROVING THE DESIGN

The table structures are cleaned up to eliminate the troublesome initial partial and transitive dependencies. You can now focus on improving the database's ability to provide information and on enhancing its operational characteristics. In the next few paragraphs, you will learn about the different types of issues you need to address to produce a good normalised set of tables. Please note that, due to space issues, each section presents just one example – the designer must apply the principle to all remaining tables in the design. Remember that normalisation cannot, by itself, be relied on to make good designs. Instead, normalisation is valuable because its use helps eliminate data redundancies. At a minimum, all designs should be in third normal form, unless intentionally left in lower normal forms for performance reasons, as discussed later.

7.4.1 Evaluate PK Assignments

As the number of employees grows, a JOB_CLASS value must be entered each time a new employee is entered into the EMPLOYEE table. Unfortunately, it is too easy to make data-entry errors that lead to referential integrity violations. For example, a JOB_CLASS entry of DB Designer, rather than Database Designer, into the EMPLOYEE table will trigger such a violation. Therefore, it would be better to add a JOB_CODE attribute to create a unique identifier. The addition of a JOB_CODE attribute produces the dependency:

JOB_CODE → JOB_CLASS, CHG_HOUR

This new attribute does produce a transitive dependency, if you assume that the JOB_CODE is a proper primary key, because it produces the dependency:

JOB_CLASS → CHG_HOUR

A transitive dependency exists because a non-key attribute – the JOB_CLASS – determines the value of another non-key attribute – the CHG_HOUR. However, that transitive dependency is an easy price to pay because the presence of JOB_CODE greatly decreases the likelihood of referential integrity violations. Note that the new JOB table now has two candidate keys (JOB_CODE and JOB_CLASS).

In this case, JOB_CODE is the chosen primary key as well as a surrogate key. A **surrogate key** is an artificial PK introduced by the designer with the purpose of simplifying the assignment of primary keys to tables. Surrogate keys are usually numeric, they are often automatically generated by the DBMS, they are free of semantic content (they have no special meaning), and they are usually hidden from the end users. You learnt about PK characteristics and assignment in Chapter 6, Data Modelling Advanced Concepts.

7.4.2 Evaluate Naming Conventions

It is best to adhere to the naming conventions outlined in Chapter 2, Data Models. Therefore, CHG_HOUR will be changed to JOB_CHG_HOUR to indicate its association with the JOB table. In addition, the attribute name JOB_CLASS does not quite describe entries such as Systems Analyst, Database Designer and so on; the label JOB_DESCRIPTION fits the entries better. Also, you may have noticed that HOURS was changed to ASSIGN_HOURS in the conversion from 1NF to 2NF. That change lets you associate the hours worked with the ASSIGNMENT table.

7.4.3 Refine Attribute Atomicity

It generally is good practice to pay attention to the *atomicity* requirement. (An **atomic attribute** is one that cannot be usefully further subdivided. Such an attribute is said to display **atomicity**.) Clearly, the use of the EMP_NAME in the EMPLOYEE table is not atomic because EMP_NAME can be decomposed into a last name, a first name and an initial. By improving the degree of atomicity, you also gain querying flexibility. For example, if you use EMP_LNAME, EMP_FNAME, and EMP_INITIAL, you can easily generate phone lists by sorting last names, first names and initials. Such a task would be very difficult if the name components were within a single attribute. In general, designers prefer to use simple, single-valued attributes as indicated by the business rules and processing requirements.

7

7.4.4 Identify New Attributes

If the EMPLOYEE table were used in a real-world environment, several other attributes would have to be added. For example, year-to-date gross salary payments and UIF (Unemployment Insurance Fund) payments would be desirable. Adding an employee hire date attribute (EMP_HIREDATE) could be used to track an employee's length of employment and serve as a basis for awarding bonuses to long-term employees and for other morale-enhancing measures. The same principle must be applied to all other tables in your design.

7.4.5 Identify New Relationships

The system's ability to supply detailed information about each project's manager is ensured by using the EMP_NUM as a foreign key in PROJECT. That action ensures that you can access the details of each PROJECT's manager data without producing unnecessary and undesirable data duplication. The designer must take care to place the right attributes in the right tables by using normalisation principles.

7.4.6 Refine Primary Keys as Required for Data Granularity

Granularity refers to the level of detail represented by the values stored in a table's row. Data stored at their lowest level of granularity are said to be *atomic data*. In Figure 7.5, the ASSIGNMENT table in 3NF uses the ASSIGN_HOURS attribute to represent the hours worked by a given employee on a given project. However, are those values recorded at their lowest level of granularity? In other words, do the ASSIGN_HOURS represent the *hourly* total, *daily* total, *weekly* total, *monthly* total or *yearly* total? Clearly, ASSIGN_HOURS requires more careful definition. In this case, the relevant question would be as follows: For what time frame – hour, day, week, month and so on – do you want to record the ASSIGN_HOURS data?

For example, assume that the combination of EMP_NUM and PROJ_NUM is an acceptable (composite) primary key in the ASSIGNMENT table. That primary key is useful in representing only the total number of hours an employee worked on a project since its start. Using a surrogate primary key such as ASSIGN_NUM provides lower granularity and yields greater flexibility. For example, assume that the EMP_NUM and PROJ_NUM combination is used as the primary key and an employee makes two 'hours worked' entries in the ASSIGNMENT table. That action violates the entity integrity requirement. Even if you add the ASSIGN_DATE as part of a composite PK, an entity integrity violation is still generated if any employee makes two or more entries for the same project on the same day. (The employee may have worked on the project a few hours in the morning and then worked on it again later in the day.) The same data entry yields no problems when ASSIGN_NUM is used as the primary key.

NOTE

In an ideal (database design) world, the level of desired granularity is determined at the conceptual design or the requirements gathering phase. However, as you have already seen in this chapter, many database designs involve the refinement of existing data requirements, thus triggering design modifications. In a real-world environment, changing granularity requirements may dictate changes in primary key selection. And those changes may ultimately require the use of surrogate keys.

7.4.7 Maintain Historical Accuracy

Writing the job charge per hour into the ASSIGNMENT table is crucial to maintaining the historical accuracy of the data in the ASSIGNMENT table. It would be appropriate to name this attribute ASSIGN_CHG_HOUR. Although this attribute would appear to have the same value as JOB_CHG_HOUR, that is true *only* if the JOB_CHG_HOUR value remains forever the same. However, it is reasonable to assume that the job charge per hour will change over time. However, suppose that the charges to each project were calculated (and billed) by multiplying the hours worked on the project found in the ASSIGNMENT table and the charge per hour found in the JOB table. Those charges would always show the current charge per hour stored in the JOB table, rather than the charge per hour that was in effect at the time of the assignment. (See Chapter 3, Section 3.6, for a more detailed discussion on how historical data accuracy is maintained within the database.)

7.4.8 Evaluate Using Derived Attributes

Finally, you can use a derived attribute in the ASSIGNMENT table to store the actual charge made to a project. That derived attribute, to be named ASSIGN_CHARGE, is the result of multiplying the ASSIGN_HOURS by the ASSIGN_CHG_HOUR. From a strictly database point of view, such derived attribute values can be calculated when they are needed to write reports or invoices. However, storing the derived attribute in the table makes it easy to write the application software to produce the desired results. Also, if many transactions must be reported and/or summarised, the availability of the derived attribute will save reporting time. (If the calculation is done at the time of data entry, it will be completed when the end user presses the Enter key, thus speeding up the process.)

The enhancements described in the preceding sections are illustrated in the tables shown in Figure 7.6.

Figure 7.6 is a vast improvement over the original database design. If the application software is designed properly, the most active table (ASSIGNMENT) requires the entry of only the PROJ_NUM, EMP_NUM and ASSIGN_HOURS values. The values for the attributes ASSIGN_NUM and ASSIGN_DATE can

FIGURE 7.6 The completed database

Database name: Ch07_ConstructCo

Table name: PROJECT

PROJ_NUM	PROJ_NAME	EMP_NUM
15	Evergreen	105
18	Amber Wave	104
22	Rolling Tide	113
25	Starflight	101

Table name: JOB

JOB_CODE	JOB_DESCRIPTION	JOB_CHG_HOUR
500	Programmer	€28.24
501	Systems Analyst	€76.43
502	Database Designer	€82.95
503	Electrical Engineer	€66.76
504	Mechanical Engineer	€53.64
505	Civil Engineer	€44.07
506	Clerical Support	€21.23
507	DSS Analyst	€36.30
508	Applications Designer	€38.00
509	Bio Technician	€27.29
510	General Support	€14.50

Table name: ASSIGNMENT

ASSIGN_ NUM	ASSIGN_ DATE	PROJ_ NUM	EMP_ NUM	ASSIGN_ HOURS	ASSIGN_CHG_ HOUR	ASSIGN_ CHARGE
1001	04-Mar-18	15	103	2.60	€67.55	€175.63
1002	04-Mar-18	18	118	1.40	€14.50	€20.30
1003	05-Mar-18	15	101	3.60	€82.95	€298.62
1004	05-Mar-18	22	113	2.50	€38.00	€95.00
1005	05-Mar-18	15	103	1.90	€67.55	€128.35
1006	05-Mar-18	25	115	4.20	€76.43	€321.01
1007	05-Mar-18	22	105	5.20	€82.95	€431.34
1008	05-Mar-18	25	101	1.70	€82.95	€141.02
1009	05-Mar-18	15	105	2.00	€82.95	€165.90
1010	06-Mar-18	15	102	3.80	€76.43	€290.43
1011	06-Mar-18	22	104	2.60	€76.43	€198.72
1012	06-Mar-18	15	101	2.30	€82.95	€190.79

ASSIGN_NUM	ASSIGN_DATE	PROJ_NUM	EMP_NUM	ASSIGN_HOURS	ASSIGN_CHG_HOUR	ASSIGN_CHARGE
1013	06-Mar-19	25	114	1.80	€38.00	€68.40
1014	06-Mar-19	22	111	4.00	€21.23	€84.92
1015	06-Mar-19	25	114	3.40	€38.00	€129.20
1016	06-Mar-19	18	112	1.20	€36.30	€43.56
1017	06-Mar-19	18	118	2.00	€14.50	€29.00
1018	06-Mar-19	18	104	2.60	€76.43	€198.72
1019	06-Mar-19	15	103	3.00	€67.55	€202.65
1020	07-Mar-19	22	105	2.70	€82.95	€223.97
1021	08-Mar-19	25	108	4.20	€76.43	€321.01
1022	07-Mar-19	25	114	5.80	€38.00	€220.40
1023	07-Mar-19	22	106	2.40	€28.24	€67.78

Table name: EMPLOYEE

EMP_NUM	EMP_LNAME	EMP_FNAME	EMP_INITIAL	EMP_HIREDATE	JOB_CODE
101	News	John	G	08-Nov-10	502
102	Moonsamy	Kavyara	H	12-Jul-99	501
103	Baloyi	Mzwandile	E	01-Dec-07	503
104	Maseki	Noxolo	K	15-Nov-98	501
105	Johnson	Alice	K	01-Feb-04	502
106	Smithfield	William		22-Jun-15	500
107	Alonzo	Maria	D	10-Oct-04	500
108	Khan	Krishshanth	B	22-Aug-99	501
109	Smith	Larry	W	18-Jul-09	501
110	Olenko	Gerald	A	11-Dec-06	505
111	Wabash	Geoff	B	04-Apr-99	506
112	Smithson	Darlene	M	23-Oct-05	507
113	Joenbrood	Delbert	K	15-Nov-04	508
114	Jones	Annelise		20-Aug-01	508
115	Bawangi	Travis	B	25-Jan-00	501
116	Pratt	Gerald	L	05-Mar-05	510
117	Williamson	Angie	H	19-Jun-04	509
118	Frommer	James	J	04-Jan-16	510

be generated by the application. For example, the ASSIGN_NUM can be created by using a counter, and the ASSIGN_DATE can be the system date read by the application and automatically entered into the ASSIGNMENT table. In addition, the application software can automatically insert the correct ASSIGN_CHG_HOUR value by writing the appropriate JOB table's JOB_CHG_HOUR value into the ASSIGNMENT table. (The JOB and ASSIGNMENT tables are related through the JOB_CODE.) If the JOB table's

JOB_CHG_HOUR value changes, the next insertion of that value into the ASSIGNMENT table will reflect the change automatically. The table structure thus minimises the need for human intervention. In fact, if the system requires the employees to enter their own work hours, they can scan their EMP_NUM into the ASSIGNMENT table by using a magnetic card reader that enters their identity. Thus, the ASSIGNMENT table's structure can set the stage for maintaining some desired level of security.

7.5 SURROGATE KEY CONSIDERATIONS

Although this design meets the vital entity and referential integrity requirements, the designer still must address some concerns. For example, a composite primary key may become too cumbersome to use as the number of attributes grows. (It becomes difficult to create a suitable foreign key when the related table uses a composite primary key. In addition, a composite primary key makes it more difficult to write search routines.) Or a primary key attribute may simply have too much descriptive content to be usable – which is why the JOB_CODE attribute was added to the JOB table to serve as that table's primary key. When, for whatever reason, the primary key is considered to be unsuitable, designers use surrogate keys.

At the implementation level, a surrogate key is a system-defined attribute generally created and managed via the DBMS. Usually, a system-defined surrogate key is numeric and its value is automatically incremented for each new row. For example, Microsoft Access uses an AutoNumber data type, MS SQL Server uses an identity column, and Oracle uses a sequence object.

Recall from Section 7.4 that the JOB_CODE attribute was designated to be the JOB table's primary key. However, remember that the JOB_CODE does not prevent duplicate entries from being made, shown in the JOB table in Table 7.3.

TABLE 7.3 Duplicate entries in the job table

JOB_CODE	JOB_DESCRIPTION	JOB_CHG_HOUR
511	Programmer	€26.66
512	Programmer	€26.66

Clearly, the data entries in Table 7.3 are inappropriate because they duplicate existing records – yet there has been no violation of either entity integrity or referential integrity. This 'multiple duplicate records' problem was created when the JOB_CODE attribute was added as the PK. (When the JOB_DESCRIPTION was initially designated to be the PK, the DBMS would ensure unique values for all job description entries when it was asked to enforce entity integrity. However, that option created the problems that caused use of the JOB_CODE attribute in the first place!) In any case, if JOB_CODE is to be the surrogate PK, you must still ensure the existence of unique values in the JOB_DESCRIPTION *through the use of a unique index*.

Note that all of the remaining tables (PROJECT, ASSIGNMENT and EMPLOYEE) are subject to the same limitations. For example, if you use the EMP_NUM attribute in the EMPLOYEE table as the PK, you can make multiple entries for the same employee. To avoid that problem, you might create a unique index for EMP_LNAME, EMP_FNAME, and EMP_INITIAL. But how would you then deal with two employees named Joe B. Smith? In that case, you might use another (preferably externally defined) attribute, such as ID number, to serve as the basis for a unique index.

It is worth repeating that database design often involves trade-offs and the exercise of professional judgement. In a real-world environment, you need to strike a balance between design integrity and flexibility. For example, you might design the ASSIGNMENT table to use a unique index on PROJ_NUM, EMP_NUM and ASSIGN_DATE if you want to limit an employee to only one ASSIGN_HOURS entry per date. That limitation would ensure that employees couldn't enter the same hours multiple times for any given date. Unfortunately, that limitation is likely to be undesirable from a managerial point of view. After all, if an employee works several different times on a project during any given day, it must be possible to make multiple entries for that same employee and the same project during that day. In that case, the best solution might be to add a new externally defined attribute – such as a stub, voucher or ticket number – to ensure uniqueness. In any case, frequent data audits would be appropriate.

7.6 HIGHER-LEVEL NORMAL FORMS

Tables in 3NF will perform suitably in business transactional databases. However, there are occasions when higher normal forms are useful. In this section, you learn about a special case of 3NF, known as Boyce-Codd normal form (BCNF), and about 4NF.

7.6.1 The Boyce-Codd Normal Form (BCNF)

A table is in **Boyce-Codd normal form (BCNF)** when every determinant in the table is a candidate key. (Recall from Chapter 3 that a candidate key has the same characteristics as a primary key, but for some reason, it was not chosen to be the primary key.) Clearly, when a table contains only one candidate key, the 3NF and the BCNF are equivalent. Putting that proposition another way, BCNF can be violated only when the table contains more than one candidate key.

NOTE

A table is in BCNF when every determinant in the table is a candidate key.

Most designers consider the BCNF as a special case of the 3NF. In fact, if the techniques shown here are used, most tables conform to the BCNF requirements once the 3NF is reached. So, how can a table be in 3NF and not be in BCNF? To answer that question, you must keep in mind that a transitive dependency exists when one non-prime attribute is dependent on another non-prime attribute.

In other words, a table is in 3NF when it is in 2NF and there are no transitive dependencies. However, what about a case in which a non-key attribute is the determinant of a key attribute? That condition does not violate 3NF, yet it fails to meet the BCNF requirements because BCNF requires that every determinant in the table be a candidate key.

The situation just described (a 3NF table that fails to meet BCNF requirements) is shown in Figure 7.7.

FIGURE 7.7 A table that is in 3NF but not in BCNF

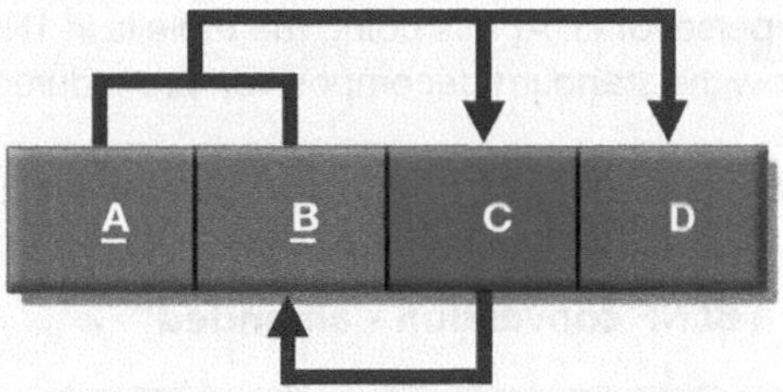

As you examine Figure 7.7, note these functional dependencies:

A + B → C, D

C → B

The table structure shown in Figure 7.7 has no partial dependencies, nor does it contain transitive dependencies. (The condition C → B indicates that *a non-key attribute determines part of the primary key* – and *that* dependency is *not* transitive!) Thus, the table structure in Figure 7.7 meets the 3NF requirements. Yet the condition C → B causes the table to fail to meet the BCNF requirements.

FIGURE 7.8 Decomposition to BCNF

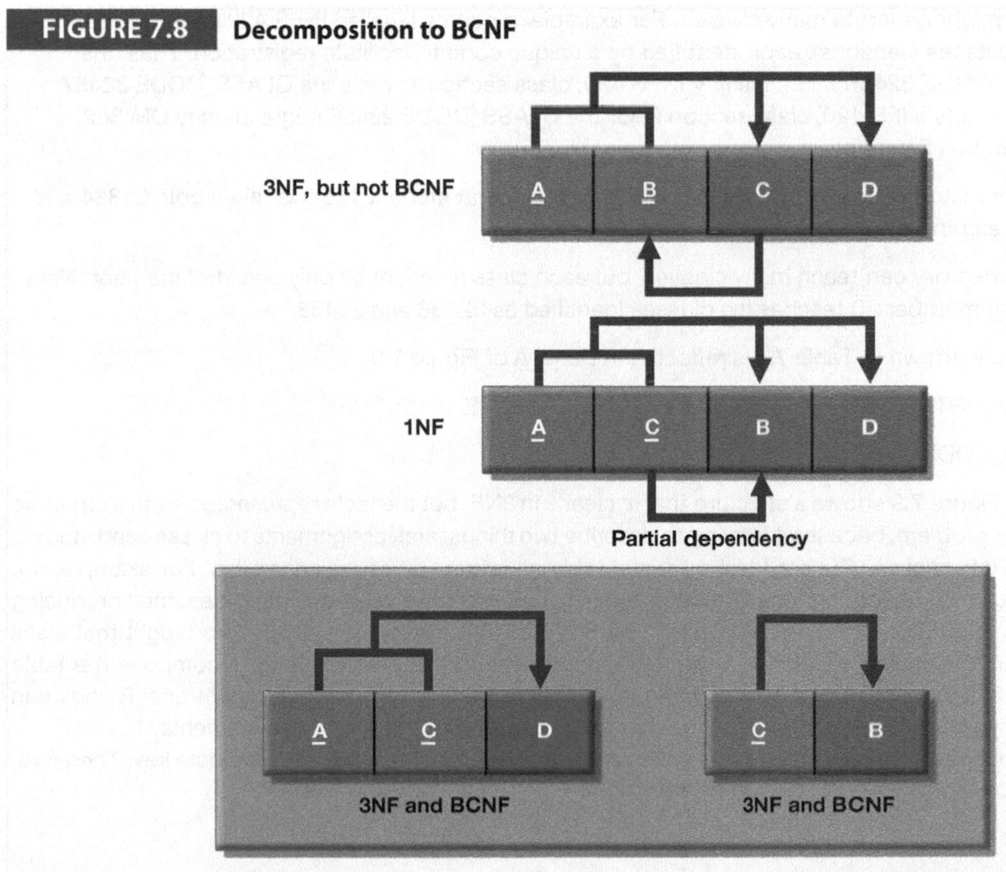

To convert the table structure in Figure 7.7 into table structures that are in 3NF and in BCNF, first change the primary key to A + C. That is an appropriate action because the dependency C → B means that C is, in effect, a superset of B. At this point, the table is in 1NF because it contains a partial dependency C → B. Next, follow the standard decomposition procedures to produce the results shown in Figure 7.8.

To see how this procedure can be applied to an actual problem, examine the sample data in Table 7.4.

TABLE 7.4 Sample data for a BCNF conversion – amended

STU_ID	STAFF_ID	CLASS_CODE	ENROL_GRADE
125	25	21334	A
125	20	32456	C
135	20	28458	B
144	25	27563	C
144	20	32456	B

7

Table 7.4 reflects the following conditions:

- Each CLASS_CODE identifies a class uniquely. This condition illustrates the case in which a course might generate many classes. For example, a course labelled INFS 420 might be taught in two classes (sections), each identified by a unique code to facilitate registration. Thus, the CLASS_CODE 32456 might identify INFS 420, class section 1, while the CLASS_CODE 32457 might identify INFS 420, class section 2. Or the CLASS_CODE 28458 might identify QM 362, class section 5.
- A student can take many classes. Note, for example, that student 125 has taken both 21334 and 32456, earning the grades A and C, respectively.
- A staff member can teach many classes, but each class is taught by only one staff member. Note that staff member 20 teaches the classes identified as 32456 and 28458.

The structure shown in Table 7.4 is reflected in Panel A of Figure 7.9:

STU_ID + STAFF_ID → CLASS_CODE, ENROL_GRADE

CLASS_CODE → STAFF_ID

Panel A of Figure 7.9 shows a structure that is clearly in 3NF, but the table represented by this structure has a major problem, because it is trying to describe two things: staff assignments to classes and student enrolment information. Such a 'dual purpose' table structure will cause anomalies. For example, if a different staff member is assigned to teach class 32456, two rows will require updates, thus producing an update anomaly. And if student 135 drops class 28458, information about who taught that class is lost, thus producing a deletion anomaly. The solution to the problem is to decompose the table structure, following the procedure outlined earlier. Note that the decomposition of Panel B shown in Figure 7.9 yields two table structures that conform to both 3NF and BCNF requirements.

Remember that a table is in BCNF when every determinant in that table is a candidate key. Therefore, when a table contains only one candidate key, 3NF and BCNF are equivalent.

FIGURE 7.9 Another BCNF decomposition

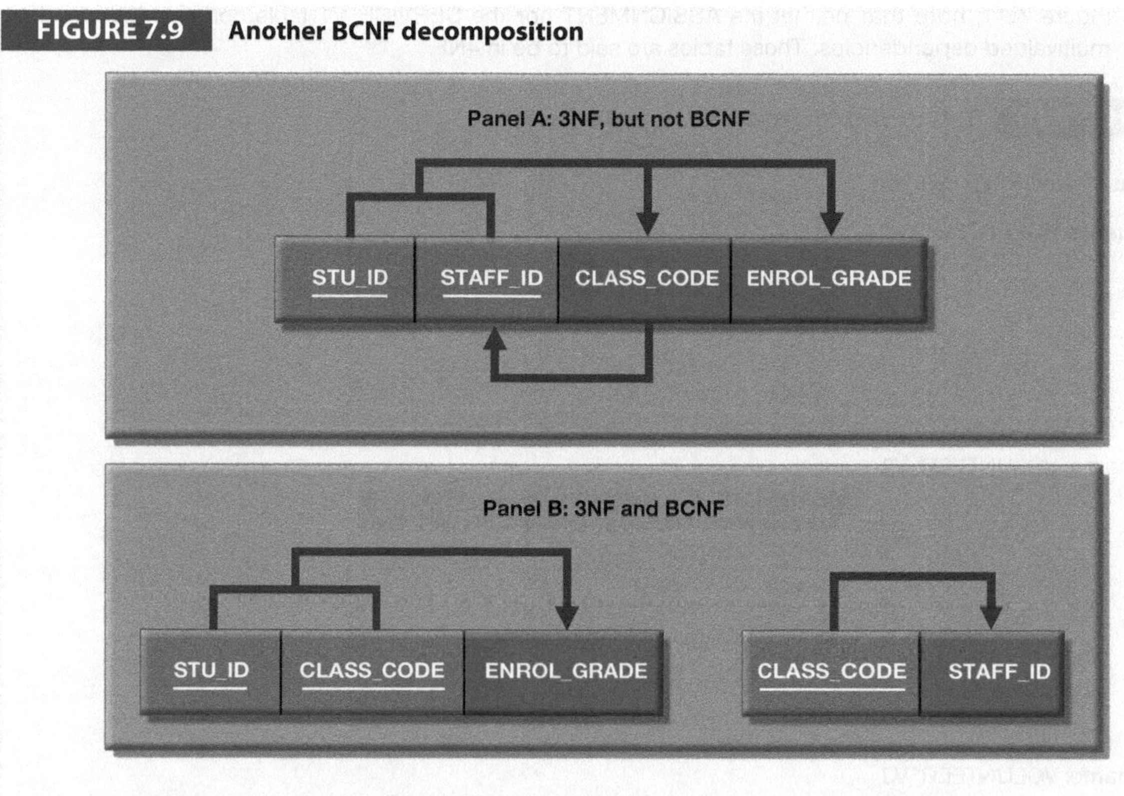

7

7.6.2 Fourth Normal Form (4NF)

You may encounter poorly designed databases in which a number of multivalued attributes exist. For example, consider the possibility that an employee can have multiple assignments and can also be involved in multiple service organisations. Suppose employee 10123 does volunteer work for the Red Cross and United Way. In addition, the same employee might be assigned to work on three projects: 1, 3 and 4. Figure 7.10 illustrates how that set of facts can be recorded in very different ways.

If you examine the tables in Figure 7.10, there seems to be a problem. The attributes ORG_CODE and ASSIGN_NUM may each have many different values. That is, the tables contain two sets of independent multivalued dependencies. (One employee can have many service entries and many assignment entries.) The presence of multiple sets of independent multivalued dependencies means that, if versions 1 and 2 (Table VOLUNTEER_V1 and VOLUNTEER_V2) are implemented, the tables are likely to contain quite a few null values; in fact, the tables do not even have a viable candidate key. (The EMP_NUM values are not unique, so they cannot be PKs. No combination of the attributes in table versions 1 and 2 can be used to create a PK because some of them contain nulls.) Such a condition is not desirable, especially when there are thousands of employees, many of whom may have multiple job assignments and many service activities. Version 3 (VOLUNTEER_V3) at least has a PK, but it is composed of all of the attributes in the table. In fact, version 3 meets 3NF requirements, yet it contains many redundancies that are clearly undesirable.

The solution is to eliminate the problems caused by independent multivalued dependencies. You do this by creating the ASSIGNMENT and SERVICE_V1 tables depicted in Figure 7.11. As you examine

Figure 7.11, note that neither the ASSIGNMENT nor the SERVICE_V1 table contains independent multivalued dependencies. Those tables are said to be in 4NF.

FIGURE 7.10 Tables with multivalued dependencies

Database name: Ch07_Service

Table name: VOLUNTEER_V1

EMP_NUM	ORG_CODE	ASSIGN_NUM
10123	RC	1
10123	UW	3
10123		4

Table name: VOLUNTEER_V2

EMP_NUM	ORG_CODE	ASSIGN_NUM
10123	RC	
10123	UW	
10123		1
10123		3
10223		4

Table name: VOLUNTEER_V3

EMP_NUM	ORG_CODE	ASSIGN_NUM
10123	RC	1
10123	RC	3
10123	UW	4

NOTE

A table is in **fourth normal form (4NF)** when it is in 3NF and has no multiple sets of multivalued dependencies.

If you follow the proper design procedures illustrated in this book, you shouldn't encounter the previously described problem. Specifically, the discussion of 4NF is largely academic if you make sure that your tables conform to the following two rules:

1. All attributes must be dependent on the primary key, but they must be independent of each other.
2. No row may contain two or more multivalued facts about an entity.

FIGURE 7.11 A set of tables in 4NF

Relational Diagram

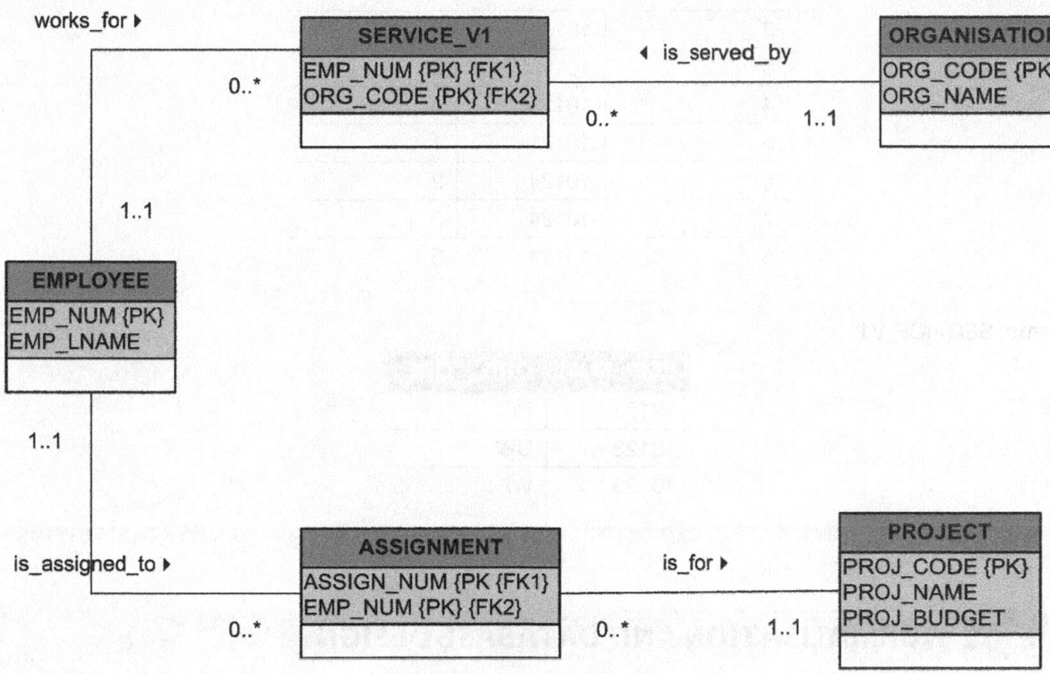

Database name: Ch07_Service

Table name: EMPLOYEE

EMP_NUM	EMP_LNAME
10121	Rogers
10122	O'Leery
10123	Panera
10124	Johnson

Table name: PROJECT

PROJ_CODE	PROJ_NAME	PROJ_BUDGET
1	BeThere	€808 363.55
2	BlueMoon	€15 956 900.32
3	GreenThumb	€2 555 220.24
4	GoFast	€4 482 460.00
5	GoSlow	€791 975.00

Table name: ORGANISATION

ORG_CODE	ORG_NAME
RC	Red Cross
UW	United Way
WF	Wildlife Fund

Table name: ASSIGNMENT

ASSIGN_NUM	EMP_NUM	PROJ_CODE
1	10123	1
2	10121	2
3	10123	3
4	10123	4
5	10121	1
6	10124	2
7	10124	3
8	10124	5

Table name: SERVICE_V1

EMP_NUM	ORG_CODE
10123	RC
10123	UW
10123	WF

7.7 NORMALISATION AND DATABASE DESIGN

The tables shown in Figure 7.6 illustrate how normalisation procedures can be used to produce good tables from poor ones. You will likely have ample opportunity to put this skill into practice when you begin to work with real-world databases. *Normalisation should be part of the design process.* Therefore, make sure that proposed entities meet the required normal form *before* the table structures are created. Keep in mind that, if you follow the design procedures discussed in Chapter 3, Relational Model Characteristics, and Chapter 5, Data Modelling with Entity Relationship Diagrams, the likelihood of data anomalies will be small. (But even the best database designers are known to make occasional mistakes that come to light during normalisation checks.) However, many of the real-world databases you encounter will have been improperly designed or burdened with anomalies if they were improperly modified during the course of time. And that means you may be asked to redesign and modify existing databases that are, in effect, anomaly traps. Therefore, you should be aware of good design principles and procedures as well as normalisation procedures.

First, an ERD is created through an iterative process. You begin by identifying relevant entities, their attributes and their relationships. Then you use the results to identify additional entities and attributes. The ERD provides the big picture, or macro view, of an organisation's data requirements and operations.

Second, normalisation focuses on the characteristics of specific entities; that is, normalisation represents a micro-view of the entities within the ERD. And as you learnt in the previous sections of this chapter, the normalisation process may yield additional entities and attributes to be incorporated into the ERD. Therefore, it is difficult to separate the normalisation process from the ER modelling process; the two techniques are used in an iterative and incremental process.

To illustrate the proper role of normalisation in the design process, let's re-examine the operations of the contracting company whose tables were normalised in the preceding sections. Those operations can be summarised by using the following business rules:

- The company manages many projects.
- Each project requires the services of many employees.
- An employee may be assigned to several different projects.
- Some employees are not assigned to a project and perform duties not specifically related to a project. Some employees are part of a labour pool, to be shared by all project teams. For example, the company's executive secretary would not be assigned to any one particular project.
- Each employee has a single primary job classification. That job classification determines the hourly billing rate.
- Many employees can have the same job classification. For example, the company employs more than one electrical engineer.

Given that simple description of the company's operations, two entities and their attributes are initially defined:

- PROJECT (PROJ_NUM, PROJ_NAME)
- EMPLOYEE (EMP_NUM, EMP_LNAME, EMP_FNAME, EMP_INITIAL, JOB_DESCRIPTION, JOB_CHG_HOUR)

Those two entities constitute the initial ERD shown in Figure 7.12.

FIGURE 7.12 **Initial contracting company ERD**

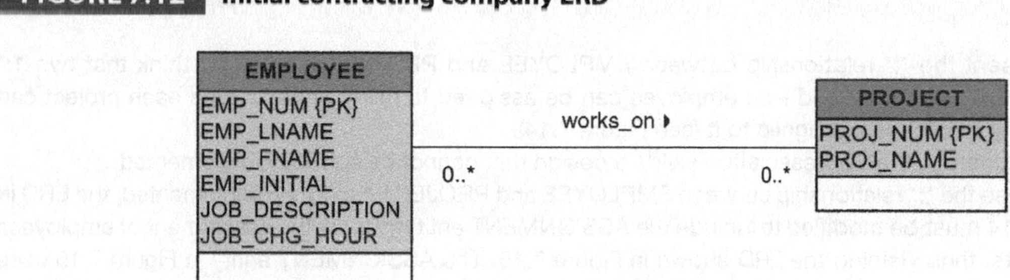

After creating the initial ERD shown in Figure 7.12, the normal forms are defined:

- PROJECT is in 3NF and needs no modification at this point.
- EMPLOYEE requires additional scrutiny. The JOB_DESCRIPTION attribute defines job classifications such as systems analyst, database designer and programmer. In turn, those classifications determine the billing rate, JOB_CHG_HOUR. Therefore, EMPLOYEE contains a transitive dependency.

The removal of EMPLOYEE's transitive dependency yields three entities:

- PROJECT (PROJ_NUM, PROJ_NAME)
- EMPLOYEE (EMP_NUM, EMP_LNAME, EMP_FNAME, EMP_INITIAL, JOB_CODE)
- JOB (JOB_CODE, JOB_DESCRIPTION, JOB_CHG_HOUR)

7

Because the normalisation process yields an additional entity (JOB), the initial ERD is modified as shown in Figure 7.13.

FIGURE 7.13 **Modified contracting company ERD**

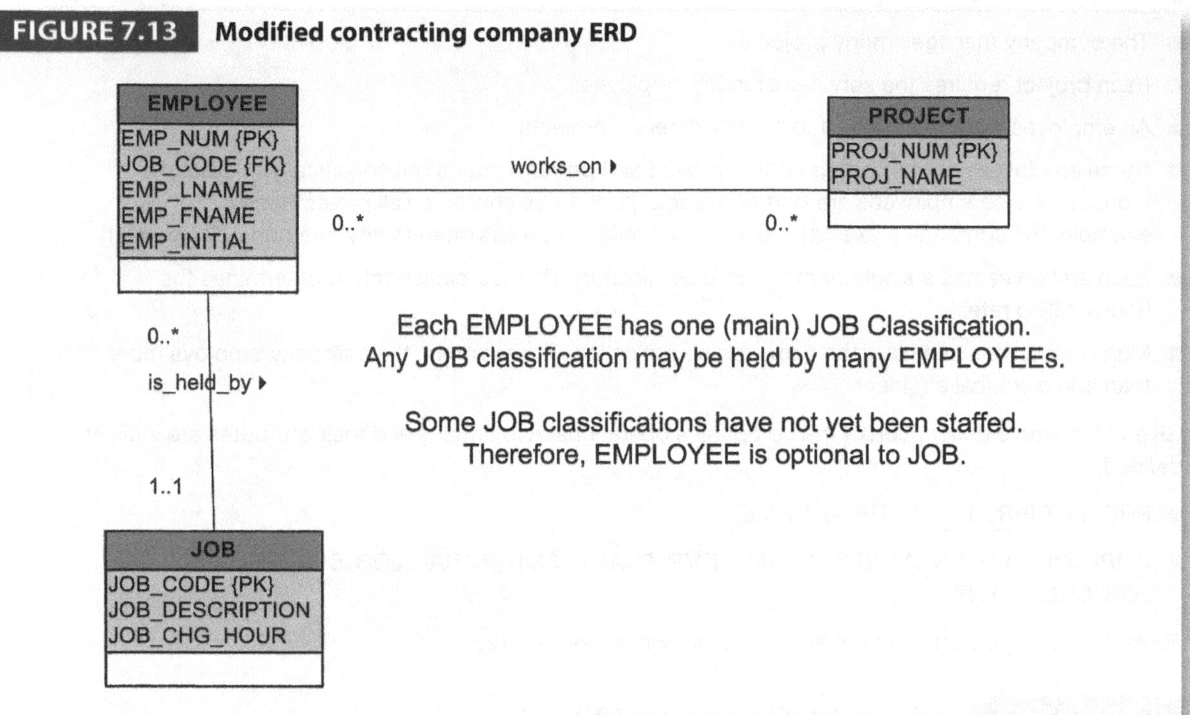

To represent the *:* relationship between EMPLOYEE and PROJECT, you might think that two 1:* relationships could be used – an employee can be assigned to many projects, and each project can have many employees assigned to it (see Figure 7.14).

Unfortunately, that representation yields a design that cannot be correctly implemented.

Because the *:* relationship between EMPLOYEE and PROJECT cannot be implemented, the ERD in Figure 7.14 must be modified to include the ASSIGNMENT entity to track the assignment of employees to projects, thus yielding the ERD shown in Figure 7.15. The ASSIGNMENT entity in Figure 7.15 uses the primary keys from the entities PROJECT and EMPLOYEE to serve as its foreign keys. However, note that in this implementation, the ASSIGNMENT entity's surrogate primary key is ASSIGN_NUM, to avoid the use of a composite primary key. Therefore, the *enters* relationship between EMPLOYEE and ASSIGNMENT and the *requires* relationship between PROJECT and ASSIGNMENT are in fact weak or non-identifying relationships.

NOTE

In Chapter 5, Data Modelling with Entity Relationship Diagrams, it was discussed that UML notation does not make a distinction between weak and strong relationships.

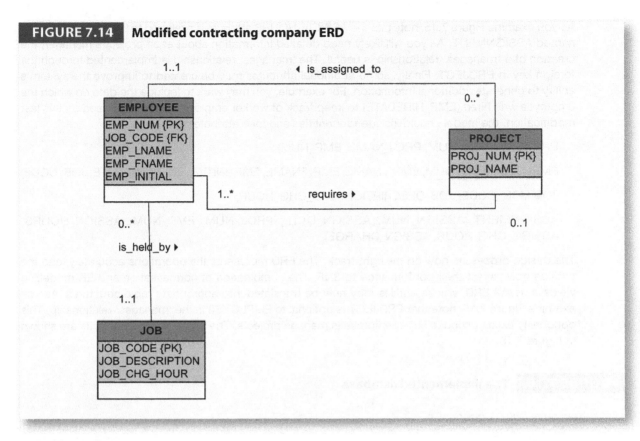

FIGURE 7.14 Modified contracting company ERD

EMPLOYEE
EMP_NUM {PK}
JOB_CODE {FK}
EMP_LNAME
EMP_FNAME
EMP_INITIAL

PROJECT
PROJ_NUM {PK}
PROJ_NAME

JOB
JOB_CODE {PK}
JOB_DESCRIPTION
JOB_CHG_HOUR

1..1 ◂ is_assigned_to 0..*
1..* requires ▸ 0..1
0..* is_held_by ▸ 1..1

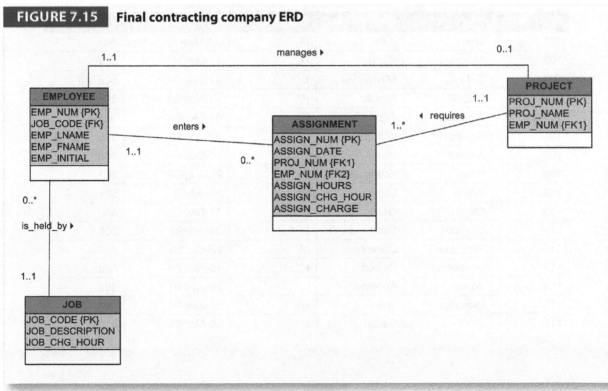

FIGURE 7.15 Final contracting company ERD

EMPLOYEE
EMP_NUM {PK}
JOB_CODE {FK}
EMP_LNAME
EMP_FNAME
EMP_INITIAL

ASSIGNMENT
ASSIGN_NUM {PK}
ASSIGN_DATE
PROJ_NUM {FK1}
EMP_NUM {FK2}
ASSIGN_HOURS
ASSIGN_CHG_HOUR
ASSIGN_CHARGE

PROJECT
PROJ_NUM {PK}
PROJ_NAME
EMP_NUM {FK1}

JOB
JOB_CODE {PK}
JOB_DESCRIPTION
JOB_CHG_HOUR

1..1 manages ▸ 0..1
enters ▸ 1..1 0..*
1..1 ◂ requires 1..*
0..* is_held_by ▸ 1..1

7

As you examine Figure 7.15, note that the ASSIGN_HOURS attribute is assigned to the composite entity named ASSIGNMENT. As you will likely need detailed information about each project's manager, the creation of a 'manages' relationship is useful. The 'manages' relationship is implemented through the foreign key in PROJECT. Finally, some additional attributes may be created to improve the system's ability to generate additional information. For example, you may want to include the date on which the employee was hired (EMP_HIREDATE) to keep track of worker employment length. Based on this last modification, the model should include four entities and their attributes:

PROJECT (PROJ_NUM, PROJ_NAME, EMP_NUM)

EMPLOYEE (EMP_NUM, EMP_LNAME, EMP_FNAME, EMP_INITIAL, EMP_HIREDATE, JOB_CODE)

JOB (JOB_CODE, JOB_DESCRIPTION, JOB_CHG_HOUR)

ASSIGNMENT (ASSIGN_NUM, ASSIGN_DATE, PROJ_NUM, EMP_NUM, ASSIGN_HOURS, ASSIGN_CHG_HOUR, ASSIGN_CHARGE)

The design process is now on the right track. The ERD represents the operations accurately, and the entities now reflect their conformance to 3NF. The combination of normalisation and ER modelling yields a useful ERD, whose entities may now be translated into appropriate table structures. As you examine Figure 7.15, note that PROJECT is optional to EMPLOYEE in the 'manages' relationship. This optionality exists because not all employees manage projects. The final database contents are shown in Figure 7.16.

FIGURE 7.16 The implemented database

Database name: Ch07_ConstructCo

Table name: EMPLOYEE

EMP_NUM	EMP_LNAME	EMP_FNAME	EMP_INITIAL	EMP_HIREDATE	JOB_CODE
101	News	John	G	08-Nov-10	502
102	Moonsamy	Kavyara	H	12-Jul-99	501
103	Baloyi	Mzwandile	E	01-Dec-07	503
104	Maseki	Noxolo	K	15-Nov-98	501
105	Johnson	Alice	K	01-Feb-04	502
106	Smithfield	William		22-Jun-15	500
107	Alonzo	Maria	D	10-Oct-04	500
108	Khan	Krishshanth	B	22-Aug-99	501
109	Smith	Larry	W	18-Jul-09	501
110	Olenko	Gerald	A	11-Dec-06	505
111	Wabash	Geoff	B	04-Apr-99	506
112	Smithson	Darlene	M	23-Oct-05	507
113	Joenbrood	Delbert	K	15-Nov-04	508
114	Jones	Annelise		20-Aug-01	508
115	Bawangi	Travis	B	25-Jan-00	501
116	Pratt	Gerald	L	05-Mar-05	510

EMP_NUM	EMP_LNAME	EMP_FNAME	EMP_INITIAL	EMP_HIREDATE	JOB_CODE
117	Williamson	Angie	H	19-Jun-2004	509
118	Frommer	James	J	04-Jan-2016	510

Table name: JOB

JOB_CODE	JOB_DESCRIPTION	JOB_CHG_HOUR
500	Programmer	€28.24
501	Systems Analyst	€76.43
502	Database Designer	€82.95
503	Electrical Engineer	€66.76
504	Mechanical Engineer	€53.64
505	Civil Engineer	€44.07
506	Clerical Support	€21.23
507	DSS Analyst	€36.30
508	Applications Designer	€38.00
509	Bio Technician	€27.29
510	General Support	€14.50

Table name: PROJECT

PROJ_NUM	PROJ_NAME	EMP_NUM
15	Evergreen	105
18	Amber Wave	104
22	Rolling Tide	113
25	Starflight	101

Table name: ASSIGNMENT

ASSIGN_ NUM	ASSIGN_ DATE	PROJ_ NUM	EMP_ NUM	ASSIGN_ HOURS	ASSIGN_CHG HOUR	ASSIGN CHARGE
1001	04-Mar-19	15	103	2.60	€67.55	€175.63
1002	04-Mar-19	18	118	1.40	€14.50	€20.30
1003	05-Mar-19	15	101	3.60	€82.95	€298.62
1004	05-Mar-19	22	113	2.50	€38.00	€95.00
1005	05-Mar-19	15	103	1.90	€67.55	€128.35
1006	05-Mar-19	25	115	4.20	€76.43	€321.01
1007	05-Mar-19	22	105	5.20	€82.95	€431.34
1008	05-Mar-19	25	101	1.70	€82.95	€141.02
1009	05-Mar-19	15	105	2.00	€82.95	€165.90
1010	06-Mar-19	15	102	3.80	€76.43	€290.43

ASSIGN_ NUM	ASSIGN_ DATE	PROJ_ NUM	EMP_ NUM	ASSIGN_ HOURS	ASSIGN_CHG_ HOUR	ASSIGN_ CHARGE
1011	06-Mar-19	22	104	2.60	€76.43	€198.72
1012	06-Mar-19	15	101	2.30	€82.95	€190.79
1013	06-Mar-19	25	114	1.80	€38.00	€68.40
1014	06-Mar-19	22	111	4.00	€21.23	€84.92
1015	06-Mar-19	25	114	3.40	€38.00	€129.20
1016	06-Mar-19	18	112	1.20	€36.30	€43.56
1017	06-Mar-19	18	118	2.00	€14.50	€29.00
1018	06-Mar-19	18	104	2.60	€76.43	€198.72
1019	06-Mar-19	15	103	3.00	€67.55	€202.65
1020	07-Mar-19	22	105	2.70	€82.95	€223.97
1021	08-Mar-19	25	108	4.20	€76.43	€321.01
1022	07-Mar-19	25	114	5.80	€38.00	€220.40
1023	07-Mar-19	22	106	2.40	€28.24	€67.78

7

7.8 DENORMALISATION

Although the creation of normalised relations is an important database design goal, it is only one of many such goals. Good database design also considers processing requirements. As tables are decomposed to conform to normalisation requirements, the number of database tables expands. Joining the larger number of tables takes additional input/output (I/O) operations and processing logic, thereby reducing system speed. Consequently, occasional circumstances may allow some degree of denormalisation so processing speed can be increased.

Keep in mind that the advantage of higher processing speed must be carefully weighed against the disadvantage of data anomalies. On the other hand, some anomalies are of only theoretical interest. For example, should people in a real-world database environment worry that a POST_CODE determines CITY in a CUSTOMER table whose primary key is the customer number? Is it really practical to produce a separate table for:

POST_CODE (POST_CODE, CITY)

to eliminate a transitive dependency from the CUSTOMER table? (Perhaps your answer to that question changes if you are in the business of producing mailing lists.) The advice is simple: use common sense during the normalisation process.

Normalisation purity is often difficult to sustain in the modern database environment. The conflicts between design efficiency, information requirements and processing speed are often resolved through compromises that may include denormalisation. You will also learn (in Chapter 15, Databases for Business Intelligence) that lower normalisation forms occur (and are even required) in specialised databases known as data warehouses. Such specialised databases reflect the ever-growing demand for greater scope and depth in the data on which decision-support systems increasingly rely. You will discover that the data warehouse routinely uses 2NF structures in its complex, multilevel, multisource data environment. In short, although normalisation is very important, especially in the so-called production database environment, 2NF is no longer disregarded as it once was.

Although 2NF tables cannot always be avoided, the problem of working with tables that contain partial and/or transitive dependencies in a production database environment should not be minimised. Aside from the possibility of troublesome data anomalies being created, unnormalised tables in a production database tend to suffer from these defects:

- Data updates are less efficient because programs that read and update tables must deal with larger tables.
- Indexing is more cumbersome. It simply is not practical to build all of the indexes required for the many attributes that may be located in a single unnormalised table.
- Unnormalised tables yield no simple strategies for creating virtual tables known as *views*. (You will learn how to create and use views in Chapter 8, Beginning Structured Query Language.)

Remember that good design cannot be created in the application programs that use a database. Also keep in mind that unnormalised database tables often lead to various data redundancy disasters in production databases such as the ones examined thus far. In other words, use denormalisation cautiously and make sure that you can explain why – under some circumstances – the unnormalised tables are a better choice than their normalised counterparts.

SUMMARY

- Normalisation is a technique used to design tables in which data redundancies are minimised. The first three normal forms (1NF, 2NF and 3NF) are most commonly encountered. From a structural point of view, higher normal forms are better than lower normal forms because higher normal forms yield relatively fewer data redundancies in the database. Almost all business designs use 3NF as the ideal normal form. (A special, more restricted 3NF is known as Boyce-Codd normal form, or BCNF.)
- A table is in 1NF when all key attributes are defined and when all remaining attributes are dependent on the primary key. However, a table in 1NF can still contain both partial and transitive dependencies. (A partial dependency is one in which an attribute is functionally dependent on only a part of a multi-attribute primary key. A transitive dependency is one in which one non-key attribute is functionally dependent on another non-key attribute.) A table with a single-attribute primary key cannot exhibit partial dependencies.
- A table is in 2NF when it is in 1NF and contains no partial dependencies. Therefore, a 1NF table is automatically in 2NF when its primary key is based on only a single attribute, i.e. it is not a composite primary key. A table in 2NF may still contain transitive dependencies.
- A table is in 3NF when it is in 2NF and contains no transitive dependencies. Given that definition of 3NF, the Boyce-Codd normal form (BCNF) is merely a special 3NF case in which all determinant keys are candidate keys. When a table has only a single attribute candidate key, a 3NF table is automatically in BCNF.
- A table that is not in 3NF may be split into new tables until all of the tables meet the 3NF requirements. The process is illustrated in Figures 7.17 to 7.19.
- Normalisation is an important part – but only a part – of the design process. As entities and attributes are defined during the ER modelling process, subject each entity (set) to normalisation

checks and form new entity (sets) as required. Incorporate the normalised entities into the ERD and continue the iterative ER process until all entities and their attributes are defined and all equivalent tables are in 3NF.

- A table in 3NF may contain multivalued dependencies that produce either numerous null values or redundant data. Therefore, it may be necessary to convert a 3NF table to the fourth normal form (4NF) by splitting the table to remove the multivalued dependencies. Thus, a table is in 4NF when it is in 3NF and contains no multivalued dependencies.
- The larger the number of tables, the more additional I/O operations are required to join them and the greater the amount of processing logic. Therefore, tables are sometimes denormalised to yield less I/O in order to increase processing speed. Unfortunately, with larger tables, you pay for the increased processing speed by making the data updates less efficient, by making indexing more cumbersome, and by introducing data redundancies that are likely to yield data anomalies. In the design of production databases, use denormalisation sparingly and cautiously.

FIGURE 7.17 The initial 1NF structure

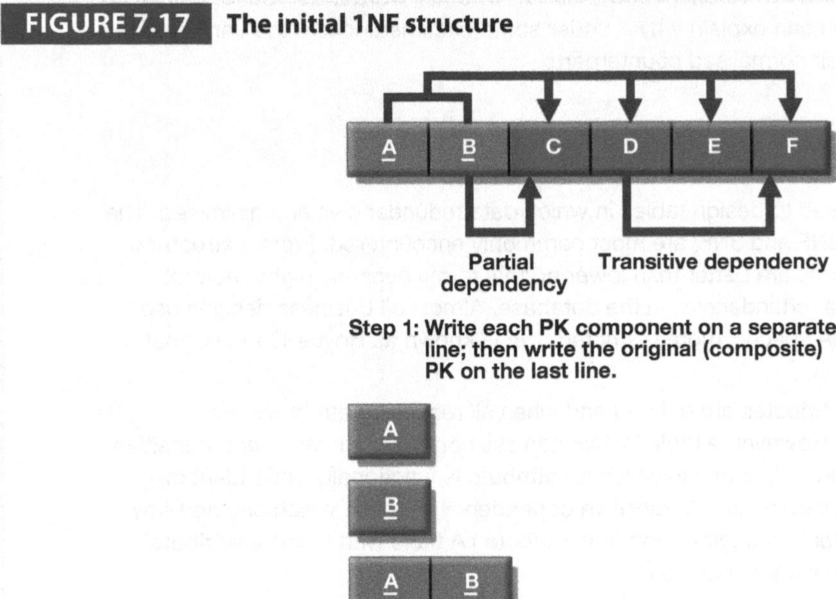

FIGURE 7.18 Identifying possible PK attributes

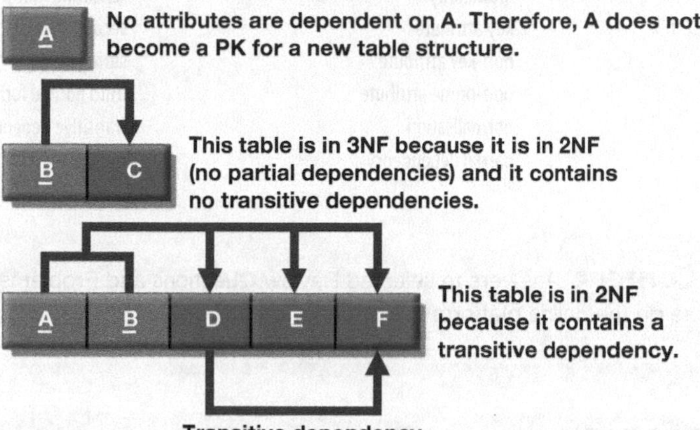
Step 2: Place all dependent attributes with the PK attributes identified in Step 1.
A
No attributes are dependent on A. Therefore, A does not become a PK for a new table structure.
B C
This table is in 3NF because it is in 2NF (no partial dependencies) and it contains no transitive dependencies.
A B D E F
This table is in 2NF because it contains a transitive dependency.
Transitive dependency

FIGURE 7.19 Table structures based on the selected PKs

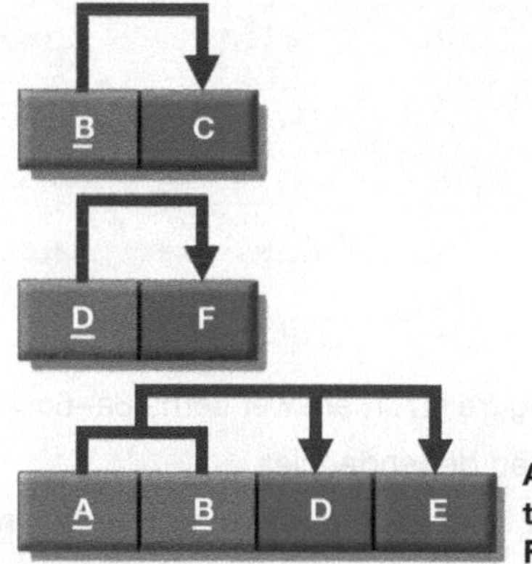
Step 3: Remove all transitive dependencies identified in Step 2 and retain all 3NF structures.
All tables are in 3NF because they are in 2NF (no partial dependencies) and they do not contain transitive dependencies.
B C
D F
A B D E
Attribute D is retained in this table structure to serve as the FK to the second table.

KEY TERMS

atomic attribute
atomicity
Boyce-Codd normal form (BCNF)
denormalisation
dependency diagram
determinant
first normal form (1NF)
fourth normal form (4NF)
granularity
key attribute
non-key attribute
non-prime attribute
normalisation
partial dependency
prime attribute
repeating group
second normal form (2NF)
surrogate key
third normal form (3NF)
transitive dependency

Online Content Answers to selected Review Questions and Problems for this chapter are available on the online platform accompanying this book.

FURTHER READING

Ambler, S. *Agile Database Techniques*. John Wiley & Sons Inc, 2003.

Codd, E.F. *Further Normalizations of the Database Relational Model. Data Base Systems*. Prentice Hall, 1972.

Fagin, R. 'Multi-valued dependencies and a new normal form for relational databases'. *ACM Transactions* 2(3), 1977.

Fagin, R. 'Normal forms and relational database operators'. In *Proceedings of ACM Sigmoid International Conference on Management of Data*, pp. 153–160, 1979.

Maier, D. *The Theory of Relational Databases*. NY Computer Science Press, 1983.

REVIEW QUESTIONS

1. What is normalisation?
2. When is a table in 1NF?
3. When is a table in 2NF?
4. When is a table in 3NF?
5. When is a table in BCNF?
6. Given the dependency diagram shown in Figure Q7.1, answer Items 6a–6c.
   a. Identify and discuss each of the indicated dependencies.
   b. Create a database whose tables are at least in 2NF, showing the dependency diagrams for each table.
   c. Create a database whose tables are at least in 3NF, showing the dependency diagrams for each table.
7. What is a partial dependency? With which normal form is it associated?
8. Which three data anomalies are likely to be the result of data redundancy? How can such anomalies be eliminated?

FIGURE Q7.1 **Dependency diagram for Question 6**

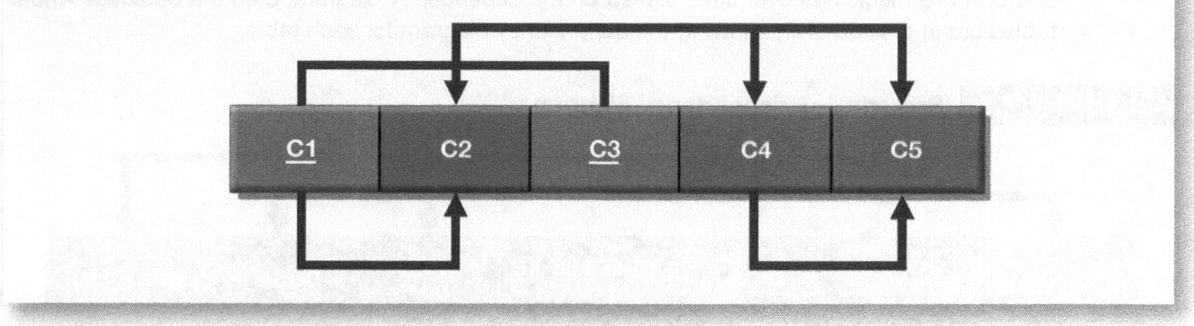

C1 | C2 | C3 | C4 | C5

9 Define and discuss the concept of transitive dependency.

10 What is a surrogate key, and when should you use one?

11 Why is a table whose primary key consists of a single attribute automatically in 2NF when it is in 1NF?

12 How would you describe a condition in which one attribute is dependent on another attribute when neither attribute is part of the primary key?

13 Suppose that someone tells you that an attribute that is part of a composite primary key is also a candidate key. How would you respond to that statement?

14 A table is in _______ normal form when it is in __________ and there are no transitive dependencies.

15 The dependency diagram in Figure Q7.2 indicates that authors are paid royalties for each book they write for a publisher. The amount of the royalty can vary by author, by book, and by edition of the book.

FIGURE Q7.2 **Book royalty dependency diagram**

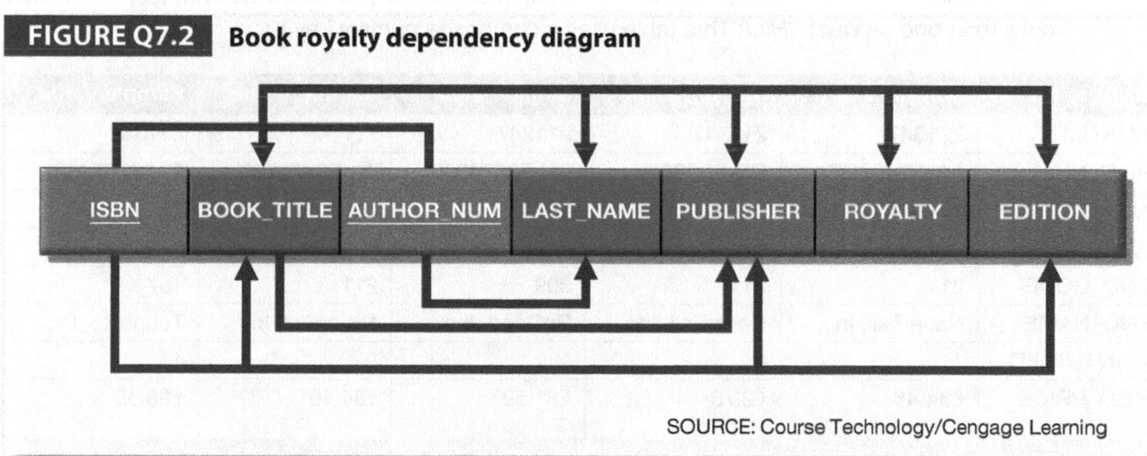

SOURCE: Course Technology/Cengage Learning

a Based on the dependency diagram, create a database whose tables are at least in 2NF, showing the dependency diagram for each table.

b Create a database whose tables are at least in 3NF, showing the dependency diagram for each table.

16 The dependency diagram in Figure Q7.3 indicates that a patient can receive many prescriptions for one or more medicines over time. Based on the dependency diagram, create a database whose tables are in at least 2NF, showing the dependency diagram for each table.

FIGURE Q7.3 Prescription dependency diagram

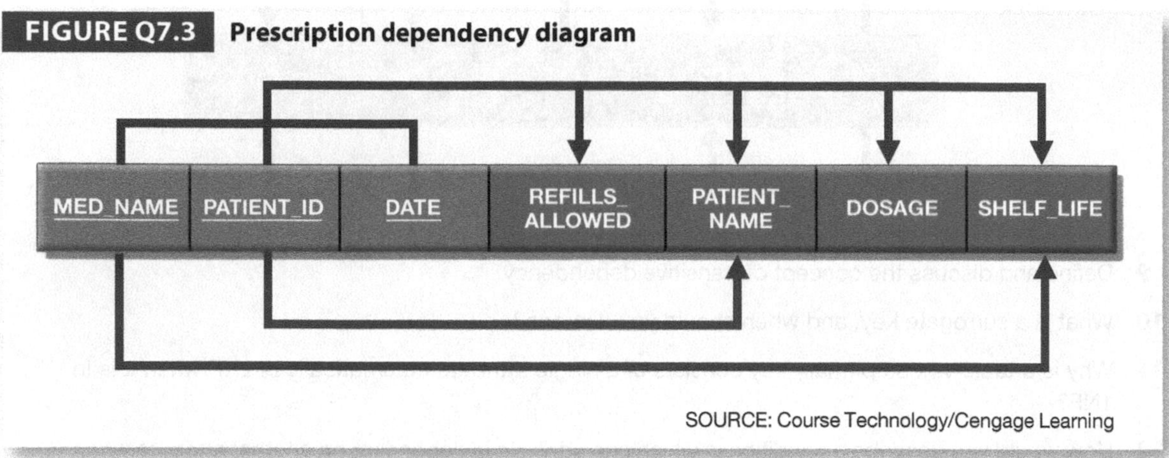

SOURCE: Course Technology/Cengage Learning

Suppose someone tells you that an attribute that is part of a composite primary key is also a candidate key. How would you respond to that statement?

PROBLEMS

1 Using the INVOICE table structure shown below, write the relational schema, draw its dependency diagram, and identify all dependencies (including all partial and transitive dependencies). You can assume that the table does not contain repeating groups and that an invoice number references more than one product. (*Hint*: This table uses a composite primary key.)

Attribute Name	Sample Value	Sample Value	Sample Value	Sample Value	Sample Value
INV_NUM	211347	211347	211347	211348	211349
PROD_NUM	AA-E3422QW	QD-300932X	RU-995748G	AA-E3422QW	GH-778345P
SALE_DATE	15-Jan-2019	15-Jan-2019	15-Jan-2019	15-Jan-2019	16-Jan-2019
PROD_LABEL	Rotary sander	0.25-in. drill bit	Band saw	Rotary sander	Power drill
VEND_CODE	211	211	309	211	157
VEND_NAME	NeverFail, Inc.	NeverFail, Inc.	BeGood, Inc.	NeverFail, Inc.	ToughGo, Inc.
QUANT_SOLD	1	8	1	2	1
PROD_PRICE	€34.46	€2.73	€31.59	€34.46	€69.32

2 Using the answer to Problem 1, remove all partial dependencies, write the relational scheme and draw the new dependency diagrams. Identify the normal forms for each table structure you created.

> **NOTE**
>
> You can assume that any given product is supplied by a single vendor, but a vendor can supply many products. Therefore, it is proper to conclude that the following dependency exists:
>
> PROD_NUM → PROD_DESCRIPTION, PROD_PRICE, VEND_CODE, VEND_NAME
>
> (*Hint*: Your actions should produce three dependency diagrams.)

3 Using the answer to Problem 2, remove all transitive dependencies, write the relational schema and draw the new dependency diagrams. Identify the normal forms for each table structure you created.

4 Using the results of Problem 3, draw the ERD using UML class notation.

5 Using the STUDENT table structure shown here, write the relational schema and draw its dependency diagram. Identify all dependencies (including all transitive dependencies).

Attribute Name	Sample Value	Sample Value	Sample Value	Sample Value	Sample Value
STU_NUM	211343	200128	199876	199876	223456
STU_LNAME	Stephanos	Smith	Jones	Ortiz	McKulski
STU_MAJOR	Accounting	Accounting	Marketing	Marketing	Statistics
DEPT_CODE	ACCT	ACCT	MKTG	MKTG	MATH
DEPT_NAME	Accounting	Accounting	Marketing	Marketing	Mathematics
DEPT_PHONE	4350	4350	4378	4378	3420
COLLEGE_NAME	Business Admin	Business Admin	Business Admin	Business Admin	Arts & Sciences
ADVISOR_ LNAME	Grastrand	Grastrand	Gentry	Tillery	Chen
ADVISOR_ OFFICE	T201	T201	T228	T356	J331
ADVISOR_BLDG	Torre Building	Torre Building	Torre Building	Torre Building	Jones Building
ADVISOR_ PHONE	2115	2115	2123	2159	3209
STU_GPA	3.87	2.78	2.31	3.45	3.58
STU_HOURS	75	45	117	113	87
STU_CLASS	UG1	UG2	UG3	UG3	UG1

6 Using the answer to Problem 5, write the relational schema and draw the dependency diagram to meet the 3NF requirements to the greatest practical extent possible. If you believe that practical considerations dictate using a 2NF structure, explain why your decision to retain 2NF is appropriate. If necessary, add or modify attributes to create appropriate determinants and to adhere to the naming conventions.

> **NOTE**
>
> Although the completed student hours (STU_HOURS) do determine the student classification (STU_CLASS), this dependency is not as obvious as you might initially assume it to be. For example, a student is considered a junior if that student has completed between 61 and 90 credit hours. Therefore, a student who is classified as a junior may have completed 66, 72 or 87 hours, or any other number of hours within the specified range of 61–90 hours. In short, any hour value within a specified range will define the classification.

7 Using the results of Problem 6, draw the ERD using UML notation.

> **NOTE**
>
> This ERD constitutes a small segment of a university's full-blown design. For example, this segment might be combined with the Tiny University presentation in Chapter 5, Data Modelling with Entity Relationship Diagrams.

7

8 To keep track of office furniture, computers, printers and so on, the FOUNDIT company uses the following table structure:

Attribute Name	Sample Value	Sample Value	Sample Value
ITEM_ID	231134-678	342245-225	254668-449
ITEM_LABEL	HP DeskJet 3755	HP Toner	DT Scanner
ROOM_NUMBER	325	325	123
BLDG_CODE	NTC	NTC	CSF
BLDG_NAME	Nottooclear	Nottoclear	Canseefar
BLDG_MANAGER	I. B. Rightonit	I. B. Rightonit	May B. Next

Given that information, write the relational schema and draw the dependency diagram. Make sure that you label the transitive and/or partial dependencies.

9 Using the answer to Problem 8, write the relational schema and create a set of dependency diagrams that meet 3NF requirements. Rename attributes to meet the naming conventions and create new entities and attributes as necessary.

10 Using the results of Problem 9, draw the ERD using UML notation.

> **NOTE**
>
> Problems 11–13 may be combined to serve as a case or a mini-project.

11 The table structure shown below contains many unsatisfactory components and characteristics. (For example, there are several multivalued attributes, naming conventions are violated and some attributes are not atomic.)

Attribute Name	Sample Value	Sample Value	Sample Value	Sample Value
EMP_NUM	1003	1018	1019	1023
EMP_LNAME	Willaker	Smith	McGuire	McGuire
EMP_EDUCATION	BBA, MBA	BBA		BS, MS, Ph.D.
JOB_CLASS	SLS	SLS	JNT	DBA
EMP_DEPENDANTS	Gerald (spouse), Mary (daughter), John (son)		JoAnne (spouse)	George (spouse) Jill (daughter)
DEPT_CODE	MKTG	MKTG	SVC	INFS
DEPT_NAME	Marketing	Marketing	General Service	Info. Systems
DEPT_MANAGER	Jill H. Martin	Jill H. Martin	Hank B. Jones	David G. Dlamini
EMP_TITLE	Sales Agent	Sales Agent	Janitor	DB Admin
EMP_DOB	23-Dec-1978	28-Mar-1989	18-May-1992	20-Jul-1969
EMP_HIRE_DATE	14-Oct-2007	15-Jan-2016	21-Apr-2013	15-Jul-2009
EMP_TRAINING	L1, L2	L1	L1	L1, L3, L8, L15
EMP_BASE_SALARY	€30 221.45	€24 095.00	€15 602.50	€101 041.00
EMP_COMMISSION_RATE	0.015	0.010		

Given that structure, write the relational schema and draw its dependency diagram. Label all transitive and/or partial dependencies.

12 Using the answer to Problem 11, draw the dependency diagrams that are in 3NF. (*Hint*: You might have to create a few new attributes. Also make sure that the new dependency diagrams contain attributes that meet proper design criteria; that is, make sure that there are no multivalued attributes, that the naming conventions are met, and so on.)

13 Using the results of Problem 12, draw the UML ERD.

> **NOTE**
>
> Problems 14–16 may be combined to serve as a case or a mini-project.

14 Suppose you are given the following business rules to form the basis for a database design. The database must enable the manager of a company dinner club to mail invitations to the club's members, to plan the meals, to keep track of who attends the dinners and so on:

- Each dinner serves many members, and each member may attend many dinners.
- A member receives many invitations, and each invitation is mailed to many members.

- A dinner is based on a single entrée, but an entrée may be used as the basis for many dinners. For example, a dinner may be composed of a fish entrée, rice and corn. Or the dinner may be composed of a fish entrée, a baked potato and string beans.
- A member may attend many dinners, and each dinner may be attended by many members.

Because the manager is not a database expert, the first attempt at creating the database uses the structure shown in the following table.

Attribute Name	Sample Value	Sample Value	Sample Value
MEMBER_NUM	214	235	214
MEMBER_NAME	Alice B. VanderVoort	Gerald M. Gallega	Alice B. VanderVoort
MEMBER_ADDRESS	325 Meadow Park	123 Rose Court	325 Meadow Park
MEMBER_CITY	Murkywater	Highlight	Murkywater
MEMBER_POSTCODE	12345	12349	12345
INVITE_NUM	8	9	10
INVITE_DATE	23-Feb-2020	12-Mar-2020	23-Feb-2020
ACCEPT_DATE	27-Feb-2020	15-Mar-2020	27-Feb-2020
DINNER_DATE	15-Mar-2020	17-Mar-2020	15-Mar-2020
DINNER_ATTENDED	Yes	Yes	No
DINNER_CODE	DI5	DI5	DI2
DINNER_DESCRIPTION	Glowing Sea Delight	Glowing Sea Delight	Ranch Superb
ENTREE_CODE	EN3	EN3	EN5
ENTREE_DESCRIPTION	Stuffed crab	Stuffed crab	Marinated steak
DESSERT_CODE	DE8	DE5	DE2
DESSERT_DESCRIPTION	Chocolate mousse with raspberry sauce	Cherries Jubilee	Apple pie with honey crust

Given that structure, write the relational schema and draw its dependency diagram. Label all transitive and/or partial dependencies. (Hint: This structure uses a composite primary key.)

15 Break up the dependency diagram you drew in Problem 14 to produce dependency diagrams that are in 3NF and write the relational schema. (*Hint*: You might have to create a few new attributes. Also make sure that the new dependency diagrams contain attributes that meet proper design criteria; that is, make sure that there are no multivalued attributes, that the naming conventions are met and so on.)

16 Using the results of Problem 15, draw the ERD.

NOTE

Problems 17–19 may be combined to serve as a case or a mini-project.

17 The manager of a consulting firm has asked you to evaluate a database that contains the table structure shown in the following table.

Attribute Name	Sample Value	Sample Value	Sample Value
CLIENT_NUM	298	289	289
CLIENT_NAME	Marianne R. Brown	James D. Smith	James D. Smith
CLIENT_REGION	Gauteng	Western Cape	Western Cape
CONTRACT_DATE	10-Feb-2018	15-Feb-2018	12-Mar-2018
CONTRACT_NUMBER	5841	5842	5843
CONTRACT_AMOUNT	a2 358 150.00	a529 537.00	a987 500.00
CONSULT_CLASS_1	Database Administration	Internet Services	Database Design
CONSULT_CLASS_2	Web Applications		Database Administration
CONSULT_CLASS_3			Network Installation
CONSULT_CLASS_4			
CONSULTANT_NUM_1	29	34	25
CONSULTANT_NAME_1	Rachel G. Carson	Gerald K. Ricardo	Angela M. Jamison
CONSULTANT_REGION_1	Gauteng	Western Cape	Western Cape
CONSULTANT_NUM_2	56	38	34
CONSULTANT_NAME_2	Karl M. Spenser	Anne T. Dimarco	Gerald K. Ricardo
CONSULTANT_REGION_2	Gauteng	Western Cape	Western Cape
CONSULTANT_NUM_3	22	45	
CONSULTANT_NAME_3	Julian H. Donatello	Geraldo J. Rivera	
CONSULTANT_REGION_3	Gauteng	Western Cape	
CONSULTANT_NUM_4		18	
CONSULTANT_NAME_4		Donald Chen	
CONSULTANT_REGION_4		Eastern Cape	

This table was created to enable the manager to match clients with consultants. The objective is to match a client within a given region with a consultant in that region and to make sure that the client's need for specific consulting services is properly matched to the consultant's expertise. For example, if the client needs help with database design and he or she is located in the Western Cape, the objective is to make a match with a consultant who is located in the Western Cape and whose expertise is in database design. (Although the consulting company manager tries to match consultant and client locations to minimise travel expense, it is not always possible to do so.) The following basic business rules are maintained:

- Each client is located in one region.
- A region can contain many clients.
- Each consultant can work on many contracts.
- Each contract may require the services of many consultants.
- A client can sign more than one contract, but each contract is signed by one client.
- Each contract may cover multiple consulting classifications. (For example, a contract may list consulting services in database design and networking.)

- Each consultant is located in one region.
- A region can contain many consultants.
- Each consultant has one or more areas of expertise (class). For example, a consultant may be classified as an expert in both database design and networking.
- Each area of expertise (class) can have many consultants in it. For example, the consulting company may employ many consultants who are networking experts.

Given that brief description of the requirements and the business rules, write the relational schema and draw the dependency diagram for the preceding (and very poor) table structure. Label all transitive and/or partial dependencies.

18 Break up the dependency diagram you drew in Problem 17 to produce dependency diagrams that are in 3NF and write the relational schema. (*Hint*: You may have to create a few new attributes. Also make sure that the new dependency diagrams contain attributes that meet proper design criteria; that is, make sure that there are no multivalued attributes, that the naming conventions are met and so on).

19 Using the results of Problem 18, draw the ERD using UML notation.

20 Given the sample records in the CHARTER table that follows, write the relational schema and draw the dependency diagram for the table structure. Make sure that you label all dependencies. CHAR_PAX indicates the number of passengers carried. The CHAR_MILES entry is based on round-trip miles, including pickup points. (*Hint*: Look at the data values to determine the nature of the relationships. For example, note that employee Melton has flown two charter trips as pilot and one trip as copilot.)

Attribute Name	Sample Value	Sample Value	Sample Value	Sample Value
CHAR_TRIP	10232	10233	10234	10235
CHAR_DATE	15-Jan-2019	15-Jan-2019	16-Jan-2019	17-Jan-2019
CHAR_CITY	STL	MIA	TYS	ATL
CHAR_MILES	580	1 290	524	768
CUST_NUM	784	231	544	784
CUST_LNAME	Brown	Hanson	Bryana	Brown
CHAR_PAX	5	12	2	5
CHAR_CARGO	235 kg	18 940 kg	348 kg	155 kg
PILOT	Melton	Chen	Henderson	Melton
COPILOT		Henderson	Melton	
FLT_ENGINEER		O'Shaski		
LOAD_MASTER		Benkasi		
AC_NUMBER	1234Q	3456Y	1234Q	2256W
MODEL_CODE	PA31-350	CV-580	PA31-350	PA31-350
MODEL_SEATS	10	38	10	10
MODEL_CHG_MILE	€2.13	€18.45	€2.20	€2.20

21 Decompose the dependency diagram in Problem 20 to create table structures that are in 3NF and write the relational schema. Make sure that you label all dependencies.

22 Draw the ERD to reflect the properly decomposed dependency diagrams you created in Problem 21. Make sure that the ERD produces a database that can track all of the data shown in Problem 20.

NOTE

Use the dependency diagram shown in Figure P7.1 to work on Problems 23–24.

FIGURE P7.1 **Initial dependency diagram for Problems 23–24**

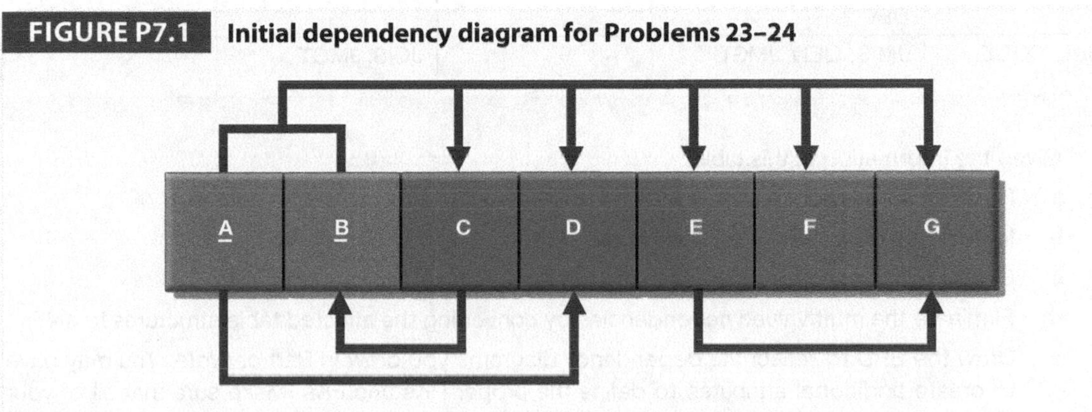

23 Break up the dependency diagram to create two new dependency diagrams, one in 3NF and one in 2NF.

24 Modify the dependency diagrams you created in Problem 23 to produce a set of dependency diagrams that are in 3NF. To keep the entire collection of attributes together, copy the 3NF dependency diagram from Problem 23; then show the new dependency diagrams that are also in 3NF. (*Hint*: One of your dependency diagrams will be in 3NF but not in BCNF.)

25 Modify the dependency diagrams in Problem 24 to produce a collection of dependency diagrams that are in 3NF and BCNF. To ensure that all attributes are accounted for, copy the 3NF dependency diagrams from Problem 24; then show the new 3NF and BCNF dependency diagrams.

26 Suppose you have been given the table structure and data shown here, which was imported from an Excel spreadsheet. The data reflect that a lecturer can have multiple advisees, can serve on multiple committees and can edit more than one journal.

Attribute Name	Sample Value	Sample Value	Sample Value	Sample Value
EMP_NUM	123	104	118	
LECT_RANK	Professor	Asst. Lecturer	Lecturer	Lecturer
EMP_NAME	Ghee	Rankin	Ortega	Smith
DEPT_CODE	CIS	CHEM	CIS	ENG
DEPT_NAME	Computer Info. Systems	Chemistry	Computer Info. Systems	English
PROF_OFFICE	KDD-567	BLF-119	KDD-562	PRT-345
ADVISEE	1215, 2312, 3233, 2218, 2098	3102, 2782, 3311, 2008, 2876, 2222, 3745, 1783, 2378	2134, 2789, 3456, 2002, 2046, 2018, 2764	2873, 2765, 2238, 2901, 2308
COMMITTEE_CODE	PROMO, TRAF, APPL, DEV	DEV	SPR, TRAF	PROMO, SPR, DEV
JOURNAL_CODE	JMIS, QED, JMGT		JCIS, JMGT	

7

Given the information in this table:

- **a** Draw the dependency diagram.
- **b** Identify the multivalued dependencies.
- **c** Create the dependency diagrams to yield a set of table structures in 3NF.
- **d** Eliminate the multivalued dependencies by converting the affected table structures to 4NF.
- **e** Draw the ERD to reflect the dependency diagrams you drew in Part c. (*Note:* You may have to create additional attributes to define the proper PKs and FKs. Make sure that all of your attributes conform to the naming conventions.)

27 Using the descriptions of the attributes given in Figure P7.2, convert the ERD into a dependency diagram that is in at least 3NF.

FIGURE P7.2 Appointment for ERD for Problem 27

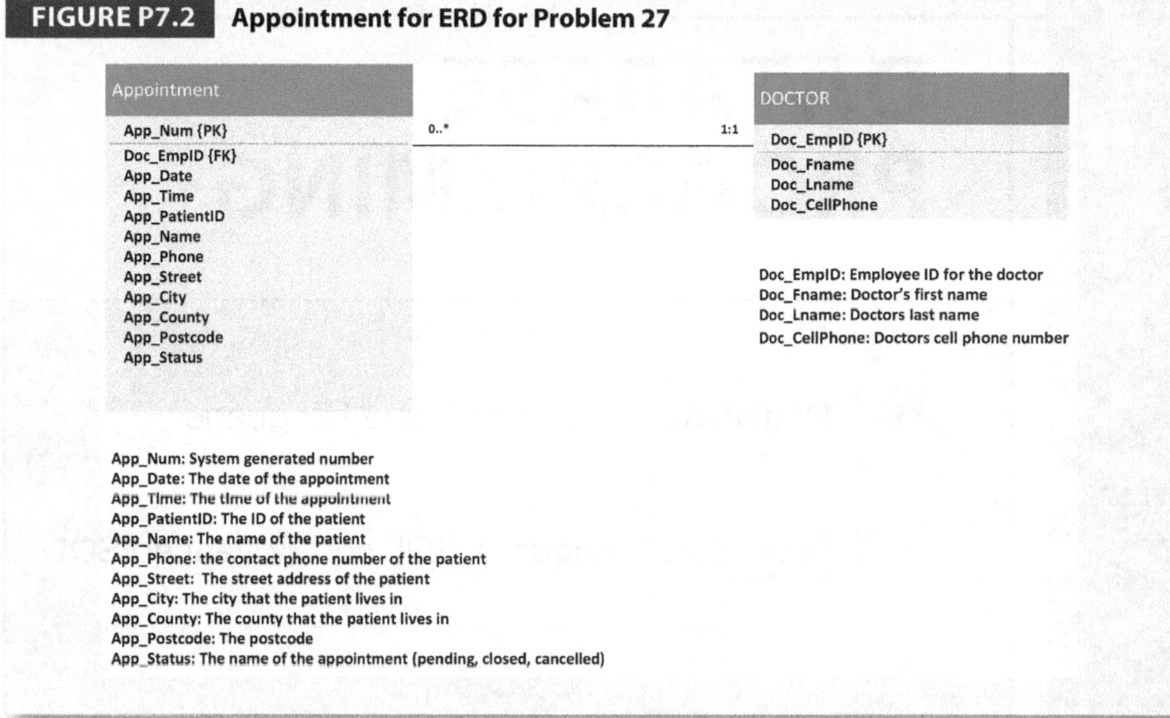

28 Using the descriptions of the attributes given in Figure P7.3, convert the ERD into a dependency diagram that is in at least 3NF.

FIGURE P7.3 Presentation ERD for Problem 28

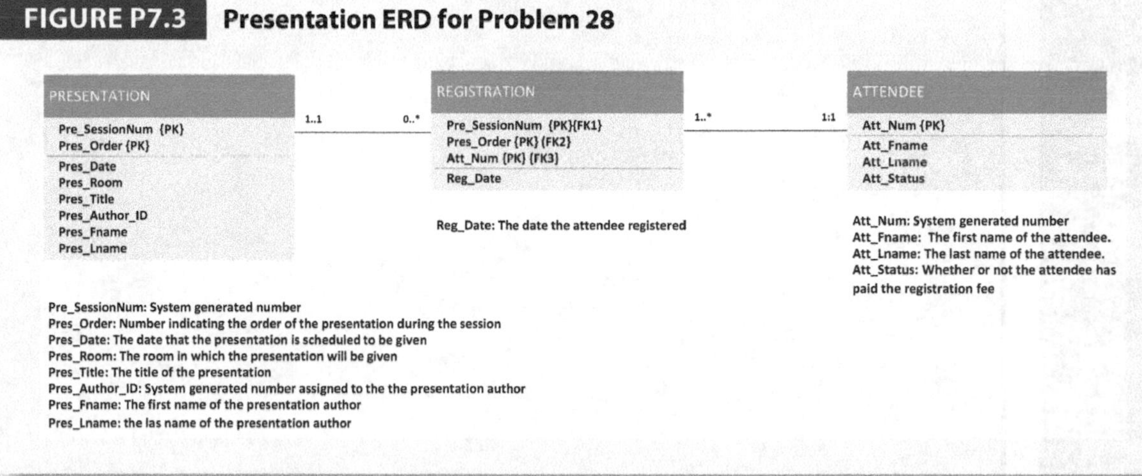

Part III

DATABASE PROGRAMMING

BUSINESS VIGNETTE

OPEN SOURCE DATABASES

With Oracle acquiring MySQL in 2009, are open source database management systems still significantly growing? An interesting question that perhaps can be answered by MySQL still being ranked the world's most popular database platform.[1] In general, organisations have been moving, and continue to move, towards open source databases due to the costs of software licensing. Oracle and IBM have both often been criticised for their expensive and complex licensing procedures, which have led customers to look for alternatives and switch to open source DBMSs. For example, in 2011, the French Government switched to the open source database management system PostgreSQL[2] for its Social Security system 'Caisse Nationale d'Allocations Familiales (CNAF)'.[3] France's Social Security system deals with allocating benefits amounting to more than €69 billion to over 11 million people. The decision to switch to an open source DBMS was made to reduce licensing costs. On evaluation, PostgreSQL was found to have all the essential features and the necessary levels of reliability and performance required. Migration from the existing DBMS took 18 months and involved 168 individual databases containing 4 terabytes of data.[3] Today, the PostgreSQL system runs almost a billion SQL queries every day.

The BBC news website began to use a MySQL open source database in 2006 in order to monitor reader interest. The aim was to produce a dynamic real-time system, 'which would give audiences a real sense of the news stories on the website being picked up most by other users'. The idea was that news stories from all time zones throughout the world could be fed to the site, which currently attracts over 35 million users. As the budget was tight, the solution was to develop the BBC News Live Stats system using the Linux operating system and a MySQL database. The database comprises 24 tables and about 8 million rows, and processes about 30 000 data inserts per minute and 4 000 requests per hour.[4]

There is an increasing number of success stories from organisations that have chosen to develop using open source databases. However, in terms of business intelligence, these open source databases still have a way to go to match the capabilities of the commercial vendors such as Oracle and IBM.

---

1 The Most Popular Databases 2019. Available: www.explore-group.com/blog/the-most-popular-databases-2018/bp46/

2 Open Source Database Engine for France's Social Security. Available: www.linuxbsdos.com/2010/11/25/open-source-database-new-engine-of-frances-social-security/

3 PostgreSQL. Available: www.postgresql.org/

4 'BBC News Website uses MySQL to Monitor Reader Interest'. Available: www-it.mysql.com/whymysql/case-studies/

CHAPTER 8

Beginning Structured Query Language

IN THIS CHAPTER, YOU WILL LEARN:

- The basic commands and functions of SQL
- How to use SQL for data administration (to create tables, indexes and views)
- How to use SQL for data manipulation (to add, modify, delete and retrieve data)
- How to use SQL to query a database to extract useful information

PREVIEW

In this chapter, you learn the basics of Structured Query Language (SQL). SQL, pronounced S-Q-L or 'sequel', is composed of commands that enable users to create database and table structures, perform various types of data manipulation and data administration, and query the database to extract useful information. All relational DBMS software supports SQL, and many software vendors have developed extensions to the basic SQL command set.

SQL's vocabulary is simple, so the language is relatively easy to learn. Its simplicity is enhanced by the fact that much of its work takes place behind the scenes. For example, a single command creates the complex table structures required to store and manipulate data successfully. Furthermore, SQL is a non-procedural language; that is, the user specifies what must be done, but not how it is to be done. To issue SQL commands, end users and programmers do not need to know the physical data storage format or the complex activities that take place when a SQL command is executed.

Although quite useful and powerful, SQL is not meant to stand alone in the applications arena. Data entry with SQL is possible but awkward, as are data corrections and additions. SQL itself does not create menus, special report forms, overlays, pop-ups or any of the other utilities and screen devices that end users usually expect. Instead, those features are available as vendor-supplied enhancements. SQL focuses on data definition (creating tables, indexes and views) and data manipulation (adding, modifying, deleting and retrieving data), the basic functions presented in this chapter. In spite of its limitations, SQL is a powerful tool for extracting information and managing data.

8.1 INTRODUCTION TO SQL

Ideally, a database language allows you to create database and table structures, to perform basic data management chores (add, delete and modify), and to perform complex queries designed to transform the raw data into useful information. Moreover, a database language must perform such basic functions with minimal user effort, and its command structure and syntax must be easy to learn. Finally, it must be portable; that is, it must conform to some basic standard so that an individual does not have to relearn the basics when moving from one RDBMS to another. SQL meets those ideal database language requirements well.

SQL functions fit into several broad categories:

- It is a *data definition language (DDL)*: SQL includes commands to create database objects such as tables, indexes and views, as well as commands to define access rights to those database objects. The data definition commands you will learn in this chapter are listed in Table 8.1.
- It is a *data manipulation language (DML)*: It includes commands to insert, update, delete and retrieve data within the database tables. The data manipulation commands you will learn in this chapter are listed in Table 8.2.
- It is a *transaction control language (TCL)*: The DML commands in SQL are executed within the context of a transaction, which is a logical unit of work composed of one or more SQL commands. SQL provides commands to control the processing of these statements in an indivisible unit of work. This will be discussed further in Chapter 9.
- It is a *data control language (DCL)*: Data control commands are used to control access to data objects, such as giving a specific user permission to view the PRODUCT table. Common TCL and DCL commands are shown in Table 8.3.

TABLE 8.1 SQL data definition commands

Command or Option	Description
CREATE SCHEMA AUTHORISATION	Creates a database schema
CREATE TABLE	Creates a new table in the user's database schema
NOT NULL	Ensures that a column will not have null values
UNIQUE	Ensures that a column will not have duplicate values
PRIMARY KEY	Defines a primary key for a table
FOREIGN KEY	Defines a foreign key for a table
DEFAULT	Defines a default value for a column (when no value is given)
CHECK	Constraint used to validate data in an attribute
CREATE INDEX	Creates an index for a table
CREATE VIEW	Creates a dynamic subset of rows/columns from one or more tables
ALTER TABLE	Modifies a table's definition (adds, modifies or deletes attributes or constraints)
CREATE TABLE AS	Creates a new table based on a query in the user's database schema
DROP TABLE	Permanently deletes a table (and thus its data)
DROP INDEX	Permanently deletes an index
DROP VIEW	Permanently deletes a view

TABLE 8.2 SQL data manipulation commands

Command or Option	Description
INSERT	Inserts row(s) into a table
SELECT	Selects attributes from rows in one or more tables or views
WHERE	Restricts the selection of rows based on a conditional expression
GROUP BY	Groups the selected rows based on one or more attributes
HAVING	Restricts the selection of grouped rows based on a condition
ORDER BY	Orders the selected rows based on one or more attributes
UPDATE	Modifies an attributes values in one or more tables rows
DELETE	Deletes one or more rows from a table
COMMIT	Permanently saves data changes
ROLLBACK	Restores data to their original values
Comparison operators	
=, <, >, <=, >=, <>	Used in conditional expressions
Logical operators	
AND/OR/NOT	Used in conditional expressions
Special operators	Used in conditional expressions
BETWEEN	Checks whether an attribute value is within a range
IS NULL	Checks whether an attribute value is null
LIKE	Checks whether an attribute value matches a given string pattern
IN	Checks whether an attribute value matches any value within a value list
EXISTS	Checks whether a subquery returns any rows
DISTINCT	Limits values to unique values
Aggregate functions	Used with SELECT to return mathematical summaries on columns
COUNT	Returns the number of rows with non-null values for a given column
MIN	Returns the minimum attribute value found in a given column
MAX	Returns the maximum attribute value found in a given column
SUM	Returns the sum of all values for a given column
AVG	Returns the average of all values for a given column

SQL is relatively easy to learn. Its basic command set has a vocabulary of fewer than 100 words. Better yet, SQL is a non-procedural language: you merely command *what* is to be done; you don't have to worry about *how* it is to be done. The American National Standards Institute (ANSI) prescribes a standard SQL – the most recent version is SQL:2011, which was formally adopted in December 2011. The ANSI SQL standards are also accepted by the International Organization for Standardization (ISO), a consortium composed of national standards bodies of more than 150 countries. Although adherence to the ANSI/ISO SQL standard is usually required in commercial and government contract database specifications, many RDBMS vendors add their own special enhancements. Consequently, it is seldom possible to move a SQL-based application from one RDBMS to another without making some changes.

However, even though there are several different SQL 'dialects', the differences among them are minor. Whether you use Oracle, Microsoft SQL Server, IBM's DB2, Microsoft Access or any other well-established RDBMS, a software manual should be sufficient to get you up to SQL speed if you know the material presented in this chapter.

NOTE

Throughout this book SQL examples will be given using both Oracle 11g Release 2 (11.2) and MySQL Community Edition RDBMS. Both of these RDBMSs comply with the ISO SQL:2011 standard to different degrees so there are small differences between the SQL dialects. It is, however, important to note that the ISO standards such as SQL:2011 are very complex and comprise several parts. Users are interested to know how a RDBMS complies with standards so that they can assess the portability of databases between different RDBMs and the functionality that each RDBMS offers. For example, SQL within Oracle 11g Release 2 (11.2) is compliant with the Core SQL:2011 Standard, which is defined in Part 2, SQL/Foundation, and Part 11, SQL/Schemata.

Whereas Oracle is a commercial DBMS, MySQL started life as an open source RDBMS in 1995 and was sponsored by a Swedish company called MySQL AB. One of the aims of MySQL over the years has been to work towards compliance with the ISO standards whil at the same time adding additional SQL extensions. The aim of the MySQL development community has been to enhance the usability of the MySQL DBMS by adding extensions to SQL and support for non-SQL features.

In 2009 Oracle acquired MySQL as part of its takeover of Sun. Currently, Oracle offer a number of editions of MySQL, one of which is the free open source Community Edition, which is supported by open source developers. If an organisation wishes to use a commercial version of MySQL, Oracle has made a number of versions available depending on the business requirements, each for a price. Oracle reap the benefits from both open source development and revenue generated by commercial versions of MySQL. Whether a version of MySQL will remain open source in the future is up for debate.

TABLE 8.3 Other SQL commands

Command or option	Definition
Transaction control language	
COMMIT	Permanently saves data changes
ROLLBACK	Restores data to its original values
Data control language	
GRANT	Gives a user permission to take a system action or access a data object
REVOKE	Removes a previously granted permission from a user

At the heart of SQL is the query. In Chapter 1, The Database Approach, you learned that a query is a spur-of-the-moment question. Actually, in the SQL environment, the word *query* covers both questions and actions. Most SQL queries are used to answer questions such as these: Which products currently held in inventory are priced over €100, and what is the quantity on hand of each of those products? How many employees have been hired since 1 January 2019 by each of the company's departments? However, many SQL queries are used to perform actions such as adding or deleting table rows or changing attribute values within tables. Still other SQL queries create new tables or indexes. In short, for a DBMS, a query is simply a SQL statement that must be executed. However, before you can use SQL to query a database, you must define the database environment for SQL with its data definition commands.

8

8.2 DATA DEFINITION COMMANDS

Before examining the SQL syntax for creating and defining tables and other elements, let's first examine the simple database model and the database tables that will form the basis of the many SQL examples you'll explore in this chapter.

8.2.1 The Database Model

A simple database composed of the following tables is used to illustrate the SQL commands in this chapter: CUSTOMER, INVOICE, LINE, PRODUCT and VENDOR. This database model is shown in Figure 8.1.

FIGURE 8.1 The database model

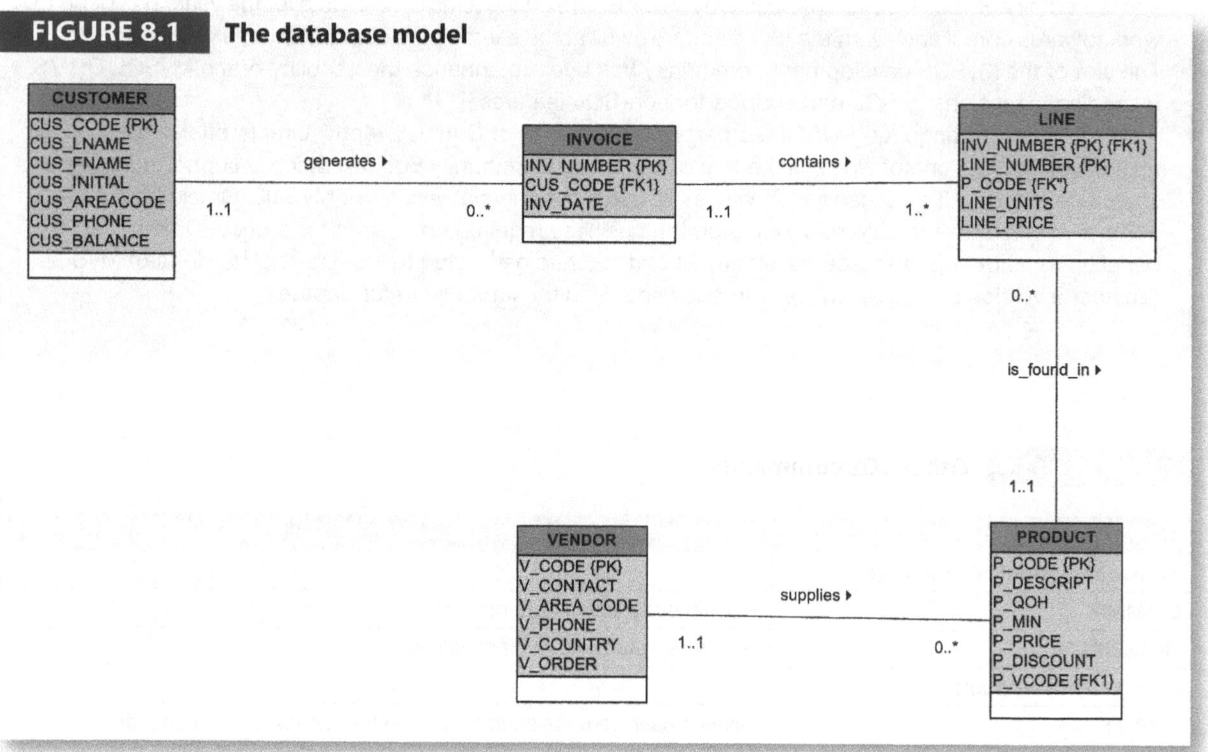

The database model in Figure 8.1 reflects the following business rules:

- A customer may generate many invoices. Each invoice is generated by one customer.
- An invoice contains one or more invoice lines. Each invoice line is associated with one invoice.
- Each invoice line references one product. A product may be found in many invoice lines. (You can sell more than one hammer to more than one customer.)
- A vendor *may* supply many products. Some vendors do not yet supply products. (For example, a vendor list may include *potential* vendors.)
- If a product is vendor supplied, that product is supplied by only a single vendor.
- Some products are not supplied by a vendor. (For example, some products may be produced in-house or may have been bought on the open market.)

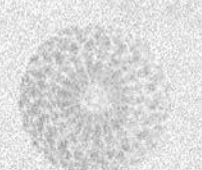

Online Content The database model in Figure 8.1 is implemented in the Microsoft Access 'Ch08_SaleCo' database located on the online platform for this book. (This database contains a few additional tables that are not reflected in Figure 8.1. These tables are used for discussion purposes only.) If you use Microsoft Access, you can use the database available on the online platform accompanying this book. However, it is strongly suggested that you create your own database structures so you can practice the SQL commands illustrated in this chapter. If you are using the Oracle or MySQL DBMS, SQL script files for creating the tables and loading the data in the database are also available online. How you connect to the Oracle database depends on how the Oracle software was installed on your server and on the access paths and methods defined and managed by the database administrator. Follow the instructions provided by your instructor, college or university.

As you can see in Figure 8.1, the database model contains many tables. However, to illustrate the initial set of data definition commands, the focus of attention will be the PRODUCT and VENDOR tables. You will have the opportunity to use the remaining tables later in this chapter and in the problem section.

So that you have a point of reference for understanding the effect of the SQL queries, the contents of the PRODUCT and VENDOR tables are listed in Figure 8.2.

Note the following about these tables. (The features correspond to the business rules reflected in the ERD shown in Figure 8.1.)

8

FIGURE 8.2 The VENDOR and PRODUCT tables

Database name: Ch8_SaleCo

Table name: VENDOR

V_CODE	V_NAME	V_CONTACT	V_POSTAL_CODE	V_PHONE	V_Country	V_ORDER
21225	Bryson, Inc.	Smithson	0181	223-3234	UK	Y
21226	SuperLoo, Inc.	Flushing	0113	215-8995	SA	N
21231	D&E Supply	Singh	0181	228-3245	UK	Y
21344	Jabavu Bros	Khumalo	0181	889-2546	SA	N
22567	Dome Supply	Smith	7253	678-1419	FR	N
23119	Randsets Ltd.	Anderson	7253	678-3998	FR	Y
24004	Brackman Bros.	Browning	0181	228-1410	UK	N
24288	ORDVA, Inc.	Dandala	0181	898-1234	SA	Y
25443	B&K, Inc.	Smith	0113	227-0093	SA	N
25501	Damal Supplies	Gounden	0181	890-3529	SA	N
25595	Rubicon Systems	Du Toit	0113	456-0092	SA	Y

Table name: PRODUCT

P_CODE	P_DESCRIPT	P_INDATE	P_QOH	P_MIN	P_PRICE	P_DISCOUNT	V_CODE
11QER/31	Power painter, 15 psi., 3-nozzle	03-Nov-18	8	5	109.99	0.00	25595
13-Q2/P2	18cm pwr. saw blade	13-Dec-18	32	15	14.99	0.05	21344

P_CODE	P_DESCRIPT	P_INDATE	P_QOH	P_MIN	P_PRICE	P_DISCOUNT	V_CODE
14-Q1/L3	22 cm pwr. saw blade	13-Nov-18	18	12	17.49	0.00	21344
1546-QQ2	Hrd. cloth, 0.6 cm, 2x50	15-Jan-19	15	8	39.95	0.00	23119
1558-QW1	Hrd. cloth, 1.25 cm, 3x50	15-Jan-19	23	5	43.99	0.00	23119
2232/QTY	B&D jigsaw, 30 cm blade	30-Dec-18	8	5	109.92	0.05	24288
2232/QWE	B&D jigsaw, 20 cm blade	24-Dec-18	6	5	99.87	0.05	24288
2238/QPD	B&D cordless drill, 1.25 cm	20-Jan-19	12	5	38.95	0.05	25595
23109-HB	Claw hammer	20-Jan-19	23	10	9.95	0.10	21225
23114-AA	Sledge hammer, 7 kg	02-Jan-19	8	5	14.40	0.05	
54778-2T	Rat-tail file, 0.5 cm fine	15-Dec-18	43	20	4.99	0.00	21344
89-WRE-Q	Hicut chain saw, 40 cm	07-Feb-19	11	5	256.99	0.05	24288
PVC23DRT	PVC pipe, 9 cm, 2.5 m	20-Feb-19	188	75	5.87	0.00	
SM-18277	3 cm metal screw, 25	01-Mar-19	172	75	6.99	0.00	21225
SW-23116	6 cm wd. screw, 50	24-Feb-19	237	100	8.45	0.00	21231
WR3/TT3	Steel matting, 10 cm × 20 cm × 0.5 cm ×1.25 cm mesh	17-Jan-19	18	5	119.95	0.10	25595

8

The VENDOR table contains vendors who are not referenced in the PRODUCT table. Database designers note that possibility by saying that PRODUCT is *optional* to VENDOR because a vendor may exist without a reference to a product. You examined such optional relationships in detail in Chapter 5, Data Modelling with Entity Relationship Diagrams.

- Existing V_CODE values in the PRODUCT table must (and do) have a match in the VENDOR table to ensure referential integrity.
- A few products are supplied factory direct, a few are made in-house, and a few may have been bought in a special warehouse sale. In other words, a product is not necessarily supplied by a vendor. Therefore, VENDOR is optional to PRODUCT.

A few of the conditions just described were made for the sake of illustrating specific SQL features. For example, null V_CODE values were used in the PRODUCT table to illustrate (later) how you can track such nulls using SQL.

8.2.2 Creating the Database

Before you can use a new RDBMS, you must complete two tasks: first, create the database structure; second, create the tables that will hold the end-user data. To complete the first task, the RDBMS creates the physical files that will hold the database. When you create a new database, the RDBMS automatically creates the data dictionary tables – to store the metadata – and creates a default database administrator. Creating the physical files that will hold the database means interacting with the operating system and the file systems supported by the operating system. Therefore, creating the database structure is the one feature that tends to differ substantially from one RDBMS to another. The good news is that it is relatively easy to create a database structure, regardless of which RDBMS you use.

If you use Microsoft Access, creating the database is simple: start Access, select File/New/Blank Database, specify the folder in which you want to store the database and name the database. However, if you work in the database environment typically used by larger organisations, you will probably use an enterprise RDBMS such as Oracle, SQL Server or DB2. Given their security requirements and greater complexity, those database products require a more elaborate database creation process.

You will be relieved to discover that, *with the exception of the database creation process*, most RDBMS vendors use SQL that deviates little from the ANSI standard SQL. For example, most RDBMSs require that any SQL command end with a semicolon. However, some SQL implementations do not use a semicolon. Important syntax differences among implementations will be highlighted in Note boxes.

If you are using an enterprise RDBMS such as Oracle, DB2 or SQL Server, before you can start creating tables you must be authenticated by the RDBMS. **Authentication** is the process through which the DBMS verifies that only registered users may access the database. To be authenticated, you must log on to the RDBMS using a user ID and a password created by the database administrator. In an enterprise RDBMS, every user ID is associated with a database schema.

8.2.3 The Database Schema

In the SQL environment, a **schema** is a group of database objects – such as tables and indexes – that are related to each other. Usually, the schema belongs to a single user or application. A single database can hold multiple schemas belonging to different users or applications. Think of a schema as a logical grouping of database objects, such as tables, indexes and views. Schemas are useful in that they group tables by owner (or function) and enforce a first level of security by allowing the user to see only the tables that belong to him or her.

ANSI SQL standards define a command to create a database schema: 8

```
CREATE SCHEMA AUTHORISATION {creator};
```

Therefore, if the creator is JONES, use the command:

```
CREATE SCHEMA AUTHORISATION JONES;
```

Most enterprise RDBMSs support that command. However, the command is seldom used directly – that is, from the command line. (When a user is created, the DBMS automatically assigns a schema to that user.) When the DBMS *is* used, the CREATE SCHEMA AUTHORISATION command must be issued by the user who owns the schema. That is, if you log on as JONES, you can use only CREATE SCHEMA AUTHORISATION JONES.

For most RDBMSs, the CREATE SCHEMA AUTHORISATION is optional. That is why this chapter focuses on the ANSI SQL commands required to create and manipulate tables.

8.2.4 Data Types

After the database schema has been created, you are ready to define the PRODUCT and VENDOR table structures within the database. The table-creating SQL commands used in the example are based on the data dictionary shown in Table 8.4.

TABLE 8.4 Data dictionary for the Ch8_SaleCo database

Table Name	Attribute Name	Contents	Data Type	Format	Range	Required	PK or FK	FK Referenced Table
PRODUCT	P_CODE	Product code	CHAR(10)	XXXXXXXXXX	NA	Y	PK	
	P_DESCRIPT	Product description	VARCHAR(35)	Xxxxxxxxxxxx	NA	Y		

Table Name	Attribute Name	Contents	Data Type	Format	Range	Required	PK or FK	FK Referenced Table
	P_INDATE	Stocking date	DATE	DD-MON-YYYY	NA	Y		
	P_QOH	Units available	SMALLINT	####	0-9999	Y		
	P_MIN	Minimum units	SMALLINT	####	0-9999	Y		
	P_PRICE	Product price	NUMBER(8,2)	####.##	0.00-9999.00	Y		
	P_DISCOUNT	Discount rate	NUMBER(4,2)	0.##	0.00-0.20	Y		
	V_CODE	Vendor code	INTEGER	###	100-999	N	FK	VENDOR
VENDOR	V_CODE	Vendor code	INTEGER	#####	1000-9999	Y	PK	
	V_NAME	Vendor name	CHAR(35)	Xxxxxxxxxxxxxx	NA	Y		
	V_CONTACT	Contact person	CHAR(25)	Xxxxxxxxxxxxxx	NA	Y		
	V_AREACODE	Area code	CHAR(5)	99999	NA	Y		
	V_PHONE	Phone number	CHAR(12)	999-999-9999	NA	Y		
	V_COUNTRY	Country	CHAR(2)	XX	NA	Y		
	V_ORDER	Previous order	CHAR(1)	X	Y or N	Y		

FK = Foreign key

PK = Primary key

CHAR = Fixed character length data, 1 to 255 characters

VARCHAR = Variable character length data, 1 to 2 000 characters. May be labelled VARCHAR2 in Oracle

NUMBER = Numeric data. NUMBER(9,2) is used to specify numbers with two decimal places and up to nine digits long, including the decimal places. Some RDBMSs permit the use of a MONEY or a CURRENCY data type

INTEGER = Integer values only. Represented by NUMBER in Oracle

SMALLINT = Small integer values only. Represented by NUMBER in Oracle

DATE formats may vary. Commonly accepted formats are DD-MON-YYYY, DD-MON-YY, MM/DD/YYYY, and MM/DD/YY

* Not all of the ranges shown here will be illustrated in this chapter. However, you can use these constraints to practise writing your own.

As you examine the data dictionary in Table 8.4, note particularly the data types selected. Keep in mind that data type selection is usually dictated by the nature of the data and by the intended use. For example:

- P_PRICE clearly requires some kind of numeric data type; defining it as a character field is not acceptable.
- Just as clearly, a vendor name is an obvious candidate for a character data type. For example, VARCHAR2(35) fits well because vendor names are 'variable-length' character strings, and in this case, such strings may be up to 35 characters long.
- Country abbreviations are always two characters, so CHAR(2) is a logical choice.
- Selecting P_INDATE to be a (Julian) DATE field rather than a character field is desirable because the Julian dates allow you to make simple date comparisons and to perform date arithmetic. For instance, *if you have used DATE fields,* you can determine how many days are between 1 March, 2018 and 15 April, 2019 by using 15-APR-2019 - 01-MAR-2018.

If you use DATE fields, you can also determine what the date will be 60 days from 15 February 2018 by using 15-FEB-2018 + 60. Or you can use the RDBMS's system date – SYSDATE in Oracle, Date() in Microsoft Access – to determine the answer to questions such as, What will be the date 60 days from today? For example, you might use SYSDATE + 60 (in Oracle) or Date() + 60 (in Access).

Date arithmetic capability is particularly useful in billing. Perhaps you want your system to start charging interest on a customer balance 60 days after the invoice is generated. Such simple date arithmetic would be impossible if you used a character data type.

On the other hand, data type selection can require professional judgement. For example, you need to make a decision about the V_CODE's data type as follows:

- If you want the computer to generate new vendor codes by adding one to the largest recorded vendor code, you must classify V_CODE as a numeric attribute. (You cannot perform mathematical procedures on character data.) The designation INTEGER will ensure that only the counting numbers (integers) can be used. Most SQL implementations also permit the use of SMALLINT for integer values up to six digits.
- If you do not want to perform mathematical procedures based on V_CODE, you should classify it as a character attribute, even though it is composed entirely of numbers. Character data are 'quicker' to process in queries. Therefore, when there is no need to perform mathematical procedures on the attribute, store it as a character attribute.

The first option is used to demonstrate the SQL procedures in this chapter.

When you define the attribute's data type, you need to pay close attention to the expected use of the attributes for sorting and data retrieval purposes. For example, in a real estate application, an attribute that represents the numbers of bathrooms in a home (H_BATH_NUM) could be assigned the CHAR(3) data type because it is highly unlikely that the application will do any addition, multiplication or division with the number of bathrooms. Based on the CHAR(3) data type definition, valid H_BATH_NUM values would be '2','1','2.5','10'. However, this data type decision creates potential problems. For example, if an application sorts the homes by number of bathrooms, a query would 'see' the value '10' as less than '2', which is clearly incorrect. Clearly, you must give some thought to the expected use of the data in order to define the attribute data type properly.

The data dictionary in Table 8.4 contains only a few of the data types supported by SQL. For teaching purposes, the selection of data types is limited to ensure that almost any RDBMS can be used to implement the examples. If your RDBMS is fully ANSI SQL compliant, it supports many more data types than the ones shown in Table 8.5. And many RDBMSs support data types beyond the ones specified in ANSI SQL.

TABLE 8.5 **Some common SQL data types**

Data Type	Format	Comments
Numeric	NUMBER(L,D)	The declaration NUMBER(7,2) indicates that numbers that will be stored with two decimal places and may be up to seven digits long, including the sign and the decimal place (for example, 12.32, or -134.99).
	INTEGER	May be abbreviated as INT. Integers are (whole) counting numbers, so they cannot be used if you want to store numbers that require decimal places.
	SMALLINT	Like INTEGER but limited to integer values up to six digits. If your integer values are relatively small, use SMALLINT instead of INT.
	DECIMAL(L,D)	Like the NUMBER specification, but the storage length is a *minimum* specification. That is, greater lengths are acceptable, but smaller ones are not. DECIMAL(9,2), DECIMAL(9) and DECIMAL are all acceptable.

8

Data Type	Format	Comments
	FLOAT(L,D)	Float is similar to DECIMAL and is used more often in MySQL.
Character	CHAR(L)	Fixed-length character data for up to 255 characters. If you store strings that are not as long as the CHAR parameter value, the remaining spaces are left unused. Therefore, if you specify CHAR(25), strings such as *Smith* and *Katzenjammer* are each stored as 25 characters. However, US area code is always three digits long, so CHAR(3) would be appropriate if you wanted to store such codes.
	VARCHAR(L) or VARCHAR2(L)	Variable-length character data. The designation VARCHAR2(25) will let you store characters up to 25 characters long. However, VARCHAR will not leave unused spaces. Oracle automatically converts VARCHAR to VARCHAR2.
Date	DATE	Stores dates in the Julian date format.

In addition to the data types shown in Table 8.5, SQL supports several other data types, including TIME, TIMESTAMP, REAL, DOUBLE, FLOAT and intervals such as INTERVAL DAY TO HOUR. Many RDBMSs also have expanded the list to include other types of data, such as LOGICAL, CURRENCY, AutoNumber (Access) and sequence (Oracle). However, because this chapter is designed to introduce the SQL basics, the discussion is limited to the data types summarised in Table 8.5.

8

8.2.5 Creating Table Structures

Now you are ready to implement the PRODUCT and VENDOR table structures with the help of SQL, using the **CREATE TABLE** syntax shown next.

CREATE TABLE *tablename* (

column1 *data type* [*constraint*] [,

column2 *data type*[*constraint*]] [,

PRIMARY KEY (*column1* [, *column2*])] [,

FOREIGN KEY (*column1* [, *column2*]) REFERENCES *tablename*] [,

CONSTRAINT *constraint*]);

Online Content For Oracle users, all the SQL commands you will see in this chapter are available on the online platform for this book. You can copy and paste the SQL commands into Oracle SQL Developer or Oracle APEX.

To make the SQL code more readable, most SQL programmers use one line per column (attribute) definition. In addition, spaces line up the attribute characteristics and constraints. Finally, both table and attribute names are fully capitalised. Those conventions are used in the following examples that create VENDOR and PRODUCT tables and throughout the book.

NOTE ABOUT SQL SYNTAX

Syntax notation for SQL commands used in this book:

CAPITALS	Required SQL command keywords
Italics	An end-user-provided parameter (generally required)
{a | b | ..}	A mandatory parameter; use one option from | separated option list
[......]	An optional parameter; anything inside square brackets is optional
tablename	The name of a table
column	The name of an attribute in a table
data type	A valid data type definition
constraint	A valid constraint definition
condition	A valid conditional expression (evaluates to true or false)
columnlist	One or more column names or expressions separated by commas
tablelist	One or more table names separated by commas
conditionlist	One or more conditional expressions separated by logical operators
expression	A simple value (that is, 76 or Married) or a formula (that is, P_PRICE - 10)

8

```
CREATE TABLE VENDOR (
V_CODE          INTEGER         NOT NULL        UNIQUE,
V_NAME          VARCHAR(35)     NOT NULL,
V_CONTACT       VARCHAR(15)     NOT NULL,
V_AREACODE      CHAR(5)         NOT NULL,
V_PHONE         CHAR(12)        NOT NULL,
V_Country       CHAR(2)         NOT NULL,
V_ORDER         CHAR(1)         NOT NULL,
PRIMARY KEY (V_CODE));
```

NOTE

- Because the PRODUCT table contains a foreign key that references VENDOR, create the VENDOR table first. (In fact, the * side of a relationship always references the 1 side. Therefore, in a 1:* relationship, you must *always* create the table for the 1 side first.)
- If your RDBMS does not support the VARCHAR2 and FCHAR format, use CHAR.
- Oracle accepts the VARCHAR data type and automatically converts it to VARCHAR2.
- If your RDBMS does not support SINT or SMALLINT, use INTEGER or INT. If INTEGER is not supported, use NUMBER.
- If you use Microsoft Access, you can use the NUMBER data type, but you cannot use the number delimiters at the SQL level. For example, NUMBER(8,2) to indicate numbers with up to eight characters and two decimal places is fine in Oracle, but you cannot use it in Access; instead, use NUMBER without the delimiters.

- If your RDBMS does not support primary and foreign key designations or the UNIQUE specification, delete them from the SQL code shown here.
- If you use the PRIMARY KEY designation in Oracle, you do not need the NOT NULL and UNIQUE specifications.
- The ON UPDATE CASCADE clause is part of the ANSI standard, but it may not be supported by your RDBMS. In that case, delete the ON UPDATE CASCADE clause.

```
CREATE TABLE PRODUCT (
P_CODE       VARCHAR(10)    NOT NULL       UNIQUE,
P_DESCRIPT   VARCHAR(35)    NOT NULL,
P_INDATE     DATE    NOT NULL,
P_QOH        SMALLINT NOT   NULL,
P_MIN        SMALLINT NOT   NULL,
P_PRICE      NUMBER(8,2)    NOT NULL,
P_DISCOUNT   NUMBER(4,2)    NOT NULL,
V_CODE       INTEGER,
PRIMARY KEY (P_CODE),
FOREIGN KEY (V_CODE) REFERENCES VENDOR
ON UPDATE CASCADE);
```

8

As you examine the preceding SQL table-creating command sequences, note the following features:

- The NOT NULL specifications for the attributes ensure that a data entry is made. When it is crucial to have the data available, the NOT NULL specification will not allow the end user to leave the attribute empty (with no data entry at all). Because this specification is made at the table level and stored in the data dictionary, application programs can use this information to create the data dictionary validation automatically.
- The UNIQUE specification creates a unique index in the respective attribute. Use it to avoid duplicated values in a column.
- The primary key attributes contain both a NOT NULL and a UNIQUE specification. Those specifications enforce the entity integrity requirements. If the NOT NULL and UNIQUE specifications are not supported, use PRIMARY KEY without the specifications. (For example, if you designate the PK in Microsoft Access, the NOT NULL and UNIQUE specifications are automatically assumed and are not spelled out.)
- The entire table definition is enclosed in parentheses. A comma is used to separate each table element (attributes, primary key and foreign key) definition.

NOTE

If you are working with a composite primary key, all of the primary key's attributes are contained within the parentheses and are separated with commas. For example, the LINE table in Figure 8.1 has a primary key that consists of the two attributes INV_NUMBER and LINE_NUMBER. Therefore, you would define the primary key by typing:

> PRIMARY KEY (INV_NUMBER, LINE_NUMBER),
>
> *The order of the primary key components is important* because the indexing starts with the first-mentioned attribute, then proceeds with the next attribute, and so on. In this example, the line numbers would be ordered within each of the invoice numbers:
>
> | INV_NUMBER | LINE_NUMBER |
> |---|---|
> | 1001 | 1 |
> | 1001 | 2 |
> | 1002 | 1 |
> | 1003 | 1 |
> | 1003 | 2 |

- The ON UPDATE CASCADE specification ensures that if you make a change in any VENDOR's V_CODE, that change is automatically applied to all foreign key references throughout the system (cascade) to ensure that referential integrity is maintained. (Although the ON UPDATE CASCADE clause is part of the ANSI standard, some RDBMSs, such as Oracle, do not support ON UPDATE CASCADE. If your RDBMS does not support the clause, delete it from the code shown here.)
- An RDBMS automatically enforces referential integrity for foreign keys. That is, you cannot have an invalid entry in the foreign key column; at the same time, you cannot delete a vendor row as long as a product row references that vendor.
- The command sequence ends with a semicolon. (Remember, your RDBMS may require that you omit the semicolon.)

NOTE ABOUT COLUMN NAMES

Do *not* use mathematical symbols such as +, −, and /. For example, PER-NUM may generate an error message, but PER_NUM is acceptable. Also, do *not* use reserved words. **Reserved words** are words used by SQL to perform specific functions. For example, in some RDBMSs, the column name INITIAL generates the message 'invalid column name'.

NOTE TO ORACLE USERS

If you are using command line SQL to create tables in Oracle, when you press the Enter key after typing each line, a line number is automatically generated as long as you do not type a semicolon before pressing the Enter key. Line numbers are also automatically generated when using Oracle's SQL Developer. For example, Oracle's execution of the CREATE TABLE command looks like this:

```
CREATE TABLE PRODUCT (
2       P_CODE VARCHAR2(10)
3       CONSTRAINT PRODUCT_P_CODE_PK PRIMARY KEY,
4       P_DESCRIPT  VARCHAR2(35)        NOT NULL,
5       P_INDATE  DATE NOT NULL,
6       P_QOH  NUMBER  NOT NULL,
7       P_MIN NUMBER  NOT NULL,
```

```
8     P_PRICE NUMBER(8,2)  NOT NULL,
9     P_DISCOUNT  NUMBER(5,2)   NOT NULL,
10    V_CODE NUMBER,
11    CONSTRAINT PRODUCT_V_CODE_FK
12    FOREIGN KEY V_CODE REFERENCES VENDOR);
```

As you examine the preceding SQL command sequence, note the following:

- The attribute definition for P_CODE starts in line 2 and ends with a comma at the end of line 3.
- The CONSTRAINT clause (line 3) allows you to define and name a constraint in Oracle. You can name the constraint to meet your own naming conventions. In this case, the constraint was named PRODUCT_P_CODE_PK.
- Examples of constraints are NOT NULL, UNIQUE, PRIMARY KEY, FOREIGN KEY and CHECK. For additional details about constraints, see below.
- To define a PRIMARY KEY constraint, you could also use the following syntax: P_CODE VARCHAR2(10) PRIMARY KEY, in this case, Oracle automatically names the constraint.
- Lines 11 and 12 define a FOREIGN KEY constraint name PRODUCT_V_CODE_FK for the attribute V_CODE. The CONSTRAINT clause is generally used at the end of the CREATE TABLE command sequence.
- *If you do not name the constraints yourself, Oracle automatically assigns a name. Unfortunately, the Oracle-assigned name makes sense only to Oracle, so you will have a difficult time deciphering it later. You should assign a name that makes sense to human beings!*

8.2.6 SQL Constraints

In Chapter 3, Relational Model Characteristics, you learnt that adherence to entity integrity and referential integrity rules is crucial in a relational database environment. Fortunately, most SQL implementations support both integrity rules. Entity integrity is enforced automatically when the primary key is specified in the CREATE TABLE command sequence. For example, you can create the VENDOR table structure and set the stage for the enforcement of entity integrity rules by using:

```
PRIMARY KEY (V_CODE)
```

As you look at the PRODUCT table's CREATE TABLE sequence, note that referential integrity has been enforced by specifying in the PRODUCT table:

```
FOREIGN KEY (V_CODE) REFERENCES VENDOR ON UPDATE CASCADE
```

That foreign key constraint definition ensures that:

- You cannot delete a vendor from the VENDOR table if at least one product row references that vendor. This is the default behaviour for the treatment of foreign keys.
- On the other hand, if a change is made in an existing VENDOR table's V_CODE, that change must be reflected automatically in any PRODUCT table V_CODE reference (ON UPDATE CASCADE).
  That restriction makes it impossible for a V_CODE value to exist in the PRODUCT table pointing to a non-existent VENDOR table V_CODE value. In other words, the ON UPDATE CASCADE specification ensures the preservation of referential integrity. (Oracle does not support ON UPDATE CASCADE.)

Online Content For a more detailed discussion of the options for the ON DELETE and ON UPDATE clauses, see Appendix D, Converting an ER Model into a Database Structure, Section D.2, General Rules Governing Relationships Among Tables. Appendix D is available to download on the online platform for this book.

NOTE ABOUT REFERENTIAL CONSTRAINT ACTIONS

The support for the referential constraint actions varies from product to product. For example:

- MySQL, SQL Server and Oracle support ON DELETE CASCADE.
- MySQL and SQL Server support ON UPDATE CASCADE.
- Oracle does not support ON UPDATE CASCADE.
- Oracle supports SET NULL.
- MySQL and SQL Server do not support SET NULL.
- Refer to your product manuals for additional information on referential constraints.

While MySQL does not support ON DELETE CASCADE or ON UPDATE CASCADE at the SQL command-line level, it does support them through the relationship window interface. In fact, whenever you try to establish a relationship between two tables in Access, the relationship window interface automatically pops up.

In general, ANSI SQL permits the use of ON DELETE and ON UPDATE clauses to cover any of the following actions: CASCADE, SET NULL or SET DEFAULT.

Besides the PRIMARY KEY and FOREIGN KEY constraints, the ANSI SQL standard also defines the following constraints:

- The NOT NULL constraint is used to ensure that a column does not accept nulls.
- The UNIQUE constraint is used to ensure that all values in a column are unique.
- The DEFAULT constraint is used to assign a value to an attribute when a new row is added to a table. The end user may, of course, enter a value other than the default value.
- The CHECK constraint is used to validate data when an attribute value is entered. The CHECK constraint does precisely what its name suggests: it checks to see that a specified condition exists. Examples of such constraints include the following:
  - *The minimum order value must be at least ten.*
  - *The date must be after 15 April 2019.*

If the CHECK constraint is met for the specified attribute (that is, the condition is true), the data are accepted for that attribute. If the condition is found to be false, an error message is generated and the data are not accepted.

Note that the CREATE TABLE command lets you define constraints in two different places:

- When you create the column definition (known as a *column constraint*).
- When you use the CONSTRAINT keyword (known as a *table constraint*).

A column constraint applies to just one column; a table constraint may apply to many columns. Those constraints are supported at varying levels of compliance by enterprise RDBMSs.

In this chapter, Oracle is used to illustrate SQL constraints. For example, note that the following SQL command sequence uses the DEFAULT and CHECK constraints to define the table named CUSTOMER.

```
CREATE TABLE CUSTOMER (
CUS_CODE        NUMBER                  PRIMARY KEY,
CUS_LNAME       VARCHAR(15)             NOT NULL,
CUS_FNAME       VARCHAR(15)             NOT NULL,
CUS_INITIAL     CHAR(1),
CUS_AREACODE    CHAR(5)                 DEFAULT '0181' NOT NULL
                CHECK(CUS_AREACODE IN
                ('0181','0161','7253')),
CUS_PHONE       CHAR(12)                NOT NULL,
CUS_BALANCE     NUMBER(9,2)             DEFAULT 0.00,
CONSTRAINT CUS_UI1 UNIQUE (CUS_LNAME, CUS_FNAME));
```


In that case, the CUS_AREACODE attribute is assigned a default value of '0181'. Therefore, if a new CUSTOMER table row is added and the end user makes no entry for the area code, the '0181' value is recorded. Also note that the CHECK condition restricts the values for the customer's area code to 0181, 0161 and 7253; any other values are rejected.

It is important to note that the DEFAULT value applies only when new rows are added to a table and then only when no value is entered for the customer's area code. (The default value is not used when the table is modified.) In contrast, the CHECK condition is validated whether a customer row is added *or modified*. However, while the CHECK condition may include any valid expression, it applies only to the attributes in the table being checked. If you want to check for conditions that include attributes in other tables, you must use triggers. (See Chapter 9, Procedural Language SQL and Advanced SQL.) Finally, the last line of the CREATE TABLE command sequence creates a unique index constraint (named CUS_UI1) on the customer's last name and first name. The index prevents the entry of two customers with the same last name and first name. (This index merely illustrates the process. Clearly, it should be possible to have more than one person named John Smith in the CUSTOMER table.)

NOTE TO MICROSOFT ACCESS USERS

Microsoft Access will not accept the DEFAULT or CHECK constraints. However, Microsoft Access will accept the CONSTRAINT CUS_UI1 UNIQUE (CUS_LNAME, CUS_FNAME) line and create the unique index.

In the following SQL command to create the INVOICE table, the DEFAULT constraint assigns a default date to a new invoice and the CHECK constraint validates that the invoice date is greater than 1 January 2019.

```
CREATE TABLE INVOICE (
INV_NUMBER          NUMBER          PRIMARY KEY,
CUS_CODE            NUMBER          NOT NULL REFERENCES
```

```
                    CUSTOMER(CUS_CODE),
INV_DATE            DATE            DEFAULT SYSDATE NOT NULL,
CONSTRAINT INV_CK1 CHECK (INV_DATE > TO_DATE('01-JAN-2019','DD-MON-YYYY')));
```

In this case, notice the following:

- The CUS_CODE attribute definition contains REFERENCES CUSTOMER (CUS_CODE) to indicate that the CUS_CODE is a foreign key. This is another way to define a foreign key.
- The DEFAULT constraint uses the SYSDATE special function. This function always returns today's date.
- The invoice date (INV_DATE) attribute is automatically given today's date (returned by SYSDATE) when a new row is added and no value is given for the attribute.
- A CHECK constraint is used to validate that the invoice date is greater than '1 January 2019'. When comparing a date to a manually entered date in a CHECK clause, Oracle requires the use of the TO_DATE function. The TO_DATE function takes two parameters, the literal date and the date format used.

The final SQL command sequence creates the LINE table. The LINE table has a composite primary key (INV_NUMBER, LINE_NUMBER) and uses a UNIQUE constraint in INV_NUMBER and P_CODE to ensure that the same product is not ordered twice in the same invoice.

```
CREATE TABLE LINE (
INV_NUMBER          NUMBER                      NOT NULL,
LINE_NUMBER         NUMBER(2,0)                 NOT NULL,
P_CODE              VARCHAR(10)                 NOT NULL,
LINE_UNITS          NUMBER(9,2) DEFAULT 0.00    NOT NULL,
LINE_PRICE          NUMBER(9,2) DEFAULT 0.00    NOT NULL,
PRIMARY KEY (INV_NUMBER,LINE_NUMBER),
FOREIGN KEY (INV_NUMBER) REFERENCES INVOICE ON DELETE CASCADE,
FOREIGN KEY (P_CODE) REFERENCES PRODUCT(P_CODE),
CONSTRAINT LINE_UI1 UNIQUE(INV_NUMBER, P_CODE));
```

In the creation of the LINE table, note that a UNIQUE constraint is added to prevent the duplication of an invoice line. A UNIQUE constraint is enforced through the creation of a unique index. Also note that the ON DELETE CASCADE foreign key action enforces referential integrity. The use of ON DELETE CASCADE is recommended for weak entities to ensure that the deletion of a row in the strong entity automatically triggers the deletion of the corresponding rows in the dependent weak entity. In that case, the deletion of an INVOICE row automatically deletes all of the LINE rows related to the invoice. In the following section, you will learn more about indexes and how to use SQL commands to create them.

NOTE

The current release of MySQL is currently 8.0, The community edition of InnoDB storage engine was integrated as the default storage engine for tables created with MySQL. This meant that the MySQL Data Manipulation Language (DML) operations followed the standard ACID (Atomicity, Consistency, Isolation and Durability) properties of database transactions in line with other major RDBMS such as Oracle. (ACID properties will be covered in more detail in Chapter 12, Managing Transactions and Concurrency.)

MySQL maintains data integrity through the InnoDB engine by supporting FOREIGN KEY constraints. This ensures that consistency is maintained across all tables when data is inserted, updated or deleted.

To summarise, MySQL version 8.0 (and beyond) supports the following SQL constraints:

- UNIQUE
- PRIMARY KEY
- FOREIGN KEY

It is important to note that the CHECK constraint can actually be added when a table is created, but it has no effect when data is actually entered into the table. Currently, CHECK is not supported.

Consider the CUSTOMER table that has been created in this section using Oracle SQL. Below is the corresponding MySQL command sequence to create the CUSTOMER table:

```
CREATE TABLE CUSTOMER (
CUS_CODE INTEGER PRIMARY KEY,
CUS_LNAME VARCHAR(15) NOT NULL,
CUS_FNAME VARCHAR(15) NOT NULL,
CUS_INITIAL CHAR(1),
CUS_AREACODE CHAR(5) NOT NULL DEFAULT '0181',
CUS_PHONE CHAR(12) NOT NULL,
CUS_BALANCE NUMBER(9,2) NOT NULL DEFAULT 0.00,
UNIQUE (CUS_LNAME, CUS_FNAME));
```

8

8.2.7 SQL Indexes

You learnt in Chapter 3, Relational Model Characteristics, that indexes can be used to improve the efficiency of searches and to avoid duplicate column values. In the previous section, you saw how to declare unique indexes on selected attributes when the table is created. In fact, when you declare a primary key, the DBMS automatically creates a unique index. Even with this feature, you often need additional indexes. The ability to create indexes quickly and efficiently is important. Using the **CREATE INDEX** command, SQL indexes can be created on the basis of any selected attribute. The syntax is:

CREATE [UNIQUE] INDEX *indexname* ON *tablename*(*column1* [, *column2*])

For example, based on the attribute P_INDATE stored in the PRODUCT table, the following command creates an index named P_INDATEX:

```
CREATE INDEX P_INDATEX ON PRODUCT(P_INDATE);
```

SQL does not let you overwrite an existing index without warning you first, thus preserving the index structure within the data dictionary. Using the UNIQUE index qualifier, you can even create an index that prevents you from using a value that has been used before. Such a feature is especially useful when the index attribute is a primary key (PK) whose values must not be duplicated:

```
CREATE UNIQUE INDEX P_CODEX ON PRODUCT(P_CODE);
```

If you now try to enter a duplicate P_CODE value, SQL produces the error message 'duplicate value in index'. Many RDBMSs, including Access, automatically create a unique index on the PK attribute(s) when you declare the PK.

A common practice is to create an index on any field that is used as a search key or in comparison operations in a conditional expression, or when you want to list rows in a specific order. For example, if you want to create a report of all products by vendor, it would be useful to create an index on the V_CODE attribute in the PRODUCT table. Remember that a vendor can supply many products. Therefore, you should *not* create a UNIQUE index in this case. Better yet, to make the search as efficient as possible, a composite index is recommended.

Unique composite indexes are often used to prevent data duplication. For example, consider the case illustrated in Table 8.6, in which required employee test scores are stored. (An employee can take a test only once on a given date.) Given the structure of Table 8.6, the PK is EMP_NUM + TEST_NUM. The third test entry for employee 111 meets entity integrity requirements – the combination 111,3 is unique – yet the WEA test entry is clearly duplicated.

TABLE 8.6 A duplicated test record

EMP_NUM	TEST_NUM	TEST_CODE	TEST_DATE	TEST_SCORE
110	1	WEA	15-May-2018	93
110	2	WEA	12-May-2018	87
111	1	HAZ	14-Dec-2018	91
111	2	WEA	18-Feb-2019	95
111	3	WEA	18-Feb-2019	95
112	1	CHEM	17-Aug-2018	91

Such duplication could have been avoided through the use of a unique composite index, using the attributes EMP_NUM, TEST_CODE and TEST_DATE:

```
CREATE UNIQUE INDEX EMP_TESTDEX ON TEST(EMP_NUM, TEST_CODE, TEST_DATE);
```

By default, all indexes produce results that are listed in ascending order, but you can create an index that yields output in descending order. For example, if you routinely print a report that lists all products ordered by price from highest to lowest, you could create an index named PROD_PRICEX by typing:

```
CREATE INDEX PROD_PRICEX ON PRODUCT(P_PRICE DESC);
```

To delete an index, use the **DROP INDEX** command:

DROP INDEX *indexname*

For example, if you want to eliminate the PROD_PRICEX index, type:

```
DROP INDEX PROD_PRICEX;
```

After creating the tables and some indexes, you are ready to start entering data. The following sections use two tables (VENDOR and PRODUCT) to demonstrate most of the data manipulation commands.

8.3 DATA MANIPULATION COMMANDS

In this section, you will learn how to use the basic SQL data manipulation commands INSERT, SELECT, COMMIT, UPDATE, ROLLBACK and DELETE.

8

8

8.3.1 Adding Table Rows

SQL requires the use of the **INSERT** command to enter data into a table. The INSERT command's basic syntax looks like this:

INSERT INTO *tablename* VALUES (*value1, value2, ... , valuen*)

Because the PRODUCT table uses its V_CODE to reference the VENDOR table's V_CODE, an integrity violation occurs if those VENDOR table V_CODE values don't yet exist. Therefore, you need to enter the VENDOR rows before the PRODUCT rows. Given the VENDOR table structure defined earlier and the sample VENDOR data shown in Figure 8.2, you would enter the first two data rows as follows:

```
INSERT INTO VENDOR

VALUES (21225,'Bryson, Inc.','Smithson','0181','223-3234','UK','Y');

INSERT INTO VENDOR

VALUES (21226,'Superloo, Inc.','Flushing','0113','215-8995','SA','N');
```

and so on, until all of the VENDOR table records have been entered.

(To see the contents of the VENDOR table, type SELECT * FROM VENDOR;)

Enter the PRODUCT table rows in the same fashion, using the PRODUCT data shown in Figure 8.2. For example, the first two data rows would be entered as follows, pressing Enter at the end of each line:

```
INSERT INTO PRODUCT

VALUES ('11QER/31','Power painter, 15 psi., 3-nozzle','03-Nov-18',8,5,109.99,0.00,25595);

INSERT INTO PRODUCT

VALUES ('13-Q2/P2','7.25-in. pwr. saw blade','13-Dec-18',32,15,14.99, 0.05, 21344);
```

(To see the contents of the PRODUCT table, type: SELECT * FROM PRODUCT;)

NOTE

Date entry is a function of the date format expected by the DBMS. For example, 25 March 2019 might be shown as 25-Mar-2019 in Microsoft Access and Oracle or in other presentation formats depending on your RDBMS. In MySQL, the default date format would be 2019-03-25, for example. Microsoft Access requires the use of # delimiters when performing any computations or comparisons based on date attributes, as in P_INDATE >= #25-Mar-19#.

As you examine the preceding data entry lines, observe that:

- The row contents are entered between parentheses. Note that the first character after VALUES is a parenthesis and that the last character in the command sequence is also a parenthesis.
- Character (string) and date values must be entered between apostrophes (').
- Numerical entries are *not* enclosed in apostrophes.
- Attribute entries are separated by commas.
- A value is required for each column in the table.

This version of the INSERT commands adds one table row at a time.

Inserting Rows with Null Attributes

Thus far, you have entered rows in which all of the attribute values are specified. But what do you do if a product does not have a vendor or if you don't yet know the vendor code? In those cases, you want to leave the vendor code null. To enter a null, use the following syntax:

```
INSERT INTO PRODUCT
VALUES ('BRT-345','Titanium drill bit','18-Oct-18', 75, 10, 4.50, 0.06, NULL);
```

Incidentally, note that the NULL entry is accepted only because the V_CODE attribute is optional – the NOT NULL declaration was not used in the CREATE TABLE statement for this attribute.

Inserting Rows with Optional Attributes

There may be occasions when more than one attribute is optional. Rather than declaring each attribute as NULL in the INSERT command, you can indicate just the attributes that have required values. You do that by listing the attribute names inside parentheses after the table name. For the purpose of this example, assume that the only required attributes for the PRODUCT table are P_CODE and P_DESCRIPT:

```
INSERT INTO PRODUCT(P_CODE, P_DESCRIPT) VALUES ('BRT-345','Titanium drill bit');
```


8.3.2 Saving Table Changes

Any changes made to the table contents are not physically saved on disk until you close the database, close the program you are using, or use the **COMMIT** command. If you are using the database and a power outage or some other interruption occurs before you issue the COMMIT command, your changes are lost and only the original table contents are retained. The syntax for the COMMIT command is:

```
COMMIT [WORK]
```

The COMMIT command will permanently save *any* changes – such as rows added, attributes modified, and rows deleted – made to any table in the database. Therefore, if you intend to make your changes to the PRODUCT table permanent, it is a good idea to save those changes by using:

```
COMMIT;
```

NOTE TO MICROSOFT ACCESS USERS

Microsoft Access doesn't support the COMMIT command. Access automatically saves changes after the execution of each SQL command.

NOTE TO MYSQL USERS

MySQL version 5.6 and onwards supports the use of the COMMIT command. When started, the storage engine defaults to the autocommit mode. As soon as any DML statement is executed that updates a table, MySQL automatically commits the transaction, making it permanent.

However, the COMMIT command's purpose is not just to save changes. In fact, the ultimate purpose of the COMMIT and ROLLBACK commands (see Section 8.3.5) is to ensure database update integrity in transaction management (You will see how such issues are addressed in Chapter 12, Managing Transactions and Concurrency.)

8.3.3 Listing Table Rows

Use the **SELECT** command to list the contents of a table. The syntax of the SELECT command is as follows:

SELECT *columnlist* FROM *tablename*

The *columnlist* represents one or more attributes, separated by commas. You could use the * (asterisk) as a wildcard character to list all attributes. (A **wildcard character** is a symbol that can be used as a general substitute for other characters or commands.) For example, to list all attributes and all rows of the PRODUCT table, use:

NOTE

The SELECT command is based on the relational operator SELECT, which was introduced in Chapter 4, Relational Algebra and Calculus. For example, the statement

```
SELECT * FROM PRODUCT;
```

Can be written in relational algebra as

σ *(PRODUCT)*

```
SELECT * FROM PRODUCT;
```

8

Figure 8.3 shows the output generated by that command. (Figure 8.3 shows all of the rows in the PRODUCT table that serve as the basis for subsequent discussions. If you entered only the PRODUCT table's first two records, as shown in the preceding section, the output of the preceding SELECT command would show only the rows you entered. Don't worry about the difference between your SELECT output and the output shown in Figure 8.3. When you complete the work in this section, you will have created and populated your VENDOR and PRODUCT tables with the correct rows for use in future sections.)

NOTE

Your listing may not be in the order shown in Figure 8.3. The listings shown in the figure are the result of system-controlled primary-key-based index operations. You will learn later how to control the output so that it conforms to the order you have specified.

FIGURE 8.3 The contents of the PRODUCT table

P_CODE	P_DESCRIPT	P_INDATE	P_QOH	P_MIN	P_PRICE	P_DISCOUNT	V_CODE
11QER/31	Power painter, 15 psi., 3-nozzle	03-Nov-18	8	5	109.99	0.00	25595
13-Q2/P2	7.25 cm pwr. saw blade	13-Dec-18	32	15	14.99	0.05	21344
14-Q1/L3	9.00 cm pwr. saw blade	13-Nov-18	18	12	17.49	0.00	21344
1546-QQ2	Hrd. cloth, 1/4 cm, 2 × 50	15-Jan-19	15	8	39.95	0.00	23119
1558-QW1	Hrd. cloth, 1/2 cm, 3 × 50	15-Jan-19	23	5	43.99	0.00	23119
2232/QTY	B&D jigsaw, 12 cm blade	30-Dec-18	8	5	109.92	0.05	24288
2232/QWE	B&D jigsaw, 8 cm blade	24-Dec-18	6	5	99.87	0.05	24288
2238/QPD	B&D cordless drill, 1/2 cm	20-Jan-19	12	5	38.95	0.05	25595
23109-HB	Claw hammer	20-Jan-19	23	10	9.95	0.10	21225
23114-AA	Sledge hammer, 12 kg	02-Jan-19	8	5	14.40	0.05	
54778-2T	Rat-tail file, 1/8 cm fine	15-Dec-18	43	20	4.99	0.00	21344
89-WRE-Q	Hicut chain saw, 16 cm	07-Feb-19	11	5	256.99	0.05	24288
PVC23DRT	PVC pipe, 3.5 cm, 8 m	20-Feb-19	188	75	5.87	0.00	
SM-18277	1.25 cm metal screw, 25	01-Mar-19	172	75	6.99	0.00	21225
SW-23116	2.5 cm wd. screw, 50	24-Feb-19	237	100	8.45	0.00	21231
WR3/TT3	Steel matting, 4 m × 8 m × 1/6 m, .5 m mesh	17-Jan-19	18	5	119.95	0.10	25595

NOTE TO ORACLE USERS

Some SQL implementations (such as Oracle) cut the attribute labels to fit the width of the column. However, Oracle lets you set the width of the display column to show the complete attribute name. You can also change the display format, regardless of how the data are stored in the table. For example, if you want to display the euro symbols and commas in the P_PRICE output, you can declare:

```
COLUMN P_PRICE FORMAT €99,999.99
```

to change the output 12347.67 to €12,347.67.

In the same manner, to display only the first 12 characters of the P_DESCRIPT attribute, use:

```
COLUMN P_DESCRIPT FORMAT A12 TRUNCATE
```

Although SQL commands can be grouped together on a single line, complex command sequences are best shown on separate lines, with space between the SQL command and the command's components. Using that formatting convention makes it much easier to see the components of the SQL statements, making it easy to trace the SQL logic and, if necessary, to make corrections. The number of spaces used in the indention is up to you. For example, note the following format for a more complex statement:

```
SELECT      P_CODE, P_DESCRIPT, P_INDATE, P_QOH, P_MIN, P_PRICE, P_DISCOUNT,
            V_CODE
FROM        PRODUCT;
```

When you run a SELECT command on a table, the RDBMS returns a set of one or more rows that have the same characteristics as a relational table. In addition, the SELECT command lists all rows from the table you specified in the FROM clause. This is a very important characteristic of SQL commands. By default, most SQL data manipulation commands operate over an entire table (or relation). That is why SQL commands are said to be *set-orientated* commands. A SQL set-orientated command works over a set of rows. The set may include one or more columns and zero or more rows from one or more tables.

8.3.4 Updating Table Rows

Use the **UPDATE** command to modify data in a table. The syntax for this command is:

UPDATE *tablename*

SET *columnname* = *expression* [, *columnname* = *expression*]

[WHERE *conditionlist*];

For example, if you want to change P_INDATE from 13 December 2018 to 18 January 2019 in the second row of the PRODUCT table (see Figure 8.3), use the primary key (13-Q2/P2) to locate the correct (second) row. Therefore, type:

```
UPDATE      PRODUCT
SET         P_INDATE = '18-JAN-2019'
WHERE       P_CODE = '13-Q2/P2';
```

If more than one attribute is to be updated in the row, separate the corrections with commas:

```
UPDATE      PRODUCT
SET         P_INDATE = '18-JAN-2019', P_PRICE = 17.99, P_MIN = 10
WHERE       P_CODE = '13-Q2/P2';
```

What would have happened if the previous UPDATE command had not included the WHERE condition? Answer: The P_INDATE, P_PRICE and P_MIN values would have been changed in *all* rows of the PRODUCT table. Remember, the UPDATE command is a set-oriented operator. Therefore, if you don't specify a WHERE condition, the UPDATE command applies the changes to *all* rows in the specified table.

Confirm the correction(s) by using this command to check the PRODUCT table's listing:

```
SELECT      *       FROM    PRODUCT;
```

8.3.5 Restoring Table Contents

If you have not yet used the COMMIT command to store the changes permanently in the database, you can restore the database to its previous condition with the **ROLLBACK** command. ROLLBACK undoes any changes and brings the data back to the values that existed before the changes were made. To restore the data to their 'prechange' condition, type:

```
ROLLBACK;
```

and press Enter. Use the SELECT statement again to see that the ROLLBACK did, in fact, restore the data to their original values. The COMMIT and ROLLBACK commands are examined in greater detail in Chapter 9.

COMMIT and ROLLBACK work only with data manipulation commands that are used to add, modify or delete table rows. For example, assume that you perform these actions:

- CREATE a table called SALES.
- INSERT ten rows in the SALES table.
- UPDATE two rows in the SALES table.
- Execute the ROLLBACK command.

Will the SALES table be removed by the ROLLBACK command? No, the ROLLBACK command will undo *only* the results of the INSERT and UPDATE commands. All data definition commands (CREATE TABLE) are automatically committed to the data dictionary and cannot be rolled back.

NOTE TO MICROSOFT ACCESS USERS

Microsoft Access doesn't support the ROLLBACK command. The lack of commands such as ROLLBACK, COMMIT, etc. illustrates one of the key differences between Microsoft Access and enterprise databases such as MySQL and Oracle. Enterprise databases are designed to support large multi-user environments and need to have robust data integrity controls.

8

Some RDBMSs, such as Oracle, automatically COMMIT data changes when issuing data definition commands. For example, if you had used the CREATE INDEX command after updating the two rows in the previous example, all previous changes would have been committed automatically; doing a ROLLBACK afterwards wouldn't have undone anything. *Check your RDBMS manual to understand these subtle differences.*

8.3.6 Deleting Table Rows

It is easy to delete a table row using the **DELETE** statement; the syntax is:

DELETE FROM *tablename*

[WHERE*conditionlist*];

For example, if you want to delete from the PRODUCT table the product that you added earlier whose product code (P_CODE) is 'BRT-345', use:

DELETE FROM PRODUCT WHERE P_CODE = 'BRT-345';

In that example, the primary key value lets SQL find the exact record to be deleted. However, deletions are not limited to a primary key match; any attribute may be used. For example, if you examine your PRODUCT table you will see that there are several products for which the P_MIN attribute is equal to 5. Use the following command to delete all rows from the PRODUCT table for which the P_MIN is equal to 5:

DELETE FROM PRODUCT WHERE P_MIN = 5;

Check the PRODUCT table's contents again to verify that all products with P_MIN equal to 5 have been deleted.

Finally, remember that DELETE is a set-oriented command. And keep in mind that the WHERE condition is optional. Therefore, if you do not specify a WHERE condition, *all* rows from the specified table are deleted!

8.3.7 Inserting Table Rows with a Select Subquery

You learnt in Section 8.3.1 how to use the INSERT statement to add rows to a table. In that section, you added rows one at a time. In this section, you learn how to add multiple rows to a table, using another table as the source of the data. The syntax for the INSERT statement is:

INSERT INTO *tablename* SELECT *columnlist* FROM *tablename*;

In that case, the INSERT statement uses a SELECT subquery. A **subquery**, also known as a *nested query* or an *inner query*, is a query that is embedded (or nested) inside another query. The inner query is always executed first by the RDBMS. Given the previous SQL statement, the INSERT portion represents the outer query and the SELECT portion represents the inner query or subquery. You can nest queries (place queries inside queries) many levels deep; in every case, the output of the inner (lower-level) query is used as the input for the outer (higher-level) query. In Chapter 9, Procedural Language SQL and Advanced SQL, you will learn more about the different types of subqueries.

The values returned by the SELECT subquery should match the attributes and data types of the table in the INSERT statement. If the table into which you are inserting rows has one date attribute, one number attribute and one character attribute, the SELECT subquery should return one or more rows in which the first column has date values, the second column has number values and the third column has character values.

8

Populating the VENDOR and PRODUCT Tables

The following steps guide you through the process of populating the VENDOR and PRODUCT tables with the data to be used in the rest of the chapter. To accomplish that task, two tables named V and P are used as the data source. V and P have the same table structure (attributes) as the VENDOR and PRODUCT tables.

Online Content The following sections assume that the database has been restored to its original condition. Therefore, you *must* do the following:

- If you are using Oracle or MySQL, run the **sqlintrodbinit.sql** script file located in either the MySQL or Oracle folder hosted on the online platform, to create all tables and load the data in the database. To connect to the database, follow the instructions specific to your school setup provided by your instructor.
- If you are using Microsoft Access, copy the original 'Ch08_SaleCo.mdb' file available to download from the online platform for this book.

Use the following steps to populate your VENDOR and PRODUCT tables. (If you haven't already created the PRODUCT and VENDOR tables to practise the SQL commands in the previous sections, do so before completing these steps.)

- Delete all rows from the PRODUCT and VENDOR tables.
  - DELETE FROM PRODUCT;
  - DELETE FROM VENDOR;
- Add the rows to VENDOR by copying all rows from V.
  - If you are using Microsoft Access, type: INSERT INTO VENDOR SELECT * FROM V;
  - If you are using Oracle or MySQL, type: INSERT INTO VENDOR SELECT * FROM TEACHER.V;
- Add the rows to PRODUCT by copying all rows from P.
  - If you are using Microsoft Access, type: INSERT INTO PRODUCT SELECT * FROM P;
  - If you are using Oracle or MySQL, type: INSERT INTO PRODUCT SELECT * FROM TEACHER.P;
- Oracle users must permanently save the changes: COMMIT;

If you followed those steps correctly, you now have the VENDOR and PRODUCT tables populated with the data that are used in the remaining sections of the chapter.

Online Content If you are using Oracle or MySQL, you can run the **sqlintrodbinit.sql** script file located in either the MySQL or Oracle folder hosted on the online platform to create all tables and load the data in the database. This script file populates the remaining tables (CUSTOMER, INVOICE, LINE, EMP and EMPLOYEE). To connect to the database, follow the instructions specific to your college or university setup provided by your instructor.

8.4 SELECT QUERIES

In this section, you will learn how to fine-tune the SELECT command by adding restrictions to the search criteria. SELECT, coupled with appropriate search conditions, is an incredibly powerful tool that enables you to transform data into information. For example, in the following sections, you learn how to create queries that can be used to answer questions such as these: 'Which products were supplied by a particular vendor?', 'Which products are priced below €10?', 'How many products supplied by a given vendor were sold between 5 January 2019 and 20 March 2019?'

8.4.1 Selecting Rows with Conditional Restrictions

You can select partial table contents by placing restrictions on the rows to be included in the output. To do this, add conditional restrictions to the SELECT statement, using the WHERE clause. The following syntax enables you to specify which rows to select:

SELECT *columnlist*
FROM *tablelist*
[WHERE *conditionlist*];

The SELECT statement retrieves all rows that match the specified condition(s) – also known as the *conditional criteria* – you specified in the WHERE clause. The *conditionlist* in the WHERE clause of the SELECT statement is represented by one or more conditional expressions separated by logical operators. The WHERE clause is optional. If no rows match the specified criteria in the WHERE clause, you may see a blank screen or a message that tells you that no rows were retrieved. For example, the query:

```
SELECT    P_DESCRIPT, P_INDATE, P_PRICE, V_CODE
FROM      PRODUCT
WHERE     V_CODE = 21344;
```

returns the description, date, and price of products with a vendor code of 21344, as shown in Figure 8.4.

FIGURE 8.4 Selected PRODUCT table attributes for vendor code 21344

P_DESCRIPT	P_PRICE	V_CODE
7.25 cm pwr. saw blade	14.99	21344
9.00 cm pwr. saw blade	17.49	21344
Rat-tail file, 1/8-in. fine	4.99	21344

8

NOTE

The query:

```
SELECT    P_DESCRIPT, P_INDATE, P_PRICE, V_CODE
FROM      PRODUCT
WHERE     V_CODE = 21344;
```

comprises both the SELECT and PROJECT relational algebra operators and can be written in relational algebra as:

$$\Pi_{p\_descript,\ p\_indate,\ p\_price,\ v\_code}(\sigma_{v\_code\ =\ 21344}(PRODUCT))$$

For more information on the SELECT and PROJECT operators, see Sections 4.1.1 and 4.1.2 in Chapter 4, Relational Algebra and Calculus.

Microsoft Access users can use the Access QBE (query by example) query generator. Although the Access QBE generates its own 'native' version of SQL, you can also choose to type standard SQL in the Access SQL window, as shown at the bottom of Figure 8.5. Figure 8.5 shows the Access QBE screen, the SQL window's QBE-generated SQL, and the listing of the modified SQL.

NOTE TO MICROSOFT ACCESS USERS

The Microsoft Access QBE interface automatically designates the data source by using the table name as a prefix. You will discover later that the table name prefix is used to avoid ambiguity when the same column name appears in multiple tables. For example, both the VENDOR and the PRODUCT tables contain the V_CODE attribute. Therefore, if both tables are used as they would be in a join, the source of the V_CODE attribute must be specified.

FIGURE 8.5 The Microsoft Access QBE and its SQL

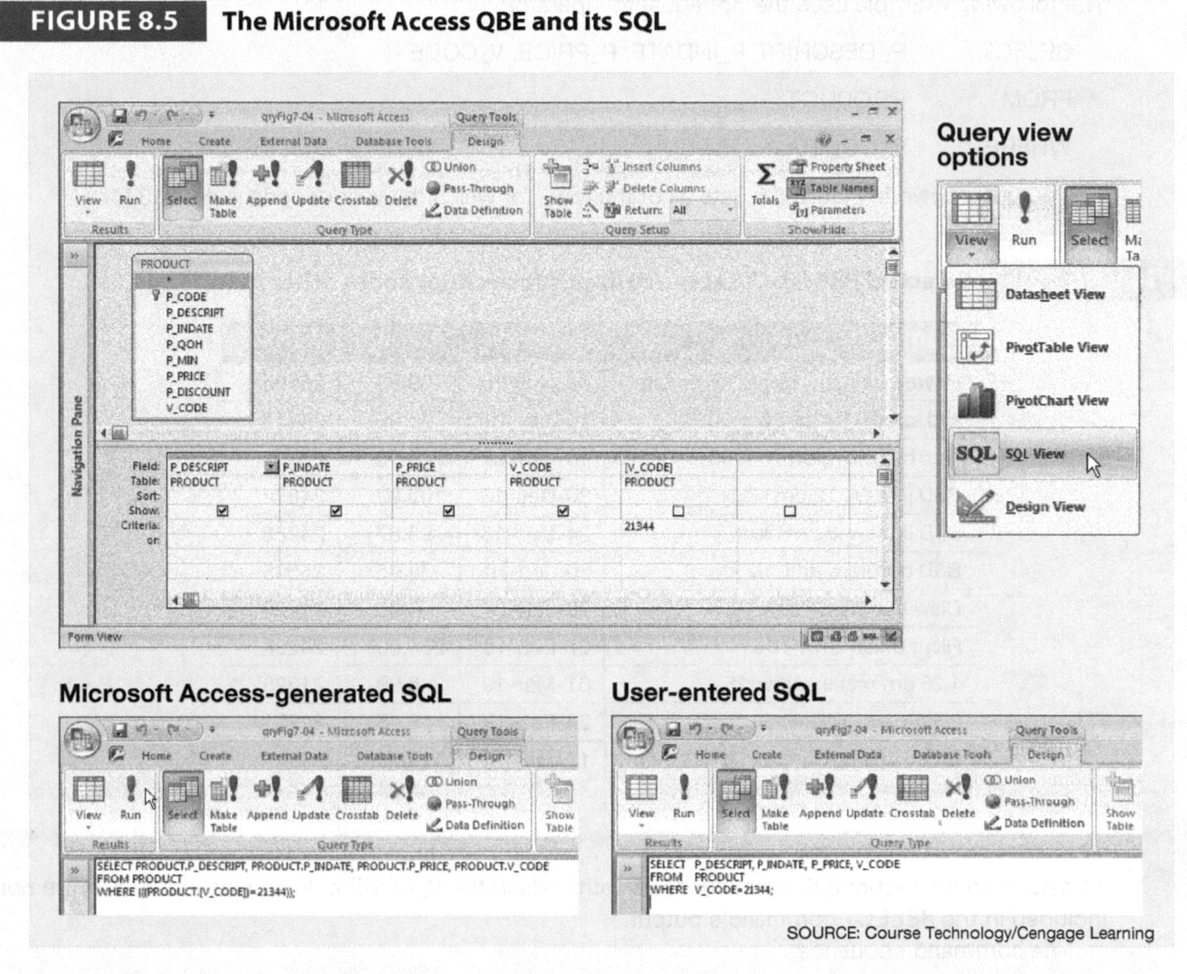

SOURCE: Course Technology/Cengage Learning

Numerous conditional restrictions can be placed on the selected table contents. For example, use the comparison operators shown in Table 8.7 to restrict output.

TABLE 8.7 Comparison operators

Symbol	Meaning
=	Equal to
<	Less than
<=	Less than or equal to
>	Greater than
>=	Greater than or equal to
<> or !=	Not equal to

The following example uses the 'not equal to' operator:

```
SELECT    P_DESCRIPT, P_INDATE, P_PRICE, V_CODE
FROM      PRODUCT
WHERE     V_CODE <> 21344;
```

The output, shown in Figure 8.6, lists all of the rows for which the vendor code is *not* 21344.

FIGURE 8.6 Selected PRODUCT table attributes for vendor codes other than 21344

P_DESCRIPT	P_INDATE	P_PRICE	V_CODE
Power painter, 15 psi., 3-nozzle	03-Nov-18	109.99	25595
Hrd. cloth, 1/4 cm, 2 × 50	15-Jan-19	39.95	23119
Hrd. cloth, 1/2 cm, 3 × 50	15-Jan-19	43.99	23119
B&D jigsaw, 12 cm blade	30-Dec-18	109.92	24288
B&D jigsaw, 3 cm blade	24-Dec-18	99.87	24288
B&D cordless drill, 1/2 cm	20-Jan-19	38.95	25595
Claw hammer	20-Jan-19	9.95	21225
Hicut chain saw, 16 cm	07-Feb-19	256.99	24288
1.25 cm metal screw, 25	01-Mar-19	6.99	21225
2.5 cm wd. screw, 50	24-Feb-19	8.45	21231
Steel matting, 4 × 8 × 1/6 × 5 cm mesh	17-Jan-19	119.95	25595

8

As you examine Figure 8.6, note that rows with nulls in the V_CODE column (see Figure 8.3) are not included in the SELECT command's output.

The command sequence:

```
SELECT    P_DESCRIPT, P_QOH, P_MIN, P_PRICE
FROM      PRODUCT
WHERE     P_PRICE <= 10;
```

yields the output shown in Figure 8.7.

FIGURE 8.7 Selected PRODUCT table attributes with a P_PRICE restriction

P_DESCRIPT	P_QOH	P_MIN	P_PRICE
Claw hammer	23	10	9.95
Rat-tail file, 1/8 cm fine	43	20	4.99
PVC pipe, 3.5 cm, 8 m	188	75	5.87
1.25 cm metal screw, 25	172	75	6.99
2.5 cm wd. screw, 50	237	100	8.45

Using Comparison Operators on Character Attributes

Because computers identify all characters by their (numeric) American Standard Code for Information Interchange (ASCII) codes, comparison operators may even be used to place restrictions on character-based attributes. Therefore, the command:

```
SELECT    P_CODE, P_DESCRIPT, P_QOH, P_MIN, P_PRICE
FROM      PRODUCT
WHERE     P_CODE < '1558-QW1';
```

would be correct and would yield a list of all rows in which the P_CODE is alphabetically less than 1558-QW1. (Because the ASCII code value for the letter *B* is greater than the value of the letter *A*, it follows that *A* is less than *B*.) Therefore, the output is generated as shown in Figure 8.8.

FIGURE 8.8 Selected PRODUCT table attributes; the ASCII code effect

P_CODE	P_DESCRIPT	P_QOH	P_MIN	P_PRICE
11QER/31	Power painter, 15 psi., 3-nozzle	8	5	109.99
13-Q2/P2	7.25 cm pwr. saw blade	32	15	14.99
14-Q1/L3	9.00 cm pwr. saw blade	18	12	17.49
1546-QQ2	Hrd. cloth, 1/4 cm, 2 × 50	15	8	39.95

8

String (character) comparisons are made from left to right. This left-to-right comparison is especially useful when attributes such as names are to be compared. For example, the string 'Ardmore' would be judged *greater than* the string 'Aarenson' but *less than* the string 'Brown'; use such results to generate alphabetical listings like those found in a phone directory. If the characters 0–9 are stored as strings, the same left-to-right string comparisons can lead to apparent anomalies. For example, the ASCII code for the character '5' is, as expected, *greater than* the ASCII code for the character '4'. Yet the same '5' will also be judged *greater than* the string '44' because the *first* character in the string '44' is less than the string '5'. For that reason, you may get some unexpected results from comparisons when dates or other numbers are stored in character format. For example, the left-to-right ASCII character comparison would force the conclusion that the date '01/01/2019' occurred *before* '12/31/2018'. Since the leftmost character '0' in '01/01/2019' is *less than* the leftmost character '1' in '12/31/2018', '01/01/2019' is *less than* '12/31/2018'. Naturally, if date strings are stored in a yyyy/mm/dd format, the comparisons will yield appropriate results, but this is a non-standard date presentation. That's why all current RDBMSs support 'date' data types, and that's why you should use them. In addition, using 'date' data types gives you the benefit of date arithmetic.

Using Comparison Operators on Dates

Date procedures are often more software specific than other SQL procedures. For example, the query to list all of the rows in which the inventory stock dates occur on or after 20 January, 2019, will look like this:

```
SELECT    P_DESCRIPT, P_QOH, P_MIN, P_PRICE, P_INDATE
FROM      PRODUCT
WHERE     P_INDATE >= '20-Jan-2019';
```

(Remember that Microsoft Access users must use the # delimiters for dates. For example, you would use #20-Jan-19# in the above WHERE clause). The date-restricted output is shown in Figure 8.9.

FIGURE 8.9 Selected PRODUCT table attributes: date restriction

P_DESCRIPT	P_QOH	P_MIN	P_PRICE	P_INDATE
B&D cordless drill, 1.25 cm	12	5	38.95	20-Jan-19
Claw hammer	23	10	9.95	20-Jan-19
Hicut chain saw, 40 cm	11	5	256.99	07-Feb-19
PVC pipe, 9 cm, 2.5 m	188	75	5.87	20-Feb-19
3 cm metal screw, 25	172	75	6.99	01-Mar-19
6 cm wd. screw, 50	237	100	8.45	24-Feb-19

Using Computed Columns and Column Aliases

Suppose you want to determine the total value of each of the products currently held in inventory. Logically, that determination requires the multiplication of each product's quantity on hand by its current price. You can accomplish this task with the following command:

```
SELECT    P_DESCRIPT, P_QOH, P_PRICE, P_QOH * P_PRICE
FROM      PRODUCT;
```

8

Entering that SQL command in Access generates the output shown in Figure 8.10.

FIGURE 8.10 SELECT statement with a computed Column in Access

P_DESCRIPT	P_QOH	P_PRICE	Expr1
Power painter, 15 psi., 3-nozzle	8	109.99	879.92
7.25-cm. pwr. saw blade	32	14.99	479.68
9.00-cm. pwr. saw blade	18	17.49	314.82
Hrd. cloth, 1/4-cm., 2x50	15	39.95	599.25
Hrd. cloth, 1/2-cm., 3x50	23	43.99	1011.77
B&D jigsaw, 12-cm. blade	8	109.92	879.36
B&D jigsaw, 8-cm. blade	6	99.87	599.22
B&D cordless drill, 1/2-cm.	12	38.95	467.40
Claw hammer	23	9.95	228.85
Sledge hammer, 6kg.	8	14.40	115.20
Rat-tail file, 1/8-cm. fine	43	4.99	214.57
Hicut chain saw, 16 cm.	11	256.99	2826.89
PVC pipe, 3.5-cm., 4m	188	5.87	1103.56
1.25-cm. metal screw, 25	172	6.99	1202.28
2.5-cm. wd. screw, 50	237	8.45	2002.65
Steel matting, 4x8x1/6, .5m mesh	18	119.95	2159.10
	0	0.00	

SQL accepts any valid expressions (or formulas) in the computed columns. Such formulas can contain any valid mathematical operators and functions that are applied to attributes in any of the tables specified in the FROM clause of the SELECT statement. Note also that Access automatically adds an Expr label to all computed columns. (The first computed column would be labelled Expr1; the second, Expr2; and so on.) Oracle uses the actual formula text as the label for the computed column.

To make the output more readable, the SQL standard permits the use of aliases for any column in a SELECT statement. An **alias** is an alternative name given to a column or table in any SQL statement. For example, you can rewrite the previous SQL statement as:

```
SELECT    P_DESCRIPT, P_QOH, P_PRICE, P_QOH * P_PRICE AS TOTVALUE
FROM      PRODUCT;
```

The output of that command is shown in Figure 8.11.

FIGURE 8.11 **SELECT statement with a computed column and an alias**

P_DESCRIPT	P_QOH	P_PRICE	TOTVALUE
Power painter, 15 psi., 3-nozzle	8	109.99	879.92
7.25 cm pwr. saw blade	32	14.99	479.68
9.00 cm pwr. saw blade	18	17.49	314.82
Hrd. cloth, 1/4 cm, 2 × 50	15	39.95	599.25
Hrd. cloth, 1/2 cm, 3 × 50	23	43.99	1011.77
B&D jigsaw, 12 cm blade	8	109.92	879.36
B&D jigsaw, 8 cm blade	6	99.87	599.22
B&D cordless drill, 1/2 cm	12	38.95	467.40
Claw hammer	23	9.95	228.85
Sledge hammer, 12 kg	8	14.40	115.20
Rat-tail file, 1/8 cm fine	43	4.99	214.57
Hicut chain saw, 16 cm	11	256.99	2826.89
PVC pipe, 3.5 cm, 8 m	188	5.87	1103.56
1.25 cm metal screw, 25	172	6.99	1202.28
2.5 cm wd. screw, 50	237	8.45	2002.65
Steel matting, 4 × 8 × 1/6 cm, .5 cm mesh	18	119.95	2159.10

You could also use a computed column, an alias and date arithmetic in a single query. For example, assume that you want to get a list of 'out-of-warranty' products that have been stored more than 90 days. In that case, the P_INDATE is at least 90 days less than the current (system) date. The Microsoft Access version of this query is shown as:

```
SELECT    P_CODE, P_INDATE, DATE() - 90 AS CUTDATE
FROM      PRODUCT
WHERE     P_INDATE <= DATE() - 90;
```

The Oracle version of the same query is shown below:

```
SELECT    P_CODE, P_INDATE, SYSDATE - 90 AS CUTDATE
FROM      PRODUCT
WHERE     P_INDATE <= SYSDATE - 90;
```

Note that DATE() and SYSDATE are special functions that return today's date in Microsoft Access and Oracle, respectively. You could use the DATE() and SYSDATE functions anywhere a date literal is expected, such as in the value list of an INSERT statement, in an UPDATE statement when changing

8

the value of a date attribute or in a SELECT statement as shown here. Of course, the previous query output changes based on today's date.

Suppose a manager wants a list of all products, the dates they were received and the warranty expiration date (90 days from when the product was received). To generate that list, type:

```
SELECT      P_CODE, P_INDATE, P_INDATE + 90 AS EXPDATE
FROM        PRODUCT;
```

Note that you can use all arithmetic operators with date attributes as well as with numeric attributes.

8.4.2 Arithmetic Operators: The Rule of Precedence

As you saw in the previous example, you can use arithmetic operators with table attributes in a column list or in a conditional expression. In fact, SQL commands are often used in conjunction with the arithmetic operators shown in Table 8.8.

TABLE 8.8 The arithmetic operators

Arithmetic Operator	Description
+	Add
−	Subtract
*	Multiply
/	Divide
^	Raise to the power of (some applications use ** instead of ^)

Do not confuse the multiplication symbol (*) with the wildcard symbol used by some SQL implementations such as Microsoft Access; the latter is used only in string comparisons, while the former is used in conjunction with mathematical procedures.

As you perform mathematical operations on attributes, remember the rules of precedence. As the name suggests, the **rules of precedence** are the rules that establish the order in which computations are completed. For example, note the order of the following computational sequence:

1. Perform operations within parentheses
2. Perform power operations
3. Perform multiplications and divisions
4. Perform additions and subtractions

The application of the rules of precedence will tell you that 8 + 2 * 5 = 8 + 10 = 18, but (8 + 2) * 5 = 10 * 5 = 50. Similarly, 4 + 5^2 * 3 = 4 + 25 * 3 = 79 but (4 + 5)^2 * 3 = 81 * 3 = 243, while the operation expressed by (4 + 5^2) * 3 yields the answer (4 + 25) * 3 = 29 * 3 = 87.

8.4.3 Logical Operators: And, Or, and Not

In the real world, a search of data normally involves multiple conditions. For example, when you are buying a new house, you look for a certain area, three bedrooms, two and a half bathrooms, two stories and so on. In the same way, SQL allows you to have multiple conditions in a query through the use of logical operators. The logical operators are AND, OR and NOT. For example, if you want a list of the table contents for either the V_CODE = 21344 **OR** the V_CODE = 24288, you can use the following command sequence:

```
SELECT    P_DESCRIPT, P_INDATE, P_PRICE, V_CODE
FROM      PRODUCT
WHERE     V_CODE = 21344 OR V_CODE = 24288;
```

That command generates the six rows shown in Figure 8.12 that match the logical restriction.

FIGURE 8.12 **Select PRODUCT table attributes: logical OR**

P_DESCRIPT	P_INDATE	P_PRICE	V_CODE
18 cm pwr. saw blade	13-Dec-18	14.99	21344
22 cm pwr. saw blade	13-Nov-18	17.49	21344
B&D jigsaw, 30 cm blade	30-Dec-18	109.92	24288
B&D jigsaw, 20 cm blade	24-Dec-18	99.87	24288
Rat-tail file, 0.3 cm fine	15-Dec-18	4.99	21344
Hicut chain saw, 40 cm	07-Feb-19	256.99	24288

The logical **AND** has the same SQL syntax requirement. The following command generates a list of all rows for which P_PRICE is less than €50 AND for which P_INDATE is a date occurring after 15 January 2019:

```
SELECT    P_DESCRIPT, P_INDATE, P_PRICE, V_CODE
FROM      PRODUCT
WHERE     P_PRICE < 50
AND P_INDATE > '15-Jan-2019';
```

This command produces the output shown in Figure 8.13.

FIGURE 8.13 **Select PRODUCT table attributes: logical AND**

P_DESCRIPT	P_INDATE	P_PRICE	V_CODE
B&D cordless drill, 1.25 cm	20-Jan-19	38.95	25595
Claw hammer	20-Jan-19	9.95	21225
PVC pipe, 9 cm, 2.5 m	20-Feb-19	5.87	
3 cm metal screw, 25	01-Mar-19	6.99	21225
6 cm wd. screw, 50	24-Feb-19	8.45	21231

You can combine the logical OR with the logical AND to place further restrictions on the output. For example, suppose you want a table listing for the following conditions:

- The P_INDATE is after 15 January 2019, and the P_PRICE is less than €50.
- Or the V_CODE is 24288.

To produce the required listing use:

```
SELECT      P_DESCRIPT, P_INDATE, P_PRICE, V_CODE
FROM        PRODUCT
WHERE       (P_PRICE < 50 AND P_INDATE > '15-Jan-2019')
            OR V_CODE = 24288;
```

Note the use of parentheses to combine logical restrictions. Where you place the parentheses depends on how you want the logical restrictions to be executed. Conditions listed within parentheses are always executed first. The preceding query yields the output shown in Figure 8.14.

FIGURE 8.14 Select PRODUCT table attributes: logical AND and OR

P_DESCRIPT	P_INDATE	P_PRICE	V_CODE
B&D jigsaw, 30 cm blade	30-Dec-18	109.92	24288
B&D jigsaw, 20 cm blade	24-Dec-18	99.87	24288
B&D cordless drill, 1.25 cm	20-Jan-19	38.95	25595
Claw hammer	20-Jan-19	9.95	21225
Hicut chain saw, 40 cm	07-Feb-19	256.99	24288
PVC pipe, 9 cm, 2.5 m	20-Feb-19	5.87	
3 cm metal screw, 25	01-Mar-19	6.99	21225
6 cm wd. screw, 50	24-Feb-19	8.45	21231

Note that the three rows with the V_CODE = 24288 are included regardless of the P_INDATE and P_PRICE entries for those rows.

The use of the logical operators OR and AND can become quite complex when numerous restrictions are placed on the query. In fact, a specialty field in mathematics known as **Boolean algebra** is dedicated to the use of logical operators.

The logical operator **NOT** is used to negate the result of a conditional expression. That is, in SQL, all conditional expressions evaluate to true or false. If an expression is true, the row is selected; if an expression is false, the row is not selected. The NOT logical operator is typically used to find the rows that *do not* match a certain condition. For example, if you want to see a listing of all rows for which the vendor code is not 21344, use the command sequence:

```
SELECT      *
FROM        PRODUCT
WHERE       NOT (V_CODE = 21344);
```

Note that the condition is enclosed in parentheses; that practice is optional, but it is highly recommended for clarity. The logical NOT can be combined with AND and OR.

> **NOTE**
>
> If your SQL version does not support the logical NOT, you can generate the required output by using the condition:
>
> ```
> WHERE V_CODE <> 21344
> ```
>
> If your version of SQL does not support <>, use:
>
> ```
> WHERE V_CODE != 21344
> ```

8.4.4 Special Operators

ANSI-standard SQL allows the use of special operators in conjunction with the WHERE clause. These special operators include:

- **BETWEEN** – Used to check whether an attribute value is within a range.
- **IS NULL** – Used to check whether an attribute value is null.
- **LIKE** – Used to check whether an attribute value matches a given string pattern.
- **IN** – Used to check whether an attribute value matches any value within a value list.
- **EXISTS** – Used to check whether a subquery returns any rows.

The BETWEEN Special Operator

If you use software that implements a standard SQL, the operator BETWEEN may be used to check whether an attribute value is within a range of values. For example, if you want to see a listing for all products whose prices are between €50 and €100, use the following command sequence:

```
SELECT    *
FROM      PRODUCT
WHERE     P_PRICE BETWEEN 50.00 AND 100.00;
```

> **NOTE TO ORACLE AND MYSQL USERS**
>
> Always specify the lower range value first when using the BETWEEN special operator. If you list the higher range value first, Oracle returns an empty result set.

If your DBMS does not support BETWEEN, you can use:

```
SELECT    *
FROM      PRODUCT
WHERE     P_PRICE > 50.00 AND P_PRICE < 100.00;
```

The IS NULL Special Operator

Standard SQL allows the use of IS NULL to check for a null attribute value. For example, suppose you want to list all products that do not have a vendor assigned (V_CODE is null). To find such a null entry use the command sequence:

```
SELECT    P_CODE, P_DESCRIPT, V_CODE
FROM      PRODUCT
WHERE     V_CODE IS NULL;
```

Similarly, if you want to check a null date entry, the command sequence is:

```
SELECT    P_CODE, P_DESCRIPT, P_INDATE
FROM      PRODUCT
WHERE     P_INDATE IS NULL;
```

Note that SQL uses a special operator to test for nulls. Why couldn't you just enter a condition such as 'V_CODE = NULL'? No. Technically, NULL is not a 'value' (such as the number 0 (zero) or the blank space), but a special property of an attribute that represents precisely the absence of any value.

The LIKE Special Operator

8

The LIKE special operator is used in conjunction with wildcards to find patterns within string attributes. Standard SQL allows you to use the per cent sign (%) and underscore (_) wildcard characters to make matches when the entire string is not known:

- % means any and all *following* characters are eligible. For example,
  'J%' includes Johnson, Jones, Jernigan, July, and J-231Q
  'Jo%' includes Johnson and Jones
- _ means any *one* character may be substituted for the underscore. For example,
  '_23-456-6789' includes 123-456-6789, 223-456-6789, and 323-456-6789
  '_23-_56-678_' includes 123-156-6781, 123-256-6782, and 823-956-6788
  '_o_es' includes Jones, Cones, Cokes, totes, and roles

NOTE

Some RDBMSs, such as Microsoft Access, use the wildcard characters * and ? instead of % and _.

For example, the following query would find all VENDOR rows for contacts whose last names begin with *Smith*.

```
SELECT    V_NAME, V_CONTACT, V_AREACODE, V_PHONE
FROM      VENDOR
WHERE     V_CONTACT LIKE 'Smith%';
```

If you check the original VENDOR data in Figure 8.2 again, you'll see that this SQL query yields three records: two Smiths and one Smithson.

Keep in mind that most SQL implementations yield case-sensitive searches. For example, Oracle will not yield a return that includes *Jones* if you use the wildcard search delimiter 'jo%' in a search for last names. The reason is because *Jones* begins with a capital *J* and your wildcard search starts with a lowercase *j*. On the other hand, Microsoft Access searches are not case sensitive.

For example, suppose you typed the following query in Oracle:

```
SELECT    V_NAME, V_CONTACT, V_AREACODE, V_PHONE
FROM      VENDOR
WHERE     V_CONTACT LIKE 'SMITH%';
```

No rows are returned because character-based queries may be case sensitive. That is, an uppercase character has a different ASCII code from a lowercase character, thus causing *SMITH, Smith,* and *smith* to be evaluated as different (unequal) entries. Because the table contains no vendor whose last name begins with (uppercase) *SMITH,* the (uppercase) 'SMITH%' used in the query cannot make a match. Matches can be made only when the query entry is written exactly like the table entry.

Some RDBMSs, such as Microsoft Access, automatically make the necessary conversions to eliminate case sensitivity. Others, such as Oracle, provide a special UPPER function to convert both table and query character entries to uppercase. (The conversion is done in the computer's memory only; the conversion has no effect on how the value is actually stored in the table.) So if you want to avoid a no-match result based on case sensitivity and if your RDBMS allows the use of the UPPER function, you can generate the same results by using the query:

```
SELECT    V_NAME, V_CONTACT, V_AREACODE, V_PHONE
FROM      VENDOR
WHERE     UPPER(V_CONTACT) LIKE 'SMITH%';
```

The preceding query produces a list including all rows that contain a last name that begins with *Smith*, regardless of uppercase or lowercase letter combinations such as *Smith, smith* and *SMITH*.

The logical operators may be used in conjunction with the special operators. For instance, the query:

```
SELECT    V_NAME, V_CONTACT, V_AREACODE, V_PHONE
FROM      VENDOR
WHERE     V_CONTACT NOT LIKE 'Smith%';
```

will yield an output of all vendors whose names do not start with *Smith*.

Suppose you do not know whether a person's name is spelled Johnson or Johnsen. The wildcard character _ lets you find a match for either spelling. The proper search would be instituted by the query:

```
SELECT    *
FROM      VENDOR
WHERE     V_CONTACT LIKE 'Johns_n'
```

Thus, the wildcards allow you to make matches when only approximate spellings are known. Wildcard characters may be used in combinations. For example, the wildcard search based on the string '_l%' can yield the strings Al, Alton, Elgin, Blakeston, blank, bloated and eligible.

The IN Special Operator

Many queries that would require the use of the logical OR can be more easily handled with the help of the special operator IN. For example, the query:

8

```
SELECT      *
FROM        PRODUCT
WHERE       V_CODE = 21344
OR          V_CODE = 24288;
```

can be handled more efficiently with:

```
SELECT      *
FROM        PRODUCT
WHERE       V_CODE IN (21344, 24288);
```

Note that the IN operator uses a value list. All of the values in the list must be of the same data type. Each of the values in the value list is compared to the attribute – in this case, V_CODE. If the V_CODE value matches any of the values in the list, the row is selected. In this example, the rows selected will be only those in which the V_CODE is either 21344 or 24288.

If the attribute used is of a character data type, the list values must be enclosed in single quotation marks. For instance, if the V_CODE had been defined as CHAR(5) during the table-creation process, the preceding query would have read:

```
SELECT      *
FROM        PRODUCT
WHERE       V_CODE IN ('21344', '24288');
```


The IN operator is especially valuable when it is used in conjunction with subqueries. For example, suppose you want to list the V_CODE and V_NAME of only those vendors who provide products. In that case, you could use a subquery within the IN operator to generate the value list automatically. The query is:

```
SELECT      V_CODE, V_NAME
FROM        VENDOR
WHERE       V_CODE IN (SELECT V_CODE FROM PRODUCT);
```

The preceding query is executed in two steps:

The inner query or subquery generates a list of V_CODE values from the PRODUCT tables. Those V_CODE values represent the vendors who supply products.

The IN operator compares the values generated by the subquery to the V_CODE values in the VENDOR table and selects only the rows with matching values – that is, the vendors who provide products.

The IN special operator receives additional attention in Chapter 9, Procedural Language SQL and Advanced SQL, where you will learn more about subqueries.

The EXISTS Special Operator

EXISTS can be used whenever there is a requirement to execute a command based on the result of another query. That is, if a subquery returns any rows, run the main query; otherwise, don't. For example, the following query will list all vendors, but only if there are products to order:

```
SELECT      *
FROM        VENDOR
WHERE       EXISTS (SELECT * FROM PRODUCT WHERE P_QOH <= P_MIN);
```

The EXISTS special operator is used in the following example to list all vendors, but only if there are products with the quantity on hand, less than double the minimum quantity:

```
SELECT     *
FROM       VENDOR
WHERE      EXISTS (SELECT * FROM PRODUCT WHERE P_QOH < P_MIN * 2);
```

The EXISTS special operator will receive additional attention in the next chapter, where you will learn more about subqueries.

8.5 ADVANCED DATA DEFINITION COMMANDS

In this section, you will learn how to change (alter) table structures by changing attribute characteristics and by adding columns. Then you will learn how to do advanced data updates to the new columns. Finally, you will learn how to copy tables or parts of tables and how to delete tables.

All changes in the table structure are made by using the **ALTER TABLE** command, followed by a keyword that produces the specific change you want to make. Three options are available: ADD, MODIFY and DROP. ADD enables you to add a column, and MODIFY enables you to change column characteristics. DROP allows you delete a column from a table. Most RDBMSs do not allow you to delete a column (unless the column does not contain any values) because such an action may delete crucial data that are used by other tables. The basic syntax to add or modify columns is:

ALTER TABLE *tablename*

{ADD | MODIFY}(*columnname datatype* [{ADD | MODIFY} *columnname datatype*]);

You can also use the ALTER TABLE command to add table constraints. In these cases, the syntax is:

ALTER TABLE *tablename*

ADD *constraint* [ADD *constraint*] ;

where *constraint* refers to a constraint definition similar to those you learned in Section 8.2.6.
You could also use the ALTER TABLE command to remove a column or table constraint. The syntax is:

ALTER TABLE *tablename*

DROP{PRIMARY KEY | COLUMN *columnname* | CONSTRAINT *constraintname* };

Notice that, when removing a constraint, you need to specify the name given to the constraint. That is one reason why you should always name your constraints in your CREATE TABLE or ALTER TABLE statement.

8.5.1 Changing a Column's Data Type

Using the ALTER syntax, the (integer) V_CODE in the PRODUCT table can be changed to a character V_CODE by using:

```
ALTER TABLE PRODUCT
MODIFY (V_CODE CHAR(5));
```

Some RDBMSs, such as Oracle, do not let you change data types unless the column to be changed is empty. For example, if you want to change the V_CODE field from the current number definition to a character definition, the above command will yield an error message because the V_CODE column already contains data. The error message is easily explained. If you change the V_CODE data type, remember that the V_CODE in PRODUCT references the V_CODE in VENDOR. If the data types don't match, there is a referential integrity violation, thus triggering the error message. If the V_CODE column does not contain data, the preceding command sequence produces the expected table structure alteration if the foreign key reference was not specified during the creation of the PRODUCT table.

8.5.2 Changing a Column's Data Characteristics

If the column to be changed already contains data, you can make changes in the column's characteristics if those changes do not alter the data *type*. For example, if you want to increase the width of the P_PRICE column to nine digits, use the command:

```
ALTER TABLE PRODUCT
MODIFY (P_PRICE DECIMAL(9,2));
```

If you now list the table contents, you see that the column width of P_PRICE has increased by one digit.

8

NOTE

Some DBMSs impose limitations on when it's possible to change attribute characteristics. For example, Oracle lets you increase (but not decrease) the size of a column. The reason for this restriction is that an attribute modification affects the integrity of the data in the database. In fact, some attribute changes can be done only when there are no data in any rows for the affected attribute.

8.5.3 Adding a Column

You can alter an existing table by adding one or more columns. In the following example, you add the column named P_SALECODE to the PRODUCT table. (This column will be used later to determine whether goods that have been in inventory for a certain length of time should be placed on special sale.)

Suppose you expect the P_SALECODE entries to be 1, 2 or 3. Because there will be no arithmetic performed with the P_SALECODE, the P_SALECODE is classified as a single-character attribute. Note the inclusion of all required information in the following ALTER command:

```
ALTER TABLE PRODUCT
ADD (P_SALECODE CHAR(1));
```

Online Content If you are using the Microsoft Access databases provided on the online platform accompanying this book, you can track each of the updates in the following sections. For example, look at the copies of the PRODUCT table in the 'Ch08_SaleCo' database, one named PRODUCT_2 and one named PRODUCT_3. Each of the two copies includes the new P_SALECODE column. If you want to see the *cumulative* effect of all UPDATE commands, you can continue using the PRODUCT table with the P_SALECODE modification and all of the changes you will make in the following sections. (You may even want to use both options, first to examine the individual effects of the update queries and then to examine the cumulative effects.)

When adding a column, be careful not to include the NOT NULL clause for the new column. Doing so causes an error message; if you add a new column to a table that already has rows, the existing rows will default to a value of null for the new column. Therefore, it is not possible to add the NOT NULL clause for this new column. (You can, of course add the NOT NULL clause to the table structure after all of the data for the new column have been entered and the column no longer contains nulls.)

8.5.4 Dropping a Column

Occasionally, you may want to modify a table by deleting a column. Suppose you want to delete the V_ORDER attribute from the VENDOR table. To accomplish that, you would use the following command:

```
ALTER TABLE VENDOR
DROP COLUMN V_ORDER;
```

8

Again, some RDBMSs impose restrictions on attribute deletion. For example, you may not drop attributes that are involved in foreign key relationships, nor may you delete an attribute of a table that contains only that one attribute.

8.5.5 Advanced Data Updates

To make data entries in an existing row's columns, SQL employs the UPDATE command. The UPDATE command updates only data in existing rows. For example, to enter the P_SALECODE value '2' in the fourth row, use the UPDATE command together with the primary key P_CODE '1546-QQ2'. To enter the value use the command sequence:

```
UPDATE    PRODUCT
SET       P_SALECODE = '2'
WHERE     P_CODE = '1546-QQ2';
```

Enter subsequent data can be entered the same way, defining each entry location by its primary key (P_CODE) and its column location (P_SALECODE). For example, if you want to enter the P_SALECODE value '1' for the P_CODE values '2232/QWE' and '2232/QTY', you use:

```
UPDATE    PRODUCT
SET       P_SALECODE = '1'
WHERE     P_CODE IN ('2232/QWE', '2232/QTY');
```

If your RDBMS does not support IN, use the following command:

```
UPDATE    PRODUCT
SET       P_SALECODE = '1'
WHERE     P_CODE = '2232/QWE' OR P_CODE = '2232/QTY';
```

To check the results of your efforts use:

```
SELECT     P_CODE, P_DESCRIPT, P_INDATE, P_PRICE, P_SALECODE
FROM       PRODUCT;
```

Although the UPDATE sequences just shown allow you to enter values into specified table cells, the process is very cumbersome. Fortunately, if a relationship can be established between the entries and the existing columns, it can be used to assign values to their appropriate slots. For example, suppose you want to place sales codes based on the P_INDATE into the table, using the following schedule:

P_INDATE	P_SALECODE
before 25 December 2018	2
between 16 January 2019 and 10 February 2019	1

Using the PRODUCT table, the following two command sequences make the appropriate assignments:

```
UPDATE     PRODUCT
SET        P_SALECODE = '2'
WHERE      P_INDATE < '25-Dec-2018';

UPDATE     PRODUCT
SET        P_SALECODE = '1'
WHERE      P_INDATE >= '16-Jan-2019'
AND P_INDATE <='10-Feb-2019';
```

To check the results of those two command sequences, use:

```
SELECT     P_CODE, P_DESCRIPT, P_INDATE, P_PRICE, P_SALECODE
FROM       PRODUCT;
```

If you have made *all* of the updates shown in this section using Oracle, your PRODUCT table should look like Figure 8.15. *Make sure that you issue a COMMIT statement to save these changes.*

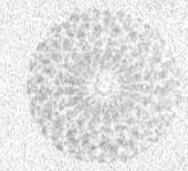

Online Content The screen shots provided in Chapter 8, Beginning Structured Query Language and Chapter 9, Procedural Language SQL and Advanced SQL, were taken from Oracle SQL Developer [5] within Oracle APEX.[6] Oracle SQL Developer is a graphical tool for database development which is provided by Oracle. It is free to use and can be used with any Oracle Database version 10g and later and runs on Windows, Linux and Mac OSX. Throughout Chapters 8 and 9, it will be used as an editor to explore the use of DML and DDL commands. A guide for how to use SQL Developer can be found on the online platform accompanying this book in Appendix N. Your college or university may be part of the Oracle Academy programme. If so, you may be using Oracle Application Express (APEX) a cloud-based software which can be used to learn SQL and PL/SQL. All Oracle scripts provided with this book will also work on Oracle APEX. Learn more about the Oracle Academy here: https://academy.oracle.com/en/oa-web-overview.html

5 Getting Started with Oracle SQL Developer. Available: www.oracle.com/database/technologies/appdev/sql-developer.html

6 Developing Applications with Oracle APEX. Available: www.oracle.com/database/technologies/appdev/apex.html

The arithmetic operators are particularly useful in data updates. For example, if the quantity on hand in your PRODUCT table has dropped below the minimum desirable value, you'll order more of the product. Suppose, for example, you have ordered 20 units of product 2232/QWE. When the 20 units arrive, you'll want to add them to inventory, using:

```
UPDATE      PRODUCT
SET         P_QOH = P_QOH + 20
WHERE       P_CODE = '2232/QWE';
```

FIGURE 8.15 The cumulative effect of multiple updates in the PRODUCT table (Oracle-APEX)

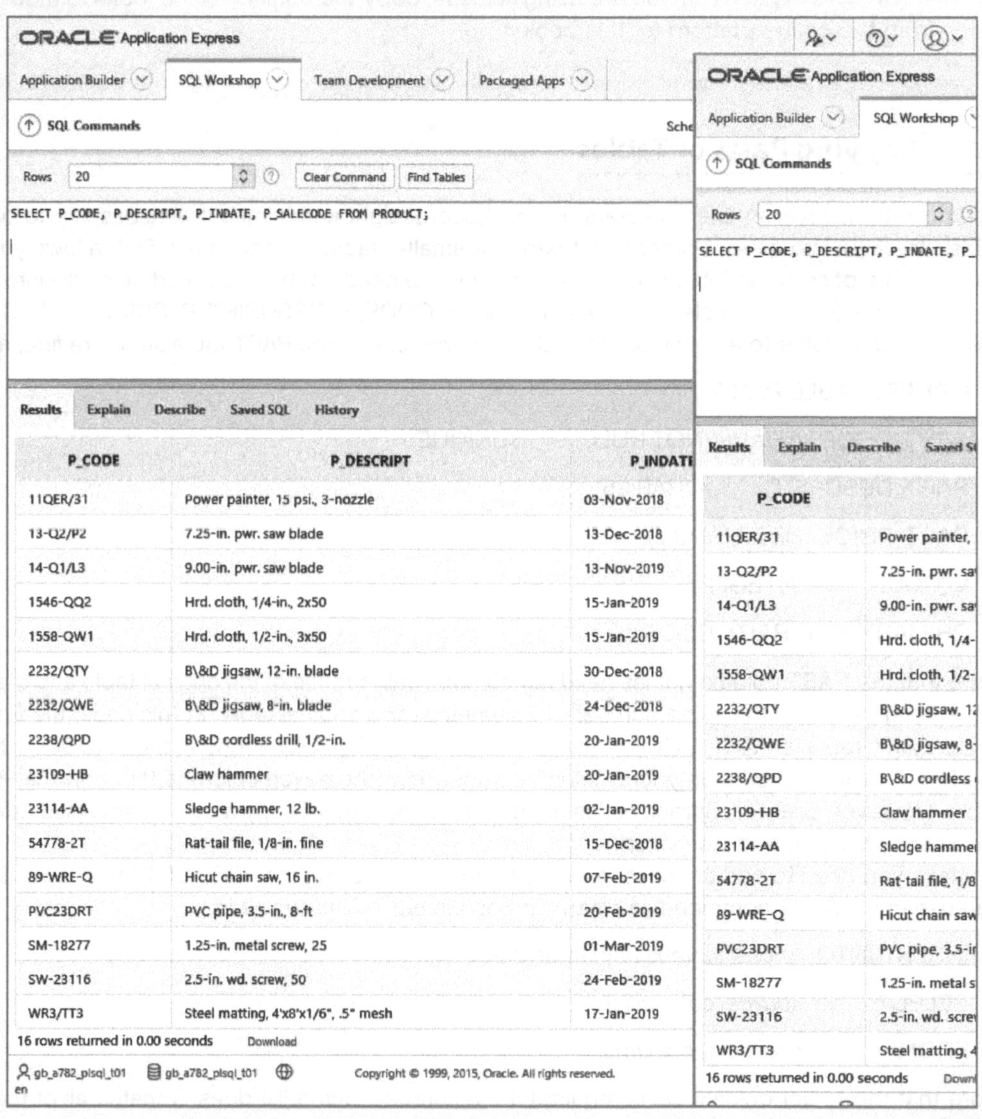

P_CODE	P_DESCRIPT	P_INDATE
11QER/31	Power painter, 15 psi., 3-nozzle	03-Nov-2018
13-Q2/P2	7.25-in. pwr. saw blade	13-Dec-2018
14-Q1/L3	9.00-in. pwr. saw blade	13-Nov-2019
1546-QQ2	Hrd. cloth, 1/4-in., 2x50	15-Jan-2019
1558-QW1	Hrd. cloth, 1/2-in., 3x50	15-Jan-2019
2232/QTY	B\&D jigsaw, 12-in. blade	30-Dec-2018
2232/QWE	B\&D jigsaw, 8-in. blade	24-Dec-2018
2238/QPD	B\&D cordless drill, 1/2-in.	20-Jan-2019
23109-HB	Claw hammer	20-Jan-2019
23114-AA	Sledge hammer, 12 lb.	02-Jan-2019
54778-2T	Rat-tail file, 1/8-in. fine	15-Dec-2018
89-WRE-Q	Hicut chain saw, 16 in.	07-Feb-2019
PVC23DRT	PVC pipe, 3.5-in., 8-ft	20-Feb-2019
SM-18277	1.25-in. metal screw, 25	01-Mar-2019
SW-23116	2.5-in. wd. screw, 50	24-Feb-2019
WR3/TT3	Steel matting, 4'x8'x1/6", .5" mesh	17-Jan-2019

If you want to add 10 per cent to the price for all products that have current prices below €50, you can use:

```
UPDATE      PRODUCT
SET         P_PRICE = P_PRICE * 1.10
WHERE       P_PRICE < 50.00;
```

NOTE

If you fail to roll back the changes of the preceding UPDATE queries, the output of the subsequent queries will not match the results shown in the figures. Therefore, if you are using Oracle, use the ROLLBACK command to restore the database to its previous state.

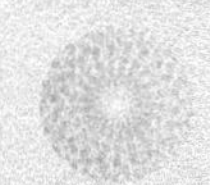

Online Content If you are using Access, copy the original 'Ch08_SaleCo.mdb' file from the online platfom for this book.

8.5.6 Copying Parts of Tables

8

As you will discover in later chapters on database design, sometimes it is necessary to break up a table structure into several component parts (or smaller tables). Fortunately, SQL allows you to copy the contents of selected table columns so that the data need not be re-entered manually into the newly created table(s). For example, if you want to copy P_CODE, P_DESCRIPT, P_PRICE and V_CODE from the PRODUCT table to a new table named PART, you create the PART table structure first, as follows:

```
CREATE TABLE PART(
PART_CODE     CHAR(8) NOT NULL     UNIQUE,
PART_DESCRIPT      CHAR(35),
PART_PRICE    DECIMAL(8,2),
V_CODE        INTEGER,
PRIMARY KEY (PART_CODE));
```

Note that the PART column names need not be identical to those of the original table and that the new table need not have the same number of columns as the original table. In this case, the first column in the PART table is PART_CODE, rather than the original P_CODE found in the PRODUCT table. And the PART table contains only four columns rather than the seven columns found in the PRODUCT table. However, column characteristics must match; you cannot copy a character-based attribute into a numeric structure and vice versa.

Next, you need to add the rows to the new PART table, using the PRODUCT table rows. To do that, you use the INSERT command you learnt in Section 8.3.7. The syntax is:

INSERT INTO *target_tablename*[(*target_columnlist*)]

SELECT *source_columnlist*

FROM *source_tablename*;

Note that the target column list is required if the source column list doesn't match all of the attribute names and characteristics of the target table (including the order of the columns). Otherwise, you do not need to specify the target column list. In this example, you must specify the target column list in the INSERT command below because the column names of the target table are different:

```
INSERT INTO PART (PART_CODE, PART_DESCRIPT, PART_PRICE, V_CODE)
SELECT P_CODE, P_DESCRIPT, P_PRICE, V_CODE FROM PRODUCT;
```

The contents of the PART table can now be examined by using the query:

```
SELECT * FROM PART;
```

to generate the new PART table's contents, shown in Figure 8.16.

FIGURE 8.16 PART table attributes copied from the PRODUCT table

PART_CODE	PART_DESCRIPT	PART_PRICE	V_CODE
11QER/31	Power painter, 15 psi., 3-nozzle	109.99	25595
13-Q2/P2	7.25 cm pwr. saw blade	14.99	21344
14-Q1/L3	9.00 cm pwr. saw blade	17.49	21344
1546-QQ2	Hrd. cloth, 1/4 cm, 2 × 50	39.95	23119
1558-QW1	Hrd. cloth, 1/2 cm, 3 × 50	43.99	23119
2232/QTY	B&D jigsaw, 12 cm blade	109.92	24288
2232/QWE	B&D jigsaw, 8 cm blade	99.87	24288
2238/QPD	B&D cordless drill, 1/2 cm	38.95	25595
23109-HB	Claw hammer	9.95	21225
23114-AA	Sledge hammer, 12 kg	14.40	
54778-2T	Rat-tail file, 1/8 cm fine	4.99	21344
89-WRE-Q	Hicut chain saw, 16 cm	256.99	24288
PVC23DRT	PVC pipe, 3.5 cm, 8 m	5.87	
SM-18277	1.25 cm metal screw, 25	6.99	21225
SW-23116	2.5 cm wd. screw, 50	8.45	21231
WR3/TT3	Steel matting, 4 × 8 × 1/6 m, .5 m mesh	119.95	25595

8

SQL also provides another way to rapidly create a new table based on selected columns and rows of an existing table. In this case, the new table copies the attribute names, data characteristics and rows of the original table. The Oracle version of the command is:

```
CREATE TABLE PART AS
SELECT     P_CODE AS PART_CODE, P_DESCRIPT AS PART_DESCRIPT,
P_PRICE AS PART_PRICE, V_CODE
FROM       PRODUCT;
```

If the PART table already exists, Oracle will not let you overwrite the existing table. To run this command, you must first delete the existing PART table. (See Section 8.5.8.)

The Microsoft Access version of this command is:

```
SELECT P_CODE AS PART_CODE, P_DESCRIPT AS PART_DESCRIPT,
P_PRICE AS PART_PRICE, V_CODE INTO PART
FROM PRODUCT;
```

If the PART table already exists, Microsoft Access will ask if you want to delete the existing table and continue with the creation of the new PART table.

The SQL command just shown creates a new PART table with PART_CODE, PART_DESCRIPT, PART_PRICE, and V_CODE columns. In addition, all of the data rows (for the selected columns) are copied automatically. *But note that no entity integrity (primary key) or referential integrity (foreign key) rules are automatically applied to the new table.* In the next section, you will learn how to define the PK and FK to enforce entity and referential integrity, respectively.

8.5.7 Adding Primary and Foreign Key Designations

When you create a new table based on another table, the new table does not include integrity rules from the old table. (In particular, there is no primary key.) To define the primary key for the new PART table, use the following command:

```
ALTER TABLE PART
ADD PRIMARY KEY (PART_CODE);
```

Aside from the fact that the integrity rules are not automatically transferred to a new table that derives its data from one or more other tables, several other scenarios could leave you without entity and referential integrity. For example, you might have forgotten to define the primary and foreign keys when you created the original tables. Or, if you imported tables from a different database, you might have discovered that the importing procedure did not transfer the integrity rules. In any case, you can re-establish the integrity rules by using the ALTER command. For example, if the PART table's foreign key has not yet been designated, it can be designated by:

8

```
ALTER TABLE PART
ADD        FOREIGN KEY (V_CODE) REFERENCES VENDOR;
```

Alternatively, if neither the PART table's primary key nor its foreign key has been designated, you can incorporate both changes at once, using:

```
ALTER TABLEPART
ADD        PRIMARY KEY (PART_CODE)
ADD        FOREIGN KEY (V_CODE) REFERENCES VENDOR;
```

Even composite primary keys and multiple foreign keys can be designated in a single SQL command. For example, if you want to enforce the integrity rules for the LINE table shown in Figure 8.1, you can use:

```
ALTER TABLE LINE
ADD        PRIMARY KEY (INV_NUMBER, LINE_NUMBER)
ADD        FOREIGN KEY (INV_NUMBER) REFERENCES INVOICE
ADD        FOREIGN KEY (PROD_CODE) REFERENCES PRODUCT;
```

8.5.8 Deleting a Table From the Database

Use the **DROP TABLE** command to delete a table from the database. For example, you can delete the PART table you just created with:

```
DROP TABLE PART;
```

You can drop a table only if that table is not participating as the 'one' side of any relationship. If you try to drop a table otherwise, the RDBMS generates an error message indicating that a foreign key integrity violation has occurred.

8.6 ADVANCED SELECT QUERIES

One of the most important advantages of SQL is its ability to produce complex free-form queries. The logical operators that were introduced earlier to update table contents work just as well in the query environment. In addition, SQL provides useful functions that count, find minimum and maximum values, calculate averages, and so on. Better yet, SQL allows the user to limit queries to only those entries that have no duplicates or entries whose duplicates can be grouped.

8.6.1 Ordering a Listing

The **ORDER BY** clause is especially useful when the listing order is important to you. The syntax is:

```
SELECT       columnlist
FROM         tablelist
[WHERE       conditionlist ]
[ORDER BY    columnlist [ASC | DESC] ] ;
```

Although you have the option of declaring the order type – ascending or descending – the default order is ascending. For example, if you want the contents of the PRODUCT table listed by P_PRICE in ascending order, use:

```
SELECT       P_CODE, P_DESCRIPT, P_INDATE, P_PRICE
FROM         PRODUCT
ORDER BY     P_PRICE;
```

The output is shown in Figure 8.17. Note that ORDER BY yields an ascending price listing.

Comparing the listing in Figure 8.17 to the actual table contents shown earlier in Figure 8.2, you will see that, in Figure 8.17, the lowest-priced product is listed first, followed by the next lowest-priced product, and so on. However, although ORDER BY produces a sorted output, the actual table contents are unaffected by the ORDER command.

To produce the list in descending order, you would enter:

```
SELECT       P_CODE, P_DESCRIPT, P_INDATE, P_PRICE
FROM         PRODUCT
ORDER BY     P_PRICE DESC;
```

Ordered listings are used frequently. For example, suppose you want to create a phone directory. It would be helpful if you could produce an ordered sequence (last name, first name, initial) in three stages:

1 ORDER BY last name.

2 Within the last names, ORDER BY first name.

3 Within the order created in Step 2, ORDER BY middle initial.

FIGURE 8.17 **Selected PRODUCT table attributes: ordered by (ascending) P_PRICE**

P_CODE	P_DESCRIPT	P_INDATE	P_PRICE
54778-2T	Rat-tail file, 0.5 cm fine	15-Dec-18	4.99
PVC23DRT	PVC pipe, 9 cm, 2.5 m	20-Feb-19	5.87
SM-18277	3 cm metal screw, 25	01-Mar-19	6.99
SW-23116	6 cm wd. screw, 50	24-Feb-19	8.45
23109-HB	Claw hammer	20-Jan-19	9.95
23114-AA	Sledge hammer, 7 kg	02-Jan-19	14.40
13-Q2/P2	7.25 cm pwr. saw blade	13-Dec-18	14.99
14-Q1/L3	9.00 cm pwr. saw blade	13-Nov-18	17.49
2238/QPD	B&D cordless drill, 1/2 cm	20-Jan-19	38.95
1546-QQ2	Hrd. cloth, 1/4 cm, 2 × 50	15-Jan-19	39.95
1558-QW1	Hrd. cloth, 1/2 cm, 3 × 50	15-Jan-19	43.99
2232/QWE	B&D jigsaw, 8 cm blade	24-Dec-18	99.87
2232/QTY	B&D jigsaw, 12 cm blade	30-Dec-18	109.92
11QER/31	Power painter, 15 psi., 3-nozzle	03-Nov-18	109.99
WR3/TT3	Steel matting, 4 × 8 × 1/6 m, .5 m mesh	17-Jan-19	119.95
89-WRE-Q	Hicut chain saw, 16 cm	07-Feb-19	256.99

Such a multilevel ordered sequence is known as a **cascading order sequence**, and it can be created easily by listing several attributes, separated by commas, after the ORDER BY clause. The cascading order sequence is the basis for any telephone directory. To illustrate a cascading order sequence, use the following SQL command on the EMPLOYEE table:

```
SELECT EMP_LNAME, EMP_FNAME, EMP_INITIAL, EMP_AREACODE, EMP_PHONE
FROM EMPLOYEE
ORDER BY EMP_LNAME, EMP_FNAME, EMP_INITIAL;
```

That command yields the results shown in Figure 8.18.

The ORDER BY clause is useful in many applications, especially because the DESC qualifier can be invoked. For example, listing the most recent items first is a standard procedure. Typically, invoice due dates are listed in descending order. Or if you want to examine budgets, it's probably useful to start by looking at the largest budget line items.

You can use the ORDER BY clause in conjunction with other SQL commands, too. For example, note the use of restrictions on date and price in the following command sequence:

```
SELECT    P_DESCRIPT, V_CODE, P_INDATE, P_PRICE
FROM      PRODUCT
WHERE     P_INDATE < '21-Jan-2019' AND
P_PRICE <= 50.00
ORDER BY V_CODE, P_PRICE DESC;
```

FIGURE 8.18 **Selected PRODUCT table attributes: ordered by (ascending) P_PRICE**

EMP_LNAME	EMP_FNAME	EMP_INITIAL	EMP_REACODE	EMP_PHONE
Brandon	Marie	G	7325	882-0845
Diante	Jorge	D	0181	890-4567
Genkazi	Leighla	W	7235	569-0093
Johnson	Edward	E	0181	898-4387
Jones	Anne	M	0181	898-3456
Cela	Nkosi	D	0181	324-5456
Lange	John	P	7325	504-4430
Lewis	Rhonda	G	0181	324-4472
Saranda	Hermine	R	0181	324-5505
Smith	George	A	0181	890-2984
Smith	George	K	7235	504-3339
Smith	Jeanine	K	0181	324-7883
Gounden	Melanie	P	0181	324-9006
Vandam	Rhett		7325	675-8993
Washington	Rupert	E	0181	890-4925
Wiesenbach	Paul	R	0181	897-4358
Williams	Robert	D	0181	890-3220

8

The output is shown in Figure 8.19. Note that within each V_CODE, the P_PRICE values are in descending order.

FIGURE 8.19 **A query based on multiple restrictions**

P_DESCRIPT	V_CODE	P_INDATE	P_PRICE
Sledge hammer, 12 kg		02-Jan-19	14.40
Claw hammer	21225	20-Jan-19	9.95
9.00 cm pwr. saw blade	21344	13-Nov-18	17.49
7.25 cm pwr. saw blade	21344	13-Dec-18	14.99
Rat-tail file, 1/8 cm fine	21344	15-Dec-18	4.99
Hrd. cloth, 1/2 cm, 3 × 50	23119	15-Jan-19	43.99
Hrd. cloth, 1/4 cm, 2 × 50	23119	15-Jan-19	39.95
B&D cordless drill, 1/2 cm	25595	20-Jan-19	38.95

NOTE

- If the ordering column has nulls, they are listed either first or last (depending on the RDBMS).
- The ORDER BY clause must always be listed last in the SELECT command sequence.

8.6.2 Listing Unique Values

How many *different* vendors are currently represented in the PRODUCT table? A simple listing (SELECT) is not very useful if the table contains several thousand rows and you have to sift through the vendor codes manually. Fortunately, SQL's **DISTINCT** clause is designed to produce a list of only those values that are different from one another. For example, the command:

```
SELECT    DISTINCT V_CODE
FROM      PRODUCT;
```

yields only the different (distinct) vendor codes (V_CODE) that are encountered in the PRODUCT table, as shown in Figure 8.20. Note that the first output row shows the null. (By default, Access places the null V_CODE at the top of the list, while Oracle places it at the bottom. The placement of nulls does not affect the list contents. In Oracle, you could use ORDER BY V_CODE NULLS FIRST to place nulls at the top of the list.)

FIGURE 8.20 A listing of distinct (different) V_CODE values in the PRODUCT table

V_CODE
21225
21231
21344
23119
24288
25595

8

8.6.3 Aggregate Functions

SQL can perform various mathematical summaries for you, such as counting the number of rows that contain a specified condition, finding the minimum or maximum values for some specified attribute, summing the values in a specified column, and averaging the values in a specified column. Those aggregate functions are shown in Table 8.9.

TABLE 8.9 Some basic SQL aggregate functions

Function	Output
COUNT	The number of rows containing non-null values
MIN	The minimum attribute value encountered in a given column
MAX	The maximum attribute value encountered in a given column
SUM	The sum of all values for a given column
AVG	The arithmetic mean (average) for a specified column

To illustrate another standard SQL command format, most of the remaining input and output sequences are presented using the Oracle RDBMS.

COUNT

Use the **COUNT** function to tally the number of non-null values of an attribute. COUNT can be used in conjunction with the DISTINCT clause. For example, suppose you want to find out how many different vendors are in the PRODUCT table. The answer, generated by the first SQL code set shown in Figure 8.21, is 6. The answer indicates that six different VENDOR codes are found in the PRODUCT table. (Note that the nulls are not counted as V_CODE values.)

FIGURE 8.21 **COUNT function output example**

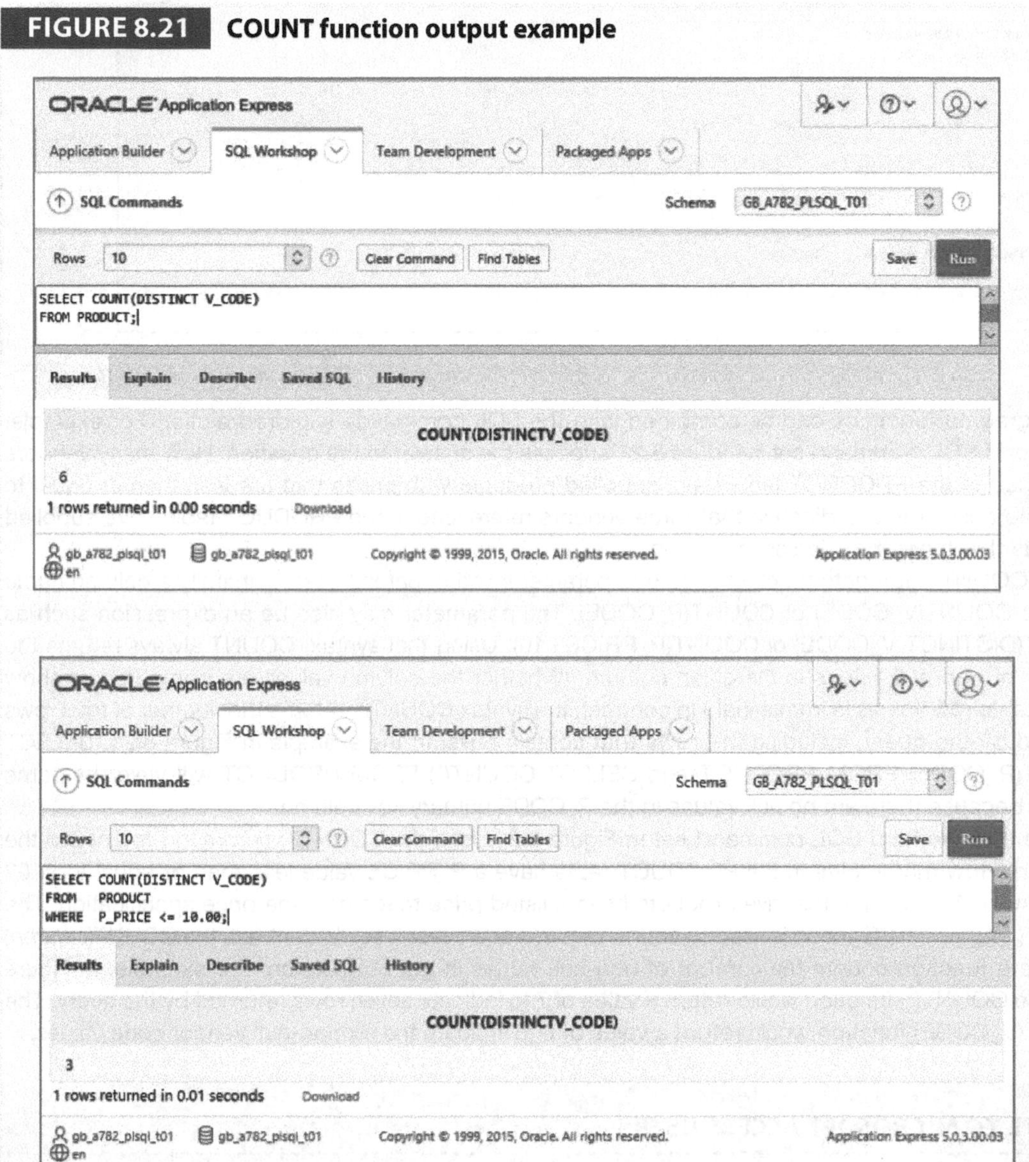

8

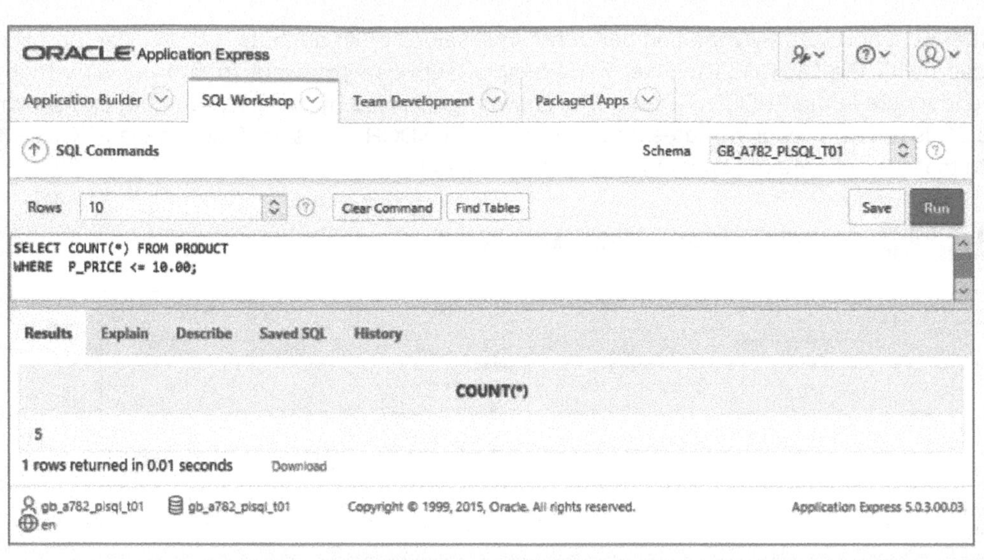

The aggregate functions can be combined with the SQL commands explored earlier. For example, the second SQL command set in Figure 8.21 supplies the answer to the question, How many vendors referenced in the PRODUCT table have supplied products with prices that are less than or equal to €10? The answer is 3, indicating that three vendors referenced in the PRODUCT table have supplied products that meet the price specification.

The COUNT aggregate function uses one parameter within parentheses, generally a column name such as COUNT(V_CODE) or COUNT(P_CODE). The parameter may also be an expression such as COUNT(DISTINCT V_CODE) or COUNT(P_PRICE+10). Using that syntax, COUNT always returns the number of non-null values in the given column. (Whether the column values are computed or show stored table row values is immaterial.) In contrast, the syntax COUNT(*) returns the number of total rows returned by the query, including the rows that contain nulls. In the example in Figure 8.21, SELECT COUNT(P_CODE) FROM PRODUCT and SELECT COUNT(*) FROM PRODUCT will yield the same answer because there are no null values in the P_CODE primary key column.

Note that the third SQL command set in Figure 8.21 uses the COUNT(*) command to answer the question, How many rows in the PRODUCT table have a P_PRICE value less than or equal to €10? The answer, 5, indicates that five products have a listed price that meets the price specification. The COUNT(*) aggregate function is used to count rows in a query result set. In contrast, the COUNT(*column*) aggregate function counts the number of non-null values in a given column. For example, in Figure 8.20, the COUNT(*) function would return a value of 7 to indicate seven rows returned by the query. The COUNT(V_CODE) function would return a value of 6 to indicate the six non-null vendor code values.

NOTE TO MICROSOFT ACCESS USERS

Microsoft Access does not support the use of COUNT with the DISTINCT clause. If you want to use such queries in Microsoft Access, you must create subqueries with DISTINCT and NOT NULL clauses. For example, the equivalent Microsoft Access queries for the first two queries shown in Figure 8.21 are:

```
SELECT      COUNT(*)
FROM        (SELECT DISTINCT V_CODE FROM PRODUCT WHERE V_CODE IS NOT NULL)
```

and

```
SELECT      COUNT(*)
FROM        (SELECT DISTINCT(V_CODE)
            FROM
            (SELECT V_CODE, P_PRICE FROM PRODUCT
            WHERE V_CODE IS NOT NULL AND P_PRICE < 10))
```

Those two queries can be found on the online platform in the 'Ch8_SaleCo' (Access) database. Microsoft Access does add a trailer at the end of the query after you have executed it, but you can delete that trailer the next time you use the query.

MAX and MIN

The **MAX** and **MIN** functions help you find answers to problems such as the:

- Highest (maximum) price in the PRODUCT table.
- Lowest (minimum) price in the PRODUCT table.

The highest price, €256.99, is supplied by the first SQL command set in Figure 8.22. The second SQL command set shown in Figure 8.22 yields the minimum price of €4.99.

FIGURE 8.22 MIN and MAX function output examples

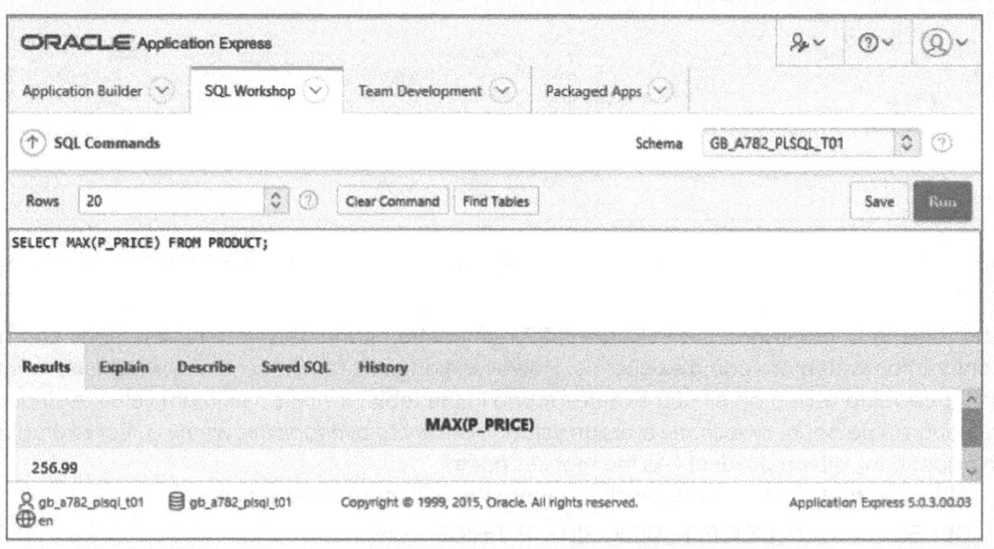

8

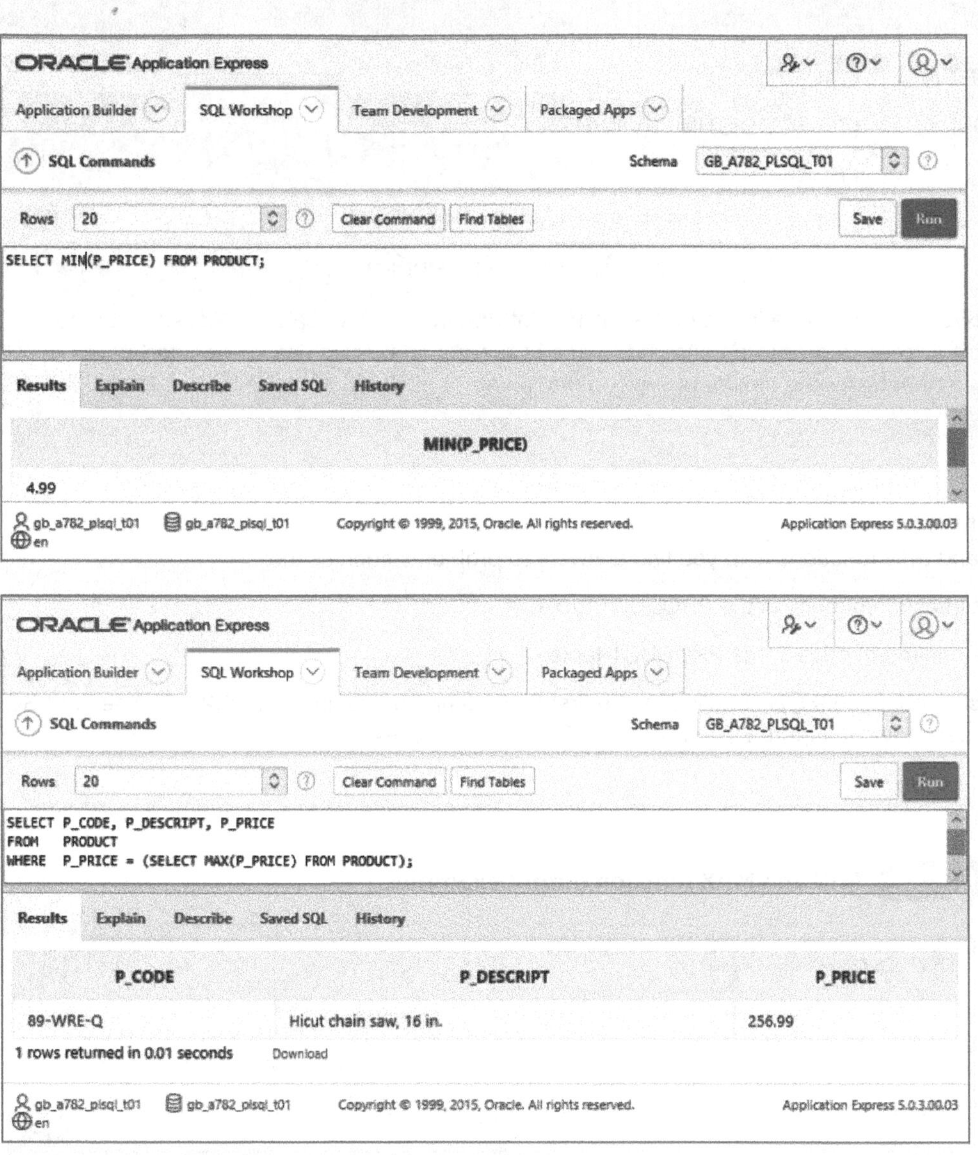

The third SQL command set in Figure 8.22 demonstrates that the numeric functions can be used in conjunction with more complex queries. However, you must remember that *the numeric functions yield only one value* based on all of the values found in the table: a single maximum value, a single minimum value, a single count or a single average value. *It is easy to overlook this warning.* For example, examine the question, Which product has the highest price?

Although that query seems simple enough, the SQL command sequence:

```
SELECT    P_CODE, P_DESCRIPT, P_PRICE
FROM      PRODUCT
WHERE     P_PRICE = MAX(P_PRICE);
```

does not yield the expected results because the use of MAX(P_PRICE) to the right side of a comparison operator is incorrect, thus producing an error message. The aggregate function MAX(*columnname*) can be used only in the column list of a SELECT statement. Also, in a comparison that uses an equality symbol, you can use only a single value to the right of the equals sign.

To answer the question, therefore, you must compute the maximum price first, then compare it to each price returned by the query. To do that, you need a nested query. In this case, the nested query is composed of two parts:

- The *inner query*, which is executed first.
- The *outer query*, which is executed last. (The outer query is always the first SQL command you encounter – in this case, SELECT – in the command sequence.)

Using the following command sequence as an example, note that the inner query first finds the maximum price value, which is stored in memory. Since the outer query now has a value to which to compare each P_PRICE value, the query executes properly:

```
SELECT      P_CODE, P_DESCRIPT, P_PRICE
FROM        PRODUCT
WHERE       P_PRICE = (SELECT MAX(PRICE) FROM PRODUCT);
```

The execution of that nested query yields the correct answer shown below the third (nested) SQL command set in Figure 8.22.

The MAX and MIN aggregate functions can also be used with date columns. For example, to find the product that has the oldest date, you would use MIN(P_INDATE). In the same manner, to find the most recent product, you would use MAX(P_INDATE).

8

NOTE

You can use expressions anywhere a column name is expected. Suppose you want to know which product has the highest inventory value. To find the answer, you can write the following query:

```
SELECT *
FROM PRODUCT
WHERE P_QOH * P_PRICE = (SELECT MAX(P_QOH*P_PRICE) FROM PRODUCT);
```

SUM

The **SUM** function computes the total sum for any specified attribute, using whichever condition(s) you have imposed. For example, if you want to compute the total amount owed by your customers, you could use the following command:

```
SELECT      SUM(CUS_BALANCE) AS TOTBALANCE
FROM        CUSTOMER;
```

You could also compute the sum total of an expression. For example, if you want to find the total value of all items carried in inventory, you could use:

```
SELECT      SUM(P_QOH * P_PRICE) AS TOTVALUE
FROM        PRODUCT;
```

because the total value is the sum of the product of the quantity on hand and the price for all items. (See Figure 8.23.)

FIGURE 8.23 The total value of all items in the PRODUCT table

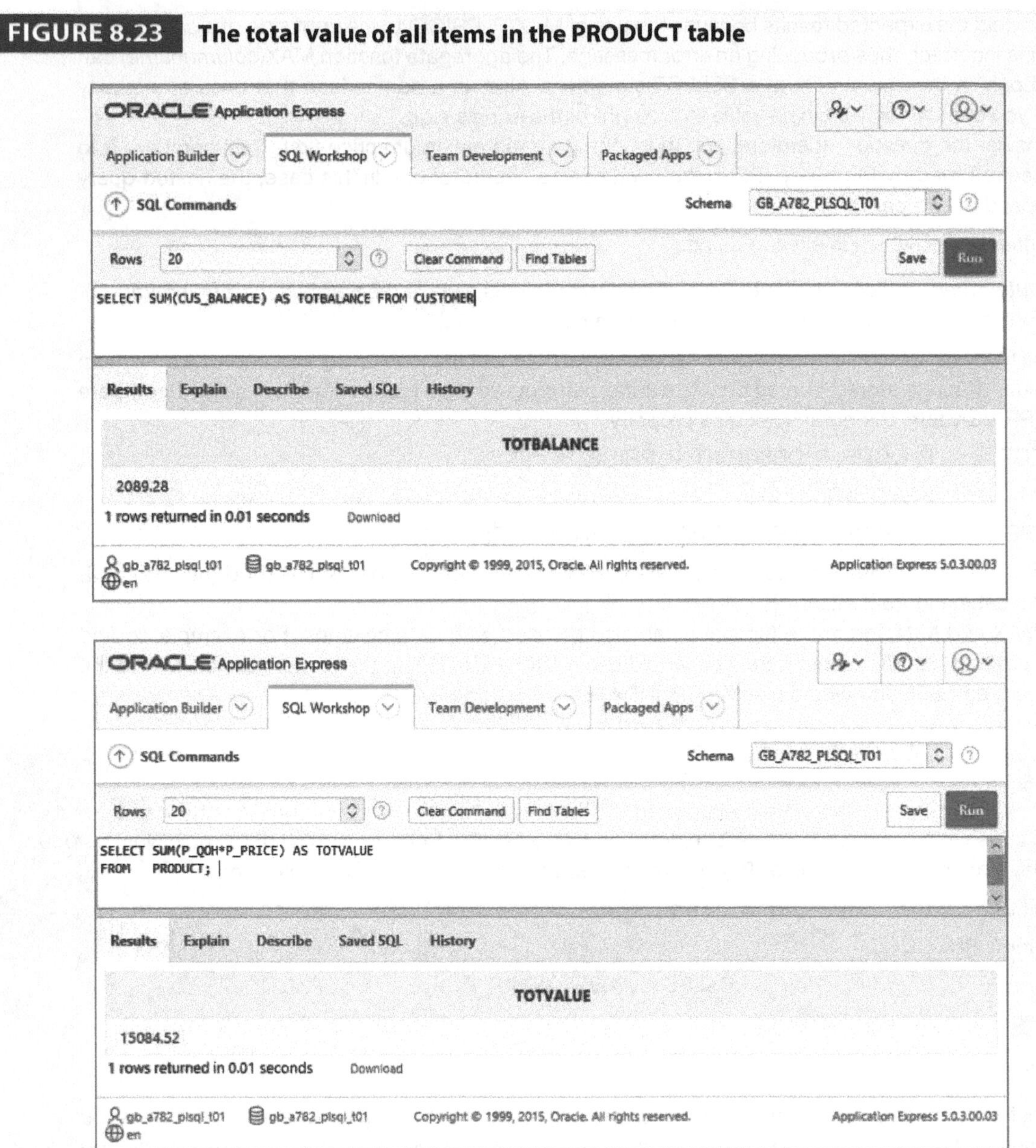

8

AVG

The **AVG** function format is similar to that of MIN and MAX and is subject to the same operating restrictions. The first SQL command set shown in Figure 8.24 shows how a simple average P_PRICE value can be generated to yield the computed average price of 56.42125. The second SQL command set in Figure 8.24 produces five output lines that describe products whose prices exceed the average product price. Note that the second query uses nested SQL commands and the ORDER BY clause examined earlier.

FIGURE 8.24 **AVG function output examples**

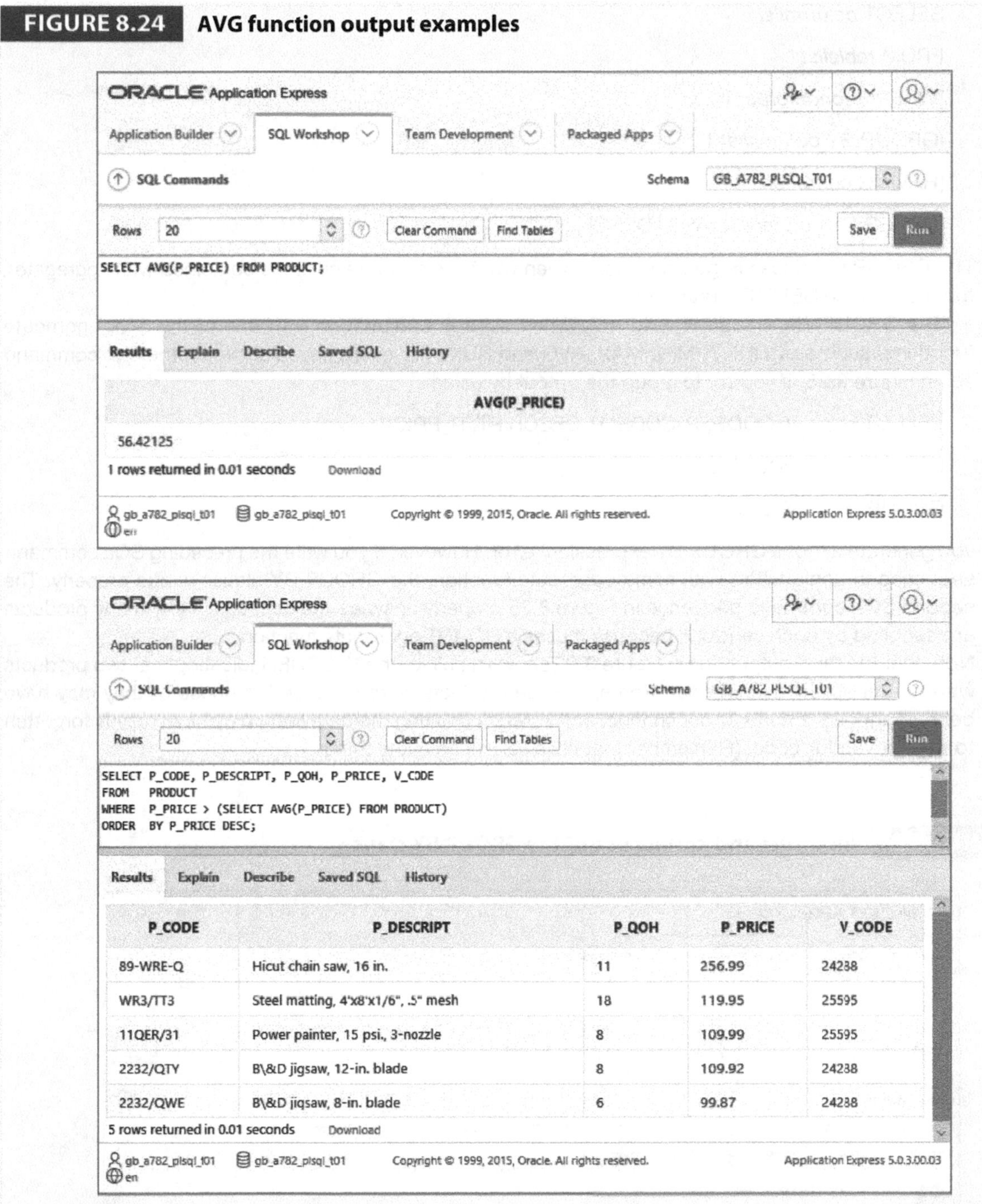

P_CODE	P_DESCRIPT	P_QOH	P_PRICE	V_CODE
89-WRE-Q	Hicut chain saw, 16 in.	11	256.99	24288
WR3/TT3	Steel matting, 4'x8'x1/6", .5" mesh	18	119.95	25595
11QER/31	Power painter, 15 psi., 3-nozzle	8	109.99	25595
2232/QTY	B\&D jigsaw, 12-in. blade	8	109.92	24288
2232/QWE	B\&D jigsaw, 8-in. blade	6	99.87	24288

8.6.4 Grouping Data

Frequency distributions can be created quickly and easily using the **GROUP BY** clause within the SELECT statement. The syntax is:

```
SELECT columnlist
FROM tablelist
[WHERE conditionlist ]
[GROUP BY columnlist ]
[HAVING conditionlist ]
[ORDER BY columnlist [ASC | DESC] ] ;
```

The GROUP BY clause is generally used when you have attribute columns combined with aggregate functions in the SELECT statement.

The GROUP BY clause is valid only when used in conjunction with one of the SQL aggregate functions, such as COUNT, MIN, MAX, AVG and SUM. For example, as shown in the first command set in Figure 8.25, if you try to group the output by using:

```
SELECT      V_CODE, P_CODE, P_DESCRIPT, P_PRICE
FROM        PRODUCT
GROUP BY    V_CODE;
```

you generate a 'not a GROUP BY expression' error. However, if you write the preceding SQL command sequence in conjunction with some aggregate function, the GROUP BY clause works properly. The second SQL command sequence in Figure 8.25 properly answers the question, 'How many products are supplied by each vendor?' because it uses a COUNT aggregate function.

Note that the third output line in Figure 8.25 shows a null for the V_CODE, indicating that two products were not supplied by a vendor. Perhaps those products were produced in-house or they may have been bought via a non-vendor channel or the person making the data entry may have merely forgotten to enter a vendor code. (Remember that nulls can mean many things.)

FIGURE 8.25 **Incorrect and correct use of the GROUP BY clause**

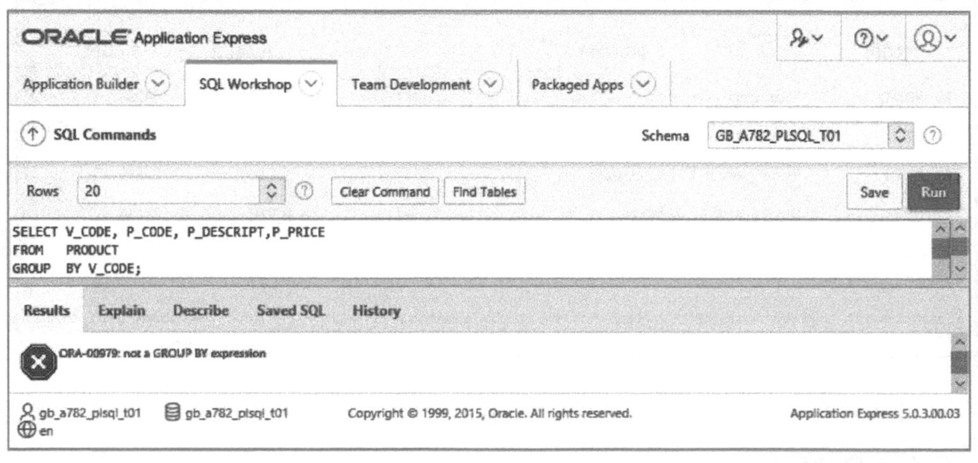

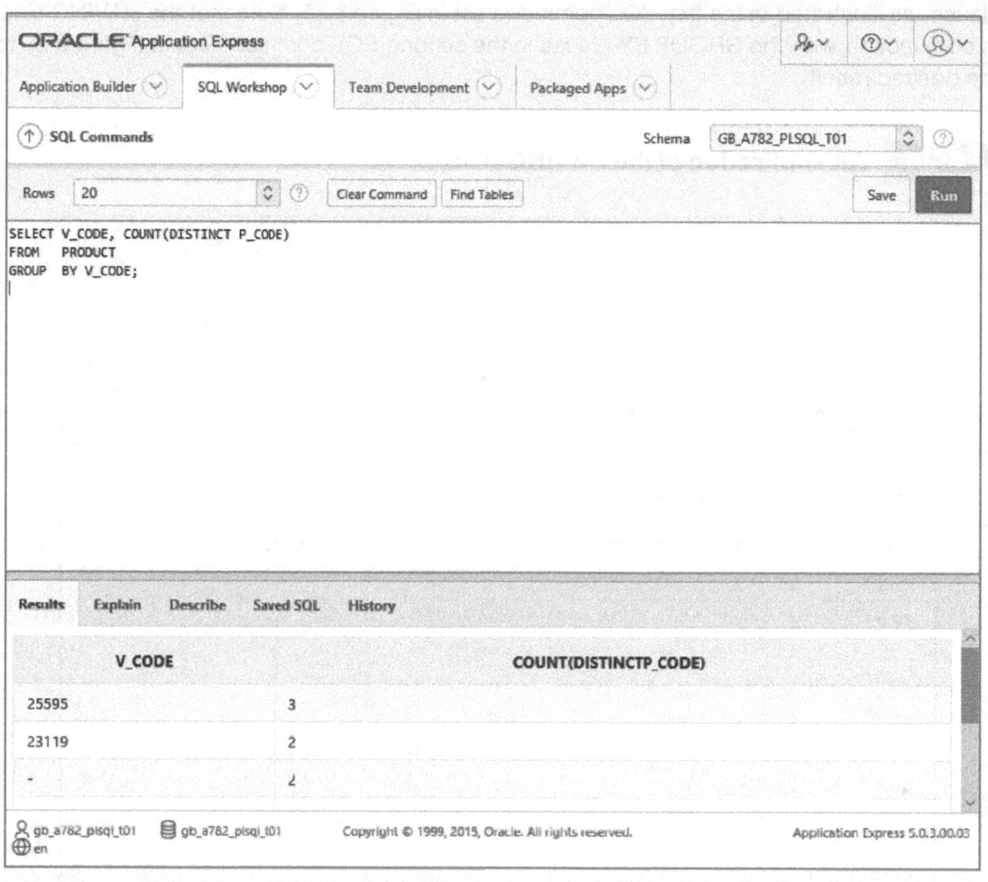

8

> **NOTE**
>
> When using the GROUP BY clause with a SELECT statement:
>
> - The SELECT's *columnlist* must include a combination of column names and aggregate functions.
> - The GROUP BY clauses *columnlist* must include all non aggregate function columns specified in the SELECTs *columnlist*. If required, you could also group by any aggregate function columns that appear in the SELECTs *columnlist*.
> - The GROUP BY clause *columnlist* can include any columns from the tables in the FROM clause of the SELECT statement, even if they do not appear in the SELECTs *columnlist*.

The GROUP BY Feature's HAVING Clause

A particularly useful extension of the GROUP BY feature is the **HAVING** clause. Basically, HAVING operates like the WHERE clause in the SELECT statement. However, the WHERE clause applies to columns and expressions for individual rows, while the HAVING clause is applied to the output of a GROUP BY operation. For example, suppose you want to generate a listing of the number of products in the inventory supplied by each vendor. But this time you want to limit the listing to products whose prices average below €10. The first part of that requirement is satisfied with the help of the GROUP BY clause, as illustrated in the first SQL command set in Figure 8.26. Note that the HAVING clause is used in conjunction with the GROUP BY clause in the second SQL command set in Figure 8.26 to generate the desired result.

FIGURE 8.26 **An application of the HAVING clause**

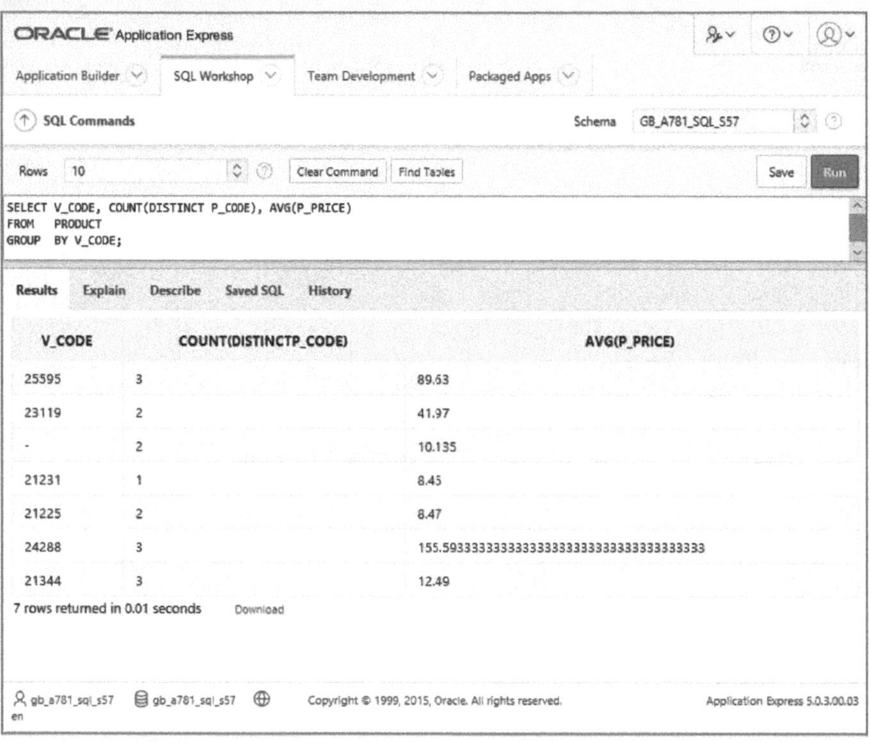

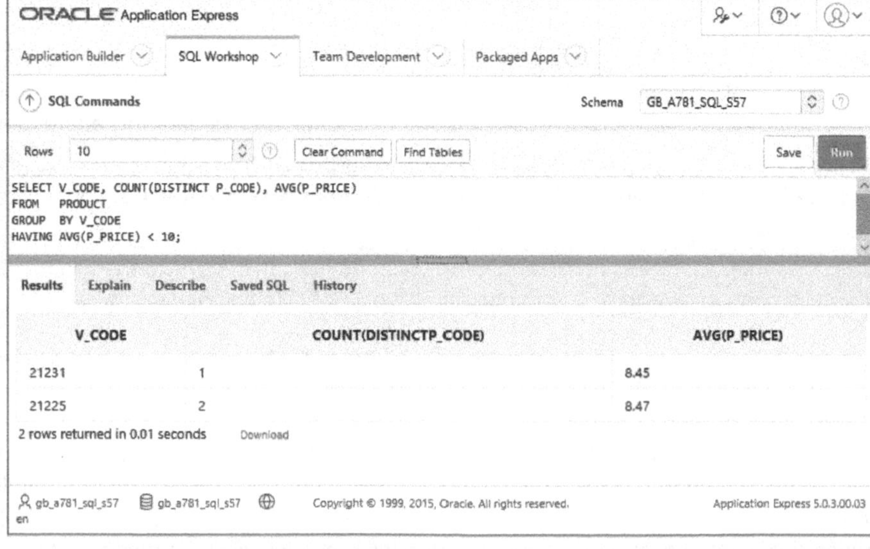

Using the WHERE clause – instead of the HAVING clause – in the second SQL command set in Figure 8.26 produces an error message.

You can also combine multiple clauses and aggregate functions. For example, the following SQL statement will:

- Aggregate the total cost of products grouped by V_CODE.
- Select only the rows having totals that exceed €500.
- List the results in descending order by the total cost.

```
SELECT      V_CODE, SUM(P_QOH * P_PRICE) AS TOTCOST
FROM        PRODUCT
GROUP BY    V_CODE
HAVING (SUM(P_QOH * P_PRICE) > 500)
ORDER BY SUM(P_QOH * P_PRICE) DESC;
```

Note the syntax used in the HAVING and ORDER BY clauses; in both cases, you must specify the column expression (formula) used in the SELECT statement's column list, rather than the column alias (TOTCOST). Some RDBMSs allow you to substitute the column expression with the column alias, while others do not.

8.7 VIRTUAL TABLES: CREATING A VIEW

As you learnt earlier, the output of a relational operator (such as SELECT) is another relation (or table). Suppose that, at the end of every day, you would like to get a list of all products to reorder, that is, products with a quantity on hand that is less than or equal to the minimum quantity. Instead of typing the same query at the end of every day, wouldn't it be better to save that query permanently in the database? That's the function of a relational view. A **view** is a virtual table based on a SELECT query. The query can contain columns, computed columns, aliases and aggregate functions from one or more tables. The tables on which the view is based are called **base tables**.

You can create a view by using the **CREATE VIEW** command:

CREATE VIEW *viewname* AS SELECT *query*

The CREATE VIEW statement is a data definition command that stores the subquery specification – the SELECT statement used to generate the virtual table – in the data dictionary.

The first SQL command set in Figure 8.27 shows the syntax used to create a view named PRICEGT50. This view contains only the designated three attributes (P_DESCRIPT, P_QOH and P_PRICE) and only rows in which the price is over €50. The second SQL command sequence in Figure 8.27 shows the rows that make up the view.

NOTE TO MICROSOFT ACCESS USERS

The CREATE VIEW command is not directly supported in Microsoft Access. To create a view in Microsoft Access, you just need to create a SQL query and then save it. While this is not as versatile as an actual view, which can be treated like a table, it achieves the same result.

FIGURE 8.27 Creating a virtual table with the CREATE VIEW command

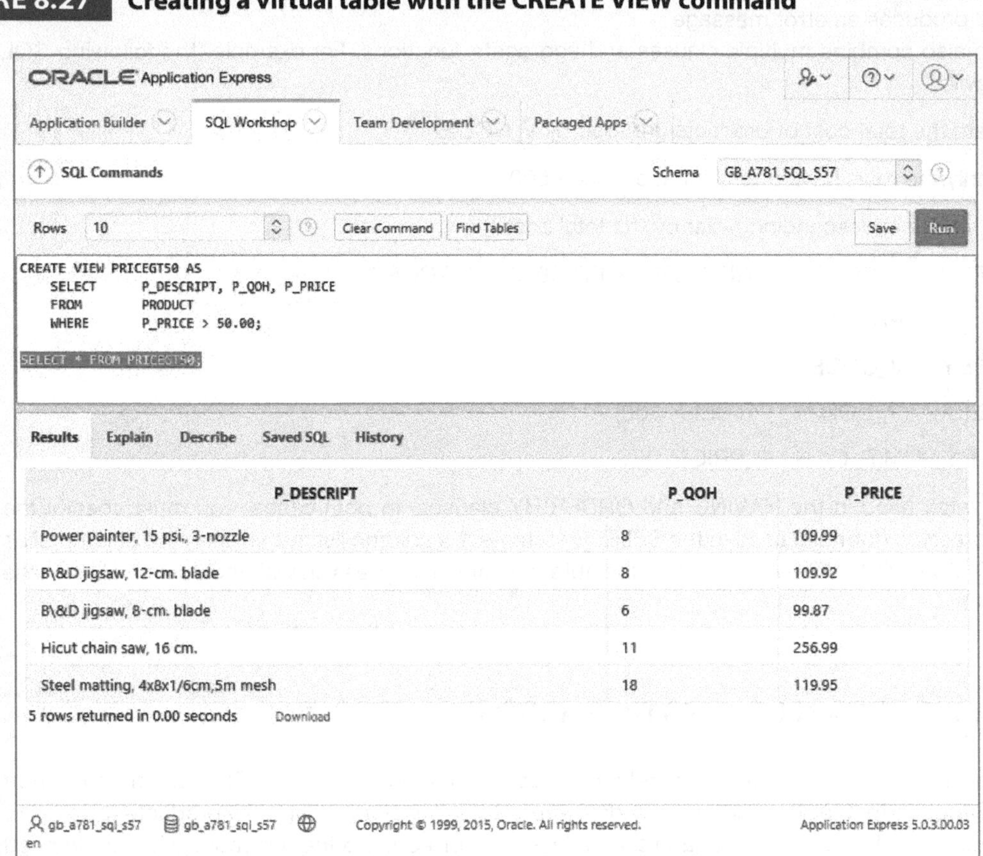

A relational view has several special characteristics:

- You can use the name of a view anywhere a table name is expected in a SQL statement.
- Views are dynamically updated. That is, the view is re-created on demand each time it is invoked. Therefore, if new products are added (or deleted) to meet the criterion P_PRICE > 50.00, those new products automatically appear (or disappear) in the PRICEGT50 view the next time it is invoked.
- Views provide a level of security in the database because the view can restrict users to specified columns and specified rows in a table. For example, if you have a company with hundreds of employees in several departments, you could give the secretary of each department a view of only certain attributes and only for the employees that belong to the secretary's department.
- Views may also be used as the basis for reports. For example, if you need a report that shows a summary of total product cost and quantity-on-hand statistics grouped by vendor, you could create a PROD_STATS view as:

```
CREATE VIEW PROD_STATS AS
SELECT      V_CODE, SUM(P_QOH*P_PRICE) AS TOTCOST,
            MAX(P_QOH) AS MAXQTY, MIN(P_QOH) AS MINQTY,
            AVG(P_QOH) AS AVGQTY
FROM PRODUCT
GROUP BY V_CODE;
```

In Chapter 9, you will learn more about views and, in particular, about updating data in base tables through views.

8.8 JOINING DATABASE TABLES

The ability to combine (join) tables on common attributes is perhaps the most important distinction between a relational database and other databases. A join is performed when data are retrieved from more than one table at a time. (If necessary, review the join definitions and examples in Chapter 4, Relational Algebra and Calculus.)

To join tables, you simply enumerate the tables in the FROM clause of the SELECT statement. The DBMS will create the Cartesian product of every table in the FROM clause. (Review Chapter 3 to revisit these terms, if necessary.) However, to get the correct result – that is, a natural join – you must select only the rows in which the common attribute values match. That is done with the WHERE clause. Use the WHERE clause to indicate the common attributes that are used to link the tables (sometimes referred to as the *join condition*).

The join condition is generally composed of an equality comparison between the foreign key and the primary key of related tables. For example, suppose you want to join the two tables, VENDOR and PRODUCT. Because V_CODE is the foreign key in the PRODUCT table and the primary key in the VENDOR table, the link is established on V_CODE. (See Table 8.10.)

TABLE 8.10 Creating links through foreign keys

Table	Attributes to be shown	Linking attribute
PRODUCT	P_DESCRIPT, P_PRICE	V_CODE
VENDOR	V_COMPANY, V_PHONE	V_CODE

When the same attribute name appears in more than one of the joined tables, the source table of the attributes listed in the SELECT command sequence must be defined. To join the PRODUCT and VENDOR tables, you would use the following, which produces the output shown in Figure 8.28:

```
SELECT      P_DESCRIPT, P_PRICE, V_NAME, V_CONTACT, V_AREACODE, V_PHONE
FROM        PRODUCT, VENDOR
WHERE       PRODUCT.V_CODE = VENDOR.V_CODE;
```

Your output might be presented in a different order because the SQL command produces a listing in which the order of the columns is not relevant. In fact, you are likely to get a different order of the same

8

listing the next time you execute the command. However, you can generate a more predictable list by using an ORDER BY clause:

```
SELECT      P_DESCRIPT, P_PRICE, V_NAME, V_CONTACT, V_AREACODE, V_PHONE
FROM        PRODUCT, VENDOR
WHERE       PRODUCT.V_CODE = VENDOR.V_CODE
ORDER BY    P_PRICE;
```

FIGURE 8.28 The results of a join

P_DESCRIPT	P_PRICE	V_NAME	V_CONTACT	V_AREACODE	V_PHONE
Claw hammer	9.95	Bryson, Inc.	Smithson	0181	223-3234
1.25 cm metal screw, 25	6.99	Bryson, Inc.	Smithson	0181	223-3234
2.5 cm wd. screw, 50	8.45	D&E Supply	Singh	0181	228-3245
7.25 cm pwr. saw blade	14.99	Jabavu Bros.	Khumalo	0181	889-2546
9.00 cm pwr. saw blade	17.49	Jabavu Bros.	Khumalo	0181	889-2546
Rat-tail file, 1/8 cm fine	4.99	Jabavu Bros.	Khumalo	0181	889-2546
Hrd. cloth, 1/4 cm, 2 × 50	39.95	Randsets Ltd.	Anderson	7253	678-3998
Hrd. cloth, 1/2 cm, 3 × 50	43.99	Randsets Ltd.	Anderson	7253	678-3998
B&D jigsaw, 12 cm blade	109.92	ORDVA, Inc.	Hakford	0181	898-1234
B&D jigsaw, 8 cm blade	99.87	ORDVA, Inc.	Hakford	0181	898-1234
Hicut chain saw, 16 cm	256.99	ORDVA, Inc.	Hakford	0181	898-1234
Power painter, 15 psi., 3-nozzle	109.99	Rubicon Systems	Du Toit	0113	456-0092
B&D cordless drill, 1/2 cm	38.95	Rubicon Systems	Du Toit	0113	456-0092
Steel matting, 4 × 8 × 1/6 m, .5 m mesh	119.95	Rubicon Systems	Du Toit	0113	456-0092

NOTE

Table names were used as prefixes in the preceding SQL command sequence. For example, PRODUCT.P_PRICE was used rather than P_PRICE. Most current-generation RDBMSs do not require table names to be used as prefixes unless the same attribute name occurs in several of the tables being joined. In that case, V_CODE is used as a foreign key in PRODUCT and as a primary key in VENDOR; therefore, you must use the table names as prefixes in the WHERE clause. In other words, you can write the previous query as:

```
SELECT      P_DESCRIPT, P_PRICE, V_NAME, V_CONTACT, V_AREACODE, V_PHONE
FROM        PRODUCT, VENDOR
WHERE       PRODUCT.V_CODE = VENDOR.V_CODE;
```

Naturally, if an attribute name occurs in several places, its origin (table) must be specified. If you fail to provide such a specification, SQL generates an error message to indicate that you have been ambiguous about the attribute's origin. In that case, your listing will always be arranged from the lowest price to the highest price.

The preceding SQL command sequence joins a row in the PRODUCT table with a row in the VENDOR table in which the V_CODE values are the same, as indicated in the WHERE clause's condition. Because any vendor can deliver any number of ordered products, the PRODUCT table may contain multiple V_CODE entries for each V_CODE entry in the VENDOR table. In other words, each V_CODE in VENDOR can be matched with many V_CODE rows in PRODUCT.

If you do not specify the WHERE clause, the result will be the Cartesian product of PRODUCT and VENDOR. Because the PRODUCT table contains 16 rows and the VENDOR table contains 11 rows, the Cartesian product would produce a listing of (16 × 11) = 176 rows. (Each row in PRODUCT would be joined to each row in the VENDOR table.)

All of the SQL commands can be used on the joined tables. For example, the following command sequence is quite acceptable in SQL and produces the output shown in Figure 8.29:

```
SELECT      P_DESCRIPT, P_PRICE, V_NAME, V_CONTACT, V_AREACODE, V_PHONE
FROM        PRODUCT, VENDOR
WHERE       PRODUCT.V_CODE = VENDOR.V_CODE
AND P_INDATE > '15-Jan-2019';
```

FIGURE 8.29 An ordered and limited listing after a join

P_DESCRIPT	P_PRICE	V_NAME	V_CONTACT	V_AREACODE	V_PHONE
1.25 cm metal screw, 25	6.99	Bryson, Inc.	Smithson	0181	223-3234
2.5 cm wd. screw, 50	8.45	D&E Supply	Singh	0181	228-3245
Claw hammer	9.95	Bryson, Inc.	Smithson	0181	223-3234
B&D cordless drill, 1/2 cm	38.95	Rubicon Systems	Du Toit	0113	456-0092
Steel matting, 4 × 8 × 1/6 m, .5 m mesh	119.95	Rubicon Systems	Du Toit	0113	456-0092
Hicut chain saw, 16 cm	256.99	ORDVA, Inc.	Hakford	0181	898-1234

NOTE

In Chapter 4, Relational Algebra and Calculus, you learnt that a JOIN is used to combine two relations in a specified way. In SQL, the natural-join is used to join tables together. The SQL statement:

```
SELECT      P_DESCRIPT, P_PRICE, V_NAME, V_CONTACT, V_AREACODE, V_PHONE
FROM        PRODUCT, VENDOR
WHERE       PRODUCT.V_CODE = VENDOR.V_CODE
AND P_INDATE > '15-Jan-2019';
```

can be written in relational algebra as:

$$\Pi_{P\_DESCRIPT,\ P\_PRICE,\ V\_NAME,\ V\_CONTACT,\ V\_AREACODE,\ V\_PHONE}((\sigma_{p\_indate\ =\ '15\text{-}Jan\text{-}2019'}(PRODUCT))\ |X|\ VENDOR)$$

For more information on JOIN operators, see Section 4.2 in Chapter 4, Relational Algebra and Calculus.

When joining three or more tables, you need to specify a join condition for each pair of tables. The number of join conditions will always be N-1, where N represents the number of tables listed in the

FROM clause. For example, if you have three tables, you must have two join conditions; if you have five tables, you must have four join conditions; and so on.

Remember, the join condition will match the foreign key of a table to the primary key of the related table. For example, using Figure 8.1, if you want to list the customer last name, invoice number, invoice date and product descriptions for all invoices for customer 10014, you must type the following:

```
SELECT      CUS_LNAME, INV_NUMBER, INV_DATE, P_DESCRIPT
FROM        CUSTOMER, INVOICE, LINE, PRODUCT
WHERE       CUSTOMER.CUS_CODE = INVOICE.CUS_CODE AND
            INVOICE.INV_NUMBER = LINE.INV_NUMBER AND
            LINE.P_CODE = PRODUCT.P_CODE AND
            CUSTOMER.CUS_CODE = 10014
ORDER BY    INV_NUMBER;
```

Finally, be careful not to create circular join conditions. For example, if Table A is related to Table B, Table B is related to Table C and Table C is also related to Table A, create only two join conditions: join A with B and B with C. Do not join C with A!

8.8.1 Joining Tables with an Alias

An alias may be used to identify the source table from which the data are taken. The aliases P and V are used to label the PRODUCT and VENDOR tables in the next command sequence. Any legal table name may be used as an alias. (Also notice that there are no table name prefixes because the attribute listing contains no duplicate names in the SELECT statement.)

```
SELECT      P_DESCRIPT, P_PRICE, V_NAME, V_CONTACT, V_AREACODE, V_PHONE
FROM        PRODUCT P, VENDOR V
WHERE       P.V_CODE = V.V_CODE
ORDER BY    P_PRICE;
```

8.8.2 Self-Joins

An alias is especially useful when a table must be joined to itself in a **recursive query**. In order to join a table to itself, a self-join is used. For example, suppose you are working with the EMP table shown in Figure 8.30.

FIGURE 8.30 The contents of the EMP table

EMP_NUM	EMP_TITLE	EMP_LNAME	EMP_FNAME	EMP_INITIAL	EMP_DOB	EMP_HIRE_DATE	EMP_AREACODE	EMP_PHONE	EMP_MGR
100	Mr	Cela	Nkosi	D	15-Jun-52	15-Mar-95	0181	324-5456	
101	Ms	Lewis	Rhonda	G	19-Mar-75	25-Apr-96	0181	324-4472	100
102	Mr	Vandam	Rhett		14-Nov-68	20-Dec-00	7253	675-8993	100
103	Ms	Jones	Anne	M	16-Oct-84	28-Aug-04	0181	898-3456	100
104	Mr	Lange	John	P	08-Nov-81	20-Oct-04	7253	504-4430	105

EMP_NUM	EMP_TITLE	EMP_LNAME	EMP_FNAME	EMP_INITIAL	EMP_DOB	EMP_HIRE_DATE	EMP_AREACODE	EMP_PHONE	EMP_MGR
105	Mr	Williams	Robert	D	14-Mar-85	08-Nov-08	0181	890-3220	
106	Mrs	Smith	Jeanine	K	12-Feb-78	05-Jan-99	0181	324-7883	105
107	Mr	Diante	Jorge	D	21-Aug-84	02-Jul-04	0181	890-4567	105
108	Mr	Wiesenbach	Paul	R	14-Feb-76	18-Nov-02	0181	897-4358	
109	Mr	Smith	George	K	18-Jun-71	14-Apr-99	7253	504-3339	108
110	Mrs	Genkazi	Leighla	W	19-May-80	01-Dec-00	7253	569-0093	108
111	Mr	Washington	Rupert	E	03-Jan-76	21-Jun-03	0181	890-4925	105
112	Mr	Johnson	Edward	E	14-May-71	01-Dec-93	0181	898-4387	100
113	Ms	Gounden	Melanie	P	15-Sep-80	11-May-09	0181	324-9006	105
114	Ms	Brandon	Marie	G	02-Nov-66	15-Nov-89	7253	882-0845	108
115	Mrs	Saranda	Hermine	R	25-Jul-82	23-Apr-03	0181	324-5505	105
116	Mr	Smith	George	A	08-Nov-75	10-Dec-98	0181	890-2984	108

Using the data in the EMP table, you can generate a list of all employees with their managers' names by joining the EMP table to itself. In that case, you would also use aliases to differentiate the tables. The SQL command sequence would look like this:

```
SELECT      E.EMP_MGR, M.EMP_LNAME, E.EMP_NUM, E.EMP_LNAME
FROM        EMP E, EMP M
WHERE       E.EMP_MGR=M.EMP_NUM
ORDER BY    E.EMP_MGR;
```

The output of the above command sequence is shown in Figure 8.31.

FIGURE 8.31 Using an alias to join a table to itself

EMP_MGR	M.EMP_LNAME	EMP_NUM	E.EMP_LNAME
100	Cela	112	Johnson
100	Cela	103	Jones
100	Cela	102	Vandam
100	Cela	101	Lewis
105	Williams	115	Saranda
105	Williams	113	Gounden
105	Williams	111	Washington
105	Williams	107	Diante
105	Williams	106	Smith
105	Williams	104	Lange
108	Wiesenbach	116	Smith
108	Wiesenbach	114	Brandon
108	Wiesenbach	110	Genkazi
108	Wiesenbach	109	Smith

8

NOTE

In Microsoft Access, add AS to the previous SQL command sequence, making it read:

```
SELECT      E.EMP_MGR, M.EMP_LNAME, E.EMP_NUM, E.EMP_LNAME
FROM        EMP AS E, EMP AS M
WHERE       E.EMP_MGR=M.EMP_NUM
ORDER BY    E.EMP_MGR;
```

8.8.3 Outer Joins

8

Figure 8.28 showed the results of joining the PRODUCT and VENDOR tables. If you examine the output, note that 14 product rows are listed. If you compare the output to the PRODUCT table in Figure 8.2, you will note that two products are missing. Why? The reason is that there are two products with nulls in the V_CODE attribute. Because there is no matching null 'value' in the VENDOR table's V_CODE attribute, the products do not show up in the final output based on the join. Also, if you examine the VENDOR table in Figure 8.2, you will notice that several vendors have no matching V_CODE in the PRODUCT table. To include those rows in the final join output, you must use an outer join.

There are two types of outer joins: left and right. (See Chapter 4.) Given the contents of the PRODUCT and VENDOR tables, the following left outer join will show all VENDOR rows and all matching PRODUCT rows:

```
SELECT      P_CODE, VENDOR.V_CODE, V_NAME

FROM        VENDOR LEFT JOIN  PRODUCT

ON VENDOR.V_CODE = PRODUCT.V_CODE;
```

Figure 8.32 shows the output generated by the left outer join command in Microsoft Access. Both Oracle and MySQL yield the same result, but show the output in a different order.

FIGURE 8.32 The left outer join results

P_CODE	V_CODE	V_NAME
23109-HB	21225	Bryson, Inc.
SM-18277	21225	Bryson, Inc.
	21226	SuperLoo, Inc.
SW-23116	21231	D&E Supply
13-Q2/P2	21344	Jabavu Bros.
14-Q1/L3	21344	Jabavu Bros.
54778-2T	21344	Jabavu Bros.
	22567	Dome Supply
1546-QQ2	23119	Randsets Ltd.

P_CODE	V_CODE	V_NAME
1558-QW1	23119	Randsets Ltd.
	24004	Brackman Bros.
2232/QTY	24288	ORDVA, Inc.
2232/QWE	24288	ORDVA, Inc.
89-WRE-Q	24288	ORDVA, Inc.
	25443	B&K, Inc.
	25501	Damal Supplies
11QER/31	25595	Rubicon Systems
2238/QPD	25595	Rubicon Systems
WR3/TT3	25595	Rubicon Systems

The right outer join will join both tables and show all product rows with all matching vendor rows. The SQL command for the right outer join is:

```
SELECT      PRODUCT.P_CODE, VENDOR.V_CODE, V_NAME
FROM        VENDOR RIGHT JOIN PRODUCT
ON VENDOR.V_CODE = PRODUCT.V_CODE;
```

Figure 8.33 shows the output generated by the right outer join command sequence in Microsoft Access. Again, both Oracle and MySQL yield the same result, but show the output in a different order.

FIGURE 8.33 The right outer join results

P_CODE	V_CODE	V_NAME
23114-AA		
PVC23DRT		
23109-HB	21225	Bryson, Inc.
SM-18277	21225	Bryson, Inc.
SW-23116	21231	D&E Supply
13-Q2/P2	21344	Jabavu Bros.
14-Q1/L3	21344	Jabavu Bros.
54778-2T	21344	Jabavu Bros.
1546-QQ2	23119	Randsets Ltd.
1558-QW1	23119	Randsets Ltd.
2232/QTY	24288	ORDVA, Inc.
2232/QWE	24288	ORDVA, Inc.
89-WRE-Q	24288	ORDVA, Inc.
11QER/31	25595	Rubicon Systems
2238/QPD	25595	Rubicon Systems
WR3/TT3	25595	Rubicon Systems

In Chapter 9, Procedural Language SQL and Advanced SQL, you will learn more about joins and how to use the latest ANSI SQL standard syntax.

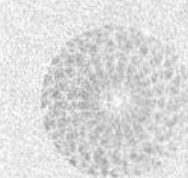

Online Content For a complete walk-through example of converting an ER model into a database structure and using SQL commands to create tables, see Appendix D, Converting an ER Model into a Database Structure, on the online platform for this book.

SUMMARY

- The SQL commands can be divided into two overall categories: data definition language (DDL) commands and data manipulation language (DML) commands.
- The ANSI standard data types are supported by all RDBMS vendors in different ways. The basic data types are NUMBER, INTEGER, CHAR, VARCHAR and DATE.
- The basic data definition commands allow you to create tables, indexes and views. Many SQL constraints can be used with columns. The commands are CREATE TABLE, CREATE INDEX, CREATE VIEW, ALTER TABLE, DROP TABLE, DROP VIEW and DROP INDEX.
- DML commands allow you to add, modify, and delete rows from tables. The basic DML commands are SELECT, INSERT, UPDATE, DELETE, COMMIT and ROLLBACK.
- The INSERT command is used to add new rows to tables. The UPDATE command is used to modify data values in existing rows of a table. The DELETE command is used to delete rows from tables. The COMMIT and ROLLBACK commands are used to permanently save or roll back changes made to the rows. Once you COMMIT the changes, you cannot undo them with a ROLLBACK command.
- The SELECT statement is the main data retrieval command in SQL. A SELECT statement has the following syntax:

  SELECT *columnlist*

  FROM *tablelist*

  [WHERE *conditionlist*]

  [GROUP BY *columnlist*]

  [HAVING *conditionlist*]

  [ORDER BY *columnlist* [ASC | DESC]] ;
- The column list represents one or more column names separated by commas. The column list may also include computed columns, aliases and aggregate functions. A computed column is represented by an expression or formula (for example, P_PRICE * P_QOH). The FROM clause contains a list of table names or view names.
- The WHERE clause can be used with the SELECT, UPDATE and DELETE statements to restrict the rows affected by the DDL command. The condition list represents one or more conditional expressions separated by logical operators (AND/OR/NOT). The conditional expression can contain any comparison operators (=, >, <, >=, <=, <>) as well as special operators (BETWEEN, IS NULL, LIKE, IN and EXISTS).

- Aggregate functions (COUNT, MIN, MAX, AVG) are special functions that perform arithmetic computations over a set of rows. The aggregate functions are usually used in conjunction with the GROUP BY clause to group the output of aggregate computations by one or more attributes. The HAVING clause is used to restrict the output of the GROUP BY clause by selecting only the aggregate rows that match a given condition.
- The ORDER BY clause is used to sort the output of a SELECT statement. The ORDER BY clause can sort by one or more columns and use either ascending or descending order.
- You can join the output of multiple tables with the SELECT statement. The join operation is performed every time you specify two or more tables in the FROM clause and use a join condition in the WHERE clause to match the foreign key of one table to the primary key of the related table. If you do not specify a join condition, the DBMS automatically performs a Cartesian product of the tables you specify in the FROM clause.
- The natural join uses the join condition to match only rows with equal values in the specified columns. You could also do a right outer join and left outer join to select the rows that have no matching values in the other related table.

KEY TERMS

alias
ALTER TABLE
AND
authentication
AVG
base tables
BETWEEN
Boolean algebra
cascading order sequence
COMMIT
COUNT
CREATE INDEX
CREATE TABLE
CREATE VIEW
DELETE
DISTINCT
DROP INDEX
DROP TABLE
EXISTS
GROUP BY
HAVING
IN
INSERT
IS NULL
LIKE
MAX
MIN
NOT
OR
ORDER BY
recursive query
reserved words
ROLLBACK
rules of precedence
schema
SELECT
subquery
SUM
UPDATE
view
wildcard character

FURTHER READING

Allison, C. and Berkowitz, N. *SQL for Microsoft Access.* Wordware Applications Library, Wordware Publishing Inc., 2005.

Freeman, R. *Oracle Database 12c Release 2 New Features (Oracle Press).* McGraw-Hill Education, 2017.

Murach, J. *Murach's MySQL,* 3rd Edition. Mike Murach & Associates Inc., 2019.

Jacobs, P. 'SQL: Comprehensive Beginners Guide to SQL Programming with Exercises and Case Studies', 2018.

Meier, A. and Kaufmann, M. *SQL & Nosql Databases: Models, Languages, Consistency Options and Architectures for Big Data Management,* Springer Vieweg, 2019.

8

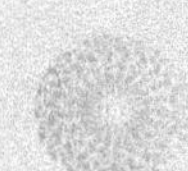

Online Content Answers to selected Review Questions and Problems for this chapter are available on the online platform for this book.

REVIEW QUESTIONS

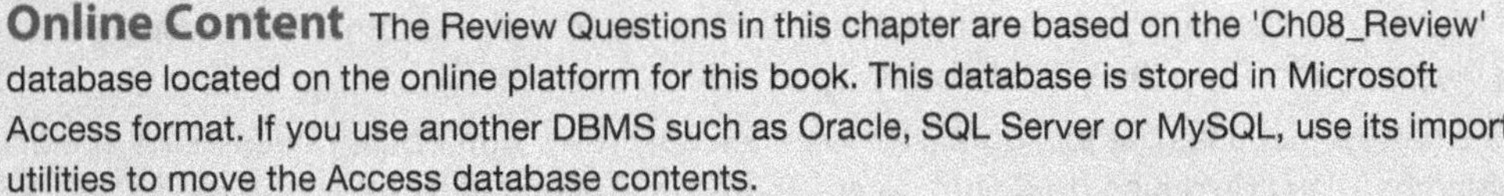

Online Content The Review Questions in this chapter are based on the 'Ch08_Review' database located on the online platform for this book. This database is stored in Microsoft Access format. If you use another DBMS such as Oracle, SQL Server or MySQL, use its import utilities to move the Access database contents.

The Ch08_Review database stores data for a consulting company that tracks all charges to projects. The charges are based on the hours each employee works on each project. The structure and contents of the Ch08_Review database are shown in Figure Q8.1.

FIGURE Q8.1 The Ch8_Review database

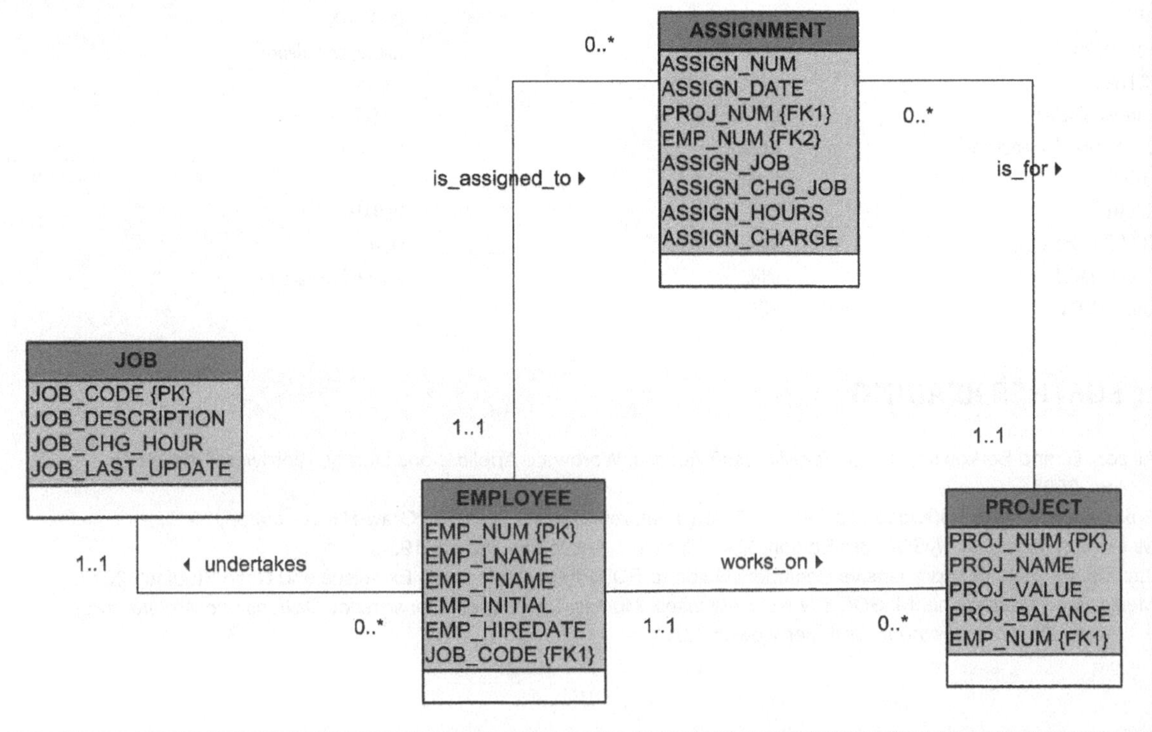

ASSIGNMENT
ASSIGN_NUM
ASSIGN_DATE
PROJ_NUM {FK1}
EMP_NUM {FK2}
ASSIGN_JOB
ASSIGN_CHG_JOB
ASSIGN_HOURS
ASSIGN_CHARGE

JOB
JOB_CODE {PK}
JOB_DESCRIPTION
JOB_CHG_HOUR
JOB_LAST_UPDATE

EMPLOYEE
EMP_NUM {PK}
EMP_LNAME
EMP_FNAME
EMP_INITIAL
EMP_HIREDATE
JOB_CODE {FK1}

PROJECT
PROJ_NUM {PK}
PROJ_NAME
PROJ_VALUE
PROJ_BALANCE
EMP_NUM {FK1}

0..*
is_assigned_to ▸
1..1
0..*
is_for ▸
1..1
1..1
◂ undertakes
0..*
works_on ▸
1..1
0..*

Table name: EMPLOYEE

EMP_NUM	EMP_LNAME	EMP_FNAME	EMP_INITIAL	EMP_HIREDATE	JOB_CODE	EMP_YEARS
101	News	John	G	08-Nov-10	502	4
102	Moonsamy	Kavyara	H	12-Jul-99	501	15
103	Baloyi	Mzwandile	E	01-Dec-06	503	8
104	Maseki	Noxolo	K	15-Nov-97	501	17
105	Johnson	Alice	K	01-Feb-03	502	12
106	Smithfield	William		22-Jun-14	500	0
107	Alonzo	Maria	D	10-Oct-03	500	11
108	Khan	Krishshanth	B	22-Aug-01	501	13
109	Smith	Larry	W	18-Jul-07	501	7
110	Olenko	Gerald	A	11-Dec-05	505	9
111	Wabash	Geoff	B	04-Apr-01	506	14
112	Smithson	Darlene	M	23-Oct-04	507	10
113	Joenbrood	Delbert	K	15-Nov-06	508	8
114	Jones	Annelise		20-Aug-03	508	11
115	Bawangi	Travis	B	25-Jan-02	501	13
116	Pratt	Gerald	L	05-Mar-07	510	8
117	Williamson	Angie	H	19-Jun-06	509	8
118	Frommer	James	J	04-Jan-15	510	0

Table name: ASSIGNMENT

ASSIGN_ NUM	ASSIGN_ DATE	PROJ_ NUM	EMP_ NUM	ASSIGN_ JOB	ASSIGN_ CHG_HR	ASSIGN_ HOURS	ASSIGN_ CHARGE
1001	22-Mar-19	18	103	503	84.50	3.50	295.75
1002	22-Mar-19	22	117	509	34.55	4.20	145.11
1003	22-Mar-19	18	117	509	34.55	2.00	69.10
1004	22-Mar-19	18	103	503	84.50	5.90	498.55
1005	22-Mar-19	25	108	501	96.75	2.20	212.85
1006	22-Mar-19	22	104	501	96.75	4.20	406.35
1007	22-Mar-19	25	113	508	50.75	3.80	192.85
1008	22-Mar-19	18	103	503	84.50	0.90	76.05
1009	23-Mar-19	15	115	501	96.75	5.60	541.80
1010	23-Mar-19	15	117	509	34.55	2.40	82.92
1011	23-Mar-19	25	105	502	105.00	4.30	451.50
1012	23-Mar-19	18	108	501	96.75	3.40	328.95
1013	23-Mar-19	25	115	501	96.75	2.00	193.50
1014	23-Mar-19	22	104	501	96.75	2.80	270.90
1015	23-Mar-19	15	103	503	84.50	6.10	515.45
1016	23-Mar-19	22	105	502	105.00	4.70	493.50

ASSIGN_NUM	ASSIGN_DATE	PROJ_NUM	EMP_NUM	ASSIGN_JOB	ASSIGN_CHG_HR	ASSIGN_HOURS	ASSIGN_CHARGE
1017	23-Mar-19	18	117	509	34.55	3.80	131.29
1018	23-Mar-19	25	117	509	34.55	2.20	76.01
1019	24-Mar-19	25	104	501	110.50	4.90	541.45
1020	24-Mar-19	15	101	502	125.00	3.10	387.50
1021	24-Mar-19	22	108	501	110.50	2.70	298.35
1022	24-Mar-19	22	115	501	110.50	4.90	541.45
1023	24-Mar-19	22	105	502	125.00	3.50	437.50
1024	24-Mar-19	15	103	503	84.50	3.30	278.85
1025	24-Mar-19	18	117	509	34.55	4.20	145.11

Table name: JOB

JOB_CODE	JOB_DESCRIPTION	JOB_CHG_HOUR	JOB_LAST_UPDATE
500	Programmer	35.75	20-Nov-18
501	Systems Analyst	96.75	20-Nov-18
502	Database Designer	125.00	24-Mar-19
503	Electrical Engineer	84.50	20-Nov-19
504	Mechanical Engineer	67.90	20-Nov-19
505	Civil Engineer	55.78	20-Nov-19
506	Clerical Support	26.87	20-Nov-19
507	DSS Analyst	45.95	20-Nov-19
508	Applications Designer	48.10	24-Mar-19
509	Bio Technician	34.55	20-Nov-18
510	General Support	18.36	20-Nov-18

Table name: PROJECT

PROJ_NUM	PROJ_NAME	PROJ_VALUE	PROJ_BALANCE	EMP_NUM
15	Evergreen	1453500.00	1002350.00	103
18	Amber Wave	3500500.00	2110346.00	108
22	Rolling Tide	805000.00	500345.20	102
25	Starflight	2650500.00	2309880.00	107

As you examine Figure Q8.1, note that the ASSIGNMENT table stores the JOB_CHG_HOUR values as an attribute (ASSIGN_CHG_HR) to maintain historical accuracy of the data. The JOB_CHG_HOUR values are likely to change over time. In fact, a JOB_CHG_HOUR change is reflected in the ASSIGNMENT table. And, naturally, the employee primary job assignment may change, so the ASSIGN_JOB is also stored. Because those attributes are required to maintain the historical accuracy of the data, they are *not* redundant.

Given the structure and contents of the Ch8_Review database shown in Figure Q8.1, use SQL commands to answer questions 1–25.

1 Write the SQL code that will create the table structure for a table named EMP_1. This table is a subset of the EMPLOYEE table. The basic EMP_1 table structure is summarised in the table below. (Note that the JOB_CODE is the FK to JOB).

Attribute (Field) Name	Data Declaration
EMP_NUM	CHAR(3)
EMP_LNAME	VARCHAR(15)
EMP_FNAME	VARCHAR(15)
EMP_INITIAL	CHAR(1)
EMP_HIREDATE	DATE
JOB_CODE	CHAR(3)

2 Having created the table structure in Question 1, write the SQL code to enter the first two rows for the table shown in Figure Q8.2.

FIGURE Q8.2 The contents of the EMP_1 table

EMP_NUM	EMP_LNAME	EMP_FNAME	EMP_INITIAL	EMP_HIREDATE	JOB_CODE
101	News	John	G	08-Nov-10	502
102	Moonsamy	Kavyara	H	12-Jul-99	501
103	Baloyi	Mzwandile	E	01-Dec-06	500
104	Maseki	Noxolo	K	15-Nov-07	501
105	Johnson	Alice	K	01-Feb-03	502
106	Smithfield	William		22-Jun-14	500
107	Alonzo	Maria	D	10-Oct-03	500
108	Khan	Krishshanth	B	22-Aug-01	501
109	Smith	Larry	W	18-Jul-07	501

3 Assuming the data shown in the EMP_1 table have been entered, write the SQL code that will list all attributes for a job code of 502.

4 Write the SQL code that will save the changes made to the EMP_1 table.

5 Write the SQL code to change the job code to 501 for the person whose employee number is 107. After you have completed the task, examine the results, then reset the job code to its original value.

6 Write the SQL code to delete the row for the person named William Smithfield, who was hired on 22 June, 2014, and whose job code classification is 500. (*Hint*: Use logical operators to include all of the information given in this problem.)

7 Write the SQL code that will restore the data to its original status; that is, the table should contain the data that existed before you made the changes in Questions 5 and 6.

8 Write the SQL code to create a copy of EMP_1, naming the copy EMP_2. Then write the SQL code that will add the attributes EMP_PCT and PROJ_NUM to its structure. The EMP_PCT is the bonus percentage to be paid to each employee. The new attribute characteristics are:

EMP_PCT NUMBER(4,2)

PROJ_NUM CHAR(3)

9 Write the SQL code to change the EMP_PCT value to 3.85 for the person whose employee number (EMP_NUM) is 103. Next, write the SQL command sequences to change the EMP_PCT values as shown in Figure Q8.3.

10 Using a single command sequence, write the SQL code that will change the project number (PROJ_NUM) to 18 for all employees whose job classification (JOB_CODE) is 500.

11 Using a single command sequence, write the SQL code that will change the project number (PROJ_NUM) to 25 for all employees whose job classification (JOB_CODE) is 502 or higher. When you finish questions 10 and 11, the EMP_2 table will contain the data shown in Figure Q8.4.

(You may assume that the table has been saved again at this point.)

FIGURE Q8.3 The contents of the EMP_2 table

EMP_NUM	EMP_LNAME	EMP_FNAME	EMP_INITIAL	EMP_HIREDATE	JOB_CODE	EMP_PCT	PROJ_NUM
101	News	John	G	08-Nov-10	502	5.00	
102	Moonsamy	Kavyara	H	12-Jul-99	501	8.00	
103	Baloyi	Mzwandile	E	01-Dec-06	500	3.85	
104	Maseki	Noxolo	K	15-Nov-97	501	10.00	
105	Johnson	Alice	K	01-Feb-03	502	5.00	
106	Smithfield	William		22-Jun-14	500	6.20	
107	Alonzo	Maria	D	10-Oct-03	500	5.15	
108	Khan	Krishshanth	B	22-Aug-01	501	10.00	
109	Smith	Larry	W	18-Jul-07	501	2.00	

FIGURE Q8.4 **The contents of the EMP_2 table after the modification**

EMP_NUM	EMP_LNAME	EMP_FNAME	EMP_INITIAL	EMP_HIREDATE	JOB_CODE	EMP_PCT	PROJ_NUM
101	News	John	G	08-Nov-10	502	5.00	25
102	Moonsamy	Kavyara	H	12-Jul-99	501	8.00	
103	Baloyi	Mzwandile	E	01-Dec-06	500	3.85	18
104	Maseki	Noxolo	K	15-Nov-97	501	10.00	
105	Johnson	Alice	K	01-Feb-03	502	5.00	25
106	Smithfield	William		22-Jun-14	500	6.20	18
107	Alonzo	Maria	D	10-Oct-03	500	5.15	18
108	Khan	Krishshanth	B	22-Aug-01	501	10.00	
109	Smith	Larry	W	18-Jul-07	501	2.00	

12 Write the SQL code that will change the PROJ_NUM to 14 for those employees who were hired before 1 January 2004, and whose job code is at least 501. (You may assume that the table will be restored to its condition preceding this question.)

13 Write the two SQL command sequences required to:

- **a** Create a temporary table named TEMP_1 whose structure is composed of the EMP_2 attributes EMP_NUM and EMP_PCT.
- **b** Copy the matching EMP_2 values into the TEMP_1 table.

14 Write the SQL command that will delete the newly created TEMP_1 table from the database.

15 Write the SQL code required to list all employees whose last names start with *Smith*. In other words, the rows for both Smith and Smithfield should be included in the listing. Assume case sensitivity.

16 Using the EMPLOYEE, JOB, and PROJECT tables in the Ch08_Review database (see Figure Q8.1), write the SQL code that will produce the results shown in Figure Q8.5.

FIGURE Q8.5 **The query results for Question 16**

PROJ_NAME	PROJ_VALUE	PROJ_BALANCE	EMP_LNAME	EMP_FNAME	EMP_INITIAL	JOB_CODE	JOB_DESCRIPTION	JOB_CHG_HOUR
Rolling Tide	805000.00	500345.20	Moonsamy	Kavyara	H	501	Systems Analyst	96.75
Evergreen	1453500.00	1002350.00	Baloyi	Mzwandile	E	500	Programmer	35.75
Starflight	2650500.00	2309880.00	Alonzo	Maria	D	500	Programmer	35.75
Amber Wave	3500500.00	2110346.00	Khan	Krishshanth	B	501	Systems Analyst	96.75

17 Write the SQL code that produces a virtual table named REP_1, containing the same information that was shown in Question 16.

18 Write the SQL code to find the average bonus percentage in the EMP_2 table you created in Question 8.

19 Write the SQL code that produces a listing for the data in the EMP_2 table in ascending order by the bonus percentage.

20 Write the SQL code that will list only the different project numbers found in the EMP_2 table.

21 Write the SQL code to calculate the ASSIGN_CHARGE values in the ASSIGNMENT table in the Ch08_Review database. (See Figure Q8.1.) Note that ASSIGN_CHARGE is a derived attribute that is calculated by multiplying ASSIGN_CHG_HR by ASSIGN_HOURS.

22 Using the data in the ASSIGNMENT table, write the SQL code that will yield the total number of hours worked for each employee and the total charges stemming from those hours worked. The results of running that query are shown in Figure Q8.6.

FIGURE Q8.6 **Total hours and charges by employee**

EMP_NUM	EMP_LNAME	SumOfASSIGN_HOURS	SumOfASSIGN_CHARGE
101	News	3.1	387.50
103	Baloyi	19.7	1664.65
104	Maseki	11.9	1218.70
105	Johnson	12.5	1382.50
108	Khan	8.3	840.15
113	Joenbrood	3.8	192.85
115	Bawangi	12.5	1276.75
117	Williamson	18.8	649.54

23 Write a query to produce the total number of hours and charges for each of the projects represented in the ASSIGNMENT table. The output is shown in Figure Q8.7.

FIGURE Q8.7 **Total hours and charges by project**

PROJ_NUM	SumOfASSIGN_HOURS	SumOfASSIGN_CHARGE
15	20.5	1806.52
18	23.7	1544.80
22	27	2593.16
25	19.4	1668.16

24 Write the SQL code to generate the total hours worked and the total charges made by all employees. The results are shown in Figure Q8.8. (*Hint:* This is a nested query. If you use Microsoft Access, you can generate the result by using the query output shown in Figure Q8.6 as the basis for the query that will produce the output shown in Figure Q8.8).

FIGURE Q8.8 **Total hours and charges, all employees**

SumOfSumOfASSIGN_HOURS	SumOfSumOfASSIGN_CHARGE
90.6	7612.64

25 Write the SQL code to generate the total hours worked and the total charges made to all projects. The results should be the same as those shown in Figure Q8.8. (*Hint:* This is a nested query. If you use Microsoft Access, you can generate the result by using the query output as the basis for this query.)

26 Explain why it would be preferable to use a DATE data type to store date data instead of a character data type.

27 Explain why the following command would create an error and which changes could be made to fix the error:

```
SELECT V_CODE, SUM(P_QOH) FROM PRODUCT;
```

28 Explain the difference between an ORDER BY clause and a GROUP BY clause.

29 Explain why the following two commands produce different results:

```
SELECT DISTINCT COUNT (V_CODE) FROM PRODUCT;
SELECT COUNT (DISTINCT V_CODE) FROM PRODUCT;
```

30 What is the difference between the COUNT aggregate function and the SUM aggregate function?

31 In a SELECT query, what is the difference between a WHERE clause and a HAVING clause?

32 Rewrite the following WHERE clause without the use of the IN operator:

```
WHERE v_COUNTRY IN ('UK', 'SA', 'USA')
```

PROBLEMS

Online Content Problems 1–15 are based on the 'Ch08_AviaCo' database located on the online platform for this book. This database is stored in Microsoft Access format. If you use another DBMS such as Oracle, SQL Server or MySQL, use its import utilities to move the Access database contents.

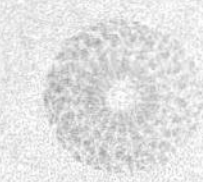

Before you attempt to write any SQL queries, familiarise yourself with the Ch08_AviaCo database structure and contents shown in Figure P8.1. Although the relational schema does not show optionalities, keep in mind that all pilots are employees but not all employees are flight crew members. (Although, in this database, the crew member assignments all involve pilots and copilots, the design is sufficiently flexible to accommodate crew member assignments – such as loadmasters and flight attendants – of people who are not pilots. That's why the relationship between CHARTER and EMPLOYEE is implemented through CREW.) Note also that this design implementation does not include multivalued attributes. For example, multiple ratings such as Instrument and Certified Flight Instructor ratings are stored in the (composite) EARNEDRATINGS table. Nor does the CHARTER table include multiple crew assignments, which are properly stored in the CREW table.

FIGURE P8.1 The Ch08_AviaCo database

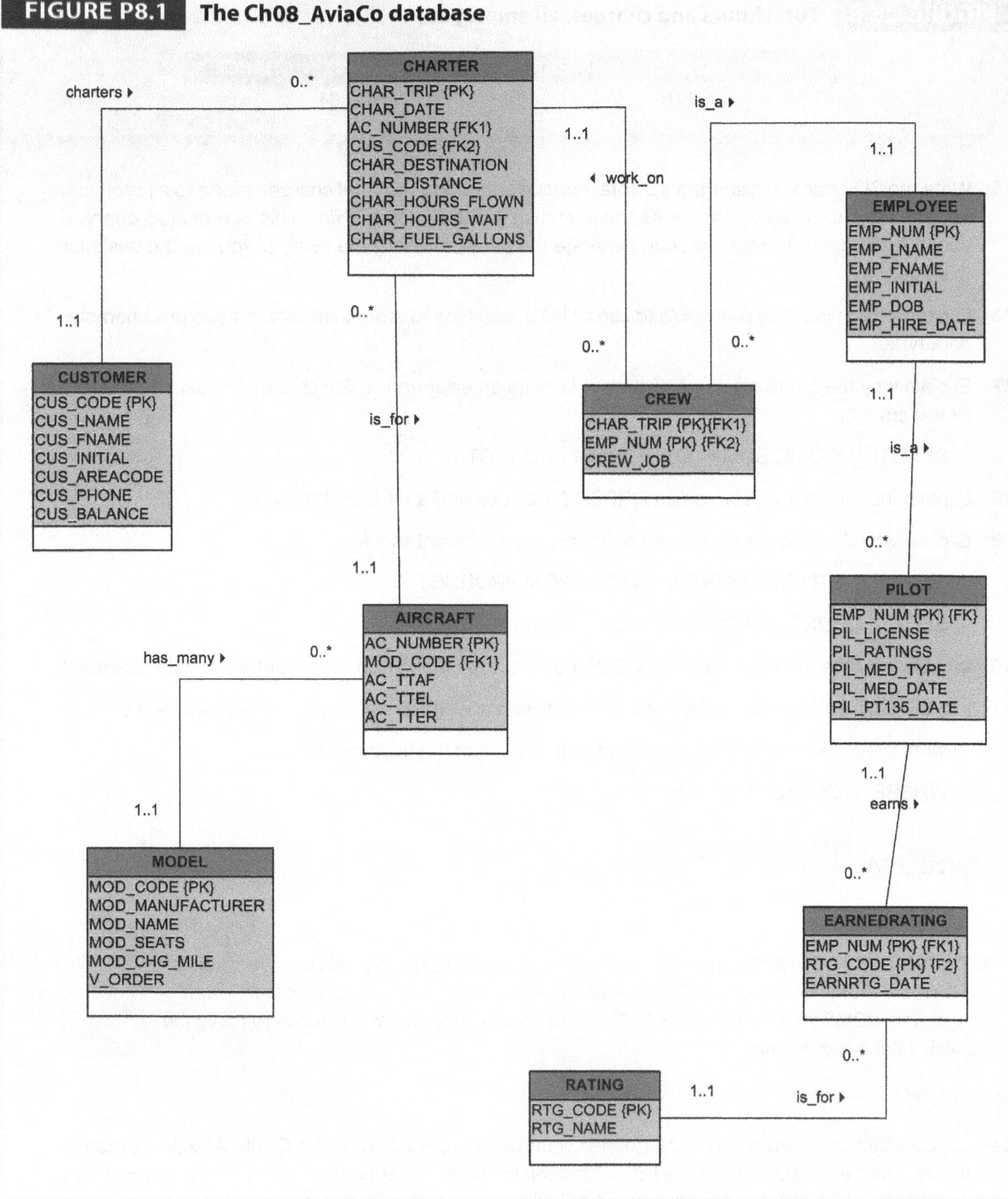

Table name: CREW

CHAR_TRIP	EMP_NUM	CREW_JOB
10001	104	Pilot
10002	101	Pilot
10003	105	Pilot
10003	109	Copilot
10004	106	Pilot
10005	101	Pilot
10006	109	Pilot
10007	104	Pilot
10007	105	Copilot
10008	106	Pilot
10009	105	Pilot
10010	108	Pilot
10011	101	Pilot
10011	104	Copilot
10012	101	Pilot
10013	105	Pilot
10014	106	Pilot
10015	101	Copilot
10015	104	Pilot
10016	105	Copilot
10016	109	Pilot
10017	101	Pilot
10018	104	Copilot
10018	105	Pilot

Table name: RATING

RTG_CODE	RTG_NAME
CFI	Certified Flight Instructor
CFII	Certified Flight Instructor, Instrument
INSTR	Instrument
MEL	Multiengine Land
SEL	Single Engine, Land
SES	Single Engine, Sea

Table name: EMPLOYEE

EMP_NUM	EMP_TITLE	EMP_LNAME	EMP_FNAME	EMP_INITIAL	EMP_DOB	EMP_HIRE_DATE
100	Mr	Nkosi	Cela	D	15-Jun-52	15-Mar-98
101	Ms	Lewis	Rhonda	G	19-Mar-75	25-Apr-96
102	Mr	Vandam	Rhett		14-Nov-68	18-May-03
103	Ms	Jones	Anne	M	11-May-84	26-Jul-09
104	Mr	Lange	John	P	12-Jul-81	20-Aug-00
105	Mr	Williams	Robert	D	14-Mar-85	19-Jun-13
106	Mrs	Duzak	Jeanine	K	12-Feb-78	13-Mar-99
107	Mr	Diante	Jorge	D	01-May-85	02-Jul-07
108	Mr	Wiesenbach	Paul	R	14-Feb-76	03-Jun-03
109	Ms	Travis	Elizabeth	K	18-Jun-71	14-Feb-16
110	Mrs	Genkazi	Leighla	W	19-May-80	29-Jun-00

Table name: PILOT

EMP_NUM	PIL_LICENSE	PIL_RATINGS	PIL_MED_TYPE	PIL_MED_DATE	PIL_PT135_DATE
101	ATP	SEL/MEL/Instr/CFII	1	12-Apr-2018	15-Jun-2018
104	ATP	SEL/MEL/Instr	1	10-Jun-2018	23-Mar-2019
105	COM	SEL/MEL/Instr/CFI	2	25-Feb-2019	12-Feb-2019
106	COM	SEL/MEL/Instr	2	02-Apr-2019	24-Dec-2019
109	COM	SEL/MEL/SES/Instr/ CFII	1	14-Apr-2019	21-Apr-2019

Table name: EARNEDRATING

EMP_NUM	RTG_CODE	EARNRTG_DATE
101	CFI	18-Feb-08
101	CFII	15-Dec-15
101	INSTR	08-Nov-03
101	MEL	23-Jun-04
101	SEL	21-Apr-03
104	INSTR	15-Jul-06
104	MEL	29-Jan-07
104	SEL	12-Mar-05
105	CFI	18-Nov-07
105	INSTR	17-Apr-05
105	MEL	12-Aug-05
105	SEL	23-Sep-04
106	INSTR	20-Dec-05
106	MEL	02-Apr-06

EMP_NUM	RTG_CODE	EARNRTG_DATE
106	SEL	10-Mar-04
109	CFI	05-Nov-08
109	CFII	21-Jun-13
109	INSTR	23-Jul-06
109	MEL	15-Mar-07
109	SEL	05-Feb-06
109	SES	12-May-06

Table name: CUSTOMER

CUS_CODE	CUS_LNAME	CUS_FNAME	CUS_INITIAL	CUS_AREACODE	CUS_PHONE	CUS_BALANCE
10010	Ramas	Alfred	A	0181	844-2573	0.00
10011	Dunne	Leona	K	0161	894-1238	0.00
10012	Smith	Kathy	W	0181	894-2285	896.54
10013	Pieterse	Jaco	F	0181	894-2180	1285.19
10014	Orlando	Myron		0181	222-1672	673.21
10015	O'Brian	Amy	B	0161	442-3381	1014.56
10016	Brown	James	G	0181	297-1228	0.00
10017	Williams	George		0181	290-2556	0.00
10018	Farriss	Anne	G	0161	382-7185	0.00
10019	Smith	Olette	K	0181	297-3809	453.98

Table name: CHARTER

CHAR_TRIP	CHAR_DATE	AC_NUMBER	CHAR_DESTINATION	CHAR_DISTANCE	CHAR_HOURS_FLOWN	CHAR_HOURS_WAIT	CHAR_FUEL_GALLONS	CHAR_OIL_QTS	CUS_CODE
10001	05-Feb-19	2289L	ATL	936.00	5.1	2.2	354.1	1	10011
10002	05-Feb-19	2778V	BNA	320.00	1.6	0	72.6	0	10016
10003	05-Feb-19	4278Y	GNV	1574.00	7.8	0	339.8	2	10014
10004	06-Feb-19	1484P	STL	472.00	2.9	4.9	97.2	1	10019
10005	06-Feb-19	2289L	ATL	1023.00	5.7	3.5	397.7	2	10011
10006	06-Feb-19	4278Y	STL	472.00	2.6	5.2	117.1	0	10017
10007	06-Feb-19	2778V	GNV	1574.00	7.9	0	348.4	2	10012
10008	07-Feb-19	1484P	TYS	644.00	4.1	0	140.6	1	10014
10009	07-Feb-19	2289L	GNV	1574.00	6.6	23.4	459.9	0	10017
10010	07-Feb-19	4278Y	ATL	998.00	6.2	3.2	279.7	0	10016
10011	07-Feb-19	1484P	BNA	352.00	1.9	5.3	66.4	1	10012
10012	08-Feb-19	2778V	MOB	884.00	4.8	4.2	215.1	0	10010

8

CHAR_TRIP	CHAR_DATE	AC_NUMBER	CHAR_DESTINATION	CHAR_DISTANCE	CHAR_HOURS_FLOWN	CHAR_HOURS_WAIT	CHAR_FUEL_GALLONS	CHAR_OIL_QTS	CUS_CODE
10013	08-Feb-19	4278Y	TYS	644.00	3.9	4.5	174.3	1	10011
10014	09-Feb-19	4278Y	ATL	936.00	6.1	2.1	302.6	0	10017
10015	09-Feb-19	2289L	GNV	1645.00	6.7	0	459.5	2	10016
10016	09-Feb-19	2778V	MQY	312.00	1.5	0	67.2	0	10011
10017	10-Feb-19	1484P	STL	508.00	3.1	0	105.5	0	10014
10018	10-Feb-19	4278Y	TYS	644.00	3.8	4.5	167.4	0	10017

Table name: AIRCRAFT

AC_NUMBER	MOD_CODE	AC_TTAF	AC_TTEL	AC_TTER
1484P	PA23-250	1833.10	1833.10	101.80
2289L	C-90A	4243.80	768.90	1123.40
2778V	PA31-350	7992.90	1513.10	789.50
4278Y	PA31-350	2147.30	622.10	243.20

Table name: MODEL

MOD_CODE	MOD_MANUFACTURER	MOD_NAME	MOD_SEATS	MOD_CHG_MILE
C-90A	Beechcraft	KingAir	8	2.67
PA23-250	Piper	Aztec	6	1.93
PA31-350	Piper	Navajo Chieftain	10	2.35

1 Write the SQL code that will list the values for the first four attributes in the CHARTER table.

2 Using the contents of the CHARTER table, write the SQL query that will produce the output shown in Figure P8.2. Note that the output is limited to selected attributes for aircraft number 2778V.

FIGURE P8.2 Problem 2 query results

CHAR_DATE	AC_NUMBER	CHAR_DESTINATION	CHAR_DISTANCE	CHAR_HOURS_FLOWN
05-Feb-19	2778V	BNA	320.00	1.60
06-Feb-19	2778V	GNV	1574.00	7.90
08-Feb-19	2778V	MOB	884.00	4.80
09-Feb-19	2778V	MQY	312.00	1.50

3 Create a virtual table (named AC2778V) containing the output presented in Problem 2.

4 Produce the output shown in Figure P8.3 for aircraft 2778V. Note that this output includes data from the CHARTER and CUSTOMER tables. (*Hint:* Use a JOIN in this query.)

FIGURE P8.3 **Problem 4 query results**

CHAR_DATE	AC_NUMBER	CHAR_DESTINATION	CUS_LNAME	CUS_AREACODE	CUS_PHONE
08-Feb-19	2778V	MOB	Ramas	0181	844-2573
09-Feb-19	2778V	MQY	Dunne	0161	894-1238
06-Feb-19	2778V	GNV	Smith	0181	894-2285
05-Feb-19	2778V	BNA	Brown	0181	297-1228

5 Produce the output shown in Figure P8.4. The output, derived from the CHARTER and MODEL tables, is limited to 6 February 2019. (*Hint:* The join passes through another table. Note that the 'connection' between CHARTER and MODEL requires the existence of AIRCRAFT because the CHARTER table does not contain a foreign key to MODEL. However, CHARTER does contain AC_NUMBER, a foreign key to AIRCRAFT, which contains a foreign key to MODEL.)

FIGURE P8.4 **Problem 5 query results**

CHAR_DATE	CHAR_DESTINATION	AC_NUMBER	MOD_NAME	MOD_CHG_MILE
06-Feb-19	STL	1484P	Aztec	1.93
06-Feb-19	ATL	2289L	KingAir	2.67
06-Feb-19	STL	4278Y	Navajo Chieftain	2.35
06-Feb-19	GNV	2778V	Navajo Chieftain	2.35

6 Modify the query in Problem 5 to include data from the CUSTOMER table. This time the output is limited to charter records generated since 9 February 2019. (The query results are shown in Figure P8.5.)

FIGURE P8.5 **Problem 6 query results**

CHAR_DATE	CHAR_DESTINATION	AC_NUMBER	MOD_NAME	MOD_CHG_MILE	CUS_LNAME
09-Feb-19	ATL	4278Y	Navajo Chieftain	2.35	Williams
09-Feb-19	MQY	2778V	Navajo Chieftain	2.35	Dunne
09-Feb-19	GNV	2289L	KingAir	2.67	Brown
10-Feb-19	TYS	4278Y	Navajo Chieftain	2.35	Williams
10-Feb-19	STL	1484P	Aztec	1.93	Orlando

7 Modify the query in Problem 6 to produce the output shown in Figure P8.6. The date limitation in Problem 6 applies to this problem, too. Note that this query includes data from the CREW and EMPLOYEE tables. (*Note:* You may wonder why the date restriction seems to generate more records than it did in Problem 6. Actually, the number of (CHARTER) records is the same, but several records are listed twice to reflect a crew of two: a pilot and a copilot. For example, the record for the 09-Feb-2019 flight to GNV, using aircraft 2289L, required a crew consisting of a pilot (Lange) and a copilot (Lewis).)

8

FIGURE P8.6 **Problem 7 query results**

CHAR_ DATE	CHAR_ DESTINATION	AC_ NUMBER	MOD_CHG_ MILE	CHAR_ DISTANCE	EMP_ NUM	CREW_ JOB	EMP_ LNAME
09-Feb-19	GNV	2289L	2.67	1645.00	104	Pilot	Lange
09-Feb-19	GNV	2289L	2.67	1645.00	101	Copilot	Lewis
09-Feb-19	MQY	2778V	2.35	312.00	109	Pilot	Travis
09-Feb-19	MQY	2778V	2.35	312.00	105	Copilot	Williams
09-Feb-19	ATL	4278Y	2.35	936.00	106	Pilot	Duzak
10-Feb-19	STL	1484P	1.93	508.00	101	Pilot	Lewis
10-Feb-19	TYS	4278Y	2.35	644.00	105	Pilot	Williams
10-Feb-19	TYS	4278Y	2.35	644.00	104	Copilot	Lange

8 Modify the query in Problem 5 to include the computed (derived) attribute 'fuel per hour'. *Hint:* It is possible to use SQL to produce computed 'attributes' that are not stored in any table. For example, the following SQL query is perfectly acceptable:

```
SELECT CHAR_DISTANCE, CHAR_FUEL_GALLONS/CHAR_DISTANCE

FROM CHARTER;
```

(The above query produces the 'gallons per mile flown' value.) Use a similar technique on joined tables to produce the 'gallons per hour' output shown in Figure P8.7. (Note that 254.3 litres/1.5 hours produces 169.54 litres per hour.)

Query output such as the 'gallons per hour' result shown in Figure P8.7 provides managers with very important information. In this case, why is the fuel burn for the Navajo Chieftain 4278Y flown on 9-Feb-19 so much higher than the fuel burn for that aircraft on 8-Feb-18? Such a query result may lead to additional queries to find out who flew the aircraft or which special circumstances might have existed. Is the fuel burn difference due to poor fuel management by the pilot, does it reflect an engine fuel metering problem, or was there an error in the fuel recording? The ability to generate useful query output is an important management asset.

FIGURE P8.7 **Problem 8 query results**

CHAR_ DATE	AC_ NUMBER	MOD_NAME	CHAR_HOURS_ FLOWN	CHAR_FUEL_ GALLONS	Expr1
09-Feb-18	2778V	Navajo Chieftain	1.5	67.2	44.8
09-Feb-18	2289L	KingAir	6.7	459.5	68.5820895522388
09-Feb-18	4278Y	Navajo Chieftain	6.1	302.6	49.6065573770492
10-Feb-18	4278Y	Navajo Chieftain	3.8	167.4	44.0526315789474
10-Feb-18	1484P	Aztec	3.1	105.5	34.0322580645161

NOTE

The output format is determined by the RDBMS you use. In this example, the Access software defaulted to an output heading labelled Expr1 to indicate the expression resulting from the division:

[CHARTER]![CHAR_FUEL_GALLONS]/[CHARTER]![CHAR_HOURS]created by its expression builder.

Oracle defaults to the full division label. You should learn to control the output format with the help of your RDBMSs utility software.

9 Create a query to produce the output shown in Figure P8.8. Note that, in this case, the computed attribute requires data found in two different tables. (*Hint:* The MODEL table contains the charge per mile, and the CHARTER table contains the total miles flown.) Note also that the output is limited to charter records generated since 9 February 2019. In addition, the output is ordered by date and, within the date, by the customer's last name.

FIGURE P8.8 Problem 9 query results

CHAR_DATE	CUS_LNAME	CHAR_DISTANCE	MOD_CHG_MILE	Mileage Charge
09-Feb-19	Brown	1645.00	2.67	4392.15
09-Feb-19	Dunne	312.00	2.35	733.20
09-Feb-19	Williams	936.00	2.35	2199.60
10-Feb-19	Orlando	508.00	1.93	980.44
10-Feb-19	Williams	644.00	2.35	1513.40

10 Use the techniques that produced the output in Problem 9 to produce the charges shown in Figure P8.9. The total charge to the customer is computed by:

- Miles flown * charge per mile.
- Hours waited * €50 per hour.

The miles flown (CHAR_DISTANCE) value is found in the CHARTER table, the charge per mile (MOD_CHG_MILE) is found in the MODEL table, and the hours waited (CHAR_HOURS_WAIT) are found in the CHARTER table.

FIGURE P8.9 Problem 10 query results

CHAR_DATE	CUS_LNAME	Mileage Charge	Waiting Charge	Total Charge
09-Feb-19	Brown	4392.15	0.00	4392.15
09-Feb-19	Dunne	733.20	0.00	733.20
09-Feb-19	Williams	2199.60	85.00	2304.60
08-Feb-19	Orlando	980.44	0.00	980.44
08-Feb-19	Williams	1513.40	225.00	1738.40

11 Create the SQL query that will produce a list of customers who have an unpaid balance. The required output is shown in Figure P8.10. Note that the balances are listed in descending order.

FIGURE P8.10 Problem 11 query results

CUS_LNAME	CUS_FNAME	CUS_INITIAL	CUS_BALANCE
Pieterse	Jaco	F	1285.19
O'Brian	Amy	B	1014.56
Smith	Kathy	W	896.54
Orlando	Myron		673.21
Smith	Olette	K	453.98

12 Find the average customer balance, the minimum balance, the maximum balance, and the total of the unpaid balances. The resulting values are shown in Figure P8.11.

FIGURE P8.11 Problem 12 query results

Average Balance	Minimum Balance	Maximum Balance	Total Unpaid Bills
432.35	0.00	1285.19	4323.48

13 Using the CHARTER table as the source, group the aircraft data. Then use the SQL functions to produce the output shown in Figure P8.12. (Utility software was used to modify the headers, so your headers may look different.)

FIGURE P8.12 Problem 13 query results

AC_NUMBER	Number of Trips	Total Distance	Average Distance	Total Hours	Average Hours
1484P	4	1976.00	494.00	12.00	3.00
2289L	4	5178.00	1294.50	24.10	6.03
2778V	4	3090.00	772.50	15.80	3.95
4278Y	6	5268.00	878.00	30.40	5.07

14 Write the SQL code to generate the output shown in Figure P8.13. Note that the listing includes all CHARTER flights that did not include a copilot crew assignment. (*Hint:* The crew assignments are listed in the CREW table. Also note that the pilot's last name requires access to the EMPLOYEE table, while the MOD_CODE requires access to the MODEL table.)

8

FIGURE P8.13 **Problem 14 query results**

CHAR_TRIP	CHAR_DATE	AC_NUMBER	MOD_NAME	CHAR_HOURS_FLOWN	EMP_LNAME	CREW_JOB
10001	05-Feb-19	2289L	KingAir	5.1	Lange	Pilot
10002	05-Feb-19	2778V	Navajo Chieftain	1.6	Lewis	Pilot
10004	06-Feb-19	1484P	Aztec	2.9	Duzak	Pilot
10005	06-Feb-19	2289L	KingAir	5.7	Lewis	Pilot
10006	06-Feb-19	4278Y	Navajo Chieftain	2.6	Travis	Pilot
10008	07-Feb-19	1484P	Aztec	4.1	Duzak	Pilot
10009	07-Feb-19	2289L	KingAir	6.6	Williams	Pilot
10010	07-Feb-19	4278Y	Navajo Chieftain	6.2	Wiesenbach	Pilot
10012	08-Feb-19	2778V	Navajo Chieftain	4.8	Lewis	Pilot
10013	08-Feb-19	4278Y	Navajo Chieftain	3.9	Williams	Pilot
10014	09-Feb-19	4278Y	Navajo Chieftain	6.1	Duzak	Pilot
10017	10-Feb-19	1484P	Aztec	3.1	Lewis	Pilot

15 Write a query that lists the ages of the employee and the date on which the query was run. The required output is shown in Figure P8.14. (As you can tell, the query was run on 4 February 2013, so the ages of the employee are current as of that date.) 8

FIGURE P8.14 **Problem 15 query results**

EMP_NUM	EMP_LNAME	EMP_FNAME	EMP_HIRE_DATE	EMP_DOB	Age	Query Date
100	Nkosi	Cela	15-Mar-1997	15-Jun-1952	67	04-Feb-19
101	Lewis	Rhonda	25-Apr-1998	19-Mar-1975	44	04-Feb-19
102	Vandam	Rhett	20-Dec-2002	14-Nov-1968	51	04-Feb-19
103	Jones	Anne	28-Aug-2015	16-Oct-1984	35	04-Feb-19
104	Lange	John	20-Oct-2006	08-Nov-1981	38	04-Feb-19
105	Williams	Robert	08-Jan-2016	14-Mar-1985	34	04-Feb-19
106	Duzak	Jeanine	05-Jan-2001	12-Feb-1978	41	04-Feb-19
107	Diante	Jorge	02-Jul-2006	21-Aug-1984	35	04-Feb-19
108	Wiesenbach	Paul	18-Nov-2004	14-Feb-1976	43	04-Feb-19
109	Travis	Elizabeth	14-Apr-2001	18-Jun-1971	48	04-Feb-19
110	Genkazi	Leighla	01-Dec-2002	19-May-1980	39	04-Feb-19

Online Content Problems 16–33 are based on the 'Ch8_SaleCo' database located on the online platform for this book. This database is stored in Microsoft Access format. If you use another DBMS such as Oracle, SQL Server or MySQL, use its import utilities to move the Access database contents.

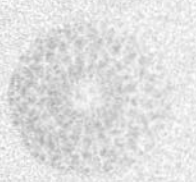

The structure and contents of the Ch8_SaleCo database are shown in Figure P8.15. Use this database to answer the following problems. Save each query as QXX, where XX is the problem number.

FIGURE P8.15 The Ch8_SaleCo database

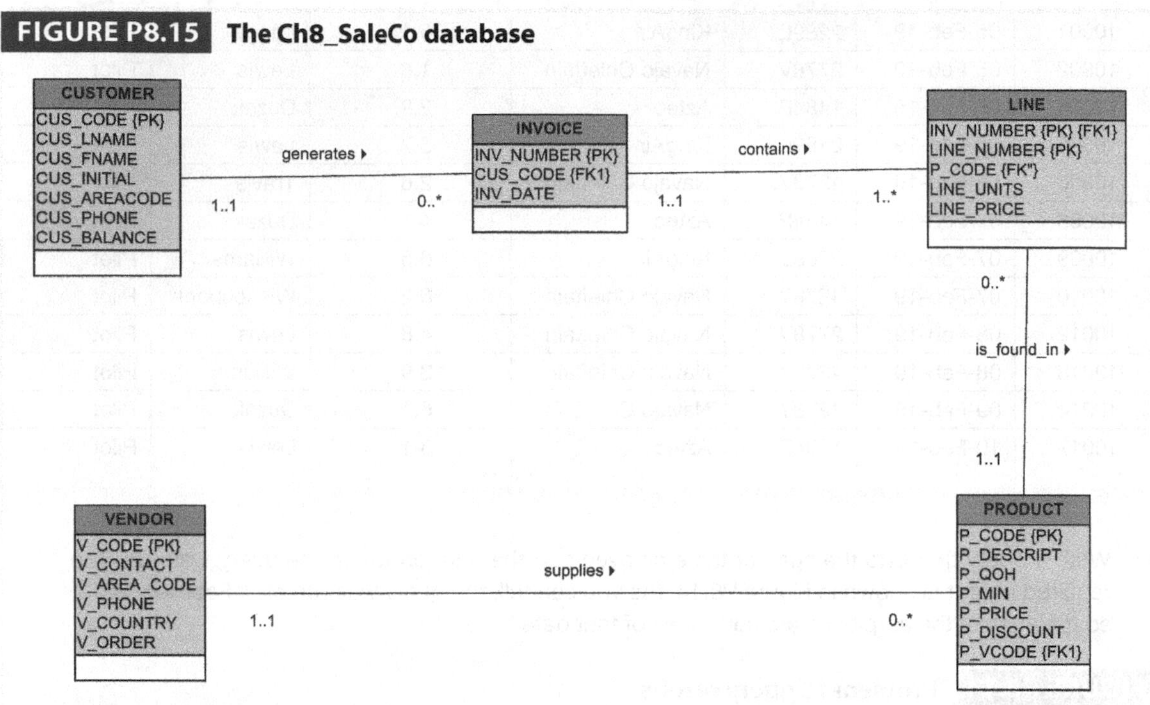

Table name: CUSTOMER

CUS_CODE	CUS_ LNAME	CUS_ FNAME	CUS_ INITIAL	CUS_ AREACODE	CUS_ PHONE	CUS_ BALANCE
10010	Ramas	Alfred	A	0181	844-2573	0.00
10011	Dunne	Leona	K	0161	894-1238	0.00
10012	Smith	Kathy	W	0181	894-2285	345.86
10013	Pieterse	Jaco	F	0181	894-2180	536.75
10014	Orlando	Myron		0181	222-1672	0.00
10015	O'Brian	Amy	B	0161	442-3381	0.00
10016	Brown	James	G	0181	297-1228	221.19
10017	Williams	George		0181	290-2556	768.93
10018	Farriss	Anne	G	0161	382-7185	216.55
10019	Smith	Olette	K	0181	297-3809	0.00

Table name: VENDOR

V_CODE	V_NAME	V_CONTACT	V_AREACODE	V_PHONE	V_COUNTRY	V_ORDER
21225	Bryson, Inc.	Smithson	0181	223-3234	UK	Y
21226	SuperLoo, Inc.	Flushing	0113	215-8995	SA	N
21231	D&E Supply	Singh	0181	228-3245	UK	Y
21344	Jabavu Bros.	Khumalo	0181	889-2546	UK	N
22567	Dome Supply	Smith	7253	678-1419	FR	N
23119	Randsets Ltd.	Anderson	7253	678-3998	FR	Y
24004	Brackman Bros.	Browning	0181	228-1410	UK	N
24288	ORDVA, Inc.	Hakford	0181	898-1234	UK	Y
25443	B&K, Inc.	Smith	0113	227-0093	SA	N
25501	Damal Supplies	Smythe	0181	890-3529	UK	N
25595	Rubicon Systems	Du Toit	0113	456-0092	SA	Y

Table name: PRODUCT

P_CODE	P_DESCRIPT	P_INDATE	P_QOH	P_MIN	P_PRICE	P_DISCOUNT	V_CODE
11QER/31	Power painter, 15 psi., 3-nozzle	03-Nov-18	8	5	109.99	0.00	25595
13-Q2/P2	7.25 cm pwr. saw blade	13-Dec-18	32	15	14.99	0.05	21344
14-Q1/L3	9.00 cm pwr. saw blade	13-Nov-18	18	12	17.49	0.00	21344
1546-QQ2	Hrd. cloth, 1/4 cm, 2x50	15-Jan-19	15	8	39.95	0.00	23119
1558-QW1	Hrd. cloth, 1/2 cm, 3x50	15-Jan-19	23	5	43.99	0.00	23119
2232/QTY	B&D jigsaw, 12 cm blade	30-Dec-18	8	5	109.92	0.05	24288
2232/QWE	B&D jigsaw, 8 cm blade	24-Dec-18	6	5	99.87	0.05	24288
2238/QPD	B&D cordless drill, 1/2 cm	20-Jan-19	12	5	38.95	0.05	25595
23109-HB	Claw hammer	20-Jan-19	23	10	9.95	0.10	21225
23114-AA	Sledge hammer, 12 kg	02-Jan-19	8	5	14.40	0.05	
54778-2T	Rat-tail file, 1/8 cm fine	15-Dec-18	43	20	4.99	0.00	21344
89-WRE-Q	Hicut chain saw, 16 cm	07-Feb-19	11	5	256.99	0.05	24288
PVC23DRT	PVC pipe, 3.5 cm, 8 m	20-Feb-19	188	75	5.87	0.00	

P_CODE	P_DESCRIPT	P_INDATE	P_QOH	P_MIN	P_PRICE	P_DISCOUNT	V_CODE
SM-18277	1.25 cm metal screw, 25	01-Mar-19	172	75	6.99	0.00	21225
SW-23116	2.5 cm wd. screw, 50	24-Feb-19	237	100	8.45	0.00	21231
WR3/TT3	Steel matting, 4 × 8 × 1/6 m, .5 m mesh	17-Jan-19	18	5	119.95	0.10	25595

Table name: INVOICE

INV_NUMBER	CUS_CODE	INV_DATE
1001	10014	16-Mar-19
1002	10011	16-Mar-19
1003	10012	16-Mar-19
1004	10011	17-Mar-19
1005	10018	17-Mar-19
1006	10014	17-Mar-19
1007	10015	17-Mar-19
1008	10011	17-Mar-19

Table name: LINE

INV_NUMBER	LINE_NUMBER	P_CODE	LINE_UNITS	LINE_PRICE
1001	1	13-Q2/P2	1	14.99
1001	2	23109-HB	1	9.95
1002	1	54778-2T	2	4.99
1003	1	2238/QPD	1	38.95
1003	2	1546-QQ2	1	39.95
1003	3	13-Q2/P2	5	14.99
1004	1	54778-2T	3	4.99
1004	2	23109-HB	2	9.95
1005	1	PVC23DRT	12	5.87
1006	1	SM-18277	3	6.99
1006	2	2232/QTY	1	109.92
1006	3	23109-HB	1	9.95
1006	4	89-WRE-Q	1	256.99
1007	1	13-Q2/P2	2	14.99
1007	2	54778-2T	1	4.99
1008	1	PVC23DRT	5	5.87
1008	2	WR3/TT3	3	119.95
1008	3	23109-HB	1	9.95

16 Write a query to count the number of invoices.

17 Write a query to count the number of customers with a customer balance over €500.

18 Generate a listing of all purchases made by the customers, using the output shown in Figure P8.16 as your guide. (*Hint:* Use the ORDER BY clause to order the resulting rows as shown in Figure P8.16.)

FIGURE P8.16 **Problem 18 query results**

CUS_CODE	INV_NUMBER	INV_DATE	P_DESCRIPT	LINE_UNITS	LINE_PRICE
10011	1002	16-Mar-19	Rat-tail file, 1/8 cm fine	2	4.99
10011	1004	17-Mar-19	Claw hammer	2	9.95
10011	1004	17-Mar-19	Rat-tail file, 1/8 cm fine	3	4.99
10011	1008	17-Mar-19	Claw hammer	1	9.95
10011	1008	17-Mar-19	PVC pipe, 3.5 cm, 8 m	5	5.87
10011	1008	17-Mar-19	Steel matting, 4 × 8 × 1/6 m, .5 m mesh	3	119.95
10012	1003	16-Mar-19	7.25 cm pwr. saw blade	5	14.99
10012	1003	16-Mar-19	B&D cordless drill, 1/2 cm	1	38.95
10012	1003	16-Mar-19	Hrd. cloth, 1/4 cm, 2 × 50	1	39.95
10014	1001	16-Mar-19	7.25 cm pwr. saw blade	1	14.99
10014	1001	16-Mar-19	Claw hammer	1	9.95
10014	1006	17-Mar-19	1.25 cm metal screw, 25	3	6.99
10014	1006	17-Mar-19	B&D jigsaw, 12 cm blade	1	109.92
10014	1006	17-Mar-19	Claw hammer	1	9.95
10014	1006	17-Mar-19	Hicut chain saw, 16 cm	1	256.99
10015	1007	17-Mar-19	7.25 cm pwr. saw blade	2	14.99
10015	1007	17-Mar-19	Rat-tail file, 1/8 cm fine	1	4.99
10018	1005	17-Mar-19	PVC pipe, 3.5 cm, 8 m	12	5.87

19 Using the output shown in Figure P8.17 as your guide, generate the listing of customer purchases, including the subtotals for each of the invoice line numbers. (*Hint:* Modify the query format used to produce the listing of customer purchases in Problem 18, delete the INV_DATE column, and add the derived (computed) attribute LINE_UNITS * LINE_PRICE to calculate the subtotals.)

8

FIGURE P8.17 **Problem 19 query results**

CUS_CODE	INV_NUMBER	P_DESCRIPT	Units Bought	Unit Price	Subtotal
10011	1002	Rat-tail file, 1/8 cm fine	2	4.99	9.98
10011	1004	Claw hammer	2	9.95	19.90
10011	1004	Rat-tail file, 1/8 cm fine	3	4.99	14.97
10011	1008	Claw hammer	1	9.95	9.95
10011	1008	PVC pipe, 3.5 cm, 8 m	5	5.87	29.35
10011	1008	Steel matting, 4 × 8 × 1/6 m, .5 m mesh	3	119.95	359.85
10012	1003	7.25cm pwr. saw blade	5	14.99	74.95
10012	1003	B&D cordless drill, 1/2 cm	1	38.95	38.95
10012	1003	Hrd. cloth, 1/4 cm, 2 × 50	1	39.95	39.95
10014	1001	7.25 cm pwr. saw blade	1	14.99	14.99
10014	1001	Claw hammer	1	9.95	9.95
10014	1006	1.25 cm metal screw, 25	3	6.99	20.97
10014	1006	B&D jigsaw, 12 cm blade	1	109.92	109.92
10014	1006	Claw hammer	1	9.95	9.95
10014	1006	Hicut chain saw, 16 cm	1	256.99	256.99
10015	1007	7.25 cm pwr. saw blade	2	14.99	29.98
10015	1007	Rat-tail file, 1/8 cm fine	1	4.99	4.99
10018	1005	PVC pipe, 3.5 cm, 8 m	12	5.87	70.44

20 Modify the query used in Problem 19 to produce the summary shown in Figure P8.18.

FIGURE P8.18 **Customer purchase summary**

CUS_CODE	CUS_BALANCE	Total Purchases
10011	0.00	444.00
10012	345.86	153.85
10014	0.00	422.77
10015	0.00	34.97
10018	216.55	70.44

21 Modify the query in Problem 20 to include the number of individual product purchases made by each customer. (In other words, if the customer's invoice is based on three products, one per LINE_NUMBER, you would count three product purchases. If you examine the original invoice data, you will note that customer 10011 generated three invoices, which contained a total of six lines, each representing a product purchase.) Your output values must match those shown in Figure P8.19.

FIGURE P8.19 Customer total purchase amounts and number of purchases

CUS_CODE	CUS_BALANCE	Total Purchases	Number of Purchases
10011	0.00	444.00	6
10012	345.86	153.85	3
10014	0.00	422.77	6
10015	0.00	34.97	2
10018	216.55	70.44	1

22 Use a query to compute the average purchase amount per product made by each customer. (*Hint:* Use the results of Problem 21 as the basis for this query.) Your output values must match those shown in Figure P8.20. Note that the average purchase amount is equal to the total purchases divided by the number of purchases.

FIGURE P8.20 Average purchase amount by customer

CUS_CODE	CUS_BALANCE	Total Purchases	Number of Purchases	Average Purchase Amount
10011	0.00	444.00	6	74.00
10012	345.86	153.85	3	51.28
10014	0.00	422.77	6	70.46
10015	0.00	34.97	2	17.48
10018	216.55	70.44	1	70.44

23 Create a query to produce the total purchase per invoice, generating the results shown in Figure P8.21. The invoice total is the sum of the product purchases in the LINE that corresponds to the INVOICE.

FIGURE P8.21 Invoice totals

INV_NUMBER	Invoice Total
1001	24.94
1002	9.98
1003	153.85
1004	34.87
1005	70.44
1006	397.83
1007	34.97
1008	399.15

8

24 Use a query to show the invoices and invoice totals as shown in Figure P8.22. (*Hint:* Group by the CUS_CODE.)

FIGURE P8.22 **Invoice totals by customer**

CUS_CODE	INV_NUMBER	Invoice Total
10011	1002	9.98
10011	1004	34.87
10011	1008	399.15
10012	1003	153.85
10014	1001	24.94
10014	1006	397.83
10015	1007	34.97
10018	1005	70.44

25 Write a query to produce the number of invoices and the total purchase amounts by customer, using the output shown in Figure P8.23 as your guide. (Compare this summary to the results shown in Problem 24.)

8

FIGURE P8.23 **Number of invoices and total purchase amounts by customer**

CUS_CODE	Number of Invoices	Total Customer Purchases
10011	3	444.00
10012	1	153.85
10014	2	422.77
10015	1	34.97
10018	1	70.44

26 Using the query results in Problem 25 as your basis, write a query to generate the total number of invoices, the invoice total for all of the invoices, the smallest invoice amount, the largest invoice amount and the average of all of the invoices. (*Hint:* Check the figure output in Problem 25.) Your output must match Figure P8.24.

FIGURE P8.24 **Number of invoices; invoice totals; minimum, maximum and average sales**

Total # of Invoices	Total Sales	Minimum Sale	Largest Sale	Average Sale
8	1 126.03	34.97	444.00	225.21

27 List the balance characteristics of the customers who have made purchases during the current invoice cycle – that is, for the customers who appear in the INVOICE table. The results of this query are shown in Figure P8.25.

FIGURE P8.25 **Balances of customers who made purchases**

CUS_CODE	CUS_BALANCE
10011	0.00
10012	345.86
10014	0.00
10015	0.00
10018	216.55

28 Using the results of the query created in Problem 27, provide a summary of customer balance characteristics as shown in Figure P8.26.

FIGURE P8.26 **Balance summary for customers who made purchases**

Minimum Balance	Maximum Balance	Average Balance
0.00	345.86	112.48

29 Create a query to find the customer balance characteristics for all customers, including the total of the outstanding balances. The results of this query are shown in Figure P8.27.

FIGURE P8.27 **Balance summary for all customers**

Total Balance	Minimum Balance	Maximum Balance	Average Balance
2089.28	0.00	768.93	208.93

30 Find the listing of customers who did not make purchases during the invoicing period. Your output must match the output shown in Figure P8.28.

FIGURE P8.28 **Balances of customers who did not make purchases**

CUS_CODE	CUS_BALANCE
10010	0.00
10013	536.75
10016	221.19
10017	768.93
10019	0.00

31 Find the customer balance summary for all customers who have not made purchases during the current invoicing period. The results are shown in Figure P8.29.

FIGURE P8.29 Balance summary for customers who did not make purchases

Total Balance	Minimum Balance	Maximum Balance	Average Balance
1526.87	0.00	768.93	305.37

32 Create a query to produce the summary of the value of products currently in inventory. Note that the value of each product is produced by the multiplication of the units currently in inventory and the unit price. Use the ORDER BY clause to match the order shown in Figure P8.30.

FIGURE P8.30 Value of products currently in inventory

P_DESCRIPT	P_QOH	P_PRICE	Subtotal
Power painter, 15 psi., 3-nozzle	8	109.99	879.92
7.25 cm pwr. saw blade	32	14.99	479.68
9.00 cm pwr. saw blade	18	17.49	314.82
Hrd. cloth, 1/4 cm, 2 × 50	15	39.95	599.25
Hrd. cloth, 1/2 cm, 3 × 50	23	43.99	1011.77
B&D jigsaw, 12 cm blade	8	109.92	879.36
B&D jigsaw, 8 cm blade	6	99.87	599.22
B&D cordless drill, 1/2 cm	12	38.95	467.40
Claw hammer	23	9.95	228.85
Sledge hammer, 12 kg	8	14.40	115.20
Rat-tail file, 1/8 cm fine	43	4.99	214.57
Hicut chain saw, 16 cm	11	256.99	2826.89
PVC pipe, 3.5 cm, 8 m	188	5.87	1103.56
1.25 cm metal screw, 25	172	6.99	1202.28
2.5 cm wd. screw, 50	237	8.45	2002.65
Steel matting, 4 × 8 × 1/6 m, .5 m mesh	18	119.95	2159.10

33 Using the results of the query created in Problem 32, find the total value of the product inventory. The results are shown in Figure P8.31.

FIGURE P8.31 Total value of all products in inventory

Total value of inventory
15084.52

Online Content Problems 34–42 are based on the 'Ch8_ThemePark' database located on the online platform for this book. This database is stored in Microsoft Access format. If you use another DBMS such as Oracle, SQL Server or MySQL use its import utilities to move the Access database contents.

The structure and contents of the Ch8_ThemePark database are shown in Figure P8.32. Use this database to answer the following problems. Save each query as QXX, where XX is the problem number.

FIGURE P8.32 The Ch8_ThemePark database

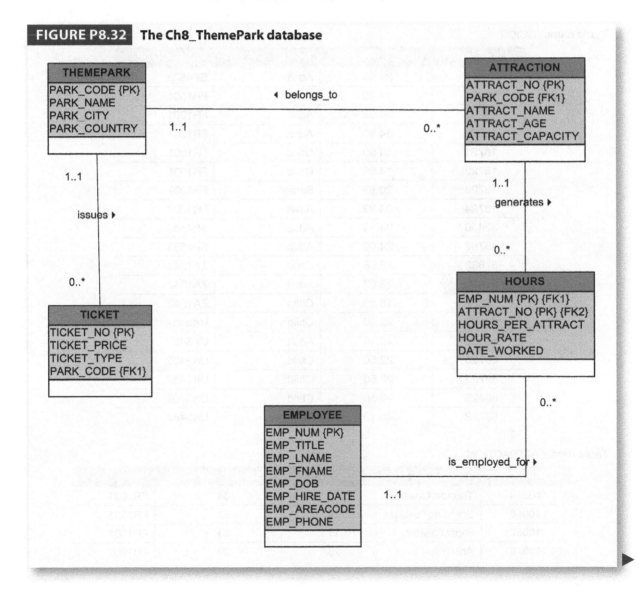

Table name: THEMEPARK

PARK_CODE	PARK_NAME	PARK_CITY	PARK_COUNTRY
FR1001	FairyLand	PARIS	FR
NL1202	Efling	NOORD	NL
SP4533	AdventurePort	BARCELONA	SP
SW2323	Labyrinthe	LAUSANNE	SW
UK2622	MiniLand	WINDSOR	UK
UK3452	PleasureLand	STOKE	UK
ZA1342	GoldTown	JOHANNESBURG	ZA

Table name: TICKET

TICKET_NO	TICKET_PRICE	TICKET_TYPE	PARK_CODE
4668	24.99	Adult	SP4533
13001	14.99	Child	FR1001
13002	34.99	Adult	FR1001
13003	34.99	Adult	FR1001
18721	14.99	Child	FR1001
18722	14.99	Child	FR1001
18723	20.99	Senior	FR1001
18724	34.99	Adult	FR1001
32450	24.99	Adult	SP4533
45767	24.99	Adult	SP4533
67832	18.56	Child	ZA1342
67833	28.67	Adult	ZA1342
67855	18.56	Child	ZA1342
88567	22.50	Child	UK3452
88568	42.10	Adult	UK3452
89720	22.50	Child	UK3452
89723	22.50	Child	UK3452
89725	22.50	Child	UK3452
89728	42.10	Adult	UK3452

Table name: ATTRACTION

ATTRACT_NO	ATTRACT_NAME	ATTRACT_AGE	ATTRACT_CAPACITY	PARK_CODE
10034	ThunderCoaster	11	34	FR1001
10056	SpinningTeacups	4	62	FR1001
10067	FlightToStars	11	24	FR1001
10078	Ant-Trap	23	30	FR1001

ATTRACT_NO	ATTRACT_NAME	ATTRACT_AGE	ATTRACT_CAPACITY	PARK_CODE
10098	Carnival	3	120	FR1001
20056	3D-Lego_Show	3	200	UK2622
30011	BlackHole2	12	34	UK3452
30012	Pirates	10	42	UK3452
30044	UnderSeaWord	4	80	UK3452
98764	GoldRush	5	80	ZA1342

Table name: HOURS

EMP_NUM	ATTRACT_NO	HOURS_PER_ATTRACT	HOUR_RATE	DATE_WORKED
100	10034	6	6.5	18/05/2019
100	10034	6	6.5	20/05/2019
101	10034	6	6.5	18/05/2019
102	30012	3	5.99	23/05/2019
102	30044	6	5.99	22/05/2019
102	30044	3	5.99	23/06/2019
104	30011	6	7.2	21/05/2019
104	30012	6	7.2	22/05/2019
105	10078	3	8.5	18/05/2019
105	10098	3	8.5	18/05/2019
105	10098	6	8.5	19/05/2019

Table name: EMPLOYEE

EMP_NUM	EMP_TITLE	EMP_LNAME	EMP_FNAME	EMP_DOB	EMP_HIRE_DATE	EMP_AREACODE	EMP_PHONE
100	Ms	Calderdale	Emma	15-Jun-82	15-Mar-02	0181	324-9134
101	Ms	Ricardo	Marshel	19-Mar-88	25-Apr-06	0181	324-4472
102	Mr	Arshad	Arif	14-Nov-79	20-Dec-00	7253	675-8993
103	Ms	Roberts	Anne	16-Oct-84	16-Aug-04	0181	898-3456
104	Mr	Denver	Enrica	08-Nov-90	20-Oct-11	7253	504-4434
105	Ms	Namowa	Mirrelle	14-Mar-00	08-Nov-16	0181	890-3243
106	Mrs	Smith	Gemma	12-Feb-78	05-Jan-99	0181	324-7845

34 Write the SQL code which lists all the attractions in each theme park.

35 Write the SQL code to display the attraction name and the capacity for all attractions in the theme park 'FairyLand'. The results are shown in Figure P8.33.

8

FIGURE P8.33 Attractions and their capacities in theme park FairyLand

ATTRACT_NAME	ATTRACT_CAPACITY
ThunderCoaster	34
SpinningTeacups	62
FlightToStars	24
Ant-Trap	30
Carnival	120

36 Using the output in Figure P8.34 as your guide, display the total number of hours worked by each employee on each attraction.

FIGURE P8.34 Number of hours worked on each attraction by employees

EMP_FNAME	EMP_LNAME	ATTRACT_NAME	SumOfHOURS_PER_ATTRACT
Arif	Arshad	Pirates	3
Arif	Arshad	UnderSeaWord	9
Emma	Calderdale	ThunderCoaster	12
Enrica	Denver	BlackHole2	6
Enrica	Denver	Pirates	6
Marshel	Ricardo	ThunderCoaster	6
Mirrelle	Namowa	Ant-Trap	3
Mirrelle	Namowa	Carnival	9

37 Write a query which shows the total price of all adult tickets sold at all theme parks. Label the total price column as 'Total Adult Ticket Sales' and round up the total price to two decimal places. The results of this query are shown in Figure P8.35.

FIGURE P8.35 Total adult ticket sales in each theme park

PARK_NAME	Total Adult Ticket Sales
AdventurePort	74.97
FairyLand	104.97
GoldTown	28.67
PleasureLand	84.20

38 Write a query to show the last names, area codes and phone numbers of all employees who worked on 18 May 2019. Your query should output the rows shown in Figure P8.36.

FIGURE P8.36 Employees who worked on 18 May 2019

EMP_LNAME	EMP_AREACODE	EMP_PHONE	ATTRACT_NAME
Calderdale	0181	324-9134	ThunderCoaster
Ricardo	0181	324-4472	ThunderCoaster
Namowa	0181	890-3243	Carnival
Namowa	0181	890-3243	Ant-Trap

39 Using Figure P8.37 as a guide, show the number of tickets sold at each theme park.

FIGURE P8.37 Total tickets sold at each theme park

PARK_NAME	TOTAL_TICKETS_SOLD
AdventurePort	3
FairyLand	7
GoldTown	3
PleasureLand	6

40 Write a query to show the details of all employees who have not worked on any attractions as shown in Figure P8.38.

FIGURE P8.38 Employees who have not worked on any attractions

EMP_LNAME	EMP_FNAME	EMP_DOB	EMP_HIRE_DATE	EMP_AREACODE	EMP_PHONE
Roberts	Anne	16-Oct-84	16-Aug-04	0181	898-3456
Smith	Gemma	12-Feb-78	05-Jan-99	0181	324-7845

41 Write a query that will list the length of service in years of each employee. Sample output is shown in Figure P8.39 when this query was run on 5 February 2019. Remember, your output will be different.

FIGURE P8.39 The length of service of each employee

EMP_NUM	EMP_LNAME	EMP_FNAME	EMP_HIRE_DATE	EMP_DOB	Length_of_Service
100	Calderdale	Emma	15-Mar-02	15-Jun-82	14
101	Ricardo	Marshel	25-Apr-06	19-Mar-88	10
102	Arshad	Arif	20-Dec-00	14-Nov-79	16
103	Roberts	Anne	16-Aug-04	16-Oct-84	12
104	Denver	Enrica	20-Oct-11	08-Nov-90	5
105	Namowa	Mirrelle	08-Nov-16	14-Mar-00	0
106	Smith	Gemma	05-Jan-99	12-Feb-78	18

42 Write the SQL code that will produce a VIEW named EMP_PARIS, containing all the information of employees who work in PARIS.

8

CHAPTER 9

Procedural Language SQL and Advanced SQL

IN THIS CHAPTER, YOU WILL LEARN:

- About the relational set operators UNION, UNION ALL, INTERSECT and MINUS
- How to use the advanced SQL JOIN operator syntax
- About the different types of subqueries and correlated queries
- How to use SQL functions to manipulate dates, strings and other data
- How to create and use updatable views
- Use Procedural Language (PL/SQL) to create triggers, stored procedures and PL/SQL functions
- How to create embedded SQL

PREVIEW

In Chapter 8, Beginning Structured Query Language, you learnt the basic SQL data definition and data manipulation commands used to create and manipulate relational data. In this chapter, you build on what you learnt in Chapter 8 and learn how to use more advanced SQL features.

In this chapter, you will learn about the SQL relational set operators (UNION, INTERSECT and MINUS) and how those operators are used to merge the results of multiple queries. Joins are at the heart of SQL. Therefore, you need to learn how to use the SQL JOIN statement to extract information from multiple tables. In the previous chapter, you learnt how cascading queries inside other queries can be useful in certain circumstances. In this chapter, you will also learn about the different styles of subqueries that can be implemented in a SELECT statement. Finally, you learn more of SQL's many functions to extract information from data, including manipulation of dates and strings as well as computations based on stored or even derived data.

In the real world, business procedures require the execution of clearly defined actions when a specific event occurs, such as the addition of a new invoice or a student's enrolment in a class. Such procedures can be applied within the DBMS through the use of triggers and stored procedures. In addition, SQL facilitates the application of business procedures when it is embedded in a programming language such as Visual Basic, .NET, C# or Java.

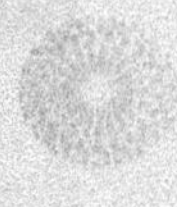

Online Content Most of the examples used in this chapter are based on Oracle. If you want to see the examples in action, you need to load the required database tables. The Oracle SQL script files for creating the tables and loading the data in the database are located on the online platform for this book. How you connect to the Oracle database depends on how the Oracle software is installed on your server and on the access paths and methods defined and managed by the database administrator. Follow the instructions provided by your instructor or your college or university's technology department.

9.1 RELATIONAL SET OPERATORS

In Chapter 3, Relational Model Characteristics, you learnt about the eight general relational operators. In this section, you will learn how to use SQL commands (UNION, INTERSECT and MINUS) to implement the union, intersection and difference relational operators.

In previous chapters, you learnt that SQL data manipulation commands are set-orientated; that is, they operate over entire sets of rows and columns (tables) at once. Using sets, you can combine two or more sets to create new sets (or relations). That's precisely what the UNION, INTERSECT and MINUS statements do. In relational database terms, you can use the words, sets, relations and tables interchangeably because they all provide a conceptual view of the data set as it is presented to the relational database user.

NOTE

The SQL-2011 standard defines the operations that all DBMSs must perform on data, but it leaves the implementation details to the DBMS vendors. Therefore, some advanced SQL features may not work on all DBMS implementations. Also, some DBMS vendors may implement additional features not found in the SQL standard.

UNION, INTERSECT and MINUS are the names of the SQL statements implemented in Oracle. The SQL standard uses the keyword EXCEPT to refer to the difference (MINUS) relational operator. Other RDBMS vendors may use a different command name or might not implement a given command at all. For example, MySQL version 8.0 supports the UNION operator and not INTERSECT.

To learn more about the ANSI/ISO SQL standards, check the ANSI website (*www.ansi.org*) to find out how to obtain the latest standard documents in electronic form.

UNION, INTERSECT and MINUS work properly only if relations are *union-compatible*. In SQL terms, *union-compatible* means that the names of the relation attributes must be the same and their data types must be identical. In practice, some RDBMS vendors require the data types to be 'compatible' but not necessarily 'exactly the same'. For example, compatible data types are VARCHAR(35) and CHAR(15). In that case, both attributes store character (string) values; the only difference is the string size. Another example of compatible data types is NUMBER and SMALLINT. Both data types are used to store numeric values.

NOTE

Some DBMS products may require union-compatible tables to have *identical* data types.

9.1.1 UNION

Suppose SaleCo has bought another company. SaleCo's management wants to make sure that the acquired company's customer list is properly merged with SaleCo's customer list. Because it is quite possible that some customers have purchased goods from both companies, the two lists may contain common customers. SaleCo's management wants to make sure that customer records are not duplicated when the two customer lists are merged. The UNION query is a perfect tool for generating a combined listing of customers – one that excludes duplicate records.

Online Content The 'Ch09_SaleCo' database used to illustrate the UNION commands is located on the online platform for this book.

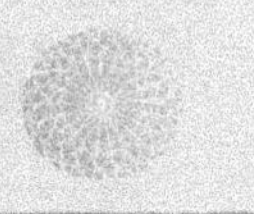

The UNION statement combines rows from two or more queries *without including duplicate rows*. The syntax of the UNION statement is:

query UNION *query*

In other words, the UNION statement combines the output of two SELECT queries. (Remember that the SELECT statements must be union-compatible. That is, they must return the same attribute names and similar data types.)

To demonstrate the use of the UNION statement in SQL, let's use the CUSTOMER and CUSTOMER_2 tables in the Ch09_SaleCo database. To show the combined CUSTOMER and CUSTOMER_2 records without the duplicates, the UNION query is written as follows:

```
SELECT    CUS_LNAME, CUS_FNAME, CUS_INITIAL, CUS_AREACODE, CUS_PHONE
FROM      CUSTOMER
UNION
SELECT    CUS_LNAME, CUS_FNAME, CUS_INITIAL, CUS_AREACODE, CUS_PHONE
FROM      CUSTOMER_2;
```

Figure 9.1 shows the contents of the CUSTOMER and CUSTOMER_2 tables and the result of the UNION query.

FIGURE 9.1 **UNION query results**

Database name: Ch09_SaleCo

Table name: CUSTOMER

CUS_CODE	CUS_ LNAME	CUS_ FNAME	CUS_ INITIAL	CUS_ AREACODE	CUS_ PHONE	CUS_BALANCE
10010	Ramas	Alfred	A	0181	844-2573	0.00
10011	Dunne	Leona	K	0161	894-1238	0.00
10012	Moloi	Marlene	W	0181	894-2285	345.86
10013	Pieterse	Jaco	F	0181	894-2180	536.75
10014	Orlando	Myron		0181	222-1672	0.00
10015	O'Brian	Amy	B	0161	442-3381	0.00
10016	Brown	James	G	0181	297-1228	221.19
10017	Williams	George		0181	290-2556	768.93
10018	Padayachee	Vinaya	G	0161	382-7185	216.55
10019	Moloi	Mlilo	K	0161	297-3809	0.00

Table name: CUSTOMER_2

CUS_CODE	CUS_LNAME	CUS_FNAME	CUS_INITIAL	CUS_AREACODE	CUS_PHONE
345	Terrell	Justine	H	0181	322-9870
347	Pieterse	Jaco	F	0181	894-2180
351	Hernandez	Carlos	J	8192	123-7654
352	McDowell	George		8192	123-7768
365	Tirpin	Khaleed	G	8192	123-9876
368	Lewis	Marie	J	8192	332-1789
369	Dunne	Leona	K	0161	894-1238

Query: CUSTOMER UNION CUSTOMER_2

CUS_LNAME	CUS_FNAME	CUS_INITIAL	CUS_AREACODE	CUS_PHONE
Brown	James	G	0181	297-1228
Dunne	Leona	K	0161	894-1238
Padayachee	Vinaya	G	0161	382-7185
Hernandez	Carlos	J	8192	123-7654
Lewis	Marie	J	8192	332-1789
McDowell	George		8192	123-7768
O'Brian	Amy	B	0161	442-3381
Pieterse	Jaco	F	0181	894-2180
Orlando	Myron		0181	222-1672
Ramas	Alfred	A	0181	844-2573
Moloi	Marlene	W	0181	894-2285
Moloi	Mlilo	K	0161	297-3809
Terrell	Justine	H	0181	322-9870
Tirpin	Khaleed	G	8192	123-9876
Williams	George		0181	290-2556

As you examine Figure 9.1, note the following:

- The CUSTOMER table contains ten rows, while the CUSTOMER_2 table contains seven rows.
- Customers Dunne and Pieterse are included in the CUSTOMER table as well as in the CUSTOMER_2 table.
- The UNION query yields 15 records because the duplicate records of customers Dunne and Pieterse are not included. In short, the UNION query yields a unique set of records.

NOTE

You were first introduced to the UNION operator in Chapter 4, Relational Algebra and Calculus, when you learnt how to combine all tuples from two relations. We could therefore write the SQL query:

```
SELECT    CUS_LNAME, CUS_FNAME, CUS_INITIAL, CUS_AREACODE, CUS_PHONE
FROM      CUSTOMER
UNION
SELECT    CUS_LNAME, CUS_FNAME, CUS_INITIAL, CUS_AREACODE, CUS_PHONE
FROM      CUSTOMER_2;
```

as the following relational algebra statement:

$$\Pi_{\text{CUS\_LNAME, CUS\_FNAME, CUS\_INITIAL, CUS\_AREACODE, CUS\_PHONE}} (\text{CUSTOMER}) \cup \Pi_{\text{CUS\_LNAME, CUS\_FNAME, CUS\_INITIAL, CUS\_AREACODE, CUS\_PHONE}} (\text{CUSTOMER\_2})$$

NOTE

The SQL standard calls for the elimination of duplicate rows when the UNION SQL statement is used. However, some DBMS vendors may not adhere to that standard. Check your DBMS manual to see if the UNION statement is supported and, if so, *how* it is supported. For example, the latest version of MySQL 8.0 and Oracle 18c both support the UNION SQL statement.

9

The UNION statement can be used to unite more than just two queries. For example, assume that you have four union-compatible queries named T1, T2, T3 and T4. With the UNION statement, you can combine the output of all four queries into a single result set. The SQL statement will be similar to this:

```
SELECT column-list FROM T1
UNION
SELECT column-list FROM T2
UNION
SELECT column-list FROM T3
UNION
SELECT column-list FROM T4;
```

9.1.2 UNION ALL

If SaleCo's management wants to know how many customers are on *both* the CUSTOMER and CUSTOMER_2 lists, a UNION ALL query can be used to produce a relation that retains the duplicate rows. Therefore, the following query will keep all rows from both queries (including the duplicate rows) and return 17 rows.

```
SELECT      CUS_LNAME, CUS_FNAME, CUS_INITIAL, CUS_AREACODE, CUS_PHONE
FROM        CUSTOMER
UNION ALL
SELECT      CUS_LNAME, CUS_FNAME, CUS_INITIAL, CUS_AREACODE, CUS_PHONE
FROM        CUSTOMER_2;
```

Running the preceding UNION ALL query produces the result shown in Figure 9.2.

FIGURE 9.2 UNION ALL query results

Database name: Ch09_SaleCo

CUS_LNAME	CUS_FNAME	CUS_INITIAL	CUS_AREACODE	CUS_PHONE
Ramas	Alfred	A	0181	844-2573
Dunne	Leona	K	0161	894-1238
Moloi	Marlene	W	0181	894-2285
Pieterse	Jaco	F	0181	894-2180
Orlando	Myron		0181	222-1672
O'Brian	Amy	B	0161	442-3381
Brown	James	G	0181	297-1228
Williams	George		0181	290-2556
Padayachee	Vinaya	G	0161	382-7185
Moloi	Mlilo	K	0161	297-3809
Terrell	Justine	H	0181	322-9870
Pieterse	Jaco	F	0181	894-2180
Hernandez	Carlos	J	8192	123-7654
McDowell	George		8192	123-7768
Tirpin	Khaleed	G	8192	123-9876
Lewis	Marie	J	8192	332-1789
Dunne	Leona	K	0161	894-1238

Like the UNION statement, the UNION ALL statement can be used to unite more than just two queries.

9.1.3 INTERSECT

If SaleCo's management wants to know which customer records are duplicated in the CUSTOMER and CUSTOMER_2 tables, the INTERSECT statement can be used to combine rows from two queries, returning only the rows that appear in both sets. The syntax for the INTERSECT statement is:

query INTERSECT *query*

To generate the list of duplicate customer records, you can use:

```
SELECT      CUS_LNAME, CUS_FNAME, CUS_INITIAL, CUS_AREACODE, CUS_PHONE
FROM        CUSTOMER
INTERSECT
SELECT      CUS_LNAME, CUS_FNAME, CUS_INITIAL, CUS_AREACODE, CUS_PHONE
FROM        CUSTOMER_2;
```

> **NOTE**
>
> The SQL query you have just seen can be written using the relational algebra INTERSECT operator as follows:
>
> $\Pi_{\text{CUS\_LNAME, CUS\_FNAME, CUS\_INITIAL, CUS\_AREACODE, CUS\_PHONE}}$ (CUSTOMER) $\cap$ $\Pi_{\text{CUS\_LNAME, CUS\_FNAME, CUS\_INITIAL, CUS\_AREACODE, CUS\_PHONE}}$ (CUSTOMER_2)

The INTERSECT statement can be used to generate additional useful customer information. For example, the following query returns the customer codes for all customers who are located in area code 0181 and who have made purchases. (If a customer has made a purchase, there must be an invoice record for that customer.)

```
SELECT      CUS_CODE FROM CUSTOMER WHERE CUS_AREACODE = '0181'
INTERSECT
SELECT      DISTINCT CUS_CODE FROM INVOICE;
```

Figure 9.3 shows both sets of SQL statements and their output.

> **NOTE**
>
> Microsoft Access does not support the INTERSECT query, nor does it support other complex queries you'll explore in this chapter. At least, in some cases, Access might be able to give you the desired results if you use an alternative query format or procedure. For example, although Access does not support SQL triggers and stored procedures, you can use Visual Basic code to perform similar actions. However, the objective here is to show you how to use some important standard SQL features.

FIGURE 9.3 **INTERSECT query results**

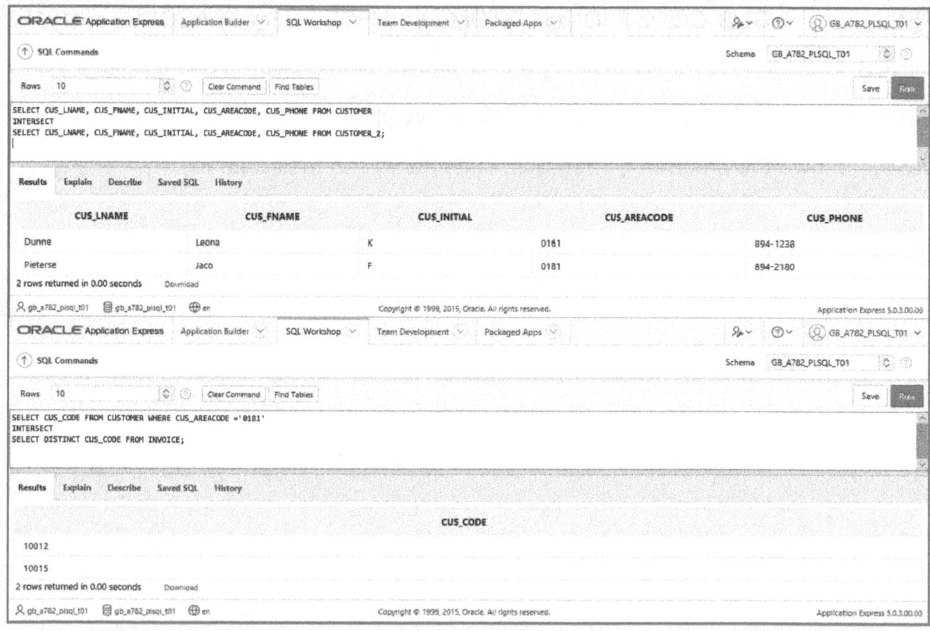

9.1.4 MINUS

The MINUS statement in SQL combines rows from two queries and returns only the rows that appear in the first set but not in the second. The syntax for the MINUS statement is:

query MINUS *query*

For example, if the SaleCo managers want to know what customers in the CUSTOMER table are not found in the CUSTOMER_2 table, they can use:

```
SELECT    CUS_LNAME, CUS_FNAME, CUS_INITIAL, CUS_AREACODE, CUS_PHONE
FROM      CUSTOMER
MINUS
SELECT    CUS_LNAME, CUS_FNAME, CUS_INITIAL, CUS_AREACODE, CUS_PHONE
FROM      CUSTOMER_2;
```

If the managers want to know which customers in the CUSTOMER_2 table are not found in the CUSTOMER table, they merely switch the table designations:

```
SELECT    CUS_LNAME, CUS_FNAME, CUS_INITIAL, CUS_AREACODE, CUS_PHONE
FROM      CUSTOMER_2
MINUS
SELECT    CUS_LNAME, CUS_FNAME, CUS_INITIAL, CUS_AREACODE, CUS_PHONE
FROM      CUSTOMER;
```

You can extract much useful information by combining MINUS with various clauses such as WHERE. For example, the following query returns the customer codes for all customers located in area code 0181 minus the ones who have made purchases, leaving the customers in area code 0181 who have not made purchases.

```
SELECT    CUS_CODE FROM CUSTOMER WHERE CUS_AREACODE = '0181'
MINUS
SELECT    DISTINCT CUS_CODE FROM INVOICE;
```

Figure 9.4 shows the preceding three SQL statements and their output.

FIGURE 9.4 **MINUS query results**

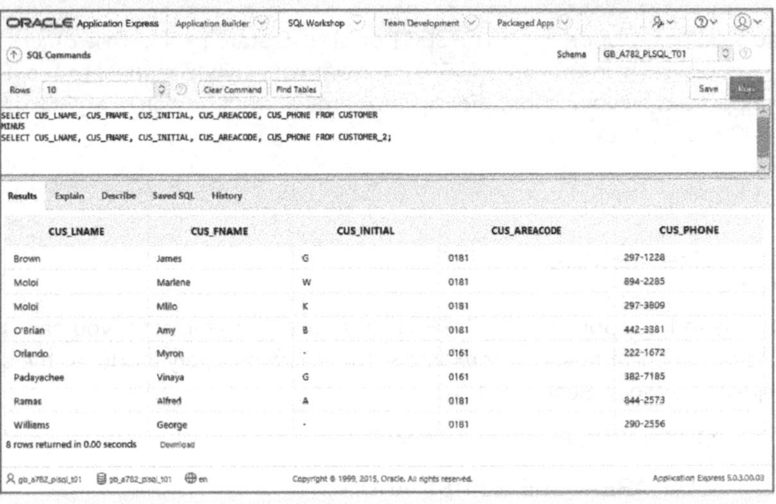

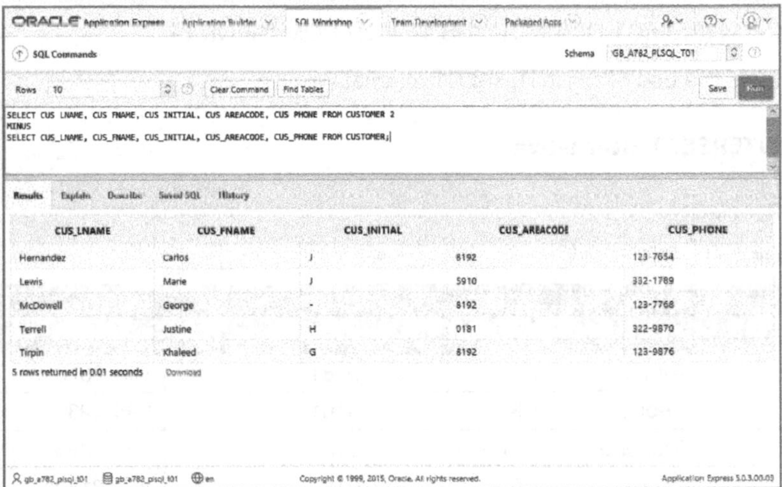

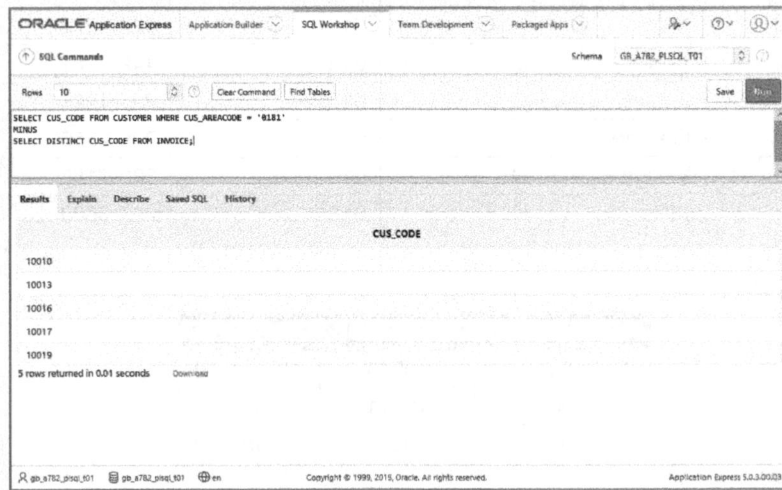

9

NOTE

Some DBMS products do not support the INTERSECT or MINUS statements, while others may implement the difference relational operator in SQL as EXCEPT. Consult your DBMS manual to see if the statements illustrated here are supported by your DBMS. For example, the current version of MySQL does not support INTERSECT or MINUS statements.

9.1.5 Syntax Alternatives

If your DBMS doesn't support the INTERSECT and MINUS statements, you can use IN and NOT IN subqueries to obtain similar results. For example, the following query produces the same results as the INTERSECT query shown in Section 9.1.3.

```
SELECT    CUS_CODE FROM CUSTOMER
WHERE     CUS_AREACODE = '0181' AND
CUS_CODE IN (SELECT DISTINCT CUS_CODE FROM INVOICE);
```

Figure 9.5 shows the use of the INTERSECT alternative.

9

FIGURE 9.5 INTERSECT alternative

Database name: Ch09_SaleCo

Table name: CUSTOMER

CUS_ CODE	CUS_ LNAME	CUS_ FNAME	CUS_ INITIAL	CUS_ AREACODE	CUS_ PHONE	CUS_ BALANCE
10010	Ramas	Alfred	A	0181	844-2573	0.00
10011	Dunne	Leona	K	0161	894-1238	0.00
10012	Moloi	Marlene	W	0181	894-2285	345.86
10013	Pieterse	Jaco	F	0181	894-2180	536.75
10014	Orlando	Myron		0181	222-1672	0.00
10015	O'Brian	Amy	B	0161	442-3381	0.00
10016	Brown	James	G	0181	297-1228	221.19
10017	Williams	George		0181	290-2556	768.93
10018	Padayachee	Vinaya	G	0161	382-7185	216.55
10019	Moloi	Mlilo	K	0181	297-3809	0.00

Table name: INVOICE

INV_NUMBER	CUS_CODE	INV_DATE
1001	10014	16-Jan-19
1002	10011	16-Jan-19
1003	10012	16-Jan-19

INV_NUMBER	CUS_CODE	INV_DATE
1004	10011	17-Jan-19
1005	10018	17-Jan-19
1006	10014	17-Jan-19
1007	10015	17-Jan-19
1008	10011	17-Jan-19

Query result:

CUS_CODE
10012
10014

NOTE

Microsoft Access generates an input request for the CUS_AREACODE if you use apostrophes around the area code. (If you supply the 0181 area code, the query will execute properly.) To eliminate that problem, use standard double quotation marks, writing the WHERE clause in the second line of the preceding SQL statement as:

WHERE CUS_AREACODE = '0181' AND

Microsoft Access will also accept single quotation marks.

9

Using the same alternative to the MINUS statement, you can generate the output for the third MINUS query shown in Section 9.1.4 by using:

```
SELECT     CUS_AREACODE = '0181' AND CUS_CODE NOT IN (SELECT DISTINCT CUS_CODE
           FROM INVOICE);
```

The results of that query are shown in Figure 9.6. Note that the query output includes only the customers in area code 0181 who have not made any purchases and, therefore, have not generated invoices.

FIGURE 9.6 MINUS alternative

Database name: Ch09_SaleCo

Table name: CUSTOMER

CUS_CODE	CUS_LNAME	CUS_FNAME	CUS_INITIAL	CUS_AREACODE	CUS_PHONE	CUS_BALANCE
10010	Ramas	Alfred	A	0181	844-2573	0.00
10011	Dunne	Leona	K	0161	894-1238	0.00
10012	Moloi	Marlene	W	0181	894-2285	345.86
10013	Pieterse	Jaco	F	0181	894-2180	536.75
10014	Orlando	Myron		0181	222-1672	0.00

CUS_CODE	CUS_LNAME	CUS_FNAME	CUS_INITIAL	CUS_AREACODE	CUS_PHONE	CUS_BALANCE
10015	O'Brian	Amy	B	0161	442-3381	0.00
10016	Brown	James	G	0181	297-1228	221.19
10017	Williams	George		0181	290-2556	768.93
10018	Padayachee	Vinaya	G	0161	382-7185	216.55
10019	Moloi	Mlilo	K	0181	297-3809	0.00

Table name: INVOICE

INV_NUMBER	CUS_CODE	INV_DATE
1001	10014	16-Jan-19
1002	10011	16-Jan-19
1003	10012	16-Jan-19
1004	10011	17-Jan-19
1005	10018	17-Jan-19
1006	10014	17-Jan-19
1007	10015	17-Jan-19
1008	10011	17-Jan-19

Query result:

CUS_CODE
10010
10013
10016
10017
10019

9.2 SQL JOIN OPERATORS

The relational join operation merges rows from two tables and returns the rows with one of the following conditions:

- Have common values in common columns (natural join).
- Meet a given join condition (equality or inequality).
- Have common values in common columns or have no matching values (outer join).

In Chapter 8, Beginning Structured Query Language, you learnt how to use the SELECT statement in conjunction with the WHERE clause to join two or more tables. For example, you can join the PRODUCT and VENDOR tables through their common V_CODE by writing:

```
SELECT    P_CODE, P_DESCRIPT, P_PRICE, V_NAME
FROM      PRODUCT, VENDOR
WHERE     PRODUCT.V_CODE = VENDOR.V_CODE;
```

The preceding SQL join syntax is sometimes referred as an 'old-style' join. Note that the FROM clause contains the tables being joined and that the WHERE clause contains the join condition(s) used to join the tables.

As you examine the preceding query, note the following points:

- The FROM clause indicates which tables are to be joined. If three or more tables are included, the join operation takes place two tables at a time, starting from left to right. For example, if you are joining tables T1, T2 and T3, first table T1 is joined to T2; the results of that join are then joined to table T3.
- The join condition in the WHERE clause tells the SELECT statement which rows will be returned. In this case, the SELECT statement returns all rows for which the V_CODE values in the PRODUCT and VENDOR tables are equal.
- The number of join conditions is always equal to the number of tables being joined minus one. For example, if you join three tables (T1, T2 and T3), you will have two join conditions (j1 and j2). All join conditions are connected through an AND logical operator. The first join condition (j1) defines the join criteria for T1 and T2. The second join condition (j2) defines the join criteria for the output of the first join and table T3.
- Generally, the join condition will be an equality comparison of the primary key in one table and the related foreign key in the second table.

Join operations can be classified as inner joins and outer joins. The **inner join** is the traditional join in which only rows that meet a given criteria are selected. The join criteria can be an equality condition (natural join or equijoin) or an inequality condition (theta join). An **outer join** returns not only the matching rows, but also the rows with unmatched attribute values for one table or both tables to be joined. The SQL standard also introduces a special type of join that returns the same result as the Cartesian product of two sets or tables.

In this section, you will learn different ways to express join operations that meet the ANSI SQL standard (see Table 9.1.). It is useful to remember that not all DBMS vendors provide the same level of SQL support and that some do not support the join styles shown in this section. Oracle 11g is used to demonstrate the use of the following queries. Refer to your DBMS manual if you are using a different DBMS.

9

TABLE 9.1 SQL join expression styles

Join Classification	Join Type	SQL Syntax Example	Description
CROSS	CROSS JOIN	SELECT * FROM T1, T2	Returns the Cartesian product of T1 and T2 (old style).
		SELECT * FROM T1 CROSS JOIN T2	Returns the Cartesian product of T1 and T2.
INNER	Old-Style JOIN	SELECT * FROM T1, T2 WHERE T1.C1=T2.C1	Returns only the rows that meet the join condition in the WHERE clause old style. Only rows with matching values are selected.
	NATURAL JOIN	SELECT * FROM T1 NATURAL JOIN T2	Returns only the rows with matching values in the matching columns. The matching columns must have the same names and similar data types.
	JOIN USING	SELECT * FROM T1 JOIN T2 USING (C1)	Returns only the rows with matching values in the columns indicated in the USING clause.
	JOIN ON	SELECT * FROM T1 JOIN T2 ON T1.C1=T2=C1	Returns only the rows that meet the join condition indicated in the ON clause.

Join Classification	Join Type	SQL Syntax Example	Description
OUTER	LEFT JOIN	SELECT * FROM T1 LEFT OUTER JOIN T2 ON T1.C1=T2.C1	Returns rows with matching values and includes all rows from the left table (T1) with unmatched values.
	RIGHT JOIN	SELECT * FROM T1 RIGHT OUTER JOIN T2 ON T1.C1=T2.C1	Returns rows with matching values and includes all rows from the right table (T2) with unmatched values.
	FULL JOIN	SELECT * FROM T1 FULL OUTER JOIN T2 ON T1.C1=T2.C1	Returns rows with matching values and includes all rows from both tables (T1 and T2) with unmatched values.

9.2.1 Cross Join

A **cross join** performs a relational product (also known as the Cartesian product) of two tables. The cross join syntax is:

SELECT *column-list* FROM *table1* CROSS JOIN *table2*

For example,

```
SELECT * FROM INVOICE CROSS JOIN LINE;
```

performs a cross join of the INVOICE and LINE tables. That CROSS JOIN query generates 144 rows. (There were eight invoice rows and 18 line rows, thus yielding $8 \times 18 = 144$ rows.)

You can also perform a cross join that yields only specified attributes. For example, you can specify:

```
SELECT      INVOICE.INV_NUMBER, CUS_CODE, INV_DATE, P_CODE
FROM        INVOICE CROSS JOIN LINE;
```

The results generated through that SQL statement can also be generated by using the following syntax:

```
SELECT      INVOICE.INV_NUMBER, CUS_CODE, INV_DATE, P_CODE
FROM        INVOICE, LINE;
```

9.2.2 Natural Join

Recall from Chapter 3, Relational Model Characteristics, that a natural join returns all rows with matching values in the matching columns and eliminates duplicate columns. That style of query is used when the tables share one or more common attributes with common names. The natural join syntax is:

SELECT *column-list* FROM *table1* NATURAL JOIN *table2*

The natural join will perform the following tasks:

- Determine the common attribute(s) by looking for attributes with identical names and compatible data types.
- Select only the rows with common values in the common attribute(s).
- If there are no common attributes, return the relational product of the two tables.

The following example performs a natural join of the CUSTOMER and INVOICE tables and returns only selected attributes:

```
SELECT      CUS_CODE, CUS_LNAME, INV_NUMBER, INV_DATE
FROM        CUSTOMER NATURAL JOIN INVOICE;
```

The SQL code and its results are shown at the top of Figure 9.7.

FIGURE 9.7 NATURAL JOIN query results

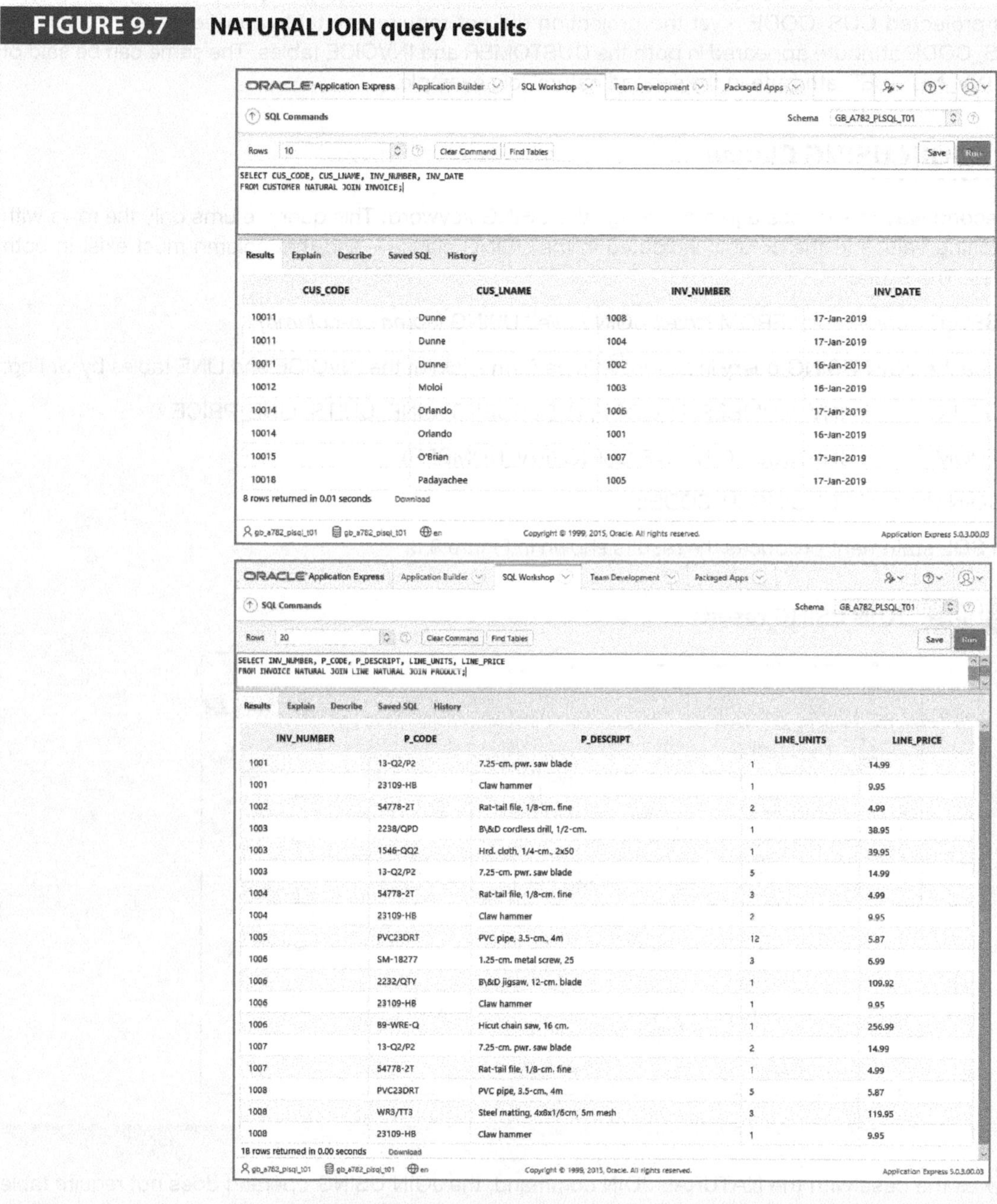

```
SELECT CUS_CODE, CUS_LNAME, INV_NUMBER, INV_DATE
FROM CUSTOMER NATURAL JOIN INVOICE;
```

CUS_CODE	CUS_LNAME	INV_NUMBER	INV_DATE
10011	Dunne	1008	17-Jan-2019
10011	Dunne	1004	17-Jan-2019
10011	Dunne	1002	16-Jan-2019
10012	Moloi	1003	16-Jan-2019
10014	Orlando	1006	17-Jan-2019
10014	Orlando	1001	16-Jan-2019
10015	O'Brian	1007	17-Jan-2019
10018	Padayachee	1005	17-Jan-2019

8 rows returned in 0.01 seconds

```
SELECT INV_NUMBER, P_CODE, P_DESCRIPT, LINE_UNITS, LINE_PRICE
FROM INVOICE NATURAL JOIN LINE NATURAL JOIN PRODUCT;
```

INV_NUMBER	P_CODE	P_DESCRIPT	LINE_UNITS	LINE_PRICE
1001	13-Q2/P2	7.25-cm. pwr. saw blade	1	14.99
1001	23109-HB	Claw hammer	1	9.95
1002	54778-2T	Rat-tail file, 1/8-cm. fine	2	4.99
1003	2238/QPD	B\&D cordless drill, 1/2-cm.	1	38.95
1003	1546-QQ2	Hrd. cloth, 1/4-cm., 2x50	1	39.95
1003	13-Q2/P2	7.25-cm. pwr. saw blade	5	14.99
1004	54778-2T	Rat-tail file, 1/8-cm. fine	3	4.99
1004	23109-HB	Claw hammer	2	9.95
1005	PVC23DRT	PVC pipe, 3.5-cm., 4m	12	5.87
1006	SM-18277	1.25-cm. metal screw, 25	3	6.99
1006	2232/QTY	B\&D jigsaw, 12-cm. blade	1	109.92
1006	23109-HB	Claw hammer	1	9.95
1006	89-WRE-Q	Hicut chain saw, 16 cm.	1	256.99
1007	13-Q2/P2	7.25-cm. pwr. saw blade	2	14.99
1007	54778-2T	Rat-tail file, 1/8-cm. fine	1	4.99
1008	PVC23DRT	PVC pipe, 3.5-cm., 4m	5	5.87
1008	WR3/TT3	Steel matting, 4x8x1/6cm, 5m mesh	3	119.95
1008	23109-HB	Claw hammer	1	9.95

18 rows returned in 0.00 seconds

You are not limited to two tables. For example, you can perform a natural join of the INVOICE, LINE and PRODUCT tables and project only selected attributes by writing:

```
SELECT    INV_NUMBER, P_CODE, P_DESCRIPT, LINE_UNITS, LINE_PRICE
FROM      INVOICE NATURAL JOIN LINE NATURAL JOIN PRODUCT;
```

The SQL code and its results are shown at the bottom of Figure 9.7.

One important difference between the natural join and the 'old-style' join syntax is that the natural join does not require the use of a table qualifier for the common attributes. In the first natural join example, you projected CUS_CODE – yet the projection did not require any table qualifier, even though the CUS_CODE attribute appeared in both the CUSTOMER and INVOICE tables. The same can be said of the INV_NUMBER attribute in the second natural join example.

9.2.3 JOIN USING Clause

A second way to express a join is through the USING keyword. This query returns only the rows with matching values in the column indicated in the USING clause – and that column must exist in both tables. The syntax is:

SELECT *column-list* FROM *table1* JOIN *table2* USING (*common-column*)

To see the JOIN USING query in action, let's perform a join of the INVOICE and LINE tables by writing:

```
SELECT    INV_NUMBER, P_CODE, P_DESCRIPT, LINE_UNITS, LINE_PRICE
FROM      INVOICE JOIN LINE USING (INV_NUMBER)
JOIN PRODUCT USING (P_CODE);
```

The SQL statement produces the results shown in Figure 9.8.

FIGURE 9.8 JOIN USING results

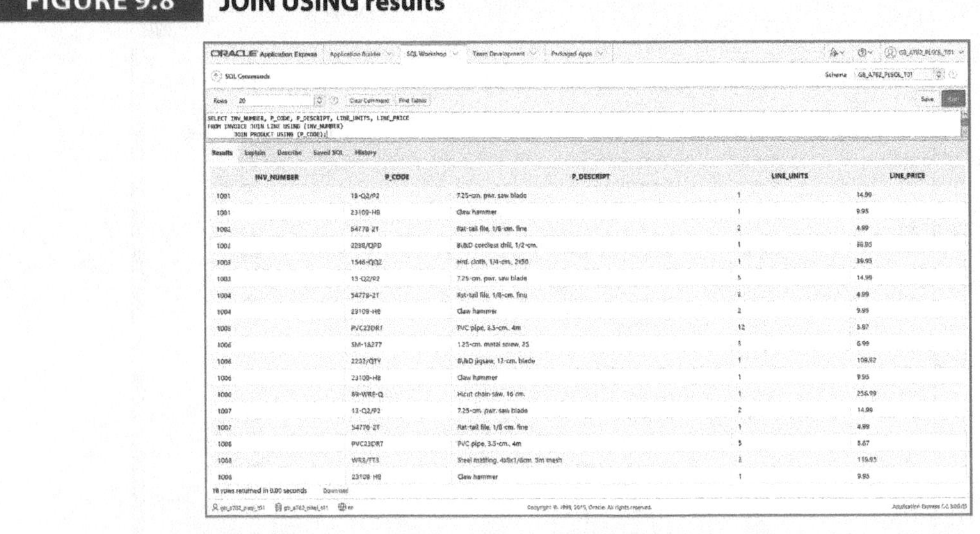

As was the case with the NATURAL JOIN command, the JOIN USING operand does not require table qualifiers. As a matter of fact, Oracle will return an error if you specify the table name in the USING clause.

9.2.4 JOIN ON Clause

The previous two join styles used common attribute names in the joining tables. Another way to express a join when the tables have no common attribute names is to use the JOIN ON operand. That query will return only the rows that meet the indicated join condition. The join condition will typically include an equality comparison expression of two columns. (The columns may or may not share the same name but, obviously, must have comparable data types.) The syntax is:

SELECT *column-list* FROM *table1* JOIN *table2* ON *join-condition*

The following example performs a join of the INVOICE and LINE tables, using the ON clause. The result is shown in Figure 9.9.

```
SELECT    INVOICE.INV_NUMBER, P_CODE, P_DESCRIPT, LINE_UNITS, LINE_PRICE
FROM      INVOICE JOIN LINE ON INVOICE.INV_NUMBER = LINE.INV_NUMBER
JOIN PRODUCT ON LINE.P_CODE = PRODUCT.P_CODE;
```

FIGURE 9.9 JOIN ON results

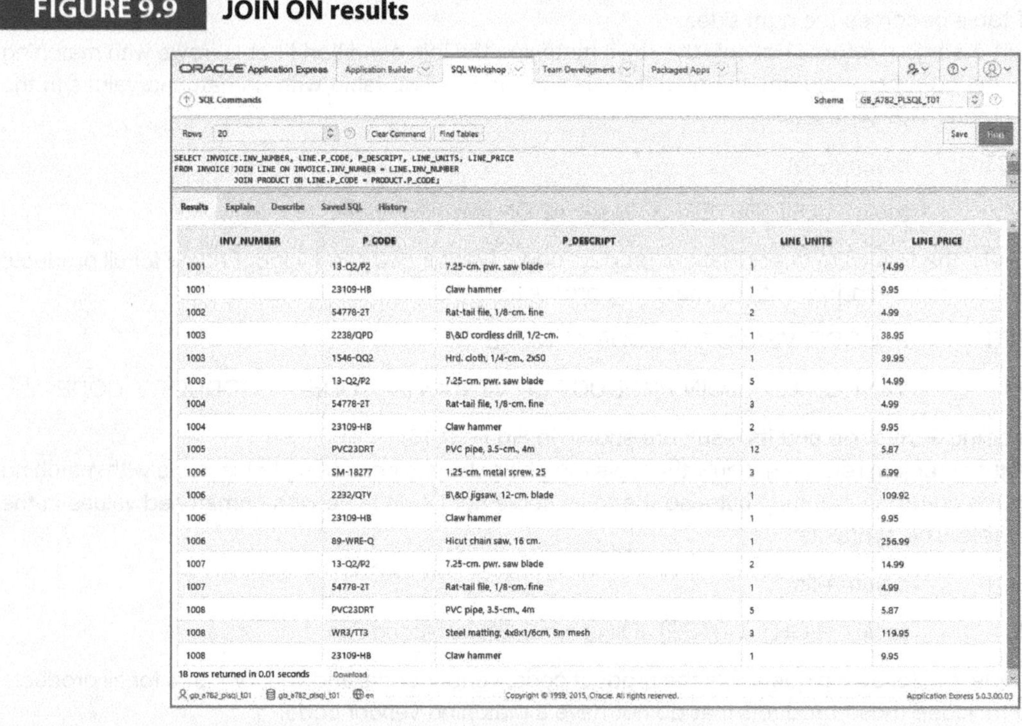

INV_NUMBER	P_CODE	P_DESCRIPT	LINE_UNITS	LINE_PRICE
1001	13-Q2/P2	7.25-cm. pwr. saw blade	1	14.99
1001	23109-HB	Claw hammer	1	9.95
1002	54778-2T	Rat-tail file, 1/8-cm. fine	2	4.99
1003	2238/QPD	B\&D cordless drill, 1/2-cm.	1	38.95
1003	1546-QQ2	Hrd. cloth, 1/4-cm., 2x50	1	39.95
1003	13-Q2/P2	7.25-cm. pwr. saw blade	5	14.99
1004	54778-2T	Rat-tail file, 1/8-cm. fine	3	4.99
1004	23109-HB	Claw hammer	2	9.95
1005	PVC23DRT	PVC pipe, 3.5-cm., 4m	12	5.87
1006	SM-18277	1.25-cm. metal screw, 25	3	6.99
1006	2232/QTY	B\&D jigsaw, 12-cm. blade	1	109.92
1006	23109-HB	Claw hammer	1	9.95
1006	89-WRE-Q	Hicut chain saw, 16 cm.	1	256.99
1007	13-Q2/P2	7.25-cm. pwr. saw blade	2	14.99
1007	54778-2T	Rat-tail file, 1/8-cm. fine	1	4.99
1008	PVC23DRT	PVC pipe, 3.5-cm., 4m	5	5.87
1008	WR3/TT3	Steel matting, 4x8x1/6cm, 5m mesh	3	119.95
1008	23109-HB	Claw hammer	1	9.95

18 rows returned in 0.01 seconds

Note that, unlike the NATURAL JOIN and the JOIN USING operands, the JOIN ON clause requires a table qualifier for the common attributes. If you do not specify the table qualifier, you will get a 'column ambiguously defined' error message.

Keep in mind that the JOIN ON syntax lets you perform a join even when the tables do not share a common attribute name. For example, to generate a list of all employees with the managers' names, you can use the following (recursive) query:

```
SELECT      E.EMP_MGR, M.EMP_LNAME, E.EMP_NUM, E.EMP_LNAME
FROM        EMP E JOIN EMP M ON E.EMP_MGR = M.EMP_NUM
ORDER BY    E.EMP_MGR;
```

9.2.5 Outer Joins

An outer join returns not only the rows matching the join condition (that is, rows with matching values in the common columns), but also the rows with unmatched values. The ANSI standard defines three types of outer joins: left, right and full. The left and right designations reflect the order in which the tables are processed by the DBMS. Remember that join operations take place two tables at a time. The first table named in the FROM clause will be the left side, and the second table named will be the right side. If three or more tables are being joined, the result of joining the first two tables becomes the left side; the third table becomes the right side.

The left outer join returns not only the rows matching the join condition (that is, rows with matching values in the common column), but also the rows in the left side table with unmatched values in the right side table. The syntax is:

```
SELECT      column-list
FROM        table1 LEFT [OUTER] JOIN table2 ON join-condition
```

9

For example, the following query lists the product code, vendor code and vendor name for all products and includes those vendors with no matching products:

```
SELECT      P_CODE, VENDOR.V_CODE, V_NAME
FROM        VENDOR LEFT JOIN PRODUCT ON VENDOR.V_CODE = PRODUCT.V_CODE;
```

The preceding SQL code and its result are shown in Figure 9.10.

The right outer join returns not only the rows matching the join condition (that is, rows with matching values in the common column), but also the rows in the right side table with unmatched values in the left side table. The syntax is:

```
SELECT      column-list
FROM        table1 RIGHT [OUTER] JOIN table2 ON join-condition
```

For example, the following query lists the product code, vendor code, and vendor name for all products and also includes those products that do not have a matching vendor code:

```
SELECT      P_CODE, VENDOR.V_CODE, V_NAME
FROM        VENDOR RIGHT JOIN PRODUCT ON VENDOR.V_CODE = PRODUCT.V_CODE;
```

The SQL code and its output are shown in Figure 9.11.

FIGURE 9.10 LEFT JOIN results

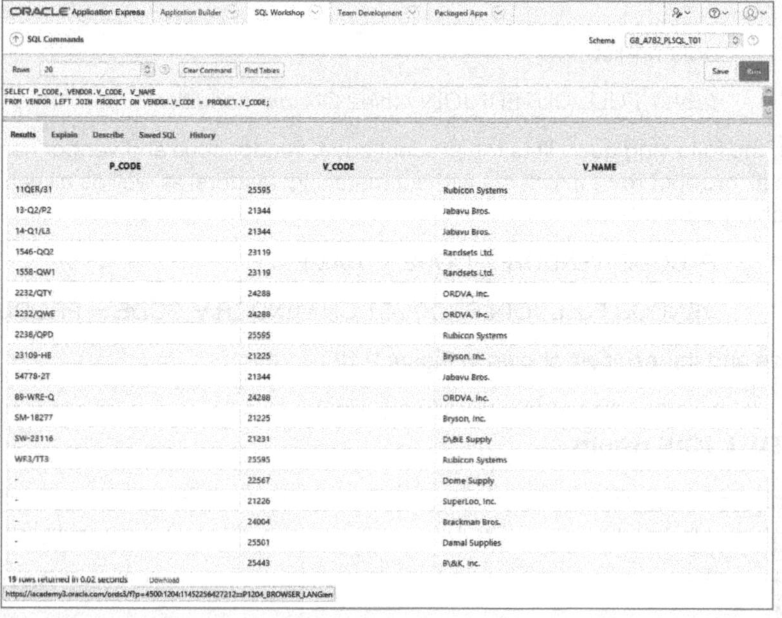

FIGURE 9.11 RIGHT JOIN results

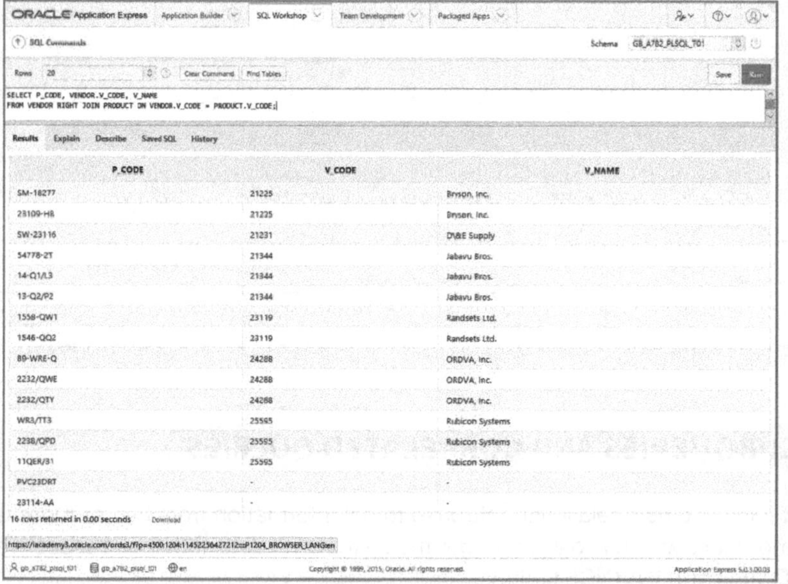

The full outer join returns not only the rows matching the join condition (that is, rows with matching values in the common column), but also all of the rows with unmatched values in either side table. The syntax is:

SELECT column-list

FROM *table1* FULL [OUTER] JOIN *table2* ON *join-condition*

For example, the following query lists the product code, vendor code and vendor name for all products and includes all product rows (products without matching vendors) as well as all vendor rows (vendors without matching products):

```
SELECT    P_CODE, VENDOR.V_CODE, V_NAME
FROM      VENDOR FULL JOIN PRODUCT ON VENDOR.V_CODE = PRODUCT.V_CODE;
```

The SQL code and its result are shown in Figure 9.12.

FIGURE 9.12 FULL JOIN results

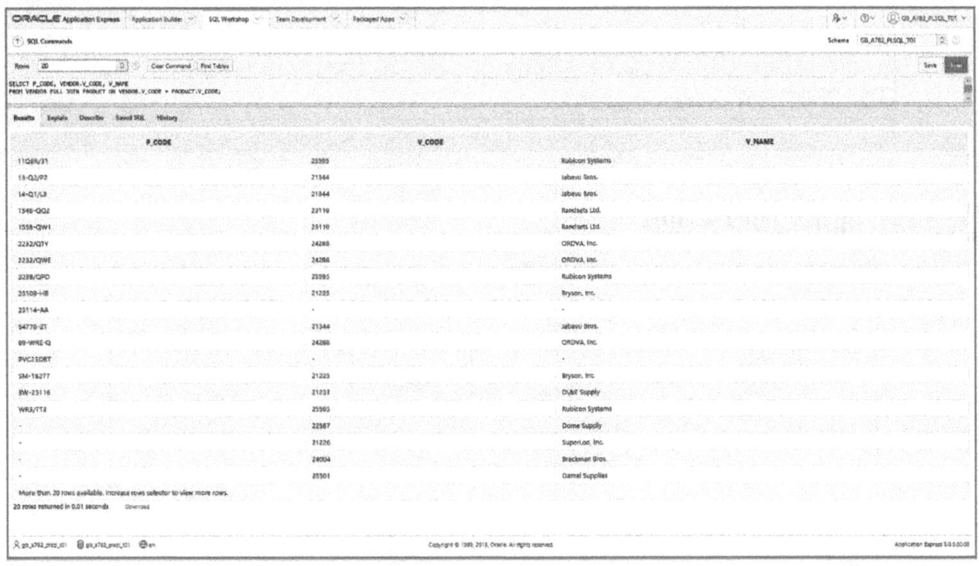

9.3 SUBQUERIES AND CORRELATED QUERIES

The use of joins allows a relational database to get information from two or more tables. For example, the following query would allow you to get the customers' data with their respective invoices by joining the CUSTOMER and INVOICE tables.

```
SELECT    INV_NUMBER, INVOICE.CUS_CODE, CUS_LNAME, CUS_FNAME
FROM      CUSTOMER, INVOICE
WHERE     CUSTOMER.CUS_CODE = INVOICE.CUS_CODE;
```

In the previous query, the data from both tables (CUSTOMER and INVOICE) are processed at once, matching rows with shared CUS_CODE values.

However, it is often necessary to process data based on *other* processed data. Suppose, for example, you want to generate a list of vendors who provide products. (Recall that not all vendors in the VENDOR table have provided products – some of them are only *potential* vendors.) In Chapter 8, Beginning Structured Query Language, you learnt that you could generate such a list by writing the following query:

```
SELECT      V_CODE, V_NAME
FROM VENDOR
WHERE       V_CODE NOT IN (SELECT V_CODE FROM PRODUCT);
```

Similarly, to generate a list of all products with a price greater than or equal to the average product price, you can write the following query:

```
SELECT      P_CODE, P_PRICE
FROM PRODUCT
WHERE       P_PRICE >= (SELECT AVG(P_PRICE) FROM PRODUCT);
```

In both of those cases, you needed to get information that was not previously known:

- Which vendors provide products?
- What is the average price of all products?

In both cases, you used a subquery to generate the required information that could then be used as input for the originating query.

Although you learnt how to use subqueries in Chapter 8, let's review the basic characteristics of a subquery:

- A subquery is a query (SELECT statement) inside a query.
- A subquery is normally expressed inside parentheses.
- The first query in the SQL statement is known as the *outer query*.
- The query inside the SQL statement is known as the *inner query*.
- The inner query is executed first.
- The output of an inner query is used as the input for the outer query.
- The entire SQL statement is sometimes referred to as a *nested query*.

In this section, you will learn more about the practical use of subqueries. You already know that a subquery is based on the use of the SELECT statement to return one or more values to another query. But subqueries have a wide range of uses. For example, you can use a subquery within a SQL data manipulation language (DML) statement (INSERT, UPDATE or DELETE) where a value or a list of values (such as multiple vendor codes or a table) is expected. Table 9.2 uses simple examples to summarise the use of SELECT subqueries in DML statements.

TABLE 9.2 SELECT subquery examples

SELECT Subquery Examples	Explanation
INSERT INTO PRODUCT SELECT * FROM P;	Inserts all rows from Table P into the PRODUCT table. Both tables must have the same attributes. The subquery returns all rows from Table P.
UPDATE PRODUCT SET P_PRICE = (SELECT AVG(P_PRICE) FROM PRODUCT) WHERE V_CODE IN (SELECT V_CODE FROM VENDOR WHERE V_AREACODE = '0181')	Updates the product price to the average product price, but only for the products that are provided by vendors who have an area code equal to 0181. The first subquery returns the average price; the second subquery returns the list of vendors with an area code equal to 0181.
DELETE FROM PRODUCT WHERE V_CODE IN (SELECT V_CODE FROM VENDOR WHERE V_AREACODE = '0181')	Deletes the PRODUCT table rows that are provided by vendors with area code equal to 0181. The subquery returns the list of vendors codes with an area code equal to 0181.

Using the examples shown in Table 9.2, note that the subquery is always at the right side of a comparison or assigning expression. Also, a subquery can return one value or multiple values. To be precise, the subquery can return:

9

- *One single value (one column and one row).* This subquery is used anywhere a single value is expected, as in the right side of a comparison expression (such as in the UPDATE example above when you assign the average price to the product's price). Obviously, when you assign a value to an attribute, that value is a single value, not a list of values. Therefore, the subquery must return only one value (one column, one row). If the query returns multiple values, the DBMS will generate an error.
- *A list of values (one column and multiple rows).* This type of subquery is used anywhere a list of values is expected, such as when using the IN clause (that is, when comparing the vendor code to a list of vendors). Again, in this case, there is only one column of data with multiple value instances. This type of subquery is used frequently in combination with the IN operator in a WHERE conditional expression.
- *A virtual table (multicolumn, multirow set of values).* This type of subquery can be used anywhere a table is expected, such as when using the FROM clause. You will see this type of query later in this chapter.

It is important to note that a subquery can return no values at all; it is a NULL. In such cases, the output of the outer query may result in an error or a null empty set depending where the subquery is used (in a comparison, an expression or a table set).

In the following sections, you will learn how to write subqueries within the SELECT statement to retrieve data from the database.

9.3.1 WHERE Subqueries

The most common type of subquery uses an inner SELECT subquery on the right side of a WHERE comparison expression. For example, to find all products with a price greater than or equal to the average product price, you write the following query:

```
SELECT    P_CODE, P_PRICE FROM PRODUCT
WHERE     P_PRICE >= (SELECT AVG(P_PRICE) FROM PRODUCT);
```

The output of the preceding query is shown in Figure 9.13. Note that this type of query, when used in a >, <, =, >=, or <= conditional expression, requires a subquery that returns only one single value (one column, one row). The value generated by the subquery must be of a 'comparable' data type; if the attribute to the left of the comparison symbol is a character type, the subquery must return a character string. Also, if the query returns more than a single value, the DBMS will generate an error.

FIGURE 9.13 WHERE subquery examples

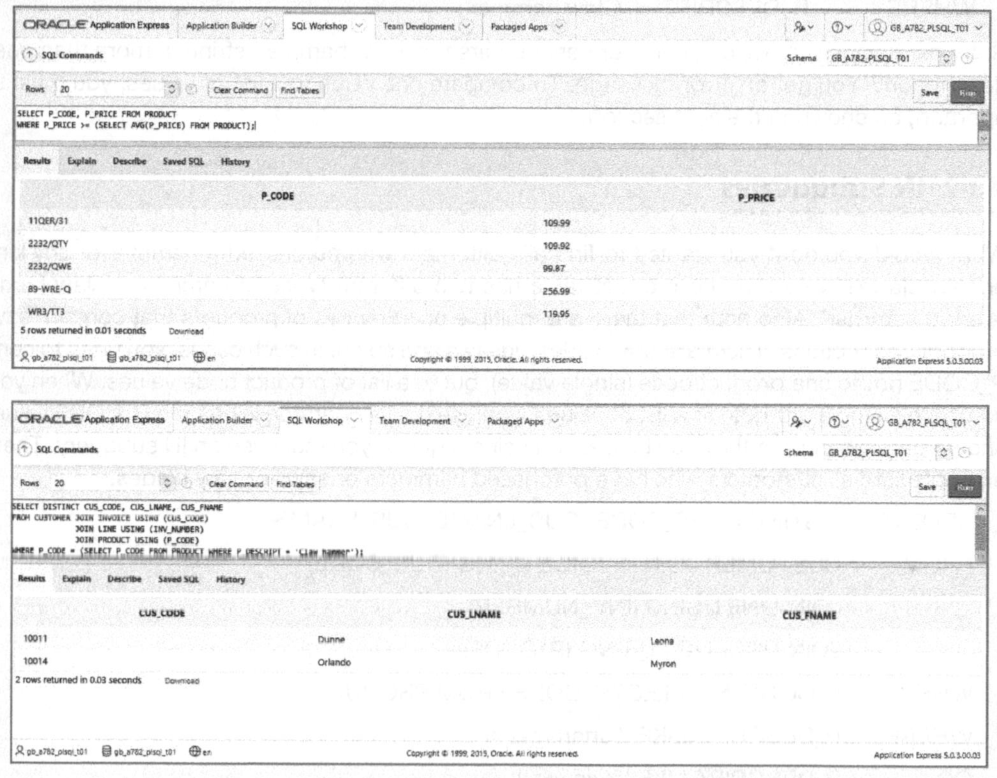

Subqueries can also be used in combination with joins. For example, the following query lists all of the customers who ordered the product 'claw hammer':

```
SELECT    DISTINCT CUS_CODE, CUS_LNAME, CUS_FNAME
FROM      CUSTOMER    JOIN INVOICE USING (CUS_CODE)
          JOIN LINE USING (INV_NUMBER)
          JOIN PRODUCT USING (P_CODE)
WHERE     P_CODE = (SELECT P_CODE FROM PRODUCT WHERE P_DESCRIPT = 'Claw
          hammer');
```

The result of that query is also shown in Figure 9.13.

In the preceding example, the inner query finds the P_CODE for the product 'claw hammer'. The P_CODE is then used to restrict the selected rows to only those where the P_CODE in the LINE table matches the P_CODE for 'Claw hammer.' Note that the previous query could have been written this way:

```
SELECT      DISTINCT CUS_CODE, CUS_LNAME, CUS_FNAME
FROM        CUSTOMER JOIN INVOICE USING (CUS_CODE)
            JOIN LINE USING (INV_NUMBER)
            JOIN PRODUCT USING (P_CODE)
WHERE       P_DESCRIPT = 'Claw hammer';
```

But what happens if the original query encounters the 'claw hammer' string in more than one product description? You get an error message. To compare one value to a list of values, you must use an IN operand, as shown in the next section.

9.3.2 IN Subqueries

What would you do if you wanted to find all customers who purchased a hammer or any kind of saw or saw blade? Note that the product table has two different types of hammers: 'claw hammer' and 'sledge hammer'. Also note that there are multiple occurrences of products that contain 'saw' in their product descriptions. There are saw blades, jigsaws and so on. In such cases, you need to compare the P_CODE not to one product code (single value), but to a list of product code values. When you want to compare a single attribute to a list of values, you use the IN operator. When the P_CODE values are not known beforehand but they can be derived using a query, you must use an IN subquery. The following example lists all customers who have purchased hammers or saws or saw blades.

```
SELECT    DISTINCT CUS_CODE, CUS_LNAME, CUS_FNAME
FROM      CUSTOMER JOIN INVOICE USING (CUS_CODE)
          JOIN LINE USING (INV_NUMBER)
          JOIN PRODUCT USING (P_CODE)
WHERE     P_CODE IN (SELECTP_CODE FROM PRODUCT
WHERE     P_DESCRIPT LIKE '%hammer%'
OR        P_DESCRIPT LIKE '%saw%');
```

The result of that query is shown in Figure 9.14.

FIGURE 9.14 IN subquery examples

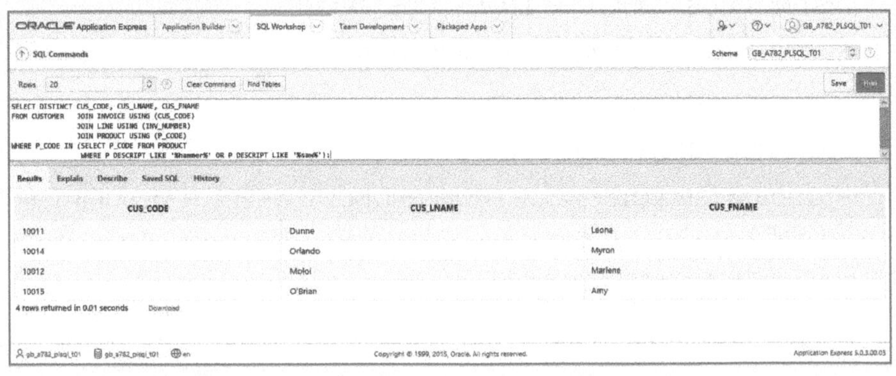

9.3.3 HAVING Subqueries

Just as you can use subqueries with the WHERE clause, you can use a subquery with a HAVING clause. Remember that the HAVING clause restricts the output of a GROUP BY query by applying a conditional criteria to the grouped rows. For example, to list all products with the total quantity sold greater than the average quantity sold, you would write the following query:

```
SELECT      P_CODE, SUM(LINE_UNITS)
FROM        LINE
GROUP BY    P_CODE
HAVING      SUM(LINE_UNITS) > (SELECT AVG(LINE_UNITS) FROM LINE);
```

The result of that query is shown in Figure 9.15.

FIGURE 9.15 **HAVING subquery examples**

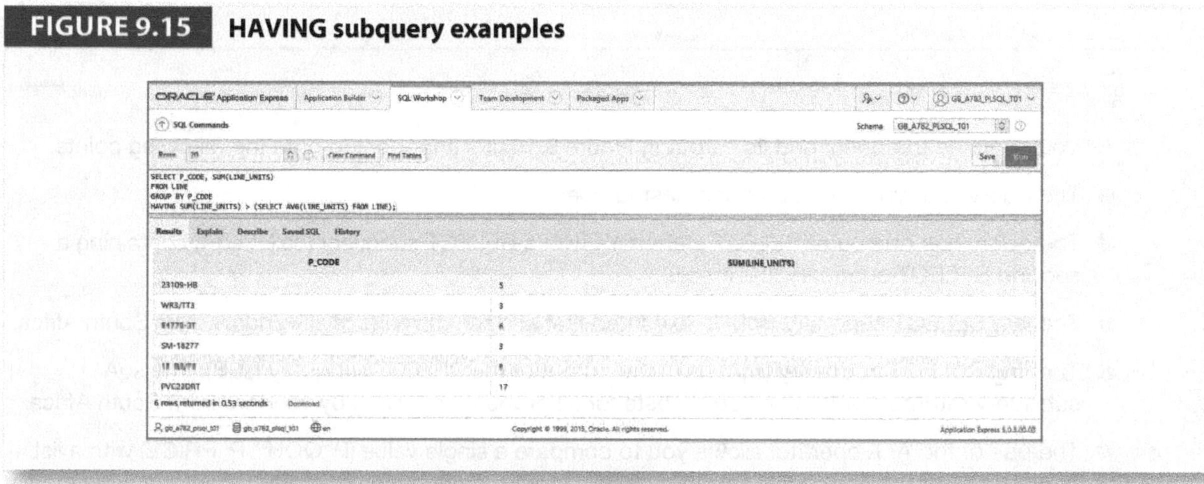

9.3.4 Multirow Subquery Operators: ANY and ALL

So far, you have learnt that you use an IN subquery when you need to compare a value to a list of values. But the IN subquery uses an equality operator; that is, it selects only those rows that match (are equal to) at least one of the values in the list. What happens if you need to do an inequality comparison (> or <) of one value to a list of values?

For example, suppose you want to know which products have a product cost that is greater than all individual product costs for products provided by vendors from South Africa (SA).

```
SELECT      P_CODE, P_QOH * P_PRICE
FROM        PRODUCT
WHERE       P_QOH * P_PRICE > ALL (SELECT P_QOH * P_PRICE
            FROM PRODUCT
            WHERE       V_CODE IN (SELECT V_CODE
            FROM        VENDOR
            WHERE       V_COUNTRY = 'SA'));
```

The result of that query is shown in Figure 9.16.

FIGURE 9.16 **Multirow subquery operator example**

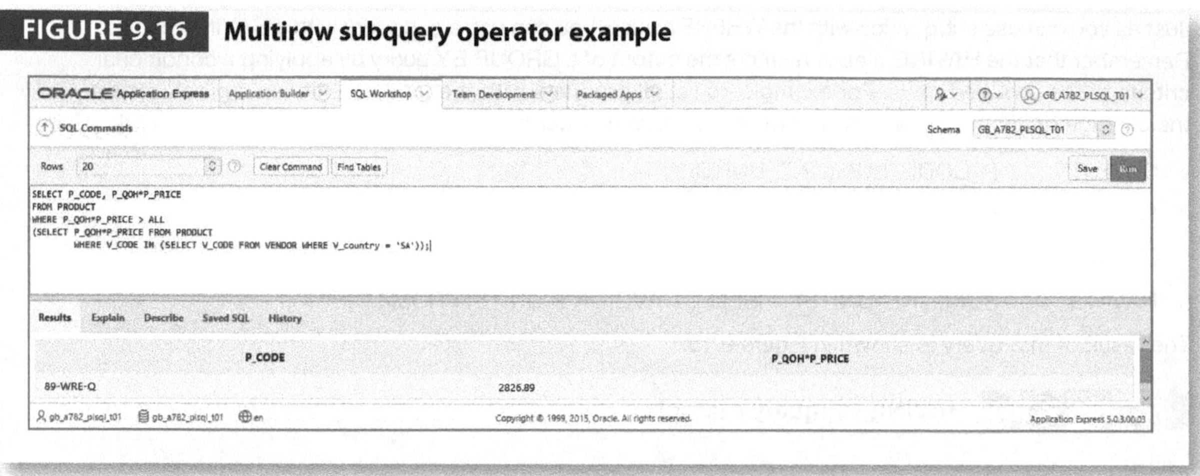

As you examine the query and its output in Figure 9.16, it's important to note the following points:

- The query is a typical example of a nested query.
- The query has one outer SELECT statement with a SELECT subquery (call it sqA) containing a second SELECT subquery (call it sqB).
- The last SELECT subquery (sqB) is executed first and returns a list of all vendors from South Africa.
- The first SELECT subquery (sqA) uses the output of the SELECT subquery (sqB). The sqA subquery returns the list of product costs for all products provided by vendors from South Africa.
- The use of the ALL operator allows you to compare a single value (P_QOH * P_PRICE) with a list of values returned by the first subquery (sqA), using a comparison operator other than equals.
- For a row to appear in the result set, it has to meet the criterion P_QOH * P_PRICE > ALL of the individual values returned by the subquery sqA. The values returned by sqA are a list of product costs. In fact, 'greater than ALL' is equivalent to 'greater than the highest product cost of the list'. In the same way, a condition of 'less than ALL' is equivalent to 'less than the lowest product cost of the list'.

Another powerful operator is the ANY multirow operator (near cousin of the ALL multirow operator). The ANY operator allows you to compare a single value to a list of values and select only the rows for which the inventory cost is greater than any value of the list or less than any value of the list. You could use the equal to ANY operator, which would be the equivalent of the IN operator.

9.3.5 FROM Subqueries

So far, you have seen how the SELECT statement uses subqueries within WHERE, HAVING and IN statements and how the ANY and ALL operators are used for multirow subqueries. In all of those cases, the subquery was part of a conditional expression and it always appeared at the right side of the expression. In this section, you will learn how to use subqueries in the FROM clause.

As you already know, the FROM clause specifies the table(s) from which the data are drawn. Because the output of a SELECT statement is another table (or more precisely a 'virtual' table), you could use a SELECT subquery in the FROM clause. For example, assume that you want to know all customers who have purchased products 13-Q2/P2 *and* 23109-HB. All product purchases are stored in the LINE table. It is easy to find out who purchased any given product by searching the P_CODE attribute in the

LINE table. But in this case, you want to know all customers who purchased both products, not just one. You could write the following query:

```
SELECT      DISTINCT CUSTOMER.CUS_CODE, CUSTOMER.CUS_LNAME
FROM        CUSTOMER,
            (SELECT INVOICE.CUS_CODE FROM INVOICE NATURAL JOIN LINE
            WHERE P_CODE = '13-Q2/P2') CP1,
            (SELECT INVOICE.CUS_CODE FROM INVOICE NATURAL JOIN LINE
            WHERE P_CODE = '23109-HB') CP2
WHERE       CUSTOMER.CUS_CODE = CP1.CUS_CODE AND CP1.CUS_CODE = CP2.
            CUS_CODE;
```

The result of that query is shown in Figure 9.17.

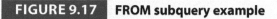

FIGURE 9.17 FROM subquery example

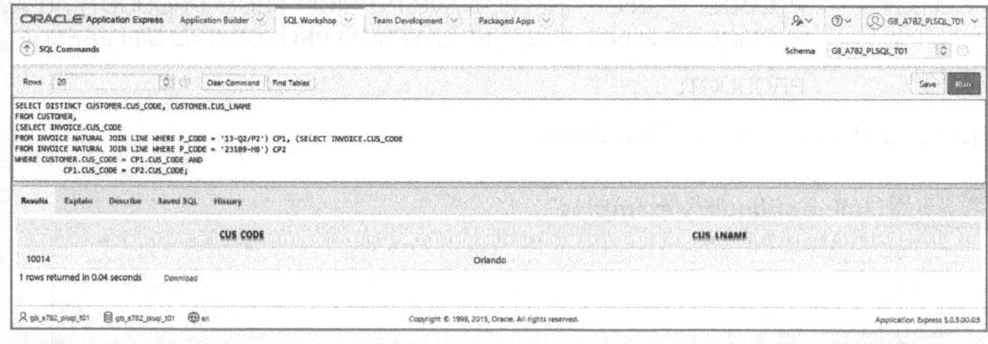

As you examine Figure 9.17, note that the first subquery returns all customers who purchased product 13-Q2/P2, while the second subquery returns all customers who purchased product 23109-HB. So, in this FROM subquery, you are joining the CUSTOMER table with two virtual tables. The join condition selects only the rows with matching CUS_CODE values in each table (base or virtual).

In the previous chapter, you learnt that a view is also a virtual table; therefore, you can use a view name anywhere a table is expected. So, you could create two views: one listing all customers who purchased product 13-Q2/P2 and another listing all customers who purchased product 23109-HB. Doing so, you would write the query as:

```
CREATE VIEW CP1 AS
            SELECT INVOICE.CUS_CODE FROM INVOICE NATURAL JOIN LINE
            WHERE P_CODE = '13-Q2/P2';
CREATE VIEW CP2 AS
            SELECT INVOICE.CUS_CODE FROM INVOICE NATURAL JOIN LINE
            WHERE P_CODE = '23109-HB';
SELECT      DISTINCT CUS_CODE, CUS_LNAME
FROM                 CUSTOMER NATURAL JOIN CP1 NATURAL JOIN CP2;
```

You may be tempted to speculate that the above query could also be written using the following syntax:

```
SELECT      CUS_CODE, CUS_LNAME
FROM        CUSTOMER NATURAL JOIN INVOICE NATURAL JOIN LINE
WHERE       P_CODE = '13-Q2/P2' AND P_CODE = '23109-HB';
```

However, if you examine that query carefully, you will note that a P_CODE cannot be equal to two different values at the same time. Therefore, the query will not return any rows.

9.3.6 Attribute List Subqueries

The SELECT statement uses the attribute list to indicate which columns to project in the resulting set. Those columns can be attributes of base tables or computed attributes or the result of an aggregate function. The attribute list can also include a subquery expression, also known as an inline subquery. A subquery in the attribute list must return one single value; otherwise, an error code is raised. For example, a simple inline query can be used to list the difference between each product's price and the average product price:

```
SELECT      P_CODE, P_PRICE, (SELECT AVG(P_PRICE) FROM PRODUCT) AS AVGPRICE,
            P_PRICE – (SELECT AVG(P_PRICE) FROM PRODUCT) AS DIFFERENCE
FROM        PRODUCT;
```

Figure 9.18 shows the result of that query.

9

FIGURE 9.18 **Inline subquery examples**

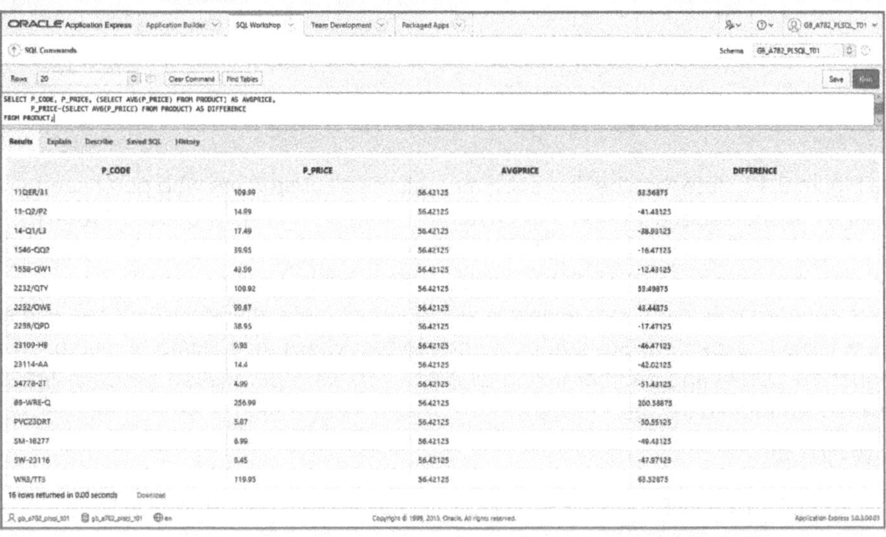

In Figure 9.18, note that the inline query output returns one single value (the average product's price) and that the value is the same in every row. Note also that the query used the full expression instead of the column aliases when computing the difference. In fact, if you try to use the alias in the difference expression, you get an error message. The column alias cannot be used in computations in the attribute list when the alias is defined in the same attribute list. That DBMS requirement is due to the way the DBMS parses and executes queries.

Another example will help you understand the use of attribute list subqueries and column aliases. For example, suppose you want to know the product code, the total sales by product, and the contribution by employee of each product's sales. To get the sales by product, you need to use only the LINE table. To compute the contribution by employee you need to know the number of employees (from the EMPLOYEE table). As you study the tables' structures, you can see that the LINE and EMPLOYEE tables do not share a common attribute. In fact, you don't need a common attribute. You need to know only the total number of employees, not the total employees related to each product. So to answer the query, you would write the following code:

```
SELECT      P_CODE, SUM(LINE_UNITS * LINE_PRICE) AS SALES,
            (SELECT COUNT(*) FROM EMPLOYEE) AS ECOUNT,
            ROUND(SUM(LINE_UNITS * LINE_PRICE)/(SELECT COUNT(*) FROM
            EMPLOYEE),2) AS CONTRIB
FROM        LINE
GROUP BY    P_CODE;
```

The result of that query is shown in Figure 9.19. Notice that the CONTRIB column has been rounded up to two decimal places using the SQL ROUND function.

FIGURE 9.19 Another example of an inline subquery

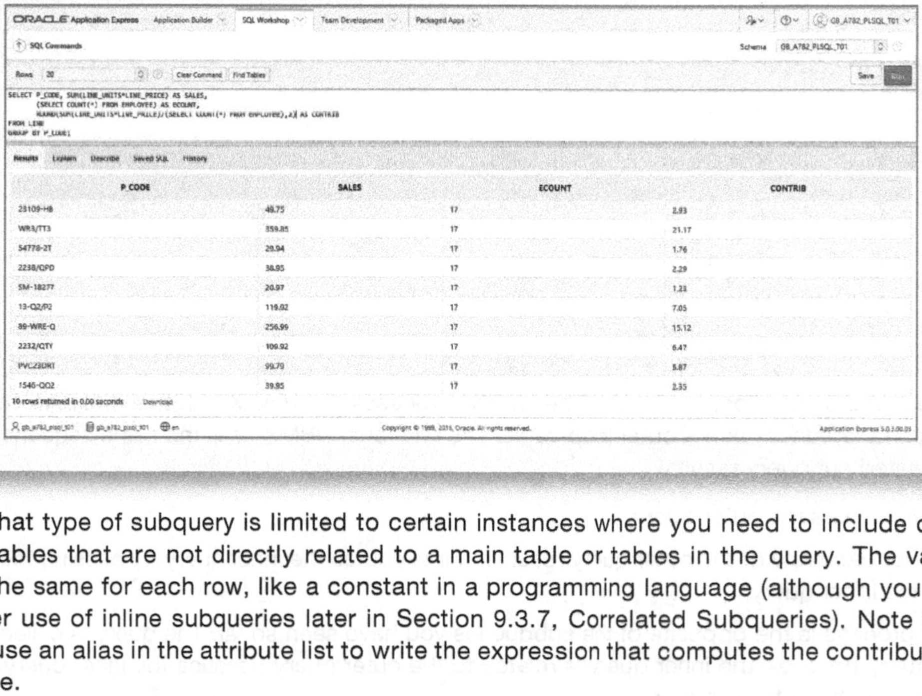

P_CODE	SALES	ECOUNT	CONTRIB
23109-HB	49.75	17	2.93
WR3/TT3	359.85	17	21.17
54778-2T	29.94	17	1.76
2238/QPD	38.95	17	2.29
SM-18277	20.97	17	1.23
13-Q2/P2	119.92	17	7.05
89-WRE-Q	256.99	17	15.12
2232/QTY	109.92	17	6.47
PVC23DRT	99.79	17	5.87
1546-QQ2	39.95	17	2.35

10 rows returned in 0.00 seconds

The use of that type of subquery is limited to certain instances where you need to include data from other tables that are not directly related to a main table or tables in the query. The value will remain the same for each row, like a constant in a programming language (although you will learn another use of inline subqueries later in Section 9.3.7, Correlated Subqueries). Note that you cannot use an alias in the attribute list to write the expression that computes the contribution per employee.

Another way to write the same query by using column aliases requires the use of a subquery in the FROM clause, as follows:

```
SELECT      P_CODE, SALES, ECOUNT, SALES/ECOUNT AS CONTRIB
FROM        (SELECT  P_CODE, SUM(LINE_UNITS * LINE_PRICE) AS SALES, (SELECT COUNT(*)
            FROM EMPLOYEE) AS ECOUNT
            FROM          LINE
            GROUP BY      P_CODE);
```

In that case, you are actually using two subqueries. The subquery in the FROM clause executes first and returns a virtual table with three columns: P_CODE, SALES and ECOUNT. The FROM subquery contains an inline subquery that returns the number of employees as ECOUNT. Because the outer query receives the output of the inner query, you can now refer to the columns in the outer subquery, using the column aliases.

9.3.7 Correlated Subqueries

Until now, all subqueries you have learnt about execute independently. That is, each subquery in a command sequence executes in a serial fashion, one after another. The inner subquery executes first; its output is used by the outer query, which then executes until the last outer query executes (the first SQL statement in the code).

In contrast, a **correlated subquery** is a subquery that executes once for each row in the outer query. That process is similar to the typical nested loop in a programming language. For example:

```
FOR X = 1 TO 2
        FOR Y = 1 TO 3
                PRINT 'X = 'X, 'Y = 'Y
        END
END
```

will yield the output

```
X = 1      Y = 1
X = 1      Y = 2
X = 1      Y = 3
X = 2      Y = 1
X = 2      Y = 2
X = 2      Y = 3
```

Note that the outer loop X = 1 TO 2 begins the process by setting X = 1; then the inner loop Y = 1 TO 3 is completed for each X outer loop value. The relational DBMS uses the same sequence to produce correlated subquery results:

1. It initiates the outer query.
2. For each row of the outer query result set, it executes the inner query by passing the outer row to the inner query.

That process is the opposite of the subqueries you have seen so far. The query is called a *correlated* subquery because the inner query is *related* to the outer query because the inner query references a column of the outer subquery.

To see the correlated subquery in action, suppose you want to know all product sales in which the units sold value is greater than the average units sold value for *that* product (as opposed to the average for *all* products). In that case, complete the following procedure:

1. Compute the average-units-sold value for a product.
2. Compare the average computed in Step 1 to the units sold in each sale row; then select only the rows in which the number of units sold is greater.

The following correlated query completes the preceding two-step process:

```
SELECT      INV_NUMBER, P_CODE, LINE_UNITS
FROM        LINE LS
WHERE       LS.LINE_UNITS > (SELECTAVG(LINE_UNITS)
            FROM LINE LA
            WHERE           LA.P_CODE = LS.P_CODE);
```

The first example in Figure 9.20 shows the result of that query.

FIGURE 9.20 Correlated subquery examples

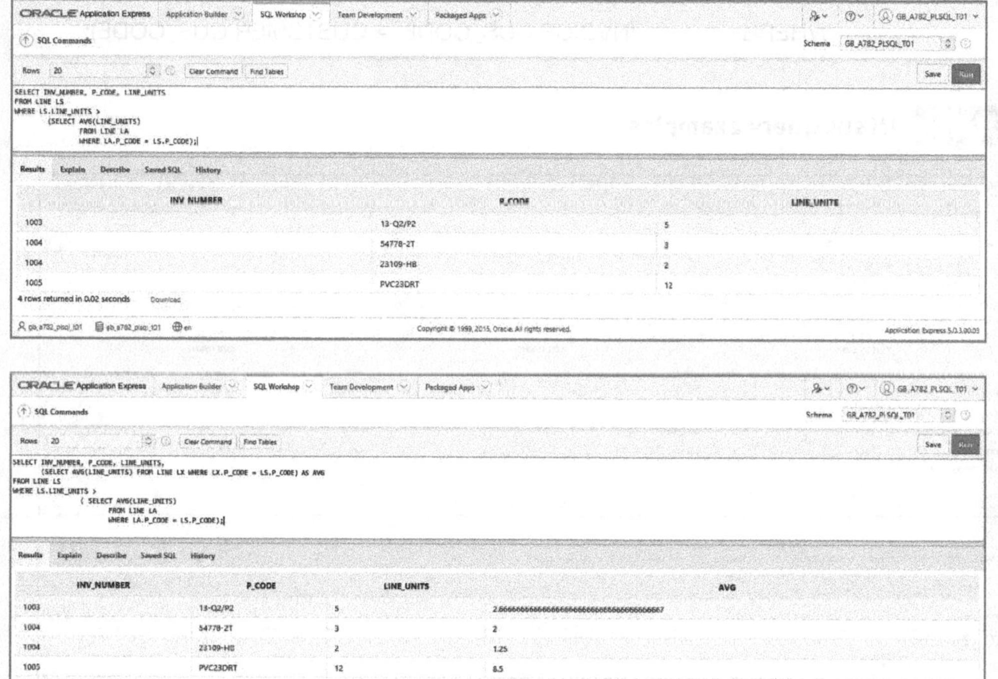

As you examine the top query and its result in Figure 9.20, note that the LINE table is used more than once; so, you need to use table aliases. In that case, the inner query computes the average units sold of the product that matches the P_CODE of the outer query P_CODE. That is, the inner query runs once using the first product code found in the (outer) LINE table and returns the average sale for that product. When the number of units sold in that (outer) LINE row is greater than the average computed, the row is added to the output. Then the inner query runs again, this time using the second product code found in the (outer) LINE table. The process repeats until the inner query has run for all rows in the (outer) LINE table. In that case, the inner query is repeated as many times as there are rows in the outer query.

To verify the results and to provide an example of how you can combine subqueries, you can add a correlated inline subquery to the previous query. That correlated inline subquery shows the average units sold column for each product. (See the second query and its results in Figure 9.20.) As you can see, the new query contains a correlated inline subquery that computes the average units sold for each product. You not only get an answer, but also can verify that the answer is correct.

You can also use correlated subqueries with the EXISTS special operator. For example, suppose you want to know all customers who have placed an order lately. In that case, you could use a correlated subquery like the first one shown in Figure 9.21:

```
SELECT      CUS_CODE, CUS_LNAME, CUS_FNAME
FROM        CUSTOMER
WHERE       EXISTS (SELECT CUS_CODE FROM INVOICE
            WHERE        INVOICE.CUS_CODE = CUSTOMER.CUS_CODE);
```

FIGURE 9.21 **IN subquery examples**

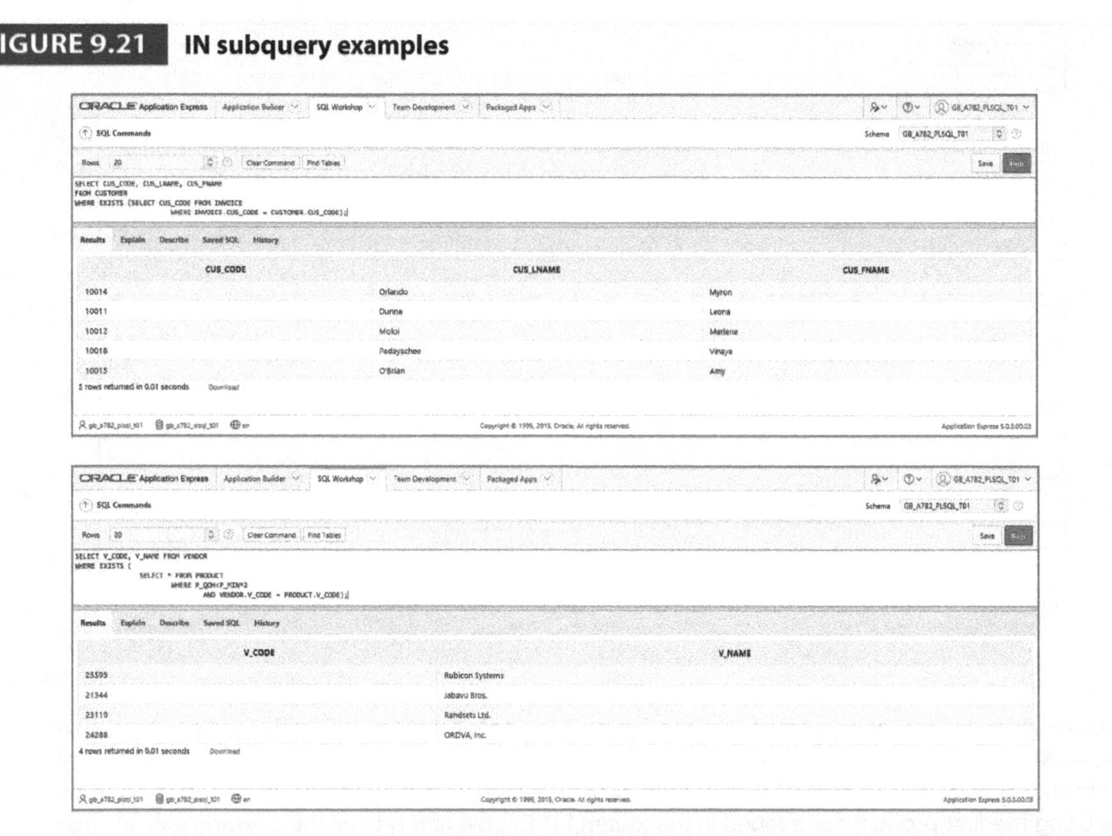

The second example of an EXISTS correlated subquery in Figure 9.21 will help you understand how to use correlated queries. For example, suppose you want to know which vendors you must contact to start ordering products that are approaching the minimum quantity-on-hand value. In particular, you want to know the vendor code and name of vendors for products having a quantity on hand that is less than double the minimum quantity. The query that answers that question is as follows:

```
SELECT    V_CODE, V_NAME
FROM              VENDOR
WHERE     EXISTS (SELECT*
FROM PRODUCT
WHERE     P_QOH < P_MIN * 2
AND               VENDOR.V_CODE = PRODUCT.V_CODE);
```

As you examine the second query in Figure 9.21, note that:

1 The inner correlated subquery runs using the first vendor.
2 If any products match the condition (quantity on hand is less than double the minimum quantity), the vendor code and name are listed in the output.
3 The correlated subquery runs using the second vendor, and the process repeats itself until all vendors are used.

9.4 SQL FUNCTIONS

The data in databases are the basis of critical business information. Generating information from data often requires many data manipulations. Sometimes, such data manipulation involves the decomposition of data elements. For example, an employee's date of birth can be subdivided into a day, a month and a year. A product manufacturing code (for example, SE-05-2-09-1234-1-3/12/04-19:26:48) may be designed to record the manufacturing region, plant, shift, production line, employee number, date and time. For years, conventional programming languages have had special functions that enabled programmers to perform data transformations like those data decompositions. If you know a modern programming language, it's very likely that the SQL functions in this section will look familiar.

SQL functions are useful tools. You'll need to use functions when you want to list all employees ordered by year of birth or when your marketing department wants you to generate a list of all customers ordered by postal code and the first four digits of their telephone numbers. In both of those cases, you'll need to use data elements that are not present as such in the database, instead using a SQL function that can be derived from an existing attribute. Functions always use a numerical, date or string value. The value may be part of the command itself (a constant or literal) or it may be an attribute located in a table. Therefore, a function may appear anywhere in a SQL statement where a value or an attribute can be used.

There are many types of SQL functions, such as arithmetic, trigonometric, string, date and time functions. This section will not explain all of those types of functions in detail, but it will give you a brief overview of the most useful ones.

NOTE

Although the main DBMS vendors support the SQL functions covered here, the syntax or degree of support may differ. In fact, DBMS vendors invariably add their own functions to products to lure new customers. The functions covered in this section represent just a small portion of functions supported by your DBMS. Read your DBMS SQL reference manual for a complete list of available functions.

9.4.1 Date and Time Functions

All SQL-standard DBMSs support date and time functions. All date functions take one parameter (of a date or character data type) and return a value (character, numeric or date type). Unfortunately, date/time data types are implemented differently by different DBMS vendors. The problem occurs because the ANSI SQL standard defines date data types but does not say how those data types are to be stored; instead, it lets the vendor deal with that issue.

Because date/time functions differ from vendor to vendor, this section will cover basic date/time functions for Microsoft Access/SQL Server and for Oracle. Table 9.3 shows a list of selected Microsoft Access/SQL Server date/time functions.

TABLE 9.3 Selected Microsoft Access/SQL Server date/time functions

Function	Example(s)
YEAR Returns a four-digit year Syntax: YEAR(date_value)	Lists all employees born in 1966: SELECT EMP_LNAME, EMP_FNAME, EMP_DOB, YEAR(EMP_DOB) AS YEAR FROM EMPLOYEE WHERE YEAR(EMP_DOB) = 1966;
MONTH Returns a two-digit month code Syntax: MONTH(date_value)	Lists all employees born in November: SELECT EMP_LNAME, EMP_FNAME, EMP_DOB, MONTH(EMP_DOB) AS MONTH FROM EMPLOYEE WHERE MONTH(EMP_DOB) = 11;
DAY Returns the number of the day Syntax: DAY(date_value)	Lists all employees born on the 14th day of the month: SELECT EMP_LNAME, EMP_FNAME, EMP_DOB, DAY(EMP_DOB) AS DAY FROM EMPLOYEE WHERE DAY(EMP_DOB) = 14;
DATE() Microsoft Access **GETDATE() SQL Server** Returns today's date	Lists how many days are left until Christmas: SELECT #25-Dec-2019# – DATE(); Note two features: ■ There is no FROM clause, which is acceptable in Microsoft Access. ■ The Christmas date is enclosed in number signs (#) because you are doing date arithmetic. In SQL Server: Use GETDATE() to get the current system date. To compute the difference between dates, use the DATEDIFF function (see below).

9

Function	Example(s)
DATEADD SQL Server Adds a number of selected time periods to a date Syntax: **DATEADD(datepart, number, date)**	Adds a number of dateparts to a given date. Dateparts can be minutes, hours, days, weeks, months, quarters, or years. For example: SELECT DATEADD(day,90, P_INDATE) AS DueDate FROM PRODUCT; The preceding example adds 90 days to P_INDATE. In Microsoft Access, use the following: SELECT P_INDATE+90 AS DueDate FROM PRODUCT;
DATEDIFF SQL Server Subtracts two dates Syntax: **DATEDIFF(datepart, startdate, enddate)**	Returns the difference between two dates expressed in a selected datepart. For example: SELECT DATEDIFF(day, P_INDATE, GETDATE()) AS DaysAgo FROM PRODUCT; In Microsoft Access, use the following: SELECT DATE() - P_INDATE AS DaysAgo FROM PRODUCT;

Table 9.4 shows the equivalent date/time functions used in Oracle. Note that Oracle uses the same function (TO_CHAR) to extract the different parts of a date. Also, another function (TO_DATE) is used to convert character strings to a valid Oracle date format that can be used in date arithmetic. Finally, Table 9.5 shows selected date/time functions for MySQL version 5.6. It is worth noting that, due to Oracle's acquisition of MySQL, it is likely that there will be an overlap of a number of MySQL and Oracle functions in the future. It is therefore advisable that the you refer to the appropriate DBMS SQL reference manual for a current list of up-to-date functions.

TABLE 9.4 Selected Oracle date/time functions

Function	Example(s)
TO_CHAR Returns a character string or a formatted string from a date value Syntax: TO_CHAR(date_value, fmt) fmt = format used; can be: MONTH: name of month MON: three-letter month name MM: two-digit month name D: number for day of week DD: number of day of month DAY: name of day of week YYYY: four-digit year value YY: two-digit year value	Lists all employees born in 1992: SELECT EMP_LNAME, EMP_FNAME, EMP_DOB, TO_CHAR(EMP_DOB,'YYYY') AS YEAR FROM EMPLOYEE WHERE TO_CHAR(EMP_DOB,'YYYY') = '1992'; Lists all employees born in November: SELECT EMP_LNAME, EMP_FNAME, EMP_DOB, TO_CHAR(EMP_DOB,'MM') AS MONTH FROM EMPLOYEE WHERE TO_CHAR(EMP_DOB,'MM') = '11'; Lists all employees born on the 14th day of the month: SELECT EMP_LNAME, EMP_FNAME, EMP_DOB, TO_CHAR(EMP_DOB,'DD') AS DAY FROM EMPLOYEE WHERE TO_CHAR(EMP_DOB,'DD') = '14';

Function	Example(s)
TO_DATE Returns a date value using a character string and a date format mask; also used to translate a date between formats Syntax: TO_DATE(char_value, fmt) fmt = format used; can be: MONTH: name of month MON: three-letter month name MM: two-digit month name D: number for day of week DD: number of day of month DAY: name of day of week YYYY: four-digit year value YY: two-digit year value	Lists the approximate age of the employees on the company's tenth anniversary date (11/25/2018): SELECT EMP_LNAME, EMP_FNAME, EMP_DOB, '11/25/2018' AS ANIV_DATE, (TO_DATE('11/25/2008','MM/DD/YYYY') EMP_DOB)/365 AS YEARS FROM EMPLOYEE ORDER BY YEARS; Note the following: ■ '11/25/2018' is a text string, not a date. ■ The TO_DATE function translates the text string to a valid Oracle date used in date arithmetic. How many days between Thanksgiving and Christmas 2018? SELECT TO_DATE('2018/12/25','YYYY/MM/DD') – TO_DATE('NOVEMBER 23, 2018','MONTH DD, YYYY') FROM DUAL; Note the following: ■ The TO_DATE function translates the text string to a valid Oracle date used in date arithmetic. ■ DUAL is Oracle's pseudo table used only for cases where a table is not really needed.
SYSDATE Returns today's date	Lists how many days are left until Christmas: SELECT TO_DATE('25-Dec-2018','DD-MON-YYYY') SYSDATE FROM DUAL; Notice two things: ■ DUAL is Oracle's pseudo table used only for cases where a table is not really needed. ■ The Christmas date is enclosed in a TO_DATE function to translate the date to a valid date format.
ADD_MONTHS Adds a number of months to a date; useful for adding months or years to a date Syntax: ADD_MONTHS(date_value, n) n = number of months	Lists all products with their expiration date (two years from the purchase date): SELECT P_CODE, P_INDATE, ADD_MONTHS(P_INDATE,24) FROM PRODUCT ORDER BY ADD_MONTHS(P_INDATE,24);
LAST_DAY Returns the date of the last day of the month given in a date Syntax: LAST_DAY(date_value)	Lists all employees who were hired within the last seven days of a month: SELECT EMP_LNAME, EMP_FNAME, EMP_HIRE_DATE FROM EMPLOYEE WHERE EMP_HIRE_DATE >= LAST_DAY(EMP_HIRE_DATE)-7;

TABLE 9.5 Selected MySQL date/time functions

Function	Examples
Date_Format Returns a character string or a formatted string from a date value Syntax: DATE_FORMAT(date_value, fmt) fmt = format used; can be: %M: name of month %m: two-digit month number %b: abbreviated month name %d: number of day of month %W: weekday name %a: abbreviated weekday name %Y: four-digit year %y: two-digit year	Displays the product code and date the product was last received into stock for all products: SELECT P_CODE, DATE_FORMAT(P_INDATE, '%m/%d/%y') FROM PRODUCT; SELECT P_CODE, DATE_FORMAT(P_INDATE, '%M %d, %Y') FROM PRODUCT;
YEAR Returns a four-digit year Syntax: YEAR(date_value)	Lists all employees born in 1982: SELECT EMP_LNAME, EMP_FNAME, EMP_DOB, YEAR(EMP_DOB) AS YEAR FROM EMPLOYEE WHERE YEAR(EMP_DOB) = 1982;
MONTH Returns a two-digit month code Syntax: MONTH(date_value)	Lists all employees born in November: SELECT EMP_LNAME, EMP_FNAME, EMP_DOB, MONTH(EMP_DOB) AS MONTH FROM EMPLOYEE WHERE MONTH(EMP_DOB) = 11;
DAY Returns the number of the day Syntax: DAY(date_value)	Lists all employees born on the 14th day of the month: SELECT EMP_LNAME, EMP_FNAME, EMP_DOB, DAY(EMP_DOB) AS DAY FROM EMPLOYEE WHERE DAY(EMP_DOB) = 14;
ADDDATE Adds a number of days to a date Syntax: ADDDATE(date_value, n) n = number of days **DATE_ADD** Adds a number of days, months, or years to a date. This is similar to ADDDATE except it is more robust. It allows the user to specify the date unit to add. Syntax: DATE_ADD(date, INTERVAL n unit) n = number to add unit = date unit, can be: DAY: add n days WEEK: add n weeks MONTH: add n months YEAR: add n years	List all products with the date they will have been on the shelf for 30 days. SELECT P_CODE, P_INDATE, ADDDATE(P_INDATE, 30) FROM PRODUCT ORDER BY ADDDATE(P_INDATE, 30); Lists all products with their expiration date (two years from the purchase date): SELECT P_CODE, P_INDATE, DATE_ADD(P_INDATE, INTERVAL 2 YEAR) FROM PRODUCT ORDER BY DATE_ADD(P_INDATE, INTERVAL 2 YEAR);

Function	Examples
LAST_DAY Returns the date of the last day of the month given in a date Syntax: LAST_DAY(date_value)	Lists all employees who were hired within the last seven days of a month: SELECT EMP_LNAME, EMP_FNAME, EMP_HIRE_DATE FROM EMPLOYEE WHERE EMP_HIRE_DATE >= DATE_ADD(LAST_DAY (EMP_HIRE_DATE), INTERVAL -7 DAY);

9.4.2 Numeric Functions

Numeric functions can be grouped in many different ways, such as algebraic, trigonometric and logarithmic. In this section, you will learn two very useful functions. Do not confuse the SQL aggregate functions you saw in the previous chapter with the numeric functions in this section. The first group operates over a set of values (multiple rows – hence, the name *aggregate functions*), while the numeric functions covered here operate over a single row. Numeric functions take one numeric parameter and return one value. Table 9.6 shows a selected group of numeric functions available in an Oracle DBMS.

TABLE 9.6 Selected Oracle numeric functions

Function	Example(s)
ABS Returns the absolute value of a number Syntax: ABS(numeric_value)	Lists absolute values: SELECT 1.95, -1.93, ABS(1.95), ABS(-1.93) FROM DUAL;
ROUND Rounds a value to a specified precision (number of digits) Syntax: ROUND(numeric_value, p) p = precision	Lists the product prices rounded to one and zero decimal places: SELECT P_CODE, P_PRICE, ROUND(P_PRICE,1) AS PRICE1, ROUND(P_PRICE,0) AS PRICE0 FROM PRODUCT;
TRUNC Truncates a value to a specified precision (number of digits) Syntax: TRUNC(numeric_value, p) p = precision	Lists the product price rounded to one and zero decimal places and truncated: SELECT P_CODE, P_PRICE, ROUND (P_PRICE,1) AS PRICE1, ROUND(P_PRICE,0) AS PRICE0, TRUNC(P_PRICE,0) AS PRICEX FROM PRODUCT;

Function	Example(s)
CEIL/FLOOR Returns the smallest integer greater than or equal to a number or returns the largest integer equal to or less than a number, respectively Syntax; CEIL(numeric_value) FLOOR(numeric_value)	Lists the product price, smallest integer greater than or equal to the product price, and the largest integer equal to or less than the product price: SELECT P_PRICE, CEIL(P_PRICE), FLOOR(P_PRICE) FROM PRODUCT;

9.4.3 String Functions

String manipulations are among the most-used functions in programming. If you have ever created a report using any programming language, you know the importance of properly concatenating strings of characters, printing names in uppercase, or knowing the length of a given attribute. Table 9.7 shows a subset of useful string manipulation functions.

TABLE 9.7 Selected string functions

Function	Example(s)
Concatenation || Oracle + Microsoft Access and SQL Server Concatenates data from two different character columns and returns a single column Syntax: strg_value || strg_value strg__value + strg_value	Lists all employee names (concatenated). In Oracle, use the following: SELECT EMP_LNAME || ', ' || EMP_FNAME AS NAME FROM EMPLOYEE; In Microsoft Access and SQL Server, use the following: SELECT EMP_LNAME + ', ' + EMP_FNAME AS NAME FROM EMPLOYEE;
UPPER and LOWER Returns a string in all capital or all lowercase letters Syntax: UPPER(strg_value) LOWER(strg_value)	Lists all employee names in all capital letters (concatenated). In Oracle, use the following: SELECT UPPER(EMP_LNAME) || ', ' || UPPER(EMP_FNAME) AS NAME FROM EMPLOYEE; In SQL Server, use the following: SELECT UPPER (EMP_LNAME) + ', ' + UPPER(EMP_FNAME), AS NAME FROM EMPLOYEE; Lists all employee names in all lowercase letters (concatenated). In Oracle, use the following: SELECT LOWER(EMP_LNAME) || ', ' || LOWER(EMP_FNAME) AS NAME FROM EMPLOYEE; In SQL Server, use the following: SELECT LOWER(EMP_LNAME) + ', ' + LOWER(EMP_FNAME) AS NAME FROM EMPLOYEE; Not supported by Microsoft Access.

Function	Example(s)
SUBSTRING Returns a substring or part of a given string parameter Syntax: SUBSTR(strg_value, p, l) Oracle SUBSTRING(strg_value,p,l) SQL Server p = start position l = length of characters	Lists the first three characters of all employee phone numbers. In Oracle, use the following: SELECT EMP_PHONE, SUBSTR(EMP_PHONE,l ,3) AS PREFIX FROM EMPLOYEE; In SQL Server, use the following: SELECT EMP_PHONE, SUBSTRING(EMP_PHONE,1,3) AS PREFIX FROM EMPLOYEE; Not supported by Microsoft Access.
LENGTH Returns the number of characters in a string value Syntax: LENGTH(strg_value) Oracle LEN(strg_value) SQL Server	Lists all employee last names and the length of their names in descending order by last name length. In Oracle, use the following: SELECT EMP_LNAME, LENGTH(EMP_LNAME) AS NAMESIZE FROM EMPLOYEE; In Microsoft Access and SQL Server, use the following: SELECT EMP_LNAME, LEN(EMP_LNAME) AS NAMESIZE FROM EMPLOYEE;

9.4.4 Conversion Functions

9

Conversion functions allow you to take a value of a given data type and convert it to the equivalent value in another data type. In Section 9.4.1, you learnt about two of the basic conversion functions: TO_CHAR and TO_DATE. Note that the TO_CHAR function takes a date value and returns a character string representing a day, a month or a year. In the same way, the TO_DATE function takes a character string representing a date and returns an actual date in Oracle format.

In this section, you will see how to use the TO_CHAR function to convert numbers to a formatted character string and how to use the TO_NUMBER function to convert text strings to numeric values. A summary of the selected functions is shown in Table 9.8.

TABLE 9.8 Selected conversion functions

Function	Example(s)
Numeric to Character: **TO_CHAR Oracle** **CAST SQL Server** **CONVERT SQL Server** Returns a character string from a numeric value. Syntax: Oracle: TO_CHAR(numeric_value, fmt)	Lists all product prices, quantity on hand, per cent discount, and total inventory cost using formatted values. In Oracle, use the following: SELECT P_CODE, TO_CHAR(P_PRICE,'999.99') AS PRICE, TO_CHAR(P_QOH,'9,999.99') AS QUANTITY, TO_CHAR(P_DISCOUNT,'0.99') AS DISC, TO_CHAR(P_PRICE*P_QOH,'99,999.99') AS TOTAL_COST FROM PRODUCT;

Function	Example(s)
SQL Server: CAST (numeric AS varchar (length)) CONVERT(varchar(length), numeric)	In SQL Server, use the following: SELECT P_CODE, CAST(P_PRICE AS VARCHAR(8)) AS PRICE, CONVERT(VARCHAR(4),P_QOH) AS QUANTITY, CAST(P_DISCOUNT AS VARCHAR(4)) AS DISC, CAST(P_PRICE*P_QOH AS VARCHAR(10)) AS TOTAL_COST FROM PRODUCT; Not supported in Microsoft Access.
Date to Character: **TO_CHAR Oracle** **CAST SQL Server** **CONVERT SQL Server** Returns a character string or a formatted character string from a date value Syntax: Oracle: TO_CHAR(date_value, fmt) SQL Server: CAST (date AS varchar(length)) CONVERT(varchar(length), date)	Lists all employee dates of birth, using different date formats. In Oracle, use the following: SELECT EMP_LNAME, EMP_DOB, TO_CHAR(EMP_DOB, DAY, MONTH DD, YYYY) AS DATEOFBIRTH FROM EMPLOYEE; SELECT EMP_LNAME, EMP_DOB, TO_CHAR(EMP_DOB, YYYY/MM/DD) AS DATEOFBIRTH FROM EMPLOYEE; In SQL Server, use the following: SELECT EMP_LNAME, EMP_DOB, CONVERT(varchar(11), EMP_DOB) AS DATE OF BIRTH FROM EMPLOYEE; SELECT EMP_LNAME, EMP_DOB, CAST(EMP_DOB as varchar(11)) AS DATE OF BIRTH FROM EMPLOYEE; Not supported in Microsoft Access.
String to Number: **TO_NUMBER** Returns a formatted number from a character string, using a given format Syntax: Oracle: TO_NUMBER(char_value, fmt) fmt = format used; can be: 9 = displays a digit 0 = displays a leading zero , = displays the comma . = displays the decimal point $ = displays the dollar sign B = leading blank S = leading sign MI = trailing minus sign	Converts text strings to numeric values when importing data to a table from another source in text format; for example, the query shown below uses the TO_NUMBER function to convert text formatted to Oracle default numeric values using the format masks given. In Oracle, use the following: SELECT TO_NUMBER('-123.99', 'S999.99'), TO_NUMBER('99.78-','B999.99MI') FROM DUAL; In SQL Server, use the following: SELECT CAST('-123.99' AS NUMERIC(8,2)), CAST('-99.78' AS NUMERIC(8,2)) The SQL Server CAST function does not support the trailing sign on the character string. Not supported in Microsoft Access.
CASE SQL Server **DECODE Oracle** Compares an attribute or expression with a series of values and returns an associated value or a default value if no match is found	The following example returns the sales tax rate for specified countries: ■ Compares V_COUNTRY to 'SA'; if the values match, it returns .08. ■ Compares V_COUNTRY to 'FR'; if the values match, it returns .05. ■ Compares V_COUNTRY to 'UK'; if the values match, it returns .085.

9

Function	Example(s)
Syntax: Oracle: DECODE(e, x, y, d) *e* = attribute or expression *x* = value with which to compare e *y* = value to return in e = x *d* = default value to return if e is not equal to x SQL Server: CASE When condition THEN value1 ELSE value2 END	If there is no match, it returns 0.00 (the default value). SELECT V_CODE, V_COUNTRY, DECODE(V_COUNTRY,'SA',.08,'FR',.05, 'UK',.085, 0.00) AS TAX FROM VENDOR; In SQL Server, use the following: SELECT V_CODE, V_COUNTRY, CASE WHEN V_COUNTRY = 'SA' THEN .08 WHEN V_COUNTRY = 'FR' THEN .05 WHEN V_COUNTRY = 'UK' THEN .085 ELSE 0.00 END AS TAX FROM VENDOR Not supported in Microsoft Access.

9.5 ORACLE SEQUENCES

If you use Microsoft Access, you might be familiar with the Autonumber data type. In Microsoft Access, you can use the Autonumber data type to define a column in your table that will be automatically populated with unique numeric values. In fact, if you create a table in Microsoft Access and forget to define a primary key, Microsoft Access offers to create a primary key column; if you accept, you will notice that Microsoft Access creats a column named *ID* with an Autonumber data type. After you define a column as an Autonumber type, every time you insert a row in the table, Microsoft Access automatically adds a value to that column, starting with 1 and increasing the value by 1 in every new row you add. Also, you cannot include that column in your INSERT statements – Microsoft Access will not let you edit that value at all.

Similarly, in Oracle, you can use a 'sequence' to assign values to a column on a table. But an Oracle sequence is very different from the Access Autonumber data type and deserves close scrutiny:

- Oracle sequences are an independent object in the database. (Sequences are not a data type.)
- Oracle sequences have a name and can be used anywhere a value is expected.
- Oracle sequences are not tied to a table or a column.
- Oracle sequences generate a numeric value that can be assigned to any column in any table.
- The table attribute to which you assign a value based on a sequence can be edited and modified.
- An Oracle sequence can be created and deleted any time.

The basic syntax to create a sequence in Oracle is:

CREATE SEQUENCE *name* [START WITH *n*] [INCREMENT BY *n*] [CACHE | NOCACHE]

where:

- *name* is the name of the sequence.
- *n* is an integer value that can be positive or negative.
- START WITH specifies the initial sequence value. (The default value is 1.)
- INCREMENT BY determines the value by which the sequence is incremented. (The default increment value is 1. The sequence increment can be positive or negative to enable you to create ascending or descending sequences.)

- The CACHE or NOCACHE clause indicates whether Oracle will pre-allocate sequence numbers in memory. (Oracle pre-allocates 20 values by default.)

For example, you could create a sequence to assign values to the customer code automatically each time a new customer is added and another sequence to assign values to the invoice number automatically each time a new invoice is added. The SQL code to accomplish those tasks is:

```
CREATE SEQUENCE CUS_CODE_SEQ START WITH 20010 NOCACHE;

CREATE SEQUENCE INV_NUMBER_SEQ START WITH 4010 NOCACHE;
```

To check all of the sequences you have created, use the following SQL command, illustrated in Figure 9.22:

```
SELECT * FROM USER_SEQUENCES;
```

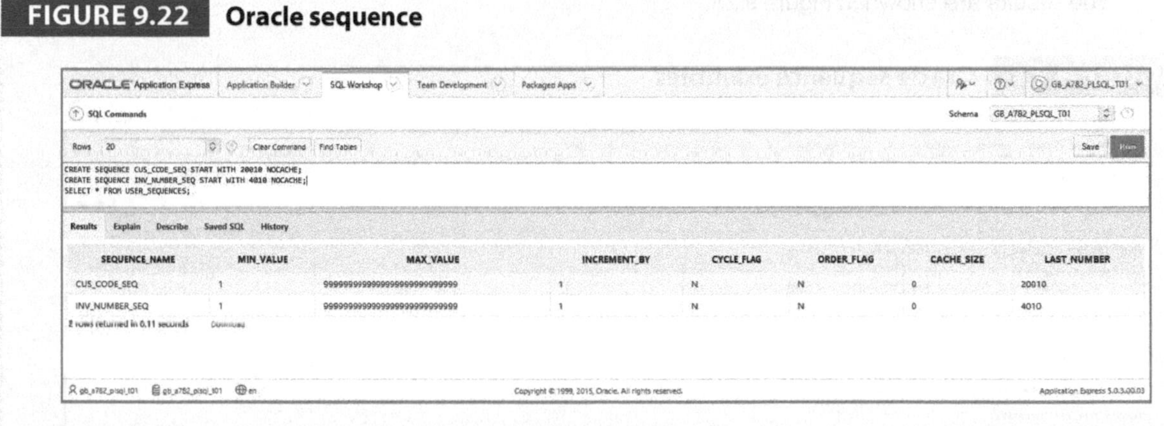

FIGURE 9.22 Oracle sequence

To use sequences during data entry, you must use two special pseudo columns: NEXTVAL and CURRVAL. NEXTVAL retrieves the next available value from a sequence. CURRVAL retrieves the current value of a sequence. For example, you can use the following code to enter a new customer:

```
INSERT INTO CUSTOMER

VALUES (CUS_CODE_SEQ.NEXTVAL, 'Connery', 'Sean', NULL, '0181', '898-2008', 0.00);
```

The preceding SQL statement adds a new customer to the CUSTOMER table and assigns the value 20010 to the CUS_CODE attribute. Let's examine some important sequence characteristics:

- CUS_CODE_SEQ.NEXTVAL retrieves the next available value from the sequence.
- Each time you use NEXTVAL, the sequence is incremented.
- Once a sequence value is used (through NEXTVAL), it cannot be used again. If, for some reason, your SQL statement rolls back, *the sequence value does not roll back*. If you issue another SQL statement (with another NEXTVAL), the next available sequence value is returned to the user – it will look as though the sequence skips a number.
- You can issue an INSERT statement without using the sequence.

CURRVAL retrieves the current value of a sequence, that is, the last sequence number used, which was generated with a NEXTVAL. You cannot use CURRVAL unless a NEXTVAL was issued previously in the same session. The main use for CURRVAL is to enter rows in dependent tables. For example, the INVOICE and LINE tables in the Ch09_SaleCo database are related in a one-to-many relationship through the INV_NUMBER attribute. You can use the INV_NUMBER_SEQ sequence to generate invoice numbers automatically. Then, using CURRVAL, you can get the latest INV_NUMBER used and assign it to the related INV_NUMBER foreign key attribute in the LINE table. For example:

```
INSERT INTO INVOICE VALUES (INV_NUMBER_SEQ.NEXTVAL, 20010, SYSDATE);

INSERT INTO LINE VALUES (INV_NUMBER_SEQ.CURRVAL, 1, '13-Q2/P2', 1, 14.99);

INSERT INTO LINE VALUES (INV_NUMBER_SEQ.CURRVAL, 2, '23109-HB', 1, 9.95);

COMMIT;
```

The results are shown in Figure 9.23.

FIGURE 9.23 **Oracle sequence examples**

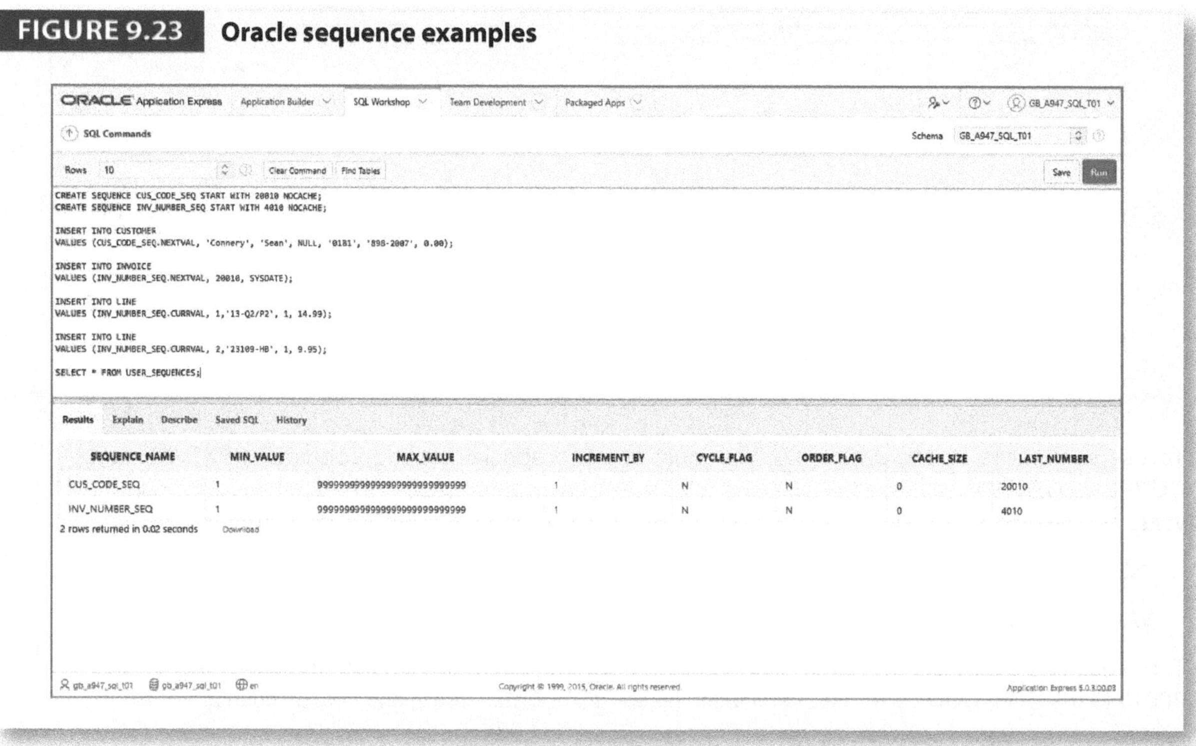

In the example shown in Figure 9.23, INV_NUMBER_SEQ.NEXTVAL retrieves the next available sequence number (4011) and assigns it to the INV_NUMBER column in the INVOICE table. Also note the use of the SYSDATE attribute to automatically insert the current date in the INV_DATE attribute.

Next, the following two INSERT statements add the products being sold to the LINE table. In this case, INV_NUMBER_SEQ.CURRVAL refers to the last-used INV_NUMBER_SEQ sequence number (4011). In this way, the relationship between INVOICE and LINE is established automatically. The COMMIT statement at the end of the command sequence makes the changes permanent. Of course, you can also issue a ROLLBACK, in which case the rows you inserted in INVOICE and LINE tables are rolled back (but the sequence number is not). Once you use a sequence number (with NEXTVAL), there is no way to reuse it! This 'no-reuse' characteristic is designed to guarantee that the sequence always generates unique values.

Remember these points when you think about sequences:

- The use of sequences is optional. You can enter the values manually.
- A sequence is not associated with a table. If you recall the examples in Figure 9.23, two distinct sequences were created (one for customer code values and one for invoice number values), but you could have created just one sequence and used it to generate unique values for both tables.

Finally, you can drop a sequence from a database with a DROP SEQUENCE command. For example, to drop the sequences created earlier, you type:

```
DROP SEQUENCE CUS_CODE_SEQ;

DROP SEQUENCE INV_NUMBER_SEQ;
```

Dropping a sequence does not delete the values you assigned to table attributes (CUS_CODE and INV_NUMBER); it deletes only the sequence object from the database. The *values* you assigned to the table columns (CUS_CODE and INV_NUMBER) remain in the database.

Because the CUSTOMER and INVOICE tables are used in subsequent examples, you should keep the original data set. Therefore, you can delete the customer, invoice and line rows you just added by using the following commands:

```
DELETE FROM INVOICE WHERE INV_NUMBER = 4011;

DELETE FROM CUSTOMER WHERE CUS_CODE = 20010;

COMMIT;
```

Those commands delete the recently added invoice and all of the invoice line rows associated with the invoice (the LINE table's INV_NUMBER foreign key was defined with the ON DELETE CASCADE option) and the recently added customer. The COMMIT statement saves all changes to permanent storage.

NOTE

At this point, you'll need to re-create the CUS_CODE_SEQ and INV_NUMBER_SEQ sequences, as they will be used again later in the chapter. Enter:

```
CREATE SEQUENCE CUS_CODE_SEQ START WITH 20010 NOCACHE;

CREATE SEQUENCE INV_NUMBER_SEQ START WITH 4011 NOCACHE;
```

9

9.6 UPDATABLE VIEWS

In Chapter 8, Beginning Structured Query Language, you learnt how to create a view and why and how views are used. As mentioned in Chapter 8, Microsoft Access does not support views. While views can be simulated using a SQL query, as is seen here, a view is far more versatile. You will now look at how to make views serve common data management tasks executed by database administrators.

One of the most common operations in production database environments is using batch update routines to update a master table attribute (field) with transaction data. As the name implies, a **batch update routine** pools multiple transactions into a single batch to update a master table field *in a single operation*. For example, a batch update routine is commonly used to update a product's quantity on hand based on summary sales transactions. Such routines are typically run as overnight batch jobs to update the quantity on hand of products in inventory. The sales transactions performed, for example, by travelling salespeople in remote areas were entered during periods when the system was offline.

To demonstrate a batch update routine, let's begin by defining the master product table (PRODMASTER) and the product monthly sales totals table (PRODSALES) shown in Figure 9.24. As you examine the tables, note the 1:1 relationship between the two tables.

FIGURE 9.24 The PRODMASTER and PRODSALES tables

Table name: PRODMASTER

PROD_ID	PROD_DESC	PROD_QOH
A123	SCREWS	60
BX34	NUTS	37
C583	BOLTS	50

Table name: PRODSALES

PROD_ID	PS_QTY
A123	7
BX34	3

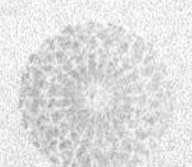

Online Content For Microsoft Access users, the PRODMASTER and PRODSALES tables are located in the 'Ch09_UV' database, which is located on the online platform for this book. For Oracle users, all SQL commands you see in this section are located in the student companion. After you locate the script files (uv01.sql through uv04.sql), you can copy and paste the command sequences into your SQL*Plus program.

Using the tables in Figure 9.24, let's update the PRODMASTER table by subtracting the PRODSALES table's product monthly sales quantity (PS_QTY) from the PRODMASTER table's PROD_QOH. To produce the required update, the update query is written like this:

```
UPDATE    PRODMASTER, PRODSALES
SET       PRODMASTER.PROD_QOH = PROD_QOH – PS_QTY
WHERE     PRODMASTER.PROD_ID = PRODSALES.PROD_ID;
```

Note that the update statement reflects the following sequence of events:

- Join the PRODMASTER and PRODSALES tables.
- Update the PROD_QOH attribute in each row of the PRODMASTER table with the matching PROD_ID in the PRODSALES table.

To be used in a batch update, the PRODSALES data must be stored in a base table rather than in a view. That query works in Microsoft Access, but Oracle returns the error message shown in Figure 9.25.

Oracle produced the error message because Oracle expects to find a single table name in the UPDATE statement. In fact, if you use Oracle, you cannot join tables in the UPDATE statement. To solve that problem, you have to create an *updatable* view. As its name suggests, an **updatable view** is a view used to update attributes in the base table(s) that is (are) used in the view. You must realise that *not all views are updatable*. Actually, several restrictions govern updatable views, and some of them are vendor-specific.

FIGURE 9.25 **The Oracle UPDATE error message**

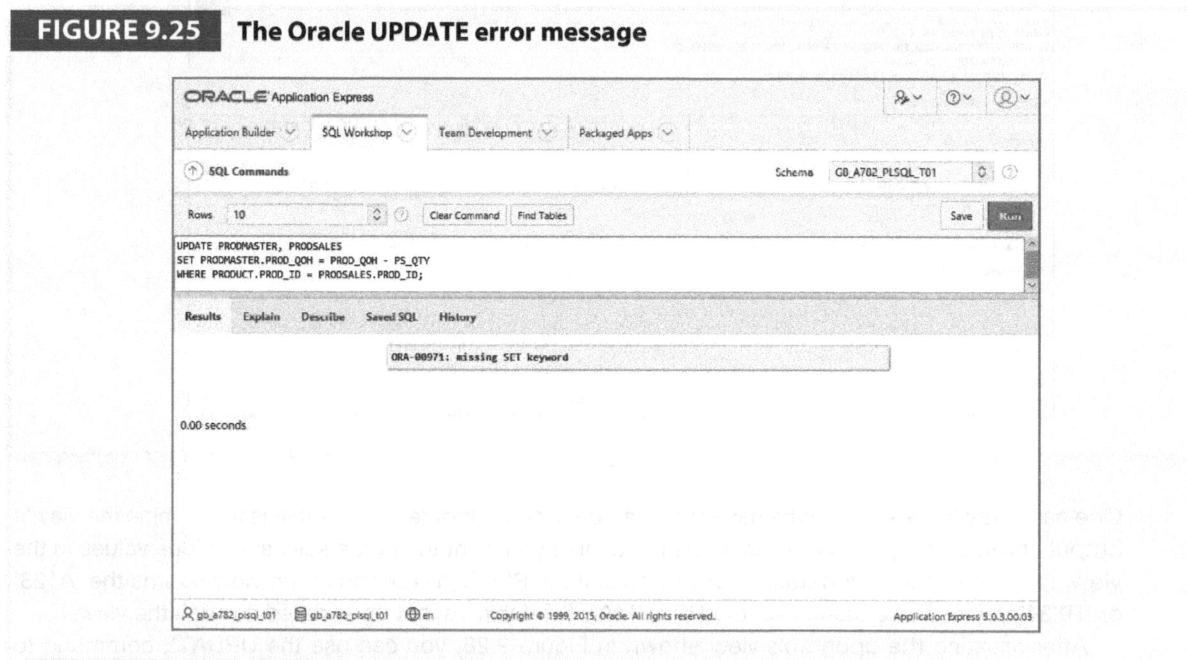

NOTE

Keep in mind that the examples in this section are generated in Oracle. To see which restrictions are placed on updatable views by the DBMS you are using, check the appropriate DBMS manual. MySQL version 8.0 supports both updatable and insertable views. For more information on the syntax, consult the MySQL 8.0 reference manual.

The most common updatable view restrictions are as follows:

- GROUP BY expressions or aggregate functions cannot be used in the updatable views.
- You cannot use set operators such as UNION, INTERSECT and MINUS.
- Most restrictions are based on the use of JOINs or group operators in views.

To meet the Oracle limitations, an updatable view named PSVUPD has been created, as shown in Figure 9.26.

FIGURE 9.26 Creating an updateable view in Oracle

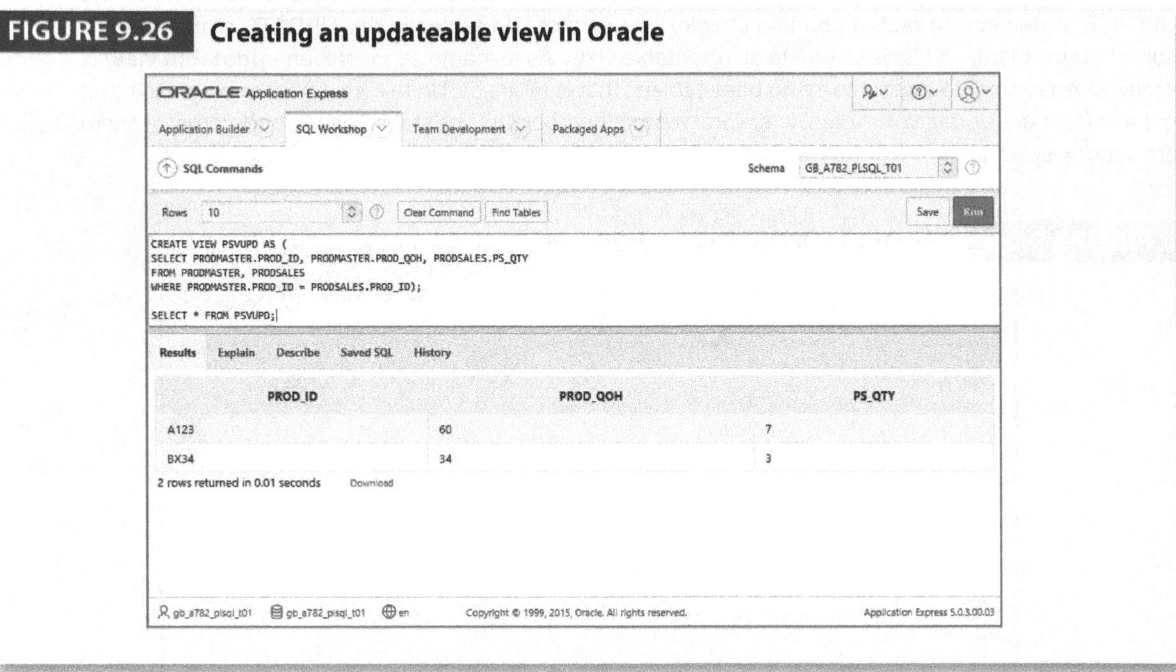

One easy way to determine whether a view can be used to update a base table is to examine the view's output. If the primary key columns of the base table you want to update still have unique values in the view, the base table is updatable. For example, if the PROD_ID column of the view returns the 'A123' or 'BX34' values more than once, the PRODMASTER table cannot be updated through the view.

After creating the updatable view shown in Figure 9.26, you can use the UPDATE command to update the view, thereby updating the PRODMASTER table. Figure 9.27 shows how the UPDATE command is used and shows the final contents of the PRODMASTER table are after the UPDATE is executed.

FIGURE 9.27 PRODMASTER table update, using an updatable view

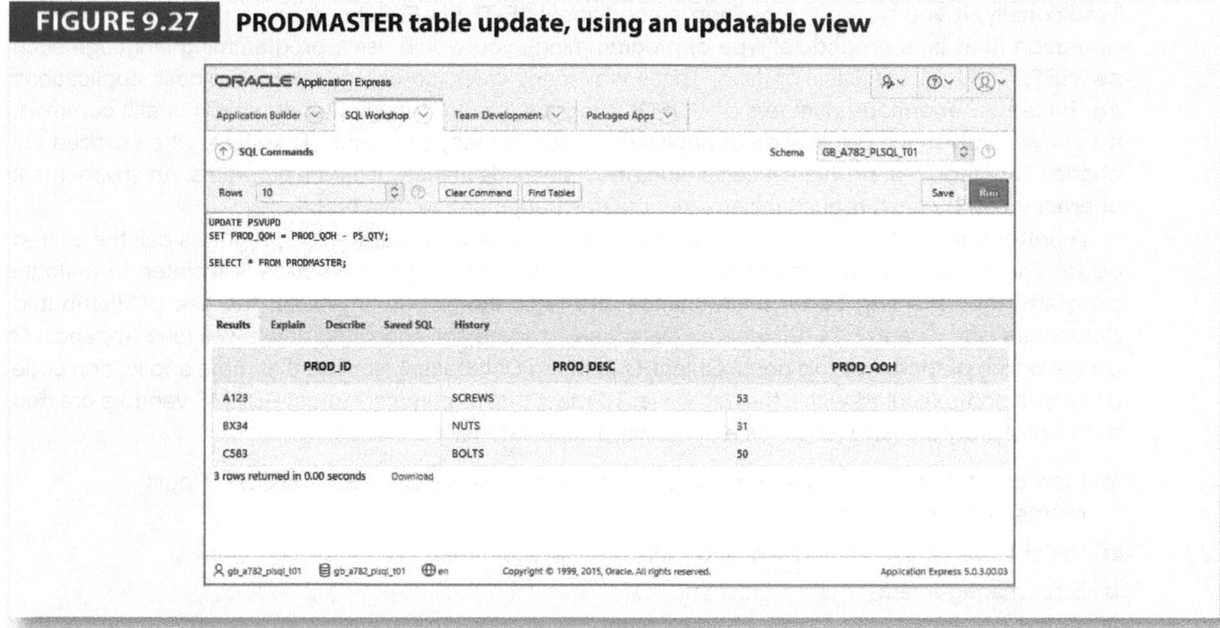

Although the batch update procedure just illustrated meets the goal of updating a master table with data from a transaction table, the preferred, real-world solution to the update problem is to use procedural SQL. You'll learn about procedural SQL in the next section.

9.7 PROCEDURAL SQL

Thus far, you have learnt to use SQL to read, write and delete data in the database. For example, you learnt to update values in a record, to add records and to delete records. Unfortunately, SQL does not support the *conditional* execution of procedures that are typically supported by a programming language using the general format:

IF <condition>

  THEN <perform procedure>

  ELSE <perform alternate procedure>

END IF

SQL also fails to support the looping operations in programming languages that permit the execution of repetitive actions typically encountered in a programming environment. The typical format is:

DO WHILE

  <perform procedure>

END DO

Traditionally, if you wanted to perform a conditional (IF-THEN-ELSE) or looping (DO-WHILE) type of operation (that is, a procedural type of programming), you would use a programming language such as .NET, C# C, Visual Basic or Java. That's why many older (so-called legacy) business applications are based on enormous numbers of COBOL program lines. Although that approach is still common, it usually involves the duplication of application code in many programs. Therefore, when procedural changes are required, program modifications must be made in many different programs. An environment characterised by such redundancies often creates data management problems.

A better approach is to isolate critical code and then have all application programs call the shared code. The advantage of that modular approach is that the application code is isolated in a single program, thus yielding better maintenance and logic control. In any case, the rise of distributed databases (see Chapter 14, Distributed Databases) and object-orientated databases (see Appendix G on the online platform for this book, Object-Orientated Databases) required that more application code be stored and executed within the database. To meet that requirement, most RDBMS vendors created numerous programming language extensions. Those extensions include:

- Flow control procedural programming structures (IF-THEN-ELSE, DO-WHILE) for logic representation.
- Variable declaration and designation within the procedures.
- Error management.

To remedy the lack of procedural functionality in SQL and to provide some standardisation within the many vendor offerings, the SQL-99 standard defined the use of persistent stored modules. A **persistent stored module** (**PSM**) is a block of code (containing standard SQL statements and procedural extensions) that is stored and executed at the DBMS server. The PSM represents business logic that can be encapsulated, stored and shared among multiple database users. A PSM lets an administrator assign specific access rights to a stored module to ensure that only authorised users can use it. Support for persistent stored modules is left to each vendor to implement. In fact, for many years, some RDBMSs (such as Oracle, SQL Server and DB2) supported stored procedure modules within the database before the official standard was promulgated.

9

Oracle implements PSMs through its procedural SQL language. **Procedural SQL** (**PL/SQL**) is a language that makes it possible to use and store procedural code and SQL statements within the database. Procedural SQL makes it possible to merge SQL and traditional programming constructs such as variables, conditional processing (IF-THEN-ELSE), basic loops (FOR and WHILE loops) and error trapping. The procedural code is executed as a unit by the DBMS when it is invoked (directly or indirectly) by the end user. End users can use PL/SQL to create:

- Anonymous PL/SQL blocks.
- Triggers (covered in Section 9.7.1).
- Stored procedures (covered in Section 9.7.2 and Section 9.7.3).
- PL/SQL functions (covered in Section 9.7.4).

Do not confuse PL/SQL functions with SQL's built-in aggregate functions such as MIN and MAX. SQL built-in functions can be used only within SQL statements, while PL/SQL functions are mainly invoked within PL/SQL programs such as triggers and stored procedures. Functions can also be called within SQL statements, provided they conform to very specific rules that are dependent on your DBMS environment.

> **NOTE**
>
> PL/SQL, triggers and stored procedures are illustrated within the context of an Oracle DBMS. All examples in the following sections assume the use of Oracle RDBMS.

Using Oracle SQL*Plus, you can write a PL/SQL code block by enclosing the commands inside BEGIN and END clauses. For example, the following PL/SQL block inserts a new row in the VENDOR table. (See Figure 9.28.)

FIGURE 9.28 Anonymous PL/SQL block examples

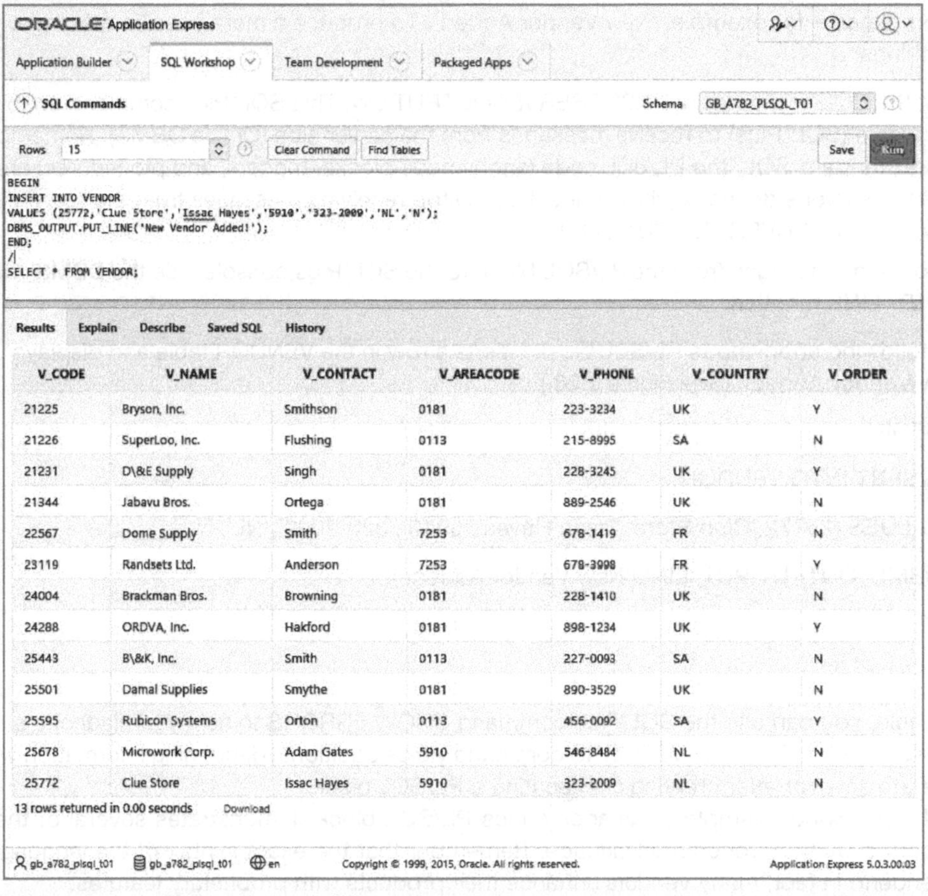

V_CODE	V_NAME	V_CONTACT	V_AREACODE	V_PHONE	V_COUNTRY	V_ORDER
21225	Bryson, Inc.	Smithson	0181	223-3234	UK	Y
21226	SuperLoo, Inc.	Flushing	0113	215-8995	SA	N
21231	D\&E Supply	Singh	0181	228-3245	UK	Y
21344	Jabavu Bros.	Ortega	0181	889-2546	UK	N
22567	Dome Supply	Smith	7253	678-1419	FR	N
23119	Randsets Ltd.	Anderson	7253	678-3998	FR	Y
24004	Brackman Bros.	Browning	0181	228-1410	UK	N
24288	ORDVA, Inc.	Hakford	0181	898-1234	UK	Y
25443	B\&K, Inc.	Smith	0113	227-0093	SA	N
25501	Damal Supplies	Smythe	0181	890-3529	UK	N
25595	Rubicon Systems	Orton	0113	456-0092	SA	Y
25678	Microwork Corp.	Adam Gates	5910	546-8484	NL	N
25772	Clue Store	Issac Hayes	5910	323-2009	NL	N

```
BEGIN
INSERT INTO VENDOR
VALUES (25678,'Microwork Corp.', 'Adam Gates','5910','546-8484','NL','N');
END;
/
```

The PL/SQL block shown in Figure 9.28 is known as an **anonymous PL/SQL block** because it has not been given a specific name. (Incidentally, note that the block's last line uses a forward slash ('/') to indicate the end of the command-line entry.) That type of PL/SQL block executes as soon as you press the Enter key after typing the forward slash. Following the PL/SQL block's execution, you see the message 'PL/SQL procedure successfully completed'.

But suppose you want a more specific message displayed on the SQL*Plus screen after a procedure is completed – for example, 'New Vendor Added'. To produce a more specific message, you must do two things:

- At the SQL > prompt, type SET SERVEROUTPUT ON. This SQL*Plus command enables the client console (SQL*Plus) to receive messages from the server side (Oracle DBMS). Remember, just like standard SQL, the PL/SQL code (anonymous blocks, triggers, and procedures) are executed at the server side, not at the client side. (To stop receiving messages from the server, you would enter SET SERVEROUT PUT OFF.)
- To send messages from the PL/SQL block to the SQL*Plus console, use the DBMS_OUTPUT. PUT_LINE function.

The following anonymous PL/SQL block inserts a row in the VENDOR table and displays the message 'New Vendor Added!' (See Figure 9.28.)

```
BEGIN
INSERT INTO VENDOR
VALUES (25772,'Clue Store','Issac Hayes','5910','323-2009','NL','N');
DBMS_OUTPUT.PUT_LINE('New Vendor Added!');
END;
/
```

In Oracle, you can use the SQL*Plus command SHOW ERRORS to help you diagnose errors found in PL/SQL blocks. The SHOW ERRORS command yields additional debugging information whenever you generate an error after creating or executing a PL/SQL block.

The following example of an anonymous PL/SQL block demonstrates several of the constructs supported by the procedural language. Remember that the exact syntax of the language is vendor-dependent; in fact, many vendors enhance their products with proprietary features.

```
DECLARE
    W_P1 NUMBER(3) := 0;
    W_P2 NUMBER(3) := 10;
    W_NUM NUMBER(2) := 0;
```

```
BEGIN
    WHILE W_P2 < 300 LOOP
    SELECT COUNT(P_CODE) INTO W_NUM FROM PRODUCT
    WHERE P_PRICE BETWEEN W_P1 AND W_P2;
    DBMS_OUTPUT.PUT_LINE('There are ' || W_NUM || ' Products with price between ' || W_P1 ||
    ' and ' || W_P2);
    W_P1 := W_P2 + 1;
    W_P2 := W_P2 + 50;
END LOOP;
END;
/
```

The block's code and execution are shown in Figure 9.29.

FIGURE 9.29 Anonymous PL/SQL block with variables and loops

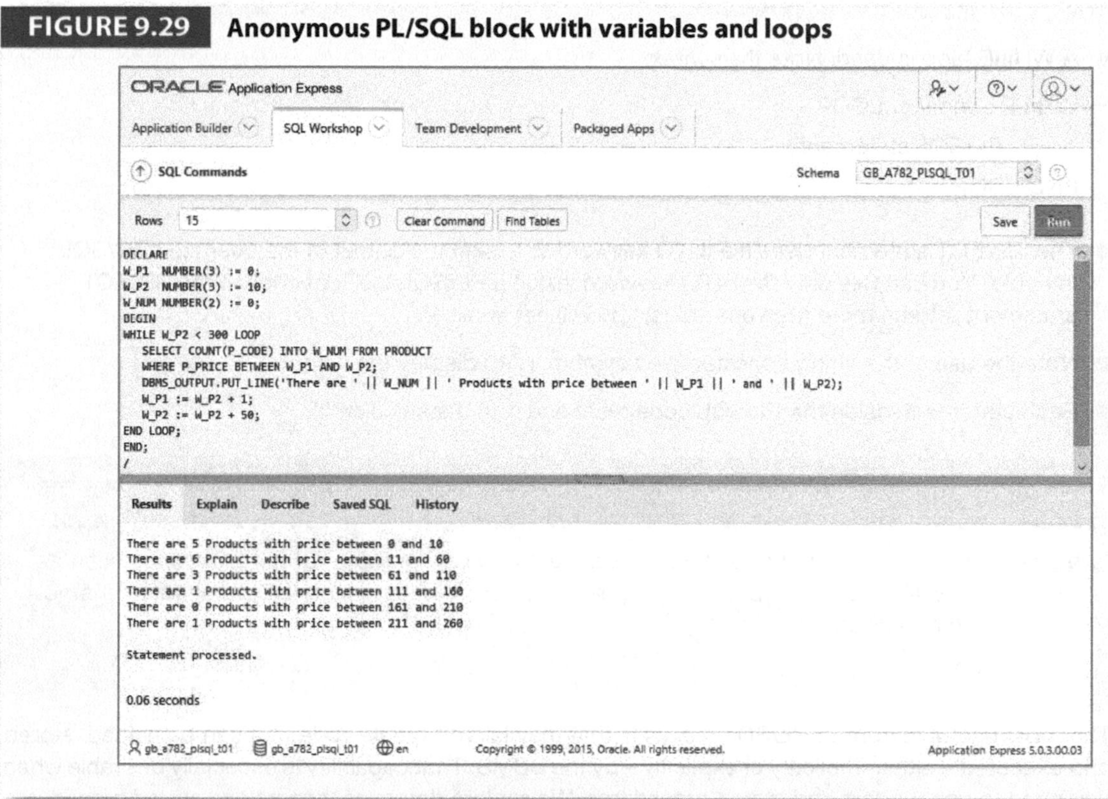

The PL/SQL block shown in Figure 9.29 has the following characteristics:

- The PL/SQL block starts with the DECLARE section in which you declare the variable names; the data types; and, if desired, an initial value. Supported data types are shown in Table 9.9.

TABLE 9.9 PL/SQL basic data types

Data Type	Description
CHAR	Character values of a fixed length; for example: W_PCODE CHAR(5)
VARCHAR2	Variable length character values; for example: W_FNAME VARCHAR2(15)
NUMBER	Numeric values; for example: W_PRICE NUMBER(6,2)
DATE	Date values; for example: W_EMP_DOB DATE
%TYPE	Inherits the data type from a variable that you declared previously or from an attribute of a database table; for example: W_PRICE PRODUCT.P_PRICE%TYPE Assigns W_PRICE the same data type as the P_PRICE column in the PRODUCT table

- A WHILE loop is used. Note the syntax:

  WHILE *condition* LOOP

  PL/SQL statements;

  END LOOP

9

- The SELECT statement uses the INTO keyword to assign the output of the query to a PL/SQL variable. You can use only the INTO keyword inside a PL/SQL block of code. If the SELECT statement returns more than one value, you will get an error.
- Note the use of the string concatenation symbol '| |' to display the output.
- Each statement inside the PL/SQL code must end with a semicolon ';'.

NOTE

PL/SQL blocks can contain only standard SQL data manipulation language (DML) commands such as SELECT, INSERT, UPDATE and DELETE. The use of data definition language (DDL) commands is not directly supported in a PL/SQL block.

The most useful feature of PL/SQL blocks is that they let you create code that can be named, stored and executed – either implicitly or explicitly – by the DBMS. That capability is especially desirable when you need to use triggers and stored procedures. We explore database triggers and stored procedures in the next sections.

9.7.1 Triggers

Automating business procedures and automatically maintaining data integrity and consistency are critical in a modern business environment. One of the most critical business procedures is proper inventory management. For example, you want to make sure that current product sales can be supported with sufficient product availability. Microsoft Access does not support triggers. While the functionality of triggers can be supported at the application level, this does not create the same level of data integrity provided by triggers. Using triggers to embed business logic into the database ensures that the correct updates are always propagated. When triggers are implemented at the application layer, it is possible for edits to be made directly to the database without the appropriate updates being propagated. Therefore, it is necessary to ensure that a product order be written to a vendor when that product's inventory drops below its minimum allowable quantity on hand. Better yet, how about ensuring that the task is completed automatically?

To accomplish automatic product ordering, you first need to make sure that the product's quantity on hand reflects an up-to-date and consistent value. After the appropriate product availability requirements have been set, two key issues must be addressed:

- Business logic requires an update of the product quantity on hand each time there is a sale of that product.
- If the product's quantity on hand falls below its minimum allowable inventory (quantity-on-hand) level, the product must be reordered.

To accomplish those two tasks, you could write multiple SQL statements: one to update the product quantity on hand and another to update the product reorder flag. Next, you would have to run each statement in the correct order each time there was a new sale. Such a multistage process would be inefficient because a series of SQL statements must be written and executed each time a product is sold. Even worse, that SQL environment requires that somebody must remember to perform the SQL tasks.

A **trigger** is procedural SQL code that is *automatically* invoked by the RDBMS upon the occurrence of a given data manipulation event. It is useful to remember that:

- A trigger is invoked before or after a data row is inserted, updated or deleted.
- A trigger is associated with a database table.
- Each database table may have one or more triggers.
- A trigger is executed as part of the transaction that triggered it.

9

Triggers tend to follow an **Event-Condition-Action (ECA) model**. An event can be any operation that changes the state of the database, for example an update operation. The condition is what determines whether the trigger (or rule) is to be executed after the event occurred. The action is what is undertaken by the trigger, such as a SQL command being executed or an external program being called.

Triggers are critical to proper database operation and management. For example:

- Triggers can enforce constraints that cannot be enforced at the DBMS design and implementation levels.
- Triggers add functionality by automating critical actions and providing appropriate warnings and suggestions for remedial action. In fact, one of the most common uses for triggers is to facilitate the enforcement of referential integrity.
- Triggers can be used to update table values, insert records in tables and call other stored procedures.

Triggers play a critical role in making the database truly useful; they also add processing power to the RDBMS and to the database system as a whole. Oracle recommends triggers for:

- Auditing purposes (creating audit logs).
- Automatic generation of derived column values.
- Enforcement of business or security constraints.
- Creation of replica tables for backup purposes.

To see how a trigger is created and used, let's examine a simple inventory management problem. For example, if a product's quantity on hand is updated when the product is sold, the system should automatically check whether the quantity on hand falls below its minimum allowable quantity. To demonstrate that process, let's use the PRODUCT table in Figure 9.30. Note the use of the minimum order quantity (P_MIN_ORDER) and the product reorder flag (P_REORDER) columns. The P_MIN_ORDER indicates the minimum quantity for restocking a order. The P_REORDER column is a numeric field that indicates whether the product needs to be reordered (1 = Yes, 0 = No). The initial P_REORDER values are set to 0 (No) to serve as the basis for the initial trigger development.

FIGURE 9.30 The PRODUCT Table

SELECT * FROM PRODUCT;

P_CODE	P_DESCRIPT	P_INDATE	P_QOH	P_MIN	P_PRICE	P_DISCOUNT	V_CODE	P_MIN_ORDER	P_REORDER
11QER/31	Power painter, 15 psi., 3-nozzle	03-Nov-2018	8	5	109.99	0	25595	25	0
13-Q2/P2	7.25-cm. pwr. saw blade	13-Dec-2018	32	15	14.99	.05	21344	50	0
14-Q1/L3	9.00-cm. pwr. saw blade	13-Nov-2018	18	12	17.49	0	21344	50	0
1546-QQ2	Hrd. cloth, 1/4-cm., 2x50	15-Jan-2019	15	8	39.95	0	23119	35	0
1558-QW1	Hrd. cloth, 1/2-cm., 3x50	15-Jan-2019	23	5	43.99	0	23119	25	0
2232/QTY	B\&D jigsaw, 12-cm. blade	30-Dec-2018	8	5	109.92	.05	24288	15	0
2232/QWE	B\&D jigsaw, 8-cm. blade	24-Dec-2018	6	5	99.87	.05	24288	15	0
2238/QPD	B\&D cordless drill, 1/2-cm.	20-Jan-2019	12	5	38.95	.05	25595	12	0
23109-HB	Claw hammer	20-Jan-2019	23	10	9.95	.1	21225	25	0
23114-AA	Sledge hammer, 6kg.	02-Jan-2019	8	5	14.4	.05	-	12	0
54778-2T	Rat-tail file, 1/8-cm. fine	15-Dec-2018	43	20	4.99	0	21344	25	0
89-WRE-Q	Hicut chain saw, 16 cm.	07-Feb-2019	11	5	256.99	.05	24288	10	0
PVC23DRT	PVC pipe, 3.5-cm., 4m	20-Feb-2019	188	75	5.87	0	-	50	0
SM-18277	1.25-cm. metal screw, 25	01-Mar-2019	172	75	6.99	0	21225	50	0
SW-23116	2.5-cm. wd. screw, 50	24-Feb-2019	237	100	8.45	0	21231	100	0

More than 15 rows available. Increase rows selector to view more rows.

15 rows returned in 0.00 seconds

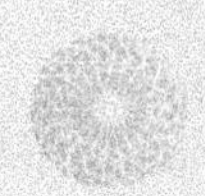

Online Content Oracle users can run the PRODLIST.SQL script file to format the output of the PRODUCT table shown in Figure 9.30. The script file is located on the online platform for this book. (The PRODUCT table is also shown in the 'Ch09_SaleCo' database that is stored in Microsoft Access format.)

Given the PRODUCT table listing shown in Figure 9.30, let's create a trigger to evaluate the product's quantity on hand, P_QOH. If the quantity on hand is below the minimum quantity shown in P_MIN, the trigger sets the P_REORDER column to 1. (Remember that the number 1 in the P_REORDER column represents 'Yes'.) The syntax to create a trigger in Oracle is:

CREATE OR REPLACE TRIGGER *trigger_name*

[BEFORE / AFTER] [DELETE / INSERT / UPDATE OF *column_name*] ON *table_name*

[FOR EACH ROW]

[DECLARE]

  [*variable_namedata type*[:=*initial_value*]]

BEGIN

  PL/SQL instructions;

  ....

END;

As you can see, a trigger definition contains the following parts:

- The triggering timing: BEFORE or AFTER. This timing indicates when the trigger's PL/SQL code executes – in this case, before or after the triggering statement is complete.
- The triggering event: The statement that causes the trigger to execute (INSERT, UPDATE, or DELETE).
- The triggering level: There are two types of triggers, statement-level triggers and row-level triggers.
    - A **statement-level trigger** is assumed if you omit the FOR EACH ROW keywords. This type of trigger is executed once, before or after the triggering statement is completed. This is the default case.
    - A **row-level trigger** requires use of the FOR EACH ROW keywords. This type of trigger is executed once for each row affected by the triggering statement. (In other words, if you update ten rows, the trigger executes ten times.)
- The triggering action: The PL/SQL code enclosed between the BEGIN and END keywords. Each statement inside the PL/SQL code must end with a semicolon ';'.

In the PRODUCT table's case, you will create a statement-level trigger that is implicitly executed AFTER an UPDATE of the P_QOH and P_MIN attributes for an existing row or AFTER an INSERT of a new row in the PRODUCT table. The trigger action executes an UPDATE statement that compares the P_QOH with the P_MIN column. If the value of P_QOH is equal to or less than P_MIN, the trigger updates the P_REORDER to 1.

The trigger code is shown in Figure 9.31.

FIGURE 9.31 The TRG_PRODUCT_REORDER trigger

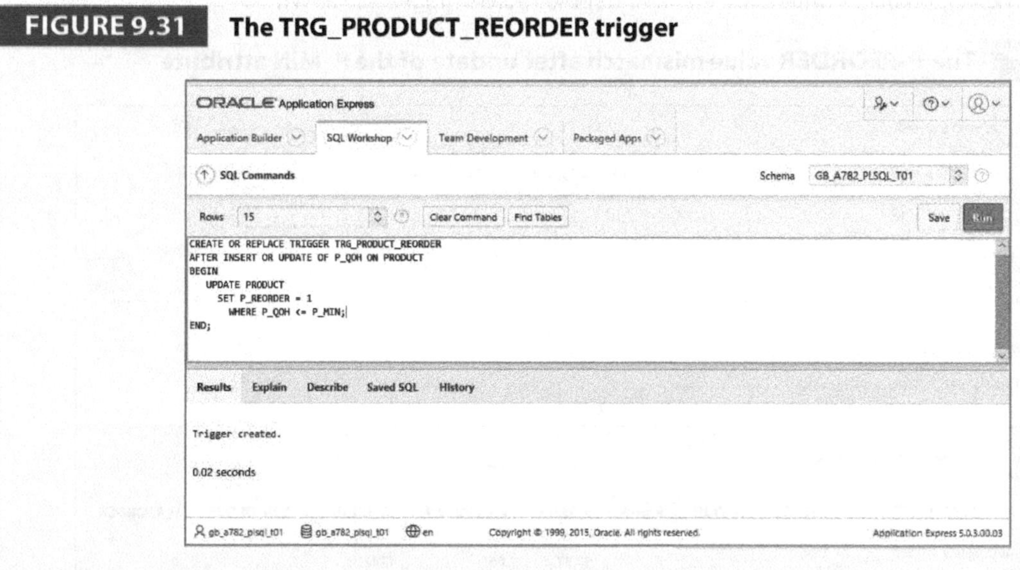

To test this trigger version, let's change the minimum quantity for product '23114-AA' to 8. After that update, the trigger makes sure that the reorder flag is properly set for all of the products in the PRODUCT table. (See Figure 9.32.)

FIGURE 9.32 Successful trigger execution after the P_MIN value is updated

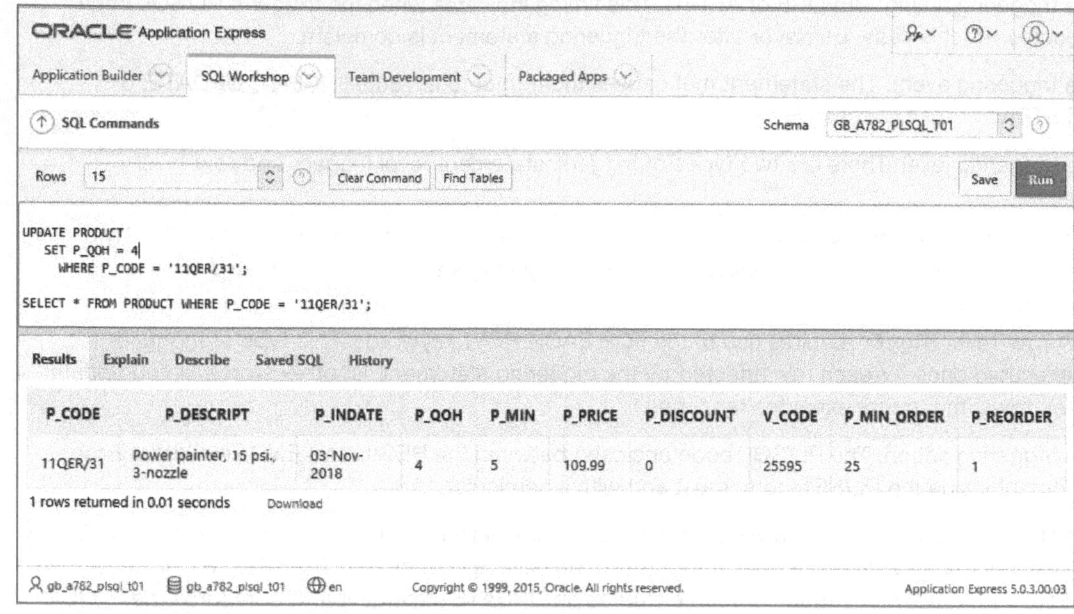

This trigger seems to work well, but what happens if you reduce the minimum quantity of product 2232/QWE? Figure 9.33 shows that when you update the minimum quantity on hand of the product 2232/QWE, it falls below the new minimum, but the reorder flag is still 0. Why?

FIGURE 9.33 The P-REORDER value mismatch after update of the P_MIN attribute

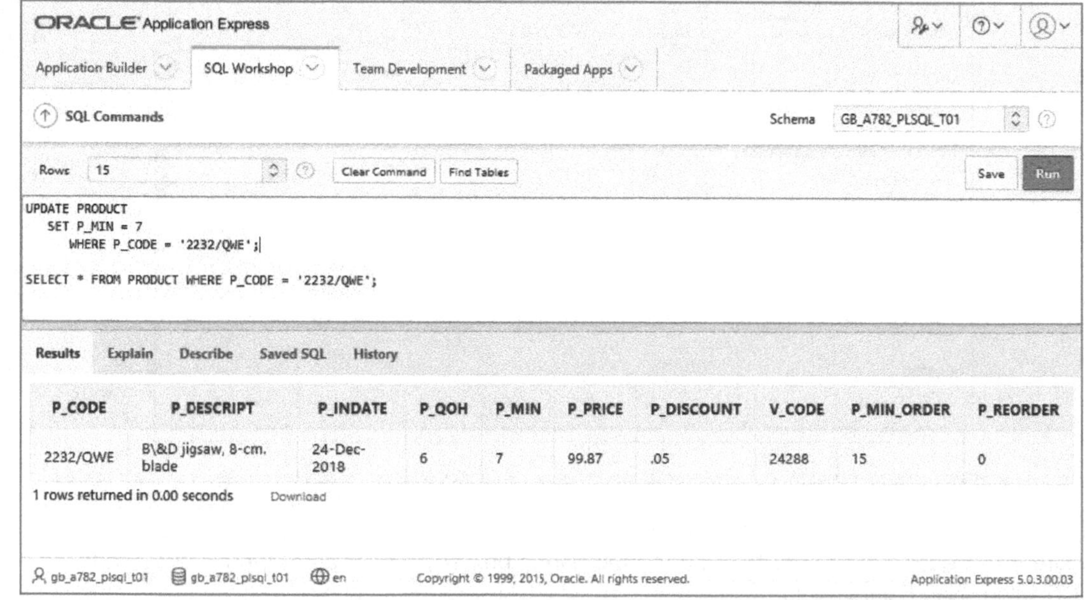

The answer is that the trigger does not consider all possible cases. Let's examine the TRG_PRODUCT_REORDER trigger code (Figure 9.31) in more detail:

- The trigger fires after the triggering statement is completed. Therefore, the DBMS always executes two statements (INSERT plus UPDATE or UPDATE plus UPDATE). That is, after you do an update of P_MIN or P_QOH or you insert a new row in the PRODUCT table, the trigger executes another UPDATE statement automatically.
- The triggering action performs an UPDATE that updates *all* of the rows in the PRODUCT table, *even if the triggering statement updates just one row!* This can affect the performance of the database. Imagine what happens if you have a PRODUCT table with 519,128 rows and you insert just one product. The trigger will update all 519,129 rows (519,128 original rows plus the one you inserted), including the rows that do not need an update!
- The trigger sets the P_REORDER value only to 1; it does not reset the value to 0, even if such an action is clearly required when the inventory level is back to a value greater than the minimum value.

Now let's modify the trigger to handle all update scenarios, as shown in Figure 9.34.

FIGURE 9.34 The second version of the TRG_PRODUCT_REORDER trigger

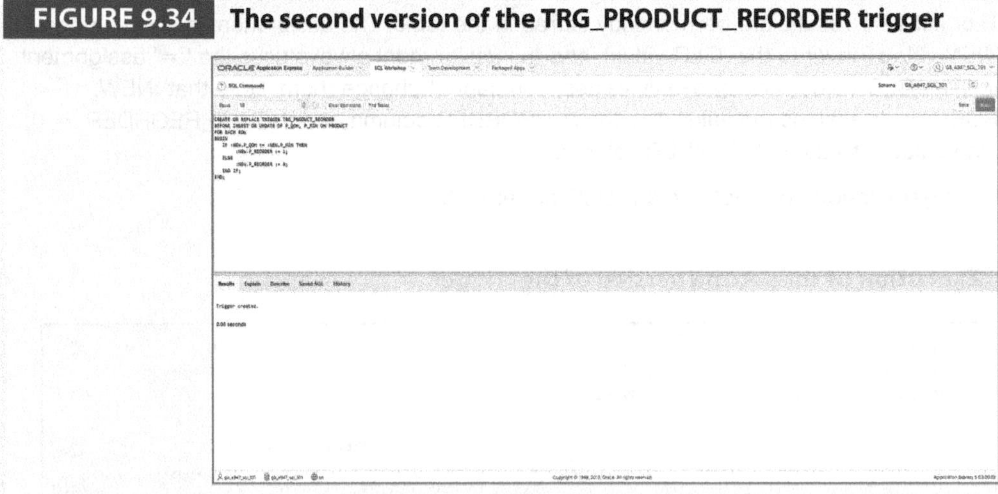

The trigger in Figure 9.34 sports several new features:

- The trigger is executed *before* the actual triggering statement is completed. In Figure 9.34, the triggering timing is defined in line 2, BEFORE INSERT OR UPDATE. This clearly indicates that the triggering statement is executed before the INSERT or UPDATE completes, unlike the previous trigger examples.
- The trigger is a row-level trigger instead of a statement-level trigger. The FOR EACH ROW keywords make the trigger a row-level trigger. Therefore, this trigger executes once for each row affected by the triggering statement.
- The trigger action uses the ':NEW' attribute reference to change the value of the P_REORDER attribute.

The use of the :NEW attribute references deserves a more detailed explanation. To understand its use, you must first consider a basic computing tenet: *all changes are done first in primary memory, then to permanent memory*. In other words, the computer cannot change anything directly in permanent storage (disk). It must first read the data from permanent storage to primary memory; then it makes the change in primary memory; finally, it writes the changed data back to permanent memory (disk).

The DBMS does exactly the same thing, in addition to something more. To ensure data integrity, the DBMS makes two copies of every row being changed by a DML (INSERT, UPDATE or DELETE) statement. (You will learn more about this in Chapter 12, Managing Transactions and Concurrency). The first copy contains the original ('old') values of the attributes before the changes. The second copy contains the changed ('new') values of the attributes that are permanently saved to the database (after any changes made by an INSERT, UPDATE or DELETE). You can use ':OLD' to refer to the original values; you can use :NEW to refer to the changed values (the values that are stored in the table). You can use :NEW and :OLD attribute references only within the PL/SQL code of a database trigger action. For example:

- IF :NEW.P_QOH < = :NEW.P_MIN compares the quantity on hand with the minimum quantity of a product. Remember that this is a row-level trigger. Therefore, this comparison is done for each row that is updated by the triggering statement.
- Although the trigger is a BEFORE trigger, this does not mean that the triggering statement hasn't executed yet. On the contrary, the triggering statement has already taken place; otherwise, the trigger would not have fired and the :NEW values would not exist. Remember, BEFORE means *before* the changes are permanently saved to disk, but *after* the changes are made in memory.
- The trigger uses the :NEW reference to assign a value to the P_REORDER column before the UPDATE or INSERT results are permanently stored in the table. The assignment is always done to the :NEW value (never to the :OLD value), and the assignment always uses the ':=' assignment operator. The :OLD values are *read-only* values; you cannot change them. Note that :NEW. P_REORDER := 1; assigns the value 1 to the P_REORDER column and :NEW.P_REORDER := 0; assigns the value 0 to the P_REORDER column.
- This new trigger version does not use any DML statement!

FIGURE 9.35 Execution of the second version of the trigger

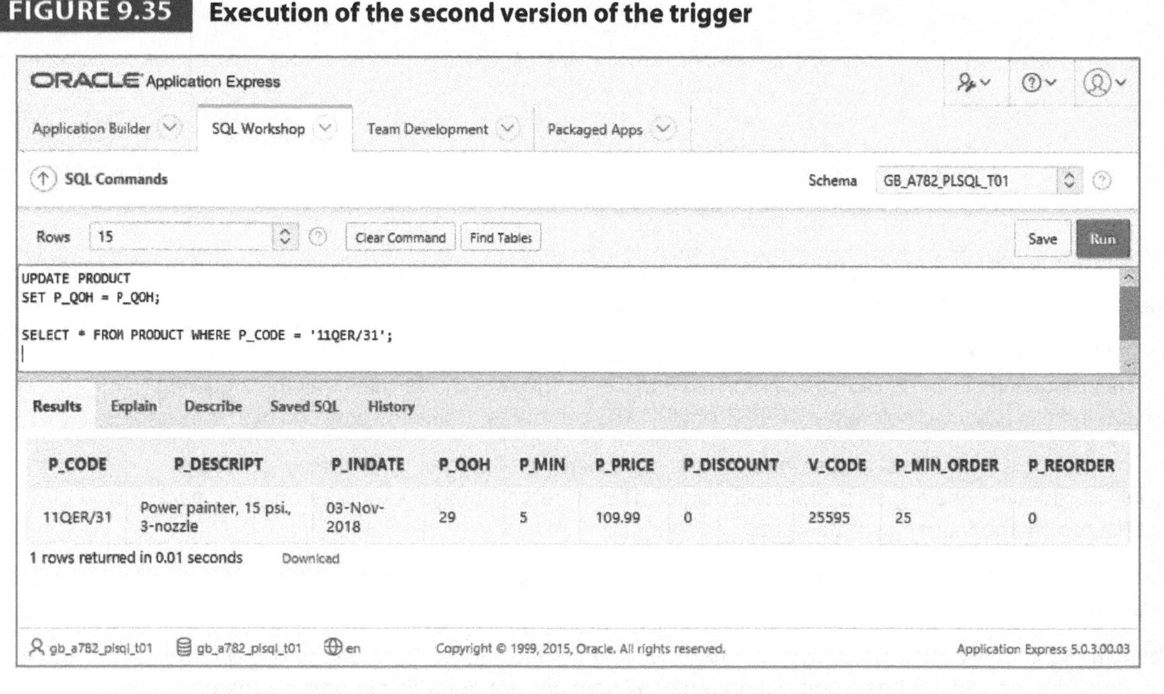

Before testing the new trigger, note that product '11QER/31' currently has a quantity on hand that is above the minimum quantity, yet the reorder flag is set to 1. Given that condition, the reorder flag must be 0. After you create the new trigger, you can execute an UPDATE statement to fire it, as shown in Figure 9.35.

As you examine Figure 9.35, note the following important features:

- The trigger is automatically invoked for each affected row – in this case, all rows of the PRODUCT table. If your triggering statement would have affected only three rows, not all PRODUCT rows would have the correct P_REORDER value set. That's the reason the triggering statement was set up as shown in Figure 9.35.
- The trigger will run only if you insert a new product row or update P_QOH or P_MIN. If you update any other attribute, the trigger won't run.

The use of triggers facilitates the automation of multiple data management tasks. Although triggers are independent objects, they are associated with database tables. When you delete a table, all trigger objects are deleted with it. However, if you need to delete a trigger without deleting the table, you could use the following command:

DROP TRIGGER *trigger_name*

9.7.2 Stored Procedures

A **stored procedure** is a named collection of procedural and SQL statements. Just like database triggers, stored procedures are stored in the database. Microsoft Access does not support stored procedures. As with triggers, this would need to be implemented at the application layer and as such would not have the same integrity robustness as stored procedures. One of the major advantages of stored procedures is that they can be used to encapsulate and represent business transactions. For example, you can create a stored procedure to represent a product sale, a credit update or the addition of a new customer. By doing that, you can encapsulate SQL statements within a single stored procedure and execute them as a single transaction. There are two clear advantages to the use of stored procedures:

- Stored procedures substantially reduce network traffic and increase performance. Because the stored procedure is stored at the server, there is no transmission of individual SQL statements over the network. The use of stored procedures improves system performance because all transactions are executed locally on the RDBMS, and each SQL statement does not have to travel over the network.
- Stored procedures help reduce code duplication by means of code isolation and code sharing (creating unique PL/SQL modules that are called by application programs), thereby minimising the chance of errors and the cost of application development and maintenance. To create a stored procedure, use the following syntax:

  CREATE OR REPLACE PROCEDURE *procedure_name* [(*argument* [IN/OUT] *data-type*, ...)] [IS/AS]

  [*variable_name data type*[:=*initial_value*]]

  BEGIN

  PL/SQL or SQL statements;

  ...

  END;

Note the following important points about stored procedures and their syntax:

- *Argument* specifies the parameters that are passed to the stored procedure. A stored procedure could have zero or more arguments or parameters.

9

- *IN/OUT* indicates whether the parameter is for input or output or both.
- *Data-type* is one of the procedural SQL data types used in the RDBMS. The data types normally match those used in the RDBMS table-creation statement.
- Variables can be declared between the keywords IS and BEGIN. You must specify the variable name, its data type, and (optionally) an initial value.

To illustrate stored procedures, assume that you want to create a procedure (PRC_PROD_DISCOUNT) to assign an additional 5 per cent discount for all products when the quantity on hand is more than or equal to twice the minimum quantity. Figure 9.36 shows how the stored procedure is created.

FIGURE 9.36 Creating the PRC_PROD_DISCOUNT stored procedure

ORACLE Application Express

Application Builder | SQL Workshop | Team Development | Packaged Apps

SQL Commands — Schema: GB_A782_PLSQL_T01

Rows 15 | Clear Command | Find Tables | Save | Run

```
CREATE OR REPLACE PROCEDURE PRC_PROD_DISCOUNT
AS BEGIN
   UPDATE PRODUCT
      SET P_DISCOUNT = P_DISCOUNT + .05
        WHERE P_QOH >= P_MIN*2;
   DBMS_OUTPUT.PUT_LINE ('* * Update finished * *');
END;
```

Results | Explain | Describe | Saved SQL | History

```
Procedure created.
```

0.02 seconds

gb_a782_plsql_t01 | gb_a782_plsql_t01 | en | | Application Express 5.0.3.00.03

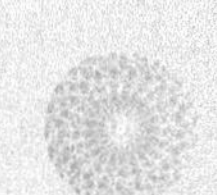

Online Content The source code for all of the stored procedures shown in this section can be found on the online platform for this book.

As you examine Figure 9.36, note that the PRC_PROD_DISCOUNT stored procedure uses the DBMS_OUTPUT.PUT_LINE function to display a message when the procedure executes. (This action assumes you previously ran SET SERVEROUTPUT ON.)

To execute the stored procedure, you must use the following code:

```
BEGIN
 PRC_PROD_DISCOUNT;
END;
/
```

Note that if you are using the SQL* Plus command line, you can also execute stored procedures using the following syntax:

EXEC procedure_name[(parameter_list)];

For example, to see the results of running the PRC_PROD_DISCOUNT stored procedure, you can use the EXEC PRC_PROD_DISCOUNT command shown in Figure 9.37.

FIGURE 9.37 **Results of the PRC_PROD_DISCOUNT stored PROCEDURE**

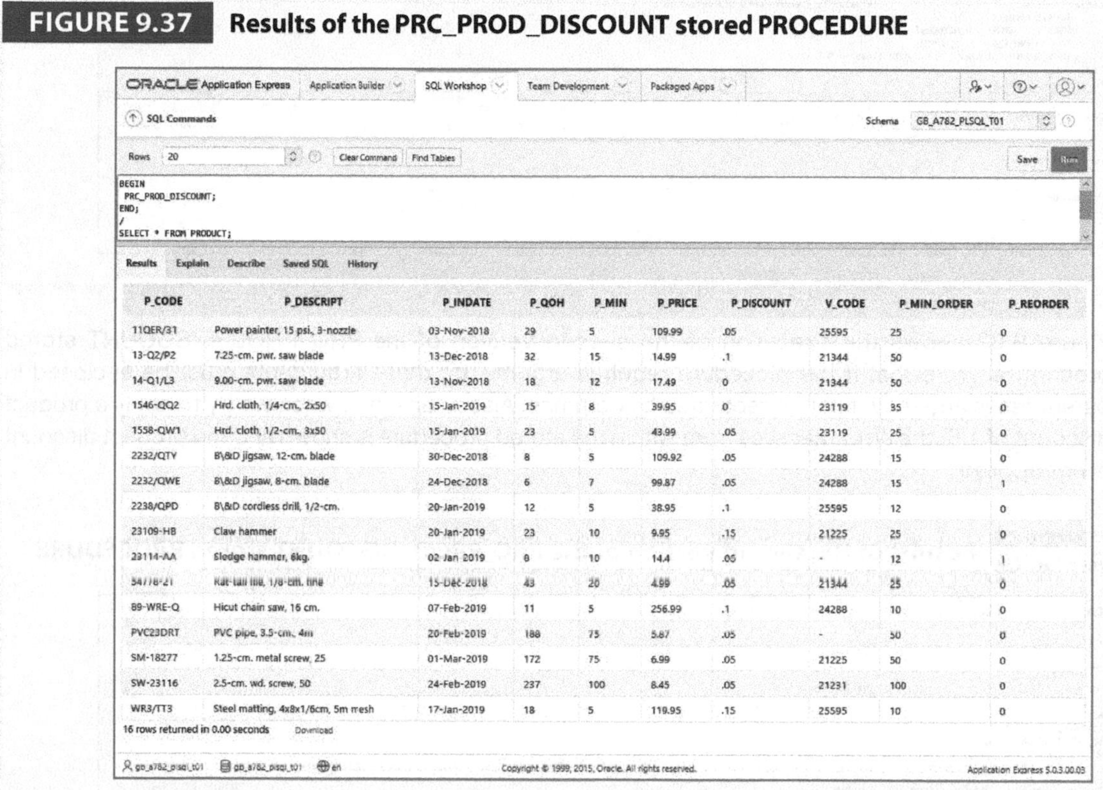

P_CODE	P_DESCRIPT	P_INDATE	P_QOH	P_MIN	P_PRICE	P_DISCOUNT	V_CODE	P_MIN_ORDER	P_REORDER
11QER/31	Power painter, 15 psi., 3-nozzle	03-Nov-2018	29	5	109.99	.05	25595	25	0
13-Q2/P2	7.25-cm. pwr. saw blade	13-Dec-2018	32	15	14.99	.1	21344	50	0
14-Q1/L3	9.00-cm. pwr. saw blade	13-Nov-2018	18	12	17.49	0	21344	50	0
1546-QQ2	Hrd. cloth, 1/4-cm., 2x50	15-Jan-2019	15	8	39.95	0	23119	35	0
1558-QW1	Hrd. cloth, 1/2-cm., 3x50	15-Jan-2019	23	5	43.99	.05	23119	25	0
2232/QTY	B\&D jigsaw, 12-cm. blade	30-Dec-2018	8	5	109.92	.05	24288	15	0
2232/QWE	B\&D jigsaw, 8-cm. blade	24-Dec-2018	6	7	99.87	.05	24288	15	1
2238/QPD	B\&D cordless drill, 1/2-cm.	20-Jan-2019	12	5	38.95	.1	25595	12	0
23109-HB	Claw hammer	20-Jan-2019	23	10	9.95	.15	21225	25	0
23114-AA	Sledge hammer, 6kg.	02 Jan 2019	8	10	14.4	.05	-	12	1
54778-2T	Rat-tail file, 1/8-cm. fine	15-Dec-2018	43	20	4.99	.05	21344	25	0
89-WRE-Q	Hicut chain saw, 16 cm.	07-Feb-2019	11	5	256.99	.1	24288	10	0
PVC23DRT	PVC pipe, 3.5-cm., 4m	20-Feb-2019	188	75	5.87	.05	-	50	0
SM-18277	1.25-cm. metal screw, 25	01-Mar-2019	172	75	6.99	.05	21225	50	0
SW-23116	2.5-cm. wd. screw, 50	24-Feb-2019	237	100	8.45	.05	21231	100	0
WR3/TT3	Steel matting, 4x8x1/6cm, 5m mesh	17-Jan-2019	18	5	119.95	.15	25595	10	0

Using Figure 9.37 as your guide, you can see how the product discount attribute for all products with a quantity on hand of more than or equal to twice the minimum quantity was increased by 5 per cent. (Compare the first PRODUCT table listing to the second PRODUCT table listing.)

One of the main advantages of procedures is that you can pass values to them. For example, the previous PRC_PRODUCT_DISCOUNT procedure worked fine, but what if you wanted to make the percentage increase an input variable? In that case, you can pass an argument to represent the rate of increase to the procedure. Figure 9.38 shows the code for that procedure.

FIGURE 9.38 **Second version of the PRC_PROD_DISCOUNT stored PROCEDURE**

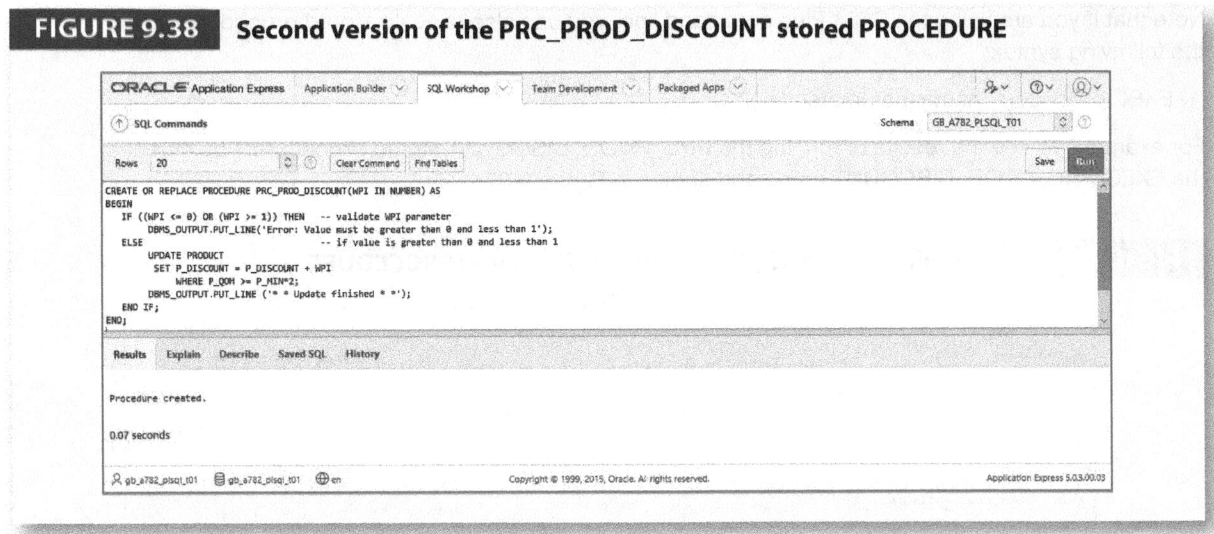

Figure 9.39 shows the execution of the second version of the PRC_PROD_DISCOUNT stored procedure. Note that if the procedure requires arguments, those arguments must be enclosed in parentheses and they must be separated by commas. Also notice that, when we try to apply a product discount of 1.5, the error message from within the stored procedure is shown and the product discount is not applied.

9

FIGURE 9.39 **Results of the second version of the PRC_PROD_DISCOUNT stored PROCEDURE**

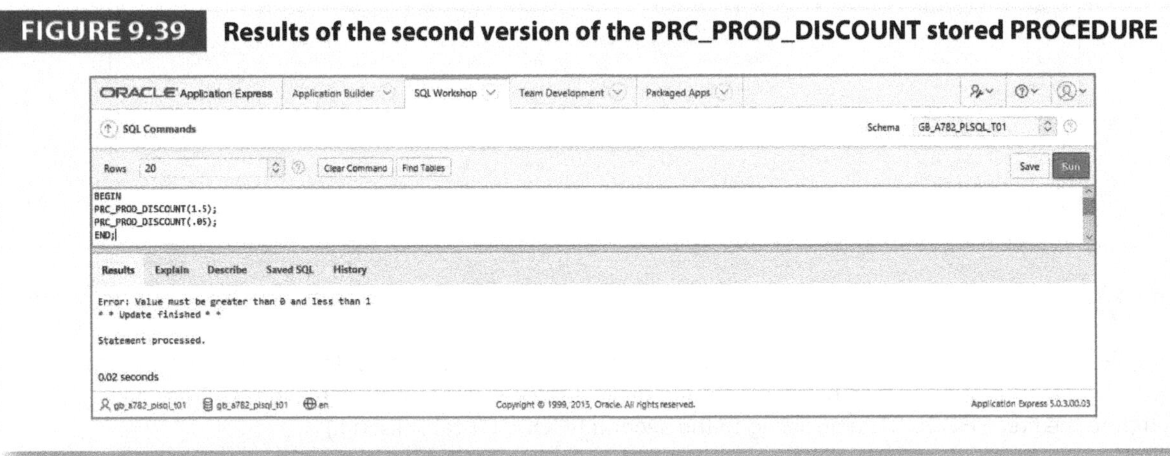

Stored procedures are also useful for encapsulating shared code to represent business transactions. For example, you can create a simple stored procedure to add a new customer. By using a stored procedure, all programs can call the stored procedure by name each time a new customer is added. Naturally, if new customer attributes are added later, you would need to modify the stored procedure. However, the programs that use the stored procedure would not need to know the name of the newly added attribute and would need to add only a new parameter to the procedure call. (Take a look at the PRC_CUS_ADD stored procedure shown in Figure 9.40.)

FIGURE 9.40 The PRC_CUS_ADD stored PROCEDURE

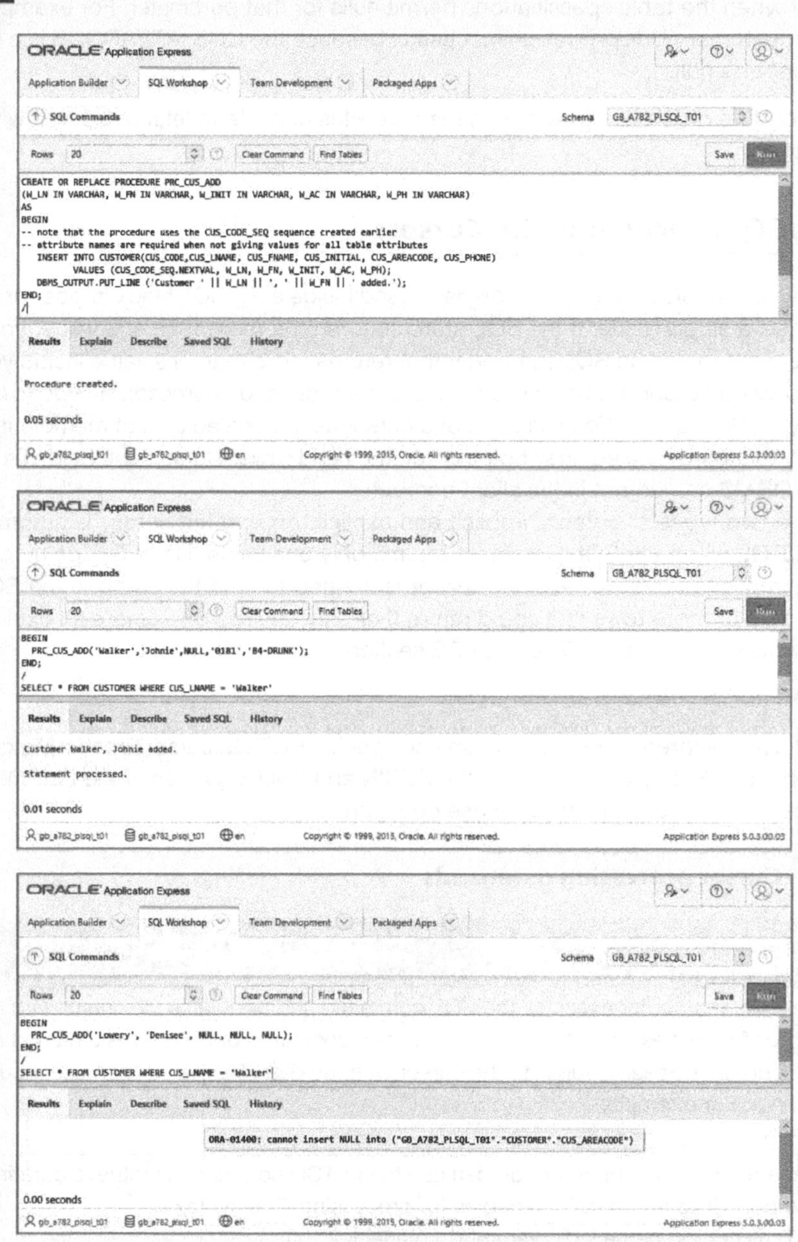

As you examine Figure 9.40, note these features:

- The PRC_CUS_ADD procedure uses several parameters, one for each required attribute in the CUSTOMER table.
- The stored procedure uses the CUS_CODE_SEQ sequence to generate a new customer code.

- The required parameters – those specified in the table definition – must be included and can be null *only* when the table specifications permit nulls for that parameter. For example, note that the second customer addition was unsuccessful because the CUS_AREACODE is a required attribute and cannot be null.
- The procedure displays a message in the SQL*Plus console to let the user know that the customer was added.

9.7.3 PL/SQL Processing with Cursors

Until now, all of the SQL statements you have used inside a PL/SQL block (trigger or stored procedure) have returned a single value. If the SQL statement returns more than one value, you will generate an error. If you want to use an SQL statement that returns more than one value inside your PL/SQL code, you need to use a cursor. A **cursor** is a special construct used in procedural SQL to hold the data rows returned by an SQL query. You can think of a cursor as a reserved area of memory in which the output of the query is stored, like an array holding columns and rows. Cursors are held in a reserved memory area in the DBMS server, not in the client computer.

There are two types of cursors: implicit and explicit. An **implicit cursor** is automatically created in procedural SQL when the SQL statement returns only one value. Up to this point, all of the examples created an implicit cursor. An **explicit cursor** is created to hold the output of an SQL statement that may return two or more rows (but could return 0 or only one row). To create an explicit cursor, use the following syntax inside a PL/SQL DECLARE section:

CURSOR *cursor_name* IS *select-query*;

9

Once you have declared a cursor, you can use specific PL/SQL cursor processing commands (OPEN, FETCH, and CLOSE) anywhere between the BEGIN and END keywords of the PL/SQL block. Table 9.10 summarises the main use of each of those commands.

TABLE 9.10 Cursor processing commands

Cursor Command	Explanation
OPEN	Opening the cursor executes the SQL command and populates the cursor with data, opening the cursor for processing. The cursor declaration command only reserves a named memory area for the cursor; it doesn't populate the cursor with the data. Before you can use a cursor, you need to open it. For example: OPEN *cursor_name*
FETCH	Once the cursor is opened, you can use the FETCH command to retrieve data from the cursor and copy it to the PL/SQL variables for processing. The syntax is: FETCH cursor_name INTO variable1 [, variable2, …] The PL/SQL variables used to hold the data must be declared in the DECLARE section and must have data types compatible with the columns retrieved by the SQL command. If the cursors SQL statement returns five columns, there must be five PL/SQL variables to receive the data from the cursor. This type of processing resembles the one-record-at-a-time processing used in previous database models. The first time you fetch a row from the cursor, the first row of data from the cursor is copied to the PL/SQL variables; the second time you fetch a row from the cursor, the second row of data is placed in the PL/SQL variables; and so on.
CLOSE	The CLOSE command closes the cursor for processing.

Cursor-style processing involves retrieving data from the cursor one row at a time. Once you open a cursor, it becomes an active data set. That data set contains a 'current' row pointer. Therefore, after opening a cursor, the current row is the first row of the cursor.

When you fetch a row from the cursor, the data from the 'current' row in the cursor is copied to the PL/SQL variables. After the fetch, the 'current' row pointer moves to the next row in the set and continues until it reaches the end of the cursor.

How do you know which number of rows are in the cursor? Or how do you know when you have reached the end of the cursor data set? You know because cursors have special attributes that convey important information. Table 9.11 summarises the cursor attributes.

TABLE 9.11 Cursor attributes

Attribute	Description
%ROWCOUNT	Returns the number of rows fetched so far. If the cursor is not OPEN, it returns an error. If no FETCH has been done but the cursor is OPEN, it returns 0.
%FOUND	Returns TRUE if the last FETCH returned a row. Returns FALSE if the last FETCH did not return any row. If the cursor is not OPEN, it returns an error. If no FETCH has been done, it contains NULL.
%NOTFOUND	Returns TRUE if the last FETCH did not return any row. Returns FALSE if the last FETCH returned a row. If the cursor is not OPEN, it returns an error. If no FETCH has been done, it contains NULL.
%ISOPEN	Returns TRUE if the cursor is open (ready for processing) or FALSE if the cursor is closed. Remember, before you can use a cursor, you must open it.

9

To illustrate the use of cursors, let's use a simple stored procedure example that lists all products that have a quantity on hand greater than the average quantity on hand for all products. The code is shown in Figure 9.41.

As you examine the stored procedure code shown in Figure 9.41, note the following important characteristics:

- The %TYPE data type in the variable definition section. As indicated in Table 9.9, the %TYPE data type is used to indicate that the given variable inherits the data type from a variable previously declared or from an attribute of a database table. In this case, you are using the %TYPE to indicate that the W_P_CODE and W_P_DESCRIPT will have the same data type as the respective columns in the PRODUCT table. This way, you ensure that the PL/SQL variable will have a compatible data type.
- The PROD_CURSOR cursor is declared as: CURSOR PROD_CURSOR
- To open the PROD_CURSOR cursor and populate it, the following command is executed: OPEN PROD_CURSOR;

FIGURE 9.41 A simple PRC_CURSOR_EXAMPLE

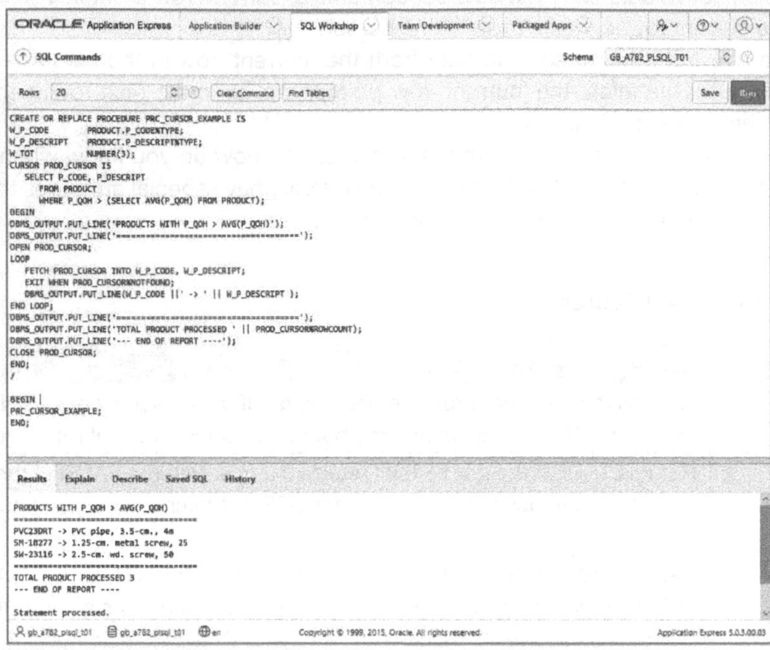

9

- The LOOP statement is used to loop through the data in the cursor, fetching one row at a time.
- The FETCH command is used to retrieve a row from the cursor and place it in the respective PL/SQL variables.
- The EXIT command is used to evaluate when there are no more rows in the cursor (using the %NOTFOUND cursor attribute) and to exit the loop.
- The %ROWCOUNT cursor attribute is used to obtain the total number of rows processed.
- The CLOSE PROD_CURSOR command is used to close the cursor.

The use of cursors, combined with standard SQL, makes relational databases very desirable because they enable programmers to work in the best of both worlds: set-oriented processing and record-orientated processing. Any experienced programmer knows to use the tool that best fits the job. Sometimes you may be better off manipulating data in a set-orientated environment; at other times, it may be better to use a record-orientated environment. Procedural SQL lets you have your proverbial cake and eat it, too. Procedural SQL provides functionality that enhances the capabilities of the DBMS while maintaining a high degree of manageability.

9.7.4 PL/SQL Stored Functions

Using programmable or procedural SQL, you can also create your own stored functions. Stored procedures and functions are very similar. A **stored function** is basically a named group of procedural and SQL statements that returns a value (indicated by a RETURN statement in its program code). To create a function, you use the following syntax:

```
CREATE FUNCTION function_name (argument IN data-type, ... ) RETURN data-type [IS]
BEGIN
    PL/SQL statements;
    ...
RETURN (value or expression);
END;
```

Stored functions can be invoked only from within stored procedures or triggers and cannot be invoked from SQL statements (unless the function follows some very specific compliance rules). Remember not to confuse built-in SQL functions (such as MIN, MAX and AVG) with stored functions.

9.8 EMBEDDED SQL

There is little doubt that SQL's popularity as a data manipulation language is in part due to its ease of use and its powerful data-retrieval capabilities. But in the real world, database systems are related to other systems and programs, and you still need a conventional programming language such as Visual Basic, .Net, C # or COBOL to integrate database systems with other programs and systems. If you are developing Web applications, you are most likely familiar with Java, ASP and .NET. Yet, almost regardless of the programming tools you use, if your Web application or Windows-based GUI system requires access to a database such as Microsoft Access, SQL Server, Oracle or DB2 you will likely need to use SQL to manipulate the data in the database.

Embedded SQL is a term used to refer to SQL statements that are contained within an application programming language such as VB.Net, C# and Java. The program being developed may be a standard binary executable in Windows or Linux, or it may be a Web application designed to run over the internet. No matter which language you use, if it contains embedded SQL statements it is called the **host language**. Embedded SQL is still the most common approach to maintaining procedural capabilities in DBMS-based applications. However, mixing SQL with procedural languages requires that you understand some key differences between SQL and procedural languages:

- *Run-time mismatch*: Remember that SQL is a non-procedural, interpreted language; that is, each instruction is parsed, its syntax is checked and it is executed one instruction at a time.[1] All of the processing takes place at the server side. Meanwhile, the host language is generally a binary-executable program (also known as a compiled program). The host program typically runs at the client side in its own memory space (different from the DBMS environment).
- *Processing mismatch*: Conventional programming languages (COBOL, Ada, FORTRAN, Pascal, C++, and PL/I) process one data element at a time. Although you can use arrays to hold data, you still process the array elements one row at a time. This is especially true for file manipulation, where the host language typically manipulates data one record at a time. However, newer programming environments such as Visual Studio .NET have adopted several object-oriented extensions that help the programmer manipulate data sets in a cohesive manner.

---

1 The authors are particularly grateful for the thoughtful comments provided by Emil T. Cipolla, who teaches at Mount Saint Mary College and whose IBM experience is the basis for his considerable and practical expertise.

- *Data type mismatch*: SQL provides several data types, but some of those data types may not match data types used in different host languages (for example, date and varchar2 data types).

To bridge the differences, the Embedded SQL Standard[2] defines a framework to integrate SQL within several programming languages. The Embedded SQL framework defines the following:

- A standard syntax to identify embedded SQL code within the host language (EXEC SQL/ END-EXEC).
- A standard syntax to identify host variables. Host variables are variables in the host language that receive data from the database (through the embedded SQL code) and process the data in the host language. All host variables are preceded by a colon (':').
- A communication area used to exchange status and error information between SQL and the host language. This communication area contains two variables – SQLCODE and SQLSTATE.

Another way to interface host languages and SQL is through the use of a call level interface (CLI),[3] in which the programmer writes to an application programming interface (API). A common CLI in Windows is provided by the Open Database Connectivity (ODBC) interface.

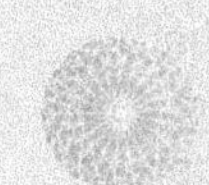

Online Content The source code for all of the stored procedures shown in this section is available on the online platform for this book.

9

Before continuing, let's explore the process required to create and run an executable program with embedded SQL statements. If you have ever programmed in COBOL or C++, you will be familiar with the multiple steps required to generate the final executable program. Although the specific details vary among language and DBMS vendors, the following general steps are standard:

- The programmer writes embedded SQL code within the host language instructions. The code follows the standard syntax required for the host language and embedded SQL.
- A preprocessor is used to transform the embedded SQL into specialised procedure calls that are DBMS- and language-specific. The preprocessor is provided by the DBMS vendor and is specific to the host language.
- The program is compiled using the host language compiler. The compiler creates an object code module for the program containing the DBMS procedure calls.
- The object code is linked to the respective library modules and generates the executable program. This process binds the DBMS procedure calls to the DBMS run-time libraries. Additionally, the binding process typically creates an 'access plan' module that contains instructions to run the embedded code at run time.
- The executable is run, and the embedded SQL statement retrieves data from the database.

---

2 https://crate.io/docs/sql-99/en/latest/chapters/39.html
3 www.oracle.com/database/technologies/appdev/oci.html

Note that you can embed individual SQL statements or even an entire PL/SQL block. Up to this point in the book, you have used a DBMS-provided application (SQL*Plus) to write SQL statements and PL/SQL blocks in an interpretive mode to address one-time or ad hoc data requests. However, it is extremely difficult and awkward to use ad hoc queries to process transactions inside a host language. Programmers typically embed SQL statements within a host language that it is compiled once and executed as often as needed. To embed SQL into a host language, follow this syntax:

```
EXEC SQL
    SQL statement;
END-EXEC.
```

The preceding syntax works for SELECT, INSERT, UPDATE and DELETE statements. For example, the following embedded SQL code will delete employee 109, George Smith, from the EMPLOYEE table:

```
EXEC SQL
    DELETE FROM EMPLOYEE WHERE EMP_NUM = 109;
END-EXEC.
```

Remember, the preceding embedded SQL statement is compiled to generate an executable statement. Therefore, the statement is fixed permanently and cannot change unless, of course, the programmer changes it. Each time the program runs, it deletes the same row. In short, the preceding code is good only for the first run; all subsequent runs will likely generate an error. Clearly, this code would be more useful if you could specify a variable to indicate the employee number to be deleted.

In embedded SQL, all host variables are preceded by a colon (':'). The host variables may be used to send data from the host language to the embedded SQL, or they may be used to receive the data from the embedded SQL. To use a host variable, you must first declare it in the host language. Common practice is to use similar host variable names as the SQL source attributes. For example, if you are using COBOL, you would define the host variables in the Working Storage section. Then you would refer to them in the embedded SQL section by preceding them with a colon (':'). For example, to delete an employee whose employee number is represented by the host variable W_EMP_NUM, you would write the following code:

```
EXEC SQL
    DELETE FROM EMPLOYEE WHERE EMP_NUM = :W_EMP_NUM;
END-EXEC.
```

At run time, the host variable value is used to execute the embedded SQL statement. What happens if the employee you are trying to delete doesn't exist in the database? How do you know that the statement has been completed without errors? As mentioned previously, the embedded SQL standard defines a SQL communication area to hold status and error information. In COBOL, such an area is known as the SQLCA area and is defined in the Data Division as follows:

```
EXEC SQL
    INCLUDE SQLCA
END-EXEC.
```

The SQLCA area contains two variables for status and error reporting. Table 9.12 shows some of the main values returned by the variables and their meaning.

9

TABLE 9.12 SQL status and error reporting variables

Variable Name	Value	Explanation
SQLCODE		Old-style error reporting supported for backward compatibility only; returns an integer value (positive or negative).
	0	Successful completion of command.
	100	No data; the SQL statement did not return any rows or did not select, update, or delete any rows.
	-999	Any negative value indicates that an error occurred.
SQLSTATE		Added by SQL-92 standard to provide predefined error codes; defined as a character string (5 characters long).
	00000	Successful completion of command.
		Multiple values in the format XXYYY where: XX-> represents the class code. YYY-> represents the subclass code.

The following embedded SQL code illustrates the use of the SQLCODE within a COBOL program.

```
EXEC SQL
EXEC SQL
     SELECT EMP_LNAME, EMP_LNAME INTO :W_EMP_FNAME, :W_EMP_LNAME
     WHERE EMP_NUM = :W_EMP_NUM;
END-EXEC.
IF SQLCODE = 0 THEN
     PERFORM DATA_ROUTINE
ELSE
     PERFORM ERROR_ROUTINE
END-IF.
```


In that example, the SQLCODE host variable is checked to determine whether the query completed successfully. If that is the case, the DATA_ROUTINE is performed; otherwise, the ERROR_ROUTINE is performed.

Just as with PL/SQL, embedded SQL requires the use of cursors to hold data from a query that returns more than one value. If COBOL is used, the cursor can be declared either in the Working Storage Section or in the Procedure Division. The cursor must be declared and processed, as you learnt earlier in this chapter. To declare a cursor, you use the syntax shown in the following example:

```
EXEC SQL
     DECLARE PROD_CURSOR FOR
     SELECT P_CODE, P_DESCRIPT FROM PRODUCT
     WHERE P_QOH > (SELECT AVG(P_QOH) FROM PRODUCT);
END-EXEC.
```

Next, you open the cursor to make the cursor ready for processing:

```
EXEC SQL
        OPEN PROD_CURSOR;
END-EXEC.
```

To process the data rows in the cursor, you use the FETCH command to retrieve one row of data at a time and place the values in the host variables. The SQLCODE must be checked to ensure that the FETCH command completed successfully. This section of code typically constitutes part of a routine in the COBOL program. Such a routine is executed with the PERFORM command. For example:

```
EXEC SQL
        FETCH PROD_CURSOR INTO :W_P_CODE, :W_P_DESCRIPT;
END-EXEC.
IF SQLCODE = 0 THEN
        PERFORM DATA_ROUTINE
ELSE
        PERFORM ERROR_ROUTINE
END-IF.
```

When all rows have been processed, you close the cursor as follows:

```
EXEC SQL
        CLOSE PROD_CURSOR;
END-EXEC.
```

Thus far, you have seen examples of embedded SQL in which the programmer used predefined SQL statements and parameters. Therefore, the end users of the programs are limited to the actions that were specified in the application programs. That style of embedded SQL is known as **static SQL**, meaning that the SQL statements will not change while the application is running. For example, the SQL statement may read like this:

```
SELECT P_CODE, P_DESCRIPT, P_QOH, P_PRICE
FROM PRODUCT
WHERE P_PRICE > 100;
```

Note that the attributes, tables and conditions are known in the preceding SQL statement. Unfortunately, end users seldom work in a static environment. They are more likely to require the flexibility of defining their data access requirements on the fly. Therefore, the end user requires that SQL be as dynamic as the data access requirements.

Dynamic SQL is a term used to describe an environment in which the SQL statement is not known in advance; instead, the SQL statement is generated at run time. At run time in a dynamic SQL environment, a program can generate the SQL statements that are required to respond to ad hoc queries. In such an environment, neither the programmer nor the end user is likely to know precisely what kind of queries are to be generated or how those queries are to be structured. For example, a dynamic SQL equivalent of the preceding example could be:

9

```
SELECT :W_ATTRIBUTE_LIST
FROM :W_TABLE
WHERE :W_CONDITION;
```

Note that the attribute list and the condition are not known until the end user specifies them. W_TABLE, W_ATTRIBUTE_LIST and W_CONDITION are text variables that contain the end-user input values used in the query generation. Because the program uses the end-user input to build the text variables, the end user can run the same program multiple times to generate different outputs. For example, in one instance, the end user might want to know which products have a price less than €100; in another case, the end user might want to know how many units of a given product are available for sale at any given moment.

Although dynamic SQL is clearly flexible, such flexibility carries a price. Dynamic SQL tends to be much slower that static SQL, and dynamic SQL requires more computer resources (overhead). In addition, you are more likely to find different levels of support and incompatibilities among DBMS vendors.

NOTE

Appendix O, Building a Simple Object-Relational Database using Oracle Objects, expands on the procedural language and advanced SQL that was introduced in this chapter to illustrate how an object relational database may be developed. The appendix briefly introduces the concepts of Oracle objects and highlights some of the object features that have been incorporated into Oracle's data model. This appendix will show how a simple example can be implemented using Oracle objects.

SUMMARY

- SQL provides relational set operators to combine the output of two queries to generate a new relation. The UNION and UNION ALL set operators combine the output of two (or more) queries and produce a new relation with all unique (UNION) or duplicate (UNION ALL) rows from both queries. The INTERSECT relational set operator selects only the common rows. The MINUS set operator selects only the rows that are different. UNION, INTERSECT and MINUS require union-compatible relations.
- Operations that join tables can be classified as inner joins and outer joins. An inner join is the traditional join in which only rows that meet a given criteria are selected. An outer join returns the matching rows as well as the rows with unmatched attribute values for one table or both tables to be joined.
- A natural join returns all rows with matching values in the matching columns and eliminates duplicate columns. This style of query is used when the tables share a common attribute with a common name. One important difference between the natural join and the 'old-style' join syntax is that the natural join does not require the use of a table qualifier for the common attributes.
- Joins may use keywords such as USING and ON. If the USING clause is used, the query will return only the rows with matching values in the column indicated in the USING clause; that column must exist in both tables. If the ON clause is used, the query will return only the rows that meet the specified join condition.
- Subqueries and correlated queries are used when it is necessary to process data based on *other* processed data. That is, the query uses results that were previously unknown and that are generated by another query. Subqueries may be used with the FROM, WHERE, IN and HAVING clauses in a SELECT statement. A subquery may return a single row or multiple rows.

- Most subqueries are executed in a serial fashion. That is, the outer query initiates the data request; then the inner subquery is executed. In contrast, a correlated subquery is a subquery that is executed once for each row in the outer query. That process is similar to the typical nested loop in a programming language. A correlated subquery is so named because the inner query is related to the outer query because the inner query references a column of the outer subquery.
- SQL functions are used to extract or transform data. The most frequently used functions are date and time functions. The results of the function output can be used to store values in a database table, to serve as the basis for the computation of derived variables or to serve as a basis for data comparisons. Function formats can be vendor-specific. Aside from time and date functions, there are numeric and string functions and conversion functions that convert one data format to another.
- Oracle sequences may be used to generate values to be assigned to a record. For example, a sequence may be used to number invoices automatically. Microsoft Access uses an Autonumber data type to generate numeric sequences.
- Procedural SQL (PL/SQL) can be used to create triggers, stored procedures and PL/SQL functions. A trigger is procedural SQL code that is automatically invoked by the DBMS upon the occurrence of a specified data manipulation event (UPDATE, INSERT or DELETE). Triggers are critical to proper database operation and management. They help automate various transaction and data management processes, and they can be used to enforce constraints that are not enforced at the DBMS design and implementation levels.
- A stored procedure is a named collection of SQL statements. Just like database triggers, stored procedures are stored in the database. One of the major advantages of stored procedures is that they can be used to encapsulate and represent complete business transactions. Use of stored procedures substantially reduces network traffic and increases system performance. Stored procedures help reduce code duplication by creating unique PL/SQL modules that are called by the application programs, thereby minimising the chance of errors and the cost of application development and maintenance.
- When SQL statements are designed to return more than one value inside the PL/SQL code, a cursor is needed. You can think of a cursor as a reserved area of memory in which the output of the query is stored, like an array holding columns and rows. Cursors are held in a reserved memory area in the DBMS server, rather than in the client computer. There are two types of cursors: implicit and explicit.
- Embedded SQL refers to the use of SQL statements within an application programming language such as Visual Basic, .NET, C#, Python or Java. The language in which the SQL statements are embedded is called the host language. Embedded SQL is still the most common approach to maintaining procedural capabilities in DBMS-based applications.

KEY TERMS

anonymous PL/SQL block
batch update routine
correlated subquery
cross join
cursor
dynamic SQL
embedded SQL
Event-Condition-Action (ECA) model
explicit cursor
host language
implicit cursor
inner join
outer join
persistent stored module (PSM)
procedural SQL (PL/SQL)
row-level trigger
statement-level trigger
static SQL
stored function
stored procedure
trigger
updatable view

Online Content Answers to selected Review Questions and Problems for this chapter are available on the online platform for this book.

FURTHER READING

MySQL 8.0 Reference Manual [online]. Available: https://dev.mysql.com/doc/refman/8.0/en/ (2019).

Oracle Database 18c PL/SQL [online]. Available: www.oracle.com/technetwork/database/features/plsql/index.html, 2019.

Malepati, T. Shah, B. and Vanier, E. *Advanced MySQL 8*. O'Reilly, 2019.

REVIEW QUESTIONS

1 The relational set operators UNION, INTERSECT and MINUS work properly only when the relations are union-compatible. What does *union-compatible* mean, and how would you check for this condition?

2 What is the difference between UNION and UNION ALL? Write the syntax for each.

3 Suppose you have two tables: EMPLOYEE and EMPLOYEE_1. The EMPLOYEE table contains the records for three employees: Alice Cordoza, John Cretchakov and Anne McDonald. The EMPLOYEE_1 table contains the records for employees John Cretchakov and Mary Chen. Given that information, what is the query output for the UNION query? (List the query output.)

4 Given the employee information in Question 3, what is the query output for the UNION ALL query? (List the query output.)

5 Given the employee information in Question 3, what is the query output for the INTERSECT query? (List the query output.)

6 Given the employee information in Question 3, what is the query output for the MINUS query? (List the query output.)

7 What is a CROSS JOIN? Give an example of its syntax.

8 Which three join types are included in the OUTER JOIN classification?

9 Using tables named T1 and T2, write a query example for each of the three join types you described in Question 8. Assume that T1 and T2 share a common column named C1.

10 What is a subquery, and what are its basic characteristics?

11 What is a correlated subquery? Give an example.

12 Which Microsoft Access/SQL Server function should you use to calculate the number of days between the current date and 25 January 2019?

13 Which Oracle function should you use to calculate the number of days between the current date and 25 January 2019?

14 Suppose a PRODUCT table contains two attributes, PROD_CODE and VEND_CODE. Those two attributes have values of ABC, 125, DEF, 124, GHI, 124, and JKL, 123, respectively. The VENDOR table contains a single attribute, VEND_CODE, with values 123, 124, 125 and 126, respectively. (The VEND_CODE attribute in the PRODUCT table is a foreign key to the VEND_CODE in the VENDOR table.) Given that information, what would be the query output for:

- **a** A UNION query based on the two tables?
- **b** A UNION ALL query based on the two tables?
- **c** An INTERSECT query based on the two tables?
- **d** A MINUS query based on the two tables?

15 Which Oracle string function should you use to list the first three characters of a company's EMP_LNAME values? Give an example using a table named EMPLOYEE.

16 What is an Oracle sequence? Write its syntax.

17 What is a trigger, and what is its purpose? Give an example.

18 What is a stored procedure, and why is it particularly useful? Give an example.

19 Give an example of a stored function. How would the function be called?

20 What are the four occasions on which Oracle recommends you use a trigger?

PROBLEMS

Online Content The 'Ch09_SimpleCo' database is located on the online platform for this book, as are the script files to duplicate this data set in Oracle.

Use the database tables in Figure P9.1 as the basis for Problems 1–18.

FIGURE P9.1 Ch09_SimpleCo database tables

Database name: Ch09_SimpleCo

Table name: CUSTOMER

CUST_NUM	CUST_LNAME	CUST_FNAME	CUST_BALANCE
1000	Smith	Jeanne	1050.11
1001	Ortega	Juan	840.92

Table name: CUSTOMER_2

CUST_NUM	CUST_LNAME	CUST_FNAME
2000	McPherson	Anne
2001	Ortega	Juan
2002	Kowalski	Jan
2003	Chen	George

Table name: INVOICE

INV_NUM	CUST_NUM	INV_DATE	INV_AMOUNT
8000	1000	23-Mar-19	235.89
8001	1001	23-Mar-19	312.82
8002	1001	30-Mar-19	528.10
8003	1000	12-Apr-19	194.78
8004	1000	23-Apr-19	619.44

1 Create the tables. (Use Figure P9.1 to see which table names and attributes to use.)

2 Insert the data into the tables you created in Problem 1.

3 Write the query that will generate a combined list of customers (from the tables CUSTOMER and CUSTOMER_2) that do not include the duplicate customer records. (Note that only the customer named Juan Ortega shows up in both customer table).

4 Write the query that will generate a combined list of customers to include the duplicate customer records.

5 Write the query that will show only the duplicate customer records.

6 Write the query that will generate only the records that are unique to the CUSTOMER_2 table.

7 Write the query to show the invoice number, the customer number, the customer name, the invoice date and the invoice amount for all customers with a customer balance of €1 000 or more.

8 Write the query that will show the invoice number, the invoice amount, the average invoice amount and the difference between the average invoice amount and the actual invoice amount.

9 Write the query that will write Oracle sequences to produce automatic customer number and invoice number values. Start the customer numbers at 1000 and the invoice numbers at 5000.

10 Modify the CUSTOMER table to included two new attributes: CUST_DOB and CUST_AGE. Customer 1000 was born on 15 March 1969, and customer 1001 was born on 22 December 1978.

11 Assuming you completed Problem 10, write the query that lists the names and ages of your customers.

12 Assuming the CUSTOMER table contains a CUST_AGE attribute, write the query to update the values in that attribute. (*Hint:* Use the results of the previous query.)

13 Write the query that will list the average age of your customers. (Assume that the CUSTOMER table has been modified to include the CUST_DOB and the derived CUST_AGE attribute.)

14 Write the trigger to update the CUST_BALANCE in the CUSTOMER table when a new invoice record is entered. (Assume that the sale is a credit sale.) Test the trigger, using the following new INVOICE record:

8005, 1001, '27-APR-19', 225.40

Name the trigger trg_updatecustbalance.

9

15 Write a stored procedure to add a new customer to the CUSTOMER table. Use the following values in the new record:

1002, 'Rauthor', 'Peter', 0.00

Name the procedure prc_cust_add. Run a query to see if the record has been added.

16 Write a procedure to add a new invoice record to the INVOICE table. Use the following values in the new record:

8006, 1000, '30-APR-19', 301.72

Name the procedure prc_invoice_add. Run a query to see if the record has been added.

17 Write a trigger to update the customer balance when an invoice is deleted. Name the trigger trg_updatecustbalance2.

18 Write a procedure to delete an invoice, giving the invoice number as a parameter. Name the procedure prc_inv_delete. Test the procedure by deleting invoices 8005 and 8006.

Use the database tables in Figure P9.2 as the basis for Problems 19–26.

FIGURE P 9.2 Ch09_Publishing database tables

Table name: BOOK

ISBN	TITLE	NUMBER_PAGES	PRICE	TYPE
72121333	Cell	496	6.99	Fiction
8990765	Rough Guide to Prague	245	10.45	Reference
912122048	Oracle 18c Reference Guide	976	34.99	Reference
912934511	Oracle Backup & Recovery	399	54.50	Reference
935642189	Introduction to SQL	4990	19.99	Reference

Table name: AUTHOR

AUTHOR_ID	FIRST_NAME	LAST_NAME
1	Stephen	King
2	Michael	Abbey
3	Michael	Robinson
4	Kenny	Smith
5	Steph	Haisley
6	Mandla	Langa
7	Rushford	Majoy
8	Farmyi	Madagore

9

Table name: AUTHOR_BOOK

ISBN	AUTHOR_ID
72121333	1
8990765	6
8990765	7
912122048	2
912122048	3
912934511	4
912934511	5
935642189	8

Table name: STOCK

ISBN	STATUS	STATUS_DATE	QUANTITY
72121333	IN STOCK		54
8990765	IN STOCK		9
912122048	ON ORDER	12/05/2019	20
912934511	FUTURE	30/03/2019	32
935642189	ON ORDER	15/04/2019	50

9

19 Create the tables. (Use Figure P9.2 to see which table names and attributes to use.)

20 Insert the data into the tables you created in Problem 19.

21 Modify the BOOK table to include a new attribute that records the DATE_PUBLISHED. Write the SQL code required to update the DATE_PUBLISHED for the following books.

ISBN	DATE_PUBLISHED
72121333	12-MAR-19
912122048	23-NOV-19
912934511	12-MAY-19
935642189	11-JUNE-19

22 Write the query that will display the ISBN and title of all books that have been published for more than two years.

23 Write a query that creates a list of unique author–book ids, using the first five characters of the author's last name and the first eight characters of the book title. Label the column AUTHOR_BOOK_ID.

24 Write an anonymous PL/SQL block that displays the maximum author_id currently held in the database and displays it to the screen.

25 Write an anonymous PL/SQL block to display the status date entered in the STOCK table for the book titled 'Oracle 18c Reference Guide'.

26 Write an anonymous PL/SQL block that contains a simple cursor to display only the first three titles from the BOOK table. (*Hint:* use the cursor function %ROWCOUNT.)

NOTE

The following problem sets can serve as the basis for a class project or case.

Use the Ch09_SaleCo2 database to work Problems 27–31 (Figure P9.3).

FIGURE P9.3 Ch09_SaleCo database tables

Table name: CUSTOMER

CUS_CODE	CUS_LNAME	CUS_FNAME	CUS_INITIAL	CUS_AREACODE	CUS_PHONE	CUS_BALANCE
10010	Ramas	Alfred	A	0181	844-2573	0.00
10011	Dunne	Leona	K	0161	894-1238	0.00
10012	Moloi	Marlene	W	0181	894-2285	345.86
10013	Pieterse	Jaco	F	0181	894-2180	536.75
10014	Orlando	Myron		0181	222-1672	0.00
10015	O'Brian	Amy	B	0161	442-3381	0.00
10016	Brown	James	G	0181	297-1228	221.19
10017	Williams	George		0181	290-2556	768.93
10018	Padayachee	Vinaya	G	0161	382-7185	216.55
10019	Moloi	Mlilo	K	0181	297-3809	0.00

Table name: PRODUCT

P_CODE	P_DESCRIPT	P_INDATE	P_QOH	P_MIN	P_PRICE	P_DISCOUNT	V_CODE
11QER/31	Power painter, 15 psi., 3-nozzle	03-Nov-18	8	5	109.99	0.00	25595
13-Q2/P2	7.25 cm pwr. saw blade	13-Dec-18	32	15	14.99	0.05	21344
14-Q1/L3	9.00 cm pwr. saw blade	13-Nov-18	18	12	17.49	0.00	21344
1546-QQ2	Hrd. cloth, 1/4 cm, 2 × 50	15-Jan-19	15	8	39.95	0.00	23119
1558-QW1	Hrd. cloth, 1/2 cm, 3 × 50	15-Jan-19	23	5	43.99	0.00	23119
2232/QTY	B&D jigsaw, 12 cm blade	30-Dec-18	8	5	109.92	0.05	24288
2232/QWE	B&D jigsaw, 8 cm blade	24-Dec-18	6	5	99.87	0.05	24288
2238/QPD	B&D cordless drill, 1/2 cm	20-Jan-19	12	5	38.95	0.05	25595
23109-HB	Claw hammer	20-Jan-19	23	10	9.95	0.10	21225

P_CODE	P_DESCRIPT	P_INDATE	P_QOH	P_MIN	P_PRICE	P_DISCOUNT	V_CODE
23114-AA	Sledge hammer, 12 kg	02-Jan-19	8	5	14.40	0.05	
54778-2T	Rat-tail file, 1/8 cm fine	15-Dec-18	43	20	4.99	0.00	21344
89-WRE-Q	Hicut chain saw, 16 cm	07-Feb-19	11	5	256.99	0.05	24288
PVC23DRT	PVC pipe, 3.5 cm, 8 m	20-Feb-19	188	75	5.87	0.00	
SM-18277	1.25 cm metal screw, 25	01-Mar-19	172	75	6.99	0.00	21225
SW-23116	2.5 cm wd. screw, 50	24-Feb-19	237	100	8.45	0.00	21231
WR3/TT3	Steel matting, 4 × 8 × 1/6 m, .5 m mesh	17-Jan-19	18	5	119.95	0.10	25595

Table name: VENDOR

V_CODE	V_NAME	V_CONTACT	V_AREACODE	V_PHONE	V_COUNTRY	V_ORDER
21225	Bryson, Inc.	Smithson	0181	223-3234	UK	Y
21226	SuperLoo, Inc.	Flushing	0113	215-8995	SA	N
21231	D&E Supply	Singh	0181	228-3245	UK	Y
21344	Jabavu Bros.	Ortega	0181	889-2546	SA	N
22567	Dome Supply	Smith	7253	678-1419	FR	N
23119	Randsets Ltd.	Anderson	7253	678-3998	FR	Y
24004	Brackman Bros.	Browning	0181	228-1410	UK	N
24288	ORDVA, Inc.	Hakford	0181	898-1234	UK	Y
25443	B&K, Inc.	Smith	0113	227-0093	SA	N
25501	Damal Supplies	Smythe	0181	890-3529	UK	N
25595	Rubicon Systems	Orton	0113	456-0092	SA	Y

Table name: INVOICE

INV_NUMBER	CUS_CODE	INV_DATE	INV_SUBTOTAL	INV_TAX	INV_TOTAL
1001	10014	16-Jan-19	24.90	1.99	26.89
1002	10011	16-Jan-19	9.98	0.80	10.78
1003	10012	16-Jan-19	153.85	12.31	166.16
1004	10011	17-Jan-19	34.97	2.80	37.77
1005	10018	17-Jan-19	70.44	5.64	76.08
1006	10014	17-Jan-19	397.83	31.83	429.66
1007	10015	17-Jan-19	34.97	2.80	37.77
1008	10011	17-Jan-19	399.15	31.93	431.08

Table name: LINE

INV_NUMBER	LINE_NUMBER	P_CODE	LINE_UNITS	LINE_PRICE	LINE_TOTAL
1001	1	13-Q2/P2	1	14.99	14.99
1001	2	23109-HB	1	9.95	9.95
1002	1	54778-2T	2	4.99	9.98
1003	1	2238/QPD	1	38.95	38.95
1003	2	1546-QQ2	1	39.95	39.95
1003	3	13-Q2/P2	5	14.99	74.95
1004	1	54778-2T	3	4.99	14.97
1004	2	23109-HB	2	9.95	19.90
1005	1	PVC23DRT	12	5.87	70.44
1006	1	SM-18277	3	6.99	20.97
1006	2	2232/QTY	1	109.92	109.92
1006	3	23109-HB	1	9.95	9.95
1006	4	89-WRE-Q	1	256.99	256.99
1007	1	13-Q2/P2	2	14.99	29.98
1007	2	54778-2T	1	4.99	4.99
1008	1	PVC23DRT	5	5.87	29.35
1008	2	WR3/TT3	3	119.95	359.85
1008	3	23109-HB	1	9.95	9.95

Online Content The 'Ch09_SaleCo2' database used in Problems 27–31 is located on the online platform for this book, as are the script files to duplicate this data set in Oracle.

27 Create a trigger named trg_line_total to write the LINE_TOTAL value in the LINE table every time you add a new LINE row. (The LINE_TOTAL value is the product of the LINE_UNITS and the LINE_PRICE values.)

28 Create a trigger named trg_line_prod that will automatically update the product quantity on hand for each product sold after a new LINE row is added.

29 Create a stored procedure named prc_inv_amounts to update the INV_SUBTOTAL, INV_TAX and INV_TOTAL. The procedure takes the invoice number as a parameter. The INV_SUBTOTAL is the sum of the LINE_TOTAL amounts for the invoice, the INV_TAX is the product of the INV_SUBTOTAL and the tax rate (8%), and the INV_TOTAL is the sum of the INV_SUBTOTAL and the INV_TAX.

Use the Ch09_AviaCo database to work Problems 31–42 (Figure P9.4).

FIGURE P9.4 Ch11_AviaCo database tables

Table name: CHARTER

CHAR_TRIP	CHAR_DATE	AC_NUMBER	CHAR_DESTINATION	CHAR_DISTANCE	CHAR_HOURS_FLOWN	CHAR_HOURS_WAIT	CHAR_FUEL_GALLONS	CHAR_OIL_QTS	CUS_CODE
10001	05-Feb-19	2289L	ATL	936.00	5.1	2.2	354.1	1	10011
10002	05-Feb-19	2778V	BNA	320.00	1.6	0.0	72.6	0	10016
10003	05-Feb-19	4278Y	GNV	1574.00	7.8	0.0	339.8	2	10014
10004	06-Feb-19	1484P	STL	472.00	2.9	4.9	97.2	1	10019
10005	06-Feb-19	2289L	ATL	1023.00	5.7	3.5	397.7	2	10011
10006	06-Feb-19	4278Y	STL	472.00	2.6	5.2	117.1	0	10017
10007	06-Feb-19	2778V	GNV	1574.00	7.9	0.0	348.4	2	10012
10008	07-Feb-19	1484P	TYS	644.00	4.1	0.0	140.6	1	10014
10009	07-Feb-19	2289L	GNV	1574.00	6.6	23.4	459.9	0	10017
10010	07-Feb-19	4278Y	ATL	998.00	6.2	3.2	279.7	0	10016
10011	07-Feb-19	1484P	BNA	352.00	1.9	5.3	66.4	1	10012
10012	08-Feb-19	2778V	MOB	884.00	4.8	4.2	215.1	0	10010
10013	08-Feb-19	4278Y	TYS	644.00	3.9	4.5	174.3	1	10011
10014	09-Feb-19	4278Y	ATL	936.00	6.1	2.1	302.6	0	10017
10015	09-Feb-19	2289L	GNV	1645.00	6.7	0.0	459.5	2	10016
10016	09-Feb-19	2778V	MQY	312.00	1.5	0.0	67.2	0	10011
10017	10-Feb-19	1484P	STL	508.00	3.1	0.0	105.5	0	10014
10018	10-Feb-19	4278Y	TYS	644.00	3.8	4.5	167.4	0	10017

Table name: CUSTOMER

CUS_CODE	CUS_LNAME	CUS_FNAME	CUS_INITIAL	CUS_AREACODE	CUS_PHONE	CUS_BALANCE
10010	Ramas	Alfred	A	0181	844-2573	0.00
10011	Dunne	Leona	K	0161	894-1238	0.00
10012	Moloi	Marlene	W	0181	894-2285	896.54
10013	Pieterse	Jaco	F	0181	894-2180	1285.19
10014	Orlando	Myron		0181	222-1672	673.21
10015	O'Brian	Amy	B	0161	442-3381	1014.56
10016	Brown	James	G	0181	297-1228	0.00
10017	Williams	George		0181	290-2556	0.00
10018	Padayachee	Vinaya	G	0161	382-7185	0.00
10019	Moloi	Mlilo	K	0181	297-3809	453.98

Table name: EMPLOYEE

EMP_NUM	EMP_TITLE	EMP_LNAME	EMP_FNAME	EMP_INITIAL	EMP_DOB	EMP_HIRE_DATE
100	Mr	Kolmycz	George	D	15-Jun-1952	15-Mar-1997
101	Ms	Lewis	Rhonda	G	19-Mar-1975	25-Apr-1998
102	Mr	Vandam	Rhett		14-Nov-1968	20-Dec-2002
103	Ms	Jones	Anne	M	16-Oct-1984	28-Aug-2015
104	Mr	Lange	John	P	08-Nov-1981	20-Oct-2006
105	Mr	Williams	Robert	D	14-Mar-1985	08-Jan-2016
106	Mrs	Duzak	Jeanine	K	12-Feb-1978	05-Jan-2001
107	Mr	Diante	Jorge	D	21-Aug-1984	02-Jul-2006
108	Mr	Wiesenbach	Paul	R	14-Feb-1976	18-Nov-2004
109	Ms	Travis	Elizabeth	K	18-Jun-1971	14-Apr-2001
110	Mrs	Genkazi	Leighla	W	19-May-1980	01-Dec-2002

Table name: CREW

CHAR_TRIP	EMP_NUM	CREW_JOB
10001	104	Pilot
10002	101	Pilot
10003	105	Pilot
10003	109	Copilot
10004	106	Pilot
10005	101	Pilot
10006	109	Pilot
10007	104	Pilot
10007	105	Copilot
10008	106	Pilot
10009	105	Pilot
10010	108	Pilot
10011	101	Pilot
10011	104	Copilot
10012	101	Pilot
10013	105	Pilot
10014	106	Pilot
10015	101	Copilot
10015	104	Pilot
10016	105	Copilot
10016	109	Pilot
10017	101	Pilot
10018	104	Copilot
10018	105	Pilot

Table name: AIRCRAFT

AC_NUMBER	MOD_CODE	AC_TTAF	AC_TTEL	AC_TTER
1484P	PA23-250	1833.10	1833.10	101.80
2289L	C-90A	4243.80	768.90	1123.40
2778V	PA31-350	7992.90	1513.10	789.50
4278Y	PA31-350	2147.30	622.10	243.20

Table name: PILOT

EMP_NUM	PIL_LICENSE	PIL_MED_TYPE	PIL_MED_DATE	PIL_PT135_DATE
101	ATP	1	12-Apr-2018	15-Jun-2018
104	ATP	1	10-Jun-2018	23-Mar-2019
105	COM	2	25-Feb-2018	12-Feb-2018
106	COM	2	02-Apr-2018	24-Dec-2019
109	COM	1	14-Apr-2018	21-Apr-2018

Table name: RATING

RTG_CODE	RTG_NAME
CFI	Certified Flight Instructor
CFII	Certified Flight Instructor, Instrument
INSTR	Instrument
MEL	Multiengine Land
SEL	Single Engine, Land
SES	Single Engine, Sea

Table name: MODEL

MOD_CODE	MOD_MANUFACTURER	MOD_NAME	MOD_SEATS	MOD_CHG_MILE
C-90A	Beechcraft	KingAir	8	2.67
PA23-250	Piper	Aztec	6	1.93
PA31-350	Piper	Navajo Chieftain	10	2.35

Table name: EARNED_RATING

EMP_NUM	RTG_CODE	EARNRTG_DATE
101	CFI	18-Feb-08
101	CFII	15-Dec-15
101	INSTR	08-Nov-03
101	MEL	23-Jun-04
101	SEL	21-Apr-03
104	INSTR	15-Jul-06
104	MEL	29-Jan-07
104	SEL	12-Mar-05

EMP_NUM	RTG_CODE	EARNRTG_DATE
105	CFI	18-Nov-07
105	INSTR	17-Apr-05
105	MEL	12-Aug-05
105	SEL	23-Sep-04
106	INSTR	20-Dec-05
106	MEL	02-Apr-06
106	SEL	10-Mar-04
109	CFI	05-Nov-08
109	CFII	21-Jun-13
109	INSTR	23-Jul-06
109	MEL	15-Mar-07
109	SEL	05-Feb-06
109	SES	12-May-06

30 Create a procedure named prc_cus_balance_update that will take the invoice number as a parameter and update the customer balance. (*Hint:* You can use the DECLARE section to define a TOTINV numeric variable that holds the computed invoice total.)

Online Content The 'Ch09_AviaCo' database used for Problems 31–42 is located on the online platform for this book, as are the script files to duplicate this data set in Oracle.

31 Modify the MODEL table to add the attribute and insert the values shown in the following table.

Attribute Name	Attribute Description	Attribute Type	Attribute Values
MOD_WAIT_CHG	Waiting charge per hour for each model	Numeric	€100 for C-90A €50 for PA23-250 €75 for PA31-350

32 Write the queries to update the MOD_WAIT_CHG attribute values based on Problem 31.

33 Modify the CHARTER table to add the attributes shown in the following table.

Attribute Name	Attribute Description	Attribute Type
CHAR_WAIT_CHG	Waiting charge for each model (copied from the MODEL table)	Numeric
CHAR_FLT_CHG_HR	Flight charge per mile for each model (copied from the MODEL table using the MOD_CHG_MILE attribute)	Numeric
CHAR_FLT_CHG	Flight charge (calculated by CHAR_HOURS_FLOWN × CHAR_FLT_CHG_HR)	Numeric
CHAR_TAX_CHG	CHAR_FLT_CHG × tax rate (8%)	Numeric
CHAR_TOT_CHG	CHAR_FLT_CHG + CHAR_TAX_CHG	Numeric
CHAR_PYMT	Amount paid by customer	Numeric
CHAR_BALANCE	Balance remaining after payment	Numeric

34 Write the sequence of commands required to update the CHAR_WAIT_CHG attribute values in the CHARTER table. (*Hint:* Use either an updatable view or a stored procedure.)

35 Write the sequence of commands required to update the CHAR_FLT_CHG_HR attribute values in the CHARTER table. (*Hint*: Use either an updatable view or a stored procedure.)

36 Write the command required to update the CHAR_FLT_CHG attribute values in the CHARTER table.

37 Write the command required to update the CHAR_TAX_CHG attribute values in the CHARTER table.

9

38 Write the command required to update the CHAR_TOT_CHG attribute values in the CHARTER table.

39 Modify the PILOT table to add the attribute shown in the following table.

Attribute Name	Attribute Description	Attribute Type
PIL_PIC_HRS	Pilot in command (PIC) hours; updated by adding the CHARTER tables CHAR_HOURS_FLOWN to the PIL_PIC_HRS when the CREW table shows the CREW_JOB to be pilot	Numeric

40 Create a trigger named trg_char_hours that automatically updates the AIRCRAFT table when a new CHARTER row is added. Use the CHARTER table's CHAR_HOURS_FLOWN to update the AIRCRAFT table's AC_TTAF, AC_TTEL, and AC_TTER values.

41 Create a trigger named trg_pic_hours that automatically updates the PILOT table when a new CREW row is added and the CREW table uses a 'pilot' CREW_JOB entry. Use the CHARTER table's CHAR_HOURS_FLOWN to update the PILOT table's PIL_PIC_HRS only when the CREW table uses a 'pilot' CREW_JOB entry.

42 Create a trigger named trg_cust_balance that automatically updates the CUSTOMER table's CUST_BALANCE when a new CHARTER row is added. Use the CHARTER table's CHAR_TOT_CHG as the update source. (Assume that all charter charges are charged to the customer balance.)

CASE

EliteVideo is a start-up company providing a concierge DVD kiosk service in upscale neighbourhoods. EliteVideo can own several copies (VIDEO) of each movie (MOVIE). For example, a kiosk may have 10 copies of the movie *Cry, the Beloved Country*. In the database, *Cry, the Beloved Country* would be one MOVIE, and each copy would be a VIDEO. A rental transaction (RENTAL) involves one or more videos being rented to a member (MEMBERSHIP). A video can be rented many times over its lifetime; therefore, there is an M:N relationship between RENTAL and VIDEO. DETAILRENTAL is the bridge table to resolve this relationship. The complete ERD is provided in Figure P9.5.

FIGURE P9.5 **The Ch09_MovieCo ERD**

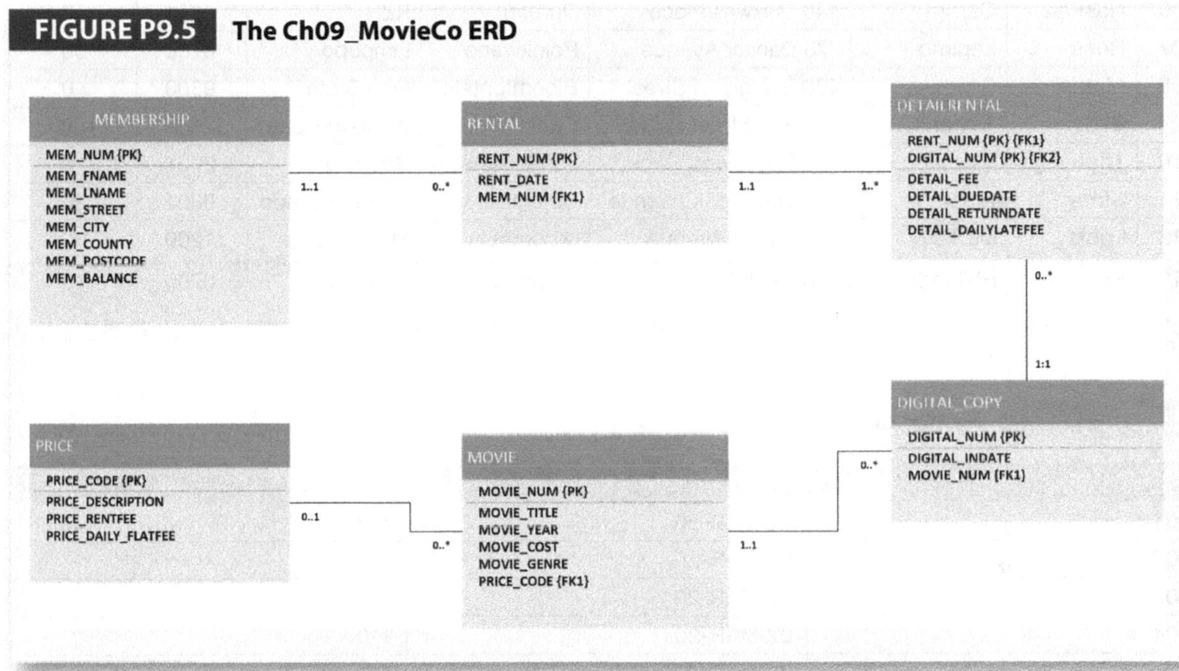

43 Write the SQL code to create the table structures for the entities shown in Figure P9.5. The structures should contain the attributes specified in the ERD. Use data types that are appropriate for the data that will need to be stored in each attribute. Enforce primary key and foreign key constraints as indicated by the ERD.

44 The following tables provide a very small portion of the data that will be kept in the database. The data needs to be inserted into the database for testing purposes. Write the INSERT commands necessary to place the following data in the tables that were created in Problem 43. (If required by your DBMS, be certain to save the rows permanently.)

TABLE P9.1 **Membership table**

MEM NUM	MEM_ FNAME	MEM_ LNAME	MEM-STREET	MEM_CITY	MEM_PROV	MEM_ POSTAL CODE	MEM_ BALANCE
102	Tami	Dawson	26 Takli Circle	East London	Eastern Cape	5200	110
103	Koert	Wessels	45 Cornell Court	Durban	KZN	4001	60
104	Jamal	Melendez	78 East 145th Avenue	Pretoria	Gauteng	0001	0
105	Palesa	Mamorobela	60 Musket Ball Circle	Cape Town	Western Cape	7100	150
106	Nasima	Carrim	446 Maxwell Place	Durban	KZN	4001	0
107	Rose	Ledimo	78 Danner Avenue	Polokwane	Limpopo	0700	50
108	Mattie	Smith	430 Evergreen Street	Bloemfontein	Free State	9300	0
109	Clint	Taylor	171 Elm Street	Cape Town	Western Cape	7100	100
110	Thabang	Moroe	24 Southwind Circle	Johannesburg	Gauteng	2001	0
111	Stacy	Mann	89 East Cook Avenue	Upington	Northern Cape	8801	80
112	Louis	Du Toit	26 Melvin Avenue	Mbombela	Mpumalanga	1200	30
113	Sulaiyman	Philander	430 Vasili Drive	Polokwane	Limpopo	0700	0

9

TABLE P9.2 **Rental table**

RENT_NUM	RENT_DATE	MEM_NUM
1001	01-MAR-20	103
1002	01-MAR-20	105
1003	02-MAR-20	102
1004	02-MAR-20	110
1005	02-MAR-20	111
1006	02-MAR-20	107
1007	02-MAR-20	104
1008	03-MAR-20	105
1009	03-MAR-20	111

TABLE P9.3 **DetailRental table**

RENT_NUM	VID_NUM	DETAIL_FEE	DETAIL_ DUEDATE	DETAIL_ RETURNDATE	DETAIL_ DAILYLATEFEE
1001	34342	20	04-MAR-20	02-MAR-20	
1001	61353	20	04-MAR-20	03-MAR-20	10
1002	59237	35	04-MAR-20	04-MAR-20	30

RENT_NUM	VID_NUM	DETAIL_FEE	DETAIL_ DUEDATE	DETAIL_ RETURNDATE	DETAIL_ DAILYLATEFEE
1003	54325	35	04-MAR-20	09-MAR-20	30
1003	61369	20	06-MAR-20	09-MAR-20	10
1003	61388	0	06-MAR-20	09-MAR-20	10
1004	44392	35	05-MAR-20	07-MAR-20	30
1004	34367	35	05-MAR-20	07-MAR-20	30
1004	34341	20	07-MAR-20	07-MAR-20	10
1005	34342	20	07-MAR-20	05-MAR-20	10
1005	44397	35	05-MAR-20	05-MAR-20	30
1006	34366	35	05-MAR-20	04-MAR-20	30
1006	61367	20	07-MAR-20		10
1007	34368	35	05-MAR-20		30
1008	34369	35	05-MAR-20	05-MAR-20	30
1009	54324	35	05-MAR-20		30
1001	34366	35	04-MAR-20	02-MAR-20	30

TABLE P9.4 **Video table**

VID_NUM	VID_INDATE	MOVIE_NUM
54321	18-JUN-19	1234
54324	18-JUN-19	1234
54325	18-JUN-19	1234
34341	22-JAN-18	1235
34342	22-JAN-18	1235
34366	02-MAR-20	1236
34367	02-MAR-20	1236
34368	02-MAR-20	1236
34369	02-MAR-20	1236
44392	21-OCT-19	1237
44397	21-OCT-19	1237
59237	14-FEB-20	1237
61388	25-JAN-18	1239
61353	28-JAN-17	1245
61354	28-JAN-17	1245
61367	30-JUL-19	1246
61369	30-JUL-19	1246

TABLE P9.5 **Movie table**

MOVIE_NUM	MOVIE_TITLE	MOVIE_YEAR	MOVIE_COST	MOVIE_GENRE	PRICE_CODE
1234	The Cesar Family Christmas	2016	39.95	FAMILY	2
1235	Smokey Mountain Wildlife	2013	59.95	ACTION	1
1236	Richard Goodhope	2017	59.95	DRAMA	2
1237	Beatnik Fever	2016	29.95	COMEDY	2
1238	Constant Companion	2017	89.95	DRAMA	
1239	Where Hope Dies	2007	25.49	DRAMA	3
1245	Time to Burn	2014	45.49	ACTION	1
1246	What He Doesn't Know	2015	58.29	COMEDY	1

TABLE P9.6 **Price table**

PRICE_CODE	PRICE_DESCRIPTION	PRICE_RENTFEE	PRICE_DAILYLATEFEE
1	Standard	20	10
2	New Release	35	30
3	Discount	15	10
4	Weekly Special	10	05

For Questions 45–59, use the tables that were created in Problem 43 and the data that was loaded into those tables in Problem 44.

45 Write the SQL command to change the movie year for movie number 1245 to 2014.

46 Write the SQL command to change the price code for all action movies to price code 3.

47 Write a single SQL command to increase all price rental fee values in the PRICE table by ZAR7.00.

48 Alter the DETAILRENTAL table to include a derived attribute named DETAIL_DAYS-LATE to store integers of up to three digits. The attribute should accept null values.

49 Update the DETAILRENTAL table to set the values in DETAIL_RETURNDATE to include a time component. Make each entry match the values shown in the following table.

TABLE P9.7 Updates for the DetailRental table

RENT_NUM	VID_NUM	DETAIL_RETURNDATE
1001	34342	02-MAR-20 10:00am
1001	61353	03-MAR-20 11:30am
1002	59237	04-MAR-20 03:30pm
1003	54325	09-MAR-20 04:00pm
1003	61369	09-MAR-20 04:00pm
1003	61388	09-MAR-20 04:00pm
1004	44392	07-MAR-20 09:00am
1004	34367	07-MAR-20 09:00am
1004	34341	07-MAR-20 09:00am
1005	34342	05-MAR-20 12:30pm
1005	44397	05-MAR-20 12:30pm
1006	34366	04-MAR-20 10:15pm
1006	61367	
1007	34368	
1008	34369	05-MAR-20 09:30pm
1009	54324	
1001	34366	02-MAR-20 10:00am

9

50 Alter the VIDEO table to include an attribute named VID_STATUS to store character data up to four characters long. The attribute should have a constraint to enforce the domain ('IN', 'OUT' and 'LOST') and have a default value of 'IN'.

51 Update the VID_STATUS attribute of the VIDEO table using a subquery to set the VID_STATUS to 'OUT' for all videos that have a null value in the DETAIL_RETURNDATE attribute of the DETAILRENTAL table.

52 Alter the PRICE table to include an attribute named PRICE_RENTDAYS to store integers of up to two digits. The attribute should not accept null values, and it should have a default value of 3.

53 Update the PRICE table to place the values shown in the following table in the PRICE_RENTDAYS attribute.

TABLE P9.8 Updates for the price table

PRICE_CODE	PRICE_RENTDAYS
1	50
2	30
3	50
4	70

54 Create a trigger named trg_late_return that will write the correct value to DETAIL_ DAYSLATE in the DETAILRENTAL table whenever a video is returned. The trigger should execute as a BEFORE trigger when the DETAIL_RETURNDATE or DETAIL_DUEDATE attributes are updated. The trigger should satisfy the following conditions:

- If the return date is null, then the days late should also be null.
- If the return date is not null, then the days late should determine if the video is returned late.
- If the return date is noon of the day after the due date or earlier, then the video is not considered late, and the days late should have a value of zero (0).
- If the return date is past noon of the day after the due date, then the video is considered late, so the number of days late must be calculated and stored.

55 Create a trigger named trg_mem_balance that will maintain the correct value in the membership balance in the MEMBERSHIP table when videos are returned late. The trigger should execute as an AFTER trigger when the due date or return date attributes are updated in the DETAILRENTAL table. The trigger should satisfy the following conditions:

- Calculate the value of the late fee prior to the update that triggered this execution of the trigger. The value of the late fee is the days late multiplied by the daily late fee. If the previous value of the late fee was null, then treat it as zero (0).
- Calculate the value of the late fee after the update that triggered this execution of the trigger. If the value of the late fee is now null, then treat it as zero (0).
- Subtract the prior value of the late fee from the current value of the late fee to determine the change in late fee for this video rental.
- If the amount calculated in Part c is not zero (0), then update the membership balance by the amount calculated for the membership associated with this rental.

56 Create a sequence named rent_num_seq to start with 1100 and increment by 1. Do not cache any values.

57 Create a stored procedure named prc_new_rental to insert new rows in the RENTAL table. The procedure should satisfy the following conditions:

- The membership number will be provided as a parameter.
- Use a Count() function to verify that the membership number exists in the MEMBERSHIP table. If it does not exist, then a message should be displayed that the membership does not exist and no data should be written to the database.
- If the membership does exist, then retrieve the membership balance and display a message that the balance amount is the previous balance. (For example, if the membership has a balance of R5.00, then display 'Previous balance: R5.00'.)
- Insert a new row in the rental table using the rent_num_seq sequence created above to generate the value for RENT_NUM, the current system date for the RENT_DATE value, and the membership number provided as the value for MEM_NUM.

58 Create a stored procedure named prc_new_detail to insert new rows in the DETAILRENTAL table. The procedure should satisfy the following requirements:

- The video number will be provided as a parameter.
- Verify that the video number exists in the VIDEO table. If it does not exist, then display a message that the video does not exist, and do not write any data to the database.

- If the video number does exist, then verify that the VID_STATUS for the video is 'IN'. If the status is not 'IN', then display a message that the video's return must be entered before it can be rented again, and do not write any data to the database.
- If the status is 'IN', then retrieve the values of the video's PRICE_RENTFEE, PRICE_DAILYLATEFEE, and PRICE_RENTDAYS from the PRICE table.
- Calculate the due date for the video rental by adding the number of days in PRICE_RENTDAYS to 11:59:59PM (hours:minutes:seconds) in the current system date.
- Insert a new row in the DETAILRENTAL table using the previous value returned by RENT_NUM_SEQ as the RENT_NUM, the video number provided in the parameter as the VID_NUM, the PRICE_RENTFEE as the value for DETAIL_FEE, the due date calculated above for the DETAIL_DUEDATE, PRICE_DAILYLATEFEE as the value for DETAIL_DAILYLATEFEE, and null for the DETAIL_RETURNDATE.

59 Create a stored procedure named prc_return_video to enter data about the return of videos that have been rented. The procedure should satisfy the following requirements:

- The video number will be provided as a parameter.
- Verify that the video number exists in the VIDEO table. If it does not exist, display a message that the video number provided was not found and do not write any data to the database.
- If the video number does exist, then use a Count() function to ensure that the video has only one record in DETAILRENTAL for which it does not have a return date. If more than one row in DETAILRENTAL indicates that the video is rented but not returned, display an error message that the video has multiple outstanding rentals and do not write any data to the database.
- If the video does not have any outstanding rentals, then update the video status to 'IN' for the video in the VIDEO table, and display a message that the video had no outstanding rentals but is now available for rental. If the video has only one outstanding rental, then update the return date to the current system date, and update the video status to 'IN' for that video in the VIDEO table. Then display a message that the video was successfully returned.

Part IV

DATABASE DESIGN

BUSINESS VIGNETTE

EM-DAT: THE INTERNATIONAL DISASTER DATABASE FOR DISASTER PREPAREDNESS

In 1998, the first emergency events database known as EM-DAT was set up by the WHO Collaborating Centre for Research on the Epidemiology of Disasters (CRED) with support from the Belgian Government. The purpose of the database was to aid in decision making for 'disaster preparedness, as well as provide an objective base for vulnerability assessment and priority setting'[1]. During the last few years EM-DAT has become the main global reference database.

EM-DAT stores information on over 22 000 disasters that have occurred across the world from 1900 to the present day. Data is collected from many sources such as the United Nations, governments and the International Red Cross. The data is of various quality so is constantly checked for inconsistencies, data redundancy and incompleteness. Each natural disaster is recorded using a unique disaster number identifier, the disaster type, subtypes, associated disasters, start and end dates, and location. Disasters are classified into 15 types of natural disasters (and more than 30 subtypes) and technological disasters which cover 15 disaster types. This now means that if a natural disaster affects a number of countries all the data that are collected from each country can be recorded under one unique reference number. For example, the 2004 tsunami in South East Asia affected 13 different countries but is recorded as one single event.

From the database, disaster-related economic damage estimates can be obtained and also details of international aid contributions for specific disasters. Each year EM-DAT aids CRED in conducting a review of disaster events throughout the year, e.g., 'In 2018, there were 281 climate-related and geophysical events recorded in the EM-DAT with 10 733 deaths, and over 60 million people affected across *the* world'.[2] Data analytics is used to produce summary tables of people in different geographical locations who have been affected by specific disaster types. The 2018

1 Information about EM-DAT is available: www.emdat.be/database

2 2018 Review Of Disaster Events, Centre for Research on the Epidemiology of Disasters, 2019.

review concludes that in 2018 the death toll was lower than in previous years, attributing this to better disaster management and living standards. However, the report acknowledges that there is a need to ensure that complete and consistent data collection should be a focus.

The EM-DAT website provides statistics of the occurrences and effects of global natural disasters which are then used to aid in the development of disaster reduction measures.[3] The information allows vulnerable populations to be identified and provides a tool for governments to use in order to determine the funding required for disaster planning. The intention is to mitigate the loss of human life through effective measures and education in reducing risk. Margareta Wahlström, United Nations Special Representative of the Secretary-General for Disaster Risk Reduction states that 'Access to information is critical to successful disaster risk management. You cannot manage what you cannot measure'.

The UN Office for Disaster Risk Reduction (UNISDR), currently is implementing the Sendai Framework for Disaster Risk Reduction 2015–2030 which adopts a people-centred approach to reducing disaster risk reduction. The four action priorities are: 'Priority 1. Understanding disaster risk . . . Priority 2. Strengthening disaster risk governance to manage disaster risk . . . Priority 3. Investing in disaster risk reduction for resilience, and Priority 4. Enhancing disaster preparedness for effective response and to 'Build Back Better in recovery, rehabilitation and reconstruction'.[4] Central to completing these actions is data. Hence, it has never been more important to ensure data is of good quality, is recorded accurately and from trustworthy sources to enable its true worth to be utilised effectively.

3 International Strategy for Disaster Reduction. Available: www.unisdr.org/disaster-statistics/introduction.htm

4 Sendai Framework for Disaster Risk Reduction. Available: www.unisdr.org/we/coordinate/sendai-framework

CHAPTER 10

Database Development Process

IN THIS CHAPTER, YOU WILL LEARN:

- That successful database design must reflect the information system of which the database is a part
- That successful information systems are developed within a framework known as the Systems Development Life Cycle (SDLC)
- That, within the information system, the most successful databases are subject to frequent evaluation and revision within a framework known as the Database Life Cycle (DBLC)
- How to conduct evaluation and revision within the SDLC and DBLC frameworks
- About database design strategies: top-down vs bottom-up design and centralised vs decentralised design
- Common threats to the security of the data and which security measures could be put in place
- The importance of database administration in an organisation
- The technical and managerial roles of the database administrator (DBA)

PREVIEW

Databases are a part of a larger picture called an *information system*. Database designs that fail to recognise that the database is part of this larger whole are not likely to be successful. That is, database designers must recognise that the database is a critical means to an end rather than an end in itself. Managers want the database to serve their management needs, but too many databases seem to require that managers alter their routines to fit the database requirements.

Information systems don't just happen; they are the product of a carefully staged development process. Systems analysis is used to determine the need for an information system and to establish its limits. Within systems analysis, the actual information system is created through a process known as systems development.

The creation and evolution of information systems follows an iterative pattern called the *Systems Development Life Cycle*, a continuous process of creation, maintenance, enhancement and replacement of the information system. A similar cycle applies to databases. The database is created, maintained and enhanced, and eventually replaced.

This chapter also briefly explores two very important issues: database administration and data security. Data is a corporate resource and is critical to the organisation. Therefore, a breach in data security could have serious implications. You will learn which threats can affect the security of the data and about measures that can be adopted to protect the data. Database administration must be fully understood and accepted within an organisation before a sound data administration strategy can be implemented. In this chapter, you will learn about important data management issues by looking at the managerial and technical roles of the database administrator (DBA).

10.1 THE INFORMATION SYSTEM

A *database* is a carefully designed and constructed repository of facts. The fact repository is a part of a larger whole, known as an information system. An **information system** provides for data collection, storage and retrieval. It also facilitates the transformation of data into information and the management of both data and information. Thus, a complete information system is composed of people, hardware, software, the database(s), application programs and procedures. **Systems analysis** is the process that establishes the need for and the scope of an information system. The process of creating an information system is known as **systems development**.

> **NOTE**
>
> This chapter is not meant to cover all aspects of systems analysis and development – these are usually covered in a separate course or book. However, this chapter should help you develop a better understanding of database design, implementation and management issues that are affected by the information system in which the database is a critical component.

Within the framework of systems development, applications transform data into the information that forms the basis of decision making. Applications usually produce formal reports, tabulations and graphic displays designed to produce insight. Figure 10.1 illustrates that every application is composed of two parts: the data and the code (program instructions) by which the data are transformed into information. Data and code work together to represent real-world business functions and activities. At any given moment, physically stored data represent a 'snapshot' of the business. But the picture is not complete without an understanding of the business activities that are represented by the code.

10

FIGURE 10.1 Generating information for decision making

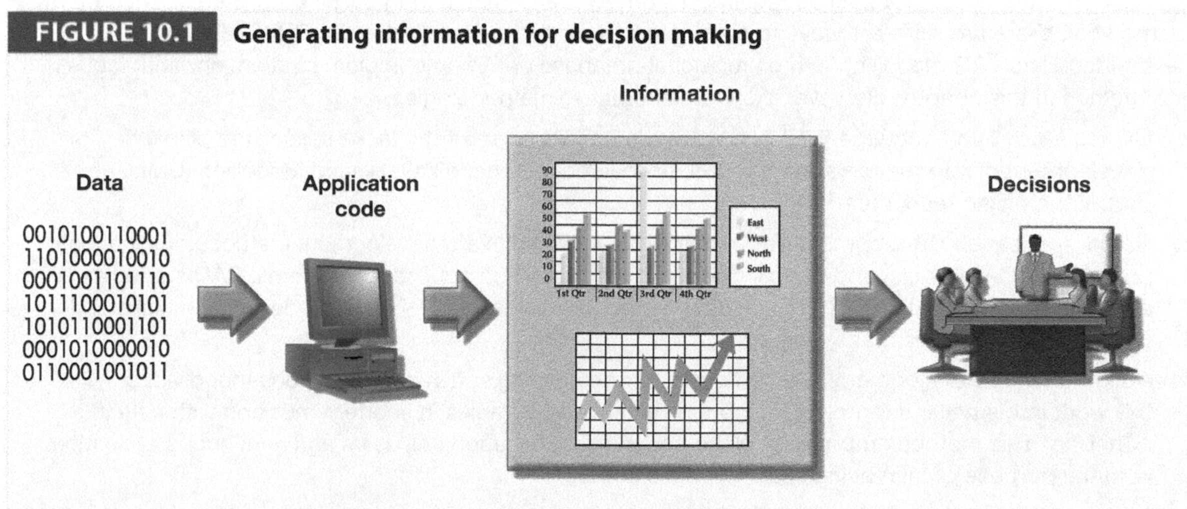

The performance of an information system depends on a triad of factors:

- Database design and implementation.
- Application design and implementation.
- Administrative procedures.

Although this book emphasises the database design and implementation segment of the triad (arguably most important), failure to address the other two segments will likely yield a poorly functioning information system. Creating a sound information system is hard work: systems analysis and development require much planning to ensure that all of the activities interface with one another, that they complement one another, and that they are completed on time.

In a broad sense, the term **database development** describes the process of database design and implementation. The primary objective in database design is to create complete, normalised, nonredundant (to the extent possible) and fully integrated conceptual, logical and physical database models. The implementation phase includes creating the database storage structure, loading data into the database and providing for data management.

To make the procedures discussed in this chapter broadly applicable, the chapter focuses on the elements that are common to all information systems. Most of the processes and procedures described in this chapter do not depend on the size, type or complexity of the database being implemented. For example, you must plan, analyse and design any size or type of database. However, the procedures used to design a small database, such as one for a local shoe shop, do not precisely scale up to the procedures needed to design a database for a large corporation or even a segment of such a corporation. To use an analogy, building a small house requires a blueprint, just as building Moses Mabhida stadium does, but the stadium requires more complex and far-ranging planning, analysis and design than the house.

The next sections trace the overall systems development life cycle and the related database life cycle. Once you are familiar with those processes and procedures, you will learn about different general approaches to database design, such as top-down vs bottom-up and centralised vs decentralised design.

NOTE

The Systems Development Life Cycle (SDLC) is a general framework through which you can track and come to understand the activities required to develop and maintain information systems. Within that framework, there are different ways to complete various tasks specified in the SDLC. For example, this text's focus is on ER modelling and on relational database design and implementation, and that focus is maintained in this chapter. However, there are alternative methodologies:

- Unified Modelling Language (UML) provides the tools to support the tasks associated with the development of information systems. UML is covered in Appendix G, Unified Modelling (UML), as part of the online resources.
- Rapid Application Development (RAD)[5] is an interactive software development methodology that uses prototypes, CASE tools, and flexible management to develop application systems. RAD started as an alternative to traditional structured development, which suffered from long deliverable times and unfulfilled requirements.
- Agile Software Development[6] is a framework for developing software applications that divides the work into smaller subprojects to obtain valuable deliverables in shorter times and with better cohesion. This method emphasises close communication among all users and continuous evaluation with the purpose of increasing customer satisfaction.

Although the development methodologies may change, the basic framework within which they are used does not change.

---

5 See James Martin, *Rapid Application Development*. Prentice-Hall, Macmillan College Division, 1991.
6 For more information about Agile Software Development, go to www.agilealliance.org.

10.2 THE SYSTEMS DEVELOPMENT LIFE CYCLE (SDLC)

The **Systems Development Life Cycle** (**SDLC**) traces the history (life cycle) of an information system. Perhaps more important to the system designer, the SDLC provides the big picture within which the database design and application development can be mapped out and evaluated.

FIGURE 10.2 The Systems Development Life Cycle (SDLC)

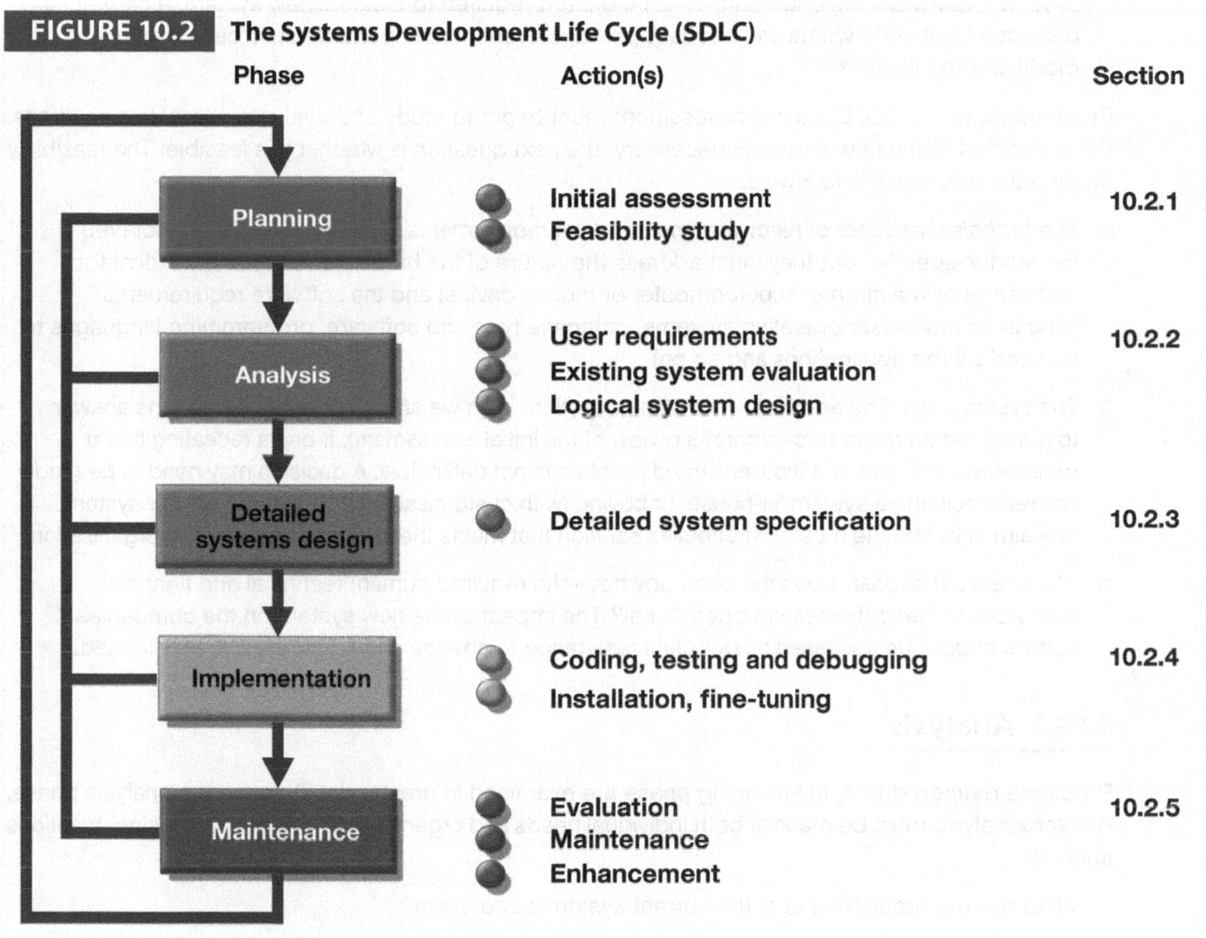

As illustrated in Figure 10.2, the traditional SDLC is divided into five phases: planning, analysis, detailed systems design, implementation and maintenance. The SDLC is an iterative rather than a sequential process. For example, the details of the feasibility study might help refine the initial assessment, and the details discovered during the user requirements portion of the SDLC might help refine the feasibility study.

Because the Database Life Cycle (DBLC) fits into and resembles the SDLC, a brief description of the SDLC is in order.

10.2.1 Planning

The SDLC planning phase yields a general overview of the company and its objectives. An initial assessment of the information-flow-and-extent requirements must be made during this discovery portion of the SDLC. Such an assessment should answer some important questions:

- *Should the existing system be continued?* If the information generator does its job well, there is no point in modifying or replacing it. To quote an old saying, 'If it's not broken, don't fix it'.

- *Should the existing system be modified?* If the initial assessment indicates deficiencies in the extent and flow of the information, minor (or even major) modifications may be in order. When considering modifications, the participants in the initial assessment must keep in mind the distinction between wants and needs.
- *Should the existing system be replaced?* The initial assessment might indicate that the current system's flaws are beyond fixing. Given the effort required to create a new system, a careful distinction between wants and needs is perhaps even more important in this case than it is in modifying the system.

Participants in the SDLC's initial assessment must begin to study and evaluate alternative solutions. If it is decided that a new system is necessary, the next question is whether it is feasible. The feasibility study must address the following:

- *The technical aspects of hardware and software requirements.* The decisions might not (yet) be vendor-specific, but they must address the nature of the hardware requirements (desktop, mid-range or mainframe, supercomputer or mobile device) and the software requirements (single- or multi-user operating systems, database type and software, programming languages to be used by the applications and so on).
- *The system cost.* The admittedly mundane question, 'Can we afford it?' is crucial (and the answer to that question might force a careful review of the initial assessment). It bears repeating that a million-rand solution to a thousand-rand problem is not defensible. A decision may need to be made between building a system 'in-house' or buying (with customisation) a third-party vendor system. The aim is to find the most cost effective solution that meets the business needs of the organisation.
- *The operational cost.* Does the company have the required human, technical and financial resources to keep the system operational? The impact of the new system on the companies culture should be assessed as people's resistance to change should not be underestimated.

10.2.2 Analysis

Problems defined during the planning phase are examined in greater detail during the analysis phase. A macroanalysis must be made of both individual needs and organisational needs, addressing questions such as:

- What are the requirements of the current system's end users?
- Do those requirements fit into the overall information requirements?

The analysis phase of the SDLC is, in effect, a thorough *audit* of user requirements.

The existing hardware and software systems are also studied during the analysis phase. The result of analysis should be a better understanding of the system's functional areas, actual and potential problems and opportunities.

End users and the system designer(s) must work together to identify processes and to uncover potential problem areas. Such cooperation is vital to defining the appropriate performance objectives by which the new system can be judged.

Along with a study of user requirements and the existing systems, the analysis phase also includes the creation of a logical systems design. The logical design must specify the appropriate conceptual data model, inputs, processes and expected output requirements.

When creating a logical design, the designer might use tools such as data flow diagrams (DFDs), hierarchical input process output (HIPO) diagrams and entity relationship (ER) diagrams. The database design's data-modelling activities take place at this point to discover and describe all entities and their attributes and the relationships among the entities within the database.

Defining the logical system also yields functional descriptions of the system's components (modules) for each process within the database environment. All data transformations (processes) are described and documented using such systems analysis tools as DFDs. The conceptual data model is validated against those processes.

10.2.3 Detailed Systems Design

In the detailed systems design phase, the designer completes the design of the system's processes. The design includes all necessary technical specifications for the screens, menus, reports and other devices that might be used to help make the system a more efficient information generator. The steps are laid out for conversion from the old to the new system. Training principles and methodologies are also planned and must be submitted for management's approval.

NOTE

Because attention has been focused on the details of the systems design process, this book has not until this point explicitly recognised the fact that management's approval is needed at all stages of the process. Such approval is needed because a GO decision requires funding. There are many GO/NO GO decision points along the way to a completed systems design!

10.2.4 Implementation

During the implementation phase, the hardware, DBMS software and application programs are installed and the database design is implemented. During the initial stages of the implementation phase, the system enters into a cycle of coding, testing and debugging until it is ready to be delivered. The actual database is created, and the system is customised by the creation of tables and views, user authorisations and so on.

The database contents may be loaded interactively or in batch mode, using a variety of methods and devices:

- Customised user programs.
- Database interface programs.
- Conversion programs that import the data from a different file structure, using batch programs, a database utility or both.

The system is subjected to exhaustive testing until it is ready for use. Traditionally, the implementation and testing of a new system took 50 to 60 per cent of the total development time. However, the advent of sophisticated application generators and debugging tools has substantially decreased coding and testing time. After testing is concluded, the final documentation is reviewed and printed, and end users are trained. The system is in full operation at the end of this phase but will be continuously evaluated and fine-tuned.

10.2.5 Maintenance

Almost as soon as the system is operational, end users begin to request changes in it. Those changes generate system maintenance activities, which can be grouped into three types:[7]

- *Corrective maintenance* in response to systems errors.
- *Adaptive maintenance* due to changes in the business environment.
- *Perfective maintenance* to enhance the system.

Because every request for structural change requires retracing the SDLC steps, the system is, in a sense, always at some stage of the SDLC.

Each system has a predetermined operational life span. The actual operational life span of a system depends on its perceived utility. There are several reasons for reducing the operational life of certain systems. Rapid technological change is one reason, especially for systems based on processing speed and expandability. Another common reason is the cost of maintaining a system.

If the system's maintenance cost is high, its value becomes suspect. **Computer-aided systems engineering** (**CASE**) technology, such as System Architect or Visio Professional, helps make it possible to produce better systems within a reasonable amount of time and at a reasonable cost. In addition, the more structured, better-documented and especially *standardised* implementation of CASE-produced applications tends to prolong the operational life of systems by making them easier and cheaper to update and maintain.

10.3 THE DATABASE LIFE CYCLE (DBLC)

10

Within the larger information system, the database, too, is subject to a life cycle. The **Database Life Cycle** (**DBLC**) contains six phases (Figure 10.3): database initial study, database design, implementation and loading, testing and evaluation, operation, and maintenance and evolution.

10.3.1 The Database Initial Study

If a designer has been called in, chances are the current system has failed to perform functions deemed vital by the company (you don't call the plumber unless the pipes leak). So, in addition to examining the current system's operation within the company, the designer must determine how and why the current system fails. That means spending a lot of time talking with (but mostly listening to) end users.

---

7 See E. Reed Doke and Neil E. Swanson, 'Software maintenance revisited: a product life cycle perspective', *Information Executive*, 4(1), Winter 1991, pp. 8–11. The date on this reference may cause you to consider it outdated, but it remains relevant today. Although the software environment changes with dizzying frequency, especially with respect to its interface, most of the underlying principles of software design, implementation and management have enjoyed remarkable longevity.

FIGURE 10.3 The Database Life Cycle (DBLC)

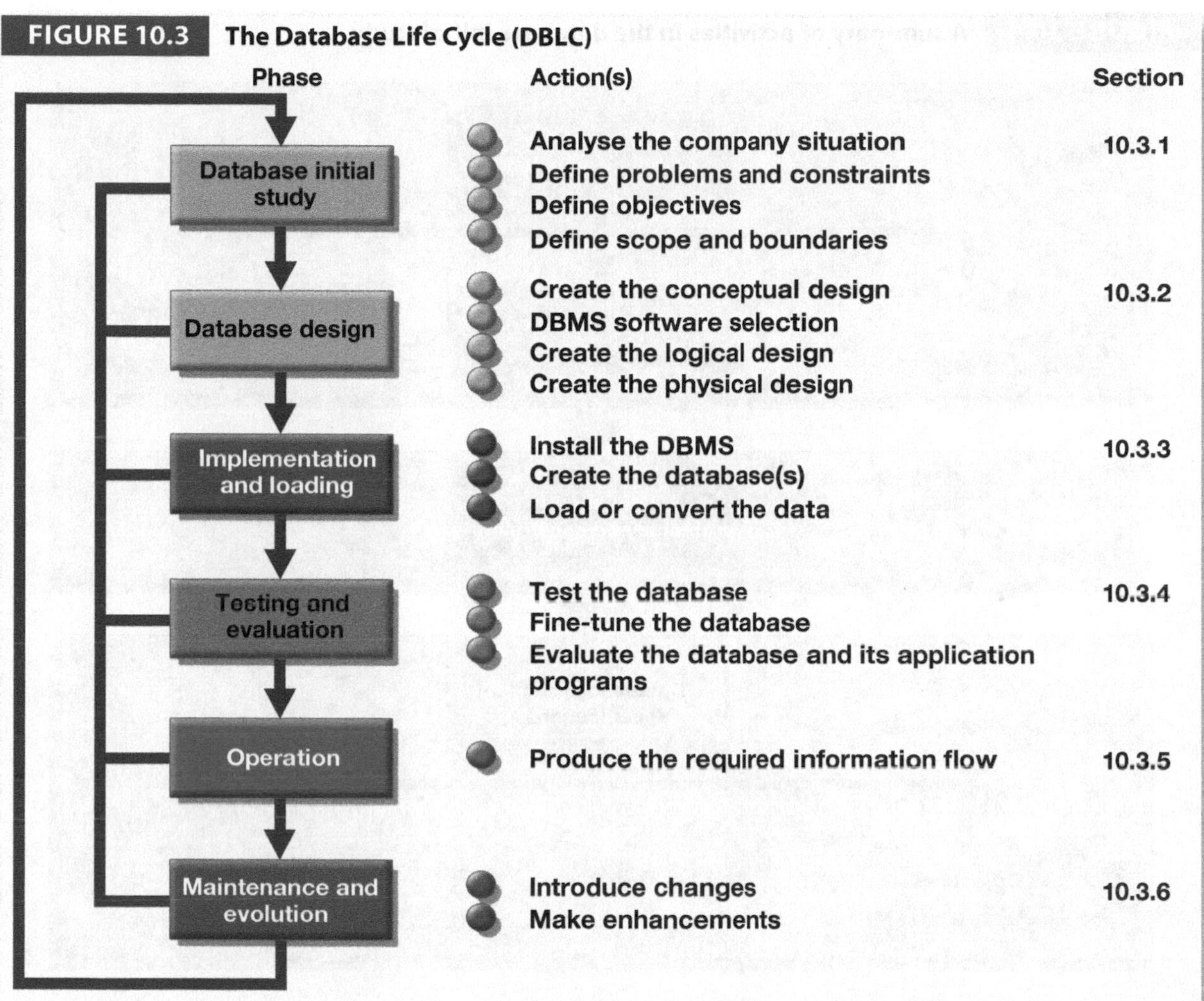

Although database design is a technical business, it is also people-orientated. Database designers must be excellent communicators, and they must have finely tuned interpersonal skills.

Depending on the complexity and scope of the database environment, the database designer might be a lone operator or part of a systems development team composed of a project leader, one or more senior systems analysts and one or more junior systems analysts. The word *designer* is used generically here to cover a wide range of design team compositions.

The overall purpose of the database initial study is to:

- Analyse the company situation.
- Define problems and constraints.
- Define objectives.
- Define scope and boundaries.

Figure 10.4 depicts the interactive and iterative processes required to complete the first phase of the DBLC successfully. As you examine Figure 10.4, note that the database initial study phase leads to the development of the database system objectives. Using Figure 10.4 as a discussion template, let's examine each of its components in greater detail.

FIGURE 10.4 A summary of activities in the database initial study

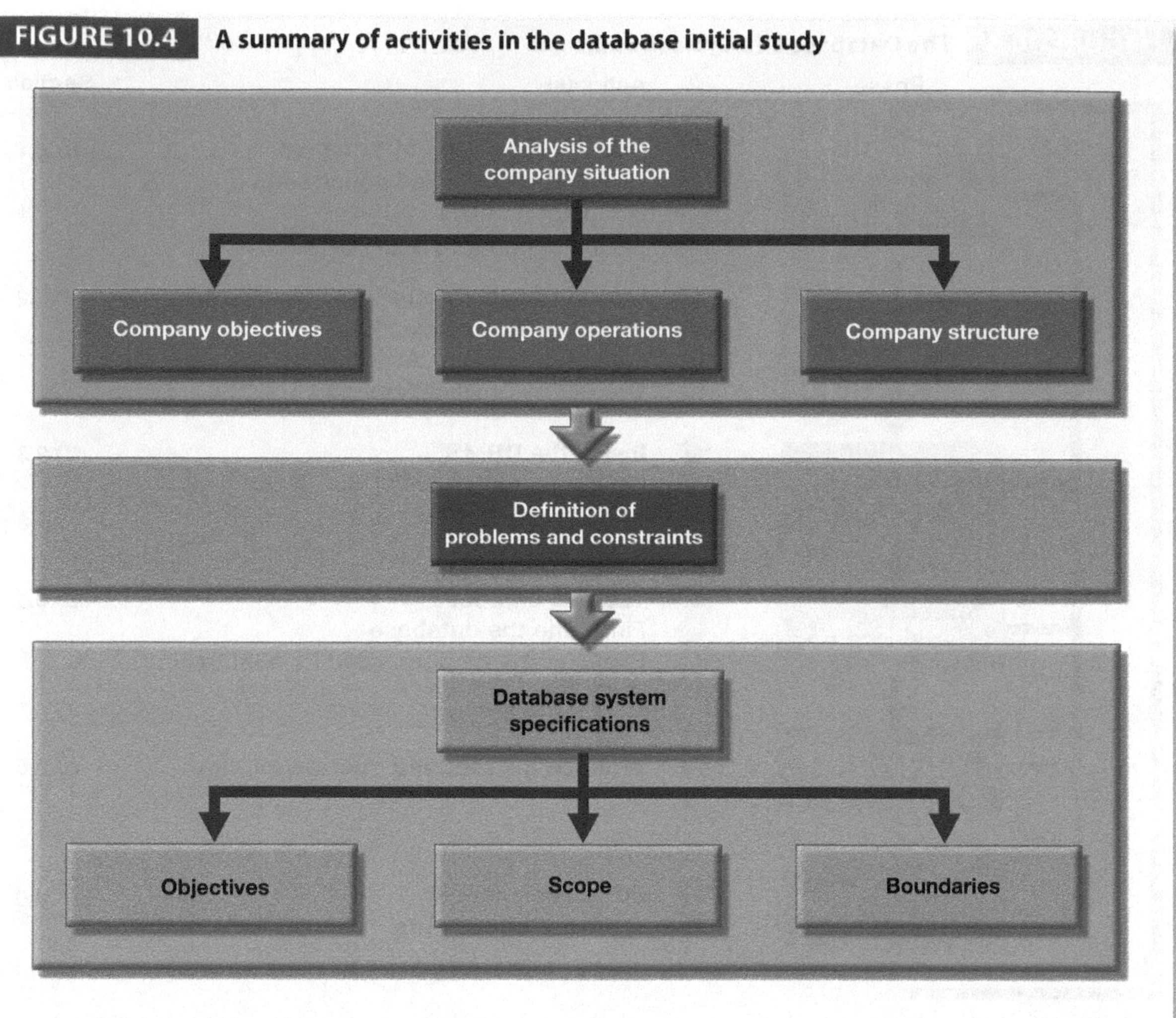

10

Analyse the Company Situation

The *company situation* describes the general conditions in which a company operates, its organisational structure and its mission. To analyse the company situation, the database designer must discover what the company's operational components are, how they function and how they interact.

These issues must be resolved:

- *What is the organisation's general operating environment, and what is its mission within that environment?* The design must satisfy the operational demands created by the organisation's mission. For example, a mail-order business is likely to have operational requirements involving its database that are quite different from those of a manufacturing business.

- *What is the organisation's structure?* Knowing who controls what and who reports to whom is quite useful when you are trying to define required information flows, specific report and query formats and so on.

Define Problems and Constraints

The designer has both formal and informal sources of information. If the company has existed for any length of time, it already has some kind of system in place (either manual or computer-based). How does the existing system function? What input does the system require? Which documents does the system generate? How is the system output used? By whom? Studying the paper trail can be very informative. Aside from the official version of the system's operation, there is also the more informal real version; the designer must be clever enough to see how these differ.

The problem definition process might initially appear to be unstructured. Company end users are often unable to describe precisely the larger scope of company operations or to identify the real problems encountered during company operations. Often the managerial view of a company's operation is different from that of the end users who perform the actual routine work.

Finding precise answers is important, especially concerning the operational relationships among business units. If a proposed system will solve the marketing department's problems but exacerbate those of the production department, not much progress will have been made. Using an analogy, suppose your home water bill is too high. You have determined the problem: the taps leak. The solution? You step outside and turn off the water supply to the house. Is that an adequate solution? Or would the replacement of the tap washers do a better job of solving the problem? You may find the leaky tap scenario simplistic, yet almost any experienced database designer can find similar instances of so-called database problem solving (admittedly more complicated and less obvious).

Even the most complete and accurate problem definition does not always lead to the perfect solution. The real world usually intrudes to limit the design of even the most elegant database by imposing constraints. Such constraints include time, budget, personnel, and more. If you must have a solution within a month and within a R20 000 budget, a solution that takes two years to develop at a cost of R800 000 is not a solution. The designer must learn to distinguish between what's perfect and what's possible.

NOTE

When trying to develop solutions, the database designer must look for the *source* of the problems. There are many cases of database systems that failed to satisfy the end users because they were designed to treat the *symptoms* of the problems rather than their source.

Define Objectives

A proposed database system must be designed to help solve at least the major problems identified during the problem discovery process. As the list of problems unfolds, several common sources are likely to be discovered.

Note that the initial study phase also yields proposed problem solutions. The designer's job is to make sure that the database system objectives, as seen by the designer, correspond to those envisioned by the end user(s). In any case, the database designer must begin to address the following questions:

- What is the proposed system's initial objective?
- Will the system interface with other existing or future systems in the company?
- Will the system share the data with other systems or users?

Define Scope and Boundaries

The designer must recognise the existence of two sets of limits: scope and boundaries. The system's **scope** defines the extent of the design according to operational requirements. Will the database design encompass the entire organisation, one or more departments within the organisation, or one or more functions of a single department? The designer must know the 'size of the field'. Knowing the database design scope helps in defining the required data structures, the type and number of entities, the physical size of the database and so on.

The proposed system is also subject to limits known as **boundaries**, which are external to the system. Has any designer ever been told, 'We have all the time in the world' or 'Use an unlimited budget and use as many people as needed to make the design come together'? Boundaries are also imposed by existing hardware and software. Ideally, the designer can choose the hardware and software that will best accomplish the system goals. In fact, software selection is an important aspect of the systems development life cycle. Unfortunately, in the real world, a system often must be designed around existing hardware. Thus, the scope and boundaries become the factors that force the design into a specific mould, and the designer's job is to design the best system possible within those constraints. Note that problem definitions and the objectives sometimes must be reshaped to meet the system scope and boundaries.

10.3.2 Database Design

The second phase focuses on the design of the database model that will support company operations and objectives. This is arguably the most critical DBLC phase: making sure that the final product meets user and system requirements. In the process of database design, you must concentrate on the data characteristics required to build the database model. At this point, there are two views of the data within the system: the business view of data as a source of information and the designer's view of the data structure, its access, and the activities required to transform the data into information. Figure 10.5 contrasts those views. Note that you can summarise the different views by looking at the terms *what* and *how*. Defining data is an integral part of the DBLC's second phase.

FIGURE 10.5 Two views of data: business manager and designer

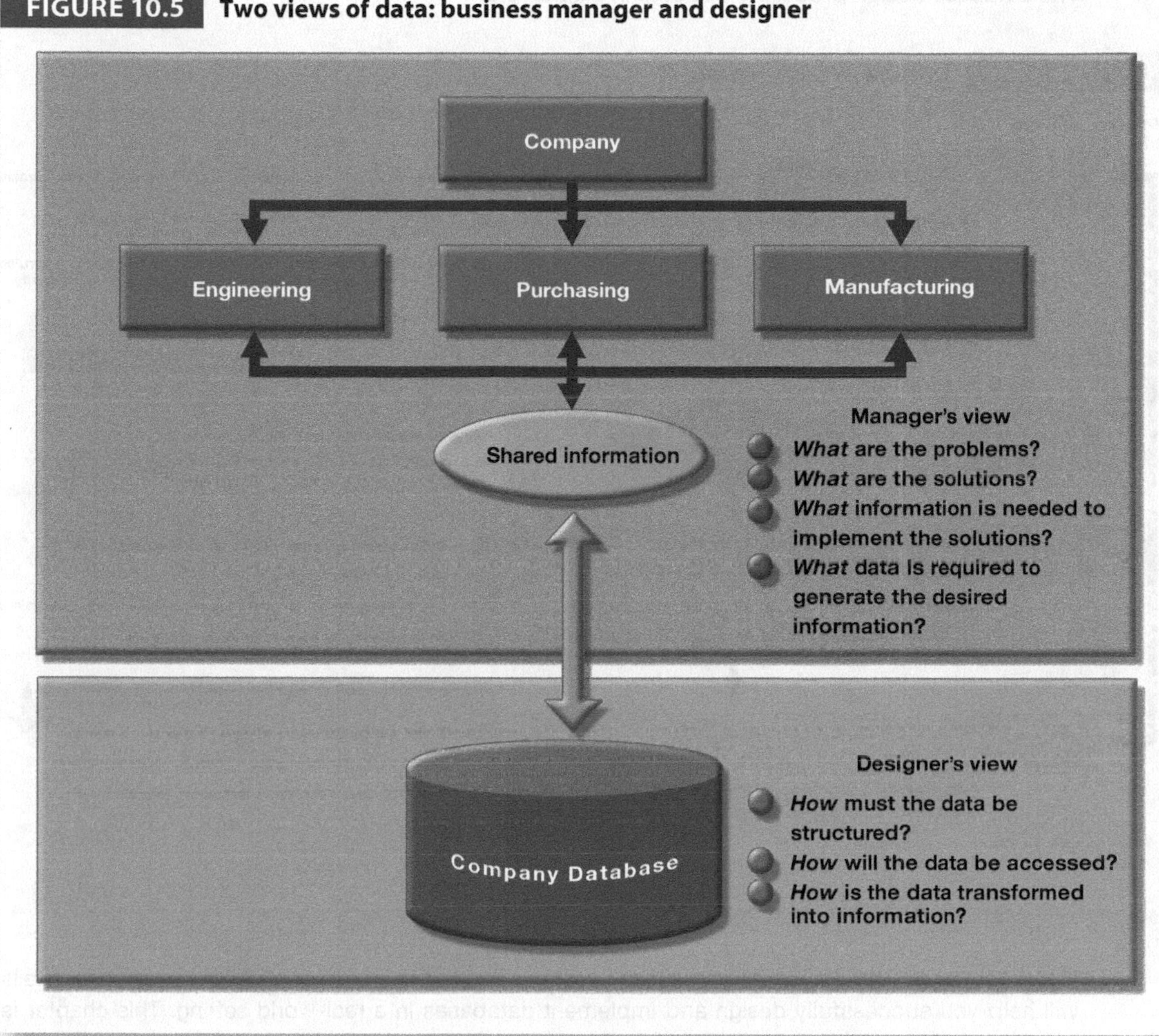

As you begin to examine the procedures required to complete the design phase in the DBLC, remember these points:

- The process of database design is loosely related to the analysis and design of a larger system. The data component is only one element of a larger information system.
- The systems analysts or systems programmers are in charge of designing the other system components. Their activities create the procedures that will help transform the data within the database into useful information.
- The database design does not constitute a sequential process. Rather, it is an iterative process that provides continuous feedback designed to trace previous steps.

The database design process is depicted in Figure 10.6.

FIGURE 10.6 Database design process

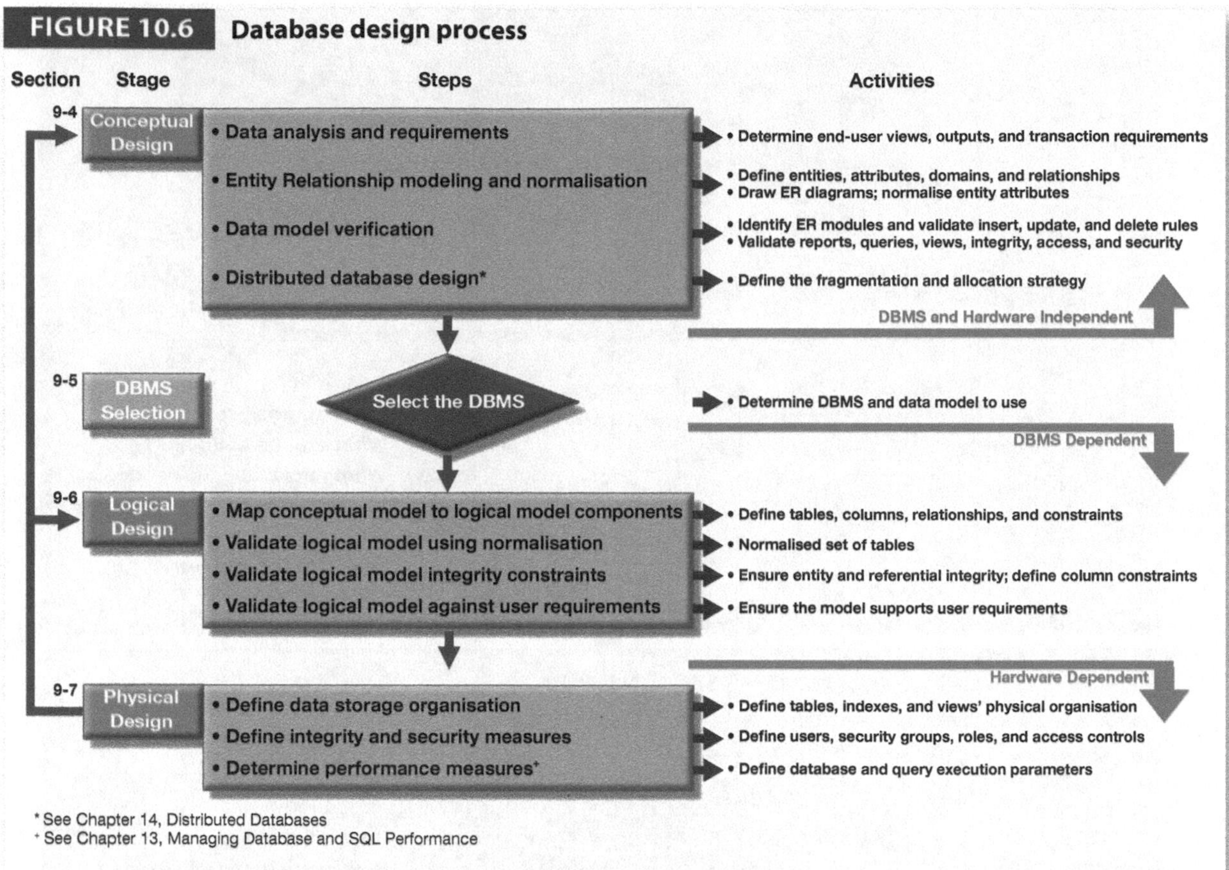

10

In this section you will learn briefly about each of the components in Figure 10.6. Knowing those details will help you successfully design and implement databases in a real-world setting. This chapter is only intended to provide an overview of these areas. In Chapter 11, Conceptual, Logical, and Physical Database Design, you will learn about each component in greater detail.

I. Conceptual Design

In the **conceptual design** stage, data modelling is used to create an abstract database structure that represents real-world objects in the most realistic way possible. The conceptual model must embody a clear understanding of the business and its functional areas. At this level of abstraction, the type of hardware and/or database model to be used might not yet have been identified. Therefore, the design must be software and hardware independent so the system can be set up within any hardware and software platform chosen later.

Keep in mind the following **minimal data rule**:

All that is needed is there, and all that is there is needed.

In other words, make sure that all data needed are in the model and that all data in the model are needed. All data elements required by the database transactions must be defined in the model, and all data elements defined in the model must be used by at least one database transaction.

However, as you apply the minimal data rule, avoid an excessive short-term bias. Focus not only on the immediate data needs of the business, but also on the future data needs. Thus, the database design must leave room for future modifications and additions, ensuring that the business's investment in information resources will endure.

As you examine Figure 10.6, note that conceptual design requires the following four steps:

- Data analysis and requirements
- Entity relationship modelling and normalisation
- Data model verification
- Distributed database design

Each of these steps will be explained in detail in Chapter 11, Conceptual, Logical, and Physical Database Design.

II. DBMS Software Selection

The selection of DBMS software is critical to the information system's smooth operation. Consequently, the advantages and disadvantages of the proposed DBMS software should be carefully studied. To avoid false expectations, the end user must be made aware of the limitations of both the DBMS and the database.

Although the factors affecting the purchasing decision vary from company to company, some of the most common are:

- *Cost*. Purchase, maintenance, operational, licence, installation, training and conversion costs.
- *DBMS features and tools*. Some database software includes a variety of tools that facilitate the application development task. For example, the availability of query by example (QBE), screen painters, report generators, application generators, data dictionaries, and so on, helps to create a more pleasant work environment for both the end user and the application programmer. Database administrator facilities, query facilities, ease of use, performance, security, concurrency control, transaction processing and third-party support also influence DBMS software selection.
- *Underlying model*. Hierarchical, network, relational, object/relational, or object-orientated.
- *Portability*. Across platforms, systems and languages.
- *DBMS hardware requirements*. Processor(s), RAM, disk space, and so on.

III. Logical Design

The second stage in the database design cycle is known as **logical design**. The aim of the logical design stage is to map the conceptual model into a logical model that can then be implemented on a relational DBMS. The logical design stage consists of the following phases:

1. Creating the logical data model.
2. Validating the logical data model using normalisation.
3. Assigning and validating integrity constraints.
4. Merging logical models constructed for different parts for the database.
5. Reviewing the logical data model with the user.

You will learn in detail about logical design in Chapter 11, Conceptual, Logical, and Physical Database Design.

The right to use the database is also specified during the logical design phase. Who will be allowed to use the tables, and which portion(s) of the table(s) will be available to which users? Within a relational framework, the answers to those questions require the definition of appropriate access rights and views.

The logical design translates the software-independent conceptual model into a software-dependent model by defining the appropriate domain definitions, the required tables and the necessary access restrictions. The stage is now set to define the physical requirements that allow the system to function within the selected hardware environment.

IV. Physical Design

Physical design is the process of selecting the data storage and data access characteristics of the database. The storage characteristics are a function of the types of devices supported by the hardware, the type of data access methods supported by the system, and the DBMS. Physical design affects not only the location of the data in the storage device(s), but also the performance of the system.

Physical database design can be broken down into a number of stages:

1. Analyse data volume and database usage.
2. Translate each relation identified in the logical data model into tables.
3. Determine a suitable file organisation.
4. Define indexes.
5. Define user views.
6. Estimate data storage requirements.
7. Determine database security for users.

You will learn about each of these stages in more detail in Chapter 11, Conceptual, Logical, and Physical Database Design.

10

Physical design is a very technical job, more typical of the client/server and mainframe world than of the desktop world. Yet even in the more complex mid-range and mainframe environments, modern database software has assumed much of the burden of the physical portion of the design and its implementation.

Online Content Physical design is particularly important in the older hierarchical and network models described in Appendices I and J, The Hierarchical Database Model and The Network Database Model, respectively, available on the online platform for this book. Relational databases are more insulated from physical details than the older hierarchical and network models.

In spite of the fact that relational models tend to hide the complexities of the computer's physical characteristics, the performance of relational databases is affected by physical-level characteristics. For example, performance can be affected by the characteristics of the storage media, such as seek time, sector and block (page) size, buffer pool size and number of disk platters and read/write heads. In addition, factors such as the creation of an index can have a considerable effect on the relational database's performance, that is, data access speed and efficiency.

Even the type of data request must be analysed carefully to determine the optimum access method for meeting the application requirements, establishing the data volume to be stored and estimating the performance. Some DBMSs automatically reserve the space required to store the database definition and the user's data in permanent storage devices. This ensures that the data are stored in sequentially adjacent locations, thereby reducing data access time and increasing system performance. (Database performance tuning is covered in detail in Chapter 13, Managing Database and SQL Performance.)

Physical design becomes more complex when data are distributed at different locations because the performance is affected by the communication media's throughput. Given such complexities, it is not surprising that designers favour database software that hides as many of the physical-level activities as possible.

The preceding sections have separated the discussions of logical and physical design activities. In fact, logical and physical design can be carried out in parallel, on a table-by-table (or file-by-file) basis. Logical and physical design can also be carried out in parallel when the designer is working with hierarchical and network models. Such parallel activities require the designer to have a thorough understanding of the software and hardware in order to take full advantage of both software and hardware characteristics.

10.3.3 Implementation and Loading

The output of the database design phase is a series of instructions detailing the creation of tables, attributes, domains, views, indexes, security constraints, and storage and performance guidelines. In this phase, you actually implement all these design specifications.

Install the DBMS

This step is required only when a new dedicated instance of the DBMS is necessary for the system. In many cases, the organisation will have made a particular DBMS the standard to leverage investments in the technology and the skills that employees have already developed. The DBMS may be installed on a new server or on existing servers. One current trend is called virtualisation. **Virtualisation** is a technique that creates logical representations of computing resources that are independent of the underlying physical computing resources. The technique is used in many areas of computing, such as the creation of virtual services, virtual storage and virtual private networks. In a database environment, database virtualisation refers to the installation of a new instance of the DBMS on a virtual server running on shared hardware. This is normally a task that involves system and network administrators to create appropriate user groups and services in the server configuration and networks routing. Another common trend is the use of cloud database services such as Microsoft SQL Database Service or Amazon Relational Database Services (RDS). This new generation of services allows users to create databases that can be easily managed, tested and scaled up as needed.

Create the Database(s)

In most modern relational DBMSs, a new database implementation requires the creation of special storage-related constructs to house the end-user tables. The constructs usually include the storage group (or file groups), the table spaces and the tables. Figure 10.7 shows that a storage group can contain more than one table space and that a table space can contain more than one table.

For example, the implementation of the logical design in IBM's DB2 would require the following:

1. The system administrator (SYSADM) would create the database storage group. This step is mandatory for such mainframes as DB2. Other DBMS software may create equivalent storage groups automatically when a database is created. (See Step 2.) Consult your DBMS documentation to see whether you need to create a storage group and, if so, what the command syntax must be.
2. The SYSADM creates the database within the storage group.
3. The SYSADM assigns the rights to use the database to a database administrator (DBA).
4. The DBA creates the table space(s) within the database.

5 The DBA creates the table(s) within the table space(s).

6 The DBA assigns access rights to the table spaces and to the tables within specified table spaces. Access rights may be limited to views rather than to whole tables. The creation of views is not required for database access in the relational environment, but views are desirable from a security standpoint. For example, using the following command, access rights to a table named PROFESSOR may be granted to the user Miriam Ledimo, whose identification code is MLEDIMO:

GRANT SELECT ON PROFESSOR TO USER MLEDIMO;

FIGURE 10.7 Physical organisation of a DB2 database environment

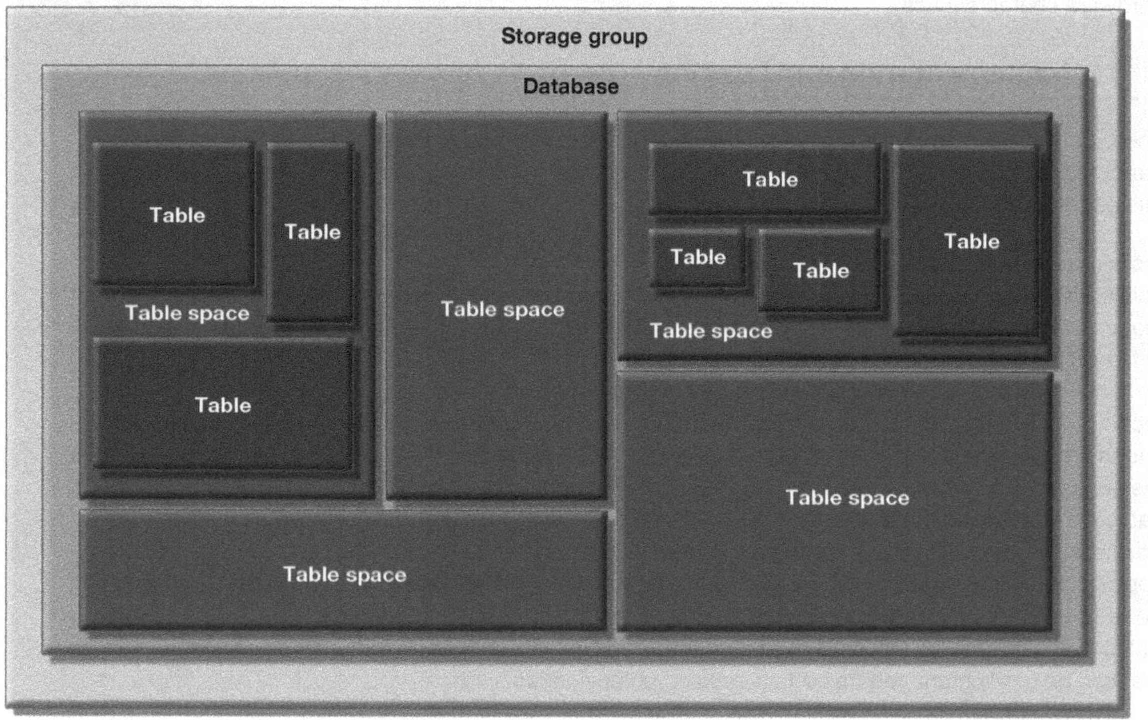

Load or Convert the Data

After the database has been created, the data must be loaded into the database tables. Typically, the data will have to be migrated from the prior version of the system. Often, data to be included in the system must be aggregated from multiple sources. In a best-case scenario, all of the data will be in a relational database so that it can be readily transferred to the new database. however, in some cases data may have to be imported from other relational databases, non-relational databases, flat files, legacy systems, or even manual paper-and-pencil systems. If the data format does not support direct importing into the new database, conversion programs may have to be created to reformat the data for importing. In a worst-case scenario, much of the data may have to be manually entered into the database. Once the data has been loaded, the DBA works with the application developers to test and evaluate the database.

Loading existing data into a cloud-based database service can sometimes be expensive. The reason for this is that most cloud services are priced based not only on the volume of data to be stored but also on the amount of data that travels over the network. In such cases, loading a 1 TB database could be a very expensive proposition. Therefore, system administrators must be very careful in reading and negotiating the terms of the cloud service contracts to ensure that there will be no 'hidden' costs.

10.3.4 Database Security

Data stored in the company database must be protected from access by unauthorised users. It does not take much imagination to predict the likely results when students have access to a student database or when employees have access to payroll data! Any misuse or damage to the data may have a serious impact on the organisation. Security is a major concern for any kind of computer system with the aim of protecting the data against intentional or accidental loss, destruction or misuse. This section will highlight only the basic ideas of security, so you should undertake further reading in this area. When developing the system it is important to establish the security goals. It is important to ask questions such as, what are we trying to protect the database from? What security related problems are we trying to prevent? The most common security goals relate to the integrity, confidentiality and the availability of data. Within database design, it is essential that security measures are developed to meet the security goals and in doing so protect the data from any kind of threat. Threats are any set of circumstances that have the potential to cause loss, misuse or harm to the system and/or its data. Threats can cause:

- The loss of the integrity of data through unauthorised modification. For example, a person gaining unauthorised access to a bank account and removing some money from the account.
- The loss of availability of the data. For example, a hacker causes the database system to stop being operational, which stops authorised users of the data from accessing it.
- The loss of confidentiality of the data (also referred to as the privacy of data). This could be caused by a person gaining access to private information such as a password or a bank account balance.

Threats can occur internally and externally to an organisation and are of various levels of severity. Some examples of threats and their effects on the security goals are:

- *Theft and fraud of data*. Activities such as these are likely to be perpetrated by humans, often by electronic means. An example would be a salesperson working for a large company who resigns and then takes your customer database with him or her so that he or she can start his or her own business. Both theft and fraud can occur both inside and outside the organisation and each have to be treated differently. Consider the case where an employee has legitimate access to the organisation's database system but he or she steals specific data that he or she is unauthorised to see. This internal breach is different from a person not connected to the organisation actually breaking in and stealing data.
- *Human error that causes accidental loss of data*. This is often caused by humans not following polices and procedures such as user authorisation. However, it is important for an organisation to ensure that it has excellent security policies and procedures in place to begin with. In addition, data can be lost by poor staff training. If employees do not know the procedures surrounding data security then it will be impossible for them to be followed.

- *Electronic infections*. There are four general categories of electronic infections:
  - *Viruses*. A virus is a malicious piece of software that is capable of copying itself and spreading across a network. As viruses are usually attached to a program or application, they cannot be 'caught' without human intervention, such as opening an email attachment or running an infected program.
  - *Email viruses*. This kind of virus attaches itself to email messages and replicates itself by automatically mailing itself to all people in the receiver's email address book.
  - *Worms* are also small pieces of software that replicate themselves using any form of telecommunication networks or hole in security. They are different from viruses in that they travel between systems without any human intervention and can replicate themselves very quickly through networks.
  - *Trojan horses*. The Trojan horse is a computer program that claims to perform one task or action. It remains dormant until run and then begins to do damage such as erase a hard disk.

The introduction of a virus to a computer network can result in both the loss of integrity of the data and the loss of availability of the system resulting in serious consequences to the business.

- The occurrence of natural disasters such as storms, fires or floods. These are unpredictable and not deliberate actions but would still result in the loss of integrity and availability of data. In addition, data could be corrupted due to power surges and hardware would become physically damaged.
- Unauthorised access and modification of data. The phrase often used for gaining unauthorised access is hacking. Hacking is usually defined as the act of illegally entering a computer system, and making unauthorised changes to the files and data contained within. Obtaining unauthorised access to a database may involve a person browsing unauthorised data to gain information that could be used to that person's benefit or against the organisation. Unauthorised modification could result in the data being changed or even deleted.
- Employee sabotage is concerned with deliberate acts of malice against the organisation. This would include not only any computer system but also the property, reputation and safety of a business and its employees. Unauthorised access and modification of data, physically damaging hardware and the theft of data are also covered by this threat.
- Poor database administration. This could be caused by the database administrator (DBA) not having enough knowledge through lack of training. One example is the DBA granting excessive privileges to a user who exceeds the requirements of his or her job within the organisation. The user then goes on to abuses these privileges. Another example would be that the DBA has only set up weak authentication schemes, which allow attackers to steal or obtain login information and then assume the identity of genuine database users.

The above list of threats is by no means exhaustive and a summary is provided in Figure 10.8. However it does highlight the need for an organisation to have a comprehensive data security plan. The plan should contain a number of data security measures to protect both the data and the hardware. The DBMS is only part of the computer system infrastructure within an organisation and will often rely on the security measures used in other parts of the system. You will now look at some of the common data security measures.

FIGURE 10.8 A non-exhaustive summary of security threats

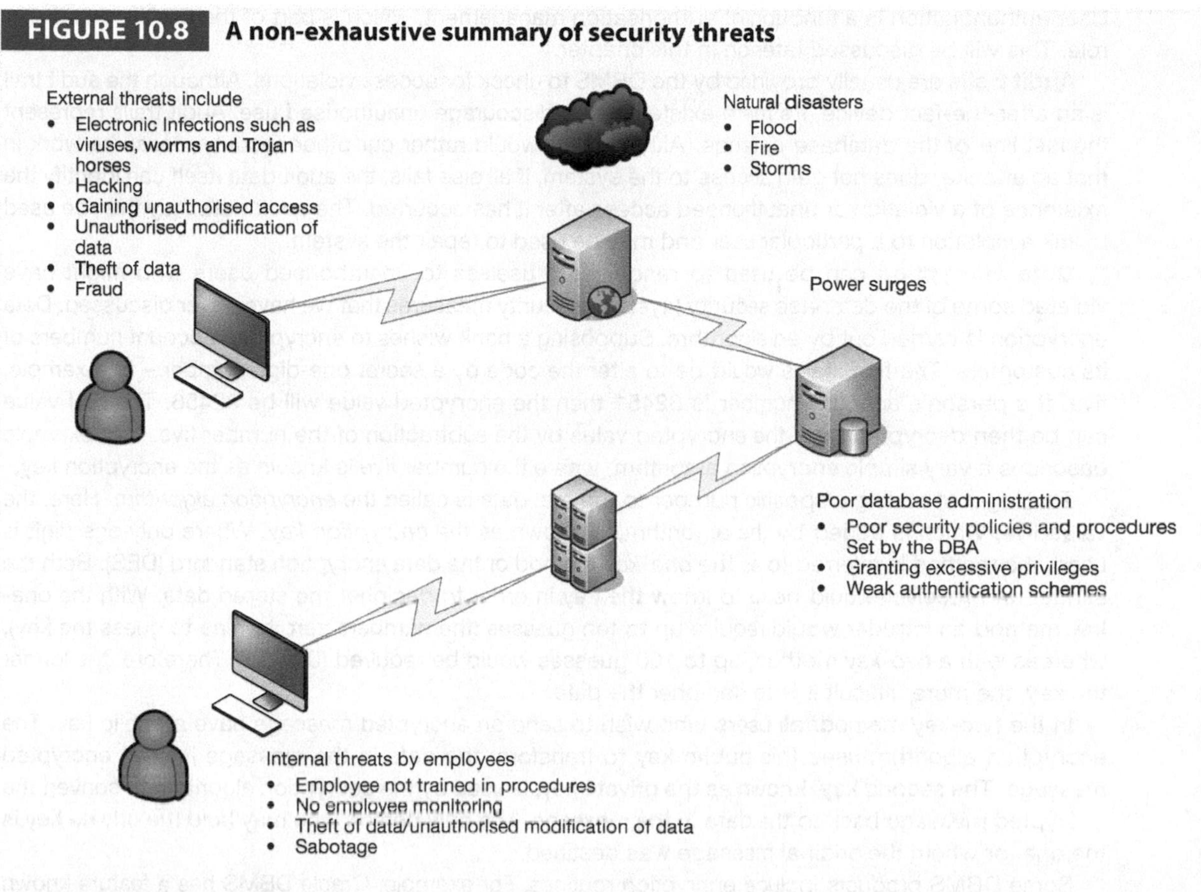
External threats include
• Electronic Infections such as viruses, worms and Trojan horses
• Hacking
• Gaining unauthorised access
• Unauthorised modification of data
• Theft of data
• Fraud
Natural disasters
• Flood
• Fire
• Storms
Power surges
Poor database administration
• Poor security policies and procedures Set by the DBA
• Granting excessive privileges
• Weak authentication schemes
Internal threats by employees
• Employee not trained in procedures
• No employee monitoring
• Theft of data/unauthorised modification of data
• Sabotage

Data Security Measures

Physical security allows only authorized personnel physical access to specific areas. Depending on the type of database implementation, however, establishing physical security may not always be practical. For example, a university student research database is not a likely candidate for physical security. The existence of large multiserver microcomputer networks often makes physical security impractical. In terms of guarding against the loss of data and hardware due to a natural disaster, the placement of the hardware in a building could be carefully considered. For example do not locate in the basement of a building due to the possibility of floods. Physical access to rooms can be controlled by push-button security controls, swipe cards or biometric systems. Recently, biometric systems have been seen to be one of the most secure and convenient authentication tools as they contain a digital imprint of an individual's physical and, in some cases, behavioural characteristics to recognise or authenticate a person's identity. The most common physical biometrics include fingerprints, a person's retina or iris and the use of hand geometry.

User authentication is a way of identifying the user and verifying that the user is allowed to access restricted data or applications. This can be achieved through the use of passwords and access rights:

- *Password security* allows the assignment of access rights to specific authorised users. Password security is usually enforced at logon time at the operating system level.
- *Access rights* can be established through the use of database software. The assignment of access rights may restrict operations (CREATE, UPDATE, DELETE and so on) on predetermined objects such as databases, tables, views, queries and reports.

User authentication is a function of authorisation management, which is part of the DBA's managerial role. This will be discussed later on in this chapter.

Audit trails are usually provided by the DBMS to check for access violations. Although the audit trail is an after-the-fact device, its mere existence can discourage unauthorised use. Audit trails represent the last line of the database defence. Although we would rather our other security measures work in that an attacker does not gain access to the system, if all else fails, the audit data itself can identify the existence of a violation or unauthorised access after it has occurred. The audit data may then be used to link a violation to a particular user and may be used to repair the system.

Data encryption can be used to render data useless to unauthorised users who might have violated some of the database security layers or security measures that we have so far discussed. Data encryption is carried out by an algorithm. Supposing a bank wishes to encrypt the account numbers of its customers. The first stage would be to alter the code by a secret one-digit number – for example, five. If a person's account number is 32451 then the encrypted value will be 32456. The real value can be then decrypted from the encrypted value by the subtraction of the number five. This example describes a very simple encryption algorithm, where the number five is known as the encryption key.

This logic of adding a specific number to the real data is called the *encryption algorithm*. Here, the value five, which is added by the algorithm, is known as the *encryption key*. Where only one digit is used, the method is referred to as the *one-key* method or the data encryption standard (DES). Both the sender and receiver would need to know the key in order to decipher the stored data. With the one-key method an intruder would require up to ten guesses (the numbers zero to nine to guess the key), whereas with a *two-key* method, up to 100 guesses would be required (0 to 99). Therefore, the longer the key, the more difficult it is to decipher the data.

In the two-key method, all users who wish to send an encrypted message have a public key. The encryption algorithm uses this public key to transform the data in the message into an encrypted message. The second key, known as the private key, is used by the decryption algorithm to convert the encrypted message back to the data in the message. The only person who may hold the private key is the one for whom the original message was destined.

Some DBMS products include encryption routines. For example, Oracle DBMS has a feature known as Transparent Data Encryption (TDE), which allows columns in a database table to be easily encrypted without the need for writing lots of complex code. When users insert data, the database transparently encrypts and stores it in the column. Similarly, when users select the column, the database automatically decrypts it.

NOTE

The most common example of encryption at work is Secure Electronic Transactions (SET). SET is an open protocol that was designed by a large consortium of companies (VISA, MasterCard, GTE, IBM, Microsoft, Netscape, SAIC, Terisa Systems and Verisign) interested in ensuring data privacy in all electronic commerce over the internet. SET ensures the authenticity of electronic transactions and provides a guarantee that customer's transactions are protected.

A combination of private and public key encryption is used in Secure Sockets Layer (SSL) technology on the internet. SSLs create a secure connection between a user and an external server, over which any amount of data can be sent securely. The use of SSL can be seen when a person purchases goods from an internet-based store. This is normally indicated by the use of 'https' instead of 'http' before the web address.

User-defined policies and procedures should be put in place by the organisation to ensure that employees know how implement the data security measures. Such policies and procedures can cover personal controls such as training employees in security aspects and monitoring employees to ensure that they are actually following the procedures themselves. The establishment of polices and procedures is also a responsibility of the DBA, and will be discussed in more detail later in this chapter.

Backup and recovery strategies should be in place in the event of a disaster occurring. The responsibility ultimately lies with the DBA to ensure the data within the database can always be fully recovered. Data backup and recovery in the context of disaster management will be discussed later in this chapter.

Antivirus software is used by organisations to search system hard drives and media devices for any known or potential viruses. Each time a virus is discovered, antivirus software vendors record the virus's unique signature and then incorporate it into their software database. The antivirus software will check, on a real-time basis, all messages entering an organisation's network from any external source to see if a known virus is trying to enter. On request, the software can also be used to scan any media device. This measure is only useful if regularly kept up to date.

Firewalls are systems comprising of hardware devices or software applications which act as gatekeepers to an organisation's network. They are used to prevent unauthorised access by allowing you to establish a set of rules or filters to determine which messages should be allowed in or out of the organisation's network. They are most commonly used when an organisation's database can be accessed by Web applications. If a message is flagged as breaking the rules, it is not allowed through. Firewalls use one or more of three methods to control messages flowing in and out of the organisation's network:

- *Packet filtering* – each message or packet that contains data is checked against a set of filters. Packets that are accepted are allowed to be sent to the designated system and all others are discarded.
- *Proxy server* – the proxy server manages all communication between the internal network of an organisation and external networks such as the internet. There are further advantages of using a proxy server, other than security measures. It also can cache the Web pages that have been requested so that network traffic is reduced if other users request the same page. This also increases response time. In addition, the proxy server can also be used to limit the websites that users may view outside the organisation.
- *Circuit-level gateway* – blocks all incoming messages to any host but itself. Within the organisation, all the client machines will run software to allow them to establish a connection with the circuit-level gateway machine. The proxy server performs all communications with any external network , such as the internet, so that the internal client machines never actually have contact with the 'outside world'.
- *Diskless workstations* – allow end users to access the database without being able to download the information from their workstations.

NOTE

James Martin provides an excellent enumeration and description of the desirable attributes of a database security strategy that remains relevant today.[8] Martin's security strategy is based on the seven essentials of database security and may be summarised as one in which:

Data are	**Users are**
Protected	Identifiable
Reconstructable	Authorised
Auditable	Monitored
Tamperproof	

8 Martin, J., *Managing the Database Environment.* Englewood Cliffs, NJ: Prentice-Hall, 1977.

10

10.3.5 Testing and Evaluation

In the design phase, decisions were made to ensure integrity, security, performance and recoverability of the database. During implementation and loading, these plans were put into place. In testing and evaluation, the DBA tests and fine-tunes the database to ensure that it performs as expected. This phase occurs in conjunction with application programming. Programmers use database tools to prototype the applications during coding of the programs. Tools such as report generators, screen painters and menu generators are especially useful to application programmers.

Test the Database

During this step, the DBA tests the database to ensure that it maintains the integrity and security of the data. Data integrity is enforced by the DBMS through the proper use of primary and foreign key rules. Many DBMSs also support the creation of domain constraints and database triggers. Testing will ensure that these constraints are properly designed and implemented. Data integrity is also the result of properly implemented data management policies, which are part of a comprehensive data administration framework.

Evaluate the Database and Its Application Programs

As the database and application programs are created and tested, the system must also be evaluated using a more holistic approach. Testing and evaluation of the individual components should culminate in a variety of broader system tests to ensure that all of the components interact properly to meet the needs of the users. At this stage, integration issues and deployment plans are refined, user training is conducted, and system documentation is finalised. Once the system receives final approval, it must be a sustainable resource for the organisation. To ensure that the data contained in the database are protected against loss, backup and recovery plans are tested.

Timely data availability is crucial for almost every database. Unfortunately, the database can lose data through unintended deletions, power outages and other causes. Data backup and recovery procedures create a safety valve, ensuring the availability of consistent data. Typically, database vendors encourage the use of fault-tolerant components such as uninterruptible power supply (UPS) units, RAID storage devices, clustered servers and data replication technologies to ensure the continuous operation of the database in case of a hardware failure. Even with these components, backup and restore functions constitute a very important part of daily database operations. Some DBMSs provide functions that allow the database administrator to schedule automatic database backups to permanent storage devices such as disks, DVDs, tapes and online storage. Database backups can be performed at different levels:

- A full backup, or dump, of the entire database. In this case, all database objects are backed up in their entirety.
- A differential backup of the database, in which only the objects that have been updated or modified since the last full backup are backed up.
- A transaction log backup, which backs up only the transaction log operations that are not reflected in a previous backup copy of the database. In this case, no other database objects are backed up. (For a complete explanation of the transaction log, see Chapter 12, Managing Transactions and Concurrency.) The database backup is stored in a secure place, usually in a different building from the database itself, and is protected against dangers such as fire, theft, flood and other potential calamities. The main purpose of the backup is to guarantee database restoration following a hardware or software failure. Failures that plague databases and systems are generally induced by software, hardware, programming exemptions, transactions, or external factors. Table 10.1 summarises the most common sources of database failure. Depending on the

TABLE 10.1 Common sources of database failure

Source	Description	Software
Software	Software-induced failures may be traceable to the operating system, the DBMS software, application programs, or viruses and other malware.	In April 2017, a new vulnerability was found in the Oracle e-Business Suite, which allows an unauthenticated attacker to create, modify, or delete critical data.[9]
Hardware	Hardware-induced failures may include memory chip errors, disk crashes, bad disk sectors and disk-full errors.	A bad memory module or a multiple hard-disk failure in a database system can bring it to an abrupt stop.
Programming exemptions	Application programs or end users may roll back transactions when certain conditions are defined. Programming exemptions can also be caused by malicious or improperly tested code that can be exploited by hackers.	In February 2016, a group of unidentified hackers fraudulently instructed the New York Federal Reserve Bank to transfer $81 million from the central bank of Bangladesh to accounts in the Philippines. The hackers used fraudulent messages injected by malware disguised as a PDF reader.[10]
Transactions	The system detects deadlocks and aborts one of the transactions. (See Chapter 12)	Deadlock occurs when executing multiple simultaneous transactions.
External factors	Backups are especially important when a system suffers complete destruction from fire, earthquake, flood, or other natural disaster.	In August 2015, lightning struck a local utility provider's grid near Google's data centres in Belgium. Although power backup kicked in automatically, the interruption was long enough to cause permanent data loss in affected systems.

type and extent of the failure, the recovery process ranges from a minor short-term inconvenience to a major long-term rebuild. Regardless of the extent of the required recovery process, recovery is not possible without a usable backup.

Database recovery generally follows a predictable scenario. First, the type and extent of the required recovery are determined. If the entire database needs to be recovered to a consistent state, the recovery uses the most recent backup copy of the database in a known consistent state. The backup copy is then rolled forward to restore all subsequent transactions by using the transaction log information. If the database needs to be recovered but the committed portion of the database is still usable, the recovery process uses the transaction log to 'undo' all of the transactions that were not committed (see Chapter 12, Managing Transactions and Concurrency). At the end of this phase, the database completes an iterative process of testing, evaluation and modification that continues until the system is certified as ready to enter the operational phase.

10

10.3.6 Operation

Once the database has passed the evaluation stage, it is considered to be operational. At this point, the database, its management, its users and its application programs constitute a complete information system.

The beginning of the operational phase invariably starts the process of system evolution. As soon as all of the targeted end users have entered the operations phase, problems that could not have been foreseen during the testing phase begin to surface. Some of the problems are serious enough to warrant emergency 'patchwork', while others are merely minor issues. For example, if the database design is implemented to interface with the Web, the sheer volume of transactions may cause even a well-designed system to bog down. In that case, the designers have to identify the source(s) of the bottleneck(s) and produce alternative solutions. These solutions may include using load-balancing software to distribute the transactions among multiple computers, increasing the available cache for the DBMS, and so on. In any case, the demand for change is the designer's constant, which leads to the next phase: maintenance and evolution.

10.3.7 Maintenance and Evolution

The database administrator must be prepared to perform routine maintenance activities within the database. Some of the required periodic maintenance activities include:

- Preventive maintenance (backup)
- Corrective maintenance (recovery)
- Adaptive maintenance (enhancing performance, adding entities and attributes and so on)
- Assignment of access permissions and their maintenance for new and old users
- Generation of database access statistics to improve the efficiency and usefulness of system audits and to monitor system performance
- Periodic security audits based on the system-generated statistics
- Periodic (monthly, quarterly, or yearly) system-usage summaries for internal billing or budgeting purposes

The likelihood of new information requirements and the demand for additional reports and new query formats require application changes and possible minor changes in the database components and contents. Those changes can be easily implemented only when the database design is flexible and when all documentation is updated and online. Eventually, even the best-designed database environment will no longer be capable of incorporating such evolutionary changes; then the whole DBLC process begins anew.

You should not be surprised to discover that many of the activities described in the Database Life Cycle (DBLC) remind you of those in the Systems Development Life Cycle (SDLC). After all, the SDLC represents the framework within which the DBLC activities take place. A summary of the parallel activities that take place within the SDLC and the DBLC is shown in Figure 10.9.

FIGURE 10.9 Parallel activities in the DBLC and the SDLC

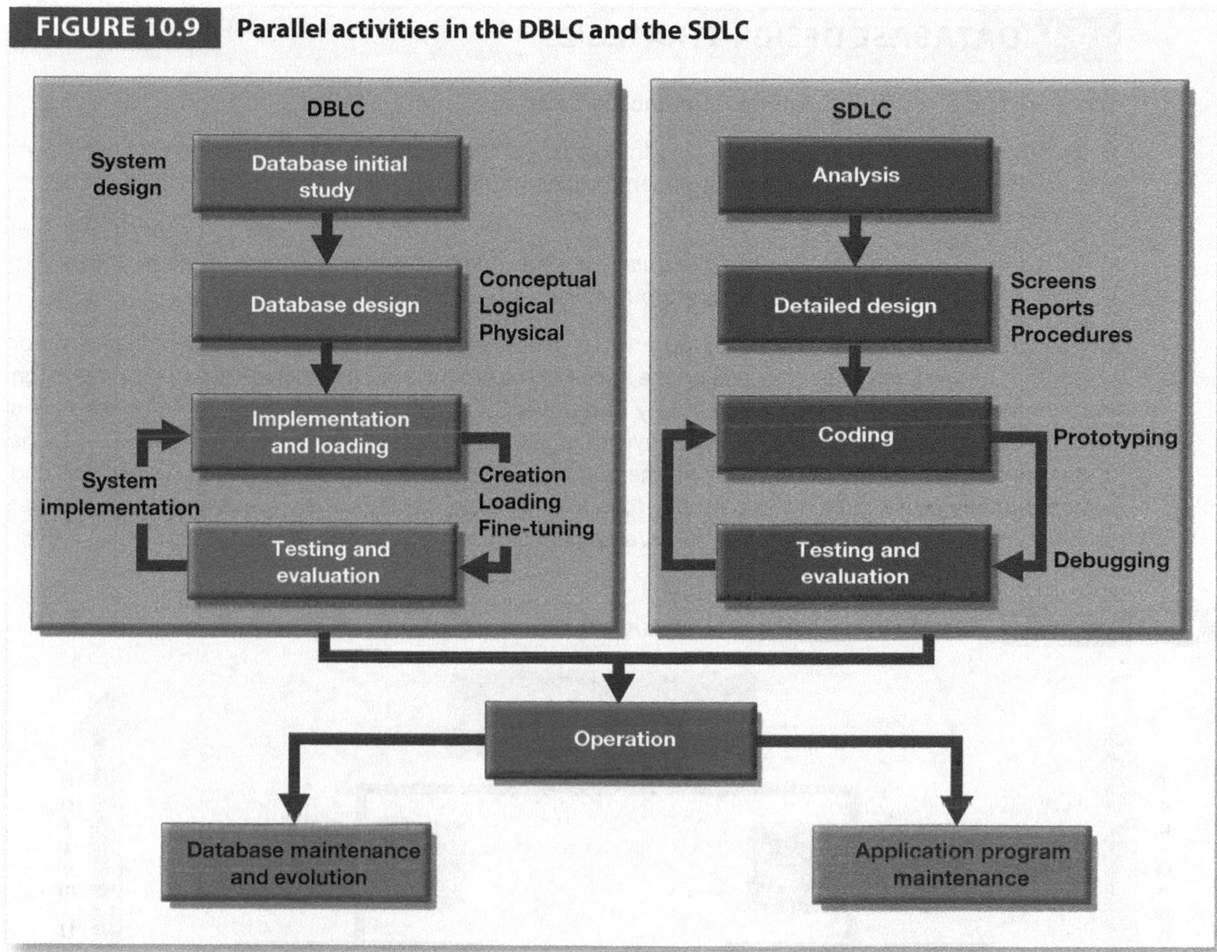

10.3.8 Determine Performance Measures

Physical design becomes more complex when data is distributed at different locations because the performance is affected by the communication media's throughput. Given such complexities, it is not surprising that designers favour database software that hides as many of the physical-level activities as possible. Despite the fact that relational models tend to hide the complexities of the computer's physical characteristics, the performance of relational databases is affected by physical storage properties. For example, performance can be affected by characteristics of the storage media, such as seek time, sector and block (page) size, buffer pool size, and the number of disk platters and read/write heads. In addition, factors such as the creation of an index can have a considerable effect on the relational database's performance – that is, data access speed and efficiency. In summary, physical design performance measurement deals with fine-tuning the DBMS and queries to ensure that they will meet end-user performance requirements.

10.4 DATABASE DESIGN STRATEGIES

There are two classical approaches to database design:

- **Top-down design** starts by identifying the data sets, then defines the data elements for each of those sets. This process involves the identification of different entity types and the definition of each entity's attributes.
- **Bottom-up design** first identifies the data elements (items), then groups them together in data sets. In other words, it first defines attributes, then groups them to form entities.

The two approaches are illustrated in Figure 10.10. The selection of a primary emphasis on top-down or bottom-up procedures often depends on the scope of the problem or on personal preferences. Although the two methodologies are complementary rather than mutually exclusive, a primary emphasis on a bottom-up approach may be more productive for small databases with few entities, attributes, relations and transactions. For situations in which the number, variety and complexity of entities, relations and transactions is overwhelming, a primarily top-down approach may be more easily managed. Most companies have standards for systems development and database design already in place.

FIGURE 10.10 **Top-down vs bottom-up design sequencing**

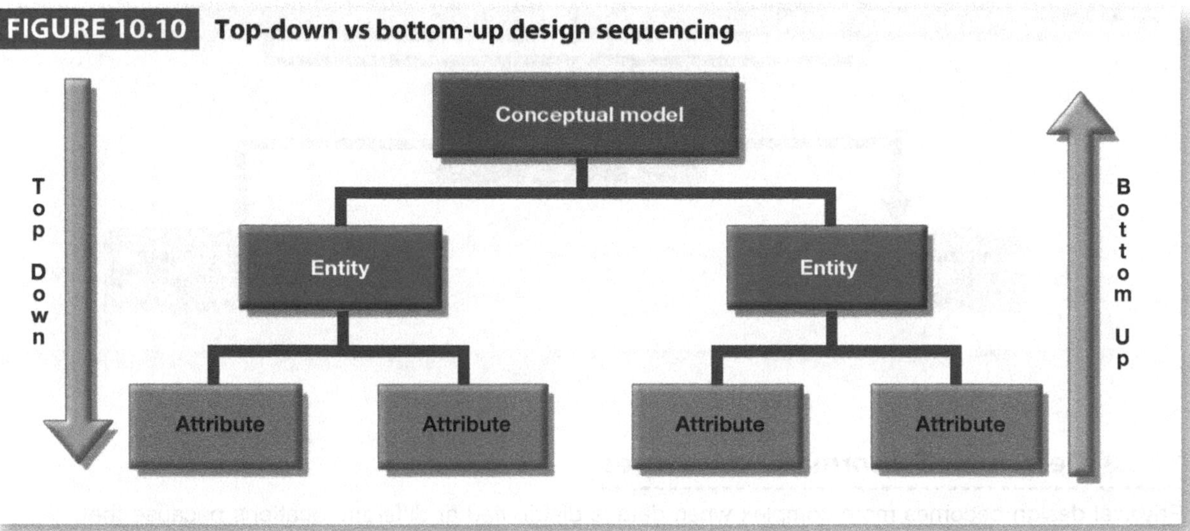

NOTE

Even when a primarily top-down approach is selected, the normalisation process that revises existing table structures is (inevitably) a bottom-up technique. ER models constitute a top-down process even when the selection of attributes and entities can be described as bottom-up. Because both the ER model and normalisation techniques form the basis for most designs, the top-down vs bottom-up debate may be based on a distinction rather than a difference.

10.5 CENTRALISED VS DECENTRALISED DESIGN

The two general approaches (bottom-up and top-down) to database design can be influenced by factors such as the scope and size of the system, the company's management style, and the company's structure (centralised or decentralised). Depending on such factors, the database design may be based on two very different design philosophies: centralised and decentralised.

Centralised design is productive when the data component is composed of a relatively small number of objects and procedures. The design can be carried out and represented in a fairly simple database. Centralised design is typical of relatively simple and/or small databases and can be successfully done by a single person (database administrator) or by a small, informal design team. The company operations and the scope of the problem are sufficiently limited to allow even a single designer to define the problem(s), create the conceptual design, verify the conceptual design with the user views, define system processes and data constraints to ensure the efficacy of the design, and ensure that the design will comply with all the requirements. Although centralised design is typical for small companies, do not make the mistake of assuming that centralised design is limited to small companies. Even large companies can operate within a relatively simple database environment. Figure 10.11 summarises the centralised design option. Note that a single conceptual design is completed and then validated in the centralised design approach.

Decentralised design might be used when the data component of the system has a considerable number of entities and complex relations on which very complex operations are performed. Decentralised design is also likely to be employed when the problem itself is spread across several operational sites and each element is a subset of the entire data set. (See Figure 10.12.)

FIGURE 10.11 Centralised design

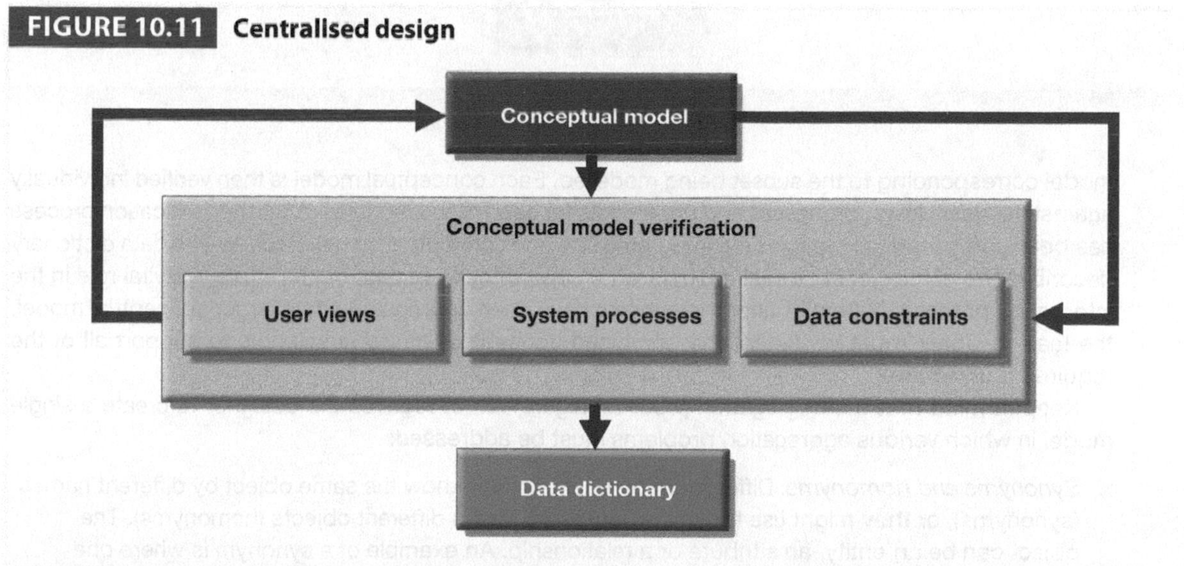

In large and complex projects, the database design typically cannot be done by only one person. Instead, a carefully selected team of database designers is employed to tackle a complex database project. Within the decentralised design framework, the database design task is divided into several modules. Once the design criteria have been established, the lead designer assigns design subsets or modules to design groups within the team.

As each design group focuses on modelling a subset of the system, the definition of boundaries and the interrelation among data subsets must be very precise. Each design group creates a conceptual data

FIGURE 10.12 **Decentralised design**

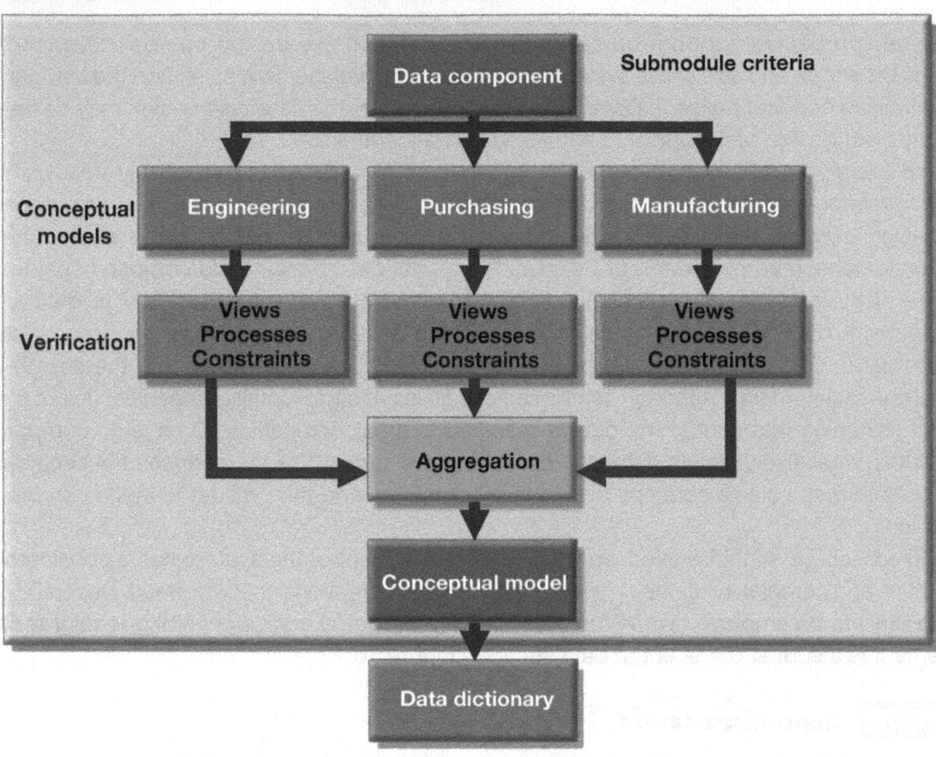

10

model corresponding to the subset being modelled. Each conceptual model is then verified individually against the user views, processes and constraints for each of the modules. After the verification process has been completed, all modules are integrated into one conceptual model. Because the data dictionary describes the characteristics of all objects within the conceptual data model, it plays a vital role in the integration process. Naturally, after the subsets have been aggregated into a larger conceptual model, the lead designer must verify that the combined conceptual model is still able to support all of the required transactions.

Keep in mind that the aggregation process (Figure 10.13) requires the designer to create a single model in which various aggregation problems must be addressed:

- *Synonyms and homonyms*. Different departments might know the same object by different names (synonyms), or they might use the same name to address different objects (homonyms). The object can be an entity, an attribute or a relationship. An example of a synonym is where one department refers to 'the client' while another refers to 'the customer'. An example of a homonym is if the IT department uses the term 'the client' to refer to a computer as in a client/server setup.
- *Entity and entity subtypes*. An entity subtype might be viewed as a separate entity by one or more departments. The designer must integrate such subtypes into a higher-level entity.
- *Conflicting object definitions*. Attributes can be recorded as different types (character, numeric), or different domains can be defined for the same attribute. Constraint definitions can also vary. The designer must remove such conflicts from the model.

FIGURE 10.13 **Summary of aggregation problems**

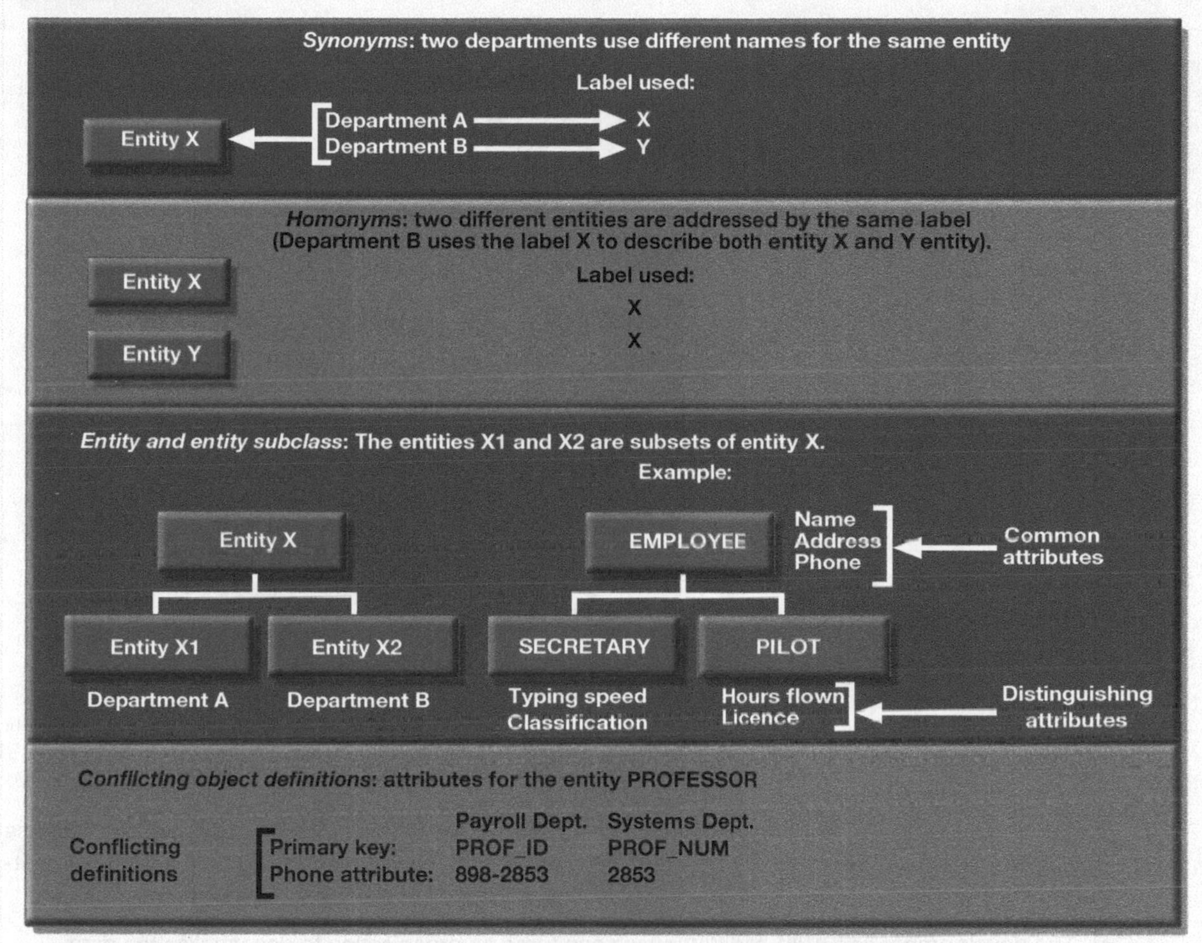

10

10.6 DATABASE ADMINISTRATION

Data is an important and valuable resource within an organisation and requires a successful database administration strategy to be implemented. Data management is a complex job and has led to the development of the database administration function. The person responsible for the control of the centralised and shared database is the **database administrator (DBA)**. The size and role of the DBA function varies from company to company, as does its placement within a company's organisational structure. On the organisation chart, the DBA function might be defined as either a staff or line position. Placing the DBA function in a staff position often creates a consulting environment in which the DBA is able to devise the data administration strategy but does not have the authority to enforce it or to resolve possible conflicts. The DBA function in a line position has both the responsibility and the authority to plan, define, implement and enforce the policies, standards and procedures used in the data administration activity. The two possible DBA function placements are illustrated in Figure 10.14.

FIGURE 10.14 The placement of the DBA function

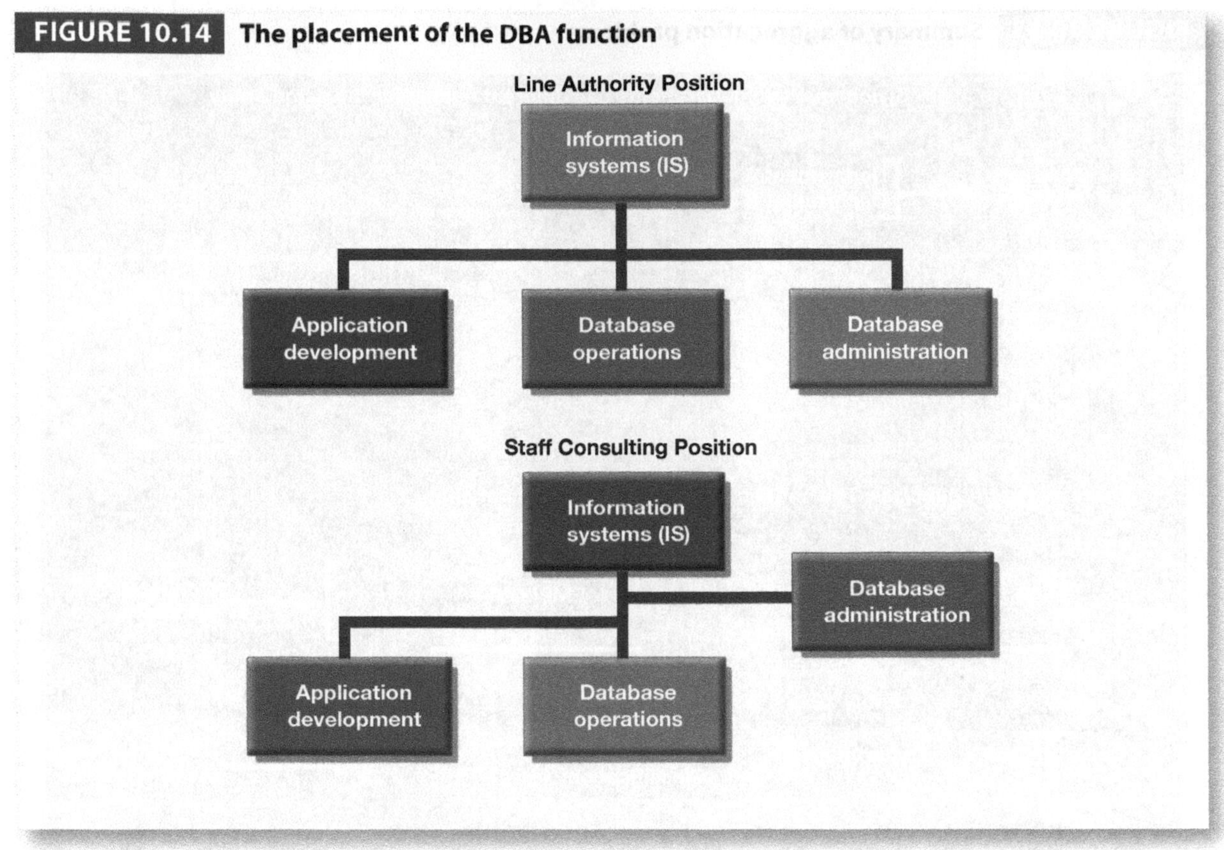

10

There is no standard for how the DBA function fits in an organisation's structure. In part, that is because the DBA function itself is probably the most dynamic of any organisation's functions. In fact, the fast-paced changes in DBMS technology dictate changing organisational styles. For example:

- The development of distributed databases can force an organisation to decentralise the data administration function further. The distributed database requires the system DBA to define and delegate the responsibilities of each local DBA, thus imposing new and more complex *coordinating* activities on the system DBA.
- The growing use of internet-ready and object-orientated databases and the growing number of data warehousing applications are likely to add to the DBA's data modelling and design activities, thus expanding and diversifying the DBA's job.
- The increasing sophistication and power of desktop-based DBMS packages provide an easy platform for the development of user-friendly, cost-effective and efficient solutions to specific departmental information needs. But such an environment also invites data duplication, not to mention the problems created by people who lack the technical qualifications to produce good database designs. In short, the new desktop environment requires the DBA to develop a new set of technical and managerial skills.

Although no current standard exists, it is common practice to define the DBA function by dividing the DBA operations according to the DBLC phases. If that approach is used, the DBA function requires personnel to cover the following activities:

- Database planning, including the definition of standards, procedures, and enforcement
- Database requirements gathering and conceptual design
- Database logical design and transaction design
- Database physical design and implementation
- Database testing and debugging
- Database operations and maintenance, including installation, conversion, and migration
- Database training and support

Figure 10.15 represents an appropriate DBA functional organisation according to that model

FIGURE 10.15 **A DBA functional organisation**

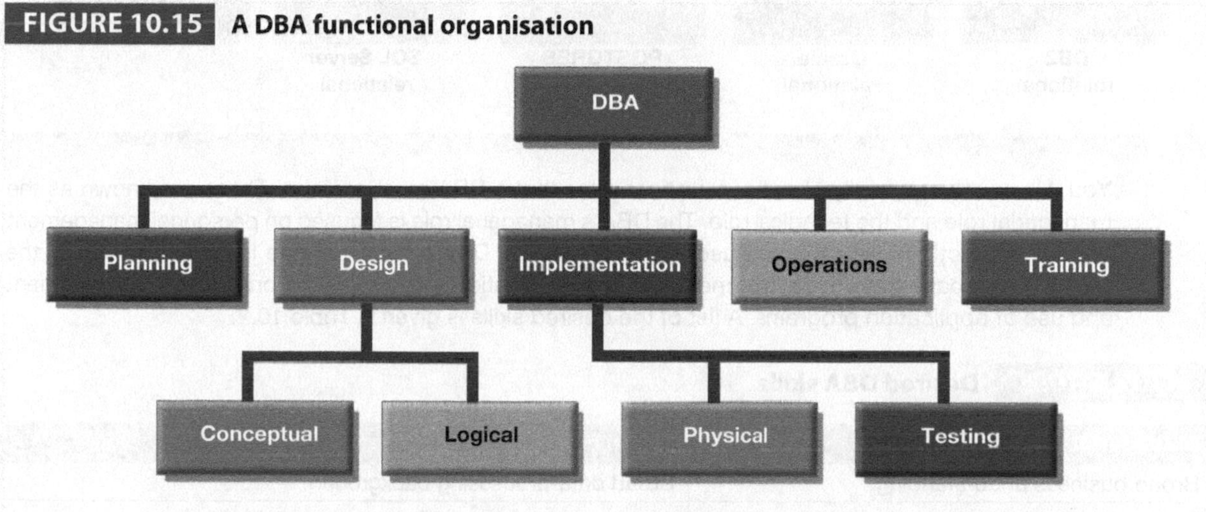

Keep in mind that a company might have several different and incompatible DBMSs installed to support different operations. For example, it is not uncommon to find corporations with a hierarchical DBMS to support the daily transactions at the operational level and a relational database to support middle and top management's ad hoc information needs. There may also be a variety of desktop DBMSs installed in the different departments. In such an environment, the company might have one DBA assigned for each DBMS. The general coordinator of all DBAs is sometimes known as the **systems administrator** (**SYSADM**); that position is illustrated in Figure 10.16.

There is a growing trend towards specialisation in the data management function. For example, the organisation charts used by some of the larger corporations make a distinction between a DBA and the **data administrator** (**DA**). The DA, also known as the **information resource manager** (**IRM**), usually reports directly to top management and is given a higher degree of responsibility and authority than the DBA, although the two roles tend to overlap to some extent.

The DA is responsible for controlling the overall corporate data resources, both computerised and manual. Thus, the DA's job description covers a larger area of operations than that of the DBA because the DA is in charge of controlling not only the computerised data, but also the data outside the scope of the DBMS. The placement of the DBA within the expanded organisational structure may vary from company to company. Depending on the structure's components, the DBA might report to the DA, the IRM, the IS manager or directly to the company's CEO. For simplicity and to avoid confusion, the label DBA is used here as a general title that encompasses all appropriate data administration functions.

FIGURE 10.16 **Multiple database administrators in an organisation**

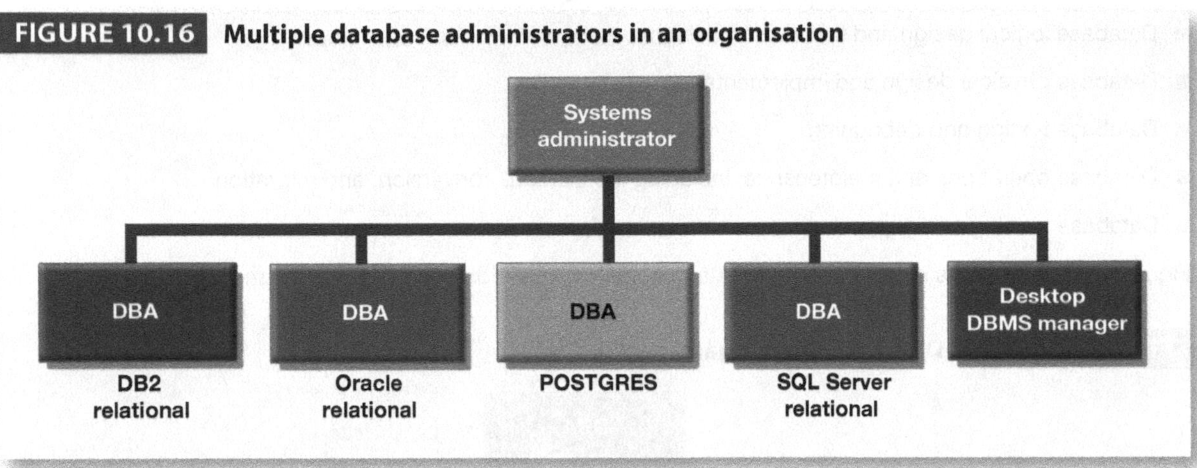

You will now learn briefly about two distinct roles that a DBA must perform. These are known as the managerial role and the technical role. The DBA's managerial role is focused on personnel management and on interactions with the end-user community. The DBA's technical role involves the use of the DBMS – database design, development and implementation – as well as the production, development and use of application programs. A list of the desired skills is given in Table 10.2.

10

TABLE 10.2 **Desired DBA skills**

Managerial	Technical
Broad business understanding	Broad data-processing background
Coordination skills	Systems development life cycle knowledge
Analytical skills	Structured methodologies: Data flow diagrams Structure charts Programming languages
Conflict resolution skills	Database life cycle knowledge
Communications skills (oral and written)	Database modelling and design skills Conceptual Logical Physical
Negotiation skills	Operational skills: database implementation, data dictionary management, security, and so on

Online Content The database administration function is covered in much greater depth in Appendix K, Database Administration, which is available on the online platform for this book.

10.6.1 The Managerial Role of the DBA

As a manager, the DBA must concentrate on the control and planning dimensions of database administration. Therefore, the DBA is responsible for:

- Coordinating, monitoring and allocating database administration resources: people and data.
- Defining goals and formulating strategic plans for the database administration function.

More specifically, the DBA's responsibilities are shown in Table 10.3.

TABLE 10.3 DBA Activities and Services

DBA Activity	DBA Service
Planning	End-user support
Organising	Policies, procedures and standards
Testing	Data security, privacy and integrity
Monitoring	Data backup and recovery
Delivering	Data distribution and use

Table 10.3 illustrates that the DBA is generally responsible for planning, organising, testing, monitoring and delivering quite a few services. Those services might be performed by the DBA or, more likely, by the DBA's personnel. Let's examine the services in greater detail.

End-User Support

The DBA interacts with the end user by providing data and information support services to the organisation's departments. Because end users usually have dissimilar computer backgrounds, end-user support services include:

- *Gathering user requirements.* The DBA must work within the end-user community to help gather the data required to identify and describe the end users' problems. The DBA's communications skills are very important at this stage because the DBA works closely with people who tend to have different computer backgrounds and communication styles. The gathering of user requirements requires the DBA to develop a precise understanding of the users' views and needs, and to identify present and future information needs.
- *Building end-user confidence.* Finding adequate solutions to end users' problems increases end-user trust and confidence in the DBA function.
- *Resolving conflicts and problems.* Finding solutions to end users' problems in one department might trigger conflicts with other departments. End users are typically concerned with their own specific data needs rather than with those of others, and they are not likely to consider how their data affect other departments within the organisation. When data/information conflicts arise, the DBA function has the authority and responsibility to resolve them.
- *Finding solutions to information needs.* The ability and authority to resolve data conflicts enable the DBA to develop solutions that will properly fit within the existing data management framework. The DBA's primary objective is to provide solutions to the end users' information needs. Given the growing importance of the internet, those solutions are likely to require the development and management of

Web browsers to interface with the databases. In fact, the explosive growth of e-commerce requires the use of *dynamic* interfaces to facilitate interactive product queries and product sales.

- *Ensuring quality and integrity of applications and data.* Once the right solution has been found, it must be properly implemented and used. Therefore, the DBA must work with both application programmers and end users to teach them the database standards and procedures required for data access and manipulation. The DBA must also make sure that the database transactions do not adversely affect the database's data quality. Certifying the quality of the application programs that access the database is a crucial DBA function. Special attention must be given to the DBMS internet interfaces because those interfaces do not provide the transaction management features that are typically found in the DBMS-managed database environment. For example, if an 'internal' application-based database transaction is required to fire a trigger, that trigger must also be fired when the transaction is generated via the internet interface.
- *Managing the training and support of DBMS users.* One of the most time-consuming DBA activities is teaching end users how to use the database properly. The DBA must ensure that all users accessing the database have a basic understanding of the functions and use of the DBMS software. The DBA coordinates and monitors all activities concerning end-user education.

Policies, Standards and Procedures

A prime component of a successful data administration strategy is the continuous enforcement of the policies, procedures and standards for correct data creation, usage, distribution and deletion within the database. The DBA must define, document and communicate the policies, procedures and standards before they can be enforced:

- **Policies** are general statements of direction or action that communicate and support DBA goals.
- **Standards** are more detailed and specific than policies and describe the minimum requirements of a given DBA activity. In effect, standards are rules that are used to evaluate the quality of the activity. For example, standards define the structure of application programs and the naming conventions programmers must use.
- **Procedures** are written instructions that describe a series of steps to be followed during the performance of a given activity. Procedures must be developed within existing working conditions, and they must support and enhance that environment.

To illustrate the distinctions among policies, standards and procedures, look at the following examples:

Policies

- All users must have passwords.
- Passwords must be changed every six months.

Standards

- A password must have a minimum of five characters.
- A password may have a maximum of 12 characters.
- ID numbers, names and birth dates cannot be used as passwords.

Procedures

- To create a password, (1) the end user sends to the DBA a written request for the creation of an account; (2) the DBA approves the request and forwards it to the computer operator; (3) the computer operator creates the account, assigns a temporary password and sends the account information to the end user; (4) a copy of the account information is sent to the DBA; and (5) the user changes the temporary password to a permanent one.

Standards and procedures defined by the DBA are used by all end users who want to benefit from the database. Standards and procedures must complement each other and must constitute an extension of data administration policies. Procedures must facilitate the work of end users and the DBA. The DBA must define, communicate and enforce procedures that cover areas such as:

- *End-user database requirements gathering.* Which documentation is required? What forms must be used?
- *Database design and modelling.* Which database design methodology to use (normalisation or object-oriented methodology)? Which tools to use (CASE tools, data dictionaries, or ER diagrams)?
- *Documentation and naming conventions.* Which documentation to use in the definition of all data elements, sets and programs that access the database?
- *Design, coding and testing of database application programs.* The DBA must define the standards for application program coding, documentation and testing. The DBA standards and procedures are given to the application programmers, and the DBA must enforce those standards.
- *Database software selection.* The selection of the DBMS package and any other software related to the database must be properly managed. For example, the DBA might require that software be properly interfaced with existing software, that it has the features needed by the organisation, and that it provides a positive return on investment. In today's internet environment, the DBA must also work with Web administrators to find proper Web-to-database connectivity solutions.
- *Database security and integrity.* The DBA must define the policies governing security and integrity. Database security is especially crucial. Security standards must be clearly defined and strictly enforced. Security procedures must be designed to handle a multitude of security scenarios to ensure that security problems are minimised. Although no system can ever be completely secure, security procedures must be designed to meet critical standards. The growing use of internet interfaces to databases opens the door to new security threats that are far more complex and difficult to manage than those encountered with more traditional internally generated and controlled interfaces. Therefore, the DBA must work closely with internet security specialists to ensure that the databases are properly protected from attacks launched inadvertently or attacks launched deliberately by unauthorised users.
- *Database backup and recovery.* Database backup and recovery procedures must include the information necessary to guarantee proper execution and management of the backups.
- *Database maintenance and operation.* The DBMS's daily operations must be clearly documented. Operators must keep job logs, and they must write operator instructions and notes. Such notes are helpful in pinpointing the causes and solutions of problems. Operational procedures must also include precise information concerning backup and recovery procedures.
- *End-user training.* A full-featured training program must be established within the organisation, and procedures governing the training must be clearly specified. The objective is to indicate

clearly who does what, when and how. Each end user must be aware of the type and extent of the available training methodology.

Procedures and standards must be revised at least annually to keep them up to date and to ensure that the organisation can adapt quickly to changes in the work environment. Naturally, the introduction of new DBMS software, the discovery of security or integrity violations, the reorganisation of the company, and similar changes require revision of the procedures and standards.

Data Security, Privacy and Integrity

The security, privacy and integrity of the data in the database are of great concern to DBAs who manage current DBMS installations. Technology has pointed the way to greater productivity through information management. Technology has also resulted in the distribution of data across multiple sites, thus making it more difficult to maintain data control, security and integrity. The multiple-site data configuration has made it imperative that the DBA use the security and integrity mechanisms provided by the DBMS to enforce the database administration policies defined in the previous section. In addition, DBAs must team up with internet security experts to build firewalls, proxy services and other security mechanisms to safeguard data from possible attacks.

Protecting the security and privacy of the data in the database is a function of authorisation management. **Authorisation management** defines procedures to protect and guarantee database security and integrity. Those procedures include, but are not limited to, user access management, view definition, DBMS access control and DBMS usage monitoring.

- *User access management.* This function is designed to limit access to the database and likely includes at least the following procedures:
  - *Define each user to the database.* This is achieved at two levels: at the operating system level and at the DBMS level. At the operating system level, the DBA can request the creation of a logon user ID that allows the end user to log on to the computer system. At the DBMS level, the DBA can either create a different user ID or employ the same user ID to authorise the end user to access the DBMS.
  - *Assign passwords to each user.* This, too, can be done at both operating system and DBMS levels. The database passwords can be assigned with predetermined expiration dates. The use of expiration dates enables the DBA to screen end users periodically and to remind users to change their passwords periodically, thus making unauthorised access less probable.
  - *Define user groups.* Classifying users into user groups according to common access needs facilitates the DBA's job of controlling and managing the access privileges of individual users.
  - *Assign access privileges.* The DBA assigns access privileges or access rights to specific users to access specified databases. An access privilege describes the type of authorised access. For example, access rights may be limited to read-only, or the authorised access may include READ, WRITE and DELETE privileges. Access privileges in relational databases are assigned through SQL GRANT and REVOKE commands.
  - *Control physical access.* Physical security can prevent unauthorised users from directly accessing the DBMS installation and facilities. Some common physical security practices found in large database installations include secured entrances, password-protected workstations, electronic personnel badges, closed-circuit video, voice recognition and biometric technology.
  - *View definition.* The DBA must define data views to protect and control the scope of the data that are accessible to an authorised user. The DBMS must provide the tools that allow the definition of views that are composed of one or more tables and the assignment of access rights to a user or a group of users. The SQL command CREATE VIEW is used in relational databases to define views.

- *DBMS access control.* Database access can be controlled by placing limits on the use of the DBMS's query and reporting tools. The DBA must make sure that those tools are used properly and only by authorised personnel.
- *DBMS usage monitoring.* The DBA must also audit the use of the data in the database. Several DBMS packages contain features that allow the creation of an **audit log**, which automatically records a brief description of the database operations performed by all users. Such audit trails enable the DBA to pinpoint access violations. The audit trails can be tailored to record all database accesses or just failed database accesses.

Security breaches can yield a database whose integrity is either preserved or corrupted:

- *Preserved:* Action is required to avoid the repetition of similar security problems, but data recovery may not be necessary. As a matter of fact, most security violations are produced by unauthorised and unnoticed access for information purposes, but such snooping does not disrupt the database.
- *Corrupted:* Action is required to avoid the repetition of similar security problems, and the database must be recovered to a consistent state. Corrupting security breaches include database access by computer viruses and by hackers whose actions are designed to destroy or alter data.

The integrity of a database might be lost because of external factors beyond the DBA's control. For example, the database might be damaged or destroyed by an explosion, a fire or an earthquake. Whatever the reason, the possibility of database corruption or destruction makes backup and recovery procedures crucial to any DBA.

Data Backup and Recovery

When data are not readily available, companies face potentially ruinous losses. Therefore, data backup and recovery procedures are critical in all database installations. The DBA must also ensure that the data in the database can be fully recovered in case of physical data loss or loss of database integrity.

Data loss can be partial or total. A partial loss can be caused when a physical loss of part of the database has occurred or when part of the database has lost integrity. A total loss might mean that the database continues to exist but its integrity is entirely lost or that the entire database is physically lost. In any case, backup and recovery procedures are the cheapest database insurance you can buy.

10

The management of database security, integrity, backup and recovery is so critical that many DBA departments have created a position staffed by the **database security officer** (**DSO**). The DSO's sole job is to ensure database security and integrity. In large database shops, the DSO's activities are often classified as *disaster management*.

Disaster management includes all of the DBA activities designed to secure data availability following a physical disaster or a database integrity failure. Disaster management includes all planning, organising and testing of database contingency plans and recovery procedures. The backup and recovery measures must include at least:

- *Periodic data and applications backups.* Some DBMSs include tools to ensure backup and recovery of the data in the database. The DBA should use those tools to render the backup and recovery tasks automatic. Products such as IBM's DB2 allow the creation of different backup types: full, incremental and concurrent. A **full backup**, also known as a database dump, produces a complete copy of the entire database. An **incremental backup** produces a backup of all data since the last backup date; a **concurrent backup** takes place while the user is working on the database.
- *Proper backup identification.* Backups must be clearly identified through detailed descriptions and date information, thus enabling the DBA to ensure that the correct backups are used to recover the database. While cloud-based backups are fast replacing tape backups, many organisations

still use tapes. As tapes require physical storage, it is vital that the storage and labelling of tapes must be done diligently by the computer operators, and the DBA must keep track of tape currency and location. However, organisations that are large enough to hire a DBA do not typically use tapes for enterprise backup. Other emerging backup solutions include optical and disk-based backup devices. Such backup solutions include online storage based on Network Attached Storage (NAS) and Storage Area Networks (SAN). Enterprise backup solutions use a layered backup approach in which the data are first backed up to fast disk media for intermediate storage and fast restoration. Later, the data is transferred to tape for archival storage.

- *Convenient and safe backup storage.* There must be multiple backups of the same data, and each backup copy must be stored in a different location. The storage locations must include sites inside and outside the organisation. (Keeping different backups in the same place defeats the purpose of having multiple backups in the first place.) The storage locations must be properly prepared and may include fire-safe and quakeproof vaults, as well as humidity and temperature controls. The DBA must establish a policy to respond to two questions: (1) Where are the backups to be stored? (2) For how long are backups to be stored?
- *Physical protection of both hardware and software.* Protection might include the use of closed installations with restricted access, as well as preparation of the computer sites to provide air conditioning, backup power and fire protection. Physical protection also includes the provision of a backup computer and DBMS for use in case of emergency.
- *Personal access control to the software of a database installation.* Multilevel passwords and privileges and hardware and software challenge/response tokens can properly identify authorised users of resources.
- *Insurance coverage for the data in the database.* The DBA or security officer must secure an insurance policy to provide financial protection in the event of a database failure. The insurance may be expensive, but it is less expensive than the disaster created by massive data loss.

Two additional points are worth making.

- Data recovery and contingency plans must be thoroughly tested and evaluated, and they must be practised frequently. So-called fire drills are not to be disparaged, and they require top-level management's support and enforcement.
- A backup and recovery program is not likely to cover all components of an information system. Therefore, it is appropriate to establish priorities concerning the nature and extent of the data recovery process.

Data Distribution and Use

Data are useful only when they reach the right users at the right time. The DBA is responsible for ensuring that the data are distributed to the right people, at the right time and in the right format. The DBA's data distribution and use tasks can become very time-consuming, especially when the data delivery capacity is based on a typical applications programming environment, where users depend on programmers to deliver the programs to access the data in the database. Although the internet and its intranet and extranet extensions have opened databases to corporate users, their use has also created a new set of challenges for the DBA.

Current data distribution philosophy makes it easy for *authorised* end users to access the database. One way to accomplish that task is to facilitate the use of a new generation of more sophisticated query tools and the new internet Web front ends. They enable the DBA to educate end users to produce the required information without being dependent on applications programmers. Naturally, the DBA must ensure that appropriate standards and procedures are adhered to.

This distribution philosophy is common today, and it is likely that it will become more common as database technology marches on. Such an environment is more flexible for the end user. Clearly, enabling end users to become relatively self-sufficient in the acquisition and use of data can lead to more efficient use of data in the decision process. Yet this 'data democracy' can also produce some troublesome side effects. Letting end users micromanage their data subsets could inadvertently sever the connection between those users and the data administration function. The DBA's job under those circumstances might become sufficiently complicated to compromise the efficiency of the data administration function. Data duplication might flourish again without checks at the organisational level to ensure the uniqueness of data elements. Thus, end users who do not completely understand the nature and sources of data might make improper use of the data elements.

10.6.2 The Technical Role of the DBA

The DBA's technical role requires a broad understanding of DBMS functions, configuration, programming languages, data modelling, and design methodologies, and other DBMS-related issues. For example, the DBA's technical activities include the selection, installation, operation, maintenance and upgrading of the DBMS and utility software, as well as the design, development, implementation and maintenance of the application programs that interact with the database.

Many of the DBA's technical activities are a logical extension of the DBA's managerial activities. For example, the DBA deals with database security and integrity, backup and recovery, and training and support. Thus, the DBA's dual role might be conceptualised as a capsule whose technical core is covered by a clear managerial shell.

The technical aspects of the DBA's job are rooted in the following areas of operation:

- Evaluating, selecting and installing the DBMS and related utilities
- Designing and implementing databases and applications
- Testing and evaluating databases and applications
- Operating the DBMS, utilities and applications
- Training and supporting users
- Maintaining the DBMS, utilities and applications

The following sections will explore the details of those operational areas.

Evaluating, Selecting and Installing the DBMS and Utilities

One of the DBA's first and most important technical responsibilities is selecting the database management system, utility software and supporting hardware for use in the organisation. Therefore, the DBA must develop and execute a plan for evaluating and selecting the DBMS, utilities and hardware. That plan must be based primarily on the organisation's needs rather than on specific software and hardware features. The DBA must recognise that the search is for solutions to problems rather than for a computer or DBMS software. Put simply, a DBMS is a management tool and not a technological toy.

The first and most important step of the evaluation and acquisition plan is to determine company needs. To establish a clear picture of those needs, the DBA must make sure that the entire end-user community, including top- and mid-level managers, is involved in the process. Once the needs are identified, the objectives of the data administration function can be clearly established and the DBMS features and selection criteria can be defined.

To match DBMS capability to the organisation's needs, the DBA would be wise to develop a checklist of desired DBMS features. That DBMS checklist should at least address these issues:

- *DBMS model.* Are the company's needs better served by a relational, object-orientated, or object/relational DBMS? If a data warehouse application is required, should a relational or multidimensional DBMS be used?
- *DBMS storage capacity.* What maximum disk and database size is required? How many disk packages must be supported? How many tape units or what other storage capacity are needed?
- *Application development support.* Which 3GLs and 4GLs are supported? Which application development tools (database schema design, data dictionary, performance monitoring, screen and menu painters) are available? Are end-user query tools provided? Does the DBMS provide Web front-end access?
- *Security and integrity.* Does the DBMS support referential and entity integrity rules, access rights, and so on? Does the DBMS support the use of audit trails to spot errors and security violations? Can the audit trail size be modified?
- *Backup and recovery.* Does the DBMS provide some automated backup and recovery tools? Does the DBMS support tape, optical disk, cloud, or network-based backups? Does the DBMS automatically back up the transaction logs?
- *Concurrency control.* Does the DBMS support multiple users? What levels of isolation (table, page, row) does the DBMS offer? How much manual coding is needed in the application programs?
- *Performance.* How many transactions per second does the DBMS support? Are additional transaction processors needed?
- *Database administration tools.* Does the DBMS offer some type of DBA management interface? What type of information does the DBA interface provide? Does the DBMS provide alerts to the DBA when errors or security violations occur?

- *Interoperability and data distribution.* Can the DBMS work with other DBMS types in the same environment? Which coexistence or interoperability level is achieved? Does the DBMS support READ and WRITE operations to and from other DBMS packages? Does the DBMS support a client/server architecture?
- *Portability and standards.* Can the DBMS run on different operating systems and platforms? Can the DBMS run on mainframes, mid-range computers and desktop computers? Can the DBMS applications run without modification on all platforms? Which national and industry standards does the DBMS follow?
- *Hardware.* Which hardware does the DBMS require?
- *Data dictionary.* Does the DBMS have a data dictionary? If so, what information is kept in it? Does the DBMS interface with any data dictionary tool? Does the DBMS support any CASE tools?
- *Vendor training and support.* Does the vendor offer in-house training? What type and level of support does the vendor provide? Is the DBMS documentation easy to read and helpful? What is the vendor's upgrade policy?
- *Available third-party tools.* Which additional tools are offered by third-party vendors (query tools, data dictionary, access management and control, and storage allocation management tools)?
- *Cost.* What costs are involved in the acquisition of the software and hardware? How many additional personnel are required and what level of expertise is required of them? What are the recurring costs? What is the expected payback period?

Pros and cons of several alternative solutions must be evaluated during the selection process. Available alternatives are often restricted because software must be compatible with the organisation's existing computer system. Remember that a DBMS is just part of the solution; it requires support from other hardware, application software and utility programs. For example, the DBMS's use is likely to be constrained by the available CPU, a front-end processor, auxiliary storage devices, data communication devices, the operating system, a transaction processor system, and so on. The costs associated with the hardware and software components must be included in the evaluations.

The selection process must also consider the site's preparation costs. For example, the DBA must include both one-time and recurring expenditures involved in the preparation and maintenance of the computer room installations.

The DBA must supervise the installation of all software and hardware designated to support the data administration strategy; must have a thorough understanding of the components being installed; and must be familiar with the installation, configuration and startup procedures of such components. The installation procedures include details such as the location of backup and transaction log files, network configuration information and physical storage details.

Keep in mind that installation and configuration details are DBMS-dependent. Therefore, such details cannot be addressed in this book. Consult the installation and configuration sections of your system's DBMS administration guide for those details.

Designing and Implementing Databases and Applications

The DBA function also provides data modelling and design services to the end-user community. Such services are often coordinated with an application development group within the data-processing department. Therefore, one of the primary activities of a DBA is to determine and enforce standards and procedures to be used. Once the appropriate standards and procedures framework is in place, the DBA must ensure that the database modelling and design activities are performed within the framework. The DBA then provides the necessary assistance and support during the design of the database at the conceptual, logical and physical levels. (Remember that the conceptual design is both DBMS- and hardware-independent, the logical design is DBMS-dependent and hardware-independent, and the physical design is both DBMS- and hardware-dependent.)

The DBA function usually requires that several people be dedicated to database modelling and design activities. These people might be grouped according to the organisational areas covered by the application. For example, database modelling and design personnel may be assigned to production systems, financial and managerial systems, or executive and decision support systems. The DBA schedules the design jobs to coordinate the data design and modelling activities. That coordination may require reassignment of available resources based on externally determined priorities.

The DBA also works with application programmers to ensure the quality and integrity of database design and transactions. Such support services include reviewing the database application design to ensure that transactions are:

- *Correct:* The transactions mirror real-world events.
- *Efficient:* The transactions do not overload the DBMS.
- *Compliant:* The transactions are compliant with integrity and standards.

These activities require personnel with broad database design and programming skills.

The implementation of the applications requires the implementation of the physical database. Therefore, the DBA must provide assistance and oversight during the physical design, including storage space determination and creation, data loading, conversion, and database migration services. The DBA's implementation tasks also include the generation, compilation and storage of the application's access plan. An **access plan** is a set of instructions generated at application completion time that predetermines how the application will access the database at run time. To be able to create and validate the access plan, the user must have the required rights to access the database.

Before an application comes online, the DBA must develop, test and implement the operational procedures required by the new system. Such operational procedures include utilising training, security, and backup and recovery plans, as well as assigning responsibility for database control and maintenance. Finally, the DBA must authorise application users to access the database from which the applications draw the required data.

The addition of a new database may require the fine-tuning and/or reconfiguring of the DBMS. Remember that the DBMS assists all applications by managing the shared corporate data repository. Therefore, when data structures are added or modified, the DBMS may require the assignment of additional resources to service the new and original users with equal efficiency.

Testing and Evaluating Databases and Applications

The DBA must also provide testing and evaluation services for all of the database and end-user applications. These services are the logical extension of the design, development and implementation services described in the preceding section. Clearly, testing procedures and standards must already be in place before any application program can be approved for use in the company.

Although testing and evaluation services are closely related to database design and implementation services, they usually are maintained independently. The reason for the separation is that applications programmers and designers are often too close to the problem being studied to detect errors and omissions.

Testing usually starts with the loading of the testbed database. That database contains test data for the applications, and its purpose is to check the data definition and integrity rules of the database and application programs.

The testing and evaluation of a database application cover all aspects of the system – from the simple collection and creation of data to its use and retirement. The evaluation process covers:

- Technical aspects of both the applications and the database. Backup and recovery, security and integrity, use of SQL and application performance must be evaluated
- Evaluation of the written documentation to ensure that the documentation and procedures are accurate and easy to follow
- Observance of standards for naming, documenting and coding
- Data duplication conflicts with existing data
- The enforcement of all data validation rules

Following the thorough testing of all applications, the database and the procedures, the system is declared operational and can be made available to end users.

Operating the DBMS, Utilities and Applications

DBMS operations can be divided into four main areas:

- System support
- Performance monitoring and tuning
- Backup and recovery
- Security auditing and monitoring

System support activities cover all tasks directly related to the day-to-day operations of the DBMS and its applications. These activities range from filling out job logs to changing tape to checking and verifying the status of computer hardware, disk packages and emergency power sources. System-related activities include periodic, occasional tasks such as running special programs and resource configurations for new and/or upgraded versions of database applications.

Performance monitoring and tuning require much of the DBA's attention and time. These activities are designed to ensure that the DBMS, utilities and applications maintain satisfactory performance levels. To carry out the performance-monitoring and tuning tasks the DBA must:

- Establish DBMS performance goals
- Monitor the DBMS to evaluate whether the performance objectives are being met
- Isolate the problem and find alternative solutions (if performance objectives are not met)
- Implement the selected performance solutions

DBMSs often include performance-monitoring tools that allow the DBA to query database usage information. If the DBMS does not include performance-monitoring tools, they are available from many different sources. DBMS utilities are provided by third-party vendors, or they may be included in operating system utilities or transaction processor facilities. Most of the performance-monitoring tools allow the DBA to focus on selected system bottlenecks. The most common bottlenecks in DBMS performance tuning are related to the use of indexes, query-optimisation algorithms and management of storage resources.

Because improper index selection can have a negative effect on system performance, most DBMS installations adhere to a carefully defined index creation and usage plan. Such a plan is especially important in a relational database environment.

To produce satisfactory performance, the DBA is likely to spend much time trying to educate programmers and end users on the proper use of SQL statements. Typically, DBMS programmers' manuals and administration manuals contain useful performance guidelines and examples that demonstrate the proper use of SQL statements, both in the command-line mode and within application programs. Since relational systems do not give the user an index choice within a query, the DBMS makes the index selection for the user. Therefore, the DBA should create indexes that can improve system performance. (See Chapter 13, Managing Database and SQL Performance, for examples of database performance tuning.)

Query-optimisation routines are usually integrated into the DBMS package, thereby allowing few tuning options. Query-optimisation routines are orientated to improving concurrent access to the database. Several database packages let the DBA specify parameters for determining the desired level of concurrency. Concurrency is also affected by the types of locks used by the DBMS and requested by the applications. Because the concurrency issue is important to the efficient operation of the system, the DBA must be familiar with the factors that influence concurrency. (See Chapter 12, Managing Transactions and Concurrency, for more information on that subject)

Available storage resources, in terms of both primary and secondary memory, must also be considered during DBMS performance tuning. The allocation of storage resources is determined when the DBMS is configured. Storage configuration parameters can be used to determine:

- The number of databases that may be opened concurrently
- The number of application programs or users supported concurrently
- The amount of primary memory (buffer pool size) assigned to each database and each database process

10

- The size and location of the log files (remember that these files are used to recover the database. The log files can be located in a separate volume to reduce the disk's head movement and to increase performance)
- Performance-monitoring issues are DBMS-specific. Therefore, the DBA must become familiar with the DBMS manuals to learn the technical details involved in the performance-monitoring task.

Since data loss is likely to be devastating to the organisation, *backup and recovery activities* are of primary concern during the DBMS operation. The DBA must establish a schedule for backing up database and log files at appropriate intervals. Backup frequency is dependent on the application type and on the relative importance of the data. All critical system components – the database, the database applications and the transaction logs – must be backed up periodically.

Most DBMS packages include utilities that schedule automated database backups, be they full or incremental. Although incremental backups are faster than full backups, an incremental backup requires the existence of a periodic full backup to be useful for recovery purposes.

Database recovery after a media or systems failure requires application of the transaction log to the correct database copy. The DBA must plan, implement, test and enforce a 'bulletproof' backup and recovery procedure.

Security auditing and monitoring assumes the appropriate assignment of access rights and the proper use of access privileges by programmers and end users. The technical aspects of security auditing and monitoring involve creating users, assigning access rights, using SQL commands to grant and revoke access rights to users and database objects, and creating audit trails to discover security violations or attempted violations. The DBA must periodically generate an audit trail report to determine whether there have been actual or attempted security violations – and, if so, from which locations and, if possible, by whom.

Training and Supporting Users

Training people to use the DBMS and its tools is included in the DBA's technical activities. In addition, the DBA provides or secures technical training in the use of the DBMS and its utilities for the applications programmers. Application programmer training covers the use of the DBMS tools as well as the procedures and standards required for database programming.

Unscheduled, on-demand technical support for end users and programmers is also included in the DBA's activities. A technical troubleshooting procedure can be developed to facilitate such support. The technical procedure might include the development of a technical database used to find solutions to common technical problems.

Part of the support is provided by interaction with DBMS vendors. Establishing good relationships with software suppliers is one way to ensure that the company has a good external support source. Vendors are the source for up-to-date information concerning new products and personnel retraining. Good vendor–company relations are also likely to give organisations an edge in determining the future direction of database development.

Maintaining the DBMS, Utilities and Applications

The maintenance activities of the DBA are an extension of the operational activities. Maintenance activities are dedicated to the preservation of the DBMS environment.

Periodic DBMS maintenance includes management of the physical or secondary storage devices. One of the most common maintenance activities is reorganising the physical location of data in the database. This is usually done as part of the DBMS fine-tuning activities. The reorganisation of a database might be designed to allocate contiguous disk-page locations to the DBMS to increase performance. The reorganisation process might also free the space allocated to deleted data, thus providing more disk space for new data.

Maintenance activities also include upgrading the DBMS and utility software. The upgrade might require the installation of a new version of the DBMS software or an internet front-end tool. Or it might create an additional DBMS gateway to allow access to a host DBMS running on a different host computer. DBMS gateway services are common in distributed DBMS applications running in a client/server environment. Also, new-generation databases include features such as spatial data support, data warehousing and star query support, and support for Java programming interfaces for internet access.

Quite often companies are faced with the need to exchange data in dissimilar formats or between databases. The maintenance efforts of the DBA include migration and conversion services for data in incompatible formats or for different DBMS software. Such conditions are common when the system is upgraded from one version to another or when the existing DBMS is replaced by an entirely new DBMS. Database conversion services also include downloading data from the host (mainframe-based) DBMS to an end user's desktop computer to allow that user to perform a variety of activities – spreadsheet analysis, charting, statistical modelling, and so on. Migration and conversion services can be done at the logical (DBMS- or software-specific) level or at the physical (storage-media- or operating-system-specific) level.

10.6.3 Developing a Data Administration Strategy

For a company to succeed, its activities must be committed to its main objectives or mission. Therefore, regardless of a company's size, a critical step for any organisation is to ensure that its information system supports its strategic plans for each of its business areas.

The database administration strategy must not conflict with the information systems plans. After all, the information systems plans are derived from a detailed analysis of the company's goals, its condition or situation, and its business needs. Several methodologies are available to ensure the compatibility of data administration and information systems plans, and to guide the strategic plan development. The most commonly used methodology is known as information engineering.

Information engineering (**IE**) allows for the translation of the company's strategic goals into the data and applications that will help the company achieve those goals. IE focuses on the description of the corporate data instead of the processes. The IE rationale is simple: business data types tend to remain fairly stable and do not change much during their existence. In contrast, processes change often and thus require the frequent modification of existing systems. By placing the emphasis on data, IE helps decrease the impact on systems when processes change.

The output of the IE process is an **information systems architecture** (**ISA**) that serves as the basis for planning, development and control of future information systems. Figure 10.17 shows the forces that affect ISA development.

FIGURE 10.17 **Forces affecting the development of the ISA**

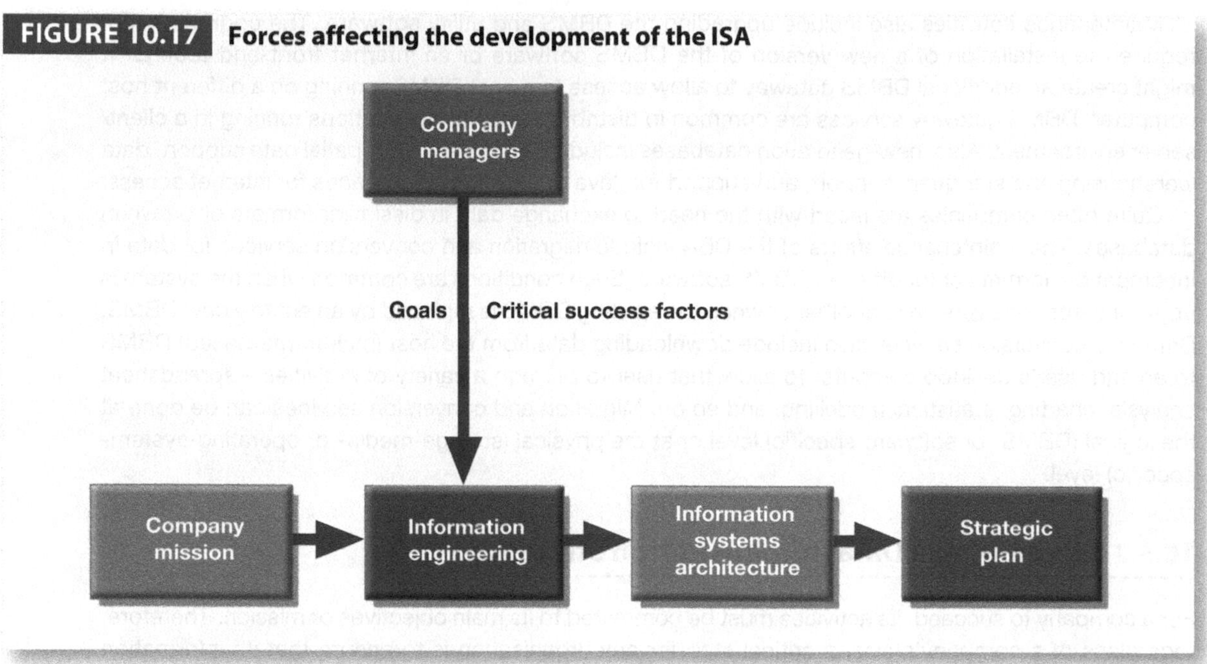

Implementing IE methodologies in an organisation is a costly process that involves planning, a commitment of resources, management liability, well-defined objectives, identification of critical factors, and control. An ISA provides a framework that includes the use of computerised, automated and integrated tools such as a DBMS and CASE tools.

10

The success of the overall information systems strategy and, therefore, of the data administration strategy depends on several critical success factors. Understanding the critical success factors helps the DBA develop a successful corporate data administration strategy. Critical success factors include managerial, technological and corporate culture issues, such as:

- *Management commitment.* Top-level management commitment is necessary to enforce the use of standards, procedures, planning, and controls. The example must be set at the top.
- *Thorough company situation analysis.* The current situation of the corporate data administration must be analysed to understand the company's position and to have a clear vision of what must be done. For example, how are database analysis, design, documentation, implementation, standards, codification, and other issues handled? Needs and problems should be identified first, then prioritized.
- *End-user involvement.* End-user involvement is another aspect critical to the success of the data administration strategy. What is the degree of organisational change involved? Successful organisational change requires that people are able to adapt to the change. Users should be given an open communication channel to upper-level management to ensure success of the implementation. Good communication channels are key to the overall process.
- *Defined standards.* Analysts and programmers must be familiar with appropriate methodologies, procedures and standards. If analysts and programmers lack familiarity, they may need to be trained in the use of the procedures and standards.

- *Training.* The vendor must train the DBA personnel in the use of the DBMS and other tools. End users must be trained to use the tools, standards and procedures to obtain and demonstrate the maximum benefit, thereby increasing end-user confidence. Key personnel should be trained first, so they can train others later.
- *A small pilot project.* A small project is recommended to ensure that the DBMS will work in the company, that the output is what was expected, and that the personnel have been trained properly.

This list of factors is not and cannot be comprehensive. Nevertheless, it does provide the initial framework for the development of a successful strategy. However, no matter how comprehensive the list of success factors is, it must be based on the notion that development and implementation of a successful data administration strategy are tightly integrated with the overall information systems planning activity of the organisation.

SUMMARY

- An information system is designed to facilitate the transformation of data into information and to manage both data and information. Thus, the database is a very important part of the information system. Systems analysis is the process that establishes the need for, and the extent of, an information system. Systems development is the process of creating an information system.
- The Systems Development Life Cycle (SDLC) traces the history (life cycle) of an application within the information system. The SDLC can be divided into five phases: planning, analysis, detailed systems design, implementation, and maintenance. The SDLC is an iterative rather than a sequential process.
- The Database Life Cycle (DBLC) describes the history of the database within the information system. The DBLC is composed of six phases: database initial study, database design, implementation and loading, testing and evaluation, operation, and maintenance and evolution. Like the SDLC, the DBLC is iterative rather than sequential.
- Threats to database security include the loss of integrity, confidentiality and availability of data. An organisation should select the relevant security measures and develop a comprehensive data security plan to protect its data.
- The conceptual portion of the design may be subject to several variations, based on two basic design philosophies: bottom-up vs top-down and centralised vs decentralised.
- The database administrator (DBA) is responsible for managing the corporate database. The internal organisation of the database administration function varies from company to company. Although no standard exists, it is common practice to divide DBA operations according to the database life-cycle phases. Some companies have created a position with a broader data management mandate to manage computerised and other data within the organisation. This broader data management activity is handled by the data administrator (DA).
- The DA and the DBA functions tend to overlap. Generally speaking, the DA is more managerially orientated than the more technically orientated DBA. Compared to the DBA function, the DA function is DBMS-independent, with a broader and longer-term focus. However, when the organisation chart does not include a DA position, the DBA executes all of the DA's functions. Because the DBA has both technical and managerial responsibilities, the DBA must have a diverse mix of skills.

10

- The managerial services of the DBA function include at least:
  - Supporting the end-user community
  - Defining and enforcing policies, procedures and standards for the database function
  - Ensuring data security, privacy and integrity
  - Providing data backup and recovery services
  - Monitoring the distribution and use of the data in the database
- The technical role requires the DBA to be involved in at least these activities:
  - Evaluating, selecting and installing the DBMS
  - Designing and implementing databases and applications
  - Testing and evaluating databases and applications
  - Operating the DBMS, utilities and applications
  - Training and supporting users
  - Maintaining the DBMS, utilities and applications
- The development of the data administration strategy is closely related to the company's mission and objectives. Therefore, the development of an organisation's strategic plan corresponds to that of data administration, requiring a detailed analysis of company goals, situation, and business needs. To guide the development of this overall plan, an integrating methodology is required. The most commonly used integrating methodology is known as information engineering (IE).

KEY TERMS

access plan
audit log
audit trail
authorisation management
bottom-up design
boundaries
centralised design
computer-aided systems engineering (CASE)
conceptual design
concurrent backup
data administrator (DA)
data encryption
database administrator (DBA)
database development
Database Life Cycle (DBLC)
database security officer (DSO)
decentralised design
disaster management
full backup
incremental backup
information resource manager (IRM)
information systems architecture (ISA)
Information engineering (IE)
information system
logical design
minimal data rule
physical design
physical security
policies
procedures
scope
standards
systems administrator (SYSADM)
systems analysis
systems development
Systems Development Life Cycle (SDLC)
top-down design
user authentication
virtualisation

FURTHER READING

Bertino, E. and Sandhu, R. 'Database Security – Concepts, Approaches, and Challenges', *IEEE Transactions on Dependable and Secure Computing*, 2(1), 2005.

Du, W. *Computer Security: A Hands-on Approach*. CreateSpace Independent Publishing Platform, 2017.

Online Content Answers to selected Review Questions and Problems for this chapter are contained on the online platform accompanying this book.

REVIEW QUESTIONS

1 What is an information system? What is its purpose?

2 How do systems analysis and systems development fit into a discussion about information systems?

3 What does the acronym SDLC mean, and what does a SDLC portray?

4 What does the acronym DBLC mean, and what does a DBLC portray?

5 Discuss the distinction between centralised and decentralised conceptual database design.

6 What is the minimal data rule in conceptual design? Why is it important?

7 Discuss the distinction between top-down and bottom-up approaches in database design.

8 What is the data dictionary's function in database design?

9 Which factors are important in a DBMS software selection?

10 Describe the DBA's responsibilities.

11 Describe and characterise the skills desired for a DBA.

12 What are the DBA's managerial roles? Describe the managerial activities and services provided by the DBA.

13 Which DBA activities are used to support the end-user community?

14 Explain the DBA's managerial role in the definition and enforcement of policies, procedures and standards.

15 Protecting data security, privacy and integrity are important database functions in authorisation management. Which activities are required in the DBA's managerial role of enforcing those functions?

16 Discuss the importance and characteristics of database backup and recovery procedures. Then describe the actions that must be detailed in backup and recovery plans.

17 Assume that your company assigned you the responsibility of selecting the corporate DBMS. Develop a checklist for the technical and other aspects involved in the selection process.

18 Describe the activities that are typically associated with the design and implementation services of the DBA technical function. Which technical skills are desirable in the DBA's personnel?

19 Briefly explain the concepts of information engineering (IE) and information systems architecture (ISA). How do those concepts affect the data administration strategy?

20 Identify and explain some of the critical success factors in the development and implementation of a successful data administration strategy.

21 What are the main categories of threats faced by an organisation in trying to protect its data?

22 What is data encryption and why is it important to data security?

PROBLEMS

1 Thabo's Car Service & Repair Centres are owned by Nationwide Car Dealers; Thabo's services and repairs only cars from Nationwide Car Dealers. Three of Thabo's Car Service & Repair Centres provide service and repair for the entire province.

Each of the three centres is independently managed and operated by a shop manager, a receptionist and at least eight mechanics. Each centre maintains a fully stocked parts inventory.

Each centre also maintains a manual file system in which each car's maintenance history is kept: repairs made, parts used, costs, service dates, owner, and so on. Files are also kept to track inventory, purchasing, billing, employees' hours and payroll.

You have been contacted by the manager of one of the centres to design and implement a computerised system. Given the preceding information, do the following:

a Indicate the most appropriate sequence of activities by labelling each of the following steps in the correct order. (For example, if you think that 'Load the database' is the appropriate first step, label it '1'.)

_____________Normalise the conceptual model.

_____________Obtain a general description of company operations.

_____________Load the database.

_____________Create a description of each system process.

_____________Test the system.

_____________Draw a data flow diagram and system flowcharts.

_____________Create a conceptual model, using ER diagrams.

_____________Create the application programs.

_____________Interview the mechanics.

_____________Create the file (table) structures.

_____________Interview the shop manager.

b Describe the different modules that you believe the system should include.

c How will a data dictionary help you develop the system? Give examples.

d Which general (system) recommendations might you make to the shop manager? For example, if the system will be integrated, which modules will be integrated? Which benefits would be derived from such an integrated system? Include several general recommendations.

e What is the best approach to conceptual database design? Why?

f Name and describe at least four reports the system should have. Explain their use. Who will use those reports?

2 Suppose you have been asked to create an information system for a manufacturing plant that produces nuts and bolts of many shapes, sizes and functions. Which questions would you ask, and how would the answers to those questions affect the database design?

3 What do you envision the SDLC to be?

4 What do you envision the DBLC to be?

5 Suppose you perform the same functions noted in Problem 2 for a larger warehousing operation. How are the two sets of procedures similar? How and why are they different?

6 Using the same procedures and concepts employed in Problem 1, how would you create an information system for the Tiny University example in Chapter 5?

7 You have been assigned to design the database for a new soccer club. Indicate the most appropriate sequence of activities by labelling each of the following steps in the correct order. (For example, if you think that 'Load the database' is the appropriate first step, label it '1'.)

____________Create the application programs.

____________Create a description of each system process.

____________Test the system.

____________Load the database.

____________Normalise the conceptual model.

____________Interview the soccer club president.

____________Create a conceptual model using ER diagrams.

____________Interview the soccer club director of coaching.

____________Create the file (table) structures.

____________Obtain a general description of the soccer club operations.

____________Draw a data flow diagram and system flowchart.

CHAPTER 11

Conceptual, Logical, and Physical Database Design

IN THIS CHAPTER, YOU WILL LEARN:

- About the three stages of database design: conceptual, logical, and physical
- How to design a conceptual model to represent the business and its key functional areas
- How the conceptual model can be transformed into a logically equivalent set of relations
- How to translate the logical data model into a set of specific DBMS table specifications
- About different types of file organisation
- How indexes can be applied to improve data access and retrieval
- How to estimate data storage requirements

PREVIEW

In Chapter 10, you learnt about the Database Life Cycle. The most critical phase of this cycle was that of the actual database design. It is essential that the data characteristics that have been captured in the database initial study are used to build a database model that accurately reflects the user requirements and the needs of the business. Such is the importance of database design; it is broken down into three distinct stages:

- *Conceptual database design* where we create the conceptual representation of the database by producing a data model that identifies the relevant entities and relationships within our system
- *Logical database design* where we design relations based on each entity and define integrity rules to ensure there are no redundant relationships within our database
- *Physical database design* where the physical database is implemented in the target DBMS. In this stage, we have to consider how each relation is stored and how the data is accessed.

Figure 11.1 shows the procedural flow of these stages and the steps within each that need to be taken.

FIGURE 11.1 The three stages of database design

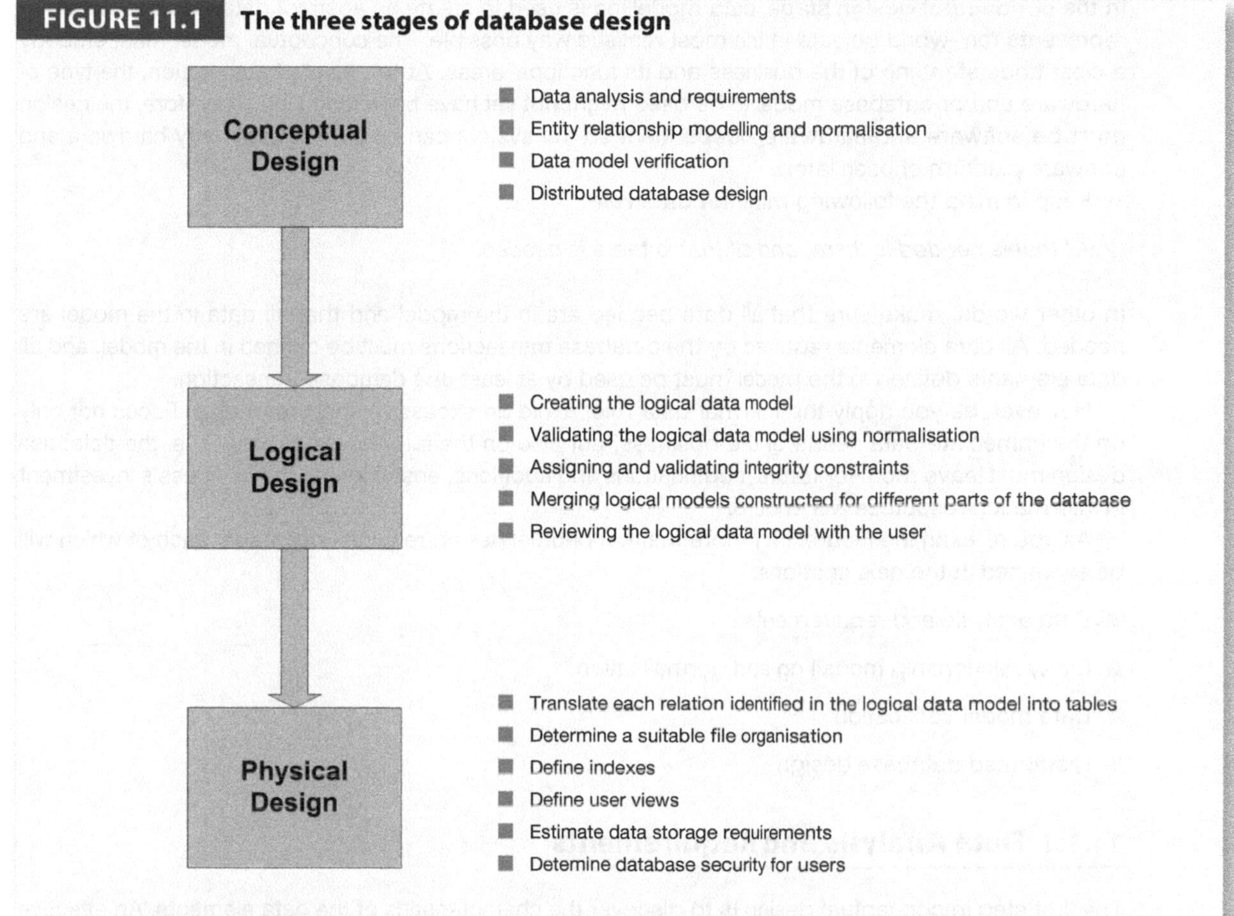

Conceptual Design
Data analysis and requirements
Entity relationship modelling and normalisation
Data model verification
Distributed database design
Logical Design
Creating the logical data model
Validating the logical data model using normalisation
Assigning and validating integrity constraints
Merging logical models constructed for different parts of the database
Reviewing the logical data model with the user
Physical Design
Translate each relation identified in the logical data model into tables
Determine a suitable file organisation
Define indexes
Define user views
Estimate data storage requirements
Detemine database security for users

These three stages of database design are not totally intuitive and obvious. There is no single quick or automated method for tackling each stage. A well-designed database takes a considerable amount of time and effort to envisage, build and refine. It cannot be stressed enough that, if the time is taken to design your databases properly, then it will provide a solid foundation in which to build a complete system. One of E.F. Codd's requirements when designing a relational database management system was that the design should maintain logical and physical data independence. The separation of these two stages is very important. Logical design is concerned with what the database looks like to the user. Physical design is concerned with how the logical design maps to the physical storage of the database in secondary storage. Codd's rules on relational database design stated that:

- if the logical structure of the database should change, then the way the user views the database should not change (logical data independence)
- if the physical methods (hardware, storage, etc.) of storing and retrieving data change, then the user interface should not be affected in any way (physical data independence).

In this chapter, you will learn about the steps required to complete conceptual, logical, and physical database design using a number of examples.

11.1 CONCEPTUAL DESIGN

In the **conceptual design** stage, data modelling is used to create an abstract database structure that represents real-world objects in the most realistic way possible. The conceptual model must embody a clear understanding of the business and its functional areas. At this level of abstraction, the type of hardware and/or database model to be used might not yet have been identified. Therefore, the design must be software and hardware independent so the system can be set up within any hardware and software platform chosen later.

Keep in mind the following **minimal data rule**:

All that is needed is there, and all that is there is needed.

In other words, make sure that all data needed are in the model and that all data in the model are needed. All data elements required by the database transactions must be defined in the model, and all data elements defined in the model must be used by at least one database transaction.

However, as you apply the minimal data rule, avoid an excessive short-term bias. Focus not only on the immediate data needs of the business, but also on the future data needs. Thus, the database design must leave room for future modifications and additions, ensuring that the business's investment in information resources will endure.

As you re-examine Figure 11.1, note that conceptual design requires four steps, each of which will be examined in the next sections:

- Data analysis and requirements
- Entity relationship modelling and normalisation
- Data model verification
- Distributed database design

11

11.1.1 Data Analysis and Requirements

The first step in conceptual design is to discover the characteristics of the data elements. An effective database is an information factory that produces key ingredients for successful decision making. Appropriate data element characteristics are those that can be transformed into appropriate information. Therefore, the designer's efforts are focused on:

- *Information needs*. What kind of information is needed – that is, what output (reports and queries) must be generated by the system, what information does the current system generate, and to what extent is that information adequate?
- *Information users*. Who will use the information? How is the information to be used? What are the different end-user data views?
- *Information sources*. Where is the information to be found? How is the information to be extracted once it is found?
- *Information constitution*. What data elements are needed to produce the information? What are the data attributes? What relationships exist among the data? What is the data volume? How frequently are the data used? What data transformations are to be used to generate the required information?

The designer obtains the answers to those questions from different sources so that he or she can compile the necessary information. Note these sources:

- *Developing and gathering end-user data views*. The database designer and the end user(s) interact to develop a precise description of end-user data views jointly. In turn, the end-user data views are used to help identify the database's main data elements.
- *Directly observing the current system: existing and desired output*. The end user usually has an existing system in place (manual or computer-based). The designer reviews the existing system to identify the data and their characteristics. The designer examines the input forms and files (tables) to discover the data type and volume. If the end user already has an automated system in place, the designer carefully examines the current and desired reports to describe the data required to support the reports.
- *Interfacing with the systems design group*. The database design process is part of the Systems Development Life Cycle (SDLC). In some cases, the systems analyst in charge of designing the new system will also develop the conceptual database model. (This is usually true in a desktop computer environment.) In other cases, the database design is considered part of the database administrator's job. The presence of a database administrator (DBA) usually implies the existence of a formal data-processing department. The DBA designs the database according to the specifications created by the systems analyst.

To develop an accurate data model, the designer must have a thorough understanding of the company's data types and their extent and uses. But data do not by themselves yield the required understanding of the total business. From a database point of view, the collection of data becomes meaningful only when business rules are defined. Remember from Chapter 2, Data Models, that a *business rule* is a brief and precise narrative description of a policy, procedure or principle within a specific organisation's environment. Business rules, derived from a detailed description of an organisation's operations, help to create and enforce actions within that organisation's environment. When business rules are written properly, they define entities, attributes, relationships, multiplicities and constraints.

To be effective, business rules must be easy to understand and they must be widely disseminated to ensure that every person in the organisation shares a common interpretation of the rules. Using simple language, business rules describe the main and distinguishing characteristics of the data *as viewed by the company*. Examples of business rules are as follows:

- A customer may make many payments on account.
- Each payment on account is credited to only one customer.
- A customer may generate many invoices.
- Each invoice is generated by only one customer.

Given their critical role in database design, business rules must not be established casually. Poorly defined or inaccurate business rules lead to database designs and implementations that fail to meet the needs of the organisation's end users.

Ideally, business rules are derived from a formal *description of operations*. As its name implies, a **description of operations** is a document that provides a precise, detailed, up-to-date and thoroughly reviewed description of the activities that define an organisation's operating environment. To the database designer, the operating environment is both the data sources and the data users. Naturally, the organisation's operating environment is dependent on the organisation's mission. For example, the operating environment of a university would be quite different from that of a steel manufacturer, an airline or a nursing home. Yet no matter how different the organisations may be, the *data analysis and requirements* component of the database design process is enhanced when the data environment and data use are described accurately and precisely within a description of operations.

In a business environment, the main sources of information for the description of operations – and, therefore, of business rules – are company managers, policy makers, department managers and written documentation such as company procedures, standards and operations manuals. A faster and more direct source of business rules is direct interviews with end users. Unfortunately, because perceptions differ, the end user can be a less reliable source when it comes to specifying business rules. For example, a maintenance department mechanic may believe that any mechanic can initiate a maintenance procedure, when actually only mechanics with inspection authorisation should perform such a task. Such a distinction may seem trivial, but it has major legal consequences. Although end users are crucial contributors to the development of business rules, it pays to verify end-user perceptions. Often, interviews with several people who perform the same job yield very different perceptions of what their job components are. While such a discovery may point to 'management problems', that general diagnosis does not help the database designer. Given the discovery of such problems, the database designer's job is to reconcile the differences and verify the results of the reconciliation to ensure that the business rules are appropriate and accurate.

Knowing the business rules enables the designer to understand fully how the business works and what role the data plays within company operations. Consequently, the designer must identify the company's business rules and analyse their impact on the nature, role and scope of data.

Business rules yield several important benefits in the design of new systems:

- They help standardise the company's view of data.
- They constitute a communications tool between users and designers.
- They allow the designer to understand the nature, role and scope of the data.
- They allow the designer to understand business processes.
- They allow the designer to develop appropriate relationship participation rules and foreign key constraints. (See Chapter 5, Data Modelling with Entity Relationship Diagrams.)

The last point is especially noteworthy: whether a given relationship is mandatory or optional is usually a function of the applicable business rule.

Example Data Analysis and Requirements for a DVD Rental Store

To illustrate the first stage of the conceptual design process, let us now consider an example based on a DVD rental store. Within this store movie titles are classified according to their type: comedy, family, documentary, action and new release. Each type contains many possible titles, and most titles within a type are available in multiple copies. For example, note the summary presented in Table 11.1.

TABLE 11.1 The DVD rental type and title relationship

Type	Title	Copy
Family	Chronicles of Narnia	1
	Chronicles of Narnia	2
	Toy Story	1
	Toy Story	2
	Toy Story	3
Comedy	Simpsons	1
	Simpsons	2
	Simpsons	3
Action	Lord of the Rings	1
	Lord of the Rings	2

You have been asked to produce a database for this store and have been provided with the following set of business rules from the manager:

- The movie type classification is standard; not all types are necessarily in stock.
- The movie list is updated as necessary; however, a movie on that list might not be ordered if the DVD shop owner decides that it is not desirable for some reason.
- The DVD rental shop does not necessarily order movies from the entire vendor list; some vendors on the vendor list are merely potential vendors from whom movies may be ordered in the future.
- Movies classified as new releases are reclassified to an appropriate type after they have been in stock for more than 30 days.
- The video shop manager wants to have an end-of-period (week, month, year) report for the number of rentals by type.
- If a customer requests a title, the shop assistant must be able to find it quickly. When a customer selects one or more titles, an invoice is written. Each invoice may thus contain charges for one or more titles. All customers pay in cash.
- When the customer checks out a title, a record is kept of the checkout date and time and the expected return date and time. Upon the return of rented titles, the shop assistant must be able to check quickly whether the return is late and to assess the appropriate late return fee.
- The DVD store owner wants to be able to generate periodic revenue reports by title and by type. The owner also wants to be able to generate periodic inventory reports and to keep track of titles on order.
- The DVD store owner, who employs two (salaried) full-time and three (hourly) part-time employees, wants to keep track of all employee work time and payroll data. Part-time employees must arrange entries in a work schedule, while all employees sign in and out on a work log.

NOTE

When capturing the requirements, the description of operations not only establishes the operational aspects of the business; it also establishes some specific system objectives we have listed next.

11

As you start to think about designing this database, remember that transaction and information requirements help drive the design by defining required entities, relationships and attributes. Also, keep in mind that the description provided by the problem leaves many possibilities for design differences. For example, consider the EMPLOYEE classification as full-time or part-time. If there are few distinguishing characteristics between the two, the situation may be handled by using an attribute EMP_CLASS (whose values might be F or P) in the EMPLOYEE table. If full-time employees earn a base salary and part-time employees earn only an hourly wage, that problem can be handled by having two attributes, EMP_HOURPAY and EMP_BASE_PAY, in EMPLOYEE. Using this approach, the HOUR_PAY is set to zero for the salaried full-time employees, while the EMP_BASE_PAY is set to zero for the part-time employees. To ensure correct pay computations, the application software selects either F or P, depending on the employee classification. On the other hand, if part-time employees are handled quite differently from full-time employees in terms of work scheduling, benefits, and so on, it would be better to use a supertype/subtype classification for FULL_TIME and PART_TIME employees. The more unique variables exist, the more sense a supertype/subtype relationship makes.

Once the basic requirements have been captured, the first ER model can be created. The ER model for the DVD rental store is presented in the next section.

11.1.2 Entity Relationship Modelling and Normalisation

Before creating the ER model, the designer must communicate and enforce appropriate standards to be used in the documentation of the design. The standards include the use of diagrams and symbols, documentation writing style, layout and any other conventions to be followed during documentation. Designers often overlook this very important requirement, especially when they are working as members of a design team. Failure to standardise documentation often means a failure to communicate later. And communications failures often lead to poor design work. In contrast, well-defined and enforced standards make design work easier and promise (but do not guarantee) a smooth integration of all system components.

Because the business rules usually define the nature of the relationship(s) among the entities, the designer must incorporate them into the conceptual model. The process of defining business rules and developing the conceptual model using ER diagrams can be described using the steps shown in Table 11.2.[1]

TABLE 11.2 Developing the conceptual model using ER diagrams

Step	Activity
1	Identify, analyse and refine the business rules.
2	Identify the main entities, using the results of Step 1.
3	Define the relationships among the entities, using the results of Steps 1 and 2.
4	Define the attributes, primary keys and foreign keys for each of the entities.
5	Normalise the entities. (Remember that entities are implemented as tables in an RDBMS.)
6	Complete the initial ER diagram.
7	Have the main end users verify the model in Step 6 against the data, information and processing requirements.
8	Modify the ER diagram, using the results of Step 7.

Some of the steps listed in Table 11.2 take place concurrently. And some, such as the normalisation process, can generate a demand for additional entities and/or attributes, thereby causing the designer to revise the ER model. For example, while identifying two main entities, the designer might also identify the composite bridge entity that represents the many-to-many relationship between those two main entities.

To review, suppose you are creating a conceptual model for the JollyGood Movie Rental Company, whose end users want to track customers' movie rentals. The simple ER diagram presented in Figure 11.2 shows a composite entity that helps track customers and their DVD rentals. Business rules define the optional nature of the relationships between the entities DVD and CUSTOMER depicted in Figure 11.2. For example, customers are not required to check out a DVD. A DVD need not be checked out in order to exist on the shelf. A customer may rent many DVDs, and a DVD may be rented by many customers. In particular, note the composite RENTAL entity that connects the two main entities.

---

1 See Alice Sandifer and Barbara von Halle, 'Linking Rules to Models', *Database Programming and Design*, 4(3), March 1991, pp. 13–16. Although the source seems dated, it remains the current standard. The technology has changed substantially, but the process has not.

FIGURE 11.2 **A composite entity**

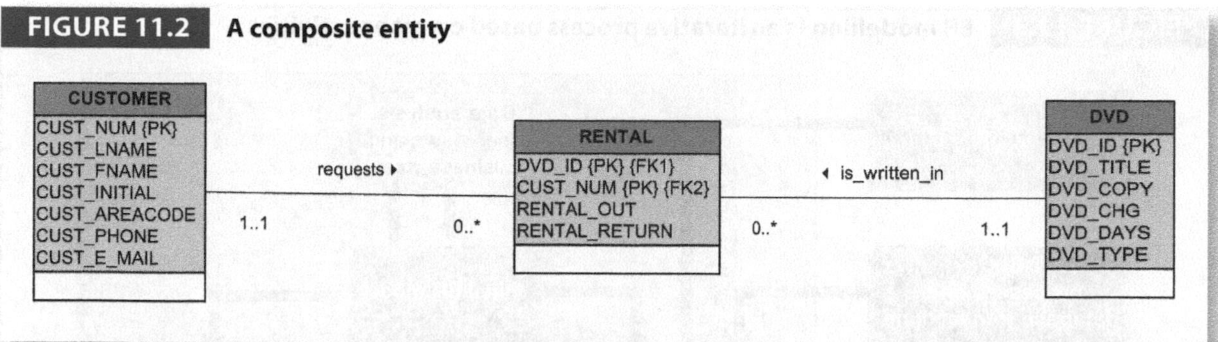

As you will likely discover, the initial ER model may be subjected to several revisions before it meets the system's requirements. Such a revision process is quite natural. Remember that the ER model is a communications tool as well as a design blueprint. Therefore, the initial ER model should give rise to questions such as, 'Is this really what you meant?' when you continue to meet with the proposed system users. For example, the ERD shown in Figure 11.2 is far from complete. Clearly, many more attributes must be defined and the dependencies must be checked before the design can be implemented. In addition, the design cannot yet support the typical DVD rental transactions environment. For example, each DVD is likely to have many copies available for rental purposes. However, if the DVD entity shown in Figure 11.2 is used to store the titles as well as the copies, the design triggers the data redundancies shown in Table 11.3.

TABLE 11.3 **Data redundancies in the DVD table**

DVD_ID	DVD_TITLE	DVD_COPY	DVD_CHG	DVD_DAYS
SF-12345FT-1	Star Wars	1	13.50	1
SF-12345FT-2	Star Wars	2	13.50	1
SF-12345FT-3	Star Wars	3	13.50	1
WE-5432GR-1	Beauty and the Beast	1	12.30	2
WE-5432GR-2	Beauty and the Beast	2	12.30	2

The initial ERD shown in Figure 11.2 must be modified to reflect the answer to the question, 'Is more than one copy available for each title?' Also, payment transactions must be supported.

From the preceding discussion, you might get the impression that ER modelling activities (entity/attribute definition, normalisation and verification) take place in a precise sequence. In fact, once you have completed the initial ER model, chances are you will move back and forth among the activities until you are satisfied that the ER model accurately represents a database design that is capable of meeting the required system demands. (The activities often take place in parallel, and the process is iterative.) Figure 11.3 summarises the ER modelling process interactions. Figure 11.4 summarises the array of design tools and information sources that the designer can use to produce the conceptual model.

FIGURE 11.3 ER modelling is an iterative process based on many activities

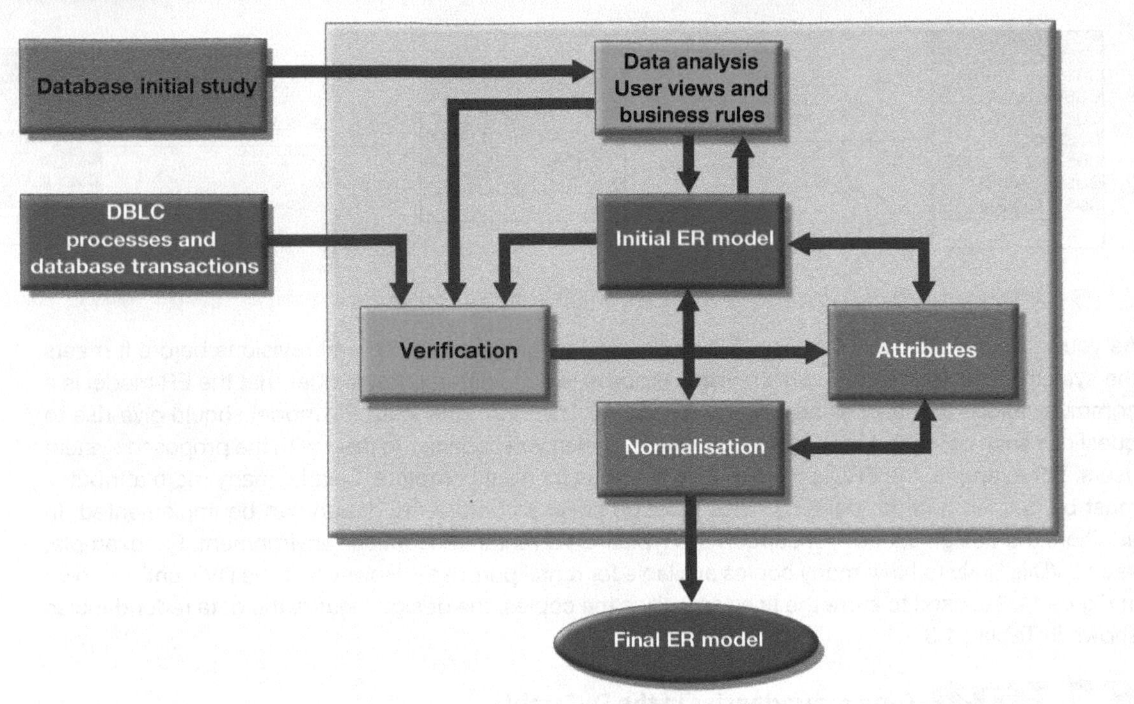

FIGURE 11.4 Conceptual design tools and information sources

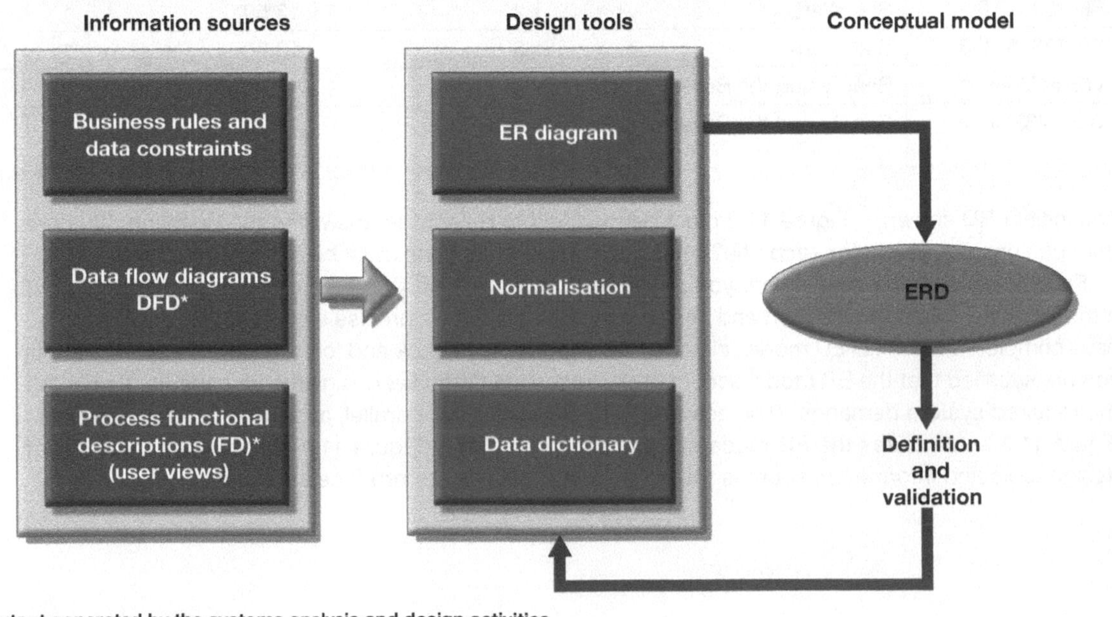

11

All objects (entities, attributes, relations, views and so on) are defined in a data dictionary, which is used in tandem with the normalisation process to help eliminate data anomalies and redundancy problems. During this ER modelling process, the designer must:

- Define entities, attributes, primary keys and foreign keys. (The foreign keys serve as the basis for the relationships among the entities.)
- Make decisions about adding new primary key attributes to satisfy end-user and/or processing requirements.
- Make decisions about the treatment of multivalued attributes.
- Make decisions about adding derived attributes to satisfy processing requirements.
- Make decisions about the placement of foreign keys in 1:1 relationships. (If necessary, review the supertype/subtype relationships in Chapter 6, Data Modelling Advanced Concepts.)
- Avoid unnecessary ternary relationships.
- Draw the corresponding ER diagram.
- Normalise the entities.
- Include all data element definitions in the data dictionary.
- Make decisions about standard naming conventions.

The naming conventions requirement is important, yet it is frequently ignored at the designer's peril. Real database design is generally accomplished by teams. Therefore, it is important to ensure that the team members work in an environment in which naming standards are defined and enforced. Proper documentation is crucial to the successful completion of the design. Therefore, it is very useful to establish procedures that are, in effect, self-documenting.

Although some useful entity and attribute naming conventions were established in Chapter 5, Data Modelling with Entity Relationship Diagrams, they will be revisited in greater detail here. This book uses naming conventions that are likely to be acceptable across a reasonably broad range of DBMSs and will meet self-documentation requirements to the greatest extent possible. As the older DBMSs fade from the scene, the naming conventions will be more broadly applicable. You should try to adhere to the following conventions:

- Use descriptive entity and attribute names wherever possible. For example, in a travel agency database, the CUSTOMER entity contains personal information about the customer who makes a BOOKING and and the HOTEL entity may be related to booking, if the customer had booked a specific hotel.
- Composite entities are usually assigned a name that describes the relationship they represent. For example, in the travel agency database, a BOOKING may consist of many TOURs and a TOUR may have many BOOKINGs made for it. Therefore, the composite (bridge) entity that links BOOKING and TOUR will be named TOUR_BOOKING. Occasionally, the designer finds it necessary to show what entities are being linked by the composite entity. In such cases, the composite entity name may borrow segments of those entity names. For example, in Tiny University, STU_CLASS may be the composite entity that links STUDENT and CLASS. However, that naming convention might make the one discussed in the next point more cumbersome, so it should be used sparingly. A better choice would be the composite entity name ENROL, to indicate that the STUDENT enrols in a CLASS.

- An attribute name should be descriptive, and it should contain a prefix that helps identify the table in which it is found. For the purposes here, the maximum prefix length will be five characters. For example, the VENDOR table might contain attributes such as VEND_ID and VEND_PHONE. Similarly, the ITEM table might contain attribute names such as ITEM_ID and ITEM_DESCRIPTION. The advantage of this naming convention is that it immediately identifies a table's foreign key(s). For example, if the EMPLOYEE table contains attributes such as EMP_ID, EMP_LNAME and DEPT_CODE, it is immediately obvious that DEPT_CODE is the foreign key that probably links EMPLOYEE to DEPARTMENT. Naturally, the existence of relationships and table names that start with the same characters might dictate that you bend this naming convention occasionally, as you can see in the next point.
- If one table is named ORDER and its weak counterpart is named ORDER_ITEM, the prefix ORD will be used to indicate an attribute originating in the ORDER table. The ITEM prefix will identify an attribute originating in the ITEM table. Clearly, you cannot use ORD as a prefix to the attributes originating in the ORDER_ITEM table, so you should use a combination of characters, such as OI, as the prefix to the ORDER_ITEM attribute names. In spite of that limitation, it is generally possible to assign prefixes that identify an attribute's origin. (Keep in mind that some RDBMSs use a 'reserved word' list. For example, ORDER may be interpreted as a reserved word in a SELECT statement. In that case, you should use a table name other than ORDER.)

As you can tell, it is not always possible to adhere strictly to the naming conventions. Sometimes the requirement to limit name lengths makes the attribute or entity names less descriptive. Also, with a large number of entities and attributes in a complex design, you might have to be somewhat inventive about using proper attribute name prefixes. But then those prefixes are less helpful in identifying the precise source of the attribute. Nevertheless, the consistent use of prefixes will reduce sourcing doubts significantly. For example, while the prefix CO does not obviously relate to the CHECK_OUT table, just as obvious is the fact that it does not originate in WITHDRAW, ITEM or USER.

Example Entity Relationship Modelling for the DVD Rental Store

Let us revisit our DVD rental store, for which we have gathered the basic requirements. Now examine the following additional requirements:

- DVDs are classified according to their TYPE (Comedy, Family, Documentary, Action and New Release), so a new entity called TYPE must be created to prevent data redundancy.
- The shop assistant must be able to find customers' requests quickly.
- This requirement is met by creating an easy way to query the DVD data (by name, type, etc.) while entering the RENTAL data.
- The shop assistant must be able to check quickly whether or not the return is late and to assess the appropriate 'late return' fee. This requirement is met by adding attributes such as expected return date, actual return date and late fees to the RENTAL entity. Note that there is no need to add a new entity, nor do we need to create an additional relationship. Keep in mind that some requirements are easily met by including the appropriate attributes in the tables and by combining those attributes through an application program that enforces the business rule. Remember that not all business rules can be represented in the database conceptual diagram.
- The store owner wants to be able to keep track of all employee work time and payroll data. This will require the creation of an EMPLOYEE entity.
- Here we must create two new entities: WORK_SCHEDULE and WORK_LOG, which will show the employee's work schedule and the actual times worked, respectively. These entities also help us generate the payroll report.

The description also specifies some of the expected reports that the database eventually produces:

- End-of-period report for the number of rentals by type. This report will use the RENTAL and DVD entities to generate all rental data for some specified period of time.
- Revenue report by title and by type. This report will use the RENTAL, DVD and TYPE entities to generate all the rental data.
- Periodic inventory reports. This report will use the DVD and TYPE entities.
- Titles on order. This report will use the ORDER, DVD and TYPE entities.
- Employee work times and payroll data. This report will use the EMPLOYEE, WORK_SCHEDULE and WORK_LOG entities.

After analysing all the requirements gathered so far, a first draft of the ER model is shown in Figure 11.5.

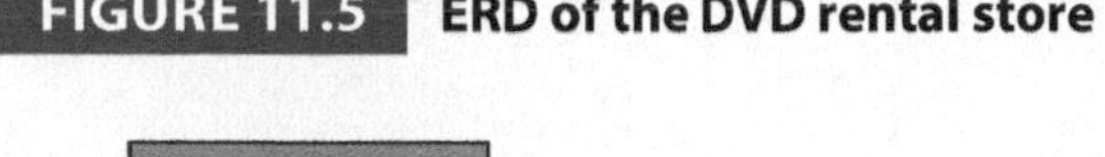

FIGURE 11.5 ERD of the DVD rental store

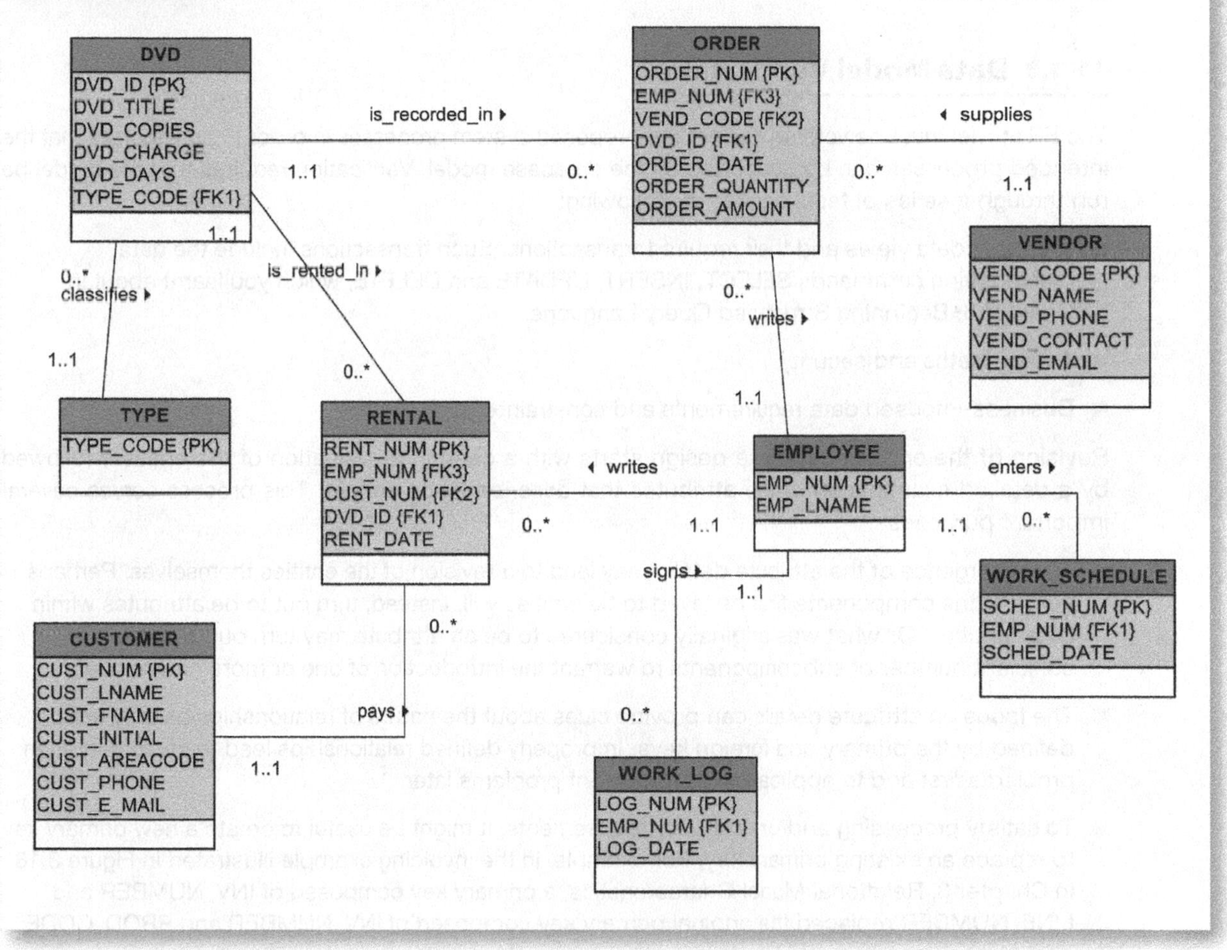

Although there is a temptation to create FULL_TIME and PART_TIME entities, which are then related to WORK_LOG and WORK_SCHEDULE, respectively, such a decision reflects a substitution of an entity for an attribute. It is far better to simply create an attribute, perhaps named EMP_TYPE, in the EMPLOYEE entity. The EMP_TYPE attribute values would then be P = part-time or F = full-time. The applications software can then be used to force entries into the WORK_LOG and WORK_SCHEDULE entities, depending on the EMP_TYPE attribute value.

At this point, the ERD has not yet been verified against the transaction requirements. For example, there is no way to check which specific video has been rented by a customer. If five customers rent copies of the same video, you don't know which customer has which copy. In addition, the work log entity's LOG_DATE is incapable of tracking when all employees logged in or out. Therefore, two dates and times are necessary, perhaps named LOG_DATE_IN and LOG_DATE_OUT. In addition, if you want to determine the hours worked by each part-time employee, it is necessary to record the time in and time out. Similarly, the work schedule cannot yet be used to track the employees' schedules. Who has worked and when? Clearly, the data model that has been produced requires additional work through the process of verification against the proposed system. You will learn how the data model is verified in the next section.

11.1.3 Data Model Verification

The ER model must be verified against the proposed system processes in order to corroborate that the intended processes can be supported by the database model. Verification requires that the model be run through a series of tests against the following:

- End-user data views and their required transactions. Such transactions include the data manipulation commands SELECT, INSERT, UPDATE and DELETE, which you learnt about in Chapter 8, Beginning Structured Query Language.
- Access paths and security.
- Business-imposed data requirements and constraints.

Revision of the original database design starts with a careful re-evaluation of the entities, followed by a detailed examination of the attributes that describe those entities. This process serves several important purposes:

- The emergence of the attribute details may lead to a revision of the entities themselves. Perhaps some of the components first believed to be entities will, instead, turn out to be attributes within other entities. Or what was originally considered to be an attribute may turn out to contain a sufficient number of subcomponents to warrant the introduction of one or more new entities.
- The focus on attribute details can provide clues about the nature of relationships as they are defined by the primary and foreign keys. Improperly defined relationships lead to implementation problems first and to application development problems later.
- To satisfy processing and/or end-user requirements, it might be useful to create a new primary key to replace an existing primary key. For example, in the invoicing example illustrated in Figure 3.18 in Chapter 3, Relational Model Characteristics, a primary key composed of INV_NUMBER and LINE_NUMBER replaced the original primary key composed of INV_NUMBER and PROD_CODE. That change ensured that the items in the invoice always appear in the same order as they were entered. To simplify queries and to increase processing speed, you may create a single-attribute surrogate primary key to replace an existing multiple-attribute primary key.

- Unless the entity details (the attributes and their characteristics) are precisely defined, it is difficult to evaluate the extent of the design's normalisation. Knowledge of the normalisation levels helps guard against undesirable redundancies.
- A careful review of the rough database design blueprint is likely to lead to revisions. Those revisions will help ensure that the design is capable of meeting end-user requirements.

Because real-world database design is generally done by teams, you should strive to organise the design's major components into modules. (A **module** is an information system component that handles a specific function, such as inventory, orders, payroll and so on. At the design level, a module is an ER segment that is an integrated part of the overall ER model.) Creating and using modules accomplishes several important ends:

- The modules (and even the segments within them) can be delegated to design groups within teams, greatly speeding up the development work.
- The modules simplify the design work. The large number of entities within a complex design can be daunting. Each module contains a more manageable number of entities.
- The modules can be prototyped quickly. Implementation and applications programming trouble spots can be identified more readily. (Quick prototyping is also a great confidence builder.)
- Even if the entire system can't be brought online quickly, the implementation of one or more modules will demonstrate that progress is being made and that at least part of the system is ready to begin serving the end users.

As useful as modules are, they represent ER model fragments. Fragmentation creates a potential problem: the fragments may not include all of the ER model's components and may, therefore, not be able to support all of the required processes. To avoid that problem, the modules must be verified against the complete ER model. That verification process is detailed in Table 11.4.

TABLE 11.4 The ER model verification process

Step	Activity
1	Identify the ER model's central entity.
2	Identify each module and its components.
3	Identify each module's transaction requirements: Internal: Updates/Inserts/Deletes/Queries/Reports External: Module interfaces
4	Verify all processes against the ER model.
5	Make all necessary changes suggested in Step 4.
6	Repeat Steps 2–5 for all modules.

11

Keep in mind that the verification process requires the continuous verification of business transactions as well as system and user requirements. The verification sequence must be repeated for each of the system's modules. Figure 11.6 illustrates the iterative nature of the process.

FIGURE 11.6 Iterative ER model verification process

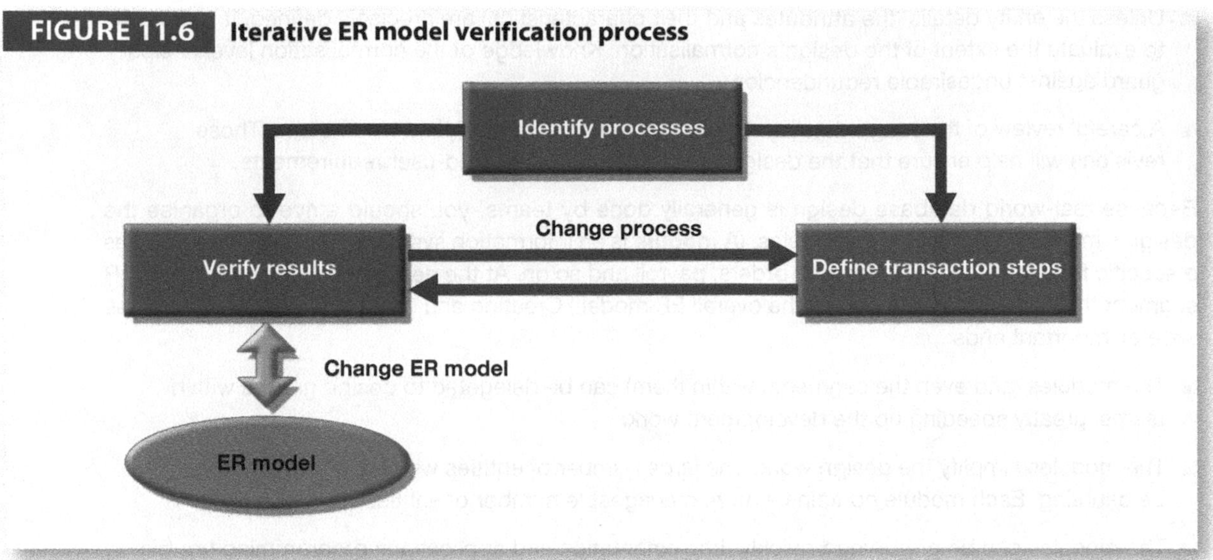

The verification process starts with selecting the central (most important) entity. The central entity is defined in terms of its participation in most of the model's relationships, and it is the focus of most of the system's operations. In other words, to identify the central entity, the designer selects the entity involved in the greatest number of relationships. (In the ER diagram, it is the entity that has more lines connected to it than any other.)

The next step is to identify the module or subsystem to which the central entity belongs and to define that module's boundaries and scope. The entity belongs to the module that uses it most frequently. Once each module is identified, the central entity is placed within the module's framework to let you focus your attention on the module's details.

Within the central entity/module framework, you need to:

- *Ensure the module's cohesivity.* The term **cohesivity** describes the strength of the relationships found among the module's entities. A module must display *high cohesivity* – that is, the entities must be strongly related, and the module must be complete and self-sufficient.
- *Analyse each module's relationships with other modules to address module coupling.* **Module coupling** describes the extent to which modules are independent of one another. Modules must display *low coupling*, indicating that they are independent of other modules. Low coupling decreases unnecessary intermodule dependencies, thereby allowing the creation of a truly modular system and eliminating unnecessary relationships among entities. Note: One of the design challenges is to achieve the right balance between cohesion and coupling. Often, the quest to have highly cohesive modules results in creating more modules that are dependent on each other, hence high coupling. Decreasing coupling has the reverse effect, resulting in low cohesion. Finding the correct balance is a key part of the database designer's job.

Processes may be classified according to their:

- Frequency (daily, weekly, monthly, yearly, or exceptions).
- Operational type (INSERT or ADD, UPDATE or CHANGE, DELETE, queries and reports, batches, maintenance and backups).

All identified processes must be verified against the ER model. If necessary, appropriate changes are implemented. The process verification is repeated for all of the model's modules. You can expect that additional entities and attributes will be incorporated into the conceptual model during its validation.

At this point, a conceptual model has been defined as hardware- and software-independent. Such independence ensures the system's portability across platforms. Portability may extend the database's life by making it possible to migrate to another DBMS and/or another hardware platform.

Example Data Model Verification for the DVD Rental Store

Applying the verification process described in Table 11.4 to the conceptual model of the DVD rental store from the previous section produces the verified data model as shown in Figure 11.7.

FIGURE 11.7 Verified ER model for the DVD rental store

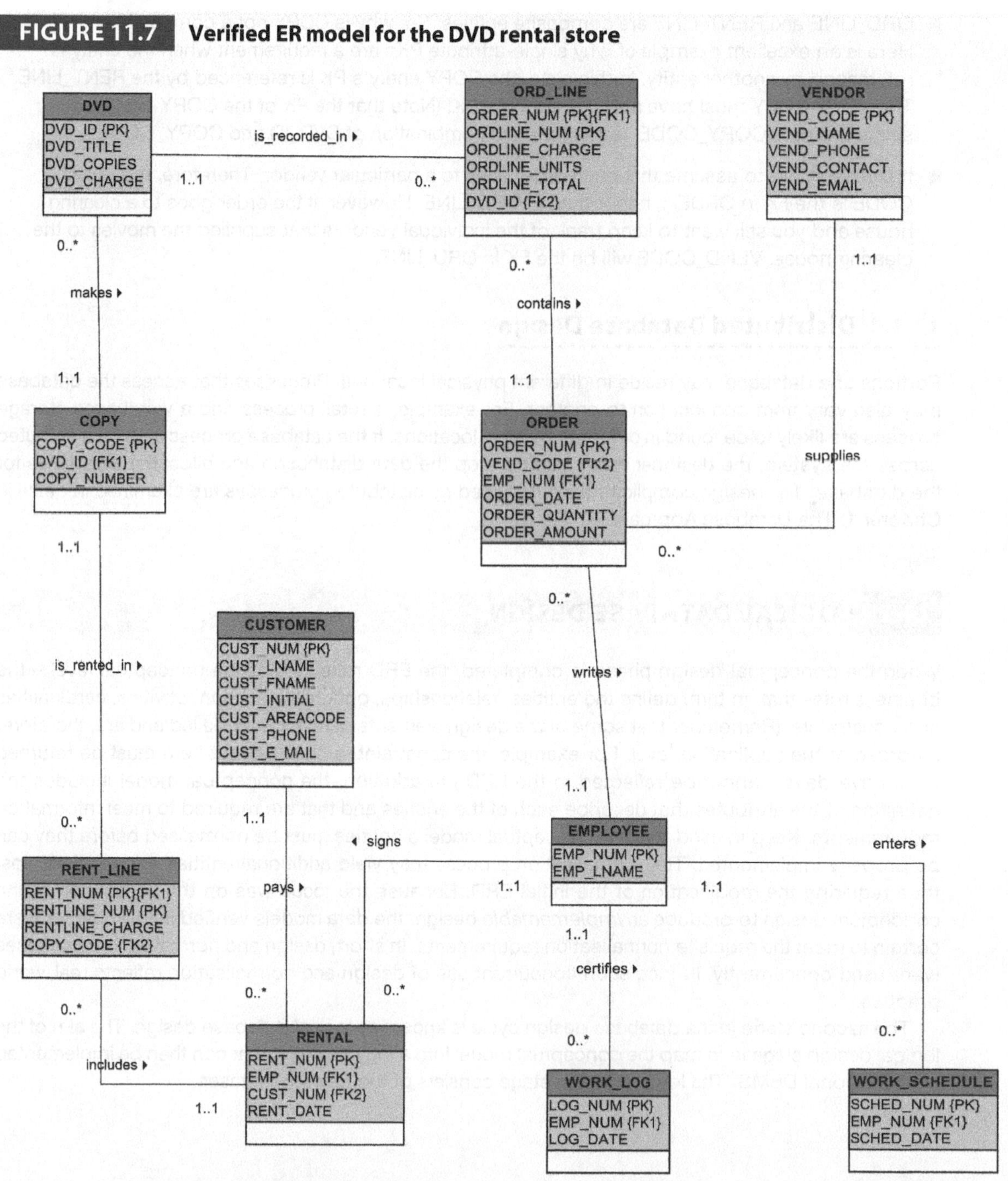

As you examine the components of the ERD model in Figure 11.7, note particularly the following points:

- All relationships are read from the parent to the related entity. Therefore, ORDER contains ORD_LINE. (The natural tendency to read from top to bottom or from left to right is not the governing factor in an ERD!)
- We can now track individual copies of each movie. If there are 12 copies of a given movie, each copy can be rented out separately.
- ORD_LINE and RENT_LINE are composite entities. So, why is COPY not a composite entity? Here is an excellent example of why single-attribute PKs are a requirement when the entity is referenced by another entity. In this case, the COPY entity's PK is referenced by the RENT_LINE. Therefore, COPY must have a single-attribute PK. (Note that the PK of the COPY entity is the single attribute COPY_CODE, rather than the combination of DVD_ID and COPY_CODE).
- It is reasonable to assume that each order goes to a particular vendor. Therefore, the VEND_CODE is the FK in ORDER, rather than in ORD_LINE. However, if the order goes to a clearing house and you still want to keep track of the individual vendors that supplied the movies to the clearing house, VEND_CODE will be the FK in ORD_LINE.

11.1.4 Distributed Database Design

Portions of a database may reside in different physical locations. Processes that access the database may also vary from one location to another. For example, a retail process and a warehouse storage process are likely to be found in different physical locations. If the database process is to be distributed across the system, the designer must also develop the data distribution and allocation strategies for the database. The design complications introduced by distributed processes are examined in detail in Chapter 1, The Database Approach.

11

11.2 LOGICAL DATABASE DESIGN

When the conceptual design phase is completed, the ERD reflects – at the conceptual level – the business rules that, in turn, define the entities, relationships, optionalities, connectivities, cardinalities and constraints. (Remember that some of the design elements cannot be modelled and are, therefore, enforced at the application level. For example, the constraint 'a checked-out item must be returned within five days' cannot be reflected in the ERD.) In addition, the conceptual model includes the definition of the attributes that describe each of the entities and that are required to meet information requirements. Keep in mind that the conceptual model's entities must be normalised before they can be properly implemented. The normalisation process may yield additional entities and relationships, thus requiring the modification of the initial ERD. Because the focus was on the verification of the conceptual design to produce an *implementable* design, the data models verified in this chapter were certain to meet the requisite normalisation requirements. In short, design and normalisation processes were used concurrently. In fact, such concurrent use of design and normalisation reflects real-world practice.

The second stage in the database design cycle is known as logical database design. The aim of the logical design stage is to map the conceptual model into a logical model that can then be implemented on a relational DBMS. The logical design stage consists of the following phases:

1 Creating the logical data model
2 Validating the logical data model using normalisation
3 Assigning and validating integrity constraints
4 Merging logical models constructed for different parts for the database
5 Reviewing the logical data model with the user

Next, you will learn about each of these phases in detail, which will help you to build a successful logical data model.

11.2.1 Creating the Logical Data Model

The first stage of logical database design is to translate the conceptual design into a set of relational database constructs. This involves converting the ER model from the conceptual design phase into a set of relations using a set of rules. A relation must be created for each entity and relationships and attributes must be created whilst at the same time meeting the required integrity constraints. Usually, relations with no dependents (e.g. not containing any foreign keys) are created first. To create the relations, the name of the relation is specified along with its associated attributes enclosed in brackets. Next, the primary key attribute(s) is (are) identified, followed by any foreign keys. So far, this sounds quite straightforward; however, let's look now at the actual steps required to convert the conceptual model in detail.

Step 1: Create Relations for Strong Entities
This rule transforms all regular entities in the ER diagram into relations. Each attribute in the entity becomes an attribute in the relation. Figure 11.8 shows the entity DVD from the DVD rental store and its corresponding relation. Notice that the primary key is indicated in the relation by underlining the attribute DVD_ID.

FIGURE 11.8 Transforming the strong entity DVD into the DVD relation

DVD ENTITY

DVD RELATION DVD (<u>DVD_ID</u>, DVD_TITLE, DVD_COPIES, DVD_CHARGE)

Step 2: Create Relations for Weak Entities
In Chapter 5, Data Modelling with Entity Relationship Diagrams, we defined a weak entity as being existence-dependent; that is, it cannot exist without the entity with which it has a relationship. In addition, a weak entity has a primary key that is partially or totally derived from the parent entity in the relationship. Step 2 states that, for each weak entity, a new relation must be created that includes all attributes from the entity.

The primary key of the relation is then determined from each owner of the entity. However, the primary key cannot be established until all the foreign key relationships with the owning entities have been identified. To do this, the primary key of the owner entity is included in the new relation as a foreign key attribute. The primary key of the new relation then becomes a composite key through combining the primary key of the owner entity and the partial identifier of the weak entity. An example of transforming the weak entity RENT_LINE from the DVD Rental Store appears in Figure 11.9.

The attributes RENT_NUM and RENTLINE_NUM are underlined to indicate the composite primary key on the RENT_LINE relation. You will also notice that foreign keys on the new relations are indicated by a '*' after the foreign key attribute.

FIGURE 11.9 Example of mapping the weak entity RENT_LINE

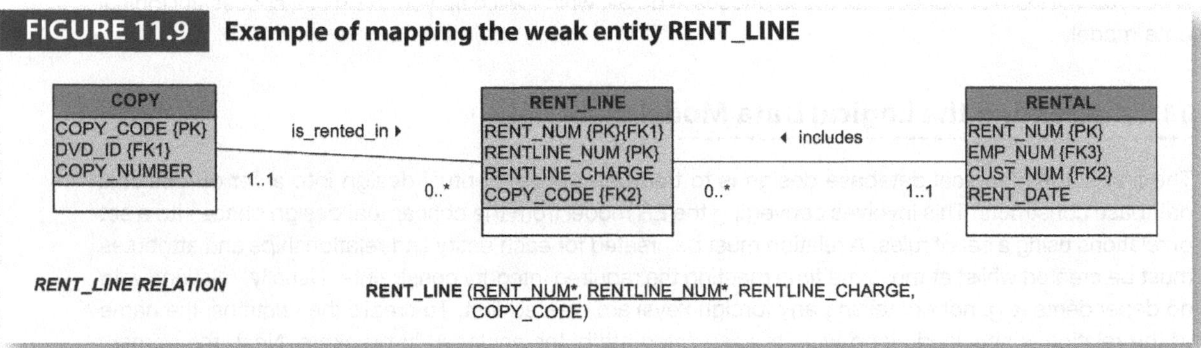

Validation of foreign keys occurs later on in the logical database design phase when we assign and validate integrity constraints.

Step 3: Map Multivalued Attributes

As part of the ER verification process, attributes that contain multiple values are identified and the database designer will have either:

- created several new attributes, one for each of the original multivalued attributes components, or
- created a new entity composed of the original multivalued attributes components.

11 Therefore, at logical database design, such attributes should not exist in the ERD. However, if they do, then for each multivalued attribute that is found within an entity, create a new relation. The new relation should have a foreign key, which is the primary key from the original entity. The primary key of the new relation is a composite key comprised of the primary key of the original entity and one or more attributes of the multivalued attribute itself.

Supposing we created an entity called CAR, where CAR_COLOUR was a multivalued attribute comprising of attributes containing information about the different colours (COL_COLOURS) that are used on different sections of the car (COL_SECTION). Figure 11.10 shows how a new entity called CAR_COLOUR is used to represent this multivalued attribute and the relations that are created.

FIGURE 11.10 Example of mapping multivalued attributes

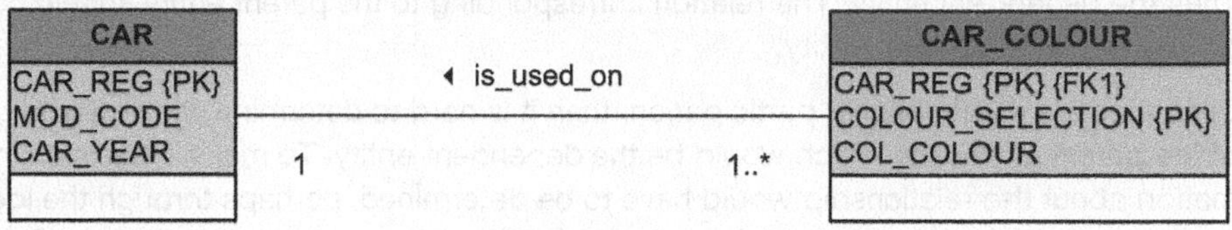

CAR RELATION **CAR** (<u>CAR_REG</u>, MOD_CODE, CAR_YEAR)

CAR_COLOUR RELATION **CAR_COLOUR** (<u>CAR_REG*</u>, <u>COLOUR_SELECTION</u>, COL_COLOUR)

Step 4: Map Binary Relations

One-to-many (1:*) Relationships

For each 1:* relationship, create the relations for each of the two entities that are participating in the relationship. To create the foreign key on the 'many' side, include the primary key attribute from the 'one' side. The 'one' side is referred to as the parent table and the 'many' side is referred to as the dependent table. For example, Figure 11.11 shows a portion of the ER diagram which represents the 'pays' one-to-many relationship between CUSTOMER and RENTAL and the corresponding relations that are created.

FIGURE 11.11 Example of mapping a 1:* relationship

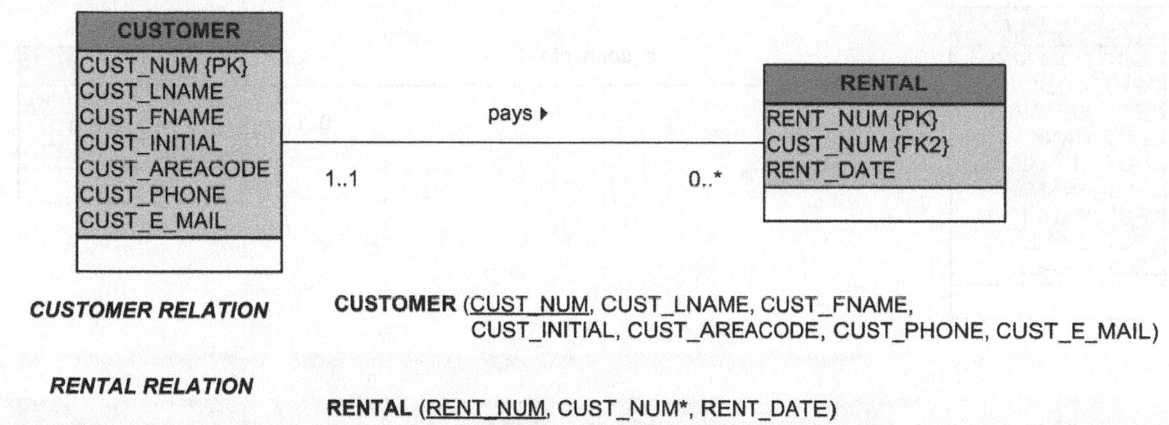

CUSTOMER RELATION **CUSTOMER** (<u>CUST_NUM</u>, CUST_LNAME, CUST_FNAME, CUST_INITIAL, CUST_AREACODE, CUST_PHONE, CUST_E_MAIL)

RENTAL RELATION **RENTAL** (<u>RENT_NUM</u>, CUST_NUM*, RENT_DATE)

One-to-one (1:1) Relationships

1:1 relationships are a special kind of relationship and each one has to be treated individually depending on the participation constraints between the two entities:

- If both entities are in a mandatory participation in a relationship and they do not participate in other relationships, it is most likely that the two entities should be part of the same entity.

- If there is mandatory participation on one side of the relationship, then the entity that has the optional participation becomes the parent entity and the entity that has the mandatory relationship becomes the dependent entity. The relation corresponding to the parent entity should contain the foreign key of the dependent entity.
- If both entities are in an optional participation, then it is hard to determine which would take the role of the parent entity and which would be the dependent entity. To make a decision, more information about the relationship would have to be determined, perhaps through the identification of more attributes. However, if no further information can be obtained, it is up to the database designer to make the decision.
- If the 1:1 relationship between the two entities is recursive (e.g. the relationship can exist between occurrences of the same entity), then you would again look at the participation constraints at each side of the relationship. If they are both mandatory, then the new relation would have two copies of the primary key. If the relationship comprises of both mandatory and optional participations or both sides are optional, then you could either create one relation with two copies of the primary key or create a further new relation to represent the relationship.

To illustrate how we would map a 1:1 relationship, consider the relationship between the entities LECTURER and SCHOOL shown in Figure 11.12. Each school must have a lecturer who is the dean of the school. Therefore, the relationship from SCHOOL to LECTURER is a mandatory participation. However, not all lecturers are the deans of a school, so the LECTURER to SCHOOL relationship is an optional one. The mapping of this 1:1 relationship is also shown in Figure 11.12. Notice that as SCHOOL is the optional participant, the foreign key is placed in this relation.

FIGURE 11.12 Example of mapping a 1:1 relationship

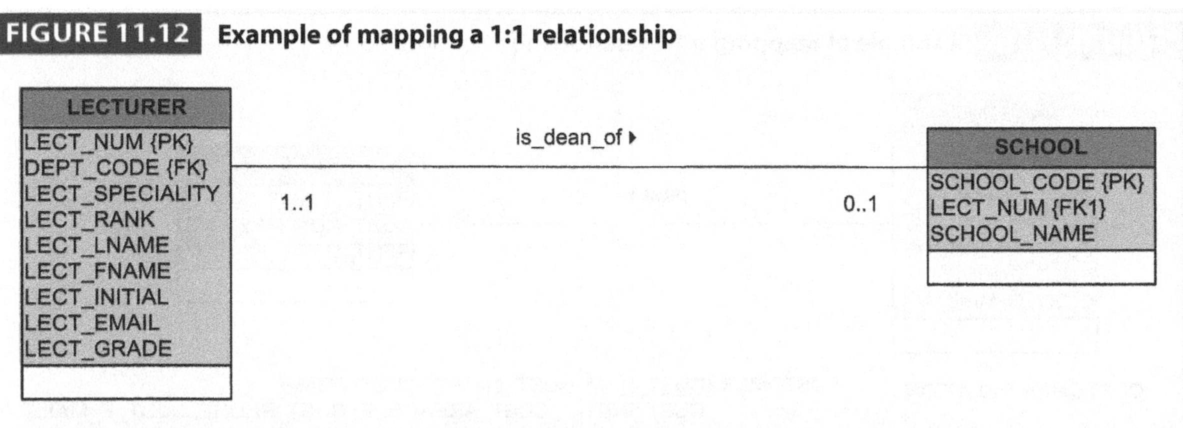

11

NOTE

Chapter 6, Data Modelling Advanced Concepts, contains more about design issues of implementing 1:1 relationships.

Many-to-many (*:*) Relationships

For each *:* relationship, create the relations for each of the two entities that are participating in the relationship. Then create a third relation to represent the actual relationship. The third relation will contain the foreign keys of the two original entries that participate in the original *:* relationship.

Figure 11.13 shows a *:* relationship between the entities TOUR and ATTRACTION. As you examine Figure 11.13, you can see that the relationship between the two entities is represented by the composite entity called ATTRACT_TOUR, which contains foreign keys to both ATTRACTION and TOUR. Figure 11.13 also shows the corresponding relations.

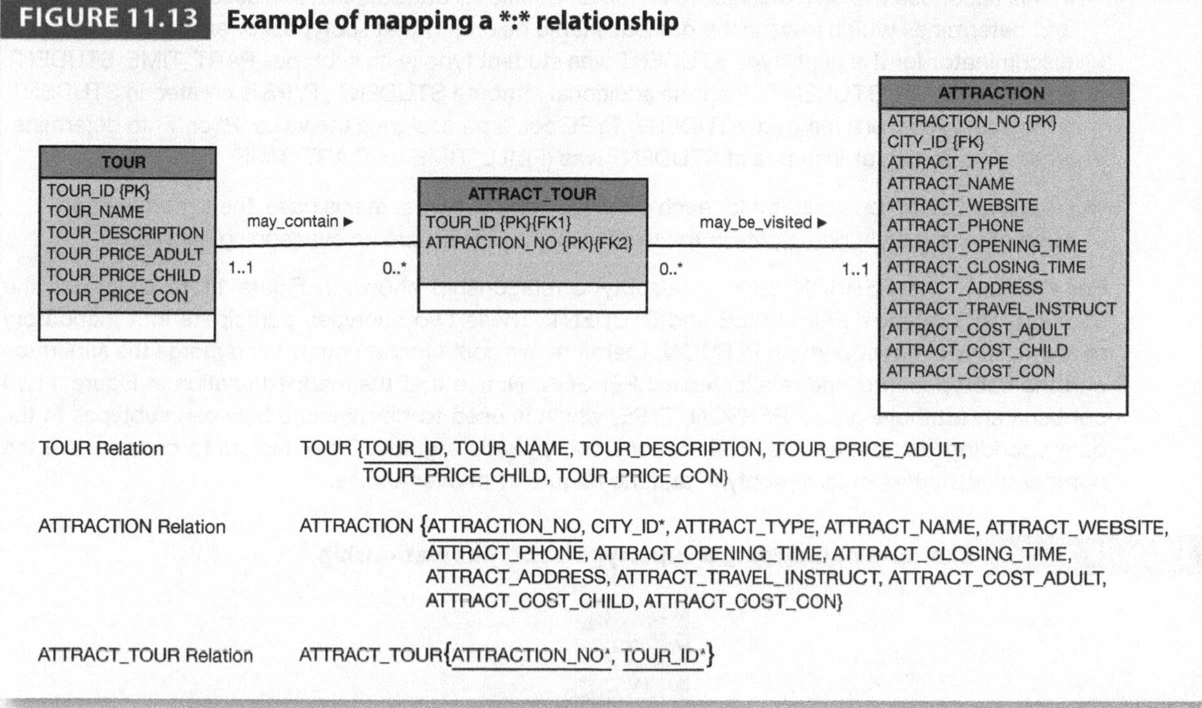

FIGURE 11.13 Example of mapping a *:* relationship

> **NOTE**
>
> Remember that, at the conceptual level, *:* relationships may have been identified and then resolved during the ER model verification process. However, if not, then all *:* relationships should be mapped to 1:* relationships during the logical database design phase.

Step 5: Map Ternary Relations

Ternary and other relationships of higher degrees amongst entities may also exist in the ERD. In the case of a ternary relationship, a fourth relation must be created to represent the relationship amongst the three entities. The primary keys of each of the entities in the ternary relationship become foreign keys in the fourth relation and may also form the composite primary key along with any additional attributes.

Step 6: Map Supertype and Subtype Relationships

There is no single set of rules available for mapping supertype and subtype relationships into a set of relations. Therefore, database designers have come up with several different techniques, which depend on a number of factors. One consideration is whether individual subtypes participate in further relationships with other entities not part of the inheritance hierarchy. Another is the type of disjoint and overlapping constraints that exist between the supertype and the subtype. Two of the most common options are:

- *Option 1*: Merge the subtypes into the supertype and create one relation. This is suitable when participation in the supertype/subtype relationship is mandatory and the subtypes can overlap. In this case, use the discriminator to create an additional attribute that is placed in the supertype and determines which rows in the database table belong to that subtype. For example, if the discriminator for the supertype STUDENT was student type (with subtypes PART_TIME_STUDENT and FULL_TIME_STUDENT), then the additional attribute STUDENT_TYPE is created in STUDENT if the subtypes were merged. STUDENT_TYPE could be assigned the value 'P' or 'F' to determine whether a particular instance of STUDENT was (F)ULL_TIME or (P)ART_TIME.
- *Option 2*: Create one relation for each supertype and subtype. In this case, the supertype and subtypes optionally participate in the relationship and there are no overlapping subtypes.

For example, the PERSON supertype/subtype relationship shown in Figure 11.14 illustrates the overlapping subtypes EMPLOYEE and STUDENT. These two subtypes participate in a mandatory relationship with the supertype PERSON. Therefore, we could follow option 1 and merge the supertype and the subtypes into one relation called PERSON. Notice that the mapped relation in Figure 11.14 contains an attribute called PERSON_TYPE, which is used to discriminate between subtypes in the corresponding database table. Both options only provide a guide. Other factors to consider are the number of attributes in each subtype and the frequency of overlapping.

FIGURE 11.14 Example of mapping a supertype/subtype relationship

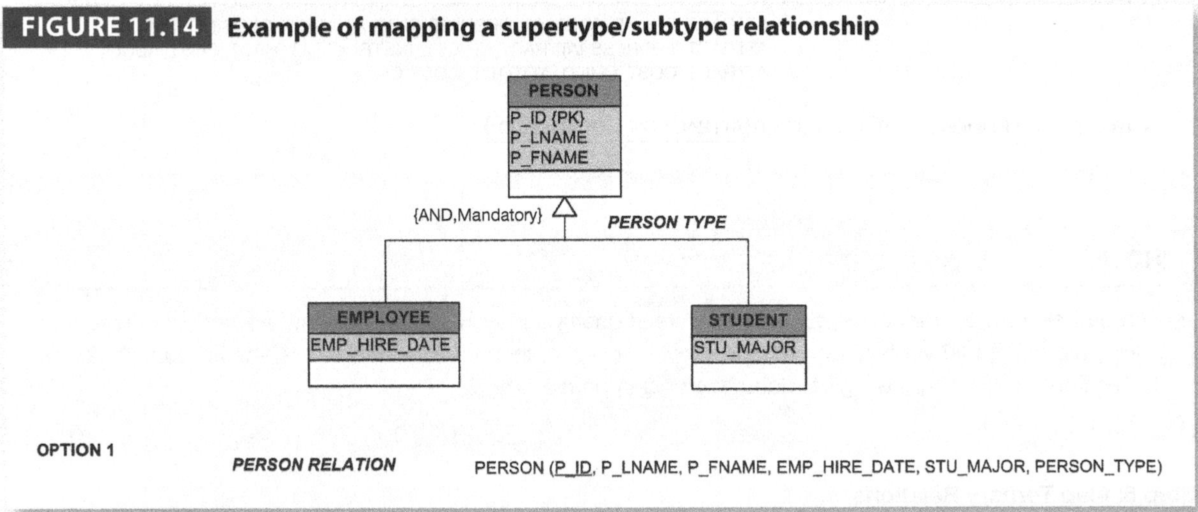

11.2.2 Validating the Logical Data Model Using Normalisation

As you will have seen in Chapter 7, Normalising Database Designs, the normalisation process helps to establish appropriate attributes, their characteristics, and their domains. Nevertheless, because the conceptual modelling process does not preclude the definition of attributes, you can reasonably argue that normalisation often straddles the line between conceptual and logical modelling. In creating the logical data model, we have so far created relations from the ERD and these relations should already be in third normal form. If they are not, then it is likely that we have made some mistake during the model verification process and it will be necessary to revisit the ERD model.

If normalisation has not been undertaken prior to logical database design, it can be used as an additional tool in which to verify the database design. After all, a normalised relational schema will avoid certain anomalies when inserting, updating or deleting data and will therefore help to keep the data in the database consistent.

11.2.3 Validate Integrity Constraints

The next stage in logical database design is to check and validate the integrity constraints on each relation. In Chapter 3, Relational Model Characteristics, you were introduced to the three main types of integrity constraints that we can impose on objects within the database. These were domain constraints, entity integrity and referential integrity. In creating the relations within the logical model, most of these integrity constraints will have been identified but it is essential that these are validated as a separate stage within the logical database design process.

First, let's look at domain constraints. All the values that are assigned to a specific attribute must be within the range of allowable values. For example, the domain constraints for the DVD relation are shown in Table 11.5.

TABLE 11.5 Domain constraints for the DVD relation

Attribute	Description	Domain
DVD_ID	Set of all possible values for movie codes	Alphanumeric character size 10
DVD_COPIES	Number of copies held of each movie	Integer 2 digits Minimum value of 1 and maximum value of 50
DVD_NAME	The name of the movie	Character size 50
DVD_CHARGE	The cost to rent a DVD	DVD_CHARGE >= €6 and DVD_CHARGE <= €16
DVD_LATE_CHG_DAY	The amount to be paid for each day the DVD is late	DVD_CHARGE >= €0.25 and DVD_CHARGE <= €25
CATEGORY	Set of all possible movie categories	Character size 6. Must be one of 'Family', 'Action', 'Comedy', 'Doc'

Entity integrity is validated by ensuring that each relation has a primary key. This constraint guarantees that no null values are inserted into the primary key. At this stage in logical database design, both singular and composite primary key values are checked.

Validating referential integrity constraints involves checking the relationships between the relations to ensure that the correct foreign keys are in place. For example, in the DVD rental store, for every row entered into the COPY relation there must be an existing row in the DVD relation so that the child and parent relationship is maintained. What may have not been identified prior to this stage is whether or not foreign keys would be allowed to contain NULL values. If every copy of a DVD requires an entry in the DVD relation and the relationship is mandatory, then the DVD_ID foreign key cannot be NULL in the COPY relation. It is possible that if the relationship was optional, then NULL values are allowed as values in the foreign key attributes. If NULLs are allowed there are a number of ways in which they can be dealt with:

1 Don't allow any movies to be deleted from the DVD relation until all values in the COPY relation associated with that movie have been deleted. This allows the user performing the delete operation

to check if they wish to proceed with the deletion and, more importantly, ensures that referential integrity is maintained.

2. When a MOVIE is deleted, then delete all associated rows in the COPY relation. This is known as a cascading delete constraint.
3. Set the foreign key value to NULL in the COPY relation. This means we may have copies of a movie in the store that are no longer listed as being available for rental. Follow this strategy with care.

It is possible that different choices will apply to different relations in the same database, so careful consideration is needed.

11.2.4 Merge Relations

In the database design process, it is likely that a number of ERDs will have been generated to represent different user views of the system. The logical database design process will so far have created relations directly from each ERD, which will inevitably lead to some duplication and redundancy amongst relations. The next stage is therefore to merge these sets of relations to remove any redundancy. For small databases, the sets of relations from each user view should be merged one at a time. For each set of relations that is merged the database designer should:

- Automatically include all relations in the new logical data model which are not duplicated.
- Identify those relations that are similar and combine them. Usually, these relations will have the same primary key, so such relations can be easily identified.
- Check all the relationships in the new merged logical data model, ensuring that all integrity constraints are maintained.

For example, in the DVD rental store, managers and sales staff will require different information from the database. Therefore, two different views of the database may have been designed for the managers and the sales staff. Consider the following two relations which have been created:

11

In the MANAGER_VIEW

MANAGER (EMP_NO, EMP_LNAME, EMP_FNAME, EMP_SALARY, AREACODE, PHONE)

In the SALES_STAFF_VIEW

SALES_STAFF (EMP_NO, EMP_LNAME, EMP_FNAME, AREACODE, PHONE)

You can see that the two relations MANAGER and SALES_STAFF have the same primary key value, EMP_NUM. In addition, they have attributes that describe the characteristic of an employee. This makes them ideal candidates for merging into one relation called EMPLOYEE.

EMPLOYEE (EMP_NO, EMP_LNAME, EMP_FNAME, AREACODE, PHONE, EMP_SALARY)

Although this process appears to be quite simple, there are a number of recognised problems that can occur surrounding the merging of relations from different views. When we merged the MANAGER and SALES_STAFF relations, we formed a new relation called EMPLOYEE. We assumed that both the MANAGER and SALES_STAFF relations referred to the same characteristics, those of employees, based upon the fact that the primary keys were the same. However, what would have been our assumption if the primary key in the SALES_STAFF relation was called EMP_ID instead of EMP_NO? We would then have two attributes with the different names but the same meaning. These are known as *synonyms* and it is up to the database designer to understand that these attributes are synonyms that represent the employee's number.

A second problem can occur if attributes with the same name in separate relations have different meanings. These kinds of attributes are known as homonyms. The two original relations MANAGER and SALES_STAFF both had attributes called AREACODE and PHONE. What would happen if the database designer discovered that these attributes in the MANAGER relation referred to a particular store's area code and phone number, whilst in the SALES_STAFF relation they referred to an individual employee's home area code and phone number? Both meanings would have to be included in the merged EMPLOYEE relation, i.e:

EMPLOYEE (EMP_NO, EMP_LNAME, EMP_FNAME, STORE_AREACODE, STORE_PHONE, EMP_AREACODE, EMP_PHONE, EMP_SALARY)

Finally, when merging relations, the database designer also needs to check that supertype/subtype relationships are represented correctly. If one of the relations contains supertype/subtypes that have already been merged when the original logical model was created, then the decision needs to be revisited if a duplicate supertype/subtype relationship exists in the merging relation. This is just to make sure that the original decision was correct.

After completing this stage, a single, validated, logical model should exist which represents the complete database system. To ensure that it is correct, all integrity constraints should be again validated before moving to the final stage in the process: reviewing the model with the user.

11.2.5 Review the Complete Logical Model with the User

So far, the users of the database should have actively participated in the conceptual design of the database by verifying the conceptual database model. The next stage involves reviewing the completed logical model with the users to ensure that all the data requirements have been modelled and all the transactions are supported within the different user views. This stage is very important as any problems need to be solved before beginning the physical database design stage, even if it requires going back a few steps and revisiting stages in the logical design process.

11.3 PHYSICAL DATABASE DESIGN

Physical database design requires the definition of specific storage or access methods that will be used by the database. In order to do this, we must translate the logical model into a set of specific DBMS specifications for storing and accessing data. In doing this, we must ensure that every logical reference to a data attribute (represented by a primary key) can be located in the physical database. In addition, we must be able to represent any relationships that occur between relations. This presents the database designer with some complex decisions regarding how the database is physically stored. The ultimate goal must be to ensure that data storage is effective to ensure integrity and security, and efficient in terms of query response time. In order to carry out physical database design, the following information needs to have been collected:

1. A set of normalised relations devised from the ER model and the normalisation process. This would have been derived from the conceptual and logical design stages and would be the logical data model.
2. An estimate of the volume of data which will be stored in each database table and the usage statistics.
3. An estimate of the physical storage requirements for each field (attribute) within the database.
4. The physical storage characteristics of the DBMS that is being used.

Physical database design can be broken down into a number of stages:

1. Analyse data volume and database usage.
2. Translate each relation identified in the logical data model into a table.
3. Determine a suitable file organisation.
4. Define indexes.
5. Define user views.
6. Estimate data storage requirements.
7. Determine database security for users.

Next you will learn about each of these phases in more detail.

11.3.1 Analyse Data Volume and Database Usage

Analysing user queries and the size of the database is usually the first stage of physical database design. The process is often carried out as part of the Systems Development Life Cycle (SDLC) that you were introduced to in Chapter 10, Database Development Process. When physically designing the database, it is very important that you know approximately the number of transactions that will take place on each table within the database and the data volume involved in the processing. Every transaction involves data usage, and has overheads and limitations based on both the number of requests to a given file and the data volume that has been requested either for viewing or modification. It is therefore essential to gather as much information as possible on at least the most important transactions that occur in order to establish performance issues that may arise. Generally, in a large system, it would be impossible to predict all the possible different types of queries that users may have, so transactions that account for 80 per cent of accesses to data are considered. This is based upon the 80/20 rule suggested by Gio Wiederhold in his 1983 book on database design, which is listed in the further reading section at the end of this chapter. Weiderhold estimated that 20 per cent of queries requested by users account for 80 per cent of data accesses. This rule is often used today in analysing data usage in existing database systems.

The steps required for carrying out this phase are:

- Identifying the most frequent and critical transactions. For example in our DVD rental store, one of the most common transactions will be a customer renting a DVD. While customers would rent DVDs every day, there may be peak times such as a Friday or Saturday evening, which might have an impact on the performance.
- Analysis of critical transactions to determine which relations in the database participate in these transactions. In order for a customer to rent a DVD, four relations (COPY, RENT_LINE, RENTAL and CUSTOMER) would need to be accessed.

Data volume and data usage statistics are usually shown on a simplified version of the ERD. This diagram is known as a **composite usage map** or a **transaction usage map**. Figure 11.15 shows the composite usage map for a section of the DVD rental store. Access frequencies to each relation are shown as dashed lines with the arrows representing the direction of the access. The numbers inside each entity represent the estimated number of records stored in each relation.

FIGURE 11.15 Composite usage map for the DVD rental store

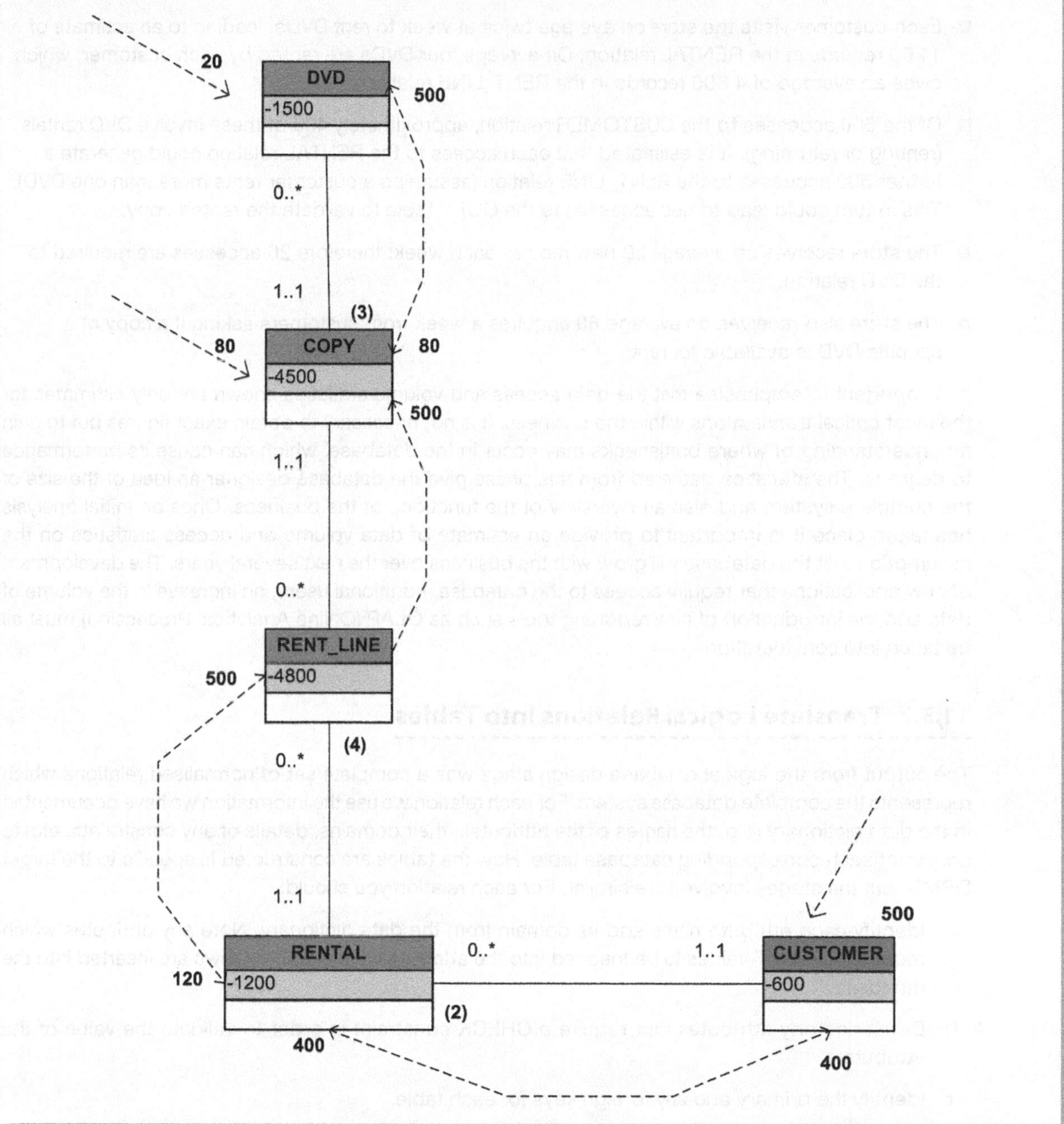

11

As you examine Figure 11.15, note the following:

- It is estimated that the store has 600 customers.
- The store holds 1 500 different movies and has on average three copies of each movie title (giving an average of 4 500 records in the COPY relation).

- There are approximately 500 accesses to the CUSTOMER relation each day. These accesses comprise customers renting and returning DVDs and new customers registering with the store.
- Each customer visits the store on average twice at week to rent DVDs, leading to an estimate of 1 200 records in the RENTAL relation. On average four DVDs are rented by each customer, which gives an average of 4 800 records in the RENT_LINE relation.
- Of the 500 accesses to the CUSTOMER relation, approximately 400 of these involve DVD rentals (renting or returning). It is estimated that each access to the RENTAL relation could generate a further 500 accesses to the RENT_LINE relation (assuming a customer rents more than one DVD). This in turn could lead to 500 accesses to the COPY table to validate the rented copy.
- The store receives on average 20 new movies each week; therefore 20 accesses are required to the DVD relation.
- The store also receives on average 80 enquires a week from customers asking if a copy of a specific DVD is available for rent.

It is important to emphasise that the data access and volume statistics shown are only estimates for the most critical transactions within the business. It is not necessary to obtain exact figures but to gain an understanding of where bottlenecks may occur in the database, which can cause its performance to degrade. The statistics gathered from this phase give the database designer an idea of the size of the complete system and also an overview of the functions of the business. Once an initial analysis has taken place it is important to provide an estimate of data volume and access statistics on the assumption that the database will grow with the business over the next several years. The development of new applications that require access to the database, additional users, an increase in the volume of data and the introduction of new reporting tools such as OLAP (Online Analytical Processing) must all be taken into consideration.

11.3.2 Translate Logical Relations into Tables

11

The output from the logical database design stage was a complete set of normalised relations which represents the complete database system. For each relation we use the information we have documented in the data dictionary (e.g. the names of the attributes, their domains, details of any constraints, etc) to construct each corresponding database table. How the tables are constructed is specific to the target DBMS, but the stages involved are similar. For each relation you should:

a Identify each attribute name and its domain from the data dictionary. Note any attributes which require DEFAULT values to be inserted into the attribute whenever new rows are inserted into the database.

b Determine any attributes that require a CHECK constraint in order to validate the value of the attribute.

c Identify the primary and any foreign keys for each table.

d Identify those attributes that are not allowed to contain NULL values and those which should be UNIQUE. You can exclude the primary key attribute(s) here as the PRIMARY KEY constraint automatically imposes the NOT NULL and UNIQUE constraints.

Once you have identified the above, the DBMS-specific SQL can be written to create the table. The order of table creation is very important. Relations that contain no foreign key dependencies should be created first, followed by those with one foreign key, then two, etc.

Let's now look at an example using two of the relations that were determined during the logical database design stage from the DVD rental store. Table 11.6 shows a portion of the data dictionary for the DVD and COPY relations and Figure 11.16 shows the SQL code used to create the two corresponding database tables where the target DBMS is Oracle.

FIGURE 11.16 Creating the DVD and COPY tables

```
CREATE TABLE DVD (
DVD_ID VARCHAR2(10),
DVD_COPIES NUMBER(3) NOT NULL,
DVD_NAME VARCHAR2(50) NOT NULL,
DVD_CHARGE NUMBER(2,2),
DVD_LATE_CHG_DAY NUMBER(2,2),
CATEGORY CHAR(6),
CONSTRAINT pk_dvd_dvdcode PRIMARY KEY(DVD_ID),
CONSTRAINT ck_dvd _category CHECK (CATEGORY IN ('Family', 'Action', 'Comedy', 'Doc')),
CONSTRAINT ck_dvd_charge CHECK (DVD_CHARGE BETWEEN 0.25 and 25),
CONSTRAINT ck_dvd_latecharge CHECK (DVD_LATE_CHG_DAY BETWEEN 6 and 16),
CONSTRAINT ck_dvd_dvdcopies CHECK (MOVIE_COPIES BETWEEN 1 AND 50));

CREATE TABLE COPY (
COPY_CODE VARCHAR2(10),
DVD_ID VARCHAR2(5),
COPY_NUM NUMBER(2) DEFAULT 1 NOT NULL,
CONSTRAINT pk_copy_copycode PRIMARY KEY(COPY_CODE),
CONSTRAINT fk_copy_movie FOREIGN KEY(MOVIE_CODE) REFERENCES MOVIE(MOVIE_CODE));
```

In Figure 11.16, notice that the constraints imposed on the attributes have been named. It is important to name constraints using a standard so that we can associate a particular constraint with a particular table. If we do not name them, the DBMS assigns an unnamed constraint that is difficult to understand. Naming them makes it easy to modify or drop constraints and quickly fix any errors as we will know which table they are related to. An example standard format for constraint naming could be:

(constraint abbreviation)_(table name)_(column_name)

where the constraint abbreviations would be PK (primary key), FK (foreign key), CK (check constraint), UK (unique constraint). Using this format you can see that the primary key constraint has been named as pk_dvd_dvdcode in Figure 11.16.

11

TABLE 11.6 Data dictionary entries for DVD and COPY rental

Table Name	Attribute Name	Description	Type	Format	Range	Required	PK or FK	Constraints CHECK / UNIQUE / NOT NULL	FK Referenced Table
DVD	DVD_ID DVD_COPIES DVD_NAME DVD_CHARGE DVD_LATE_ CHG_DAY CATEGORY	Unique DVD identifier No of copies of the DVD in store Name of the DVD Cost to rent the DVD The amount to be paid each day the DVD is late Set of all possible movie categories	VARCHAR2(10) NUMBER(3) VARCHAR2(50) NUMBER(2,2) NUMBER(2,2) CHAR(6)	X9999 99 Xxxxxxx 99.99 99.99 Xxxxxx	 0 – 99 0 – 10.00 0.00 – 99.99 'Family', 'Action', 'Comedy', 'Doc'	Y Y Y	PK	 NOT NULL NOT NULL CHECK	
COPY	COPY_CODE DVD_ID COPY_NUM	The unique copy code Unique DVD identifier The copy number	VARCHAR2(10) VARCHAR2(5) NUMBER(2)	Xxxxxxxxx X9999 99	 0 - 99	Y Y Y	PK FK	 NOT NULL DEFAULT OF 1	 MOVIE

FK = Foreign key

PK = Primary key

CHAR = Fixed character length data, 1 to 255 characters

VARCHAR2 = Variable character length data, 1 to 2 000 characters

NUMBER= Numeric data. NUMBER(9,2) is used to specify numbers with two decimal places and up to nine digits long, including the decimal places

NOTE

Both the SQL required for creating tables and the data types for each attribute are specific to each DBMS. In Chapter 8, Beginning Structured Query Language, we identified some common SQL data types.

11.3.3 Determine a Suitable File Organisation

An important aspect of physical database design is choosing how the database records are physically arranged. Techniques for physically arranging relations onto secondary storage are known as file organisation techniques. All data in a database are stored in data files. Each file may contain many rows from one single database table, or it may contain rows from many different tables. Each row represents a database record that can consist of a number of data fields. Each entity in the logical data model will correspond to a record and each attribute corresponds to a data field. For example, in the DVD rental store, the entity DVD can be represented as a record with the fields DVD_ID, DVD_TITLE, DVD_COPIES and DVD_CHARGE.

Selecting the most suitable **file organisation** is very important to ensure that the data is stored efficiently and data can be retrieved as quickly as possible. If your database contains thousands of records and one single record is required, you must be able to locate and retrieve this record as quickly as possible. To do this, the DBMS must know where this record is stored and how it can identify it. It is also important to look at the future growth of the database and whether the type of file organisation provides some protection against data loss. As you can see, there are a lot of criteria that you need to take into consideration. In a DBMS such as Oracle 12c, complex file organisation techniques are built in and often only need tuning by the database administrator. However, it is important that you have an understanding of the basic file organisation techniques. There are three categories of file organisations:

- Files that contain randomly ordered records known as heap files
- Files that are sorted by one or more fields, such as file organisations which are based on indexes
- Files hashed on one or more fields, known as hash files.

11

In the following sections, you learn in more detail about the characteristics of the most commonly used file organisation techniques. These are heap, sequential, indexed, b-trees, bitmap and join indexes, hash files and clusters.

Heap File Organisations

The most basic file organisation is that of the **heap file** where records are unordered. Records are inserted into the file as they come. Heap files are only used when a large quantity of data needs to be inserted into a table for the first time. The input sequence is often used to automatically generate a primary key for each row. Since the only way to access a record in this type of file is to search every row in the file, they become impractical if we want to provide efficient data retrieval.

Sequential File Organisations

In a **sequential file** organisation, the records are stored in a sequence based on the value of one or more fields, which is often the primary key. In order to locate a specific record, the whole file must be searched and every record in the file must be read in turn until the required record is located. In some situations, this search can be fast if all the records are ordered based on the primary key value. However, if this is not the case it can be very time-consuming to find one specific record. Inserting or modifying records usually results in rewriting the whole file, which is very impractical in a database. In addition, the deletion of records leads to storage space being wasted unless the file is reorganised. An example of a sequential file is a telephone book, as shown in Figure 11.17. Each name and phone number represents a record that is stored alphabetically.

FIGURE 11.17 Example of sequential file organisation

	LAST NAME	FIRST NAME	AREACODE	PHONE
First record in file →	Brown	James	0181	297-1228
	Dunne	Leona	0161	894-1238
	Moloi	Marlene	0171	894-2285
	Moloi	Mlilo	0181	297-3809
To locate Williams all other records must first be read	O'Brian	Amy	0161	442-3381
		Paul	0181	894-2180
	Orlando	Myron	0181	222-1672
	Padayachee	Vinaya	0161	382-7185
	Ramas	Alfred	0181	844-2573
⋯⋯→	Williams	George	0181	290-2556

Due to their deficiencies, sequential files are not used for modern database storage.

Indexed File Organisations

Accessing a record directly instead of searching through the entire file involves the use of an indexed file organisation. Records in a file supporting this type of file organisation can be stored in a sorted or unsorted sequence and an index is created to locate specific records quickly. Indexes are crucial in speeding up data access. Indexes facilitate searching, sorting and using aggregate functions and even join operations. The improvement in data access speed occurs because an index is an ordered set of values that contains the index key and pointers. The pointers are the row IDs for the actual table rows. Conceptually, a data index is similar to a book index. When you use a book index, you look up the word, similar to the index key, which is accompanied by the page number(s), similar to the pointer(s), which direct(s) you to the appropriate page(s).

An index scan is more efficient than a full table scan because the index data are already ordered and the amount of data is usually a magnitude of scale smaller. Therefore, when performing searches, it is almost always better for the DBMS to use an index to access a table than to scan all its rows sequentially. For example, Figure 11.18 shows the index representation of a CUSTOMER table with 14 786 rows and the index COUNTRY_NDX on the CUS_COUNTRY attribute.

FIGURE 11.18 Index representation for the CUSTOMER table

STATE_NDX INDEX

Key	Row
AS	1
...	....
....	....
FR	5
....	....
.....	....
UK	3
UK	4
UK	8
UK	10
.....	....

CUSTOMER TABLE (14 786 ROWS)

Row ID	CUS_CODE	CUS_LNAME	CUS_FNAME	CUS_INITIAL	CUS_AREACODE	CUS_PHONE	CUS_COUNTRY	CUS_BALANCE
1	10010	Ramas	Alfred	A	0181	844-2573	AS	0.00
2	10011	Dunne	Leona	K	0161	894-1238	SA	0.00
3	10012	Moloi	Marlene	W	0181	894-2285	UK	896.54
4	10013	Olowski	Paul	F	0181	894-2180	UK	1285.19
5	10014	Orlando	Myron		0181	222-1672	FR	673.21
6	10015	O'Brian	Amy	B	0161	442-3381	NL	1014.56
7	10016	Brown	James	G	0181	297-1228	CZ	0.00
8	10017	Williams	George		0181	290-2556	UK	0.00
9	10018	Padayachee	Vinaya	G	0161	382-7185	SW	0.00
10	10019	Moloi	Mlilo	K	0181	297-3809	UK	453.98
......	....	....	....	....	....	....	....	....
......	....	....	....	....	....	....	....	....
13245	23120	Veron	George	D	415	342-9234	UK	€675.00
......	....	....	....	....	....	....	....	....
......	....	....	....	....	....	....	....	....
14786	24560	Suraez	Victor		7898	233-8999	UK	€342.00

Suppose you submit the following query:

```
SELECT    CUS_NAME, CUS_COUNTRY
FROM      CUSTOMER
WHERE     CUS_COUNTRY = 'UK';
```

If there is no index, the DBMS must perform a full table scan, thus reading all 14 786 customer rows. Assuming that the index COUNTRY_NDX is created, the DBMS automatically uses the index to locate the first customer with a state equal to 'UK' and then reads all subsequent CUSTOMER rows, using the row IDs in the index as a guide. Assuming that only five rows meet the condition CUS_COUNTRY = 'UK', the DBMS would save 14 781 I/O requests for customer rows that do not meet the criteria. That's a lot of CPU cycles!

If indexes are so important, why not index every column in every table? It's not practical to do so. Indexing every column in every table will tax the DBMS too much in terms of index-maintenance processing, especially if the table has many attributes, has many rows and/or requires many inserts, updates and/or deletes.

Indexes are logically and physically independent of the data in the associated table. This means, of course, that they require their own storage space. How much space depends on the type of index that is applied and is an important factor that is initially decided within the physical database design stage.

Types of Indexes

There are three main types of indexes that can be used:

- *Primary index* – these indexes are placed on unique fields such as the primary key. They are used to locate a specific record pointed to by the index. A file can have at most one primary index but can have several secondary indexes.
- *Secondary index* – these indexes can be placed on any field in the file that is unordered.

- *Multilevel index* – these indexes are used where one index becomes too large and is split into a number of separate indexes in order to reduce the search. This then results in a further index, which keeps track of these additional indexes! Figure 11.19 shows an example of a two-level index on the DVD table from the DVD rental store.

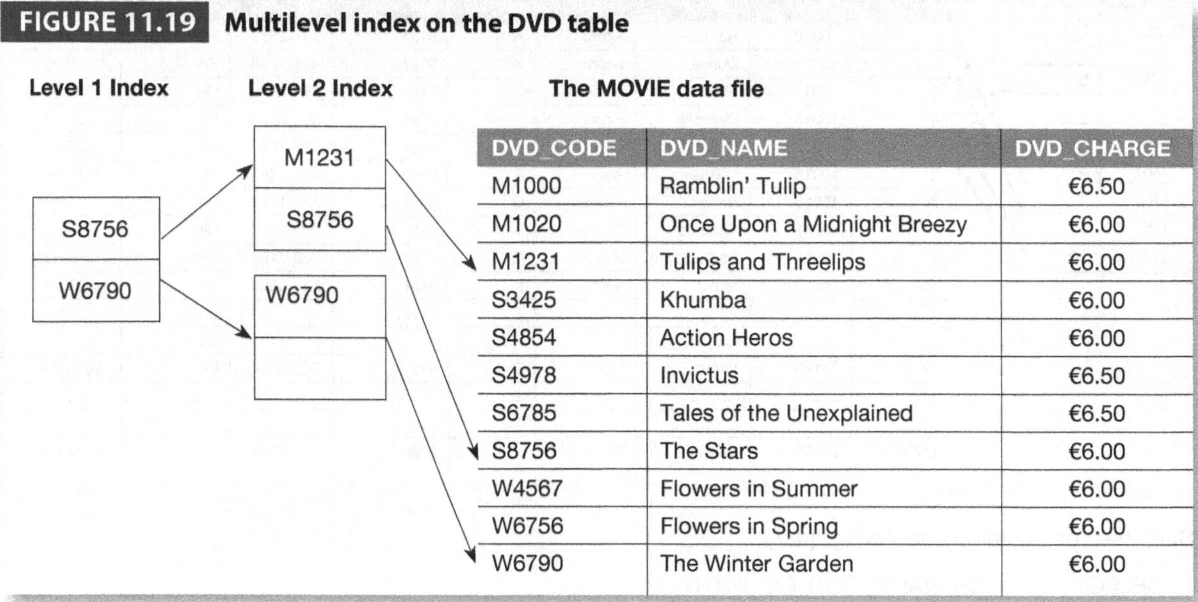

DVD_CODE	DVD_NAME	DVD_CHARGE
M1000	Ramblin' Tulip	€6.50
M1020	Once Upon a Midnight Breezy	€6.00
M1231	Tulips and Threelips	€6.00
S3425	Khumba	€6.00
S4854	Action Heros	€6.00
S4978	Invictus	€6.50
S6785	Tales of the Unexplained	€6.50
S8756	The Stars	€6.00
W4567	Flowers in Summer	€6.00
W6756	Flowers in Spring	€6.00
W6790	The Winter Garden	€6.00

FIGURE 11.19 Multilevel index on the DVD table

Each index can be defined as being sparse or dense. When using a sparse index, index pointers are created only for some of the records, whereas with a dense index, an index pointer appears for every search key value in the file. In practice, dense indexes are faster, but sparse indexes require less storage space.

In addition to these three types of index, there are a number of other types of index that are popular. You will learn about each of these indexes in the next sections.

B-trees

Within a DBMS, indexes are often stored in a data structure known as a *tree*. Trees are generally more efficient at storing indexes as they reduce the time of the search compared with other data structures such as lists. These trees are often referred to as Balanced or **B-trees** and are used to maintain an ordered set of indexes or data to allow efficient operations to select, delete and insert data. A B-tree consists of a hierarchy of nodes that contain a set of pointers that link the nodes of the B-tree together. Each B-tree that is created is said to be of the order n where n is the maximum number of children allowed for each parent node. We can say that each node in a B-tree of order n contains at most $2n$ keys and $2n + 1$ pointers.

This is true except for the root node, which provides the starting point of the B-tree. When a node does not have any children, it is called a *leaf node*. Each item (index or data) stored in a B-tree is known as a key. Each key is unique and can occur in the B-tree in only one location. The B-tree must always be balanced in that every path from the root to the leaf must be exactly the same length. The general principle is that for every node (which we will call n) in the tree:

- The left subtree of n contains only values smaller than the value in n.
- The right subtree of n contains only values greater than the value in n.

A special kind of B-tree is known as the B+-tree, where all keys reside in the leaves. This tree is most often used to represent indexes which act as a 'road map' so that each index can be quickly located. Often, B-trees are referred to as B+-trees and vice versa. Although they have similar proprieties, there are some differences. You can read more about these kinds of trees in an article by Douglas Comer, details of which are in the further reading section of this chapter. As we are dealing with choosing a suitable file organisation based upon indexes in the context of physical database design, we will concentrate on the basics of B+-trees in this section.

Figure 11.20 shows the general structure of a B+-tree, which represents country names.

The B+-tree in Figure 11.20 is of the order two so it contains at most two keys (the country names) and pointers to other nodes. To locate the data record for Germany, first look in the root node. Germany is not in the root node, so we must look for Germany in the child nodes. Alphabetically, Germany is greater than France and less than the UK, so we select the middle pointer and proceed to the second level in the tree. Here, we find a match for Germany and follow the pointer to the left of Germany to access the data record.

FIGURE 11.20 B+-tree terminology

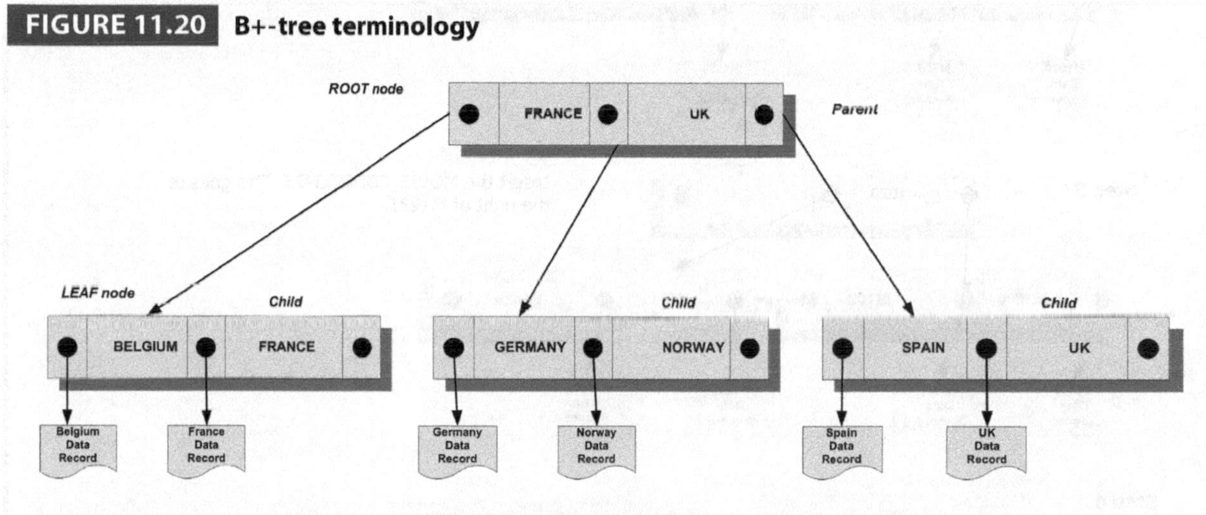

Now that we have introduced some of the basic terminology of B+-trees, let's see if we can insert a new key into the tree. Suppose we want to use the attribute DVD_IDs to act as the primary index on the DVD table. Figure 11.21 illustrates the steps required to construct a B+-tree of order two to store the DVD_IDs shown in Table 11.7.

TABLE 11.7 DVD codes

DVD_CODE
M1020
M1231
M1000
S3425
S4854

FIGURE 11.21 Creating a B+-tree

Step 1

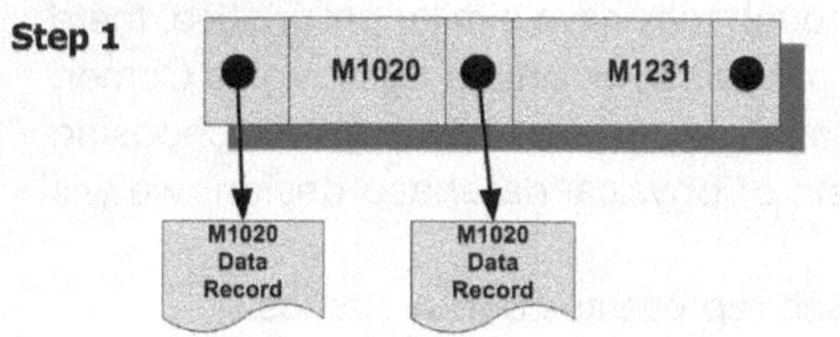

Insert the first two MOVIE CODES, M1020 and M1231

Step 2

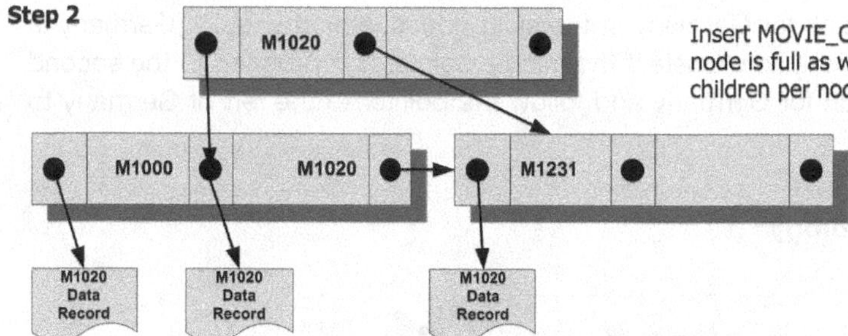

Insert MOVIE_CODE M1000. Seems simple but the node is full as we can only have two children per node. There we must create a new node.

Step 3

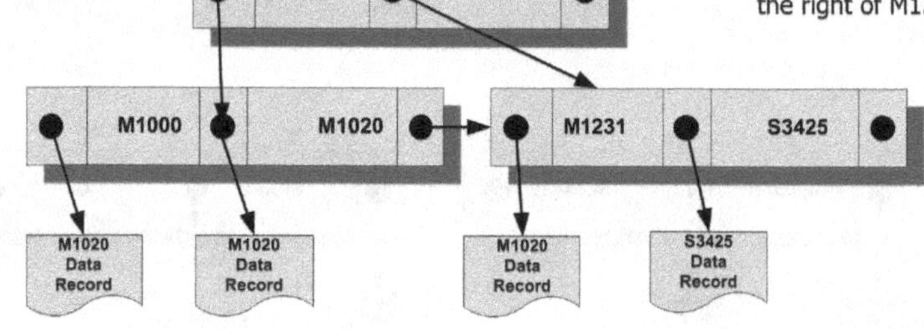

Insert the MOVIE_CODE S3425. This goes to the right of M1231.

Step 4

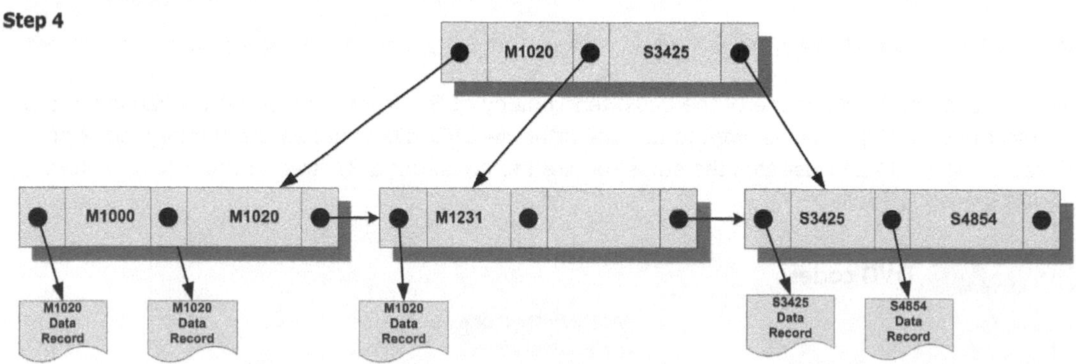

Insert MOVIE_CODE S4854. It is greater than S3425 and should therefore be placed to the right of S3425, but the node is full. So we have to split this node and promote S3425 to the parent node (which currently contains M1020). However, this will mean that the parent node becomes full, so we have to create a further child node for M1231.

As you have seen, the B-tree is a powerful way of storing indexes as it allows the quick retrieval of data, which leads to a faster response time for user queries. The B-tree automatically sustains the appropriate levels of index for the file being indexed and, through the careful management of storage space, ensures that each node is at least half used and full. There is never a case of overcrowding at a node as the tree reorganises itself as you saw in Figure 11.21.

NOTE

You may be wondering what happens to B-trees when we delete a record. While it is possible to remove leaf node pointers to records, some B-tree implementations do not perform the actual deletion of the pointer to the data record at all. The basis for this is that all files are likely to grow and therefore the leaf is likely to continue to grow again once the maximum number of children in the node has been reached.

B-tree indexes are mainly used when you know that a query refers to a column which is indexed and will retrieve only a few rows.

Bitmap Indexes

So far, we have looked at indexes that are applied to speed up data retrevial from relational database tables. Another popular type of index that is often used on multidimensional data held in data warehouses is known as the **bitmap index**. Bitmap indexes are usually applied to attributes that are sparse in their given domain. For example, if customers were required to enter personal information on an application form to join the DVD rental store, everyone would enter their name and address, but a large number would not enter their age. So, the values for age in the database would be sparse.

NOTE

You will look at how bitmap indexes can be used to optimise queries that use multidimensional data in Chapter 15, Databases for Business Intelligence.

11

In a bitmap index, a two-dimensional array is constructed. One column is generated for every row in the table that we want to index, with each column representing a distinct value within the bitmapped index. The two-dimensional array represents each value within the index multiplied by the number of rows in the table. An example of a bitmap index on the DVD_CHARGE field is shown in Figure 11.22. The DVD table also shown in Figure 11.22 currently has 11 rows and the DVD_CHARGE field has five different values {€6.00, €6.50, €7.00, €7.50, €8.00}. This bitmap index has 11 entries with five bits per entry.

FIGURE 11.22 Bitmap index on the field MOVIE_CHARGE

The MOVIE table

MOVIE_CODE	MOVIE_COPIES	MOVIE_NAME	MOVIE_CHARGE	MOVIE_LATE_CHG_DAY	CATEGORY
M3456	3	Ramblin' Tulip	€6.50	€0.25	Family
R2345	2	Once Upon a Midnight Breezy	€8.00	€0.25	Comedy
S4567	3	Tulips and Threelips	€6.00	€0.25	Family
S4854	3	Action Heros	€6.00	€0.25	Action
S4978	2	Invictus	€6.50	€0.50	Action
S6785	3	Tales of the Unexplained	€6.50	€0.25	Action
S8756	2	The Stars	€6.00	€0.50	Doc
W1234	5	Khumba	€8.00	€0.50	Family
W4567	2	Flowers in Summer	€6.00	€0.25	Doc
W6756	2	Flowers in Spring	€6.00	€0.25	Doc
W6970	3	The Winter Garden	€6.00	€25.00	Doc

Bitmap index on the field DVD_CHARGE

MOVIE_CHARGE				
€6.00	€6.50	€7.00	€7.50	€8.00
0	1	0	0	0
0	0	0	0	1
1	0	0	0	0
1	0	0	0	0
0	1	0	0	0
0	1	0	0	0
1	0	0	0	0
0	0	0	0	1
1	0	0	0	0
1	0	0	0	0
1	0	0	0	0

11

Bitmaps are more compact than B-trees and take up less storage space. However, combining multiple bitmap indexes can provide significant improvements in performance. Suppose we decide to also create a bitmap index on the CATEGORY field in the DVD table. Figure 11.23 shows the DVD table and the associated bitmap index for the CATEGORY field. This bitmap index has 11 entries with four bits per entry. Suppose we then wanted to find out the names of all movies with a movie charge of €6.00 and the category 'Family'. The SQL to retrieve this data is:

```
SELECT MOVIE_NAME
FROM MOVIE
WHERE CATEGORY = 'Family' AND MOVIE_CHARGE = 6.00;
```

To retrieve this data, we would access the first bit from the CATEGORY bitmap index and perform an AND operation with the third bit from the DVD_CHARGE bitmap index. This would then allow the retrieval of data where both bits had a matching value of 1. Not only is this an efficient way of accessing data, but bitmaps are also easy to read.

FIGURE 11.23 Bitmap index on the CATEGORY field

CATEGORY			
Family	Comedy	Action	Doc
1	0	0	0
0	1	0	0
1	0	0	0
0	0	1	0
0	0	1	0
0	0	1	0
0	0	0	1
1	0	0	0
0	0	0	1
0	0	0	1
0	0	0	1

Bitmap indexes are usually used when:

- A column in the table has low cardinality. Although all DBMSs vary, Oracle considers columns where the index has fewer than 100 distinct values.
- The table is not used often for data manipulation activities. This means that there are hardly any updates to the data in the table and few rows are inserted or deleted. Updating bitmapped indexes takes a lot of time, so, for example, if you update the data in the table regularly another type of index would be less resource intensive. As a guideline, bitmapped indexes are most suitable for large, read-only tables.
- Specific SQL queries reference a number of low cardinality values in their WHERE clauses.

11

Join Index

Like the bitmap index, the **join index** is used mainly in data warehousing and applies to columns from two or more tables whose values come from the same domain. It is often referred to as a *bitmap join index* and it is a way of saving space by reducing the volume of data that must be joined. The bitmap join stores the ROWIDs of corresponding rows in a separate table.

For example, Figure 11.24 shows two tables, CUSTOMER and EMPLOYEE, which both have columns containing area codes (CUST_AREACODE and EMP_AREACODE) that share the same domain. Each table also has a ROWID. The join index on the AREACODE column (also shown in Figure 11.24) shows the ROWIDs for the rows in each table which share the same AREACODE.

FIGURE 11.24 Join index on the AREACODE field

The customer table

ROWID	CUST_NUM	CUST_LNAME	CUST_FNAME	CUST_INITIAL	CUST_AREACODE	CUST_PHONE
50001	1001	Ramas	Alfred	A	0181	844-2573
50002	1002	Dunne	Leona	K	0161	894-1238
50003	1003	Moloi	Marlene	W	0191	894-2285
50004	1004	Olowski	Paul	F	0181	894-2180
50005	1005	Orlando	Myron		0181	222-1672
50006	1006	O'Brian	Amy	B	0161	442-3381
50007	1007	Brown	James	G	0181	297-1228
50008	1008	Williams	George		0113	290-2556
50009	1009	Padayachee	Vinaya	G	0161	382-7185
50010	1010	Moloi	Mlilo	K	0181	297-3809

The employee table

ROWID	EMP_NUM	EMP_LNAME	EMP_AREACODE	EMP_PHONE
72001	230	Smithson	0191	555-1234
72002	231	Johnson	0181	123-4536
72003	233	Wallace	0113	342-6567
72004	235	Ortozo	0161	899-3425

The join index on the common column AREACODE

ROWID	ROWID	AREACODE
50001	72002	0181
50002	72004	0161
50003	72001	0191
50004	72002	0181
50005	72002	0181
50006	72004	0161
50007	72002	0181
50008	72003	0113
50009	72004	0161
50010	72002	0181

11

This type of index is useful when dealing with large quantities of data that are typically found in data warehouses. Join indexes are less common in small relational databases. However, like bitmaps they are unsuitable when there are high-volume updates. The queries that access these indexes may also not reference any fields in the WHERE clause which are not in the join index.

Hashed File Organisations

A **hashed file** organisation uses a hashing algorithm to map a primary key value onto a specific record address in the file. Records are stored in a random order throughout the file. Thus, files that follow the hashed organisation are often referred to as *random* or *direct files*. There are many different kinds of hashing algorithms, but the aim of each is to distribute records evenly within the data storage area. Each specific hashing algorithm generates an artificial number that has no direct meaning except that it will tell the DBMS where the record is located relative to the start of the file. This artificial number is generated from a real-world logical primary key. The algorithm will usually reduce the primary key value to a shorter identifier, called a hash.

One common type of hashing algorithm is known as the division/remainder method. The steps for generating a hash using this method are:

1. Choose a prime number that is approximately 20 per cent larger than the number of records you want to store.
2. Divide the value of the logical primary key by the prime number and use the remainder as the relative record number for storing the record.

Let's look at an example. Suppose we need to store information about 800 customers. A suitable prime number would be 997 as it is approximately 20 per cent larger than 800. A customer with a customer number of 120001 would then have a hash of 362 (120001 divided by 997 gives 120 with a remainder of 362). The value 362 would then be the relative record number of customer 120001. Figure 11.25 illustrates this hashing algorithm.

FIGURE 11.25 **Hashing algorithm applied to the customer number field**

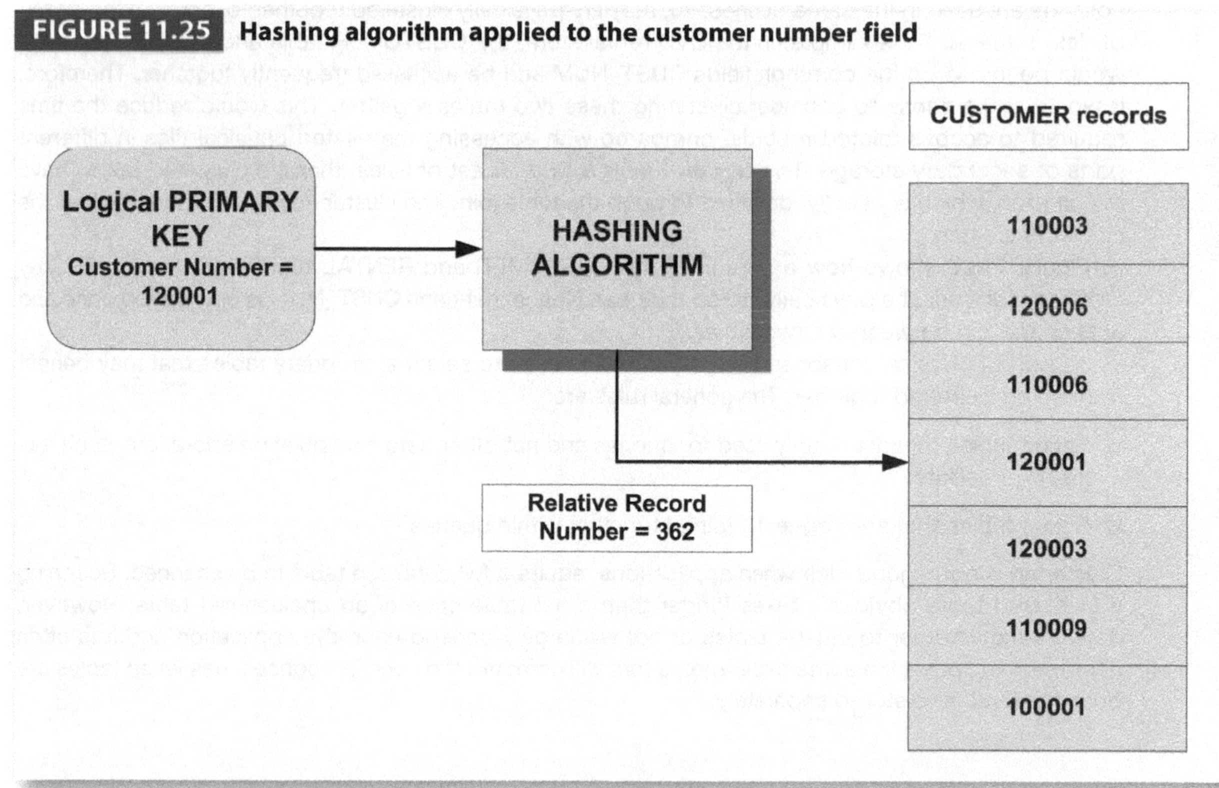

11

In hashed file organisations, each relative address that is generated is held in a storage location known as a *bucket*. If the bucket can hold more than one record, then individual records are held in a slot. If the bucket can hold several records, then the capacity of the bucket for a specific hashed file should be set to the number of records that the bucket can hold, including some free space for future modifications of records.

The main weakness with hashing algorithms is that there is no guarantee that a unique address is generated. If the algorithm generates the same hash for two different primary keys it is known as a *collision* as the hash will point to the same relative record. If a lot of collisions occur, the performance of the DBMS will decrease as the time taken to retrieve data increases. If the bucket has already been filled to capacity, the record must be stored elsewhere to prevent the bucket from overflowing. To deal with this problem, hashed file organisations have an overflow area where the overflow records are stored. In order to keep track of these overflow records, a pointer is used to point to where the overflowed record should be stored in the primary storage area. Alternatively, the logical primary key value is rehashed to produce a new location in the overflow area to store the record. If the overflow area becomes full, then another algorithm is used to put the overflowing record into the next free bucket.

Dealing with collisions may seem rather complicated, so the good news is that most DBMSs will manage all of the hashed file organisation. This type of file organisation is generally used when records are in a random order and exact matches can be obtained based upon the hash that is generated.

Clusters

User queries more often than not require data from multiple tables. Where these tables are stored in secondary storage has an impact on the query response time. Usually, tables that share common columns are used in the same queries; so, they are physically clustered together to increase the speed of data retrieval. For example, in the DVD rental store, the CUSTOMER table and the RENTAL table would be joined on the common fields CUST_NUM and be accessed frequently together. Therefore, it would make sense to consider clustering these two tables together. This would reduce the time required to access related records, compared with accessing the related physical files in different parts of secondary storage. The **cluster key** is a field, or set of fields, that the clustered tables have in common, which is usually identified through the table join. The cluster key is determined when the *cluster* is created.

Figure 11.26 shows how a portion of the CUSTOMER and RENTAL tables with the cluster key CUST_NUM would be physically stored together. Notice that each CUST_NUM is only stored once and acts as the join between the two tables.

As part of physical database design you would have to select appropriate tables that may benefit from being clustered together. The general rules are:

- Select tables that are mainly used for queries and not other data manipulation operations such as insert or update.
- Select tables that are frequently joined together within queries.

Clustering is not a good idea when applications require a full database table to be scanned. Scanning a clustered table obviously takes longer than a full table scan of an unclustered table. However, determining whether to cluster tables or not will largely depend upon the application and it is often necessary to undertake some experiments that will compare the query response times when tables are both clustered and stored separately.

FIGURE 11.26 Cluster key on the CUSTOMER and RENTAL tables

CUSTOMER TABLE | RENTAL TABLE

CUST_ LNAME	CUST_ FNAME	CUST_ INITIAL	CUST_ AREACODE	CUST_ PHONE	CUST_ NUM	RENT_ NUM	RENT_ CHARGE
Ramas	Alfred	A	0181	844-2573	1001	3	€6.00
						6	€8.00
						9	€6.00
						13	€6.00
Dunne	Leona	K	0161	894-1238	1002	1	€6.50
						8	€0.00
Moloi	Marlene	W	0191	894-2285	1003	2	€6.00
......	......	......	.....	....	.....	.....	......

Cluster Key – CUST_NUM

11.3.4 Define Indexes

As you discovered in the previous section, **indexes** can play an important role in improving the perfomance of the database system. Defining indexes is a large part of physical database design and decisions need to be made regarding the fields to be indexed and the type of index (primary or secondary) that will be applied. Each table typically has a **primary index** created for the primary key of the table. **Secondary indexes** are usually placed on additional fields that are used regularly in user queries in order to increase the speed of data retrieval.

In SQL, indexes are created using the CREATE INDEX statement. For example, if we wanted to create a primary index on the DVD_ID primary key field from the DVDs table, the SQL would be:

```
CREATE UNIQUE INDEX DVDINDEX ON DVD(DVD_ID)
```

where:

- UNIQUE specifies that the index may not have duplicate values. If the table does contain a duplicate value in the DVD_ID field, the CREATE INDEX statement will return an error message. In addition, after creation, if an attempt is made to insert any further records into the DVD table and these violate this unique constraint (e.g. have duplicate DVD_IDs), they are not inserted.
- DVDINDEX is the name of the index file that is created to store each value of the index.
- The ON clause specifies the table and the column for which the index is being created.

Secondary indexes are created using a similar SQL command. Supposing that customers frequently ring up the DVD rental store to enquire if a specific DVD is stocked by the store. They are unlikely to know the DVD_ID and will instead give the DVD_TITLE. A regular query to the database may be:

```
SELECT DVD_ID
FROM DVD
WHERE M.DVD_TITLE = 'Flowers in Winter';
```

11

To speed up results of this query, a secondary index could be created on the DVD_TITLE field:

```
CREATE INDEX DVD_TITLE_INDEX ON DVD(DVD_TITLE);
```

As it is possible that there could be two DVDs with the same title (but with different DVD codes), the UNIQUE keyword should not be used. This is true of most secondary indexes as the values of fields are often repeated and as a result there can be additional overheads. For example, every time a new record is inserted into a table that has a secondary index, a record must also be inserted into the corresponding index table.

The selection of both primary and secondary indexes is closely linked to database tuning and performance optimisation, which are covered in Chapter 13. During the physical database design process you must, however, make some initial decisions about which fields to index. Generally, you should create unique indexes for the primary key of each table. Indexes should also be considered on large tables that are regularly accessed as searching through an index is more efficient than scanning the complete table.

As a general rule, indexes are likely to be used:

- When an indexed column appears by itself in a search criterion which has a WHERE or HAVING clause.
- When an indexed column appears by itself in a GROUP BY or ORDER BY clause.
- When a MAX or MIN function is applied to an indexed column.
- When the data sparsity on the indexed column is high. Data sparsity refers to the number of different values a column could possibly have. For example, a STU_GENDER column in a STUDENT table can have only two possible values, M or F; therefore, that column is said to have low sparsity. In contrast, the STU_DOB column that stores the student date of birth can have many different date values; therefore, that column is said to have high sparsity. Knowing the sparsity helps you to decide whether the use of an index is appropriate. For example, when you perform a search in a column with low sparsity, you are likely to read a high percentage of the table rows anyway; therefore, index processing may be unnecessary work.

Indexes are also useful when you want to select a small subset of rows from a large table, based on a condition. The objective is to create indexes with high selectivity. **Index selectivity** is a measure of how likely it is that an index will be used in query processing. Here are some general guidelines for creating and using indexes:

- *Create indexes for each single attribute used in a WHERE, HAVING, ORDER BY, or GROUP BY clause*. If you create indexes for all single attributes *used in search conditions*, the DBMS accesses the table using an index scan instead of a full table scan. For example, if you have an index for P_PRICE, the condition P_PRICE > 10.00 can be handled by accessing the index instead of sequentially scanning all table rows and evaluating P_PRICE for each row. Indexes are also used in join expressions, such as in CUSTOMER.CUS_CODE = INVOICE.CUS_CODE.
- *Do not use indexes in small tables or tables with low sparsity*. Remember, small tables and low-sparsity tables are not the same thing. A search condition in a table with low sparsity may return a high percentage of table rows, making the index operation too costly and making the full table scan a viable option. Using the same logic, do not create indexes for tables with few rows and few attributes – *unless you must ensure the existence of unique values in a column*.
- *Declare primary and foreign keys so the query optimiser within a specific DBMS can use the indexes in join operations*. (Note that the query optimiser will be covered in detail in Chapter 13, Managing Database and SQL Performance.) All natural joins and old-style joins will benefit if you declare primary keys and foreign keys because the optimiser will use the available indexes at join

time. (The declaration of a PK or FK will automatically create an index for the declared column.) Also, for the same reason, it is better to write joins using the SQL JOIN syntax (see Chapter 9, Procedural Language SQL and Advanced SQL).

- *Declare indexes in join columns other than the PK/FK.* If you do join operations in columns other than the primary and foreign keys, you may be better off declaring indexes in those columns.

11.3.5 Define User Views

During the conceptual design stage, the different user views required for the database are determined. Using the relations defined in the logical data model, these views must now be defined. Views are often defined taking database security into account as they can help to define the roles of different types of users. We discuss how to define roles in section 11.3.7. You can learn more about how to create views in SQL in Chapter 8, Beginning Structured Query Language.

11.3.6 Estimate Data Storage Requirements

Allocating physical storage characteristics depends on the DBMS and the operating systems used. Most of the information necessary for defining the physical storage characteristics can be found in the technical manuals of the software you are using.

NOTE

If the DBMS does not automate the process of determining storage locations and data access paths, physical design requires well-developed technical skills and a precise knowledge of the physical-level details of the database, operating system and hardware used by the database. Fortunately, the more recent versions of relational DBMS software hide most of the complexities inherent in the physical design phase.

During the process of physical database design it is important to estimate not only the size of each table but also its long-term growth pattern. It is not necessary to be 100 per cent accurate but it should be based upon the expected growth of the business. Therefore, input into this process should be provided by the business experts within the company. They will need to answer questions such as 'How many customers are we likely to have in the next five years?' or 'Are we likely to expand the products that we currently sell?'

Next, the physical requirements of each table must be estimated. One simple way of performing this for each table is to:

1. Estimate the size of each row by summing the length in bytes for each data type.
2. Estimate the number of rows, taking into consideration the expected growth.
3. Multiply the size by the estimated number of rows.

Table 11.7 shows this calculation for the DVD table from the DVD rental store database.

TABLE 11.7 Physical storage requirements: the DVD table

Attribute Name	Data Type	Storage Requirement (Bytes)
DVD_ID	VARCHAR2(10)	10
MOVIE_COPIES	NUMBER(3)	3
MOVIE_NAME	VARCHAR2(50)	50
MOVIE_CHARGE	NUMBER(2,2)	4
MOVIE_LATE_CHG_DAY	NUMBER(2,2)	4
CATEGORY	CHAR(6)	6

Row length: 77
Number of rows: 7 590
Total space required: 584 430

The physical size of any indexes that have been specified must also be estimated. This is more difficult than estimating table sizes, because the actual size can depend on the specific DBMS.

NOTE

Oracle 18c provides a number of tools for estimating the size of database tables and indexes:

- CREATE_TABLE_COST determines the size of the table given various attributes including the average row size in bytes.
- CREATE_INDEX_COST determines the amount of storage space required to create an index on an existing table.

These tools, however, can only usually be accessed by the database administrator.

11

11.3.7 Determine Database Security for Users

In Chapter 10, Database Development Process, issues surrounding the security of the databases such as potential threats and measures that could be taken to combact these threats were discussed. As part of the Systems Development Life Cycle (SDLC), the security requirements of the database will have been identified. This will have included all the users of the database and their individual access requirements and restrictions. During physical database design, these requirements must be implemented within the target DBMS and database privileges for users will need to be established. For example, privileges may include selecting rows from specified tables or views, being able to modify or delete data in specified tables, etc.

Implementing basic data security in Oracle requires all users to be given an account comprising a user name and an associated password. Oracle has two levels of privilege (system and object) that allow the database administrator (DBA) to control how much power a specific user is granted. For example, we do not want all staff to be able to access the complete database or to drop tables when they have no right to do so. *System* privileges authorise a user account to execute SQL data definition language (DDL) commands such as CREATE TABLE. *Object* privileges allow a user account to execute SQL data manipulation language (DML) commands such as performing SELECT, INSERT, UPDATE and DELETE operations on specific tables.

The SQL commands GRANT and REVOKE are used to authorise or withdraw privileges on specific user accounts. For example, the following two SQL statements grant the account with the username 'Craig' the ability to select rows from the DVD table and the ability to create tables:

```
GRANT SELECT ON DVD TO Craig;
GRANT CREATE TABLE TO Craig;
```

Removing these privileges can be done using the following SQL statements:

```
REVOKE SELECT ON DVD FROM Craig;
REVOKE CREATE TABLE FROM Craig;
```

In any company, it is likely that there will be a very large number of users, so the DBA will have a very difficult time managing all the privileges that are required. To overcome this, the users of the database can be grouped depending on the type of privileges they require and a database role can be assigned to each group. A role is simply a collection of privileges referred to under a single name. The major benefit of roles is that a DBA can add or revoke privileges from a role at any time. These changes will then automatically apply to all the users who have been assigned that role. For example, in the DVD rental store, the sales staff need to perform SELECT and UPDATE operations on the CUSTOMER table. The SQL command CREATE ROLE is used to create the role STAFF_CUSTOMER_ROLE:

```
CREATE ROLE STAFF_CUSTOMER_ROLE;
```

Once created, privileges can then be granted on selected database objects to the new role. For example:

```
GRANT SELECT ON CUSTOMERS TO STAFF_CUSTOMER_ROLE;
GRANT UPDATE ON CUSTOMERS TO STAFF_CUSTOMER_ROLE;
```

The last stage then involves granting the role to individual users accounts, e.g. Lindiwe;

```
GRANT STAFF_CUSTOMER_ROLE TO Lindiwe;
```

If the DBA then chooses to revoke a privilege from the role, it is automatically removed from all users assigned to the role.

SUMMARY

- Conceptual database design is where the conceptual representation of the database is created by producing a data model that identifies the relevant entities and relationships within the system. This stage of the Database Life Cycle can be broken down in to four steps: data analysis and requirements, entity relationship modelling and normalisation, data model verification, and distributed database design. The final conceptual model must embody a clear understanding of the business and its functional areas.
- Data model verification is part of the conceptual database design phase where the ER model must be verified against the proposed system processes in order to corroborate that the intended processes can be supported by the database model. Verification requires that the model be run through a series of tests against end-user data views and their required transactions, access paths and security and business-imposed data requirements and constraints.
- Logical database design is the second stage in the Database Life Cycle, where relations are designed based on each entity and its relationships within the conceptual model. Creating the logical data model involves the following stages: creating the logical data model, validating the logical data model using normalisation, assigning and validating integrity constraints, merging

logical models constructed for different parts for the database, and reviewing the logical data model with the user.

- When creating the logical data model, the order in which the entities are translated into relations is important. Those with no dependents (e.g. that do not contain any foreign keys) should be translated first. To create the relations, the name of the relation is specified along with its associated attributes enclosed in brackets. Finally, the primary key attribute(s) is identified, followed by any foreign keys.
- Physical database design is where the logical data model is mapped onto the physical database tables to be implemented in the chosen DBMS. The ultimate goal must be to ensure that data storage is used effectively, to ensure integrity and security, and to improve efficiency in terms of query response time. Physical database design comprises the following seven stages: analysing data volume and database usage, translating each relation identified in the logical data model into database tables, determining the most suitable file organisation, defining indexes to speed up data access, designing user views, estimating data storage requirements, and determining appropriate database security for users.
- Selecting a suitable file organisation is important for fast data retrieval and efficient use of storage space. The three most common types of file organisation are heap files, which contain randomly ordered records; indexed sequential files, which are sorted on one or more fields using indexes; and hashed files, in which a hashing algorithm is used to determine the address of each record based upon the value of the primary key. Within a DBMS, indexes are often stored in data structures known as B-trees, which allow fast data retrieval. Two other kinds of indexes are bitmap indexes and join indexes. These are often used on multidimensional data held in data warehouses.
- Indexes are crucial for speeding up data access. Indexes facilitate searching, sorting, and using aggregate functions and even join operations. The improvement in data access speed occurs because an index is an ordered set of values that contains the index key and pointers. Data sparsity refers to the number of different values a column could possibly have. Indexes are recommended in highly sparse columns used in search conditions.

11

Online Content In Appendices B and C, available on the online platform for this book, you will have the chance to experience all the stages of the database design life cycle through the creation of two real-world database systems: the University Lab and Global Tickets Ltd, a travel e-commerce database.

KEY TERMS

B-tree
bitmap index
cluster key
cohesivity
composite usage map
conceptual design
description of operations
file organisation
hashed file
heap file
index selectivity
indexes
join index
minimal data rule
module
module coupling
primary index
secondary index
sequential file
transaction usage map

FURTHER READING

Comer, D. 'The Ubiquitous B-Tree', *ACM Computing Surveys,* 11(2), pp. 121–137, 1979.

Garmany, J., Walker, J. and Clark, T. *Logical Database Design Principles (Foundations of Database Design)*. AUERBACH, 2005.

Pavlovic, Z. and Veselica, M., *Oracle Database 12c Security Cookbook*. Packt Publishing, 2016.

Lightstone, S., Teorey, T. and Nadeau, T. *Physical Database Design: The Database Professional's Guide to Exploiting Indexes, Views, Storage, and More*, 4th revised edition. Morgan Kaufmann Series in Data Management Systems, 2007.

Teorey, T. *Database Modelling and Design Logical D*, 5th edition. Morgan Kaufmann Series in Data Management Systems, 2011.

Wiederhold, G. *Database Design*, 2nd edition. McGraw-Hill, 1983.

Online Content Answers to selected Review Questions and Problems for this chapter are available on the online platform accompanying this book.

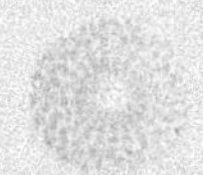

REVIEW QUESTIONS

1 What are the stages of the conceptual database design?

2 What are business rules? Why are they important to a database designer?

3 Which steps are required in the development of an ER diagram?

4 List and briefly explain the activities involved in the verification of an ER model.

5 Describe the logical database design process.

6 Describe the steps required to convert the conceptual ER model into the logical model.

7 What are the typical problems in merging relations?

8 Which integrity constraints need validating during logical database design?

9 What are the stages of physical database design?

10 Why is it important to analyse data volume and usage statistics?

11 When should indexes be used?

12 Describe the purpose of a B-tree.

13 When are factors important in selecting a bitmap index?

14 How is basic database security implemented?

15 How is entity integrity and referential integrity enforced when creating tables in SQL?

PROBLEMS

1 Write the proper sequence of activities in the design of a video rental database. (The initial ERD was shown in Figure 11.7.) The design must support all rental activities, customer payment tracking and employee work schedules, as well as track which employees checked out the videos to the customers. When you have finished writing the design activity sequence, complete the ERD to ensure that the database design can be successfully implemented. (Make sure that the design is normalised properly and that it can support the required transactions.)

2 Create the initial ER diagram for a car dealership. The dealership sells both new and used cars, and it operates a service facility. Base your design on the following business rules:

- **a** A salesperson can sell many cars, but each car is sold by only one salesperson.
- **b** A customer can buy many cars, but each car is sold to only one customer.
- **c** A salesperson writes a single invoice for each car sold.
- **d** A customer gets an invoice for each car(s) he or she buys.
- **e** A customer might come in only to have a car serviced; that is, one need not buy a car to be classified as a customer.
- **f** When a customer takes in one or more cars for repair or service, one service ticket is written for each car.
- **g** The car dealership maintains a service history for each car serviced. The service records are referenced by the car's serial number.
- **h** A car brought in for service can be worked on by many mechanics, and each mechanic can work on many cars.
- **i** A car that is serviced may or may not need parts. (For example, parts are not necessary to adjust a carburettor or to clean a fuel injector nozzle.)

3 Verify the conceptual model you created in Question 2. Create a data dictionary for the verified model.

4 Transform the ERD in Figure P11.1 into a relational schema showing all primary and foreign keys.

FIGURE P11.1 **ERD for Problem 4**

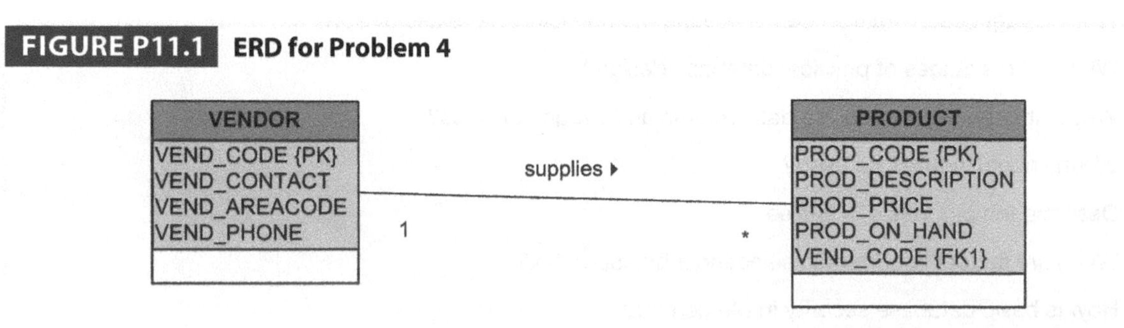

5 Show two ways in which the ERD in Figure P11.2 could be converted into a relational schema. In each case show all primary and foreign keys.

FIGURE P11.2 ERD for Problem 5

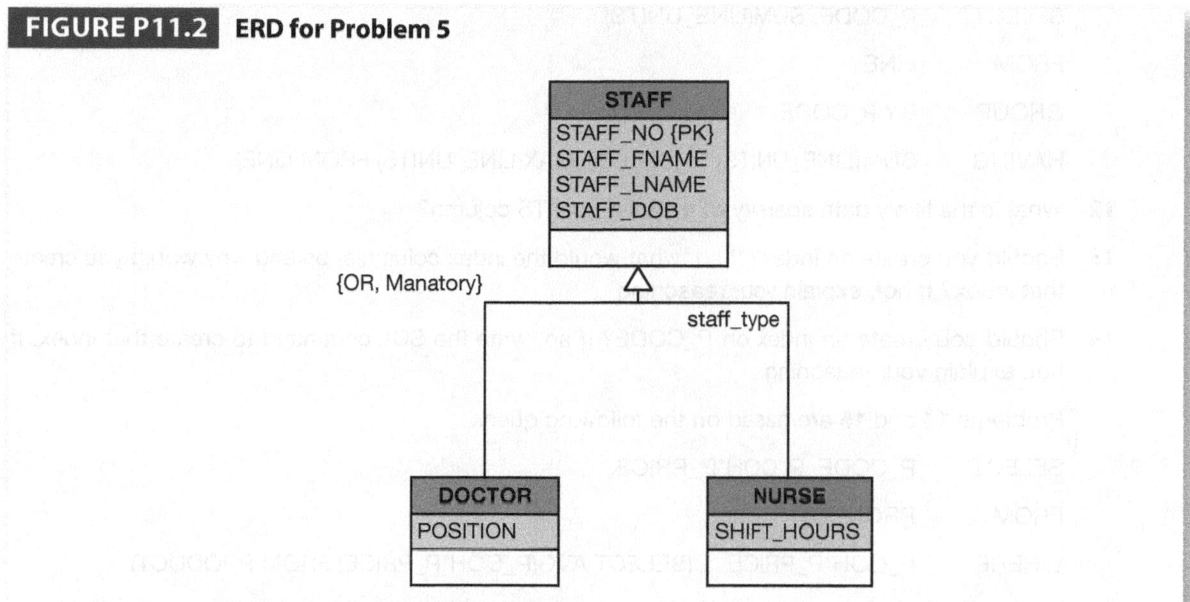

6 Transform the verified ER model shown in Figure 11.7 on p. 593 into a relational schema showing all primary and foreign keys.

7 Produce a relational schema for the ERD of the car dealership you created in Question 2.

Find the solutions to Problems 8 and 9 based on the following query:

```
SELECT    EMP_LNAME, EMP_FNAME, EMP_AREACODE, EMP_GENDER
FROM      EMPLOYEE
WHERE     EMP_GENDER = 'F' AND EMP_AREACODE = '0181'
ORDER BY  EMP_LNAME, EMP_FNAME;
```

8 What is the likely data sparsity of the EMP_GENDER column?

9 Which indexes should you create? Write the required SQL commands.

Problems 10 and 11 are based on the following query:

```
SELECT    EMP_LNAME, EMP_FNAME, EMP_DOB, YEAR(EMP_DOB) AS YEAR
FROM      EMPLOYEE
WHERE     YEAR(EMP_DOB) = 1976;
```

10 What is the likely data sparsity of the EMP_DOB column?

11 Should you create an index on EMP_DOB? Why or why not?

Problems 12 and 13 are based on the following query:

```
SELECT    P_CODE, SUM(LINE_UNITS)
FROM      LINE
GROUP     BY P_CODE
HAVING    SUM(LINE_UNITS) > (SELECT MAX(LINE_UNITS) FROM LINE);
```

12 What is the likely data sparsity of the LINE_UNITS column?

13 Should you create an index? If so, what would the index column(s) be and why would you create that index? If not, explain your reasoning.

14 Should you create an index on P_CODE? If so, write the SQL command to create that index. If not, explain your reasoning.

Problems 14 and 15 are based on the following query:

```
SELECT    P_CODE, P_QOH*P_PRICE
FROM      PRODUCT
WHERE     P_QOH*P_PRICE > (SELECT AVG(P_QOH*P_PRICE) FROM PRODUCT)
```

15 What is the likely data sparsity of the P_QOH and P_PRICE columns?

16 Should you create an index, what would the index column(s) be, and why should you create that index?

17 Consider the composite usage map shown in Figure P11.3 for a building company called BricksRUs. The composite usage map shows that there are 1000 rows in the material table (e.g. bricks, cement, etc.). There are two types of materials, full price materials and wholesale materials. Full-price materials account for 35 per cent of materials that are purchased while wholesale materials account for 70 per cent of purchases. As the same materials can be of both subtypes, the percentages can be greater than 100 per cent. When contractors wish to apply for a contract for a building

FIGURE P11.3 **Composite usage map for BricksRUs**

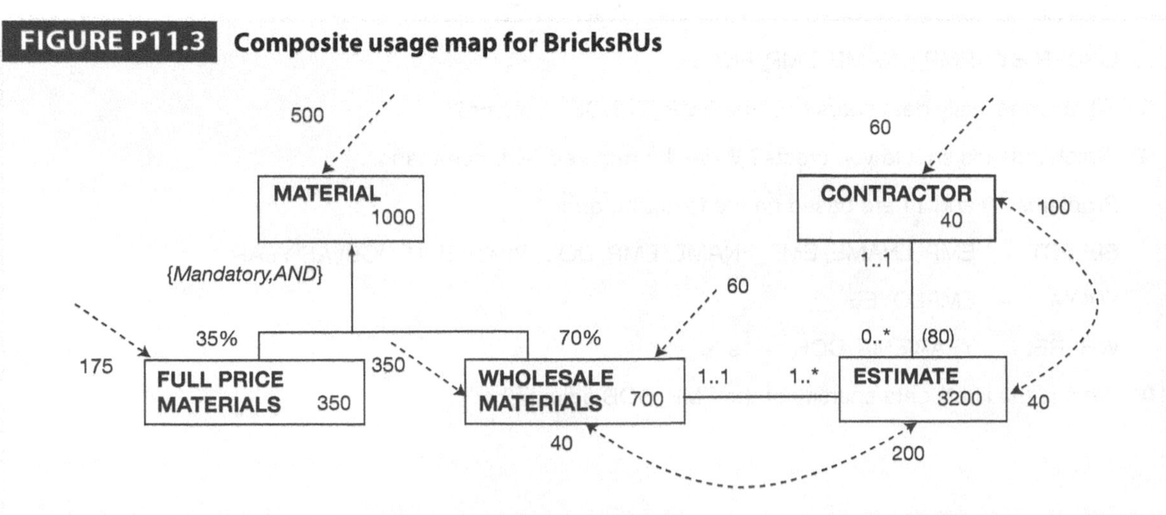

job, they send in estimates. There are roughly 40 contractors who undertake jobs for BricksRUs and, on average, they provide 80 estimates (giving a total of 3200 estimates). On average there are 500 accesses to the material table which can be broken down into 175 accesses to full-price materials and 350 accesses to wholesale materials. Of the 60 accesses to the contractor table, there are 40 subsequent accesses to the estimate table.

After a period of time, the assumptions for this usage map have changed as follows:

a The number of direct accesses to materials has decreased to 400 per hour. Out of this, 175 require subsequent accesses to the estimate table.

b Wholesale materials now account for 80 per cent of all materials.

c Full price materials now represent only 25 per cent of all materials.

d There are now an average of 60 estimates for each supplier.

Draw a new composite usage map reflecting this new information.

18 Draw a B+-tree with $n = 2$ and insert the following keys in order: A, B, C, D and E into the tree. You should show the insertions at each stage. Remember $n = 2$ means that nodes are allowed to have no more than two keys and no fewer than one key each.

19 Draw another B+-tree with $n = 2$ and insert the following keys in order: B, D, C, A, E, F. You should show the insertions at each stage.

Part V

DATABASE TRANSACTIONS AND PERFORMANCE TUNING

BUSINESS VIGNETTE

FROM DATA WAREHOUSE TO DATA LAKE

Since the early 1990s, a vast amount of data has been stored in data warehouses in order to provide a central repository for business intelligence within an organisation. The concept of a data warehouse originated from studies undertaken at MIT in the early 1970s.[1] However, the term 'information warehouse' was first used in 1986 by Barry Devlin and Paul Murphy in an article entitled 'An Architecture for a Business and Information System' in *IBM Systems Journal*.[2] They identified what was known commonly as the 'islands of information' problem. This is where organisations had many operational systems that were not integrated, data were duplicated and reporting from the global business perspective was rare. Data warehousing took off in earnest in 1991 when Bill Inmon published his book entitled *Building the Data Warehouse*.[3] While in 1996 there were more data warehouse projects initiated than in previous years, arguments began about whether data warehousing solutions were too generalised in trying to model the whole organisation. An alternative methodology to developing a data warehouse that focused on the use of data marts was championed by Ralph Kimball.[4] The development of data marts focused on the data requirements of individual departments rather than the whole organisation. The data mart proved successful as it provided a quick return on investment and introduced the concepts of the dimensional modelling of data.

It is now the norm for data warehouses to store terabytes of data. The number of users accessing a typical organisation's data warehouse has increased, along with the requirements for more complex queries and near real-time information. With the rise of Big Data, traditional data

1 Haisten, M. 'Data warehousing: what's next? Part 4: integrate the new islands of information', *DM Direct Newsletter*. Available at www.dmreview.com/article_sub.cfm?articleId=5238

2 Devlin, B. and Murphy, P. 'An architecture for a business and information system', *IBM Systems Journal* 27(1), pp. 60–80, 1998.

3 Imnon, B. *Building the Data Warehouse*, 4th edition. Hungry Minds Inc, 2005.

4 Kimball, Ralph. The Data Warehouse Toolkit: Practical Techniques for Building Dimensional Data Warehouses, Kindle Edition. John Wiley & Sons, 2010.

warehouses can sometimes be seen as rigid in structure. An alternative is a Data Lake, which allows the user to store data in its raw format in an unstructured form. Data Lakes are important for companies whose business are data driven.

Today, organisations require Smart Data, which provides a summarised, cross-functional view of the right information at the right time and in the right business context. Smart Data is likely to be extracted from Big Data where different information architectures need to be devised to cope with data larger volumes and different sizes. Furthermore, complex data analysis of this Big Data will be required to deliver timely results to organisations. Business intelligence and analytics are fundamental tools within a business. Business intelligence typically uses a data warehouse and/or a Data Lake to make decisions through a variety of tools such as multiple dimensional analyses, forecasting tools and data mining. It can be used to answer questions such as 'What if our competitors introduced an expensive advertising campaign?' to 'Which products do we think our customers might like, based upon their previous shopping habits?' Today, business intelligence is used to find new business opportunities and produce more efficient business processes.

In 2018, Forbes reported that Big Data revenues will increase from $42 billion in 2018 to $103 billion in 2027.[5] In addition, 59 per cent of executives reported that, if they used artificial intelligence alongside their company Big Data, it would deliver more value. The main driver of combining advanced analytics and artificial intelligence approaches to Big Data is to achieve greater predictive accuracy and to accelerate decision making.

5 Columbus, L. 10 Charts That Will Change Your Perspective Of Big Data's Growth, Available: www.forbes.com/sites/louiscolumbus/2018/05/23/10-charts-that-will-change-your-perspective-of-big-datas-growth/#1d6790d32926

CHAPTER 12

Managing Transactions and Concurrency

IN THIS CHAPTER, YOU WILL LEARN:

- What a database transaction is and what its properties are
- What concurrency control is and what role it plays in maintaining the database's integrity
- What locking methods are and how they work
- How stamping methods are used for concurrency control
- How optimistic methods are used for concurrency control
- How database recovery management is used to maintain database integrity
- The ANSI levels of transaction isolation

PREVIEW

Database transactions reflect real-world transactions that are triggered by events such as buying a product, registering for a course, or making a deposit in a current account. Transactions are likely to contain many parts. For example, a sales transaction may require updating the customer's account, adjusting the product inventory and updating the seller's accounts receivable. All parts of a transaction must be successfully completed to prevent data integrity problems. Therefore, executing and managing transactions are important database system activities.

The main database transaction properties are atomicity, consistency, durability, isolation and serialisability. After defining these transaction properties, this chapter shows how SQL can be used to represent transactions and how transaction logs can ensure the DBMS's ability to recover transactions.

When many transactions take place at the same time, they are called *concurrent transactions*. Managing the execution of such transactions is called *concurrency control*. As you can imagine, concurrency control is especially important in a multi-user database environment (just imagine the number of transactions routinely handled by companies that conduct sales and provide services via the Web!). This chapter discusses some of the problems that can occur with concurrent transactions such as lost updates, uncommitted data and inconsistent summaries. You will discover that such problems can be solved when a DBMS scheduler enforces concurrency control.

You will learn about the most common algorithms for concurrency control: locks, time stamping and optimistic methods. Because locks are the most widely used method, you will examine various levels and types of locks. Locks can also create deadlocks, so you will learn about strategies for managing deadlocks.

Database contents can be damaged or destroyed by critical operational errors, including transaction management failures. Therefore, you will learn how database recovery management maintains a database's contents by means of various backup procedures. Such backup procedures range from **full backups** to **transaction log backups**.

12.1 WHAT IS A TRANSACTION?

To illustrate what transactions are and how they work, let's use the Ch12_SaleCo database. The relational diagram for that database is shown in Figure 12.1.

Online Content The 'Ch12_SaleCo' database used to illustrate the material in this chapter is available on the online platform for this book.

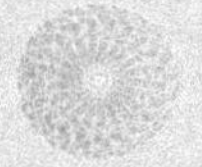

FIGURE 12.1 The Ch12_SaleCo database ERD

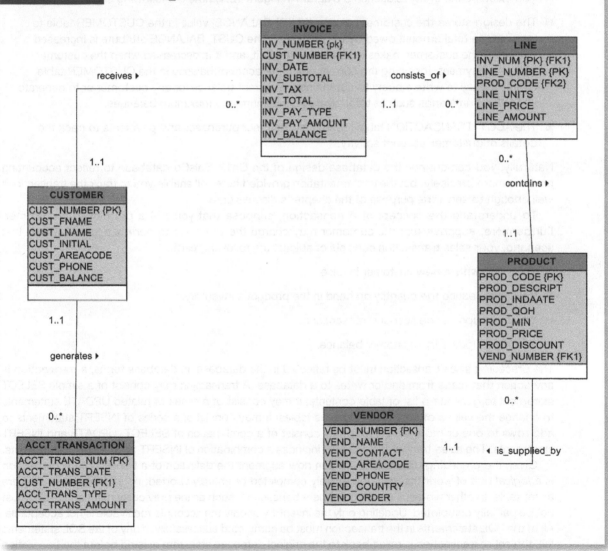

NOTE

Although SQL commands illustrate several transaction and concurrency control issues, you should be able to follow the discussions even if you have not studied Chapter 8, Beginning Structured Query Language, and Chapter 9, Procedural Language and Advanced SQL. If you don't know SQL, ignore the SQL commands and focus on the discussions. If you have a working knowledge of SQL, you can use the Ch12_SaleCo database to generate your own SELECT and UPDATE examples and to augment the material presented in Chapters 8 and 9 by writing your own triggers and stored procedures.

As you examine the entity relationship diagram in Figure 12.1, note the following simplifying features:

- The design stores the customer balance (CUST_BALANCE) value in the CUSTOMER table to indicate the total amount owed by the customer. The CUST_BALANCE attribute is increased whenever the customer makes a purchase on credit, and it is decreased when the customer makes a payment. Including the current customer account balance in the CUSTOMER table makes it easy to write a query to determine the current balance for any customer or to generate important summaries such as total, average, minimum and maximum balances.
- The ACCT_TRANSACTION table records all customer purchases and payments to track the details of customer account activity.

Naturally, you can change the database design of the Ch12_SaleCo database to reflect accounting practice more precisely, but the implementation provided here will enable you to track the transactions well enough to serve the purpose of the chapter's discussions.

To understand the concept of a transaction, suppose that you sell a product to a customer. Furthermore, suppose that the customer may charge the purchase to her/his account. Given that scenario, your sales transaction consists of at least the following parts:

- You must write a new customer invoice.
- You must reduce the quantity on hand in the product's inventory.
- You must update the account transactions.
- You must update the customer balance.

The preceding sales transaction must be reflected in the database. In database terms, a **transaction** is any action that reads from and/or writes to a database. A transaction may consist of a simple SELECT statement to generate a list of table contents; it may consist of a series of related UPDATE statements to change the values of attributes in various tables; it may consist of a series of INSERT statements to add rows to one or more tables; or it may consist of a combination of SELECT, UPDATE and INSERT statements. The sales transaction example includes a combination of INSERT and UPDATE statements.

Given the preceding discussion, you can now augment the definition of a transaction. A *transaction* is a *logical* unit of work that must be entirely completed or entirely aborted; no intermediate states are acceptable. In other words, a multi-component transaction, such as the previously mentioned sale, must not be partially completed. Updating only the inventory or only the accounts receivable is not acceptable. All of the SQL statements in the transaction must be completed successfully. If any of the SQL statements fail, the entire transaction is rolled back to the original database state that existed before the transaction started. A successful transaction changes the database from one consistent state to another. A **consistent database state** is one in which all data integrity constraints are satisfied.

To ensure consistency of the database, every transaction must begin with the database in a known consistent state. If the database is not in a consistent state, the transaction will yield an inconsistent database that violates its integrity and business rules. For that reason, subject to limitations discussed later, all transactions are controlled and executed by the DBMS to guarantee database integrity.

Most real-world database transactions are formed by two or more database requests. A **database request** is the equivalent of a single SQL statement in an application program or transaction. Therefore, if a transaction is composed of two UPDATE statements and one INSERT statement, the transaction uses three database requests. In turn, each database request generates several input/output (I/O) operations that read from or write to physical storage media.

12.1.1 Evaluating Transaction Results

Not all transactions update the database. Suppose you want to examine the current balance for customer number 10016 located in the CUSTOMER table. Such a transaction can be completed by using the SQL code:

```
SELECT    CUST_NUMBER, CUST_BALANCE
FROM      CUSTOMER
WHERE     CUST_NUMBER = 10016;
```

Although that query does not make any changes in the CUSTOMER table, the SQL code represents a transaction because it *accesses* the database. If the database existed in a consistent state before the access, the database remains in a consistent state after the access, because the transaction did not alter the database.

Remember that a transaction may consist of a single SQL statement or a collection of related SQL statements. Let's revisit the previous sales example to illustrate a more complex transaction, using the Ch12_SaleCo database. Suppose that on 18 January 2019 you register the credit sale of one unit of product 89-WRE-Q to customer 10016 in the amount of €277.55. The required transaction affects the INVOICE, LINE, PRODUCT, CUSTOMER and ACCT_TRANSACTION tables. The SQL statements that represent this transaction are as follows:

```
INSERT INTO INVOICE
VALUES (1009, 10016, '18-Jan-2019', 256.99, 20.56, 277.55, 'cred', 0.00, 277.55);
INSERT INTO LINE
VALUES (1009, 1, '89-WRE-Q', 1, 256.99, 256.99);
UPDATE PRODUCT
SET PROD_QOH = PROD_QOH – 1
WHERE PROD_CODE = '89-WRE-Q'; UPDATE CUSTOMER
SET CUST_BALANCE = CUST_BALANCE + 277.55
WHERE CUST_NUMBER = 10016;
INSERT INTO ACCT_TRANSACTION
VALUES (10007, '18-Jan-19', 10016, 'charge', 277.55);
COMMIT;
```

12

The results of the successfully completed transaction appear in Figure 12.2. (Note that all records involved in the transaction are highlighted.)

To further your understanding of the transaction results, note the following:

- A new row 1009 was added to the INVOICE table. In this row, derived attribute values were stored for the invoice subtotal, the tax, the invoice total, and the invoice balance.
- The LINE row for invoice 1009 was added to reflect the purchase of one unit of product '89-WRE-Q' with a price of €256.99. In this row, the derived attribute values for the line amount were stored.
- The product 89-WRE-Q's quantity on hand (PROD_QOH) in the PRODUCT table was reduced by one (the initial value was 12), thus leaving a quantity on hand of 11.
- The customer balance (CUST_BALANCE) for customer 10016 was updated by adding €277.55 to the existing balance (the initial value was €0.00).
- A new row was added to the ACCT_TRANSACTION table to reflect the new account transaction number 10007.
- The COMMIT statement is used to end a successful transaction. (See Section 12.1.3.)

FIGURE 12.2 **Tracing the transaction in the Ch12SaleCo database**

Table name: INVOICE

INV_NUMBER	CUST_NUMBER	INV_DATE	INV_SUBTOTAL	INV_TAX	INV_TOTAL	INV_PAY_TYPE	INV_PAY_AMOUNT	INV_BALANCE
1001	10014	16-Jan-19	54.92	4.39	59.31	cc	59.31	0.00
1002	10011	16-Jan-19	9.98	0.80	10.78	cash	10.78	0.00
1003	10012	16-Jan-19	270.70	21.66	292.36	cc	292.36	0.00
1004	10011	17-Jan-19	34.87	2.79	37.66	cc	37.66	0.00
1005	10018	17-Jan-19	70.44	5.64	76.08	cc	76.08	0.00
1006	10014	17-Jan-19	397.83	31.83	429.66	cred	100.00	329.66
1007	10015	17-Jan-19	34.97	2.80	37.77	chk	37.77	0.00
1008	10011	17-Jan-19	1033.08	82.65	1115.73	cred	500.00	615.73
1009	10016	18-Jan-19	256.99	20.56	277.55	cred	0.00	277.55

Table name: PRODUCT

PROD_CODE	PROD_DESCRIPT	PROD_INDATE	PROD_QOH	PROD_MIN	PROD_PRICE	PROD_DISCOUNT	VEND_NUMBER
11QER/31	Power painter, 15 psi., 3-nozzle	03-Nov-18	8	5	109.99	0.00	25595
13-Q2/P2	7.25 cm pwr. saw blade	13-Dec-18	32	15	14.99	0.05	21344
14-Q1/L3	9.00 cm pwr. saw blade	13-Nov-18	18	12	17.49	0.00	21344
1546-QQ2	Hrd. cloth, 1/4 cm, 2 × 50	15-Jan-19	15	8	39.95	0.00	23119
1558-QW1	Hrd. cloth, 1/2 cm, 3 × 50	15-Jan-19	23	5	43.99	0.00	23119
2232/QTY	B&D jigsaw, 12 cm blade	30-Dec-18	8	5	109.92	0.05	24288
2232/QWE	B&D jigsaw, 8 cm blade	24-Dec-18	6	5	99.87	0.05	24288
2238/QPD	B&D cordless drill, 1/2 cm	20-Jan-19	12	5	38.95	0.05	25595
23109-HB	Claw hammer	20-Jan-19	23	10	9.95	0.10	21225

PROD_CODE	PROD_DESCRIPT	PROD_INDATE	PROD_QOH	PROD_MIN	PROD_PRICE	PROD_DISCOUNT	VEND_NUMBER
23114-AA	Sledge hammer, 12 kg	02-Jan-19	8	5	14.40	0.05	
54778-2T	Rat-tail file, 1/8 cm fine	15-Dec-18	43	20	4.99	0.00	21344
89-WRE-Q	Hicut chain saw, 16 cm	07-Jan-19	11	5	256.99	0.05	24288
PVC23DRT	PVC pipe, 3.5 cm, 8 m	06-Jan-18	188	75	5.87	0.00	
SM-18277	1.25 cm metal screw, 25	01-Mar-19	172	75	6.99	0.00	21225
SW-23116	2.5 cm wd. screw, 50	24-Feb-19	237	100	8.45	0.00	21231
WR3/TT3	Steel matting, 4 m × 8 m × 1/6 m, .5 m mesh	17-Jan-19	18	5	119.95	0.10	25595

Table name: CUSTOMER

CUST_NUMBER	CUST_LNAME	CUST_FNAME	CUST_INITIAL	CUST_AREACODE	CUST_PHONE	CUST_BALANCE
10010	Ramas	Alfred	A	0181	844-2573	0.00
10011	Dunne	Leona	K	0161	894-1238	615.73
10012	Moloi	Marlene	W	0181	894-2285	0.00
10013	Pieterse	Jaco	F	0181	894-2180	0.00
10014	Orlando	Myron		0181	222-1672	0.00
10015	O'Brian	Amy	B	0161	442-3381	0.00
10016	Brown	James	G	0181	297-1228	277.55
10017	Williams	George		0181	290-2556	0.00
10018	Padayachee	Vinaya	G	0181	382-7185	0.00
10019	Moloi	Mlilo	K	0161	297-3809	0.00

Table name: LINE

INV_NUMBER	LINE_NUMBER	PROD_CODE	LINE_UNITS	LINE_PRICE	LINE_AMOUNT
1001	1	13-Q2/P2	3	14.99	44.97
1001	2	23109-HB	1	9.95	9.95
1002	1	54778-2T	2	4.99	9.98
1003	1	2238/QPD	4	38.95	155.80
1003	2	1546-QQ2	1	39.95	39.95
1003	3	13-Q2/P2	5	14.99	74.95
1004	1	54778-2T	3	4.99	14.97
1004	2	23109-HB	2	9.95	19.90
1005	1	PVC23DRT	12	5.87	70.44
1006	1	SM-18277	3	6.99	20.97
1006	2	2232/QTY	1	109.92	109.92

INV_NUMBER	LINE_NUMBER	PROD_CODE	LINE_UNITS	LINE_PRICE	LINE_AMOUNT
1006	3	23109-HB	1	9.95	9.95
1006	4	89-WRE-Q	1	256.99	256.99
1007	1	13-Q2/P2	2	14.99	29.98
1007	2	54778-2T	1	4.99	4.99
1008	1	PVC23DRT	5	5.87	29.35
1008	2	WR3/TT3	4	119.95	479.80
1008	3	23109-HB	1	9.95	9.95
1008	4	89-WRE-Q	2	256.99	513.98
1009	1	89-WRE-Q	1	256.99	256.99

Table name: ACCT_TRANSACTION

ACCT_TRANS_NUM	ACCT_TRANS_DATE	CUST_NUMBER	ACCT_TRANS_TYPE	ACCT_TRANS_AMOUNT
10003	17-Jan-19	10014	charge	329.66
10004	17-Jan-19	10011	charge	615.73
10006	29-Jan-19	10014	payment	329.66
10007	18-Jan-19	10016	charge	277.55

Now suppose that the DBMS completes the first three SQL statements. Further, suppose that during the execution of the fourth statement (the UPDATE of the CUSTOMER table's CUST_BALANCE value for customer 10016), the computer system experiences a loss of electrical power. If the computer does not have a backup power supply, the transaction cannot be completed. Therefore, the INVOICE and LINE rows were added, the PRODUCT table was updated to represent the sale of product 89-WRE-Q, but customer 10016 was not charged, nor was the required record in the ACCT_TRANSACTION table written. The database is now in an inconsistent state, and it is not usable for subsequent transactions. Assuming that the DBMS supports transaction management, *the DBMS will roll back the database to a previous consistent state.*

12

NOTE

Microsoft Access supports transaction management through its native JET engine, via an ODBC interface to an external DBMS, or via Access Data Objects (ADO) components. More sophisticated DBMSs, such as Oracle, SQL Server and DB2, do support the transaction management components discussed in this chapter.

Although the DBMS is designed to recover a database to a previous consistent state when an interruption prevents the completion of a transaction, the transaction itself is defined by the end user or programmer and must be semantically correct. *The DBMS cannot guarantee that the semantic meaning of the transaction truly represents the real-world event.* For example, suppose that following the sale of ten units of product 89-WRE-Q, the inventory UPDATE commands were written this way:

```
UPDATE    PRODUCT
SET       OD_QOH = PROD_QOH + 10
WHERE     OD_CODE = '89-WRE-Q';
```

The sale should have *decreased* the PROD_QOH value for product 89-WRE-Q by ten. Instead, the UPDATE *added* ten to product 89-WRE-Q's PROD_QOH value.

Although the UPDATE command's syntax is correct, its use yields incorrect results. Yet the DBMS will execute the transaction anyway. The DBMS cannot evaluate whether the transaction represents the real-world event correctly; that is the end user's responsibility. End users and programmers are capable of introducing many errors in this fashion. Imagine the consequences of reducing the quantity on hand for product 1546-QQ2 instead of product 89-WRE-Q or of crediting the CUST_BALANCE value for customer 10012 rather than customer 10016.

Clearly, improper or incomplete transactions can have a devastating effect on database integrity. Some DBMSs – *especially* the relational variety – provide means by which the user can define enforceable constraints based on business rules. Other integrity rules, such as those governing referential and entity integrity, are enforced automatically by the DBMS when the table structures are properly defined, thereby letting the DBMS validate some transactions. For example, if a transaction inserts a new customer into a customer table and the customer number being inserted already exists, the DBMS will end the transaction with an error code to indicate a violation of the primary key integrity rule.

12.1.2 Transaction Properties

All transactions must display *atomicity*, *consistency*, *isolation, durability* and *serialisability*. These properties are sometimes referred to as the ACIDS test. Let's look briefly at each of these properties:

- **Atomicity** requires that *all* operations (SQL requests) of a transaction be completed; if not, the transaction is aborted. If a transaction T1 has four SQL requests, all four requests must be successfully completed; otherwise, the entire transaction is aborted. In other words, a transaction is treated as a single, indivisible, logical unit of work.
- **Consistency** indicates the permanence of the database's consistent state. A transaction takes a database from one consistent state to another. When a transaction is completed, the database reaches a consistent state. If any of the transaction parts violates an integrity constraint, the entire transaction is aborted.
- **Isolation** means that the data used during the execution of a transaction cannot be used by a second transaction until the first one is completed. In other words, if a transaction T1 is being executed and is using the data item X, that data item cannot be accessed by any other transaction (T2 ... T*n*) until T1 ends. This property is particularly useful in multi-user database environments because several different users can access and update the database at the same time.
- **Durability** ensures that once transaction changes are done (committed), they cannot be undone or lost, even in the event of a system failure.
- **Serialisability** ensures that the concurrent execution of several transactions yields consistent results. More specifically, the concurrent execution of transactions T1, T2 and T3 yields results that appear to have been executed in serial order (one after another). This property is important in multi-user and distributed databases, where multiple transactions are likely to be executed concurrently. Naturally, if only a single transaction is executed, serialisability is not an issue.

By its very nature, a single-user database system automatically ensures serialisability and isolation of the database, because only one transaction is executed at a time. The atomicity and the durability of transactions must be guaranteed by the single-user DBMSs. (Even a single-user DBMS must manage recovery from errors created by operating-system-induced interruptions, power interruptions and improper application execution.)

Multi-user databases, whether mainframe- or LAN-based, are typically subject to multiple concurrent transactions. Therefore, the multi-user DBMS must implement controls to ensure serialisability and isolation of transactions – in addition to atomicity and durability – to guard the database's consistency and integrity. For example, if several concurrent transactions are executed over the same data set and the second transaction updates the database before the first transaction is finished, the isolation property is violated and the database is no longer consistent. The DBMS must manage the transactions by using concurrency control techniques to avoid such undesirable situations.

12.1.3 Transaction Management with SQL

The American National Standards Institute (ANSI) has defined standards that govern SQL database transactions. Transaction support is provided by two SQL statements: COMMIT and ROLLBACK. ANSI standards require that, when a transaction sequence is initiated by a user or an application program, the sequence must continue through all succeeding SQL statements until one of the following four events occurs:

1. A COMMIT statement is reached, in which case all changes are permanently recorded within the database. The COMMIT statement automatically ends the SQL transaction.
2. A ROLLBACK statement is reached, in which case all changes are aborted and the database is rolled back to its previous consistent state.
3. The end of a program is successfully reached, in which case all changes are permanently recorded within the database. This action is equivalent to COMMIT.
4. The program is abnormally terminated, in which case the changes made in the database are aborted and the database is rolled back to its previous consistent state. This action is equivalent to ROLLBACK.

The use of COMMIT is illustrated in the following simplified sales example, which updates a product's quantity on hand (PROD_QOH) and the customer's balance when the customer buys two units of product 1558-QW1 priced at €43.99 per unit (for a total of €87.98) and charges the purchase to his or her account:

12

```
UPDATE      PRODUCT
SET         PROD_QOH = PROD_QOH - 2
WHERE       PROD_CODE = '1558-QW1';

UPDATE      CUSTOMER
SET         CUST_BALANCE = CUST_BALANCE + 87.98
WHERE       CUST_NUMBER = '10011';
COMMIT;
```

(Note that the example is simplified to make it easy to trace the transaction. In the Ch12_SaleCo database, the transaction would involve several additional table updates.)

Actually, the COMMIT statement used in that example is not necessary if the UPDATE statement is the application's last action and the application terminates normally. However, good programming practice dictates that you include the COMMIT statement at the end of a transaction declaration.

A transaction begins implicitly when the first SQL statement is encountered. Not all SQL implementations follow the ANSI standard; some (such as SQL Server) use transaction management statements such as:

```
BEGIN TRANSACTION;
```

to indicate the beginning of a new transaction. Other SQL implementations, such as VAX/SQL, allow you to assign characteristics for the transactions as parameters to the BEGIN statement. For example, the Oracle RDBMS uses the SET TRANSACTION statement to declare a new transaction start and its properties.

12.1.4 The Transaction Log

A DBMS uses a **transaction log** to keep track of all transactions that update the database. The information stored in this log is used by the DBMS for a recovery requirement triggered by a ROLLBACK statement, a program's abnormal termination, or a system failure such as a network discrepancy or a disk crash. Some RDBMSs use the transaction log to recover a database *forward* to a currently consistent state. After a server failure, for example, Oracle automatically rolls back uncommitted transactions and rolls forward transactions that were committed but not yet written to the physical database.

While the DBMS executes transactions that modify the database, it also automatically updates the transaction log. The transaction log stores:

- A record for the beginning of the transaction
- For each transaction component (SQL statement):
  - The type of operation (update, delete, insert)
  - The names of the objects affected by the transaction (the name of the table)
  - The 'before' and 'after' values for the fields being updated
  - Pointers to the previous and next transaction log entries for the same transaction
- The ending (COMMIT) of the transaction.

Although using a transaction log increases the processing overhead of a DBMS, the ability to restore a corrupted database is worth the price. (*Note:* Microsoft Access does not support advanced transaction management options such as COMMIT, ROLLBACK, etc. As such it is not as resilient to failure recovery as enterprise databases like Oracle.)

Table 12.1 illustrates a simplified transaction log that reflects a basic transaction composed of two SQL UPDATE statements. If a system failure occurs, the DBMS will examine the transaction log for all uncommitted or incomplete transactions and restore (ROLLBACK) the database to its previous state on the basis of that information. When the recovery process is complete, the DBMS writes in the log all committed transactions that were not physically written to the database before the failure occurred.

TABLE 12.1 A transaction log

TRL_ID	TRX_ NUM	PREV PTR	NEXT PTR	OPERATION	TABLE	ROW ID	ATTRIBUTE	BEFORE VALUE	AFTER VALUE
341	101	Null	352	START	****Start Transaction				
352	101	341	363	UPDATE	PRODUCT	1558-QW1	PROD_QOH	25	23
363	101	352	365	UPDATE	CUSTOMER	10011	CUST_ BALANCE	525.75	615.73
365	101	363	Null	COMMIT	**** End of Transaction				

TRL_ID = Transaction log record ID
TRX_NUM = Transaction number
(Note: The transaction number is automatically assigned by the DBMS.)
PTR = Pointer to a transaction log record ID

If a ROLLBACK is issued before the termination of a transaction, the DBMS will restore the database only for that particular transaction, rather than for all transactions, to maintain the *durability* of the previous transactions. In other words, committed transactions are not rolled back.

The transaction log is itself a database, and it is managed by the DBMS like any other database. The transaction log is subject to common database dangers such as disk-full conditions and disk crashes. As the transaction log contains some of the most critical data in a DBMS, some implementations support logs on several different disks to reduce the risk of a system failure.

12.2 CONCURRENCY CONTROL

12

The coordination of the simultaneous execution of transactions in a multi-user database system is known as **concurrency control**. The objective of concurrency control is to ensure the serialisability of transactions in a multi-user database environment. Concurrency control is important because the simultaneous execution of transactions over a shared database can create several data integrity and consistency problems. The three main problems are lost updates, uncommitted data and inconsistent retrievals.

12.2.1 Lost Updates

The lost update problem occurs when two concurrent transactions, T1 and T2, are updating the same data element and one of the updates is lost (overwritten by the other transaction). To see an illustration of **lost updates**, let's examine a simple PRODUCT table. One of the PRODUCT table's attributes is a product's quantity on hand (PROD_QOH). Assume that you have a product whose current PROD_QOH value is 35. Also assume that two concurrent transactions, T1 and T2, occur that update the PROD_QOH value for some item in the PRODUCT table. The transactions are:

Transaction	Computation
T1: Purchase 100 units	PROD_QOH = PROD_QOH + 100
T2: Sell 30 units	PROD_QOH = PROD_QOH − 30

Table 12.2 shows the serial execution of those transactions under normal circumstances, yielding the correct answer PROD_QOH = 105.

TABLE 12.2 Normal execution of two transactions

Time	Transaction	Step	Stored Value
1	T1	Read PROD_QOH	35
2	T1	PROD_QOH = 35 + 100	
3	T1	Write PROD_QOH	135
4	T2	Read PROD_QOH	135
5	T2	PROD_QOH = 135 − 30	
6	T2	Write PROD_QOH	105

However, suppose that a transaction is able to read a product's PROD_QOH value from the table *before* a previous transaction (using the *same* product) has been committed. The sequence depicted in Table 12.3 shows how the lost update problem can arise. Note that the first transaction (T1) has not yet been committed when the second transaction (T2) is executed. Therefore, T2 still operates on the value 35, and its subtraction yields 5 in memory. In the meantime, T1 writes the value 135 to disk, which is promptly overwritten by T2. In short, the addition of 100 units is 'lost' during the process.

TABLE 12.3 Lost updates

Time	Transaction	Step	Stored Value
1	T1	Read PROD_QOH	35
2	T2	Read PROD_QOH	35
3	T1	PROD_QOH = 35 + 100	
4	T2	PROD_QOH = 35 − 30	
5	T1	Write PROD_QOH **(Lost update)**	135
6	T2	Write PROD_QOH	5

12.2.2 Uncommitted Data

The phenomenon of **uncommitted data** occurs when two transactions, T1 and T2, are executed concurrently and the first transaction (T1) is rolled back after the second transaction (T2) has already accessed the uncommitted data – thus violating the isolation property of transactions. To illustrate this possibility, let's use the same transactions described during the lost updates discussion. T1 has two atomic parts to it, one of which is the update of the inventory, the other possibly being the update of the invoice total (not shown). T1 is forced to roll back due to an error during the update of the invoice total; hence, it rolls back all the way, undoing the inventory update as well. This time the T1 transaction is rolled back to eliminate the addition of the 100 units. Because T2 subtracts 30 from the original 35 units, the correct answer should be 5.

Transaction	Computation
T1: Purchase 100 units	PROD_QOH = PROD_QOH + 100 (**Rolled back**)
T2: Sell 30 units	PROD_QOH = PROD_QOH – 30

Table 12.4 shows how, under normal circumstances, the serial execution of those transactions yields the correct answer.

TABLE 12.4 Correct execution of two transactions

Time	Transaction	Step	Stored Value
1	T1	Read PROD_QOH	35
2	T1	PROD_QOH = 35 + 100	
3	T1	Write PROD_QOH	135
4	T1	*****ROLLBACK *****	35
5	T2	Read PROD_QOH	35
6	T2	PROD_QOH = 35 – 30	
7	T2	Write PROD_QOH	5

Table 12.5 shows how the uncommitted data problem can arise when the ROLLBACK is completed after T2 has begun its execution.

TABLE 12.5 An uncommitted data problem

Time	Transaction	Step	Stored Value
1	T1	Read PROD_QOH	35
2	T1	PROD_QOH = 35 + 100	
3	T1	Write PROD_QOH	135
4	T2	Read PROD_QOH (**Read uncommitted data**)	135
5	T2	PROD_QOH = 135 – 30	
6	T1	***** ROLLBACK *****	35
7	T2	Write PROD_QOH	105

12

12.2.3 Inconsistent Retrievals

Inconsistent retrievals occur when a transaction accesses data before and after one or more other transactions finish working with such data. For example, an inconsistent retrieval would occur if transaction T1 calculated a summary (using SQL aggregate functions) over a set of data while transaction, T2, was updating the same data. The problem is that the transaction might read some data before they are changed and other data *after* they are changed, thereby yielding inconsistent results.

To illustrate that problem, assume the following conditions:

1. T1 calculates the total quantity on hand of the products stored in the PRODUCT table.
2. At the same time, T2 updates the quantity on hand (PROD_QOH) for two of the PRODUCT table's products.

The two transactions are shown in Table 12.6.

TABLE 12.6 Retrieval during update

transaction T1	Transaction T2
SELECT SUM(PROD_QOH) FROM PRODUCT	UPDATE PRODUCT SET PROD_QOH = PROD_QOH + 10 WHERE PROD_CODE = 1546-QQ2
	UPDATE PRODUCT SET PROD_QOH = PROD_QOH − 10 WHERE PROD_CODE = 1558-QW1
	COMMIT;

While T1 calculates the total quantity on hand (PROD_QOH) for all items, T2 represents the correction of a typing error: the user added ten units to product 1558-QW1's PROD_QOH, but *meant* to add the ten units to product 1546-QQ2's PROD_QOH. To correct the problem, the user adds ten to product 1546-QQ2's PROD_QOH and subtracts ten from product 1558-QW1's PROD_QOH. (See the two UPDATE statements in Table 12.6.) The initial and final PROD_QOH values are reflected in Table 12.7. (Only a few of the PROD_CODE values for the PRODUCT table are shown. To illustrate the point, the sum for the PROD_QOH values is given for those few products.)

TABLE 12.7 Transaction results: data entry correction

	Before	After
PROD_CODE	PROD_QOH	PROD_QOH
11QER/31	8	8
13-Q2/P2	32	32
1546-QQ2	15	(15 + 10) → 25
1558-QW1	23	(23 – 10) →13
2232-QTY	8	8
2232-QWE	6	6
Total	92	92

12

Although the final results shown in Table 12.7 are correct after the adjustment, Table 12.8 demonstrates that inconsistent retrievals are possible during the transaction execution, making the result of T1's execution incorrect. The 'After' summation shown in Table 12.8 reflects the fact that the value of 25 for product 1546-QQ2 was read *after* the write statement was completed. Therefore, the 'After' total is 40 + 25 = 65. The 'Before' total reflects the fact that the value of 23 for product 1558-QW1 was read *before* the next write statement was completed to reflect the corrected update of 13. Therefore, the 'Before' total is 65 + 23 = 88.

TABLE 12.8 **Inconsistent retrievals**

Time	Transaction	Action	Value	Total
1	T1	Read PROD_QOH for PROD_CODE = '11QER/31'	8	8
2	T1	Read PROD_QOH for PROD_CODE = '13-Q2/P2'	32	40
3	T2	Read PROD_QOH for PROD_CODE = '1546-QQ2'	15	
4	T2	PROD_QOH = 15 + 10		
5	T2	Write PROD_QOH for PROD_CODE = '1546-QQ2'	25	
6	T1	Read PROD_QOH for PROD_CODE = '1546-QQ2'	25	(After) 65
7	T1	Read PROD_QOH for PROD_CODE = '1558-QW1'	23	(Before) 88
8	T2	Read PROD_QOH for PROD_CODE = '1558-QW1'	23	
9	T2	PROD_QOH = 23 − 10		
10	T2	Write PROD_QOH for PROD_CODE = '1558-QW1'	13	
11	T2	***** COMMIT *****		
12	T1	Read PROD_QOH for PROD_CODE = '2232-QTY'	8	96
13	T1	Read PROD_QOH for PROD_CODE = '2232-QWE'	6	102

The computed answer of 102 is obviously wrong because you know from Table 12.7 that the correct answer is 92. Unless the DBMS exercises concurrency control, a multi-user database environment can create havoc within the information system.

12.2.4 The Scheduler

You now know that severe problems can arise when two or more concurrent transactions are executed. You also know that a database transaction involves a series of database I/O operations that take the database from one consistent state to another. Finally, you know that database consistency can be ensured only before and after the execution of transactions. A database always moves through an unavoidable temporary state of inconsistency during a transaction's execution. That temporary inconsistency exists because a computer cannot execute two operations at the same time and must therefore execute them serially. During this serial process, the isolation property of transactions prevents them from accessing the data not yet released by other transactions.

12

In previous examples, the operations within a transaction were executed in an arbitrary order. As long as two transactions, T1 and T2, access *unrelated* data, there is no conflict and the order of execution is irrelevant to the final outcome. However, if the transactions operate on related (or the same) data, conflict is possible among the transaction components and the selection of one operational order over another may have some undesirable consequences. So, how is the correct order determined, and who determines that order? Fortunately, the DBMS handles that tricky assignment by using a built-in scheduler.

The **scheduler** is a special DBMS program that establishes the order in which the operations within concurrent transactions are executed. The scheduler *interleaves* the execution of database operations to ensure serialisability and isolation of transactions. To determine the appropriate order, the scheduler bases its actions on concurrency control algorithms, such as locking or time stamping methods, which are explained in the next sections.

The scheduler also makes sure that the computer's central processing unit (CPU) is used efficiently. If there were no way to schedule the execution of transactions, all transactions would be executed on a first-come, first-served basis. The problem with that approach is that processing time is wasted when the CPU waits for a READ or WRITE operation to finish, thereby losing several CPU cycles. In short, first-come, first-served scheduling tends to yield unacceptable response times within the multi-user DBMS environment. Therefore, some other scheduling method is needed to improve the efficiency of the overall system.

Additionally, the scheduler facilitates data isolation to ensure that two transactions do not update the same data element at the same time. Database operations may require READ and/or WRITE actions that produce conflicts. For example, Table 12.9 shows the possible conflict scenarios when two transactions, T1 and T2, are executed concurrently over the same data. Using the summary in Table 12.9, note that two operations are in conflict when they access the same data and at least one of them is a WRITE operation.

TABLE 12.9 Read/write conflict scenarios: conflicting database operations matrix

	Transactions		
	T1	T2	Result
Operations	Read	Read	No conflict
	Read	Write	Conflict
	Write	Read	Conflict
	Write	Write	Conflict

Several methods have been proposed to schedule the execution of conflicting operations in concurrent transactions. Those methods have been classified as locking, time stamping and optimistic. Locking methods are used most frequently.

12.3 CONCURRENCY CONTROL WITH LOCKING METHODS

A **lock** guarantees exclusive use of a data item to a current transaction. In other words, transaction T2 does not have access to a data item that is currently being used by transaction T1. A transaction acquires a lock prior to data access; the lock is released (unlocked) when the transaction is complete so that another transaction can lock the data item for its exclusive use. This series of locking actions assumes that concurrent transactions might attempt to manipulate the same data at the same time. The use of locks is based on the assumption that conflict between transactions is likely and is known as pessimistic locking.

Recall from the earlier discussion that data consistency cannot be guaranteed *during* a transaction; the database may be in a temporary inconsistent state when several updates are executed. Therefore, locks are required to prevent another transaction from reading inconsistent data.

Most multi-user DBMSs automatically initiate and enforce locking procedures. All lock information is managed by a **lock manager**, which is responsible for assigning and policing the locks used by the transactions.

12.3.1 Lock Granularity

Lock granularity indicates the level of lock use. Locking can take place at the following levels: database, table, page, row or even field (attribute).

Database Level

In a **database-level lock**, the entire database is locked, thus preventing the use of any tables in the database by transaction T2 while transaction Tl is being executed. This level of locking is good for batch processes, but it is unsuitable for online multi-user DBMSs. You can imagine how slow the data access would be if thousands of transactions had to wait for the previous transaction to be completed before the next one could reserve the entire database. Figure 12.3 illustrates the database-level lock. Note that transactions T1 and T2 cannot access the same database concurrently *even when they use different tables.*

FIGURE 12.3 Database-level locking sequence

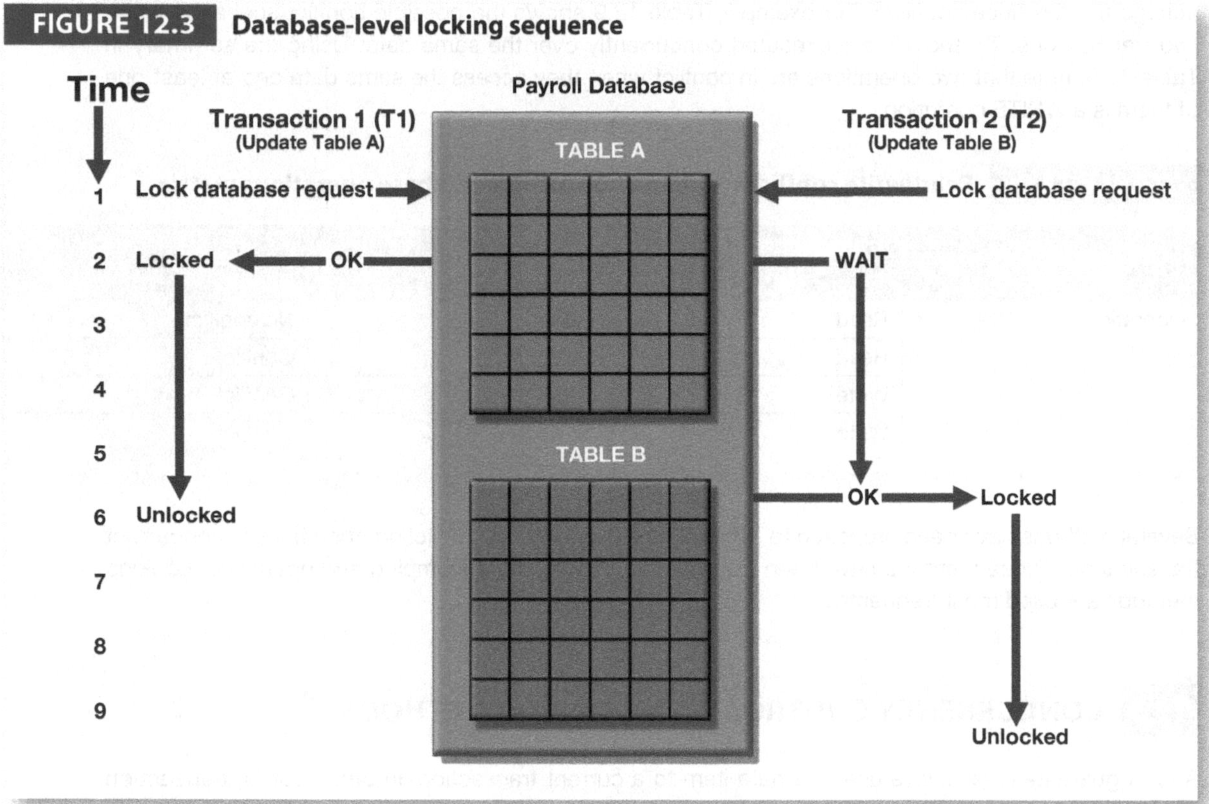

Table Level

In a **table-level lock**, the entire table is locked, preventing access to any row by transaction T2 while transaction T1 is using the table. If a transaction requires access to several tables, each table may be locked. However, two transactions can access the same database as long as they access different tables.

Table-level locks, while less restrictive than database-level locks, cause traffic jams when many transactions are waiting to access the same table. Such a condition is especially irksome if the lock forces a delay when different transactions require access to different parts of the same table, that is, when the transactions would not interfere with each other. Consequently, table-level locks are not suitable for multi-user DBMSs. Figure 12.4 illustrates the effect of a table-level lock. As you examine Figure 12.4, note that transactions T1 and T2 cannot access the same table even when they try to use different rows; T2 must wait until T1 unlocks the table.

FIGURE 12.4 An example of a table-level lock

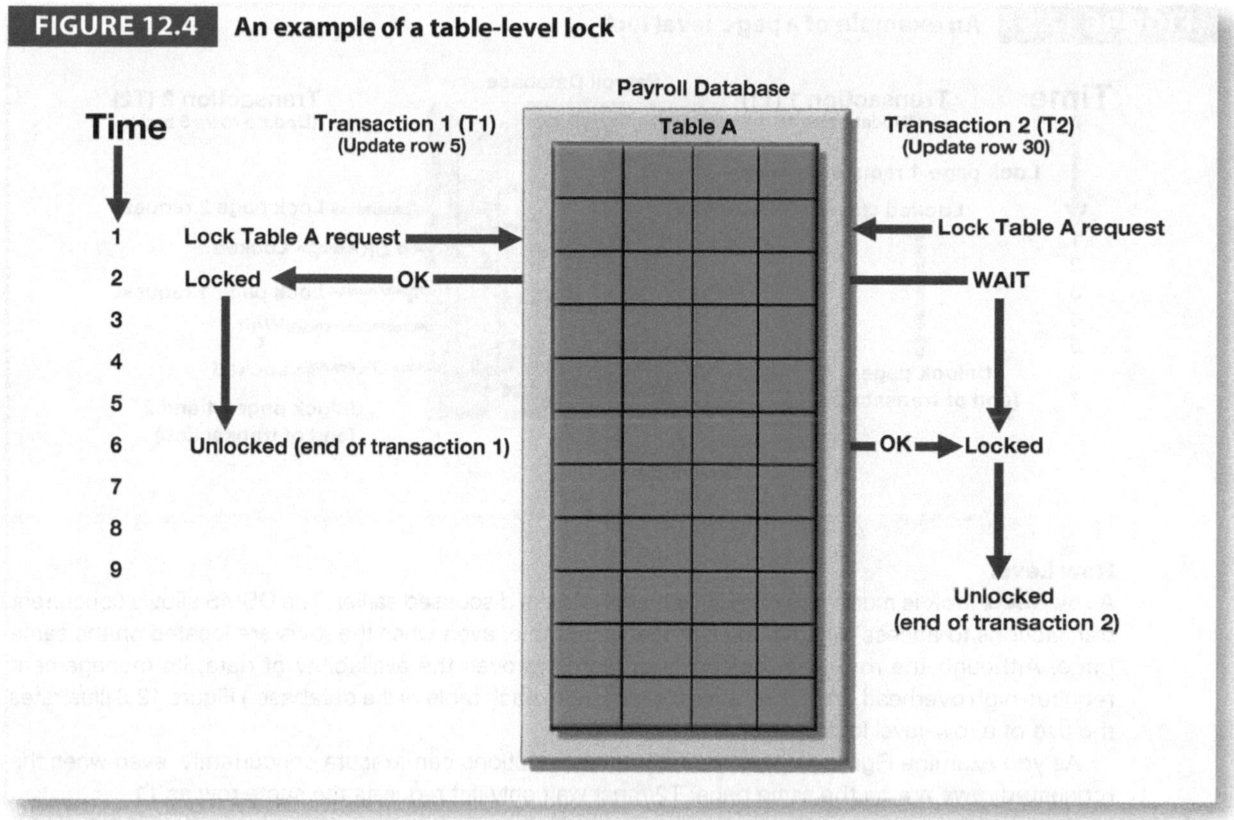

Page Level

In a **page-level lock**, the DBMS locks an entire diskpage. A *diskpage*, or **page**, is the equivalent of a *diskblock*, which can be described as a directly addressable section of a disk. A page has a fixed size, such as 4K, 8K or 16K. For example, if you want to write only 73 bytes to a 4K page, the entire 4K page must be read from disk, updated in memory and written back to disk. A table can span several pages, and a page can contain several rows of one or more tables. Page-level locks are currently the most frequently used multiuser DBMS locking method. An example of a page-level lock is shown in Figure 12.5. As you examine Figure 12.5, note that T1 and T2 access the same table while locking different diskpages. If T2 requires the use of a row located on a page that is locked by T1, T2 must wait until the page is unlocked by T1.

FIGURE 12.5 An example of a page-level lock

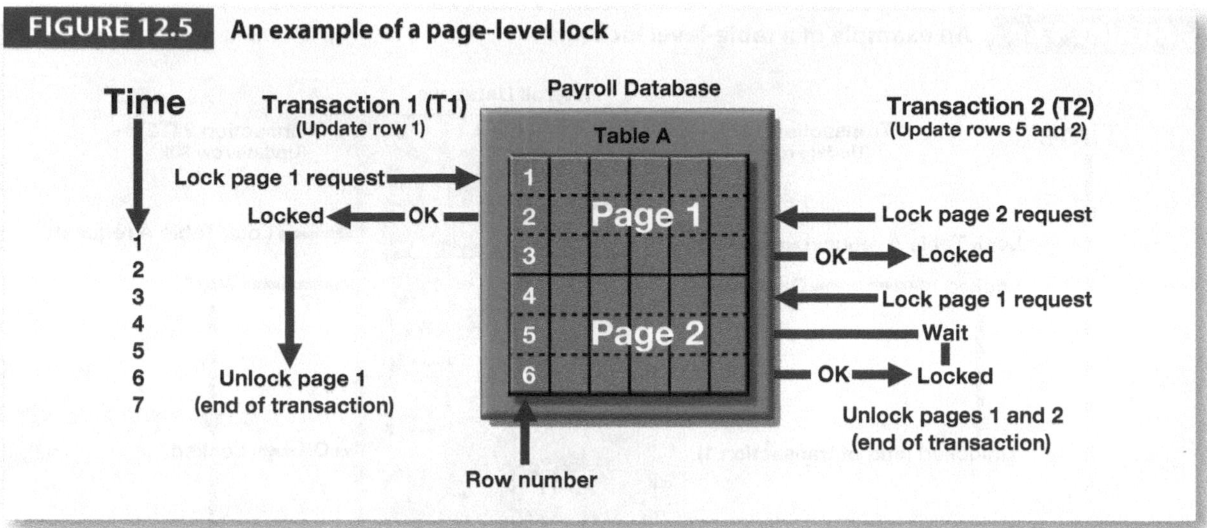

Row Level

A **row-level lock** is much less restrictive than the locks discussed earlier. The DBMS allows concurrent transactions to access different rows of the same table, even when the rows are located on the same page. Although the row-level locking approach improves the availability of data, its management requires high overhead. (A lock exists for each row in each table of the database.) Figure 12.6 illustrates the use of a row-level lock.

As you examine Figure 12.6, note that both transactions can execute concurrently, even when the requested rows are on the same page. T2 must wait only if it requests the same row as T1.

FIGURE 12.6 An example of a row-level lock

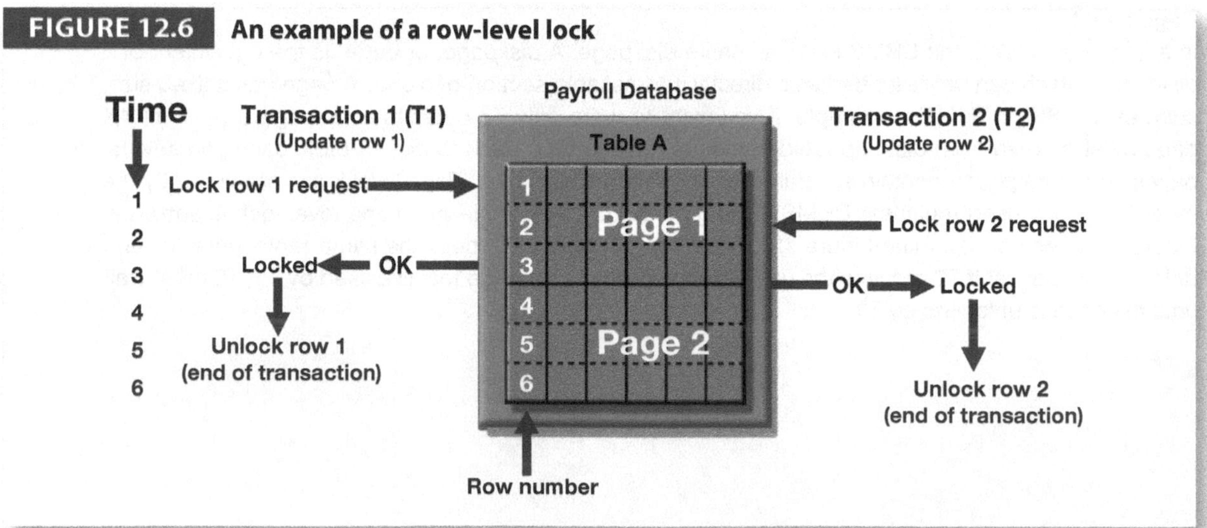

12

Field Level

The **field-level lock** allows concurrent transactions to access the same row as long as they require the use of different fields (attributes) within that row. Although field-level locking clearly yields the most flexible multi-user data access, it is rarely done because it requires an extremely high level of computer overhead.

12.3.2 Lock Types

Regardless of the level of locking, the DBMS may use different lock types: binary or shared/exclusive.

Binary Locks

A **binary lock** has only two states: locked (1) or unlocked (0). If an object – that is, a database, table, page or row – is locked by a transaction, no other transaction can use that object. If an object is unlocked, any transaction can lock the object for its use. Every database operation requires that the affected object be locked. As a rule, a transaction must unlock the object after its termination. Therefore, every transaction requires a lock and unlock operation for each data item that is accessed. Such operations are automatically managed and scheduled by the DBMS; the user does not need to be concerned about locking or unlocking data items. (Every DBMS has a default locking mechanism. If the end user wants to override the default, the LOCK TABLE and other SQL commands are available for that purpose.)

The binary locking technique is illustrated in Table 12.10, using the lost updates problem you encountered in Table 12.3. As you examine Table 12.10, note that the lock and unlock features eliminate the lost update problem. (The lock is not released until the write statement is completed. Therefore a PROD_QOH value cannot be used until it has been properly updated.) However, binary locks are now considered too restrictive to yield optimal concurrency conditions. For example, the DBMS will not allow two transactions to read the same database object even though neither transaction updates the database (and, therefore, no concurrency problems can occur). Remember from Table 12.9 that concurrency conflicts occur only when two transactions execute concurrently and one of them updates the database.

TABLE 12.10 An example of a binary lock

Time	Transaction	Step	Stored Value
1	T1	Lock PRODUCT	
2	T1	Read PROD_QOH	15
3	T1	PROD_QOH = 15 + 10	
4	T1	Write PROD_QOH	25
5	T1	Unlock PRODUCT	
6	T2	Lock PRODUCT	
7	T2	Read PROD_QOH	23
8	T2	PROD_QOH = 23 – 10	
9	T2	Write PROD_QOH	13
10	T2	Unlock PRODUCT	

Shared/Exclusive Locks

An **exclusive lock** exists when access is reserved specifically for the transaction that locked the object. The exclusive lock must be used when the potential for conflict exists (see Table 12.9). A **shared lock** exists when concurrent transactions are granted Read access on the basis of a common lock. A shared lock produces no conflict as long as all the concurrent transactions are read-only.

A shared lock is issued when a transaction wants to read data from the database and no exclusive lock is held on that data item. An exclusive lock is issued when a transaction wants to update (write) a data item and no locks are currently held on that data item by any other transaction. Using the shared/exclusive locking concept, a lock can have three states: unlocked, shared (Read) and exclusive (Write).

As you saw in Table 12.9, two transactions conflict only when at least one of them is a Write transaction. Because the two Read transactions can be safely executed at once, shared locks allow several Read transactions to read the same data item concurrently. For example, if transaction T1 has a shared lock on data item X and transaction T2 wants to read data item X, T2 may also obtain a shared lock on data item X.

If transaction T2 updates data item X, an exclusive lock is required by T2 over data item X. *The exclusive lock is granted if and only if no other locks are held on the data item.* Therefore, if a shared or exclusive lock is already held on data item X by transaction T1, an exclusive lock cannot be granted to transaction T2, and T2 must wait to begin until T1 commits. This condition is known as the **mutually exclusive rule**: only one transaction at a time can own an exclusive lock on the same object.

Although the possibility of shared locks renders data access more efficient, a shared/exclusive lock schema increases the lock manager's overhead, for several reasons:

- The type of lock held must be known before a lock can be granted.
- Three lock operations exist: READ_LOCK (to check the type of lock), WRITE_LOCK (to issue the lock) and UNLOCK (to release the lock).
- The schema has been enhanced to allow a lock upgrade (from shared to exclusive) and a lock downgrade (from exclusive to shared).

Although locks prevent serious data inconsistencies, they can lead to two major problems:

- The resulting transaction schedule may not be serialisable.
- The schedule may create deadlocks. A database **deadlock**, which is equivalent to traffic gridlock in a big city, is caused when two transactions wait for each other to unlock data.

Fortunately, both problems can be managed: serialisability is guaranteed through a locking protocol known as two-phase locking, and deadlocks can be managed using deadlock detection and prevention techniques. Those techniques are examined in the next two sections.

12.3.3 Two-Phase Locking to Ensure Serialisability

12

Two-phase locking defines how transactions acquire and relinquish locks. Two-phase locking guarantees serialisability, but it does not prevent deadlocks. The two phases are:

1. A growing phase, in which a transaction acquires all required locks without unlocking any data. Once all locks have been acquired, the transaction is in its locked point.
2. A shrinking phase, in which a transaction releases all locks and cannot obtain any new lock.

The two-phase locking protocol is governed by the following rules:

- Two transactions cannot have conflicting locks.
- No unlock operation can precede a lock operation in the same transaction.
- No data are affected until all locks are obtained – that is, until the transaction is in its locked point.

Figure 12.7 depicts the two-phase locking protocol.

FIGURE 12.7 Two-phase locking protocol

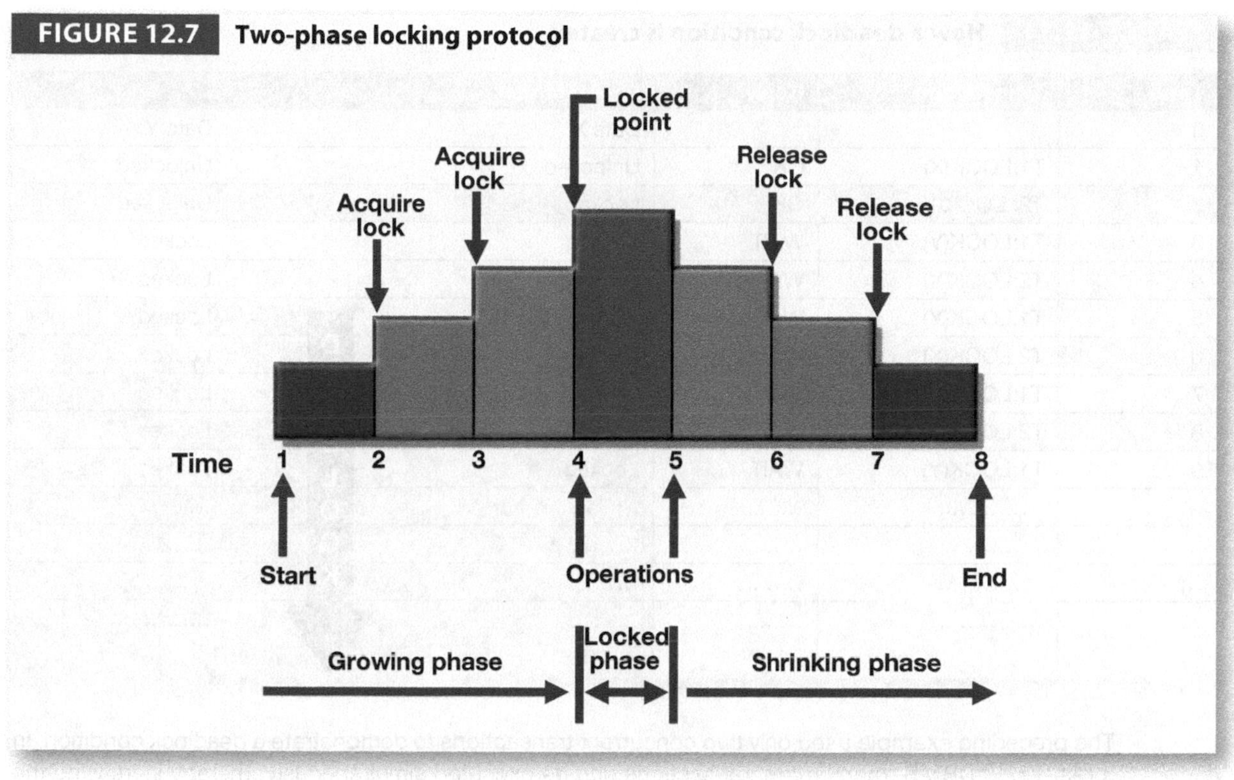

In this example, the transaction acquires all of the locks it needs until it reaches its locked point. (In this example, the transaction requires two locks.) When the locked point is reached, the data are modified to conform to the transaction requirements. Finally, the transaction is completed as it releases all of the locks it acquired in the first phase.

Two-phase locking increases the transaction processing cost and may cause additional undesirable effects. One undesirable effect is the possibility of creating deadlocks.

12.3.4 Deadlocks

A deadlock occurs when two transactions wait for each other to unlock data. For example, a deadlock occurs when two transactions, T1 and T2, exist in the following mode:

T1 = access data items X and Y

T2 = access data items Y and X

If T1 has not unlocked data item Y, T2 cannot begin; if T2 has not unlocked data item X, T1 cannot continue. Consequently, T1 and T2 wait indefinitely, each waiting for the other to unlock the required data item. Such a deadlock is also known as a **deadly embrace**. Table 12.11 demonstrates how a deadlock condition is created.

TABLE 12.11 How a deadlock condition is created

Time	Transaction	Reply	Lock Status	
0			Data X	Data Y
1	T1:LOCK(X)	OK	Unlocked	Unlocked
2	T2: LOCK(Y)	OK	Locked	Unlocked
3	T1:LOCK(Y)	WAIT	Locked	Locked
4	T2:LOCK(X)	WAIT	Locked	Locked
5	T1:LOCK(Y)	WAIT	Locked	Locked
6	T2:LOCK(X)	WAIT	Locked	Locked
7	T1:LOCK(Y)	WAIT	Locked	Locked
8	T2:LOCK(X)	WAIT	Locked	Locked
9	T1:LOCK(Y)	WAIT	Locked	Locked
...	....	....	....	....
...	....	....	....	....
...	....	....	....	....
...	....	....	....	....

DEADLOCK

The preceding example used only two concurrent transactions to demonstrate a deadlock condition. In a real-world DBMS, many more transactions can be executed simultaneously, thereby increasing the probability of generating deadlocks. Note that deadlocks are possible only when one of the transactions wants to obtain an exclusive lock on a data item; no deadlock condition can exist among *shared* locks.

The three basic techniques to control deadlocks are:

- *Deadlock prevention*. A transaction requesting a new lock is aborted when there is the possibility that a deadlock can occur. If the transaction is aborted, all changes made by this transaction are rolled back and all locks obtained by the transaction are released. The transaction is then rescheduled for execution. Deadlock prevention works because it avoids the conditions that lead to deadlocking.
- *Deadlock detection*. The DBMS periodically tests the database for deadlocks. If a deadlock is found, one of the transactions (the 'victim') is aborted (rolled back and restarted) and the other transaction continues.
- *Deadlock avoidance*. The transaction must obtain all of the locks it needs before it can be executed. This technique avoids the rollback of conflicting transactions by requiring that locks be obtained in succession. However, the serial lock assignment required in deadlock avoidance increases action response times.

The choice of the best deadlock control method depends on the database environment. For example, if the probability of deadlocks is low, deadlock detection is recommended. However, if the probability of deadlocks is high, deadlock prevention is recommended. If response time is not high on the system's priority list, deadlock avoidance might be employed.

12.4 CONCURRENCY CONTROL WITH TIME STAMPING METHODS

The **time stamping** approach to scheduling concurrent transactions assigns a global, unique time stamp to each transaction. The time stamp value produces an explicit order in which transactions are submitted to the DBMS. Time stamps must have two properties: uniqueness and monotonicity. **Uniqueness** ensures that no equal time stamp values can exist, and **monotonicity**[6] ensures that time stamp values always increase.

All database operations (Read and Write) within the same transaction must have the same time stamp. The DBMS executes conflicting operations in time stamp order, thereby ensuring serialisability of the transactions. If two transactions conflict, one is stopped, rolled back, rescheduled and assigned a new time stamp value.

The disadvantage of the time stamping approach is that each value stored in the database requires two additional time stamp fields: one for the last time the field was read and one for the last update. Time stamping thus increases memory needs and the database's processing overhead. Time stamping tends to demand considerable system resources because many transactions may have to be stopped, rescheduled and restamped.

12.4.1 Wait/Die and Wound/Wait Schemes

You have learnt that time stamping methods are used to manage concurrent transaction execution. In this section, you will learn about two schemes used to decide which transaction is rolled back and which continues executing: the wait/die scheme and the wound/wait scheme.[7] An example illustrates the difference. Assume that you have two conflicting transactions, T1 and T2, each with a unique time stamp. Suppose T1 has a time stamp of 11548789 and T2 has a time stamp of 19562545. You can deduce from the time stamps that T1 is the older transaction (the lower time stamp value) and T2 is the newer transaction. Given that scenario, the four possible outcomes are shown in Table 12.12.

TABLE 12.12 Wait/die and wound/wait concurrency control schemes

Transaction Requesting Lock	Transaction Owning Lock	Wait/Die Scheme	Wound/Wait Scheme
T1 (11548789)	T2 (19562545)	■ T1 waits until T2 is completed and T2 releases its locks.	T1 preempts (rolls back) T2. T2 is rescheduled using the same time stamp.
T2 (19562545)	T1 (11548789)	■ T2 dies (rolls back). ■ T2 is rescheduled using the same time stamp.	T2 waits until T1 is completed and T1 releases its locks.

Using the wait/die scheme:

- If the transaction requesting the lock is the older of the two transactions, it will *wait* until the other transaction is completed and the locks are released.

12

6 The term *monotonicity* is part of the standard concurrency control vocabulary. The authors' first introduction to this term and to its proper use was in an article written by W.H. Kohler, 'A survey of techniques for synchronization and recovery in decentralized computer systems', *Computer Surveys* 3(2), June 1981, pp. 149–283.

7 The procedure was first described by R.E. Stearnes and P.M. Lewis II in 'System-level concurrency control for distributed database systems', *ACM Transactions on Database Systems*, 2, June 1978, pp. 178–98.

- If the transaction requesting the lock is the younger of the two transactions, it will *die* (roll back) and is rescheduled using the same time stamp.

In short, in the **wait/die** scheme, the older transaction waits and the younger is rolled back and rescheduled.

In the wound/wait scheme:

- If the transaction requesting the lock is the older of the two transactions, it will pre-empt (*wound*) the younger transaction (by rolling it back). T1 pre-empts T2 when T1 rolls back T2. The younger preempted transaction is rescheduled using the same time stamp.
- If the transaction requesting the lock is the younger of the two transactions, it will wait until the other transaction is completed and the locks are released.

In short, in the **wound/wait** scheme, the older transaction rolls back the younger transaction and reschedules it.

In both schemes, one of the transactions waits for the other transaction to finish and release the locks. However, in many cases, a transaction requests multiple locks. How long does a transaction have to wait for each lock request? Obviously, that scenario can cause some transactions to wait indefinitely, causing a deadlock. To prevent that type of deadlock, each lock request has an associated time-out value. If the lock is not granted before the time-out expires, the transaction is rolled back.

12.5 CONCURRENCY CONTROL WITH OPTIMISTIC METHODS

The **optimistic approach** is based on the assumption that the majority of the database operations do not conflict. The optimistic approach does not require locking or time stamping techniques. Instead, a transaction is executed without restrictions until it is committed. Using an optimistic approach, each transaction moves through two or three phases. The phases are *Read*, *validation* and *Write*.[8]

- During the *Read phase*, the transaction reads the database, executes the needed computations and makes the updates to a private copy of the database values. All update operations of the transaction are recorded in a temporary update file, which is not accessed by the remaining transactions.
- During the *validation phase*, the transaction is validated to ensure that the changes made will not affect the integrity and consistency of the database. If the validation test is positive, the transaction goes to the Write phase. If the validation test is negative, the transaction is restarted and the changes are discarded.
- During the *Write phase*, the changes are permanently applied to the database.

The optimistic approach is acceptable for most read or query database systems that require few update transactions.

In a heavily used DBMS environment, the management of deadlocks – their prevention and detection – constitutes an important DBMS function. The DBMS will use one or more of the techniques discussed, as well as variations on those techniques. However, the deadlock is sometimes worse

8 The optimistic approach to concurrency control is described in an article by H.T. King and J.T. Robinson, 'Optimistic methods for concurrency control', *ACM Transactions on Database Systems* 6(2), June 1981, pp. 213–26. Even the most current software is built on conceptual standards that were developed more than two decades ago.

than the disease that locks are supposed to cure. Therefore, it may be necessary to employ database recovery techniques to restore the database to a consistent state. To further understand how transaction management is implemented in a database, it is important that you learn about the transaction isolation levels as defined in ANSI SQL 1992 standard.

12.6 ANSI LEVELS OF TRANSACTION ISOLATION

The ANSI SQL standard (1992) defines transaction management based on transaction isolation levels. Transaction isolation levels refer to the degree to which transaction data is 'protected or isolated' from other concurrent transactions. The isolation levels are described based on which data other transactions can see (read) during execution. More precisely, the transaction isolation levels are described by the type of 'read' that a transaction allows or not. The types of read operations are:

- *Dirty read:* A transaction can read data that is not yet committed.
- *Non-repeatable read:* A transaction reads a given row at time t1, and then it reads the same row at time t2, yielding different results. The original row may have been updated or deleted.
- *Phantom read:* A transaction executes a query at time t1, and then it runs the same query at time t2, yielding additional rows that satisfy the query.

Based on the above operations, ANSI defined four levels of transaction isolation: Read Uncommitted, Read Committed, Repeatable Read, and Serialisable. Table 12.13 shows the four ANSI transaction isolation levels. The table also shows an additional level of isolation provided by Oracle and MS SQL Server databases.

Read Uncommitted will read uncommitted data from other transactions. At this isolation level, the database does not place any locks on the data, which increases transaction performance but at the cost of data consistency. **Read Committed** forces transactions to read only committed data. This is the default mode of operation for most databases (including Oracle and SQL Server). At this level, the database will use exclusive locks on data, causing other transactions to wait until the original transaction commits. The **Repeatable Read** isolation level ensures that queries return consistent results. This type of isolation level uses shared locks to ensure that other transactions do not update a row after the original query reads it. However, new rows are read (phantom read) as these rows did not exist when the first query ran. The **Serialisable** isolation level is the most restrictive level defined by the ANSI SQL standard. However, it is important to note that even with a Serialisable isolation level, deadlocks are always possible. Most databases use a deadlock detection approach to transaction management and, therefore, they will detect deadlocks during the transaction validation phase and reschedule the transaction.

The reason for the different levels of isolation is to increase transaction concurrency. The isolation levels go from the least restrictive (Read Uncommitted) to the more restrictive (Serialisable). The higher the isolation level, the more locks (shared and exclusive) are required to improve data consistency, at the expense of transaction concurrency performance. The isolation level of a transaction is defined in the transaction statement, for example using general ANSI SQL syntax:

BEGIN TRANSACTION ISOLATION LEVEL READ COMMITTED ... SQL STATEMENTS ... COMMIT TRANSACTION;

Oracle and MS SQL Server use the SET TRANSACTION ISOLATION LEVEL statement to define the level of isolation. SQL Server supports all four ANSI isolation levels. Oracle by default provides consistent statement-level reads to ensure Read Committed and Repeatable Read transactions. MySQL

TABLE 12.13 Transaction isolation levels

	Isolation Level	Allowed			Comment
		Dirty Read	Non-Repeatable Read	Phantom Read	
Less restrictive	Read Uncommitted	Y	Y	Y	The transaction reads uncommitted data, allows non-repeatable reads and phantom reads.
	Read Committed	N	Y	Y	Does not allow uncommitted data reads but allows non-repeatable reads and phantom reads.
β More restrictive	Repeatable Read	N	N	N	Only allows phantom reads.
	Serialisable	N	N	N	Does not allow dirty reads, non-repeatable reads or phantom reads.
Oracle/SQL Server only	Read Only/ Snapshot	N	N	N	Supported by Oracle and SQL Server. The transaction can only see the changes that were committed at the time the transaction started.

12

uses START TRANSACTION WITH CONSISTENT SNAPSHOT to provide transactions with consistent reads; that is, the transaction can only see the committed data at the time the transaction started.

As you can see from the previous discussion, transaction management is a complex subject and databases make use of various techniques to manage the concurrent execution of transactions. However, it may be necessary sometimes to employ database recovery techniques to restore the database to a consistent state.

12.7 DATABASE RECOVERY MANAGEMENT

Database recovery restores a database from a given state, usually inconsistent, to a previously consistent state. Recovery techniques are based on the **atomic transaction property**: all portions of the transaction must be treated as a single, logical unit of work in which all operations are applied and completed to produce a consistent database. If, for some reason, any transaction operation cannot be completed, the transaction must be aborted and any changes to the database must be rolled back (undone). In short, transaction recovery reverses all of the changes that the transaction made to the database before it was aborted.

Although this chapter has emphasised the recovery of *transactions*, recovery techniques also apply to the *database* or the *system* after some type of critical error has occurred.

Examples of critical events are:

- Hardware/software failures. A failure of this type could be a hard disk media failure, a bad capacitor on a motherboard, or a failing memory bank. Other causes of errors under this category include application program or operating system errors that cause data to be overwritten, deleted, or lost. Some database administrators argue that this is one of the most common sources of database problems.
- Human-caused incidents. This type of event can be categorised as unintentional or intentional.
    - An unintentional failure is caused by a careless end user. Such errors include deleting the wrong rows from a table, pressing the wrong key on the keyboard, or shutting down the main database server by accident.
    - Intentional events are of a more severe nature and normally indicate that the company data is at serious risk. Under this category are security threats caused by hackers trying to gain unauthorised access to data resources and virus attacks caused by disgruntled employees trying to compromise the database operation and damage the company.
- Natural disasters. This category includes fires, earthquakes, floods and power failures. Whatever the cause, a critical error can render the database into an inconsistent state.

The following section introduces the various techniques used to recover the database from an inconsistent state to a consistent state.

12.7.1 Transaction Recovery

In Section 12.1.4, you learnt about the transaction log structure and how it contains data for database recovery purposes. Database transaction recovery focuses on the different methods used to recover a database from an inconsistent to a consistent state by using the data in the transaction log.

Before continuing, let's examine four important concepts that affect the recovery process:

- The **write-ahead-log protocol**. This protocol ensures that transaction logs are always written *before* any database data are actually updated. This protocol ensures that, in case of a failure, the database can later be recovered to a consistent state, using the data in the transaction log.
- **Redundant transaction logs**. Most DBMSs keep several copies of the transaction log to ensure that a physical disk failure will not impair the DBMS's ability to recover data.
- Database **buffers**. A buffer is a temporary storage area in primary memory used to speed up disk operations. To improve processing time, the DBMS software reads the data from the physical disk and stores a copy of it on a 'buffer' in primary memory. When a transaction updates data, it actually updates the copy of the data in the buffer because that process is much faster than accessing the physical disk every time. Later on, all buffers that contain updated data are written to a physical disk during a single operation, thereby saving significant processing time.
- Database **checkpoints**. A database checkpoint is an operation in which the DBMS writes all of its updated buffers to disk. While this is happening, the DBMS does not execute any other requests. A checkpoint operation is also registered in the transaction log. As a result of this operation,

the physical database and the transaction log will be 'in sync'. This synchronisation is required because update operations update the copy of the data in the buffers and not in the physical database. Checkpoints are automatically scheduled by the DBMS several times per hour. As you will see next, checkpoints also play an important role in transaction recovery.

The database recovery process involves bringing the database to a consistent state after a failure. Transaction recovery procedures generally make use of deferred-write and write-through techniques.

When the recovery procedure uses **deferred write** or **deferred update**, the transaction operations do not immediately update the physical database. Instead, only the transaction log is updated. The database is physically updated only after the transaction reaches its commit point, using the transaction log information. If the transaction aborts before it reaches its commit point, no changes (no ROLLBACK or undo) need to be made to the database because the database was never updated. The recovery process for all started and committed transactions (before the failure) follows these steps:

1. Identify the last checkpoint in the transaction log. This is the last time transaction data was physically saved to disk.
2. For a transaction that started and committed before the last checkpoint, nothing needs to be done, because the data are already saved.
3. For a transaction that performed a COMMIT operation after the last checkpoint, the DBMS uses the transaction log records to redo the transaction and to update the database, using the 'after' values in the transaction log. The changes are made in ascending order, from oldest to newest.
4. For any transaction that had a ROLLBACK operation after the last checkpoint or that was left active (with neither a COMMIT nor a ROLLBACK) before the failure occurred, nothing needs to be done because the database was never updated.

When the recovery procedure uses **write-through** or **immediate update**, the database is immediately updated by transaction operations during the transaction's execution, even before the transaction reaches its commit point. If the transaction aborts before it reaches its commit point, a ROLLBACK or undo operation needs to be done to restore the database to a consistent state. In that case, the ROLLBACK operation uses the transaction log 'before' values. The recovery process follows these steps:

1. Identify the last checkpoint in the transaction log. This is the last time transaction data were physically saved to disk.
2. For a transaction that started and committed before the last checkpoint, nothing needs to be done because the data are already saved.
3. For a transaction that committed after the last checkpoint, the DBMS redoes the transaction, using the 'after' values of the transaction log. Changes are applied in ascending order, from oldest to newest.
4. For any transaction that had a ROLLBACK operation after the last checkpoint or that was left active (with neither a COMMIT nor a ROLLBACK) before the failure occurred, the DBMS uses the transaction log records to ROLLBACK or undo the operations, using the 'before' values in the transaction log. Changes are applied in reverse order, from newest to oldest.

You may use the transaction log in Table 12.14 to trace a simple database recovery process. To make sure you understand the recovery process, a simple transaction log is used that includes three transactions and one checkpoint. This transaction log includes the transaction components used earlier

TABLE 12.14 A transaction log for transaction recovery examples

TRL ID	TRX NUM	PREV PTR	NEXT PTR	Operation	Table	ROW ID	Attribute	Before Value	After Value
341	101	Null	352	START	**** Start Transaction				
352	101	341	363	UPDATE	PRODUCT	54778-2T	PROD_QOH	45	43
363	101	352	365	UPDATE	CUSTOMER	10011	CUST_BALANCE	615.73	675.62
365	101	363	Null	COMMIT	**** End of Transaction				
397	106	Null	405	START	**** Start Transaction				
405	106	397	415	INSERT	INVOICE	1009			1009,10016, …
415	106	405	419	INSERT	LINE	1009,1			1009,1, 89-WRE-Q,1, …
419	106	415	427	UPDATE	PRODUCT	89-WRE-Q	PROD_QOH	12	11
423				CHECKPOINT					
427	106	419	431	UPDATE	CUSTOMER	10016	CUST_BALANCE	0.00	277.55
431	106	427	457	INSERT	ACCT_TRANSACTION	10007			1007,18-JAN-2014, …
457	106	431	Null	COMMIT	**** End of Transaction				
521	155	Null	525	START	**** Start Transaction				
525	155	521	528	UPDATE	PRODUCT	2232/QWE	PROD_QOH	6	26
528	155	525	Null	COMMIT	**** End of Transaction				

***** C *R*A* S* H ***

12

in the chapter, so you should already be familiar with the basic process. Given the transaction, the transaction log has the following characteristics:

- Transaction 101 consists of two UPDATE statements that reduce the quantity on hand for product 54778-2T and increase the customer balance for customer 10011 for a credit sale of two units of product 54778-2T.
- Transaction 106 is the same credit sales event you saw in Section 12.1.1. This transaction represents the credit sale of one unit of product 89-WRE-Q to customer 10016 in the amount of €277.55. This transaction consists of five SQL DML (three INSERT and two UPDATE) statements.
- Transaction 155 represents a simple inventory update. This transaction consists of one UPDATE statement that increases the quantity on hand of product 2232/QWE from 6 units to 26 units.
- A database checkpoint wrote all updated database buffers to disk. The checkpoint event writes only the changes for all previously committed transactions. In this case, the checkpoint applies all changes done by transaction 101 to the database data files.

Using Table 12.14, you can now trace the database recovery process for a DBMS, using the deferred update method as follows:

1. Identify the last checkpoint. In this case, the last checkpoint was TRL ID 423. This was the last time database buffers were physically written to disk.
2. Note that transaction 101 started and finished before the last checkpoint. Therefore, all changes were already written to disk, and no additional action needs to be taken.
3. For each transaction that committed after the last checkpoint (TRL ID 423), the DBMS uses the transaction log data to write the changes to disk, using the after values. For example, for transaction 106:
   - Find COMMIT (TRL ID 457).
   - Use the previous pointer values to locate the start of the transaction (TRL ID 397).
   - Use the next pointer values to locate each DML statement and apply the changes to disk, using the after values. (Start with TRL ID 405, then 415, 419, 427 and 431.) Remember that TRL ID 457 was the COMMIT statement for this transaction.
   - Repeat the process for transaction 155.
4. Any other transactions are ignored. Therefore, for transactions that ended with ROLLBACK or that were left active (do not end with a COMMIT or ROLLBACK) nothing is done because no changes were written to disk.

SUMMARY

- A transaction is a sequence of database operations that access the database. A transaction represents real-world events. A transaction must be a logical unit of work; that is, no portion of the transaction can exist by itself. Either all parts are executed, or the transaction is aborted. A transaction takes a database from one consistent state to another. A consistent database state is one in which all data integrity constraints are satisfied.
- Transactions have five main properties: *atomicity* (all parts of the transaction are executed; otherwise, the transaction is aborted), *consistency* (maintaining the permanence of the database's consistent state), *isolation* (data being used by one transaction cannot be accessed by another

transaction until the first transaction is completed) *durability* (the changes made by a transaction cannot be rolled back once the transaction is committed) and *serialisability* (the result of the concurrent execution of transactions is the same as that of the transactions being executed in serial order).

- SQL provides support for transactions through the use of two statements: COMMIT (saves changes to disk) and ROLLBACK (restores the previous database state).
- SQL transactions are formed by several SQL statements or database requests. Each database request originates several I/O database operations.
- The transaction log keeps track of all transactions that modify the database. The information stored in the transaction log is used for recovery (ROLLBACK) purposes.
- Concurrency control coordinates the simultaneous execution of transactions. The concurrent execution of transactions can result in three main problems: lost updates, uncommitted data and inconsistent retrievals.
- The scheduler is responsible for establishing the order in which the concurrent transaction operations are executed. The transaction execution order is critical and ensures database integrity in multi-user database systems. Locking, time stamping and optimistic methods are used by the scheduler to ensure the serialisability of transactions.
- A lock guarantees unique access to a data item by a transaction. The lock prevents one transaction from using the data item while another transaction is using it. There are several levels of locking: database, table, page, row and field.
- Two types of locks can be used in database systems: binary locks and shared/exclusive locks. A binary lock can have only two states: 1 (locked) or 0 (unlocked). A shared lock is used when a transaction wants to read data from a database and no other transaction is updating the same data. Several shared or 'Read' locks can exist for a particular item. An exclusive lock is issued when a transaction wants to update (write to) the database and no other locks (shared or exclusive) are held on the data.
- Serialisability of schedules is guaranteed through the use of two-phase locking. The two-phase locking schema has a growing phase, in which the transaction acquires all of the locks that it needs without unlocking any data, and a shrinking phase, in which the transaction releases all of the locks without acquiring new locks.
- When two or more transactions wait indefinitely for each other to release a lock, they are in a deadlock, or a deadly embrace. There are three deadlock control techniques: prevention, detection and avoidance.
- Concurrency control with time stamping methods assigns a unique time stamp to each transaction and schedules the execution of conflicting transactions in time stamp order. Two schemes are used to decide which transaction is rolled back and which continues executing: the wait/die scheme and the wound/wait scheme.
- Concurrency control with optimistic methods assumes that the majority of database transactions do not conflict and that transactions are executed concurrently, using private, temporary copies of the data. At commit time, the private copies are updated to the database. The ANSI standard defines four transaction isolation levels: Read Uncommitted, Read Committed, Repeatable Read, and Serialisable.
- Database recovery restores the database from a given state to a previous consistent state. Database backups are permanent copies of the database; they are stored in a safe place and are to be used in case of a critical error in the master database.

KEY TERMS

atomicity
atomic transaction property
binary lock
buffer
checkpoint
concurrency control
consistency
consistent database state
database-level lock
database recovery
database request
deadlock
deadly embrace
deferred update
deferred write
differential backup
durability
exclusive lock
field-level lock
full backup
immediate update
inconsistent retrievals
isolation
lock
lock granularity
lock manager
lost updates
monotonicity
mutually exclusive rule
optimistic approach
page
page-level lock
Read Committed
Read Uncommited
redundant transaction logs
repeatable read
row-level lock
scheduler
serialisability
serialisable
shared lock
table-level lock
time stamping
transaction
transaction log
transaction log backup
two-phase locking
uncommitted data
uniqueness
wait/die
wound/wait
write-ahead-log protocol
write-through

FURTHER READING

Assaf, W., West, R., Aelterman, S. and Curnutt, M. *SQL Server 2017 Administration Inside Out*. Microsoft Press, 2017.

Brumm, B. *Beginning Oracle SQL for Oracle Database 18c: From Novice to Professional,* 1st edition. Apress, 2019.

Seppo, S., and Soisalon-Soininen, S. *Transaction Processing: Management of the Logical Database and its Underlying Physical Structure, Data-Centric Systems and Applications*. Springer, 2016.

Online Content Answers to selected Review Questions and Problems for this chapter are available on the online platform for this book.

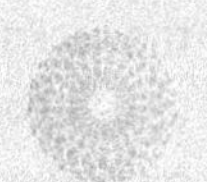

REVIEW QUESTIONS

1 Explain the following statement: A transaction is a logical unit of work.

2 What is a consistent database state, and how is it achieved?

3 The DBMS does not guarantee that the semantic meaning of the transaction truly represents the real-world event. What are the possible consequences of that limitation? Give an example.

4 List and discuss the four transaction properties.

5 What is a transaction log, and what is its function?

6 What is a scheduler, what does it do and why is its activity important to concurrency control?

7 What is a lock, and how, in general, does it work?

8 What is concurrency control, and what is its objective?

9 What is an exclusive lock, and under which circumstances is it granted?

10 What is a deadlock, and how can it be avoided? Discuss several deadlock avoidance strategies.

11 Which three levels of backup may be used in database recovery management? Briefly describe what each of those three backup levels does.

12 What are the four ANSI transaction isolation levels? Which type of reads does each level allow?

13 What does serialisability of transactions mean?

PROBLEMS

1 Suppose you are a manufacturer of product ABC, which is composed of parts A, B and C. Each time a new product ABC is created, it must be added to the product inventory, using the PROD_QOH in a table named PRODUCT. And each time the product is created, the parts inventory, using PART_QOH in a table named PART, must be reduced by one each of parts A, B and C. The sample database contents are shown in the following tables.

Table name: PRODUCT	
PROD_CODE	PROD_QOH
ABC	1205

Table name: PART	
PART_CODE	PART_QOH
A	567
B	98
C	549

Given that information, answer questions a–e.

- a How many database requests can you identify for an inventory update for both PRODUCT and PART?
- b Using SQL, write each database request you identified in Step a.
- c Write the complete transaction(s).
- d Write the transaction log, using Table 12.1 on p. 646 as your template.
- e Using the transaction log you created in Step d, trace its use in database recovery.

2 Describe the three most common concurrent transaction execution problems. Explain how concurrency control can be used to avoid those problems.

3 Which DBMS component is responsible for concurrency control? How is this feature used to resolve conflicts?

12

4 Using a simple example, explain the use of binary and shared/exclusive locks in a DBMS.

5 Suppose your database system has failed. Describe the database recovery process and the use of deferred-write and write-through techniques.

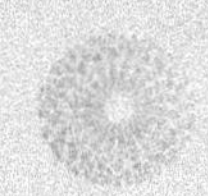

Online Content The 'Ch12_ABC_Markets' database is available on the online platform for this book.

6 ABC Markets sell products to customers. The entity relationship diagram shown in Figure P12.6 represents the main entities for ABC's database. Note the following important characteristics:

- A customer may make many purchases, each one represented by an invoice.
- The CUS_BALANCE is updated with each credit purchase or payment and represents the amount the customer owes.
- The CUS_BALANCE is increased (+) with every credit purchase and decreased (−) with every customer payment.
- The date of last purchase is updated with each new purchase made by the customer.
- The date of last payment is updated with each new payment made by the customer.

FIGURE P12.6 The ABC Markets Relational Diagram

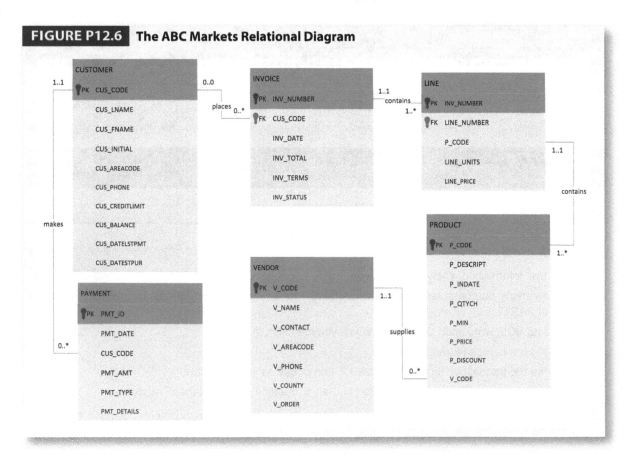

- An invoice represents a product purchase by a customer.
- An INVOICE can have many invoice LINEs, one for each product purchased.
- The INV_TOTAL represents the total cost of the invoice, including taxes.
- The INV_TERMS can be '30', '60' or '90' (representing the number of days of credit) or 'CASH', 'CHEQUE' or 'CC'.
- The invoice status can be 'OPEN', 'PAID' or 'CANCEL'.
- A product's quantity on hand (P_QTYOH) is updated (decreased) with each product sale.
- A customer may make many payments. The payment type (PMT_TYPE) can be one of the following:
  - 'CASH' for cash payments.
  - 'CHEQUE' for cheque payments.
  - 'CC' for credit card payments.
- The payment details (PMT_DETAILS) are used to record data about check or credit card payments:
  - The bank, account number and cheque number for cheque payments.
  - The issuer, credit card number and expiration date for credit card payments.

Note: Not all entities and attributes are represented in this example. Use only the attributes indicated.

Using this database, write the SQL code to represent each of the following transactions. Use BEGIN TRANSACTION and COMMIT to group the SQL statements in logical transactions.

a On 11 May 2019 customer 10010 makes a credit purchase (30 days) of one unit of product 11QER/31 with a unit price of €110.00; the tax rate is 8 per cent. The invoice number is 10983, and this invoice has only one product line.

b On 3 June 2019 customer 10010 makes a payment of €100 in cash. The payment ID is 3428.

c Create a simple transaction log (using the format shown in Table 12.14) to represent the actions of the two previous transactions.

7 Create a simple transaction log (using the format shown in Table 12.14) to represent the actions of the transactions in Problems 6a and 6b.

8 Assuming that pessimistic locking is being used but the two-phase locking protocol is not, create a chronological list of locking, unlocking and data manipulation activities that would occur during the complete processing of the transaction described in Problem 6a.

9 Assuming that pessimistic locking is being used with the two-phase locking protocol, create a chronological list of locking, unlocking and data manipulation activities that would occur during the complete processing of the transaction described in Problem 6a.

10 Assuming that pessimistic locking is being used but the two-phase locking protocol is not, create a chronological list of locking, unlocking and data manipulation activities that would occur during the complete processing of the transaction described in Problem 6b.

11 Assuming that pessimistic locking is being used with the two-phase locking protocol, create a chronological list of locking, unlocking and data manipulation activities that would occur during the complete processing of the transaction described in Problem 6b.

12

CHAPTER 13

Managing Database and SQL Performance

IN THIS CHAPTER, YOU WILL LEARN:

- Basic database performance-tuning concepts
- How a DBMS processes SQL queries
- About the importance of indexes in query processing
- About the types of decisions the query optimiser has to make
- Some common practices used to write efficient SQL code
- How to formulate queries and tune the DBMS for optimal performance

PREVIEW

Database performance optimisation is a critical topic, yet it usually receives minimal coverage in the database curriculum. Most databases used in classrooms have only a few records per table. As a result, the focus often is on making SQL queries perform an intended task, without considering the efficiency of the query process. In fact, even the most efficient query environment gives no visible performance improvements over the least efficient query environment when only 20 or 30 table rows (records) are queried. Unfortunately, the lack of attention to query efficiency can give unacceptably slow results when, in the real world, queries are executed over tens of millions of records. In this chapter, you learn what it takes to create a more efficient query environment.

NOTE

As this book focuses on databases, this chapter covers only those factors directly affecting *database* performance. Also, because performance-tuning techniques can be DBMS-specific, the material in this chapter may not be applicable under all circumstances, nor will it necessarily pertain to all DBMS types. This chapter is designed to build a foundation for the general understanding of database performance-tuning issues and to help you choose appropriate performance-tuning strategies. (For the most current information about tuning your database, consult the vendor's documentation.)

13.1 DATABASE PERFORMANCE-TUNING CONCEPTS

One of the main functions of a database system is to provide answers to end users when they are required. End users and the DBMS interact through the use of queries to generate information, using the following sequence:

1. The end-user (client-end) application generates a query.
2. The query is sent to the DBMS (server end).
3. The DBMS (server end) executes the query.
4. The DBMS sends the resulting data set to the end-user (client-end) application.

End users expect their queries to return results as quickly as possible. How do you know whether the performance of a database is good? Good database performance is hard to evaluate. How do you know if a 1.06-second query response time is good enough? It's easier to identify bad database performance than good database performance – all it takes is end-user complaints about slow query results. Unfortunately, the same query may perform well one day and not so well two months later. Regardless of end-user perceptions, *the goal of database performance is to execute queries as fast as possible*. Therefore, database performance must be closely monitored and regularly tuned. **Database performance tuning** refers to a set of activities and procedures designed to reduce the response time of the database system, that is, to try to ensure that an end-user query is processed by the DBMS in the minimum amount of time.

The time required by a query to return a *result set* depends on many factors. These factors tend to be wide-ranging and to vary from environment to environment and from vendor to vendor. The performance of a typical DBMS is constrained by three main factors: CPU processing power, available primary memory (RAM) and input/output (hard disk and network) throughput. Table 13.1 lists some system components and summarises general guidelines for achieving better query performance.

TABLE 13.1 General guidelines for better system performance

	System Resources	Client	Server
Hardware	CPU	The fastest possible	Multiple processors. The fastest possible, i.e. quad-core or higher. Cluster of networked computers. Virtualised server technology.
	RAM	The maximum possible	The maximum possible to avoid OS memory to disk swapping.
	Storage	Fast SATA/EIDE hard disk with sufficient free hard disk space. Solid state drives (SSDs) for faster speed)	Multiple high-speed, high-capacity disks (SCSI/SATA/Firewire/Fibre Channel) in RAID configuration). Solid state drives (SSDs) for faster speed. Separate disks for OS, DBMS and data spaces.
	Network	High-speed connection	High-speed connection.
Software	Operating system	Fine-tuned for best client application performance	64-bit OS for larger address spaces. Fine-tuned for best server application possible.
	Network	Fine-tuned for best throughput	Fine-tuned for best throughput.
	Application	Optimise SQL in client application	Optimise DBMS for best performance.

Naturally, the system performs best when its hardware and software resources are optimised. However, in the real world, unlimited resources are not the norm; internal and external constraints always exist. Therefore, the hardware and software components should be optimised to obtain the best throughput possible with existing (and often limited) resources, which is why database performance tuning is important.

Fine-tuning the performance of a system requires a holistic approach. That is, *all* factors must be checked to ensure that each one operates at its optimum level and has sufficient resources to minimise the occurrence of bottlenecks. As database design is such an important factor in determining the database system's performance efficiency, it is worth repeating this book's ethos:

Good database performance starts with good database design. *No amount of fine-tuning will make a poorly designed database perform as well as a well-designed database*. This is true when an existing database is redesigned and the end user expects a unrealistic performance gain from older databases.

13.1.1 Performance Tuning: Client and Server

In general, database performance-tuning activities can be divided into those taking place either on the client side or on the server side:

- On the client side, the objective is to generate a SQL query that returns the correct answer in the least amount of time, using the minimum amount of resources at the server end. The activities required to achieve that goal are commonly referred to as **SQL performance tuning**.
- On the server side, the DBMS environment must be properly configured to respond to clients' requests in the fastest way possible, while making optimum use of existing resources. The activities required to achieve that goal are commonly referred to as **DBMS performance tuning**.

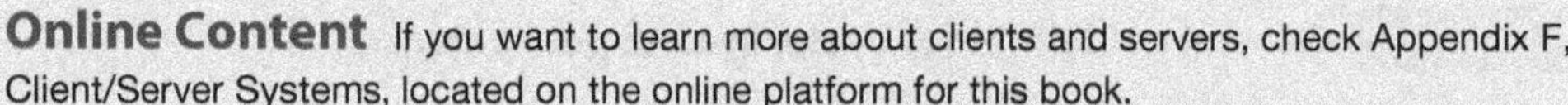

Online Content If you want to learn more about clients and servers, check Appendix F, Client/Server Systems, located on the online platform for this book.

Keep in mind that DBMS implementations are typically more complex than just a two-tier client/server configuration. However, even in multi-tier (client front-end, application middleware and database server back-end) client/server environments, performance-tuning activities are frequently subdivided into subtasks to ensure the fastest possible response time between any two component points.

This chapter covers SQL performance-tuning practices on the client side and DBMS performance-tuning practices on the server side. However, before you can start learning about the tuning processes, you must first learn more about the DBMS architectural components and processes, and how those processes interact to respond to end-user requests.

13.1.2 DBMS Architecture

The architecture of a DBMS is represented by the processes and structures (in memory and in permanent storage) used to manage a database. Such processes collaborate with one another to perform specific functions. Figure 13.1 illustrates the basic DBMS architecture.

FIGURE 13.1 **Basic DBMS architecture**

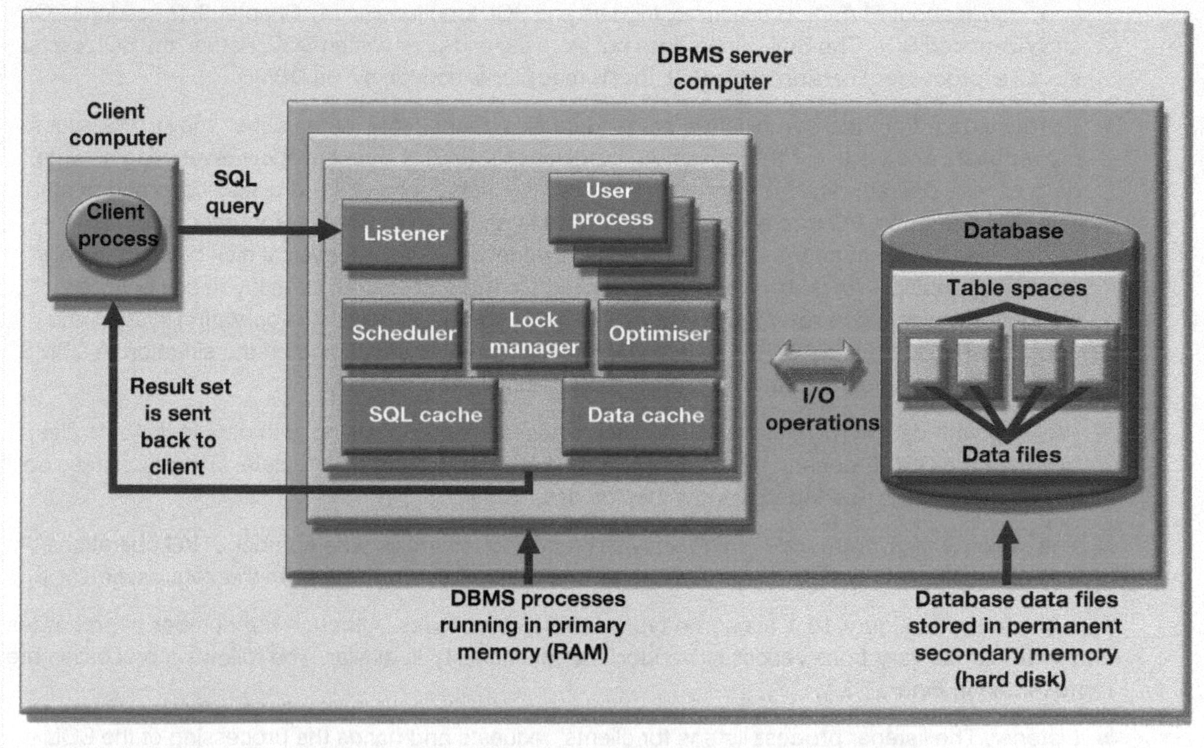

As you examine Figure 13.1, note the following components and functions:

- All data in a database are stored in **data files**. A typical enterprise database is normally composed of several data files. A data file can contain rows from one single table, or it can contain rows from many different tables. A database administrator (DBA) determines the initial size of the data files that make up the database; however, as required, the data files can automatically expand in predefined increments known as **extends**. For example, if more space is required, the DBA can define that each new extend will be in 10 KB or 10 MB increments.
- Data files are generally grouped in file groups creating table spaces. A **table space** or **file group** is a logical grouping of several data files that store data with similar characteristics. For example, you may have a *system* table space where the data dictionary table data are stored; a *user data* table space to store the user-created tables; an *index* table space to hold all indexes; or a *temporary* table space to do temporary sorts, grouping, and so on. Each time you create a new database, the DBMS automatically creates a minimum set of table spaces.
- To work with the data, the DBMS must retrieve the data from permanent storage (data files in which the data are stored) and place it in RAM (data cache).
- The **data cache** or **buffer cache** is a shared, reserved memory area that stores the most recently accessed data blocks in RAM. The data cache is where the data read from the database data files are stored after the data have been read or before the data are written to the database data files. The data cache also caches system catalogue data and the contents of the indexes.

13

- The **SQL cache** or **procedure cache** is a shared, reserved memory area that stores the most recently executed SQL statements or PL/SQL procedures, including triggers and functions. (If you want to know more about PL/SQL procedures, triggers and SQL functions, study Chapter 9, Procedural SQL and Advanced SQL. The SQL cache does not store the end-user written SQL. Rather, the SQL cache stores a 'processed' version of the SQL that is ready for execution by the DBMS.
- To move data from the permanent storage (data files) to the RAM (data cache), the DBMS issues I/O requests and waits for the replies. An **input/output (I/O) request** is a low-level (read or write) data access operation to/from computer devices (such as memory, hard disks, video and printer). The purpose of the I/O operation is to move data to and from different computer components or devices. Note that an I/O disk read operation retrieves an entire physical disk block, generally containing multiple rows, from permanent storage to the data cache, even if you use only one attribute from only one row. The physical disk block size depends on the operating system and could be 4K, 8K, 16K, 32K, 64K or even larger. Furthermore, depending on the situation, A DBMS might issue a singleblock read request or a multi-block read request.
- Working with data in the data cache is many times faster than working with data in the data files, because the DBMS doesn't have to wait for the hard disk to retrieve the data. (That's because no I/O operations are needed to work within the data cache.)
- The majority of performance-tuning activities focus on minimising the number of I/O operations, because using I/O operations is many times slower than reading data from the data cache.

Also illustrated in Figure 13.1 are some typical DBMS processes. Although the number of processes and their names vary from vendor to vendor, the functionality is similar. The following processes are represented in Figure 13.1:

- *Listener*. The listener process listens for clients' requests and hands the processing of the SQL requests to other DBMS processes. Once a request is received, the listener passes the request to the appropriate user process.
- *User*. The DBMS creates a user process to manage each client session. Therefore, when you log on to the DBMS, you are assigned a user process. This process will handle all requests you submit to the server. There are many user processes, at least one per each logged-in client.
- *Scheduler*. The scheduler process schedules the concurrent execution of SQL requests. (See Chapter 12, Managing Transactions and Concurrency.)
- *Lock manager*. This process manages all locks placed on database objects. (See Chapter 12, Managing Transactions and Concurrency.)
- *Optimiser*. The optimiser process analyses SQL queries and finds the most efficient way to access the data. You will learn more about this process later in the chapter.

13.1.3 Database Query Optimisation Modes

Most of the algorithms proposed for query optimisation are based on two principles:

- The selection of the optimum execution order
- The selection of sites to be accessed to minimise communication costs

Within those two principles, a query optimisation algorithm can be evaluated on the basis of its operation mode or the timing of its optimisation. Operation modes can be classified as manual or automatic. **Automatic query optimisation** means that the DBMS finds the most cost-effective access path without user intervention. Manual query optimisation requires that the optimisation be selected and scheduled by the end user or programmer. Automatic query optimisation is clearly more desirable from the end user's point of view, but the cost of such convenience is the increased overhead that it imposes on the DBMS.

Query optimisation algorithms can also be classified according to when the optimisation is done. Within this timing classification, query optimisation algorithms can be static or dynamic.

Static query optimisation takes place at compilation time. In other words, the best optimisation strategy is selected when the query is compiled by the DBMS. This approach is common when SQL statements are embedded in procedural programming languages such as C# or Visual Basic .NET. When the program is submitted to the DBMS for compilation, it creates the plan necessary to access the database. When the program is executed, the DBMS uses that plan to access the database.

Dynamic query optimisation takes place at execution time. Database access strategy is defined when the program is executed. Therefore, access strategy is dynamically determined by the DBMS at run time, using the most up-to-date information about the database. Although dynamic query optimisation is efficient, its cost is measured by run-time processing overhead. The best strategy is determined every time the query is executed which could happen several times in the same program.

Finally, query optimisation techniques can be classified according to the type of information that is used to optimise the query. For example, queries may be based on statistically based or rule-based algorithms.

A **statistically based query optimisation algorithm** uses statistical information about the database. The statistics provide information about database characteristics such as size, number of records, average access time, number of requests serviced and number of users with access rights. These statistics are then used by the DBMS to determine the best access strategy. Within statistically based optimisers, some DBMSs allow setting a goal to specify that the optimiser should attempt to minimize the time to retrieve the first row or the last row. Minimising the time to retrieve the first row is often used in transaction systems and interactive client environments. In these cases, the goal is to present the first several rows to the user as quickly as possible. Then, while the DBMS waits for the user to scroll through the data, it can fetch the other rows for the query.

Setting the optimiser goal to minimise retrieval of the last row is typically done in embedded SQL and inside stored procedures. In these cases, the control will not pass back to the calling application until all of the data have been retrieved; therefore, it is important to retrieve all of the data to the last row as quickly as possible so control can be returned.

The statistical information is managed by the DBMS and is generated in one of two different modes: dynamic or manual. In the **dynamic statistical generation mode**, the DBMS automatically evaluates and updates the statistics after each access. In the **manual statistical generation mode**, the statistics must be updated periodically through a user-selected utility which is specific to the a particular DBMS.

A **rule-based query optimisation algorithm** is based on a set of user-defined rules to determine the best query access strategy. The rules are entered by the end user or database administrator, and they are typically general in nature.

Because database statistics play a crucial role in query optimisation, this topic is explored in more detail in the next section.

13

13.1.4 Database Statistics

Another DBMS process that plays an important role in query optimisation is gathering database statistics. *Database statistics* refers to a number of measurements about database objects such as tables, indexes and available resources such as number of processors used, processor speed and temporary space available. These statistics give a snapshot of database characteristics.

As you will learn later in this chapter, the DBMS uses the statistics to make critical decisions about improving query processing efficiency. Database statistics can be gathered on request by the DBA or automatically by the DBMS. For example, many DBMS vendors support the ANALYZE command in SQL to gather statistics. In addition, many vendors have their own routines to gather statistics. For example, IBM's DB2 uses the RUNSTATS procedure, while Microsoft's SQL Server uses the UPDATE STATISTICS procedure and provides the Auto-Update and Auto-Create Statistics options in its initialisation parameters. A sample of measurements that the DBMS may gather about different database objects is shown in Table 13.2.

TABLE 13.2 Sample database statistics measurements

Database Object	Sample Measurements
Table	Number of rows, number of disk blocks used, row length, number of columns in each row, number of distinct values in each column, maximum value in each column, minimum value in each column and columns that have indexes.
Indexes	Number and name of columns in the index key, number of key values in the index, number of distinct key values in the index key and histogram of key values in an index.
Environment Resources	Logical and physical disk block size, location and size of data files and number of extends per data file.

If the object statistics exist, the DBMS uses them in query processing as is described in detail later. Although some of the newer DBMSs (such as Oracle, SQL Server and DB2) automatically gather statistics, others require the DBA to gather statistics on request. To generate the database object statistics on request, you could use the following syntax:

```
ANALYZE <TABLE/INDEX> object_name COMPUTE STATISTICS;
```

For example, to generate statistics for the VENDOR table, you would use the following command:

```
ANALYZE TABLE VENDOR COMPUTE STATISTICS;
```

When you generate statistics for a table, all related indexes are also analysed. However, you could generate statistics for a single index with the following command:

```
ANALYZE INDEX VEND_NDX COMPUTE STATISTICS;
```

(In this example, VEND_NDX is the name of the index.)

13

Database statistics are stored in the system catalogue in specially designated tables. It is common periodically to regenerate the statistics for database objects, especially those database objects that are subject to frequent change. For example, if you are the owner of a video store and you have a video rental DBMS, your system will likely use a RENTAL table to store the daily video rentals. That RENTAL table (and its associated indexes) would be subject to constant inserts and updates as you record your daily rentals and returns. Therefore, the RENTAL table statistics you generated last week do not depict an accurate picture of the table as it exists today. The more current the statistics, the better the chances are for the DBMS to find the fastest way to execute a given query.

Now that you know the basic architecture of DBMS processes and memory structures, you are ready to learn how the DBMS processes a SQL query request.

13.2 QUERY PROCESSING

What happens at the DBMS server end when the client's SQL statement is received? In simple terms, the DBMS processes queries in three phases:

1 *Parsing*. The DBMS parses the SQL query and chooses the most efficient access/execution plan.

2 *Execution*. The DBMS executes the SQL query, using the chosen execution plan.

3 *Fetching*. The DBMS fetches the data and sends the result set back to the client.

The processing of SQL DDL statements (such as CREATE TABLE) is different from the processing required by DML statements. The difference is that a DDL statement actually updates the data dictionary tables or system catalog, while a DML statement (SELECT, INSERT, UPDATE and DELETE) mostly manipulates end-user data. Figure 13.2 shows the steps required for query processing. Each of the steps are discussed in the following sections.

FIGURE 13.2 Query processing

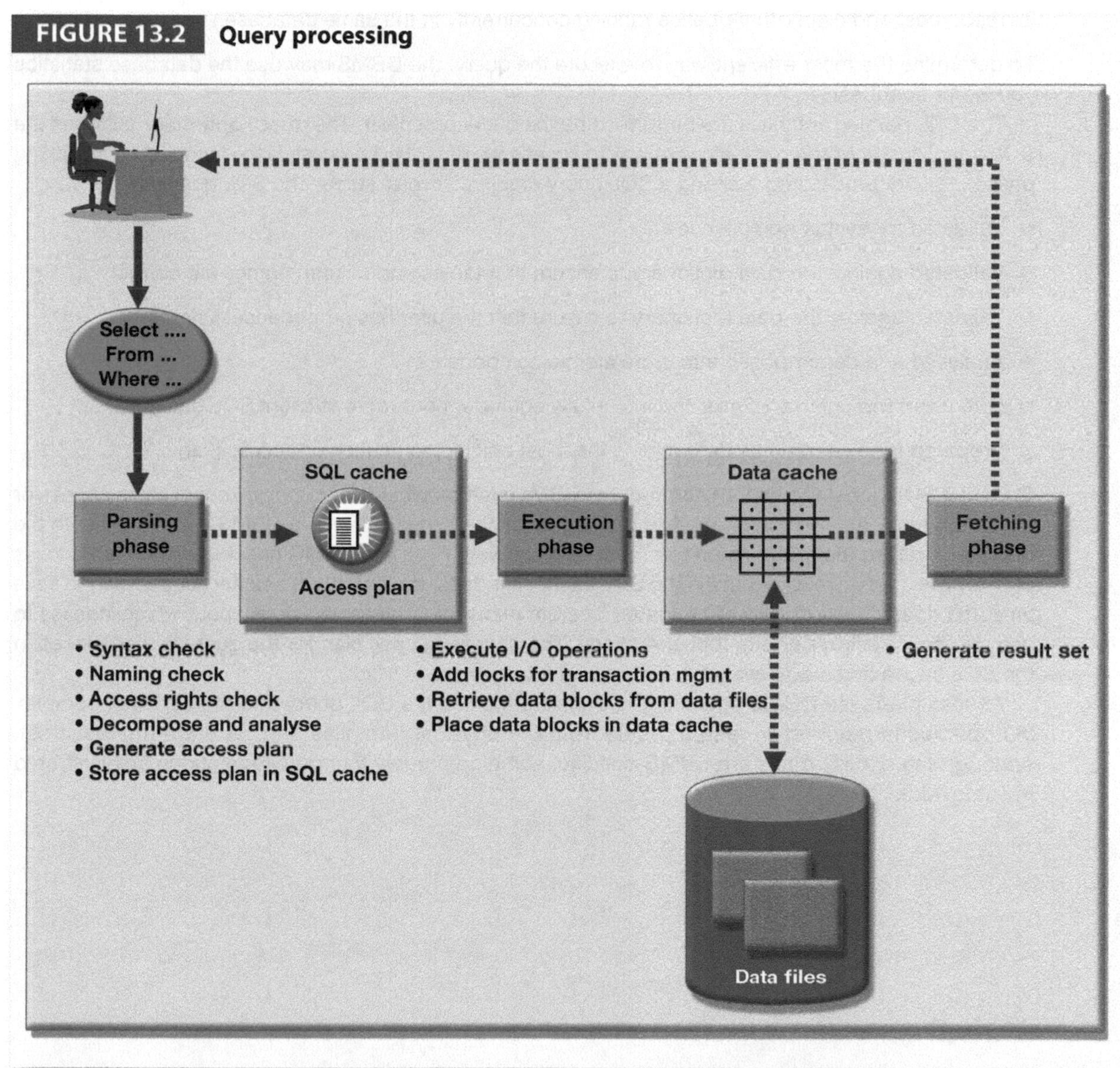

13.2.1 SQL Parsing Phase

The optimisation process includes breaking down – parsing – the query into smaller units and transforming the original SQL query into a slightly different version of the original SQL code, but one that is fully equivalent and more efficient.

- *Fully equivalent* means that the optimised query results are always the same as the original query.
- *More efficient* means that the optimised query will almost always execute faster than the original query. (Note that it *almost* always executes faster because, as explained earlier, many factors affect the performance of a database. Those factors include the network, the client computer's resources, and even other queries running concurrently in the same database.)

To determine the most efficient way to execute the query, the DBMS may use the database statistics you learnt about earlier.

The SQL parsing activities are performed by the query optimiser. The **query optimiser** analyses the SQL query and finds the most efficient way to access the data. This process is the most time-consuming phase in query processing. Parsing a SQL query requires several steps. The SQL query is:

- Validated for syntax compliance
- Validated against the data dictionary to ensure that tables and column names are correct
- Validated against the data dictionary to ensure that the user has proper access rights
- Analysed and decomposed into more atomic components
- Optimised through transformation into a fully equivalent but more efficient SQL query
- Prepared for execution by determining the most efficient execution or access plan.

Once the SQL statement is transformed, the DBMS creates what is commonly known as an access or execution plan. An **access/execution plan** contains the series of steps a DBMS uses to execute the query and return the result set in the most efficient way. First, the DBMS checks to see if an access plan for the query already exists in the SQL cache. If it does, the DBMS reuses the access plan to save time. If it doesn't, the optimiser evaluates different plans and makes decisions about which indexes to use and how best to perform join operations. The chosen access plan for the query is then placed in the SQL cache and made available for use and future reuse.

Access plans are DBMS-specific and translate the client's SQL query into the series of complex I/O operations required to read the data from the physical data files and generate the result set. Although the access plans are DBMS-specific, some commonly found I/O operations are illustrated in Table 13.3.

TABLE 13.3 Sample DBMS access plan I/O operations

Operation	Description
Table Scan (Full)	Reads the entire table sequentially, from the first row to the last row, one row at a time (slowest).
Table Access (Row ID)	Reads a table row directly, using the row ID value (fastest).
Index Scan (Range)	Reads the index first to obtain the row IDs and then accesses the table rows directly (faster than a full table scan).
Index Access (Unique)	Used when a table has a unique index in a column.
Nested Loop	Reads and compares a set of values to another set of values, using a nested loop style (slow).
Merge	Merges two data sets (slow).
Sort	Sorts a data set (slow).

Table 13.3 shows just a few database access I/O operations. (This illustration is based on an Oracle RDBMS.) However, Table 13.3 does illustrate the type of I/O operations that most DBMSs perform when accessing and manipulating data sets.

As you examine Table 13.3, note that a table access using a row ID is the fastest method. A row ID is a unique identification for every row saved in permanent storage and can be used to access the row directly. A row ID is like the row address. Conceptually, it is similar to the parking slip you get when you park your car in an airport parking space. The parking slip contains the section number and space number. Using that information, you can go directly to your car without having to go through every single section and space.

13.2.2 SQL Execution Phase

In this phase, all I/O operations indicated in the access plan are executed. When the execution plan is run, the proper locks are – if needed – acquired for the data to be accessed and the data are retrieved from the data files and placed in the DBMSs data cache. All transaction management commands are processed during the parsing and execution phases of query processing.

13.2.3 SQL Fetching Phase

13

After the parsing and execution phases are completed, all rows that match the specified condition(s) are retrieved, sorted, grouped and/or (if required) aggregated. During the fetching phase, the rows of the resulting query result set are returned to the client. During this phase, the DBMS may use temporary table space to store temporary data.

13.2.4 Query Processing Bottlenecks

The main objective of query processing is to execute a given query in the fastest way possible with the fewest resources. As you have seen, the execution of a query requires the DBMS to break down the query into a series of interdependent I/O operations to be executed in a collaborative manner. The more complex a query is, the more complex the operations are, which means that bottlenecks are more likely. A **query processing bottleneck** is a delay introduced in the processing of an I/O operation that causes the overall system to slow down. In the same way, the more components a system has, the more interfacing is required among the components, increasing the likelihood of bottlenecks. Within a DBMS, five components typically cause bottlenecks:

- CPU – the CPU processing power of the DBMS should match the system's expected workload. A high CPU utilisation might indicate that the processor speed is too slow for the amount of work performed. However, heavy CPU utilisation can be caused by other factors, such as a defective component, not enough RAM (the CPU spends too much time swapping memory blocks), a badly written device driver or a rogue process. A CPU bottleneck will affect not only the DBMS but all processes running in the system.
- RAM – the DBMS allocates memory for specific usage, such as data cache and SQL cache. RAM must be shared among all running processes, including the operating system and DBMS. If there is not enough RAM available, moving data among components that are competing for scarce RAM can create a bottleneck.
- Hard disk – hard disk space is used for more than just storing end-user data. Current operating systems also use the hard disk for virtual memory, which refers to copying areas of RAM to the hard disk as needed to make room in RAM for more urgent tasks. Therefore, the more hard disk storage space available and the ability to have faster data transfer rates reduce the likelihood of bottlenecks.
- Network – in a database environment, the database server and the clients are connected via a network. All networks have a limited amount of bandwidth that is shared among all clients. When many network nodes access the network at the same time, bottlenecks are likely.
- Application code – two of the most common sources of bottlenecks are inferior application code and poorly designed databases. Inferior code can be improved with code optimisation techniques, as long as the underlying database design is sound. However, no amount of coding will make a poorly designed database perform better.

Learning how to avoid these bottlenecks and optimise database performance is the main focus of this chapter.

13.3 INDEXES AND QUERY OPTIMISATION

13

In Chapter 11, Conceptual, Logical, and Physical Database Design, you learnt that indexes are crucial in the process that speeds up data access. Indexes facilitate searching, sorting and using aggregate functions and even join operations. The improvement in data access speed occurs because an index is an ordered set of values that contains the index key and pointers. In addition, you also learnt that indexes are recommended where high-sparsity columns are used in search conditions. The careful selection of indexes in the physical database design stage will play a huge part in query optimisation. In section 13.5, you will learn how indexes impact SQL performance tuning.

NOTE

You can learn how to select indexes in Chapter 11, Conceptual, Logical, and Physical Database Design (Section 11.3.3.).

13.4 OPTIMISER CHOICES

Query optimisation is the central activity during the parsing phase in query processing. In this phase, the DBMS must choose what indexes to use, how to perform join operations, which table to use first, and so on. Each DBMS has its own algorithms for determining the most efficient way to access the data. The query optimiser can operate in one of two modes:

- A **rule-based optimiser** uses a set of preset rules and points to determine the best approach to execute a query. The rules assign a 'fixed cost' to each SQL operation; the costs are then added to yield the cost of the execution plan. For example, a full table scan will have a set cost of ten, while a table access by row ID will have a set cost of three.
- A **cost-based optimiser** uses sophisticated algorithms based on the statistics about the objects being accessed to determine the best approach to execute a query. In this case, the optimiser process adds up the processing cost, the I/O costs, and the resource costs (RAM and temporary space) to come up with the total cost of a given execution plan.

The optimiser objective is to find alternative ways to execute a query, to evaluate the 'cost' of each alternative and then to choose the one with the lowest cost. To understand the function of the query optimiser, let's use a simple example. Assume that you want to list all products provided by a vendor based in South Africa (SA). To acquire that information, you could write the following query:

```
SELECT    P_CODE, P_DESCRIPT, P_PRICE, V_NAME, V_STATE
FROM      PRODUCT, VENDOR
WHERE     PRODUCT.V_CODE = VENDOR.V_CODE
AND       VENDOR.V_COUNTRY = 'SA';
```

Furthermore, let's assume that the database statistics indicate that:

1 The PRODUCT table has 7000 rows.

2 The VENDOR table has 300 rows.

3 Ten vendors come from South Africa.

4 One thousand products come from vendors in South Africa.

It's important to point out that only items 1 and 2 are available to the optimiser. Items 3 and 4 are assumed to illustrate the choices that the optimiser must make. Armed with the information in items 1 and 2, the optimiser would try to find the most efficient way to access the data. The primary factor in determining the most efficient access plan is the I/O cost. (Remember, the DBMS will always try to minimize I/O operations.) Table 13.4 shows two sample access plans for the previous query and their respective I/O costs.

TABLE 13.4 Comparing access plans and I/O costs

Plan	Step	Operation	I/O Operations	I/O Cost	Resulting Set Rows	Total I/O Cost
A	A1	Cartesian product A1 = (PRODUCT X VENDOR)	7 000 + 300	7 300	2 100 000	7 300
	A2	Select rows in A1 with matching vendor codes A2 = σ PRODUCT.v_code = VENDOR.v_code(A1)	2 100 000	2 100 000	7 000	2 107 300
	A3	Select rows in A2 with V_COUNTRY = 'SA' A3 = (σ V_COUNTRY = 'SA' (A2))	7 000	7 000	1 000	**2 114 300**
B	B1	Select rows in VENDOR with V_COUNTRY = 'SA' B1 = σ V_COUNTRY = 'SA' (VENDOR)	300	300	10	300
	B2	Cartesian Product B2 = (PRODUCT X B1)	7 000 + 10	7 010	70 000	7 310
	B3	Select rows in B2 with matching vendor codes B3 = σ PRODUCT.v_code = B1.v_code(B2)	70 000	70 000	1 000	**77 310**

To make the example easier to understand, the I/O Operations and I/O Cost columns in Table 13.4 estimate only the number of I/O disk reads the DBMS must perform. For simplicity's sake, it is assumed that there are no indexes and that each row read has an I/O cost of 1. For example, in Step A1, the DBMS must perform a Cartesian product of PRODUCT and VENDOR. To do that, the DBMS must read all rows from PRODUCT (7 000) and all rows from VENDOR (300), giving a total of 7 300 I/O operations. The same computation is done in all steps. In Table 13.4, you can see how plan A has a total I/O cost that is almost 30 times higher than plan B. In this case, the optimiser will choose plan B to execute the SQL.

13

NOTE

Not all DBMSs optimise SQL queries the same way. As a matter of fact, Oracle parses queries differently from the way described in several sections in this chapter. Always read the documentation to examine the optimisation requirements for your DBMS implementation.

Given the right conditions, some queries could be answered entirely with only an index. For example, assume the PRODUCT table with an index PQOH_NDX in the P_QOH attribute. Then a query such as SELECT MIN(P_QOH) FROM PRODUCT could be resolved by reading only the first entry in the PQOH_NDX index, without the need to access any of the data blocks for the PRODUCT table. (Remember that the index defaults to ascending order.)

You learnt in Chapter 11, Conceptual, Logical, and Physical Database Design, that columns with low sparsity are not good candidates for index creation. However, there are cases where an index in a low sparsity column would be helpful. For example, assume that the EMPLOYEE table has 122 483 rows. If you want to find out how many female employees are in the company, you would write a query such as:

```
SELECT COUNT(EMP_GENDER) FROM EMPLOYEE WHERE EMP_GENDER = 'F';
```

If you do not have an index for the EMP_GENDER column, the query would have to perform a full table scan to read all EMPLOYEE rows – and each full row includes attributes you do not need. However, if you have an index on EMP_GENDER, the query could be answered by reading only the index data, without the need to access the employee data at all.

13.4.1 Using Hints to Affect Optimiser Choices

Although the optimiser generally performs well under most circumstances, in some instances the optimiser may not choose the best execution plan. Remember, the optimiser makes decisions based on the existing statistics. If the statistics are old, the optimiser may not do a good job in selecting the best execution plan. Even with current statistics, the optimiser choice may not be the most efficient one. There are some occasions when the end user would like to change the optimiser mode for the current SQL statement. In order to do that, you need to use hints. **Optimiser hints** are special instructions for the optimiser that are embedded inside the SQL command text. Table 13.5 summarises a few of the most common optimiser hints used in standard SQL.

TABLE 13.5 Optimiser hints

Hint	Usage
ALL_ROWS	Instructs the optimiser to minimise the overall execution time, that is, to minimise the time it takes to return all rows in the query result set. This hint is generally used for batch mode processes. For example: SELECT /*+ ALL_ROWS */ * FROM PRODUCT WHERE P_QOH < 10;
FIRST_ROWS	Instructs the optimiser to minimise the time it takes to process the first set of rows, that is, to minimize the time it takes to return only the first set of rows in the query result set. This hint is generally used for interactive mode processes. For example: SELECT /*+ FIRST_ROWS */ * FROM PRODUCT WHERE P_QOH < 10;
INDEX(name)	Forces the optimiser to use the P_QOH_NDX index to process this query. For example: SELECT /*+ INDEX(P_QOH_NDX) */ * FROM PRODUCT WHERE P_QOH < 10;

Now that you are familiar with the way the DBMS processes SQL queries, let's turn our attention to some general SQL coding recommendations to facilitate the work of the query optimiser.

13.5 SQL PERFORMANCE TUNING

SQL performance tuning is evaluated from the client perspective. Therefore, the goal is to illustrate some common practices used to write efficient SQL code. A few words of caution are appropriate:

1 Most current-generation relational DBMSs perform automatic query optimisation at the server end.

2 Most SQL performance optimisation techniques are DBMS-specific and, therefore, are rarely portable, even across different versions of the same DBMS. Part of the reason for this behaviour is the constant advancement in database technologies.

Does this mean that you should not worry about how a SQL query is written because the DBMS will always optimise it? No, because there is considerable room for improvement. (The DBMS uses *general* optimisation techniques, rather than focusing on specific techniques dictated by the special circumstances of the query execution.) A poorly written SQL query can, *and usually will*, bring the database system to its knees from a performance point of view. The majority of current database performance problems are related to poorly written SQL code. Therefore, although a DBMS provides general optimizing services, a carefully written query almost always outperforms a poorly written one.

Although SQL data manipulation statements include many different commands (such as INSERT, UPDATE, DELETE and SELECT), most recommendations in this section are related to the use of the SELECT statement and, in particular, the use of indexes and how to write conditional expressions.

13.5.1 Index Selectivity

Indexes are the most important technique used in SQL performance optimisation. As you learnt from Chapter 11, Conceptual, Logical, and Physical Database Design, **index selectivity** is a measure of how likely an index is to be used in query processing. To recap, the general guidelines for creating and using indexes are:

- Create indexes for each single attribute used in a WHERE, HAVING, ORDER BY or GROUP BY clause.
- Create an index when the data sparsity on the indexed column is high.
- When a MIN or MAX function is applied to an indexed column.
- Declare all primary and foreign keys so the optimiser can use the indexes in join operations.
- Declare indexes in join columns other than PK/FK.

However, you cannot always use an index to improve performance. For example, using the data shown in Table 13.6 in the next section, the creation of an index for P_MIN will not help the search condition P_QOH > P_MIN * 1.10. The reason is because *indexes are ignored when you use functions in the table attributes*.

How many indexes should you create? It bears repeating that you should not create an index for every column in a table. Too many indexes will slow down INSERT, UPDATE and DELETE operations, especially if the table contains many thousands of rows. Furthermore, some query optimisers will choose only one index to be the driving index for a query, even if your query uses conditions in many different indexed columns. Which index does the optimiser use? If you use the cost-based optimiser, the answer will change with time as new rows are added or deleted from the tables. In any case, you should create indexes in all search columns and then let the optimiser choose. A proper procedure will be the constant evaluation of the index usage – monitor, test, evaluate and improve if performance is not adequate.

13.5.2 Conditional Expressions

A conditional expression is normally expressed within the WHERE or HAVING clauses of a SQL statement. A conditional expression (also known as conditional criteria) restricts the output of a query to only the rows matching the conditional criteria. Generally, the conditional criteria have the form shown in Table 13.6.

TABLE 13.6 Conditional criteria

Operand1	Conditional Operator	Operand2
P_PRICE	>	10.00
V_COUNTRY	=	'SA'
V_CONTACT	LIKE	'Moloi%'
P_QOH	>	P_MIN * 1.10

As you examine Table 13.6, note that an operand can be:

- A simple column name such as P_PRICE or V_COUNTRY
- A literal or a constant such as the value 10.00 or the text 'SA'.
- An expression such as P_MIN * 1.10.

Most of the query optimisation techniques mentioned next are designed to make the optimiser's work easier. Let's examine some common practices used to write efficient conditional expressions in SQL code:

- *Use simple columns or literals as operands in a conditional expression – avoid the use of conditional expressions with functions whenever possible.* Comparing the contents of a single column to a literal is faster than comparing to expressions. For example, P_PRICE > 10.00 will be faster than P_QOH > P_MIN * 1.10 because the DBMS must evaluate the P_MIN * 1.10 expression first. The use of functions in expressions will also add to the total query execution time. For example, if your condition is UPPER (V_NAME) = 'JIM', try to use V_NAME = 'Jim' if all names in the V_NAME column are stored with proper capitalisation.
- *Numeric field comparisons are faster than character, date and NULL comparisons.* In search conditions, comparing a numeric attribute to a numeric literal is faster than comparing a character attribute to a character literal. In general, the CPU handles numeric comparisons (integer, decimal) faster than character and date comparisons. As indexes do not store references to null values, NULL conditions involve additional processing and, therefore, tend to be the slowest of all conditional operands.
- *Equality comparisons are faster than inequality comparisons.* As a general rule, equality comparisons are processed faster than inequality comparisons. For example, P_PRICE = 10.00 is processed faster because the DBMS can do a direct search using the index in the column. If there are no exact matches, the condition is evaluated as false. However, if you use an inequality symbol (>, >=, <, <=), the DBMS must perform additional processing to complete the request. The reason is because there will almost always be more 'greater than' or 'less than' values and perhaps only a few exactly 'equal' values in the index. The slowest (with the exception of NULL) of all comparison operators is LIKE with wildcard symbols, such as in V_CONTACT LIKE '%glo%'. Also, using the 'not equal' symbol (<>) yields slower searches, especially when the sparsity of the data is high, that is, when there are many more different values than there are equal values.
- *Whenever possible, transform conditional expressions to use literals.* For example, if your condition is P_PRICE – 10 = 7, change it to read P_PRICE = 17.
- *When using multiple conditional expressions, write the equality conditions first.* If you have a composite condition such as:

  P_QOH < P_MIN AND P_MIN = P_REORDER AND P_QOH = 10

change it to read:

P_QOH = 10 AND P_MIN = P_REORDER AND P_MIN > 10

Remember, equality conditions are faster to process than inequality conditions. Although most RDBMSs will automatically do this for you, paying attention to this detail lightens the load for the query optimiser. (The optimiser won't have to do what you have already done.)

- *If you use multiple AND conditions, write the condition most likely to be false first*. If you use this technique, the DBMS will stop evaluating the rest of the conditions as soon as it finds a conditional expression that is evaluated to be false. Remember, for multiple AND conditions to be found true, all conditions must be evaluated as true. If one of the conditions evaluates to false, everything else will be evaluated as false. Therefore, if you use this technique, the DBMS won't waste time unnecessarily evaluating additional conditions. Naturally, the use of this technique implies an implicit knowledge of the sparsity of the data set. For example, look at the following condition list:

  P_PRICE > 10 AND V_COUNTRY= 'SA'

  If you know that only a few vendors are located in South Africa, you could rewrite this condition as:

  V_COUNTRY = 'SA' AND P_PRICE > 10

- *When using multiple OR conditions, put the condition most likely to be true first*. By doing this, the DBMS will stop evaluating the remaining conditions as soon as it finds a conditional expression that is evaluated to be true. Remember, for multiple OR conditions to evaluate to true, only one of the conditions must be evaluated to true.

NOTE

Oracle evaluates queries in an opposite way from what is described here. That is, Oracle evaluates conditions from last to first.

- *Whenever possible, try to avoid the use of the NOT logical operator*. It is best to transform a SQL expression containing a NOT logical operator into an equivalent expression. For example:

  NOT (P_PRICE > 10.00) can be written as P_PRICE <= 10.00.

  Also, NOT (EMP_GENDER = 'M') can be written as EMP_GENDER = 'F'.

13.6 QUERY FORMULATION

Queries are usually written to answer questions. For example, if an end user gives you a sample output and tells you to match that output format, you must write the SQL required to generate the output. To get the job done, you must carefully evaluate which columns, tables and computations are required to generate the desired output. To do that, you must have a good understanding of the database environment and of the database that will be the focus of your SQL code.

This section will focus on SELECT queries because they are the queries you will find in most applications. To formulate a query, you would normally follow the steps outlined below:

1 *Identify which columns and computations are required*. The first step is to determine clearly which data values you want to return. Do you want to return just the names and addresses, or do you also want to include some computations? Remember that all columns in the SELECT statement should return single values.

- Do you need simple expressions? That is, do you need to multiply the price times the quantity on hand to generate the total inventory cost? You may need some single attribute functions such as DATE(), SYSDATE() or ROUND().
- Do you need aggregate functions? If you need to compute the total sales by product, you should use a GROUP BY clause. In some cases, you may need to use a subquery.
- Determine the granularity of the raw data required for your output. The granularity is the level of detail within the data. Data with maximum granularity is known as atomic data. You will learn more about granularity in Chapter 15, Databases for Business intelligence.
- Sometimes, you may need to summarise data that are not readily available on any table. In such cases, you may consider breaking the query into multiple subqueries and storing those subqueries as views. Then you could create a top-level query that joins those views and generates the final output.

2 *Identify the source tables*. Once you know which columns are required, you can determine the source tables used in the query. Some attributes appear in more than one table. In those cases, try to use the fewest tables in your query to minimise the number of join operations.

3 *Determine how to join the tables*. Once you know which tables you need in your query statement, you must properly identify how to join the tables. In most cases, you will use some type of natural join, but in some instances, you may need to use an outer join.

4 *Determine which selection criteria are needed*. Most queries involve some type of selection criteria. In this case, you must determine which operands and operators are needed in your criteria. Ensure that the data type and granularity of the data in the comparison criteria are correct:

- *Simple comparison*. In most cases, you will be comparing single values. For example: P_PRICE > 10
- *Single value to multiple values*. If you are comparing a single value to multiple values, you may need to use an IN comparison operator. For example: V_COUNTRY IN ('FR', 'UK', 'SA');
- *Nested comparisons*. Also, in other cases, you may need to have some nested selection criteria involving subqueries. For example: P_PRICE > = (SELECT AVG(P_PRICE) FROM PRODUCT);
- *Grouped data selection*. On other occasions, the selection criteria may apply not to the raw data, but to the aggregate data. In those cases, you need to use the HAVING clause.

5 *Determine in which order to display the output*. Finally, the required output may be ordered by one or more columns. In those cases, you need to use the ORDER BY clause.

13.7 DBMS PERFORMANCE TUNING

DBMS performance tuning includes global tasks such as managing the DBMS processes in primary memory (allocating memory for caching purposes) and the structures in physical storage (allocating space for the data files).

Fine-tuning the performance of the DBMS also includes applying several practices examined in the previous section. For example, the DBA must work with developers to ensure that the queries perform as expected. In that case, the DBA is responsible for creating the indexes to speed up query response time and for generating the database statistics required by cost-based optimisers.

DBMS performance tuning at the server end focuses on setting the parameters used for:

- *Data cache*. The data cache must be set large enough to permit as many data requests to be serviced from the cache as possible. Each DBMS has settings that control the size of the data cache; this cache is shared among all database users. The majority of primary memory resources are allocated to the data cache.

- *SQL cache*. The SQL cache stores the most recently executed SQL statements (after the SQL statements have been parsed by the optimiser). Generally, if you have an application with multiple users accessing a database, the *same* query will likely be submitted by many different users. In these cases, the DBMS will parse the query only once and execute it many times, using the same access plan. In that way, the second and subsequent SQL requests for the same query are served from the SQL cache, skipping the parsing phase.
- *Sort cache*. The sort cache is used as a temporary storage area for ORDER BY or GROUP BY operations, as well as for index-creation functions.
- *Optimiser mode*. Most DBMSs operate in one of two optimisation modes: cost-based or rule-based. Others automatically determine the optimisation mode based on whether database statistics are available. For example, the DBA is responsible for generating the database statistics that are used by the cost-based optimiser. If the statistics are not available, the DBMS uses a rule-based optimiser.

From the performance point of view, it would be optimal to have the entire database stored in primary memory to minimise costly disk access. This is why several database vendors offer in-memory database options for their main products. **In-memory database** systems are optimised to store large portions (if not all) of the database in primary (RAM) storage rather than secondary (disk) storage. These systems are becoming popular because of increased performance demands from modern database applications (such as Business Analytics and Big Data), diminishing costs, and technology advances of components (such as flash memory and solid state drives). Even though these type of databases 'eliminate' disk access bottlenecks, they are still subject to query optimisation and performance tuning rules, especially when faced with poorly designed databases or poorly written SQL statements. Although in-memory databases are carving a niche in selected markets, most database implementations still rely on data stored on disk drives. That is why managing the physical storage details of the data files plays an important role in DBMS performance tuning. Note the following general recommendations for physical storage of databases:

- Use **I/O accelerators**. This type of device uses flash solid state drives (SSDs) to store the database. An SSD does not have any moving parts and, therefore performs I/O operations at a higher speed than traditional rotating disk drives. I/O accelerators deliver high transaction performance rates and reduce contention caused by typical storage drives.
- Use **RAID** (Redundant Array of Independent Disks) to provide balance between performance and fault tolerance. RAID systems use multiple disks to create virtual disks (storage volumes) formed by several individual disks. RAID systems provide performance improvement and fault tolerance. Table 13.7 shows the most common RAID configurations.

TABLE 13.7 Common RAID configurations

RAID Level	Description
0	The data blocks are spread over separate drives. Also known as a striped array. Provides increased performance but no fault tolerance. Fault tolerance means that, in case of failure, data could be reconstructed and retrieved. Requires a minimum of two drives.
1	The same data blocks are written (duplicated) to separate drives. Also referred to as mirroring or duplexing. Provides increased read performance and fault tolerance via data redundancy. Requires a minimum of two drives.

RAID Level	Description
3	The data are striped across separate drives, and parity data are computed and stored in a dedicated drive. Parity data are specially generated data that permit the reconstruction of corrupted or missing data. Provides good read performance and fault tolerance via parity data. Requires a minimum of three drives.
5	The data and the parity are striped across separate drives. Provides good read performance and fault tolerance via parity data. Requires a minimum of three drives.
1+0	The data blocks are spread over separate drives and mirrored. This arrangement provides both speed and fault tolerance. This is recommended RAID configuration for most database installations (if cost is not an issue).

- Minimise disk contention. Use multiple, independent storage volumes with independent spindles (a spindle is a rotating disk) to minimise hard disk cycles. Remember, a database is composed of many table spaces, each with a particular function. In turn, each table space is composed of several data files (in which the data are actually stored). A database should have at least the following table spaces:
  - *System table space*. Used to store the data dictionary tables. It is the most frequently accessed table space and should be stored in its own volume.
  - *User data table space*. Used to store end-user data. You should create as many user data table spaces and data files as are required. You can create and assign a different user data table space for each application and/or for each group of users.
  - *Index table space*. Used to store indexes. You can create and assign a different index table space for each application and/or for each group of users. The index table space data files should be stored on a storage volume that is separate from user data files or system data files.
  - *Temporary table space*. Used as a temporary storage area for merge, sort or set aggregate operations. You can create and assign a different temporary table space for each application and/or for each group of users.
  - *Rollback segment table space*. Used for transaction-recovery purposes.
- Put high-usage tables in their own table spaces. By doing this, the database minimises conflict with other tables.
- Take advantage of the various table storage organisations available in the database. For example, in Oracle, consider the use of index-organised tables (IOT); in SQL Server, consider clustered index tables. An **index-organised table** (or **clustered index table**) is a table that stores the end-user data and the index data in consecutive locations on permanent storage. This type of storage organisation provides a performance advantage to tables that are commonly accessed through a given index order, because the index contains the index key as well as the data rows. Therefore, the DBMS tends to perform fewer I/O operations.
- Assign separate files in separate storage volumes for the indexes, system and high-usage tables. This ensures that index operations will not conflict with end-user data or data dictionary table access operations.
- Partition tables based on usage. Some RDBMSs support horizontal partitioning of tables based on attributes. (See Chapter 14, Distributed Databases.) By doing so, a single SQL request could be processed by multiple data processors. Put the table partitions closest to where they are used the most.

- Use denormalised tables where appropriate. Another performance-improving technique involves taking a table from a higher normal form to a lower normal form – typically, from third to second normal form. This technique causes data duplication, but it minimises join operations. (Denormalisation was discussed in Chapter 7, Normalising Database Designs.)
- Store computed and aggregate attributes in tables. In short, use derived attributes in your tables. For example, you might add the invoice subtotal, the amount of tax and the total in the INVOICE table. Using derived attributes minimises computations in queries and join operations.

13.8 QUERY OPTIMISATION EXAMPLE

Now that you have learnt the basis of query optimisation, you are ready to test your new knowledge. Let's use a simple example to illustrate how the query optimiser works and how you can help it do its work. The example is based on the QOVENDOR and QOPRODUCT tables. Those tables are similar to the ones you used in previous chapters. However, the QO prefix is used for the table name to ensure that you do not overwrite previous tables.

Online Content The databases and scripts used in this chapter can be found on the online platform for this book.

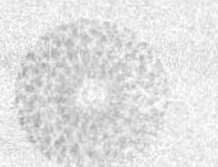

To perform this query optimisation illustration, you will be using the Oracle SQL*Plus interface. Some preliminary work must be done before you can start testing query optimisation. The following steps will guide you through this preliminary work:

1. Log in to Oracle SQL*Plus. using the username and password provided by your instructor.
2. Create a fresh set of tables, using the QRYOPTDATA.SQL script file located on the online platform for this book. This step is necessary so that Oracle has a new set of tables and the new tables contain no statistics. At the SQL> prompt, type:

   @path\ QRYOPTDATA.SQL

   where *path* is the location of the file in your computer.
3. Create the PLAN_TABLE. The PLAN_TABLE is a special table used by Oracle to store the access plan information for a given query. End users can then query the PLAN_TABLE to see how Oracle will execute the query. To create the PLAN_TABLE, run the UTLXPLAN.SQL script file located in the RDBMS\ADMIN folder of your Oracle RDBMS installation. The UTLXPLAN.SQL script file is also found on the online platform for this book. At the SQL prompt, type:

   @path\UTLXPLAN.SQL

You use the EXPLAIN PLAN command to store the execution plan of a SQL query in the PLAN_TABLE. Then, you would use the SELECT * FROM TABLE(DBMS_XPLAN.DISPLAY) command to display the access plan for a given SQL statement.

> **NOTE**
>
> Oracle, MySQL and SQL server all default to cost-based optimisation. In Oracle, if table statistics are not available, the DBMS will fall back to a rule-based optimiser. The examples in this section were generated using ORACLE 11g through the Oracle SQL*Plus interface. The examples will give different outputs depending on the version of ORACLE you are using.

To see the access plan used by the DBMS to execute your query, use the EXPLAIN PLAN and SELECT statements as shown in Figure 13.3. Then, you use the SELECT * FROM TABLE (DBMS_XPLAN. DISPLAY) command to display the access plan for a given SQL statement.

Note that the first SQL statement generates the statistics for the QOVENDOR table. Also, the initial access plan in Figure 13.3 uses a full table scan on the QOVENDOR table, and the cost of the plan is 3.

FIGURE 13.3 **INITIAL EXPLAIN PLAN (Oracle 11g)**

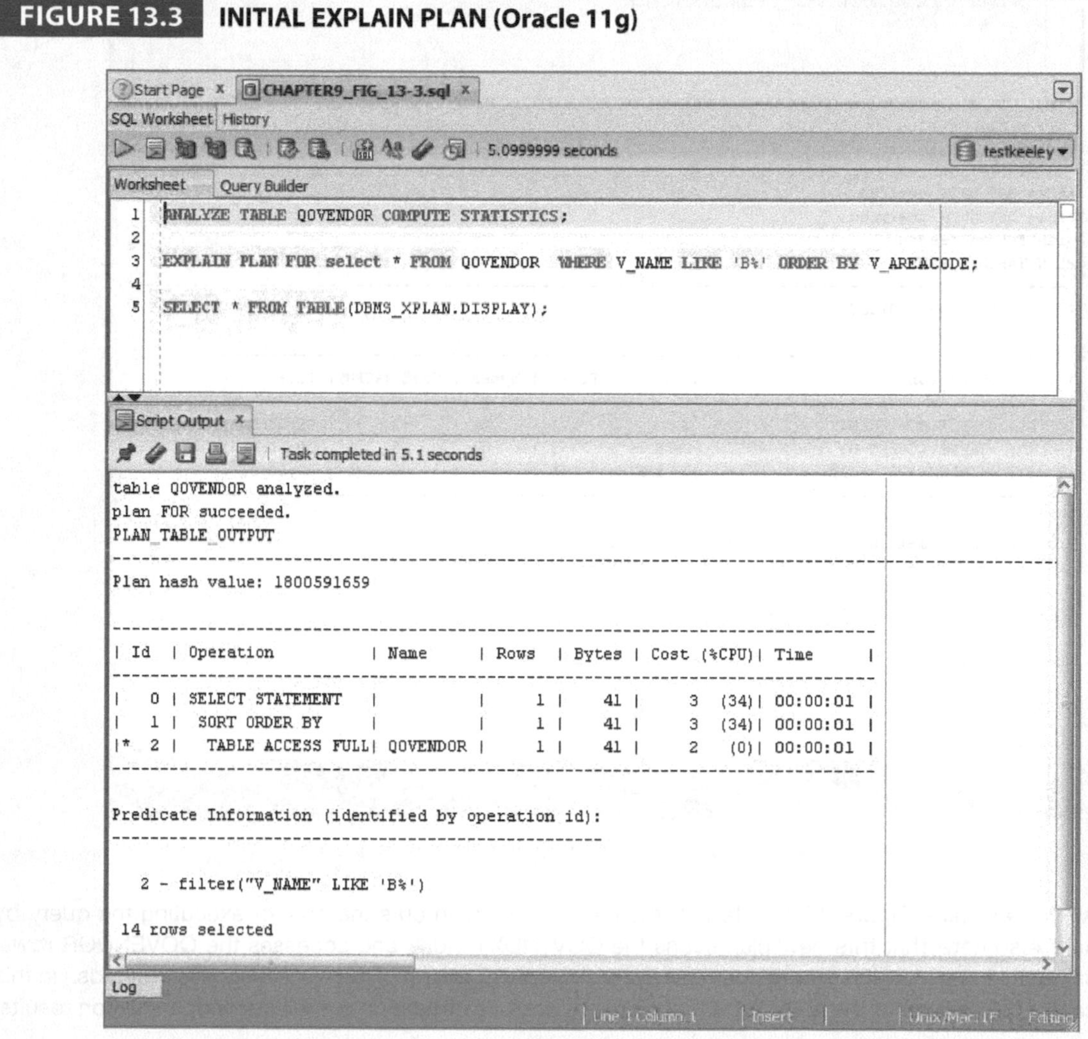

Let's now create an index on V_AREACODE (note that V_AREACODE is used in the ORDER BY clause) and see how that affects the access plan generated by the cost-based optimiser. The results are shown in Figure 13.4.

FIGURE 13.4 EXPLAIN PLAN after index on V_AREACODE (Oracle 11g)

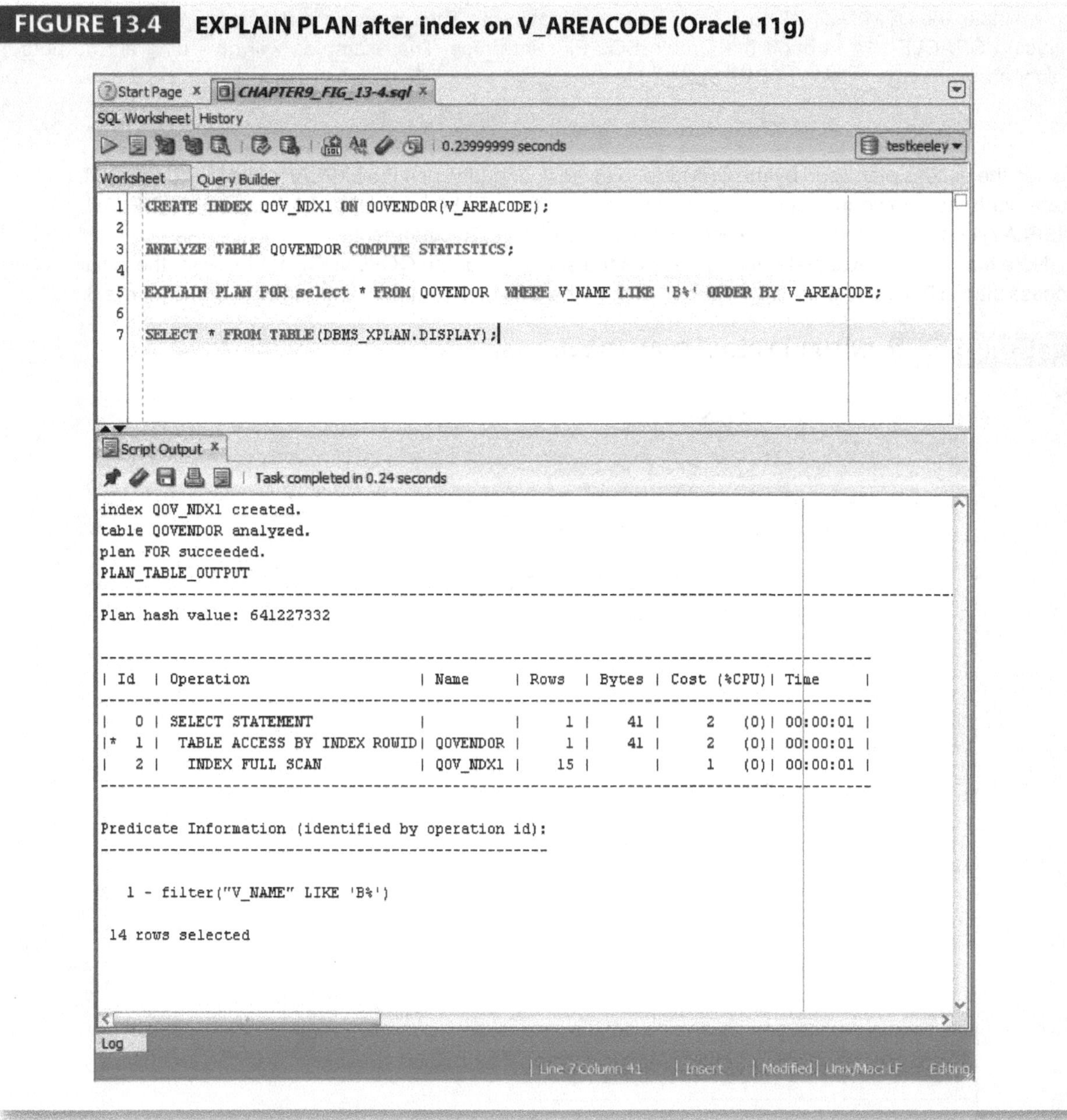

As you examine Figure 13.4, note that the new access plan cuts the cost of executing the query by half! Also note that this new plan scans the QOV_NDX1 index and accesses the QOVENDOR rows, using the index row ID. (Remember that access by row ID is one of the fastest access methods.) In this case, the creation of the QOV_NDX1 index had a positive impact on overall query optimisation results.

At other times, indexes do not necessarily help in query optimisation. This is the case when you have indexes on small tables or when the query accesses a high percentage of table rows anyway. Let's see what happens when you create an index on V_NAME. The new access plan is shown in Figure 13.5. (Note that V_NAME is used on the WHERE clause as a conditional expression operand.)

FIGURE 13.5 EXPLAIN PLAN after index on V_NAME (Oracle 11g)

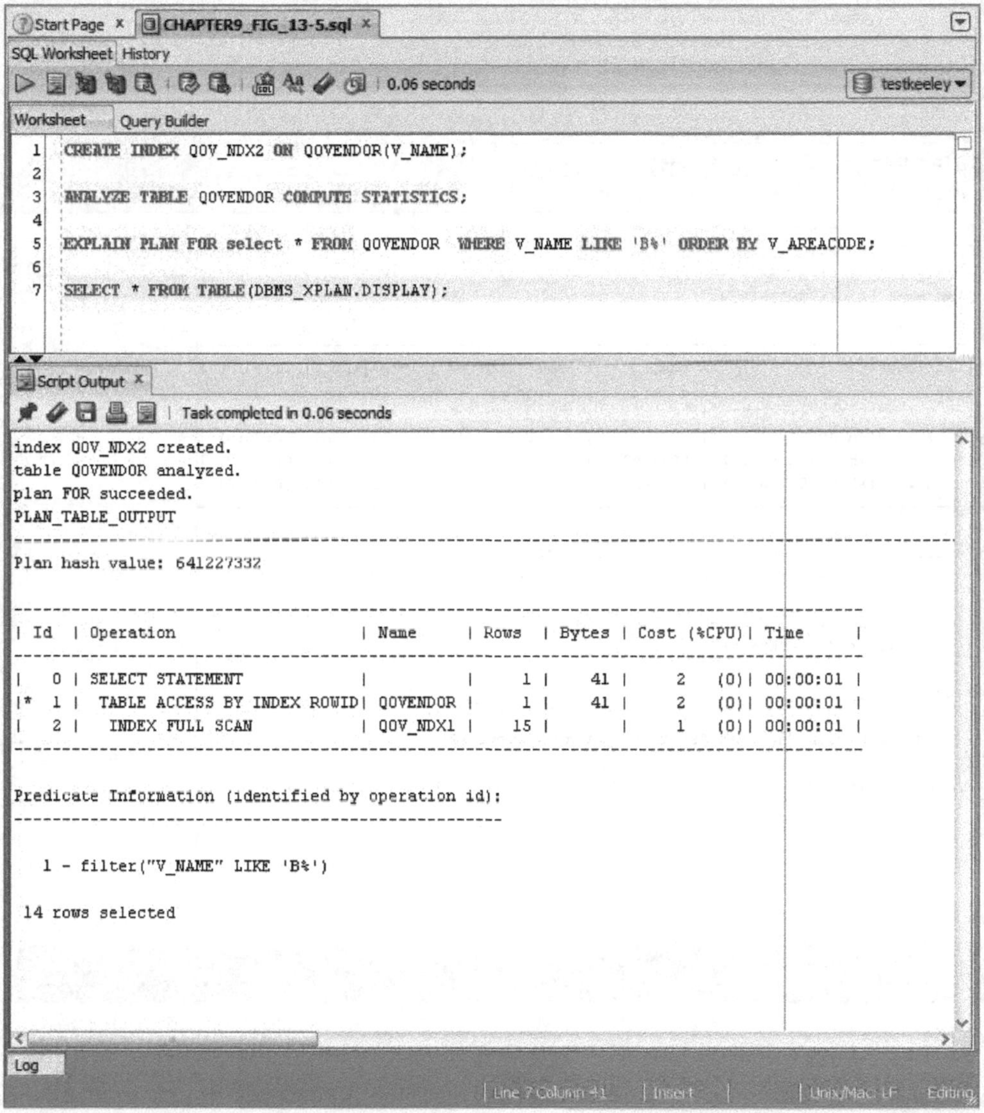

```
CREATE INDEX QOV_NDX2 ON QOVENDOR(V_NAME);

ANALYZE TABLE QOVENDOR COMPUTE STATISTICS;

EXPLAIN PLAN FOR select * FROM QOVENDOR WHERE V_NAME LIKE 'B%' ORDER BY V_AREACODE;

SELECT * FROM TABLE(DBMS_XPLAN.DISPLAY);
```



```
index QOV_NDX2 created.
table QOVENDOR analyzed.
plan FOR succeeded.
PLAN_TABLE_OUTPUT
-----------------------------------------------------------------------------------
Plan hash value: 641227332

-----------------------------------------------------------------------------------
| Id  | Operation                    | Name     | Rows  | Bytes | Cost (%CPU)| Time     |
-----------------------------------------------------------------------------------
|   0 | SELECT STATEMENT             |          |     1 |    41 |     2   (0)| 00:00:01 |
|*  1 |  TABLE ACCESS BY INDEX ROWID| QOVENDOR |     1 |    41 |     2   (0)| 00:00:01 |
|   2 |   INDEX FULL SCAN            | QOV_NDX1 |    15 |       |     1   (0)| 00:00:01 |
-----------------------------------------------------------------------------------

Predicate Information (identified by operation id):
---------------------------------------------------

   1 - filter("V_NAME" LIKE 'B%')

 14 rows selected
```


As you can see in Figure 13.5, creation of the second index did not help the query optimisation. However, there are occasions when an index could be used by the optimiser, but it is not selected because of the way in which the query is written. For example, Figure 13.6 shows the access plan for a different query using the V_NAME column.

FIGURE 13.6 ACCESS PLAN using index on V_NAME (Oracle 11g)

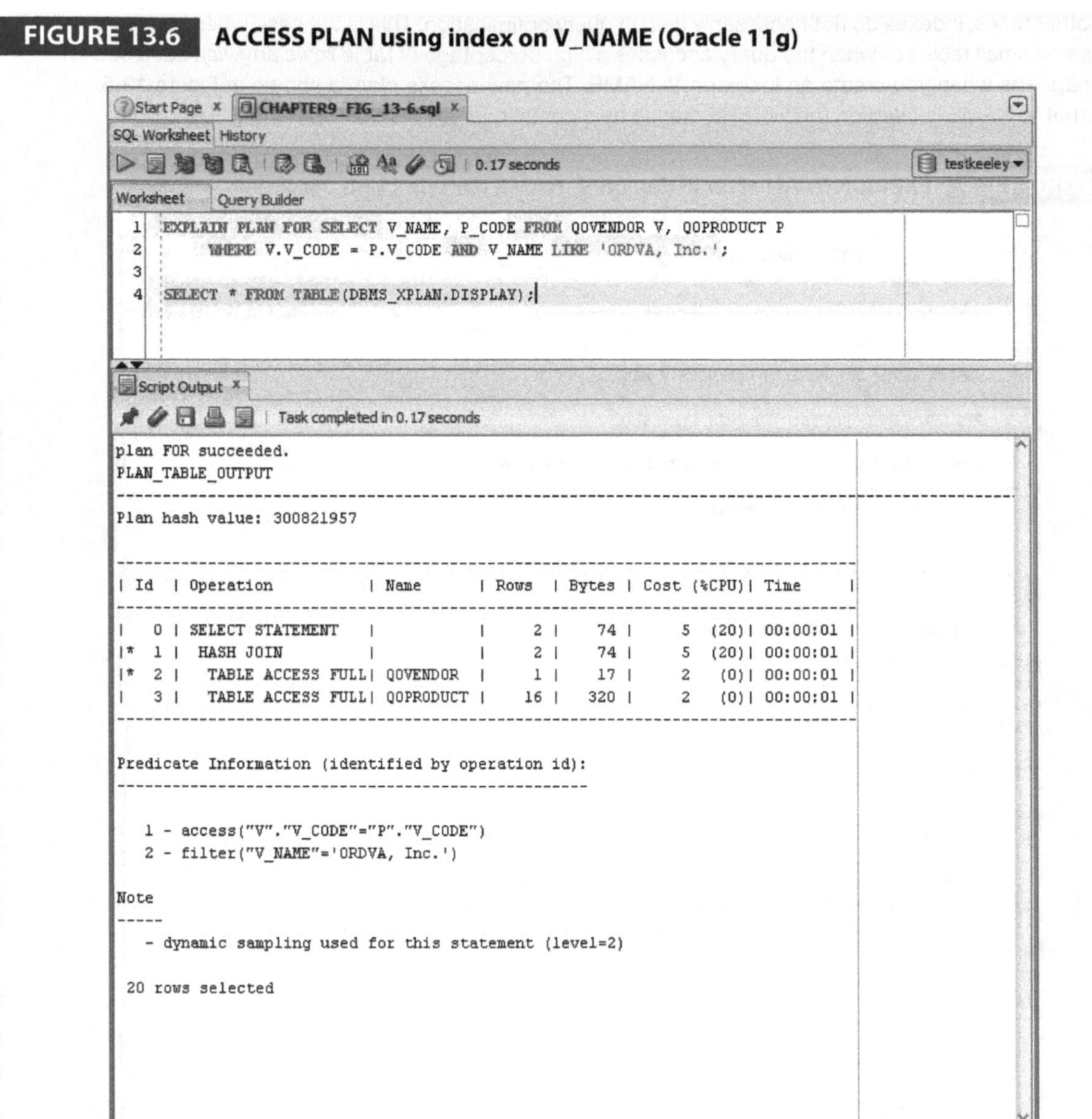

In Figure 13.6, note that the access plan for this new query uses the QOV_NDX2 index on the V_NAME column.

Let's now use the table QOPRODUCT to demonstrate how an index can help when aggregate function queries are being run. For example, Figure 13.7 shows the access plan for a SELECT statement using the MAX(P_PRICE) aggregate function. Note that this plan uses a full table scan with a total cost of 3.

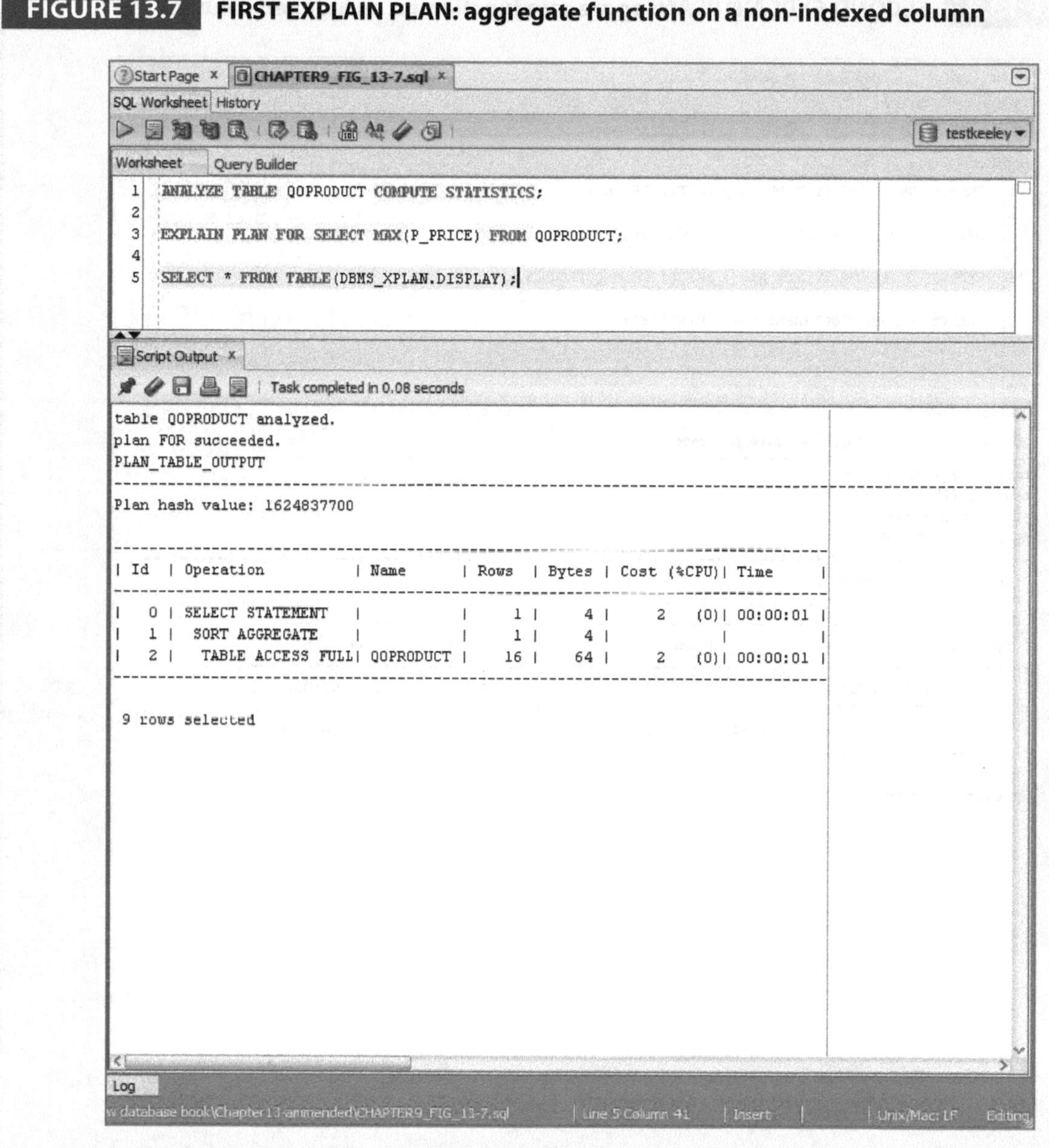

FIGURE 13.7 **FIRST EXPLAIN PLAN: aggregate function on a non-indexed column**

A cost of 2 is very low already, but could you improve it? Yes, you could improve the previous query performance by creating an index on P_PRICE. Figure 13.8 shows how the plan cost is reduced by two-thirds after the index is created and the QOPRODUCT table is analysed. Also note that the second version of the access plan uses only the index QOP_NDX2 to answer the query; *the QOPRODUCT table* is *never accessed*.

FIGURE 13.8 SECOND EXPLAIN PLAN: aggregate function on an indexed column

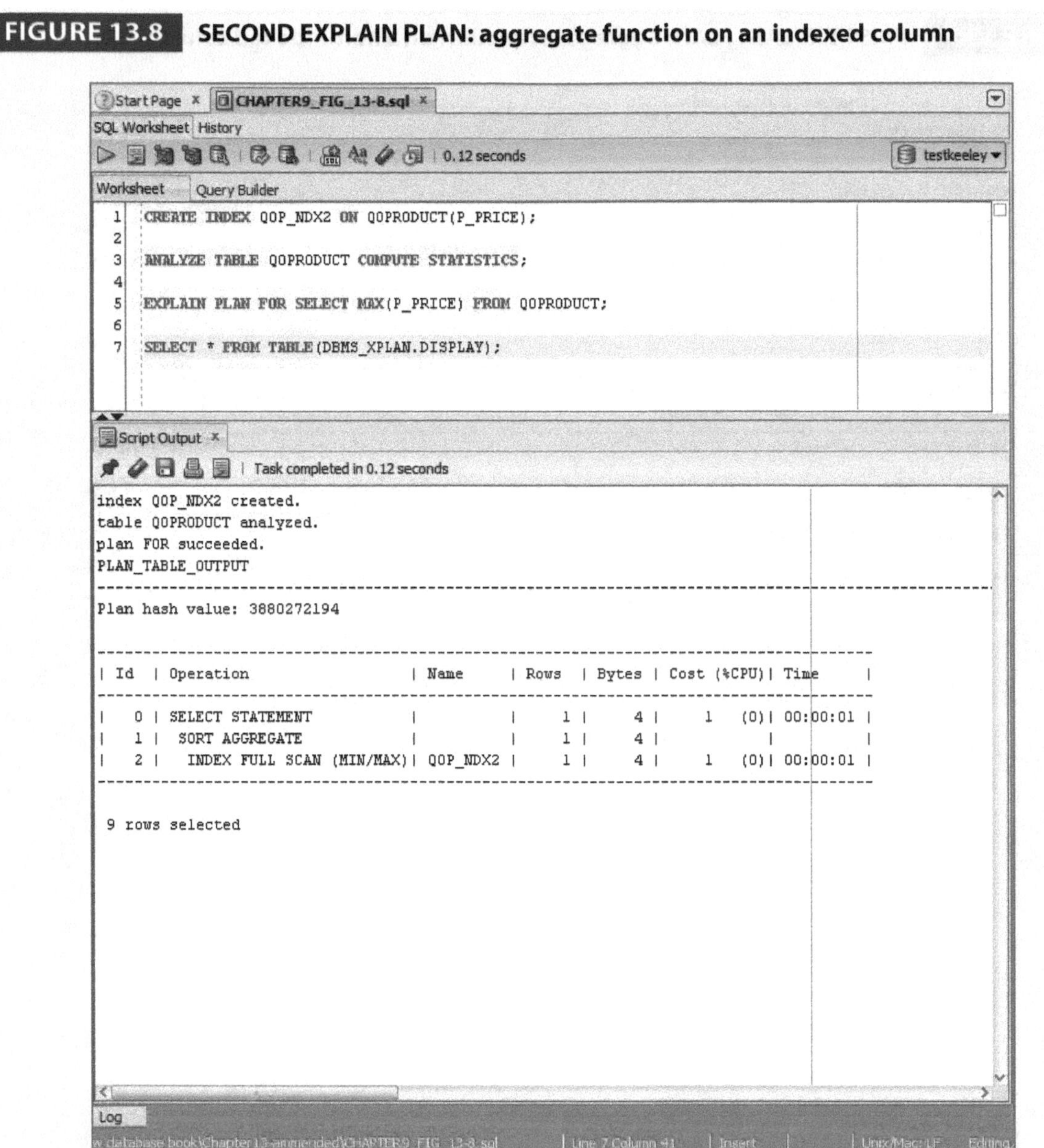

Although the few examples in this section show how important proper index selection is for query optimisation, you also saw examples in which index creation does not improve query performance. As a DBA, you should be aware that the main goal is to optimise overall database performance – not just for a single query, but for all requests and query types. Most database systems provide advanced graphical tools for performance monitoring and testing.

SUMMARY

- Database performance tuning refers to a set of activities and procedures designed to ensure that an end-user query is processed by the DBMS in the minimum amount of time.
- SQL performance tuning refers to the activities on the client side designed to generate SQL code that returns the correct answer in the least amount of time, using the fewest resources at the server end.
- DBMS performance tuning refers to activities on the server side orientated to ensure that the DBMS is properly configured to respond to clients' requests in the fastest way possible while making optimum use of existing resources.
- Database statistics refers to a number of measurements gathered by the DBMS that describe a snapshot of the database objects' characteristics. The DBMS gathers statistics about objects such as tables, indexes, and available resources such as number of processors used, processor speed and temporary space available. The DBMS uses the statistics to make critical decisions about improving the query processing efficiency.
- The DBMS processes queries in three phases:
  - *Parsing*. The DBMS parses the SQL query and chooses the most efficient access/execution plan.
  - *Execution*. The DBMS executes the SQL query, using the chosen execution plan.
  - *Fetching*. The DBMS fetches the data and sends the result set back to the client.
- Indexes are crucial to the process that speeds up data access and should be carefully selected during physical database design in order to facilitate the searching, sorting and use of aggregate functions and join operations.
- During query optimisation, the DBMS must choose which indexes to use, how to perform join operations, which table to use first, and so on. Each DBMS has its own algorithms for determining the most efficient way to access the data. The two most common approaches are rule-based optimisation and cost-based optimisation.
- A rule-based optimiser uses a set of preset rules and points to determine the best approach to execute a query. The rules assign a 'fixed cost' to each SQL operation; the costs are then added to yield the cost of the execution plan.
- A cost-based optimiser uses sophisticated algorithms based on the statistics about the objects being accessed to determine the best approach to execute a query. In this case, the optimiser process adds up the processing cost, the I/O costs and the resource costs (RAM and temporary space) to come up with the total cost of a given execution plan. 13
- Hints are used to change the optimiser mode for the current SQL statement. Hints are special instructions for the optimiser that are embedded inside the SQL command text.
- SQL performance tuning deals with writing queries that make good use of the statistics. In particular, queries should make good use of indexes. Indexes are very useful when you want to select a small subset of rows from a large table based on a condition. When an index exists for the column used in the selection, the DBMS may choose to use it. The objective is to create indexes with high selectivity. Index selectivity is a measure of how likely an index will be used in query processing.

- Query formulation deals with how to translate business questions into specific SQL code to generate the required results. To do this, you must carefully evaluate which columns, tables and computations are required to generate the desired output.
- DBMS performance tuning includes tasks such as managing the DBMS processes in primary memory (allocating memory for caching purposes) and the structures in physical storage (allocating space for the data files).

KEY TERMS

access/execution plan
automatic query optimisation
cluster-indexed table
cost-based optimiser
data cache or buffer cache
data files
database performance tuning
DBMS performance tuning
dynamic statistical generation mode
dynamic query optimisation
extends
index-organised table
index selectivity
in-memory database
input/output (I/O) request
I/O accelerators
manual statistical generation mode
optimiser hints
query optimiser
query processing bottleneck
RAID
rule-based optimiser
rule-based query optimisation algorithm
SQL cache or procedure cache
SQL performance tuning
static query optimisation
statistically based query optimisation algorithm
table space or file group

Online Content Answers to selected Review Questions and Problems for this chapter are contained on the online platform accompanying this book.

FURTHER READING

Fritchey, G. *SQL Server 2017 Query Performance Tuning: Troubleshoot and Optimize Query Performance*, 5th edition. Apress, 2018.

Niemiec, R. *Oracle Database 12c Release 2 Performance Tuning Tips & Techniques*, Oracle Press, 2017.

REVIEW QUESTIONS

13

1 What is SQL performance tuning?

2 What is database performance tuning?

3 What is the focus of most performance-tuning activities, and why does that focus exist?

4 What are database statistics, and why are they important?

5 How are database statistics obtained?

6 Which database statistics measurements are typical of tables, indexes and resources?

7 How is the processing of SQL DDL statements (such as CREATE TABLE) different from the processing required by DML statements?

8 In simple terms, the DBMS processes queries in three phases. What are those phases, and what is accomplished in each phase?

9 If indexes are so important, why not index every column in every table?

10 What is the difference between a rule-based optimiser and a cost-based optimiser?

11 What are optimiser hints, and how are they used?

12 Most of the query optimisation techniques are designed to make the optimiser's work easier. Which factors should you keep in mind if you intend to write conditional expressions in SQL code?

13 Which recommendations would you make for managing the data files in a DBMS with many tables and indexes?

14 What does RAID stand for, and what are some commonly used RAID levels?

PROBLEMS

Find the solutions to Problems 1 to 3 based on the following query:

```
SELECT    EMP_LNAME, EMP_FNAME, EMP_AREACODE, EMP_GENDER
FROM      EMPLOYEE
WHERE     EMP_GENDER = 'F' AND EMP_AREACODE = '0181'
ORDERBY EMP_LNAME, EMP_FNAME;
```

1 What is the likely sparsity of the EMP_GENDER column?

2 Which indexes should you create? Write the required SQL commands.

3 Using Table 13.4 as an example, create two alternative access plans. Use the following assumptions:

- a There are 8 000 employees.
- b There are 4 150 female employees.
- c There are 370 employees in area code 0181.
- d There are 190 female employees in area code 0181.

Problems 4 to 6 are based on the following query:

```
SELECT    EMP_LNAME, EMP_FNAME, EMP_DOB, YEAR(EMP_DOB) AS YEAR
FROM      EMPLOYEE
WHERE     YEAR(EMP_DOB) = 1976;
```

4 4 What is the likely data sparsity of the EMP-DOB column?

5 5 Should you create an index on EMP_DOB? Why or why not?

6 What type of database I/O operations will likely be used by the query? (See Table 13.3.)

13

Problems 7 to 10 are based on the ER model shown in Figure P13.1. Given the following query:

```
SELECT    P_CODE, P_PRICE
FROM      PRODUCT
WHERE     P_PRICE >= (SELECT AVG(P_PRICE) FROM PRODUCT);
```

7 Assuming that there are no table statistics, what type of optimisation will the DBMS use?

8 What type of database I/O operations will likely be used by the query? (See Figure P13.1.)

9 What is the likely data sparsity of the P_PRICE column?

10 Should you create an index? Why or why not?

FIGURE P13.1 **The Ch11-SaleCo ER model**

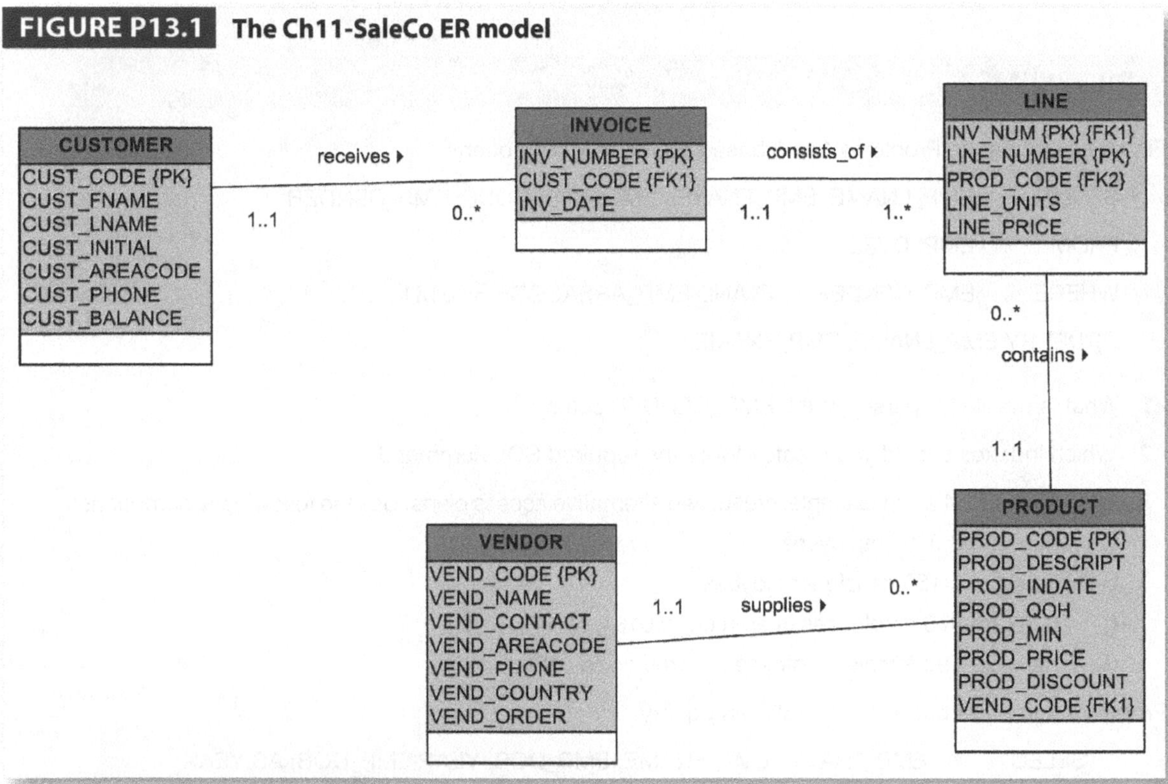

Problems 11 to 14 are based on the following query:

```
SELECT    P_CODE, SUM(LINE_UNITS)
FROM      LINE
GROUPBY   P_CODE
HAVING    SUM(LINE_UNITS) > (SELECT MAX(LINE_UNITS) FROM LINE);
```

11 What is the likely data sparsity of the LINE_UNITS column?

12 Should you create an index? If so, what would the index column(s) be, and why would you create the index? If not, explain your reasoning.

13 Discuss whether or not you should create an index on P_CODE. Justify your answer.

14 Write the command to create statistics for this table.

Problems 15 to 19 are based on the following query:

```
SELECT     V_CODE, V_NAME, V_CONTACT, V_COUNTRY
FROM       VENDOR
WHERE      V_COUNTRY = 'UK'
ORDERBY    V_NAME;
```

15 Which indexes should you create and why? Write the SQL command to create the indexes.

16 Assume that 10 000 vendors are distributed as shown in the table below. What percentage of rows will be returned by the query?

Country	Number of Vendors	Country	Number of Vendors
AB	15	HG	47
AN	55	IC	358
AU	100	IT	25
BE	3244	LV	645
BL	345	LC	16
BH	995	LT	821
BU	75	LX	62
CR	68	MC	425
CY	89	MO	12
CR	12	MN	65
DK	19	NL	74
ES	45	NW	113
FI	29	PL	589
FR	208	SA	36
GM	745	UK	375
GR	35	VC	258

17 What type of I/O database operations would most likely be used to execute that query?

18 Using Table 13.4 as an example, create two alternative access plans.

13

19 Assume that you have 10 000 different products stored in the PRODUCT table and that you are writing a Web-based interface to list all products with a quantity on hand (P_QOH) that is less than or equal to the minimum quantity, P_MIN. Which optimiser hint would you use to ensure that your query returns the result set to the Web interface in the least time possible? Write the SQL code.

Problems 20 to 21 are based on the following query:

```
SELECT      P_CODE, P_DESCRIPT, P_PRICE, P.V_CODE, V_COUNTRY
FROM        PRODUCT P, VENDOR V
WHERE       P.V_CODE = V.V_CODE
AND         V_COUNTRY= 'UK'
AND         V_AREACODE = '0181'
ORDER BY    P_PRICE;
```

20 Which indexes would you recommend?

21 Write the command(s) used to generate the statistics for the PRODUCT and VENDOR tables.

Problems 22 and 23 are based on the following query:

```
SELECT      P_CODE, P_DESCRIPT, P_QOH, P_PRICE, V_CODE
FROM        PRODUCT
WHERE       V_CODE = '21344'
ORDER BY    P_CODE;
```

22 Which index would you recommend, and which command would you use?

23 How should you rewrite the query to ensure that it uses the index you created in your solution to Problem 22?

Problems 24 and 25 are based on the following query:

```
SELECT      P_CODE, P_DESCRIPT, P_QOH, P_PRICE, V_CODE
FROM        PRODUCT
WHERE       P_QOH < P_MIN
AND         P_MIN = P_REORDER
AND         P_REORDER = 50
ORDER BY    P_QOH;
```


24 Use the recommendations given in Section 13.5.2 to rewrite the query to produce the required results more efficiently.

25 Which indexes would you recommend?

Problems 26 to 29 are based on the following query:

```
SELECT    CUS_CODE, MAX(LINE_UNITS*LINE_PRICE)
FROM      CUSTOMER NATURAL JOIN INVOICE NATURAL JOIN LINE
WHERE     CUS_AREACODE = '0181'
GROUPBY   CUS_CODE;
```

26 Assuming that you generate 15 000 invoices per month, what recommendation would you give the designer about the use of derived attributes?

27 Assuming that you follow the recommendations you gave in Problem 26, how would you rewrite the query?

28 Which indexes would you recommend for the query you wrote in Problem 27, and what SQL commands would you use?

29 How would you rewrite the query to ensure that the index you created in Problem 28 is used?

Part VI

DATABASE MANAGEMENT

BUSINESS VIGNETTE

THE FACEBOOK–CAMBRIDGE ANALYTICA DATA SCANDAL AND THE GDPR

In 2018, Facebook faced international investigations into illegally collecting users' personal data. The data was collected by Cambridge Analytica, which was a political consultation company that supported President Trump's 2016 election campaign. It was suggested that Cambridge Analytica had collected data from up to 87 million users across the globe and then used this data: firstly, to profile the candidate people were likely to vote for in the US election, and secondly, to target advertisements at users to try to influence who they would vote for. The data was collected through a Facebook app called 'thisisyourdigitallife', where users consented to take part in a personality study. However, the app also extracted personal data from linked Facebook friends without their consent. However, all the data obtained was used without knowledge to develop a software program to influence the US elections, which was sold to Trump campaigners. The major concern, even today, is that Facebook does not know which data the app shared with Cambridge Analytica.

In 2019, lawsuits against Facebook continue, with US judges requesting that all Facebook's data privacy records be made available after the company's lawyers argued that users 'have no expectation of privacy'. What this scandal demonstrated was the power of Big Data analytics and how collecting personal data to profile individuals for the purpose of automated profiling could be used to mislead people and generate fake news. It raises a debate about giving a company consent to collect your personal data and what exactly this data will be used for. In the field of data mining – where hidden patterns are discovered in data that can be used to make inferences about a person's behaviour and perform predictive analytics – new knowledge can be discovered about a person that he or she does not even know about. So, this raises the questions: Who owns this knowledge, and was consent ever obtained to use it for a purpose unknown at the time of collection?

Better protection for users of data is now in place, thanks to the General Data Protection Regulation (GDPR),[1] which become a legal requirement for all organisations in Europe from 25 May 2018, that collect and process data. One of the major changes detailed in Article 22 of the GDPR includes the rights of an individual not to be subject to automated decision making, which includes profiling, unless explicit consent is given. Article 4(4) of the GDPR defines which forms of data processing could be considered 'profiling'. This includes any form of automated processing of personal data, and utilising this personal data to evaluate certain personal aspects relating to a natural person – for example, analysing or predicting 'aspects concerning that natural person's performance at work, economic situation, health, personal preferences, interests, reliability, behaviour, location or movements'.[1] Recital 71 provides a lengthy definition of what is meant by the term profiling especially in relation to any personal aspect 'concerning the data subject's performance at work, economic situation, health, personal preferences or interests, reliability or behaviour, location or movements, where it produces legal effects concerning him or her or similarly significantly affects him or her'. The penalty for an organisation that breaches the regulation is a fine of up to 4 per cent of annual global turnover or €20 million (whichever is greater).[1] Given that the GDPR applies to all organisations and companies that process the personal data of European Union citizens, the challenge will be to ensure that all organisations know exactly what personal data they store and where it is stored, and ensure they have the consent to use it for the purpose for which it was collected. Could the GDPR have stopped the Cambridge Analytica scandal? It is unlikely, but if the news had broken two months later then Facebook might now be facing fines for violation of GDPR rules.

14

1 The GDPR Portal (2019), [online]. Available: https://eugdpr.org/

CHAPTER 14

Distributed Databases

IN THIS CHAPTER, YOU WILL LEARN:

- What a distributed database management system (DDBMS) is and what its components are
- How database implementation is affected by different levels of data and process distribution
- How transactions are managed in a distributed database environment
- How database design is affected by the distributed database environment

PREVIEW

A single database can be divided into several fragments. The fragments can be stored on different computers within a network. Processing, too, can be dispersed among several different network sites, or nodes. The multi-site database forms the core of the distributed database system.

The growth of distributed database management systems has been fostered by the increased globalisation of business operations, the growth of Big Data and technological changes that have made distributed network-based services practical. more reliable and cost effective.

The distributed database management system (DDBMS) treats a distributed database as a single logical database; therefore, the basic design concepts you learnt in earlier chapters apply. However, the distribution of data among different sites in a computer network clearly adds to a system's complexity. For example, the design of a distributed database must consider the location of the data and the partitioning of the data into database fragments, and replication of those fragments. In today's Web-centric environment, any distributed data system must be highly scalable; in other words, it must grow dynamically as demand increases. As demand grows, so do the system's processing needs and inherent complexity. To accommodate such dynamic growth, trade-offs must be made to achieve some desirable properties.

14.1 THE EVOLUTION OF DISTRIBUTED DATABASE MANAGEMENT SYSTEMS

A **distributed database management system** (**DDBMS**) governs the storage and processing of logically related data over interconnected computer systems in which both data and processing functions are distributed among several sites. To understand how and why the DDBMS is different from the DBMS, it is useful to examine briefly the changes in the database environment that set the stage for the development of the DDBMS.

During the 1970s, corporations implemented centralised database management systems to meet their structured information needs. Structured information is usually presented as regularly issued formal reports in a standard format. Such information, generated by 3GL programming languages, is created by specialists in response to precisely channelled requests. Thus, structured information needs are well served by centralised systems.

Basically, the use of a centralised database required that corporate data be stored in a single central site, usually a mainframe or midrange computer. Data access was provided through dumb terminals. The centralised approach, illustrated in Figure 14.1, worked well to fill the structured information needs of corporations, but it fell short when quickly moving events required faster response times and equally quick access to information. The slow progression from information request to approval, to specialist, to user, simply did not serve decision makers well in a dynamic environment. What was needed was quick, unstructured access to databases, using ad hoc queries to generate on-the-spot information.

FIGURE 14.1 Centralised database management system

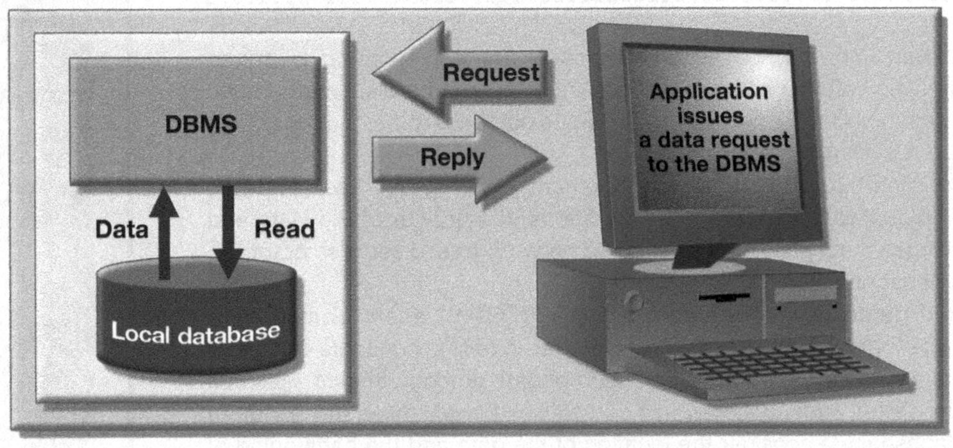

14

Database management systems based on the relational model could provide the environment in which unstructured information needs would be met by employing ad hoc queries. End users would be given the ability to access data when needed. Unfortunately, the early relational model implementations did not yet deliver acceptable throughput when compared to the well-established hierarchical or network database models.

The past three decades gave birth to a series of crucial social and technological changes that have affected database development and design. Among those changes were:

- Business operations became global; with this change, competition expanded from the shop on the next corner to the Web store in cyberspace.
- Customer demands and market needs favoured an on-demand transaction style, mostly based on Web-based services.
- Rapid social and technological changes fuelled by low-cost, smart mobile devices increased the demand for complex and fast networks to interconnect them. As a consequence, corporations have increasingly adopted advanced network technologies as the platform for their computerised solutions.
- Data realms are converging in the digital world more frequently. As a result, applications must manage multiple types of data, such as voice, video, music and images. Such data tend to be geographically distributed and remotely accessed from diverse locations via location-aware mobile devices.

These factors created a dynamic business environment in which companies had to respond quickly to competitive and technological pressures. As large business units restructured to form leaner-and-meaner, quickly reacting, dispersed operations, two database requirements became obvious:

- Rapid ad hoc data access became crucial in the quick-response decision-making environment.
- The decentralisation of management structures based on the decentralisation of business units made decentralised multiple-access and multiple-location databases a necessity.

During recent years, the factors just described became even more firmly entrenched. However, the way those factors were addressed was strongly influenced by:

- The growing acceptance of the internet – particularly, the World Wide Web (WWW – as the platform for data access and distribution. The WWW is, in effect, the *repository* for distributed data.
- The mobile wireless revolution. The widespread use of mobile wireless digital devices includes smartphones such as Apple's iPhone and Google's Pixel, and tablets such as Apple's iPad, and Samsung's Galaxy. These devices have created high demand for data access. They access data from geographically dispersed locations and require varied data exchanges in multiple formats, such as data, voice, video, music and pictures. Although distributed data access does not necessarily imply distributed databases, performance and failure tolerance requirements often lead to the use of data replication techniques similar to those in distributed databases.
- The accelerated growth of companies using 'applications as a service'. This new type of service provides remote applications to companies that want to outsource their application development, maintenance and operations. The company data are generally stored on central servers and are not necessarily distributed. Just as with mobile data access, this type of service may not require fully distributed data functionality; however, other factors such as performance and failure tolerance often require the use of data replication techniques similar to those in distributed databases.
- The increased focus on mobile business intelligence. More and more companies are embracing mobile technologies within their business plans. As companies use social networks to get closer to customers, the need for on-the-spot decision making increases. Although a data warehouse

is not usually a distributed database, it does rely on techniques such as data replication and distributed queries that facilitate data extraction and integration.

- Emphasis on Big Data analytics. The era of mobile communications gave us data from many sources and of many different data types. Today's customers have significant influence on the spending habits of communities, and organisations are investing in ways to harvest such data to 'discover' new ways to effectively and efficiently reach customers.

Online Content To learn more about the internet's impact on data access and distribution, see Appendix H, Databases in e-Commerce, available on the online platform for this book.

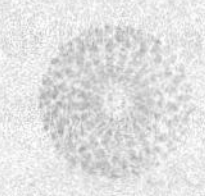

At this point in time, the long-term impact of the internet and the mobile revolution on *distributed* database design and management is unclear. Perhaps the internet and mobile technologies' success will foster the use of distributed databases as bandwidth becomes a more troublesome bottleneck. Perhaps the resolution of bandwidth problems will simply confirm the centralised database standard. In any case, distributed databases exist today and many distributed database operating concepts and components are likely to find a place in future database development.

The distributed database is especially desirable because centralised database management is subject to problems such as:

- *Performance degradation* due to a growing number of remote locations over greater distances
- *High costs* associated with maintaining and operating large central (mainframe) database systems
- *Reliability problems* created by dependence on a central site (single point of failure syndrome) and the need for data replication
- *Scalability problems* associated with the physical limits imposed by a single location, such as physical space, temperature conditioning and power consumption
- *Organisational rigidity* imposed by the database, which means it might not support the flexibility and agility required by modern global organisations.

The dynamic business environment and the centralised database's shortcomings spawned a demand for applications based on accessing data from different sources at multiple locations. Such a multiple-source/multiple-location database environment is managed by a DDBMS.

14

14.2 DDBMS ADVANTAGES AND DISADVANTAGES

Distributed database management systems deliver several advantages over traditional systems. At the same time, they are subject to some problems. Table 14.1 summarises the advantages and disadvantages associated with a DDBMS.

TABLE 14.1 Distributed DBMS advantages and disadvantages

Advantages	Disadvantages
■ *Data are located near the greatest demand site*. The data in a distributed database system are dispersed to match business requirements. ■ *Faster data access*. End users often work with only a locally stored subset of the company's data. ■ *Faster data processing*. A distributed database system spreads out the systems workload by processing data at several sites. ■ *Growth facilitation*. New sites can be added to the network without affecting the operations of other sites. ■ *Improved communications*. Because local sites are smaller and located closer to customers, local sites foster better communication among departments and between customers and company staff. ■ *Reduced operating costs*. It is more cost-effective to add workstations to a network than to update a mainframe system. Development work is done more cheaply and more quickly on low-cost PCs than on mainframes. ■ *User-friendly interface*. PCs and workstations are usually equipped with an easy-to-use graphical user interface (GUI). The GUI simplifies use and training for end users. ■ *Less danger of a single-point failure*. When one of the computers fails, the workload is picked up by other workstations. Data are also distributed at multiple sites. ■ *Processor independence*. The end user is able to access any available copy of the data, and an end user's request is processed by any processor at the data location.	■ *Complexity of management and control*. Applications must recognise data location, and they must be able to 'stitch' together data from different sites. Database administrators must have the ability to coordinate database activities to prevent database degradation due to data anomalies. Transaction management, concurrency control, security, backup, recovery, query optimisation, access path selection and so on, must all be addressed and resolved. ■ *Security*. The probability of security lapses increases when data are located at multiple sites. The responsibility of data management will be shared by different people at several sites. ■ *Lack of standards*. There are no standard communication protocols *at the database level*. For example, different database vendors employ different and often incompatible techniques to manage the distribution of data and processing in a DDBMS environment. ■ *Increased storage requirements*. Multiple copies of data are required at different sites, thus requiring additional disk storage space. ■ *Increased training cost*. Training costs are generally higher in a distributed model than they would be in a centralised model, sometimes even to the extent of offsetting operational and hardware savings. ■ *Higher costs*. Distributed databases require duplicated infrastructure to operate, such as physical location, environment, personnel, software and licensing.

Distributed databases are used successfully but have a long way to go before they can yield the full flexibility and power of which they are theoretically capable. The inherently complex distributed data environment increases the urgency for standard protocols governing transaction management, concurrency control, security, backup, recovery, query optimisation, access path selection, and so on. Such issues must be addressed and resolved before DDBMS technology is widely embraced.

The remainder of this chapter will explore the basic components and concepts of the distributed database. Because the distributed database is usually based on the relational database model, relational terminology is used to explain the basic distributed concepts and components.

14.3 DISTRIBUTED PROCESSING AND DISTRIBUTED DATABASES

In **distributed processing**, a database's logical processing is shared among two or more physically independent sites that are connected through a network. For example, the data input/output (I/O), data selection and data validation might be performed on one computer, and a report based on that data might be created on another computer.

A basic distributed processing environment is illustrated in Figure 14.2. It shows that a distributed processing system shares the database processing chores among three sites connected through a communications network. Although the database resides at only one site (London), each site can access the data and update the database. The database is located on Computer A, a network computer known as the *database server*.

FIGURE 14.2 Distributing processing environment

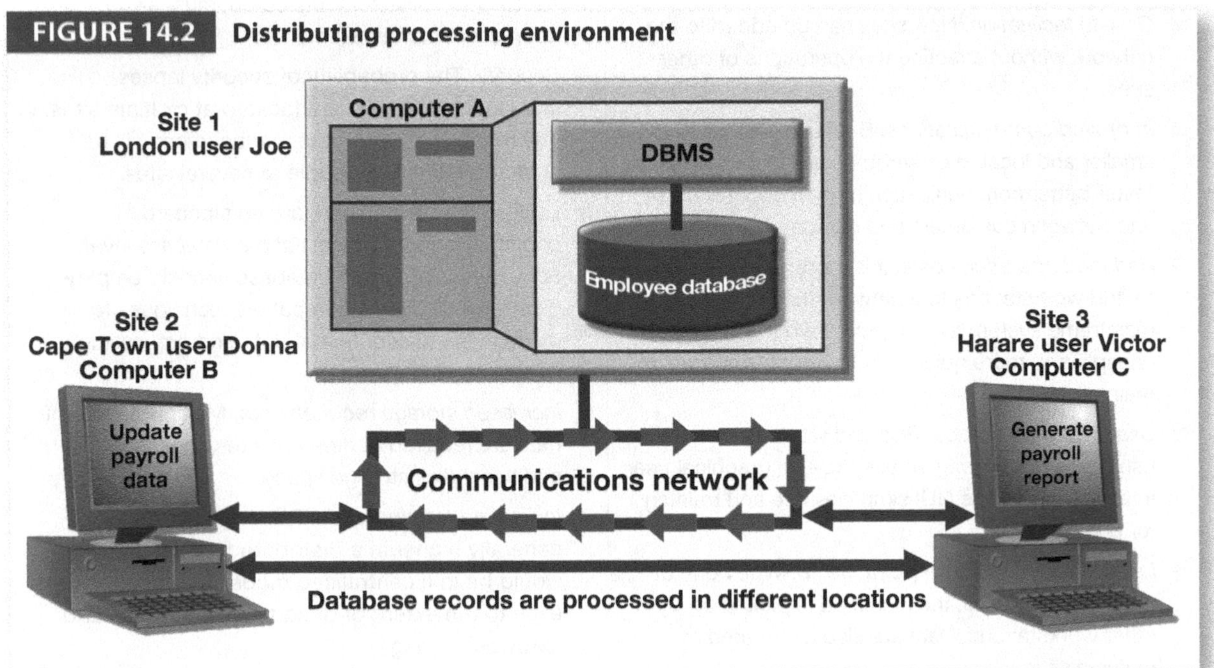

A **distributed database**, on the other hand, stores a logically related database over two or more physically independent sites. The sites are connected via a computer network. In contrast, the distributed processing system uses only a single-site database but shares the processing chores among several sites. In a distributed database system, a database is composed of several parts known as **database fragments**. The database fragments are located at different sites and can be replicated among various sites. An example of a distributed database environment is shown in Figure 14.3.

FIGURE 14.3 Distributed database environment

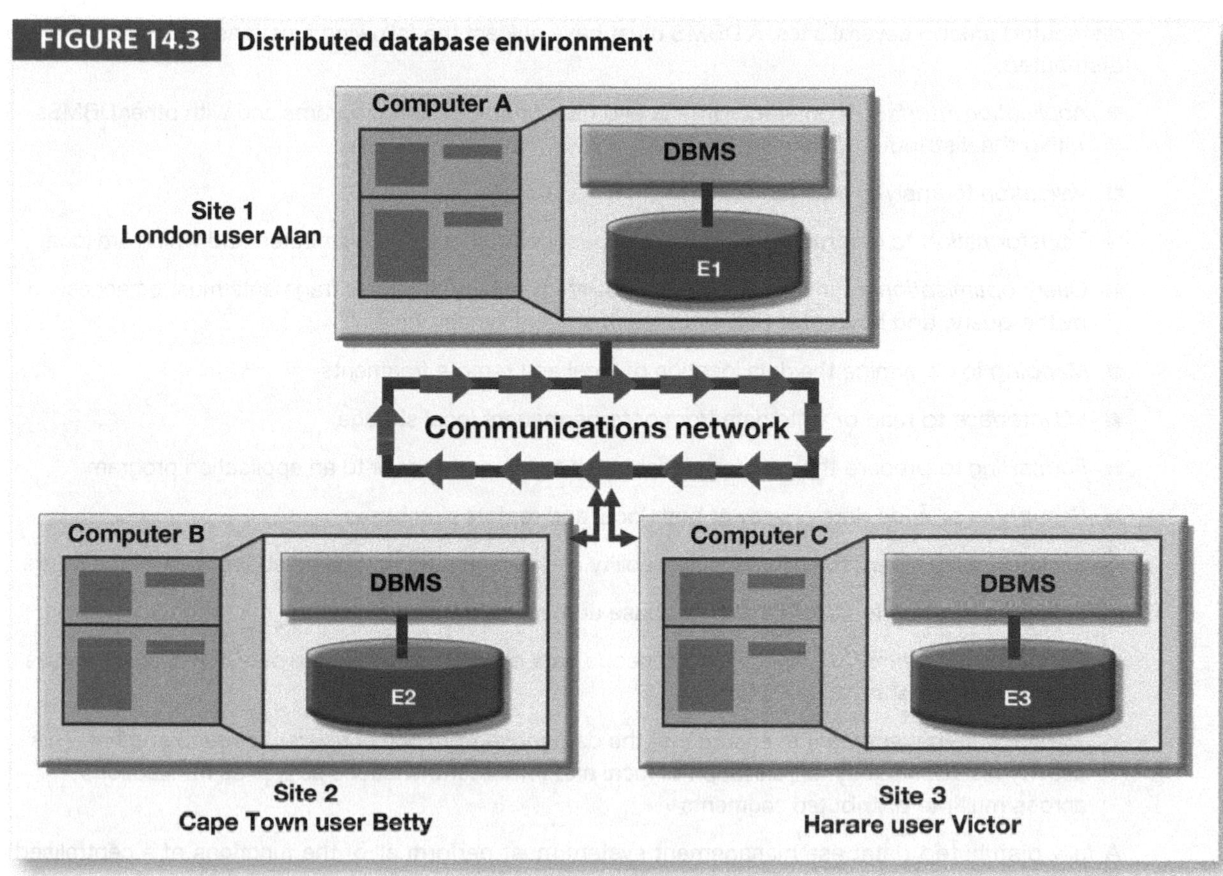

The database in Figure 14.3 is divided into three database fragments (E1, E2 and E3) located at different sites. The computers are connected through a network system. In a fully distributed database, the users Alan, Betty and Victor do not need to know the name or location of each database fragment in order to access the database. Also, the users may be located at sites other than London, Cape Town, or Harare, and still be able to access the database as a single logical unit.

As you examine and contrast Figures 14.2 and 14.3, you should keep the following points in mind:

- Distributed processing does not require a distributed database, but a distributed database requires distributed processing.
- Distributed processing may be based on a single database located on a single computer. For the management of distributed data to occur, copies or parts of the database processing functions must be distributed to all data storage sites.
- Both distributed processing and distributed databases require a network of interconnected components.

14

14.4 CHARACTERISTICS OF DISTRIBUTED DATABASE MANAGEMENT SYSTEMS

A distributed database management system (DDBMS) governs the storage and processing of logically related data over interconnected computer systems in which both data and processing functions are distributed among several sites. A DBMS must have at least the following functions to be classified as distributed:

- *Application interface* to interact with the end user or application programs and with other DBMSs within the distributed database
- *Validation* to analyse data requests
- *Transformation* to determine which data request components are distributed and which are local
- *Query optimisation* to find the best access strategy (which database fragments must be accessed by the query, and how must data updates, if any, be synchronised?)
- *Mapping* to determine the data location of local and remote fragments
- *I/O interface* to read or write data from or to permanent local storage
- *Formatting* to prepare the data for presentation to the end user or to an application program
- *Security* to provide data privacy at both local and remote databases
- *Backup and recovery* to ensure the availability and recoverability of the database in case of a failure
- *DB administration* features for the database administrator
- *Concurrency control* to manage simultaneous data access and to ensure data consistency across database fragments in the DDBMS
- *Transaction management* to ensure that the data move from one consistent state to another. This activity includes the synchronisation of local and remote transactions as well as transactions across multiple distributed segments

A fully distributed database management system must perform all of the functions of a centralised DBMS, as follows:

1. Receive an application's (or an end user's) request
2. Validate, analyse and decompose the request. The request may include mathematical and/or logical operations such as the following: 'Select all customers with balance greater than €1 000'. The request may require data from only a single table, or it may require access to several tables
3. Map the request's logical-to-physical data components
4. Decompose the request into several disk I/O operations
5. Search for, locate, read and validate the data
6. Ensure database consistency, security and integrity
7. Validate the data for the conditions, if any, specified by the request
8. Present the selected data in the required format

In addition, a distributed DBMS must handle all necessary functions imposed by the distribution of data and processing. And it must perform those additional functions *transparently* to the end user. The DDBMS's transparent data access features are illustrated in Figure 14.4.

FIGURE 14.4 **A fully distributed database management system**

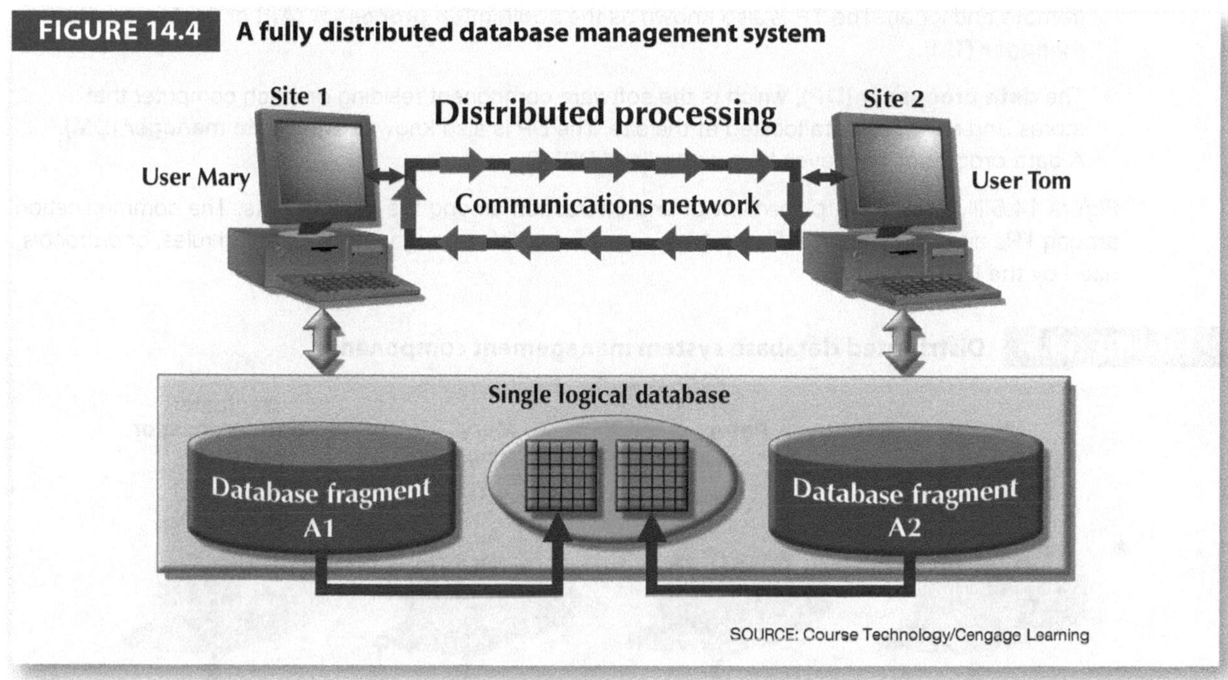

The single logical database in Figure 14.4 consists of two database fragments, A1 and A2, located at sites 1 and 2, respectively. Mary can query the database as if it were a local database; so can Tom. Both users 'see' only one logical database and *do not need to know the names of the fragments*. In fact, the end users do not even need to know that the database is divided into separate fragments, *nor do they need to know where the fragments are located*.

To better understand the different types of distributed database scenarios, let's first define the distributed database system's components.

14.5 DDBMS COMPONENTS

The DDBMS must include at least the following components:

- *Computer workstations* (sites or nodes) that form the network system. The distributed database system must be independent of the computer system hardware.
- *Network hardware and software* components that reside in each workstation. The network components allow all sites to interact and exchange data. As the components – computers, operating systems, network hardware and so on – are likely to be supplied by different vendors, it is best to ensure that distributed database functions can be run on multiple platforms.
- *Communications media* that carry the data from one workstation to another. The DDBMS must be communications-media-independent; that is, it must be able to support several types of communications media.
- The **transaction processor (TP)**, which is the software component found in each computer that requests data. The transaction processor receives and processes the application's data requests

(remote and local). The TP is also known as the **application processor (AP)** or the **transaction manager (TM)**.

- The **data processor (DP)**, which is the software component residing on each computer that stores and retrieves data located at the site. The DP is also known as the **data manager (DM)**. A data processor may even be a centralised DBMS.

Figure 14.5 illustrates the placement of and interaction among the components. The communication among TPs and DPs shown in Figure 14.5 is made possible through a specific set of rules, or *protocols*, used by the DDBMS.

FIGURE 14.5 Distributed database system management components

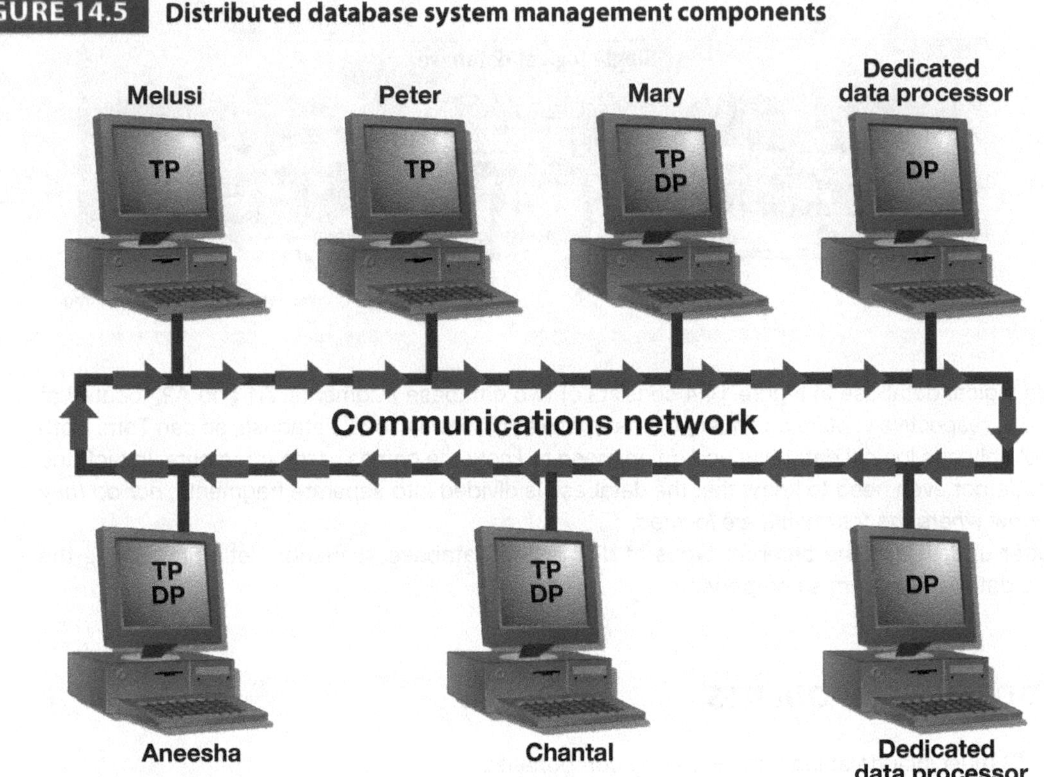

Note: Each TP can access data on any DP, and each DP handles all requests for local data from any TP.

The protocols determine how the distributed database system will:

- Interface with the network to transport data and commands between DPs and TPs
- Synchronise all data received from DPs (TP side) and route retrieved data to the appropriate TPs (DP side)
- Ensure common database functions in a distributed system. Such functions include security, concurrency control, backup and recovery.

DPs and TPs can be added to the system without affecting the operation of the other components. A TP and a DP can reside on the same computer, allowing the end user to access local as well as remote data transparently. In theory, a DP can be an independent centralised DBMS with proper interfaces to support remote access from other independent DBMSs in the network.

14.6 LEVELS OF DATA AND PROCESS DISTRIBUTION

Current database systems can be classified on the basis of how process distribution and data distribution are supported. For example, a DBMS may store data in a single site (centralised DB) or in multiple sites (distributed DB) and may support data processing at a single site or at multiple sites. Table 14.2 uses a simple matrix to classify database systems according to data and process distribution. These types of processes are discussed in the sections that follow.

TABLE 14.2 Database systems: levels of data and process distribution

	Single-Site Data	Multiple-Site Data
Single-site process	Host DBMS	Not applicable (Requires multiple processes)
Multiple-site process	File server Client/server DBMS (LAN DBMS)	Fully distributed Client/server DDBMS

FIGURE 14.6 Single-site-processing, single-site data (centralised)

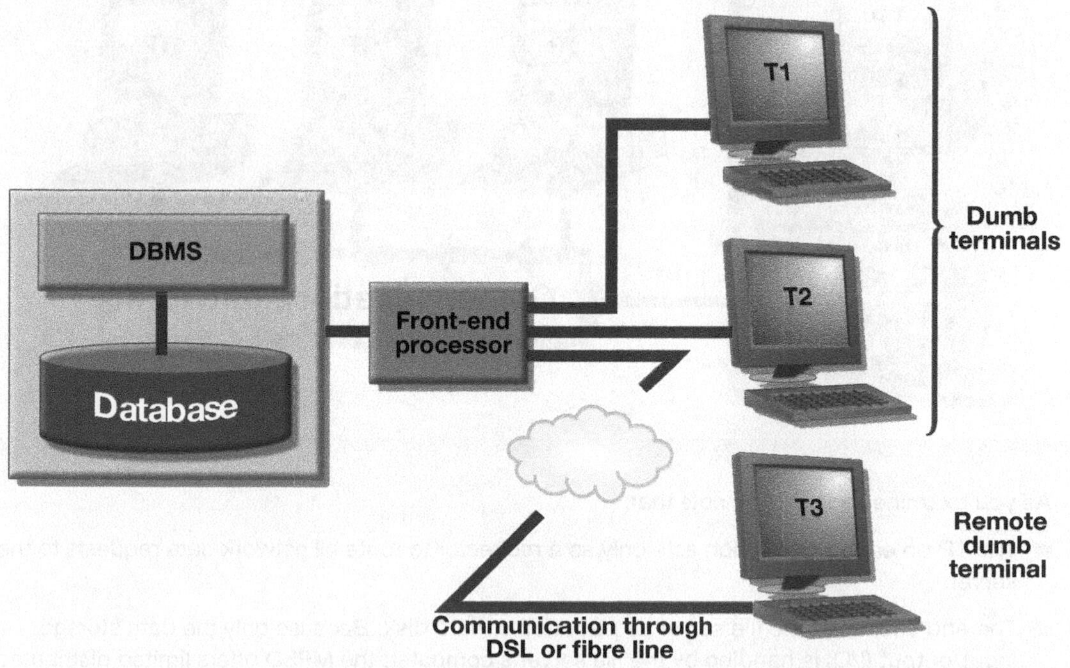

14.6.1 Single-Site Processing, Single-Site Data (SPSD)

In the **single-site processing, single-site data (SPSD)** scenario, all processing is done on a single host computer and all data are stored on the host computer's local disk. Processing cannot be done on the end user's side of the system. Such a scenario is typical of most mainframe and midrange computer DBMSs. The DBMS is located on the host computer, which is accessed by dumb terminals connected to it. (See Figure 14.6.) This scenario is also typical of the first generation of single-user microcomputer databases.

Using Figure 14.6 as an example, the functions of the TP and the DP are embedded within the DBMS located on a single computer. The DBMS usually runs under a time-sharing, multitasking operating system, which allows several processes to run concurrently on a host computer accessing a single DP. All data storage and data processing are handled by a single host computer.

14.6.2 Multiple-Site Processing, Single-Site Data (MPSD)

Under the **multiple-site processing, single-site data (MPSD)** scenario, multiple processes run on different computers sharing a single data repository. Typically, the MPSD scenario requires a network file server running conventional applications that are accessed through a network. Many multi-user accounting applications running under a personal computer network fit such a description. (See Figure 14.7.)

FIGURE 14.7 Multiple-site-processing, single-site data

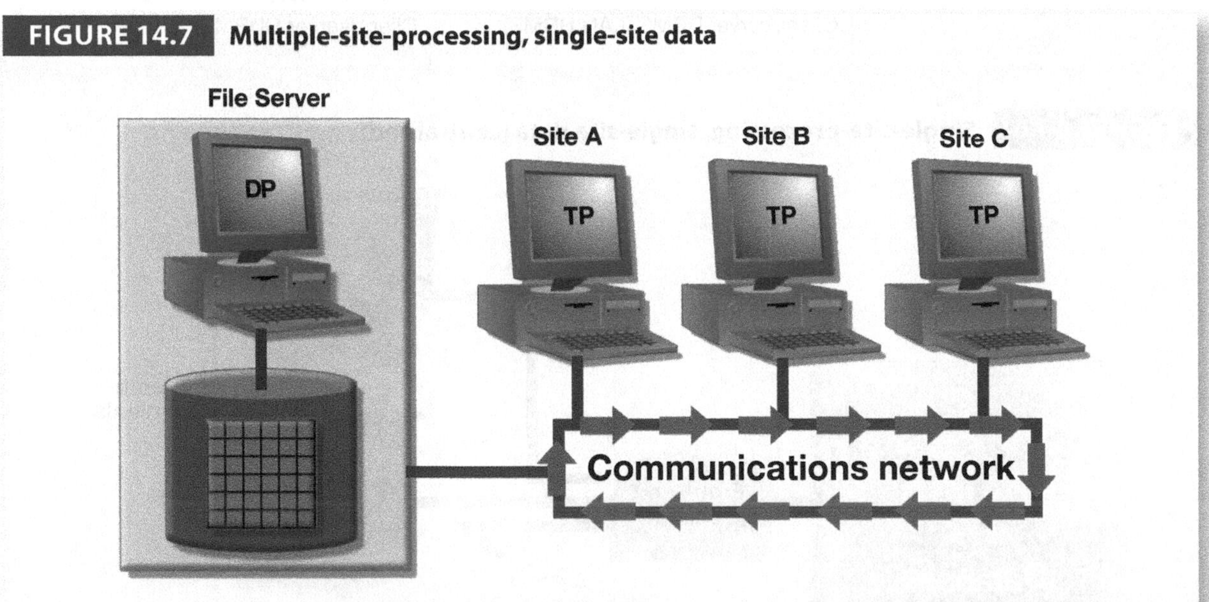

14

As you examine Figure 14.7, note that:

- The TP on each workstation acts only as a redirector to route all network data requests to the file server.
- The end user sees the file server as just another hard disk. Because only the data storage input/output (I/O) is handled by the file server's computer, the MPSD offers limited distributed processing capabilities.

- The end user must make a direct reference to the file server in order to access remote data. All record- and file-locking activity is done at the end-user location.
- All data selection, search and update functions take place at the workstation, thus requiring that entire files travel through the network for processing at the workstation. Such a requirement increases network traffic, slows response time and increases communication costs.

The inefficiency of the last condition can be illustrated easily. For example, suppose the file server computer stores a CUSTOMER table containing 10 000 data rows, 50 of which have balances greater than €1 000. If site A issues the SQL query:

```
SELECT    *
FROM      CUSTOMER
WHERE     CUS_BALANCE > 1000;
```

All 10 000 CUSTOMER rows must travel through the network to be evaluated at site A.

A variation of the multiple-site processing, single-site data approach is known as **client/server architecture**. Client/server architecture is similar to that of the network file server *except that all database processing is done at the server site, thus reducing network traffic*. Although both the network file server and the client/server systems perform multiple-site processing, the latter's processing is distributed. Note that the network file server approach requires the database to be located at a single site. In contrast, the client/server architecture is capable of supporting data at multiple sites.

Online Content Appendix F, Client/Server Systems, is located on the online platform for this book.

14.6.3 Multiple-Site Processing, Multiple-Site Data (MPMD)

The **multiple-site processing, multiple-site data (MPMD)** scenario describes a fully distributed DBMS with support for multiple data processors and transaction processors at multiple sites. Depending on the level of support for different types of centralised DBMSs, DDBMSs are classified as either homogeneous or heterogeneous.

Homogeneous DDBMSs integrate multiple instances of the same database over a network. Thus, the same DBMS will be running on different mainframes, minicomputers and microcomputers. In contrast, **heterogeneous DDBMSs** integrate different types of centralised DBMSs over a network. A **fully heterogeneous DDBMS** will support different DBMSs that may even support different data models (relational, hierarchical or network) running over a network.

No DDBMS currently provides full support for the scenario depicted in Figure 14.8 or for the fully heterogeneous environment. Some DDBMS implementations support several platforms, operating systems and networks, and allow remote data access to another DBMS. However, such DDBMSs still are subject to certain restrictions. For example:

- Remote access is on a read-only basis and does not support write privileges.
- Restrictions are placed on the number of remote tables that may be accessed in a single transaction.

14

- Restrictions are placed on the number of distinct databases that may be accessed.
- Restrictions are placed on the database model that may be accessed. Thus, access may be provided to relational databases but not to network or hierarchical databases.

FIGURE 14.8 Heterogeneous distributed database scenario

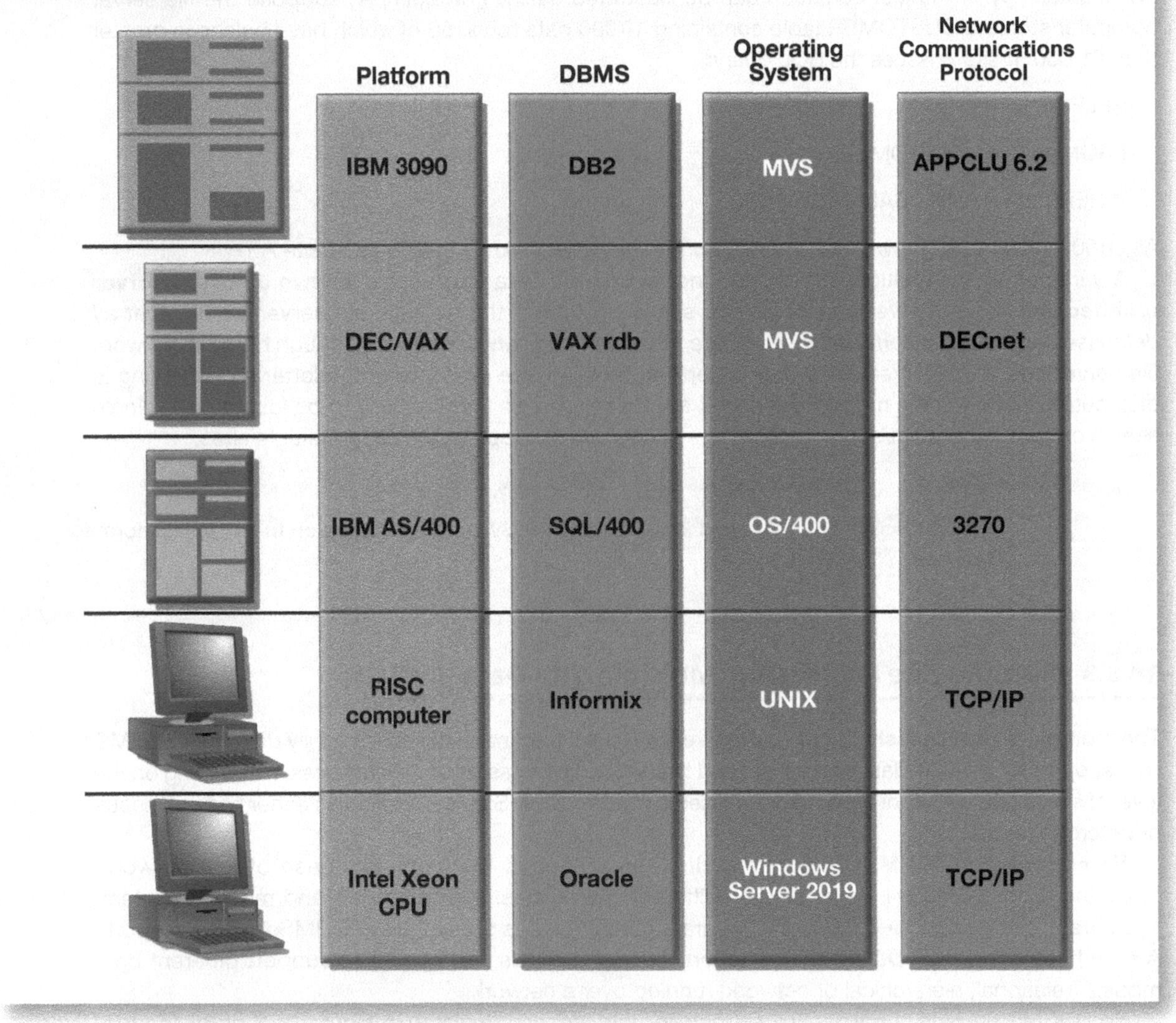

Platform	DBMS	Operating System	Network Communications Protocol
IBM 3090	DB2	MVS	APPCLU 6.2
DEC/VAX	VAX rdb	MVS	DECnet
IBM AS/400	SQL/400	OS/400	3270
RISC computer	Informix	UNIX	TCP/IP
Intel Xeon CPU	Oracle	Windows Server 2019	TCP/IP

The preceding list of restrictions is by no means exhaustive. The DDBMS technology continues to change rapidly, and new features are added frequently. Managing data at multiple sites leads to a number of issues that must be addressed and understood. Therefore, the next section will examine several key features of distributed database management systems.

14.7 DISTRIBUTED DATABASE TRANSPARENCY FEATURES

A distributed database system requires functional characteristics that can be grouped and described as transparency features. DDBMS transparency features have the common property of allowing the end user to feel like the database's only user. In other words, the user believes that he or she is working with a centralised DBMS; all complexities of a distributed database are hidden, or transparent, to the user.

The DDBMS transparency features are:

- **Distribution transparency**, which allows a distributed database to be treated as a single logical database. If a DDBMS exhibits distribution transparency, the user does not need to know:
  - That the data are partitioned, meaning that the table's rows and columns are split vertically or horizontally and stored on multiple sites.
  - That the data are geographically dispersed among multiple sites.
  - That the data are replicated among multiple sites.
- **Transaction transparency**, which allows a transaction to update data at several network sites. Transaction transparency ensures that the transaction will be either entirely completed or aborted, thus maintaining database integrity.
- **Failure transparency**, which ensures that the system will continue to operate in the event of a node failure. Functions that were lost because of the failure will be picked up by another network node. This is a critical feature particularly in organisations that depend on a Web presence as the backbone for maintaining trust in their business.
- **Performance transparency**, which allows the system to perform as if it were a centralised DBMS. The system will not suffer any performance degradation due to its use on a network or due to the network's platform differences. Performance transparency also ensures that the system will find the most cost-effective path to access remote data. The systems should be able to scale out in a transparent manner or increase performance capacity by adding more transaction or data processing nodes, without affecting the overall performance of the system.
- **Heterogeneity transparency**, which allows the integration of several different local DBMSs (relational, network and hierarchical) under a common, or global, schema. The DDBMS is responsible for translating the data requests from the global schema to the local DBMS schema.

Distribution, transaction and performance transparency features will be examined in greater detail in the next few sections.

14.8 DISTRIBUTION TRANSPARENCY

Distribution transparency allows a physically dispersed database to be managed as though it were a centralised database. The level of transparency supported by the DDBMS varies from system to system. Three levels of distribution transparency are recognised:

- **Fragmentation transparency** is the highest level of transparency. The end user or programmer does not need to know that a database is partitioned. Therefore, neither fragment names nor fragment locations are specified prior to data access.
- **Location transparency** exists when the end user or programmer must specify the database fragment names but does not need to specify where those fragments are located.
- **Local mapping transparency** exists when the end user or programmer must specify both the fragment names and their locations.

Transparency features are summarised in Table 14.3.

TABLE 14.3 A summary of transparency features

If the SQL statement requires:			
Fragment name?	**Location name?**	**Then the DBMS supports**	**Level of distributon transparency**
Yes	Yes	Local mapping transparency	Low
Yes	No	Location transparency	Medium
No	No	Fragmentation transparency	High

As you examine Table 14.3, you might ask why there is no reference to a situation in which the fragment name is 'No' and the location name is 'Yes'. The reason for not including that scenario is simple: you cannot have a location name that fails to reference an existing fragment. (If you don't need to specify a fragment name, its location is clearly irrelevant.)

To illustrate the use of various transparency levels, suppose you have an EMPLOYEE table containing the attributes EMP_NAME, EMP_DOB, EMP_ADDRESS, EMP_DEPARTMENT and EMP_SALARY. The EMPLOYEE data are distributed over three different locations: London, Cape Town and Harare. The table is divided by location; that is, the London employee data are stored in fragment E1, Cape Town employee data are stored in fragment E2 and Harare employee data are stored in fragment E3. (See Figure 14.9.)

FIGURE 14.9 Fragment locations

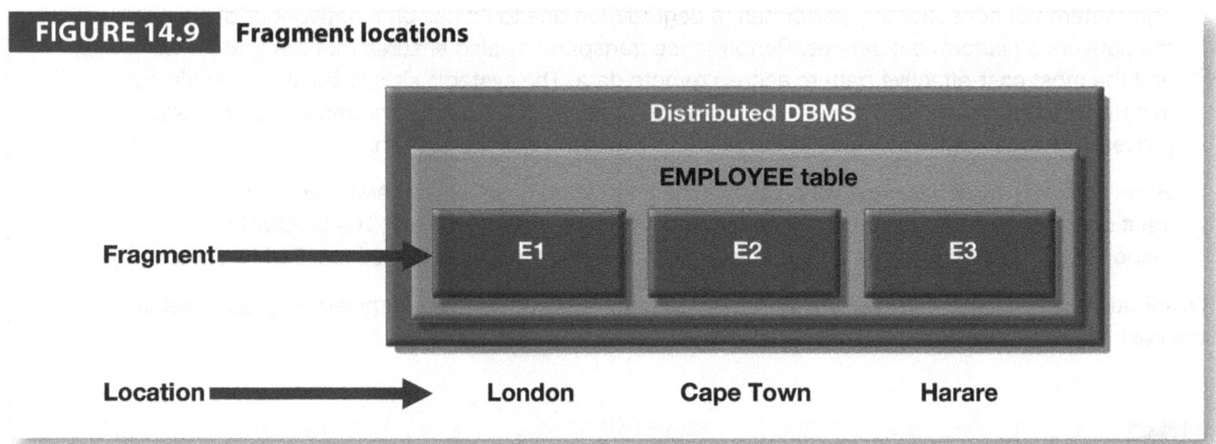

Now suppose the end user wants to list all employees with a date of birth prior to 1 January, 1970. To focus on the transparency issues, also suppose the EMPLOYEE table is fragmented and each fragment is unique. The **unique fragment** condition indicates that each row is unique, regardless of the fragment in which it is located. Finally, assume that no portion of the database is replicated at any other site on the network.

Depending on the level of distribution transparency support, you may examine three query cases.

Case 1: The Database Supports Fragmentation Transparency

The query conforms to a non-distributed database query format; that is, it does not specify fragment names or locations. The query reads:

```
SELECT    *
FROM      EMPLOYEE
WHERE     EMP_DOB < '01-JAN-1970';
```

Case 2: The Database Supports Location Transparency
Fragment names must be specified in the query, but fragment location is not specified. The query reads:

```
SELECT    *
FROM      E1
WHERE     EMP_DOB < '01-JAN-1970';
UNION
SELECT    *
FROM      E2
WHERE     EMP_DOB < '01-JAN-1970';
UNION
SELECT    *
FROM      E3
WHERE     EMP_DOB < '01-JAN-1970';
```

Case 3: The Database Supports Local Mapping Transparency
Both the fragment name and location must be specified in the query. Using pseudo-SQL:

```
SELECT    *
FROM      E1 NODE LONDON
WHERE     EMP_DOB < '01-JAN-1970';
UNION
SELECT    *
FROM      E2 NODE CAPE TOWN
WHERE     EMP_DOB < '01-JAN-1970';
UNION
SELECT    *
FROM      E3 NODE HARARE
WHERE     EMP_DOB < '01-JAN-1970';
```

14

NOTE

NODE indicates the location of the database fragment. NODE is used for illustration purposes and is not part of the standard SQL syntax.

As you examine the preceding query formats, you can see how distribution transparency affects the way end users and programmers interact with the database.

Distribution transparency is supported by a **distributed data dictionary (DDD)**, or a **distributed data catalogue (DDC)**. The DDC contains the description of the entire database as seen by the database administrator. The database description, known as the **distributed global schema**, is the common database schema used by local TPs to translate user requests into subqueries (remote requests) that are processed by different DPs. The DDC is itself distributed, and it is replicated at the network nodes. Therefore, the DDC must maintain consistency through updating at all sites.

Keep in mind that some of the current DDBMS implementations impose limitations on the level of transparency support. For instance, you might be able to distribute a database, but not a table, across multiple sites. Such a condition indicates that the DDBMS supports location transparency but not fragmentation transparency.

14.9 TRANSACTION TRANSPARENCY

Transaction transparency is a DDBMS property that ensures that database transactions maintain the distributed database's integrity and consistency. Remember that a DDBMS database transaction can update data stored in many different computers connected in a network. Transaction transparency ensures that the transactions are completed only when all database sites involved in the transaction complete their part of the transaction.

Distributed database systems require complex mechanisms to manage transactions and to ensure the database's consistency and integrity. To understand how the transactions are managed, you should know the basic concepts governing remote requests, remote transactions, distributed transactions and distributed requests.

14.9.1 Distributed Requests and Distributed Transactions[2]

Whether or not a transaction is distributed, it is formed by one or more database requests. The basic difference between a non-distributed transaction and a distributed transaction is that the latter can update or request data from several different remote sites on a network. To better illustrate the distributed transaction concepts, let's begin by establishing the difference between remote and distributed transactions, using the BEGIN WORK and COMMIT WORK transaction format. Assume the existence of location transparency to avoid having to specify the data location.

FIGURE 14.10 A remote request

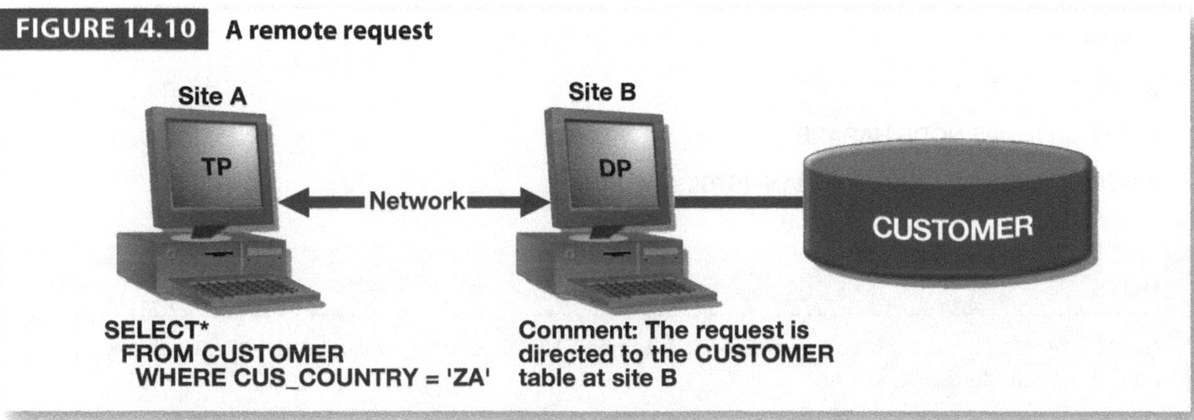
Site A
TP
Network
Site B
DP
CUSTOMER
SELECT*
FROM CUSTOMER
WHERE CUS_COUNTRY = 'ZA'
Comment: The request is
directed to the CUSTOMER
table at site B

14

2 The details of distributed requests and transactions were originally described in David McGoveran and Colin White, 'Clarifying Client/Server', *DBMS* 3(14), November 1990, pp. 78–89.

A **remote request**, illustrated in Figure 14.10, lets a single SQL statement access the data that are to be processed by a single remote database processor. In other words, the SQL statement (or request) can reference data at only one remote site.

Similarly, a **remote transaction** composed of several requests, accesses data at a single remote site. A remote transaction is illustrated in Figure 14.11.

FIGURE 14.11 **A remote transaction**

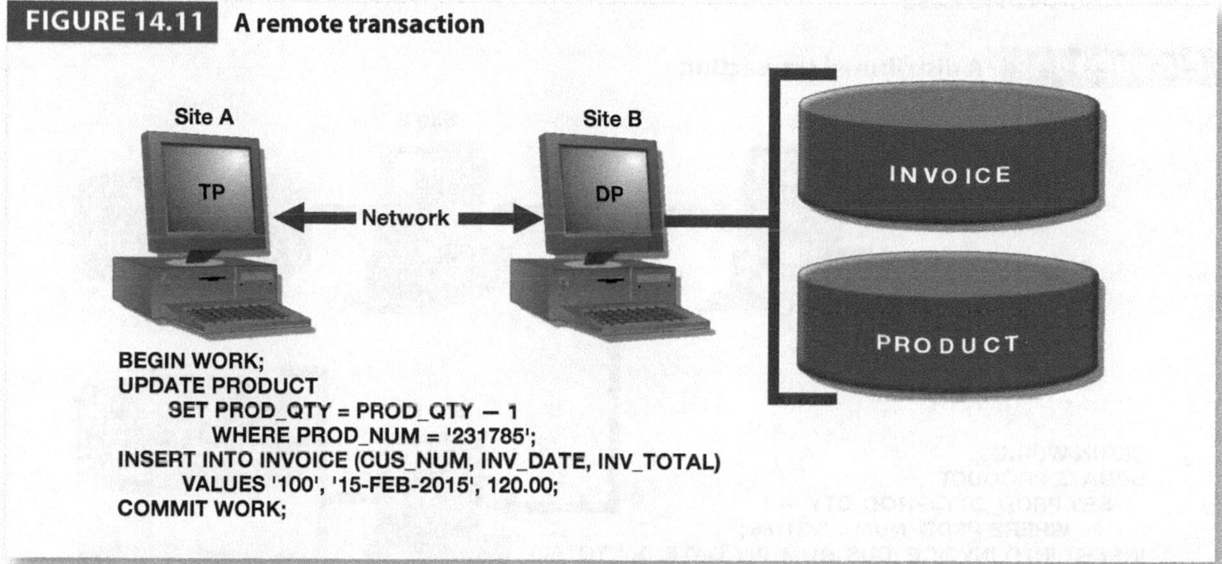
Site A
TP
Network
Site B
DP
INVOICE
PRODUCT
BEGIN WORK;
UPDATE PRODUCT
SET PROD_QTY = PROD_QTY – 1
WHERE PROD_NUM = '231785';
INSERT INTO INVOICE (CUS_NUM, INV_DATE, INV_TOTAL)
VALUES '100', '15-FEB-2015', 120.00;
COMMIT WORK;

As you examine Figure 14.11, note the following remote transaction features:

- The transaction updates the PRODUCT and INVOICE tables (located at site B).
- The remote transaction is sent to and executed at the remote site B.
- The transaction can reference only one remote DP.
- Each SQL statement (or request) can reference only one (the same) remote DP at a time, and the entire transaction can reference and be executed at only one remote DP.

A **distributed transaction** allows a transaction to reference several different local or remote DP sites. Although each single request can reference only one local or remote DP site, the transaction as a whole can reference multiple DP sites because each request can reference a different site. The distributed transaction process is illustrated in Figure 14.12.

Note the following features in Figure 14.12:

- The transaction references two remote sites (B and C).
- The first two requests (UPDATE PRODUCT and INSERT INTO INVOICE) are processed by the DP at the remote site C, and the last request (UPDATE CUSTOMER) is processed by the DP at the remote site B.
- Each request can access only one remote site at a time.

The third characteristic may create problems. For example, suppose the table PRODUCT is divided into two fragments, PRODI and PROD2, located at sites B and C, respectively. Given that scenario, the preceding distributed transaction cannot be executed because the request:

```
SELECT    *
FROM      PRODUCT
WHERE     PROD_NUM = '231785';
```

cannot access data from more than one remote site. Therefore, the DBMS must be able to support a distributed request.

FIGURE 14.12 **A distributed transaction**

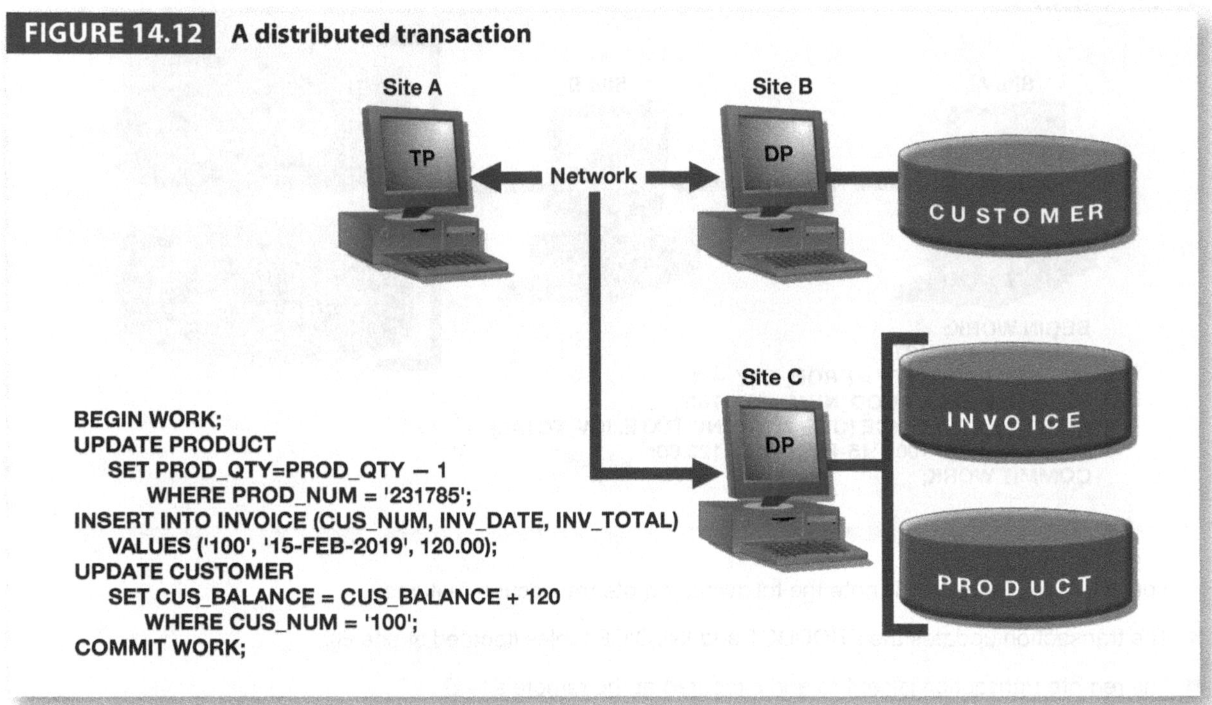
Site A
TP
Network
Site B
DP
CUSTOMER
Site C
DP
INVOICE
PRODUCT
BEGIN WORK;
UPDATE PRODUCT
SET PROD_QTY=PROD_QTY – 1
WHERE PROD_NUM = '231785';
INSERT INTO INVOICE (CUS_NUM, INV_DATE, INV_TOTAL)
VALUES ('100', '15-FEB-2019', 120.00);
UPDATE CUSTOMER
SET CUS_BALANCE = CUS_BALANCE + 120
WHERE CUS_NUM = '100';
COMMIT WORK;

A **distributed request** lets a single SQL statement reference data located at several different local or remote DP sites. Because each request (SQL statement) can access data from more than one local or remote DP site, a transaction can access several sites. The ability to execute a distributed request provides fully distributed database processing capabilities because of the ability to:

- partition a database table into several fragments
- reference one or more of those fragments with only one request. In other words, there is fragmentation transparency.

14

The location and partition of the data should be transparent to the end user. Figure 14.13 illustrates a distributed request. As you examine Figure 14.13, note that the transaction uses a single SELECT statement to reference two tables, CUSTOMER and INVOICE. The two tables are located at two different sites, B and C.

The distributed request feature also allows a single request to reference a physically partitioned table. For example, suppose a CUSTOMER table is divided into two fragments, C1 and C2, located at sites B and C, respectively. Further suppose the end user wants to obtain a list of all customers whose balances exceed €250. The request is illustrated in Figure 14.14. Full fragmentation transparency support is provided only by a DDBMS that supports distributed requests.

Understanding the different types of database requests in distributed database systems helps you address the transaction transparency issue more effectively. Transaction transparency ensures that distributed transactions are treated as centralised transactions, ensuring serialisability of transactions. (Review Chapter 12, Managing Transactions and Concurrency, if necessary.) That is, the execution of concurrent transactions, whether or not they are distributed, will take the database from one consistent state to another.

FIGURE 14.13 **A distributed request**

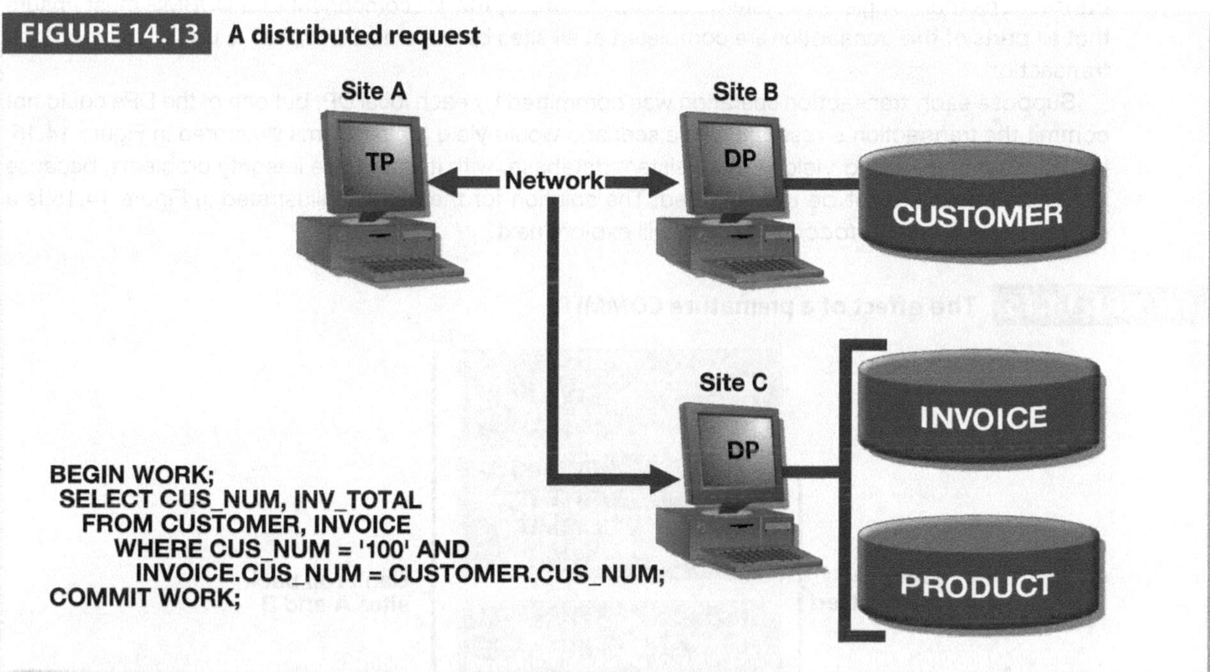
Site A
TP
Network
Site B
DP
CUSTOMER
Site C
DP
INVOICE
PRODUCT
BEGIN WORK;
SELECT CUS_NUM, INV_TOTAL
FROM CUSTOMER, INVOICE
WHERE CUS_NUM = '100' AND
INVOICE.CUS_NUM = CUSTOMER.CUS_NUM;
COMMIT WORK;

FIGURE 14.14 **Another distributed request**

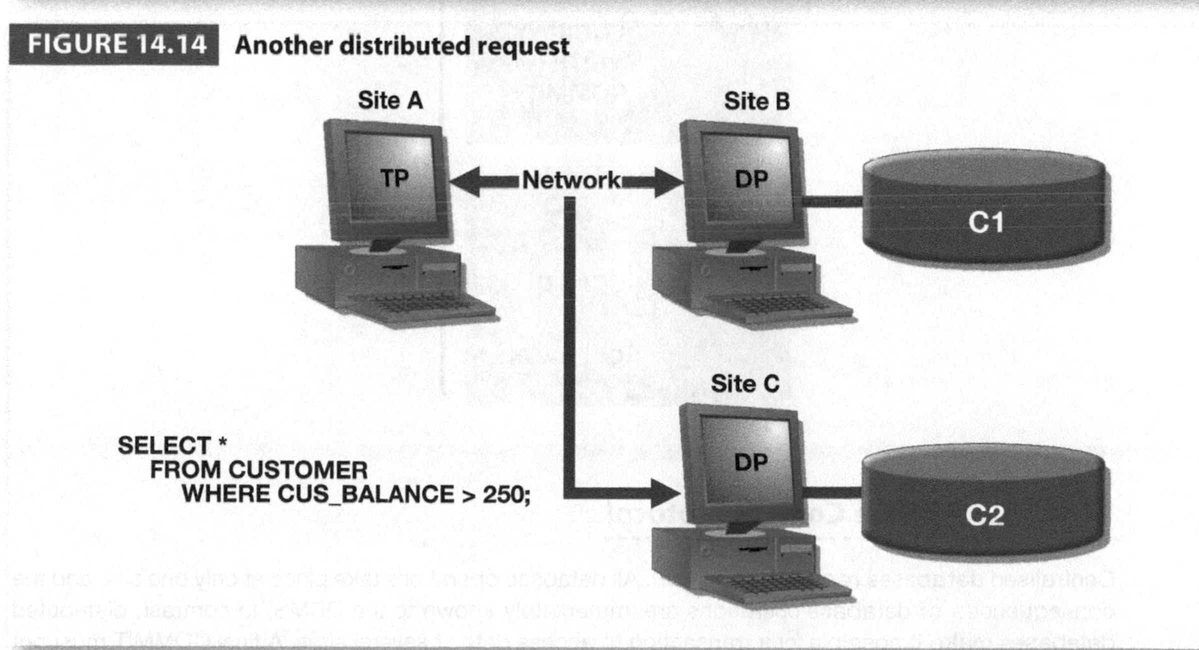
Site A
TP
Network
Site B
DP
C1
Site C
DP
C2
SELECT *
FROM CUSTOMER
WHERE CUS_BALANCE > 250;

14.9.2 Distributed Concurrency Control

Concurrency control becomes especially important in the distributed database environment because multi-site, multiple-process operations are more likely to create data inconsistencies and deadlocked transactions than single-site systems are. For example, the TP component of a DDBMS must ensure that all parts of the transaction are completed at all sites before a final COMMIT is issued to record the transaction.

Suppose each transaction operation was committed by each local DP, but one of the DPs could not commit the transaction's results. Such a scenario would yield the problems illustrated in Figure 14.15: the transaction(s) would yield an inconsistent database, with its inevitable integrity problems, because committed data cannot be uncommitted! The solution for the problem illustrated in Figure 14.15 is a *two-phase commit protocol*, which you will explore next.

FIGURE 14.15 **The effect of a premature COMMIT**

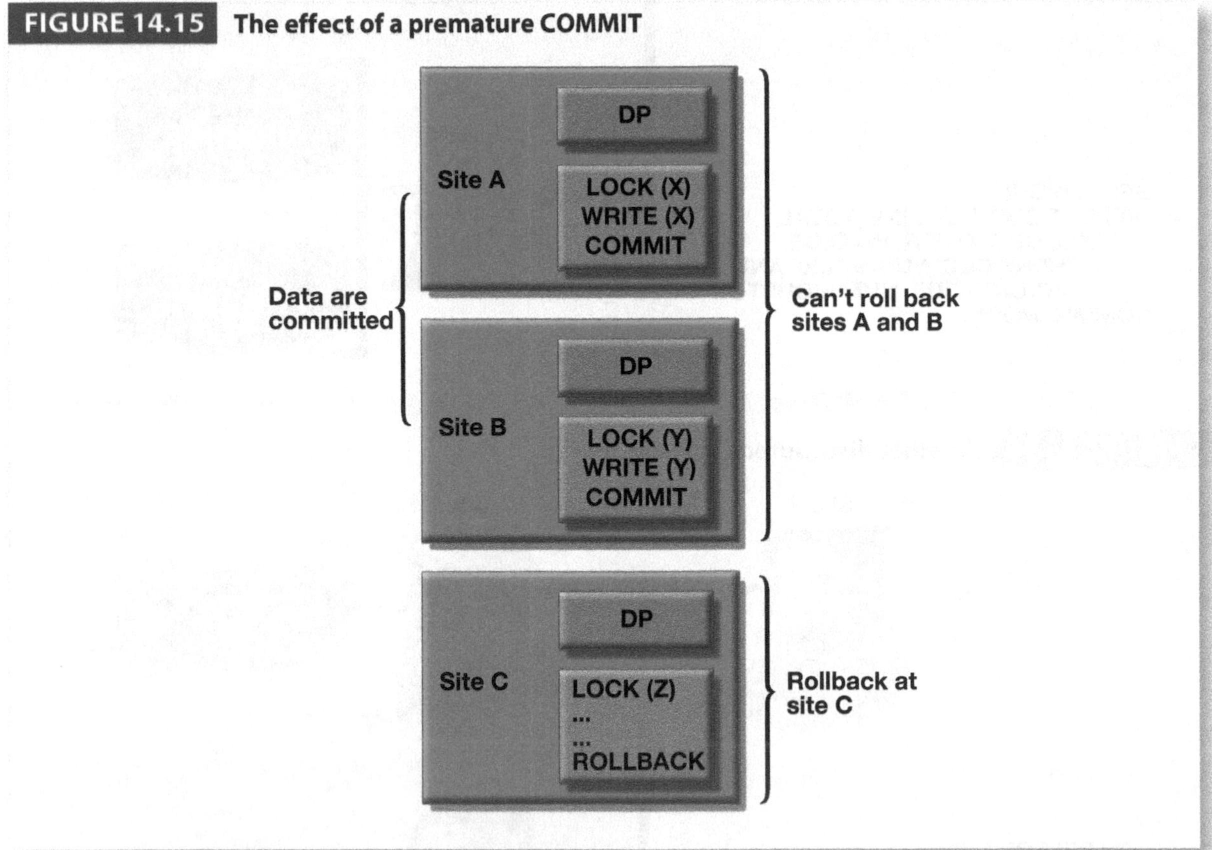

14.9.3 Two-Phase Commit Protocol

Centralised databases require only one DP. All database operations take place at only one site, and the consequences of database operations are immediately known to the DBMS. In contrast, distributed databases make it possible for a transaction to access data at several sites. A final COMMIT must not be issued until all sites have committed their parts of the transaction. The **two-phase commit protocol** guarantees that, if a portion of a transaction operation cannot be committed, all changes made at the other sites participating in the transaction will be undone to maintain a consistent database state.

Each DP maintains its own transaction log. The two-phase commit protocol requires that the transaction entry log for each DP be written before the database fragment is actually updated. (See Chapter 12, Managing Transactions and Concurrency, Section 12.6.) Therefore, the two-phase commit protocol requires a DO-UNDO-REDO protocol and a write-ahead protocol.

The **DO-UNDO-REDO protocol** is used by the DP to roll back and/or roll forward transactions with the help of the system's transaction log entries. The DO-UNDO-REDO protocol defines three types of operations:

- DO performs the operation and records the 'before' and 'after' values in the transaction log.
- UNDO reverses an operation, using the log entries written by the DO portion of the sequence.
- REDO redoes an operation, using the log entries written by the DO portion of the sequence.

To ensure that the DO, UNDO and REDO operations can survive a system crash while they are being executed, a write-ahead protocol is used. The **write-ahead protocol** forces the log entry to be written to permanent storage before the actual operation takes place.

The two-phase commit protocol defines the operations between two types of nodes: the **coordinator** and one or more **subordinates**, or *cohorts*. The participating nodes agree on a coordinator. Generally, the coordinator role is assigned to the node that initiates the transaction. However, different systems implement various, more sophisticated election methods. The protocol is implemented in two phases:

Phase 1: Preparation

1. The coordinator sends a PREPARE TO COMMIT message to all subordinates.
2. The subordinates receive the message; write the transaction log, using the write-ahead protocol; and send an acknowledgement (YES/PREPARED TO COMMIT or NO/NOT PREPARED) message to the coordinator.
3. The coordinator makes sure that all nodes are ready to commit, or it aborts the action.

If all nodes are PREPARED TO COMMIT, the transaction goes to phase 2. If one or more nodes reply NO or NOT PREPARED, the coordinator broadcasts an ABORT message to all subordinates.

Phase 2: The Final COMMIT

1. The coordinator broadcasts a COMMIT message to all subordinates and waits for the replies.
2. Each subordinate receives the COMMIT message, then updates the database using the DO protocol.
3. The subordinates reply with a COMMITTED or NOT COMMITTED message to the coordinator.

If one or more subordinates did not commit, the coordinator sends an ABORT message, thereby forcing them to UNDO all changes.

The objective of the two-phase commit is to ensure that all nodes commit their part of the transaction; otherwise, the transaction is aborted. If one of the nodes fails to commit, the information necessary to recover the database is in the transaction log, and the database can be recovered with the DO-UNDO-REDO protocol. (Remember that the log information was updated using the write-ahead protocol.)

14.10 PERFORMANCE AND FAILURE TRANSPARENCY

One of the most important functions of a database is its ability to make data available. Web-based distributed data systems demand high availability, which means not only that data are accessible but that requests are processed in a timely manner. For example, the average Google search has a sub-second response time. When was the last time you entered a Google query and waited more than a couple of seconds for the results? Performance transparency allows a DDBMS to perform as if it were a centralised database. In other words, no performance degradation should be incurred due to data distribution. Failure transparency ensures that the system will continue to operate in the case of a node or network failure. Although these are two separate issues, they are interrelated in that a failing node or congested network path could cause performance problems. Therefore, both issues are addressed in this section.

The objective of a query optimisation routine is to minimise the total cost associated with the execution of a request. The costs associated with a request are a function of the:

- access time (I/O) cost involved in accessing the physical data stored on disk
- communication cost associated with the transmission of data among nodes in distributed database systems
- CPU time cost associated with the processing overhead of managing distributed transactions.

Although costs are often classified as either communication or processing costs, it is difficult to separate the two. Not all query optimisation algorithms use the same parameters, and not all algorithms assign the same weight to each parameter. For example, some algorithms minimise total time; others minimise the communication time; and still others do not factor in the CPU time, considering it insignificant relative to other cost sources.

NOTE

Chapter 13, Managing Database and SQL Performance, provides additional details about query optimisation.

Resolving data requests in a distributed data environment must take the following points into consideration:

- *Data distribution*. In a DDBMS, query translation is more complicated because the DDBMS must decide which fragment to access. (Distribution transparency was explained earlier in this chapter.) In this case, a TP executing a query must choose what fragments to access, create multiple data requests to the chosen remote DPs, combine the DP responses and present the data to the application.
- *Data replication*. In addition, the data may also be replicated at several different sites. The data replication makes the access problem even more complex because the database must ensure that all copies of the data are consistent. Therefore, an important characteristic of query optimisation in distributed database systems is that it must provide replica transparency. **Replica transparency** refers to the DDBMS's ability to hide multiple copies of data from the user. This ability is particularly important with data update operations. If a read-only request is being processed, it can be satisfied by accessing any available remote DP. However, processing a

write request also involves 'synchronising' all existing fragments to maintain data consistency. The two-phase commit protocol you learnt about in Section 14.9.3 ensures that the transaction will complete successfully. However, if data are replicated at other sites, the DDBMSs must also ensure the consistency of all the fragments – that is, all fragments should be mutually consistent. To accomplish this, a DP captures all changes and pushes them to each remote replica. This introduces delays in the system and basically means that not all data changes are immediately seen by all replicas.

- *Network and node availability*. The response time associated with remote sites cannot be easily predetermined because some nodes finish their part of the query in less time than others and network path performance varies because of bandwidth and traffic loads. Hence, to achieve performance transparency, the DDBMS should consider issues such as **network latency**, the delay imposed by the amount of time required for a data packet to make a round trip from point A to point B; or **network partitioning**, the delay imposed when nodes become suddenly unavailable due to a network failure.

Carefully planning how to partition a database and where to locate the database fragments can help ensure the performance and consistency of a distributed database. The following section discusses issues for distributed database design.

14.11 DISTRIBUTED DATABASE DESIGN

Whether the database is centralised or distributed, the design principles and concepts described in Chapter 3, Relational Model Characteristics; Chapter 5, Data Modelling with Entity Relationship Diagrams; and Chapter 7, Normalising Database Designs, are still applicable. However, the design of a distributed database introduces three new issues:

- How to partition the database into fragments
- Which fragments to replicate
- Where to locate those fragments and replicas

Data fragmentation and *data replication* deal with the first two issues, and *data allocation* deals with the third issue.

14.11.1 Data Fragmentation

Data fragmentation allows you to break a single object into two or more segments or fragments. The object might be a user's database, a system database or a table. Each fragment can be stored at any site over a computer network. Information about data fragmentation is stored in the distributed data catalogue (DDC), from where it is accessed by the TP to process user requests.

Data fragmentation strategies, as discussed here, are based at the table level and consist of dividing a table into logical fragments. You will explore three types of data fragmentation strategies: *horizontal*, *vertical* and *mixed*. (Keep in mind that a fragmented table can always be recreated from its fragmented parts by a combination of unions and joins.)

- **Horizontal fragmentation** refers to the division of a relation into subsets (fragments) of tuples (rows). Each fragment is stored at a different node, and each fragment has unique rows. However, the unique rows all have the same attributes (columns). In short, each fragment represents the equivalent of a SELECT statement, with the WHERE clause on a single attribute.

- **Vertical fragmentation** refers to the division of a relation into attribute (column) subsets. Each subset (fragment) is stored at a different node, and each fragment has unique columns – with the exception of the key column, which is common to all fragments. This is the equivalent of the PROJECT statement in SQL.
- **Mixed fragmentation** refers to a combination of horizontal and vertical strategies. In other words, a table may be divided into several horizontal subsets (rows), each one having a subset of the attributes (columns).

To illustrate the fragmentation strategies, let's use the CUSTOMER table for the XYZ Company, depicted in Figure 14.16. The table contains the attributes CUS_NUM, CUS_NAME, CUS_ADDRESS, CUS_COUNTRY, CUS_LIMIT, CUS_BAL, CUS_RATING and CUS_DUE.

FIGURE 14.16 A sample customer table

Table name: CUSTOMER

CUS_NUM	CUS_NAME	CUS_ADDRESS	CUS_COUNTRY	CUS_LIMIT	CUS_BAL	CUS_RATING	CUS_DUE
10	Sinex, Inc.	12 Main St.	UK	3500.00	2700.00	3	1245.00
11	Martin Corp.	321 Sunset Blvd.	SA	6000.00	1200.00	1	0.00
12	Mynux Corp.	910 Eagle St.	UK	4000.00	3500.00	3	3400.00
13	BTBC, Inc.	Rue du Monde	SA	6000.00	5890.00	3	1090.00
14	Victory, Inc.	123 Maple St.	SA	1200.00	550.00	1	0.00
15	NBCC Corp.	909 High Ave.	NL	2000.00	350.00	2	50.00

Online Content The databases used to illustrate the material in this chapter are found on the online platform for this book.

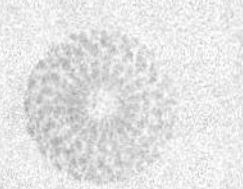

Horizontal Fragmentation

There are various ways to partition a table horizontally:

- *Round-robin partitioning*. Rows are assigned to a given fragment in a round-robin fashion (F1, F2, F3, ..., F*n*) to ensure an even distribution of rows among all fragments. However, this is not a good strategy if you require 'location awareness' – the ability to determine which DP node will process a query based on the geospatial location of the requester. For example, you would want all queries from UK customers to be resolved from a fragment that stores only UK customers and this fragment to be located in a node close to UK.
- *Range partitioning based on a partition key*. A **partition key** is one or more attributes in a table that determine the fragment in which a row will be stored. For example, if you want to provide location awareness, a good partition key would be the customer state field. This is the most common and useful data partitioning strategy.

Suppose XYZ Company's corporate management requires information about its customers in all three countries, but company locations in each country (UK, SA and NL) require data regarding local customers only. Based on such requirements, you decide to distribute the data by country. Therefore, you define the horizontal fragments to conform to the structure shown in Table 14.4.

TABLE 14.4 Horizontal fragmentation of the customer table by country

Fragment Name	Location	Condition	Node Name	Customer Numbers	Number of Rows
CUST_H1	United Kingdom	CUS_COUNTRY = 'UK'	NAS	10, 14	2
CUST_H2	The Netherlands	CUS_COUNTRY = 'NL'	ATL	15	1
CUST_H3	South Africa	CUS_COUNTRY = 'SA'	TAM	11, 13, 14	3

The partition key will be the CUS_COUNTRY field. Each horizontal fragment may have a different number of rows, but each fragment must have the same attributes. The resulting fragments yield the three tables depicted in Figure 14.17.

FIGURE 14.17 Table fragments in three locations

Table name: CUST_H1 Location: United Kingdom Node: NAS

CUS_NUM	CUS_NAME	CUS_ADDRESS	CUS_COUNTRY	CUS_LIMIT	CUS_BAL	CUS_RATING	CUS_DUE
10	Sinex, Inc.	12 Main St.	UK	3500.00	2700.00	3	1245.00
12	Mynux Corp.	910 Eagle St.	UK	4000.00	3500.00	3	3400.00

Table name: CUST_H2 Location: The Netherlands Node: ATL

CUS_NUM	CUS_NAME	CUS_ADDRESS	CUS_COUNTRY	CUS_LIMIT	CUS_BAL	CUS_RATING	CUS_DUE
15	NBCC Corp.	909 High Ave.	NL	2000.00	350.00	2	50.00

Table name: CUST_H3 Location: South Africa Node: TAM

CUS_NUM	CUS_NAME	CUS_ADDRESS	CUS_COUNTRY	CUS_LIMIT	CUS_BAL	CUS_RATING	CUS_DUE
11	Martin Corp.	321 Sunset Blvd.	SA	6000.00	1200.00	1	0.00
13	BTBC, Inc.	Rue du Monde	SA	6000.00	5890.00	3	1090.00
14	Victory, Inc.	123 Maple St.	SA	1200.00	550.00	1	0.00

14

Vertical Fragmentation

You may also divide the CUSTOMER relation into vertical fragments that are composed of a collection of attributes. For example, suppose the company is divided into two departments: the service department and the collections department. Each department is located in a separate building, and each has an interest in only a few of the CUSTOMER table's attributes. In this case, the fragments are defined as shown in Table 14.5.

TABLE 14.5 Vertical fragmentation of the CUSTOMER table

Fragment name	Location	Node Name	Attribute Names
CUST_V1	Service Bldg	SVC	CUS_NUM, CUS_NAME, CUS_ADDRESS, CUS_COUNTRY
CUST_V2	Collection Bldg	ARC	CUS_NUM, CUS_LIMIT, CUS_BAL, CUS_RATING, CUS_DUE

Each vertical fragment must have the same number of rows, but the inclusion of the different attributes depends on the key column. The vertical fragmentation results are displayed in Figure 14.18. Note that the key attribute (CUS_NUM) is common to both fragments CUST_V1 and CUST_V2.

FIGURE 14.18 Vertically fragmented table contents

Table name: CUST_V1 Location: Service Building Node: SVC

CUS_NUM	CUS_NAME	CUS_ADDRESS	CUS_COUNTRY
10	Sinex, Inc.	12 Main St.	UK
11	Martin Corp.	321 Sunset Blvd.	SA
12	Mynux Corp.	910 Eagle St.	UK
13	BTBC, Inc.	Rue du Monde	SA
14	Victory, Inc.	123 Maple St.	SA
15	NBCC Corp.	909 High Ave.	NL

Table name: CUST_V2 Location: Collection Building Node: ARC

CUS_NUM	CUS_LIMIT	CUS_BAL	CUS_RATING	CUS_DUE
10	3500.00	2700.00	3	1245.00
11	6000.00	1200.00	1	0.00
12	4000.00	3500.00	3	3400.00
13	6000.00	5890.00	3	1090.00
14	1200.00	550.00	1	0.00
15	2000.00	350.00	2	50.00

14

Mixed Fragmentation

The XYZ Company's structure requires that the CUSTOMER data be fragmented horizontally to accommodate the different company locations; within the locations, the data must be fragmented vertically to accommodate the different departments (service and collection). In short, the CUSTOMER table requires mixed fragmentation.

Mixed fragmentation requires a two-step procedure. First, horizontal fragmentation is introduced for each site based on the location within a country (CUS_COUNTRY). The horizontal fragmentation yields the subsets of customer tuples (horizontal fragments) that are located at each site. As the departments are located in different buildings, vertical fragmentation is used within each horizontal fragment to divide the attributes, thus meeting each department's information needs at each sub site. Mixed fragmentation yields the results displayed in Table 14.6.

TABLE 14.6 Mixed fragmentation of the CUSTOMER table

Fragment name	Location	Horizontal Criteria	Node Name	Resulting Rows at Site	Vertical Criteria Attributes at Each Fragment
CUST_M1	UK-Service	CUS_COUNTRY = 'UK'	NAS-S	10, 14	CUS_NUM, CUS_NAME, CUS_ADDRESS, CUS_COUNTRY
CUST_M2	UK-Collection	CUS_COUNTRY = 'UK'	NAS-C	10, 14	CUS_NUM, CUS_LIMIT, CUS_BAL, CUS_RATING, CUS_DUE
CUST_M3	NL-Service	CUS_COUNTRY = 'NL'	ATL-S	15	CUS_NUM, CUS_NAME, CUS_ADDRESS, CUS_COUNTRY
CUST_M4	NL-Collection	CUS_COUNTRY = 'NL'	ATL-C	15	CUS_NUM, CUS_LIMIT, CUS_BAL, CUS_RATING, CUS_DUE
CUST_M5	SA-Service	CUS_COUNTRY = 'SA'	TAM-S	11, 13, 14	CUS_NUM, CUS_NAME, CUS_ADDRESS, CUS_COUNTRY
CUST_M6	SA-Collection	CUS_COUNTRY = 'SA'	TAM-C	11, 13, 14	CUS_NUM, CUS_LIMIT, CUS_BAL, CUS_RATING, CUS_DUE

Each fragment displayed in Table 14.6 contains customer data by country and, within each country, by department location, to fit each department's data requirements. The tables corresponding to the fragments listed in Table 14.6 are shown in Figure 14.19.

FIGURE 14.19 Table contents after the mixed fragmentation process

Table name: CUST_M1 Location: UK-Service Node: NAS-S

CUS_NUM	CUS_NAME	CUS_ADDRESS	CUS_COUNTRY
10	Sinex, Inc.	12 Main St.	UK
12	Mynux Corp.	910 Eagle St.	UK

Table name: CUST_M2 Location: UK-Collection Node: NAS-C

CUS_NUM	CUS_LIMIT	CUS_BAL	CUS_RATING	CUS_DUE
10	3500.00	2700.00	3	1245.00
12	4000.00	3500.00	3	3400.00

Table name: CUST_M3 Location: NL-Service Node: ATL-S

CUS_NUM	CUS_NAME	CUS_ADDRESS	CUS_COUNTRY
15	NBCC Corp.	909 High Ave.	NL

14

Table name: CUST_M4 Location: NL-Collection Node: ATL-C

CUS_NUM	CUS_LIMIT	CUS_BAL	CUS_RATING	CUS_DUE
15	2000.00	350.00	2	50.00

Table name: CUST_M5 Location: SA-Service Node: TAM-S

CUS_NUM	CUS_NAME	CUS_ADDRESS	CUS_COUNTRY
11	Martin Corp.	321 Sunset Blvd.	SA
13	BTBC, Inc.	Rue du Monde	SA
14	Victory, Inc.	123 Maple St.	SA

Table name: CUST_M6 Location: SA-Collection Node: TAM-C

CUS_NUM	CUS_LIMIT	CUS_BAL	CUS_RATING	CUS_DUE
11	6000.00	1200.00	1	0.00
13	6000.00	5890.00	3	1090.00
14	1200.00	550.00	1	0.00

14.11.2 Data Replication

Data replication refers to the storage of data copies at multiple sites served by a computer network. Fragment copies can be stored at several sites to serve specific information requirements. Since the existence of fragment copies can enhance data availability and response time, data copies can help to reduce communication and total query costs.

Suppose database A is divided into two fragments, A1 and A2. Within a replicated distributed database, the scenario depicted in Figure 14.20 is possible: fragment A1 is stored at sites S1 and S2, while fragment A2 is stored at sites S2 and S3.

Replicated data are subject to the mutual consistency rule. The **mutual consistency rule** requires that all copies of data fragments be identical. Therefore, to maintain data consistency among the replicas, the DDBMS must ensure that a database update is performed at all sites where replicas exist.

There are basically two styles of replication:

- *Push replication*. After a data update, the originating DP node sends the changes to the replica nodes to ensure that data are immediately updated. This type of replication focuses on maintaining data consistency. However, it decreases data availability due to the latency involved in ensuring data consistency at all nodes.
- *Pull replication*. After a data update, the originating DP node sends 'messages' to the replica nodes to notify them of the update. The replica nodes decide when to apply the updates to their local fragment. In this type of replication, data updates propagate more slowly to the replicas. The focus is on maintaining data availability. However, this style of replication allows for temporary data inconsistencies.

Although replication has some benefits, it also imposes additional DDBMS processing overhead because each data copy must be maintained by the system. To illustrate the replica overhead imposed on a DDBMS, consider the processes that the DDBMS must perform to use the database:

FIGURE 14.20 **Data replication**

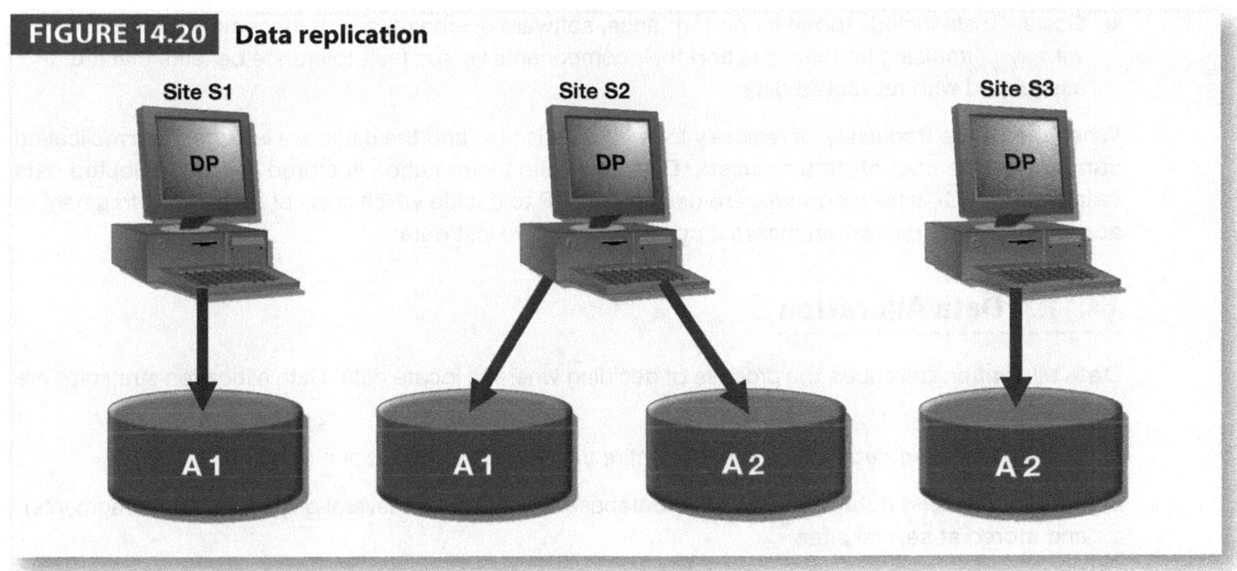

- If the database is fragmented, the DDBMS must decompose a query into *subqueries* to access the appropriate fragments.
- If the database is replicated, the DDBMS must decide which copy to access. A READ operation selects the *nearest copy* to satisfy the transaction. A WRITE operation requires that *all copies* be selected and updated to satisfy the mutual consistency rule.
- The TP sends a data request to each selected DP for execution.
- The DP receives and executes each request and sends the data back to the TP.
- The TP assembles the DP responses.

The problem becomes more complex when you consider additional factors such as network topology and communication throughputs.

Three replication scenarios exist: a database can be *fully replicated*, *partially replicated*, or *unreplicated*:

- A **fully replicated database** stores multiple copies of *each* database fragment at multiple sites. In this case, all database fragments are replicated. A fully replicated database can be impractical due to the amount of overhead it imposes on the system.
- A **partially replicated database** stores multiple copies of *some* database fragments at multiple sites. Most DDBMSs are able to handle the partially replicated database well.
- An **unreplicated database** stores each database fragment at a single site. Therefore, there are no duplicate database fragments.

Several factors influence the decision to use data replication:

- *Database size*. The amount of data replicated will have an impact on the storage requirements and the data transmission costs. Replicating large amounts of data requires a window of time and higher network bandwidth that could affect other applications.
- *Usage frequency*. The frequency of data usage determines how frequently the data needs to be updated.

- *Costs*. Costs include those for performance, software overhead, and management associated with synchronising transactions and their components versus fault-tolerance benefits that are associated with replicated data.

When the usage frequency of remotely located data is high and the database is large, data replication can reduce the cost of data requests. Data replication information is stored in the distributed data catalogue (DDC), whose contents are used by the TP to decide which copy of a database fragment to access. The data replication makes it possible to restore lost data.

14.11.3 Data Allocation

Data allocation describes the process of deciding where to locate data. Data allocation strategies are as follows:

- With **centralised data allocation**, the entire database is stored at one site.
- With **partitioned data allocation**, the database is divided into several disjointed parts (fragments) and stored at several sites.
- With **replicated data allocation**, copies of one or more database fragments are stored at several sites.

Data distribution over a computer network is achieved through data partition, data replication, or a combination of both. Data allocation is closely related to the way a database is divided or fragmented. Most data allocation studies focus on one issue: *which* data to locate *where*.

Data allocation algorithms take into consideration a variety of factors, including:

- Performance and data availability goals
- Size, number of rows and number of relations that an entity maintains with other entities
- Types of transactions to be applied to the database and the attributes accessed by each of those transactions
- Disconnected operation for mobile users

Most algorithms include data such as network topology, network bandwidth and throughput, data size and location. Some algorithms include external data, such as network topology or network throughput. No optimal or universally accepted algorithm exists yet, and very few algorithms have been implemented to date.

14.12 THE CAP THEOREM

In a 2000 symposium on distributed computing, Dr Eric Brewer stated in his presentation that 'in any highly distributed data system there are three commonly desirable properties: consistency, availability, and partition tolerance. However, it is impossible for a system to provide all three properties at the same time'.[3] The initials *CAP* stand for the three desirable properties. Consider these three properties in more detail:

---

3 'Towards Robust Distributed Systems', Eric A. Brewer, University of California at Berkeley and Inktomi Corporation, presentation at the Principles of Distributed Computing, ACM Symposium, July 2000. This theorem was later proven by Seth Gilbert and Nancy Lynch of MIT in their paper 'Brewer's Conjecture and the Feasibility of Consistent, Available, Partition-Tolerant Web Services', ACM SIGACT News, vol. 33, Issue 2, pp. 51–59, 2002.

- *Consistency*. In a distributed database, consistency takes a bigger role. All nodes should see the same data at the same time, which means that the replicas should be immediately updated. However, this involves dealing with latency and network partitioning delays, as you learnt in Section 14.10.
- *Availability*. Simply speaking, a request is always fulfilled by the system. No received request is ever lost. If you are buying tickets online, you do not want the system to stop in the middle of the operation. This is a paramount requirement of all Web-centric organisations.
- *Partition tolerance*. The system continues to operate even in the event of a node failure. This is the equivalent of failure transparency in distributed databases (see Section 14.7). The system will fail only if all nodes fail.

Although the CAP theorem focuses on highly distributed Web-based systems, its implications are widespread for all distributed systems, including databases. In Chapter 12, you learnt that there are five database transaction properties: atomicity, consistency, isolation, durability, and serialisability. The ACIDS properties ensure that all successful transactions result in a consistent database state – one in which all data operations always return the same results. For centralised and small distributed databases, latency is not an issue. As the business grows and the need for availability increases, database latency becomes a bigger problem. It is more difficult for a highly distributed database to ensure ACIDS transactions without paying a high price in network latency or data contention (delays imposed by concurrent data access).

For example, imagine that you are using Computicket to buy tickets for the Kaizer Chiefs–Orlando Pirates soccer game at the FNB Stadium in Johannesburg. You may spend a few minutes browsing through the available tickets and checking the stadium website to see which seats have the best view. At the same time, other users from all over the world may be doing exactly the same thing. By the time you click the checkout button, the tickets you selected may already have been purchased by someone else! In this case, you will start again and select other tickets until you get the ones you want. The website is designed to work this way on purpose because Computicket prefers the small probability of having a few customers restart their transactions than locking the database to ensure consistency and have thousands of customers waiting for their Web pages to refresh. If you have noticed the small countdown clock when using Webtickets to buy concert tickets, you have seen the same principle at work.

As this example shows, when dealing with highly distributed systems, some companies tend to forfeit the consistency and isolation components of the ACIDS properties to achieve higher availability. This trade-off between consistency and availability has generated a new type of distributed data systems in which data are **basically available, soft state, eventually consistent (BASE)**. BASE refers to a data consistency model in which data changes are not immediate but propagate slowly through the system until all replicas are eventually consistent. For example, **NoSQL** databases provide a highly distributed database with eventual consistency (see Chapter 2). In practice, the emergence of NoSQL distributed databases now provides a spectrum of consistency that ranges from the highly consistent (ACIDS) to the eventually consistent (BASE), as shown in Table 14.7.

NewSQL databases attempt to merge the best of relational and NoSQL data models. For example, the Google Cloud Spanner data service provides highly scalable distributed databases with support for ACIDS transactions. This new type of database provides consistency and high availability with relaxed partition tolerance support. In practice, the emergence of NoSQL and NewSQL distributed databases now provides a spectrum of consistency that ranges from ACIDS to the eventually consistent BASE.

TABLE 14.7 Distributed database spectrum

DBMS Type	Consistency	Availability	Partition Tolerance	Transaction Model	Trade-off
Centralised DBMS	High	High	N/A	ACIDS	No distributed data processing
Relational DBMS	High	Relaxed	High	ACIDS (2PC)	Sacrifices availability to ensure consistency and isolation
NoSQL DDBMS	Relaxed	High	High	BASE	Sacrifices consistency to ensure availability
NewSQL DDBMS	High	High	Relaxed	ACIDS	Sacrifices partition tolerance to ensure transaction consistency and availability

14.13 DATABASE SECURITY

Maintaining data security in a DDBMS is far more complex than in a centralised DBMS, as the underlying network has also to be made secure. Typically the DDBMS database will support all of the security features described in Chapter 10, Database Development Process, i.e. password authentication for users and roles. In addition, specific vendors will offer additional features. For example, Oracle provides features to access a distributed database via authentication through database links.[4] To make a link public, the PUBLIC keyword is used when creating the actual link. Consider the following SQL statement:

```
CREATE PUBLIC DATABASE LINK customer USING 'travel';
```

This statement creates a public, non-authenticated link that all users could access by referencing the 'customer' pointer to the remote database 'travel'.

For more specific information about DDMBS security, refer to the vendor-specific reference manual.

14.14 DISTRIBUTED DATABASES WITHIN THE CLOUD

Current trends in distributed data systems cannot fail to discuss cloud computing. **Cloud computing** is a new style of delivering applications, data and resources to users over the Web. It provides an alternative for organisations that do not wish to provide their own information technology (IT) infrastructure to host their own databases or software. Instead, they rely on a third party cloud provider that uses a number of interconnected and virtualised computers to supply a range of IT services that are standardised. Each third party cloud provider will have its own flexible pricing model for each service it provides, which can be negotiated with the organisation. This is often called a **service level agreement**. The main benefits to an organisation of using cloud infrastructure are:

14

- *Cost-effectiveness.* As the third party cloud provider is likely to be hosting services for many organisations, only one IT infrastructure is required, which reduces the cost to the individual

4 Oracle® Database Administrator's Guide, 11g Release 2 (11.2), Part Number E25494-02. Available: https://docs.oracle.com/cd/E11882_01/nav/portal_4.htm

organisation. Under the negotiated service level agreement, an organisation will also only pay for what it requires.

- *Latest software*. Most third party cloud providers will ensure that their software is always the latest version available to remain competitive.
- *Scalable architecture*. If the data requirements of the organisation expand, it is easy to increase the database capacity and/or change the underlying data model.
- *Mobile access*. Data and software within the cloud can be accessed generally from anywhere, which allows greater flexibility for employees in terms of where they work.

NOTE

You will learn more about cloud computing services in Chapter 17, Database Connectivity and Web Technologies.

It is clear that traditional DDBMS will face problems when trying to operate in a cloud environment. For example, a DDBMS typically has control over all data requests (through queries) and associated hardware resources to ensure data is consistent. This is in contrast to a DDBMS operating within a cloud where hardware resources are allocated dynamically based upon service requirements at a given time.[5]

One solution is to use NoSQL databases to store and manage data within the cloud. Current NoSQL solutions include **column stores** and **document stores**:

- *Column stores* are for large-scale distributed systems that store petrabytes of data across hundreds, if not thousands, of servers. Google, for example, uses Bigtable to store its structured data for applications such as Google Earth. Google defines Bigtable as a parse, distributed, persistent multidimensional sorted map where the map is indexed by a row key, column key and a time stamp.
- *Document stores* move away from storing data in tables. Instead, each document is stored differently depending upon its size and format. Document stores are referred to as document-orientated databases. An example is Apache's CouchDB, which is a distributed database system where replica copies of the same database can exist on multiple servers or offline clients. In addition, all users are offered the ability to query, update, insert or delete data.

A further example of a vendor-specific NoSQL database solution is Amazon's SimpleDB, which is a non-relational data store that operates within a cloud environment. Thus, the data can be geographically distributed with replication, which allows high availability. Traditional relational database queries can be used to query data using Web service requests. The underlying data model can be changed quickly, and data is automatically indexed and optimised for performance.

Cloud computing seeks ultimately to offer unlimited scalability, but do cloud infrastructures follow the CAP theorem? As data is stored and accessed using Web services, it is a necessity that the cloud can deal with failure of individual servers (nodes within the cloud) so the property of partition tolerance is met. High availability of data is also essential. So, a cloud can be said to support only two properties of the CAP theorem and is often referred to as an AP system. In 2012, Dr Daniel Abadi stated 'that a distributed system often cannot support synchronous replication because many applications require low latency. Thus, consistency is sacrificed even when there is no network partition'.[6]

---

5 Singh, T. and Sandhu, P., Cloud Computing Databases: Latest Trends and Architectural Concepts, *World Academy of Science, Engineering and Technology*, 73, pp. 1042–45, 2011.

6 Shim, S., The CAP Theorem's Growing Impact, *IEEE Computer Society*, 45(2), 21–2, 2012.

When a third party manages all your data, how good is the security of that data? In 2019, big public cloud providers such as Microsoft Azure, Google Cloud, Amazon Web Services (AWS), IBM, Alibaba and Oracle are set to grow bigger. This growth makes them more of a target for malicious attacks. Oracle predicts that the number of security-related events will increase dramatically on a daily basis and that one solution will be to use cloud-based artificial intelligence to defend against these threats.[7]

14.15 C.J. DATE'S 12 COMMANDMENTS FOR DISTRIBUTED DATABASES

No discussion of distributed databases is complete unless it includes C.J. Date's distributed database commandments.[8] Date's commandments describe a fully distributed database and, although no current DDBMS conforms to all of them, the rules do constitute a useful distributed database target. The 12 rules are as follows:

1. *Local site independence.* Each local site can act as an independent, autonomous, centralised DBMS. Each site is responsible for security, concurrency control, backup and recovery.
2. *Central site independence.* No site in the network relies on a central site or any other site. All sites have the same capabilities.
3. *Failure independence.* The system is not affected by node failures. The system is in continuous operation, even in the case of a node failure or an expansion of the network.
4. *Location transparency.* The user does not need to know the location of the data in order to retrieve those data.
5. *Fragmentation transparency.* The user sees only one logical database. Data fragmentation is transparent to the user. The user does not need to know the name of the database fragments in order to retrieve them.
6. *Replication transparency.* The user sees only one logical database. The DDBMS transparently selects the database fragment to access. To the user, the DDBMS manages all fragments transparently.
7. *Distributed query processing.* A distributed query may be executed at several different DP sites. Query optimisation is performed transparently by the DDBMS.
8. *Distributed transaction processing.* A transaction may update data at several different sites. The transaction is transparently executed at several different DP sites.
9. *Hardware independence.* The system must run on any hardware platform.
10. *Operating system independence.* The system must run on any operating system software platform.
11. *Network independence.* The system must run on any network platform.
12. *Database independence.* The system must support any vendor's database product.

14

7 Oracle's top 10 Cloud Predictions 2019 [online], available: www.oracle.com/assets/oracle-cloud-predictions-2019-5244106.pdf, 2019

8 Date, C.J., 'Twelve Rules for a Distributed Database', *Computer World*, 2 (23), pp. 77–81, 8 June, 1987.

SUMMARY

- A distributed database stores logically related data in two or more physically independent sites connected via a computer network. The database is divided into fragments, which can be horizontal (a set of rows) or vertical (a set of attributes). Each fragment can be allocated to a different network node.
- Distributed processing is the division of logical database processing among two or more network nodes. Distributed databases require distributed processing. A distributed database management system (DDBMS) governs the processing and storage of logically related data through interconnected computer systems.
- The main components of a DDBMS are the transaction processor (TP) and the data processor (DP). The transaction processor component is the software that resides on each computer node that requests data. The data processor component is the software that resides on each computer that stores and retrieves data.
- Current database systems can be classified by the extent to which they support processing and data distribution. Three major categories are used to classify distributed database systems: (1) single-site processing, single-site data (SPSD); (2) multiple-site processing, single-site data (MPSD); and (3) multiple-site processing, multiple-site data (MPMD).
- A homogeneous distributed database system integrates only one particular type of DBMS over a computer network. A heterogeneous distributed database system integrates several different types of DBMSs over a computer network.
- DDBMS characteristics are best described as a set of transparencies: distribution, transaction, failure, heterogeneity and performance. All transparencies share the common objective of making the distributed database behave as though it were a centralised database system; that is, the end user sees the data as part of a single logical centralised database and is unaware of the system's complexities.
- A transaction is formed by one or more database requests. An undistributed transaction updates or requests data from a single site. A distributed transaction can update or request data from multiple sites.
- Distributed concurrency control is required in a network of distributed databases. A two-phase COMMIT protocol is used to ensure that all parts of a transaction are completed.
- A distributed DBMS evaluates every data request to find the optimum access path in a distributed database. The DDBMS must optimise the query to reduce access, communications and CPU costs associated with the query.
- The design of a distributed database must consider the fragmentation and replication of data. The designer must also decide how to allocate each fragment or replica to obtain better overall response time and to ensure data availability to the end user.
- A database can be replicated over several different sites on a computer network. The replication of the database fragments has the objective of improving data availability, thus decreasing access time. A database can be partially, fully, or not replicated. Data allocation strategies are designed to determine the location of the database fragments or replicas.
- The CAP theorem states that a highly distributed data system has some desirable properties of consistency, availability and partition tolerance. However, a system can only provide two of these properties at a time.

KEY TERMS

application processor (AP)
basically available, soft state, eventually consistent (BASE)
centralised data allocation
client/server architecture
cloud computing
column stores
coordinator
data allocation
data fragmentation
data manager (DM)
data processor (DP)
data replication
database fragments
distributed data catalogue (DDC)
distributed data dictionary (DDD)
distributed database
distributed database management system (DDBMS)
distributed global schema
distributed processing
distributed request
distributed transaction
distribution transparency
document stores
DO-UNDO-REDO protocol
failure transparency
fragmentation transparency
fully heterogeneous DDBMS
fully replicated database
heterogeneity transparency
heterogeneous DDBMS
homogeneous DDBMS
horizontal fragmentation
local mapping transparency
location transparency
mixed fragmentation
multiple-site processing, multiple-site data (MPMD)
multiple-site processing, single-site data (MPSD)
mutual consistency rule
network latency
network partitioning
NewSQL
NoSQL
partially replicated database
partition key
partitioned data allocation
performance transparency
remote request
remote transaction
replica transparency
replicated data allocation
service level agreement
single-site processing, single-site data (SPSD)
subordinates
transaction manager (TM)
transaction processor (TP)
transaction transparency
two-phase commit protocol
unique fragment
unreplicated database
vertical fragmentation
write-ahead protocol

FURTHER READING

Jain, A., *The Cloud DBA-Oracle: Managing Oracle Database in the Cloud*. Apress, 2017.

Online Content Answers to selected Review Questions and Problems for this chapter are contained in the online platform for this book.

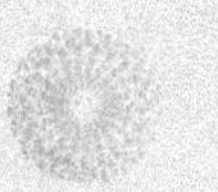

14

REVIEW QUESTIONS

1. Describe the evolution from centralised DBMS to distributed DBMSs.
2. List and discuss some of the factors that influenced the evolution of the DDBMS.
3. What are the advantages of the DDBMS?
4. What are the disadvantages of the DDBMS?
5. Explain the difference between a distributed database and distributed processing.

6 What is a fully distributed database management system?

7 What are the components of a DDBMS?

8 Explain the transparency features of a DDBMS.

9 Define and explain the different types of distribution transparency.

10 Describe the different types of database requests and transactions.

11 Explain the need for the two-phase commit protocol. Then describe the two phases.

12 What is the objective of query optimisation functions?

13 To which transparency feature are the query optimisation functions related?

14 What are the different types of query optimisation algorithms?

15 Describe the three data fragmentation strategies. Give some examples.

16 What is data replication, and what are the three replication strategies?

17 How does a BASE system differ from a traditional distributed database system?

18 What are the three proprieties of the CAP theorem?

19 What are the main benefits to an organisation of using a cloud infrastructure?

PROBLEMS

The following problem is based on the DDBMS scenario in Figure P14.1.

FIGURE P14.1 The DDBMS scenario for Problem 1

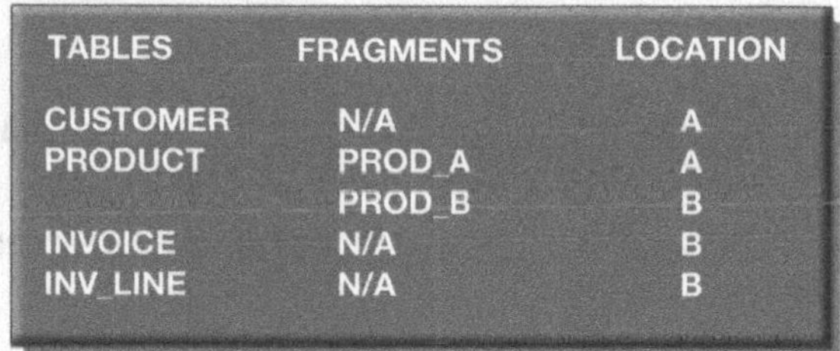

TABLES	FRAGMENTS	LOCATION
CUSTOMER	N/A	A
PRODUCT	PROD_A	A
	PROD_B	B
INVOICE	N/A	B
INV_LINE	N/A	B

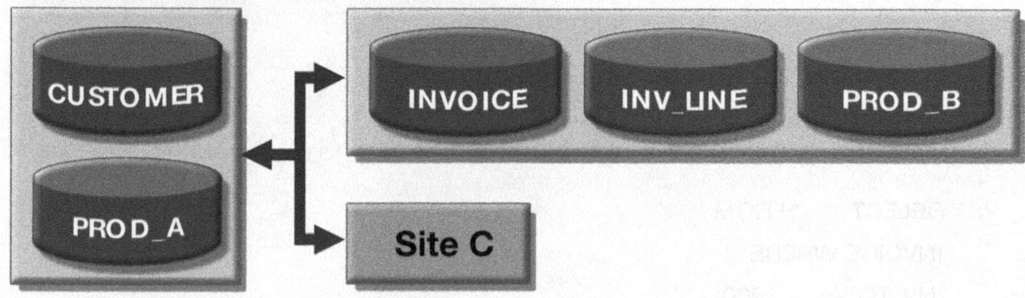

1 Specify the minimum type(s) of operation(s) the database must support (remote request, remote transaction, distributed transaction, or distributed request) to perform the following operations:

At Site C

a
```
SELECT *
FROM      CUSTOMER;
```

b
```
SELECT    *
FROM      INVOICE
WHERE     INV_TOT . 1000;
```

c
```
SELECT    *
FROM      PRODUCT
WHERE     PROD_ QOH < 10;
```

d
```
BEGIN WORK;
UPDATE    CUSTOMER
SET       CUS_BAL = CUS_BAL + 100
WHERE     CUS_NUM = '10936';
INSERT    INTO INVOICE(INV_NUM, CUS_NUM, INV_DATE, INV_TOTAL) VALUES ('986391',
          '10936', '15-FEB-2019', 100);
INSERT    INTO LINE(INV_NUM, PROD_NUM, LINE_PRICE) VALUES('986391', '1023', 100);
UPDATE    PRODUCT
SET       PROD_QOH = PROD_ QOH –1
WHERE     PROD_NUM = '1023';
COMMIT WORK;
```

e
```
BEGIN WORK;
INSERT    INTO CUSTOMER(CUS_NUM, CUS_NAME, CUS_ADDRESS, CUS_BAL)VALUES
          ('34210', 'Victor Ephanor', '143 Main St.', 0.00);
INSERT    INTO INVOICE(INV_NUM, CUS_NUM, INV_DATE, INV_TOTAL) VALUES ('986434',
          '34210', '10-AUG-2018', 2.00);
COMMIT WORK;
```

At Site A

f
```
SELECT    CUS_NUM,CUS_NAME,INV_TOTAL
FROM      CUSTOMER, INVOICE
WHERE     CUSTOMER.CUS_NUM = INVOICE.CUS_NUM;
```

g
```
SELECT    * FROM
INVOICE WHERE
INV_TOTAL > 1000;
```

h
```
SELECT    *
FROM PRODUCT
WHERE     PROD_QOH < 10;
```

At Site B

i
```
SELECT   *
FROM     CUSTOMER;
```

j
```
SELECT   CUS_NAME, INV_TOTAL
FROM     CUSTOMER, INVOICE
WHEREINV_TOTAL > 1000 AND CUSTOMER.CUS_NUM =
INVOICE.CUS_NUM;
```

k
```
SELECT   *
FROM     PRODUCT
WHERE    PROD_QOH<10;
```

2 The following data structure and constraints exist for a magazine publishing company:

- **a** The company publishes one regional magazine in each country: France (FR), South Africa (SA), the Netherlands (NL) and the United Kingdom (UK).
- **b** The company has 300 000 customers (subscribers) distributed throughout the four countries listed in Part a.
- **c** On the first of each month, an annual subscription INVOICE is printed and sent to each customer whose subscription is due for renewal. The INVOICE entity contains a REGION attribute to indicate the country (FR, SA, NL, UK) in which the customer resides:

  CUSTOMER (CUS_NUM, CUS_NAME, CUS_ADDRESS, CUS_CITY, CUS_REGION, CUS_POSTCODE, CUS_SUBSDATE) INVOICE (INV_NUM, INV_REGION, CUS_NUM, INV_DATE, INV_TOTAL)

  The company's management is aware of the problems associated with centralised management and has decided to decentralise management of the subscriptions into the company's four regional subsidiaries. Each subscription site will handle its own customer and invoice data. The management at company headquarters, however, will have access to customer and invoice data to generate annual reports and to issue ad hoc queries such as:

  - List all current customers by region.
  - List all new customers by region.
  - Report all invoices by customer and by region.

  Given those requirements, how must you partition the database?

3 Given the scenario and the requirements in Problem 2, answer the following questions:

- **a** Which recommendations will you make regarding the type and characteristics of the required database system?
- **b** What type of data fragmentation is needed for each table?
- **c** Which criteria must be used to partition each database?
- **d** Design the database fragments. Show an example with node names, location, fragment names, attribute names and demonstration data.
- **e** What type of distributed database operations must be supported at each remote site?
- **f** What type of distributed database operations must be supported at the headquarters site?

CHAPTER 15

Databases for Business Intelligence

IN THIS CHAPTER, YOU WILL LEARN:

- How business intelligence provides a comprehensive business decision support framework
- About business intelligence architecture, its evolution and reporting styles
- About the data warehouse life cycle
- How to prepare data for the data warehouse using the Extraction, Transformation and Loading Process.
- How to develop star and snowflake schemas for decision-making purposes
- About the role and functions of data analytics and data mining
- About the characteristics and capabilities of online analytical processing (OLAP)
- How SQL analytic functions are used to support data analytics
- About data visualisation and how it supports business intelligence

PREVIEW

Business intelligence (BI) is the collection of best practices and software tools developed to support business decision making in this age of globalisation, emerging markets, rapid change and increasing regulation. The complexity and range of information required to support business decisions has increased, and operational database structures were unable to support all of these requirements. Therefore, a new data storage facility, called a data warehouse, developed. The data warehouse extracts its data from operational databases as well as from external sources, providing a more comprehensive data pool. Additionally, new ways to analyse and present decision support data were developed.

Online analytical processing (OLAP) provides advanced data analysis and visualisation tools, including multidimensional data analysis. This chapter explores the main concepts and components of business intelligence and decision support systems that gather, generate and present information for business decision makers, focusing especially on the use of data warehouses, data analytics and data visualisation.

15.1 THE NEED FOR DATA ANALYSIS

Organisations tend to grow and prosper as they gain a better understanding of their environment. Typically, business managers must be able to track daily transactions to evaluate how the business is performing. By tapping into the operational database, management can develop strategies to meet organisational goals. In addition, data analysis can provide information about short-term tactical evaluations and strategies such as: Are our sales promotions working? What market percentage are we controlling? Are we attracting new customers? Tactical and strategic decisions are also shaped by constant pressure from external and internal forces, including globalisation, the cultural and legal environment, and, perhaps most importantly, technology.

Given the many and varied competitive pressures, managers are always looking for a competitive advantage through product development and maintenance, service, market positioning, sales promotion and so on. Thanks to the internet, customers are more informed about the products they want and how much they are willing to pay. Technological advances allow customers to place orders from their smartphones while they commute to work. Decision makers can no longer wait a couple of days for a report to be generated; quick decisions must be made for the business to remain competitive. Every day, advertisements offer, for example, instant price matching, and the question is, How can a company survive on lower margins and still make a profit? The key is having the right data at the right time to support the decision-making process.

Different managerial levels require different decision support needs. For example, transaction-processing systems, based on operational databases, are tailored to serve the information needs of people who deal with short-term inventory, accounts payable and purchasing. Middle-level managers, general managers, vice presidents and presidents focus on strategic and tactical decision making. Those managers require summarised information designed to help them make decisions in a complex business environment. Companies and software vendors addressed these multilevel decision support needs by creating autonomous applications for particular groups of users – for example, those in finance, customer relationship management, etc. Applications were also developed for different industries such as education, healthcare and finance. The approach started to work well, but changes in the way in which business was conducted, e.g. globalisation, expanding markets, merges and acquisitions, increased regulation and new technologies, called for new ways of integrating and managing decision support across levels, sectors and geographical locations. This more comprehensive and integrated decision support framework became known as business intelligence.

15.2 BUSINESS INTELLIGENCE

Business intelligence (BI)[1] is a term that describes a comprehensive, cohesive, and integrated set of tools and processes used to capture, collect, integrate, store and analyse data with the purpose of generating and presenting information to support business decision making. This intelligence is based on learning and understanding the facts about the business environment. BI is a framework 15

1 In 1989, while working at Gartner Inc., Howard Dresner popularised BI as an umbrella term to describe a set of concepts and methods to improve business decision making by using fact-based support systems (www.computerworld.com/action/article.do?command=viewArticleBasic&articleId=266298).

that allows a business to transform data into information, information into knowledge, and knowledge into wisdom. BI has the potential to affect a company's culture positively by creating continuous business performance improvement through active decision support at all levels in an organisation. This business insight empowers users to make sound decisions based on the accumulated knowledge of the business.

BI's initial adopters were high-volume industries such as financial services, insurance and healthcare companies. As BI technology evolved, its usage spread to other industries such as telecommunications, retail/merchandising, manufacturing, media, government, and even education. Table 15.1 lists some companies that have implemented BI tools and shows how the tools have benefited the companies. You will learn about these tools later in the chapter.

TABLE 15.1 Solving business problems and adding value with BI tools

Company	Problem	Benefit
CiCi's Enterprises Eighth-largest pizza chain in the US; operates 650 pizza restaurants in 30 states Source: Cognos Corp. *www.cognos.com*	■ Information access was cumbersome and time-consuming ■ Needed to increase accuracy in the creation of marketing budgets ■ Needed an easy, reliable and efficient way to access daily data	■ Provided accurate, timely budgets in less time ■ Provided analysts with access to data for decision-making purposes ■ Received in-depth view of product performance by store to reduce waste and increase profits
Nasdaq Largest US electronic stock market trading organisation Source: Oracle *www.oracle.com*	■ Inability to provide real-time, ad hoc query and standard reporting for executives, business analysts and other users ■ Excessive storage costs for many terabytes of data	■ Reduced storage costs by moving to a multitier storage solution ■ Implemented new data warehouse centre with support for ad hoc query and reporting, and near real-time data access for end users
Pfizer Global pharmaceutical company Source: Oracle *www.oracle.com*	■ Needed a way to control costs and adjust to tougher market conditions, international competition and increasing government regulations ■ Needed better analytical capabilities and flexible decision-making framework	■ Ability to get and integrate financial data from multiple sources in a reliable way ■ Streamlined, standards-based financial analysis to improve forecasting process ■ Faster and smarter decision making for business strategy formulation
Swisscom Switzerland's leading telecommunications provider Source: Microsoft *www.microsoft.com*	■ Needed a tool to help employees monitor service-level compliance ■ Had a time-consuming process to generate performance reports ■ Needed a way to integrate data from 200 different systems	■ Ability to monitor performance using dashboard technology ■ Quick and easy access to real-time performance data ■ Managers have closer and better control over costs

Implementing BI in an organisation involves capturing not only internal and external business data, but also the metadata, or knowledge about the data. In practice, BI is a complex proposition that requires a deep understanding and alignment of the business processes, business data and information needs of users at all levels in an organisation. (See Appendix L, Data Warehouse Implementation Factors, available on the online platform for this book.)

BI is not a product by itself, but a framework of concepts, practices, tools and technologies that help a business better understand its core capabilities, provide snapshots of the company situation and identify key opportunities to create competitive advantage. In general, BI provides a framework for:

1. Collecting and storing operational data
2. Aggregating the operational data into decision support data
3. Analysing decision support data to generate information
4. Presenting such information to the end user to support business decisions
5. Making business decisions, which in turn generate more data that are collected, stored, and so on (restarting the process)
6. Monitoring results to evaluate outcomes of the business decisions, which again provides more data to be collected, stored, and so on
7. Predicting future behaviours and outcomes with a high degree of accuracy.

The seven preceding points represent a system-wide view of the flow of data, processes and outcomes within the BI framework. In practice, the first point, collecting and storing operational data, does not fall into the realm of a BI system per se; rather, it is the function of an operational system. However, the BI system will use the operational data as input material from which information will be derived. The rest of the processes and outcomes explained in the preceding points are orientated towards generating knowledge, and they are the focus of the BI system. In the following section, you will learn about the basic BI architecture.

15.2.1 Business Intelligence Architecture

BI covers a range of technologies and applications to manage the entire data life cycle from acquisition to storage, transformation, integration, presentation, analysis, monitoring and archiving. BI functionality ranges from simple data gathering and transformation to very complex data analysis and presentation. BI architecture ranges from highly integrated single-vendor systems to loosely integrated, multivendor environments. However, some common functions are expected in most BI implementations.

Like any critical business IT infrastructure, the BI architecture is composed of data, people, processes, technology and the management of such components. Figure 15.1 depicts how all these components fit together within the BI framework.

FIGURE 15.1 Business intelligence framework

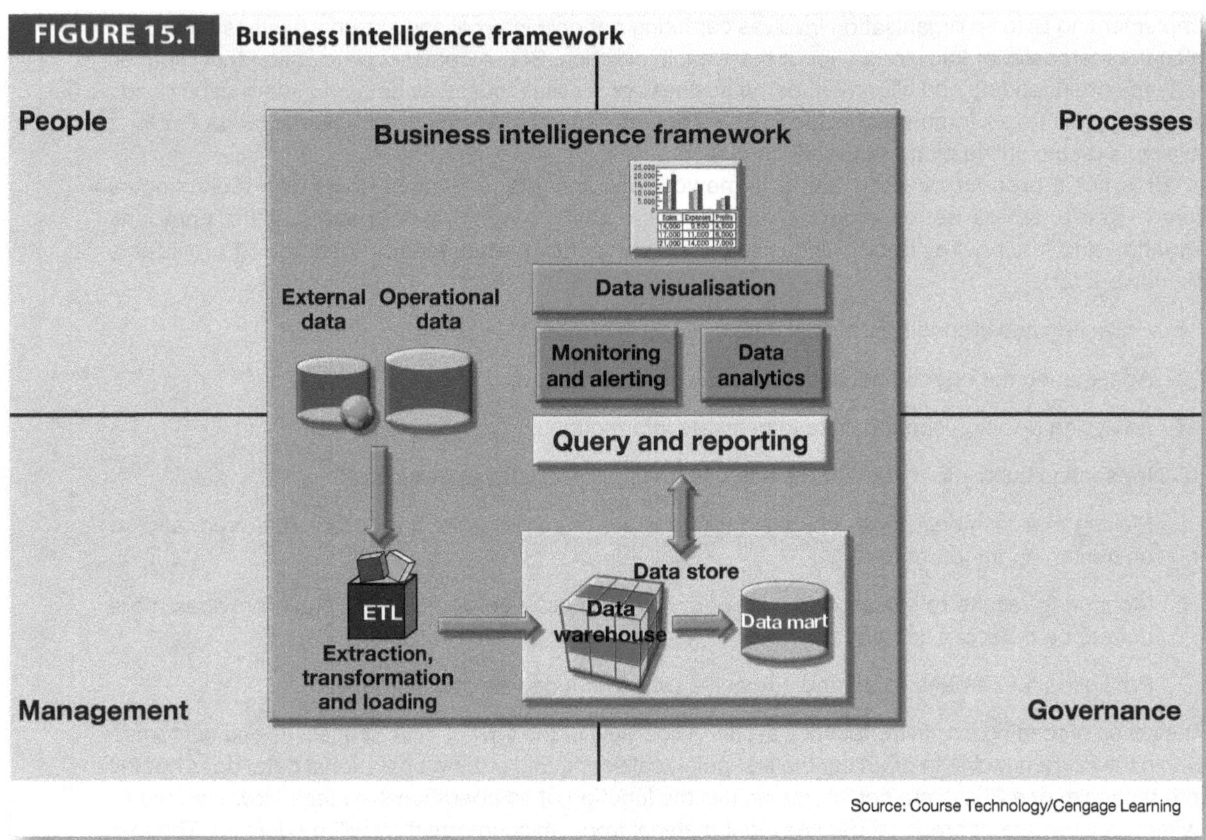

Source: Course Technology/Cengage Learning

The general BI framework depicted in Figure 15.1 has six basic components that encompass the functionality required in most current-generation BI systems. You will learn more about these components later in this chapter. The components are briefly described in Table 15.2.

TABLE 15.2 Basic BI architectural components

Component	Description
ETL tools	Data **extraction, transformation and loading (ETL)** tools collect, filter, integrate and aggregate internal and external data to be saved into a data store optimised for decision support. Internal data are generated by the company during its day-to-day operations, such as product sales history, invoicing and payments. The external data sources provide data that cannot be found within the company but are relevant to the business, such as stock prices, market indicators, marketing information (such as demographics) and competitors' data. Such data are generally located in external databases provided by industry groups or companies that market the data.
Data store	The **data store** is optimised for decision support and is generally represented by a *data warehouse* or a *data mart*. The data are stored in structures that are optimised for data analysis and query speed.

Component	Description
Query and reporting	This component performs data selection and retrieval, and is used by the data analyst to create queries that access the database and create the required reports. Depending on the implementation, the query and reporting tool accesses the operational database, or more commonly, the data store.
Data visualisation	This component presents data to the end user in a variety of meaningful and innovative ways. This tool helps the end user to select the most appropriate presentation format, such as summary reports, maps, pie or bar graphs, mixed graphs, or dashboards.
Data monitoring and alerting	This component allows real-time monitoring of business activities. The BI system will present the concise information in a single integrated view for the data analyst. This integrated view could include specific metrics about the system performance or activities, such as number of orders placed in the past four hours, number of customer complaints by product by month, and total revenue by region. Alerts can be placed on a given metric; once the value of a metric goes below or above a certain baseline, the system will perform a given action, such as emailing shop floor managers, presenting visual alerts or starting an application.
Data analytics	This component performs data analysis and data-mining tasks using the data in the data store. This tool advises the user about which data analysis tool to select and how to build a reliable business data model. Business models are generated by special algorithms that identify and enhance the understanding of business situations and problems. Data analysis can be either explanatory or predictive. Explanatory analysis uses the existing data in the data store to discover relationships and their types, and predictive analysis creates statistical models of the data that allow predictions of future values and events.

Each BI component shown in Table 15.2 has generated a fast-growing market for specialised tools. Thanks to technological advancements, the components can interact with other components to form a truly open architecture. As a matter of fact, you can integrate multiple tools from different vendors into a single BI framework. Table 15.3 shows a sample of common BI tools and vendors.

TABLE 15.3 Sample of business intelligence tools

Tool	Description	Sample Vendors
Dashboards and business activity monitoring	**Dashboards** use Web-based technologies to present key business performance indicators or information in a single integrated view, generally using graphics that are clear, concise and easy to understand.	Salesforce IBM/Cognos BusinessObjects Information Builders iDashboards Tableau
Portals	**Portals** provide a unified, single point of entry for information distribution. Portals are a Web-based technology that use a Web browser to integrate data from multiple sources into a single Web page. Many different types of BI functionality can be accessed through a portal.	Oracle Portal Actuate Microsoft SAP

Tool	Description	Sample Vendors
Data analysis and reporting tools	These advanced tools are used to query multiple and diverse data sources to create integrated reports.	Microsoft Reporting Services MicroStrategy SAS Web Report Studio
Data-mining tools	These tools provide advanced statistical analysis to uncover problems and opportunities hidden within business data.	SAP Teradata MicroStrategy Hadoop
Data warehouses (DW)	The data warehouse is the foundation of a BI infrastructure. Data are captured from the production system and placed in the DW on a near real-time basis. BI provides company-wide integration of data and the capability to respond to business issues in a timely manner.	Amazon Redshift Oracle Exadata IBM DB2 Azure
OLAP tools	Online analytical processing provides multidimensional data analysis.	IBM/Cognos Micro Strategy ioCube Apache Kylin
Data visualisation	These tools provide advanced visual analysis and techniques to enhance understanding and create additional insight into business data and its true meaning.	Dundas Tableau QlikView Actuate

As depicted in Figure 15.1, BI integrates people and processes using technology to add value to the business. Such value is derived from how end users apply such information in their daily activities, and particularly in their daily business decision making.

The focus of traditional information systems was on operational automation and reporting; in contrast, BI tools focus on the strategic and tactical use of information. To achieve this goal, BI recognises that technology alone is not enough. Therefore, BI uses an arrangement of best management practices to manage data as a corporate asset. One of the most recent developments in this area is the use of master data management techniques. **Master data management (MDM)** is a collection of concepts, techniques and processes for the proper identification, definition and management of data elements within an organisation. MDM's main goal is to provide a comprehensive and consistent definition of all data within an organisation. MDM ensures that all company resources (people, procedures and IT systems) that work with data have uniform and consistent views of the company's data.

An added benefit of this meticulous approach to data management and decision making is that it provides a framework for business governance. **Governance** is a method or process of government. In this case, BI provides a method for controlling and monitoring business health and for consistent decision making. Furthermore, having such governance creates accountability for business decisions. In the present age of business flux, accountability is increasingly important. Had governance been as pivotal to business operations in previous years, crises precipitated by Enron, WorldCom, Arthur Andersen and the 2008 financial meltdown might have been avoided.

Monitoring a business's health is crucial to understanding where the company is and where it is headed. To do this, BI makes extensive use of a special type of metrics known as key performance indicators. **Key performance indicators (KPIs)** are quantifiable numeric or scale-based measurements that assess the company's effectiveness or success in reaching its strategic and operational goals. Many different KPIs are used by different industries. Some examples of KPIs are:

- *General*. Year-to-year measurements of profit by line of business, same-store sales, product turnovers, product recalls, sales by promotion and sales by employee
- *Finance*. Earnings per share, profit margin, revenue per employee, percentage of sales to account receivable and assets to sales
- *Human resources*. Applicants to job openings, employee turnover and employee longevity
- *Education*. Graduation rates, number of incoming first-years, student retention rates, publication rates and teaching evaluation scores

KPIs are determined after the main strategic, tactical and operational goals are defined for a business. To tie the KPI to the strategic master plan of an organisation, a KPI is compared to a desired goal within a specific time frame. For example, if you are in an academic environment, you might be interested in ways to measure student satisfaction or retention. In this case, a sample goal would be to increase the final exam grades of graduating high school seniors by autumn 2022. Another sample KPI would be to increase the returning student rate from first year to second year from 60 per cent to 75 per cent by 2022. In this case, such performance indicators would be measured and monitored on a year-to-year basis, and plans to achieve such goals would be set in place.

Although BI has an unquestionably important role in modern business operations, the manager must initiate the decision support process by asking the appropriate questions. The BI environment exists to support the manager; it does not replace the management function. If the manager fails to ask the appropriate questions, problems will not be identified and solved, and opportunities will be missed. In spite of the very powerful BI presence, the human component is still at the centre of business technology.

The main BI architectural components were illustrated in Figure 15.1 and further explained in Tables 15.2 and 15.3. However, the heart of the BI system is its advanced information generation and decision support capabilities. A BI system's advanced decision support functions come to life via its intuitive and informational user interface, and particularly its reporting capabilities. A modern BI system provides three distinctive reporting styles:

- *Advanced reporting*. A BI system presents insightful information about the organisation in a variety of presentation formats. Furthermore, the reports provide interactive features that allow the end user to study the data from multiple points of view – from highly summarised to very detailed data. The reports present key actionable information used to support decision making.
- *Monitoring and alerting*. After a decision has been made, the BI system offers ways to monitor the decision's outcome. The BI system provides the end user with ways to define metrics and other key performance indicators to evaluate different aspects of an organisation. In addition, exceptions and alerts can be set to warn managers promptly about deviations or problem areas.
- *Advanced data analytics*. A BI system provides tools to help the end user discover relationships, patterns and trends hidden within the organisation's data. These tools are used to create two types of data analysis: explanatory and predictive. Explanatory analysis provides ways to discover relationships, trends and patterns among data, while predictive analysis provides the end user with ways to create models that predict future outcomes.

Understanding the architectural components of a BI framework is the first step in properly implementing BI in an organisation. A good BI infrastructure promises many benefits to an organisation, as outlined in the next section.

15.2.2 Business Intelligence Benefits

As you have learnt in previous sections, a properly implemented BI architecture could provide a framework for continuous performance improvements and business decision making. Improved decision making is the main goal of BI, but BI provides other benefits:

- *Integrating architecture*. Like any other IT project, BI has the potential of becoming the integrating umbrella for a disparate mix of IT systems within an organisation. This architecture could support all types of company-generated data from operational to executive, as well as diverse hardware such as mainframes, servers, desktops, laptops and mobile devices.
- *Common user interface for data reporting and analysis*. BI front ends can provide up-to-the-minute consolidated information using a common interface for all company users. IT departments no longer have to provide multiple training options for diverse interfaces. End users benefit from similar or common interfaces in different devices that use multiple clever and insightful presentation formats.
- *Common data repository fosters single version of company data*. In the past, multiple IT systems supported different aspects of an organisation's operations. Such systems collected and stored data in separate data stores. Keeping the data synchronised and up-to-date has always been difficult. BI provides a framework to integrate such data under a common environment and present a single version of the data.
- *Improved organisational performance*. BI can provide competitive advantages in many different areas, from customer support to manufacturing processes. Such advantages can be reflected in added efficiency, reduced waste, increased sales, reduced employee and customer turnover, and most importantly, an increased bottom line for the business.

Achieving all these benefits takes a lot of human, financial and technological resources, not to mention time. BI benefits are not achieved overnight, but are the result of a focused company-wide effort that could take a long time. As a matter of fact, as you will learn in the next section, the BI field has evolved over a long period of time itself.

15.2.3 Business Intelligence Evolution

Providing useful information to end users has been a priority of IT systems since mainframe computing became an integral part of corporations. Business decision support has evolved over many decades. Following computer technology advances, business intelligence started with centralised reporting systems and evolved into today's highly integrated BI environments. Table 15.4 summarises the evolution of BI systems.

TABLE 15.4 **Business intelligence evolution**

System Type	Data Source	Data Extraction/ Integration Process	Data Store	End User Query Tool	End User Presentation Tool
Traditional mainframe-based online transaction processing (OLTP)	Operational data	None Reports read and summarise data directly from operational data	None Temporary files used for reporting purposes	Very basic Predefined reporting formats Basic sorting, totalling, and averaging	Very basic Menu-driven, predefined reports, text and numbers only
Managerial information system (MIS)	Operational data	Basic extraction and aggregation Read, filter and summarise operational data into intermediate data store	Lightly aggregated data in RDBMS	Same as above, in addition to some ad hoc reporting using SQL	Same as above, in addition to some ad hoc columnar report definitions
First-generation departmental decision support system (DSS)	Operational data External data	Data extraction and integration process populates DSS data store Run periodically	First DSS database generation Usually RDBMS	Query tool with some analytical capabilities and predefined reports	Spreadsheet style Advanced presentation tools with plotting and graphics capabilities
First generation BI	Operational data External data	Advanced data extraction and integration Access diverse data sources, filters, aggregations, classifications, scheduling and conflict resolution	Data warehouse RDBMS technology Optimised for query purposes Star schema model	Same as above	Same as above, in addition to multidimensional presentation tools with drill-down capabilities
Second-generation BI Online analytical processing (OLAP)	Same as above	Same as above	Data warehouse stores data in MDBMS cubes with multiple dimensions	Adds support for end-user-based data analytics	Same as above, but uses cubes and multidimensional matrixes; limited by terms of cube size Dashboards Scorecards Portals
Third-generation Mobile BI Cloud-based Big Data	Same as above but includes social media, IoT and machine-generated data	Same as above Cloud-based	Same as above Cloud-based Hadoop and NoSQL databases	Advanced analytics Flexible interactions via data visualisation	Mobile devices: iPhone, iPad, Pixel, Galaxy Note

Using Table 15.4 as a guide, you can trace business intelligence from the mainframe environment to the desktop and then to the more current cloud-based, mobile BI environments. (Chapter 17, Database Connectivity and Web Technologies, provides a detailed discussion of cloud-based systems.)

The precursor of the modern BI environment was the first-generation decision support system. A **decision support system (DSS)** is an arrangement of computerised tools used to assist managerial decision making. A DSS typically has a much narrower focus and reach than a BI solution. At first, decision support systems were the realm of a few selected managers in an organisation. Over time, and with the introduction of the desktop computer, decision support systems migrated to more agile platforms, such as minicomputers, high-end servers, commodity servers, appliances and cloud-based offerings. This evolution effectively changed the reach of decision support systems; BI is no longer limited to a small group of top-level managers with training in statistical modelling. Instead, BI is now available to all users in an organisation, from line managers to the shop floor to mobile agents in the field.

You can also use Table 15.4 to track the evolution of information dissemination styles used in business intelligence:

- Starting in the late 1970s, the need for information distribution was filled by centralised reports running on mainframes, minicomputers or even central server environments. Such reports were predefined and took considerable time to process.
- With the introduction of desktop computers in the 1980s, a new style of information distribution, the spreadsheet, emerged as the dominant format for decision support systems. In this environment, managers downloaded information from centralised data stores and manipulated the data in desktop spreadsheets.
- As the use of spreadsheets multiplied, IT departments tried to manage the flow of data in a more formal way using enterprise reporting systems. These systems were developed in the early 1990s and basically integrated all data into an IT umbrella that started with the first-generation DSS. The systems still used spreadsheet-like features with which end users were familiar.
- Once DSSs were established, the evolution of business intelligence flourished with the introduction of the data warehouse and online analytical processing systems (OLAPs) in the mid-1990s. You can find out more about OLAP in Section 15.7 of this chapter.
- Rapid changes in information technology and the internet revolution led to the introduction of advanced BI systems such as Web-based dashboards in the early 2000s and mobile BI later in the decade. With mobile BI, end users access BI reports via native applications that run on a mobile smart device, such as the iPhone, Google Pixel or iPad.

Figure 15.2 depicts the evolution of BI information dissemination.

FIGURE 15.2 Evolution of BI information dissemination formats

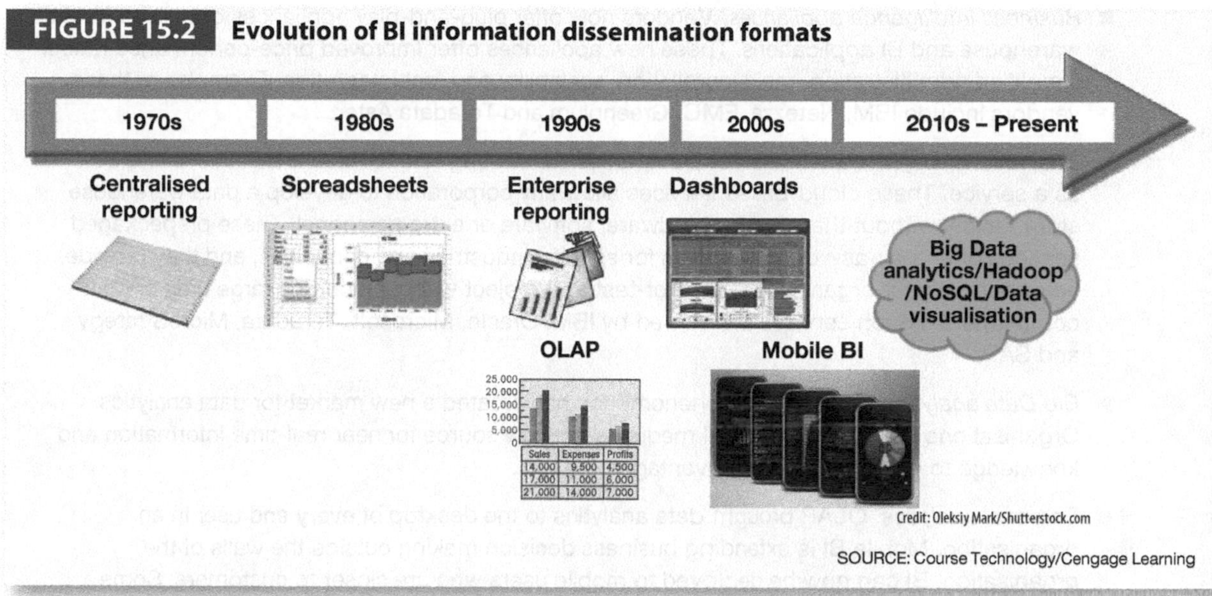

SOURCE: Course Technology/Cengage Learning

Although still in its infancy, mobile BI technology is poised to have a significant impact on the way BI information is disseminated and processed. If the number of students using smart phones to communicate with friends, update their Facebook status and send tweets on Twitter is any indicator, you can expect the next generation of consumers and workers to be highly mobile. Leading corporations are therefore starting to push decision making to agents in the field to facilitate customer relationships, sales and ordering, and product support. Such mobile technologies are so portable and interactive that some users call them 'disruptive' technologies.

BI information technology has evolved from centralised reporting styles to the current, mobile BI style in just over a decade. The rate of technological change is not slowing down; to the contrary, technology advancements are accelerating the adoption of BI to new levels. The next section illustrates some BI technology trends.

15.2.4 Business Intelligence Technology Trends

Several technological advances are driving the growth of business intelligence technologies. These advances create new generations of more affordable products and services that are faster and easier to use. In turn, such products and services open new markets and work as driving forces in the increasing adoption of business intelligence technologies within organisations. Some of the more remarkable technological trends are:

- *Data storage improvements*. New data storage technologies, such as solid state drives (SSDs) and Serial Advanced Technology Attachment (SATA) drives, offer increased performance and larger capacity that make data storage faster and more affordable. Currently, you can buy single drives with a capacity approaching 16 terabytes.

- *Business intelligence appliances*. Vendors now offer plug-and-play appliances optimised for data warehouse and BI applications. These new appliances offer improved price-performance ratios, simplified administration, rapid installation, scalability and fast integration. Examples of these vendors include IBM, Netezza, EMC, Greenplum and Teradata Aster.
- *Business intelligence as a service*. Companies are starting to offer data warehouses and BI as a service. These cloud-based services allow any corporation to develop a data warehouse store rapidly without the need for hardware, software or extra personnel. These prepackaged services offer 'pay-as-you-go' models for specific industries and capacities, and they provide an opportunity for organisations to pilot-test a BI project without incurring large time or cost commitments. Such services are offered by IBM, Oracle, Microsoft, Teradata, MicroStrategy and SAP.
- *Big Data analytics*. The Big Data phenomenon has created a new market for data analytics. Organisations are turning to social media as the new source for near real-time information and knowledge to gain competitive advantages.
- *Personal analytics*. OLAP brought data analytics to the desktop of every end user in an organisation. Mobile BI is extending business decision making outside the walls of the organisation. BI can now be deployed to mobile users who are closer to customers. Some personal analytics vendors include MicroStrategy and Tableau. There is a growing trend for self-service personalised data analytics.

One constant in this relentless technological evolution is the need for better decision support data and the importance of understanding the difference between decision support data and operational data.

15.3 DECISION SUPPORT DATA

Although BI is used at strategic and tactical managerial levels within an organisation, its effectiveness depends on the quality of the data gathered at the operational level. Yet operational data is seldom well suited to decison support tasks. The differences between operational data and decision support data are examined in the following section.

15.3.1 Operational Data vs Decision Support Data

Operational data and decision support data serve different purposes. Therefore, it is not surprising to learn that their formats and structures differ.

Most operational data are stored in a relational database in which the structures (tables) tend to be highly normalised. Operational data storage is optimised to support transactions that represent daily operations. For example, each time an item is sold, it must be accounted for. Customer data, inventory data, and so on are in a frequent update mode. To provide effective update performance, operational systems store data in many tables, each with a minimum number of fields. Thus, a simple sales transaction might be represented by five or more different tables (for example, INVOICE, INVOICE LINE, DISCOUNT, STORE and DEPARTMENT). Although such an arrangement is excellent in an operational database, it is not query-friendly. For example, to extract a simple invoice, you would have to join several tables. Whereas operational data capture daily business transactions, DSS data give tactical and strategic business meaning to the operational data. From the data analyst's point of view, DSS data differ from operational data in three main areas: time span, granularity and dimensionality.

- *Time span.* Operational data cover a short time frame. In contrast, decision support data tend to cover a longer time frame. Managers are seldom interested in a specific sales invoice to customer X; rather, they tend to focus on sales generated during the past month, the past year or the past five years.
- *Granularity (level of aggregation).* DSS data must be presented at different levels of aggregation, from highly summarised to near-atomic. For example, if managers need to analyse sales by region, they must be able to access data showing the sales by region, by city within the region, by store within the city within the region, and so on. In this case, managers require summarised data to compare the regions, but they also need data in a structure that enables them to **drill down**, or decompose, the data into more atomic components (that is, finer-grained data at lower levels of aggregation). In contrast, when you **roll up** the data, you are aggregating the data to a higher level.
- *Dimensionality.* Operational data focus on representing individual transactions rather than on the effects of the transactions over time. In contrast, data analysts tend to include many data dimensions and are interested in how the data relate over those dimensions. For example, an analyst might want to know how product X fared relative to product Z during the past six months by region, province, city, store and customer. In that case, both place and time are part of the picture.

Figure 15.3 shows how decision support data can be examined from multiple dimensions (such as product, region and year), using a variety of filters to produce each dimension. The ability to analyse, extract and present information in meaningful ways is one of the differences between decision support data and transaction-at-a-time operational data.

FIGURE 15.3 **Transforming operational data into decision support data**

Operational data

	A	B	C	D	E
3	Year	Region	Agent	Product	Value
4	2014	East	Carlos	Erasers	50
5	2014	East	Tere	Erasers	12
6	2014	North	Carlos	Widgets	120
7	2014	North	Tere	Widgets	100
8	2014	North	Carlos	Widgets	30
9	2014	South	Victor	Balls	145
10	2014	South	Victor	Balls	34
11	2014	South	Victor	Balls	80
12	2014	West	Mary	Pencils	89
13	2014	West	Mary	Pencils	56
14	2015	East	Carlos	Pencils	45
15	2015	East	Victor	Balls	55
16	2015	North	Mary	Pencils	60
17	2015	North	Victor	Erasers	20
18	2015	South	Carlos	Widgets	30
19	2015	South	Mary	Widgets	75
20	2015	South	Mary	Widgets	50
21	2015	South	Tere	Balls	70
22	2015	South	Tere	Erasers	90
23	2015	West	Carlos	Widgets	25
24	2015	West	Tere	Balls	100

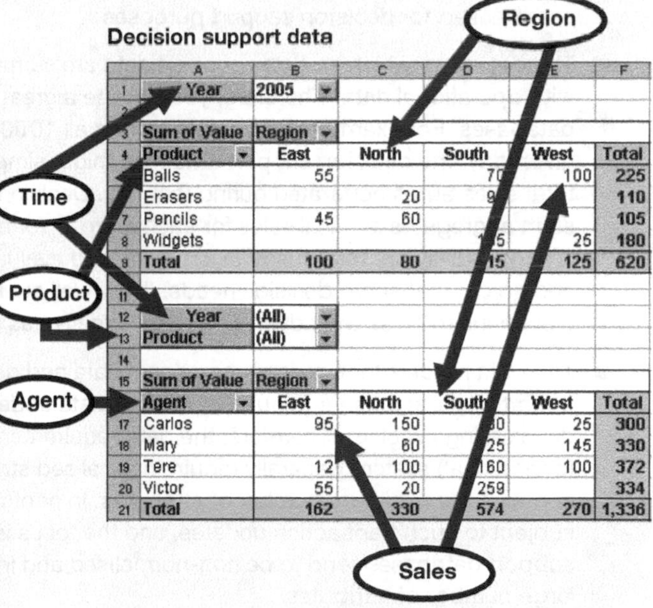

	A	B	C	D	E	F
1	Year	2005				
2						
3	Sum of Value	Region				
4	Product	East	North	South	West	Total
5	Balls	55		70	100	225
6	Erasers		20	9[illegible]		110
7	Pencils	45	60			105
8	Widgets			1[illegible]5	25	180
9	Total	100	80	[illegible]15	125	620
11						
12	Year	(All)				
13	Product	(All)				
14						
15	Sum of Value	Region				
16	Agent	East	North	South	West	Total
17	Carlos	95	150	[illegible]0	25	300
18	Mary		60	[illegible]25	145	330
19	Tere	12	100	160	100	372
20	Victor	55	20	259		334
21	Total	162	330	574	270	1,336

Operational data have a narrow time span, low granularity and single focus. Such data are usually presented in tabular format, in which each row represents a single transaction. This format often makes it difficult to derive useful information.

Decision support system (DSS) data focus on a broader timespan, tend to have high levels of granularity, and can be examined in multiple dimensions. For example, note these possible aggregations:

- Sales by product, region, agent, etc.
- Sales for all years or only a few selected years.
- Sales for all products or only a few selected products.

15

Online Content The operational data in Figure 15.3 are found on the online platform for this book. The decision support data in Figure 15.3 show the output for the solution to Problem 2 at the end of this chapter.

From the designer's point of view, the differences between operational and decision support data are as follows:

- Operational data represent transactions as they happen, in real time. Decision support data are a snapshot of the operational data at a given point in time. Therefore, decision support data are historic, representing a time slice of the operational data.
- Operational and decision support data are different in terms of the transaction *type* and transaction *volume*. Whereas operational data are characterised by update transactions, DSS data are mainly characterised by *query* (read-only) transactions. Decision support data also require *periodic* updates to load new data that are summarised from the operational data. Finally, the transaction volume in operational data tends to be very high when compared with the low-to-medium levels found in decision support data.
- Operational data are commonly stored in many tables, and the stored data represent the information about a given transaction only. Decision support data are generally stored in a few tables that store data derived from the operational data. The decision support data do not include the details of each operational transaction. Instead, decision support data represent transaction *summaries*; therefore, the decision support stores data that are integrated, aggregated and summarised for decision support purposes.
- The degree to which decision support data are summarised is very high when contrasted with operational data. Therefore, you will see a great deal of derived data in decision support databases. For example, rather than storing all 10 000 sales transactions for a given store on a given day, the decision support database might simply store the total number of units sold and the total sales euros generated during that day. Decision support data might be collected to monitor such aggregates as total sales for each store or for each product. The purpose of the summaries is simple: they are to be used to establish and evaluate sales trends, product sales comparisons, and so on, that serve decision needs. (How well are items selling? Should this product be discontinued? Has the advertising been effective as measured by increased sales?)
- The data models that govern operational data and decision support data are different. The operational database's frequent and rapid data updates make data anomalies a potentially devastating problem. Therefore, the data requirements in a typical relational transaction (operational) system generally require normalised structures that yield many tables, each of which contains the minimum number of attributes. In contrast, the decision support database is not subject to such transaction updates, and the focus is on querying capability. Therefore, decision support databases tend to be non-normalised and include few tables, each of which contains a large number of attributes.

- Query activity (frequency and complexity) in the operational database tends to be low to allow additional processing cycles for the more crucial update transactions. Therefore, queries against operational data typically are narrow in scope, low in complexity and speed-critical. In contrast, decision support data exist for the sole purpose of serving query requirements. Queries against decision support data typically are broad in scope, high in complexity and less speed-critical.

- Finally, decision support data are characterised by large amounts of data. The large data volume is the result of two factors. First, data are stored in non-normalised structures that are likely to display many data redundancies and duplications. Second, the same data can be categorised in many different ways to represent different snapshots. For example, sales data might be stored in relation to product, store, customer, region and manager.

Table 15.5 summarises the differences between operational and decision support data from the database designer's point of view.

TABLE 15.5 Contrasting operational and decision support data characteristics

Characteristic	Operational Data	Decision Support Data
Data currency	Current operations Real-time data	Historic data Snapshot of company data Time component (week/month/year)
Granularity	Atomic-detailed data	Summarised data
Summarisation level	Low; some aggregate yields	High; many aggregation levels
Data model	Highly normalised Mostly relational DBMS	Non-normalised Complex structures Some relational, but mostly multidimensional DBMS
Transaction type	Mostly updates	Mostly query
Transaction volumes	High update volumes	Periodic loads and summary calculations
Transaction speed	Updates are critical	Retrievals are critical
Query activity	Low to medium	High
Query scope	Narrow range	Broad range
Query complexity	Simple to medium	Very complex
Data volumes	Hundreds of gigabytes	Hundreds of terabytes to petabytes

The many differences between operational data and decision support data are good indicators of the requirements of the decision support database, described in the next section.

15.3.2 Decision Support Database Requirements

A decision support database is a specialised DBMS tailored to provide fast answers to complex queries. There are four main requirements for a decision support database: the database schema, data extraction and loading, the end-user analytical interface and database size.

Database Schema

The decision support database schema must support complex (non-normalised) data representations. As noted earlier, the decision support database must contain data that are aggregated and summarised. In addition to meeting those requirements, the queries must be able to extract multidimensional time slices. If you are using an RDBMS, the conditions suggest using non-normalised and even duplicated data. To see why this must be true, take a look at the ten-year sales history for a single store containing a single department. At this point, the data are fully normalised within the single table, as shown in Table 15.6.

TABLE 15.6 Ten-year sales history for a single department, millions of euros

Year	Sales
2010	8 227
2011	9109
2012	10104
2013	11553
2014	10018
2015	11875
2016	12699
2017	14875
2018	16301
2019	19986

This structure works well when you have only one store with only one department. However, it is very unlikely that such a simple environment has much need for a decision support. One would suppose that a decision support becomes a factor when dealing with more than one store, each of which has more than one department. To support all of the decision support requirements, the database must contain data for all of the stores and all of their departments – and the database must be able to support multidimensional queries that track sales by stores, by departments, and over time. For simplicity, suppose there are only two stores (A and B) and two departments (1 and 2) within each store. Let's also change the time dimension to include yearly data. Table 15.7 shows the sales figures under the specified conditions. Only 2010, 2014 and 2019 are shown; ellipses (...) indicate that data values were omitted. If

TABLE 15.7 Yearly sales summaries, two stores and two departments per store, millions of euros

Year	Store	Department	Sales
2010	A	1	1985
2010	A	2	2401
2010	B	1	1879
2010	B	2	1962
...	...	...	...
2014	A	1	3912
2014	A	2	4158
2014	B	1	3426
2014	B	2	1203
...	...	...	...
2019	A	1	7683
2019	A	2	6912
2019	B	1	3768
2019	B	2	1623

you examine Table 15.7, you can see that the number of rows and attributes already multiplies quickly and that the table exhibits multiple redundancies.

Now suppose that the company has ten departments per store and 20 stores nationwide. And suppose you want to access *yearly* sales summaries. Now you are dealing with 200 rows and 12 monthly sales attributes per row. (Actually, there are 15 attributes per row if you add each store's sales total for each year.)

The decision support database schema must also be optimised for query (read-only) retrievals. To optimise query speed, the DBMS must support features such as bitmap indexes and data partitioning to increase search speed. In addition, the DBMS query optimiser must be enhanced to support the non-normalised and complex structures found in decision support databases.

Data Extraction and Filtering

The decision support database is created largely by extracting data from the operational database and by importing additional data from external sources. Thus, the DBMS must support advanced data extraction and filtering tools. To minimise the impact on the operational database, the data extraction capabilities should allow batch and scheduled data extraction. The data extraction capabilities should also support different data sources: flat files and hierarchical, network and relational databases, as well as multiple vendors. **Data filtering** capabilities must include the ability to check for inconsistent data or data validation rules. Finally, to filter and integrate the operational data into the DSS database, the DBMS must support advanced data integration, aggregation and classification.

Using data from multiple external sources also usually means having to solve data-formatting conflicts. For example, dates and ID numbers may occur in different formats, measurements may be based on different scales, and the same data elements may have different names. In short, data must be filtered and purified to ensure that only the pertinent decision support data are stored in the database and that they are stored in a standard format.

Database Size

Decision support databases tend to be enormous; terabyte and petabyte ranges are not unusual. For example, in 2017, Wal-Mart had more than 40 petabytes of data in its data warehouses. Therefore, the DBMS must be capable of supporting **very large databases (VLDBs)**. To support a VLDB adequately, the DBMS might be required to use advanced hardware, such as multiple disk arrays, and, even more importantly, to support multiple-processor technologies, such as a symmetric multiprocessor (SMP) or a massively parallel processor (MPP).

The complex information requirements and the ever-growing demand for sophisticated data analysis sparked the creation of a new type of data repository. This repository, called a data warehouse, contains data in formats that facilitate data extraction, data analysis and decision making.

15.4 THE DATA WAREHOUSE

Bill Inmon, the acknowledged 'father of the **data warehouse**', defines the term as 'an *integrated, subject-oriented, time-variant, nonvolatile* collection of data that provides support for decision making'.[2] To understand that definition, let's take a more detailed look at its components.

2 Inmon, B. and Kelley, C. 'The twelve rules of data warehouse for a client/server world', *Data Management Review*, 4(5), pp. 6–16, May 1994.

- *Integrated.* The data warehouse is a centralised, consolidated database that integrates data derived from the entire organisation and from multiple sources with diverse formats. Data integration implies that all business entities, data elements, data characteristics and business metrics *are described in the same way throughout the enterprise*. Although this requirement sounds logical, you would be amazed to discover how many different measurements for 'sales performance' can exist within an organisation; the same scenario holds true for any other business element. For instance, the status of an order might be indicated with text labels such as 'open', 'received', 'cancel' and 'closed' in one department and as '1', '2', '3' and '4' in another department. A student's status might be defined as 'undergraduate year 1', 'undergraduate year 2', 'undergraduate year 3' or 'postgraduate' in the accounting department and as 'UG1', 'UG2', 'UG3' or 'PG' in the computer information systems department. To avoid the potential format tangle, the data in the data warehouse must conform to a common format acceptable throughout the organisation. This integration can be time-consuming, but once accomplished, it enhances decision making and helps managers better understand the company's operations. This understanding can be translated into recognition of strategic business opportunities.
- *Subject-orientated.* Data warehouse data are arranged and optimised to provide answers to questions coming from diverse functional areas within a company. Data warehouse data are organised and summarised by topic, such as sales, marketing, finance, distribution and transportation. For each topic, the data warehouse contains specific subjects of interest – products, customers, departments, regions, promotions and so on. This form of data organisation is quite different from the more functional or process-orientated organisation of typical transaction systems. For example, an invoicing system designer concentrates on designing normalised data structures (relational tables) to support the business process by storing invoice components in two tables: INVOICE and INVLINE. In contrast, the data warehouse has a *subject* orientation. Data warehouse designers focus specifically on the data rather than on the processes that modify the data. (After all, data warehouse data are not subject to numerous real-time data updates!) Therefore, instead of storing an invoice, the data warehouse stores its 'sales by product' and 'sales by customer' components because decision support activities require the retrieval of sales summaries by product or customer.
- *Time-variant.* In contrast to operational data, which focus on current transactions, warehouse data represent the flow of data through time. The data warehouse can even contain projected data, generated through statistical and other models. It is also time-variant in the sense that once data are periodically uploaded to the data warehouse, all time-dependent aggregations are recomputed. For example, when data for previous weekly sales are uploaded to the data warehouse, the weekly, monthly, yearly and other time-dependent aggregates for products, customers, stores and other variables are also updated. As data in a data warehouse constitute a snapshot of the company history as measured by its variables, the time component is crucial. The data warehouse contains a time ID that is used to generate summaries and aggregations by week, month, quarter, year and so on. Once the data enter the data warehouse, the time ID assigned to the data cannot be changed.

- *Non-volatile.* Once data enter the data warehouse, they are never removed. Because the data in the warehouse represent the company's history, the operational data, representing the near-term history, are always added to it. Data are never deleted and new data are continually added, so the data warehouse is always growing. That is why the DSS DBMS must be able to support multigigabyte and even multiterabyte databases and multiprocessor hardware.

In contrast to Bill Inmon's definition, Ralph Kimball provided a more comprehensive description of a data warehouse saying it was '... a copy of transaction data specifically structured for query and analysis'.[3] In this definition, Kimball only focuses on the functionality of the data warehouse and not how it should be developed.

Bill Inmon's approach to data warehouse development is often referred to as the Top Down approach and revolves around the creation of a large centralised enterprise-wide data warehouse, which is linked to a number of departmental databases known as data marts. (You will learn about data marts in more detail in Section 15.4.2.) In contrast, Ralph Kimball adopts a Bottom Up approach by first building several data marts within different departments in an organisation and then virtually integrating these dart marts to ensure one consistent enterprise view of the organisation. A further comparison can be made between the two approaches in terms of how the data in the warehouse is structured. Bill Inmon's method structures data using the relational model in third normal form, whereas Ralph Kimball's method creates multidimensional models of the data, i.e. the star schema (Section 15.5).

Despite the differences, both Ralph Kimball and Bill Inmon's approaches to data warehouse development have been successfully implemented in large organisations. With the advent of Big Data, data warehousing has to transform to be able to facilitate big data analytics. Ralph Kimball recognises the need for 'new development paradigms'[4] that are required for the enterprise data warehouse to expand and encompass the challenges of Big Data.

Table 15.8 summarises the differences between data warehouses and operational databases.

TABLE 15.8 A comparison of data warehouse and operational database characteristics

Characteristic	Operational Database Data	Data Warehouse Data
Integrated	Similar data can have different representations or meanings. For example, ID numbers may be stored as ######-####-### or as #############, and a given condition may be labelled as T/F or 0/1 or Y/N. A sales value may be shown in thousands or in millions.	Provide a unified view of all data elements with a common definition and representation for all business units.
Subject-orientated	Data are stored with a functional, or process, orientation. For example, data may be stored for invoices, payments and credit amounts.	Data are stored with a subject orientation that facilitates multiple views of the data and facilitates decision making. For example, sales may be recorded by product, by division, by manager, or by region.
Time-variant	Data are recorded as current transactions. For example, the sales data may be the sale of a product on a given date, such as €342.78 on 12-MAY-2013.	Data are recorded with a historical perspective in mind. Therefore, a time dimension is added to facilitate data analysis and various time comparisons.
Non-volatile	Data updates are frequent and common. For example, an inventory amount changes with each sale. Therefore, the data environment is fluid.	Data cannot be changed. Data are added only periodically from historical systems. Once the data are properly stored, no changes are allowed. Therefore, the data environment is relatively static.

3 Kimball, R. *The Data Warehouse Lifecycle Toolkit: Practical Techniques for Building Data Warehouse and Business Intelligence Systems, 2nd Edition.* John Wiley & Sons, 2008.

4 Kimball, R. The Evolving Role of the Enterprise Data Warehouse in the Era of Big Data Analytics. Available: www.kimballgroup.com/

In summary, the data warehouse is usually a read-only database optimised for data analysis and query processing. Typically, data are extracted from various sources and are then transformed and integrated – in other words, passed through a data filter – before being loaded into the data warehouse. As mentioned, this process is known as ETL. Figure 15.4 illustrates the ETL process to create a data warehouse from operational data.

FIGURE 15.4 **Creating a data warehouse**

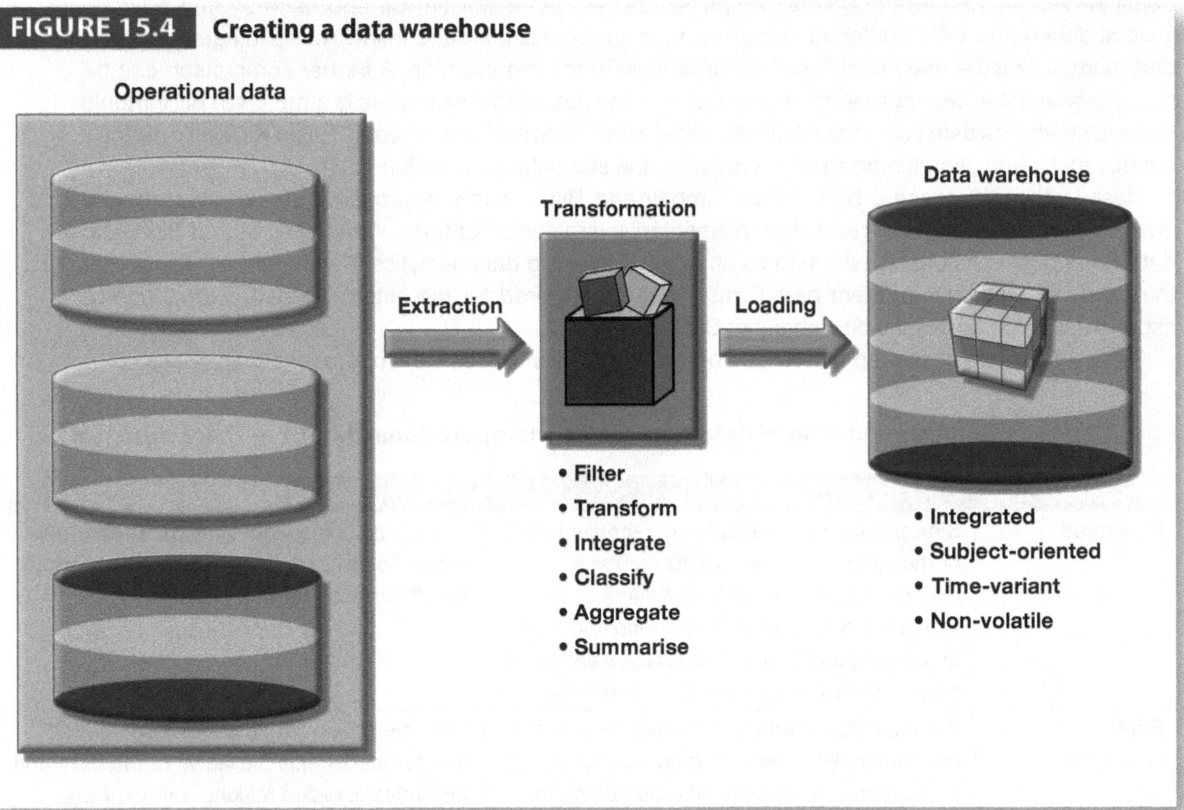

Although the centralised and integrated data warehouse can be an attractive proposition that yields many benefits, managers may be reluctant to embrace this strategy. Creating a data warehouse requires time, money and considerable managerial effort. Therefore, it is not surprising that many companies begin their foray into data warehousing by focusing on more manageable data sets that are targeted to meet the special needs of small groups within the organisation. These smaller data stores are called data marts.

15.4.1 Twelve Rules that Define a Data Warehouse

In 1994, William H. Inmon and Chuck Kelley created 12 rules defining a data warehouse, which summarise many of the points made in this chapter about data warehouses.[5]

1 The data warehouse and operational environments are separated.

2 The data warehouse data are integrated.

3 The data warehouse contains historical data over a long time horizon.

5 Inmon, B., and Kelley, C. 'The twelve rules of data warehouse for a client/server world', *Data Management Review*, 4(5), pp. 6–16, May 1994.

4 The data warehouse data are snapshot data captured at a given point in time.

5 The data warehouse data are subject-oriented.

6 No online updates are allowed.

7 The data warehouse development life cycle differs from classical systems development. The data warehouse development is data-driven; the classical approach is process-driven.

8 The data warehouse contains data with several levels of detail: current detail data, old detail data, lightly summarised data and highly summarised data.

9 The data warehouse environment is characterised by read-only transactions to very large data sets. The operational environment is characterised by numerous update transactions to a few data entities at a time.

10 The data warehouse environment has a system that traces data sources, transformations and storage.

11 The data warehouse's metadata are a critical component of this environment. The metadata identify and define all data elements. The metadata provide the source, transformation, integration, storage, usage, relationships and history of each data element.

12 The data warehouse contains a chargeback mechanism for resource usage that enforces optimal use of the data by end users.

Note how those 12 rules capture the complete data warehouse life cycle – from its introduction as an entity separate from the operational data store to its components, functionality and management processes. Most data warehouse implementations are based on the relational database model, and their market share suggests that their popularity will not fade anytime soon. Relational data warehouses use the star schema design technique to handle multidimensional data.

Online Content Further considerations about data warehouse development can be found in Appendix L, Data Warehouse Implementation Factors, located on the online platform for this book.

15.4.2 Data Marts

A **data mart** is a small, single-subject data warehouse subset that provides decision support to a small group of people. A data mart could also be created from the data extracted from a larger data warehouse for the specific purpose of supporting faster data access to a target group or function.

Some organisations choose to implement data marts not only because of the lower cost and shorter implementation time, but also because of the current technological advances and inevitable 'people issues' that make data marts attractive. Powerful computers can provide a customised DSS to small groups in ways that might not be possible with a centralised system. Also, a company's culture may predispose its employees to resist major changes, but they might quickly embrace relatively minor changes that lead to demonstrably improved decision support. In addition, people at different organisational levels are likely to require data with different summarisation, aggregation and presentation formats. Data marts can serve as a test vehicle for companies exploring the potential benefits of data warehouses. By migrating gradually from data marts to data warehouses, a specific department's decision support needs can be addressed within a reasonable time frame (six months to one year), as compared to the longer time frame usually required to implement a data warehouse (one to three years). Information technology (IT) departments also benefit from this approach because their personnel have the opportunity to learn the issues and develop the skills required to create a data warehouse.

The only difference between a data mart and a data warehouse is the size and scope of the problem being solved. Therefore, the problem definitions and data requirements are essentially the same for both.

15.4.3 Designing and Implementing a Data Warehouse

Organisation-wide information system development is subject to many constraints. Some of the constraints are based on available funding. Others are a function of management's view of the role played by an IS department and of the extent and depth of the information requirements. Add the constraints imposed by corporate culture, and you understand why no single formula can describe perfect data warehouse development. Therefore, rather than proposing a single data warehouse design and implementation methodology, this section will identify a few factors that appear to be common to data warehousing.

The Data Warehouse as an Active Decision Support Framework

Perhaps the first thing to remember is that a data warehouse is not a static database. Instead, it is a dynamic framework for decision support that is, almost by definition, always a work in progress. Because it is the foundation of business intelligence activities, the design and implementation of the data warehouse means that you are involved in the design and implementation of a complete database-system-development infrastructure for company-wide decision support. Although it is easy to focus on the data warehouse database as the central data repository, you must remember that the decision support infrastructure includes hardware, software, people and procedures, as well as data. Therefore, its design and implementation must be examined in light of the entire infrastructure.

A Company-Wide Effort That Requires User Involvement

Designing a data warehouse means being given an opportunity to help develop an integrated data model that captures the data that are considered to be essential to the organisation, from both end user and business perspectives. Data warehouse data cross departmental lines and geographical boundaries. Because the data warehouse represents an attempt to model all of the organisation's data, you are likely to discover that organisational components (divisions, departments, support groups and so on) often have conflicting goals, and it certainly is easy to find data inconsistencies and damaging redundancies. Information is power, and the control of its sources and uses is likely to trigger turf battles, end-user resistance and power struggles at all levels. Building the perfect data warehouse is not just a matter of knowing how to create a star schema; it requires managerial skills to deal with conflict resolution, mediation and arbitration. In short, the designer must:

- Involve end users in the process.
- Secure end users' commitment from the beginning.
- Create continuous end-user feedback.
- Manage end-user expectations.
- Establish procedures for conflict resolution.

Great managerial skills are not, of course, solely sufficient. The technical aspects of the data warehouse must be addressed as well. The old adage of input-process-output repeats itself here. The data warehouse designer must satisfy:

- Data integration and loading criteria.
- Data analysis capabilities with acceptable query performance.
- End-user data analysis needs.

The foremost technical concern in implementing a data warehouse is to provide end-user decision support with advanced data analysis capabilities – at the right moment, in the right format, with the right data, and at the right cost.

Apply Database Design Procedures

You learnt about the database life cycle and the database design process in Chapters 10 and 11, so perhaps it is wise to begin with a review of the traditional database design procedures. These design procedures must then be adapted to fit the data warehouse requirements. If you remember that the data warehouse derives its data from operational databases, you will understand why a solid foundation in operational database design is important. It's difficult to produce good data warehouse data when the operational database data are corrupted. Figure 15.5 depicts a simplified process for implementing the data warehouse.

FIGURE 15.5 Data warehouse design and implementation road map

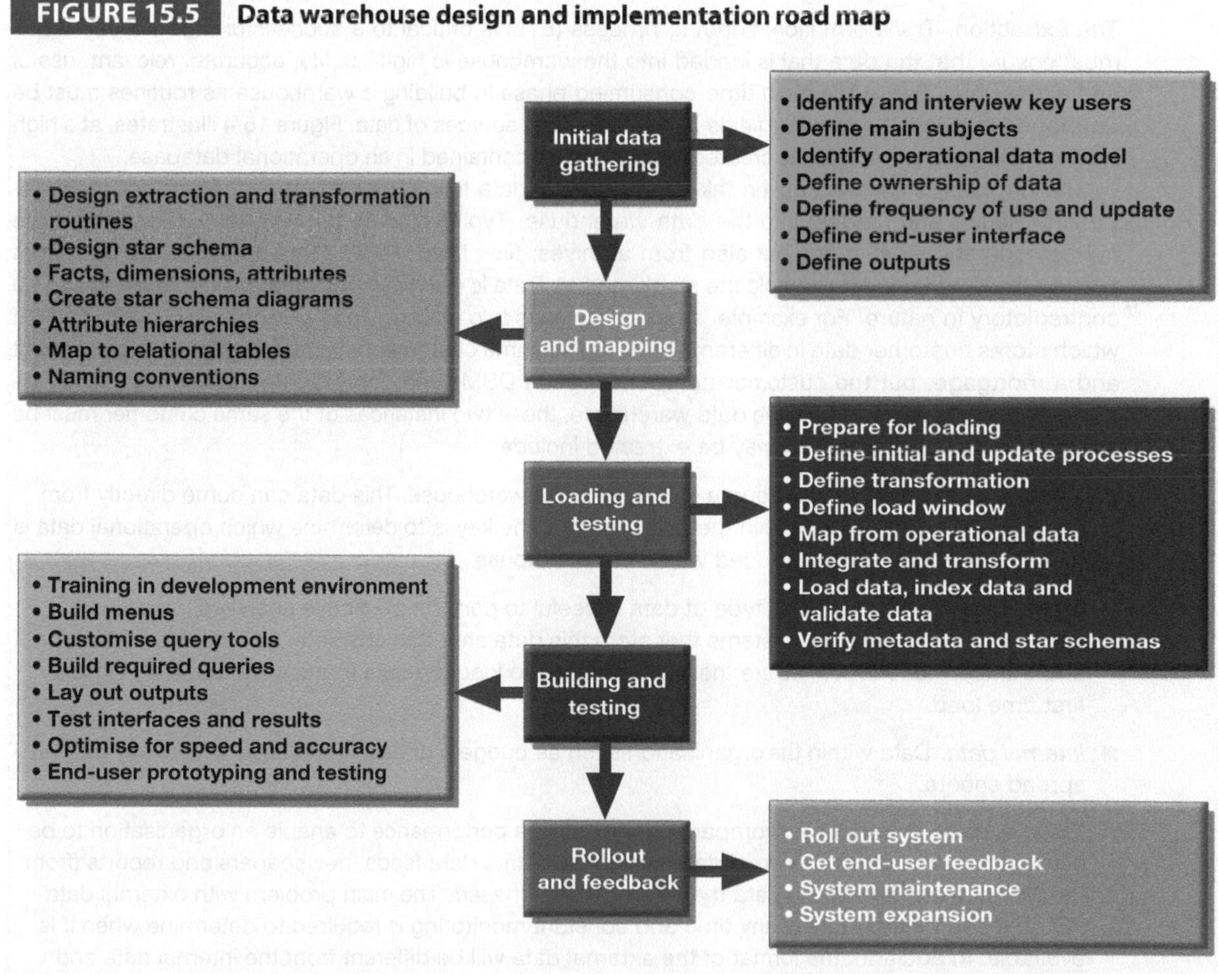
Initial data gathering
• Identify and interview key users
• Define main subjects
• Identify operational data model
• Define ownership of data
• Define frequency of use and update
• Define end-user interface
• Define outputs
Design and mapping
• Design extraction and transformation routines
• Design star schema
• Facts, dimensions, attributes
• Create star schema diagrams
• Attribute hierarchies
• Map to relational tables
• Naming conventions
Loading and testing
• Prepare for loading
• Define initial and update processes
• Define transformation
• Define load window
• Map from operational data
• Integrate and transform
• Load data, index data and validate data
• Verify metadata and star schemas
Building and testing
• Training in development environment
• Build menus
• Customise query tools
• Build required queries
• Lay out outputs
• Test interfaces and results
• Optimise for speed and accuracy
• End-user prototyping and testing
Rollout and feedback
• Roll out system
• Get end-user feedback
• System maintenance
• System expansion

15

One of the key differences from the traditional database design process is the level of detail required in defining the business model. Each business process that is to be modelled within the data warehouse must be described in detail in order to:

- Identify business measures. For example, a sales business measure may be the number of a particular product that has been sold in a week.
- Identify the level of detail or granularity of the data. For example, does the organisation need to know how many of a particular product were sold on a daily basis or an hourly basis? The general rule of thumb is to design for one grain finer than what the users require.
- Check all data sources to ensure that the level of data required can actually be obtained from the existing source systems.

Only when this has been completed can the dimensional model be created and the ETL processes be defined. The following sections will explore ETL process design issues and one option of how to create the dimensional model using a star schema.

15.4.4 The Extraction, Transformation, Loading Process

The Extraction, Transformation, Loading process (ETL) is critical to a successful data warehouse. It must ensure that the data that is loaded into the warehouse is high-quality, accurate, relevant, useful and accessible. This is the most time-consuming phase in building a warehouse as routines must be developed to select the required fields from often many sources of data. Figure 15.4 illustrates, at a high level, how a data warehouse is created from the data contained in an operational database.

The process of data extraction takes preselected data fields from a number of sources ready for transformation and loading into the data warehouse. Typically, data is not just extracted from the current operational systems but also from archives, files from old systems and external data from outside the company, for example the stock market. Data is often in many different formats and can be contradictory in nature. For example, a bank may have two departments, Savings and Loans, each of which stores customer data in different DBMSs. The same customer may have both a savings account and a mortgage, but the customer numbers in each DBMS may be different. In order to store the customer as a 'subject' within the data warehouse, these two instances of the same customer must be associated. Types of data that may be extracted include:

- *Operational data*. The main source of data into the warehouse. This data can come directly from any DBMS or application within the organisation. The key is to determine which operational data is relevant as not all will be included within the warehouse.
- *Historical archived data*. This type of data is useful to perform predictive analytics (discussed in section 15.6.2). However, systems that store this data are often obsolete. Unique data extraction and transformation routines are therefore required to load the data in the warehouse during the first time load.
- *Internal data*. Data within the organisation such as budgets or sales forecasts, which may exist in spread sheets.
- *External data*. Important for comparing the business performance to enable an organisation to be competitive. Sources of external data include real-time data feeds, newspapers and reports (from the internet) and marketing data that has been purchased. The main problem with external data is that it can be available at any time and constant monitoring is required to determine when it is available. In addition, the format of the external data will be different from the internal data and may require unique one-off transformations.

An organisation may choose to buy tools to extract data or may write individual routines in-house. The main issue is cost.

Once the data has been determined, each selected attribute must be mapped into the data warehouse. In each case, it may be necessary to apply a transformation rule, for example if the field from the source system is in a different format from the mapped field in the data warehouse. This is known as mapping.

The process of data transformation aims to eliminate any data anomalies found in the extracted data, especially when it is from an operational source. Transformation also scrubs (or cleans) the data and ensures it is in a standardised format ready for being presented as subject-oriented data.

Some common source data anomalies include:

Name and Address Inconsistencies

Storing names and addresses within a DBMS and a data warehouse provides many unique challenges for the designer. There is often no unique key and values may be missing. A person may have more than one address, which could be down to a data entry error or the fact that the person has moved house and, instead of updating the details, a new record has been created. Two or more people may be stored under the same address, and both names and addresses may be spelt incorrectly. For example, consider the two tables shown in Figure 15.6, which exist in two separate databases within

FIGURE 15.6 Name and address data anomalies

Database 1: Customer Sales table

Name	Address	Gender	Location
Roy Rogers	6 State Rd, North West,Manchester, M23	M	L100
Roy Rogers	6 State Road, NW, M22	M	L100
Clare A. Peterson	4 West Street, M33	F	L121
Jane Smiley	12–14 Range Warehouse		L333

Database 2: Customer Marketing table

Name	Marketing Addresses	Gender	Location	Supplier_ID
Rogers, R		Male	L100	Z123
Peterson, A Claire	14 West St, M33	Female	L121	Z45
Smiley, Jane	12 to 14 Range Warehouse	Female	L333	

A solution to this problem is to ensure that the name and address are broken down into their component parts. For example, an agreed format for names and addresses within the data warehouse could be:

Title	Mr
First_name	Roy
Middle_name	
Last_name	Rodgers
Street No. or house name	6
Address_line1	State Road
Address_line2	
Country	Manchester
Postal code	M23 4FR
Country	United Kingdom
……..	……..

an organisation. Customer Roy Rogers appears in both the Customer Sales table and the Customer Marketing table in a total of three rows, yet in each case his address is different or not entered at all. In the address field, Road is also stored as Rd and the postal code is both M23 and M22.

In order to resolve such problems, the data warehouse developer needs to ensure that each component part of the name and address appears in a standardised format, e.g. Rd becomes Road. Accuracy of the address should be checked against external sources. For example, a postal code database could be used to check that M23 4FR is a valid postal code in the city of Manchester, UK. Rules should also be in place to ensure that, when data is entered, a person with the same name does not already exist – if one does, then both the existing record and the record to be inserted should be flagged for further analysis. Finally, it is necessary to check whether there is not already a person living at that address. This is a difficult situation to analyse. The address entered may be incorrect or a person may have moved house and the correct details may not have been recorded. In this case, again, both records should be flagged for further analysis.

Multiple Encoding Problems

Multiple encoding problems typically occur when merging data from a number of operations systems. In Figure 15.6, the Gender field has been encoded differently in each of the two databases. In the Customer Sales table it is stored as 'M' and 'F' while in the Customer Marketing table it is stored as 'Male' and 'Female'. The solution is to agree on a format for each file in the data warehouse and write routines to transform the data values into the correct format. It is very important that these rules also pick up erroneous data and flag records where fields cannot be standardised.

Different Country Standards

Multiple country standards are likely to exist in global organisations. Standards cover the type of currency, the format of the date (dd/mm/yyyy as opposed to mm/dd/yyyy) and measurements. For example, if measurements are to be stored within the data warehouse, should these be in metric, which is suitable for the UK, Europe and South Africa, or imperial, which is used in the US? Often, one standard is agreed on, and then routines exist to perform automatic conversions of the data as it is transported from the source file into the data warehouse.

Missing Values

Often, when you extract individual fields into the data warehouse, values may be missing. Sometimes, information may not have been collected. For example, people may decline to give their age and weight or fields may not be applicable to all cases. In addition, values may be missing due to human error, no data available at the input stage in the source system, or data may simply have been mismatched from being selected across a number of sources. How to deal with missing values depends upon the significance of the field within the data warehouse. If the data contained within the field is not critical, in terms of the BI function, the missing value could be simply ignored. If critical, then the record containing the missing field could be flagged and an attempt made to establish the missing field value by going back to the original source. However, if the missing value within the record is time-dependent, for example, waiting for some action to be completed, then an alternative is to not extract the record until all fields are complete.

Referential Integrity

In Chapter 3, Relational Model Characteristics, you learnt that referential integrity must be enforced in a relational database. Referential integrity states that a foreign key must have a null entry or an entry that matches the primary key value in a table to which it is related. Referential integrity checks must be made on all data that is extracted from source systems prior to insertion into the data warehouse. As data is combined from different databases, violations of referential integrity constraints are more likely to occur. To ensure that this does not happen, a set of data warehouse referential integrity rules are applied to each relationship that will determine the status of foreign key columns when records are first extracted and then inserted into the data warehouse.

It is very important that all transformation routines such as referential integrity fixes and rules for handling missing values etc. are documented within the data warehouse metadata (data about data). In order to support business intelligence, it is essential to know exactly which data is available within the warehouse to enable effective data analysis.

The final stage of the ETL process is known as loading, in which the data is moved into the data warehouse. Loading data can be a very time-consuming process and is usually done in two stages. The first stage, known as the *first time load*, takes place only once and is used initially to load historical data into the data warehouse. Due to unique extraction and transformation routines being used (that is, older systems not being in use) and the large volume of data and processing required, the first time load is very time and resource intensive.

Once the data warehouse is live, it will need to be updated or refreshed at regular intervals. How often it is updated is dependent on the organisation's business cycle and the scheduling of its business intelligence activities. The update of a data warehouse is less complex than the first time load. The extraction and transformation routines are less intricate and, of course, there is less data. However, the update will put pressure on the organisation's systems and networks, and therefore the load window (the time it takes to update the warehouse) should be scheduled during non-business hours.

15.5 STAR SCHEMAS

The **star schema** is a data modelling technique used to map multidimensional decision support data into a relational database. In effect, the star schema creates the near equivalent of a multidimensional database schema from the existing relational database. The star schema was developed because existing relational modelling techniques, ER and normalisation did not yield a database structure that served advanced data analysis requirements well.

Star schemas yield an easily implemented model for multidimensional data analysis while still preserving the relational structures on which the operational database is built. The basic star schema has four components: facts, dimensions, attributes and attribute hierarchies.

15.5.1 Facts

Facts are numeric measurements (values) that represent a specific business aspect or activity. For example, sales figures are numeric measurements that represent product and/or service sales. Facts commonly used in business data analysis are units, costs, prices and revenues. Facts are normally stored in a fact table that is the centre of the star schema. The **fact table** contains facts that are linked through their dimensions (covered in the next section).

Facts can also be computed or derived at run time. Such computed or derived facts are sometimes called **metrics** to differentiate them from stored facts. The fact table is updated periodically with data from operational databases.

15.5.2 Dimensions

Dimensions are qualifying characteristics that provide additional perspectives to a given fact. Recall that dimensions are of interest because *DSS data are almost always viewed in relation to other data*. For instance, sales might be compared by product from region to region and from one time period to the next. The kind of problem typically addressed by a DSS might be as follows: make a comparison of the sales of unit X by region for the first quarters of 2014 to 2018. In that example, sales have product, location and time dimensions. In effect, dimensions are the magnifying glass through which you study the facts. Such dimensions are normally stored in **dimension tables**. Figure 15.7 depicts a star schema for sales with product, location and time dimensions.

FIGURE 15.7 Simple star schema

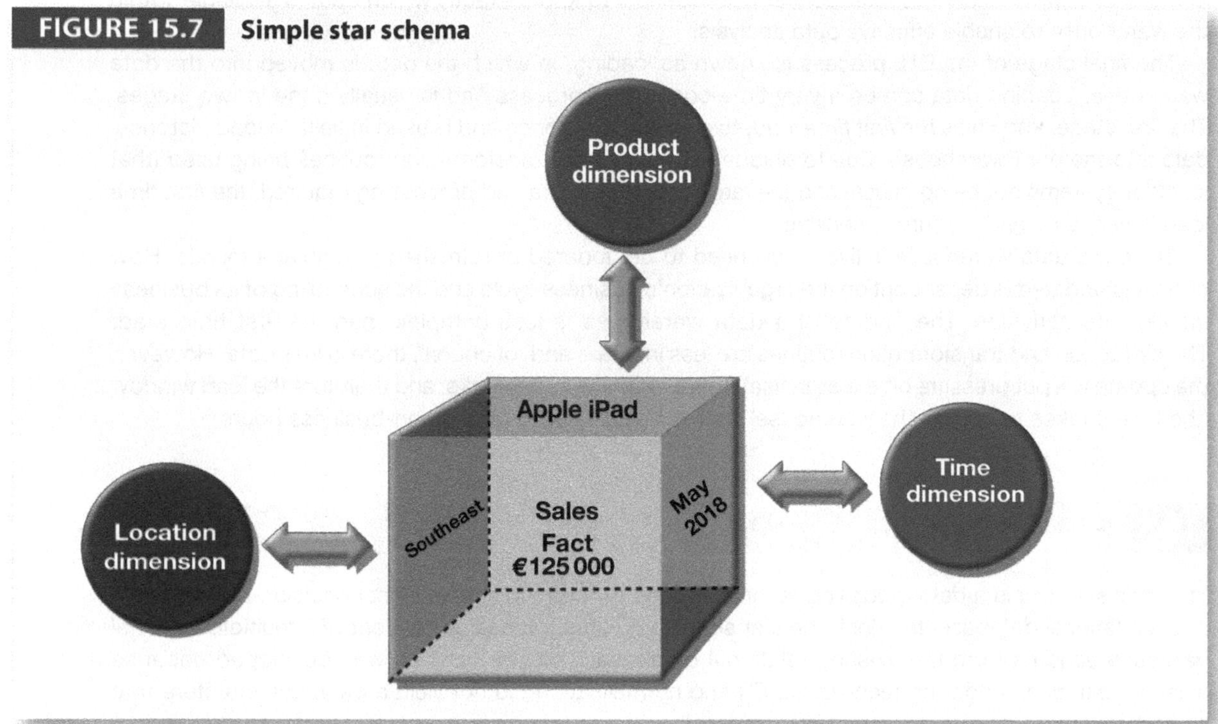

15.5.3 Attributes

Each dimension table contains attributes. Attributes are often used to search, filter or classify facts. *Dimensions provide descriptive characteristics about the facts through their attributes*. Therefore, the data warehouse designer must define common business attributes that will be used by the data analyst to narrow a search, group information or describe dimensions. Using a sales example, some possible attributes for each dimension are illustrated in Table 15.9.

TABLE 15.9 Possible attributes for sales dimensions

Dimension Name	Description	Possible Attributes
Location	Anything that provides a description of the location. Example: East London, Store 101, Eastern Cape and SA	Region, country, city, store and so on
Product	Anything that provides a description of the product sold. For example, hair care product, shampoo, Natural Essence brand, 150 ml bottle and blue liquid	Product type, product ID, brand, package, presentation, colour, size and so on
Time	Anything that provides a time frame for the sales fact. For example, the year 2018, the month of July, the date 29/07/2018, and the time 4:46 p.m.	Year, quarter, month, week, day, time of day, and so on

15

These product, location and time dimensions add a business perspective to the sales facts. The data analyst can now group the sales figures for a given product, in a given region and at a given time. The star schema, through its facts and dimensions, can provide the data in the required format when the data are needed. And it can do so without imposing the burden of the additional and unnecessary data (such as order number, purchase order number and status) that commonly exist in operational databases.

Conceptually, the sales example's multidimensional data model is best represented by a three-dimensional cube. Of course, this does not imply that there is a limit on the number of dimensions that can be associated to a fact table. There is no mathematical limit to the number of dimensions used. However, using a three-dimensional model makes it easy to visualise the problem. In this three-dimensional example, using the multidimensional data analysis jargon, the cube illustrated in Figure 15.8 represents a view of sales dimensioned by product, location and time.

FIGURE 15.8 **Three-dimensional view of sales**

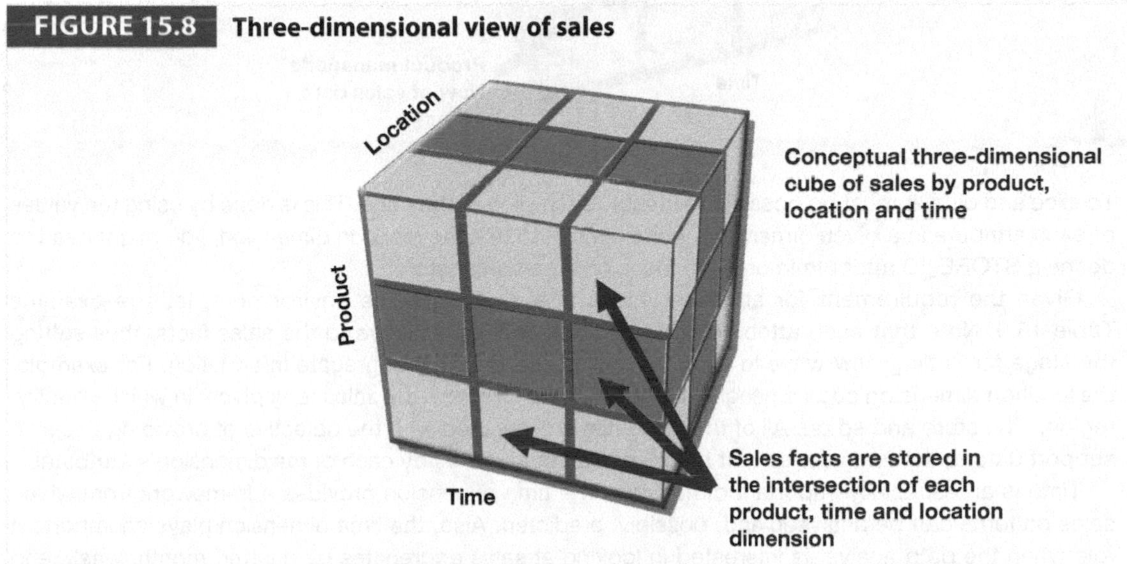
Location
Product
Time
Conceptual three-dimensional cube of sales by product, location and time
Sales facts are stored in the intersection of each product, time and location dimension

Note that each sales value stored in the cube in Figure 15.8 is associated with the location, product and time dimensions. However, keep in mind that this cube is only a *conceptual* representation of multidimensional data, and it does not show how the data are physically stored in a data warehouse.

Whatever the underlying database technology, one of the main features of multidimensional analysis is its ability to focus on specific 'slices' of the cube. For example, the product manager may be interested in examining the sales of a product, while the store manager is interested in examining the sales made by a particular store. Using multidimensional jargon, the ability to focus on slices of the cube to perform a more detailed analysis is known as **slice and dice**. Figure 15.9 illustrates the slice-and-dice concept. As you look at Figure 15.9, note that each cut across the cube yields a slice. Intersecting slices produce small cubes that constitute the 'dice' part of the 'slice-and-dice' operation.

FIGURE 15.9 Slice-and-dice view of sales

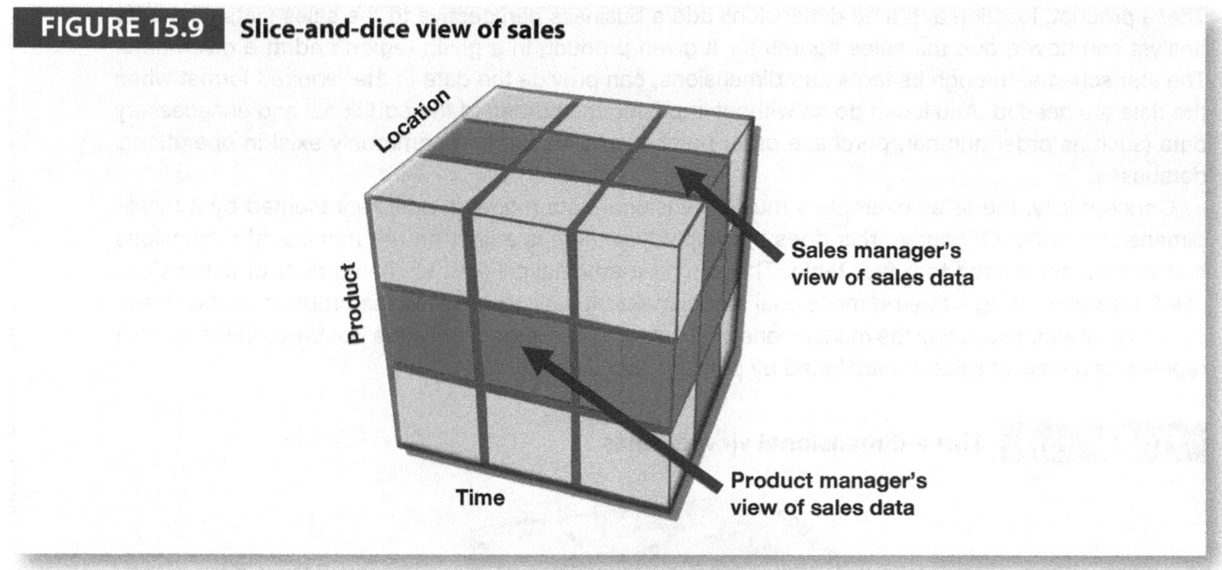

To slice and dice, it must be possible to identify each slice of the cube. This is done by using the values of each attribute in a given dimension. For example, to use the location dimension, you might need to define a STORE_ID attribute in order to focus on a particular store.

Given the requirement for attribute values in a slice-and-dice environment, let's re-examine Table 15.9. Note that each attribute adds an additional perspective to the sales facts, thus setting the stage for finding new ways to search, classify and possibly aggregate information. For example, the location dimension adds a geographic perspective of where the sales took place: in which country, region, city, store and so on. All of the attributes are selected with the objective of providing decision support data to the end user so that he or she can study sales by each of the dimension's attributes.

Time is an especially important dimension. The time dimension provides a framework from which sales patterns can be analysed and, possibly, predicted. Also, the time dimension plays an important role when the data analyst is interested in looking at sales aggregates by quarter, month, week, and so on. Given the importance and universality of the time dimension from a data analysis perspective, many vendors have added automatic time dimension management features to their data warehousing products.

15.5.4 Attribute Hierarchies

Attributes within dimensions can be ordered in a well-defined attribute hierarchy. The **attribute hierarchy** provides a top-down data organisation that is used for two main purposes: aggregation and drill-down/roll-up data analysis. For example, Figure 15.10 shows how the location dimension attributes can be organised in a hierarchy by country, region, city and store.

15

FIGURE 15.10 Location attribute hierarchy

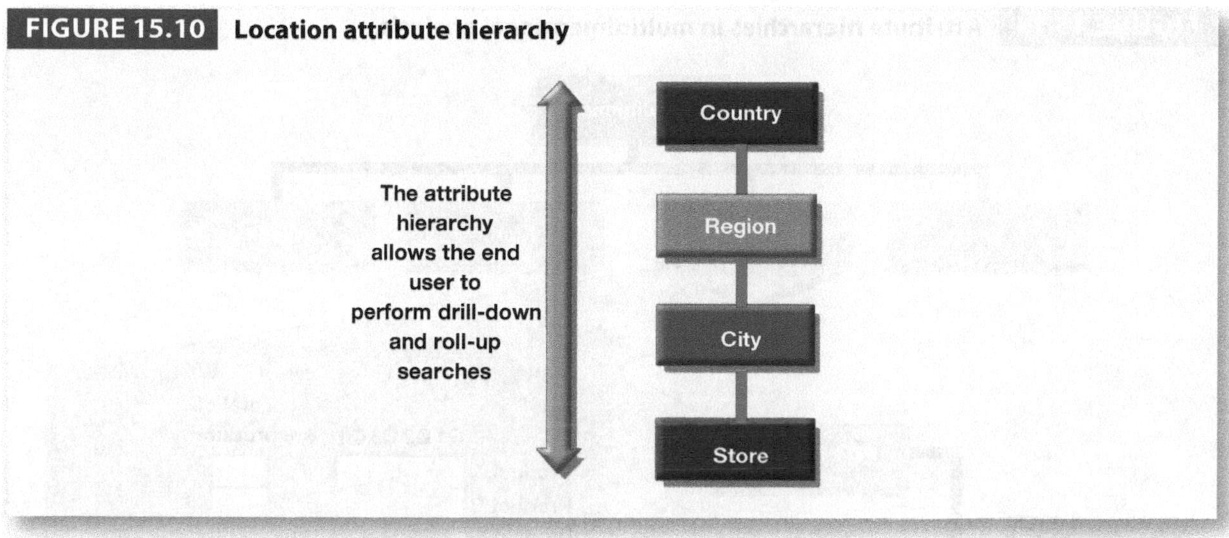

The attribute hierarchy provides the capability to perform drill-down and roll-up searches in a data warehouse. For example, suppose a data analyst looks at the answers to the query, 'How does the 2013 month-to-date sales performance compare to the 2019 month-to-date sales performance?' The data analyst spots a sharp sales decline for March 2019. The data analyst might decide to drill down inside the month of March to see how sales by region compared to those of the previous year. By doing that, the analyst can determine whether the low March sales were reflected in all regions within a specific country or in only a particular region. This type of drill-down operation can even be extended until the data analyst identifies the store that is performing below the norm.

The just-described scenario is possible because the attribute hierarchy allows the data warehouse and OLAP systems to have a defined path that will identify how data are to be decomposed and aggregated for drill-down and roll-up operations. It is not necessary for all attributes to be part of an attribute hierarchy; some attributes exist merely to provide narrative descriptions of the dimensions. But keep in mind that the attributes from different dimensions can be grouped to form a hierarchy. For example, after you drill down from city to store, you may want to drill down using the product dimension so the manager can identify slow products in the store. The product dimension can be based on the product group (dairy, meat, and so on) or on the product brand (Brand A, Brand B, and so on).

Figure 15.11 illustrates a scenario in which the data analyst studies sales facts, using the product, time and location dimensions. In this example, the product dimension is set to 'All products', meaning that the data analyst will see all products on the y-axis. The time dimension (x-axis) is set to 'Quarter', meaning that the data are aggregated by quarters (for example, total sales of products A, B and C in Q1, Q2, Q3 and Q4). Finally, the location dimension is initially set to 'Country', thus ensuring that each cell contains the total sales for each country for a given product in a given quarter.

FIGURE 15.11 Attribute hierarchies in multidimensional analysis

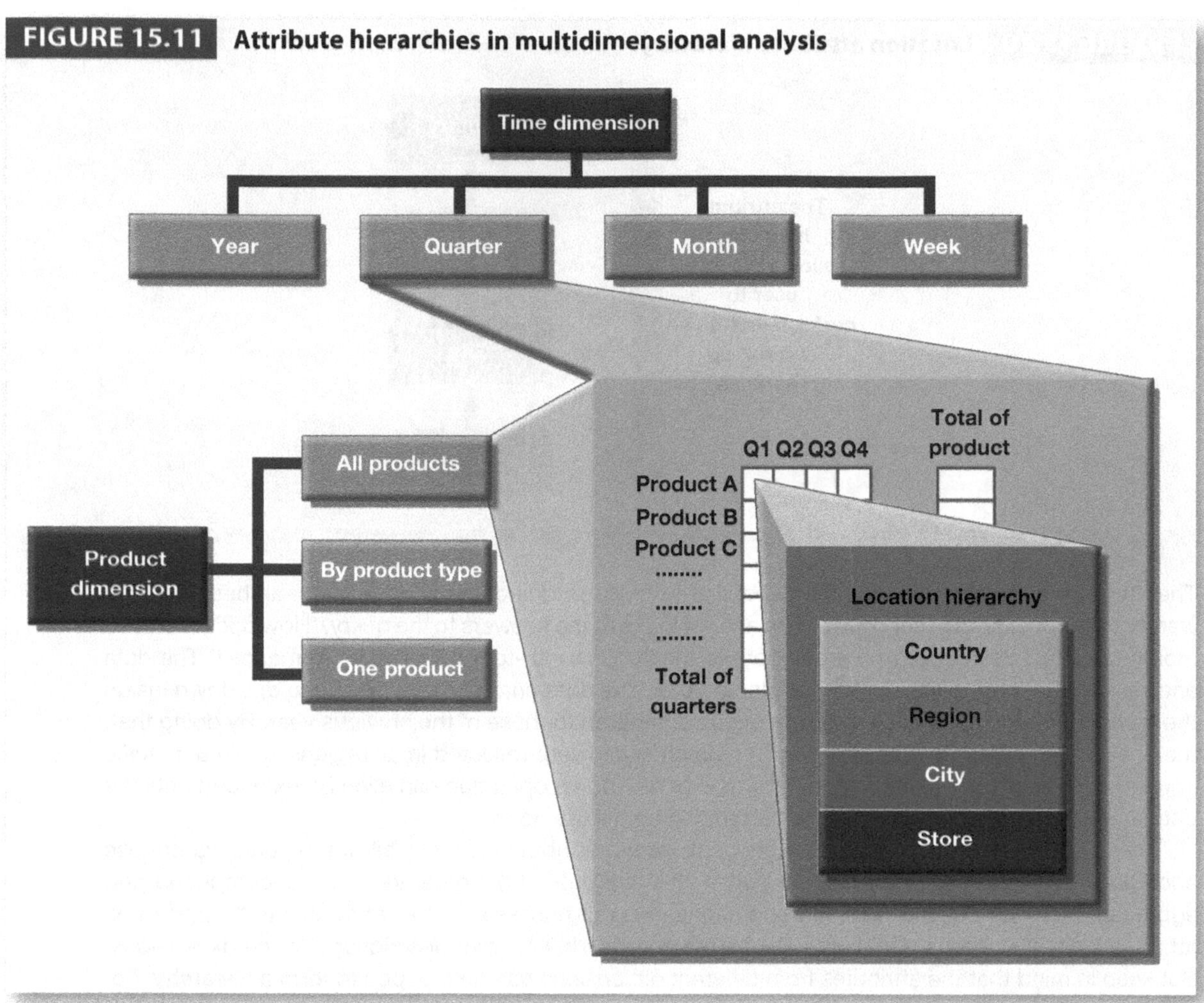

The simple data analysis scenario illustrated in Figure 15.11 provides the data analyst with three different information paths. On the product dimension (the y-axis), the data analyst can request to see all products, products grouped by type, or just one product. On the time dimension (the x-axis), the data analyst can request time-variant data at different levels of aggregation: year, quarter, month or week. Each sales value initially shows the total sales, by country, of each product. When a GUI is used, the data analyst clicks on the country cell to drill down to see sales by region within the country. Clicking again on one of the region values gives the sales for each city in the region, and so forth.

As the preceding examples illustrate, attribute hierarchies determine how the data in the data warehouse are extracted and presented. The attribute hierarchy information is stored in the DBMS's data dictionary and is used by the OLAP tool to access the data warehouse properly. Once such access is ensured, query tools must be closely integrated with the data warehouse's metadata and they must support powerful analytical capabilities.

15

15.5.5 Star Schema Representation

Facts and dimensions are normally represented by physical tables in the data warehouse database. The fact table is related to each dimension table in a many-to-one (*:1) relationship. In other words, many fact rows are related to each dimension row. Using the sales example, you can conclude that each product appears many times in the sales fact table.

Fact and dimension tables are related by foreign keys and are subject to the familiar primary key/ foreign key constraints. The primary key on the '1' side, the dimension table, is stored as part of the primary key on the 'many' side, the fact table. *Because the fact table is related to many dimension tables, the primary key of the fact table is a composite primary key.* Figure 15.12 illustrates the relationships among the sales fact table and the product, location and time dimension tables. To show you how easily the star schema can be expanded, a customer dimension has been added to the mix. Adding the customer dimension merely required including the CUST_ID in the SALES fact table and adding the CUSTOMER table to the database.

FIGURE 15.12 Star schema for SALES

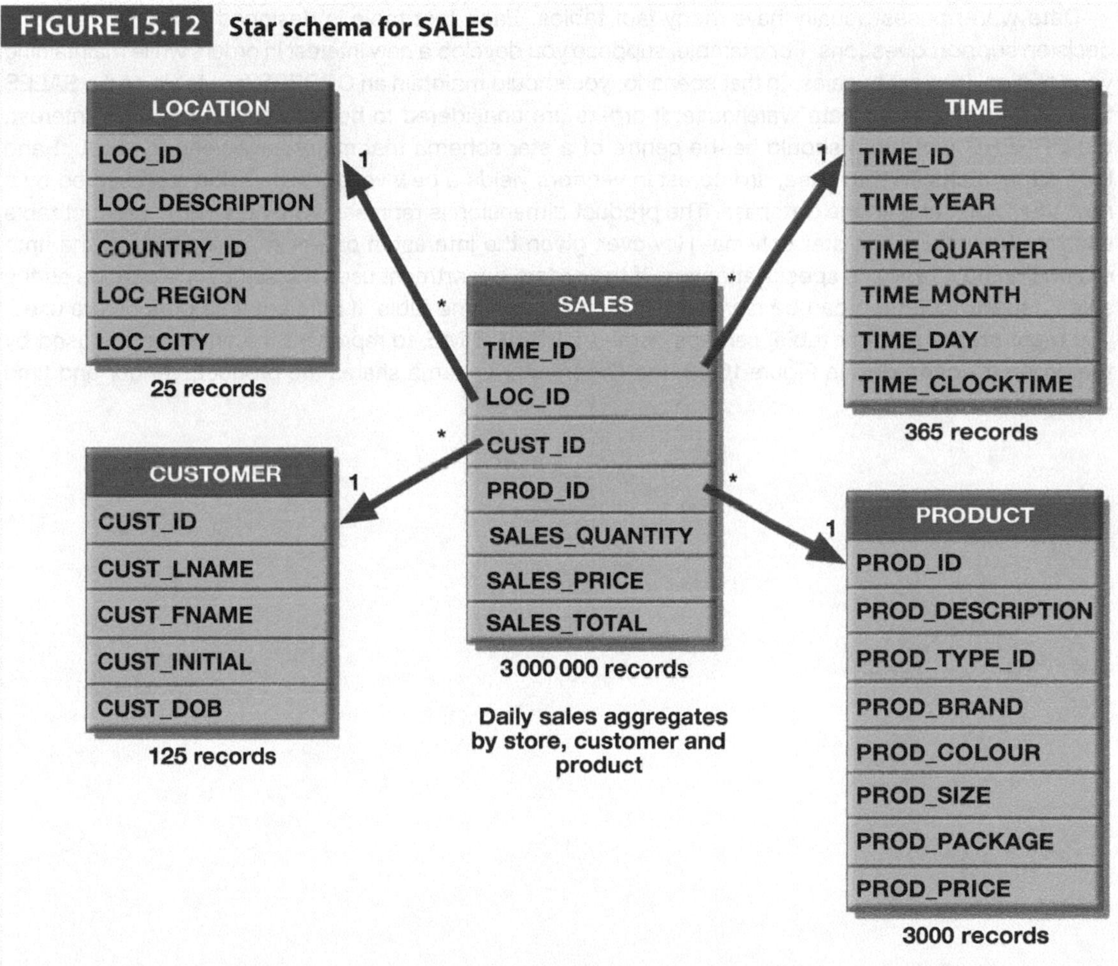

The composite primary key for the SALES fact table is composed of TIME_ID, LOCATION_ID, CUST_ID and PRODUCT_ID. Each record in the SALES fact table is uniquely identified by the combination of values for each of the fact tables' foreign keys. *By default, the fact table's primary key is always formed by combining the foreign keys pointing to the dimension tables to which they are related*. In this case, each sales record represents each product sold to a specific customer, at a specific time and in a specific location. In this schema, the time dimension table represents daily periods, so the SALES fact table represents daily sales aggregates by product and by customer. Since fact tables contain the actual values used in the decision support process, those values are repeated many times in the fact tables. Therefore, the fact tables are always the largest tables in the star schema. Since the dimension tables contain only non-repetitive information (all unique salespersons, all unique products, and so on), the dimension tables are always smaller than the fact tables.

In a typical star schema, each dimension record is related to thousands of fact records. For example, 'widget' appears only once in the product dimension, but it has thousands of corresponding records in the SALES fact table. That characteristic of the star schema facilitates data retrieval functions because most of the time the data analyst will look at the facts through the dimension's attributes. Therefore, a DSS-optimised data warehouse DBMS first searches the smaller dimension tables before accessing the larger fact tables.

Data warehouses usually have many fact tables. Each fact table is designed to answer specific decision support questions. For example, suppose you develop a new interest in orders while maintaining your original interest in sales. In that scenario, you should maintain an ORDERS fact table and a SALES fact table in the same data warehouse. If orders are considered to be an organisation's key interest, the ORDERS fact table should be the centre of a star schema that might have vendor, product and time dimensions. In that case, an interest in vendors yields a new vendor dimension represented by a new VENDOR table in the database. The product dimension is represented by the same product table used in the initial sales star schema. However, given the interest in orders as well as sales, the time dimension now requires special attention. If the orders department uses the same time periods as the sales department, time can be represented by the same time table. If different time periods are used, you must create another table, perhaps named ORDER_TIME, to represent the time periods used by the orders department. In Figure 15.13, the Orders star schema shares the product, vendor and time dimensions.

FIGURE 15.13 Orders star schema

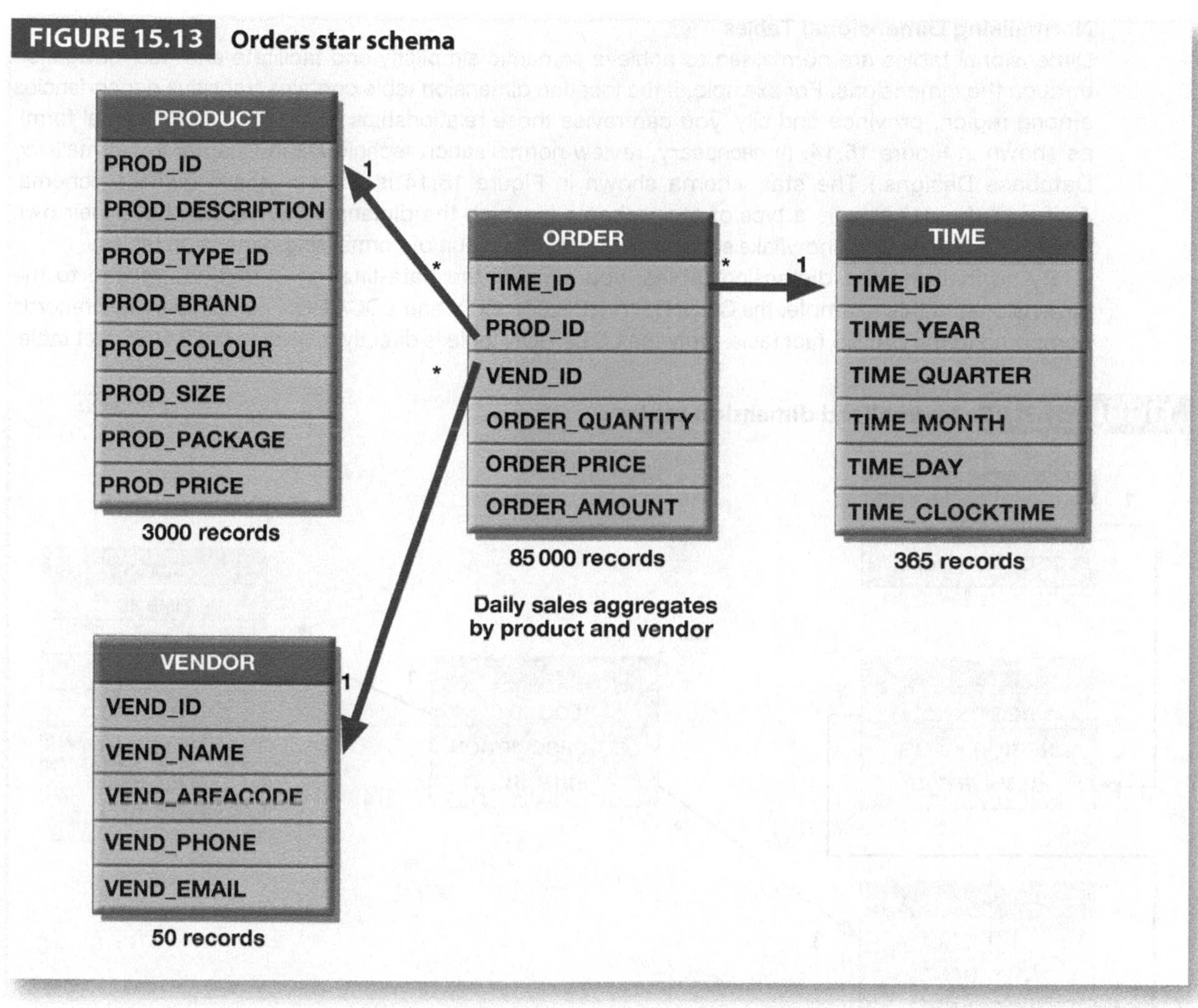

Multiple fact tables can also be created for performance and semantic reasons. The following section will explain several performance-enhancing techniques that can be used within the star schema.

15.5.6 Star Schema Performance-Improving Techniques

The creation of a database that provides fast and accurate answers to data analysis queries is the data warehouse design's prime objective. Therefore, performance-enhancement actions might target query speed through the facilitation of SQL code as well as through better semantic representation of business dimensions. Four techniques are often used to optimise data warehouse design:

- Normalising dimensional tables
- Maintaining multiple fact tables to represent different aggregation levels
- Denormalising fact tables
- Partitioning and replicating tables

Normalising Dimensional Tables

Dimensional tables are normalised to achieve semantic simplicity and facilitate end-user navigation through the dimensions. For example, if the location dimension table contains transitive dependencies among region, province and city, you can revise those relationships to the 3NF (third normal form), as shown in Figure 15.14. (If necessary, review normalisation techniques in Chapter 7, Normalising Database Designs.) The star schema shown in Figure 15.14 is known as a snowflake schema. A **snowflake schema** is a type of star schema in which the dimension tables can have their own dimension tables. The snowflake schema is usually the result of normalising dimension tables.

By normalising the dimension tables, you simplify the data-filtering operations related to the dimensions. In this example, the COUNTRY, REGION, CITY and LOCATION contain very few records compared to the SALES fact table. Only the LOCATION table is directly related to the SALES fact table.

FIGURE 15.14 Normalised dimension tables

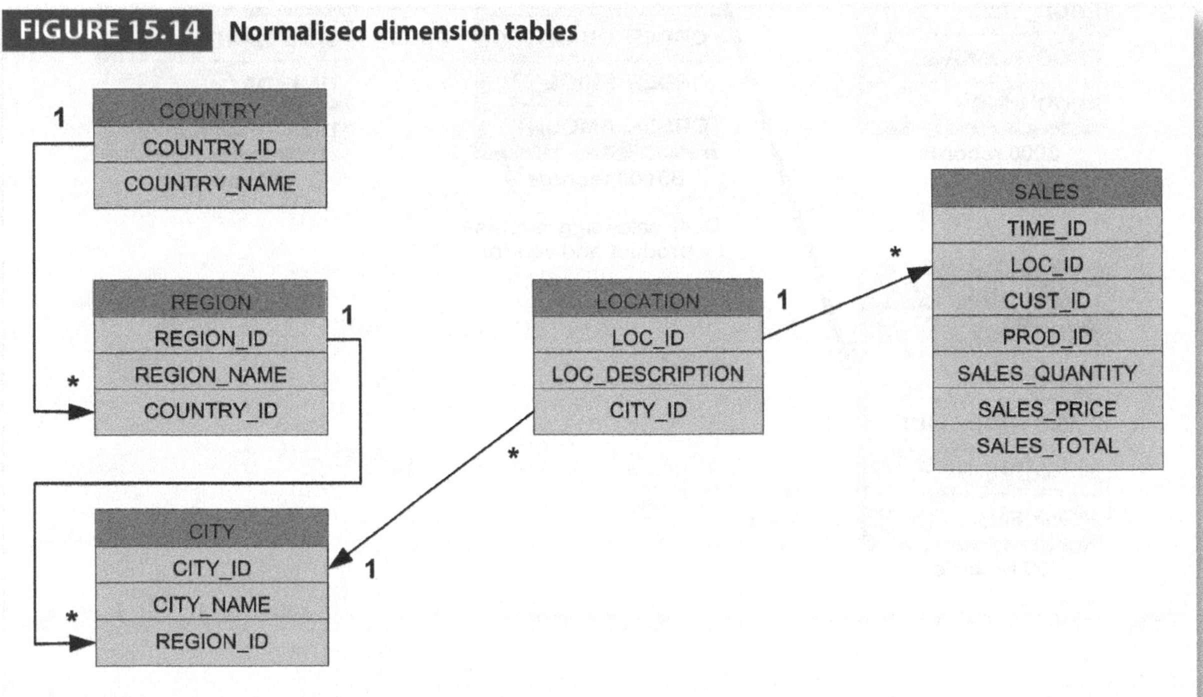

NOTE

Although using the dimension tables shown in Figure 15.14 gains structural simplicity, there is a price to pay for that simplicity. For example, if you want to aggregate the data by country, you must use a four-table join, thus increasing the complexity of the SQL statements. The star schema in Figure 15.12 uses a LOCATION dimension table that greatly facilitates data retrieval by eliminating multiple join operations. This is yet another example of the trade-offs that designers must consider.

Maintaining Multiple Fact Tables Representing Different Aggregation Levels

You can also speed up query operations by creating and maintaining multiple fact tables related to each level of aggregation (country, region and city) in the location dimension. These aggregate tables are precomputed at the data-loading phase rather than at run time. The purpose of this technique is to save processor cycles at run time, thereby speeding up data analysis. An end-user query tool optimised for decision analysis then properly accesses the summarised fact tables instead of computing the values by accessing a lower level of detail fact table. This technique is illustrated in Figure 15.15, which adds aggregate fact tables for country, region and city to the initial sales example.

FIGURE 15.15 Multiple fact tables

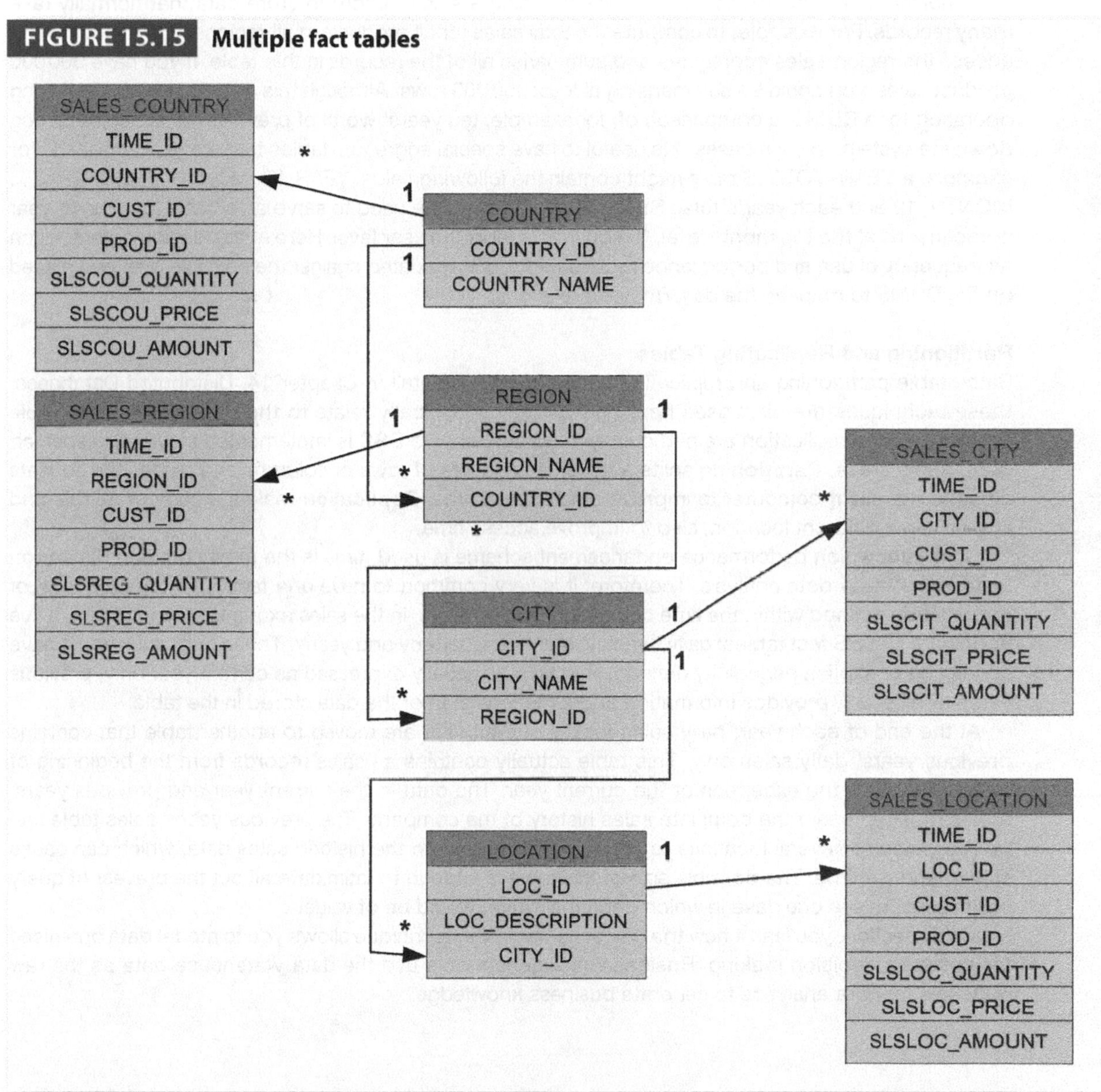

The data warehouse designer must identify which levels of aggregation to pre-compute and store in the database. These multiple aggregate fact tables are updated during each load cycle in batch mode. And because the objective is to minimise access and processing time, according to the expected frequency of use and the processing time required to calculate a given aggregation level at run time, the data warehouse designer must select which aggregation fact tables to create.

Denormalising Fact Tables

Denormalising fact tables improves data access performance and saves data storage space. The latter objective, however, is becoming less of an issue. Data storage costs decrease almost daily, and DBMS limitations that restrict database and table size limits, and record size limits and the maximum number of records in a single table, have far more negative effects than raw storage space costs.

Denormalisation improves performance by using a single record to store data that normally take many records. For example, to compute the total sales for all products in all regions, you might have to access the region sales aggregates and summarise all of the records in this table. If you have 300 000 product sales, you could be summarising at least 300 000 rows. Although this might not be a very taxing operation for a DBMS, a comparison of, for example, ten years' worth of previous sales begins to bog down the system. In such cases, it is useful to have special aggregate tables that are denormalised. For example, a YEAR_TOTALS table might contain the following fields: YEAR_ID, MONTH_1, MONTH_2 ... MONTH_12 and each year's total. Such tables can easily be used to serve as a basis for year-to-year comparisons at the top month level, the quarter level or the year level. Here again, design criteria, such as frequency of use and performance requirements, are evaluated against the possible overload placed on the DBMS to manage the denormalised relations.

Partitioning and Replicating Tables

Since table partitioning and replication were covered in detail in Chapter 14, Distributed Databases, these techniques are discussed here only as they specifically relate to the data warehouse. Table partitioning and replication are particularly important when a DSS is implemented in widely dispersed geographic areas. **Partitioning** splits a table into subsets of rows or columns and places the subsets close to the client computer to improve data access time. **Replication** makes a copy of a table and places it in a different location, also to improve access time.

No matter which performance-enhancement scheme is used, time is the most common dimension used in business data analysis. Therefore, it is very common to have one fact table for each level of aggregation defined within the time dimension. For example, in the sales example, you might have five aggregate SALES fact tables: daily, weekly, monthly, quarterly and yearly. Those fact tables must have an implicit or explicit periodicity defined. **Periodicity**, usually expressed as current year only, previous years or all years, provides information about the timespan of the data stored in the table.

At the end of each year, daily sales for the current year are moved to another table that contains previous years' daily sales only. This table actually contains all sales records from the beginning of operations, with the exception of the current year. The data in the current year and previous years' tables thus represent the complete sales history of the company. The previous years' sales table can be replicated at several locations to avoid remote access to the historic sales data, which can cause slow response time. The possible size of this table is enough to intimidate all but the bravest of query optimisers. This is one case in which denormalisation would be of value!

In this section, you learnt how the star schema design technique allows you to model data optimised for business decision making. Business intelligence tools use the data warehouse data as the raw materials for data analytics to generate business knowledge.

15.6 DATA ANALYTICS

Data analytics is a subset of BI functionality that encompasses a wide range of mathematical, statistical and modelling techniques with the purpose of extracting knowledge from data. Data analytics is used at all levels within the BI framework, including queries and reporting, monitoring and alerting, and data visualisation. Hence, data analytics is a 'shared' service that is crucial to what BI adds to an organisation. Data analytics represents what business managers really want from BI: the ability to extract actionable business insight from current events and foresee future problems or opportunities.

Data analytics discovers characteristics, relationships, dependencies or trends in the organisation's data, and then explains the discoveries and predicts future events based on the discoveries. In practice, data analytics is better understood as a continuous spectrum of knowledge acquisition that goes from discovery to explanation to prediction. The outcomes of data analytics then become part of the information framework on which decisions are built. Based on the previous discussion, data analytics tools can be grouped into two separate (but closely related and often overlapping) areas:

- **Explanatory analytics** focuses on discovering and explaining data characteristics and relationships based on existing data. Explanatory analytics uses statistical tools to formulate hypotheses, test them, and answer the how and why of such relationships – for example, how do past sales relate to previous customer promotions?
- **Predictive analytics** focuses on predicting future data outcomes with a high degree of accuracy. Predictive analytics uses sophisticated statistical tools to help the end user create advanced models that answer questions about future data occurrences – for example, what would next month's sales be based on a given customer promotion?

You can think of explanatory analytics as explaining the past and present, while predictive analytics forecasts the future. However, you need to understand that both sciences work together; predictive analytics uses explanatory analytics as a stepping stone to create predictive models. Data analytics has evolved over the years from simple statistical analysis of business data to dimensional analysis with OLAP tools, and then from data mining that discovers data patterns, relationships and trends to its current status of predictive analytics. The next sections illustrate the basic characteristics of data mining and predictive analytics.

15.6.1 Data Mining

Data mining refers to analysing massive amounts of data to uncover hidden trends, patterns and relationships; to form computer models to simulate and explain the findings; and then to use such models to support business decision making. In other words, data mining focuses on the discovery and explanation stages of knowledge acquisition.

To put data mining in perspective, look at the pyramid in Figure 15.16, which represents how knowledge is extracted from data. *Data* form the pyramid base and represent what most organisations collect in their operational databases. The second level contains *information* that represents the purified and processed data. Information forms the basis for decision making and business understanding. *Knowledge* is found at the pyramid's apex and represents highly specialised information.

FIGURE 15.16 Extracting knowledge from data

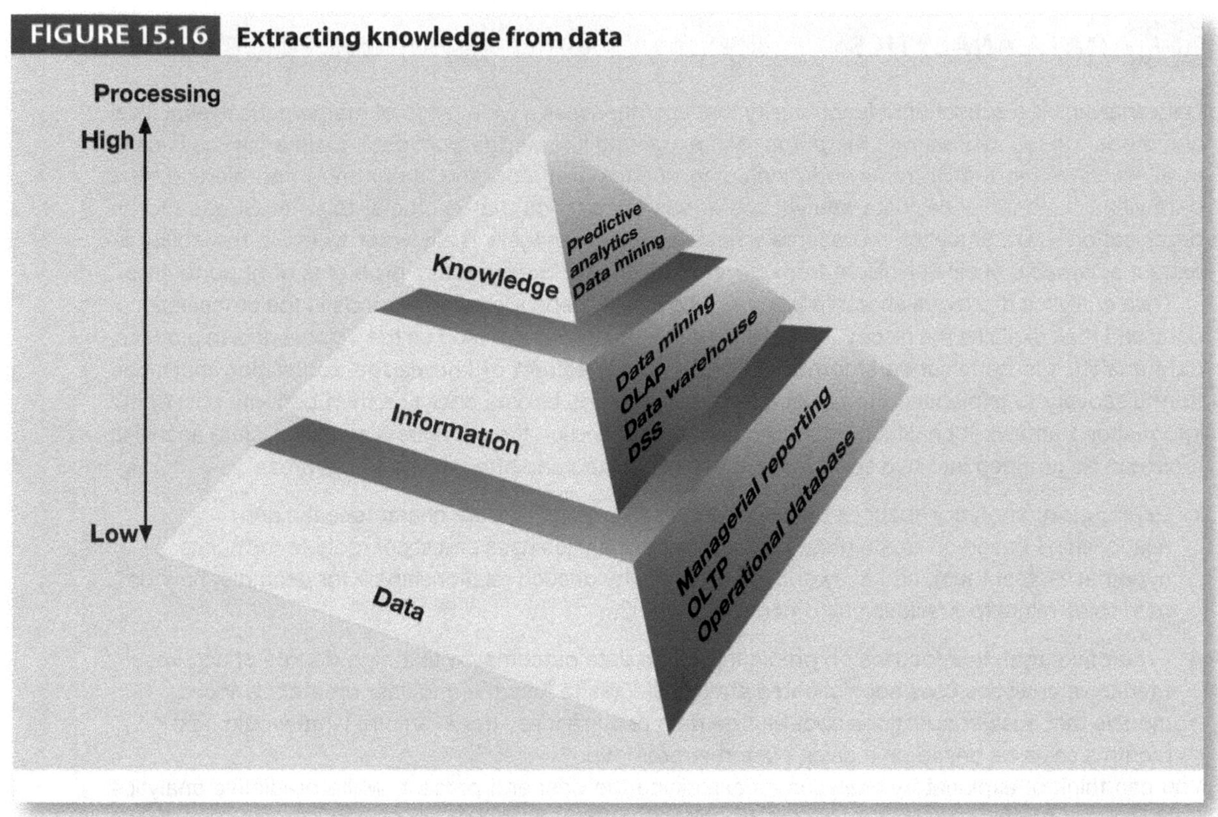

Current-generation data mining tools contain many design and application variations to fit specific business requirements. Depending on the problem domain, data mining tools focus on market niches such as banking, insurance, marketing, retailing, finance and healthcare. Within a given niche, data mining tools can use certain algorithms that are implemented in different ways and applied over different data.

In spite of the lack of precise standards, data mining is subject to four general phases:

1 Data preparation
2 Data analysis and classification
3 Knowledge acquisition
4 Prognosis.

In the *data preparation phase*, the main data sets to be used by the data mining operation are identified and cleansed of any data impurities. Because the data in the data warehouse are already integrated and filtered, the data warehouse is usually the target set for data mining operations.

15

The *data analysis and classification phase* studies the data to identify common data characteristics or patterns. During this phase, the data mining tool applies specific algorithms to find:

- Data groupings, classifications, clusters, or sequences
- Data dependencies, links, or relationships
- Data patterns, trends and deviations.

The *knowledge acquisition phase* uses the results of the data analysis and classification phase. During the knowledge acquisition phase, the data mining tool (with possible intervention by the end user) selects the appropriate modelling or knowledge acquisition algorithms. The most common algorithms used in data mining are based on neural networks, decision trees, rules induction, classification and regression trees, memory-based reasoning, and nearest neighbour and data visualisation. Hybrid algorithms also exist, for example, genetic algorithms that can be used to optimise decision trees and neural networks. A data mining tool may use many of these algorithms in any combination to generate a computer model that reflects the behaviour of the target data set.

Although many data mining tools stop at the knowledge acquisition phase, others continue to the *prognosis phase*. In that phase, the data mining findings are used to predict future behaviour and forecast business outcomes. Examples of data mining findings can be:

- Sixty-five per cent of customers who did not use a particular credit card in the past six months are 88 per cent likely to cancel that account.
- Eighty-two per cent of customers who bought a 60-inch or larger TV are 90 per cent likely to buy an entertainment centre within the next four weeks.
- If age < 30 and income $<= 25000$ and credit rating < 3 and credit amount > 25000, then the minimum loan term is ten years.

The complete set of findings can be represented in a decision tree, a neural network, a forecasting model or a visual presentation interface that is used to project future events or results. For example, the prognosis phase might project the likely outcome of a new product rollout or a new marketing promotion. Figure 15.17 illustrates the different phases of the data mining techniques.

FIGURE 15.17 Data mining phases

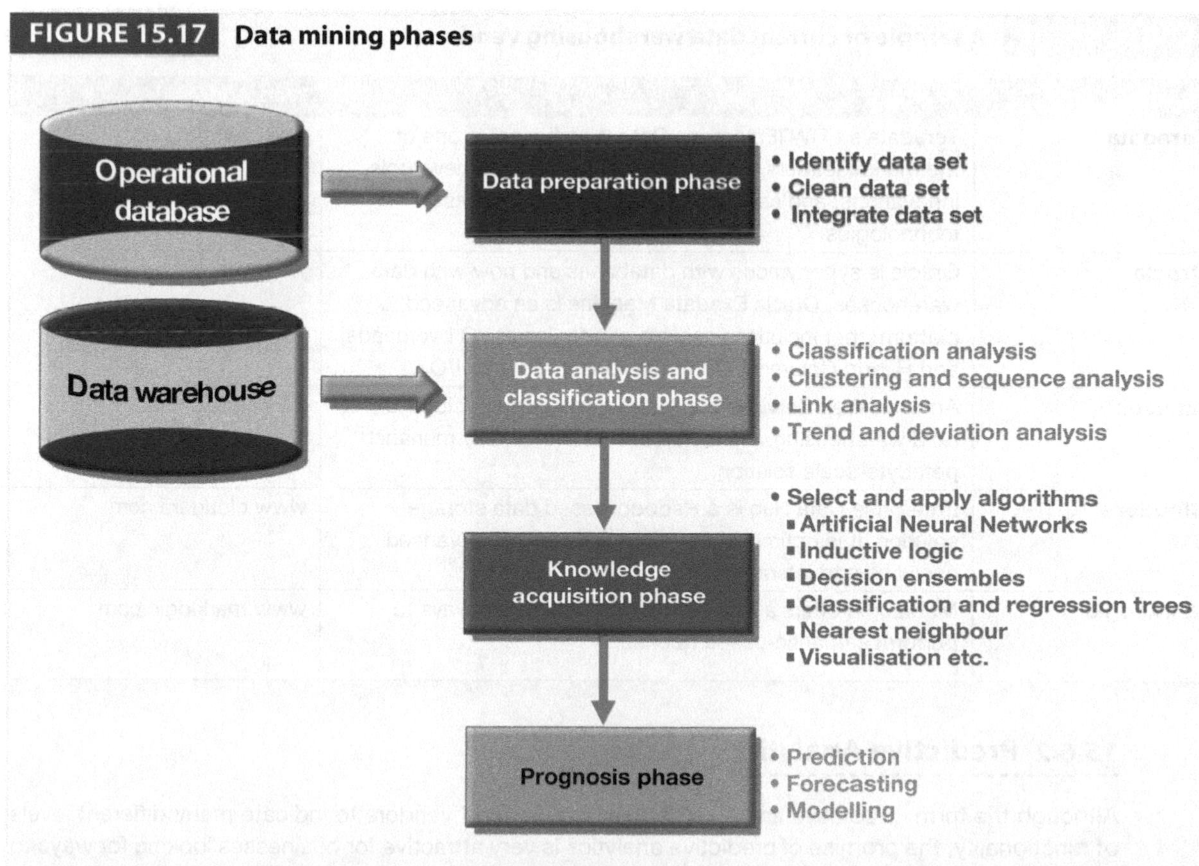

Because of the nature of the data mining process, some findings might fall outside the boundaries of what business managers expect. For example, a data mining tool might find a close relationship between a customer's favourite brand of cool drink and the brand of tyres on the customer's car. Clearly, that relationship might not be held in high regard among sales managers. (In regression analysis, these relationships are commonly described by the label 'idiot correlation'.) Fortunately, data mining usually yields more meaningful results. In fact, data mining has proven helpful in finding practical relationships among data that help define customer buying patterns, improve product development and acceptance, reduce healthcare fraud, analyse stock markets, and so on. Data mining can be run in two modes:

- *Guided*. The end user guides the data mining tool step by step to explore and explain known patterns or relationships. In this mode, the end user decides which techniques to apply to the data.
- *Automated*. In this mode, the end user sets up the data mining tool to run automatically and uncover hidden patterns, trends and relationships. The data mining tool applies multiple techniques to find significant relationships. As you learnt in this section, data mining methodologies focus on discovering and extracting information that describes and explains the data. For example, an explanatory model could create a customer profile that describes a given customer group. However, data mining can also be used as the basis to create advanced predictive data models. For example, a predictive model could be used to predict future customer behaviour, such as a customer response to a target marketing campaign. The next section explains the use of predictive analytics in more detail. Table 15.10 contains a sample of data warehouse and data mining software vendors.

TABLE 15.10 A sample of current data warehousing vendors

Vendor	Product	Web Address
Teradata	Teradata's EDW (Enterprise Data Warehouse) is one of the market leaders. The company has included new tools, innovations, and capabilities such as Hadoop-based technologies.	www.teradata.com
Oracle	Oracle is synonymous with databases and now with data warehouses. Oracle Exadata Machine is an advanced platform that includes flash storage for lower I/O overheads and Hybrid Columnar Compression for reduced I/O.	www.oracle.com
Amazon	Amazon Web Services has led the way through cloud-based data warehousing. Amazon Redshift is their fully managed petabyte-scale solution.	aws.amazon.com
Cloudera	Enterprise Data Hub is a Hadoop-based data storage solution. It is optimised for batch processing, advanced analytics and interactive SQL.	www.cloudera.com
MarkLogic	MarkLogic offers a NoSQL platform that offers ways to perform semantic-based queries.	www.marklogic.com

15.6.2 Predictive Analytics

Although the term 'predictive analytics' is used by many BI vendors to indicate many different levels of functionality, the promise of predictive analytics is very attractive for businesses looking for ways to improve their bottom line. Therefore, predictive analytics is receiving a lot of marketing buzz; vendors and businesses are dedicating extensive resources to this BI area. Predictive analytics refers to the use of advanced mathematical, statistical and modelling tools to predict future business outcomes with high degrees of accuracy. What is the difference between data mining and predictive analytics? As you learnt earlier, data mining also has predictive capabilities. In fact, data mining and predictive analytics use similar and overlapping sets of tools, but with a slightly different focus. Data mining focuses on answering the 'how' and 'what' of past data, while predictive analytics focuses on creating actionable models to predict future behaviours and events. In some ways, you can think of predictive analytics as the next logical step after data mining; once you understand your data, you can use the data to predict future behaviours. In fact, most BI vendors are dropping the term 'data mining' and replacing it with the more alluring term 'predictive analytics'.

The origins of predictive analytics can be traced back to the banking and credit card industries. The need to profile customers and predict customer buying patterns in these industries was a critical driving force for the evolution of many modelling methodologies used in BI data analytics today. For example, based on your demographic information and purchasing history, a credit card company can use data mining models to determine what credit limit to offer, which offers you are more likely to accept, and when to send those offers.

Predictive analytics received a big stimulus with the advent of social media. Companies turned to data mining and predictive analytics as a way to harvest the mountains of data stored on social media sites. Google was one of the first companies that offered targeted ads as a way to increase and personalise search experiences. Similar initiatives were used by all types of organisations to increase customer loyalty and drive up sales. Take the example of the airline and credit card industries and their frequent flyer and affinity card programs. Nowadays, many organisations use predictive analytics to profile customers in an attempt to get and keep the right ones, which in turn will increase loyalty and sales.[6]

Predictive analytics employs mathematical and statistical algorithms, neural networks, artificial intelligence and other advanced modelling tools to create actionable predictive models based on available data. The algorithms used to build the predictive model are specific to certain types of problems and work with certain types of data. Therefore, it is important that the end user, who typically is trained in statistics and understands business, applies the proper algorithms to the problem in hand. However, thanks to constant technology advances, modern BI tools automatically apply multiple algorithms to find the optimum model. Most predictive analytics models are used in areas such as customer relationships, customer service, customer retention, fraud detection, targeted marketing and optimised pricing. Predictive analytics can add value to an organisation in many different ways; for example, it can help optimise existing processes, identify hidden problems and anticipate future problems or opportunities. However, predictive analytics is not the 'secret sauce' to fix all business problems. Managers should carefully monitor and evaluate the value of predictive analytics models to determine their return on investment.

So far, you have learnt about data warehouses and star schemas to model and store decision support data, and data analytics to extract knowledge from the data. A BI system uses all the previously mentioned components to provide decision support to all organisational users. In the next section, you will learn about a widely used BI style known as online analytical processing.

6 "Analytics Insight", Available: www.analyticsinsight.net/

15.7 ONLINE ANALYTICAL PROCESSING

The need for more intensive decision support prompted the introduction of a new generation of tools. Those new tools, called **online analytical processing** (**OLAP**), create an advanced data analysis environment that supports decision making, business modelling and operations research. OLAP systems share three main characteristics. They:

- Use multidimensional data analysis techniques
- Provide advanced database support
- Provide easy-to-use end-user interfaces.

Let's examine each of those characteristics.

15.7.1 Multidimensional Data Analysis Techniques

The most distinct characteristic of modern OLAP tools is their capacity for multidimensional analysis. In multidimensional analysis, data are processed and viewed as part of a multidimensional structure. This type of data analysis is particularly attractive to business decision makers because they tend to view business data as data that are related to other business data.

To better understand this view, let's examine how a business data analyst might investigate sales figures. In this case, he or she is probably interested in the sales figures as they relate to other business variables such as customers and time. In other words, customers and time are viewed as different dimensions of sales. Figure 15.18 illustrates how the operational (one-dimensional) view differs from the multidimensional view of sales.

As you examine Figure 15.18, note that the tabular (operational) view of sales data is not well suited to decision support because the relationship between INVOICE and LINE does not provide a business perspective of the sales data. On the other hand, the end user's view of sales data *from a business perspective* is more closely represented by the multidimensional view of sales than by the tabular view of separate tables. Note also that the multidimensional view allows end users to consolidate or aggregate data at different levels: total sales figures by customers and by date. Finally, the multidimensional view of data allows a business data analyst easily to switch business perspectives (dimensions) from sales by customer to sales by division, by region, and so on.

Multidimensional data analysis techniques are augmented by the following functions:

- Advanced data presentation functions: 3-D graphics, pivot tables, crosstabs, data rotation and three-dimensional cubes. Such facilities are compatible with desktop spreadsheets, statistical packages and query and report-writer packages.
- Advanced data aggregation, consolidation and classification functions that allow the data analyst to create multiple data aggregation levels, slice-and-dice data (see section 15.5.3), and drill-down and roll-up data across different dimensions and aggregation levels. For example, aggregating data across the time dimension (by week, month, quarter and year) allows the data analyst to drill down and roll up across time dimensions.
- Advanced computational functions: Business-orientated variables (market share, period comparisons, sales margins, product margins and percentage changes), financial and accounting ratios (profitability, overhead, cost allocations and returns), and statistical and forecasting functions. These functions are provided automatically and the end user does not need to redefine their components each time they are accessed.
- Advanced data modelling functions: Support for what-if scenarios, variable assessment, variable contributions to outcome, linear programming and other modelling tools.

FIGURE 15.18 Operational vs multidimensional view of sales

Database name: Ch15_Text

Table name: DW_INVOICE

INV_NUM	INV_DATE	CUS_NAME	INV_TOTAL
2034	15-May-19	Dartonik	1400.00
2035	15-May-19	Summer Lake	1200.00
2036	16-May-19	Dartonik	1350.00
2037	16-May-19	Summer lake	3100.00
2038	16-May-19	Trydon	400.00

Table name: DW_LINE

DW_LINE					
INV_NUM	LINE_NUM	PROD_DESCRIPTION	LINE_PRICE	LINE_QUANTITY	LINE_AMOUNT
2034	1	Optical Mouse	45.00	20	900.00
2034	2	Wireless RF remote and laser pointer	50.00	10	500.00
2035	1	Everlast Hard Drive, 3TB	200.00	6	1200.00
2036	1	Optical Mouse	45.00	30	1350.00
2037	1	Optical Mouse	45.00	10	450.00
2037	2	Router	120.00	5	600.00
2037	3	Everlast Hard Drive, 3TB	205.00	10	2050.00
2038	1	NoTech Speaker Set	50.00	8	400.00

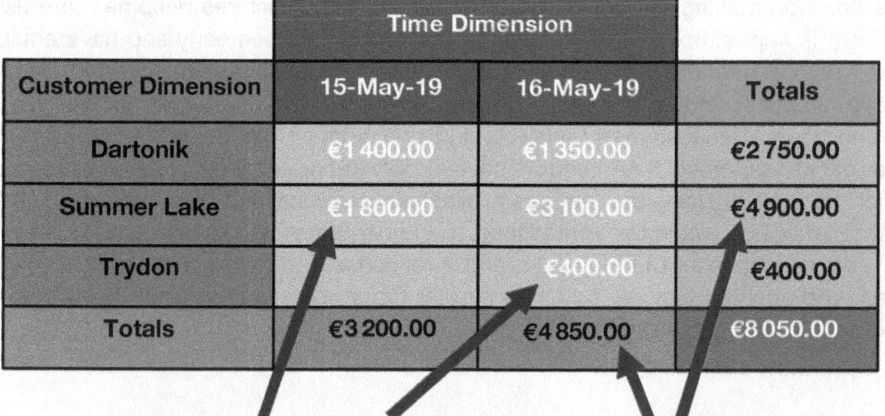

Multidimensional View of Sales
Time Dimension
Customer Dimension
15-May-19
16-May-19
Totals
Dartonik
€1 400.00
€1 350.00
€2 750.00
Summer Lake
€1 800.00
€3 100.00
€4 900.00
Trydon
€400.00
€400.00
Totals
€3 200.00
€4 850.00
€8 050.00
Sales are located in the intersection of a customer row and time column
Aggregations are provided for both dimensions

15

Predictive modeling allows the system to build advanced statistical models to predict future values (business outcomes) with a high percentage of accuracy.

15.7.2 Advanced Database Support

To deliver efficient decision support, OLAP tools must have advanced data access features. Such features include:

- Access to many different kinds of DBMSs, flat files and internal and external data sources
- Access to aggregated data warehouse data as well as to the detail data found in operational databases
- Advanced data navigation features such as drill-down and roll-up
- Rapid and consistent query response times
- The ability to map end-user requests, expressed in either business or model terms, to the appropriate data source and then to the proper data access language (usually SQL). The query code must be optimised to match the data source, regardless of whether the source is operational or data warehouse data.
- Support for very large databases. As already explained, the data warehouse can easily and quickly grow to multiple terabytes in size.

To provide a seamless interface, OLAP tools map the data elements from the data warehouse and from the operational database to their own data dictionaries. These metadata are used to translate end-user data analysis requests into the proper (optimised) query codes, which are then directed to the appropriate data source(s).

15.7.3 Easy-to-Use End-User Interface

The end-user analytical interface is one of the most critical OLAP components. When properly implemented, an analytical interface permits the user to navigate the data in a way that simplifies and accelerates decision making or data analysis. Advanced OLAP features become more useful when access to them is kept simple. OLAP tool vendors learnt this lesson early and have equipped their sophisticated data extraction and analysis tools with easy-to-use graphical interfaces. Many of the interface features are 'borrowed' from previous generations of data analysis tools that are already familiar to end users. Because many analysis and presentation functions are common to desktop spreadsheet packages, most OLAP vendors have closely integrated their systems with spreadsheets such as Microsoft Excel. Using the features available in graphical end-user interfaces, OLAP simply becomes another option within the spreadsheet menu bar, as shown in Figure 15.19. This seamless integration is an advantage for OLAP systems and spreadsheet vendors because end users gain access to advanced data analysis features by using familiar programs and interfaces. Therefore, additional training and development costs are minimised.

FIGURE 15.19 Integration of OLAP with a spreadsheet program

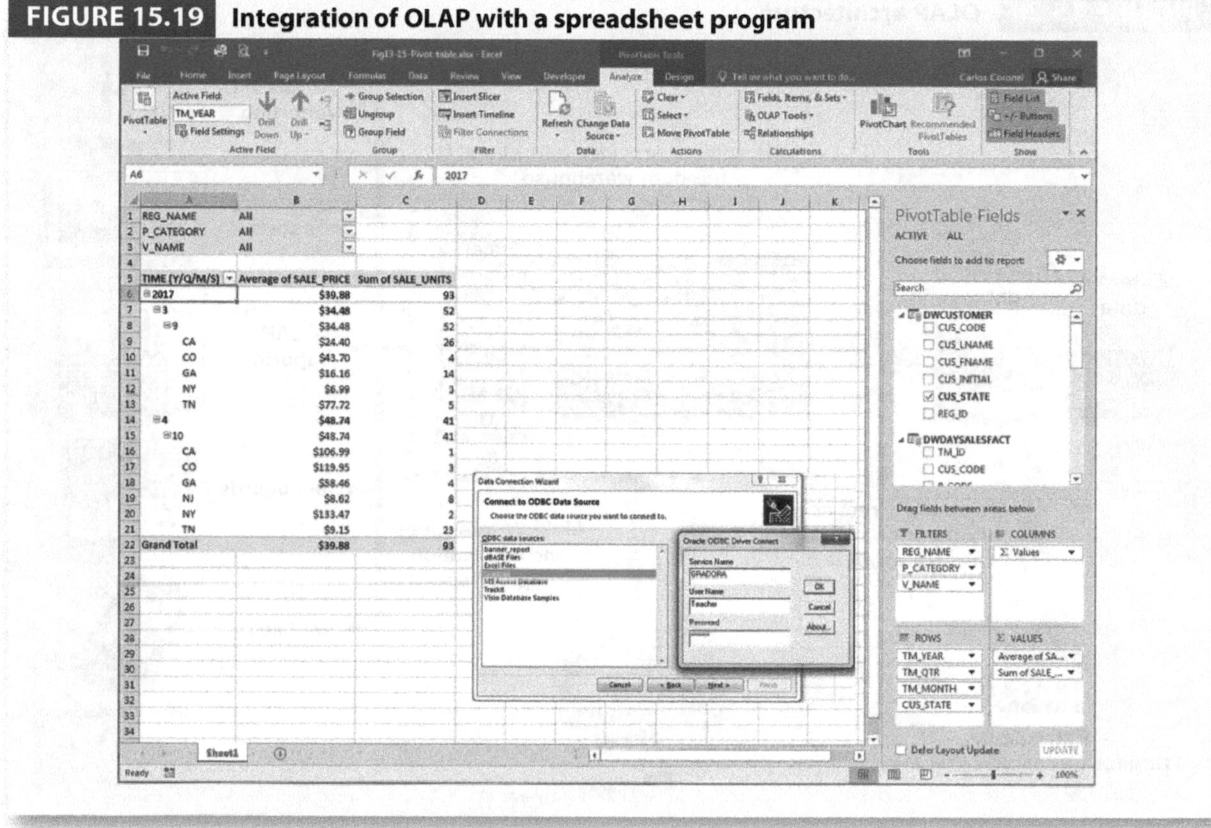

15.7.4 OLAP Architecture

OLAP operational characteristics can be divided into three main modules:

- Graphical user interface (GUI)
- Analytical processing logic
- Data processing logic.

Figure 15.20 illustrates OLAP's architectural components.

As Figure 15.20 illustrates, OLAP systems are designed to use both operational and data warehouse data. Although Figure 15.20 shows the OLAP system components located on a single computer, this single-user scenario is only one of many. In fact, one problem with the installation shown here is that each data analyst must have a powerful computer on which to store the OLAP system and perform all data processing locally. In addition, each analyst uses a separate copy of the data. Therefore, the data copies must be synchronised to ensure that analysts are working with the same data. In other words, each end user must have his or her own 'private' copy (extract) of the data and programs, thus returning to the *islands of information* problems discussed in Chapter 1, The Database Approach. This approach does not provide the benefits of a single business image shared among all users.

A more common and practical architecture is one in which the OLAP GUI runs on client workstations, while the OLAP engine, or server, composed of the OLAP analytical processing logic and OLAP data-processing logic, runs on a shared computer. In that case, the OLAP server will be a front end to the data warehouse's decision support data. This front end or middle layer (because it sits between the data warehouse and the end-user GUI) accepts and processes the data-processing requests generated

FIGURE 15.20 OLAP architecture

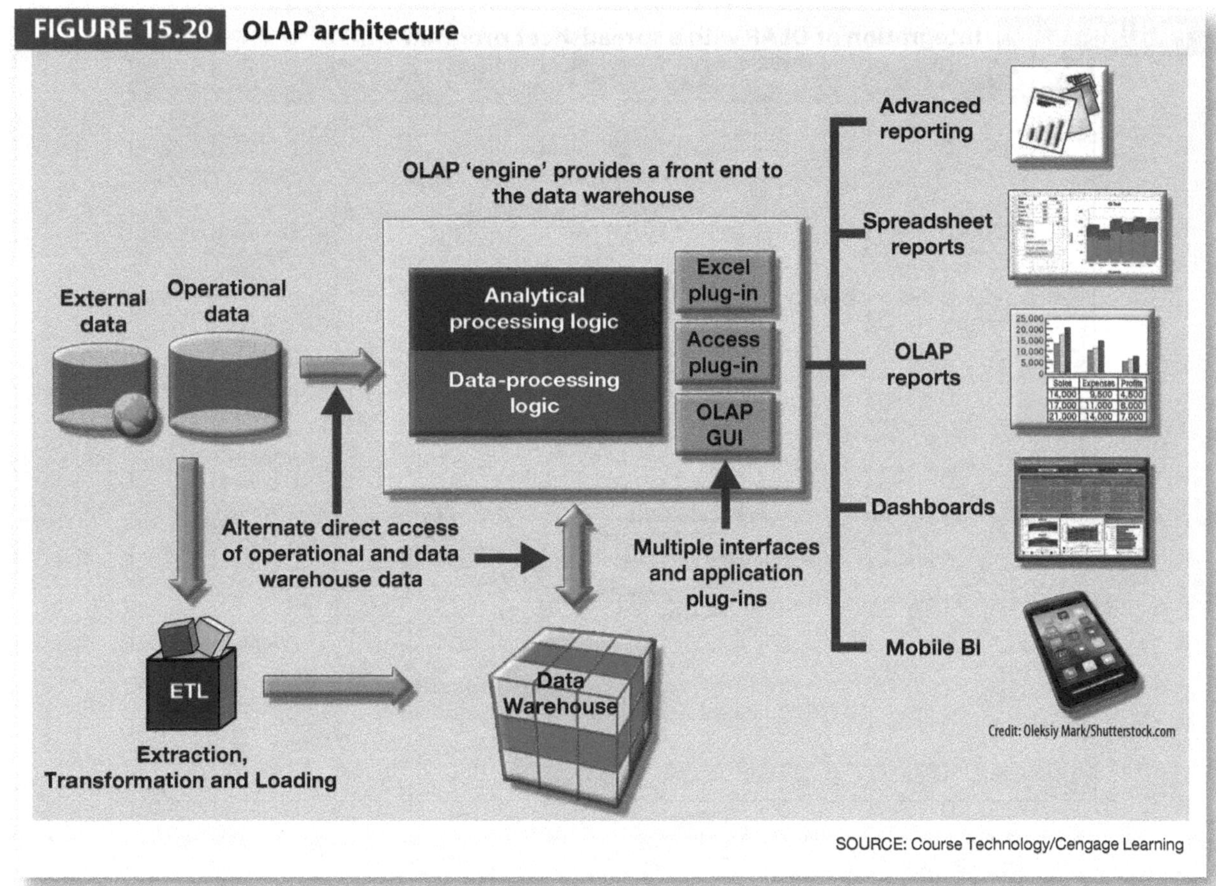

SOURCE: Course Technology/Cengage Learning

by the many end-user OLAP workstations. Figure 15.21 illustrates an OLAP server with local miniature data marts.

As illustrated in Figure 15.21, the OLAP system could merge the data warehouse and data mart approaches by storing extracts of the data warehouse at end-user workstations. The objective is to increase the speed of data access and data visualisation (the graphic representations of data trends and characteristics). The logic behind this approach is the assumption that most end users usually work with fairly small, stable data warehouse subsets. For example, a sales analyst is most likely to work with sales data, whereas a customer representative is likely to work with customer data.

Whatever the arrangement of the OLAP components, one thing is certain: multidimensional data must be used. But how are multidimensional data best stored and managed? OLAP proponents are sharply divided. Some favour the use of relational databases to store the multidimensional data; others argue for the superiority of specialised multidimensional databases to store multidimensional data. The basic characteristics of each approach will be examined next.

FIGURE 15.21 OLAP server with local miniature data marts

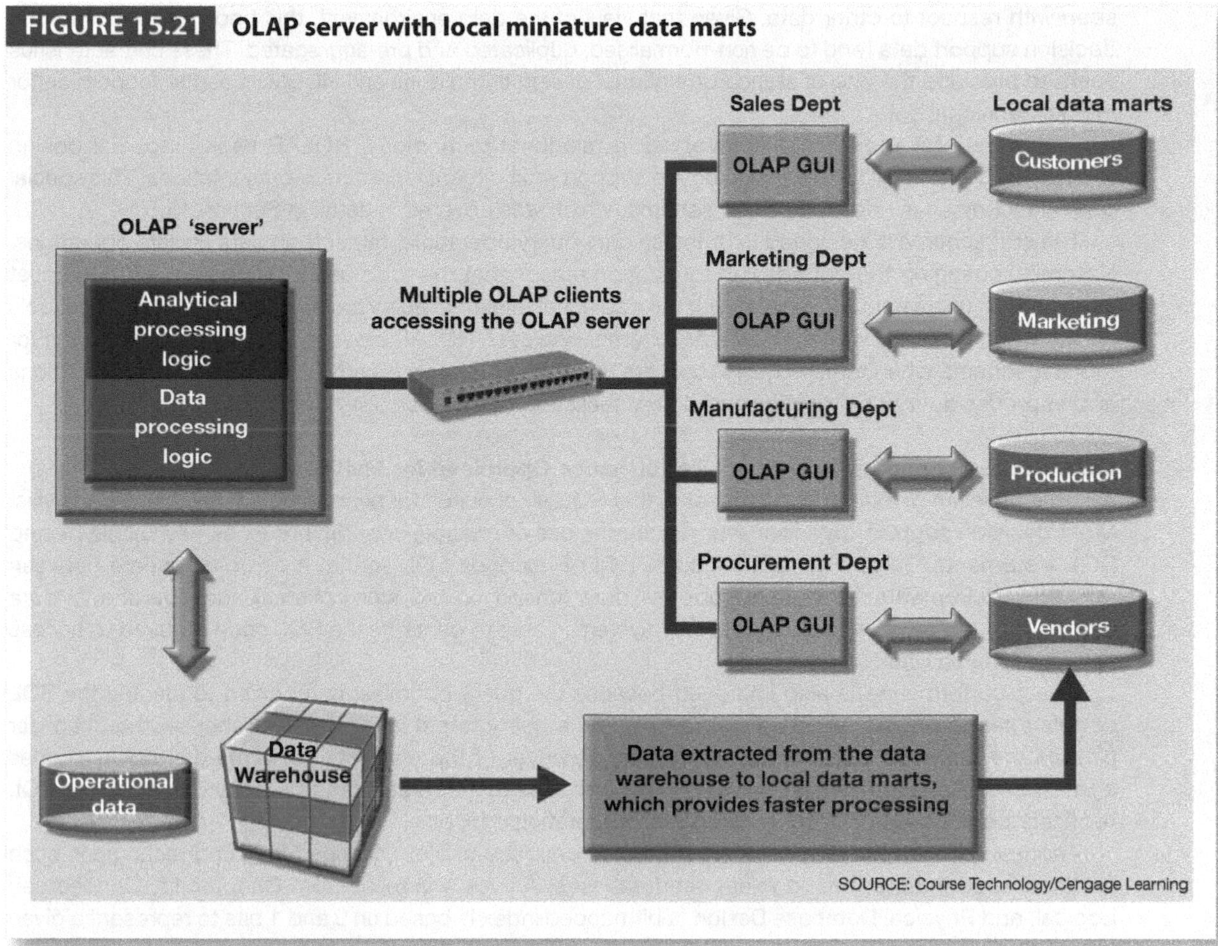

15.7.5 Relational OLAP

Relational online analytical processing (ROLAP) provides OLAP functionality by using relational databases and familiar relational query tools to store and analyse multidimensional data. That approach builds on existing relational technologies and represents a natural extension to all of the companies that already use relational database management systems within their organisations. ROLAP adds the following extensions to traditional RDBMS technology:

- Multidimensional data schema support within the RDBMS.
- Data access language and query performance that are optimised for multidimensional data.
- Support for very large databases (VLDBs).

15

Multidimensional Data Schema Support within the RDBMS

Relational technology uses normalised tables to store data. The reliance on normalisation as the design methodology for relational databases is seen as a stumbling block to its use in OLAP systems. Normalisation divides business entities into smaller pieces to produce the normalised tables. For example, sales data components might be stored in four or five different tables. The reason for using normalised tables is to reduce redundancies, thereby eliminating data anomalies and to facilitate data updates. Unfortunately, for decision support purposes, it is easier to understand data when they are seen with respect to other data. Given that view of the data environment, this book has stressed that decision support data tend to be non-normalised, duplicated and pre-aggregated. These characteristics seem to preclude the use of standard relational design techniques and RDBMSs as the foundation for multidimensional data.

Fortunately for those heavily invested in relational technology, ROLAP uses a special design technique to enable RDBMS technology to support multidimensional data representations. This special design technique is known as a star schema, which was covered in detail in Section 15.5.

The star schema is designed to optimise data query operations rather than data update operations. Naturally, changing the data design foundation means that the tools used to access such data must change. End users who are familiar with the traditional relational query tools will discover that those tools do not work efficiently with the new star schema. However, ROLAP saves the day by adding support for the star schema when familiar query tools are used. ROLAP provides advanced data analysis functions and improves query optimisation and data visualisation methods.

Data Access Language and Query Performance Optimised for Multidimensional Data

Another criticism of relational databases is that SQL is not suited for performing advanced data analysis. Most decision support data requests require the use of multiple-pass SQL queries or multiple nested SQL statements. To answer this criticism, ROLAP extends SQL so that it can differentiate between access requirements for data warehouse data (based on the star schema) and operational data (normalised tables). In that way, a ROLAP system is able to generate the SQL code required to access the star schema data.

Query performance is also improved because the query optimiser is modified to identify the SQL code's intended query targets. For example, if the query target is the data warehouse, the optimiser passes the requests to the data warehouse. However, if the end user performs drill-down queries against operational data, the query optimiser identifies that operation and properly optimises the SQL requests before passing them through to the operational DBMS.

Another source of improved query performance is the use of advanced indexing techniques such as bitmapped indexes within relational databases. As you will recall from Chapter 11, Conceptual, Logical, and Physical Database Design, a bitmapped index is based on 0 and 1 bits to represent a given condition. For example, if the REGION attribute in Figure 15.3 has only four outcomes – North, South, East and West – those outcomes may be represented as shown in Table 15.11. (Only the first ten rows from Figure 15.3 are represented in Table 15.11. The '1' represents 'bit on', and the '0' represents 'bit off'. For example, to represent a row with a REGION attribute = 'East', only the 'East' bit would be on. Note that each row must be represented in the index table.)

TABLE 15.11 Bitmap representation of region values

North	South	East	West
0	0	1	0
0	0	1	0
1	0	0	0
1	0	0	0
1	0	0	0
0	1	0	0
0	1	0	0
0	1	0	0
0	0	0	1
0	0	0	1

As you examine Table 15.11, note that the index takes a minimum amount of space. Therefore, bitmapped indexes are more efficient at handling large amounts of data than are the indexes typically found in many relational databases. However, do keep in mind that bitmapped indexes are primarily used in situations where the number of possible values for an attribute (in other words, the attribute domain) is fairly small. For example, REGION has only four outcomes in this example. Marital status – married, single, widowed, divorced – would be another good bitmapped index candidate, as would gender – M or F.

Early examples of ROLAP tools are mainly client/server products in which the end-user interface, the analytical processing, and the data processing took place on different computers. Figure 15.22 shows the interaction of the client/server ROLAP components.

FIGURE 15.22 Early traditional ROLAP client/server architecture

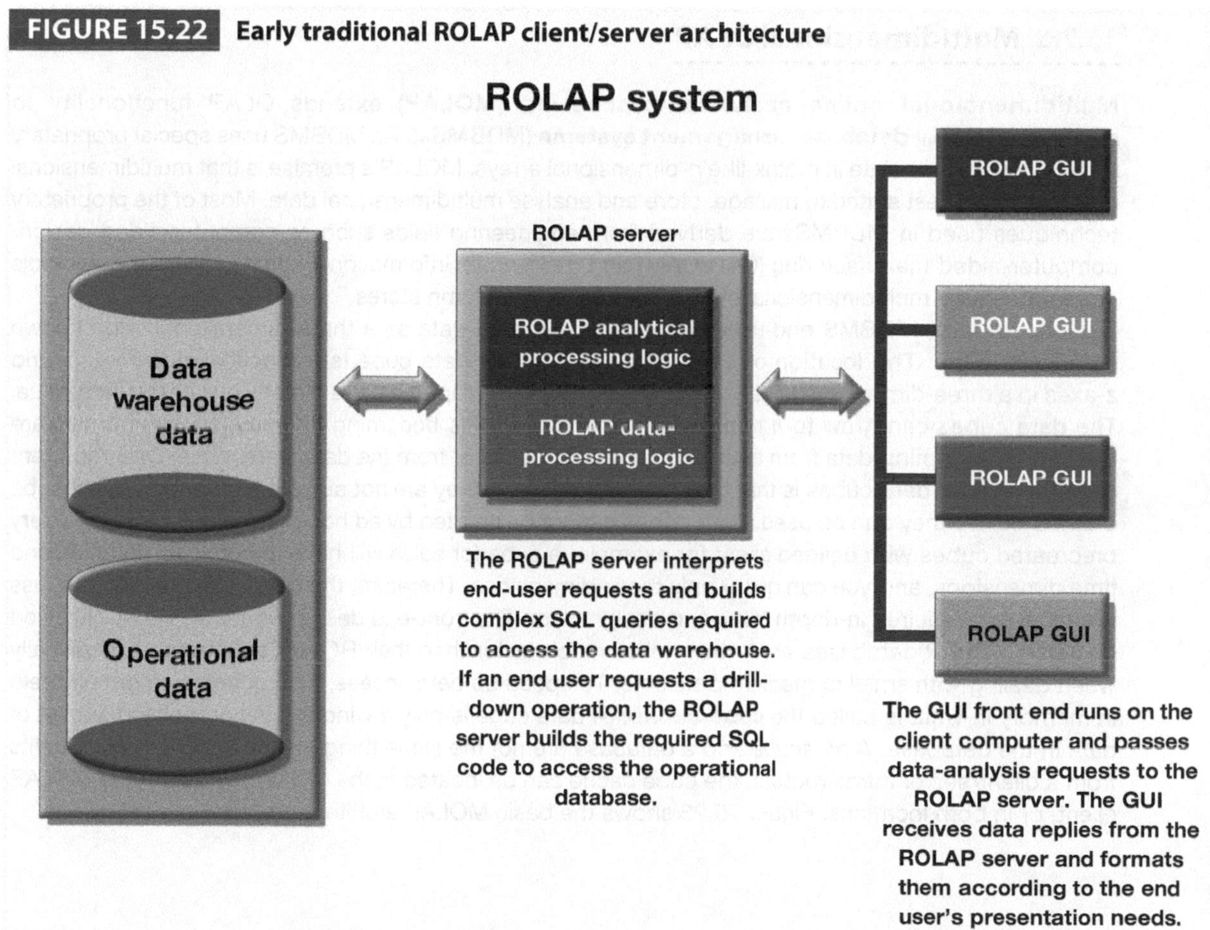
ROLAP system
ROLAP server
ROLAP analytical processing logic
ROLAP data-processing logic
Data warehouse data
Operational data
ROLAP GUI
ROLAP GUI
ROLAP GUI
ROLAP GUI
The ROLAP server interprets end-user requests and builds complex SQL queries required to access the data warehouse. If an end user requests a drill-down operation, the ROLAP server builds the required SQL code to access the operational database.
The GUI front end runs on the client computer and passes data-analysis requests to the ROLAP server. The GUI receives data replies from the ROLAP server and formats them according to the end user's presentation needs.

15

Support for Very Large Databases

Recall that support for VLDBs is a requirement for DSS databases. Therefore, when the relational database is used in a DSS role, it must also be able to store very large amounts of data. Both the storage capability and the process of loading data into the database are crucial. Therefore, the RDBMS must have the proper tools to import, integrate and populate the data warehouse with data. Decision support data are normally loaded in bulk (batch) mode from the operational data. However, batch operations require that both the source and the destination databases be reserved (locked). The speed of the data-loading operations is important, especially when you realise that most operational systems run 24 hours a day, 7 days a week, 52 weeks a year. Therefore, the window of opportunity for maintenance and batch loading is open only briefly, typically during slack periods.

With an open client/server architecture, ROLAP provides advanced decision support capabilities that are scalable to the entire enterprise. Clearly, ROLAP is a logical choice for companies that already use relational databases for their operational data. Given the size of the relational database market, it is hardly surprising that most current RDBMS vendors have extended their products to support data warehouses.

15.7.6 Multidimensional OLAP

Multidimensional online analytical processing (MOLAP) extends OLAP functionality to **multidimensional database management systems (MDBMSs)**. An MDBMS uses special proprietary techniques to store data in matrix-like *n*-dimensional arrays. MOLAP's premise is that multidimensional databases are best suited to manage, store and analyse multidimensional data. Most of the proprietary techniques used in MDBMSs are derived from engineering fields such as computer-aided design/computer-aided manufacturing (CAD/CAM) and geographic information systems (GIS). MOLAP tools store data using multidimensional arrays, row stores or column stores.

Conceptually, MDBMS end users visualise the stored data as a three-dimensional cube known as a **data cube**. The location of each data value in the data cube is a function of the x-, y- and z-axes in a three-dimensional space. The x-, y- and z-axes represent the dimensions of the data value. The data cubes can grow to *n* number of dimensions, thus becoming *hypercubes*. Data cubes are created by extracting data from the operational databases or from the data warehouse. One important characteristic of data cubes is that they are static; that is, they are not subject to change and must be created before they can be used. Data cubes cannot be created by ad hoc queries. Instead, you query precreated cubes with defined axes; for example, a cube for sales will have the product, location and time dimensions, and you can query only those dimensions. Therefore, the data cube creation process is critical and requires in-depth front-end design work. The front-end design work may be well justified because MOLAP databases are known to be much faster than their ROLAP counterparts, especially when dealing with small to medium data sets. To speed up data access, data cubes are normally held in memory in what is called the **cube cache**. (A data cube is only a window to a predefined subset of data in the database. A *datacube* and a *database* are not the same thing.) Since MOLAP also benefits from a client/server infrastructure, the cube cache can be located at the MOLAP server, at the MOLAP client, or in both locations. Figure 15.23 shows the basic MOLAP architecture.

FIGURE 15.23 MOLAP client/server architecture

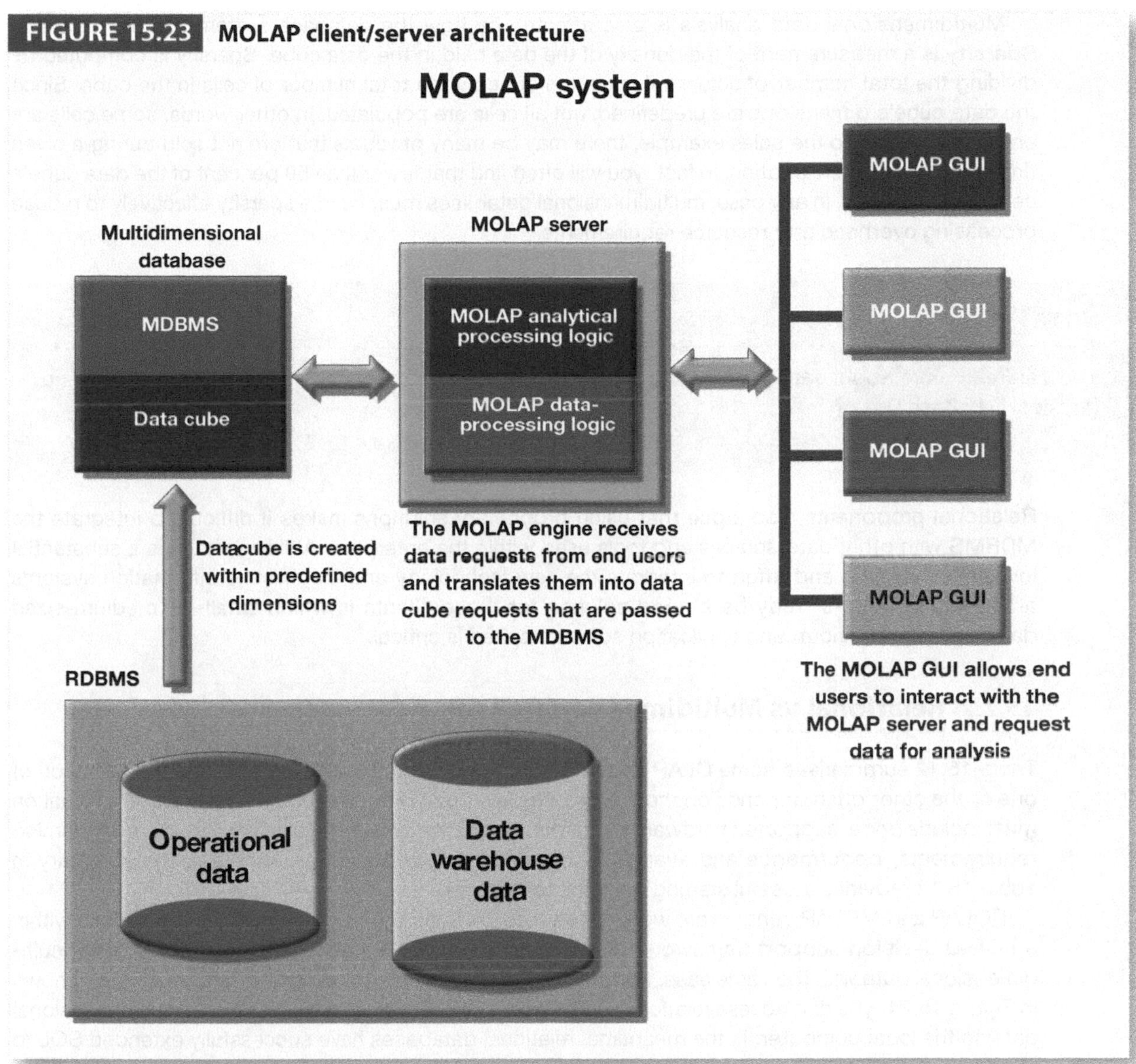
MOLAP system
Multidimensional database
MDBMS
Data cube
MOLAP server
MOLAP analytical processing logic
MOLAP data-processing logic
MOLAP GUI
MOLAP GUI
MOLAP GUI
MOLAP GUI
Datacube is created within predefined dimensions
The MOLAP engine receives data requests from end users and translates them into data cube requests that are passed to the MDBMS
The MOLAP GUI allows end users to interact with the MOLAP server and request data for analysis
RDBMS
Operational data
Data warehouse data

As the data cube is predefined with a set number of dimensions, the addition of a new dimension requires that the entire data cube be re-created. This re-creation process is a time-consuming operation. Therefore, when data cubes are created too often, the MDBMS loses some of its speed advantage over the relational database. And although MDBMSs have performance advantages over relational databases, the MDBMS is best suited to small and medium data sets. Scalability is somewhat limited because the size of the data cube is restricted to avoid lengthy data access times caused by having less work space (memory) available for the operating system and the application programs. In addition, the MDBMS makes use of proprietary data storage techniques that, in turn, require proprietary data access methods using a multidimensional query language.

Multidimensional data analysis is also affected by how the database system handles sparsity. **Sparsity** is a measurement of the density of the data held in the data cube. Sparsity is computed by dividing the total number of actual values in the cube by the total number of cells in the cube. Since the data cube's dimensions are predefined, not all cells are populated. In other words, some cells are empty. Returning to the sales example, there may be many products that are not sold during a given time period in a given location. In fact, you will often find that fewer than 50 per cent of the data cube's cells are populated. In any case, multidimensional databases must handle sparsity effectively to reduce processing overhead and resource requirements.

NOTE

You can read more about data sparsity and bitmapped indexes in Chapter 11, Conceptual, Logical, and Physical Database Design.

Relational proponents also argue that using proprietary solutions makes it difficult to integrate the MDBMS with other data sources and tools used within the enterprise. Although it takes a substantial investment of time and effort to integrate the new technology and the existing information systems architecture, MOLAP may be a good solution for those clients in which small- to medium-sized databases are the norm and application software speed is critical.

15.7.7 Relational vs Multidimensional OLAP

Table 15.12 summarises some OLAP and MOLAP pros and cons. Keep in mind that the selection of one or the other often depends on the evaluator's view point. For example, a proper OLAP evaluation must include price, supported hardware platforms, compatibility with the existing DBMS, programming requirements, performance and availability of administrative tools. Nevertheless, the summary in Table 15.12 provides a useful starting point for comparison.

ROLAP and MOLAP vendors are working towards the integration of their respective solutions within a unified decision support framework. Many OLAP products are able to handle tabular and multidimensional data with the same ease. For example, if you are using Excel OLAP functionality, as shown in Figure 15.24, you can access relational OLAP data in a SQL server as well as cube (multidimensional data) in the local computer. In the meantime, relational databases have successfully extended SQL to support many OLAP tools.

TABLE 15.12 Relational vs multidimensional OLAP

Characteristic	ROLAP	MOLAP
Schema	Uses star schema Additional dimensions can be added dynamically	Uses data cubes Multidimensional arrays, row stores, column stores. Additional dimensions require re-creation of the data cube.
Database size	Medium to large	Large
Architecture	Client/server Standards-based Open	Client/server Open or proprietary depending on vendor.

15

Characteristic	ROLAP	MOLAP
Access	Supports ad hoc requests Unlimited dimensions	Limited to predefined dimensions. Proprietary access languages.
Speed	Good with small data sets; average for medium to large data sets	Faster for large data sets with predefined dimensions.

15.8 SQL ANALYTIC FUNCTIONS

The proliferation of OLAP tools has fostered the development of SQL extensions to support multi-dimensional data analysis. Most SQL innovations are the result of vendor-centric product enhancements. However, many of the innovations have made their way into standard SQL. This section will introduce some of the new SQL extensions that have been created to support OLAP-type data manipulations.

The SaleCo snowflake schema shown in Figure 15.24 demonstrates the use of the SQL extensions. Note that this snowflake schema has a central DWSALESFACT fact table and three dimension tables: DWCUSTOMER, DWPRODUCT and DWTIME. The central fact table represents daily sales by product and customer. However, as you examine the star schema shown in Figure 15.24 more carefully, you

FIGURE 15.24 SaleCo snowflake schema

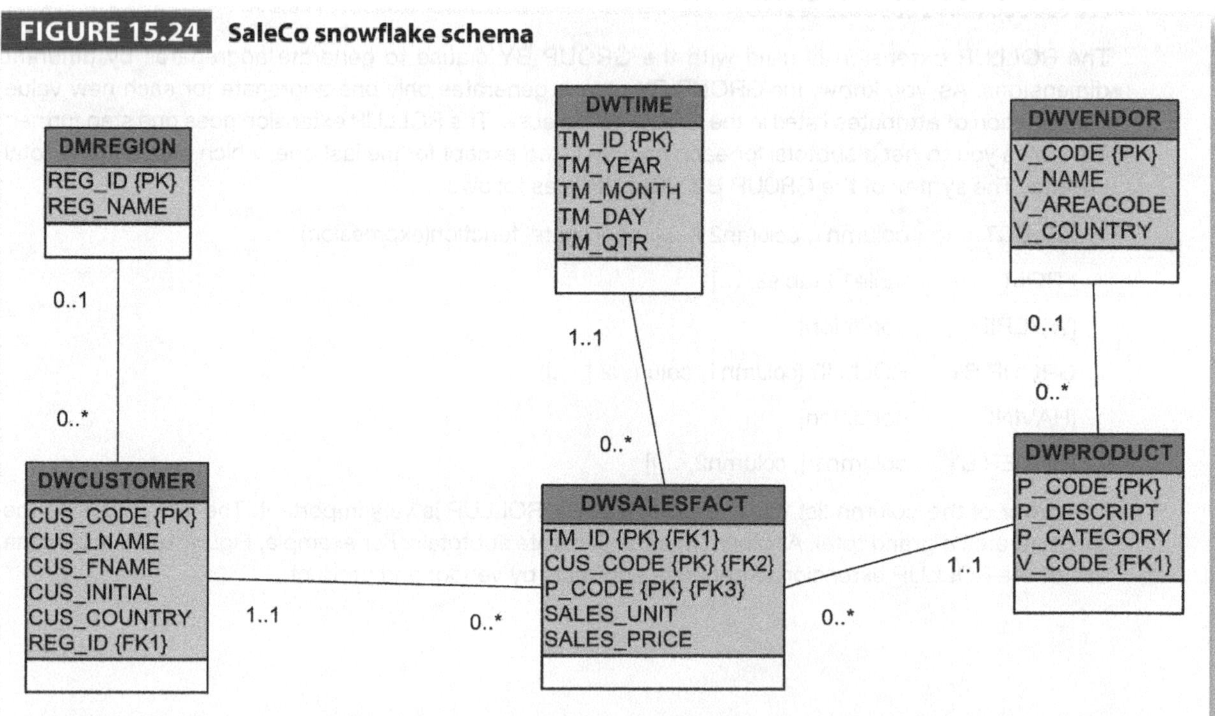

15

see that the DWCUSTOMER and DWPRODUCT dimension tables have their own dimension tables: DWREGION and DWVENDOR.

Keep in mind that a database is at the core of all data warehouses. Therefore, all SQL commands (such as CREATE, INSERT, UPDATE, DELETE and SELECT) will work in the data warehouse as expected. However, most queries you run in a data warehouse tend to include data groupings and aggregations over multiple columns. That's why this section introduces two extensions to the GROUP BY clause that are particularly useful: ROLLUP and CUBE. In addition, you will learn about using materialised views to store pre-aggregated rows in the database.

Online Content The script files used to populate the database and run the SQL commands are available on the online platform for this book.

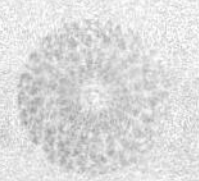

NOTE

This section uses the Oracle RDBMS to demonstrate the use of SQL extensions to support OLAP functionality. If you use a different DBMS, consult the documentation to verify whether the vendor supports similar functionality and what the proper syntax is for your DBMS.

15.8.1 The ROLLUP Extension

The ROLLUP extension is used with the GROUP BY clause to generate aggregates by different dimensions. As you know, the GROUP BY clause generates only one aggregate for each new value combination of attributes listed in the GROUP BY clause. The ROLLUP extension goes one step further; it enables you to get a subtotal for each column listed except for the last one, which gets a grand total instead. The syntax of the GROUP BY ROLLUP is as follows:

```
SELECT      column1, column2 [, ...], aggregate_function(expression)
FROM        table1 [,table2, ...]
[WHERE      condition]
GROUP BY    ROLLUP (column1, column2 [, ...])
[HAVING     condition]
[ORDER BY   column1 [, column2, ...]]
```

The order of the column list within the GROUP BY ROLLUP is very important. The last column in the list generates a grand total. All other columns generate subtotals. For example, Figure 15.25 shows the use of the ROLLUP extension to generate subtotals by vendor and product.

15

FIGURE 15.25 **ROLLUP extension**

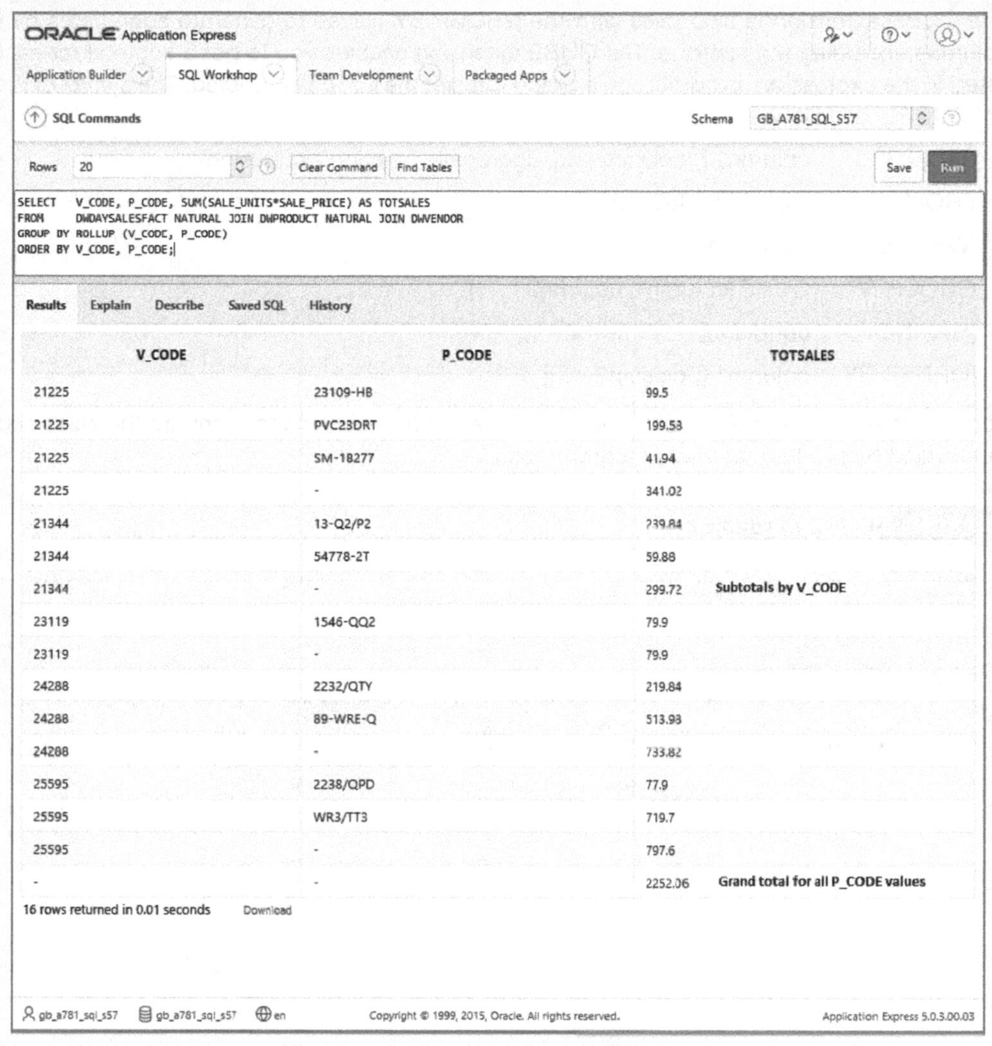

Note that Figure 15.25 shows the subtotals by vendor code and a grand total for all product codes. Contrast that with the normal GROUP BY clause that generates only the subtotals for each vendor and product combination rather than the subtotals *by vendor* and the grand total for *all products*. The ROLLUP extension is particularly useful when you want to obtain multiple nested subtotals for a dimension hierarchy. For example, within a location hierarchy, you can use ROLLUP to generate subtotals by region, province, city and store.

15.8.2 The CUBE Extension

The CUBE extension is also used with the GROUP BY clause to generate aggregates by the listed columns, including the last one. The CUBE extension enables you to get a subtotal for each column listed in the expression, in addition to a grand total for the last column listed. The syntax of the GROUP BY CUBE is as follows:

```
SELECT        column1 [, column2, ...], aggregate_function(expression)
FROM          table1 [,table2, ...]
[WHERE        condition]
GROUP BY      CUBE (column1, column2 [,....])
[HAVING       condition]
[ORDER BY     column1 [, column2, ...]]
```

For example, Figure 15.26 shows the use of the CUBE extension to compute the sales subtotals by month and by product, as well as a grand total.

FIGURE 15.26 CUBE extension

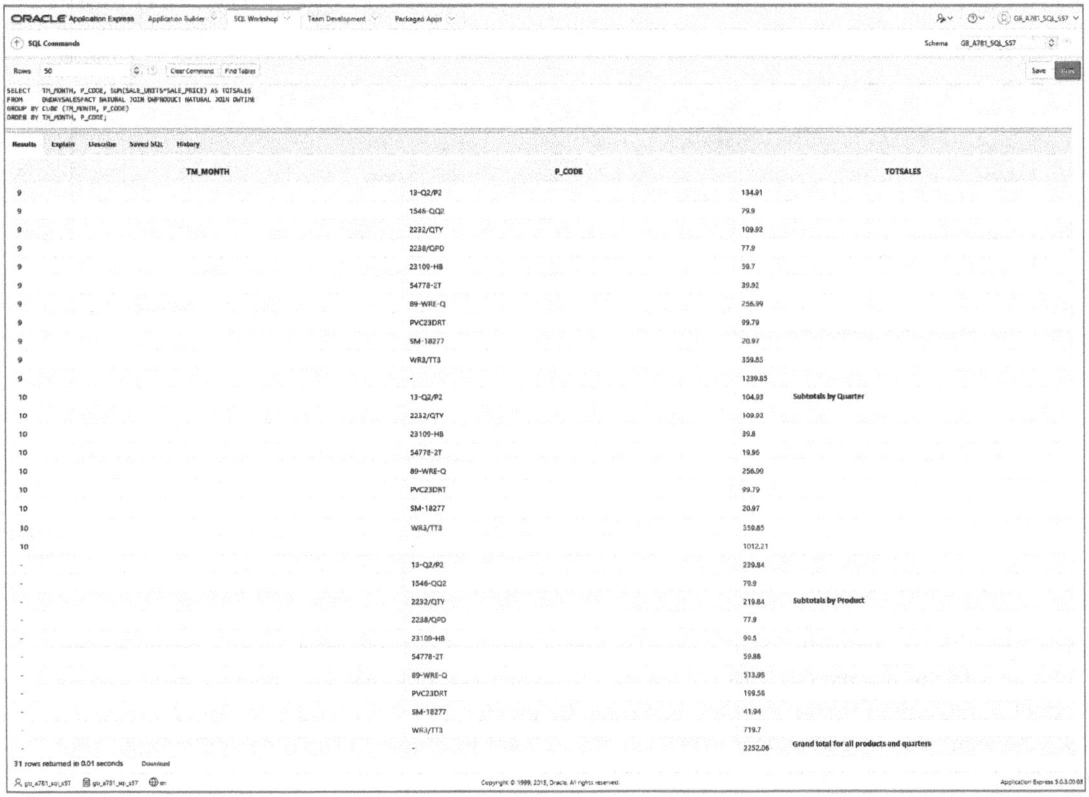

ORACLE Application Express   Application Builder   SQL Workshop   Team Development   Packaged Apps

SQL Commands

Rows 50   Clear Command   Find Tables

```
SELECT   TM_MONTH, P_CODE, SUM(SALE_UNITS*SALE_PRICE) AS TOTSALES
FROM     DWDAYSALESFACT NATURAL JOIN DWPRODUCT NATURAL JOIN DWTIME
GROUP BY CUBE (TM_MONTH, P_CODE)
ORDER BY TM_MONTH, P_CODE;
```

Results   Explain   Describe   Saved SQL   History

TM_MONTH	P_CODE	TOTSALES	
9	13-Q2/P2	134.91	
9	1546-QQ2	79.9	
9	2232/QTY	109.92	
9	2238/QPD	77.9	
9	23109-HB	59.7	
9	54778-2T	39.92	
9	89-WRE-Q	256.99	
9	PVC23DRT	99.79	
9	SM-18277	20.97	
9	WR3/TT3	359.85	
9	-	1239.85	
10	13-Q2/P2	104.93	**Subtotals by Quarter**
10	2232/QTY	109.92	
10	23109-HB	39.8	
10	54778-2T	19.96	
10	89-WRE-Q	256.99	
10	PVC23DRT	99.79	
10	SM-18277	20.97	
10	WR3/TT3	359.85	
10	-	1012.21	
-	13-Q2/P2	239.84	
-	1546-QQ2	79.9	
-	2232/QTY	219.84	**Subtotals by Product**
-	2238/QPD	77.9	
-	23109-HB	99.5	
-	54778-2T	59.88	
-	89-WRE-Q	513.98	
-	PVC23DRT	199.58	
-	SM-18277	41.94	
-	WR3/TT3	719.7	
-	-	2252.06	**Grand total for all products and quarters**

31 rows returned in 0.01 seconds   Download

In Figure 15.26, note that the CUBE extension generates the subtotals for each combination of month and product, in addition to subtotals by month and by product, as well as a grand total. The CUBE extension is particularly useful when you want to compute all possible subtotals within groupings based on multiple dimensions. Cross-tabulations are especially good candidates for application of the CUBE extension.

15.8.3 Materialised Views

The data warehouse normally contains fact tables that store specific measurements of interest to an organisation. Such measurements are organised by different dimensions. The vast majority of OLAP business analysis of 'everyday activities' is based on comparisons of data that are aggregated at different levels, such as totals by vendor, by product and by store.

Since businesses normally use a predefined set of summaries for benchmarking, it is reasonable to predefine such summaries for future use by creating summary fact tables. However, creating multiple summary fact tables that use GROUP BY queries with multiple table joins could become a resource-intensive operation. In addition, data warehouses must also be able to maintain up-to-date summarised data at all times. So, what happens with the summary fact tables after new sales data have been added to the base fact tables? Under normal circumstances, the summary fact tables are re-created. This operation requires that the SQL code be run again to re-create all summary rows, even when only a few rows needed updating. Clearly, this is a time-consuming process.

To save query processing time, most database vendors have implemented additional 'functionality' to manage aggregate summaries more efficiently. This new functionality resembles the standard SQL views for which the SQL code is predefined in the database. However, the added functionality difference is that the views also store the preaggregated rows, something like a summary table. For example, Microsoft SQL Server provides indexed views, while Oracle provides materialised views. This section explains the use of materialised views.

A **materialised view** is a dynamic table that contains not only the SQL query command to generate the rows, but also stores the actual rows. The materialised view is created the first time the query is run and the summary rows are stored in the table. The materialised view rows are automatically updated when the base tables are updated. That way, the data warehouse administrator creates the view but will not have to update the view. The use of materialised views is totally transparent to the end user. The OLAP end user can create OLAP queries, using the standard fact tables, and the DBMS query optimisation feature will automatically use the materialised views if those views provide better performance.

The basic syntax for the materialised view is:

```
CREATE MATERIALISED VIEW view_name
BUILD {IMMEDIATE | DEFERRED}
REFRESH {[FAST | COMPLETE | FORCE]} ON COMMIT
[ENABLE QUERY REWRITE]
AS select_query;
```

The BUILD clause indicates when the materialised view rows are actually populated. IMMEDIATE indicates that the materialised view rows are populated right after the command is entered. DEFERRED indicates that the materialised view rows are populated at a later time. Until then, the materialised view is in an 'unusable' state. The DBMS provides a special routine that an administrator runs to populate materialised views.

The REFRESH clause lets you indicate when and how to update the materialised view when new rows are added to the base tables. FAST indicates that whenever a change is made in the base tables, the materialised view updates only the affected rows. COMPLETE indicates that a complete update is made for all rows in the materialised view when the select query on which the view is based is rerun. FORCE indicates that the DBMS will first try to do a FAST update; otherwise, it will do a COMPLETE update. The ON COMMIT clause indicates that the updates to the materialised view will take place as part of the commit process of the underlying DML statement, that is, as part of the commit of the DML transaction that updated the base tables. The ENABLE QUERY REWRITE option allows the DBMS to use the materialised views in query optimisation.

To create materialised views, you need specified privileges and you must complete specified prerequisite steps. As always, defer to the DBMS documentation for the latest updates. In the case of Oracle versions 11g and 12c, you must create materialised view logs on the base tables of the materialised view. In order to do this you must have the appropriate privileges set by the Oracle DBA. Figure 15.27 shows the code to create the MONTH_SALES_MV materialised view in the Oracle 11g RDBMS. Note that, if you do not have Database Administer privileges (i.e. you would log into Oracle as a 'sysdba') then you will not be able to create a materialised view.

As you can see in Figure 15.27, this materialised view computes the monthly total units sold and the total sales aggregates by product. The SALES_MONTH_MV materialised view is configured to update

FIGURE 15.27 Creating a materialised view in Oracle 11g using Oracle SQL* Plus as a DBA

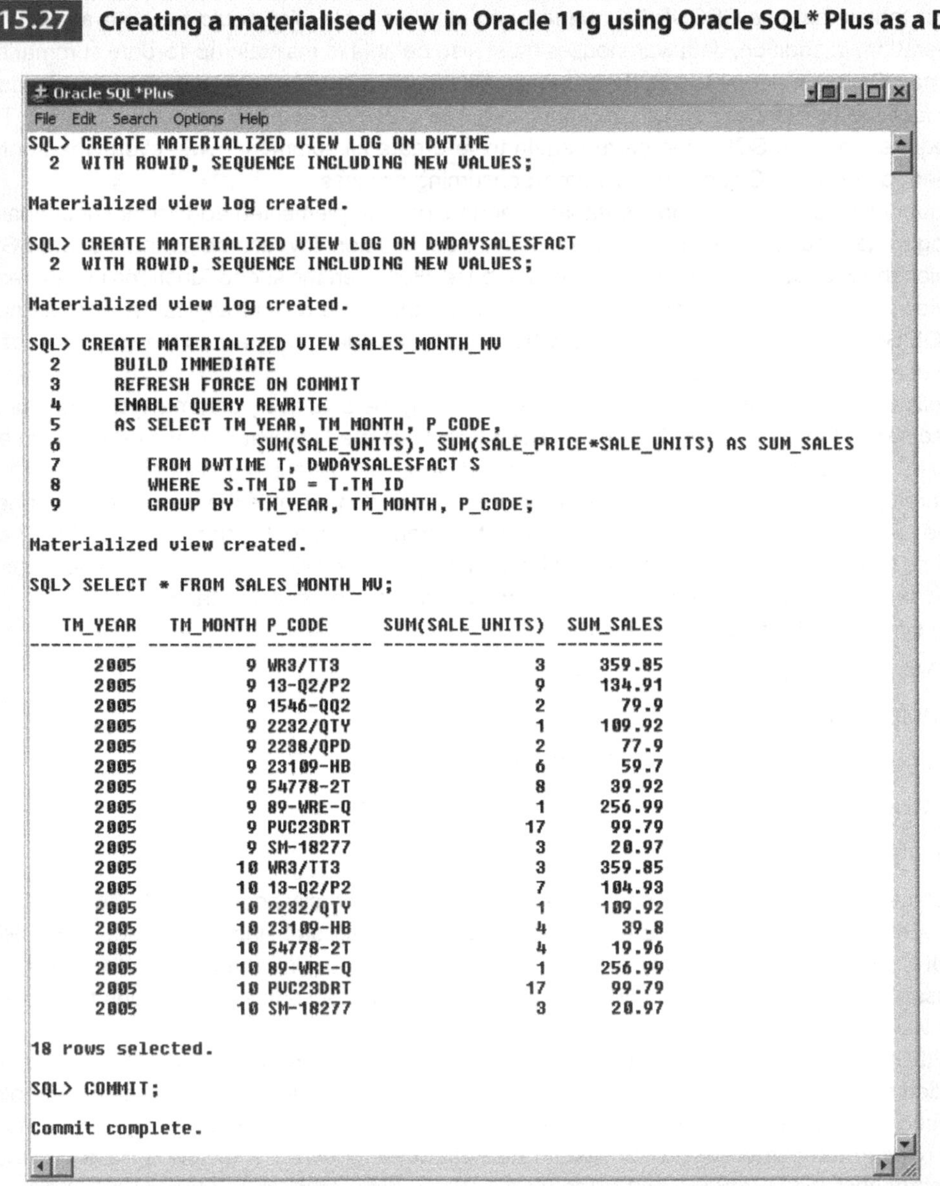

```
SQL> CREATE MATERIALIZED VIEW LOG ON DWTIME
     WITH ROWID, SEQUENCE INCLUDING NEW VALUES;

Materialized view log created.

SQL> CREATE MATERIALIZED VIEW LOG ON DWDAYSALESFACT
     WITH ROWID, SEQUENCE INCLUDING NEW VALUES;

Materialized view log created.

SQL> CREATE MATERIALIZED VIEW SALES_MONTH_MV
        BUILD IMMEDIATE
        REFRESH FORCE ON COMMIT
        ENABLE QUERY REWRITE
        AS SELECT TM_YEAR, TM_MONTH, P_CODE,
                  SUM(SALE_UNITS), SUM(SALE_PRICE*SALE_UNITS) AS SUM_SALES
           FROM DWTIME T, DWDAYSALESFACT S
           WHERE  S.TM_ID = T.TM_ID
           GROUP BY  TM_YEAR, TM_MONTH, P_CODE;

Materialized view created.

SQL> SELECT * FROM SALES_MONTH_MV;

   TM_YEAR   TM_MONTH P_CODE     SUM(SALE_UNITS)  SUM_SALES
---------- ---------- ---------- --------------- ----------
      2005          9 WR3/TT3                  3     359.85
      2005          9 13-Q2/P2                 9     134.91
      2005          9 1546-QQ2                 2       79.9
      2005          9 2232/QTY                 1     109.92
      2005          9 2238/QPD                 2       77.9
      2005          9 23109-HB                 6       59.7
      2005          9 54778-2T                 8      39.92
      2005          9 89-WRE-Q                 1     256.99
      2005          9 PVC23DRT                17      99.79
      2005          9 SM-18277                 3      20.97
      2005         10 WR3/TT3                  3     359.85
      2005         10 13-Q2/P2                 7     104.93
      2005         10 2232/QTY                 1     109.92
      2005         10 23109-HB                 4       39.8
      2005         10 54778-2T                 4      19.96
      2005         10 89-WRE-Q                 1     256.99
      2005         10 PVC23DRT                17      99.79
      2005         10 SM-18277                 3      20.97

18 rows selected.

SQL> COMMIT;

Commit complete.
```


automatically after each change in the base tables. Note that the last row of SALES_MONTH_MV indicates that, during October 2015, the sales of product 'SM-18277' are three units, for a total of €20.97.

Although all of the examples in this section focus on SQL extensions to support OLAP reporting in an Oracle DBMS, you have seen just a small fraction of the many business intelligence features currently provided by most DBMS vendors. For example, most vendors provide rich graphical user interfaces to manipulate, analyse and present the data in multiple formats. Figure 15.28 shows two sample screens, one for Oracle and one for Microsoft OLAP products.

FIGURE 15.28 Sample OLAP applications

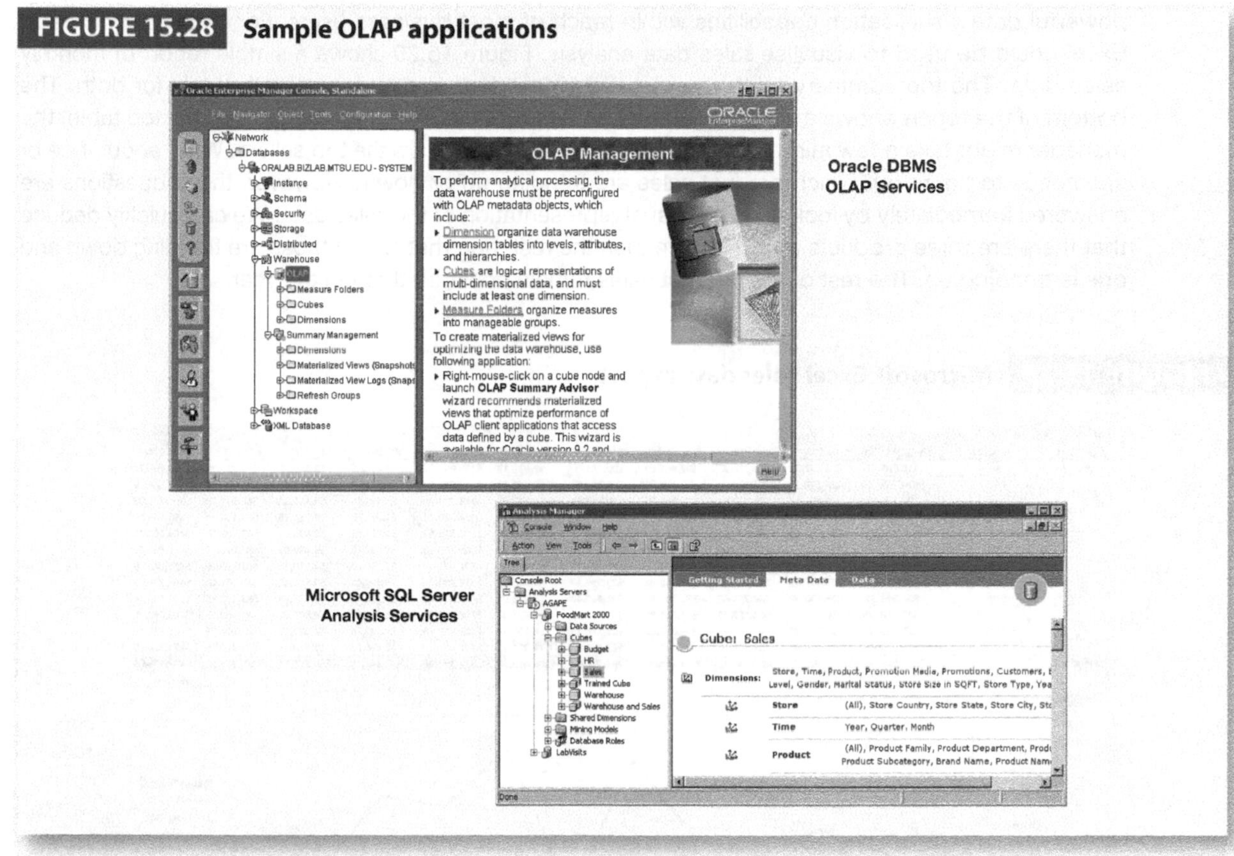

15.9 DATA VISUALISATION

Data visualisation is the process of abstracting data to provide a visual data representation that enhances the user's ability to comprehend the meaning of the data. The goal of data visualisation is to allow the user quickly and efficiently to see the data's big picture by identifying trends, patterns and relationships. We have all heard the saying 'a picture is worth a thousand words', and this has never been more accurate than in data visualisation. Tables with hundreds, thousands, or millions of rows of data cannot be processed by the human mind in a meaningful way. Providing summarised tabular data to managers does not give them enough insight into the meaning of the data to make informed decisions. Data visualisation encodes the data into visually rich formats (mostly graphical) that provide at-a-glance insight into overall trends, patterns and possible relationships. Data visualisation techniques range from simple to very complex, and many are familiar. Such techniques include pie charts, line graphs, bar charts, bubble charts, bubble maps, donut charts, scatter plots, Gantt charts, heat maps, histograms, time series plots, steps charts, waterfall charts, and many more. The tools used in data visualisation range from a simple spreadsheet (such as Microsoft Excel) to advanced data visualisation software such as Tableau, Microsoft Power BI, Domo and Google Analytics.[7]

7 'The Best Data Visualization Tools of 2019,' Oliver Rist, Pam Baker *PC Magazine*, July 24, 2018. Available: huk.pcmag.com/cloud-services/83744/the-best-data-visualization-tools.

Common productivity tools such as Microsoft Excel can often provide surprisingly powerful data visualisations. Excel has long included basic charting and PivotTable and PivotChart capabilities for visualising spreadsheet data. More recently, the introduction of the PowerPivot add-in has eliminated row and column data limitations and allows for the integration of data from multiple sources. This puts powerful data visualisation capabilities within reach of most business users. For example, Microsoft Excel could be used to visualise sales data analysis. Figure 15.29 shows a simple report of monthly sales data. The top summary table shows sales by product and by month with totals for both. The bottom of the report shows a line plot of the sales by product and month. Looking at the top table, the manager might take a few minutes to figure out which products are the top sellers. What about if he or she needs to figure out which product sales are trending up or down? However, those questions are answered immediately by looking at the visual representation of the sales data. We can quickly deduce that there are three products that sell more than the rest, and that two of those are trending down and one is trending up. The rest of the product sales remain constant through the year.

FIGURE 15.29 **Microsoft Excel sales data report**

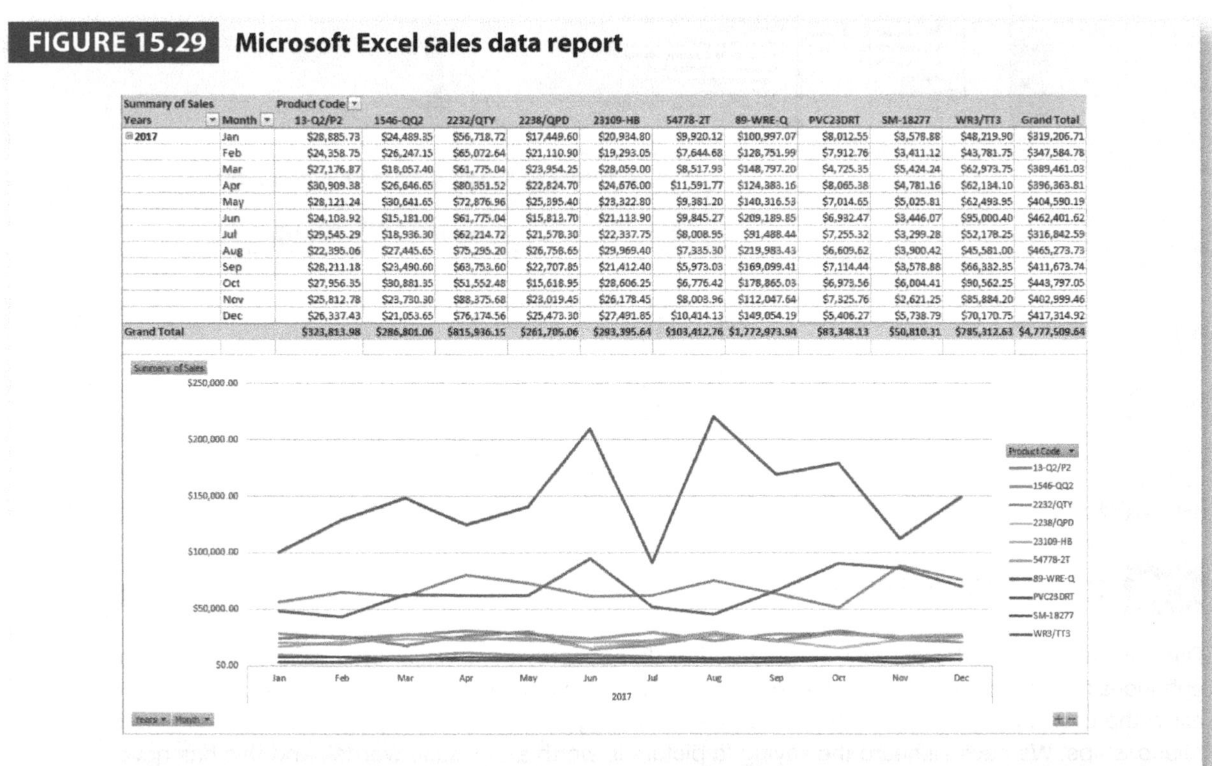

Summary of Sales		Product Code										
Years	Month	13-Q2/P2	1546-QQ2	2232/QTY	2238/QPD	23109-HB	54778-2T	89-WRE-Q	PVC23DRT	SM-18277	WR3/TT3	Grand Total
2017	Jan	$28,885.73	$24,489.35	$56,718.72	$17,449.60	$20,934.80	$9,920.12	$100,997.07	$8,012.55	$3,578.88	$48,219.90	$319,206.71
	Feb	$24,358.75	$26,247.15	$65,072.64	$21,110.90	$19,293.05	$7,644.68	$128,751.99	$7,912.76	$3,411.12	$43,781.75	$347,584.78
	Mar	$27,176.87	$18,057.40	$61,775.04	$23,954.25	$28,059.00	$8,517.93	$148,797.20	$4,725.35	$5,424.24	$62,973.75	$389,461.03
	Apr	$30,909.38	$26,646.65	$80,351.52	$22,824.70	$24,676.00	$11,591.77	$124,383.16	$8,065.38	$4,781.16	$62,134.10	$396,363.81
	May	$28,121.24	$30,641.65	$72,876.96	$25,395.40	$23,322.80	$9,381.20	$140,316.53	$7,014.65	$5,025.81	$62,493.95	$404,590.19
	Jun	$24,103.92	$15,181.00	$61,775.04	$15,813.70	$21,113.90	$9,845.27	$209,189.85	$6,932.47	$3,446.07	$95,000.40	$462,401.62
	Jul	$29,545.29	$18,936.30	$62,214.72	$21,578.30	$22,337.75	$8,008.95	$91,488.44	$7,255.32	$3,299.28	$52,178.25	$316,842.59
	Aug	$22,395.06	$27,445.65	$75,295.20	$26,758.65	$29,969.40	$7,335.30	$219,983.43	$6,609.62	$3,900.42	$45,581.00	$465,273.73
	Sep	$28,211.18	$23,490.60	$63,753.60	$22,707.85	$21,412.40	$5,973.03	$169,099.41	$7,114.44	$3,578.88	$66,332.35	$411,673.74
	Oct	$27,956.35	$30,881.35	$51,552.48	$15,618.95	$28,606.25	$6,776.42	$178,865.03	$6,973.56	$6,004.41	$90,562.25	$443,797.05
	Nov	$25,812.78	$23,730.30	$88,375.68	$23,019.45	$26,178.45	$8,003.96	$112,047.64	$7,325.76	$2,621.25	$85,884.20	$402,999.46
	Dec	$26,337.43	$21,053.65	$76,174.56	$25,473.30	$27,491.85	$10,414.13	$149,054.19	$5,406.27	$5,738.79	$70,170.75	$417,314.92
Grand Total		$323,813.98	$286,801.06	$815,936.15	$261,705.06	$293,395.64	$103,412.76	$1,772,973.94	$83,348.13	$50,810.31	$785,312.63	$4,777,509.64

The above, albeit simple, example shows the power of data visualisation; it shows how end users can quickly gain insight into their data using a simple graphical representation.

15.9.1 The Need for Data Visualisation

From the previous discussion you might think that data visualisation is nothing new, and you are correct to a certain degree. After all, spreadsheets and graphics libraries have been around for a while. What has changed is the development of Big Data and business intelligence. The reality is that, in the current business climate, companies are trying to find a competitive edge by mining large amounts of data. Tools that facilitate and enhance the understanding of large amounts of data have become the latest 'holy grail' in business analytics. The real problem with Big Data is that humans are not able to comprehend such large amounts of data quickly enough; in a sense, we are 'drowning' in data. Computers play an important role in helping humans make sense of large amounts of data.

NOTE

It is a mistake to think that data visualisation is useful only when dealing with Big Data. Any organisation (regardless of size) that collects and uses data in its daily activities can benefit from the use of data analytics and visualisation techniques.

The more data you have, the more you might discover. To illustrate this, let's expand the previous sales data example and add data for the province and zip code (postal code). Now imagine that we have a tabular report that includes such data. It may take a manager a few minutes to read and interpret the report. Now, let's take a look at the same data as shown in Figure 15.30. This data visualisation uses a simple heat map, created using Tableau (www. tableau.com), a data visualisation tool, to analyse sales for a company.

FIGURE 15.30 Visualising sales totals by zip code (postal code)

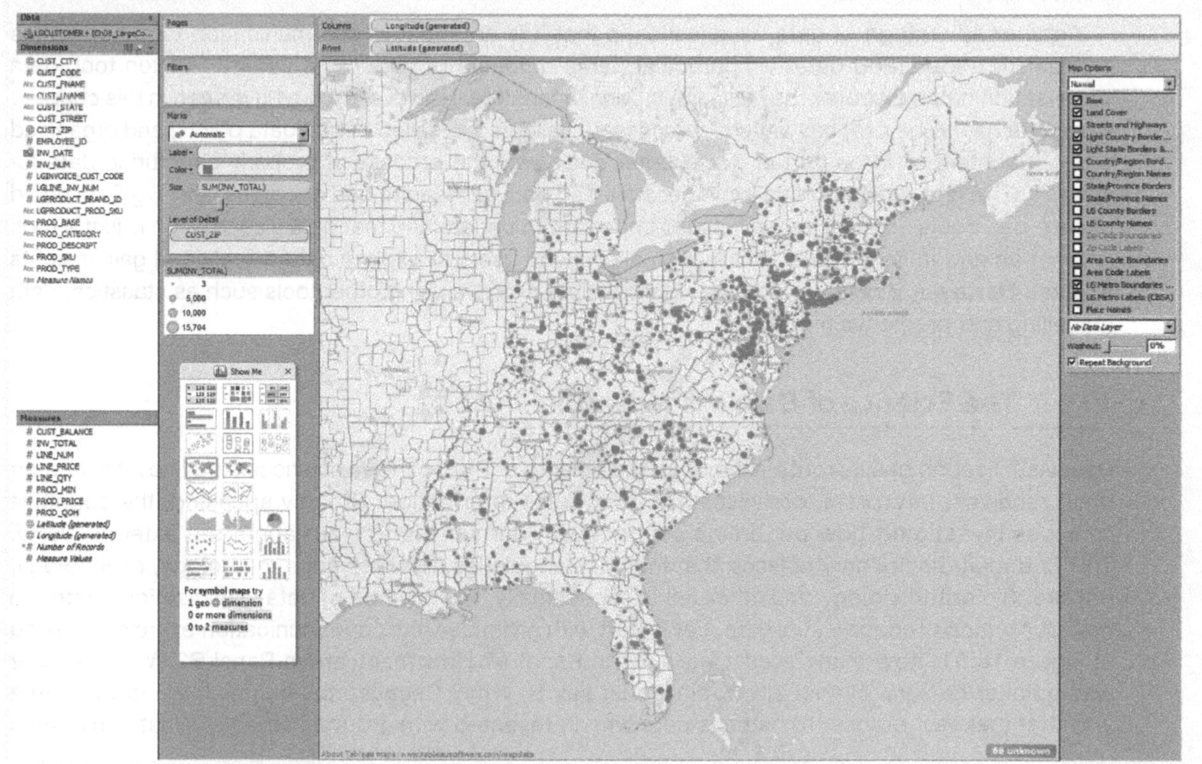

Courtesy of Tableau

This new data visualisation conveys at least two additional insights into the sales data:

- Comparative sales volumes as shown by the size of the bubbles. Larger total sales values produce larger bubbles.
- Geographic market penetration as shown by the density of the bubbles against the map. The visualisation makes it easier for a manager to identify the region (northeastern) that has the greatest sales penetration. Furthermore, the sales manager could click on any of the sales bubbles to get more detail data. Also, by clicking on the map, the end user can zoom in on a given region to get more detailed information. The ability to zoom in and out, drill down and up, filter, etc. is one of the many advantages of the current breed of data visualisation tools.

NOTE

Data visualisation plays an important role in discovering and understanding the meaning of data. New ways to present data are constantly being developed. Good data visualisations can be used in any discipline. For example, see the video from Dr Hans Rosling, (www.youtube.com/watch?v=jbkSRLYSojo) in which he uses public health data to visualise the history of world population health over the past 200 years.

Another advantage of data visualisation is that it is an effective communication tool that makes it easier to understand data – in particular, large amounts of data. As a communication tool, data visualisation helps discover the message hidden in the data. However, as we have seen in this chapter, such data has to be properly vetted – processed, validated (distilled of bad data points) and organised within a context. A large part of this chapter deals with the process of properly structuring data for analysis. This is a very important issue because bad data can lead to bad decisions, and Big Data could make a bad decision even larger! It's also important to understand that data visualisation is just a tool, and not an end in itself. Data visualisation allows end users to explore data quickly and gain insights about it. However, it does not replace rigorous data analysis using other tools such as statistics, data modelling and predictive modelling.

15.9.2 The Science of Data Visualisation

Data visualisation has its roots in the cognitive sciences. The cognitive sciences study how the human brain receives, interprets, organises and processes information. Broadly speaking, the cognitive sciences investigate how our brains connect with our senses to learn about the external world. This is a multidisciplinary science that includes linguistics, neuroscience, neurology, psychology, philosophy, anthropology and other fields. Specifically, the science of data visualisation relates to how our brains process visual data. Let's start with a simple visual communication exercise: looking at Figure 15.31, how many soccer balls are in Panel A? How many are in Panel B? Which answer was quicker/easier? Almost all people would say B. Why? Because the human brain is wired in a way that makes it quicker to process data when presented with grouped objects. What constitutes good data visualisation? That is a difficult question to answer because data visualisation can be seen as both an art and a science. In other words, data visualisation is concerned with both form and function. Form means using the proper visual construct, and function means applying the correct data transformations. Remember that the purpose of data visualisation is to communicate the meaning of data easily.

FIGURE 15.31 **The power of visual communication**

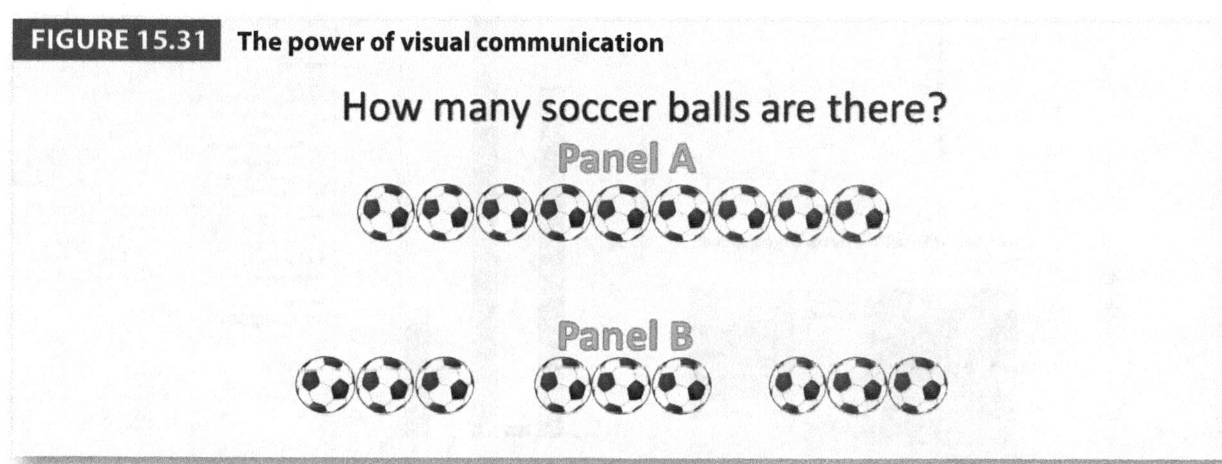

Over the past few decades, plenty of research has been done on data visualisation. Data visualisation has evolved to become a very robust discipline. As a discipline, data visualisation can be studied as a group of visual communication techniques used to explore and discover data insights by applying:

- *Pattern recognition*: Visually identifying trends, distribution and relationships
- *Spatial awareness*: Use of size and orientation to compare and relate data
- *Aesthetics*: Use of shapes and colours to highlight and contrast data composition and relationships.

In general, data visualisation uses five characteristics: shape, colour, size, position and grouping/order to convey and highlight the meaning of the data. When used correctly, data visualisation can tell the story behind the data. Here is another example that uses data visualisation to explore data and quickly provide some useful data insights. In this case, we are going to use vehicle crash data for the state of Iowa, available at https://catalog.data.gov/. The data set contains data on car accidents in the US State of Iowa from 2010 to early 2015. Figure 15.32 contains a visualisation of this data set using Tableau.

FIGURE 15.32 Vehicle crash analysis

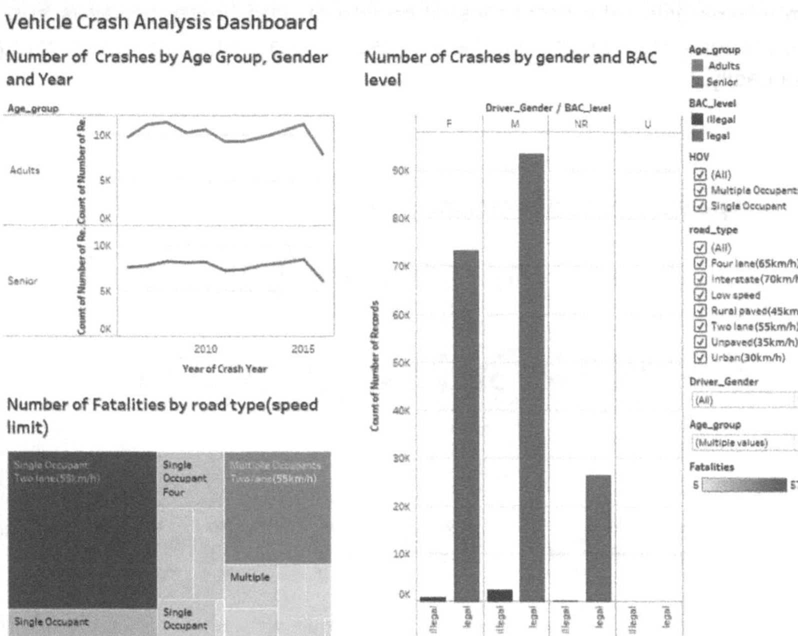

NOTE

There are several public sources of large data sets that you could use to practise visualisations. Some of the most common sources are:

- http://catalog.data.gov
- http://aws.amazon.com/datasets
- https://data.medicare.gov
- www.cdc.gov/nchs/data_access/
- http://data.worldbank.org
- http://data.worldbank.org
- www.faa.gov/data_research/
- https://data.world/

For some good examples of data visualisations, see the Centers for Disease Control and Prevention, Data Visualisation Gallery, at www.cdc.gov/nchs/data-visualization/

This visualisation includes three graphs (line, bar, and heat map) and filters. Looking at this visualisation, we can quickly determine that a significant number of car accidents involved single-occupant vehicles driving on two-lane roads where the speed limit is 90 km/h. We can also see that the majority of accidents did not involve alcohol. Finally, we could also determine that there seems to be a slight increase in vehicle crashes in the past four years. It is also important to note that, in order to do the visualisation, the data was previously processed and transformed – extracted, formatted, formulas applied, etc. For example, in this data set we used several formulas to classify drivers as child, teenager, adult or senior; determine if the BAC level was legal or illegal; determine single or multiple occupants, etc. As you can see in these examples, data visualisation implies a good understanding of the data set and its domain. You can't start analysing what you don't understand. Therefore, after you get the raw data, you usually must dedicate some time to understanding the problem domain. The next section introduces some basic notions on this topic.

15.9.3 Understanding the Data

Before you start with data visualisation, you need to understand the data. The same data can be presented in multiple ways. Some of those ways may not be the proper use of the data or the tool. In general, there are two types of data:

- *Qualitative*: Describes qualities of the data. This type of data can be subdivided into two subtypes:
  - Nominal: This is data that can be counted but not ordered or aggregated. Examples: Gender (male or female); student class (graduate or undergraduate).
  - Ordinal: This is data that can be counted and ordered but not aggregated. Examples: Rate your teacher (excellent, good, fair, poor), what is your family income (under R200 000, 200 001 to 400 000, 400 001 to 600 000, 600 001 or more).
- *Quantitative*: Describes numeric facts or measures of the data. This type of data can be counted, ordered and aggregated. Statisticians refer to this data as 'interval and ratio' data. Examples of quantitative data include age, GPA, number of accidents, etc.

You can think of qualitative data as being the dimensions on a star schema and the quantitative data as being the facts of a star schema. This is important because it means that you need to use the correct type of functions and operations with each data type, including the proper way to represent it visually. As you have learnt before, data visualisation uses shape, colour, size, position and group/order characteristics to represent and highlight data in certain ways. The way you visualise the data tells a story and has an impact on the end users. Some data visualisations can provide unknown insights and others can be a way to draw attention to an issue. As you can see in Figure 15.33, Panel A, the main characteristic of this visualisation is that the bar graph's x-axis is at the top instead of at the bottom of the graph. This was done purposely, along with using a red colour, to resonate visually with the title of the presentation.

However, you could use the same data to plot the bar graph with the x-axis at the bottom (Panel B), change the colour of the bars to blue, and it would have a different impact on the story you are trying to convey. Notice that the same data can tell two different stories depending on the visualisation.

FIGURE 15.33 **Infographics can have an impact beyond presenting the data**

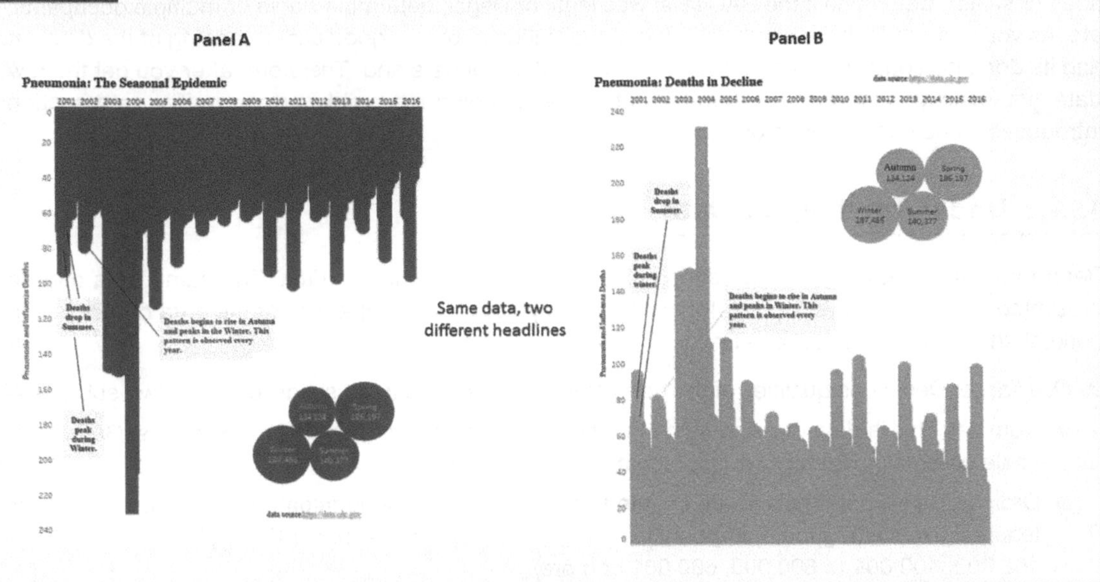

> **NOTE**
>
> If you would like to learn more about the fascinating discipline of data visualisation, *Show Me the Numbers: Designing Tables and Graphs to Enlighten* by Stephen Few and *The Visual Display of Quantitative Information* by Edward R. Tufte are good places to start.

SUMMARY

- Business intelligence (BI) is a term for a comprehensive, cohesive and integrated set of applications used to capture, collect, integrate, store and analyse data with the purpose of generating and presenting information to support business decision making.
- Decision support refers to a methodology (or a series of methodologies) designed to extract information from data and to use such information as a basis for decision making. A decision support system (DSS) is an arrangement of computerised tools used to assist managerial decision making within a business.
- Operational data are not best suited for decision support. From the end-user point of view, DSS data differ from operational data in three main areas: time span, granularity and dimensionality.
- The data warehouse is an integrated, subject-orientated, time-variant, non-volatile collection of data that provides support for decision making. The data warehouse is usually a read-only database optimised for data analysis and query processing. A data mart is a small, single-subject data warehouse subset that provides decision support to a small group of people.
- Online analytical processing (OLAP) refers to an advanced data analysis environment that supports decision making, business modelling and operations research.

- Relational online analytical processing (ROLAP) provides OLAP functionality by using relational databases and familiar relational query tools to store and analyse multidimensional data. Multidimensional online analytical processing (MOLAP) provides OLAP functionality by using multidimensional database management systems (MDBMSs) to store and analyse multidimensional data.
- The star schema is a data modelling technique used to map multidimensional decision support data into a relational database with the purpose of performing advanced data analysis. The basic star schema has four components: facts, dimensions, attributes and attribute hierarchies. Facts are numeric measurements or values representing a specific business aspect or activity. Dimensions are general qualifying categories that provide additional perspectives to a given fact. Conceptually, the multidimensional data model is best represented by a three-dimensional cube. Attributes can be ordered in well-defined attribute hierarchies. The attribute hierarchy provides a top-down organisation that is used for two main purposes: to permit aggregation and to provide drill-down/roll-up data analysis.
- Data analytics is a subset of BI functionality that provides advanced data analysis tools to extract knowledge from business data. Data analytics can be divided into explanatory and predictive analytics. Explanatory analytics focuses on discovering and explaining data characteristics and relationships. Predictive analytics focuses on creating models to predict future outcomes or events based on the existing data.
- Data mining automates the analysis of operational data with the intention of finding previously unknown data characteristics, relationships, dependencies and/or trends. The data mining process has four phases: data preparation, data analysis and classification, knowledge acquisition and prognosis.
- SQL has been enhanced with analytic functions that support OLAP type processing and data generation.
- Data visualisation provides visual representations of data that enhance the user's ability to comprehend the meaning of the data.

KEY TERMS

attribute hierarchy
business intelligence (BI)
cube cache
dashboard
data cube
data extraction
data filtering
data mart
data mining
data store
data visualisation
data warehouse
decision support system (DSS)
dimensions
dimension tables
drill-down
explanatory analytics
extraction, transformation and loading (ETL)
facts
fact table
governance
Key Performance Indicators (KPI)
master data management (MDM)
materialised view
metrics
multidimensional database management system (MDBMS)
multidimensional online analytical processing (MOLAP)
online analytical processing (OLAP)
partitioning
periodicity
portal
relational online analytical processing (ROLAP)
replication
roll-up
slice and dice
snowflake schema
sparsity
star schema
very large databases (VLDBs)

FURTHER READING

Finlay, S. *Artificial Intelligence and Machine Learning for Business: A No-Nonsense Guide to Data Driven Technologies*, 2nd edition. Relativistic, 2017.

Inmon, W. *Building the Data Warehouse*, 4th edition. Wiley Publishing, 2005.

Kimbal, R. *The Data Warehouse Toolkit*, 3rd edition. Wiley Publishing, 2013.

Witten, I. and Frank, E. *Data Mining: Practical Machine Learning Tools and Techniques* (Morgan Kaufmann Series in Data Management Systems), 2016.

Online Content Answers to selected Review Questions and Problems for this chapter are available on the online platform for this book.

REVIEW QUESTIONS

1 What is business intelligence? Give some recent examples of BI usage, using the internet for assistance. What BI benefits have companies found?

2 Describe the BI framework. Illustrate the evolution of BI.

3 What are decision support systems, and what role do they play in the business environment?

4 Explain how the main components of the BI architecture interact to form a system. Describe the evolution of BI information dissemination formats.

5 What are the most relevant differences between operational and decision support data?

6 What is a data warehouse, and what are its main characteristics?

7 Give three examples of problems likely to be encountered when operational data are integrated into the data warehouse.

Use the following scenario to answer Questions 8–14.

While working as a database analyst for a national sales organisation, you are asked to be part of its data warehouse project team.

8 Prepare a high-level summary of the main requirements for evaluating DBMS products for data warehousing.

9 Your data warehousing project group is arguing about prototyping a data warehouse before its implementation. The project group members are especially concerned about the need to acquire some data warehousing skills before implementing the enterprise-wide data warehouse. What would you recommend? Explain your recommendations.

10 Suppose you are selling the data warehouse idea to your users. How would you define multi-dimensional data analysis for them? How would you explain its advantages to them?

11 Before making a commitment, the data warehousing project group has invited you to provide an OLAP overview. The group's members are particularly concerned about the OLAP client/server architecture requirements and how OLAP will fit the existing environment. Your job is to explain to them the main OLAP client/server components and architectures.

12 One of your vendors recommends using an MDBMS. How would you explain this recommendation to your project leader?

13 The project group is ready to make a final decision, choosing between ROLAP and MOLAP. What should be the basis for this decision? Why?

14 The data warehouse project is in the design phase. Explain to your fellow designers how you would use a star schema in the design.

15 Trace the evolution of DSS from its origins to today's advanced analytical tools. Which major technologies influenced this evolution?

16 What is OLAP, and what are its main characteristics?

17 Explain ROLAP and give the reasons you would recommend its use in the relational database environment.

18 Explain the use of facts, dimensions and attributes in the star schema.

19 Explain multidimensional cubes and describe how the slice-and-dice technique fits into this model.

20 In the star schema context, what are attribute hierarchies and aggregation levels and what is their purpose?

21 Discuss the most common performance improvement techniques used in star schemas.

22 Explain some of the most important issues in data warehouse implementation.

23 What is data mining, and how does it differ from traditional DSS tools?

24 How does data mining work? Discuss the different phases in the data mining process.

25 Describe the characteristics of predictive analytics. What is the impact of Big Data in predictive analytics?

26 Describe data visualisation. What is the goal of data visualisation?

27 Is data visualisation only useful when used with Big Data? Explain and expand.

28 As a discipline, data visualisation can be studied as ______________ used to explore and discover data insights by applying: ______________, ______________ and ______________.

29 Describe the different types of data and how they map to star schemas and data analysis. Give some examples of the different data types.

30 Which five graphical data characteristics does data visualisation use to highlight and contrast data findings and convey a story?

PROBLEMS

Online Content The databases used for this problem set are found on the online platform for this book. These databases are stored in Microsoft Access 2002 format. The databases, named 'Ch15_P1.mdb', 'Ch15_P3.mdb', and 'Ch15_P4.mdb', contain the data for Problems 1, 3 and 4, respectively. The data for Problem 2 are stored in Microsoft Excel format on the online platform for this book.

15

1 The university computer lab's director keeps track of lab usage, measured by the number of students using the lab. This particular function is important for budgeting purposes. The computer lab director assigns you the task of developing a data warehouse in which to keep track of the lab usage statistics. The main requirements for this database are to:

- Show the total number of users by different time periods.
- Show usage numbers by time period, by major and by student classification.
- Compare usage for different majors and different semesters.

Use the Ch15_P1.mdb database, which includes the following tables:

- USELOG contains the student lab access data.
- STUDENT is a dimension table containing student data.
- Given the three bulleted requirements and using the Ch15_P1.MDB data, complete Problems 1a–1g.

a Define the main facts to be analysed. (*Hint:* These facts become the source for the design of the fact table.)

b Define and describe the appropriate dimensions. (*Hint:* These dimensions become the source for the design of the dimension tables.)

c Draw the lab usage star schema, using the fact and dimension structures you defined in Problems 1a and 1b.

d Define the attributes for each of the dimensions in Problem 1b.

e Recommend the appropriate attribute hierarchies.

f Implement your data warehouse design, using the star schema you created in Problem 1c and the attributes you defined in Problem 1d.

g Create the reports that will meet the requirements listed in this problem's introduction.

2 Victoria Ephanor manages a small product distribution company. Because the business is growing fast, she recognises that it is time to manage the vast information pool to help guide the accelerating growth. Ms Ephanor, who is familiar with spreadsheet software, currently employs a small sales force of four people. She asks you to develop a data warehouse application prototype that will enable her to study sales figures by year, region, salesperson and product. (This prototype is to be used as the basis for a future data warehouse database.)

Using the data supplied in the Ch15-P2.xls file, complete the following seven problems:

a Identify the appropriate fact table components.

b Identify the appropriate dimension tables.

c Draw a star schema diagram for this data warehouse.

d Identify the attributes for the dimension tables that will be required to solve this problem.

e Using a Microsoft Excel spreadsheet (or any other spreadsheet capable of producing pivot tables), generate a pivot table to show the sales by product and by region. The end user must be able to specify the display of sales for any given year. (The sample output is shown in the first pivot table in Figure P15.1.)

f Using Problem 2e as your base, add a second pivot table (see Figure P15.1) to show the sales by salesperson and by region. The end user must be able to specify sales for a given year or for all years and for a given product or for all products.

g Create a 3-D bar graph to show sales by salesperson, by product, and by region. (See the sample output in Figure P15.2.)

FIGURE P15.1 **Using a pivot table**

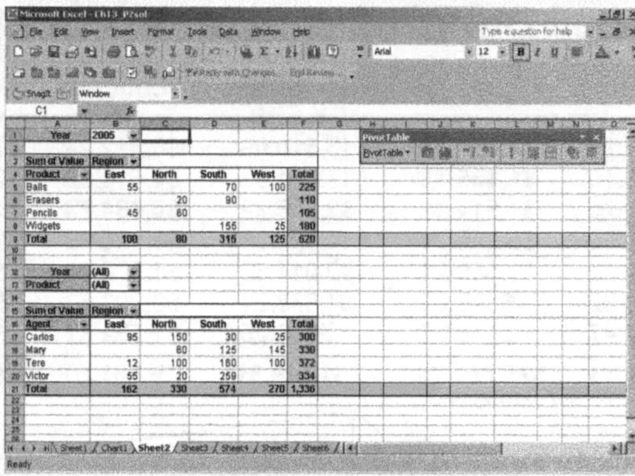

Year	2005				
Sum of Value	Region				
Product	East	North	South	West	Total
Balls	55		70	100	225
Erasers		20	90		110
Pencils	45	60			105
Widgets			155	25	180
Total	100	80	315	125	620

Year	(All)				
Product	(All)				
Sum of Value	Region				
Agent	East	North	South	West	Total
Carlos	95	150	30	25	300
Mary		60	125	145	330
Tere	12	100	160	100	372
Victor	55	20	259		334
Total	162	330	574	270	1,336

FIGURE P15.2 **3-D bar graph showing the relationships among the agent, product and region**

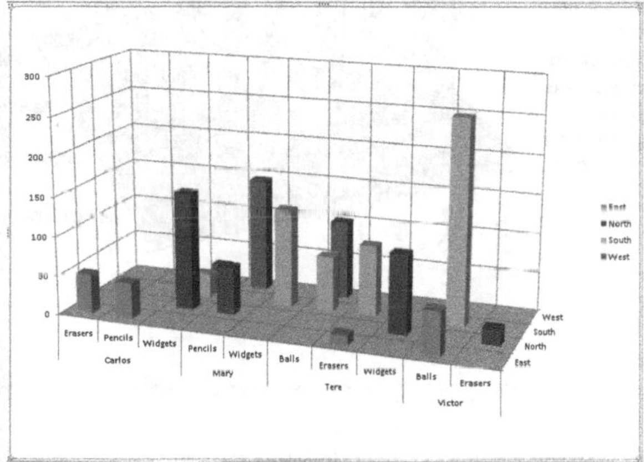

3 David Suker, the inventory manager for a marketing research company, is interested in studying the use of supplies within the different company departments. Mr Suker has heard that his friend, Ms Ephanor, has developed a small spreadsheet-based data warehouse model (see Problem 2) that she uses to analyse sales data. Mr Suker is interested in developing a small data warehouse model like Ms Ephanor's so he can analyse orders by department and by product. He will use Microsoft Access as the data warehouse DBMS and Microsoft Excel as the analysis tool.

- **a** Develop the order star schema.
- **b** Identify the appropriate dimensions attributes.
- **c** Identify the attribute hierarchies required to support the model.
- **d** Develop a crosstab report (in Microsoft Access), using a 3-D bar graph to show orders by product and by department. (The sample output is shown in Figure P15.3.)

FIGURE P15.3 Crosstab report: orders by product and department

Orders by Department and Product

Product	Accounting	Design	Marketing	Production	Row Total
Disks	$1.429.79	$17,268.80	$13,510.09	$6,312.24	**$38,520.92**
Envelopes	$329.16	$1,165.79	$17,074.33	$4,517.91	**$23,087.19**
Labels	$3,651.76	$1,514.15	$2,356.72	$8,464.79	**$15,987.42**
Paper	$1.761.90	$5,246.74	$14,222.35	$3,928.99	**$25,159.98**
Pencil	$741.83	$1,585.21	$2,014.56	$1,370.30	**$5,711.90**
Ribbons	$1.916.92	$525.00	$1,873.21	$3,203.82	**$7,518.95**
Toners	$110.47	$448.55	$358.25	$1,589.57	**$2,506.84**
	$9,941.83	**$27,754.24**	**$51,409.51**	**$29,387.62**	**$118,493.20**

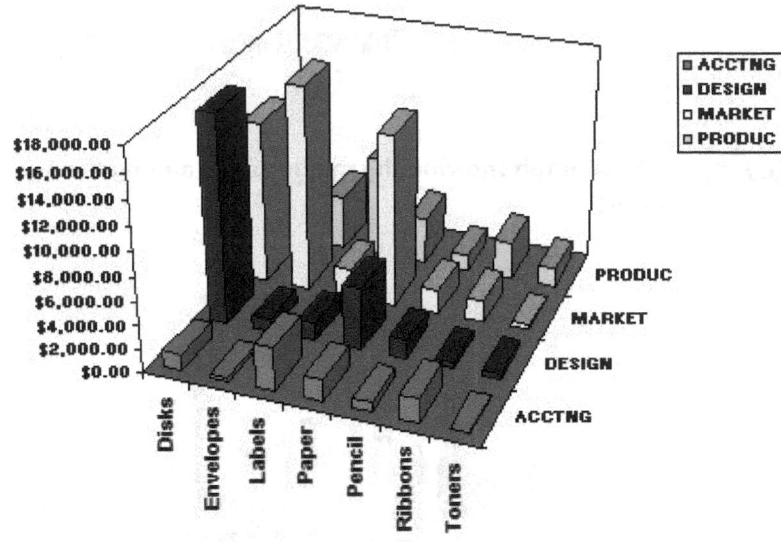

4 ROBCOR, whose sample data are contained in the database named Ch15_P4.mdb, provides 'on-demand' aviation charters, using a mix of different aircraft and aircraft types. Because ROBCOR has grown rapidly, it hires you to be its first database manager. (The company's database, developed by an outside consulting team, already has a charter database in place to help manage all of its operations.) Your first critical assignment is to develop a decision support system to analyse the charter data. (Review Problems 24–28 in Chapter 3, Relational Model Characteristics, in which the operations have been described.) The charter operations manager wants to be able to analyse charter data such as cost, hours flown, fuel used and revenue. She would also like to be able to drill down by pilot, type of aircraft and time periods.

Given those requirements, complete the following:

- **a** Create a star schema for the charter data.
- **b** Define the dimensions and attributes for the charter operation's star schema.
- **c** Define the necessary attribute hierarchies.
- **d** Implement the data warehouse design, using the design components you developed in Problems 4a–4c.
- **e** Generate the reports that will illustrate that your data warehouse meets the specified information requirements.

Using the data provided in the SaleCo snowflake schema in Figure 15.24, solve the following problems.

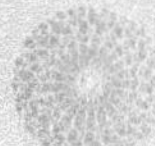

Online Content The script files used to populate the database are available on the online platform for this book. The script files assume an Oracle RDBMS. If you use a different DBMS, consult the documentation to verify whether the vendor supports similar functionality and what the proper syntax is for your DBMS.

5 What is the SQL command to list the total sales by customer and by product, with subtotals by customer and a grand total for all product sales? (*Hint:* Use the ROLLUP command.)

6 What is the SQL command to list the total sales by customer, month and product, with subtotals by customer and by month and a grand total for all product sales? (*Hint:* Use the ROLLUP command.)

7 What is the SQL command to list the total sales by region and customer, with subtotals by region and a grand total for all sales? (*Hint:* Use the ROLLUP command.)

8 What is the SQL command to list the total sales by month and product category, with subtotals by month and a grand total for all sales? (*Hint:* Use the ROLLUP command.)

9 What is the SQL command to list the number of product sales (number of rows) and total sales by month, with subtotals by month and a grand total for all sales? (*Hint:* Use the ROLLUP command.)

10 What is the SQL command to list the number of product sales (number of rows) and total sales by month and product category, with subtotals by month and product category and a grand total for all sales? (*Hint:* Use the ROLLUP command.)

11 What is the SQL command to list the number of product sales (number of rows) and total sales by month, product category and product, with subtotals by month and product category and a grand total for all sales? (*Hint:* Use the ROLLUP command.)

12 Using the answer to Problem 10 as your base, which command would you need to generate the same output but with subtotals in all columns? (*Hint:* Use the CUBE command.)

13 Create your own data analysis and visualisation presentation. The purpose of this project is for you to search for a publicly available data set using the internet and create your own presentation using what you have learnt in this chapter.

   a Search for a data set that interests you and download it. Some examples of public data sets sources are (see also Note on page 816):

   - www.data.gov
   - http://data.worldbank.org
   - http://aws.amazon.com/datasets
   - http://usgovxml.com/
   - https://data.medicare.gov/
   - www.faa.gov/data_research/

   b Use any tool available to you to analyse the data. You can use tools such as Microsoft Excel Pivot Tables, Pivot Charts, or other free tools, such as Google Fusion tables, Tableau free trial, IBM Many Eyes, etc.

   c Create a short presentation to explain some of your findings what the data sources are, where the data comes from, what the data represents, etc.

15

CHAPTER 16

Big Data and NoSQL

IN THIS CHAPTER, YOU WILL LEARN:

- The role of Big Data in modern business
- The primary characteristics of Big Data and how these go beyond the traditional '3 Vs'
- How the core components of the Hadoop framework operate
- To identify the major components of the Hadoop ecosystem
- To summarise the four major approaches of the NoSQL data model and how they differ from the relational model
- To describe the characteristics of NewSQL databases
- How to work with document databases using MongoDB
- How to work with graph databases using Neo4j

PREVIEW

In Chapter 2, Data Models, you were introduced to the emerging NoSQL data model and the Big Data problem that has led to NoSQL's development. In this chapter, you learn about these issues in much greater detail.

You will also learn about the technologies that have developed, and continue to be developed, to address Big Data. First, you learn about the low-level technologies in the Hadoop framework. Hadoop has become a standard component in organisations' efforts to address Big Data. Next, you learn about the higher-level approaches of the NoSQL data model to developing non-relational databases such as key-value databases, document databases, column-oriented databases and graph databases. You also learn about NewSQL databases, which try to bridge the gap between relational database systems and NoSQL.

Finally, you explore basic database activities in two current NoSQL products: MongoDB and Neo4j. Just as with relational databases, the ability to perform data management – storing new data, updating existing data, removing old data and retrieving specific data – is key to NoSQL databases. Online Appendixes Q and R provide hands-on coding tutorials for MongoDB and Neo4j, respectively.

The relational database model has been dominant for decades and, during that time, it has faced challenges such as object-oriented databases and the development of data warehouses. The relational model and the tools based on it have evolved to adapt to these challenges and remain dominant in the data management arena. In each case the challenge arose because technological advances changed businesses' perceptions of what is possible, and created new opportunities for organisations to create value from increased data leverage. The latest of these challenges is Big Data. Big Data is an ill-defined term that describes a new wave of data storage and manipulation possibilities and requirements. Organisations' efforts to store, manipulate and analyse this new wave of data represent one of the most urgent emerging trends in the database field. The challenges of dealing with the wave of Big Data have led to the development of NoSQL databases that reject many of the underlying assumptions of the relational model. Although the term 'Big Data' lacks a consistent definition, there is a set of characteristics generally associated with it.

16.1 BIG DATA

Big Data generally refers to a set of data that displays the characteristics of volume, velocity, variety, veracity and value (the 5 Vs) to an extent that makes the data unsuitable for management by a relational database management system. These characteristics can be defined as follows:

- **Volume** – the quantity of data to be stored
- **Velocity** – the speed at which data is entering the system
- **Variety** – the variations in the structure of the data to be stored
- **Veracity** – the trustworthiness of the data
- **Value** – the worth of the data to the business.

Notice the lack of specific values associated with these characteristics. This lack of specificity is what leads to the ambiguity in defining Big Data. What was Big Data five years ago might not be considered Big Data now. Similarly, something considered Big Data now might not be considered Big Data five years from now. The key is that the characteristics are present to an extent that the current relational database technology struggles with managing the data.

Further adding to the problem of defining Big Data is that there is some disagreement among pundits about which of the 5 Vs must be present for a data set to be considered Big Data. Originally, Big Data was conceived as shown in Figure 16.1 as a combination of the 3 Vs: volume, velocity and variety. Web data, a combination of text, graphics, video and audio sources combined into complex structures, created new challenges for data management that involve all three characteristics. After the dot-com bubble burst in the 1990s, many Web-based start-up companies failed, but the companies that survived experienced significant growth as Web commerce consolidated into a smaller set of businesses. As a result, companies like Google and Amazon experienced significant growth and were among the first to feel the pressure of managing Big Data. The success of social media giant Facebook quickly followed, and these companies became pioneers in creating new technologies to address Big Data problems. Google created the Bigtable data store, Amazon created Dynamo, and Facebook created Cassandra (technologies that are discussed later in this chapter), to deal with the growing need to store and manage large sets of data that had the characteristics of the original 3 Vs.

Although social media and Web data have been at the forefront of perceptions of Big Data issues, other organisations have Big Data issues too. More recently, changes in technology have increased the opportunities for businesses to generate and track data so that Big Data has been redefined as involving any, but not necessarily all, of the 5 Vs. Given the Volume of Big Data, the Value of the data to the business has to outweigh the cost of automatically processing and mining this data in terms of generating new revenue. However, the Veracity of the data, in terms of its accuracy and quality, must be verified before a business acts upon it. Advances in technology have led to a vast array of user-generated data and machine-generated data that can spur growth in specific areas.

FIGURE 16.1 **Original view of Big Data**

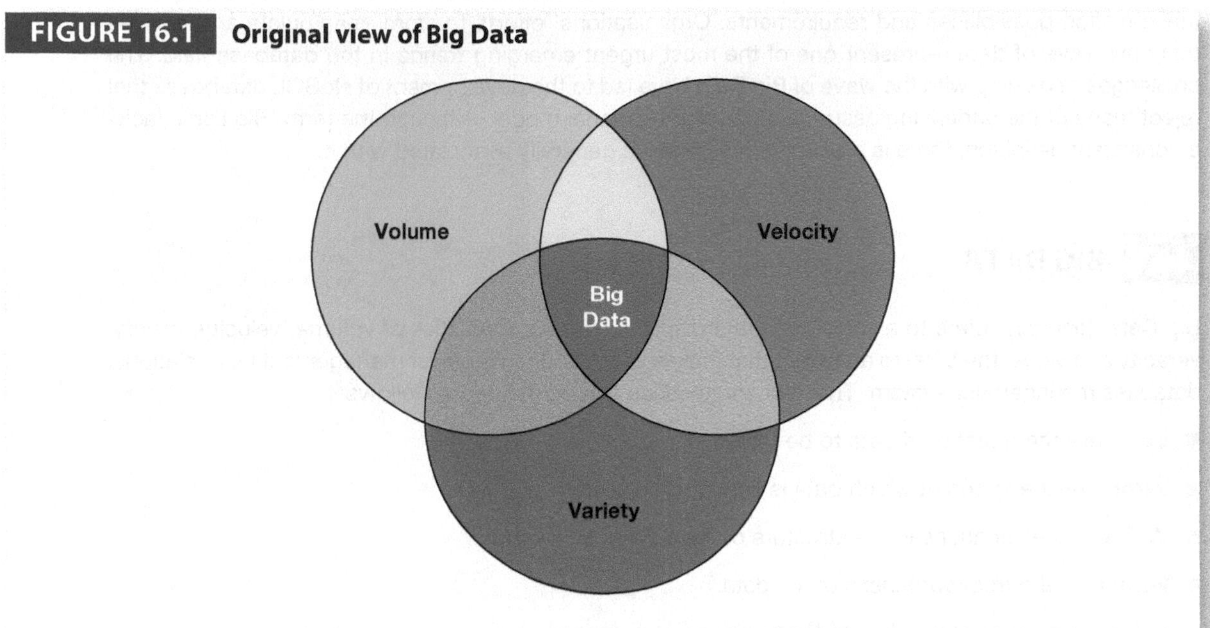

For example, Disney World has introduced 'Magic Bands' for park visitors to wear on their wrists. Each visitor's Magic Band is connected to much of the data that Disney stores about that individual. These bands use radio frequency identification (RFID) and near-field communications (NFC) to act as tickets for rides, hotel room keys, and even credit cards within the park. The bands can be tracked so that Disney systems can follow individuals as they move through the park, record with which Disney characters (who are also tracked) they interact, purchases made, wait time in lines, and more. Visitors can make reservations at a restaurant and order meals through a Disney app on their smartphones and, by tracking the Magic Bands, the restaurant staff know when the visitors arrive for their reservation, can track at which table they are seated, and deliver their meals within minutes of the guests sitting down. With the many cameras mounted throughout the park, Disney can also capture pictures and short videos of the visitors throughout their stay in the park to produce a personalised movie of their vacation experience, which can then be sold to the visitors as souvenirs. All of this involves the capture of a constant stream of data from each band, processed in real time. Considering the tens of thousands of visitors to Disney World each day, each with their own Magic Band, the volume, velocity, and variety of the data are enormous.

16.1.1 Volume

Volume, the quantity of data to be stored, is a key characteristic of Big Data. The storage capacities associated with Big Data are extremely large. Table 16.1 provides definitions for units of data storage capacity.

TABLE 16.1 Storage capacity units

Term	Capacity	Abbreviation
Bit	0 or 1 value	b
Byte	8 bits	B
Kilobyte	1 024* bytes	KB
Megabyte	1 024 KB	MB
Gigabyte	1 024 MB	GB
Terabyte	1 024 GB	TB
Petabyte	1 024 TB	PB
Exabyte	1 024 PB	EB
Zettabyte	1 024 EB	ZB
Yottabyte	1 024 ZB	YB

*Note that because bits are binary in nature and are the basis on which all other storage values are based, all values for data storage units are defined in terms of powers of 2. For example, the prefix *kilo* typically means 1000; however, in data storage, a kilobyte = 2^{10} = 1024 bytes.

Naturally, as the quantity of data needing to be stored increases, the need for larger storage devices also increases. When this occurs, systems can either scale up or scale out. **Scaling up** is keeping the same number of systems, but migrating each system to a larger system: for example, changing from a server with 16 CPU cores and a 1 TB storage system to a server with 64 CPU cores and a 100 TB storage system. Scaling up involves moving to larger and faster systems. However, there are limits to how large and fast a single system can be. Further, the costs of these high-powered systems increase at a dramatic rate.

On the other hand, **scaling out** means that, when the workload exceeds the capacity of a server, the workload is spread out across a number of servers. This is also referred to as *clustering* – creating a cluster of low-cost servers to share a workload. This can help to reduce the overall cost of the computing resources since it is cheaper to buy ten 100 TB storage systems than it is to buy a single 1 PB storage system. Make no mistake, organisations need storage capacities in these extreme sizes. Organisations such as eBay collect clickstream data that easily reaches into the dozens of petabytes. This is in addition to the enterprise data warehouses, which can also be petabytes in size and spread over hundreds of thousands of nodes.

Recall from Chapter 3 that one of the greatest advances represented by the relational model was the development of an RDBMS – a sophisticated database management system that could hide the complexity of the underlying data storage and manipulation from the user, so that the data always appears to be in tables. To carry out these functions, the DBMS acts as the 'brain' of the database system and must maintain control over all of the data within the database. As discussed in Chapter 12, it is possible to distribute a relational database over multiple servers using replication and fragmentation. However, because the DBMS must act as a single point of control for all of the data in the database, distributing the database across multiple systems requires a high degree of communication and coordination across the systems. There are significant limits associated with the ability to distribute the DBMS due to the increased performance costs of communication and coordination as the number of nodes grows. This limits the degree to which a relational database to be scaled out as data volume grows, and it makes RDBMSs ill-suited for clusters.

NOTE

Although some RDBMS products, such as SQL Server and Oracle Real Application Clusters, legitimately claim to support clusters, these clusters are limited in scope and generally rely on a single, shared data storage subsystem, such as a storage area network.

16.1.2 Velocity

Velocity, another key characteristic of Big Data, refers to the rate at which new data enters the system as well as the rate at which the data must be processed. In many ways, the issues of velocity mirror those of volume. For example, consider a web retailer such as Amazon. In the past, a retail store might capture only the data about the final transaction of a customer making a purchase. Today, a retailer like Amazon captures not only the final transaction but also every click of the mouse in the searching, browsing, comparing and purchasing process. Instead of capturing one event (the final sale) in a 20-minute shopping experience, it might capture data on 30 events during that 20-minute time frame – a 30× increase in the velocity of the data. Other advances in technology, such as RFID, GPS and NFC, add new layers of data-gathering opportunities that often generate large amounts of data that must be stored in real time. For example, RFID tags can be used to track items for inventory and warehouse management. The tags do not require line-of-sight between the tag and the reader, and the reader can read hundreds of tags simultaneously while the products are still in boxes. This means that, instead of a single record for tracking a given quantity of a product being produced, each individual product is tracked, creating an increase of several orders of magnitude in the amount of data being delivered to the system at any one time.

In addition to the speed with which data is entering the system, for Big Data to be actionable, that data must be processed at a very rapid pace. The velocity of processing can be broken down into two categories:

- Stream processing
- Feedback loop processing.

Stream processing focuses on input processing, and it requires analysis of the data stream as it enters the system. In some situations, large volumes of data can enter the system at such a rapid pace that it is not feasible to try to store all of the data. The data must be processed and filtered as it enters the system to determine which data to keep and which data to discard. For example, at the CERN Large Hadron Collider, the largest and most powerful particle accelerator in the world, experiments produce about 600 TB per second of raw data. Scientists have created **algorithms** to decide ahead of time which data will be kept. These algorithms are applied in a two-step process to filter the data down to only about 1 GB per second of data that will actually be stored.[1]

Feedback loop processing refers to the analysis of the data to produce actionable results. While stream processing could be thought of as focused on inputs, feedback loop processing can be thought of as focused on outputs. The process of capturing the data, processing it into usable information, and then acting on that information, is a feedback loop. Figure 16.2 shows a feedback loop for providing recommendations for book purchases. Feedback loop processing to provide immediate results requires analysing large amounts of data within just a few seconds so that the results of the analysis can become a part of the product delivered to the user in real time. Not all feedback loops are used for inclusion of

1 CERN, 'Processing: What to record?' http://home.web.cern.ch/about/computing/processing-what-record, August 20, 2015.

results within immediate data products. Feedback loop processing is also used to help organisations sift through terabytes and petabytes of data to inform decision makers and help them make faster strategic and tactical decisions. It is also a key component in data analytics.

FIGURE 16.2 Feedback loop processing

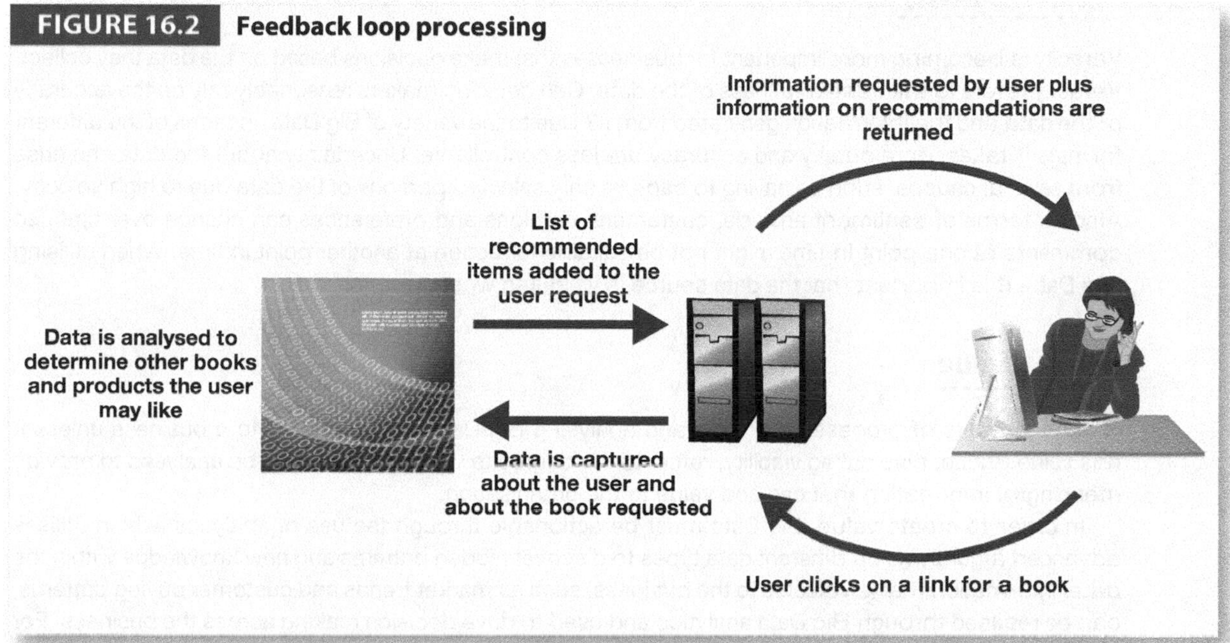
Information requested by user plus information on recommendations are returned
List of recommended items added to the user request
Data is analysed to determine other books and products the user may like
Data is captured about the user and about the book requested
User clicks on a link for a book

16.1.3 Variety

In the Big Data context, variety refers to the vast array of formats and structures in which the data may be captured. Data can be considered to be structured, unstructured, or semi-structured. **Structured data** is data that has been organised to fit a predefined data model. **Unstructured data** is data that is not organised to fit into a predefined data model. **Semi-structured data** combines elements of both – some parts of the data fit a predefined model while other parts do not. Relational databases rely on structured data. A data model is created by the database designer based on the organisation's business rules, as discussed in Chapter 4. As data enters the database, the data are decomposed and routed for storage in the corresponding tables and columns as defined in the data model. Although much of the transactional data that organisations use work well in a structured environment, most of the data in the world are semi-structured or unstructured. Unstructured data includes maps, satellite images, emails, texts, tweets, videos, transcripts, and a whole host of other data forms. Over the decades for which the relational model has been dominant, relational databases have evolved to address some forms of unstructured data. For example, most large-scale RDBMSs support a binary large object (BLOB) data type that allows the storage of unstructured objects like audio, video and graphic data as a single, atomic value. One problem with BLOB data is that the semantic value of the data, the meaning that the object conveys, is inaccessible and uninterpretable by data processing.

Big Data requires that the data be captured in whatever format it naturally exists in, without any attempt to impose a data model or structure to the data. This is one of the key differences between processing data in a relational database and Big Data processing. Relational databases impose a structure on the data when the data is captured and stored. Big Data processing imposes a structure on the data as needed for applications as a part of retrieval and processing. One advantage of providing structure during retrieval and processing is the flexibility of being able to structure the data in different ways for different applications.

16.1.4 Veracity

Veracity is becoming more important for businesses that make decisions based on the data they collect. Veracity refers to the trustworthiness of the data. Can decision makers reasonably rely on the accuracy of the data and the information generated from it? Due to the variety of Big Data, in terms of the different formats it takes, data quality and accuracy are less controllable. Uncertainty about the data can arise from several causes, such as having to capture only selected portions of the data due to high velocity. Also, in terms of sentiment analysis, customers' opinions and preferences can change over time, so comments at one point in time might not be suitable for action at another point in time. When utilising Big Data, it is important that the data source is validated where possible.

16.1.5 Value

Given the costs of processing, storing and analysing Big Data, it is of no use to a business unless it has value. Value, also called viability, refers to the degree to which the data can be analysed to provide meaningful information that can add value to the organisation.

In order to create value, Big Data must be actionable through the use of analytics, which utilises advanced algorithms on different data types to discover hidden patterns and new knowledge within the data. Information that is valuable to the business, such as market trends and customer buying patterns, can be realised through Big Data analytics and used to drive decision making across the business. For example, after analytics, an insurance company that collects data about insurance claims, all customer contacts (surveys, phone calls etc.), insured objects and persons, and website usage, can create value to the company by looking at risk distribution amongst current and new customers; increase turnover by using predictive models to cross-sell other insurance products; and even perform analytical pricing of different insurance contracts.

NOTE

While the value of Big Data is linked to measurable actions informed by Big Data analytics, it is also important to ensure that the data is used both ethically and legally. The General Data Protection Regulation (GDPR) became a legal requirement for all businesses and organisations that collect and process data on 25 May 2018. Although this is a European Union legal requirement, most businesses exchange data internationally and have to comply with its requirements. One of the major changes detailed in Article 22 of the GDPR includes the rights of an individual not to be subject to automated decision making, which includes profiling, unless explicit consent is given. A person who is subject to such decision making now has the right to ask for an explanation of how the decision is reached. For example, if a person was to apply for a bank loan online, and was automatically rejected, they would have a right to ask for an explanation of the logic used by the algorithm that made the decision.[2]

2 Crockett, K., Goltz, S. and Garratt, M. GDPR Impact on Computational Intelligence Research, IEEE International Joint conference on Artificial Neural Networks (IJCNN), DOI: 10.1109/IJCNN.2018.8489614, ISSN: 2161-4407, 2018.

16.1.6 Other Characteristics

Characterising Big Data with the 5 Vs is fairly standard. However, as the industry matures, other characteristics have been put forward as being equally important. Keeping with the spirit of the 5 Vs, these additional characteristics are typically presented as additional Vs. **Variability** refers to the changes in the meaning of the data based on context. While *variety* and *variability* are similar terms, they mean distinctly different things in Big Data. Variety is about differences in structure. Variability is about differences in meaning. Variability is especially relevant in areas such as sentiment analysis that attempt to understand the meanings of words. **Sentiment analysis** is a method of text analysis that attempts to determine whether a statement conveys a positive, negative, or neutral attitude about a topic. For example, consider the statements 'I just bought a new smartphone – I love it!' and 'The screen on my new smartphone shattered the first time I dropped it – I love it!' In the first statement, the presence of the phrase 'I love it' might help an algorithm correctly interpret the statement as expressing a positive attitude. However, the second statement uses sarcasm to express a negative attitude, so the presence of the phrase 'I love it' may cause the analysis to interpret the meaning of the phrase incorrectly.

The final characteristic of Big Data is visualisation. **Visualisation** is the ability to present the data graphically in such a way as to make it understandable. Volumes of data can leave decision makers awash in facts but with little understanding of what the facts mean. Visualisation is a way of presenting the facts so that decision makers can comprehend the meaning of the information to gain insights.

An argument could be made that these additional Vs are not necessarily characteristics of Big Data; or, perhaps more accurately, they are not characteristics of *only* Big Data. Visualisation was discussed and illustrated at length in Chapter 15 as an important tool in working with data warehouses, which are often maintained as structured data stores in RDBMS products. The important thing to remember is that these characteristics that play an important part in working with data in the relational model are universal and also apply to Big Data.

Big Data represents a new wave in data management challenges, but it does not mean that relational database technology is going away. Structured data that depends on ACIDS (atomicity, consistency, isolation, durability, and serialisability) transactions, as discussed in Chapter 12, will always be critical to business operations. Relational databases are still the best way of storing and managing this type of data. What has changed is that now, for the first time in decades, relational databases are not necessarily the best way for storing and managing *all* of an organisation's data. Since the rise of the relational model, the decision for data managers when faced with new storage requirements was not whether to use a relational database, but which relational DBMS to use. Now, the decision of whether to use a relational database at all is a real question. This has led to **polyglot persistence**—the coexistence of a variety of data storage and management technologies within an organisation's infrastructure. Scaling up, as discussed, is often considered a viable option as relational databases grow. However, it has practical limits and cost considerations that make it unfeasible for many Big Data installations. Scaling out into clusters based on low-cost commodity servers is the dominant approach that organisations are currently pursuing for Big Data management. As a result, new technologies not based on the relational model have been developed.

16.2 HADOOP

16

Big Data requires a different approach to distributed data storage that is designed for large-scale clusters. Although other implementation technologies are possible, Hadoop has become the de facto standard for most Big Data storage and processing. Hadoop is not a database. Hadoop is a Java-based framework for distributing and processing very large data sets across clusters of computers. While the Hadoop framework includes many parts, the two most important components are the Hadoop Distributed File System (HDFS) and MapReduce. HDFS is a low-level distributed file processing system, which means that it can be used directly for data storage. MapReduce is a programming model that supports processing large data sets in a highly parallel, distributed manner. While it is possible to use HDFS and MapReduce separately, the two technologies complement each other so that they work better together as a Hadoop system. Hadoop was engineered specifically to distribute and process enormous amounts of data across vast clusters of servers.

16.2.1 Hadoop Distributed File System

The **Hadoop Distributed File System (HDFS)** approach to distributing data is based on several key assumptions:

- *High volume*. The volume of data in Big Data applications is expected to be in terabytes, petabytes, or larger. Hadoop assumes that files in the HDFS will be extremely large. Data in the HDFS is organised into physical blocks, just as in other types of file storage. For example, on a typical personal computer, file storage is organised into blocks that are often 512 bytes in size, depending on the hardware and operating system involved. Relational databases often aggregate these into database blocks. By default, Oracle organises data into 8 KB physical blocks. Hadoop, on the other hand, has a default block size of 64 MB (8000 times the size of an Oracle block!), and it can be configured to even larger values. As a result, the number of blocks per file is greatly reduced, simplifying the metadata overhead of tracking the blocks in each file.
- *Write-once, read-many*. Using a write-once, read-many model simplifies concurrency issues and improves overall data throughput. Using this model, a file is created, written to the file system, and then closed. Once the file is closed, changes cannot be made to its contents. This improves overall system performance and works well for the types of tasks performed by many Big Data applications. Although existing contents of the file cannot be changed, recent advancements in the HDFS allow for files to have new data appended to the end of the file. This is a key advancement for NoSQL databases because it allows for database logs to be updated.
- *Streaming access*. Unlike transaction processing systems where queries often retrieve small pieces of data from several different tables, Big Data applications typically process entire files. Instead of optimising the file system to access individual data elements randomly, Hadoop is optimised for batch processing of entire files as a continuous stream of data.
- *Fault tolerance*. Hadoop is designed to be distributed across thousands of low-cost, commodity computers. It is assumed that, with thousands of such devices, at any point in time, some will experience hardware errors. Therefore, the HDFS is designed to replicate data across many different devices so that when one device fails, the data is still available from another device. By default, Hadoop uses a replication factor of three, meaning that each block of data is stored on three different devices. Different replication factors can be specified for each file, if desired.

Hadoop uses several types of nodes. A *node* is just a computer that performs one or more types of tasks within the system. Within the HDFS, there are three types of nodes: the client node, the name node and one or more data nodes, as depicted in Figure 16.3.

FIGURE 16.3 **Hadoop Distributed File System (HDFS)**

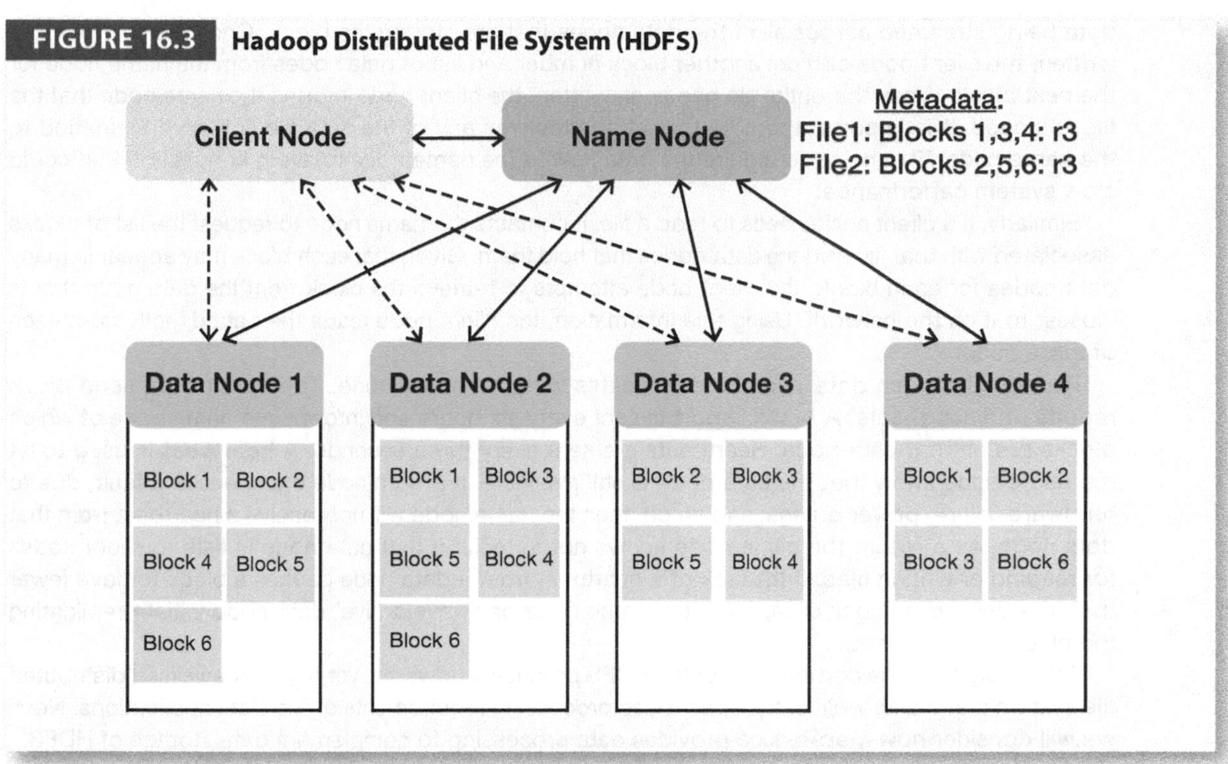

Data nodes store the actual file data within the HDFS. Recall that files in HDFS are broken into blocks and are replicated to ensure fault tolerance. As a result, each block is duplicated on more than one data node. Figure 16.3 shows the default replication factor of three, so each block appears on three data nodes.

The name node contains the metadata for the file system. There is typically only one name node within a HDFS cluster. The metadata is designed to be small, simple, and easily recoverable. Keeping the metadata small allows the name node to hold all of the metadata in memory to reduce disk accesses and improve system performance. This is important because there is only one name node so contention for the name node is minimised. The metadata is composed primarily of the name of each file, the block numbers that comprise each file, and the desired replication factor for each file. The client node makes requests to the file system, either to read files or to write new files, as needed to support the user application.

When a client node needs to create a new file, it communicates with the name node. The name node:

- Adds the new file name to the metadata
- Determines a new block number for the file
- Determines a list of which data nodes the block will be stored
- Passes that information back to the client node.

The client node contacts the first data node specified by the name node and begins writing the file on that data node. At the same time, the client node sends the data node the list of other data nodes that will be replicating the block. As the data is received from the client node, the data node contacts the next data node in the list and begins sending the data to this node for replication. This second data node then contacts the next data node in the list, and the process continues with the

16

data being streamed across all of the data nodes that are storing the block. Once the first block is written, the client node can get another block number and list of data nodes from the name node for the next block. When the entire file has been written, the client node informs the name node that the file is closed. It is important to note that at no time was any of the data file actually transmitted to the name node. This helps to reduce the data flow to the name node to avoid congestion that could slow system performance.

Similarly, if a client node needs to read a file, it contacts the name node to request the list of blocks associated with that file and the data nodes that hold them. Given that each block may appear in many data nodes for each block, the client node attempts to retrieve the block from the data node that is closest to it on the network. Using this information, the client node reads the data directly from each of these nodes.

Periodically, each data node communicates with the name node. The data nodes send block reports and heartbeats. A **block report** is sent every six hours and informs the name node of which blocks are on that data node. Heartbeats are sent every three seconds. A **heartbeat** is used to let the name node know that the data node is still available. If a data node experiences a fault, due to hardware failure, power outage, and so on, then the name node will not receive a heartbeat from that data node. As a result, the name node knows not to include that data node in lists to client nodes for reading or writing files. If the lack of a heartbeat from a data node causes a block to have fewer than the desired number of replicas, the name node can have a 'live' data node initiate replicating the block on another data node.

Taken together, the components of the HDFS produce a powerful, yet highly specialised distributed file system that works well for the specialised processing requirements of Big Data applications. Next, we will consider how MapReduce provides data processing to complement data storage of HDFS.

16.2.2 MapReduce

MapReduce is the computing framework used to process large data sets across clusters. Conceptually, MapReduce is easy to understand and follows the principle of *divide and conquer*. MapReduce takes a complex task, breaks it down into a collection of smaller subtasks, performs the subtasks all at the same time, and then combines the result of each subtask to produce a final result for the original task. As the name implies, it is a combination of a map function and a reduce function. A **map** function takes a collection of data and sorts and filters the data into a set of key-value pairs. The map function is performed by a program called a **mapper**. A **reduce** function takes a collection of key-value pairs, all with the same key value, and summarises them into a single result. The reduce function is performed by a program called a **reducer**. Recall that Hadoop is a Java-based platform; therefore, map and reduce functions are written as detailed, procedure-oriented Java programs.

Figure 16.4 provides a simple conceptual illustration of MapReduce that determines the total number of units of each product that has been sold. The original data in Figure 16.4 are stored as key-value pairs, with the invoice number as the key and the remainder of the invoice data as a value. Remember, the data in Hadoop data storage do not constitute a relational database so the data are not separated into tables and there is no form of normalisation that ensures that each fact is stored only once. Therefore, there is a great deal of duplication of data in the original data store. Note that, even in the very small subset of data that is shown in Figure 16.4, redundant data is kept for customer 10011, Leona Dunne. In the figure, map functions parse each invoice to find data about the products sold on that invoice. The result of the map function is a new list of key-value pairs in which the product code is the key and the line units are the value. The reduce function then takes that list of key-value pairs and combines them by summing the values associated with each key (product code) to produce the summary result.

FIGURE 16.4 MapReduce

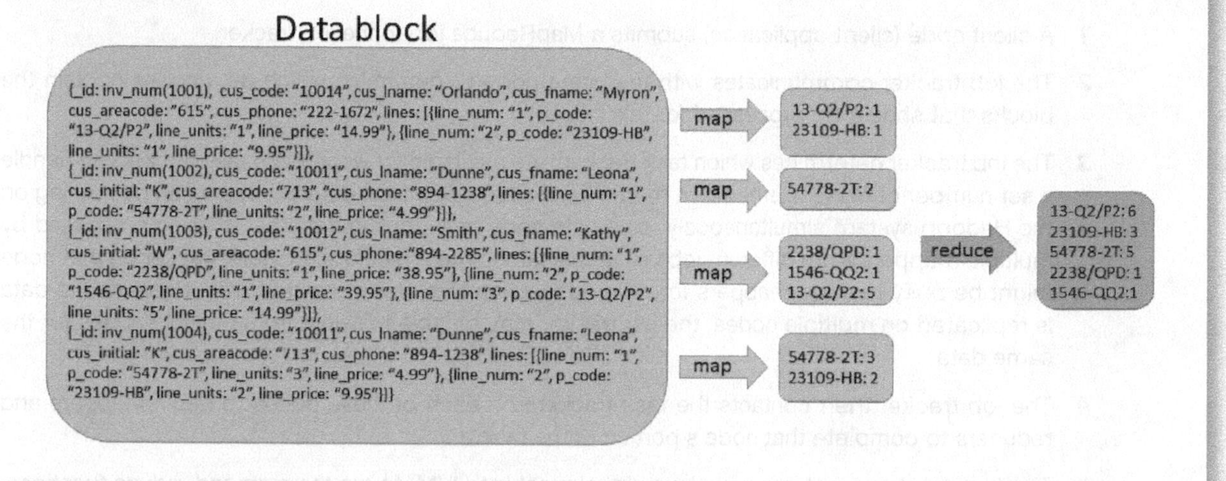

Data block

{_id: inv_num(1001), cus_code: "10014", cus_lname: "Orlando", cus_fname: "Myron", cus_areacode: "615", cus_phone: "222-1672", lines: [{line_num: "1", p_code: "13-Q2/P2", line_units: "1", line_price: "14.99"}, {line_num: "2", p_code: "23109-HB", line_units: "1", line_price: "9.95"}]},
{_id: inv_num(1002), cus_code: "10011", cus_lname: "Dunne", cus_fname: "Leona", cus_initial: "K", cus_areacode: "713", "cus_phone: "894-1238", lines: [{line_num: "1", p_code: "54778-2T", line_units: "2", line_price: "4.99"}]},
{_id: inv_num(1003), cus_code: "10012", cus_lname: "Smith", cus_fname: "Kathy", cus_initial: "W", cus_areacode: "615", cus_phone:"894-2285", lines: [{line_num: "1", p_code: "2238/QPD", line_units: "1", line_price: "38.95"}, {line_num: "2", p_code: "1546-QQ2", line_units: "1", line_price: "39.95"}, {line_num: "3", p_code: "13-Q2/P2", line_units: "5", line_price: "14.99"}]},
{_id: inv_num(1004), cus_code: "10011", cus_lname: "Dunne", cus_fname: "Leona", cus_initial: "K", cus_areacode: "713", cus_phone: "894-1238", lines: [{line_num: "1", p_code: "54778-2T", line_units: "3", line_price: "4.99"}, {line_num: "2", p_code: "23109-HB", line_units: "2", line_price: "9.95"}]}

map → 13-Q2/P2: 1, 23109-HB: 1
map → 54778-2T: 2
map → 2238/QPD: 1, 1546-QQ2: 1, 13-Q2/P2: 5
map → 54778-2T: 3, 23109-HB: 2

reduce → 13-Q2/P2: 6, 23109-HB: 3, 54778-2T: 5, 2238/QPD: 1, 1546-QQ2: 1

As previously stated, the data sets used in Big Data applications are extremely large. Transferring entire files from multiple nodes to a central node for processing would require a tremendous amount of network bandwidth, and place an incredible processing burden on the central node. Therefore, instead of the computational program retrieving the data for processing in a central location, copies of the program are 'pushed' to the nodes containing the data to be processed. Each copy of the program produces results that are then aggregated across nodes and sent back to the client. This mirrors the distribution of data in the HDFS. Typically, the Hadoop framework distributes a mapper for each block on each data node that must be processed. This can lead to a very large number of mappers. For example, if 1 TB of data is to be processed and the HDFS is using 64 MB blocks, that yields over 15 000 mapper programs. The number of reducers is configurable by the user, but best practices suggest about one reducer per data node.

NOTE

Best practices suggest that the number of mappers on a given node should be kept to 100 or less. However, there are cases of applications with simple map functions running as many as 300 mappers on a given node with satisfactory performance. Clearly, much depends on the computing resources available at each node.

The implementation of MapReduce complements the structure of the HDFS, which is an important reason why they work so well together. Just as the HDFS structure is composed of a name node and several data nodes, MapReduce uses a **job tracker** (the actual name of the program is JobTracker) and several **task trackers** (the programs are named TaskTrackers). The job tracker acts as a central control for MapReduce processing, and it normally exists on the same server that is acting as the name node. Task tracker programs reside on the data nodes. One important feature of the MapReduce framework is that the user must write the Java code for the map and reduce functions, and must specify the input and output files to be read and written for the job that is being submitted. However, the job tracker will take care of locating the data, determining which nodes to use, dividing the job into tasks for the nodes, and managing failures of the nodes. All of this is done automatically without user intervention. When a user submits a MapReduce job for processing, the general process is as follows:

1 A client node (client application) submits a MapReduce job to the job tracker.
2 The job tracker communicates with the name node to determine which data nodes contain the blocks that should be processed for this job.
3 The job tracker determines which task trackers are available for work. Each task tracker can handle a set number of tasks. Remember, many MapReduce jobs from different users can be running on the Hadoop system simultaneously, so a data node may contain data that is being processed by multiple mappers from different jobs all at the same time. Therefore, the task tracker on that node might be busy running mappers for other jobs when this new request arrives. Because the data is replicated on multiple nodes, the job tracker may be able to select from multiple nodes for the same data.
4 The job tracker then contacts the task trackers on each of those nodes to begin mappers and reducers to complete that node's portion of the task.
5 The task tracker creates a new Java virtual machine (JVM) to run the map and reduce functions. This way, if a function fails or crashes, the entire task tracker is not halted.
6 The task tracker sends heartbeat messages to the job tracker to let the job tracker know that the task tracker is still working on the job (and about the nodes availability for more jobs).
7 The job tracker monitors the heartbeat messages to determine whether a task manager has failed. If so, the job tracker can reassign that portion of the task to another node.
8 When the entire job is finished, the job tracker changes status to indicate that the job is completed.
9 The client node periodically queries the job tracker until the job status is completed.

The Hadoop system uses batch processing. **Batch processing** is when a program runs from beginning to end, either completing the task or halting with an error, without any interaction with the user. Batch processing is often used when the computing task requires an extended period of time or a large portion of the system's processing capacity. Businesses often use batch processing to run year-end financial reports in the evenings when systems may be idle, and universities might use batch processing for student fee payment processing. Batch processing is not bad, but it has limitations. As a result, a number of complementary programs have been developed to improve the integration of Hadoop within the larger IT infrastructure. The next section discusses some of these programs.

16.2.3 Hadoop Ecosystem

Hadoop is widely used by organisations tapping into the potential of analysing extremely large data sets. Unfortunately, because Hadoop is a very low-level tool requiring considerable effort to create, manage and use, it presents quite a few obstacles. As a result, a host of related applications have grown up around Hadoop to attempt to make it easier to use and more accessible to users who are not skilled at complex Java programming. Figure 16.5 shows examples of some of these types of applications. Most organisations that use Hadoop also use a set of other related products that interact and complement each other to produce an entire ecosystem of applications and tools. Like any ecosystem, the interconnected pieces are constantly evolving and their relationships are changing, so it is a rather fluid situation. The following are some of the more popular components in a Hadoop ecosystem and how they relate to each other.

FIGURE 16.5 A sample of the Hadoop ecosystem

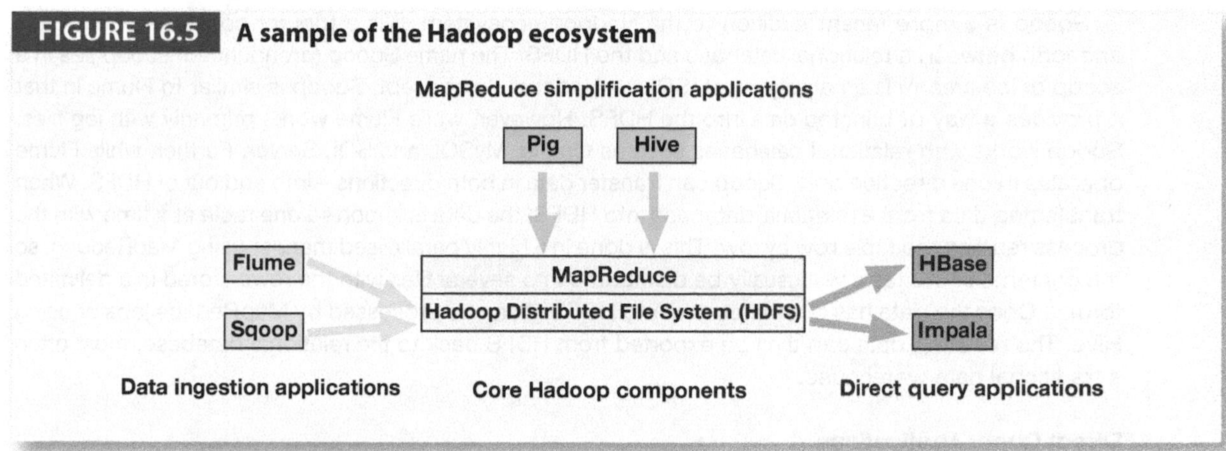

MapReduce Simplification Applications

Creating MapReduce jobs requires significant programming skills. As the mapper and reducer programs become more complex, the skill requirements increase and the time to produce the programs becomes significant. These skills are beyond the capabilities of most data users. Therefore, applications to simplify the process of creating MapReduce jobs have been developed. Two of the most popular are Hive and Pig.

Hive is a data warehousing system that sits on top of HDFS. It is not a relational database, but it supports its own SQL-like language, called HiveQL, that mimics SQL commands to run ad hoc queries. HiveQL commands are processed by the Hive query engine into sets of MapReduce jobs. As a result, the underlying processing tends to be batch-oriented, producing jobs that are very scalable over extremely large sets of data. However, the batch nature of the jobs makes Hive a poor choice for jobs that only require a small subset of data to be returned very quickly.

Pig is a tool for compiling a high-level scripting language, named Pig Latin, into MapReduce jobs for executing in Hadoop. In concept it is similar to Hive in that it provides a means of producing MapReduce jobs without the burden of low-level Java programming. The primary difference is that Pig Latin is a scripting language, which means it is procedural, while HiveQL, like SQL, is declarative. Declarative languages allow the user to specify what they want, not how to get it. This is very useful for query processing. Procedural languages require the user to specify how the data is to be manipulated. This is very useful for performing data transformations. As a result, Pig is often used for producing data pipeline tasks that transform data in a series of steps. This is often seen in ETL (Extraction, Transformation and Loading) processes as described in Chapter 15.

Data Ingestion Applications

One challenge faced by organisations that are taking advantage of Hadoop's massive data storage and data processing capabilities, is the issue of actually getting data from their existing systems into the Hadoop cluster. To simplify this task, applications have been developed to 'ingest' or gather this data into Hadoop.

Flume is a component for ingesting data into Hadoop. It is designed primarily for harvesting large sets of data from server log files, like clickstream data from Web server logs. It can be configured to import the data on a regular schedule or based on specified events. In addition to simply bringing the data into Hadoop, Flume contains a simple query-processing component so the possibility exists of performing some transformations on the data as it is being harvested. Typically, Flume would move the data into the HDFS, but it can also be configured to input the data directly into another component of the Hadoop ecosystem named HBase.

Sqoop is a more recent addition to the Hadoop ecosystem. It is a tool for converting data back and forth between a relational database and the HDFS. The name Sqoop (pronounced 'scoop', as in a scoop of ice cream) is an amalgam of 'SQL-to-Hadoop'. In concept, Sqoop is similar to Flume in that it provides a way of bringing data into the HDFS. However, while Flume works primarily with log files, Sqoop works with relational databases such as Oracle, MySQL and SQL Server. Further, while Flume operates in one direction only, Sqoop can transfer data in both directions – into and out of HDFS. When transferring data from a relational database into HDFS, the data is imported one table at a time with the process reading the table row by row. This is done in a highly parallelised manner using MapReduce, so the contents of the table will usually be distributed into several files with the rows stored in a delimited format. Once the data has been imported into HDFS, it can be processed by MapReduce jobs or using Hive. The resulting data can then be exported from HDFS back to the relational database, most often a traditional data warehouse.

Direct Query Applications

Direct query applications attempt to provide faster query access than is possible through MapReduce. These applications interact with HDFS directly, instead of going through the MapReduce processing layer.

HBase is a column-oriented NoSQL database designed to sit on top of the HDFS. One of HBase's primary characteristics is that it is highly distributed and designed to scale out easily. It does not support SQL or SQL-like languages, relying instead on lower-level languages such as Java for interaction. The system does not rely on MapReduce jobs, so it avoids the delays caused by batch processing, making it more suitable for fast processing involving smaller subsets of the data. HBase is very good at quickly processing sparse data sets. HBase is one of the more popular components of the Hadoop ecosystem and is used by Facebook for its messaging system. Column-oriented databases will be discussed in more detail in the next section.

Impala was the first SQL on Hadoop application. It was produced by Cloudera as a query engine that supports SQL queries that pull data directly from HDFS. Prior to Impala, if an organisation needed to make data from Hadoop available to analysts through an SQL interface, data would be extracted from HDFS and imported into a relational database. With Impala, analysts can write SQL queries directly against the data while they are still in HDFS. Impala makes heavy use of in-memory caching on data nodes. It is generally considered an appropriate tool for processing large amounts of data into a relatively small result set.

NOTE

Other than Impala, each of the components of the Hadoop ecosystem described in this section are all open-source, top-level projects of the Apache Software Foundation. More information on each of these projects and many others is available at *www.apache.org*.

16.3 NoSQL DATABASES

16

NoSQL is the unfortunate name given to a broad array of non-relational database technologies that have developed to address the challenges represented by Big Data. (You may recall that we first introduced NoSQL in Chapter 2, Data Models.) The name is unfortunate in that it does not describe what the NoSQL technologies are, but rather what they are not. In fact, the name also does a poor job of explaining what the technologies are not! The name was chosen as a Twitter hashtag to simplify coordinating a meeting of developers to discuss ideas about the non-relational database technologies that were being developed by organisations like Google, Amazon and Facebook to deal with the problems they were encountering as their data sets reached enormous sizes. The term *NoSQL* was never meant to imply that products in this category should never include support for SQL. In fact, many such products support query languages that mimic SQL in important ways. Although no one has yet produced a NoSQL system that implements standard SQL, given the large base of SQL users, the appeal of creating such a product is obvious. More recently, some industry observers have tried to interject that NoSQL could stand for 'Not Only SQL'. In fact, if the requirement to be considered a NoSQL product were simply that languages beyond SQL are supported, then all of the traditional RDBMS products such as Oracle, SQL Server, MySQL and Microsoft Access would qualify. Regardless, you are better off focusing on understanding the array of technologies to which the term refers than worrying about the name itself.

There are literally hundreds of products that can be considered as being under the broadly defined term NoSQL. Most of these fit roughly into one of four categories: key-value data stores, document databases, column-oriented databases and graph databases. Table 16.2 shows some popular NoSQL databases of each type. Although not all NoSQL databases have been produced as open-source software, most have been. As a result, NoSQL databases are generally perceived as a part of the open-source movement. Accordingly, they also tend to be associated with the Linux operating system. It makes sense from a cost standpoint that, if an organisation is going to create a cluster containing tens of thousands of nodes, the organisation does not want to purchase licences for Windows or MacOS for all of those nodes. The preference is to use a platform, like Linux, that is freely available and highly customisable. Therefore, most of the NoSQL products run only in a Linux or Unix environment. The following sections discuss each of the major NoSQL approaches.

TABLE 16.2 NoSQL databases

NoSQL Category	Example Databases	Developer
Key-value databases	Dynamo Riak Redis Voldemort	Amazon Basho Redis Labs LinkedIn
Document databases	MongoDB CouchDB OrientDB RavenDB	MongoDB, Inc. Apache OrientDB Ltd Hibernating Rhinos
Column-oriented databases	HBase Cassandra Hypertable	Apache Apache (originally Facebook) Hypertable, Inc.
Graph databases	Neo4J ArangoDB GraphBase	Neo4j ArangoDB, LLC FactNexus

16.3.1 Key-Value Databases

16

Key-value (KV) databases are conceptually the simplest of the NoSQL data models. A KV database is a NoSQL database that stores data as a collection of key-value pairs. The key acts as an identifier for the value. The value can be anything such as text, an XML document, or an image. The database does not attempt to understand the contents of the value component or its meaning—the database simply stores whatever value is provided for the key. It is the job of the applications that use the data to understand the meaning of the data in the value component. There are no foreign keys; in fact, relationships cannot be tracked among keys at all. This greatly simplifies the work that the DBMS must perform, making KV databases extremely fast and scalable for basic processing.

Key-value pairs are typically organised into 'buckets'. A **bucket** can roughly be thought of as the KV database equivalent of a table. A bucket is a logical grouping of keys. Key values must be unique within a bucket, but they can be duplicated across buckets. All data operations are based on the bucket plus the key. In other words, it is not possible to query the data based on anything in the value component of the key-value pair. All queries are performed by specifying the bucket and key.

Operations on KV databases are rather simple – only *get*, *store* and *delete* operations are used. *Get* or *fetch* is used to retrieve the value component of the pair. *Store* is used to place a value in a key. If the bucket + key combination does not exist, then it is added as a new key-value pair. If the bucket + key combination does exist, then the existing value component is replaced with the new value. *Delete* is used to remove a key-value pair. Figure 16.6 shows a customer bucket with three key-value pairs. Since the KV model does not allow queries based on data in the value component, it is not possible to query for a key-value pair based on customer last name, for example. In fact, the KV DBMS does not even know that there is such a thing as a customer last name because it does not understand the content of the value component. An application could issue a *get* command to have the KV DBMS return the key-value pair for bucket customer and key 10011, but it would be up to the application to know how to parse the value component to find the customer's last name, first name and other characteristics. (One important note about Figure 16.6: Be aware that, although key-value pairs appear in tabular form in the figure, the tabular format is just a convenience to help visually distinguish the components. Actual key-value pairs are not stored in a table-like structure.)

FIGURE 16.6 Key-value database storage

Bucket = Customer

Key	Value
10010	"LName Ramas FName Alfred Initial A Areacode 0161 Phone 844-2573 Balance 0"
10011	"LName Dunne FName Leona Initial K Areacode 0181 Phone 894-1238 Balance 0"
10014	"LName Orlando FName Myron Areacode 0161 Phone 222-1672 Balance 0"

16.3.2 Document Databases

Document databases are conceptually similar to key-value databases, and they can almost be considered a subtype of KV databases. A document database is a NoSQL database that stores data in tagged documents in key-value pairs. Unlike a KV database where the value component can contain any type of data, a document database always stores a document in the value component. The document can be in any encoded format, such as XML, **JavaScript Object Notation (JSON)**, or **Binary JSON (BSON)**. Another important difference is that, while KV databases do not attempt to understand the content of the value component, document databases do. Tags are named portions of a document. For example, a document may have tags to identify which text in the document represents the title, author and body of the document. Within the body of the document, there may be additional tags to indicate chapters and sections. Despite the use of tags in documents, document databases are considered schema-less, that is, they do not impose a predefined structure on the data that is stored. For a document database, being schema-less means that, although all documents have tags, not all documents are required to have the same tags, so each document can have its own structure. The tags in a document database are extremely important because they are the basis for most of the additional capabilities that document databases have over KV databases. Tags inside the document are accessible to the DBMS, which makes sophisticated querying possible.

Just as KV databases group key-value pairs into logical groups called buckets, document databases group documents into logical groups called **collections**. While a document may be retrieved by specifying the collection and key, it is also possible to query based on the contents of tags. For example, Figure 16.7 represents the same data from Figure 16.6, but in a tagged format for a document database. Because the DBMS is aware of the tags within the documents, it is possible to write queries that retrieve all of the documents where the Balance tag has the value 0. Document databases even support some aggregate functions such as summing or averaging balances in queries. You learn some basic operations in the MongoDB document database later in this chapter, and Appendix Q, Working with MongoDB, includes a hands-on tutorial (available on online platform).

FIGURE 16.7 Document database tagged format

Collection = Customer

Key	Document
10010	{LName: "Ramas", FName: "Alfred", Initial: "A", Areacode: "0161", Phone: "844-2573", Balance: "0"}
10011	{LName: "Dunne", FName: "Leona", Initial: "K", Areacode: "0181", Phone: "894-1238", Balance: "0"}
10014	{LName: "Orlando", FName: "Myron", Areacode: "0161", Phone: "222-1672", Balance: "0"}

Document databases tend to operate on an implied assumption that a document is relatively self-contained, not a fragment of the data about a given topic. Relational databases decompose complex data in the business environment into a set of related tables. For example, data about orders may be decomposed into customer, invoice, line, and product tables. A document database would expect all of the data related to an order to be in a single order document. Therefore, each order document in an Orders collection would contain data on the customer, the order itself, and the products purchased in that order, all as a single self-contained document. Document databases do not store relationships as perceived in the relational model and generally have no support for join operations.

16.3.3 Column-Oriented Databases

The term '*column-oriented database*' can refer to two different sets of technologies that are often confused with each other. In one sense, column-oriented database or columnar database can refer to traditional, relational database technologies that use **column-centric storage** instead of **row-centric storage**. Relational databases present data in logical tables; however, the data is actually stored in data blocks containing rows of data. All of the data for a given row is stored together in sequence, with many rows in the same data block. If a table has many rows of data, the rows will be spread across many data blocks. Figure 16.8 illustrates a relational table with 10 rows of data that is physically stored across five data blocks. Row-centric storage minimises the number of disk reads necessary to retrieve a row of data. Retrieving one row of data requires accessing just one data block, as shown in Figure 16.8.

FIGURE 16.8 Comparison of row-centric and column-centric storage

CUSTOMER relational table

Cus_Code	Cus_LName	Cus_FName	Cus_City	Cus_Country
10010	Ramas	Alfred	Manchester	UK
10011	Dunne	Leona	Durban	SA
10012	Smith	Kathy	Paris	FR
10013	Olowski	Paul	Manchester	UK
10014	Orlando	Myron		
10015	O'Brian	Amy	Durban	SA
10016	Brown	James		
10017	Williams	George	Utrecht	NL
10018	Farriss	Anne	Cape Town	SA
10019	Smith	Olette	Manchester	UK

Row-centric storage

Block 1
10010,Ramas,Alfred,Manchester,UK 10011,Dunne,Leona,Durban,SA

Block 2
10012,Smith,Kathy,Paris,FR 10013,Olowski,Paul,Manchester,UK

Block 3
10014,Orlando,Myron,NULL,NULL 10015,O'Brian,Amy,Durban,SA

Block 4
10016,Brown,James,NULL,NULL 10017,Williams,George,Utrecht,NL

Block 5
10018,Farriss,Anne,Cape Town,SA 10019,Smith,Olette,Manchester,UK

Column-centric storage

Block 1
10010,10011,10012,10013,10014 10015,10016,10017,10018,10019

Block 2
Ramas,Dunne,Smith,Olowski,Orlando O'Brian,Brown,Williams,Farriss,Smith

Block 3
Alfred,Leona,Kathy,Paul,Myron Amy,James,George,Anne,Olette

Block 4
Manchester,Durban,Paris,Manchester,NULL Durban,NULL,Utrecht,Cape Town,Manchester

Block 5
UK,SA,FR,UK,NULL, SA,NULL,NL,NL,UK

Remember, in transactional systems, normalisation is used to decompose complex data into related tables to reduce redundancy and to improve the speed of rapid manipulation of small sets of data. These manipulations tend to be row-oriented, so row-oriented storage works very well. However, in queries that retrieve a small set of columns across a large set of rows, a large number of disk accesses are required. For example, a query that wants to retrieve only the city and province of every customer will have to access every data block that contains a customer row to retrieve that data. In Figure 16.8, that would mean accessing five data blocks to get the city and province of every customer.

A column-oriented or columnar database stores the data in blocks by column instead of by row. A single customer's data will be spread across several blocks, but all of the data from a single column will be in just a few blocks. In Figure 16.8, all of the city data for customers will be stored together, just as all of the state data will be stored together. In that case, retrieving the city and province for every customer might require accessing only two data blocks. This type of column-centric storage works very well for databases that are primarily used to run queries over few columns but many rows, as is done in many reporting systems and data warehouses. Though Figure 16.8 shows only a few rows and data blocks, it is easy to imagine that the gains would be significant if the table size grew to millions or billions of rows across hundreds of thousands of data blocks. At the same time, column-centric storage would be very inefficient for processing transactions since insert, update, and delete activities would be very disk intensive. It is worth noting that column-centric storage can be achieved within relational database technology, meaning that it still requires structured data and has the advantage of supporting SQL for queries.

The other use of the term *column-oriented database*, also called *column family database*, is to describe a type of NoSQL database that takes the concept of column-centric storage beyond the confines of the relational model. As NoSQL databases, these products do not require the data to conform to predefined structures, nor do they support SQL for queries. This database model originated with Google's Bigtable product. Other column-oriented database products include HBase, described earlier, Hypertable, and Cassandra. Cassandra began as a project at Facebook, but Facebook released it to the open-source community, which has continued to develop Cassandra into one of the most popular column-oriented databases. A **column family database** is a NoSQL database that organises data in key-value pairs with keys mapped to a set of columns in the value component. While column family databases use many of the same terms as relational databases, the terms don't mean quite the same things. Fortunately, the column family databases are conceptually simple and are conceptually close enough to the relational model that your understanding of the relational model can help you understand the column family model. A column is a key-value pair that is similar to a cell of data in a relational database. The key is the name of the column, and the value component is the data that is stored in that column. Therefore, 'cus_lname: Ramas' is a column; *cus_lname* is the name of the column, and *Ramas* is the data value in the column. Similarly, 'cus_city: Cape Town' is another column, with *cus_city* as the column name and *Cape Town* as the data value.

NOTE

Even though column family databases do not (yet) support standard SQL, Cassandra developers have created a Cassandra query language (CQL). It is similar to SQL in many respects and is one of the more compelling reasons for adopting Cassandra.

As more columns are added, it becomes clear that some columns form natural groups, such as cus_fname, cus_lname, and cus_initial, which would logically group together to form a customer's name. Similarly, cus_street, cus_city, cus_province and cus_postcode would logically group together to form a customer's address. These groupings are used to create super columns. A **super column** is a group of columns that are logically related. Recall the discussion in Chapter 4 about simple and composite attributes in the entity relationship model. In many cases, super columns can be thought of as the composite attribute and the columns that compose the super column as the simple attributes. Just as not all simple attributes have to belong to a composite attribute, not all columns have to belong to a super column. Although this analogy is helpful in many contexts, it is not perfect. It is possible to group columns into a super column that logically belongs together for application processing reasons but does not conform to the relational idea of a composite attribute.

Row keys are created to identify objects in the environment. All of the columns or super columns that describe these objects are grouped together to create a **column family**; therefore, a column family is conceptually similar to a table in the relational model. Although a column family is similar in concept to a relational table, Figure 16.9 shows that it is structurally very different. Notice in Figure 16.9 that each row key in the column family can have different columns.

NOTE

A column family can be composed of columns or super columns, but it cannot contain both.

FIGURE 16.9 Column family database

Column Family Name	CUSTOMERS	
Key	Rowkey 1	
Columns	City	Manchester
	Fname	Alfred
	Lname	Ramas
	Country	UK
Key	Rowkey 2	
Columns	Balance	345.86
	Fname	Kathy
	Lname	Smith
Key	Rowkey 3	
Columns	Company	Local Markets, Inc.
	Lname	Dunne

16.3.4 Graph Databases

A **graph database** is a NoSQL database based on graph theory to store data about relationship-rich environments. Graph theory is a mathematical and computer science field that models relationships, or *edges*, between objects called nodes. Modelling and storing data about relationships is the focus of graph databases. Graph theory is a well-established field of study going back hundreds of years. As a result, creating a database model based on graph theory immediately provides a rich source for algorithms and applications that have helped graph databases gain in sophistication very quickly. As it also happens that much of the data explosion over the past decade has involved data that is relationship-rich, graph databases have been poised to experience significant interest in the business environment.

Interest in graph databases originated in the area of social networks. Social networks include a wide range of applications beyond the typical Facebook, Twitter and Instagram examples that immediately come to mind. Dating websites, knowledge management, logistics and routing, master data management, and identity and access management, are all areas that rely heavily on tracking complex relationships among objects. Of course, relational databases support relationships too. One of the great advances of the relational model was that relationships are easy to maintain. A relationship between a customer and an agent is as easy to implement in the relational model as adding a foreign key to create a common attribute, and the customer and agent rows are related by having the same value in the common attributes. If the customer changes to a different agent, then simply changing the value in the foreign key will change the relationship between the rows to maintain the integrity of the data. The relational model does all of these things very well. However, what if we want a 'like' option so customers can 'like' agents on our website? This would require a structural change to the database to add a new foreign key to support this second relationship. Next, what if the company wants to allow customers on its website to 'friend' each other so a customer can see which agents their friends like, or the friends of their friends? In social networking data, there can be dozens of different relationships among individuals that need to be tracked, and often the relationships are tracked many layers deep (e.g., friends, friends of friends, and friends of friends of friends). This results in a situation where the relationships become just as important as the data itself. This is the area where graph databases shine.

The primary components of graph databases are nodes, edges and properties, as shown in Figure 16.10. A node corresponds to the idea of a relational entity instance. The **node** is a specific instance of something we want to keep data about. Each node (circle) in Figure 16.10 represents a single agent. Properties are like attributes; they are the data that we need to store about the node. All agent nodes might have properties like first name and last name, but not all nodes are required to have the same properties. An **edge** is a relationship between nodes. Edges (shown as arrows in Figure 16.10) can be in one direction, or they can be bidirectional.

For example, in Figure 16.10, the *friends* relationships are bidirectional, but the *likes* relationships are not. Note that edges can also have **properties**. In Figure 16.10, the date on which customer Alfred Ramas *liked* agent Alex Alby is recorded in the graph database. A query in a graph database is called a **traversal**. Instead of *querying the database*, the correct terminology would be *traversing the graph*. Graph databases excel at traversals that focus on relationships between nodes, such as shortest path and degree of connectedness.

Graph databases share some characteristics with other NoSQL databases in that graph databases do not force data to fit predefined structures, do not support SQL, and are optimised to provide velocity of processing, at least for relationship-intensive data. However, other key characteristics do not apply to graph databases. Graph databases do not scale out very well to clusters due to differences in aggregate awareness.

FIGURE 16.10 Graph database representation

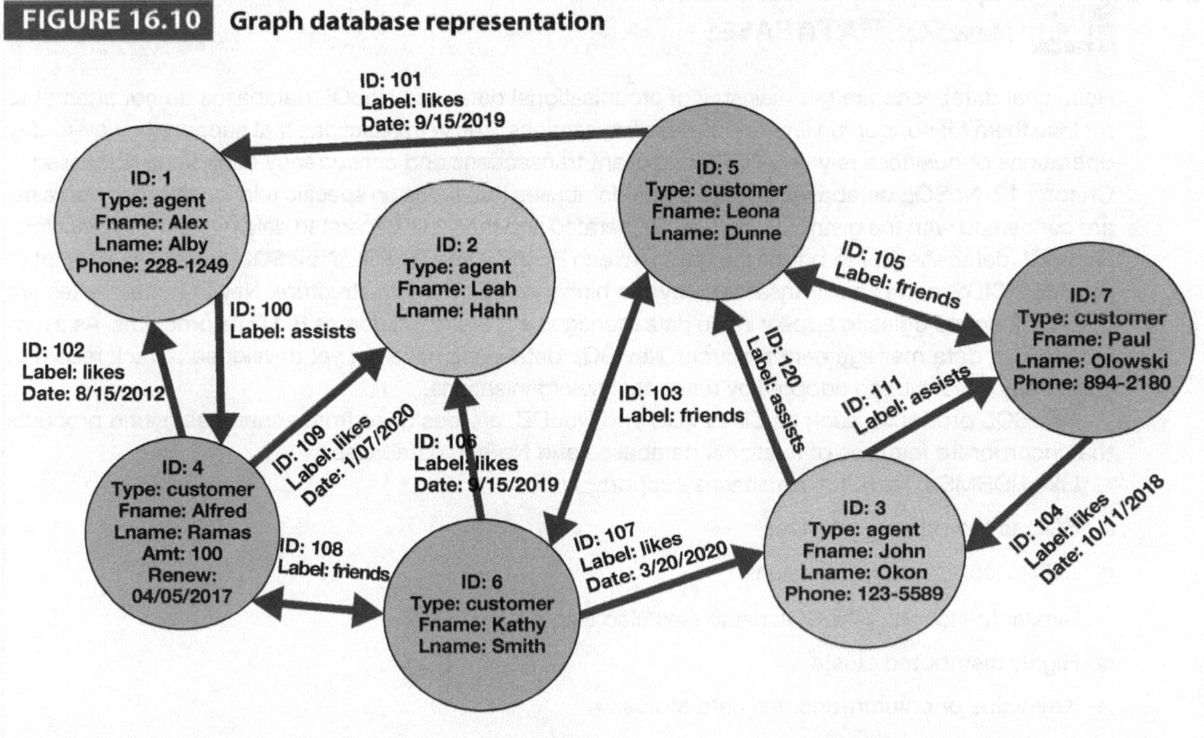

16

16.3.5 Aggregate Awareness

Key-value, document and column family databases are **aggregate aware**. Aggregate aware means that the data is collected or aggregated around a central topic or entity. For example, a blog website might organise data around individual blog posts. All data related to each blog post are aggregated into a single denormalised collection that might include data about the blog post (title, content and date posted), the poster (user name and screen name), and all comments made on the post (comment content and commenter's user name and screen name). In a normalised, relational database, this same data might call for USER, BLOGPOST and COMMENT tables. Determining the best central entity for forming aggregates is one of the most important tasks in designing most NoSQL databases, and is determined by how the application will use the data.

The aggregate-aware database models achieve clustering efficiency by making each piece of data relatively independent. That allows a key-value pair to be stored on one node in the cluster without the DBMS needing to associate it with another key-value pair that may be on a different node on the cluster. The greater the number of nodes involved in a data operation, the greater the need for coordination and centralised control of resources. Separating independent pieces of data often called *shards* across nodes in the cluster, is what allows NoSQL databases to scale out so effectively.

Graph databases, like relational databases, are **aggregate ignorant**. Aggregate-ignorant models do not organise the data into collections based on a central entity. Data about each topic is stored separately and joins are used to aggregate individual pieces of data as needed. Aggregate-ignorant databases, therefore, tend to be more flexible at allowing applications to combine data elements in a greater variety of ways. Graph databases specialise in highly related data, not independent pieces of data. As a result, graph databases tend to perform best in centralised or lightly clustered environments, similar to relational databases.

16.4 NewSQL DATABASES

Relational databases are the mainstay of organisational data, and NoSQL databases do not attempt to replace them for supporting line-of-business transactions. These transactions that support the day-to-day operations of business rely on ACIDS-compliant transactions and concurrency control, as discussed in Chapter 12. NoSQL databases (except graph databases that focus on specific relationship-rich domains) are concerned with the distribution of user-generated and machine-generated data over massive clusters. NewSQL databases try to bridge the gap between RDBMS and NoSQL. **NewSQL** databases attempt to provide ACIDS-compliant transactions over a highly distributed infrastructure. NewSQL databases are the latest technologies to appear in the data management arena to address Big Data problems. As a new category of data management products, NewSQL databases have not yet developed a track record of success and have been adopted by relatively few organisations.

NewSQL products, such as ClustrixDB and NuoDB, are designed from scratch as hybrid products that incorporate features of relational databases and NoSQL databases.

Like RDBMSs, NewSQL databases support:

- SQL as the primary interface
- ACIDS-compliant transactions.

16

Similar to NoSQL, NewSQL databases also support:

- Highly distributed clusters
- Key-value or column-oriented data stores.

As expected, no technology can perfectly provide the advantages of both RDBMS and NoSQL, so NewSQL has disadvantages (the CAP theorem covered in Chapter 14 still applies!). Principally, the disadvantages that have been discovered centre on NewSQL's heavy use of in-memory storage. Critics point to the fact that this can jeopardise the 'durability' component of ACIDS. Further, the ability to handle vast data sets can be impacted by the reliance on in-memory structures because there are practical limits to the amount of data that can be held in memory. Although in theory NewSQL databases should be able to scale out significantly, in practice little has been done to scale beyond a few dozen data nodes. While this is a marked improvement over traditional RDBMS distribution, it is far from the hundreds of nodes used by NoSQL databases.

A few NoSQL database products have experienced success in niche markets by providing solutions to specific business needs. The following sections provide a brief introduction to two widely used NoSQL databases, MongoDB and Neo4j. These two databases provide a set of functionality not yet matched by traditional relational databases. You can find more detailed hands-on examples of these databases in Appendixes Q and R, respectively, available on the online platform.

16.5 WORKING WITH DOCUMENT DATABASES USING MongoDB

This section introduces you to MongoDB, a popular document database. Among the NoSQL databases currently available, MongoDB has been one of the most successful in penetrating the database market. Therefore, learning the basics of working with MongoDB can be quite useful for database professionals.

NOTE

MongoDB is a product of MongoDB, Inc. In this book, we use the Community Server v.4.0.9 edition, which is open source and available free of charge from MongoDB, Inc. New versions are released regularly. This version of MongoDB is available for Windows, MacOS and Linux from the MongoDB website.

The name, MongoDB, comes from the word *humongous* as its developers intended their new product to support extremely large data sets. It is designed for:

- high availability
- high scalability
- high performance.

Online Content An expanded set of hands-on exercises using MongoDB can be found in Appendix Q, Working with MongoD, available on the online platform.

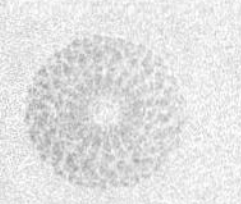

As a document database, MongoDB is schema-less and aggregate aware. Recall that being schema-less means that all documents are not required to conform to the same structure, and the structure of documents does not have to be declared ahead of time. Aggregate aware means that the documents encapsulate all relevant data related to a central entity within the same document. Data is stored in documents, documents of a similar type are stored in collections, and related collections are stored in a database.

To the users, the documents appear as JSON files, which makes them easy to read and easy to manipulate in a variety of programming languages. Recall that JavaScript Object Notation (JSON) is a data interchange format that represents data as a logical object. Objects are enclosed in curly brackets {} that contain key-value pairs. A single JSON object can contain many *key:value* pairs separated by commas. A simple JSON document to store data on a book might look like this:

```
{_id: 101, title: 'Database Principles'}
```

16

This document contains two *key:value* pairs:

- *_id* is a key with 101 as the associated value
- *title* is a key with 'Database Principles' as the associated value.

The *value* component may have multiple values that would be appropriate for a given key. In the previous example, adding a *key:value* pair for authors could have the values 'Coronel' and 'Morris'. When there are multiple values for a single key, an array is used. Arrays in JSON are placed inside square brackets []. For example, the above document could be expanded to:

```
{_id: 101, title: 'Database Systems', author: ['Coronel', 'Morris', 'Crockett', 'Blewett']}
```

When JSON documents are intended to be read by humans, they are often displayed with each *key:value* pair on a separate line to improve readability, such as:

```
{
_id: 101,
title: 'Database Principles',
author: ['Coronel', 'Morris', 'Crockett', 'Blewett']
}
```

MongoDB databases are comprised of collections of documents. Each MongoDB server can host many databases. When connected to the MongoDB server, the first task is to specify with which database object you want to work. A list of the databases available on the server can be retrieved with the command:

```
show dbs
```

All data manipulation commands in MongoDB must be directed to a particular database. Creating a new database in MongoDB is as easy as issuing the *use* command.

```
use fact
```

The use command informs the server which database is to be the target of the commands that follow. If there is a database with the name specified, then that database will be used for the subsequent commands. If there is not a database with that name, then one is created automatically.

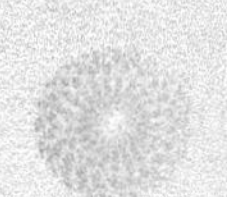

Online Content The documents for the *fact* database are available as a collection of JSON documents that can be directly imported into MongoDB. The file is named 'Ch16_Fact.json' and is available on the online platform.

16.5.1 Importing Documents in MongoDB

16

Remember that a MongoDB database is a collection of documents. The collection of documents we will use to illustrate a sample MongoDB query is based on a fact database and a patron collection. Free Access to Computer Technology (FACT) is a small library run by the Computer Information Systems department at Tiny College. The portion of the model that is being used here consists of documents with *patron* as the central entity. The documents have the following structure:

{_id: <system-generated ObjectID,

display: <the patron's full name as it will be displayed to users>,

fname: <patron's first name in all lowercase letters>,

lname: <patron's last name in all lowercase letters>,

type: <either 'faculty' or 'student'>,

age: <patron's age in years only if the patron is a student>,

checkouts: <an array of objects for the patron's checkout history>

[id: <an assigned number for this checkout object>,

year: <the year in which this checkout occurred>,

month:<the month in which this checkout occurred>,

day: <the day of the month in which this checkout occurred>,

book:<the book number of the book for this checkout>,

title:<the title of the book>,

pubyear: <the year the book was published>,

subject:<the subject of the book>]

}

Notice that the patron document collection contains information about each patron and all the books that the patron has checked out. Notice also that the checkouts subdocument is an array of objects under each patron. Finally, note that the patron's name is stored twice, once with first and last name together with capitalisation, and again with first name and last name in all lowercase letters in separate *key:value* pairs. The reason for this is that all searches in MongoDB are case sensitive by default, storing the faculty name twice facilitates searches.

NOTE

The database can be created using the Ch16_Fact.json file by using the following command at an operating system command prompt (note that the command is for use at a command prompt in the OS, not inside the MongoDB shell).

mongoimport–db fact–collection patron–type json–file Ch16_Fact.json

Mongoimport is an executable program that is installed with MongoDB that is used to import data into a MongoDB database. The above command specifies that the imported documents should be placed in the fact database (if one does not exist, it will be created) and in the patron collection (if one does not exist, it will be created). Mongoimport can work with different file types such as CSV files and JSON files. The type parameter specifies that the imported documents are already in JSON format. The file parameter specifies the name of the file to be imported. If your copy of the Ch16_Fact.json file is not in the current directory for your command prompt, you will need to provide an appropriate path for the file location.

16.5.2 Example of a MongoDB Query Using find()

Once the patron collection is imported, you are ready to query the MongoDB database. In order to manipulate collections, a MongoDB database uses methods. **Methods** are programmed functions to manipulate objects. Examples of such methods are createCollection(), getName(), insert(), update(), find(), and so on. The **find()** method retrieves objects from a collection that match the restrictions provided. The find() method has two parameters: find({<query>},{<projection>})

The <query> parameter specifies the criteria to retrieve the collection objects. The <projection> parameter is optional and specifies which *key:value* pairs to return. The value with each key in the projection object is either 0 (do not return), or 1 (return).

For example, Figure 16.11 shows the code to retrieve the _id, display the name and age for patrons that either have the last name 'barry' and are faculty, or have the last name 'hays' and are under 30 years old:

```
db.patron.find({$or: [
            {$and: [{lname: "barry"}, {type: "faculty"}]},
            {$and: [{lname: "hays"}, {age: {$lt: 30}}]}
            ]},
    {display: 1, age: 1, type: 1}).pretty()
```

FIGURE 16.11 **Example of MongoDB document query**

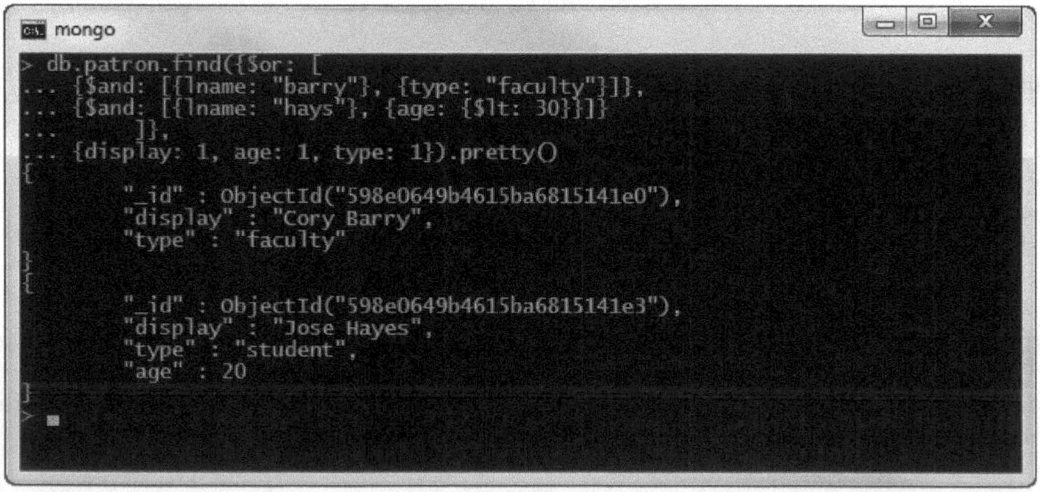

```
mongo
> db.patron.find({$or: [
... {$and: [{lname: "barry"}, {type: "faculty"}]},
... {$and: [{lname: "hays"}, {age: {$lt: 30}}]}
...     ]},
... {display: 1, age: 1, type: 1}).pretty()
{
        "_id" : ObjectId("598e0649b4615ba6815141e0"),
        "display" : "Cory Barry",
        "type" : "faculty"
}
{
        "_id" : ObjectId("598e0649b4615ba6815141e3"),
        "display" : "Jose Hayes",
        "type" : "student",
        "age" : 20
}
>
```

Notice also that this example uses the pretty() method. The **pretty()** method is a MongoDB method used to improve readability of the documents by placing *key:value* pairs on separate lines.

MongoDB is a powerful document database that is being adopted by many organisations. It was originally designed to support Web-based operations and, as such, it draws heavily on JavaScript for the structure of its documents and for its query language.

NOTE

We have introduced you to the basic concepts of a MongoDB collection and how to query it using the find() method here, but there is much more to learn if you are interested in pursuing a career in document databases. Appendix Q, Working with MongoDB, contains a more thorough tutorial on how to use this powerful document database and is located on the online platform of this book.

16.6 WORKING WITH GRAPH DATABASES USING Neo4j

Even though Neo4j is not yet as widely adopted as MongoDB, it has been one of the fastest growing NoSQL databases, with thousands of adopters including LinkedIn and Walmart. Neo4j is a graph database. Like relational databases, graph databases still work with concepts similar to entities and relationships. However, in relational databases, the focus is primarily on the entities. In graph databases, the focus is on the relationships.

Online Content An expanded set of hands-on exercises using Neo4j can be found in Appendix R, Working with Neo4j, available at on the online platform of this book.

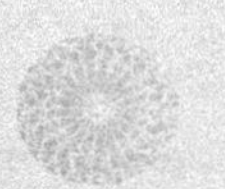

Graph databases are used in environments with complex relationships among entities. Graph databases, therefore, are heavily reliant on interdependence among their data, which is why they are the least able to scale out among the NoSQL database types. Consider an example of a social network such as LinkedIn that connects people. A person can be friends with many other people, each of whom can be friends with many people. In terms of a relational model, we could represent this as a person entity with a many-to-many unary relationship. In implementation, we would create a bridge for the relationship and end up with a two-entity solution. Imagine the person table has 10 000 people (rows) in it, and those people average 30 friends each so that the bridge table has 300 000 rows. A query to retrieve a person and the names of his or her friends would require two joins: one to link the person to their friends in the bridge and another to retrieve those friends' names from the person entity. A relational database can perform this query quickly. The problem comes when we look beyond that direct friend relationship. What if we want to know about friends of friends? Then, another join connecting the bridge table to itself will have to be included. Joining a 300 000-row table to itself is not trivial (there are 90 billion rows in the Cartesian product that the DBMS engine is contending with to construct the join). The relational database can handle that volume, but it is starting to slow. Now query for friends of friends of friends. This requires joining yet another copy of the bridge table so the query, producing a Cartesian product with 2.7×10^{16} rows! As you can see, by the time we are working the 'six degrees of separation' types of problems, relational database technology is unable to keep up. These types of highly interdependent queries about relationships that could take hours to run in a relational database, are the forte of graph databases. Graph databases can complete these queries in seconds. In fact, you often encounter the phrase 'minutes to milliseconds' when adopters describe their use of graph databases.

NOTE

Neo4j is a product of Neo4j, Inc. There are multiple versions of Neo4j available. In this book, we use the Community Server v.3.5.5 edition, which is open source and available free of charge from Neo4j, Inc. New versions are released regularly. This version of Neo4j is available for Windows (64-bit and 32-bit), MacOS and Linux from the Neo4j website.

Neo4j provides several interface options. It was originally designed with Java programming in mind, and optimised for interaction through a Java API. Later releases have included the options for a Neo4j command shell, similar to the MongoDB shell, a REST API for website interaction, and a graphical, browser-based interface for intuitive interactive sessions. In this section, you will use the Web browser interface.

16.6.1 Creating Nodes in Neo4j

NOTE

An instance of Neo4j can have only one active database at a time. However, the data path for the database can be changed in the configuration before starting the Neo4j server. If the data path is changed to point at an empty directory, Neo4j automatically creates all needed files in that directory on start-up. By keeping each database in a separate folder and changing the data path before starting the server, multiple databases can be maintained for practice.

As you learnt earlier in the chapter, graph databases are composed of nodes and edges. Roughly speaking, nodes in a graph database correspond to entity instances in a relational database. In Neo4j, a label is the closest thing to the concept of a table from the relational model. A label is a tag that is used to associate a collection of nodes as being of the same type or belonging to the same group. Just as entity instances have values for attributes to describe the characteristics of that instance, a node has properties that describe the characteristics of that node. Unlike the relational model, graph databases are schema-less so nodes with the same label are not required to have the same set of properties. In fact, nodes can have more than one label if they logically belong to more than one group.

Consider an example of a club for food critics where members share reviews of area restaurants. Each club member would be represented as a node. Each restaurant would be represented as a node. Although both members and restaurants are nodes, the members are one kind or type of node while the restaurants are another kind or type of node. To help distinguish the types of nodes both in code and in the minds of users and programmers, you can use labels. The nodes for members might get a Member label, and nodes for restaurants get a Restaurant label. This makes it more convenient in code to distinguish between the types of nodes.

16

The interactive, declarative query language in Neo4j is called **Cypher**. Cypher is declarative, like SQL, even though the syntax is very different. However, being a declarative language instead of an imperative language, Cypher is very easy to learn and a few simple commands can be used to perform basic database processing.

Nodes and relationships are created using a CREATE command. The following code creates a member node:

```
CREATE (:Member {mid: 1, fname: "Phillip", lname: "Stallings"})
```

> **NOTE**
>
> Neo4j creates an internal ID field named <id> for every node and relationship; however, this field is for internal use within the database for storage algorithms. It is not intended to be, and should not be used as, a unique key.

The previous command creates a node with the Member label. That node was given the properties *mid* with the value 1, *fname* with the value 'Phillip' and the property *lname* with the value 'Stallings'. The *mid* property is being used as a member ID field to identify the members. If there is not already a label named Member, it is created at the same time the node is.

16.6.2 Retrieving Node Data with MATCH and WHERE

Let's start by issuing a simple command to retrieve our single member node:

```
MATCH (m)
RETURN(m)
```

In this case, this command retrieves all of the nodes in the graph database. In this case, the only node is for Phillip Stallings so that is the only node to display. If many nodes existed, we could have used a command such as the following to retrieve Phillip Stallings:

```
MATCH (m {fname: "Phillip"}), (x {lname: "Stallings"})
RETURN m
```

In this case, the properties and values were embedded in the node. Alternatively, the use of a WHERE clause allows for more complex criteria, such as using comparison operators other than equality. The previous command can be rewritten using a WHERE clause as follows:

```
MATCH (m)
WHERE m.fname = "Phillip" AND m.lname = "Stallings"
RETURN m
```

Online Content The 'Ch16_FCC.txt' file used in the following section is available on the online platform of this book. The contents of the file should be copied and pasted into the Neo4j editor bar and executed using the play button in the interface.

The following section assumes that you have preloaded the Neo4j food critics database, using the Ch16_FCC.txt file, available to you online. This file contains a single, massive command that creates 78 additional members, 43 owners, 67 restaurants, and 8 cuisines. Providing the code as a single command is necessary if you are using the browser interface. Because it is designed for interactive use, it does not support script files with multiple commands. The command includes many statements that may seem unfamiliar to you. To learn more about such commands, please refer to Appendix R, Working with Neo4j, available on the online platform.

16

16.6.3 Retrieving Relationship Data with MATCH and WHERE

Beyond retrieving nodes, it is possible to retrieve data based on the relationships between nodes. As stated earlier, focusing on relationships is the primary strength of graph databases. For example, the following command retrieves every member who has reviewed the restaurant 'Tofu for You' and rated the restaurant a '4' on taste:

```
MATCH (m :Member) – [r :REVIEWED {taste: 4}] – > (res :Restaurant {name: "Tofu for You"})
RETURN m, r, res
```

When retrieving data based on a relationship, criteria for the direction of the relationship and any data characteristics of the relationship can be specified in the query. In this example, there are two nodes (*m* and *res*) and a relationship that joins them (*r*). In this case, we are matching all nodes that are members, the one node that is named 'Tofu for You', and all relationships that are labelled as REVIEWED and have a property named 'taste' equal to the value '4'.

You could add comparisons and logical operators using the WHERE clause, as shown in the following command, with the results shown in Figure 16.12:

```
MATCH (m: Member) – [r :REVIEWED] – > (res :Restaurant)

WHERE (r.value > 4 OR r.taste > 4 ) AND res.state = "KY"

RETURN m, r, res
```

FIGURE 16.12 Neo4J query using MATCH/WHERE/RETURN

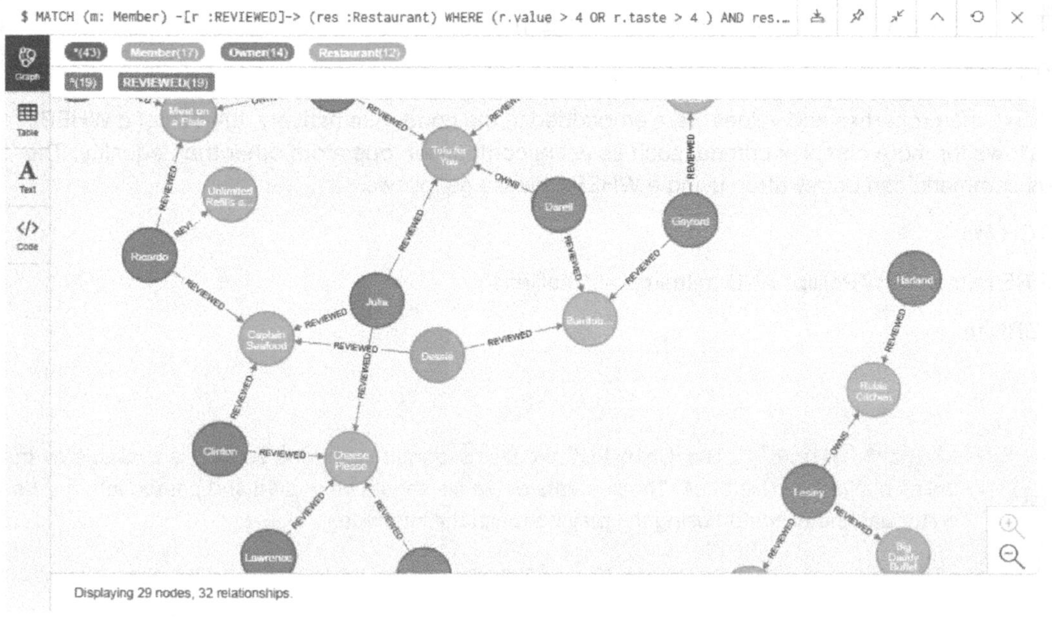

The command retrieves all members who have reviewed any restaurant in Johannesburg and rated the restaurant greater than '4', on 'value' or 'taste'. Notice that using the WHERE clause allows the use of inequalities such as greater than, and logical operators.

> **NOTE**
>
> This section is just a very brief introduction to Neo4j, but there is much more to learn if you are interested in pursuing a career in graph databases. Appendix R, Working with Neo4j, contains a more thorough tutorial on how to use this powerful graph database and is located on the online platform of this book.

In Chapter 15, you learnt about data warehouses and star schemas for modelling and storing decision support data. In this chapter, you have added to that by exploring the vast stores of data that organisations are collecting in unstructured formats and the technologies that make that data available to users. Data analytics, discussed in Chapter 15, is used to extract knowledge from all of these sources of data – NoSQL databases, Hadoop data stores, and data warehouses – to provide decision support to all organisational users. Even though relational databases are still dominant for most business transactions, and will continue to be so for the foreseeable future, the growth of Big Data must be accommodated. There is too much value in the immense amounts of unstructured data available to organisations for them to ignore it. Database professionals must be informed about these new approaches to data management to ensure that the right tool is used for each job.

SUMMARY

- Big Data is characterised by data of such volume, velocity and/or variety that the relational model struggles to adapt to it. Volume refers to the quantity of data that must be stored. Velocity refers to both the speed at which data is entering storage as well as the speed with which it must be processed. Variety refers to the lack of uniformity in the structure of the data being stored. As a result of Big Data, organisations are having to employ a variety of data storage solutions that include technologies, in addition to relational databases, a situation referred to as polyglot persistence.
- Volume, velocity, variety, veracity and value are collectively referred to as the 5 Vs of Big Data. However, these are not the only characteristics of Big Data to which data administrators must be sensitive. Additional Vs that have been suggested by the data management industry include variability and visualisation. Variability is the variation in the meaning of data that can occur over time. Further, visualisation is the requirement that the data must be able to be presented in a manner that makes it comprehensible to decision makers. Most of these additional Vs are not unique to Big Data. There are also concerns for data in relational databases.
- The Hadoop framework has quickly emerged as a standard for the physical storage of Big Data. The primary components of the framework include the Hadoop Distributed File System (HDFS) and MapReduce. HDFS is a coordinated technology for reliably distributing data over a very large cluster of commodity servers. MapReduce is a complementary process for distributing data processing across distributed data. One of the key concepts for MapReduce is to move the computations to the data instead of moving the data to the computations. MapReduce works by combining the functions of *map*, which distributes subtasks to the cluster servers that hold data to be processed, and *reduce*, which combines the map results into a single result set. The Hadoop framework also supports an entire ecosystem of additional tools and technologies, such as Hive, Pig and Flume, which work together to produce a complex system of Big Data processing.
- NoSQL is a broad term that refers to any of several non-relational database approaches to data management. Most NoSQL databases fall into one of four categories: key-value databases,

document databases, column-oriented databases, or graph databases. Due to the wide variability of products under the NoSQL umbrella, these categories are not necessarily all-encompassing, and many products can fit into multiple categories.

- Key-value databases store data in key-value pairs. In a key-value pair, the value of the key must be known to the DBMS, but the data in the value component can be of any type, and the DBMS makes no attempt to understand the meaning of the data in it. These types of databases are very fast when the data is completely independent, and the application programs can be relied on to understand the meaning of the data.
- Document databases also store data in key-value pairs, but the data in the value component is an encoded document. The document must be encoded using tags, such as in XML or JSON. The DBMS is aware of the tags in the documents, which makes querying on tags possible. Document databases expect documents to be self-contained and relatively independent of one another.
- Column-oriented databases, also called column family databases, organise data into key-value pairs in which the value component is composed of a series of columns, which themselves are key-value pairs. Columns can be grouped into super columns, similar to a composite attribute in the relational model being composed of simple attributes. All objects of a similar type are identified as rows, given a row key, and placed within a column family. Rows within a column family are not required to have the same structure, that is, they are not required to have the same columns.
- Graph databases are based on graph theory and represent data through nodes, edges and properties. A node is similar to an instance of an entity in the relational model. Edges are the relationships between nodes. Both nodes and edges can have properties, which are attributes that describe the corresponding node or edge. Graph databases excel at tracking data that is highly interrelated, such as social media data. Due to the many relationships among the nodes, it is difficult to distribute a graph database across a cluster in a highly distributed manner.
- NewSQL databases attempt to integrate features of both RDBMS (providing ACIDS-compliant transactions) and NoSQL databases (using a highly distributed infrastructure).
- MongoDB is a document database that stores documents in JSON format. The documents can be created, updated, deleted and queried using a JavaScript-like language, named MongoDB Query Language. Data retrieval is done primarily through the find() method.
- Neo4j is a graph database that stores data as nodes and relationships, both of which can contain properties to describe them. Neo4j databases are queried using Cypher, a declarative language that shares many commonalities with SQL, but is still significantly different in many ways. Data retrieval is done primarily through the MATCH command to perform pattern matching.

KEY TERMS

aggregate aware
aggregate ignorant
algorithm
batch processing
block report
BSON (Binary JSON)
bucket
collection
column-centric storage
column family
column family database
Cypher
document database
edge
feedback loop processing
find()
graph database
Hadoop Distributed File System (HDFS)
heartbeat
job tracker
JSON (JavaScript Object Notation)
key-value (KV) database
map

mapper
MapReduce
method
NewSQL
node
NoSQL
polyglot persistence
pretty()
properties
reduce
reducer
row-centric storage
scaling out
scaling up
semi-structured data
sentiment analysis
stream processing
structured data
super column
task tracker
traversal
unstructured data
value
variability
variety
velocity
veracity
visualisation
volume

REVIEW QUESTIONS

1 What is Big Data? Give a brief definition.

2 What are the traditional '3 Vs' of Big Data? Briefly, define each.

3 Explain why companies like Google and Amazon were among the first to address the Big Data problem.

4 Explain the difference between *scaling up* and *scaling out*.

5 What is stream processing, and why is it sometimes necessary?

6 How is stream processing different from feedback loop processing?

7 Explain why veracity, value and visualisation can be said to apply to relational databases as well as Big Data.

8 What is polyglot persistence, and why is it considered a new approach?

9 What are the key assumptions made by the Hadoop Distributed File System approach?

10 What is the difference between a name node and a data node in HDFS?

11 Explain the basic steps in MapReduce processing.

12 Briefly explain how HDFS and MapReduce are complementary to each other.

13 What are the four basic categories of NoSQL databases?

14 How are the value components of a key-value database and a document database different?

15 Briefly explain the difference between row-centric and column-centric data storage.

16 What is the difference between a column and a super column in a column family database?

17 Explain why graph databases tend to struggle with scaling out.

18 Explain what it means for a database to be aggregate aware.

CHAPTER 17

Database Connectivity and Web Technologies

IN THIS CHAPTER, YOU WILL LEARN:

- About the different database connectivity technologies
- What Extensible Markup Language (XML) is and why it is important for Web database development
- About the functionality and features of various database connectivity technologies: ODBC, OLE, ADO.NET and JDBC
- Which services are provided by Web application servers
- About cloud computing and how it enables the database-as-a-service model
- About the Semantic Web and how it describes concepts in a way that computers can actually understand

PREVIEW

Databases are the central repository for critical data generated by business applications, including newer channels such as the Web and mobile devices. To be useful universally, the data must be available to all business users. Those users may access the data via a spreadsheet, a user-developed Visual Basic application, a Web front end, and newer technologies such as iPads, iPhones and Android phones. In this chapter, you learn about the architectures used by applications to connect to databases.

The internet has changed how organisations of all types and origins operate. For example, buying goods and services via the internet has become commonplace. In today's environment, interconnectivity occurs not only between an application and the database, but also between applications interchanging messages and data. Extensible Markup Language (XML) provides a standard way of exchanging unstructured and structured data between applications.

Companies that want to integrate database and Web technologies within their applications portfolio can now choose from a range of internet-based services. Therefore, you will learn how organisations can benefit from cloud computing by leveraging the database-as-a-service model within their IT environments. These cloud-based services offer a quick and cost efficient way to provide new business services.

17.1 DATABASE CONNECTIVITY

Database connectivity refers to the mechanisms through which application programs connect and communicate with data repositories. Databases store data in persistent storage structures so that they can be retrieved at a later time for processing. As you have already learnt, the database management system (DBMS) functions as an intermediary between the data (stored in the database) and the end user's applications. Before learning about the various data connectivity options, it is important to review some important fundamentals you have learnt in this book:

- DBMSs provide means to interact with the data in their databases. This could be in the form of administrative tools and data manipulation tools. DBMSs also provide a proprietary way for external application programs to connect to the database by the means of an application programming interface. (See Chapter 1, The Database Approach.)
- Modern DBMSs have the option to store data locally or distributed in multiple locations. Locally stored data resides in the same processing host as the DBMS. A distributed database stores data in multiple geographically distributed nodes with data management capability. (See Chapter 14, Distributed Databases.)
- The database connectivity software we discuss in this chapter supports Structured Query Language (SQL) as the standard data manipulation language. However, depending on the type of database model, some database connectivity interfaces may support other proprietary data manipulation languages.
- Database connectivity software works in a client/server architecture, in which processing tasks are split among multiple software layers. In this model, the multiple layers exchange control messages and data. (See Chapter 14, Distributed Databases, and Appendix F, Client/Server Systems, located on the online platform of this book, for more information on this topic.) To better understand database connectivity software, we use client/server concepts in which an application is broken down into interconnected functional layers. In the case of database connectivity software, you could break down its basic functionality into three broad layers:

    1. A data layer where the data resides. You can think of this layer as the actual data repository interface. This layer resides closest to the database itself and is normally provided by the DBMS vendor.
    2. A middle layer that manages multiple connectivity and data transformation issues. This layer is in charge of dealing with data logic issues, data transformations, ways to 'talk' to the database below it, and so on. This would also include translating multiple data manipulation languages to the native language supported by the specific data repository.
    3. A top layer that interfaces with the actual external application. This mostly comes in the form of an application programming interface that publishes specific protocols for the external programs to interact with the data.

From the previous discussion, you can understand why database connectivity software is also known as **database middleware** – because it provides an interface between the application program and the database or data repository. The data repository, also known as the data source, represents the data management application, such as Oracle, SQL Server, IBM DB2, or NoSQL that will be used to store the data generated by the application program. Ideally, a data source or data repository can be located anywhere and hold any type of data. Furthermore, the same database connectivity middleware can support multiple data sources at the same time. For example, the data source could be a relational database, a NoSQL database, a spreadsheet, a Microsoft Access database, or a text data file. This multidata-source-type capability is based on the support of well-established data access standards. The need for standard database connectivity interfaces cannot be overstated. Just as SQL has become the de facto data manipulation language, a standard database connectivity interface is necessary for enabling applications to connect to data repositories. Although there are many ways to achieve database connectivity, this section covers only the following interfaces:

- Native SQL connectivity (vendor provided)
- Microsoft's Open Database Connectivity (ODBC), Data Access Objects (DAO) and Remote Data Objects (RDO)
- Microsoft's Object Linking and Embedding for Database (OLE-DB)
- Microsoft's ActiveX Data Objects (ADO.NET)
- Oracle's Java Database Connectivity (JDBC)

The data connectivity interfaces illustrated here are dominant players in the market and, more importantly, they enjoy the support of most database vendors. In fact, ODBC, OLE-DB, and ADO.NET form the backbone of Microsoft's Universal Data Access (UDA) architecture, a collection of technologies used to access any type of data source and manage the data through a common interface. As you will see, Microsoft's database connectivity interfaces have evolved over time: each interface builds on top of the other, thus providing enhanced functionality, features, flexibility and support.

17.1.1 Native SQL Connectivity

Most DBMS vendors provide their own methods for connecting to their databases, although they support more standard interfaces as well. Native SQL connectivity refers to the connection interface that is provided by the database vendor and is unique to that vendor. The best example of that type of native interface is the Oracle RDBMS. To connect a client application to an Oracle database, you must install and configure the Oracle's SQL*Net interface in the client computer. Figure 17.1 shows the configuration of Oracle SQL*Net interface on the client computer.

Native database connectivity interfaces are optimised for 'their' DBMS, and these interfaces support access to most, if not all, of the database features. However, maintaining multiple native interfaces for different databases can become a burden for the programmer. Therefore, the need for 'universal' database connectivity arises. Usually, the native database connectivity interface provided by the vendor is not the only way to connect to a database; most current DBMS products support other database connectivity standards, the most common being ODBC.

FIGURE 17.1 **Oracle native connectivity**

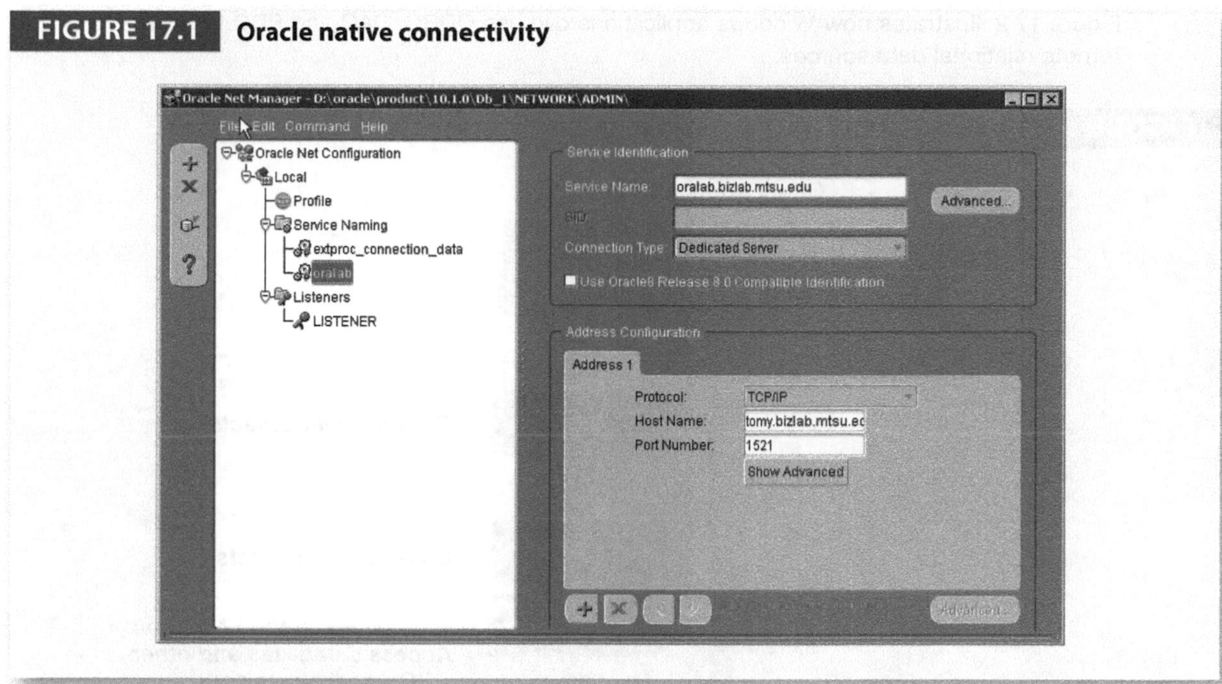

17.1.2 ODBC, DAO, RDO and UDA

Developed in the early 1990s, **Open Database Connectivity (ODBC)** is Microsoft's implementation of a superset of the SQL Access Group **Call Level Interface (CLI)** standard for database access. ODBC Is probably the most widely supported database connectivity interface. ODBC allows any Windows application to access relational data sources, using SQL via a standard application programming interface (API). The Webopedia online dictionary (*www.webopedia.com*) defines an **application programming interface (API)** as 'a set of routines, protocols and tools for building software applications'. A good API makes it easy to develop a program by providing all of the building blocks. A programmer puts the blocks together. Most operating environments, such as Microsoft Windows, provide an API so programmers can write applications consistent with the operating environment. Although APIs are designed for programmers, they are ultimately good for users because they guarantee that all programs using a common API will have similar interfaces. That makes it easy for users to learn new programs.

ODBC was the first widely adopted database middleware standard, and it enjoyed rapid adoption in Windows applications. As programming languages evolved, ODBC did not provide significant functionality beyond the ability to execute SQL to manipulate relational style data. Therefore, programmers needed a better way to access data. To answer that need, Microsoft developed two other data access interfaces:

- **Data Access Objects (DAO)** is Microsoft's API that allows access to the Microsoft Access database. DAO was Microsoft's first object-oriented API. However, while DAO is still widely used there is a move towards ActiveX Data Objects (ADO). .
- **Remote Data Objects (RDO)** was a higher level object-oriented application interface primarily used in Microsoft Visual Basic. It allowed developers to interface directly with ODBC data sources.
- Microsoft's **Universal Data Access (UDA)** model is a new framework that they have proposed. UDA is designed to bring about a single uniform API that will allow access to relational and non-relational databases.

Figure 17.2 illustrates how Windows applications can use ODBC, DAO and RDO to access local and remote relational data sources.

FIGURE 17.2 **Using ODBC, DAO and RDO to access databases**

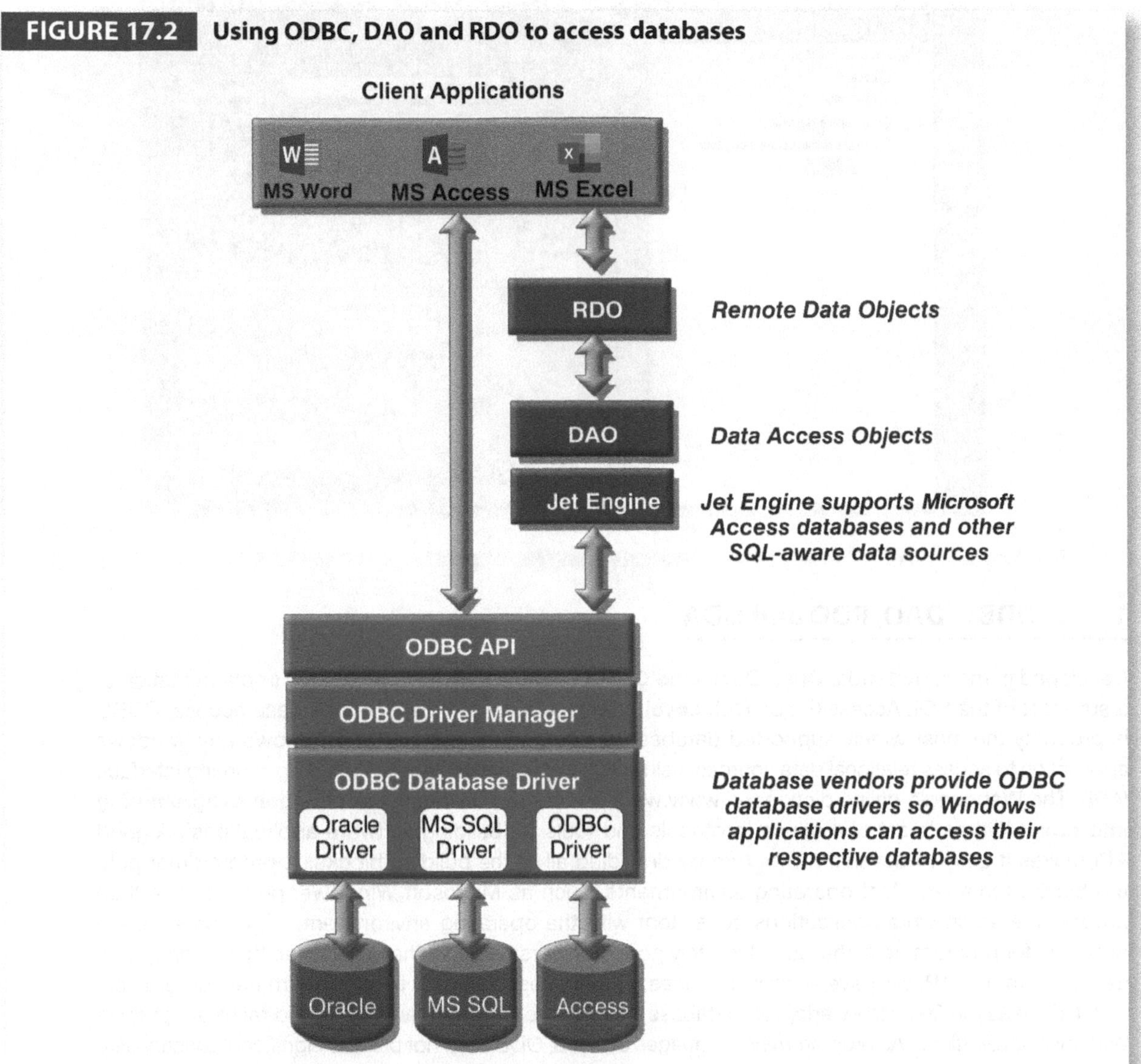

As you can tell by examining Figure 17.2, client applications can use ODBC to access relational data sources. However, the DAO and RDO object interfaces provide more functionality. DAO and RDO make use of the underlying ODBC data services. ODBC, DAO and RDO are implemented as shared code that is dynamically linked to the Windows operating environment through **dynamic link libraries (DLLs)**. DLLs are stored as files with the .dll extension. Running as a DLL, the code speeds up load and run times.

The basic ODBC architecture has three main components:

- A high-level *ODBC API* through which application programs access ODBC functionality
- A *driver manager* that is in charge of managing all database connections
- An *ODBC driver* that communicates directly with the DBMS.

Defining a data source is the first step in using ODBC. To define a data source, you must create a **data source name (DSN)** for the data source. To create a DSN, you need to provide:

- *An ODBC driver.* You need to identify the driver to use to connect to the data source. The ODBC driver is normally provided by the database vendor, although Microsoft provides several drivers that connect to most common databases. For example, if you are using an Oracle DBMS, you will select the Oracle ODBC driver provided by Oracle or, if desired, the Microsoft-provided ODBC driver for Oracle.
- A *name.* This is a unique name by which the data source will be known to ODBC and, therefore, to applications. ODBC offers two types of data sources: user and system. *User data sources* are available only to the user. *System data sources* are available to all users, including operating system services.
- *ODBC driver parameters.* Most ODBC drivers require specific parameters to establish a connection to the database. For example, if you are using a Microsoft Access database, you need to point to the location of the Microsoft Access (.mdb) file and, if necessary, provide a username and password. If you are using a DBMS server, you must provide the server name, the database name and the username and password needed to connect to the database. Figure 17.3 shows the ODBC screens required to create a system ODBC data source for an Oracle DBMS. Note that some ODBC drivers use the native driver provided by the DBMS vendor.

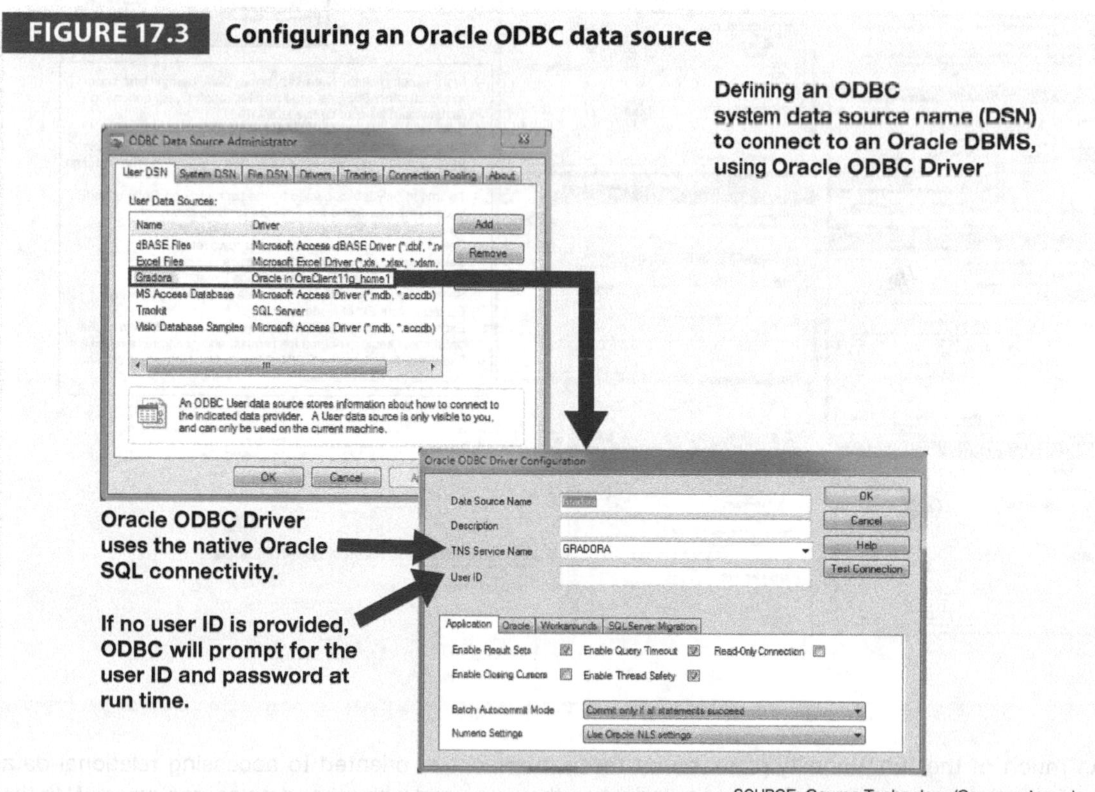

FIGURE 17.3 Configuring an Oracle ODBC data source

SOURCE: Course Technology/Cengage Learning

Once the ODBC data source is defined, application programmers can write to the ODBC API by issuing specific commands and providing the required parameters. The ODBC Driver Manager will properly route the calls to the appropriate data source. The ODBC API standard defines three levels of compliance: Core, Level-1 and Level-2. The compliance levels provide increasing features. For example, Level-1 may provide support for most SQL DDL and DML statements, including sub queries and aggregate functions, but no support for procedural SQL or cursors. The database vendors can choose which level to support. However, to interact with ODBC, the database vendor must implement all of the features indicated in that ODBC API support level.

Figure 17.4 shows how you could use Microsoft Excel to retrieve data from an Oracle RDBMS, using ODBC.

FIGURE 17.4 Microsoft EXCEL uses ODBC to connect to the ORACLE database

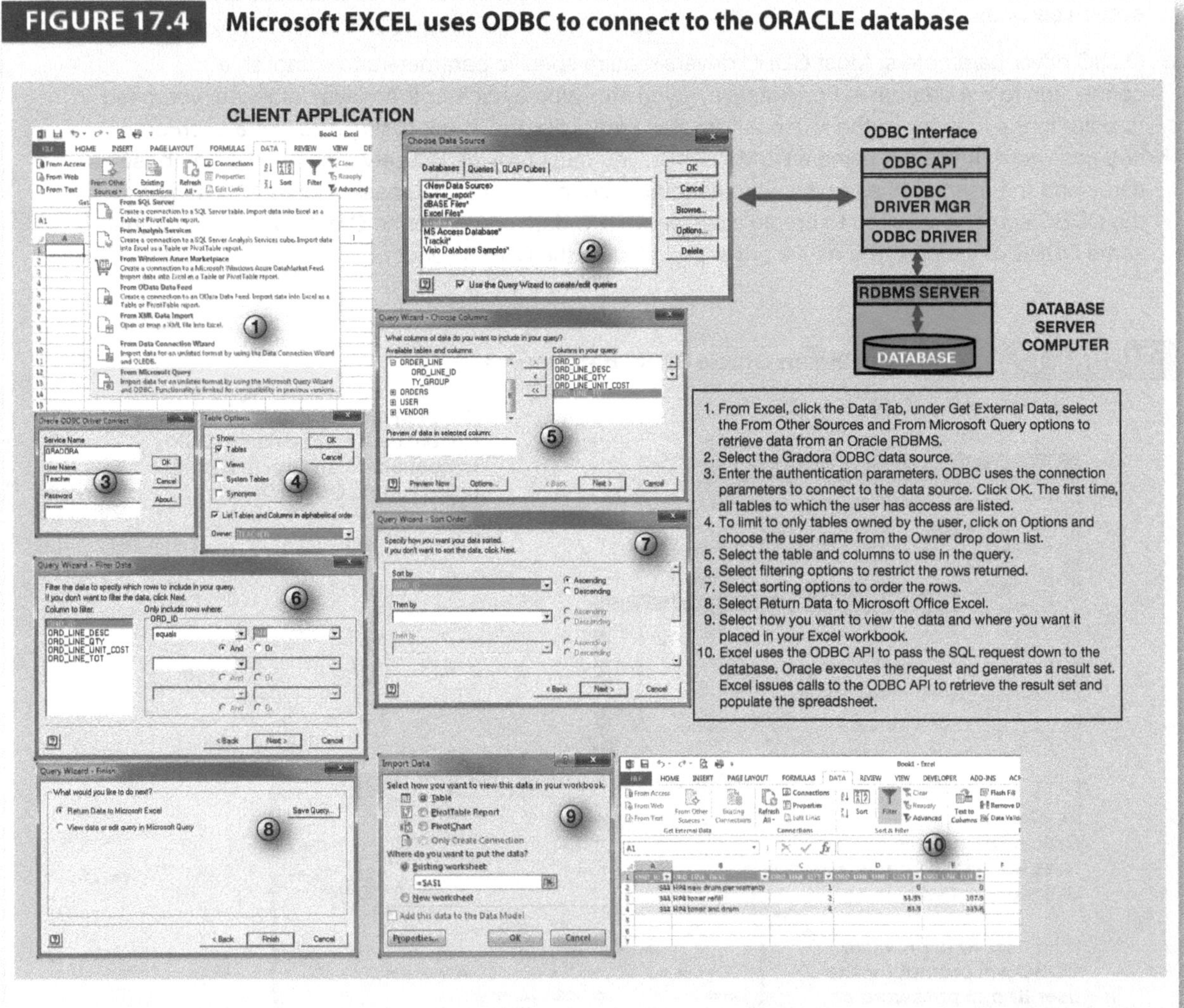

As much of the functionality provided by these interfaces is oriented to accessing relational data sources, the use of the interfaces is limited when they are used with other data source types. With the advent of object-oriented programming languages, it has become more important to provide access to other non-relational data sources.

17.1.3 OLE-DB

Although ODBC, DAO and RDO were widely used, they did not provide support for non-relational data. To answer that need and to simplify data connectivity, Microsoft developed **Object Linking and Embedding for Database (OLE-DB)**. Based on Microsoft's Component Object Model (COM), OLE-DB is database middleware that adds object-orientated functionality for access to relational and non-relational data. OLE-DB was the first part of Microsoft's strategy to provide a unified object-orientated framework for the development of next-generation applications.

OLE-DB is composed of a series of COM objects that provide low-level database connectivity for applications. Since OLE-DB is based on COM, the objects contain data and methods (also known as the interface). The OLE-DB model is better understood when you divide its functionality into two types of objects:

- *Consumers* are objects (applications or processes) that request and use data. The data consumers request data by invoking the methods exposed by the data provider objects (public interface) and passing the required parameters.
- *Providers* are objects that manage the connection with a data source and provide data to the consumers. Providers are divided into two categories: data providers and service providers.
- *Data providers* provide data to other processes. Database vendors create data provider objects that expose the functionality of the underlying data source (relational, object-oriented, text, and so on).
- *Service providers* provide additional functionality to consumers. The service provider is located between the data provider and the consumer. The service provider requests data from the data provider, transforms the data and then provides the transformed data to the data consumer. In other words, the service provider acts like a data consumer of the data provider and as a data provider for the data consumer (end-user application). For example, a service provider could offer cursor management services, transaction management services, query processing services and indexing services.

As a common practice, many vendors provide OLE-DB objects to augment their ODBC support, effectively creating a shared object layer on top of their existing database connectivity (ODBC or native) through which applications can interact. The OLE-DB objects expose functionality about the database; for example, there are objects that deal with relational data, hierarchical data and flat-file text data. Additionally, the objects implement specific tasks, such as establishing a connection, executing a query, invoking a stored procedure, defining a transaction, or invoking an OLAP function. By using OLE-DB objects, the database vendor can choose which functionality to implement in a modular way, instead of being forced to include all of the functionality all of the time. Table 17.1 shows a sample of the object-orientated classes used by OLE-DB and some of the methods (interfaces) exposed by the objects.

TABLE 17.1 Sample OLE-DB classes and interfaces

Object Class	Usage	Sample Interface
Session	Used to create an OLE-DB session between a data consumer application and a data provider.	IGetDataSource ISessionProperties
Command	Used to process commands to manipulate a data provider's data. Generally, the command object will create RowSet objects to hold the data returned by a data provider.	ICommandPrepare ICommandProperties
RowSet	Used to hold the result set returned by a relational style database or a database that supports SQL. Represents a collection of rows in a tabular format.	IRowsetInfo IRowsetFind IRowsetScroll

OLE-DB provides additional capabilities for the applications accessing the data. However, it does not provide support for scripting languages, especially the ones used for Web development, such as Active Server Pages (ASP) and ActiveX. To provide that support, Microsoft developed a new object framework called **ActiveX Data Objects (ADO)**. (A **script** is written in a programming language that is not compiled but is interpreted and executed at run time.) ADO provides a high-level application-orientated interface to interact with OLE-DB, DAO and RDO. ADO provides a unified interface to access data from any programming language that uses the underlying OLE-DB objects. Figure 17.5 illustrates the ADO/OLE-DB architecture, showing how it interacts with ODBC and native connectivity options.

FIGURE 17.5 **OLE-DB architecture**

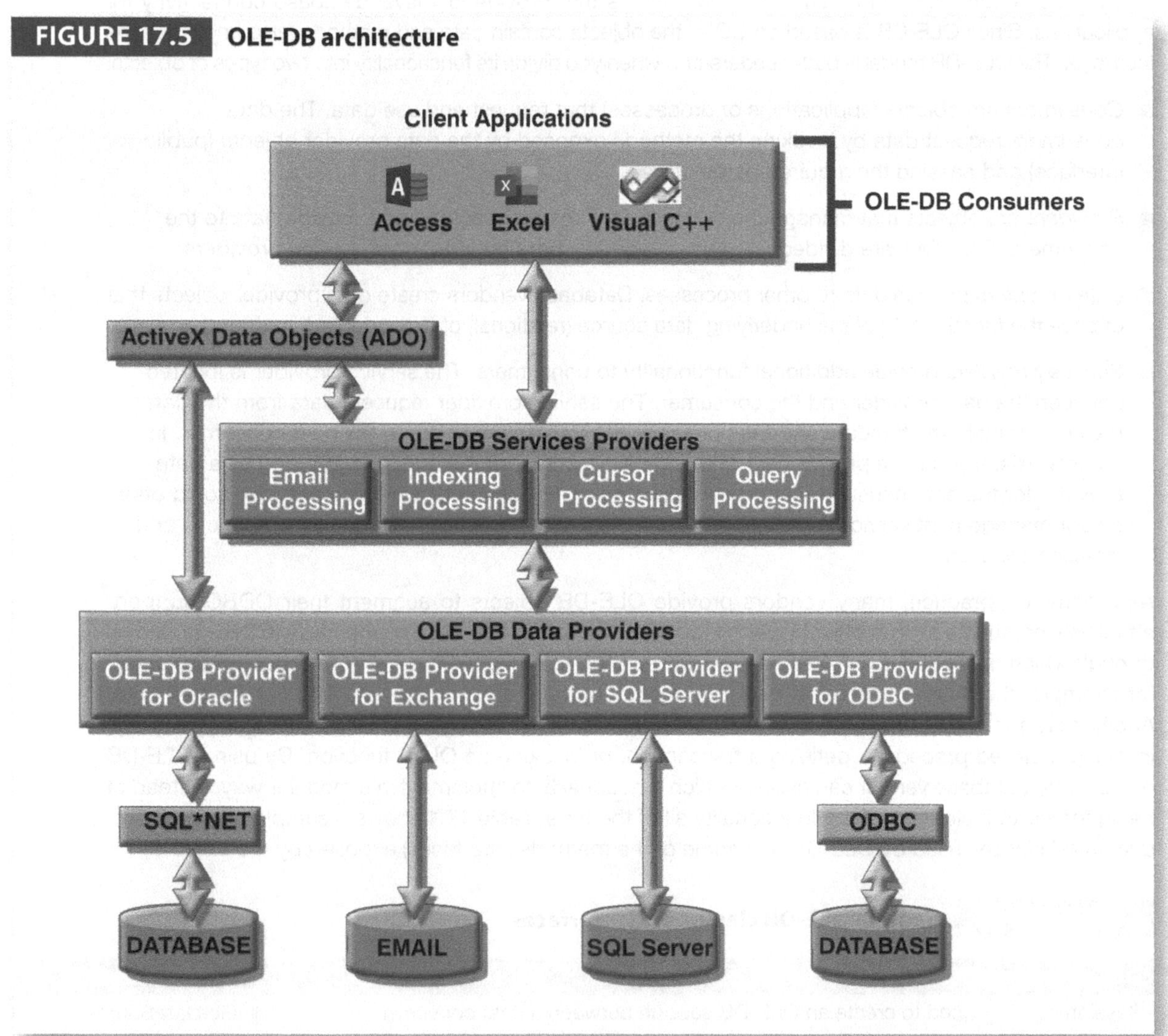

ADO introduced a simpler object model that was composed of only a few interacting objects to provide the data manipulation services required by the applications. Sample objects in ADO are shown in Table 17.2.

17

TABLE 17.2 Sample ADO objects

Object Class	Usage
Connection	Used to set up and establish a connection with a data source. ADO will connect to any OLE-DB data source. The data source can be of any type.
Command	Used to execute commands against a specific connection (data source).
Recordset	Contains the data generated by the execution of a command. It will also contain any new data to be written to the data source. The Recordset can be disconnected from the data source.
Fields	Contains a collection of Field descriptions for each column in the Recordset.

Although the ADO model is a tremendous improvement over the OLE-DB model, Microsoft is actively encouraging programmers to use its new data access framework, ADO.NET.

17.1.4 ADO.NET

Based on ADO, **ADO.NET** is the data access component of Microsoft's .NET application development framework. The **Microsoft .NET framework** is a component-based platform for developing distributed, heterogeneous, interoperable applications aimed at manipulating any type of data over any network under any operating system and programming language. Comprehensive coverage of the .NET framework is beyond the scope of this book. Therefore, this section will only introduce the basic data access component of the .NET architecture, ADO.NET.

It is important to understand that the .NET framework extends and enhances the functionality provided by the ADO/OLE-DB duo. ADO.NET introduced two new features critical for the development of distributed applications: DataSets and XML support.

To understand the importance of this new model, you should know that a **DataSet** is a disconnected memory-resident representation of the database. That is, the DataSet contains tables, columns, rows, relationships and constraints. Once the data are read from a data provider, the data are placed on a memory-resident DataSet. The DataSet is then disconnected from the data provider. The data consumer application interacts with the data in the DataSet object to make changes (inserts, updates and deletes) in the DataSet. Once the processing is done, the DataSet data are synchronised with the data source and the changes are made permanent.

The DataSet is internally stored in XML format (you will learn about XML later in this chapter), and the data in the DataSet can be made persistent as XML documents. This is critical in today's distributed environments. In short, you can think of the DataSet as an XML-based, in-memory database that represents the persistent data stored in the data source. Figure 17.6 illustrates the main components of the ADO.NET object model.

The ADO.NET framework consolidated all data access functionality under one integrated object model. In this object model, several objects interact with one another to perform specific data manipulation functions. Those objects can be grouped as data providers and consumers.

Data provider objects are provided by the database vendors. However, ADO.NET comes with two standard data providers: a data provider for OLE-DB data sources and a data provider for SQL Server. That way, ADO.NET can work with any previously supported database, including an ODBC database with an OLE-DB data provider. At the same time, ADO.NET includes a highly optimised data provider for SQL Server.

FIGURE 17.6 ADO.NET framework

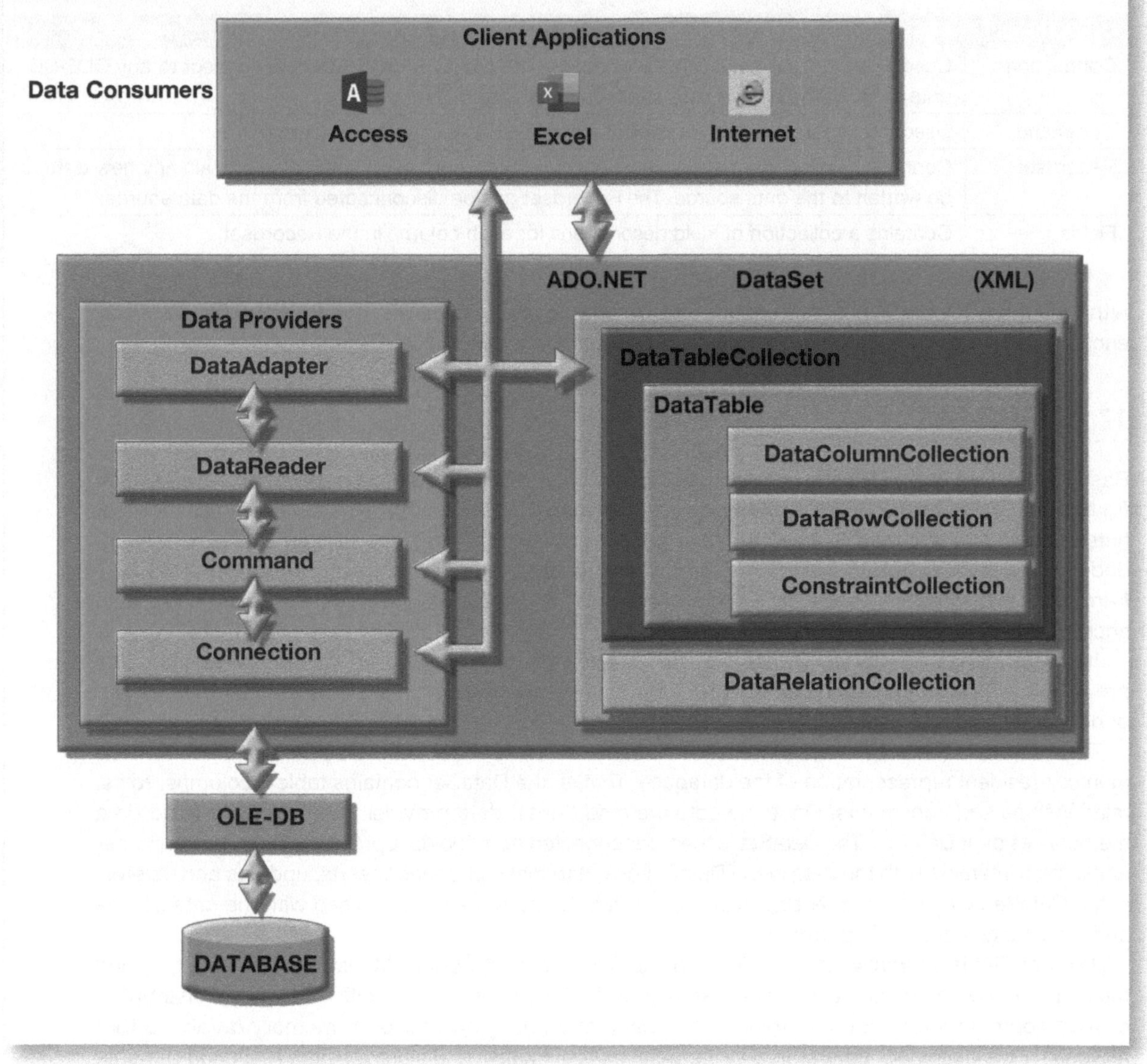

Whatever the data provider is, it must support a set of specific objects in order to manipulate the data in the data source. Some of those objects are shown in Figure 17.6. A brief description of the objects follows:

- *Connection.* The Connection object defines the data source used, the name of the server, the database, and so on. This object enables the client application to open and close a connection to a database.
- *Command*. The Command object represents a database command to be executed within a specified database connection. This object contains the actual SQL code or a stored procedure call to be run by the database. When a SELECT statement is executed, the Command object returns a set of rows and columns.

- *DataReader*. The DataReader object is a specialised object that creates a read-only session with the database to retrieve data sequentially (forward only) in a rapid manner.
- *DataAdapter*. The DataAdapter object is in charge of managing a DataSet object. This is the most specialised object in the ADO.NET framework. The DataAdapter object contains the following objects that aid in managing the data in the DataSet: SelectCommand, InsertCommand, UpdateCommand and DeleteCommand. The DataAdapter object uses those objects to populate and synchronise the data in the DataSet with the permanent data source data.
- *DataSet*. The DataSet object is the in-memory representation of the data in the database. This object contains two main objects. The DataTableCollection object contains a collection of DataTable objects that make up the 'in-memory' database, and the DataRelationCollection object contains a collection of objects describing the data relationships and ways to associate one row in a table to the related row in another table.
- *DataTable*. The DataTable object represents the data in tabular format. This object has one important property: PrimaryKey, which allows the enforcement of entity integrity. In turn, the DataTable object is composed of three main objects:
    - *DataColumnCollection* contains one or more column descriptions. Each column description has properties such as column name, data type, nulls allowed, maximum value and minimum value.
    - *DataRowCollection* contains zero rows, one row or more than one row with data as described in the DataColumnCollection.
    - *ConstraintCollection* contains the definition of the constraints for the table. Two types of constraints are supported: ForeignKeyConstraint and UniqueConstraint.

As you can see, a DataSet is, in fact, a simple database with tables, rows and constraints. Even more important, the DataSet doesn't require a permanent connection to the data source. The DataAdapter uses the SelectCommand object to populate the DataSet from a data source. However, once the DataSet is populated, it is completely independent of the data source, which is why it's called 'disconnected'.

Additionally, DataTable objects in a DataSet can come from different data sources. This means that you could have an EMPLOYEE table in an Oracle database and a SALES table in a SQL Server database. You could then create a DataSet that relates both tables as though they were located in the same database. In short, the DataSet object paves the way for truly heterogeneous distributed database support within applications.

The ADO.NET framework is optimised to work in disconnected environments. In a disconnected environment, applications exchange messages in request/reply format. The most common example of a disconnected system is the internet. Modern applications rely on the internet as the network platform and on the Web browser as the graphical user interface. In the next section, you will learn about how internet databases work.

17.1.5 Java Database Connectivity (JDBC)

Java is an object-oriented programming language developed by Sun Microsystems (acquired by Oracle in 2010) that runs on top of Web browser software. Java is one of the most common programming languages for Web development. Sun Microsystems created Java as a 'write once, run anywhere' environment, which means that a programmer can write a Java application once and then run it in multiple environments without any modification. The cross-platform capabilities of Java are based on its portable architecture. Java code is normally stored in pre-processed 'chunks' known as applets that run in a virtual machine environment in the host operating system. This environment has well-defined boundaries, and all interactivity with the host operating system is closely monitored. Sun provides Java run-time environments for most operating systems, from computers to handheld mobile devices to TV set-top boxes. Another advantage of using Java is its 'on-demand' architecture. When a Java application loads, it can dynamically download all its modules or required components via the internet.

When Java applications need to access data outside the Java run-time environment, they use predefined application programming interfaces. **Java Database Connectivity (JDBC)** is an application programming interface that allows a Java program to interact with a wide range of data sources, including relational databases, tabular data sources, spreadsheets and text files. JDBC allows a Java program to establish a connection with a data source, prepare and send the SQL code to the database server, and process the result set.

One main advantage of JDBC is that it allows a company to leverage its existing investment in technology and personnel training. JDBC allows programmers to use their SQL skills to manipulate the data in the company's databases. As a matter of fact, JDBC allows direct access to a database server or access via database middleware. Furthermore, JDBC provides a way to connect to databases through an ODBC driver. Figure 17.7 illustrates the basic JDBC architecture and the various database access styles.

FIGURE 17.7 JDBC architecture

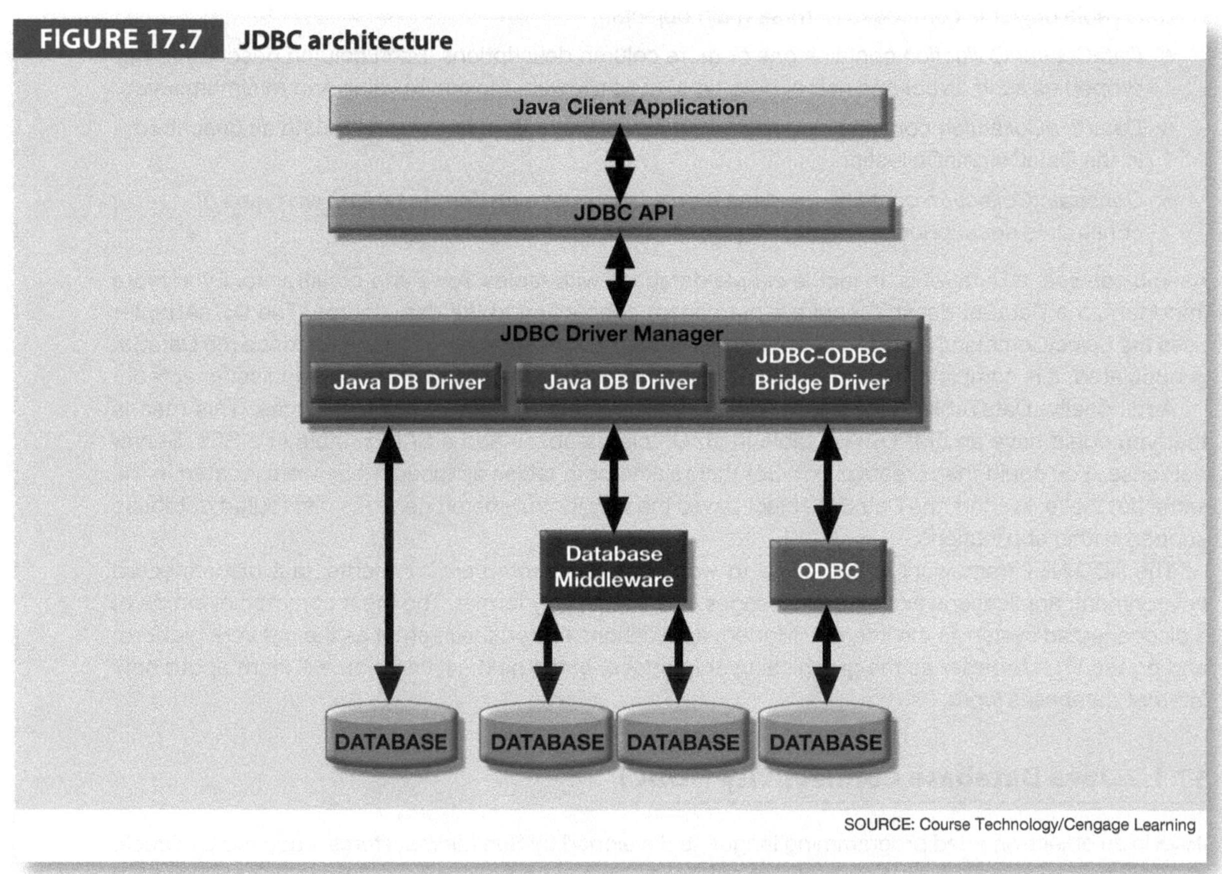

SOURCE: Course Technology/Cengage Learning

As you see in Figure 17.7, the database access architecture in JDBC is very similar to the ODBC/OLE/ADO.NET architecture. All database access middleware shares similar components and functionality. One advantage of JDBC over other middleware is that it requires no configuration on the client side. The JDBC driver is automatically downloaded and installed as part of the Java applet download. Because Java is a Web-based technology, applications can connect to a database directly using a simple URL. Once the URL is invoked, the Java architecture comes into play, the necessary applets are downloaded to the client (including the JDBC database driver and all configuration information), and then the applets are executed securely in the client's run-time environment. Every day, more and more companies are investing resources to develop and expand their Web presence and are finding ways to do more business on the internet. Such business generates increasing amounts of data to be stored in databases. Java and the .NET framework are part of the trend towards increasing reliance on the internet as a critical business resource. In fact, the internet is likely to become the development platform of the future.

17.1.6 PHP

PHP or *Hypertext Preprocessor*, is a widely-used general-purpose scripting language that is especially suited for Web development and is seen as an alternative to Microsoft's ASP. It is a Server-Side Scripting Language, which means that it is interpreted on the Web server before the Web page is sent to a Web browser to be displayed. PHP supports connectivity to a number of different databases through specific database extensions in the case of MySQL, to connecting through ODBC extensions for Oracle. In January 2019, it was reported that 78.9 per cent[1] of websites used PHP, ahead of Java. One of the key reasons for this is that PHP, along with versions of MySQL, is free to use and not difficult to learn. For example, it is possible to connect with a MySQL database using a few short statements. Another advantage is that PHP is supported almost everywhere. It can be used on all major operating systems (including Microsoft Windows, Mac OS X and Linux PHP) and it supports most Web servers today, including Apache and IIS. In addition, most websites for small to medium organisations usually have simpler requirements and have a shorter development time if PHP is used.

PHP also offers an extension module that can be used to connect to Oracle databases. The Oracle Call Interface (OCI 11) is an application programming interface that allows the creation of applications that use a series of function calls to access an Oracle database server. In addition, OCI 11 gives the developer control of all stages of SQL query execution. A typical application developed using OCI 11 must connect to one or more databases, open the cursors needed by the program to hold the data extracted by the SQL query, process any SQL statements within the application, close the cursor and then disconnect to the database. Oracle believes that OCI 11 is the most efficient way of connecting to any Oracle database as if gives greater control over how an application is designed and also a higher degree of control over program execution.

17.2 DATABASE INTERNET CONNECTIVITY

Millions of people all over the world use computers and Web browser software to access the internet, connecting to databases over the Web. Web database connectivity opens the door to new innovative services that:

- Permit rapid responses to competitive pressures by bringing new services and products to market quickly.
- Increase customer satisfaction through the creation of Web-based support services.
- Allow anywhere, anytime data access using mobile smart devices via the internet.
- Give fast and effective information dissemination through universal access from across the street or across the globe.

1 Comparison of the usage of PHP vs Java for websites, W3Techs.com, January 2019, News, Technologies, Server-Side Languages Available: https://w3techs.com/technologies/comparison/pl-java,pl-php

Given those advantages, many IS departments face the need to create universal data access architectures, based on internet standards, to streamline operations and to facilitate decision making. Table 17.3 shows a sample of internet technology characteristics and the benefits they provide.

TABLE 17.3 Characteristics and benefits of internet technologies

Internet Characteristic	Benefit
Hardware and software independence	Savings in equipment/software acquisition Ability to run on most existing equipment Platform independence and portability No need for multiple platform development
Common and simple user interface	Reduced training time and cost Reduced end-user support cost No need for multiple platform development
Location independence	Global access through internet infrastructure Reduced requirements (and costs!) for dedicated connections
Rapid development at manageable costs	Availability of multiple development tools Plug-and-play development tools (open standards) More interactive development Reduced development times Relatively inexpensive tools Free client access tools (Web browsers) Low entry costs frequent availability of free Web servers Reduced costs of maintaining private networks Distributed processing and scalability, using multiple servers

In the current business and global information environment, it is easy to see why many database professionals consider the DBMS connection to the internet to be a critical element in IS development. As you will learn in the following sections, database application development – and, in particular, the creation and management of user interfaces and database connectivity – are profoundly affected by the Web. However, having a Web-based database interface does not negate the database design and implementation issues that were addressed in the previous chapters. In the final analysis, whether you make a purchase by going online or by standing in line, the system-level transaction details are essentially the same, and they require the same basic database structures and relationships. If any immediate lesson is to be learnt, it is this: *The effects of bad database design, implementation and management are multiplied in an environment in which transactions may be measured in millions per day, rather than in hundreds per day.*

The internet is rapidly changing the way information is generated, accessed and distributed. At the core of this change is the Web's ability to access data in databases (local and remote), the simplicity of the interface, and cross-platform (heterogeneous) functionality. The Web has helped create a new information dissemination standard.

The following sections examine how Web-to-database middleware enables end users to interact with databases over the Web.

17.2.1 Web-to-Database Middleware: Server-Side Extensions

In general, the Web server is the main hub through which all internet services are accessed. For example, when an end user uses a Web browser to query a database dynamically, the client browser requests a Web page. When the Web server receives the page request, it looks for the page on the hard disk; when it finds the page (for example, a stock quote, product catalogue information or an airfare listing), the server sends it back to the client.

Online Content Client/server systems are covered in detail in Appendix F, Client/Server Systems, located on the online platform for this book.

Dynamic Web pages are at the heart of current generation websites. In this database query scenario, the Web server generates the Web page contents before it sends the page to the client Web browser. The only problem with the preceding query scenario is that the Web server must include the database query result on the page *before* it sends that page back to the client. Unfortunately, neither the Web browser nor the Web server knows how to connect to and read data from the database. Therefore, to support this type of request (database query), the Web server's capability must be extended so it can understand and process database requests. This job is done through a server-side extension.

A **server-side extension** is a program that interacts directly with the Web server to handle specific types of requests. In the preceding database query example, the server-side extension program retrieves the data from databases and passes the retrieved data to the Web server, which, in turn, sends the data to the client's browser for display purposes. The server-side extension makes it possible to retrieve and present the query results, but what's more important is that *it provides its services to the Web server in a way that is totally transparent to the client browser*. In short, the server-side extension adds significant functionality to the Web server and, therefore, to the internet.

A database server-side extension program is also known as **Web-to-database middleware**. Figure 17.8 shows the interaction between the browser, the Web server and the Web-to-database middleware.

As you examine Figure 17.8, trace the Web-to-database middleware actions:

1 The client browser sends a page request to the Web server.

2 The Web server receives and validates the request. In this case, the server passes the request to the Web-to-database middleware for processing. Generally, the requested page contains some type of scripting language to enable the database interaction.

3 The Web-to-database middleware reads, validates and executes the script. In this case, it connects to the database and passes the query, using the database connectivity layer.

4 The database server executes the query and passes the result back to the Web-to-database middleware.

5 The Web-to-database middleware compiles the result set, dynamically generates an HTML-formatted page that includes the data retrieved from the database, and sends it to the Web server.

6 The Web server returns the just-created HTML page, which now includes the query result, to the client browser.

7 The client browser displays the page on the local computer.

FIGURE 17.8 Web-to-database middleware

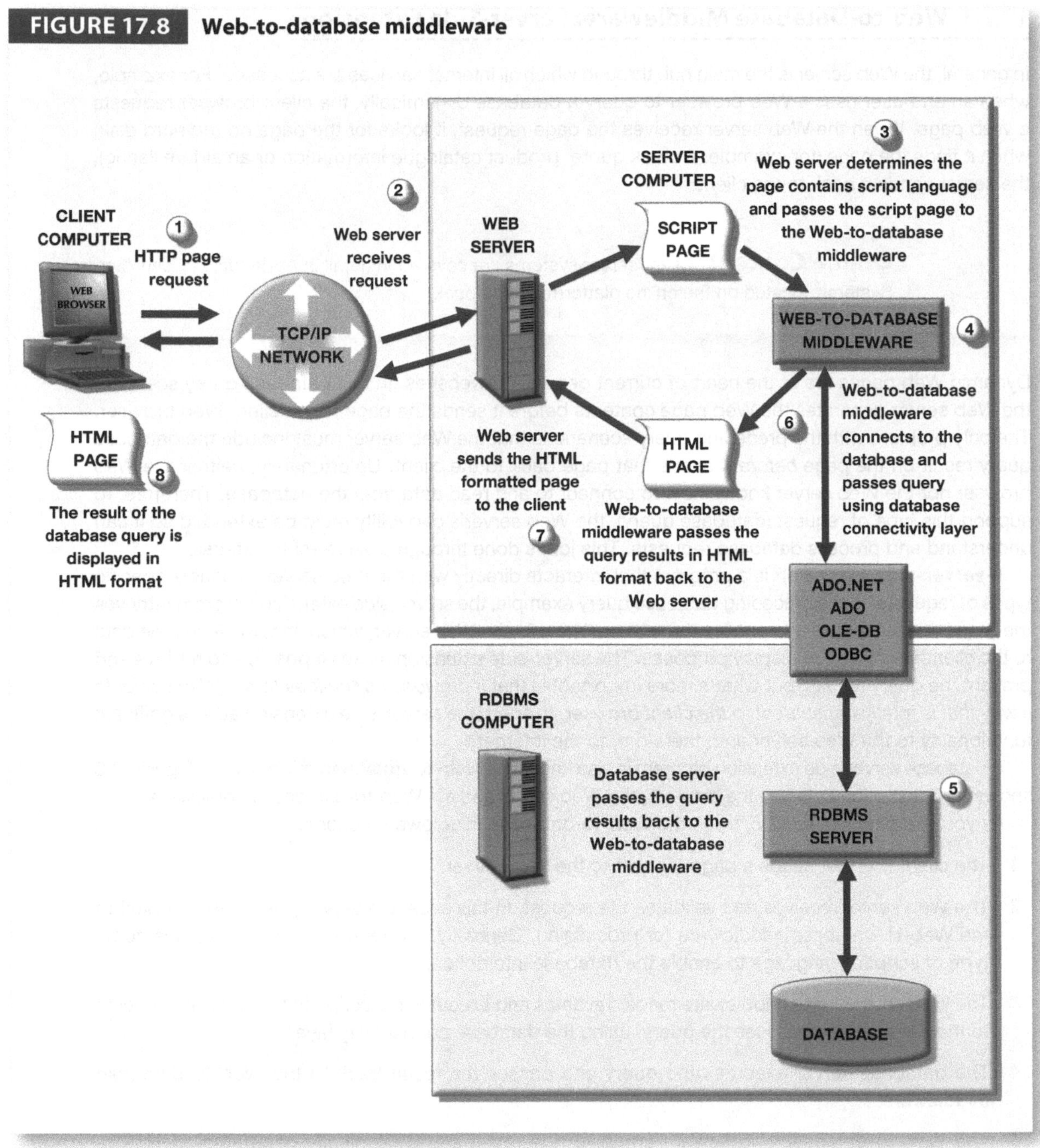

The interaction between the Web server and the Web-to-database middleware is crucial to the development of a successful internet database implementation. Therefore, the middleware must be well integrated with the other internet services and the components that are involved in its use.

17.2.2 Web Server Interfaces

Extending Web server functionality implies that the Web server and the Web-to-database middleware will properly communicate with each other. (Database professionals often use the word *interoperate* to indicate that each party to the communication can respond to the communications of the other. This book's use of *communicate* assumes interoperation.) If a Web server is to communicate successfully with an external program, both programs must use a standard way to exchange messages and to respond to requests. Currently, there are two well-defined Web server interfaces:

- Common Gateway Interface (CGI)
- Application programming interface (API).

The **Common Gateway Interface (CGI)** uses script files that perform specific functions based on the client's parameters that are passed to the Web server. The script file is a small program containing commands written in a programming language, usually Perl, C++, C# or Visual Basic. The script file's contents can be used to connect to the database and to retrieve data from it, using the parameters passed by the Web server. Next, the script converts the retrieved data to HTML format and passes the data to the Web server, which sends the HTML-formatted page to the client.

The main disadvantage of using CGI scripts is that the script file is an external program that is individually executed for each user request. That scenario decreases system performance. For example, if you have 200 concurrent requests, the script is loaded 200 *different* times, which takes significant CPU and memory resources away from the Web server. The language and method used to create the script can also affect system performance. For example, performance is degraded by using an interpreted language or by writing the script inefficiently.

An application programming interface (API) is a newer Web server interface standard that is more efficient and faster than a CGI script. APIs are more efficient because they are implemented as shared code or as dynamic link libraries (DLLs). That means the API is treated as part of the Web server program that is dynamically invoked when needed.

APIs are faster than CGI scripts because the code resides in memory and there is no need to run an external program for each request. Instead, the same API serves all requests. Another advantage is that an API can use a shared connection to the database instead of creating a new one every time, as is the case with CGI scripts.

Although APIs are more efficient in handling requests, they have some disadvantages. Because the APIs share the same memory space as the Web server, an API error can bring down the server. The other disadvantage is that APIs are specific to the Web server and to the operating system.

The Web interface architecture is illustrated in Figure 17.9.

Regardless of the type of Web server interface used, the Web-to-database middleware program must be able to connect with the database. That connection can be accomplished in one of two ways:

- Use the native SQL access middleware provided by the vendor. For example, you can use SQL*Net if you are using Oracle.
- Use the services of general database connectivity standards such as ODBC, OLE-DB, ADO, ADO.NET or JDBC.

FIGURE 17.9 Web server CGI and API interfaces

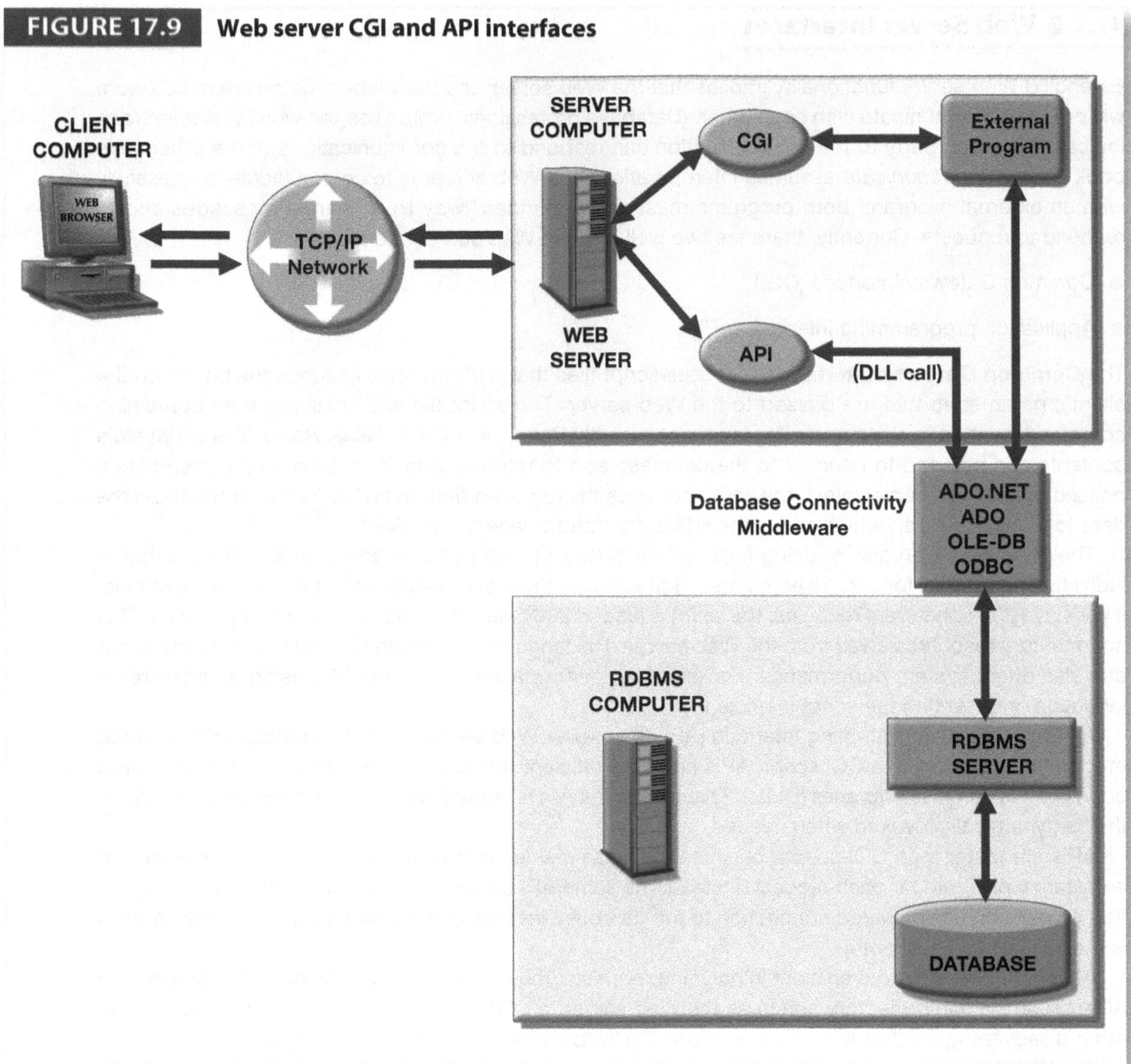

17.2.3 The Web Browser

The Web browser is the application software such as Google Chrome, Apple Safari or Mozilla Firefox that lets end users navigate (browse) the Web. Each time the end user clicks a hyperlink, the browser generates an HTTP GET page request that is sent to the designated Web server, using the TCP/IP internet protocol.

The Web browser's job is to *interpret* the HTML code that it receives from the Web server and to present the different page components in a standard formatted way. Unfortunately, the browser's interpretation and presentation capabilities are not sufficient to develop Web-based applications.

The Web is a **stateless system** – at any given time, a Web server does not know the status of any of the clients communicating with it. That is, there is no open communication line between the server and each client accessing it, which of course is impractical in a worldwide Web! Instead, client and server computers interact in very short 'conversations' that follow the request-reply model. For example, the browser is concerned only with the current page, so there is no way for the second page to know what was done in the first page. The only time the client and server computers communicate is when the client requests a page – when the user clicks a link – and the server sends the requested page to the client. Once the client receives the page and its components, the client/server communication is ended. Therefore, although you may be browsing a page and think that the communication is open, you are actually just browsing the HTML document stored in the local cache (temporary directory) of your browser. The server does not have any idea what the end user is doing with the document, which data are entered in a form, which option is selected, and so on. On the Web, if you want to act on a client's selection, you need to jump to a new page (go back to the Web server), thus losing track of what was done before.

The Web browser, through its use of HTML, does not have computational abilities beyond formatting output text and accepting form field inputs. Even when the browser accepts form field data, there is no way to perform immediate data entry validation. Therefore, to perform such crucial processing in the client, the Web defers to other Web programming languages such as PHP, Java, JavaScript and VBScript. The browser resembles a dumb terminal that displays only data and can perform only rudimentary processing such as accepting form data inputs. To improve the capabilities of the Web browser, you must use plug-ins and other client-side extensions. On the server side, Web application servers provide the necessary processing power.

17.2.4 Client-Side Extensions

Client-side extensions add functionality to the Web browser. Although client-side extensions are available in various forms, the most commonly encountered extensions are:

- Plug-ins
- Java and JavaScript
- ActiveX and VBScript

A **plug-in** is an external application that is automatically invoked by the browser when needed. Because it is an *external* application, the plug-in is operating-system-specific. The plug-in is associated with a data object – generally using the file extension – to allow the Web server to handle data properly that are not originally supported. For example, if one of the page components is a .pdf document, the Web server will receive the data, recognise it as a 'portable document format' object and launch Adobe Acrobat Reader to present and manipulate the document on the client computer.

JavaScript is a scripting language (one that enables the running of a series of commands or macros) that allows Web authors to design interactive sites. Because JavaScript is simpler to generate than Java, it is easier to learn. JavaScript code is embedded in the Web pages. It is downloaded with the Web page and is executed when a specific event takes place – such as a mouse click on an object or a page being loaded from the server into memory.

ActiveX was Microsoft's alternative to Java. ActiveX was a specification for writing programs that ran inside Microsoft's browser (Internet Explorer). However, despite Microsoft's efforts, ActiveX was not truly cross-platform compatible. ActiveX support was dropped and in 2015 Microsoft released Microsoft Edge, a replacement for Internet Explorer with no ActiveX support.

From the developer's point of view, using routines that permit data validation on the client side is an absolute necessity. For example, when data are entered on a Web form and no data validation is done on the client side, the entire data set must be sent to the Web server. That scenario requires the server to perform all data validation, thus wasting valuable CPU processing cycles. Therefore, client-side data input validation is one of the most basic requirements for Web applications. Most of the data validation routines are done in Java, JavaScript, or VBScript.

17.2.5 Web Application Servers

A Web application server is a middleware application that expands the functionality of Web servers by linking them to a wide range of services, such as databases, directory systems, and search engines. The Web application server also provides a consistent run-time environment for Web applications. Web application servers can be used to perform the following:

- Connect to and query a database from a Web page.
- Present database data in a Web page using various formats.
- Create dynamic Web search pages.
- Create Web pages to insert, update and delete database data.
- Enforce referential integrity in the application program logic.
- Use simple and nested queries and programming logic to represent business rules.

Web application servers provide features such as:

- An integrated development environment with session management and support for persistent application variables
- Security and authentication of users through user IDs and passwords
- Computational languages to represent and store business logic in the application server
- Automatic generation of HTML pages integrated with Java, JavaScript, VBScript, ASP, and so on
- Performance and fault-tolerant features
- Database access with transaction management capabilities
- Access to multiple services, such as file transfers (FTP), database connectivity, email and directory services.

Examples of Web application servers include ColdFusion/JRun by Adobe, WebSphere Application Server by IBM, WebLogic Server by Oracle, Fusion by NetObjects, Visual Studio .NET by Microsoft and WebObjects by Apple. All Web application servers offer the ability to connect Web servers to multiple data sources and other services. They vary in their range of available features, robustness, scalability, compatibility with other Web and database tools, and extent of the development environment.

17.2.6 Web Database Development

Web database development deals with the process of interfacing databases with the Web browser – in short, how to create Web pages that access data in a database. As you learnt earlier in this chapter, multiple Web environments can be used to develop Web database applications.

One of the most common web application development environments is known as **LAMP**. LAMP is made up of the Linux operating system, the Apache Web server, MySQL database and the PHP programming language (although Perl and Python can be used instead of PHP). It is often used within organisations that need an effective way of managing organisational data but do not have the time or money to invest in a large-scale, costly web development project. LAMP allows Web developers to build efficient Web applications that are reliable and stable. Examining the components of LAMP will allow us to see why:

- The Linux operating system is open source can be used to offer cross-platform compatibility. This is important to enable your website to be used across all major browsers and any mobile device.
- The Apache Web server is the leading platform in terms of its total number of domains. This is because it allows, with PHP, the development of highly interactive Web applications. In 2018, 34.8 per cent of domains were hosted on Apache Web servers. As of 2018, Microsoft's Web servers power the most sites – 40.65 per cent.[2]
- MySQL databases can be used to store data for both simple and complex websites with varying degrees of database complexity. It allows easy retrieval and capturing of data from the Web.
- The programming language PHP is used to link all the components of LAMP. PHP allows the dynamic content of the website to be obtained through accessing data within the MySQL database.

The main benefits of LAMP are that it is easy to programme and applications can be developed offline and then deployed onto the Web. Deployment is also relatively straightforward as PHP is easily integrated with the Apache Web server and MySQL. Despite the development of the LAMP components being independent, when combined they offer one of the best solutions for Web database development.

In order to illustrate the use of PHP to retrieve a data through a simple query, let's examine a PHP code example. Because this is a database book, the examples focus only on the commands used to interface with the database, rather than the specifics of HTML code.

A Microsoft Access database named Orderdb is used to illustrate the Web-to-database interface examples. The Orderdb database, whose relational diagram is shown in Figure 17.10, was designed to track the purchase orders placed by users in a multidepartment company.

2 Web Server Survey. Available: http://news.netcraft.com/archives/category/web-server-survey/

FIGURE 17.10 The Orderdb relational diagram for the Web database development examples

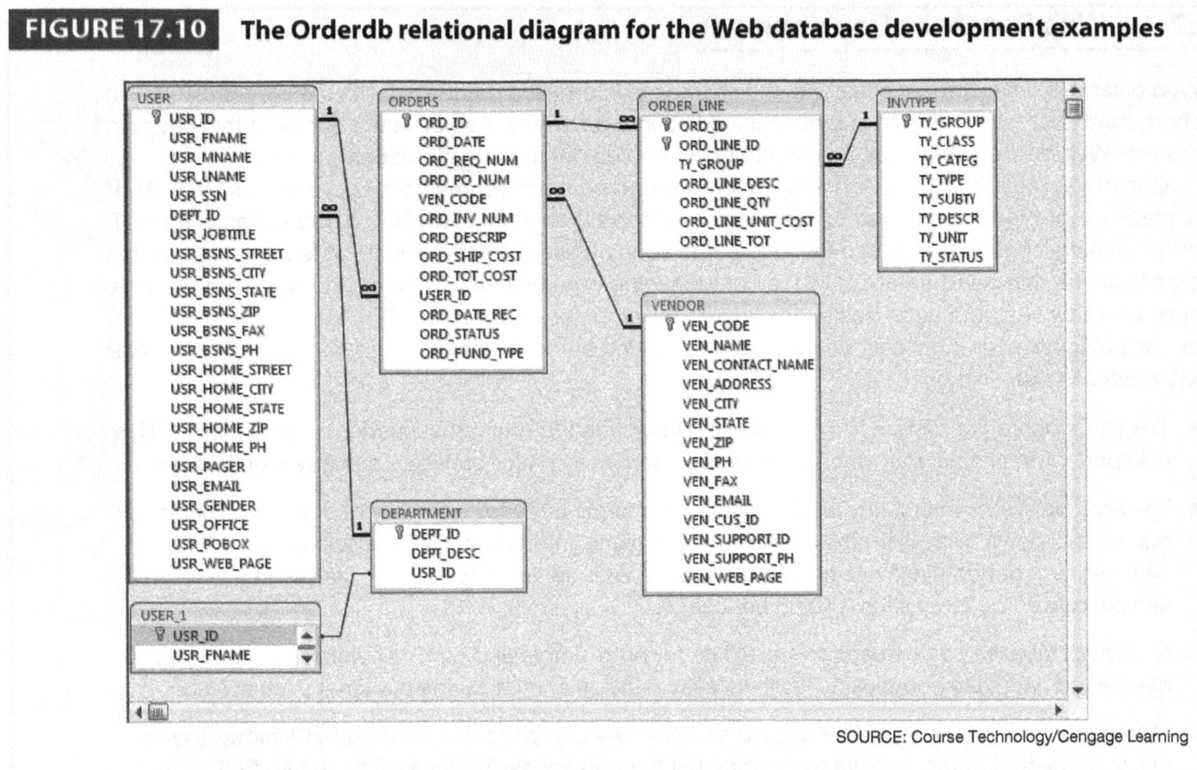

SOURCE: Course Technology/Cengage Learning

The following example will explain how to use PHP to create a simple Web page to list the VENDOR rows. The scripts used in these examples perform two basic tasks:

1 Query the database using standard SQL to retrieve a data set that contains all records in the VENDOR table. The examples will use an ODBC data source named RobCor. The ODBC data source was defined using the operating system tools shown in Section 17.1.2.

2 Format the records generated in Step 1 in HTML so they are included in the Web page that is returned to the client browser.

Figure 17.11 shows the PHP code to query the VENDOR table.

FIGURE 17.11 **PHP code to query the VENDOR table**

```
1  <HTML>
2  <HEAD>
3  <TITLE>Rob & Coronel -  PHP Example</TITLE>
4  </HEAD>
5  <BODY BGCOLOR="LIGHTBLUE">
6  <H1><CENTER><B>Simple Query using PHP and ODBC functions</B></CENTER>
7  <CENTER><B>(Vertical Output)</B></CENTER></H1>
8  <BR>
9  <HR>
10 <?php
11 $dbc = odbc_connect("RobCor","","");
12 $sql = "SELECT * FROM VENDOR ORDER BY VEN_CODE";
13 $rs  = odbc_exec( $dbc, $sql );
14 
15 while (odbc_fetch_row( $rs ))
16 {
17 $VEN_CODE         = odbc_result($rs,"VEN_CODE");
18 $VEN_NAME         = odbc_result($rs,"VEN_NAME");
19 $VEN_CONTACT_NAME = odbc_result($rs,"VEN_CONTACT_NAME");
20 $VEN_ADDRESS      = odbc_result($rs,"VEN_ADDRESS");
21 $VEN_CITY         = odbc_result($rs,"VEN_CITY");
22 $VEN_STATE        = odbc_result($rs,"VEN_STATE");
23 $VEN_ZIP          = odbc_result($rs,"VEN_ZIP");
24 $VEN_PH           = odbc_result($rs,"VEN_PH");
25 $VEN_FAX          = odbc_result($rs,"VEN_FAX");
26 $VEN_EMAIL        = odbc_result($rs,"VEN_EMAIL");
27 $VEN_CUS_ID       = odbc_result($rs,"VEN_CUS_ID");
28 $VEN_SUPPORT_ID   = odbc_result($rs,"VEN_SUPPORT_ID");
29 $VEN_SUPPORT_PH   = odbc_result($rs,"VEN_SUPPORT_PH");
30 $VEN_WEB_PAGE     = odbc_result($rs,"VEN_WEB_PAGE");
31 
32 echo "<BR>";
33 echo "VENDOR CODE:     ", $VEN_CODE . "<BR>";
34 echo "VENDOR NAME:     ", $VEN_NAME . "<BR>";
35 echo "CONTACT PERSON:  ", $VEN_CONTACT_NAME . "<BR>";
36 echo "ADDRESS:         ", $VEN_ADDRESS . "<BR>";
37 echo "CITY:            ", $VEN_CITY . "<BR>";
38 echo "STATE:           ", $VEN_STATE . "<BR>";
39 echo "ZIP:             ", $VEN_ZIP . "<BR>";
40 echo "PHONE:           ", $VEN_PH . "<BR>";
41 echo "FAX:             ", $VEN_FAX . "<BR>";
42 echo "E-MAIL:          ", $VEN_EMAIL . "<BR>";
43 echo "CUSTOMER ID:     ", $VEN_CUS_ID . "<BR>";
44 echo "SUPPORT ID:      ", $VEN_SUPPORT_ID . "<BR>";
45 echo "SUPPORT PHONE:   ", $VEN_SUPPORT_PH . "<BR>";
46 echo "VENDOR WEB PAGE:", $VEN_WEB_PAGE . "<BR>";
47 echo "<HR>";
48 }
49 odbc_close($dbc);
50 ?>
51 </BODY>
52 </HTML>
```

SOURCE: Course Technology/Cengage Learning

In the figure, note that PHP uses multiple **tags** to query and display the data returned by the query. Take a closer look at the PHP functions:

- The ODBC_CONNECT function (line 11) opens a connection to the ODBC data source. A handle to this database is set in the $dbc variable.
- The ODBC_EXEC function (line 13) executes the SQL query stored in the $sql variable against the $dbc database connection. The query's result set is stored in the $rs variable.
- The WHILE function (line 15) loops through the result set ($rs) and uses the ODBC_FETCH_ROW function to get one row at a time from the result set. Notice that PHP variables start with the dollar sign ($).

17

- The ODBC_RESULT function (lines 17–30) gets a column value from a row in the result set and stores it in a variable. This function extracts the different values for each field to be displayed and stores them in variables.
- The ECHO function (lines 32–47) outputs text to the Web page using the variables defined in the previous lines. You can also combine text (HTML code) and PHP variables (lines 33–46) using the "." delimiter.
- The ODBC_CLOSE function closes the database connection.

The previous examples are just two of the many ways you can interface Web pages and databases with Web applications. These examples only scratch the surface of the multiple features that Web application servers provide. Current-generation systems involve more than just the development of Web-enabled database applications. They also require applications that can communicate with one another and with other systems not based on the Web. Clearly, systems must be able to exchange data in a standard-based format. That is the role of XML.

17.3 EXTENSIBLE MARKUP LANGUAGE (XML)

Companies are using the internet to create new types of systems that integrate their data to increase efficiency and reduce costs. Electronic commerce (e-commerce) enables organisations – whether they are public or private, for-profit or not-for-profit – to market and sell products and services to a global market of millions of users. E-commerce transactions – the sale of products or services – can take place between businesses (business-to-business or B2B) or between a business and a consumer (business-to-consumer or B2C).

Most e-commerce transactions take place between businesses. Since B2B e-commerce integrates business processes among companies, it requires the transfer of business information among different business entities. However, the way in which businesses represent, identify and use data, tends to differ substantially from company to company. For example, is a *product code* the same thing as an *item ID*?

Until recently, a purchase order travelling over the Web was expected to be in the form of an HTML document. The HTML Web page displayed on the Web browser would include formatting as well as the order details. HTML tags describe how something looks on the Web page, such as typefaces and heading styles, and they often come in pairs to start and end formatting features. For example, the following tags in angle brackets would display FOR SALE in bold Arial font:

```
<strong><font face=Arial>FOR SALE</font></strong>
```

If an application needs to get the order data from the Web page, there is no easy way to extract details such as the order number, date, customer number, product code, quantity, or price from an HTML document. The HTML document can only describe how to display the order in a Web browser; it does not permit the manipulation of the order's data elements. To solve that problem, a new markup language known as Extensible Markup Language was developed.

Extensible Markup Language (XML) is a metalanguage used to represent and manipulate data elements. XML is designed to facilitate the exchange of structured documents, such as orders and invoices, over the internet. The World Wide Web Consortium (W3C)[3] published the first XML 1.0 standard definition in 1998. That standard sets the stage for giving XML the real-world appeal of being a true vendor-independent platform. Therefore, it is not surprising that XML is rapidly becoming the data exchange standard for e-commerce applications.

17

3 Visit the W3C Web page, located at *www.w3.org*, for additional information about the efforts that have been made to develop the XML standard.

The XML metalanguage allows the definition of new tags, such as <ProdPrice>, to describe the data elements used in an XML document. Given that feature, XML is said to be an *extensible* language. XML is derived from the Standard Generalised Markup Language (SGML). SGML is an international standard for the publication and distribution of highly complex technical documents – such as those used by the aviation industry and the military services – that are too complex and unwieldy for the Web. Just like HTML – *which was also derived from SGML* – an XML document is a text file, but it has a few – although very important – additional characteristics, as follows:

- XML allows the definition of new tags to describe data elements, such as <ProductId>.
- XML is case sensitive: <ProductID> is not the same as <Productid>.
- XML tags must be well formed; that is, each opening tag has a corresponding closing tag. For example, the product identification would require the format <ProductId>2345-AA</ProductId>.
- XML tags must be properly nested. For example, a properly nested XML tag might look like this: <Product><ProductId>2345-AA</ProductId></Product>.
- You can use the <-- and --> symbols to enter comments in the XML document.
- The *XML* and *xml* prefixes are reserved for XML only.

XML is *not* a new version or replacement for HTML. XML is concerned with the description and representation of the data, rather than the way the data are displayed. (Data display remains the job of HTML.) XML provides the semantics that facilitate the sharing, exchange and manipulation of structured documents over organisational boundaries. In short, XML and HTML perform complementary, rather than overlapping, functions. Extensible Hypertext Markup Language (XHTML) is the next generation of HTML based on the XML framework. The XHTML specification expands the HTML standard to include XML features. Although it is more powerful than HTML, XHTML requires strict adherence to syntax requirements. As an illustration of the use of XML, consider a B2B example in which Company A uses XML to exchange product data with Company B over the internet. Figure 17.12 shows the contents of the productlist.xml document.

FIGURE 17.12 Contents of the productlist.xml document

productlist.xml - Notepad

File Edit Format View Help

```
<?xml version ="1.0"?>
<ProductList>
        <Product>
                <P_CODE>23109-HB</P_CODE>
                <P_DESCRIPT>Claw hammer</P_DESCRIPT>
                <P_INDATE>08/19/2018</P_INDATE>
                <P_QOH>23</P_QOH>
                <P_MIN>10</P_MIN>
                <P_PRICE>5.95</P_PRICE>
        </Product>
        <Product>
                <P_CODE>23114-AA</P_CODE>
                <P_DESCRIPT>Sledge Hammer, 12 lb.</P_DESCRIPT>
                <P_INDATE>09/01/2018</P_INDATE>
                <P_QOH>8</P_QOH>
                <P_MIN>5</P_MIN>
                <P_PRICE>14.40</P_PRICE>
        </Product>
</ProductList>
```

The XML example shown in Figure 17.12 illustrates several important XML features, as follows:

- The first line represents the XML document declaration, and it is mandatory.
- Every XML document has a *root element*. In the example, the second line declares the ProductList root element.
- The root element contains *child elements* or sub-elements. In the example, line three declares Product as a child element of ProductList.
- Each element can contain *sub-elements*. For example, each Product element is composed of several child elements, represented by P_CODE, P_DESCRIPT, P_INDATE, P_ONHAND, P_MIN, and P_PRICE.

Once Company B receives the ProductList.xml document, it can process the document – assuming it understands the tags created by Company A. The meaning of the XML tags in the example shown in Figure 17.12 is fairly self-evident, but there is no easy way to validate the data or to check whether the data are complete. For example, you could encounter a P_INDATE value of '25/06/2019' – but is that value correct? And what happens if Company B expects a Vendor element as well? How can companies share data descriptions about their business data elements? The next section will show how document type definitions and XML schemas are used to address those concerns.

17.3.1 Document Type Definitions (DTD) and XML Schemas

Companies that use B2B transactions must have a way to understand and validate one another's tags. One way to accomplish that task is through the use of Document Type Definitions. A **Document Type Definition (DTD)** is a file with a .dtd extension that describes XML elements – in effect, a DTD file provides the composition of the database's logical model and defines the syntax rules or valid tags for each type of XML document. (The DTD component is similar to having a public data dictionary for business data.) Companies that intend to engage in e-commerce business transactions must develop and share DTDs. Figure 17.13 shows the productlist.dtd document for the productlist.xml document shown earlier in Figure 17.12.

FIGURE 17.13 **Contents of the productlist.dtd document**

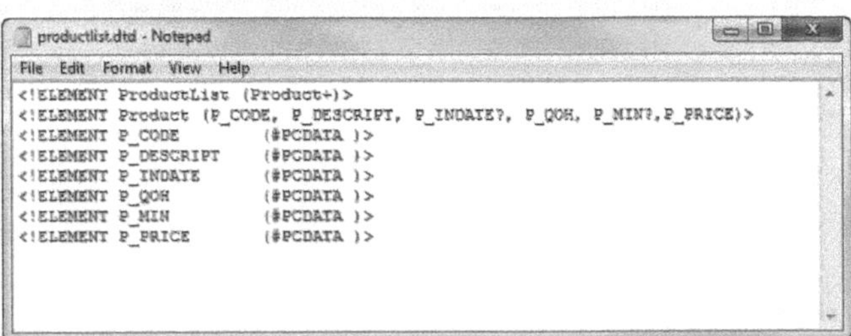

```
<!ELEMENT ProductList (Product+)>
<!ELEMENT Product (P_CODE, P_DESCRIPT, P_INDATE?, P_QOH, P_MIN?,P_PRICE)>
<!ELEMENT P_CODE        (#PCDATA )>
<!ELEMENT P_DESCRIPT    (#PCDATA )>
<!ELEMENT P_INDATE      (#PCDATA )>
<!ELEMENT P_QOH         (#PCDATA )>
<!ELEMENT P_MIN         (#PCDATA )>
<!ELEMENT P_PRICE       (#PCDATA )>
```

As you examine Figure 17.13, note that the productlist.dtd file provides definitions of the elements in the productlist.xml document. In particular, note that:

- The first line declares the ProductList root element.
- The ProductList root element has one child, the Product element.

- The plus '+' symbol indicates that Product occurs one or more times within ProductList.
- An asterisk '*' would mean that the child element occurs zero or more times.
- A question mark '?' would mean that the child element is optional.
- The second line describes the Product element.
- The question mark '?' after the P_INDATE and P_MIN indicates that they are optional elements.
- Lines three to eight show that the Product element has six children sub-elements.
- The #PCDATA keyword represents the actual text data.

To be able to use a DTD file to define elements within an XML document, the DTD must be referenced from within that XML document. Figure 17.14 shows the productlistv2.xml document that includes the reference to the productlist.dtd in the second line.

As you examine Figure 17.14, note that the P_INDATE and P_MIN do not appear in all Product definitions because they were declared to be optional elements. The DTD can be referenced by many XML documents of the same type. For example, if Company A routinely exchanges product data with Company B, it will need to create the DTD only once. All subsequent XML documents will refer to the DTD and Company B will be able to verify the data being received.

FIGURE 17.14 Contents of the productlistv2.xml document

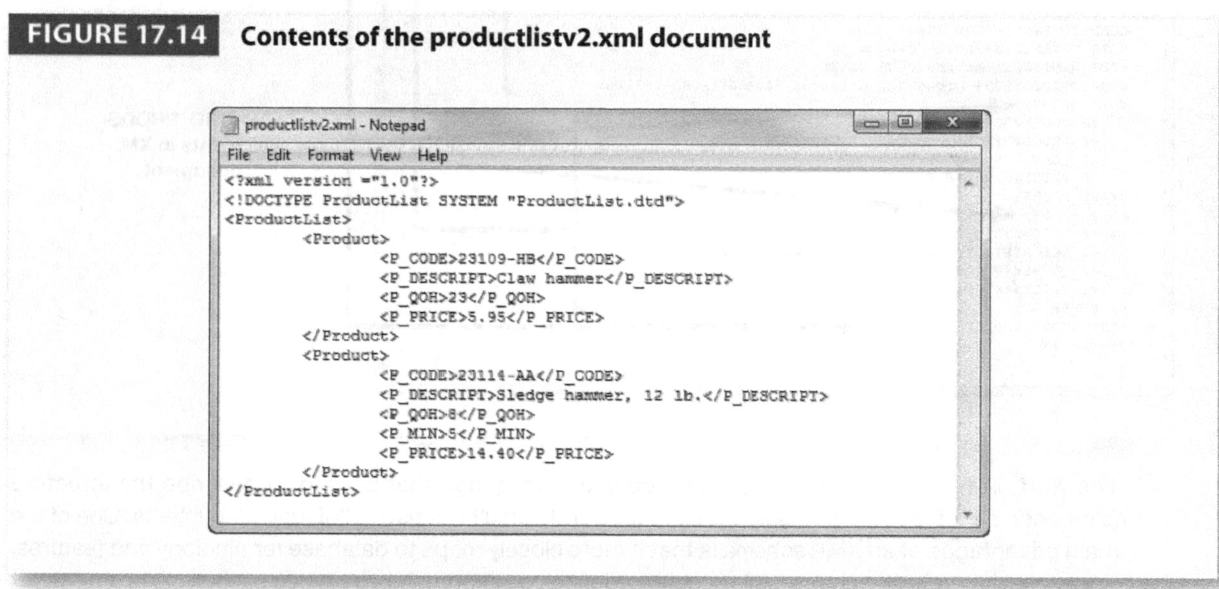

productlistv2.xml - Notepad

File Edit Format View Help

```
<?xml version ="1.0"?>
<!DOCTYPE ProductList SYSTEM "ProductList.dtd">
<ProductList>
        <Product>
                <P_CODE>23109-HB</P_CODE>
                <P_DESCRIPT>Claw hammer</P_DESCRIPT>
                <P_QOH>23</P_QOH>
                <P_PRICE>5.95</P_PRICE>
        </Product>
        <Product>
                <P_CODE>23114-AA</P_CODE>
                <P_DESCRIPT>Sledge hammer, 12 lb.</P_DESCRIPT>
                <P_QOH>8</P_QOH>
                <P_MIN>5</P_MIN>
                <P_PRICE>14.40</P_PRICE>
        </Product>
</ProductList>
```

To further demonstrate the use of XML and DTD for e-commerce business data exchanges, assume the case of two companies exchanging order data. Figure 17.15 shows the DTD and XML documents for that scenario.

Although the use of DTDs is a great improvement for data sharing over the Web, a DTD provides only descriptive information for understanding how the elements – root, parent, child, mandatory or optional – relate to one another. A DTD provides limited additional semantic value, such as data type support or data validation rules. That information is very important for database administrators who are in charge of large e-commerce databases. To solve the DTD problem, the W3C published an XML schema standard to provide a better way to describe XML data.

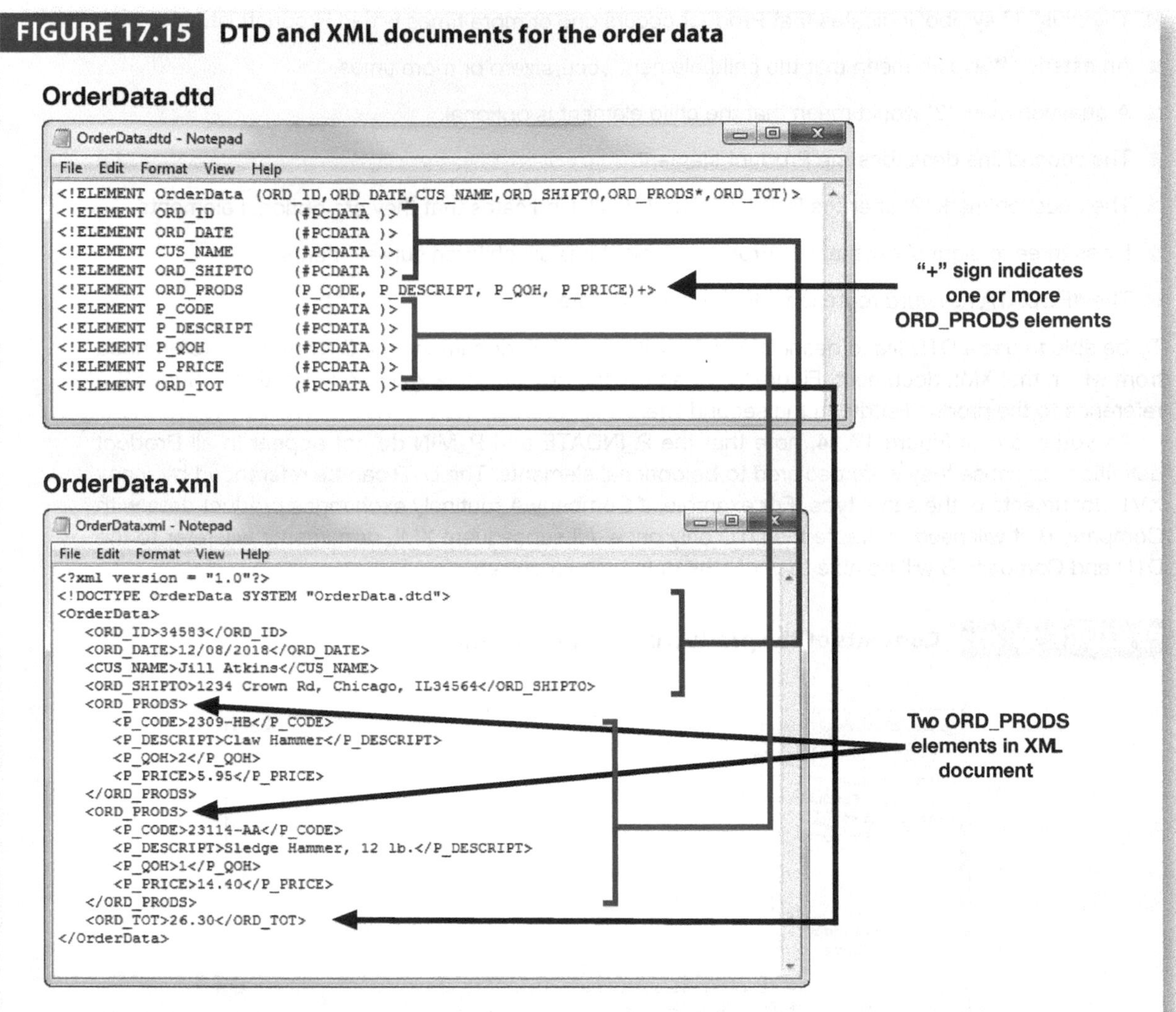

FIGURE 17.15 **DTD and XML documents for the order data**

OrderData.dtd

OrderData.dtd - Notepad

```
<!ELEMENT OrderData (ORD_ID,ORD_DATE,CUS_NAME,ORD_SHIPTO,ORD_PRODS*,ORD_TOT)>
<!ELEMENT ORD_ID        (#PCDATA )>
<!ELEMENT ORD_DATE      (#PCDATA )>
<!ELEMENT CUS_NAME      (#PCDATA )>
<!ELEMENT ORD_SHIPTO    (#PCDATA )>
<!ELEMENT ORD_PRODS     (P_CODE, P_DESCRIPT, P_QOH, P_PRICE)+>
<!ELEMENT P_CODE        (#PCDATA )>
<!ELEMENT P_DESCRIPT    (#PCDATA )>
<!ELEMENT P_QOH         (#PCDATA )>
<!ELEMENT P_PRICE       (#PCDATA )>
<!ELEMENT ORD_TOT       (#PCDATA )>
```

OrderData.xml

OrderData.xml - Notepad

```
<?xml version = "1.0"?>
<!DOCTYPE OrderData SYSTEM "OrderData.dtd">
<OrderData>
   <ORD_ID>34583</ORD_ID>
   <ORD_DATE>12/08/2018</ORD_DATE>
   <CUS_NAME>Jill Atkins</CUS_NAME>
   <ORD_SHIPTO>1234 Crown Rd, Chicago, IL34564</ORD_SHIPTO>
   <ORD_PRODS>
      <P_CODE>2309-HB</P_CODE>
      <P_DESCRIPT>Claw Hammer</P_DESCRIPT>
      <P_QOH>2</P_QOH>
      <P_PRICE>5.95</P_PRICE>
   </ORD_PRODS>
   <ORD_PRODS>
      <P_CODE>23114-AA</P_CODE>
      <P_DESCRIPT>Sledge Hammer, 12 lb.</P_DESCRIPT>
      <P_QOH>1</P_QOH>
      <P_PRICE>14.40</P_PRICE>
   </ORD_PRODS>
   <ORD_TOT>26.30</ORD_TOT>
</OrderData>
```

"+" sign indicates one or more ORD_PRODS elements
Two ORD_PRODS elements in XML document

The **XML schema** is an advanced data definition language that is used to describe the structure (elements, data types, relationship types, ranges and default values) of XML data documents. One of the main advantages of an XML schema is that it more closely maps to database terminology and features. For example, an XML schema will be able to define common database types such as date, integer or decimal, minimum and maximum values, list of valid values and required elements. Using the XML schema, a company would be able to validate the data for values that may be out of range, incorrect dates, valid values, and so on. For example, a university application must be able to specify that a grade point average (GPA) value be between zero and 4.0, and it must be able to detect an invalid birth date such as '13/16/1987'. (There is no 16th month.) Many vendors are adopting this new standard and are supplying tools to translate DTD documents into XML Schema Definition (XSD) documents. It is widely expected that XML schemas will replace DTD as the method to describe XML data.

Unlike a DTD document, which uses a unique syntax, an **XML schema definition (XSD)** file uses a syntax that resembles an XML document. Figure 17.16 shows the XSD document for the OrderData XML document.

FIGURE 17.16 **The XML schema document for the order data**

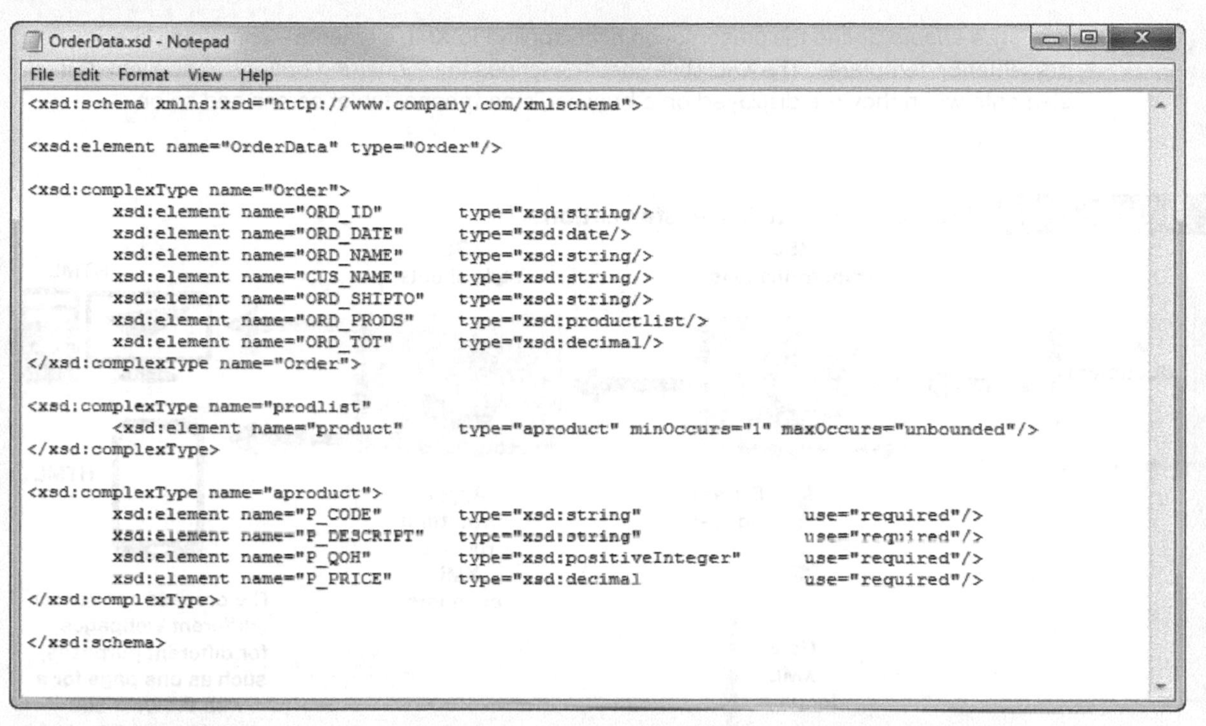
OrderData.xsd - Notepad

File Edit Format View Help

```
<xsd:schema xmlns:xsd="http://www.company.com/xmlschema">

<xsd:element name="OrderData" type="Order"/>

<xsd:complexType name="Order">
        xsd:element name="ORD_ID"        type="xsd:string/>
        xsd:element name="ORD_DATE"      type="xsd:date/>
        xsd:element name="ORD_NAME"      type="xsd:string/>
        xsd:element name="CUS_NAME"      type="xsd:string/>
        xsd:element name="ORD_SHIPTO"    type="xsd:string/>
        xsd:element name="ORD_PRODS"     type="xsd:productlist/>
        xsd:element name="ORD_TOT"       type="xsd:decimal/>
</xsd:complexType name="Order">

<xsd:complexType name="prodlist"
        <xsd:element name="product"      type="aproduct" minOccurs="1" maxOccurs="unbounded"/>
</xsd:complexType>

<xsd:complexType name="aproduct">
        xsd:element name="P_CODE"        type="xsd:string"                use="required"/>
        xsd:element name="P_DESCRIPT"    type="xsd:string"                use="required"/>
        xsd:element name="P_QOH"         type="xsd:positiveInteger"       use="required"/>
        xsd:element name="P_PRICE"       type="xsd:decimal                use="required"/>
</xsd:complexType>

</xsd:schema>
```

The code shown in Figure 17.16 is a simplified version of the XML schema document. As you can see, the XML schema syntax is similar to the XML document syntax. In addition, the XML schema introduces additional semantic information for the OrderData XML document, such as string, date and decimal data types; required elements; and minimum and maximum cardinalities for the data elements.

17.3.2 XML Presentation

One of the main benefits of XML is that it separates data structure from its presentation and processing. By separating data and presentation, you are able to present the same data in different ways – which is similar to having views in SQL. The Extensible Style Language (XSL) specification provides the mechanism to display XML data. XSL is used to define the rules by which XML data are formatted and displayed. The XSL specification is divided into two parts: Extensible Style Language Transformations (XSLT) and XSL style sheets.

- *Extensible Style Language Transformations (XSLT)* describe the general mechanism that is used to extract and process data from one XML document and enable its transformation within another document. Using XSLT, you can extract data from an XML document and convert it into a text file, an HTML Web page or a Web page that is formatted for a mobile device. What the user sees in those cases is actually a view (or HTML representation) of the actual XML data. XSLT can also be used to extract certain elements from an XML document, such as the product codes and product prices, to create a product catalogue. XSLT can even be used to transform an XML document into another XML document.

- *XSL style sheets* define the presentation rules applied to XML elements – something like presentation templates. The XSL style sheet describes the formatting options to apply to XML elements when they are displayed on a browser, smartphone, tablet screen and so on.

FIGURE 17.17 Framework for XML transformations

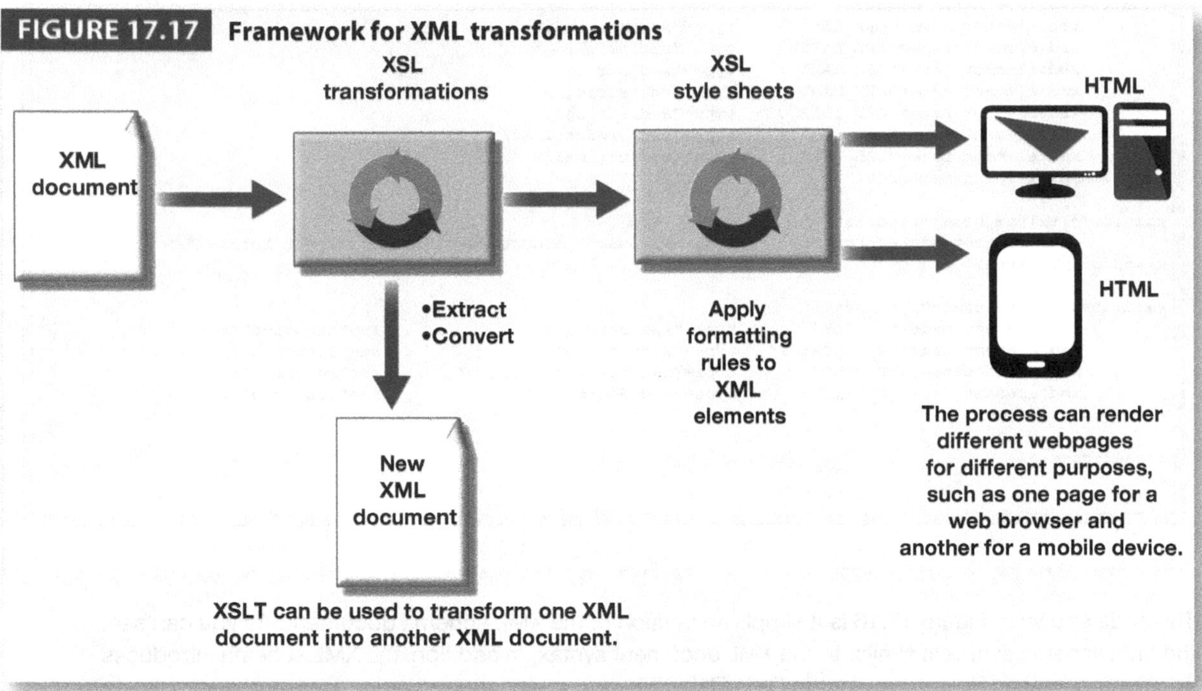

Figure 17.17 illustrates the framework used by the different components to translate XML documents into viewable Web pages, an XML document or some other document.

To display the XML document with Windows Internet Explorer (IE) 5.0 or later, enter the URL of the XML document in the browser's address bar. Figure 17.18 is based on the productlist.xml document created earlier. As you examine Figure 17.18, note that IE shows the XML data in a colour-coded, collapsible, tree-like structure. (Actually, this is the IE default style sheet that is used to render XML documents.)

FIGURE 17.18 Displaying XML documents

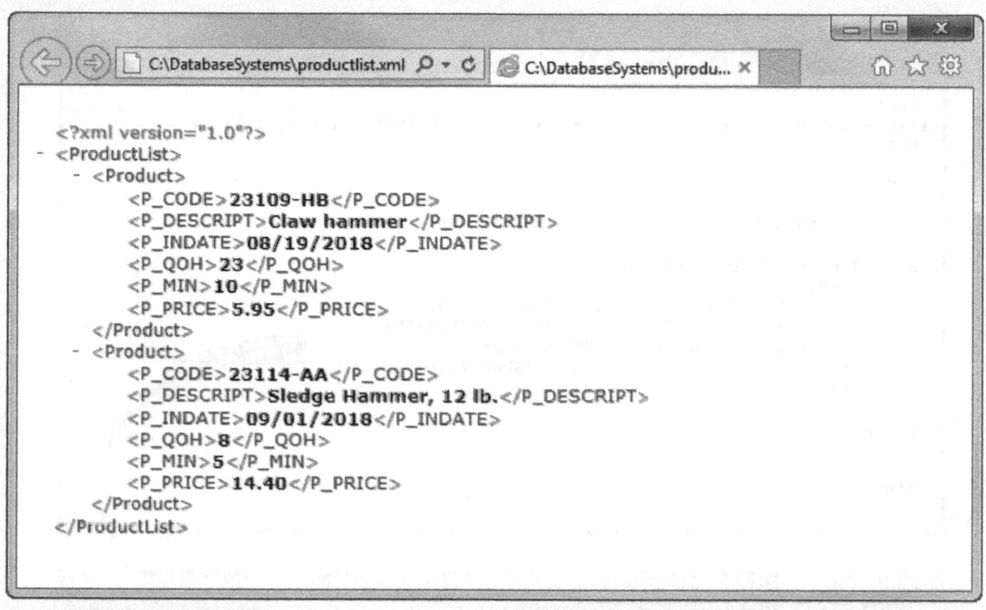

Internet Explorer also provides *data binding* of XML data to HTML documents. Figure 17.19 shows the HTML code that is used to bind an XML document to an HTML table. The example uses the <xml> tag to include the XML data in the HTML document, later to bind it to the HTML table. This example works only in IE 5.0 or later.

FIGURE 17.19 XML data binding

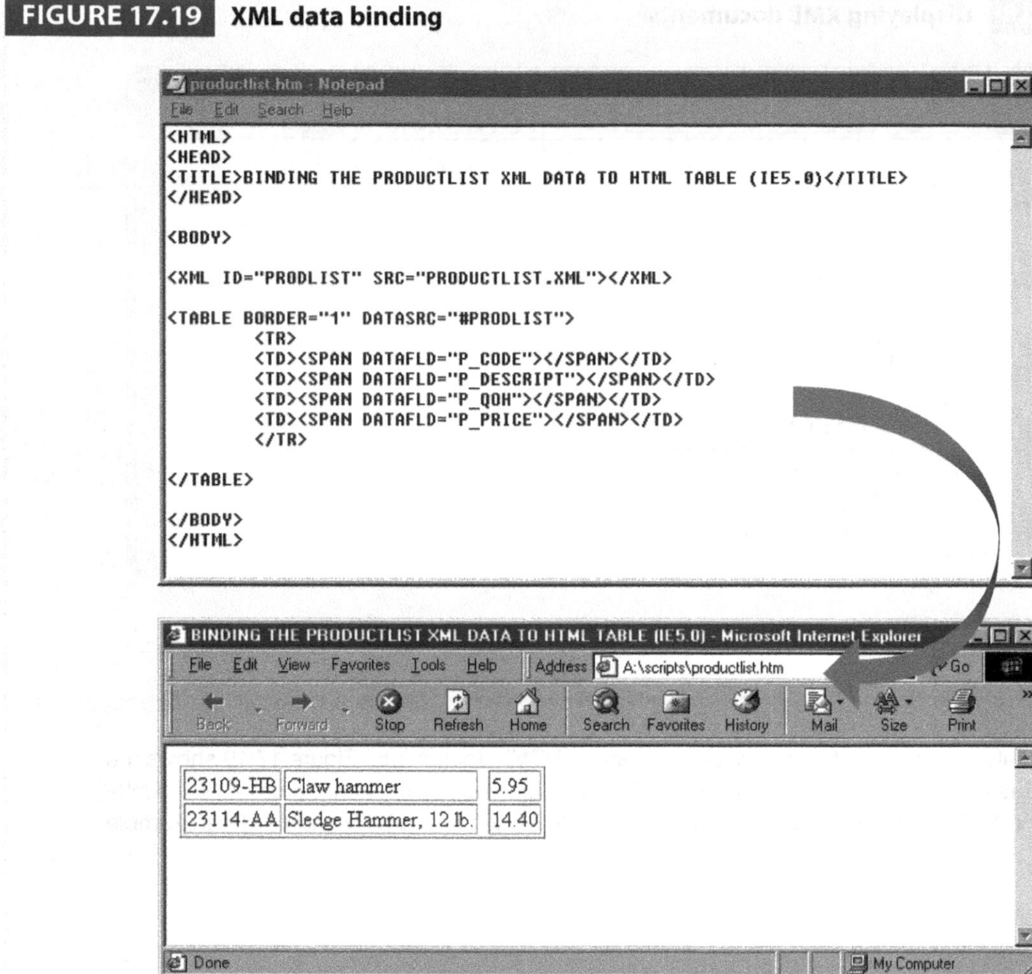

17.3.3 SQL/XML and XQuery

As you have just learnt, XML is used to transfer data from a Web-based application to the database and back again. SQL/XML and XQuery are two standard querying languages that are used to retrieve data from a relational database in the XML format. XQuery 1.0 is the W3C language designed for querying XML data and it is relatively similar to SQL, except it was designed to query semi-structured XML data. SQL/XML is an extension of SQL that is part of ANSI/ISO SQL 2011 standard. This is because only small additions have been made to the standard SQL language. These additions include:

- XML publishing functions that can be incorporated directly into the SQL query. These functions include:
    - xmlelement(), which creates an XML element with a specific name
    - xmlattributes(), which creates a set of XML attributes from the columns within the specific database table(s)
    - xmlroot(), which creates the root element of an XML document

- xmlcomment(), which allows an XML comment to be created
- xmlpi(), which allows the creation of an XML processing instruction
- xmlparse(), which parses a string as XML and returns the resulting XML value
- xmlforest(), which creates a list of XML elements from the columns within the specific database table(s)
- xmlconcat(), which combines a list of XML values into one that contains an XML forest
- xmlagg(), which aggregates a number of single XML values together to create a single XML forest.

- An XML datatype
- A set of rules to map relational data to XML.

Let's now look at an example. Consider the following SQL query:

SELECT V.VEND_CODE, V.VEND_CONTACT AS VENDOR_NAME, V.VEND_AREACODE

FROM VENDOR V;

Figure 17.20 shows the contents of the vendor table and the results of this query.

FIGURE 17.20 **The contents of the VENDOR and PRODUCT tables and results of the query**

Database Ch17_SaleCo

Table name: VENDOR

VEND_CODE	VEND_CONTACT	VEND_AREACODE	VEND_PHONE
230	Shelly K. Smithson	7325	555-1234
231	James Johnson	0181	123-4536
232	Khaya Sibiya	7325	224-2134
233	Lindiwe Molefe	0113	342-6567
234	Nijan Pillay	0181	123-3324
235	Henry Ortozo	0181	899-3425

Table name: PRODUCT

PROD_CODE	PROD_DESCRIPT	PROD_PRICE	PROD_ON_HAND	VEND_CODE
001278-AB	Claw hammer	10.23	23	232
123-21UUY	Houselite chain saw, 16 cm bar	150.09	4	235
QER-34256	Sledge hammer, 16 kg head	14.72	6	231
SRE-657UG	Rat-tail file	2.36	15	232
ZZX/3245Q	Steel tape, 12 m length	5.36	8	235

Data returned by query

SELECT V.VEND_CODE, V.VEND_CONTACT AS VENDOR_NAME, V.VEND_AREACODE

FROM VENDOR V;

VEND_CODE	VENDOR_NAME	VEND_AREACODE
230	Shelly K. Smithson	7325
231	James Johnson	0181
232	Khaya Sibiya	7325
233	Lindiwe Molefe	0113
234	Nijan Pillay	0181
235	Henry Ortozo	0181

In order to display these results as XML, the xmlelement() function can be incorporated into the SQL statement like this:

```
SELECT XMLELEMENT(NAME 'VENDOR',
XMLELEMENT(NAME 'VEND_CODE', V.VENDCODE),
XMLELEMENT(NAME 'VENDOR_NAME', V.VEND_CONTACT),
XMLELEMENT(NAME 'VEND_AREACODE', V.VEND_AREACODE))
FROM VENDOR V;
```

Each row returned by the query corresponds to one VENDOR element, which is represented as:

```
<VENDOR>
        <VEND_CODE>230</VEND_CODE>
        <VENDOR_NAME>Shelly K. Smithson</VENDOR_NAME>
        <VEND_AREACODE>7325</VEND_AREACODE>
</VENDOR>
```

As you will have seen, the SQL/XML query we have just written is quite complicated. We could rewrite this query using the publishing function xmlforest(), which creates a list of XML elements from the columns within the VENDOR table. The query would then look like this:

```
SELECT XMLELEMENT(NAME 'VENDOR',
XMLFOREST(V.VENDOR_CODE, V.VEND_CONTACT AS VENDOR_NAME, V.VEND_AREACODE))
FROM VENDOR V;
```

Producing XML from SQL queries that contain relational joins requires the use of more XML publishing functions, if we want to display the results in a way the user will understand. Suppose we wanted to list all the products that were associated with each vendor. (The contents of the PRODUCT table can be found in Figure 17.17.) This could be achieved using the following SQL query:

17

```
SELECT V.VEND_CODE, V.VEND_CONTACT AS VENDOR_NAME, P.PROD_CODE,
P.PROD_DESCRIPT

FROM VENDOR V, PRODUCT, P

WHERE V.VEND_CODE = P.VEND_CODE;
```

To represent the results of this query as XML, we want to show the vendor details once and then a list of the products that the vendor supplies. In SQL/XML this can be achieved using the publishing function xmlattributes() in a subquery that retrieves the products associated with each vendor. Subqueries in SQL/XML are only designed to return one row, so if multiple rows are to be returned they must be aggregated into one single value using the function xmlagg(). The following SQL/XML query makes use of these publishing functions to display all products associated with each vendor:

```
SELECT

XMLELEMENT(NAME VENDOR,

XMLATTRIBUTES (V.VEND_CODE AS VEND_CODE),

XMLFOREST(V.VEND_CONTACT AS VENDOR_NAME, V.VEND_AREACODE AS AREA),

XMLELEMENT(NAME PRODUCT,

(SELECT XMLAGG(XMELEMENT(NAME PRODUCT,

XMLATTRIBUTES (P.PROD_CODE AS PROD_CODE),

            XMLFOREST(P.PROD_DESCRIPT AS DESCRIPTION)))

FROM PRODUCT P

WHERE P.VEND_CODE = V.VEND_CODE)))

              AS 'PRODUCTS RELATED TO VENDORS'

FROM VENDOR V;
```

An alternative approach to SQL/XML is XQuery. XQuery is a language that can query, store, process and exchange structured or semi-structured XML data. XQuery is used in conjunction with XPath, which is used to navigate through elements and attributes in an XML document. XPath is a major component of W3C's XSLT standard. XQuery includes over 100 built-in functions including functions, for manipulating strings and comparing dates. The following is an example of an XQuery that retrieves a list of products which has been supplied by each vendor:

```
FOR V$ IN $VENDOR/ROW

RETURN

<VENDOR_CODE = '{$V/VENDOR_CODE}'>

 <VEND_NAME >{ STRING ($V/ VENDOR_CONTACT)}</VEND_NAME>

<PRODUCT>

{

              FOR $P IN $PRODUCT/ROW

              WHERE $P/VENDOR_CODE = $V/VENDOR_CODE
```

17

```
                RETURN
                        <PROD_CODE = '{$P/PROD_CODE}'
    PROD_DESCRIPT = '{$P/PROD_DESCRIPT}'/>
                }
    </PRODUCT>
    </VENDOR>
```

The XQuery performs exactly the same query as the last SQL/XML query that we looked at, but as you can see requires a more in-depth knowledge of XML programming. One of the main strengths of XQuery is that it can query data stored inside the database or directly from an XML source.

Let's consider a simpler example by using the DVDStore.xml document in Figure 17.21.

FIGURE 17.21 DVDStore.xml Document

```
<?xml version="1.0" encoding="ISO-8859-1"?>
<!—Created by KAC -->
<dvdstore>
<dvd category="Children">
        <title>ToyStory </title>
        <year>2005</year>
        <price>9.00</price>
</dvd>
<dvd category="Action">
        <title>Indiana Jones </title>
        <year>2001</year>
        <price>15.00</price>
</dvd>
</dvdstore>
```

In order to extract data from XML documents, the doc() function is used to open the dvdstore.xml file as shown below:

```
doc("dvdstore.xml")
```

In order to extract data elements, **path expressions** from XQuery are used. The following example illustrates how the title element would be extracted from the dvdstore.xml document:

```
doc("dvdstore.xml")/dvdstore/dvd/title
```

Executing this function would display the following:

```
<title>ToyStory </title>
<title>Indiana Jones </title>
```

Writing the function as /dvd/title selects the child elements of the top-level dvd element.

If we wanted to extract elements based on a specific condition, for example to select the details of DVDs costing less than twelve rand, we would write:

```
doc("dvdstore.xml")/dvdkstore/dvd[price<12]
```

17

This function would return the following:

```
<dvd category="Children">
        <title>ToyStory </title>
        <year>2005</year>
        <price>9.00</price>
</dvd>
```

FLWOR expressions are a fundamental part of XQuery. FLWOR is an acronym *for* For .. *Let .. Where .. Order By .. Return*. Each of the elements is known as a clause and only the use of the Return clause is mandatory. An example of a FLWOR expression used for retrieving DVDs costing less than twelve rand is shown below:

```
for $y in doc("dvdstore.xml")/dvdstore/dvd
where $y/price<12
order by $y/title
return $y/title
```

This expression returns the same result as the previous function, except the results are ordered. In this FLWOR expression, the for clause selects all dvd elements under the parent dvdstore element into a variable called $y. Then, the where clause selects only dvd elements with a price less than twelve rand. The order by clause orders the title results alphabetically and the return clause states what should be returned, in this case the title elements. For comparison purposes, the above FLWOR expression can also be written as the following SQL query:

```
SELECT d.title FROM dvd d WHERE d.price < 12;
```

An in-depth look at XQuery is beyond the scope of this book, but additional reading can be found in the further reading section at the end of this chapter.

17.3.4 XML Applications

Now that you have some idea of what XML is, the next question is, how can you use it? What kinds of applications lend themselves particularly well to XML? This section will list some of the uses of XML. Keep in mind that the future use of XML is limited only by the imagination and creativity of developers, designers and programmers.

- *B2B exchanges*. As noted earlier, XML enables the exchange of B2B data, providing the standard for all organisations that need to exchange data with partners, competitors, the government or customers. In particular, XML is positioned to replace Electronic Data Interchange (EDI) as the standard for the automation of the supply chain because it is less expensive and more flexible.
- *Legacy systems integration*. XML provides the 'glue' that integrates legacy system data with modern e-commerce Web systems. Web and XML technologies could be used to inject some new life in 'old but trusted' legacy applications. Another example is the use of XML to import transaction data from multiple operational databases to a data warehouse database.
- *Web page development*. XML provides several features that make it a good fit for certain Web development scenarios. For example, Web portals with large amounts of personalised data can

use XML to pull data from multiple external sources (such as news, weather and stocks) and apply different presentation rules to format pages on desktop computers as well as mobile devices.

- *Database support*. A DBMS that supports XML exchanges will be able to integrate with external systems (Web, mobile data, legacy systems, and so on) and thus enable the creation of new types of systems. These databases can import or export data in XML format or generate XML documents from SQL queries while still storing the data, using their native data model format. Alternatively, a DBMS can support a XML data type to store XML data in its native format. The implications of these capabilities are far-reaching – you would even be able to store a hierarchical-like tree structure inside a relational structure. Of course, such activities would also require that the query language be extended to support queries on XML data.
- *Database metadictionaries*. XML is also used to create metadictionaries, or vocabularies, for entire industries. Examples of metadictionaries include HR-XML for the human resources industry, the metadata encoding and transmission standard (METS) from the Library of Congress, the clinical accounting information (CLAIM) data exchange standard for patient data exchange in electronic medical record systems, and the extensible business reporting language (XBRL) standard for exchanging business and financial information.
- *XML databases*.[4] Most databases on the market support XML to manage data in some shape or form. The approaches range from simple middleware XML software to object databases with XML interfaces to full XML database engines and servers. XML databases provide for the storage of data in complex relationships. For example, an XML database would be well suited to store the contents of a book. The book's structure would dictate its database structure: a book typically consists of chapters, sections, paragraphs, figures, charts, footnotes, endnotes, and so on. Examples of XML databases are Oracle, IBM DB2 and MS SQL Server. An example of a full XML database is the Berkeley DB XML by Oracle (www.oracle.com/database/berkeley-db/xml.html).
- *XML services*. Many companies are already working on the development of a new breed of services based on XML and Web technologies. These services promise to break down the interoperability barriers among systems and companies alike. XML provides the infrastructure that facilitates heterogeneous systems to work together across the desk, the street, and the world. Services would use XML and other internet technologies to publish their interfaces. Other services, wanting to interact with existing services, would locate them and learn their vocabulary (service request and replies) to establish a 'conversation'.

One area in which internet, Web, virtualisation and XML technologies work together in innovative ways to leverage IT services is cloud computing.

17.4 CLOUD COMPUTING SERVICES

You have almost certainly heard about the 'cloud' from the thousands of publications and TV ads that have used the term over the years, although it has represented different concepts. In the late 1980s, the term *cloud* was used by telecommunication companies to describe their data networks. In the late 1990s, during the peak of internet growth, the term depicted the internet itself. Then, in 2006, Google

4 For a comprehensive analysis of XML database products, see *XML Database Products* by Ronald Bourret at *www.rpbourret.com*.

and Amazon began using the term *cloud computing* to describe a new set of innovative Web-based services. Google, Yahoo, eBay and Amazon were the early adopters of this new computing paradigm.

But what exactly is cloud computing? According to the National Institute of Standards and Technology (NIST),[5] **cloud computing** is 'a computing model for enabling ubiquitous, convenient, on-demand network access to a shared pool of configurable computer resources (e.g., networks, servers, storage, applications and services) that can be rapidly provisioned and released with minimal management effort or service provider interaction'. The term **cloud services** is used in this book to refer to the services provided by cloud computing. Cloud services allow any organisation to add information technology services such as applications, storage, servers, processing power, databases and infrastructure to its IT portfolio quickly and economically. Figure 17.22 shows a representation of cloud computing services on the internet.

FIGURE 17.22 Cloud services

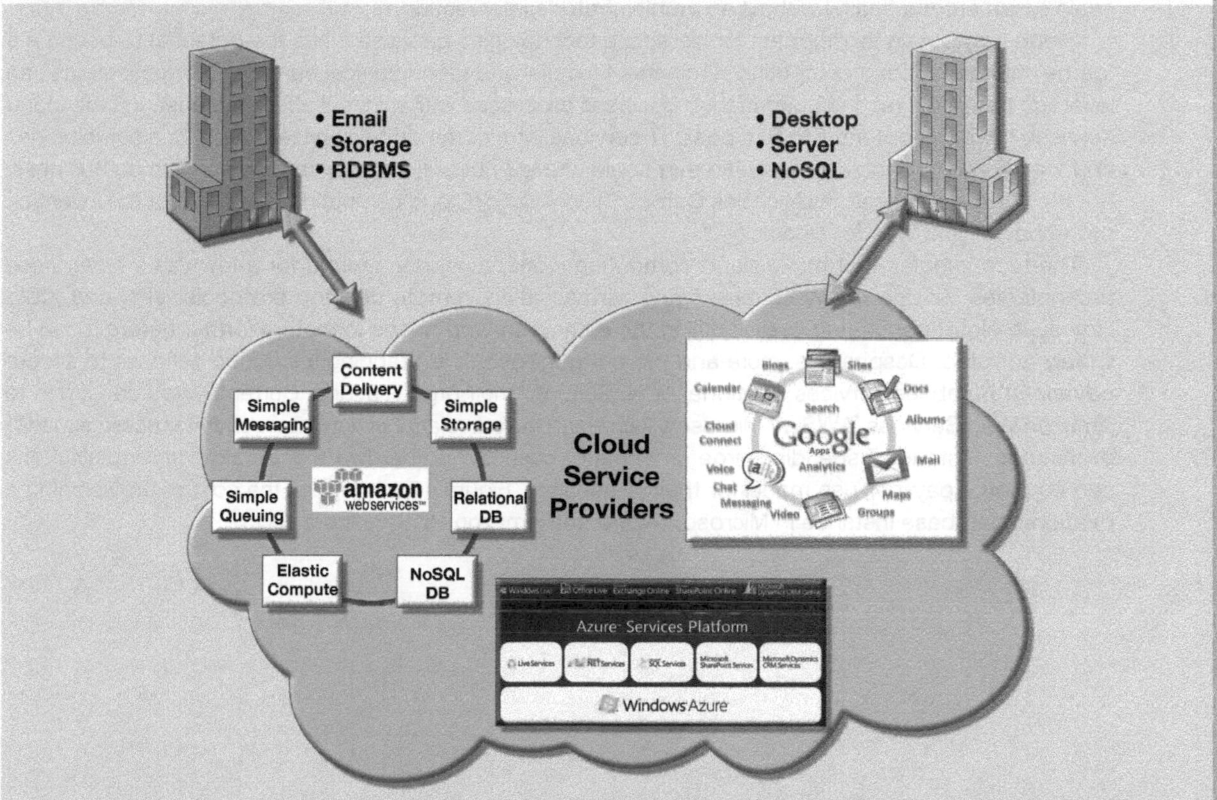

SOURCE: Course Technology/Cengage Learning

Cloud computing allows highly specialised, IT-savvy organisations such as Amazon, Google and Microsoft to build high-performance, fault-tolerant, flexible and scalable IT services. These services include applications, storage, servers, processing power, databases and email, which are delivered via the internet to individuals and organisations using a pay-as-you-go price model.

5 *Recommendations of the National Institute of Standards and Technology*, Peter Mell and Timothy Grance, Special Publication 800-145, September 2011.

For example, imagine that the chief technology officer of a non-profit organisation wants to add email services to the IT portfolio. A few years ago, this proposition would have implied building the email system's infrastructure from the ground up, including hardware, software, setup, configuration, operation and maintenance. However, in today's cloud computing era, you can use Google's G Suite for Business or Microsoft Office 365 and get a scalable, flexible and more reliable email solution for a fraction of the cost. The best part is that you do not have to worry about the daily chores of managing and maintaining the IT infrastructure, such as OS updates, patches, security, fault tolerance and recovery. What used to take months or years to implement can now be done in a matter of minutes. If you need more space, you just add another storage unit to your storage cloud. If you need more processing power to handle last-minute orders during the busy Christmas season, you simply add more processing units to your cloud servers. Even more importantly, you can scale down as easily as you scaled up. Once your need for additional processing or storage subsides, you can go back to your previous levels of usage and pay only for what you use. The beauty of cloud services is that you can scale down automatically, without an administrator's intervention.

Cloud computing is important for database technologies because it has the potential to become a 'game changer'. Cloud computing eliminates financial and technological barriers so organisations can leverage database technologies in their business processes with minimal effort and cost. In fact, cloud services have the potential to turn basic IT services into 'commodity' services, such as electricity, gas and water, and to enable a revolution that could change not only the way that companies do business, but the IT business itself. As Nicholas Carr put it so vividly: 'Cloud computing is for IT what the invention of the power grid was for electricity'.[6]

The technologies that make cloud computing work have been around for a few years now; these technologies include the Web, messaging, virtualisation, remote desktop protocols, VPN and XML. However, cloud computing itself is still in the early years and needs to mature further before it can be widely adopted. Despite this, more and more organisations are tapping into cloud services to secure advanced database services (relational or NoSQL) for their organisations. Currently, you can log in to Amazon Web Services (AWS) or Microsoft Azure and have a relational database ready for use in a matter of minutes. Instead of spending large amounts of cash buying hardware and software, organisations can employ a pay-per-use model for their IT services. Figure 17.23 depicts the cost of provisioning a relational database instance in Microsoft Azure and Amazon RDS, respectively.

6 Nicholas Carr, *The Big Switch: Rewiring the World, from Edison to Google*, W.W. Norton & Co., 2009.

FIGURE 17.23 Provisioning an RDBMS in the cloud

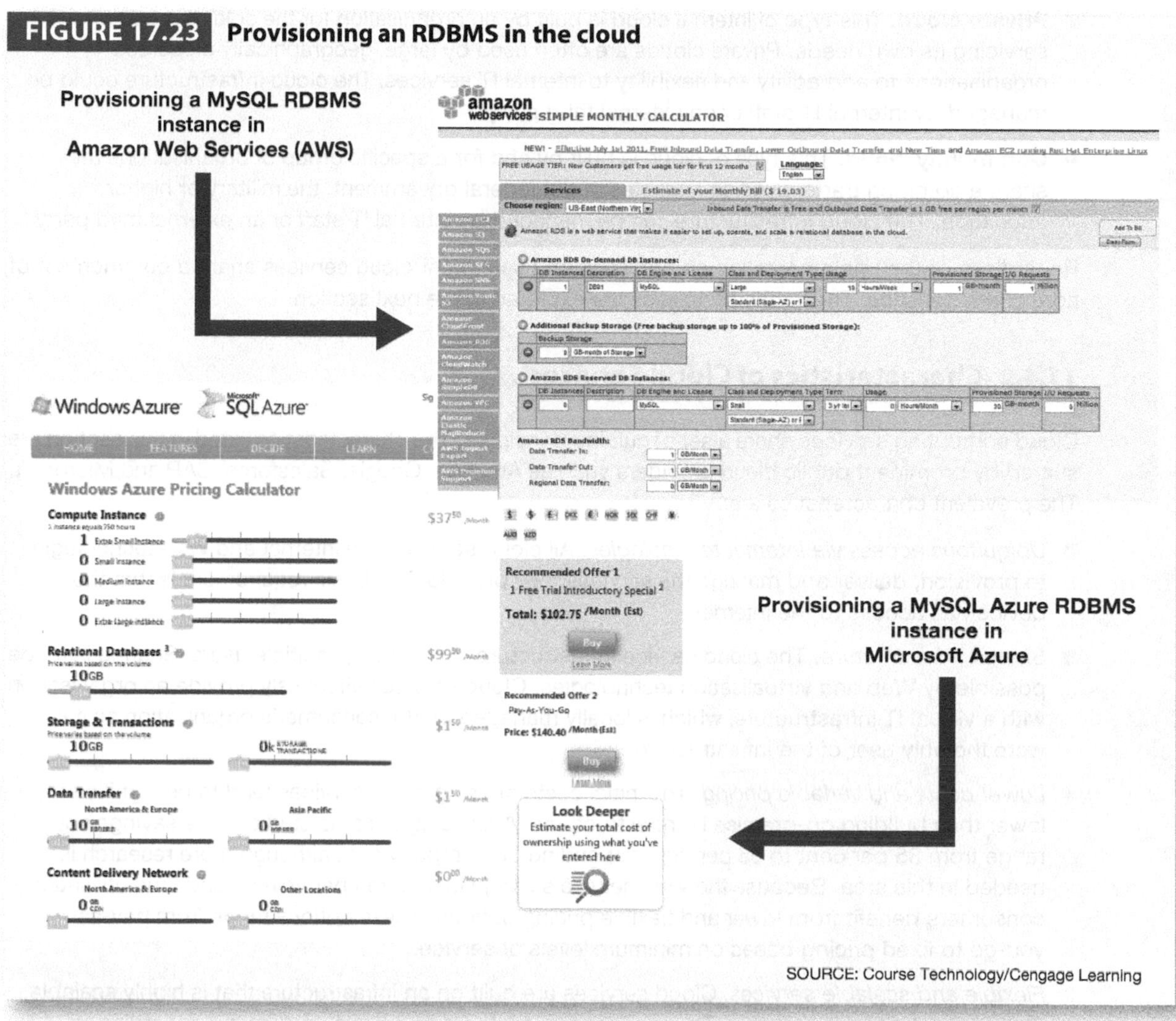

SOURCE: Course Technology/Cengage Learning

Although Figure 17.23 shows a cloud that requires some degree of customisation on the customer's part, other cloud computing services are more transparent to the user and require less customisation. For example, Dropbox is a simple cloud service that lets you synchronise your documents, photos, music and other files transparently over the internet across many devices. In 2011, Apple announced a similar service, known as iCloud. Both services work transparently behind the scenes with minimal end-user intervention. As you can see, cloud computing implementations vary; the next section explains the basic types.

17.4.1 Cloud Implementation Types

Cloud computing has different types of implementations based on who the target customers are:

- **Public cloud.** This type of cloud infrastructure is built by a third-party organisation to sell cloud services to the general public. The public cloud is the most common type of cloud implementation; examples include Amazon Web Services (AWS), Google App Engine and Microsoft Azure. In this model, cloud consumers share resources with other consumers transparently. The public cloud infrastructure is managed exclusively by the third-party provider.

- **Private cloud**. This type of internal cloud is built by an organisation for the sole purpose of servicing its own needs. Private clouds are often used by large, geographically dispersed organisations to add agility and flexibility to internal IT services. The cloud infrastructure could be managed by internal IT staff or an external third party.
- **Community cloud**. This type of cloud is built by and for a specific group of organisations that share a common trade, such as agencies of the federal government, the military or higher education. The cloud infrastructure can be managed by internal IT staff or an external third party.

Regardless of the implementation an organisation uses, most cloud services share a common set of core characteristics. These characteristics are explored in the next section.

17.4.2 Characteristics of Cloud Services

Cloud computing services share a set of guiding principles. The characteristics listed in this section are shared by prominent public cloud providers such as Amazon, Google, Salesforce, SAP and Microsoft. The prevalent characteristics are:

- *Ubiquitous access via internet technologies*. All cloud services use internet and Web technologies to provision, deliver and manage the services they provide. The basic requirement is that the device has access to the internet.
- *Shared infrastructure*. The cloud service infrastructure is shared by multiple users. Sharing is made possible by Web and virtualisation technologies. Cloud services effectively provide an organisation with a virtual IT infrastructure, which is locally managed by the consumer's organisation as if it were the only user of the infrastructure.
- *Lower costs and variable pricing*. The initial costs of using cloud services tend to be significantly lower than building on-premise IT infrastructures. According to some studies,[7] the savings could range from 35 per cent to 55 per cent depending on company size, although more research is needed in this area. Because the Web service's usage is metered per volume and time utilisation, consumers benefit from lower and flexible pricing options. These options range from pay-as-you-go to fixed pricing based on minimum levels of service.
- *Flexible and scalable services*. Cloud services are built on an infrastructure that is highly scalable, fault tolerant and very reliable. The services can scale up and down on demand according to resource demands.
- *Dynamic provisioning*. The consumer can quickly provision any needed resources, including servers, processing power, storage and email, by accessing the Web management dashboard and then adding and removing services on demand. This process can also be automated via other services.
- *Service orientation*. Cloud computing focuses on providing consumers with specific, well-defined services that use well-known interfaces. These interfaces hide the complexity from the end user, and can be delivered anytime and anywhere.
- *Managed operations*. Cloud computing minimises the need for extensive and expensive in-house IT staff. The system infrastructure is managed by the cloud provider. The consumer organisation's IT staff is free from routine management and maintenance tasks so they can focus on other tasks

7 'The Compelling TCO Case for Cloud Computing in SMB and Mid-Market Enterprises: A 4-year total cost of ownership (TCO) perspective comparing cloud and on-premise business application development', Sanjeev Aggarwal, Partner; Laurie McCabe, Partner; Hurwitz & Associates, 2009.

within the organisation. Managed operations apply to organisations that use public clouds and that outsource cloud management to an external third party.

The preceding list is not exhaustive, but it is a starting point for understanding most cloud computing offerings. Although most companies move to cloud services because of cost savings, some companies move to them because they are the best way to gain access to specific IT resources that would otherwise be unavailable. Not all cloud services are the same; in fact, there are several different types, as explained in the next section.

17.4.3 Types of Cloud Services

Cloud services come in different shapes and forms; no single type of service works for all consumers. In fact, cloud services often follow an 'à la carte' model; consumers can choose multiple service options according to their individual needs. These services can build on top of one another to provide sophisticated solutions. Based on the types of services provided, cloud services can be classified by the following categories:

- **Software as a Service (SaaS).** The cloud service provider offers turnkey applications that run in the cloud. Consumers can run the provider's applications internally in their organisations via the Web or any mobile device. The consumer can customise certain aspects of the application but cannot make changes to the application itself. The application is actually shared among users from multiple organisations. Examples of SaaS include Microsoft Office 365, Google Docs, Intuit's TurboTax Online and SCALA digital signage.
- **Platform as a Service (PaaS).** The cloud service provider offers the capability to build and deploy consumer created applications using the provider's cloud infrastructure. In this scenario, the consumer can build, deploy and manage applications using the provider's cloud tools, languages and interfaces. However, the consumer does not manage the underlying cloud infrastructure. Examples of PaaS include the Microsoft Azure platform with .NET and the Java development environment, and Google App Engine with Python or Java.
- **Infrastructure as a Service (IaaS).** In this case, the cloud service provider offers consumers the ability to provision their own resources on demand; these resources include storage, servers, databases, processing units and even a complete virtualised desktop. The consumer can then add or remove the resources as needed. For example, a consumer can use AWS and provision a server computer that runs Linux and Apache Web server using 64 GB of RAM and 1 TB of storage.

Figure 17.24 illustrates a sample of the different types of cloud services; these services can be accessed from any computing device.

Cloud computing services have evolved in their sophistication and flexibility. The merging of new technologies has enabled the creation of new options such as 'desktop as a service', which effectively creates a virtual computer on the cloud that can be accessed from any device over the internet. For

FIGURE 17.24 Types of cloud services

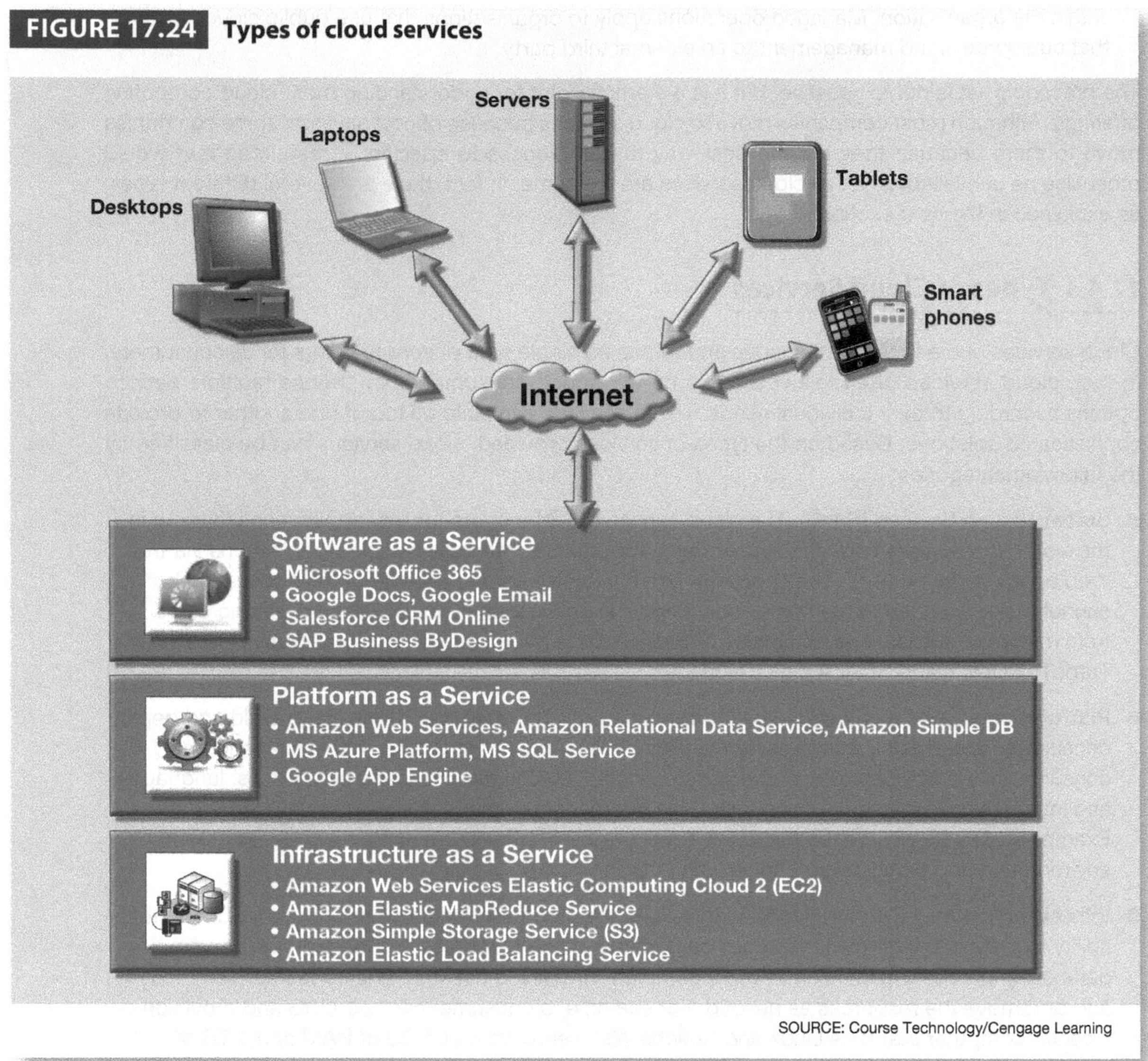

SOURCE: Course Technology/Cengage Learning

example, you can use a service such as VirtualBox (www.virtualbox.org) and get a Windows 10 desktop running over the Web for your personal use in a matter of minutes. Moreover, you can access your virtual desktop via the Web browser or using any Remote Desktop Protocol (RDP) application.

17.4.4 Cloud Services: Advantages and Disadvantages

Cloud computing has grown remarkably in the past few years. Companies of all sizes are enjoying the advantages of cloud computing, but its widespread adoption is still limited by several factors.[8] Table 17.4 summarises the main advantages and disadvantages of cloud computing.

8 Cloud Computing Market Outlook 2019 | Global Opportunities, Challenges, Forecast and Strategies To 2028, Global Banking and Finance Review, 2019, Available: www.globalbankingandfinance.com/category/news/cloud-computing-market-outlook-2019-global-opportunities-challenges-forecast-and-strategies-to-2028/

TABLE 17.4 Advantages and disadvantages of cloud computing

Advantages	Disadvantages
Low initial cost of entry. Cloud computing has lower costs of entry when compared with the alternative of building in-house.	*Issues of security, privacy and compliance*. Trusting sensitive company data to external entities is difficult for most data-cautious organisations.
Scalability/elasticity. It is easy to add and remove resources on demand.	*Hidden costs of implementation and operation*. It is hard to estimate bandwidth and data migration costs.
Support for mobile computing. Cloud computing providers support multiple types of mobile computing devices.	*Data migration is a difficult and lengthy process*. Migrating large amounts of data to and from the cloud infrastructure can be difficult and time-consuming.
Ubiquitous access. Consumers can access cloud resources from anywhere at any time, as long as they have internet access.	*Complex licensing schemes*. Organisations that implement cloud services are faced with complex licensing schemes and complicated service-level agreements.
High reliability and performance. Cloud providers build solid infrastructures that are otherwise difficult for the average organisation to leverage.	*Loss of ownership and control*. Companies that use cloud services are no longer in complete control of their data. What is the responsibility of the cloud provider if data are breached? Can the vendor use your data without your consent?
Fast provisioning. Resources can be provisioned on demand in a matter of minutes with minimal effort.	*Organisation culture*. End users tend to be resistant to change. Do the savings justify being dependent on a single provider? Will the cloud provider be around in ten years?
Managed infrastructure. Most cloud implementations are managed by dedicated internal or external staff. This allows the organisation's IT staff to focus on other areas.	*Difficult integration with internal IT system*. Configuring the cloud services to integrate transparently with internal authentication and other internal services could be a daunting task.

As the table shows, the top perceived benefit of cloud computing is the lower cost of entry. At the same time, the chief concern of cloud computing is data security and privacy, particularly in companies that deal with sensitive data and are subject to high levels of regulation and compliance.[9] This concern leads to the perception that cloud services are mainly implemented in small to medium-sized companies where the risk of service loss is minimal. In fact, some companies that are subject to strict data security regulations tend to favour private clouds rather than public ones.[10]

One of the biggest growth segments in cloud services is mobile computing. For example, Netflix,[11] the video-on-demand trailblazer, announced in 2011 that it had moved significant parts of its IT infrastructure to AWS. Netflix decided to move to the cloud because of the challenges of building IT infrastructure fast enough to keep up with its relentless growth.

9 'Are security issues delaying adoption of cloud computing?', Ellen Messmer, *Network World*, April 27, 2009.

10 'Lessons From FarmVille', Charles Babcock, *InformationWeek*, May 16, 2011.

11 'NoSQL at Netflix', Yuri Israilevsky, Director of Cloud and Systems Infrastructure at Netflix, January 28, 2011, *http://techblog.netflixx.com/2011/ nosql-at-netflix.html*.

NOTE

Cloud Reality Check: Is the Cloud Enterprise Ready?

Cloud service outages and security breach incidents are reported every year. Such incidents affect all types and sizes of organisations, from data breaches in large universities to service interruptions in cloud infrastructure providers. Some are very public, such as the iCloud security breach that allowed hackers to steal thousands of private pictures from well-known celebrities. Other incidents could affect millions of people all over the world, such as interruptions in social media services (Instagram, Facebook, Twitter, etc.). These incidents can cause service interruption, data loss, performance degradation, or cost millions of dollars in lost business. To see the up-to-date status of the most common web services, go to http://downdetector.com. There, you can find a list of the most recent problems by provider with a live outage map.

Regardless of a company's size, databases remain at the centre of all system development. Cloud computing brings a new dimension to data management that is within reach of any type of organisation.

17.4.5 SQL Data Services

As you have seen in this chapter, data access technologies have evolved from simple ODBC data retrieval to advanced remote data processing using ADO.NET and XML. At the same time, companies are looking for ways to better manage ever-growing amounts of data while controlling costs without sacrificing data management features. Cloud computing provides a relatively stable and reliable platform for developing and deploying business services; cloud vendors have expanded their business to offer SQL data services. **SQL data services (SDS)** refers to a cloud computing-based data management service that provides relational data storage, access and management to companies of all sizes without the typically high costs of in-house hardware, software, infrastructure and personnel. This type of service provides some unique benefits:

- *Hosted data management*. SDS typically uses a cluster of database servers that provide a large subset of database functionality over the internet to database administrators and users. Typically, features such as SQL queries, indexing, stored procedures, triggers, reporting and analytical functions are available to end users. Other features such as data synchronisation, data backup and restore, and data importing and exporting are available for administrative purposes.
- *Standard protocols*. SDS uses standard data communication and relational data access protocols. Typically, these services encapsulate SQL networking protocols, such as SQL-Net for Oracle databases and Tabular Data Services (TDS) for Microsoft SQL Server databases, inside the TCP/IP networking protocol.
- *A common programming interface*. SDS is transparent to application developers. Programmers continue to use familiar programming interfaces such as ADO.NET and Visual Studio.NET to manipulate the data. Programmers write embedded SQL code in their applications and connect to the database as if the data were stored locally instead of in a remote location on the internet. One potential disadvantage, however, is that some specialised data types may not be supported by SDS.

SQL data services offer the following advantages when compared with in-house systems:

- Highly reliable and scalable relational database for a fraction of the cost
- High level of failure tolerance because data are normally distributed and replicated among multiple servers

- Dynamic and automatic load balancing
- Automated data backup and disaster recovery included with the service
- Dynamic creation and allocation of database processes and storage.

Cloud providers such as Amazon, Google and Microsoft allow you to get your own database server running in a matter of minutes. Even better, you do not have to worry about backups, fault tolerance, scalability and routine maintenance tasks. The use of SQL data services enables rapid application development for businesses with limited information technology resources, and allows them to deploy business solutions rapidly. A consumer of cloud services is free to use the database to create the best solution for the problem at hand. However, having access to relational database technology via a SQL data service is just the start – you still need to be knowledgeable about database design and SQL to develop high-quality applications.

17.5 THE SEMANTIC WEB

The Semantic Web was conceived by Tim Berners-Lee, one of the founders of the WWW and director of the World Wide Web Consortium (W3C) as a mechanism for describing concepts in a way that computers can actually understand. In 2001, he published his initial vision of the future of the WWW as:

> 'If the interaction between person and hypertext could be so intuitive that the machine-readable information space gave an accurate representation of the state of people's thoughts, interactions, and work patterns, then machine analysis could become a very powerful management tool, seeing patterns in our work and facilitating our working together through the typical problems which beset the management of large organisations'.[12]

The WWW represents information using a variety of formats including images, multimedia and natural language, which is easy for the majority of human beings to understand as they comprehend the semantics of language. A traditional computer, however, can only understand the syntax of the language and cannot relate the meanings between two concepts written using different natural languages that actually have the same meaning.

In 2001, Tim Berners-Lee formally defined his idea of a Semantic Web as 'An extension of the current web in which information is given well-defined meaning, better enabling computers and people to work in cooperation'.[13]

Today, the Semantic Web is often referred to as a *Web of data*. On a daily basis, individuals use the WWW to share photographs, book holidays, manage bank accounts and view their own calendar. However, it is not always possible to link data between applications as each application manages and maintains its own data. If we had a Web of data, it would be possible to know what you were doing (via your calendar) when you took a specific photograph.

Research and work on the Sematic Web is ongoing and led by the W3C in collaboration with researchers and industry.[14] The aim is to produce a framework that allows all data to be shared and reused across applications, without any boundaries. The framework will establish common formats for integration and combination of data from different sources and develop a language for modelling how data relates to real world objects. The framework is based on the **Resource Description Framework (RDF),** which is a model that has a number of features for interchanging data over the WWW. For example, one such feature allows data from two different applications to be merged even if the underlying database schemas are different.

---

12 Berners-Lee, T. 'WWW: Past, Present, and Future', *Computer*, October 1996 (vol. 29 no. 10), pp. 69–77.
13 Berners-Lee, T., Hendler, J. and Lassila, O. 'The Semantic Web', *Scientific American*, May 2001.
14 W3C Semantic Web Activity. Available: www.w3.org/standards/semanticweb/

Technologies developed for using the Sematic Web are being used by large organisations. One of the most public uses of the Sematic Web was by the British Broadcasting Corporation (BBC) World Cup website in 2010. One of the main benefits to the BBC was in enabling' ... very rich cross-domain user journeys. This means BBC content can be discovered by users in many different ways, and content teams within the organisation have a focal point around which to organise their content.'[15] One of the key trends in 2019 is the use of semantic knowledge graphs (sometimes referred to as ontologies) to allow semantic data to be connected and navigable through a graph structure. Having data that is labelled in training sets helps machine learning algorithms to learn, virtual assistants to have conversations, and the mapping of genetic patient data in healthcare to try to detect early warning signs of disease. Such is the importance of semantics, an International Semantic Web conference is held annually where the latest research and industrial applications are showcased.

---

15 Raimond, Y., Scott, T., Sinclair, P., Miller, L., Betts, S. and McNamara, F. Case Study: Use of Semantic Web Technologies on the BBC Web Sites, 2010. Available: www.w3.org/2001/sw/sweo/public/UseCases/BBC/

SUMMARY

- Database connectivity refers to the mechanisms through which application programs connect and communicate with data repositories. Database connectivity software is also known as *database middleware.*
- Microsoft database connectivity interfaces are dominant players in the market and enjoy the support of most database vendors. In fact, ODBC, OLE-DB and ADO.NET form the backbone of Microsoft's Universal Data Access (UDA) architecture.
- Native database connectivity refers to the connection interface that is provided by the database vendor and is unique to that vendor. ODBC is probably the most widely supported database connectivity interface. ODBC allows any Windows application to access relational data sources using standard SQL. Data Access Objects (DAO) is an older, object-oriented application interface. Remote Data Objects (RDO) is a higher-level, object-oriented application interface used to access remote database servers. RDO was optimised to deal with server-based databases such as Microsoft SQL Server and Oracle.
- Object Linking and Embedding for Database (OLE-DB) is database middleware developed with the goal of adding object-oriented functionality for access to relational and non-relational data. ActiveX Data Objects (ADO) provides a high-level, application-oriented interface to interact with OLE-DB, DAO, and RDO. Based on ADO, ADO.NET is the data access component of Microsoft's. NET application development framework. Java Database Connectivity (JDBC) is the standard way to interface Java applications with data sources.
- Database access through the Web is achieved through middleware. To improve the capabilities on the client side of the Web browser, you must use plug-ins and other client-side extensions such as Java and JavaScript, or ActiveX and VBScript. On the server side, Web application servers are middleware that expand the functionality of Web servers by linking them to a wide range of services, such as databases, directory systems and search engines.
- Extensible Markup Language (XML) facilitates the exchange of B2B and other data over the internet. XML provides the semantics that facilitates the exchange, sharing and manipulation of structured documents across organisational boundaries. XML produces the description and the representation of data, thus setting the stage for data manipulation in ways that were not possible before XML. XML documents can be validated through the use of Document Type Definition (DTD) documents and XML Schema Definition (XSD) documents.

- Cloud computing is a computing model that provides ubiquitous, on-demand access to a shared pool of configurable resources that can be rapidly provisioned. SQL data services (SDS) refers to a cloud computing-based data management service that provides relational data storage, ubiquitous access and local management to companies of all sizes. This service enables rapid application development for businesses with limited information technology resources. SDS allows rapid deployment of business solutions using standard protocols and common programming interfaces.
- The Semantic Web, often referred to as a Web of data, is a framework that allows all data on the WWW to be shared and reused across applications, without any boundaries.

KEY TERMS

ActiveX
ActiveX Data Objects (ADO)
ADO.NET
application programming interface (API)
Call Level Interface (CLI)
client-side extensions
cloud computing
cloud services
common cloud
Common Gateway Interface (CGI)
Data Access Objects (DAO)
data source name (DSN)
database middleware
DataSet
Document Type Definition (DTD)
dynamic link libraries (DLLs)
Extensible Markup Language (XML)
Infrastructure as a Service (InaS)
Java
Java Database Connectivity (JDBC)
JavaScript
LAMP
Microsoft .NET framework
Object Linking and Embedding for Database (OLE-DB)
Open Database Connectivity (ODBC)
path expressions
Platform as a Service (PaaS)
plug-in
private cloud
public cloud
Remote Data Objects (RDO)
Resource Description Framework (RDF)
script
server-side extension
Software as a Service (SaaS)
SQL data services (SDS)
stateless system
tags
Universal Data Access (UDA)
VBScript
Web-to-database middleware
XML schema
XML schema definition (XSD)

FURTHER READING

Duckett, J., *PHP & MySQL: Server-side Web Development*. John Wiley & Sons, 2019.
Fawcett, J., Ayers, D. and Quin, L., *Beginning XML*, 5th revised edition. John Wiley & Sons, 2012.
Jain, A., *The Cloud DBA-Oracle: Managing Oracle Database in the Cloud*. Apress, 2017.

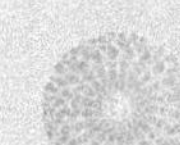

Online Content Answers to selected Review Questions and Problems for this chapter are available on the online platform for this book.

REVIEW QUESTIONS

1 Give some examples of database connectivity options and what they are used for.

2 What are ODBC, DAO and RDO? How are they related?

3 What is the difference between DAO and RDO?

17

4. What are the three basic components of the ODBC architecture?
5. Which steps are required to create an ODBC data source name?
6. What is OLE-DB used for, and how does it differ from ODBC?
7. Explain the OLE-DB model based on its two types of objects.
8. How does ADO complement OLE-DB?
9. What is ADO.NET, and what two new features make it important for application development?
10. What is a DataSet, and why is it considered to be disconnected?
11. What are Web server interfaces used for? Give some examples.
12. What does this statement mean: The Web is a stateless system. What implications does a stateless system have for database applications developers?
13. What is a Web application server, and how does it work from a database perspective?
14. What are scripts, and what is their function? (Think in terms of database applications development.)
15. What is XML, and why is it important?
16. What are Document Type Definition (DTD) documents, and what do they do?
17. What are XML Schema Definition (XSD) documents, and what do they do?
18. What is JDBC, and what is it used for?
19. What is cloud computing, and why is it a 'game changer'?
20. Name and contrast the types of cloud computing implementation.
21. Name and describe the most prevalent characteristics of cloud computing services.
22. Using the internet, search for providers of cloud services. Then, classify the types of services they provide (SaaS, PaaS and IaaS).
23. Summarise the main advantages and disadvantages of cloud computing services.
24. Define SQL data services and list their advantages.
25. What is meant by the Semantic Web?

Online Content The databases used in the Problems for this chapter can be found on the online platform for this book.

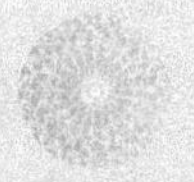

PROBLEMS

In the following exercises, you set up database connectivity using Microsoft Excel.

1. Use Microsoft Excel to connect to the Ch02_InsureCo Microsoft Access database, using ODBC, and retrieve all of the AGENTs.
2. Use Microsoft Excel to connect to the Ch02_InsureCo Microsoft Access database, using ODBC, and retrieve all of the CUSTOMERs.

3 Use Microsoft Excel to connect to the Ch02_InsureCo Microsoft Access database, using ODBC, and retrieve the customers whose AGENT_CODE is equal to 503.

4 Create an ODBC System Data Source Name Ch02_SaleCo, using the Control Panel, Administrative Tools, Data Sources (ODBC) option.

5 Use Microsoft Excel to list all of the invoice lines for Invoice 103, using the Ch02_SaleCo System DSN.

6 Create an ODBC System Data Source Name Ch02_Tinycollege, using the Control Panel, Administrative Tools, Data Sources (ODBC) option.

7 Use Microsoft Excel to list all classes taught in room KLR200, using the Ch02_TinyCollege System DSN.

8 Create a sample XML document and DTD for the exchange of customer data.

9 Create a sample XML document and DTD for the exchange of product and pricing data.

10 Create a sample XML document and DTD for the exchange of order data.

11 Create a sample XML document and DTD for the exchange of student transcript data. Use your college transcript as a sample.

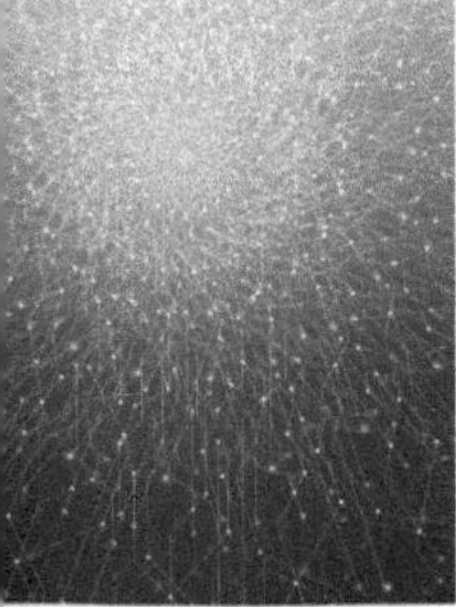

GLOSSARY

A

access plan A set of instructions generated at application compilation time that is created and managed by a DBMS. The access plan predetermines how an application's query will access the database at run time.

ActiveX Microsoft's alternative to Java. A specification for writing programs that will run inside the Microsoft client browser, Internet Explorer. Oriented mainly to Windows applications, it is not portable. It adds controls such as drop-down windows and calendars to Web pages.

ActiveX Data Objects (ADO) A Microsoft object framework that provides a high-level, application-oriented interface to OLE-DB, DAO, and RDO. ADO provides a unified interface to access data from any programming language that uses the underlying OLE-DB objects.

ad hoc query A "spur-of-the-moment" question.

ADO.NET The data access component of Microsoft's .NET application development framework, which is a component-based platform for developing distributed, heterogeneous, and interoperable applications aimed at manipulating any type of data over any network using any operating system and programming language.

aggregate aware A data model that organises data around a central entity based on the way the data will be used.

aggregate ignorant A data model that does not organise data around a central entity based on the anticipated usage of the data.

algorithms A process or set of operations in a calculation.

alias An alternative name for a column or table in a SQL statement.

ALTER TABLE The SQL command used to make changes to table structure. When the command is followed by a keyword (ADD or MODIFY), it adds a column or changes column characteristics.

American National Standards Institute (ANSI) The group that accepted the DBTG recommendations and augmented database standards in 1975 through its SPARC committee.

analytical database A database focused primarily on storing historical data and business metrics used exclusively for tactical or strategic decision making.

AND - No match found showing the function The SQL logical operator used to link multiple conditional expressions in a WHERE or HAVING clause. It requires that all conditional expressions evaluate to true.

anonymous PL/SQL block A PL/SQL block that has not been given a specific name.

application processor See *transaction processor (TP)*.

application programming interface (API) Software through which programmers interact with middleware. An API allows the use of generic SQL code, thereby allowing client processes to be database server-independent.

atomic attribute An attribute that cannot be further subdivided to produce meaningful components. For example, a person's last name attribute cannot be meaningfully subdivided.

atomic transaction property A property that requires all parts of a transaction to be treated as a single, logical unit of work in which all operations must be completed (committed) to produce a consistent database.

atomicity See *atomic transaction property*.

attribute A characteristic of an entity or object. An attribute has a name and a data type.

attribute domain See *domain*.

attribute hierarchy A top-down data organisation that is used for two main purposes: aggregation and drill-down/roll-up data analysis.

audit log A security feature of a database management system that automatically records a brief description of the database operations performed by all users.

authentication The process through which a DBMS verifies that only registered users can access the database.

authorisation management Procedures that protect and guarantee database security and integrity. Such procedures include user access management, view definition, DBMS access control, and DBMS usage monitoring.

automatic query optimisation A method by which a DBMS finds the most efficient access path for the execution of a query.

AVG A SQL aggregate function that outputs the mean average for a specified column or expression.

B

batch processing A data processing method that runs data processing tasks from beginning to end without any user interaction.

batch update routine A routine that pools transactions into a single batch to update a master table in a single operation.

BETWEEN In SQL, a special comparison operator used to check whether a value is within a range of specified values.

Big Data A movement to find new and better ways to manage large amounts of Web-generated data and derive business insight from it, while simultaneously providing high performance and scalability at a reasonable cost.

binary lock A lock that has only two states: *locked* (1) and *unlocked* (0). If a data item is locked by a transaction, no other transaction can use that data item. See also *lock*.

binary relationship An ER term for an association (relationship) between two entities. For example, PROFESSOR teaches COURSE.

bitmap index An index that uses a bit array (0s and 1s) to represent the existence of a value or condition.

block report In the Hadoop Distributed File System (HDFS), a report sent every six hours by the data node to the name node informing the name node which blocks are on that data node.

Boolean algebra A branch of mathematics that uses the logical operators OR, AND, and NOT.

bottom-up design A design philosophy that begins by identifying individual design components and then aggregates them into larger units. In database design, the process begins by defining attributes and then groups them into entities. Compare to top-down design.

boundaries The external limits to which any proposed system is subjected. These limits include budgets, personnel, and existing hardware and software.

Boyce-Codd normal form (BCNF) A special type of third normal form (3NF) in which every determinant is a candidate key. A table in BCNF must be in 3NF. See also *determinant*.

bridge entity See *composite entity*.

BSON (Binary JSON) A computer-readable format for data interchange that expands the JSON format to include additional data types including binary objects.

b-tree index An ordered data structure organised as an upside-down tree.

bucket In a key-value database, a logical collection of related key-value pairs.

business intelligence A comprehensive, cohesive, and integrated set of tools and processes used to capture, collect, integrate, store, and analyse data with the purpose of generating and presenting information to support business decision making.

business rule A description of a policy, procedure, or principle within an organisation. For example, a pilot cannot be on duty for more than 10 hours during a 24-hour period, or a professor may teach up to four classes during a semester.

C

Call Level Interface (CLI) A standard developed by the SQL Access Group for database access.

candidate key A minimal superkey; that is, a key that does not contain a subset of attributes that is itself a superkey. See *key*.

cardinality A property that assigns a specific value to connectivity and expresses the range of allowed entity occurrences associated with am single occurrence of the related entity.

cascading order sequence A nested ordering sequence for a set of rows, such as a list in which all last names are alphabetically ordered and, within the last names, all first names are ordered.

centralised data allocation A data allocation strategy in which the entire database is stored at one site. Also known as a *centralised database*.

centralised database A database located at a single site.

centralised design A process in which a single conceptual design is modelled to match an organisation's database requirements. It is typically used when a data component consists of a relatively small number of objects and procedures. Compare to decentralised design.

checkpoint In transaction management, an operation in which the database management system writes all of its updated buffers to disk.

class A collection of similar objects with shared structure (attributes) and behaviour (methods). A class encapsulates an object's data representation and a method's implementation. Classes are organised in a class hierarchy.

class diagram A diagram used to represent data and their relationships in UML object notation.

class diagram notation The set of symbols used in the creation of class diagrams.

class hierarchy The organisation of classes in a hierarchical tree in which each parent class is a *superclass* and each child class is a *subclass*. See also *inheritance*.

client/server architecture The arrangement of hardware and software components to form a system composed of clients, servers, and middleware. The client/server architecture features a user of resources, or a client, and a provider of resources, or a server.

client-side extensions Extensions that add functionality to a Web browser. The most common extensions are plug-ins, Java, JavaScript, ActiveX, and VBScript.

closure A property of relational operators that permits the use of relational algebra operators on existing tables (relations) to produce new relations.

closure A property of relational operators that permits the use of relational algebra operators on existing tables (relations) to produce new relations.

cloud computing A computing model that provides ubiquitous, on-demand access to a shared pool of configurable resources that can be rapidly provisioned.

cloud services The services provided by cloud computing. Cloud services allow any organiastion to quickly and economically add information technology services such as applications, storage, servers, processing power, databases, and infrastructure.

cohesivity The strength of the relationships between a module's components. Module cohesivity must be high.

collections In document databases, a logical storage unit that contains similar documents, roughly analogous to a table in a relational database.

column family In a column family database, a collection of columns or super columns related to a collection of rows.

column family database A NoSQL database model that organises data into key-value pairs, in which the value component is composed of a set of columns that vary by row.

column-centric storage A physical data storage technique in which data is stored in blocks, which hold data from a single column across many rows.

COMMIT The SQL command that permanently saves data changes to a database.

Common Gateway Interface (CGI) A Web server interface standard that uses script files to perform specific functions based on a client's parameters.

completeness constraint A constraint that specifies whether each entity supertype occurrence must also be a member of at least one subtype. The completeness constraint can be partial or total. Partial completeness means that some supertype occurrences might not be members of any subtype. Total completeness means that every supertype occurrence must be a member of at least one subtype.

composite attribute An attribute that can be further subdivided to yield additional attributes. For example, a phone number such as 615-898-2368 may be divided into an area code (615), an exchange number (898), and a four-digit code (2368). Compare to *simple attribute*.

composite entity An entity designed to transform an M:N relationship into two 1:M relationships. The composite entity's primary key comprises at least the primary keys of the entities that it connects. Also known as a *bridge entity*. See also *linking table*.

composite key A multiple-attribute key.

computer-aided systems engineering (CASE) Tools used to automate part or all of the Systems Development Life Cycle.

conceptual design A process that uses data-modelling techniques to create a model of a database structure that represents real-world objects as realistically as possible. The techniques are both software- and hardware-independent.

conceptual design A process that uses data-modelling techniques to create a model of a database structure that represents real-world objects as realistically as possible. The techniques are both software- and hardware-independent.

conceptual model The output of the conceptual design process. The conceptual model provides a global view of an entire database and describes the main data objects, avoiding details.

conceptual schema A representation of the conceptual model, usually expressed graphically. See also *conceptual model*.

concurrency control A DBMS feature that coordinates the simultaneous execution of transactions in a multiprocessing database system while preserving data integrity.

concurrent backup A backup that takes place while one or more users are working on a database.

connectivity The classification of the relationship between entities. Classifications include 1:1, 1:M, and M:N.

consistency A database condition in which all data integrity constraints are satisfied. To ensure consistency of a database, every transaction must begin with the database in a known consistent state. If not, the transaction will yield an inconsistent database that violates its integrity and business rules.

consistent database state A database state in which all data integrity constraints are satisfied.

constraint A restriction placed on data, usually expressed in the form of rules. For example, "A student's GPA must be between 0.00 and 4.00." Constraints are important because they help to ensure data integrity.

coordinator The transaction processor (TP) node that coordinates the execution of a two-phase COMMIT in a DDBMS. See also *data processor (DP)*, *transaction processor (TP)*, and *two-phase commit protocol*.

correlated subquery A subquery that executes once for each row in the outer query.

cost-based optimiser A query optimiser technique that uses an algorithm based on statistics about the objects being accessed, including number of rows, indexes available, index sparsity, and so on.

COUNT A SQL aggregate function that outputs the number of rows containing not null values for a given column or expression, sometimes used in conjunction with the DISTINCT clause.

CREATE INDEX A SQL command that creates indexes on the basis of a selected attribute or attributes.

CREATE TABLE A SQL command that creates a table's structures using the characteristics and attributes given.

cross join A join that performs a relational product (or Cartesian product) of two tables.

Crow's Foot notation A representation of the entity relationship diagram that uses a three-pronged symbol to represent the "many" sides of the relationship.

cube cache In multidimensional OLAP, the shared, reserved memory area where data cubes are held. Using the cube cache assists in speeding up data access.

cursor A special construct used in procedural SQL to hold the data rows returned by a SQL query. A cursor may be considered a reserved area of memory in which query output is stored, like an array holding columns and rows. Cursors are held in a reserved memory area in the DBMS server, not in the client computer.

Cypher A declarative query language used in Neo4j for querying a graph database.

D

data Raw facts, or facts that have not yet been processed to reveal their meaning to the end user.

Data Access Objects (DAO) An object-oriented application programming interface used to access MS Access, MS FoxPro, and dBase databases from Visual Basic programs. DAO provides an optimised programming interface that exposes the functionality of the Jet data engine, on which MS Access is based. The DAO interface can be used to access other relational-style data sources.

data administrator (DA) The person responsible for managing the entire data resource, whether it is computerised or not. The DA has broader authority and responsibility than the database administrator (DBA). Also known as an information resource manager (IRM).

data allocation In a distributed DBMS, the process of deciding where to locate data fragments.

data anomaly A data abnormality in which inconsistent changes have been made to a database. For example, an employee moves, but the address change is not corrected in all files in the database.

data cache or buffer cache A shared, reserved memory area that stores the most recently accessed data blocks in RAM. A buffer cache takes advantage of a computer's fast primary memory compared to the slower secondary memory, minimising the number of input/output (I/O) operations between primary and secondary memory.

data cube The multidimensional data structure used to store and manipulate data in a multidimensional DBMS. The location of each data value in the data cube is based on its x-, y-, and z-axes. Data cubes are static, meaning they must be created before they are used, so they cannot be created by an ad hoc query.

data definition language (DDL) The language that allows a database administrator to define the database structure, schema, and subschema.

data dependence A data condition in which data representation and manipulation are dependent on the physical data storage characteristics.

data dictionary A DBMS component that stores metadata—data about data. Thus, the data dictionary contains the data definition as well as their characteristics and relationships. A data dictionary may also include data that are external to the DBMS. Also known as an *information resource dictionary*.

data dictionary A DBMS component that stores metadata—data about data. Thus, the data dictionary contains the data definition as well as their characteristics and relationships. A data dictionary may also include data that are external to the DBMS. Also known as an *information resource dictionary*.

data extraction A process used to extract and validate data from an operational database and external data sources prior to their placement in a data warehouse.

data file A named physical storage space that stores a database's data. It can reside in a different directory on a hard disk or on one or more hard disks. All data in a database are stored in data files. A typical enterprise database is normally composed of several data files. A data file can contain rows from one or more tables.

data filtering A process used to extract and validate data from an operational database and external data sources prior to their placement in a data warehouse. See data extraction.

data fragmentation A characteristic of a DDBMS that allows a single object to be broken into two or more segments or fragments. The object might be a user's database, a system database, or a table. Each fragment can be stored at any site on a computer network.

data inconsistency A condition in which different versions of the same data yield different (inconsistent) results.

data independence A condition in which data access is unaffected by changes in the physical data storage characteristics.

data integrity In a relational database, a condition in which the data in the database comply with all entity and referential integrity constraints.

data management A process that focuses on data collection, storage, and retrieval. Common data management functions include addition, deletion, modification, and listing.

data manager (DM) See *data processing (DP) manager*.

data manipulation language (DML) The set of commands that allows an end user to manipulate the data in the database. The commands include SELECT, INSERT, UPDATE, DELETE, COMMIT, and ROLLBACK.

data mart A small, single-subject data warehouse subset that provides decision support to a small group of people.

data mining A process that employs automated tools to analyse data in a data warehouse and other sources and to proactively identify possible relationships and anomalies.

data model A representation, usually graphic, of a complex "real-world" data structure. Data models are used in the database design phase of the Database Life Cycle.

data processing (DP) manager A DP specialist who evolved into a department supervisor. Roles include managing technical and human resources, supervising senior programmers, and troubleshooting the program. Also known as a *data manager (DM)*.

data processor (DP) The resident software component that stores and retrieves data through a DDBMS. The DP is responsible for managing the local data in the computer and coordinating access to that data. See also *transaction processor (TP)*.

data quality A comprehensive approach to ensuring the accuracy, validity, and timeliness of data.

data redundancy A condition in which a data environment contains redundant (unnecessarily duplicated) data.

data replication The storage of duplicated database fragments at multiple sites on a DDBMS. Duplication of the fragments is transparent to the end user. Data replication provides fault tolerance and performance enhancements.

data source name (DSN) A name that identifies and defines an ODBC data source.

data store The component of the decision support system that acts as a database for storage of business data and business model data. The data in the data store have already been extracted and filtered from the external and operational data, and will be stored for access by the end-user query tool for the business data model.

data warehouse An integrated, subject-oriented, time-variant, non-volatile collection of data that provides support for decision making, according to Bill Inmon, the acknowledged "father of the data warehouse."

data warehouse An integrated, subject-oriented, time-variant, nonvolatile collection of data that provides support for decision making, according to Bill Inmon, the acknowledged "father of the data warehouse."

database administrator (DBA) The person responsible for planning, organising, controlling, and monitoring the centralised and shared corporate database. The DBA is the general manager of the database administration department.

database design The process that yields the description of the database structure and determines the database components. Database design is the second phase of the Database Life Cycle.

database development The process of database design and implementation.

database fragment A subset of a distributed database. Although the fragments may be stored at different sites within a computer network, the set of all fragments is treated as a single database. See also *horizontal fragmentation* and *vertical fragmentation*.

Database Life Cycle (DBLC) A cycle that traces the history of a database within an information system. The cycle is divided into six phases: initial study, design, implementation and loading, testing and evaluation, operation and maintenance, and evolution.

database management system (DBMS) The collection of programs that manages the database structure and controls access to the data stored in the database.

database middleware Database connectivity software through which application programs connect and communicate with data repositories.

database performance tuning A set of activities and procedures designed to reduce the response time of a database system—that is, to ensure that an end-user query is processed by the DBMS in the minimum amount of time.

database recovery The process of restoring a database to a previous consistent state.

database request The equivalent of a single SQL statement in an application program or a transaction.

database security officer The person responsible for the security, integrity, backup, and recovery of the database.

database system An organisation of components that defines and regulates the collection, storage, management, and use of data in a database environment.

database-level lock A type of lock that restricts database access to the owner of the lock and allows only one user at a time to access the database. This lock works for batch processes but is unsuitable for online multiuser DBMSs.

DataSet In ADO.NET, a disconnected, memory-resident representation of the database. The DataSet contains tables, columns, rows, relationships, and constraints.

DBMS performance tuning Activities to ensure that clients' requests are addressed as quickly as possible while making optimum use of existing resources.

deadlock A condition in which two or more transactions wait indefinitely for the other to release the lock on a previously locked data item. Also called *deadly embrace*. See also *lock*.

deadly embrace See *deadlock*.

decentralised design A process in which conceptual design is used to model subsets of an organisation's database requirements. After verification of the views, processes, and constraints, the subsets are then aggregated into a complete design. Such modular designs are typical of complex systems in which the data component has a relatively large number of objects and procedures. Compare to centralised design.

decision support system (DSS) An arrangement of computerised tools used to assist managerial decision making within a business.

deferred update In transaction management, a condition in which transaction operations do not immediately update a physical database. Also called *deferred write technique*.

deferred-write See *deferred update*.

DELETE A SQL command that allows data rows to be deleted from a table.

denormalisation A process by which a table is changed from a higher-level normal form to a lower-level normal form, usually to increase processing speed. Denormalisation potentially yields data anomalies.

dependency diagram A representation of all data dependencies (primary key, partial, or transitive) within a table.

derived attribute An attribute that does not physically exist within the entity and is derived via an algorithm.

For example, the Age attribute might be derived by subtracting the birth date from the current date.

description of operations A document that provides a precise, detailed, up-to-date, and thoroughly reviewed description of the activities that define an organisation's operating environment.

design trap A problem that occurs when a relationship is improperly or incompletely identified and therefore is represented in a way that is not consistent with the real world. The most common design trap is known as a *fan trap*.

desktop database A single-user database that runs on a personal computer.

determinant Any attribute in a specific row whose value directly determines other values in that row. See also *Boyce-Codd normal form (BCNF)*.

determination The role of a key. In the context of a database table, the statement "A determines B" indicates that knowing the value of attribute A means that the value of attribute B can be looked up.

dimension tables In a data warehouse, tables used to search, filter, or classify facts within a star schema. The fact table is in a one-to-many relationship with dimension tables.

dimensions In a star schema design, qualifying characteristics that provide additional perspectives to a given fact.

disaster management The set of DBA activities dedicated to securing data availability following a physical disaster or a database integrity failure.

disjoint subtype (non-overlapping subtype) In a specialisation hierarchy, a unique and nonoverlapping subtype entity set.

DISTINCT A SQL clause that produces only a list of values that are different from one another.

distributed data catalogue (DDC) A data dictionary that contains the description (fragment names, locations) of a distributed database. Also known as a *distributed data dictionary (DDD)*.

distributed data dictionary (DDD) See *distributed data catalogue*.

distributed database A logically related database that is stored in two or more physically independent sites.

distributed database A logically related database that is stored in two or more physically independent sites.

distributed database management system (DDBMS) A DBMS that supports a database distributed across several different sites; a DDBMS governs the storage and processing of logically related data over interconnected computer systems in which both data and processing functions are distributed among several sites.

distributed global schema The database schema description of a distributed database as seen by the database administrator.

distributed processing Sharing the logical processing of a database over two or more sites connected by a network.

distributed request A database request that allows a single SQL statement to access data in several remote data processors (DPs) in a distributed database.

distributed transaction A database transaction that accesses data in several remote data processors (DPs) in a distributed database.

distribution transparency A DDBMS feature that allows a distributed database to look like a single logical database to an end user.

Document databases A NoSQL database model that stores data in key-value pairs in which the value component is composed of a tag-encoded document.

document type definition (DTD) A file with a .DTD extension that describes XML elements; in effect, a DTD file describes a document's composition and defines the syntax rules or valid tags for each type of XML document.

domain In data modelling, the construct used to organise and describe an attribute's set of possible values.

DO-UNDO-REDO protocol A protocol used by a data processor (DP) to roll back or roll forward transactions with the help of a system's transaction log entries.

drill down To decompose data into more atomic components—that is, data at lower levels of aggregation. This approach is used primarily in a decision support system to focus on specific geographic areas, business types, and so on. See also *roll up*.

DROP A SQL command used to delete database objects such as tables, views, indexes, and users.

DROP INDEX Permanently deletes an index

DROP TABLE Permanently deletes a table (and its data)

durability The transaction property that indicates the permanence of a database's consistent state. Transactions that have been completed will not be lost in a system failure if the database has proper durability.

dynamic query optimisation The process of determining the SQL access strategy at run time, using the most up-to-date information about the database. Contrast with *static query optimisation*.

dynamic SQL An environment in which the SQL statement is not known in advance, but instead is generated at run time. In a dynamic SQL environment, a program can generate the SQL statements that are required to respond to ad hoc queries.

E

edge In a graph database, the representation of a relationship between nodes.

EER diagram (EERD) The entity relationship diagram resulting from the application of extended entity relationship concepts that provide additional semantic content in the ER model.

embedded SQL SQL statements contained within application programming languages such as COBOL, C++, ASP, Java, and ColdFusion.

end-user presentation tool A data analysis tool that organises and presents selected data compiled by the end-user query tool.

end-user query tool A data analysis tool used to create the queries that access desired information from the data store.

enterprise database The overall company data representation, which provides support for present and expected future needs.

entity A person, place, thing, concept, or event for which data can be stored. See also *attribute*.

entity cluster A "virtual" entity type used to represent multiple entities and relationships in the ERD. An entity cluster is formed by combining multiple interrelated entities into a single abstract entity object. An entity cluster is considered "virtual" or "abstract" because it is not actually an entity in the final ERD.

entity instance In ER modelling, a specific table row. Also known as an *entity occurrence*.

entity integrity The property of a relational table that guarantees each entity has a unique value in a primary key and that the key has no null values.

entity occurrence See *entity instance*.

entity relationship (ER) model (ERM) A data model that describes relationships (1:1, 1:M, and M:N) among entities at the conceptual level with the help of ER diagrams. The model was developed by P. Chen in 1975.

entity relationship diagram (ERD) A diagram that depicts an entity relationship model's entities, attributes, and relations.

entity set In a relational model, a grouping of related entities.

entity subtype In a generalisation/specialisation hierarchy, a subset of an entity supertype. The entity supertype contains the common characteristics and the subtypes contain the unique characteristics of each entity.

entity supertype In a generalisation/specialisation hierarchy, a generic entity type that contains the common characteristics of entity subtypes.

equijoin A join operator that links tables based on an equality condition that compares specified columns of the tables.

eventual consistency A model for database consistency in which updates to the database will propagate through the system so that all data copies will be consistent eventually.

exclusive lock A lock that is reserved by a transaction. An exclusive lock is issued when a transaction requests permission to update a data item and no locks are held on that data item by any other transaction. An exclusive lock does not allow other transactions to access the database. See also *shared lock*.

existence-dependent A property of an entity whose existence depends on one or more other entities. In such an environment, the existence-independent table must be created and loaded first because the existence-dependent key cannot reference a table that does not yet exist.

existence-independent A property of an entity that can exist apart from one or more related entities. Such a table must be created first when referencing an existence-dependent table.

EXISTS In SQL, a comparison operator that checks whether a subquery returns any rows.

explicit cursor In procedural SQL, a cursor created to hold the output of a SQL statement that may return two or more rows, but could return zero or only one row.

extended entity relationship model (EERM) Sometimes referred to as the enhanced entity relationship model; the result of adding more semantic constructs, such as entity supertypes, entity subtypes, and entity clustering, to the original entity relationship (ER) model.

extended relational data model (ERDM) A model that includes the object-oriented model's best features in an inherently simpler relational database structural environment.

extends In a DBMS environment, refers to the ability of data files to expand in size automatically using predefined increments.

Extensible Markup Language (XML) A metalanguage used to represent and manipulate data elements. Unlike other markup languages, XML permits the manipulation of a document's data elements. XML facilitates the exchange of structured documents such as orders and invoices over the internet.

Extensible Markup Language (XML) A metalanguage used to represent and manipulate data elements. Unlike other markup languages, XML permits the manipulation of a document's data elements. XML facilitates the exchange of structured documents such as orders and invoices over the internet.

external model The application programmer's view of the data environment. Given its business focus, an external model works with a data subset of the global database schema.

external schema The specific representation of an external view; the end user's view of the data environment.

F

fact table In a data warehouse, the star schema table that contains facts linked and classified through their common dimensions. A fact table is in a one-to-many relationship with each associated dimension table.

facts In a data warehouse, the measurements (values) that represent a specific business aspect or activity. For example, sales figures are numeric measurements that represent product or service sales. Facts commonly used in business data analysis include units, costs, prices, and revenues.

failure transparency A feature that allows continuous operation of a DDBMS, even if a network node fails.

fan trap A design trap that occurs when one entity is in two 1:M relationships with other entities, thus producing an association among the other entities that is not expressed in the model.

feedback loop processing Analysing stored data to produce actionable results.

field An alphabetic or numeric character or group of characters that defines a characteristic of a person, place, or thing. For example, a person's Social Security number, address, phone number, and bank balance all constitute fields.

field-level lock A lock that allows concurrent transactions to access the same row as long as they require the use of different fields (attributes) within that row. This type of lock yields the most flexible multiuser data access but requires a high level of computer overhead.

file A named collection of related records.

find() A MongoDB method to retrieve documents from a collection.

first normal form (1NF) The first stage in the normalisation process. It describes a relation depicted in tabular format, with no repeating groups and a primary key identified. All nonkey attributes in the relation are dependent on the primary key.

flags Special codes implemented by designers to trigger a required response, alert end users to specified conditions, or encode values. Flags may be used to prevent nulls by bringing attention to the absence of a value in a table.

foreign key (FK) An attribute or attributes in one table whose values must match the primary key in another table or whose values must be null. See *key*.

fourth normal form (4NF) A table that is in 3NF and contains no multiple independent sets of multivalued dependencies.

fragmentation transparency A DDBMS feature that allows a system to treat a distributed database as a single database even though it is divided into two or more fragments.

full backup A complete copy of an entire database saved and periodically updated in a separate memory location. A full backup ensures a full recovery of all data after a physical disaster or database integrity failure.

full functional dependence A condition in which an attribute is functionally dependent on a composite key but not on any subset of the key.

fully heterogeneous DDBMS A system that integrates different types of database management systems (hierarchical, network, and relational) over a network. It supports different database management systems that may even support different data models running under different computer systems, such as mainframes, minicomputers, and microcomputers. See also *heterogeneous DDBMS* and *homogeneous DDBMS*.

fully replicated database In a DDBMS, the distributed database that stores multiple copies of each database fragment at multiple sites. See also *partially replicated database*.

functional dependence Within a relation R, an attribute B is functionally dependent on an attribute A if and only if a given value of attribute A determines exactly one value of attribute B. The relationship "B is dependent on A" is equivalent to "A determines B," and is written as AB.

G

granularity The level of detail represented by the values stored in a table's row. Data stored at their lowest level of granularity are said to be *atomic data*.

graph database A NoSQL database model based on graph theory that stores data on relationship-rich data as a collection of nodes and edges.

GROUP BY A SQL clause used to create frequency distributions when combined with any of the aggregate functions in a SELECT statement.

H

hardware independence A condition in which a model does not depend on the hardware used in the model's implementation. Therefore, changes in the hardware will have no effect on the database design at the conceptual level.

HAVING A clause applied to the output of a GROUP BY operation to restrict selected rows.

heartbeat In the Hadoop Distributed File System (HDFS), a signal sent every three seconds from the data node to the name node to notify the name node that the data node is still available.

heterogeneity transparency A feature that allows a system to integrate several centralised DBMSs into one logical DDBMS.

heterogeneous DDBMS A system that integrates different types of centralised database management systems over a network. See also *fully heterogeneous distributed database system (fully heterogeneous DDBMS)* and *homogeneous DDBMS*.

hierarchical model An early database model whose basic concepts and characteristics formed the basis for subsequent database development. This model is based on an upside-down tree structure in which each record is called a segment. The top record is the root segment. Each segment has a 1:M relationship to the segment directly below it.

homogeneous DDBMS A system that integrates only one type of centralised database management system over a network. See also *heterogeneous DDBMS* and *fully heterogeneous distributed database system (fully heterogeneous DDBMS)*.

homonym The use of the same name to label different attributes. Homonyms generally should be avoided. Some relational software automatically checks for homonyms and either alerts the user to their existence or automatically makes the appropriate adjustments. See also *synonym*.

horizontal fragmentation The distributed database design process that breaks a table into subsets of unique rows. See also *database fragment* and *vertical fragmentation*.

host language Any language that contains embedded SQL statements.

I

identifiers In an ERM, unique names of each entity instance. In the relational model, such identifiers are mapped to primary keys in tables.

identifying relationship A relationship in which related entities are existence-dependent. Also called a *strong relationship* or *strong identifying relationship* because the dependent entity's primary key contains the primary key of the parent entity.

immediate update A database update that is performed immediately during a transaction's execution, even before the transaction reaches its commit point.

implicit cursor A cursor that is automatically created in procedural SQL when the SQL statement returns only one value.

IN In SQL, a comparison operator used to check whether a value is among a list of specified values.

inconsistent retrievals A concurrency control problem that arises when a transaction-calculating summary (aggregate)functions over a set of data while other transactions are updating the data, yielding erroneous results.

incremental backup A process that only backs up data that has changed in the database since the last incremental or full backup.

index An ordered array of index key values and row ID values (pointers). Indexes are generally used to speed up and facilitate data retrieval. Also known as an *index key*.

index key See *index*.

index selectivity A measure of how likely an index is to be used in query processing.

information The result of processing raw data to reveal its meaning. Information consists of transformed data and facilitates decision making.

information engineering (IE) A methodology that translates a company's strategic goals into helpful data and applications. IE focuses on the description of corporate data instead of the processes.

information resource manager See data administrator (DA).

information systems architecture (ISA) The output of the information engineering (IE) process that serves as the basis for planning, developing, and controlling future information systems.

Inheritance In the object-oriented data model, the ability of an object to inherit the data structure and methods of the classes above it in the class hierarchy. See also *class hierarchy*.

inheritance In the object-oriented data model, the ability of an object to inherit the data structure and methods of the classes above it in the class hierarchy.

inner join A join operation in which only rows that meet a given criterion are selected. The join criterion can be an equality condition (natural join or equijoin) or an inequality condition (theta join). The inner join is the most commonly used type of join. Contrast with *outer join*.

input/output (I/O) request A low-level operation that reads or writes data to and from computer devices such as memory, hard disks, video, and printers.

INSERT A SQL command that allows the insertion of one or more data rows into a table using a subquery.

internal model In database modelling, a level of data abstraction that adapts the conceptual model to a specific DBMS model for implementation. The internal model is the representation of a database as "seen" by the DBMS. In other words, the internal model requires a designer to match the conceptual model's characteristics and constraints to those of the selected implementation model.

internal schema A representation of an internal model using the database constructs supported by the chosen database.

IS NULL In SQL, a comparison operator used to check whether an attribute has a value.

islands of information In the old file system environment, pools of independent, often duplicated, and inconsistent data created and managed by different departments.

isolation A property of a database transaction in which a data item used by one transaction is not available to other transactions until the first one ends.

iterative process A process based on repetition of steps and procedures.

J

Java An object-oriented programming language developed by Sun Microsystems that runs on top of the Web browser software. Java applications are compiled and stored on the Web server. Java's main advantage is its ability to let application developers create their applications once and then run them in many environments.

Java Database Connectivity (JDBC) An application programming interface that allows a Java program to interact with a wide range of data sources, including relational databases, tabular data sources, spreadsheets, and text files.

JavaScript A scripting language developed by Netscape that allows Web authors to design interactive Websites. JavaScript code is embedded in Web pages, and then downloaded with the page and activated when a specific event takes place, such as a mouse click on an object.

job tracker A central control program used to accept, distribute, monitor, and report on MapReduce processing jobs in a Hadoop environment.

join column(s) Columns that join two tables. The join columns generally share similar values.

JSON (JavaScript Object Notation) A human-readable text format for data interchange that defines attributes and values in a document.

K

key An entity identifier based on the concept of functional dependence; keys may be classified in several ways. See also *superkey, candidate key, primary key (PK), secondary key*, and *foreign key*.

key attribute The attributes that form a primary key.

key attributes The attributes that form a primary key. See also prime attribute.

key performance indicators (KPIs) In business intelligence, quantifiable numeric or scale-based measurements that assess a company's effectiveness or success in reaching strategic and operational goals. Examples of KPI are product turnovers, sales by promotion, sales by employee, and earnings per share.

key-value A data model based on a structure composed of two data elements: a key and a value, in which every key has a corresponding value or set of values. The key-value data model is also called the associative or attribute-value data model.

Key-value (KV) databases A NoSQL database model that stores data as a collection of key-value pairs in which the value component is unintelligible to the DBMS.

knowledge The body of information and facts about a specific subject. Knowledge implies familiarity, awareness, and understanding of information as it applies to an environment. A key characteristic is that new knowledge can be derived from old knowledge.

L

left outer join In a pair of tables to be joined, a join that yields all the rows in the left table, including those that have no matching values in the other table. For example, a left outer join of CUSTOMER with AGENT will yield all of the CUSTOMER rows, including the ones that do not have a matching AGENT row. See also *outer join* and *right outer join*.

LIKE In SQL, a comparison operator used to check whether an attribute's text value matches a specified string pattern.

linking table In the relational model, a table that implements an M:M relationship. See also *composite entity*.

local mapping transparency A property of a DDBMS in which database access requires the end user to know both the name and location of the fragments. See also *location transparency*.

location transparency A property of a DDBMS in which database access requires the user to know only the name of the database fragments. (Fragment locations need not be known.) See also *local mapping transparency*.

lock A device that guarantees unique use of a data item in a particular transaction operation. A transaction requires a lock prior to data access; the lock is released after the operation's execution to enable other transactions to lock the data item for their own use.

lock granularity The level of lock use. Locking can take place at the following levels: database, table, page, row, and field (attribute).

lock manager A DBMS component that is responsible for assigning and releasing locks.

logical data format The way a person views data.

logical design A stage in the design phase that matches the conceptual design to the requirements of the selected DBMS and is therefore software-dependent. Logical design is used to translate the conceptual design into the internal model for a selected database management system, such as DB2, SQL Server, Oracle, IMS, Informix, Access, or Ingress.

logical design A stage in the design phase that matches the conceptual design to the requirements of the selected DBMS and is therefore software-dependent. Logical design is used to translate the conceptual design into the internal model for a selected database management system, such as DB2, SQL Server, Oracle, IMS, Informix, Access, or Ingress.

logical independence A condition in which the internal model can be changed without affecting the conceptual model. (The internal model is hardware-independent because it is unaffected by the computer on which the software is installed. Therefore, a change in storage devices or operating systems will not affect the internal model.)

lost updates A concurrency control problem in which data updates are lost during the concurrent execution of transactions.

M

mandatory participation A relationship in which one entity occurrence must have a corresponding occurrence in another entity. For example, an EMPLOYEE works in a DIVISION. (A person cannot be an employee without being assigned to a company's division.)

many-to-many (M:N or *..*) relationship Associations among two or more entities in which one occurrence of an entity is associated with many occurrences of a related entity and one occurrence of the related entity is associated with many occurrences of the first entity.

map The function in a MapReduce job that sorts and filters data into a set of key-value pairs as a subtask within a larger job.

Mapper A program that performs a map function.

materialised view A dynamic table that not only contains the SQL query command to generate rows but stores the actual rows. The materialised view is created the first time the query is run and the summary rows are stored in the table. The materialised view rows are automatically updated when the base tables are updated.

MAX A SQL aggregate function that yields the maximum attribute value in a given column.

metadata Data about data; that is, data about data characteristics and relationships. See also *data dictionary*.

method In the object-oriented data model, a named set of instructions to perform an action. Methods represent real-world actions, and are invoked through messages.

metrics In a data warehouse, numeric facts that measure a business characteristic of interest to the end user.

Microsoft .NET framework A component-based platform for the development of distributed, heterogeneous, interoperable applications aimed at manipulating any type of data over any network regardless of operating system and programming language.

MIN A SQL aggregate function that yields the minimum attribute value in a given column.

minimal data rule Defined as "All that is needed is there, and all that is there is needed." In other words, all data elements required by database transactions must be defined in the model, and all data elements defined in the model must be used by at least one database transaction.

minimal data rule Defined as "All that is needed is there, and all that is there is needed." In other words, all data elements required by database transactions must be defined in the model, and all data elements defined in the model must be used by at least one database transaction.

mixed fragmentation A combination of horizontal and vertical strategies for data fragmentation, in which a table may be divided into several rows and each row has a subset of the attributes (columns).

module (1) A design segment that can be implemented as an autonomous unit, and is sometimes linked to produce a system. (2) An information system component that handles a specific function, such as inventory, orders, or payroll.

module coupling The extent to which modules are independent of one another.

monotonicity A quality that ensures that timestamp values always increase. (The time-stamping approach to scheduling concurrent transactions assigns a global, unique timestamp to each transaction. The timestamp value produces an explicit order in which transactions are submitted to the DBMS.)

multidimensional database management system (MDBMSs) A database management system that uses proprietary techniques to store data in matrix-like arrays of *n* dimensions known as cubes.

multidimensional online analytical processing (MOLAP) An extension of online analytical processing to multidimensional database management systems.

multiple-site processing, multiple-site data (MPMD) A scenario describing a fully distributed database management system with support for multiple data processors and transaction processors at multiple sites.

multiple-site processing, single-site data (MPSD) A scenario in which multiple processes run on different computers sharing a single data repository.

multivalued attribute An attribute that can have many values for a single entity occurrence.

For example, an EMP_DEGREE attribute might store the string "BBA, MBA, PHD" to indicate three different degrees held.

mutual consistency rule A data replication rule that requires all copies of data fragments to be identical.

mutual exclusive rule A condition in which only one transaction at a time can own an exclusive lock on the same object.

N

natural join A relational operation that links tables by selecting only the rows with common values in their common attribute(s).

natural key (natural identifier) A generally accepted identifier for real-world objects. As its name implies, a natural key is familiar to end users and forms part of their day-to-day business vocabulary.

network latency The delay imposed by the amount of time required for a data packet to make a round trip from point A to point B.

network model A data model standard created in the late 1960s that represented data as a collection of record types and relationships as predefined sets with an owner record type and a member record type in a 1:M relationship.

network partitioning The delay imposed when nodes become suddenly unavailable due to a network failure.

node In a graph database, the representation of a single entity instance.

non-identifying relationship A relationship in which the primary key of the dependent (many side) entity does not contain the primary key of the related parent entity. Also known as a *weak relationship*.

non-key attribute See nonprime attribute.

non-prime attribute An attribute that is not part of a key.

normalisation A process that assigns attributes to entities so that data redundancies are reduced or eliminated.

NoSQL A new generation of database management systems that is not based on the traditional relational database model.

NoSQL A new generation of database management systems that is not based on the traditional relational database model.

NOT A SQL logical operator that negates a given predicate.

null In SQL, the absence of an attribute value. Note that a null is not a blank.

O

object An abstract representation of a real-world entity that has a unique identity, embedded properties, and the ability to interact with other objects and itself.

Object Linking and Embedding for Database (OLE-DB) Based on Microsoft's Component Object Model (COM), OLE-DB is database middleware that adds object-oriented functionality for accessing relational and non-relational data. OLE-DB was the first part of Microsoft's strategy to provide a unified object-oriented framework for the development of next-generation applications.

object/relational database management system (O/R DBMS) A DBMS based on the extended relational model (ERDM). The ERDM, championed by many relational database researchers, constitutes the relational model's response to the OODM. This model includes many of the object-oriented model's best features within an inherently simpler relational database structure.

object-oriented data model (OODM) A data model whose basic modelling structure is an object.

object-oriented database management system (OODBMS) Data management software used to manage data in an object-oriented database model.

one-to-many (1:M or 1..*) relationship Associations among two or more entities that are used by data models. In a 1:M relationship, one entity instance is associated with many instances of the related entity.

one-to-one (1:1 or 1..1) relationship Associations among two or more entities that are used by data models. In a 1:1 relationship, one entity instance is associated with only one instance of the related entity.

online analytical processing (OLAP) Decision support system (DSS) tools that use multidimensional data analysis techniques. OLAP creates an advanced data analysis environment that supports decision making, business modelling, and operations research.

online transaction processing (OLTP) The systems that support a company's day-to-day operations. Databases that support OLTP are known as OLTP databases, transactional databases, or operational databases.

Open Database Connectivity (ODBC) Database middleware developed by Microsoft to provide a database access API to Windows applications.

operational database A database designed primarily to support a company's day-to-day operations. Also known as a *transactional database* or *production database*.

optimiser hints Special instructions for the query optimiser that are embedded inside the SQL command text.

optimistic approach In transaction management, a concurrency control technique based on the assumption that most database operations do not conflict.

optional attribute In ER modelling, an attribute that does not require a value; therefore, it can be left empty.

optional participation In ER modelling, a condition in which one entity occurrence does not require a corresponding entity occurrence in a particular relationship.

OR The SQL logical operator used to link multiple conditional expressions in a WHERE or HAVING clause. It requires only one of the conditional expressions to be true.

ORDER BY A SQL clause that is useful for ordering the output of a SELECT query (for example, in ascending or descending order).

outer join A relational algebra JOIN operation that produces a table in which all unmatched pairs are retained; unmatched values in the related table are left null. Contrast with *inner join*.

outer join A relational algebra JOIN operation that produces a table in which all unmatched pairs are retained; unmatched values in the related table are left null. Contrast with *inner join*. See also *left outer join* and *right outer join*.

overlapping (non-disjoint) subtypes In a specialisation hierarchy, a condition in which each entity instance (row) of the supertype can appear in more than one subtype.

P

page In permanent storage, the equivalent of a disk block, which can be described as a directly addressable section of a disk. A diskpage has a fixed size, such as 4K, 8K, or 16K.

page-level lock In this type of lock, the database management system locks an entire diskpage, or section of a disk. A diskpage can contain data for one or more rows and from one or more tables.

partial completeness In a generalisation hierarchy, a condition in which some supertype occurrences might not be members of any subtype.

partial dependency In normalisation, a condition in which an attribute is dependent on only a portion (subset) of the primary key.

partially replicated database A distributed database in which copies of only some database fragments are stored at multiple sites. See also *fully replicated database*.

participants An ER term for entities that participate in a relationship. For example, in the relationship "PROFESSOR teaches CLASS," the *teaches* relationship is based on the participants PROFESSOR and CLASS.

partition key In partitioned databases, one or more attributes in a table that determine the fragment in which a row will be stored.

partitioned data allocation A data allocation strategy of dividing a database into two or more fragments that are stored at two or more sites.

partitioning The process of splitting a table into subsets of rows or columns.

performance transparency A DDBMS feature that allows a system to perform as though it were a centralised DBMS.

performance tuning Activities that make a database perform more efficiently in terms of storage and access speed.

periodicity Information about the time span of data stored in a table, usually expressed as current year only, previous years, or all years.

persistent stored module (PSM) A block of code with standard SQL statements and procedural extensions that is stored and executed at the DBMS server.

physical data format The way a computer "sees" (stores) data.

physical design A stage of database design that maps the data storage and access characteristics of a database. Because these characteristics are a function of the types of devices supported by the hardware, the data access methods supported by the system physical design are both hardware- and software-dependent. See also physical model.

physical independence A condition in which the physical model can be changed without affecting the internal model.

physical model A model in which physical characteristics such as location, path, and format are described for the data. The physical model is both hardware- and software-dependent.

Platform as a Service (PaaS) A model in which the cloud service provider can build and deploy consumer-created applications using the provider's cloud infrastructure.

plug-in In the World Wide Web (WWW), a client-side, external application that is automatically invoked by the browser when needed to manage specific types of data.

policies General statements of direction that are used to manage company operations through the communication and support of the organisation's objectives.

polyglot persistence The coexistence of a variety of data storage and data management technologies within an organisation's infrastructure.

predicate logic Used extensively in mathematics to provide a framework in which an assertion (statement of fact) can be verified as either true or false.

pretty() In MongoDB, a method that can be chained to the find() method to improve the readability of retrieved documents through the use of line breaks and indention.

primary key (PK) In the relational model, an identifier composed of one or more attributes that uniquely identifies a row. Also, a candidate key selected as a unique entity identifier. See also *key*.

prime attribute A key attribute; that is, an attribute that is part of a key or is the whole key. See also *key attributes*.

private cloud A form of cloud computing in which an internal cloud is built by an organisation to serve its own needs.

Procedural Language SQL (PL/SQL) A type of SQL that allows the use of procedural code and in which SQL statements are stored in a database as a single callable object that can be invoked by name.

procedures Series of steps to be followed during the performance of an activity or process.

properties In a graph database, the attributes or characteristics of a node or edge that are of interest to the users.

public cloud A form of computing in which the cloud infrastructure is built by a third-party organisation to sell cloud services to the general public.

Q

query A question or task asked by an end user of a database in the form of SQL code. A specific request for data manipulation issued by the end user or the application to the DBMS.

query language A nonprocedural language that is used by a DBMS to manipulate its data. An example of a query language is SQL.

query optimiser A DBMS process that analyses SQL queries and finds the most efficient way to access the data. The query optimiser generates the access or execution plan for the query.

query result set The collection of data rows returned by a query.

R

RAID An acronym for *R*edundant *A*rray of *I*ndependent *D*isks. RAID systems use multiple disks to create virtual disks (storage volumes) from several individual disks. RAID systems provide performance improvement, fault tolerance, and a balance between the two.

record A collection of related (logically connected) fields.

recursive query A nested query that joins a table to itself.

recursive relationship A relationship found within a single entity type. For example, an EMPLOYEE is married to an EMPLOYEE or a PART is a component of another PART.

reduce The function in a MapReduce job that collects and summarises the results of map functions to produce a single result.

reducer A program that performs a reduce function.

redundant transaction logs Multiple copies of the transaction log kept by database management systems to ensure that the physical failure of a disk will not impair the DBMS's ability to recover data.

referential integrity A condition by which a dependent table's foreign key must have either a null entry or a matching entry in the related table. Even though an attribute may not have a *corresponding* attribute, it is impossible to have an invalid entry.

relation In a relational database model, an entity set. Relations are implemented as tables. Relations are related to each other through the sharing of a common entity characteristic (a value in a column).

relational algebra A set of mathematical principles that form the basis for manipulating relational table contents; the eight main functions are SELECT, PROJECT, JOIN, INTERSECT, UNION, DIFFERENCE, PRODUCT, and DIVIDE.

relational database management system (RDBMS) A collection of programs that manages a relational database. The RDBMS software translates a user's logical requests (queries) into commands that physically locate and retrieve the requested data. A good RDBMS also creates and maintains a data dictionary to help provide data security, data integrity, concurrent and easy access, and system administration to the data through a query language (SQL) and application programs.

relational diagram A graphical representation of a relational database's entities, the attributes within those entities, and the relationships among the entities.

relational model Developed by E. F. Codd of IBM in 1970, it represented a major breakthrough for users and designers because of its conceptual simplicity. The relational model is based on mathematical set theory and represents data as independent relations. Each relation (table) is conceptually represented as a matrix of intersecting rows and columns. The relations are related to each other through the sharing of common entity characteristics (values in columns).

relational online analytical processing (ROLAP) Analytical processing functions that use relational databases and familiar relational query tools to store and analyse multidimensional data.

relational schema The organisation of a relational database as described by the database administrator.

relational schema The organisation of a relational database as described by the database administrator.

relationship An association between entities.

relationship degree The number of entities or participants associated with a relationship. A relationship degree can be unary, binary, ternary, or higher.

Remote Data Objects (RDO) A higher-level, object-oriented application interface used to access remote database servers. RDO uses the lower-level DAO and ODBC for direct access to databases. RDO was optimised to deal with server-based databases such as MS SQL Server, Oracle, and DB2.

remote request A DDBMS feature that allows a single SQL statement to access data in a single remote DP. See also *remote transaction*.

remote transaction A DDBMS feature that allows a transaction (formed by several requests) to access data in a single remote DP. See also *remote request*.

repeating group In a relation, a characteristic describing a group of multiple entries of the same type for a single key attribute occurrence. For example, a car can have multiple colors for its top, interior, bottom, trim, and so on.

replica transparency The DDBMS's ability to hide the existence of multiple copies of data from the user.

replicated data allocation A data allocation strategy in which copies of one or more database fragments are stored at several sites.

replication The process of creating and managing duplicate versions of a database. Replication is used to place copies in different locations and to improve access time and fault tolerance.

reserved words Words used by a system that cannot be used for any other purpose. For example, in Oracle SQL, the word INITIAL cannot be used to name tables or columns.

right outer join In a pair of tables to be joined, a join that yields all of the rows in the right table, including the ones with no matching values in the other table. For example, a right outer join of CUSTOMER with AGENT will yield all of the AGENT rows, including the ones that do not have a matching CUSTOMER row. See also *left outer join* and *outer join*.

roll up In SQL, an OLAP extension used with the GROUP BY clause to aggregate data by different dimensions. Rolling up the data is the exact opposite of drilling down the data. See also *drill down*.

ROLLBACK A SQL command that restores the database table contents to the condition that existed after the last COMMIT statement.

row-centric storage A physical data storage technique in which data is stored in blocks, which hold data from all columns of a given set of rows.

row-level lock A less restrictive database lock in which the DBMS allows concurrent transactions to access different rows of the same table, even when the rows are on the same page.

row-level trigger A trigger that is executed once for each row affected by the triggering SQL statement. A row-level trigger requires the use of the FOR EACH ROW keywords in the trigger declaration.

rule-based optimiser A query optimisation mode based on the rule-based query optimisation algorithm.

rule-based query optimisation algorithm A query optimisation technique that uses preset rules and points to determine the best approach to executing a query.

rules of precedence Basic algebraic rules that specify the order in which operations are performed. For example, operations within parentheses are executed first, so in the equation 2 + (3 × 5), the multiplication portion is calculated first, making the correct answer 17.

S

scaling out A method for dealing with data growth that involves distributing data storage structures across a cluster of commodity servers.

scaling up A method for dealing with data growth that involves migrating the same structure to more powerful systems.

scheduler The DBMS component that establishes the order in which concurrent transaction operations are executed. The scheduler *interleaves* the execution of database operations in a specific sequence to ensure *serialisability*.

schema A logical grouping of database objects, such as tables, indexes, views, and queries, that are related to each other. Usually, a schema belongs to a single user or application.

schema A logical grouping of database objects, such as tables, indexes, views, and queries, that are related to each other. Usually, a schema belongs to a single user or application.

scope The part of a system that defines the extent of the design, according to operational requirements.

second normal form (2NF) The second stage in the normalisation process, in which a relation is in 1NF and there are no partial dependencies (dependencies in only part of the primary key).

secondary key A key used strictly for data retrieval purposes. For example, customers are not likely to know their customer number (primary key), but the combination of last name, first name, middle initial, and telephone number will probably match the appropriate table row. See also *key*.

segment In the hierarchical data model, the equivalent of a file system's record type.

SELECT A SQL command that yields the values of all rows or a subset of rows in a table. The SELECT statement is used to retrieve data from tables.

semantic data model The first of a series of data models that more closely represented the real world, modelling both data and their relationships in a single structure known as an object. The SDM, published in 1981, was developed by M. Hammer and D. McLeod.

semi-structured data Data that have already been processed to some extent.

sentiment analysis A method of text analysis that attempts to determine if a statement conveys a positive, negative, or neutral attitude.

serialisability A property in which the selected order of transaction operations creates the same final database state that would have been produced if the transactions had been executed in a serial fashion.

server-side extension A program that interacts directly with the server process to handle specific types of requests. Server-side extensions add significant functionality to Web servers and intranets.

set theory A part of mathematical science that deals with sets, or groups of things, and is used as the basis for data manipulation in the relational model.

shared lock A lock that is issued when a transaction requests permission to read data from a database and no exclusive locks are held on the data by another transaction. A shared lock allows other read-only transactions to access the database. See also *exclusive lock*.

simple attribute An attribute that cannot be subdivided into meaningful components. Compare to *composite attribute*.

single-site processing, single-site data (SPSD) A scenario in which all processing is done on a single CPU or host computer and all data are stored on the host computer's local disk.

single-user database A database that supports only one user at a time.

single-valued attribute An attribute that can have only one value.

slice and dice The ability to cut slices off a data cube (drill down or drill up) to perform a more detailed analysis.

snowflake schema A type of star schema in which dimension tables can have their own dimension tables. The snowflake schema is usually the result of normalising dimension tables.

Software as a Service (SaaS) A model in which the cloud service provider offers turnkey applications that run in the cloud.

software independence A property of any model or application that does not depend on the software used to implement it.

sparse data A case in which the number of table attributes is very large but the number of actual data instances is low.

sparsity In multidimensional data analysis, a measurement of the data density held in the data cube.

specialisation hierarchy A hierarchy based on the top-down process of identifying lower-level, more specific entity subtypes from a higher-level entity supertype. Specialisation is based on grouping unique characteristics and relationships of the subtypes.

SQL cache A shared, reserved memory area that stores the most recently executed SQL statements or PL/SQL procedures, including triggers and functions. Also called *procedure cache*.

SQL data services (SDS) Data management services that provide relational data storage, access, and management over the internet.

SQL performance tuning Activities to help generate a SQL query that returns the correct answer in the least amount of time, using the minimum amount of resources at the server end.

standards A detailed and specific set of instructions that describes the minimum requirements for a given activity. Standards are used to evaluate the quality of the output.

star schema A data modelling technique used to map multidimensional decision support data into a relational database. The star schema represents data using a central table known as a fact table in a 1:M relationship with one or more dimension tables.

stateless system A system in which a Web server does not know the status of the clients communicating with it. The Web does not reserve memory to maintain an open communications state between the client and the server.

statement-level trigger A SQL trigger that is assumed if the FOR EACH ROW keywords are omitted. This type of trigger is executed once, before or after the triggering statement completes, and is the default case.

static query optimisation A query optimisation mode in which the access path to a database is predetermined at compilation time. Contrast with *dynamic query optimisation*.

static SQL A style of embedded SQL in which the SQL statements do not change while the application is running.

statistically based query optimisation algorithm A query optimisation technique that uses statistical information about a database. The DBMS then uses these statistics to determine the best access strategy.

stored function A named group of procedural and SQL statements that returns a value, as indicated by a RETURN statement in its program code.

stored procedure (1) A named collection of procedural and SQL statements. (2) Business logic stored on a server in the form of SQL code or another DBMS-specific procedural language.

stream processing The processing of data inputs in order to make decisions about which data to keep and which data to discard before storage.

strong relationship A relationship that occurs when two entities are existence-dependent; from a database design perspective, this relationship exists whenever the primary key of the related entity contains the primary key of the parent entity.

structural dependence A data characteristic in which a change in the database schema affects data access, thus requiring changes in all access programs.

structural independence A data characteristic in which changes in the database schema do not affect data access.

structured data Unstructured data that have been formatted to facilitate storage, use, and information generation.

Structured Query Language (SQL) A powerful and flexible relational database language composed of commands that enable users to create database and table structures, perform various types of data manipulation and data administration, and query the database to extract useful information.

subordinate In a DDBMS, a data processor (DP) node that participates in a distributed transaction using the two-phase COMMIT protocol.

subquery A query that is embedded (or nested) inside another query. Also known as a *nested query* or an *inner query*.

subschema In the network model, the portion of the database "seen" by the application programs that produce the desired information from the data in the database.

subtype discriminator The attribute in the supertype entity that determines to which entity subtype each supertype occurrence is related.

SUM A SQL aggregate function that yields the sum of all values for a given column or expression.

super column In a column family database, a column that is composed of a group of other related columns.

superkey An attribute or attributes that uniquely identify each entity in a table. See *key*.

surrogate key A system-assigned primary key, generally numeric and auto-incremented.

synonym The use of different names to identify the same object, such as an entity, an attribute, or a relationship; synonyms should generally be avoided. See also *homonym*.

system catalogue A detailed system data dictionary that describes all objects in a database.

systems administrator The person responsible for coordinating an organisation's data-processing activities.

systems analysis The process that establishes the need for an information system and its extent.

systems development The process of creating an information system.

Systems Development Life Cycle (SDLC) The cycle that traces the history of an information system. The SDLC provides the big picture within which database design and application development can be mapped out and evaluated.

T

table A matrix composed of intersecting rows (entities) and columns (attributes) that represents an entity set in the relational model. Also called a *relation*.

table space In a DBMS, a logical storage space used to group related data. Also known as a *file group*.

table-level lock A locking scheme that allows only one transaction at a time to access a table. A table-level lock locks an entire table, preventing access to any row by transaction T2 while transaction T1 is using the table.

tag In markup languages such as HTML and XML, a command inserted in a document to specify how the document should be formatted. Tags are used in server-side markup languages and interpreted by a Web browser for presenting data.

task trackers A program in the MapReduce framework responsible to running map and reduce tasks on a node.

ternary relationship An ER term used to describe an association (relationship) between three entities. For example, a CONTRIBUTOR contributes money to a FUND from which a RECIPIENT receives money.

theta join A join operator that links tables using an inequality comparison operator (<, >, <=, >=) in the join condition.

theta join A join operator that links tables using an inequality comparison operator (<, >, <=, >=) in the join condition.

third normal form (3NF) A table is in 3NF when it is in 2NF and no nonkey attribute is functionally dependent on another nonkey attribute; that is, it cannot include transitive dependencies.

time stamping In transaction management, a technique used in scheduling concurrent transactions that assigns a global unique timestamp to each transaction.

time-variant data Data whose values are a function of time. For example, time-variant data can be seen at work when a company's history of all administrative appointments is tracked.

top-down design A design philosophy that begins by defining the main structures of a system and then moves to define the smaller units within those structures. In database design, this process first identifies entities and then defines the attributes within the entities. Compare to bottom-up design.

total completeness In a generalisation/specialisation hierarchy, a condition in which every supertype occurrence must be a member of at least one subtype.

transaction A sequence of database requests that accesses the database. A transaction is a logical unit of work; that is, it must be *entirely* completed or aborted—no intermediate ending states are accepted. All transactions must have the properties of atomicity, consistency, isolation, and durability.

transaction log A feature used by the DBMS to keep track of all transaction operations that update the database. The information stored in this log is used by the DBMS for recovery purposes.

transaction manager (TM) See *transaction processor (TP)*.

transaction processor (TP) In a DDBMS, the software component on each computer that requests data. The TP is responsible for the execution and coordination of all databases issued by a local application that accesses data on any DP. Also called *transaction manager (TM)*. See also *data processor (DP)*.

transaction transparency A DDBMS property that ensures database transactions will maintain the distributed database's integrity and consistency, and that a transaction will be completed only when all database sites involved complete their part of the transaction.

transactional database A database designed to keep track of the day-to-day transactions of an organisation.

transitive dependency A condition in which an attribute is dependent on another attribute that is not part of the primary key.

traversal A query in a graph database.

trigger A procedural SQL code that is automatically invoked by the relational database management system when a data manipulation event occurs.

tuple In the relational model, a table row.

tuple In the relational model, a table row.

two-phase commit protocol In a DDBMS, an algorithm used to ensure atomicity of transactions and database consistency as well as integrity in distributed transactions.

two-phase locking A set of rules that governs how transactions acquire and relinquish locks. Two-phase locking guarantees serialisability, but it does not prevent deadlocks. The two-phase locking protocol is divided into two phases: (1) A *growing phase* occurs when the transaction acquires the locks it needs without unlocking any *existing* data locks. Once all locks have been acquired, the transaction is in its *locked* point. (2) A *shrinking phase* occurs when the transaction releases all locks and cannot obtain a new lock.

U

unary relationship An ER term used to describe an association *within* an entity. For example, a COURSE might be a prerequisite to another COURSE.

uncommitted data When you are trying to achieve concurrency control, uncommitted data cause problems with data integrity and consistency. These problems occur when two transactions are executed concurrently and the first transaction is rolled back after the second transaction has already accessed the uncommitted data, thus violating the isolation property of transactions.

Unified Modelling Language (UML) A language based on object-oriented concepts that provides tools such as diagrams and symbols to graphically model a system.

union-compatible Two or more tables that share the same column names and have columns with compatible data types or domains.

unique fragment In a DDBMS, a condition in which each row is unique, regardless of which fragment it is located in.

unique index An index in which the index key can have only one associated pointer value (row).

uniqueness In concurrency control, a property of time-stamping that ensures no equal timestamp values can exist.

Universal Data Access (UDA) Within the Microsoft application framework, a collection of technologies used to access any type of data source and to manage the data through a common interface.

unreplicated database A distributed database in which each database fragment is stored at a single site.

unstructured data Data that exist in their original, raw state; that is, in the format in which they were collected.

UPDATE A SQL command that allows attribute values to be changed in one or more rows of a table.

V

value The degree to which data can be analysed to provide meaningful insights.

variability The characteristic of Big Data for the same data values to vary in meaning over time.

variety A characteristic of Big Data that describes the variations in the structure of data to be stored.

VBScript A client-side extension in the form of a Microsoft product that extends a browser's functionality; VBScript is derived from Visual Basic.

velocity A characteristic of Big Data that describes the speed at which data enters the system and must be processed.

vertical fragmentation In distributed database design, the process that breaks a table into a subset of columns from the original table. Fragments must share a common primary key. See also *database fragment* and *horizontal fragmentation*.

very large databases (VLDBs) Databases that contain huge amounts of data—gigabyte, terabyte, and petabyte ranges are not unusual.

view A virtual table based on a SELECT query.

visualisation The ability to graphically present data in such a way as to make it understandable to users.

volume A characteristic of Big Data that describes the quantity of data to be stored.

W

wait/die A concurrency control scheme in which an older transaction must wait for the younger transaction to complete and release the locks before requesting the locks itself. Otherwise, the newer transaction dies and is rescheduled.

weak entity An entity that displays existence dependence and inherits the primary key of its parent entity. For example, a DEPENDENT requires the existence of an EMPLOYEE.

weak relationship A relationship in which the primary key of the related entity does not contain a primary key component of the parent entity. Also known as a *non-identifying relationship*.

Web-to-database middleware A database server-side extension that retrieves data from databases and passes them to the Web server, which in turn sends the data to the client's browser for display.

wildcard character A symbol that can be used as a general substitute for one or more characters in a SQL LIKE clause condition. The wildcard characters used in SQL are the _ and % symbols.

wound/wait A concurrency control scheme in which an older transaction can request the lock, pre-empt the younger transaction, and reschedule it. Otherwise, the newer transaction waits until the older transaction finishes.

write-ahead-log protocol In concurrency control, a process that ensures transaction logs are written to permanent storage before any database data are actually updated. Also called a write-ahead protocol.

write-through In concurrency control, a process that ensures a database is immediately updated by operations during the transaction's execution, even before the transaction reaches its commit point.

X

XML See *Extensible Markup Language (XML).*

XML database A database system that stores and manages semistructured XML data.

XML schema An advanced data definition language used to describe the elements, data types, relationship types, ranges, and default values of XML data documents. One of the main advantages of an XML schema is that it more closely maps to database terminology and features.

XML schema definition (XSD) A file that contains the description of an XML document.

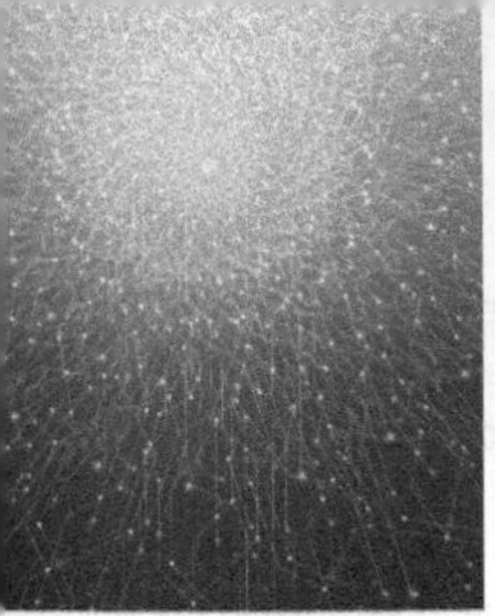

INDEX

A

B

C

D

E

F

G

H

N

O

P

Q

R

S

T